T0140441

Lecture Notes in Computer Science 13667

More information about this series at https://link.springer.com/bookseries/558

Shai Avidan · Gabriel Brostow ·
Moustapha Cissé · Giovanni Maria Farinella ·
Tal Hassner (Eds.)

Computer Vision – ECCV 2022

17th European Conference
Tel Aviv, Israel, October 23–27, 2022
Proceedings, Part VII

 Springer

Editors
Shai Avidan
Tel Aviv University
Tel Aviv, Israel

Gabriel Brostow 🆔
University College London
London, UK

Moustapha Cissé
Google AI
Accra, Ghana

Giovanni Maria Farinella 🆔
University of Catania
Catania, Italy

Tal Hassner 🆔
Facebook (United States)
Menlo Park, CA, USA

ISSN 0302-9743   ISSN 1611-3349 (electronic)
Lecture Notes in Computer Science
ISBN 978-3-031-20070-0   ISBN 978-3-031-20071-7 (eBook)
https://doi.org/10.1007/978-3-031-20071-7

This Springer imprint is published by the registered company Springer Nature Switzerland AG
The registered company address is: Gewerbestrasse 11, 6330 Cham, Switzerland

Foreword

Organizing the European Conference on Computer Vision (ECCV 2022) in Tel-Aviv during a global pandemic was no easy feat. The uncertainty level was extremely high, and decisions had to be postponed to the last minute. Still, we managed to plan things just in time for ECCV 2022 to be held in person. Participation in physical events is crucial to stimulating collaborations and nurturing the culture of the Computer Vision community.

There were many people who worked hard to ensure attendees enjoyed the best science at the 16th edition of ECCV. We are grateful to the Program Chairs Gabriel Brostow and Tal Hassner, who went above and beyond to ensure the ECCV reviewing process ran smoothly. The scientific program includes dozens of workshops and tutorials in addition to the main conference and we would like to thank Leonid Karlinsky and Tomer Michaeli for their hard work. Finally, special thanks to the web chairs Lorenzo Baraldi and Kosta Derpanis, who put in extra hours to transfer information fast and efficiently to the ECCV community.

We would like to express gratitude to our generous sponsors and the Industry Chairs, Dimosthenis Karatzas and Chen Sagiv, who oversaw industry relations and proposed new ways for academia-industry collaboration and technology transfer. It's great to see so much industrial interest in what we're doing!

Authors' draft versions of the papers appeared online with open access on both the Computer Vision Foundation (CVF) and the European Computer Vision Association (ECVA) websites as with previous ECCVs. Springer, the publisher of the proceedings, has arranged for archival publication. The final version of the papers is hosted by SpringerLink, with active references and supplementary materials. It benefits all potential readers that we offer both a free and citeable version for all researchers, as well as an authoritative, citeable version for SpringerLink readers. Our thanks go to Ronan Nugent from Springer, who helped us negotiate this agreement. Last but not least, we wish to thank Eric Mortensen, our publication chair, whose expertise made the process smooth.

October 2022

Rita Cucchiara
Jiří Matas
Amnon Shashua
Lihi Zelnik-Manor

Preface

Welcome to the proceedings of the European Conference on Computer Vision (ECCV 2022). This was a hybrid edition of ECCV as we made our way out of the COVID-19 pandemic. The conference received 5804 valid paper submissions, compared to 5150 submissions to ECCV 2020 (a 12.7% increase) and 2439 in ECCV 2018. 1645 submissions were accepted for publication (28%) and, of those, 157 (2.7% overall) as orals.

846 of the submissions were desk-rejected for various reasons. Many of them because they revealed author identity, thus violating the double-blind policy. This violation came in many forms: some had author names with the title, others added acknowledgments to specific grants, yet others had links to their github account where their name was visible. Tampering with the LaTeX template was another reason for automatic desk rejection.

ECCV 2022 used the traditional CMT system to manage the entire double-blind reviewing process. Authors did not know the names of the reviewers and vice versa. Each paper received at least 3 reviews (except 6 papers that received only 2 reviews), totalling more than 15,000 reviews.

Handling the review process at this scale was a significant challenge. To ensure that each submission received as fair and high-quality reviews as possible, we recruited more than 4719 reviewers (in the end, 4719 reviewers did at least one review). Similarly we recruited more than 276 area chairs (eventually, only 276 area chairs handled a batch of papers). The area chairs were selected based on their technical expertise and reputation, largely among people who served as area chairs in previous top computer vision and machine learning conferences (ECCV, ICCV, CVPR, NeurIPS, etc.).

Reviewers were similarly invited from previous conferences, and also from the pool of authors. We also encouraged experienced area chairs to suggest additional chairs and reviewers in the initial phase of recruiting. The median reviewer load was five papers per reviewer, while the average load was about four papers, because of the emergency reviewers. The area chair load was 35 papers, on average.

Conflicts of interest between authors, area chairs, and reviewers were handled largely automatically by the CMT platform, with some manual help from the Program Chairs. Reviewers were allowed to describe themselves as senior reviewer (load of 8 papers to review) or junior reviewers (load of 4 papers). Papers were matched to area chairs based on a subject-area affinity score computed in CMT and an affinity score computed by the Toronto Paper Matching System (TPMS). TPMS is based on the paper's full text. An area chair handling each submission would bid for preferred expert reviewers, and we balanced load and prevented conflicts.

The assignment of submissions to area chairs was relatively smooth, as was the assignment of submissions to reviewers. A small percentage of reviewers were not happy with their assignments in terms of subjects and self-reported expertise. This is an area for improvement, although it's interesting that many of these cases were reviewers hand-picked by AC's. We made a later round of reviewer recruiting, targeted at the list of authors of papers submitted to the conference, and had an excellent response which helped provide enough emergency reviewers. In the end, all but six papers received at least 3 reviews.

The challenges of the reviewing process are in line with past experiences at ECCV 2020. As the community grows, and the number of submissions increases, it becomes ever more challenging to recruit enough reviewers and ensure a high enough quality of reviews. Enlisting authors by default as reviewers might be one step to address this challenge.

Authors were given a week to rebut the initial reviews, and address reviewers' concerns. Each rebuttal was limited to a single pdf page with a fixed template.

The Area Chairs then led discussions with the reviewers on the merits of each submission. The goal was to reach consensus, but, ultimately, it was up to the Area Chair to make a decision. The decision was then discussed with a buddy Area Chair to make sure decisions were fair and informative. The entire process was conducted virtually with no in-person meetings taking place.

The Program Chairs were informed in cases where the Area Chairs overturned a decisive consensus reached by the reviewers, and pushed for the meta-reviews to contain details that explained the reasoning for such decisions. Obviously these were the most contentious cases, where reviewer inexperience was the most common reported factor.

Once the list of accepted papers was finalized and released, we went through the laborious process of plagiarism (including self-plagiarism) detection. A total of 4 accepted papers were rejected because of that.

Finally, we would like to thank our Technical Program Chair, Pavel Lifshits, who did tremendous work behind the scenes, and we thank the tireless CMT team.

October 2022

Gabriel Brostow
Giovanni Maria Farinella
Moustapha Cissé
Shai Avidan
Tal Hassner

Organization

General Chairs

Rita Cucchiara   University of Modena and Reggio Emilia, Italy
Jiří Matas   Czech Technical University in Prague, Czech
                                   Republic
Amnon Shashua   Hebrew University of Jerusalem, Israel
Lihi Zelnik-Manor   Technion – Israel Institute of Technology, Israel

Program Chairs

Shai Avidan   Tel-Aviv University, Israel
Gabriel Brostow   University College London, UK
Moustapha Cissé   Google AI, Ghana
Giovanni Maria Farinella   University of Catania, Italy
Tal Hassner   Facebook AI, USA

Program Technical Chair

Pavel Lifshits   Technion – Israel Institute of Technology, Israel

Workshops Chairs

Leonid Karlinsky   IBM Research, Israel
Tomer Michaeli   Technion – Israel Institute of Technology, Israel
Ko Nishino   Kyoto University, Japan

Tutorial Chairs

Thomas Pock   Graz University of Technology, Austria
Natalia Neverova   Facebook AI Research, UK

Demo Chair

Bohyung Han   Seoul National University, Korea

Social and Student Activities Chairs

Tatiana Tommasi	Italian Institute of Technology, Italy
Sagie Benaim	University of Copenhagen, Denmark

Diversity and Inclusion Chairs

Xi Yin	Facebook AI Research, USA
Bryan Russell	Adobe, USA

Communications Chairs

Lorenzo Baraldi	University of Modena and Reggio Emilia, Italy
Kosta Derpanis	York University & Samsung AI Centre Toronto, Canada

Industrial Liaison Chairs

Dimosthenis Karatzas	Universitat Autònoma de Barcelona, Spain
Chen Sagiv	SagivTech, Israel

Finance Chair

Gerard Medioni	University of Southern California & Amazon, USA

Publication Chair

Eric Mortensen	MiCROTEC, USA

Area Chairs

Lourdes Agapito	University College London, UK
Zeynep Akata	University of Tübingen, Germany
Naveed Akhtar	University of Western Australia, Australia
Karteek Alahari	Inria Grenoble Rhône-Alpes, France
Alexandre Alahi	École polytechnique fédérale de Lausanne, Switzerland
Pablo Arbelaez	Universidad de Los Andes, Columbia
Antonis A. Argyros	University of Crete & Foundation for Research and Technology-Hellas, Crete
Yuki M. Asano	University of Amsterdam, The Netherlands
Kalle Åström	Lund University, Sweden
Hadar Averbuch-Elor	Cornell University, USA

Hossein Azizpour	KTH Royal Institute of Technology, Sweden
Vineeth N. Balasubramanian	Indian Institute of Technology, Hyderabad, India
Lamberto Ballan	University of Padova, Italy
Adrien Bartoli	Université Clermont Auvergne, France
Horst Bischof	Graz University of Technology, Austria
Matthew B. Blaschko	KU Leuven, Belgium
Federica Bogo	Meta Reality Labs Research, Switzerland
Katherine Bouman	California Institute of Technology, USA
Edmond Boyer	Inria Grenoble Rhône-Alpes, France
Michael S. Brown	York University, Canada
Vittorio Caggiano	Meta AI Research, USA
Neill Campbell	University of Bath, UK
Octavia Camps	Northeastern University, USA
Duygu Ceylan	Adobe Research, USA
Ayan Chakrabarti	Google Research, USA
Tat-Jen Cham	Nanyang Technological University, Singapore
Antoni Chan	City University of Hong Kong, Hong Kong, China
Manmohan Chandraker	NEC Labs America, USA
Xinlei Chen	Facebook AI Research, USA
Xilin Chen	Institute of Computing Technology, Chinese Academy of Sciences, China
Dongdong Chen	Microsoft Cloud AI, USA
Chen Chen	University of Central Florida, USA
Ondrej Chum	Vision Recognition Group, Czech Technical University in Prague, Czech Republic
John Collomosse	Adobe Research & University of Surrey, UK
Camille Couprie	Facebook, France
David Crandall	Indiana University, USA
Daniel Cremers	Technical University of Munich, Germany
Marco Cristani	University of Verona, Italy
Canton Cristian	Facebook AI Research, USA
Dengxin Dai	ETH Zurich, Switzerland
Dima Damen	University of Bristol, UK
Kostas Daniilidis	University of Pennsylvania, USA
Trevor Darrell	University of California, Berkeley, USA
Andrew Davison	Imperial College London, UK
Tali Dekel	Weizmann Institute of Science, Israel
Alessio Del Bue	Istituto Italiano di Tecnologia, Italy
Weihong Deng	Beijing University of Posts and Telecommunications, China
Konstantinos Derpanis	Ryerson University, Canada
Carl Doersch	DeepMind, UK

Matthijs Douze	Facebook AI Research, USA
Mohamed Elhoseiny	King Abdullah University of Science and Technology, Saudi Arabia
Sergio Escalera	University of Barcelona, Spain
Yi Fang	New York University, USA
Ryan Farrell	Brigham Young University, USA
Alireza Fathi	Google, USA
Christoph Feichtenhofer	Facebook AI Research, USA
Basura Fernando	Agency for Science, Technology and Research (A*STAR), Singapore
Vittorio Ferrari	Google Research, Switzerland
Andrew W. Fitzgibbon	Graphcore, UK
David J. Fleet	University of Toronto, Canada
David Forsyth	University of Illinois at Urbana-Champaign, USA
David Fouhey	University of Michigan, USA
Katerina Fragkiadaki	Carnegie Mellon University, USA
Friedrich Fraundorfer	Graz University of Technology, Austria
Oren Freifeld	Ben-Gurion University, Israel
Thomas Funkhouser	Google Research & Princeton University, USA
Yasutaka Furukawa	Simon Fraser University, Canada
Fabio Galasso	Sapienza University of Rome, Italy
Jürgen Gall	University of Bonn, Germany
Chuang Gan	Massachusetts Institute of Technology, USA
Zhe Gan	Microsoft, USA
Animesh Garg	University of Toronto, Vector Institute, Nvidia, Canada
Efstratios Gavves	University of Amsterdam, The Netherlands
Peter Gehler	Amazon, Germany
Theo Gevers	University of Amsterdam, The Netherlands
Bernard Ghanem	King Abdullah University of Science and Technology, Saudi Arabia
Ross B. Girshick	Facebook AI Research, USA
Georgia Gkioxari	Facebook AI Research, USA
Albert Gordo	Facebook, USA
Stephen Gould	Australian National University, Australia
Venu Madhav Govindu	Indian Institute of Science, India
Kristen Grauman	Facebook AI Research & UT Austin, USA
Abhinav Gupta	Carnegie Mellon University & Facebook AI Research, USA
Mohit Gupta	University of Wisconsin-Madison, USA
Hu Han	Institute of Computing Technology, Chinese Academy of Sciences, China

Bohyung Han	Seoul National University, Korea
Tian Han	Stevens Institute of Technology, USA
Emily Hand	University of Nevada, Reno, USA
Bharath Hariharan	Cornell University, USA
Ran He	Institute of Automation, Chinese Academy of Sciences, China
Otmar Hilliges	ETH Zurich, Switzerland
Adrian Hilton	University of Surrey, UK
Minh Hoai	Stony Brook University, USA
Yedid Hoshen	Hebrew University of Jerusalem, Israel
Timothy Hospedales	University of Edinburgh, UK
Gang Hua	Wormpex AI Research, USA
Di Huang	Beihang University, China
Jing Huang	Facebook, USA
Jia-Bin Huang	Facebook, USA
Nathan Jacobs	Washington University in St. Louis, USA
C. V. Jawahar	International Institute of Information Technology, Hyderabad, India
Herve Jegou	Facebook AI Research, France
Neel Joshi	Microsoft Research, USA
Armand Joulin	Facebook AI Research, France
Frederic Jurie	University of Caen Normandie, France
Fredrik Kahl	Chalmers University of Technology, Sweden
Yannis Kalantidis	NAVER LABS Europe, France
Evangelos Kalogerakis	University of Massachusetts, Amherst, USA
Sing Bing Kang	Zillow Group, USA
Yosi Keller	Bar Ilan University, Israel
Margret Keuper	University of Mannheim, Germany
Tae-Kyun Kim	Imperial College London, UK
Benjamin Kimia	Brown University, USA
Alexander Kirillov	Facebook AI Research, USA
Kris Kitani	Carnegie Mellon University, USA
Iasonas Kokkinos	Snap Inc. & University College London, UK
Vladlen Koltun	Apple, USA
Nikos Komodakis	University of Crete, Crete
Piotr Koniusz	Australian National University, Australia
Philipp Kraehenbuehl	University of Texas at Austin, USA
Dilip Krishnan	Google, USA
Ajay Kumar	Hong Kong Polytechnic University, Hong Kong, China
Junseok Kwon	Chung-Ang University, Korea
Jean-Francois Lalonde	Université Laval, Canada

Ivan Laptev	Inria Paris, France
Laura Leal-Taixé	Technical University of Munich, Germany
Erik Learned-Miller	University of Massachusetts, Amherst, USA
Gim Hee Lee	National University of Singapore, Singapore
Seungyong Lee	Pohang University of Science and Technology, Korea
Zhen Lei	Institute of Automation, Chinese Academy of Sciences, China
Bastian Leibe	RWTH Aachen University, Germany
Hongdong Li	Australian National University, Australia
Fuxin Li	Oregon State University, USA
Bo Li	University of Illinois at Urbana-Champaign, USA
Yin Li	University of Wisconsin-Madison, USA
Ser-Nam Lim	Meta AI Research, USA
Joseph Lim	University of Southern California, USA
Stephen Lin	Microsoft Research Asia, China
Dahua Lin	The Chinese University of Hong Kong, Hong Kong, China
Si Liu	Beihang University, China
Xiaoming Liu	Michigan State University, USA
Ce Liu	Microsoft, USA
Zicheng Liu	Microsoft, USA
Yanxi Liu	Pennsylvania State University, USA
Feng Liu	Portland State University, USA
Yebin Liu	Tsinghua University, China
Chen Change Loy	Nanyang Technological University, Singapore
Huchuan Lu	Dalian University of Technology, China
Cewu Lu	Shanghai Jiao Tong University, China
Oisin Mac Aodha	University of Edinburgh, UK
Dhruv Mahajan	Facebook, USA
Subhransu Maji	University of Massachusetts, Amherst, USA
Atsuto Maki	KTH Royal Institute of Technology, Sweden
Arun Mallya	NVIDIA, USA
R. Manmatha	Amazon, USA
Iacopo Masi	Sapienza University of Rome, Italy
Dimitris N. Metaxas	Rutgers University, USA
Ajmal Mian	University of Western Australia, Australia
Christian Micheloni	University of Udine, Italy
Krystian Mikolajczyk	Imperial College London, UK
Anurag Mittal	Indian Institute of Technology, Madras, India
Philippos Mordohai	Stevens Institute of Technology, USA
Greg Mori	Simon Fraser University & Borealis AI, Canada

Vittorio Murino   Istituto Italiano di Tecnologia, Italy
P. J. Narayanan   International Institute of Information Technology,
                                    Hyderabad, India
Ram Nevatia   University of Southern California, USA
Natalia Neverova   Facebook AI Research, UK
Richard Newcombe   Facebook, USA
Cuong V. Nguyen   Florida International University, USA
Bingbing Ni   Shanghai Jiao Tong University, China
Juan Carlos Niebles   Salesforce & Stanford University, USA
Ko Nishino   Kyoto University, Japan
Jean-Marc Odobez   Idiap Research Institute, École polytechnique
                                    fédérale de Lausanne, Switzerland
Francesca Odone   University of Genova, Italy
Takayuki Okatani   Tohoku University & RIKEN Center for
                                    Advanced Intelligence Project, Japan
Manohar Paluri   Facebook, USA
Guan Pang   Facebook, USA
Maja Pantic   Imperial College London, UK
Sylvain Paris   Adobe Research, USA
Jaesik Park   Pohang University of Science and Technology,
                                    Korea
Hyun Soo Park   The University of Minnesota, USA
Omkar M. Parkhi   Facebook, USA
Deepak Pathak   Carnegie Mellon University, USA
Georgios Pavlakos   University of California, Berkeley, USA
Marcello Pelillo   University of Venice, Italy
Marc Pollefeys   ETH Zurich & Microsoft, Switzerland
Jean Ponce   Inria, France
Gerard Pons-Moll   University of Tübingen, Germany
Fatih Porikli   Qualcomm, USA
Victor Adrian Prisacariu   University of Oxford, UK
Petia Radeva   University of Barcelona, Spain
Ravi Ramamoorthi   University of California, San Diego, USA
Deva Ramanan   Carnegie Mellon University, USA
Vignesh Ramanathan   Facebook, USA
Nalini Ratha   State University of New York at Buffalo, USA
Tammy Riklin Raviv   Ben-Gurion University, Israel
Tobias Ritschel   University College London, UK
Emanuele Rodola   Sapienza University of Rome, Italy
Amit K. Roy-Chowdhury   University of California, Riverside, USA
Michael Rubinstein   Google, USA
Olga Russakovsky   Princeton University, USA

Mathieu Salzmann	École polytechnique fédérale de Lausanne, Switzerland
Dimitris Samaras	Stony Brook University, USA
Aswin Sankaranarayanan	Carnegie Mellon University, USA
Imari Sato	National Institute of Informatics, Japan
Yoichi Sato	University of Tokyo, Japan
Shin'ichi Satoh	National Institute of Informatics, Japan
Walter Scheirer	University of Notre Dame, USA
Bernt Schiele	Max Planck Institute for Informatics, Germany
Konrad Schindler	ETH Zurich, Switzerland
Cordelia Schmid	Inria & Google, France
Alexander Schwing	University of Illinois at Urbana-Champaign, USA
Nicu Sebe	University of Trento, Italy
Greg Shakhnarovich	Toyota Technological Institute at Chicago, USA
Eli Shechtman	Adobe Research, USA
Humphrey Shi	University of Oregon & University of Illinois at Urbana-Champaign & Picsart AI Research, USA
Jianbo Shi	University of Pennsylvania, USA
Roy Shilkrot	Massachusetts Institute of Technology, USA
Mike Zheng Shou	National University of Singapore, Singapore
Kaleem Siddiqi	McGill University, Canada
Richa Singh	Indian Institute of Technology Jodhpur, India
Greg Slabaugh	Queen Mary University of London, UK
Cees Snoek	University of Amsterdam, The Netherlands
Yale Song	Facebook AI Research, USA
Yi-Zhe Song	University of Surrey, UK
Bjorn Stenger	Rakuten Institute of Technology
Abby Stylianou	Saint Louis University, USA
Akihiro Sugimoto	National Institute of Informatics, Japan
Chen Sun	Brown University, USA
Deqing Sun	Google, USA
Kalyan Sunkavalli	Adobe Research, USA
Ying Tai	Tencent YouTu Lab, China
Ayellet Tal	Technion – Israel Institute of Technology, Israel
Ping Tan	Simon Fraser University, Canada
Siyu Tang	ETH Zurich, Switzerland
Chi-Keung Tang	Hong Kong University of Science and Technology, Hong Kong, China
Radu Timofte	University of Würzburg, Germany & ETH Zurich, Switzerland
Federico Tombari	Google, Switzerland & Technical University of Munich, Germany

Todd Zickler   Harvard University, USA
Wangmeng Zuo   Harbin Institute of Technology, China

Technical Program Committee

Davide Abati	Filippo Aleotti	Sinem Aslan
Soroush Abbasi	Konstantinos P.	Vishal Asnani
Koohpayegani	Alexandridis	Mahmoud Assran
Amos L. Abbott	Motasem Alfarra	Amir Atapour-Abarghouei
Rameen Abdal	Mohsen Ali	Nikos Athanasiou
Rabab Abdelfattah	Thiemo Alldieck	Ali Athar
Sahar Abdelnabi	Hadi Alzayer	ShahRukh Athar
Hassan Abu Alhaija	Liang An	Sara Atito
Abulikemu Abuduweili	Shan An	Souhaib Attaiki
Ron Abutbul	Yi An	Matan Atzmon
Hanno Ackermann	Zhulin An	Mathieu Aubry
Aikaterini Adam	Dongsheng An	Nicolas Audebert
Kamil Adamczewski	Jie An	Tristan T.
Ehsan Adeli	Xiang An	Aumentado-Armstrong
Vida Adeli	Saket Anand	Melinos Averkiou
Donald Adjeroh	Cosmin Ancuti	Yannis Avrithis
Arman Afrasiyabi	Juan Andrade-Cetto	Stephane Ayache
Akshay Agarwal	Alexander Andreopoulos	Mehmet Aygün
Sameer Agarwal	Bjoern Andres	Seyed Mehdi
Abhinav Agarwalla	Jerone T. A. Andrews	Ayyoubzadeh
Vaibhav Aggarwal	Shivangi Aneja	Hossein Azizpour
Sara Aghajanzadeh	Anelia Angelova	George Azzopardi
Susmit Agrawal	Dragomir Anguelov	Mallikarjun B. R.
Antonio Agudo	Rushil Anirudh	Yunhao Ba
Touqeer Ahmad	Oron Anschel	Abhishek Badki
Sk Miraj Ahmed	Rao Muhammad Anwer	Seung-Hwan Bae
Chaitanya Ahuja	Djamila Aouada	Seung-Hwan Baek
Nilesh A. Ahuja	Evlampios Apostolidis	Seungryul Baek
Abhishek Aich	Srikar Appalaraju	Piyush Nitin Bagad
Shubhra Aich	Nikita Araslanov	Shai Bagon
Noam Aigerman	Andre Araujo	Gaetan Bahl
Arash Akbarinia	Eric Arazo	Shikhar Bahl
Peri Akiva	Dawit Mureja Argaw	Sherwin Bahmani
Derya Akkaynak	Anurag Arnab	Haoran Bai
Emre Aksan	Aditya Arora	Lei Bai
Arjun R. Akula	Chetan Arora	Jiawang Bai
Yuval Alaluf	Sunpreet S. Arora	Haoyue Bai
Stephan Alaniz	Alexey Artemov	Jinbin Bai
Paul Albert	Muhammad Asad	Xiang Bai
Cenek Albl	Kumar Ashutosh	Xuyang Bai

Yang Bai
Yuanchao Bai
Ziqian Bai
Sungyong Baik
Kevin Bailly
Max Bain
Federico Baldassarre
Wele Gedara Chaminda
  Bandara
Biplab Banerjee
Pratyay Banerjee
Sandipan Banerjee
Jihwan Bang
Antyanta Bangunharcana
Aayush Bansal
Ankan Bansal
Siddhant Bansal
Wentao Bao
Zhipeng Bao
Amir Bar
Manel Baradad Jurjo
Lorenzo Baraldi
Danny Barash
Daniel Barath
Connelly Barnes
Ioan Andrei Bârsan
Steven Basart
Dina Bashkirova
Chaim Baskin
Peyman Bateni
Anil Batra
Sebastiano Battiato
Ardhendu Behera
Harkirat Behl
Jens Behley
Vasileios Belagiannis
Boulbaba Ben Amor
Emanuel Ben Baruch
Abdessamad Ben Hamza
Gil Ben-Artzi
Assia Benbihi
Fabian Benitez-Quiroz
Guy Ben-Yosef
Philipp Benz
Alexander W. Bergman

Urs Bergmann
Jesus Bermudez-Cameo
Stefano Berretti
Gedas Bertasius
Zachary Bessinger
Petra Bevandić
Matthew Beveridge
Lucas Beyer
Yash Bhalgat
Suvaansh Bhambri
Samarth Bharadwaj
Gaurav Bharaj
Aparna Bharati
Bharat Lal Bhatnagar
Uttaran Bhattacharya
Apratim Bhattacharyya
Brojeshwar Bhowmick
Ankan Kumar Bhunia
Ayan Kumar Bhunia
Qi Bi
Sai Bi
Michael Bi Mi
Gui-Bin Bian
Jia-Wang Bian
Shaojun Bian
Pia Bideau
Mario Bijelic
Hakan Bilen
Guillaume-Alexandre
  Bilodeau
Alexander Binder
Tolga Birdal
Vighnesh N. Birodkar
Sandika Biswas
Andreas Blattmann
Janusz Bobulski
Giuseppe Boccignone
Vishnu Boddeti
Navaneeth Bodla
Moritz Böhle
Aleksei Bokhovkin
Sam Bond-Taylor
Vivek Boominathan
Shubhankar Borse
Mark Boss

Andrea Bottino
Adnane Boukhayma
Fadi Boutros
Nicolas C. Boutry
Richard S. Bowen
Ivaylo Boyadzhiev
Aidan Boyd
Yuri Boykov
Aljaz Bozic
Behzad Bozorgtabar
Eric Brachmann
Samarth Brahmbhatt
Gustav Bredell
Francois Bremond
Joel Brogan
Andrew Brown
Thomas Brox
Marcus A. Brubaker
Robert-Jan Bruintjes
Yuqi Bu
Anders G. Buch
Himanshu Buckchash
Mateusz Buda
Ignas Budvytis
José M. Buenaposada
Marcel C. Bühler
Tu Bui
Adrian Bulat
Hannah Bull
Evgeny Burnaev
Andrei Bursuc
Benjamin Busam
Sergey N. Buzykanov
Wonmin Byeon
Fabian Caba
Martin Cadik
Guanyu Cai
Minjie Cai
Qing Cai
Zhongang Cai
Qi Cai
Yancheng Cai
Shen Cai
Han Cai
Jiarui Cai

Bowen Cai
Mu Cai
Qin Cai
Ruojin Cai
Weidong Cai
Weiwei Cai
Yi Cai
Yujun Cai
Zhiping Cai
Akin Caliskan
Lilian Calvet
Baris Can Cam
Necati Cihan Camgoz
Tommaso Campari
Dylan Campbell
Ziang Cao
Ang Cao
Xu Cao
Zhiwen Cao
Shengcao Cao
Song Cao
Weipeng Cao
Xiangyong Cao
Xiaochun Cao
Yue Cao
Yunhao Cao
Zhangjie Cao
Jiale Cao
Yang Cao
Jiajiong Cao
Jie Cao
Jinkun Cao
Lele Cao
Yulong Cao
Zhiguo Cao
Chen Cao
Razvan Caramalau
Marlène Careil
Gustavo Carneiro
Joao Carreira
Dan Casas
Paola Cascante-Bonilla
Angela Castillo
Francisco M. Castro
Pedro Castro

Luca Cavalli
George J. Cazenavette
Oya Celiktutan
Hakan Cevikalp
Sri Harsha C. H.
Sungmin Cha
Geonho Cha
Menglei Chai
Lucy Chai
Yuning Chai
Zenghao Chai
Anirban Chakraborty
Deep Chakraborty
Rudrasis Chakraborty
Souradeep Chakraborty
Kelvin C. K. Chan
Chee Seng Chan
Paramanand Chandramouli
Arjun Chandrasekaran
Kenneth Chaney
Dongliang Chang
Huiwen Chang
Peng Chang
Xiaojun Chang
Jia-Ren Chang
Hyung Jin Chang
Hyun Sung Chang
Ju Yong Chang
Li-Jen Chang
Qi Chang
Wei-Yi Chang
Yi Chang
Nadine Chang
Hanqing Chao
Pradyumna Chari
Dibyadip Chatterjee
Chiranjoy Chattopadhyay
Siddhartha Chaudhuri
Zhengping Che
Gal Chechik
Lianggangxu Chen
Qi Alfred Chen
Brian Chen
Bor-Chun Chen
Bo-Hao Chen

Bohong Chen
Bin Chen
Ziliang Chen
Cheng Chen
Chen Chen
Chaofeng Chen
Xi Chen
Haoyu Chen
Xuanhong Chen
Wei Chen
Qiang Chen
Shi Chen
Xianyu Chen
Chang Chen
Changhuai Chen
Hao Chen
Jie Chen
Jianbo Chen
Jingjing Chen
Jun Chen
Kejiang Chen
Mingcai Chen
Nenglun Chen
Qifeng Chen
Ruoyu Chen
Shu-Yu Chen
Weidong Chen
Weijie Chen
Weikai Chen
Xiang Chen
Xiuyi Chen
Xingyu Chen
Yaofo Chen
Yueting Chen
Yu Chen
Yunjin Chen
Yuntao Chen
Yun Chen
Zhenfang Chen
Zhuangzhuang Chen
Chu-Song Chen
Xiangyu Chen
Zhuo Chen
Chaoqi Chen
Shizhe Chen

Xiaotong Chen
Xiaozhi Chen
Dian Chen
Defang Chen
Dingfan Chen
Ding-Jie Chen
Ee Heng Chen
Tao Chen
Yixin Chen
Wei-Ting Chen
Lin Chen
Guang Chen
Guangyi Chen
Guanying Chen
Guangyao Chen
Hwann-Tzong Chen
Junwen Chen
Jiacheng Chen
Jianxu Chen
Hui Chen
Kai Chen
Kan Chen
Kevin Chen
Kuan-Wen Chen
Weihua Chen
Zhang Chen
Liang-Chieh Chen
Lele Chen
Liang Chen
Fanglin Chen
Zehui Chen
Minghui Chen
Minghao Chen
Xiaokang Chen
Qian Chen
Jun-Cheng Chen
Qi Chen
Qingcai Chen
Richard J. Chen
Runnan Chen
Rui Chen
Shuo Chen
Sentao Chen
Shaoyu Chen
Shixing Chen

Shuai Chen
Shuya Chen
Sizhe Chen
Simin Chen
Shaoxiang Chen
Zitian Chen
Tianlong Chen
Tianshui Chen
Min-Hung Chen
Xiangning Chen
Xin Chen
Xinghao Chen
Xuejin Chen
Xu Chen
Xuxi Chen
Yunlu Chen
Yanbei Chen
Yuxiao Chen
Yun-Chun Chen
Yi-Ting Chen
Yi-Wen Chen
Yinbo Chen
Yiran Chen
Yuanhong Chen
Yubei Chen
Yuefeng Chen
Yuhua Chen
Yukang Chen
Zerui Chen
Zhaoyu Chen
Zhen Chen
Zhenyu Chen
Zhi Chen
Zhiwei Chen
Zhixiang Chen
Long Chen
Bowen Cheng
Jun Cheng
Yi Cheng
Jingchun Cheng
Lechao Cheng
Xi Cheng
Yuan Cheng
Ho Kei Cheng
Kevin Ho Man Cheng

Jiacheng Cheng
Kelvin B. Cheng
Li Cheng
Mengjun Cheng
Zhen Cheng
Qingrong Cheng
Tianheng Cheng
Harry Cheng
Yihua Cheng
Yu Cheng
Ziheng Cheng
Soon Yau Cheong
Anoop Cherian
Manuela Chessa
Zhixiang Chi
Naoki Chiba
Julian Chibane
Kashyap Chitta
Tai-Yin Chiu
Hsu-kuang Chiu
Wei-Chen Chiu
Sungmin Cho
Donghyeon Cho
Hyeon Cho
Yooshin Cho
Gyusang Cho
Jang Hyun Cho
Seungju Cho
Nam Ik Cho
Sunghyun Cho
Hanbyel Cho
Jaesung Choe
Jooyoung Choi
Chiho Choi
Changwoon Choi
Jongwon Choi
Myungsub Choi
Dooseop Choi
Jonghyun Choi
Jinwoo Choi
Jun Won Choi
Min-Kook Choi
Hongsuk Choi
Janghoon Choi
Yoon-Ho Choi

Yukyung Choi
Jaegul Choo
Ayush Chopra
Siddharth Choudhary
Subhabrata Choudhury
Vasileios Choutas
Ka-Ho Chow
Pinaki Nath Chowdhury
Sammy Christen
Anders Christensen
Grigorios Chrysos
Hang Chu
Wen-Hsuan Chu
Peng Chu
Qi Chu
Ruihang Chu
Wei-Ta Chu
Yung-Yu Chuang
Sanghyuk Chun
Se Young Chun
Antonio Cinà
Ramazan Gokberk Cinbis
Javier Civera
Albert Clapés
Ronald Clark
Brian S. Clipp
Felipe Codevilla
Daniel Coelho de Castro
Niv Cohen
Forrester Cole
Maxwell D. Collins
Robert T. Collins
Marc Comino Trinidad
Runmin Cong
Wenyan Cong
Maxime Cordy
Marcella Cornia
Enric Corona
Huseyin Coskun
Luca Cosmo
Dragos Costea
Davide Cozzolino
Arun C. S. Kumar
Aiyu Cui
Qiongjie Cui

Quan Cui
Shuhao Cui
Yiming Cui
Ying Cui
Zijun Cui
Jiali Cui
Jiequan Cui
Yawen Cui
Zhen Cui
Zhaopeng Cui
Jack Culpepper
Xiaodong Cun
Ross Cutler
Adam Czajka
Ali Dabouei
Konstantinos M. Dafnis
Manuel Dahnert
Tao Dai
Yuchao Dai
Bo Dai
Mengyu Dai
Hang Dai
Haixing Dai
Peng Dai
Pingyang Dai
Qi Dai
Qiyu Dai
Yutong Dai
Naser Damer
Zhiyuan Dang
Mohamed Daoudi
Ayan Das
Abir Das
Debasmit Das
Deepayan Das
Partha Das
Sagnik Das
Soumi Das
Srijan Das
Swagatam Das
Avijit Dasgupta
Jim Davis
Adrian K. Davison
Homa Davoudi
Laura Daza

Matthias De Lange
Shalini De Mello
Marco De Nadai
Christophe De
    Vleeschouwer
Alp Dener
Boyang Deng
Congyue Deng
Bailin Deng
Yong Deng
Ye Deng
Zhuo Deng
Zhijie Deng
Xiaoming Deng
Jiankang Deng
Jinhong Deng
Jingjing Deng
Liang-Jian Deng
Siqi Deng
Xiang Deng
Xueqing Deng
Zhongying Deng
Karan Desai
Jean-Emmanuel Deschaud
Aniket Anand Deshmukh
Neel Dey
Helisa Dhamo
Prithviraj Dhar
Amaya Dharmasiri
Yan Di
Xing Di
Ousmane A. Dia
Haiwen Diao
Xiaolei Diao
Gonçalo José Dias Pais
Abdallah Dib
Anastasios Dimou
Changxing Ding
Henghui Ding
Guodong Ding
Yaqing Ding
Shuangrui Ding
Yuhang Ding
Yikang Ding
Shouhong Ding

Haisong Ding
Hui Ding
Jiahao Ding
Jian Ding
Jian-Jiun Ding
Shuxiao Ding
Tianyu Ding
Wenhao Ding
Yuqi Ding
Yi Ding
Yuzhen Ding
Zhengming Ding
Tan Minh Dinh
Vu Dinh
Christos Diou
Mandar Dixit
Bao Gia Doan
Khoa D. Doan
Dzung Anh Doan
Debi Prosad Dogra
Nehal Doiphode
Chengdong Dong
Bowen Dong
Zhenxing Dong
Hang Dong
Xiaoyi Dong
Haoye Dong
Jiangxin Dong
Shichao Dong
Xuan Dong
Zhen Dong
Shuting Dong
Jing Dong
Li Dong
Ming Dong
Nanqing Dong
Qiulei Dong
Runpei Dong
Siyan Dong
Tian Dong
Wei Dong
Xiaomeng Dong
Xin Dong
Xingbo Dong
Yuan Dong

Samuel Dooley
Gianfranco Doretto
Michael Dorkenwald
Keval Doshi
Zhaopeng Dou
Xiaotian Dou
Hazel Doughty
Ahmad Droby
Iddo Drori
Jie Du
Yong Du
Dawei Du
Dong Du
Ruoyi Du
Yuntao Du
Xuefeng Du
Yilun Du
Yuming Du
Radhika Dua
Haodong Duan
Jiafei Duan
Kaiwen Duan
Peiqi Duan
Ye Duan
Haoran Duan
Jiali Duan
Amanda Duarte
Abhimanyu Dubey
Shiv Ram Dubey
Florian Dubost
Lukasz Dudziak
Shivam Duggal
Justin M. Dulay
Matteo Dunnhofer
Chi Nhan Duong
Thibaut Durand
Mihai Dusmanu
Ujjal Kr Dutta
Debidatta Dwibedi
Isht Dwivedi
Sai Kumar Dwivedi
Takeharu Eda
Mark Edmonds
Alexei A. Efros
Thibaud Ehret

Max Ehrlich
Mahsa Ehsanpour
Iván Eichhardt
Farshad Einabadi
Marvin Eisenberger
Hazim Kemal Ekenel
Mohamed El Banani
Ismail Elezi
Moshe Eliasof
Alaa El-Nouby
Ian Endres
Francis Engelmann
Deniz Engin
Chanho Eom
Dave Epstein
Maria C. Escobar
Victor A. Escorcia
Carlos Esteves
Sungmin Eum
Bernard J. E. Evans
Ivan Evtimov
Fevziye Irem Eyiokur
    Yaman
Matteo Fabbri
Sébastien Fabbro
Gabriele Facciolo
Masud Fahim
Bin Fan
Hehe Fan
Deng-Ping Fan
Aoxiang Fan
Chen-Chen Fan
Qi Fan
Zhaoxin Fan
Haoqi Fan
Heng Fan
Hongyi Fan
Linxi Fan
Baojie Fan
Jiayuan Fan
Lei Fan
Quanfu Fan
Yonghui Fan
Yingruo Fan
Zhiwen Fan

Zicong Fan
Sean Fanello
Jiansheng Fang
Chaowei Fang
Yuming Fang
Jianwu Fang
Jin Fang
Qi Fang
Shancheng Fang
Tian Fang
Xianyong Fang
Gongfan Fang
Zhen Fang
Hui Fang
Jiemin Fang
Le Fang
Pengfei Fang
Xiaolin Fang
Yuxin Fang
Zhaoyuan Fang
Ammarah Farooq
Azade Farshad
Zhengcong Fei
Michael Felsberg
Wei Feng
Chen Feng
Fan Feng
Andrew Feng
Xin Feng
Zheyun Feng
Ruicheng Feng
Mingtao Feng
Qianyu Feng
Shangbin Feng
Chun-Mei Feng
Zunlei Feng
Zhiyong Feng
Martin Fergie
Mustansar Fiaz
Marco Fiorucci
Michael Firman
Hamed Firooz
Volker Fischer
Corneliu O. Florea
Georgios Floros

Wolfgang Foerstner
Gianni Franchi
Jean-Sebastien Franco
Simone Frintrop
Anna Fruehstueck
Changhong Fu
Chaoyou Fu
Cheng-Yang Fu
Chi-Wing Fu
Deqing Fu
Huan Fu
Jun Fu
Kexue Fu
Ying Fu
Jianlong Fu
Jingjing Fu
Qichen Fu
Tsu-Jui Fu
Xueyang Fu
Yang Fu
Yanwei Fu
Yonggan Fu
Wolfgang Fuhl
Yasuhisa Fujii
Kent Fujiwara
Marco Fumero
Takuya Funatomi
Isabel Funke
Dario Fuoli
Antonino Furnari
Matheus A. Gadelha
Akshay Gadi Patil
Adrian Galdran
Guillermo Gallego
Silvano Galliani
Orazio Gallo
Leonardo Galteri
Matteo Gamba
Yiming Gan
Sujoy Ganguly
Harald Ganster
Boyan Gao
Changxin Gao
Daiheng Gao
Difei Gao

Chen Gao
Fei Gao
Lin Gao
Wei Gao
Yiming Gao
Junyu Gao
Guangyu Ryan Gao
Haichang Gao
Hongchang Gao
Jialin Gao
Jin Gao
Jun Gao
Katelyn Gao
Mingchen Gao
Mingfei Gao
Pan Gao
Shangqian Gao
Shanghua Gao
Xitong Gao
Yunhe Gao
Zhanning Gao
Elena Garces
Nuno Cruz Garcia
Noa Garcia
Guillermo
    Garcia-Hernando
Isha Garg
Rahul Garg
Sourav Garg
Quentin Garrido
Stefano Gasperini
Kent Gauen
Chandan Gautam
Shivam Gautam
Paul Gay
Chunjiang Ge
Shiming Ge
Wenhang Ge
Yanhao Ge
Zheng Ge
Songwei Ge
Weifeng Ge
Yixiao Ge
Yuying Ge
Shijie Geng

Zhengyang Geng
Kyle A. Genova
Georgios Georgakis
Markos Georgopoulos
Marcel Geppert
Shabnam Ghadar
Mina Ghadimi Atigh
Deepti Ghadiyaram
Maani Ghaffari Jadidi
Sedigh Ghamari
Zahra Gharaee
Michaël Gharbi
Golnaz Ghiasi
Reza Ghoddoosian
Soumya Suvra Ghosal
Adhiraj Ghosh
Arthita Ghosh
Pallabi Ghosh
Soumyadeep Ghosh
Andrew Gilbert
Igor Gilitschenski
Jhony H. Giraldo
Andreu Girbau Xalabarder
Rohit Girdhar
Sharath Girish
Xavier Giro-i-Nieto
Raja Giryes
Thomas Gittings
Nikolaos Gkanatsios
Ioannis Gkioulekas
Abhiram
   Gnanasambandam
Aurele T. Gnanha
Clement L. J. C. Godard
Arushi Goel
Vidit Goel
Shubham Goel
Zan Gojcic
Aaron K. Gokaslan
Tejas Gokhale
S. Alireza Golestaneh
Thiago L. Gomes
Nuno Goncalves
Boqing Gong
Chen Gong

Yuanhao Gong
Guoqiang Gong
Jingyu Gong
Rui Gong
Yu Gong
Mingming Gong
Neil Zhenqiang Gong
Xun Gong
Yunye Gong
Yihong Gong
Cristina I. González
Nithin Gopalakrishnan
   Nair
Gaurav Goswami
Jianping Gou
Shreyank N. Gowda
Ankit Goyal
Helmut Grabner
Patrick L. Grady
Ben Graham
Eric Granger
Douglas R. Gray
Matej Grcić
David Griffiths
Jinjin Gu
Yun Gu
Shuyang Gu
Jianyang Gu
Fuqiang Gu
Jiatao Gu
Jindong Gu
Jiaqi Gu
Jinwei Gu
Jiaxin Gu
Geonmo Gu
Xiao Gu
Xinqian Gu
Xiuye Gu
Yuming Gu
Zhangxuan Gu
Dayan Guan
Junfeng Guan
Qingji Guan
Tianrui Guan
Shanyan Guan

Denis A. Gudovskiy
Ricardo Guerrero
Pierre-Louis Guhur
Jie Gui
Liangyan Gui
Liangke Gui
Benoit Guillard
Erhan Gundogdu
Manuel Günther
Jingcai Guo
Yuanfang Guo
Junfeng Guo
Chenqi Guo
Dan Guo
Hongji Guo
Jia Guo
Jie Guo
Minghao Guo
Shi Guo
Yanhui Guo
Yangyang Guo
Yuan-Chen Guo
Yilu Guo
Yiluan Guo
Yong Guo
Guangyu Guo
Haiyun Guo
Jinyang Guo
Jianyuan Guo
Pengsheng Guo
Pengfei Guo
Shuxuan Guo
Song Guo
Tianyu Guo
Qing Guo
Qiushan Guo
Wen Guo
Xiefan Guo
Xiaohu Guo
Xiaoqing Guo
Yufei Guo
Yuhui Guo
Yuliang Guo
Yunhui Guo
Yanwen Guo

Akshita Gupta
Ankush Gupta
Kamal Gupta
Kartik Gupta
Ritwik Gupta
Rohit Gupta
Siddharth Gururani
Fredrik K. Gustafsson
Abner Guzman Rivera
Vladimir Guzov
Matthew A. Gwilliam
Jung-Woo Ha
Marc Habermann
Isma Hadji
Christian Haene
Martin Hahner
Levente Hajder
Alexandros Haliassos
Emanuela Haller
Bumsub Ham
Abdullah J. Hamdi
Shreyas Hampali
Dongyoon Han
Chunrui Han
Dong-Jun Han
Dong-Sig Han
Guangxing Han
Zhizhong Han
Ruize Han
Jiaming Han
Jin Han
Ligong Han
Xian-Hua Han
Xiaoguang Han
Yizeng Han
Zhi Han
Zhenjun Han
Zhongyi Han
Jungong Han
Junlin Han
Kai Han
Kun Han
Sungwon Han
Songfang Han
Wei Han

Xiao Han
Xintong Han
Xinzhe Han
Yahong Han
Yan Han
Zongbo Han
Nicolai Hani
Rana Hanocka
Niklas Hanselmann
Nicklas A. Hansen
Hong Hanyu
Fusheng Hao
Yanbin Hao
Shijie Hao
Udith Haputhanthri
Mehrtash Harandi
Josh Harguess
Adam Harley
David M. Hart
Atsushi Hashimoto
Ali Hassani
Mohammed Hassanin
Yana Hasson
Joakim Bruslund Haurum
Bo He
Kun He
Chen He
Xin He
Fazhi He
Gaoqi He
Hao He
Haoyu He
Jiangpeng He
Hongliang He
Qian He
Xiangteng He
Xuming He
Yannan He
Yuhang He
Yang He
Xiangyu He
Nanjun He
Pan He
Sen He
Shengfeng He

Songtao He
Tao He
Tong He
Wei He
Xuehai He
Xiaoxiao He
Ying He
Yisheng He
Ziwen He
Peter Hedman
Felix Heide
Yacov Hel-Or
Paul Henderson
Philipp Henzler
Byeongho Heo
Jae-Pil Heo
Miran Heo
Sachini A. Herath
Stephane Herbin
Pedro Hermosilla Casajus
Monica Hernandez
Charles Herrmann
Roei Herzig
Mauricio Hess-Flores
Carlos Hinojosa
Tobias Hinz
Tsubasa Hirakawa
Chih-Hui Ho
Lam Si Tung Ho
Jennifer Hobbs
Derek Hoiem
Yannick Hold-Geoffroy
Aleksander Holynski
Cheeun Hong
Fa-Ting Hong
Hanbin Hong
Guan Zhe Hong
Danfeng Hong
Lanqing Hong
Xiaopeng Hong
Xin Hong
Jie Hong
Seungbum Hong
Cheng-Yao Hong
Seunghoon Hong

Yi Hong
Yuan Hong
Yuchen Hong
Anthony Hoogs
Maxwell C. Horton
Kazuhiro Hotta
Qibin Hou
Tingbo Hou
Junhui Hou
Ji Hou
Qiqi Hou
Rui Hou
Ruibing Hou
Zhi Hou
Henry Howard-Jenkins
Lukas Hoyer
Wei-Lin Hsiao
Chiou-Ting Hsu
Anthony Hu
Brian Hu
Yusong Hu
Hexiang Hu
Haoji Hu
Di Hu
Hengtong Hu
Haigen Hu
Lianyu Hu
Hanzhe Hu
Jie Hu
Junlin Hu
Shizhe Hu
Jian Hu
Zhiming Hu
Juhua Hu
Peng Hu
Ping Hu
Ronghang Hu
MengShun Hu
Tao Hu
Vincent Tao Hu
Xiaoling Hu
Xinting Hu
Xiaolin Hu
Xuefeng Hu
Xiaowei Hu

Yang Hu
Yueyu Hu
Zeyu Hu
Zhongyun Hu
Binh-Son Hua
Guoliang Hua
Yi Hua
Linzhi Huang
Qiusheng Huang
Bo Huang
Chen Huang
Hsin-Ping Huang
Ye Huang
Shuangping Huang
Zeng Huang
Buzhen Huang
Cong Huang
Heng Huang
Hao Huang
Qidong Huang
Huaibo Huang
Chaoqin Huang
Feihu Huang
Jiahui Huang
Jingjia Huang
Kun Huang
Lei Huang
Sheng Huang
Shuaiyi Huang
Siyu Huang
Xiaoshui Huang
Xiaoyang Huang
Yan Huang
Yihao Huang
Ying Huang
Ziling Huang
Xiaoke Huang
Yifei Huang
Haiyang Huang
Zhewei Huang
Jin Huang
Haibin Huang
Jiaxing Huang
Junjie Huang
Keli Huang

Lang Huang
Lin Huang
Luojie Huang
Mingzhen Huang
Shijia Huang
Shengyu Huang
Siyuan Huang
He Huang
Xiuyu Huang
Lianghua Huang
Yue Huang
Yaping Huang
Yuge Huang
Zehao Huang
Zeyi Huang
Zhiqi Huang
Zhongzhan Huang
Zilong Huang
Ziyuan Huang
Tianrui Hui
Zhuo Hui
Le Hui
Jing Huo
Junhwa Hur
Shehzeen S. Hussain
Chuong Minh Huynh
Seunghyun Hwang
Jaehui Hwang
Jyh-Jing Hwang
Sukjun Hwang
Soonmin Hwang
Wonjun Hwang
Rakib Hyder
Sangeek Hyun
Sarah Ibrahimi
Tomoki Ichikawa
Yerlan Idelbayev
A. S. M. Iftekhar
Masaaki Iiyama
Satoshi Ikehata
Sunghoon Im
Atul N. Ingle
Eldar Insafutdinov
Yani A. Ioannou
Radu Tudor Ionescu

Umar Iqbal
Go Irie
Muhammad Zubair Irshad
Ahmet Iscen
Berivan Isik
Ashraful Islam
Md Amirul Islam
Syed Islam
Mariko Isogawa
Vamsi Krishna K. Ithapu
Boris Ivanovic
Darshan Iyer
Sarah Jabbour
Ayush Jain
Nishant Jain
Samyak Jain
Vidit Jain
Vineet Jain
Priyank Jaini
Tomas Jakab
Mohammad A. A. K.
   Jalwana
Muhammad Abdullah
   Jamal
Hadi Jamali-Rad
Stuart James
Varun Jampani
Young Kyun Jang
YeongJun Jang
Yunseok Jang
Ronnachai Jaroensri
Bhavan Jasani
Krishna Murthy
   Jatavallabhula
Mojan Javaheripi
Syed A. Javed
Guillaume Jeanneret
Pranav Jeevan
Herve Jegou
Rohit Jena
Tomas Jenicek
Porter Jenkins
Simon Jenni
Hae-Gon Jeon
Sangryul Jeon

Boseung Jeong
Yoonwoo Jeong
Seong-Gyun Jeong
Jisoo Jeong
Allan D. Jepson
Ankit Jha
Sumit K. Jha
I-Hong Jhuo
Ge-Peng Ji
Chaonan Ji
Deyi Ji
Jingwei Ji
Wei Ji
Zhong Ji
Jiayi Ji
Pengliang Ji
Hui Ji
Mingi Ji
Xiaopeng Ji
Yuzhu Ji
Baoxiong Jia
Songhao Jia
Dan Jia
Shan Jia
Xiaojun Jia
Xiuyi Jia
Xu Jia
Menglin Jia
Wenqi Jia
Boyuan Jiang
Wenhao Jiang
Huaizu Jiang
Hanwen Jiang
Haiyong Jiang
Hao Jiang
Huajie Jiang
Huiqin Jiang
Haojun Jiang
Haobo Jiang
Junjun Jiang
Xingyu Jiang
Yangbangyan Jiang
Yu Jiang
Jianmin Jiang
Jiaxi Jiang

Jing Jiang
Kui Jiang
Li Jiang
Liming Jiang
Chiyu Jiang
Meirui Jiang
Chen Jiang
Peng Jiang
Tai-Xiang Jiang
Wen Jiang
Xinyang Jiang
Yifan Jiang
Yuming Jiang
Yingying Jiang
Zeren Jiang
ZhengKai Jiang
Zhenyu Jiang
Shuming Jiao
Jianbo Jiao
Licheng Jiao
Dongkwon Jin
Yeying Jin
Cheng Jin
Linyi Jin
Qing Jin
Taisong Jin
Xiao Jin
Xin Jin
Sheng Jin
Kyong Hwan Jin
Ruibing Jin
SouYoung Jin
Yueming Jin
Chenchen Jing
Longlong Jing
Taotao Jing
Yongcheng Jing
Younghyun Jo
Joakim Johnander
Jeff Johnson
Michael J. Jones
R. Kenny Jones
Rico Jonschkowski
Ameya Joshi
Sunghun Joung

Felix Juefei-Xu
Claudio R. Jung
Steffen Jung
Hari Chandana K.
Rahul Vigneswaran K.
Prajwal K. R.
Abhishek Kadian
Jhony Kaesemodel Pontes
Kumara Kahatapitiya
Anmol Kalia
Sinan Kalkan
Tarun Kalluri
Jaewon Kam
Sandesh Kamath
Meina Kan
Menelaos Kanakis
Takuhiro Kaneko
Di Kang
Guoliang Kang
Hao Kang
Jaeyeon Kang
Kyoungkook Kang
Li-Wei Kang
MinGuk Kang
Suk-Ju Kang
Zhao Kang
Yash Mukund Kant
Yueying Kao
Aupendu Kar
Konstantinos Karantzalos
Sezer Karaoglu
Navid Kardan
Sanjay Kariyappa
Leonid Karlinsky
Animesh Karnewar
Shyamgopal Karthik
Hirak J. Kashyap
Marc A. Kastner
Hirokatsu Kataoka
Angelos Katharopoulos
Hiroharu Kato
Kai Katsumata
Manuel Kaufmann
Chaitanya Kaul
Prakhar Kaushik

Yuki Kawana
Lei Ke
Lipeng Ke
Tsung-Wei Ke
Wei Ke
Petr Kellnhofer
Aniruddha Kembhavi
John Kender
Corentin Kervadec
Leonid Keselman
Daniel Keysers
Nima Khademi Kalantari
Taras Khakhulin
Samir Khaki
Muhammad Haris Khan
Qadeer Khan
Salman Khan
Subash Khanal
Vaishnavi M. Khindkar
Rawal Khirodkar
Saeed Khorram
Pirazh Khorramshahi
Kourosh Khoshelham
Ansh Khurana
Benjamin Kiefer
Jae Myung Kim
Junho Kim
Boah Kim
Hyeonseong Kim
Dong-Jin Kim
Dongwan Kim
Donghyun Kim
Doyeon Kim
Yonghyun Kim
Hyung-Il Kim
Hyunwoo Kim
Hyeongwoo Kim
Hyo Jin Kim
Hyunwoo J. Kim
Taehoon Kim
Jaeha Kim
Jiwon Kim
Jung Uk Kim
Kangyeol Kim
Eunji Kim

Daeha Kim
Dongwon Kim
Kunhee Kim
Kyungmin Kim
Junsik Kim
Min H. Kim
Namil Kim
Kookhoi Kim
Sanghyun Kim
Seongyeop Kim
Seungryong Kim
Saehoon Kim
Euyoung Kim
Guisik Kim
Sungyeon Kim
Sunnie S. Y. Kim
Taehun Kim
Tae Oh Kim
Won Hwa Kim
Seungwook Kim
YoungBin Kim
Youngeun Kim
Akisato Kimura
Furkan Osman Kınlı
Zsolt Kira
Hedvig Kjellström
Florian Kleber
Jan P. Klopp
Florian Kluger
Laurent Kneip
Byungsoo Ko
Muhammed Kocabas
A. Sophia Koepke
Kevin Koeser
Nick Kolkin
Nikos Kolotouros
Wai-Kin Adams Kong
Deying Kong
Caihua Kong
Youyong Kong
Shuyu Kong
Shu Kong
Tao Kong
Yajing Kong
Yu Kong

Zishang Kong
Theodora Kontogianni
Anton S. Konushin
Julian F. P. Kooij
Bruno Korbar
Giorgos Kordopatis-Zilos
Jari Korhonen
Adam Kortylewski
Denis Korzhenkov
Divya Kothandaraman
Suraj Kothawade
Iuliia Kotseruba
Satwik Kottur
Shashank Kotyan
Alexandros Kouris
Petros Koutras
Anna Kreshuk
Ranjay Krishna
Dilip Krishnan
Andrey Kuehlkamp
Hilde Kuehne
Jason Kuen
David Kügler
Arjan Kuijper
Anna Kukleva
Sumith Kulal
Viveka Kulharia
Akshay R. Kulkarni
Nilesh Kulkarni
Dominik Kulon
Abhinav Kumar
Akash Kumar
Suryansh Kumar
B. V. K. Vijaya Kumar
Pulkit Kumar
Ratnesh Kumar
Sateesh Kumar
Satish Kumar
Vijay Kumar B. G.
Nupur Kumari
Sudhakar Kumawat
Jogendra Nath Kundu
Hsien-Kai Kuo
Meng-Yu Jennifer Kuo
Vinod Kumar Kurmi

Yusuke Kurose
Keerthy Kusumam
Alina Kuznetsova
Henry Kvinge
Ho Man Kwan
Hyeokjun Kweon
Heeseung Kwon
Gihyun Kwon
Myung-Joon Kwon
Taesung Kwon
YoungJoong Kwon
Christos Kyrkou
Jorma Laaksonen
Yann Labbe
Zorah Laehner
Florent Lafarge
Hamid Laga
Manuel Lagunas
Shenqi Lai
Jian-Huang Lai
Zihang Lai
Mohamed I. Lakhal
Mohit Lamba
Meng Lan
Loic Landrieu
Zhiqiang Lang
Natalie Lang
Dong Lao
Yizhen Lao
Yingjie Lao
Issam Hadj Laradji
Gustav Larsson
Viktor Larsson
Zakaria Laskar
Stéphane Lathuilière
Chun Pong Lau
Rynson W. H. Lau
Hei Law
Justin Lazarow
Verica Lazova
Eric-Tuan Le
Hieu Le
Trung-Nghia Le
Mathias Lechner
Byeong-Uk Lee

Chen-Yu Lee
Che-Rung Lee
Chul Lee
Hong Joo Lee
Dongsoo Lee
Jiyoung Lee
Eugene Eu Tzuan Lee
Daeun Lee
Saehyung Lee
Jewook Lee
Hyungtae Lee
Hyunmin Lee
Jungbeom Lee
Joon-Young Lee
Jong-Seok Lee
Joonseok Lee
Junha Lee
Kibok Lee
Byung-Kwan Lee
Jangwon Lee
Jinho Lee
Jongmin Lee
Seunghyun Lee
Sohyun Lee
Minsik Lee
Dogyoon Lee
Seungmin Lee
Min Jun Lee
Sangho Lee
Sangmin Lee
Seungeun Lee
Seon-Ho Lee
Sungmin Lee
Sungho Lee
Sangyoun Lee
Vincent C. S. S. Lee
Jaeseong Lee
Yong Jae Lee
Chenyang Lei
Chenyi Lei
Jiahui Lei
Xinyu Lei
Yinjie Lei
Jiaxu Leng
Luziwei Leng

Jan E. Lenssen
Vincent Lepetit
Thomas Leung
María Leyva-Vallina
Xin Li
Yikang Li
Baoxin Li
Bin Li
Bing Li
Bowen Li
Changlin Li
Chao Li
Chongyi Li
Guanyue Li
Shuai Li
Jin Li
Dingquan Li
Dongxu Li
Yiting Li
Gang Li
Dian Li
Guohao Li
Haoang Li
Haoliang Li
Haoran Li
Hengduo Li
Huafeng Li
Xiaoming Li
Hanao Li
Hongwei Li
Ziqiang Li
Jisheng Li
Jiacheng Li
Jia Li
Jiachen Li
Jiahao Li
Jianwei Li
Jiazhi Li
Jie Li
Jing Li
Jingjing Li
Jingtao Li
Jun Li
Junxuan Li
Kai Li

Kailin Li
Kenneth Li
Kun Li
Kunpeng Li
Aoxue Li
Chenglong Li
Chenglin Li
Changsheng Li
Zhichao Li
Qiang Li
Yanyu Li
Zuoyue Li
Xiang Li
Xuelong Li
Fangda Li
Ailin Li
Liang Li
Chun-Guang Li
Daiqing Li
Dong Li
Guanbin Li
Guorong Li
Haifeng Li
Jianan Li
Jianing Li
Jiaxin Li
Ke Li
Lei Li
Lincheng Li
Liulei Li
Lujun Li
Linjie Li
Lin Li
Pengyu Li
Ping Li
Qiufu Li
Qingyong Li
Rui Li
Siyuan Li
Wei Li
Wenbin Li
Xiangyang Li
Xinyu Li
Xiujun Li
Xiu Li

Xu Li
Ya-Li Li
Yao Li
Yongjie Li
Yijun Li
Yiming Li
Yuezun Li
Yu Li
Yunheng Li
Yuqi Li
Zhe Li
Zeming Li
Zhen Li
Zhengqin Li
Zhimin Li
Jiefeng Li
Jinpeng Li
Chengze Li
Jianwu Li
Lerenhan Li
Shan Li
Suichan Li
Xiangtai Li
Yanjie Li
Yandong Li
Zhuoling Li
Zhenqiang Li
Manyi Li
Maosen Li
Ji Li
Minjun Li
Mingrui Li
Mengtian Li
Junyi Li
Nianyi Li
Bo Li
Xiao Li
Peihua Li
Peike Li
Peizhao Li
Peiliang Li
Qi Li
Ren Li
Runze Li
Shile Li

Sheng Li
Shigang Li
Shiyu Li
Shuang Li
Shasha Li
Shichao Li
Tianye Li
Yuexiang Li
Wei-Hong Li
Wanhua Li
Weihao Li
Weiming Li
Weixin Li
Wenbo Li
Wenshuo Li
Weijian Li
Yunan Li
Xirong Li
Xianhang Li
Xiaoyu Li
Xueqian Li
Xuanlin Li
Xianzhi Li
Yunqiang Li
Yanjing Li
Yansheng Li
Yawei Li
Yi Li
Yong Li
Yong-Lu Li
Yuhang Li
Yu-Jhe Li
Yuxi Li
Yunsheng Li
Yanwei Li
Zechao Li
Zejian Li
Zeju Li
Zekun Li
Zhaowen Li
Zheng Li
Zhenyu Li
Zhiheng Li
Zhi Li
Zhong Li

Zhuowei Li
Zhuowan Li
Zhuohang Li
Zizhang Li
Chen Li
Yuan-Fang Li
Dongze Lian
Xiaochen Lian
Zhouhui Lian
Long Lian
Qing Lian
Jin Lianbao
Jinxiu S. Liang
Dingkang Liang
Jiahao Liang
Jianming Liang
Jingyun Liang
Kevin J. Liang
Kaizhao Liang
Chen Liang
Jie Liang
Senwei Liang
Ding Liang
Jiajun Liang
Jian Liang
Kongming Liang
Siyuan Liang
Yuanzhi Liang
Zhengfa Liang
Mingfu Liang
Xiaodan Liang
Xuefeng Liang
Yuxuan Liang
Kang Liao
Liang Liao
Hong-Yuan Mark Liao
Wentong Liao
Haofu Liao
Yue Liao
Minghui Liao
Shengcai Liao
Ting-Hsuan Liao
Xin Liao
Yinghong Liao
Teck Yian Lim

Che-Tsung Lin
Chung-Ching Lin
Chen-Hsuan Lin
Cheng Lin
Chuming Lin
Chunyu Lin
Dahua Lin
Wei Lin
Zheng Lin
Huaijia Lin
Jason Lin
Jierui Lin
Jiaying Lin
Jie Lin
Kai-En Lin
Kevin Lin
Guangfeng Lin
Jiehong Lin
Feng Lin
Hang Lin
Kwan-Yee Lin
Ke Lin
Luojun Lin
Qinghong Lin
Xiangbo Lin
Yi Lin
Zudi Lin
Shijie Lin
Yiqun Lin
Tzu-Heng Lin
Ming Lin
Shaohui Lin
SongNan Lin
Ji Lin
Tsung-Yu Lin
Xudong Lin
Yancong Lin
Yen-Chen Lin
Yiming Lin
Yuewei Lin
Zhiqiu Lin
Zinan Lin
Zhe Lin
David B. Lindell
Zhixin Ling

Zhan Ling
Alexander Liniger
Venice Erin B. Liong
Joey Litalien
Or Litany
Roee Litman
Ron Litman
Jim Little
Dor Litvak
Shaoteng Liu
Shuaicheng Liu
Andrew Liu
Xian Liu
Shaohui Liu
Bei Liu
Bo Liu
Yong Liu
Ming Liu
Yanbin Liu
Chenxi Liu
Daqi Liu
Di Liu
Difan Liu
Dong Liu
Dongfang Liu
Daizong Liu
Xiao Liu
Fangyi Liu
Fengbei Liu
Fenglin Liu
Bin Liu
Yuang Liu
Ao Liu
Hong Liu
Hongfu Liu
Huidong Liu
Ziyi Liu
Feng Liu
Hao Liu
Jie Liu
Jialun Liu
Jiang Liu
Jing Liu
Jingya Liu
Jiaming Liu

Jun Liu
Juncheng Liu
Jiawei Liu
Hongyu Liu
Chuanbin Liu
Haotian Liu
Lingqiao Liu
Chang Liu
Han Liu
Liu Liu
Min Liu
Yingqi Liu
Aishan Liu
Bingyu Liu
Benlin Liu
Boxiao Liu
Chenchen Liu
Chuanjian Liu
Daqing Liu
Huan Liu
Haozhe Liu
Jiaheng Liu
Wei Liu
Jingzhou Liu
Jiyuan Liu
Lingbo Liu
Nian Liu
Peiye Liu
Qiankun Liu
Shenglan Liu
Shilong Liu
Wen Liu
Wenyu Liu
Weifeng Liu
Wu Liu
Xiaolong Liu
Yang Liu
Yanwei Liu
Yingcheng Liu
Yongfei Liu
Yihao Liu
Yu Liu
Yunze Liu
Ze Liu
Zhenhua Liu

Zhenguang Liu
Lin Liu
Lihao Liu
Pengju Liu
Xinhai Liu
Yunfei Liu
Meng Liu
Minghua Liu
Mingyuan Liu
Miao Liu
Peirong Liu
Ping Liu
Qingjie Liu
Ruoshi Liu
Risheng Liu
Songtao Liu
Xing Liu
Shikun Liu
Shuming Liu
Sheng Liu
Songhua Liu
Tongliang Liu
Weibo Liu
Weide Liu
Weizhe Liu
Wenxi Liu
Weiyang Liu
Xin Liu
Xiaobin Liu
Xudong Liu
Xiaoyi Liu
Xihui Liu
Xinchen Liu
Xingtong Liu
Xinpeng Liu
Xinyu Liu
Xianpeng Liu
Xu Liu
Xingyu Liu
Yongtuo Liu
Yahui Liu
Yangxin Liu
Yaoyao Liu
Yaojie Liu
Yuliang Liu

Yongcheng Liu
Yuan Liu
Yufan Liu
Yu-Lun Liu
Yun Liu
Yunfan Liu
Yuanzhong Liu
Zhuoran Liu
Zhen Liu
Zheng Liu
Zhijian Liu
Zhisong Liu
Ziquan Liu
Ziyu Liu
Zhihua Liu
Zechun Liu
Zhaoyang Liu
Zhengzhe Liu
Stephan Liwicki
Shao-Yuan Lo
Sylvain Lobry
Suhas Lohit
Vishnu Suresh Lokhande
Vincenzo Lomonaco
Chengjiang Long
Guodong Long
Fuchen Long
Shangbang Long
Yang Long
Zijun Long
Vasco Lopes
Antonio M. Lopez
Roberto Javier
    Lopez-Sastre
Tobias Lorenz
Javier Lorenzo-Navarro
Yujing Lou
Qian Lou
Xiankai Lu
Changsheng Lu
Huimin Lu
Yongxi Lu
Hao Lu
Hong Lu
Jiasen Lu

Juwei Lu
Fan Lu
Guangming Lu
Jiwen Lu
Shun Lu
Tao Lu
Xiaonan Lu
Yang Lu
Yao Lu
Yongchun Lu
Zhiwu Lu
Cheng Lu
Liying Lu
Guo Lu
Xuequan Lu
Yanye Lu
Yantao Lu
Yuhang Lu
Fujun Luan
Jonathon Luiten
Jovita Lukasik
Alan Lukezic
Jonathan Samuel Lumentut
Mayank Lunayach
Ao Luo
Canjie Luo
Chong Luo
Xu Luo
Grace Luo
Jun Luo
Katie Z. Luo
Tao Luo
Cheng Luo
Fangzhou Luo
Gen Luo
Lei Luo
Sihui Luo
Weixin Luo
Yan Luo
Xiaoyan Luo
Yong Luo
Yadan Luo
Hao Luo
Ruotian Luo
Mi Luo

Tiange Luo
Wenjie Luo
Wenhan Luo
Xiao Luo
Zhiming Luo
Zhipeng Luo
Zhengyi Luo
Diogo C. Luvizon
Zhaoyang Lv
Gengyu Lyu
Lingjuan Lyu
Jun Lyu
Yuanyuan Lyu
Youwei Lyu
Yueming Lyu
Bingpeng Ma
Chao Ma
Chongyang Ma
Congbo Ma
Chih-Yao Ma
Fan Ma
Lin Ma
Haoyu Ma
Hengbo Ma
Jianqi Ma
Jiawei Ma
Jiayi Ma
Kede Ma
Kai Ma
Lingni Ma
Lei Ma
Xu Ma
Ning Ma
Benteng Ma
Cheng Ma
Andy J. Ma
Long Ma
Zhanyu Ma
Zhiheng Ma
Qianli Ma
Shiqiang Ma
Sizhuo Ma
Shiqing Ma
Xiaolong Ma
Xinzhu Ma

Gautam B. Machiraju
Spandan Madan
Mathew Magimai-Doss
Luca Magri
Behrooz Mahasseni
Upal Mahbub
Siddharth Mahendran
Paridhi Maheshwari
Rishabh Maheshwary
Mohammed Mahmoud
Shishira R. R. Maiya
Sylwia Majchrowska
Arjun Majumdar
Puspita Majumdar
Orchid Majumder
Sagnik Majumder
Ilya Makarov
Farkhod F.
   Makhmudkhujaev
Yasushi Makihara
Ankur Mali
Mateusz Malinowski
Utkarsh Mall
Srikanth Malla
Clement Mallet
Dimitrios Mallis
Yunze Man
Dipu Manandhar
Massimiliano Mancini
Murari Mandal
Raunak Manekar
Karttikeya Mangalam
Puneet Mangla
Fabian Manhardt
Sivabalan Manivasagam
Fahim Mannan
Chengzhi Mao
Hanzi Mao
Jiayuan Mao
Junhua Mao
Zhiyuan Mao
Jiageng Mao
Yunyao Mao
Zhendong Mao
Alberto Marchisio

Diego Marcos
Riccardo Marin
Aram Markosyan
Renaud Marlet
Ricardo Marques
Miquel Martí i Rabadán
Diego Martin Arroyo
Niki Martinel
Brais Martinez
Julieta Martinez
Marc Masana
Tomohiro Mashita
Timothée Masquelier
Minesh Mathew
Tetsu Matsukawa
Marwan Mattar
Bruce A. Maxwell
Christoph Mayer
Mantas Mazeika
Pratik Mazumder
Scott McCloskey
Steven McDonagh
Ishit Mehta
Jie Mei
Kangfu Mei
Jieru Mei
Xiaoguang Mei
Givi Meishvili
Luke Melas-Kyriazi
Iaroslav Melekhov
Andres Mendez-Vazquez
Heydi Mendez-Vazquez
Matias Mendieta
Ricardo A. Mendoza-León
Chenlin Meng
Depu Meng
Rang Meng
Zibo Meng
Qingjie Meng
Qier Meng
Yanda Meng
Zihang Meng
Thomas Mensink
Fabian Mentzer
Christopher Metzler

Gregory P. Meyer
Vasileios Mezaris
Liang Mi
Lu Mi
Bo Miao
Changtao Miao
Zichen Miao
Qiguang Miao
Xin Miao
Zhongqi Miao
Frank Michel
Simone Milani
Ben Mildenhall
Roy V. Miles
Juhong Min
Kyle Min
Hyun-Seok Min
Weiqing Min
Yuecong Min
Zhixiang Min
Qi Ming
David Minnen
Aymen Mir
Deepak Mishra
Anand Mishra
Shlok K. Mishra
Niluthpol Mithun
Gaurav Mittal
Trisha Mittal
Daisuke Miyazaki
Kaichun Mo
Hong Mo
Zhipeng Mo
Davide Modolo
Abduallah A. Mohamed
Mohamed Afham
   Mohamed Aflal
Ron Mokady
Pavlo Molchanov
Davide Moltisanti
Liliane Momeni
Gianluca Monaci
Pascal Monasse
Ajoy Mondal
Tom Monnier

Aron Monszpart
Gyeongsik Moon
Suhong Moon
Taesup Moon
Sean Moran
Daniel Moreira
Pietro Morerio
Alexandre Morgand
Lia Morra
Ali Mosleh
Inbar Mosseri
Sayed Mohammad
    Mostafavi Isfahani
Saman Motamed
Ramy A. Mounir
Fangzhou Mu
Jiteng Mu
Norman Mu
Yasuhiro Mukaigawa
Ryan Mukherjee
Tanmoy Mukherjee
Yusuke Mukuta
Ravi Teja Mullapudi
Lea Müller
Matthias Müller
Martin Mundt
Nils Murrugarra-Llerena
Damien Muselet
Armin Mustafa
Muhammad Ferjad Naeem
Sauradip Nag
Hajime Nagahara
Pravin Nagar
Rajendra Nagar
Naveen Shankar Nagaraja
Varun Nagaraja
Tushar Nagarajan
Seungjun Nah
Gaku Nakano
Yuta Nakashima
Giljoo Nam
Seonghyeon Nam
Liangliang Nan
Yuesong Nan
Yeshwanth Napolean

Dinesh Reddy
    Narapureddy
Medhini Narasimhan
Supreeth
    Narasimhaswamy
Sriram Narayanan
Erickson R. Nascimento
Varun Nasery
K. L. Navaneet
Pablo Navarrete Michelini
Shant Navasardyan
Shah Nawaz
Nihal Nayak
Farhood Negin
Lukáš Neumann
Alejandro Newell
Evonne Ng
Kam Woh Ng
Tony Ng
Anh Nguyen
Tuan Anh Nguyen
Cuong Cao Nguyen
Ngoc Cuong Nguyen
Thanh Nguyen
Khoi Nguyen
Phi Le Nguyen
Phong Ha Nguyen
Tam Nguyen
Truong Nguyen
Anh Tuan Nguyen
Rang Nguyen
Thao Thi Phuong Nguyen
Van Nguyen Nguyen
Zhen-Liang Ni
Yao Ni
Shijie Nie
Xuecheng Nie
Yongwei Nie
Weizhi Nie
Ying Nie
Yinyu Nie
Kshitij N. Nikhal
Simon Niklaus
Xuefei Ning
Jifeng Ning

Yotam Nitzan
Di Niu
Shuaicheng Niu
Li Niu
Wei Niu
Yulei Niu
Zhenxing Niu
Albert No
Shohei Nobuhara
Nicoletta Noceti
Junhyug Noh
Sotiris Nousias
Slawomir Nowaczyk
Ewa M. Nowara
Valsamis Ntouskos
Gilberto Ochoa-Ruiz
Ferda Ofli
Jihyong Oh
Sangyun Oh
Youngtaek Oh
Hiroki Ohashi
Takahiro Okabe
Kemal Oksuz
Fumio Okura
Daniel Olmeda Reino
Matthew Olson
Carl Olsson
Roy Or-El
Alessandro Ortis
Guillermo Ortiz-Jimenez
Magnus Oskarsson
Ahmed A. A. Osman
Martin R. Oswald
Mayu Otani
Naima Otberdout
Cheng Ouyang
Jiahong Ouyang
Wanli Ouyang
Andrew Owens
Poojan B. Oza
Mete Ozay
A. Cengiz Oztireli
Gautam Pai
Tomas Pajdla
Umapada Pal

Simone Palazzo
Luca Palmieri
Bowen Pan
Hao Pan
Lili Pan
Tai-Yu Pan
Liang Pan
Chengwei Pan
Yingwei Pan
Xuran Pan
Jinshan Pan
Xinyu Pan
Liyuan Pan
Xingang Pan
Xingjia Pan
Zhihong Pan
Zizheng Pan
Priyadarshini Panda
Rameswar Panda
Rohit Pandey
Kaiyue Pang
Bo Pang
Guansong Pang
Jiangmiao Pang
Meng Pang
Tianyu Pang
Ziqi Pang
Omiros Pantazis
Andreas Panteli
Maja Pantic
Marina Paolanti
Joao P. Papa
Samuele Papa
Mike Papadakis
Dim P. Papadopoulos
George Papandreou
Constantin Pape
Toufiq Parag
Chethan Parameshwara
Shaifali Parashar
Alejandro Pardo
Rishubh Parihar
Sarah Parisot
JaeYoo Park
Gyeong-Moon Park

Hyojin Park
Hyoungseob Park
Jongchan Park
Jae Sung Park
Kiru Park
Chunghyun Park
Kwanyong Park
Sunghyun Park
Sungrae Park
Seongsik Park
Sanghyun Park
Sungjune Park
Taesung Park
Gaurav Parmar
Paritosh Parmar
Alvaro Parra
Despoina Paschalidou
Or Patashnik
Shivansh Patel
Pushpak Pati
Prashant W. Patil
Vaishakh Patil
Suvam Patra
Jay Patravali
Badri Narayana Patro
Angshuman Paul
Sudipta Paul
Rémi Pautrat
Nick E. Pears
Adithya Pediredla
Wenjie Pei
Shmuel Peleg
Latha Pemula
Bo Peng
Houwen Peng
Yue Peng
Liangzu Peng
Baoyun Peng
Jun Peng
Pai Peng
Sida Peng
Xi Peng
Yuxin Peng
Songyou Peng
Wei Peng

Weiqi Peng
Wen-Hsiao Peng
Pramuditha Perera
Juan C. Perez
Eduardo Pérez Pellitero
Juan-Manuel Perez-Rua
Federico Pernici
Marco Pesavento
Stavros Petridis
Ilya A. Petrov
Vladan Petrovic
Mathis Petrovich
Suzanne Petryk
Hieu Pham
Quang Pham
Khoi Pham
Tung Pham
Huy Phan
Stephen Phillips
Cheng Perng Phoo
David Picard
Marco Piccirilli
Georg Pichler
A. J. Piergiovanni
Vipin Pillai
Silvia L. Pintea
Giovanni Pintore
Robinson Piramuthu
Fiora Pirri
Theodoros Pissas
Fabio Pizzati
Benjamin Planche
Bryan Plummer
Matteo Poggi
Ashwini Pokle
Georgy E. Ponimatkin
Adrian Popescu
Stefan Popov
Nikola Popović
Ronald Poppe
Angelo Porrello
Michael Potter
Charalambos Poullis
Hadi Pouransari
Omid Poursaeed

Shraman Pramanick
Mantini Pranav
Dilip K. Prasad
Meghshyam Prasad
B. H. Pawan Prasad
Shitala Prasad
Prateek Prasanna
Ekta Prashnani
Derek S. Prijatelj
Luke Y. Prince
Véronique Prinet
Victor Adrian Prisacariu
James Pritts
Thomas Probst
Sergey Prokudin
Rita Pucci
Chi-Man Pun
Matthew Purri
Haozhi Qi
Lu Qi
Lei Qi
Xianbiao Qi
Yonggang Qi
Yuankai Qi
Siyuan Qi
Guocheng Qian
Hangwei Qian
Qi Qian
Deheng Qian
Shengsheng Qian
Wen Qian
Rui Qian
Yiming Qian
Shengju Qian
Shengyi Qian
Xuelin Qian
Zhenxing Qian
Nan Qiao
Xiaotian Qiao
Jing Qin
Can Qin
Siyang Qin
Hongwei Qin
Jie Qin
Minghai Qin

Yipeng Qin
Yongqiang Qin
Wenda Qin
Xuebin Qin
Yuzhe Qin
Yao Qin
Zhenyue Qin
Zhiwu Qing
Heqian Qiu
Jiayan Qiu
Jielin Qiu
Yue Qiu
Jiaxiong Qiu
Zhongxi Qiu
Shi Qiu
Zhaofan Qiu
Zhongnan Qu
Yanyun Qu
Kha Gia Quach
Yuhui Quan
Ruijie Quan
Mike Rabbat
Rahul Shekhar Rade
Filip Radenovic
Gorjan Radevski
Bogdan Raducanu
Francesco Ragusa
Shafin Rahman
Md Mahfuzur Rahman
    Siddiquee
Hossein Rahmani
Kiran Raja
Sivaramakrishnan
    Rajaraman
Jathushan Rajasegaran
Adnan Siraj Rakin
Michaël Ramamonjisoa
Chirag A. Raman
Shanmuganathan Raman
Vignesh Ramanathan
Vasili Ramanishka
Vikram V. Ramaswamy
Merey Ramazanova
Jason Rambach
Sai Saketh Rambhatla

Clément Rambour
Ashwin Ramesh Babu
Adín Ramírez Rivera
Arianna Rampini
Haoxi Ran
Aakanksha Rana
Aayush Jung Bahadur
    Rana
Kanchana N. Ranasinghe
Aneesh Rangnekar
Samrudhdhi B. Rangrej
Harsh Rangwani
Viresh Ranjan
Anyi Rao
Yongming Rao
Carolina Raposo
Michalis Raptis
Amir Rasouli
Vivek Rathod
Adepu Ravi Sankar
Avinash Ravichandran
Bharadwaj Ravichandran
Dripta S. Raychaudhuri
Adria Recasens
Simon Reiß
Davis Rempe
Daxuan Ren
Jiawei Ren
Jimmy Ren
Sucheng Ren
Dayong Ren
Zhile Ren
Dongwei Ren
Qibing Ren
Pengfei Ren
Zhenwen Ren
Xuqian Ren
Yixuan Ren
Zhongzheng Ren
Ambareesh Revanur
Hamed Rezazadegan
    Tavakoli
Rafael S. Rezende
Wonjong Rhee
Alexander Richard

Christian Richardt
Stephan R. Richter
Benjamin Riggan
Dominik Rivoir
Mamshad Nayeem Rizve
Joshua D. Robinson
Joseph Robinson
Chris Rockwell
Ranga Rodrigo
Andres C. Rodriguez
Carlos Rodriguez-Pardo
Marcus Rohrbach
Gemma Roig
Yu Rong
David A. Ross
Mohammad Rostami
Edward Rosten
Karsten Roth
Anirban Roy
Debaditya Roy
Shuvendu Roy
Ahana Roy Choudhury
Aruni Roy Chowdhury
Denys Rozumnyi
Shulan Ruan
Wenjie Ruan
Patrick Ruhkamp
Danila Rukhovich
Anian Ruoss
Chris Russell
Dan Ruta
Dawid Damian Rymarczyk
DongHun Ryu
Hyeonggon Ryu
Kwonyoung Ryu
Balasubramanian S.
Alexandre Sablayrolles
Mohammad Sabokrou
Arka Sadhu
Aniruddha Saha
Oindrila Saha
Pritish Sahu
Aneeshan Sain
Nirat Saini
Saurabh Saini

Takeshi Saitoh
Christos Sakaridis
Fumihiko Sakaue
Dimitrios Sakkos
Ken Sakurada
Parikshit V. Sakurikar
Rohit Saluja
Nermin Samet
Leo Sampaio Ferraz
     Ribeiro
Jorge Sanchez
Enrique Sanchez
Shengtian Sang
Anush Sankaran
Soubhik Sanyal
Nikolaos Sarafianos
Vishwanath Saragadam
István Sárándi
Saquib Sarfraz
Mert Bulent Sariyildiz
Anindya Sarkar
Pritam Sarkar
Paul-Edouard Sarlin
Hiroshi Sasaki
Takami Sato
Torsten Sattler
Ravi Kumar Satzoda
Axel Sauer
Stefano Savian
Artem Savkin
Manolis Savva
Gerald Schaefer
Simone Schaub-Meyer
Yoni Schirris
Samuel Schulter
Katja Schwarz
Jesse Scott
Sinisa Segvic
Constantin Marc Seibold
Lorenzo Seidenari
Matan Sela
Fadime Sener
Paul Hongsuck Seo
Kwanggyoon Seo
Hongje Seong

Dario Serez
Francesco Setti
Bryan Seybold
Mohamad Shahbazi
Shima Shahfar
Xinxin Shan
Caifeng Shan
Dandan Shan
Shawn Shan
Wei Shang
Jinghuan Shang
Jiaxiang Shang
Lei Shang
Sukrit Shankar
Ken Shao
Rui Shao
Jie Shao
Mingwen Shao
Aashish Sharma
Gaurav Sharma
Vivek Sharma
Abhishek Sharma
Yoli Shavit
Shashank Shekhar
Sumit Shekhar
Zhijie Shen
Fengyi Shen
Furao Shen
Jialie Shen
Jingjing Shen
Ziyi Shen
Linlin Shen
Guangyu Shen
Biluo Shen
Falong Shen
Jiajun Shen
Qiu Shen
Qiuhong Shen
Shuai Shen
Wang Shen
Yiqing Shen
Yunhang Shen
Siqi Shen
Bin Shen
Tianwei Shen

Xi Shen
Yilin Shen
Yuming Shen
Yucong Shen
Zhiqiang Shen
Lu Sheng
Yichen Sheng
Shivanand Venkanna
  Sheshappanavar
Shelly Sheynin
Baifeng Shi
Ruoxi Shi
Botian Shi
Hailin Shi
Jia Shi
Jing Shi
Shaoshuai Shi
Baoguang Shi
Boxin Shi
Hengcan Shi
Tianyang Shi
Xiaodan Shi
Yongjie Shi
Zhensheng Shi
Yinghuan Shi
Weiqi Shi
Wu Shi
Xuepeng Shi
Xiaoshuang Shi
Yujiao Shi
Zenglin Shi
Zhenmei Shi
Takashi Shibata
Meng-Li Shih
Yichang Shih
Hyunjung Shim
Dongseok Shim
Soshi Shimada
Inkyu Shin
Jinwoo Shin
Seungjoo Shin
Seungjae Shin
Koichi Shinoda
Suprosanna Shit

Palaiahnakote
  Shivakumara
Eli Shlizerman
Gaurav Shrivastava
Xiao Shu
Xiangbo Shu
Xiujun Shu
Yang Shu
Tianmin Shu
Jun Shu
Zhixin Shu
Bing Shuai
Maria Shugrina
Ivan Shugurov
Satya Narayan Shukla
Pranjay Shyam
Jianlou Si
Yawar Siddiqui
Alberto Signoroni
Pedro Silva
Jae-Young Sim
Oriane Siméoni
Martin Simon
Andrea Simonelli
Abhishek Singh
Ashish Singh
Dinesh Singh
Gurkirt Singh
Krishna Kumar Singh
Mannat Singh
Pravendra Singh
Rajat Vikram Singh
Utkarsh Singhal
Dipika Singhania
Vasu Singla
Harsh Sinha
Sudipta Sinha
Josef Sivic
Elena Sizikova
Geri Skenderi
Ivan Skorokhodov
Dmitriy Smirnov
Cameron Y. Smith
James S. Smith
Patrick Snape

Mattia Soldan
Hyeongseok Son
Sanghyun Son
Chuanbiao Song
Chen Song
Chunfeng Song
Dan Song
Dongjin Song
Hwanjun Song
Guoxian Song
Jiaming Song
Jie Song
Liangchen Song
Ran Song
Luchuan Song
Xibin Song
Li Song
Fenglong Song
Guoli Song
Guanglu Song
Zhenbo Song
Lin Song
Xinhang Song
Yang Song
Yibing Song
Rajiv Soundararajan
Hossein Souri
Cristovao Sousa
Riccardo Spezialetti
Leonidas Spinoulas
Michael W. Spratling
Deepak Sridhar
Srinath Sridhar
Gaurang Sriramanan
Vinkle Kumar Srivastav
Themos Stafylakis
Serban Stan
Anastasis Stathopoulos
Markus Steinberger
Jan Steinbrener
Sinisa Stekovic
Alexandros Stergiou
Gleb Sterkin
Rainer Stiefelhagen
Pierre Stock

Ombretta Strafforello
Julian Straub
Yannick Strümpler
Joerg Stueckler
Hang Su
Weijie Su
Jong-Chyi Su
Bing Su
Haisheng Su
Jinming Su
Yiyang Su
Yukun Su
Yuxin Su
Zhuo Su
Zhaoqi Su
Xiu Su
Yu-Chuan Su
Zhixun Su
Arulkumar Subramaniam
Akshayvarun Subramanya
A. Subramanyam
Swathikiran Sudhakaran
Yusuke Sugano
Masanori Suganuma
Yumin Suh
Yang Sui
Baochen Sun
Cheng Sun
Long Sun
Guolei Sun
Haoliang Sun
Haomiao Sun
He Sun
Hanqing Sun
Hao Sun
Lichao Sun
Jiachen Sun
Jiaming Sun
Jian Sun
Jin Sun
Jennifer J. Sun
Tiancheng Sun
Libo Sun
Peize Sun
Qianru Sun

Shanlin Sun
Yu Sun
Zhun Sun
Che Sun
Lin Sun
Tao Sun
Yiyou Sun
Chunyi Sun
Chong Sun
Weiwei Sun
Weixuan Sun
Xiuyu Sun
Yanan Sun
Zeren Sun
Zhaodong Sun
Zhiqing Sun
Minhyuk Sung
Jinli Suo
Simon Suo
Abhijit Suprem
Anshuman Suri
Saksham Suri
Joshua M. Susskind
Roman Suvorov
Gurumurthy Swaminathan
Robin Swanson
Paul Swoboda
Tabish A. Syed
Richard Szeliski
Fariborz Taherkhani
Yu-Wing Tai
Keita Takahashi
Walter Talbott
Gary Tam
Masato Tamura
Feitong Tan
Fuwen Tan
Shuhan Tan
Andong Tan
Bin Tan
Cheng Tan
Jianchao Tan
Lei Tan
Mingxing Tan
Xin Tan

Zichang Tan
Zhentao Tan
Kenichiro Tanaka
Masayuki Tanaka
Yushun Tang
Hao Tang
Jingqun Tang
Jinhui Tang
Kaihua Tang
Luming Tang
Lv Tang
Sheyang Tang
Shitao Tang
Siliang Tang
Shixiang Tang
Yansong Tang
Keke Tang
Chang Tang
Chenwei Tang
Jie Tang
Junshu Tang
Ming Tang
Peng Tang
Xu Tang
Yao Tang
Chen Tang
Fan Tang
Haoran Tang
Shengeng Tang
Yehui Tang
Zhipeng Tang
Ugo Tanielian
Chaofan Tao
Jiale Tao
Junli Tao
Renshuai Tao
An Tao
Guanhong Tao
Zhiqiang Tao
Makarand Tapaswi
Jean-Philippe G. Tarel
Juan J. Tarrio
Enzo Tartaglione
Keisuke Tateno
Zachary Teed

Ajinkya B. Tejankar
Bugra Tekin
Purva Tendulkar
Damien Teney
Minggui Teng
Chris Tensmeyer
Andrew Beng Jin Teoh
Philipp Terhörst
Kartik Thakral
Nupur Thakur
Kevin Thandiackal
Spyridon Thermos
Diego Thomas
William Thong
Yuesong Tian
Guanzhong Tian
Lin Tian
Shiqi Tian
Kai Tian
Meng Tian
Tai-Peng Tian
Zhuotao Tian
Shangxuan Tian
Tian Tian
Yapeng Tian
Yu Tian
Yuxin Tian
Leslie Ching Ow Tiong
Praveen Tirupattur
Garvita Tiwari
George Toderici
Antoine Toisoul
Aysim Toker
Tatiana Tommasi
Zhan Tong
Alessio Tonioni
Alessandro Torcinovich
Fabio Tosi
Matteo Toso
Hugo Touvron
Quan Hung Tran
Son Tran
Hung Tran
Ngoc-Trung Tran
Vinh Tran

Phong Tran
Giovanni Trappolini
Edith Tretschk
Subarna Tripathi
Shubhendu Trivedi
Eduard Trulls
Prune Truong
Thanh-Dat Truong
Tomasz Trzcinski
Sam Tsai
Yi-Hsuan Tsai
Ethan Tseng
Yu-Chee Tseng
Shahar Tsiper
Stavros Tsogkas
Shikui Tu
Zhigang Tu
Zhengzhong Tu
Richard Tucker
Sergey Tulyakov
Cigdem Turan
Daniyar Turmukhambetov
Victor G. Turrisi da Costa
Bartlomiej Twardowski
Christopher D. Twigg
Radim Tylecek
Mostofa Rafid Uddin
Md. Zasim Uddin
Kohei Uehara
Nicolas Ugrinovic
Youngjung Uh
Norimichi Ukita
Anwaar Ulhaq
Devesh Upadhyay
Paul Upchurch
Yoshitaka Ushiku
Yuzuko Utsumi
Mikaela Angelina Uy
Mohit Vaishnav
Pratik Vaishnavi
Jeya Maria Jose Valanarasu
Matias A. Valdenegro Toro
Diego Valsesia
Wouter Van Gansbeke
Nanne van Noord

Simon Vandenhende
Farshid Varno
Cristina Vasconcelos
Francisco Vasconcelos
Alex Vasilescu
Subeesh Vasu
Arun Balajee Vasudevan
Kanav Vats
Vaibhav S. Vavilala
Sagar Vaze
Javier Vazquez-Corral
Andrea Vedaldi
Olga Veksler
Andreas Velten
Sai H. Vemprala
Raviteja Vemulapalli
Shashanka
    Venkataramanan
Dor Verbin
Luisa Verdoliva
Manisha Verma
Yashaswi Verma
Constantin Vertan
Eli Verwimp
Deepak Vijaykeerthy
Pablo Villanueva
Ruben Villegas
Markus Vincze
Vibhav Vineet
Minh P. Vo
Huy V. Vo
Duc Minh Vo
Tomas Vojir
Igor Vozniak
Nicholas Vretos
Vibashan VS
Tuan-Anh Vu
Thang Vu
Mårten Wadenbäck
Neal Wadhwa
Aaron T. Walsman
Steven Walton
Jin Wan
Alvin Wan
Jia Wan

Jun Wan
Xiaoyue Wan
Fang Wan
Guowei Wan
Renjie Wan
Zhiqiang Wan
Ziyu Wan
Bastian Wandt
Dongdong Wang
Limin Wang
Haiyang Wang
Xiaobing Wang
Angtian Wang
Angelina Wang
Bing Wang
Bo Wang
Boyu Wang
Binghui Wang
Chen Wang
Chien-Yi Wang
Congli Wang
Qi Wang
Chengrui Wang
Rui Wang
Yiqun Wang
Cong Wang
Wenjing Wang
Dongkai Wang
Di Wang
Xiaogang Wang
Kai Wang
Zhizhong Wang
Fangjinhua Wang
Feng Wang
Hang Wang
Gaoang Wang
Guoqing Wang
Guangcong Wang
Guangzhi Wang
Hanqing Wang
Hao Wang
Haohan Wang
Haoran Wang
Hong Wang
Haotao Wang

Hu Wang
Huan Wang
Hua Wang
Hui-Po Wang
Hengli Wang
Hanyu Wang
Hongxing Wang
Jingwen Wang
Jialiang Wang
Jian Wang
Jianyi Wang
Jiashun Wang
Jiahao Wang
Tsun-Hsuan Wang
Xiaoqian Wang
Jinqiao Wang
Jun Wang
Jianzong Wang
Kaihong Wang
Ke Wang
Lei Wang
Lingjing Wang
Linnan Wang
Lin Wang
Liansheng Wang
Mengjiao Wang
Manning Wang
Nannan Wang
Peihao Wang
Jiayun Wang
Pu Wang
Qiang Wang
Qiufeng Wang
Qilong Wang
Qiangchang Wang
Qin Wang
Qing Wang
Ruocheng Wang
Ruibin Wang
Ruisheng Wang
Ruizhe Wang
Runqi Wang
Runzhong Wang
Wenxuan Wang
Sen Wang

Shangfei Wang
Shaofei Wang
Shijie Wang
Shiqi Wang
Zhibo Wang
Song Wang
Xinjiang Wang
Tai Wang
Tao Wang
Teng Wang
Xiang Wang
Tianren Wang
Tiantian Wang
Tianyi Wang
Fengjiao Wang
Wei Wang
Miaohui Wang
Suchen Wang
Siyue Wang
Yaoming Wang
Xiao Wang
Ze Wang
Biao Wang
Chaofei Wang
Dong Wang
Gu Wang
Guangrun Wang
Guangming Wang
Guo-Hua Wang
Haoqing Wang
Hesheng Wang
Huafeng Wang
Jinghua Wang
Jingdong Wang
Jingjing Wang
Jingya Wang
Jingkang Wang
Jiakai Wang
Junke Wang
Kuo Wang
Lichen Wang
Lizhi Wang
Longguang Wang
Mang Wang
Mei Wang

Min Wang
Peng-Shuai Wang
Run Wang
Shaoru Wang
Shuhui Wang
Tan Wang
Tiancai Wang
Tianqi Wang
Wenhai Wang
Wenzhe Wang
Xiaobo Wang
Xiudong Wang
Xu Wang
Yajie Wang
Yan Wang
Yuan-Gen Wang
Yingqian Wang
Yizhi Wang
Yulin Wang
Yu Wang
Yujie Wang
Yunhe Wang
Yuxi Wang
Yaowei Wang
Yiwei Wang
Zezheng Wang
Hongzhi Wang
Zhiqiang Wang
Ziteng Wang
Ziwei Wang
Zheng Wang
Zhenyu Wang
Binglu Wang
Zhongdao Wang
Ce Wang
Weining Wang
Weiyao Wang
Wenbin Wang
Wenguan Wang
Guangting Wang
Haolin Wang
Haiyan Wang
Huiyu Wang
Naiyan Wang
Jingbo Wang

Jinpeng Wang
Jiaqi Wang
Liyuan Wang
Lizhen Wang
Ning Wang
Wenqian Wang
Sheng-Yu Wang
Weimin Wang
Xiaohan Wang
Yifan Wang
Yi Wang
Yongtao Wang
Yizhou Wang
Zhuo Wang
Zhe Wang
Xudong Wang
Xiaofang Wang
Xinggang Wang
Xiaosen Wang
Xiaosong Wang
Xiaoyang Wang
Lijun Wang
Xinlong Wang
Xuan Wang
Xue Wang
Yangang Wang
Yaohui Wang
Yu-Chiang Frank Wang
Yida Wang
Yilin Wang
Yi Ru Wang
Yali Wang
Yinglong Wang
Yufu Wang
Yujiang Wang
Yuwang Wang
Yuting Wang
Yang Wang
Yu-Xiong Wang
Yixu Wang
Ziqi Wang
Zhicheng Wang
Zeyu Wang
Zhaowen Wang
Zhenyi Wang

Zhenzhi Wang
Zhijie Wang
Zhiyong Wang
Zhongling Wang
Zhuowei Wang
Zian Wang
Zifu Wang
Zihao Wang
Zirui Wang
Ziyan Wang
Wenxiao Wang
Zhen Wang
Zhepeng Wang
Zi Wang
Zihao W. Wang
Steven L. Waslander
Olivia Watkins
Daniel Watson
Silvan Weder
Dongyoon Wee
Dongming Wei
Tianyi Wei
Jia Wei
Dong Wei
Fangyun Wei
Longhui Wei
Mingqiang Wei
Xinyue Wei
Chen Wei
Donglai Wei
Pengxu Wei
Xing Wei
Xiu-Shen Wei
Wenqi Wei
Guoqiang Wei
Wei Wei
XingKui Wei
Xian Wei
Xingxing Wei
Yake Wei
Yuxiang Wei
Yi Wei
Luca Weihs
Michael Weinmann
Martin Weinmann

Congcong Wen
Chuan Wen
Jie Wen
Sijia Wen
Song Wen
Chao Wen
Xiang Wen
Zeyi Wen
Xin Wen
Yilin Wen
Yijia Weng
Shuchen Weng
Junwu Weng
Wenming Weng
Renliang Weng
Zhenyu Weng
Xinshuo Weng
Nicholas J. Westlake
Gordon Wetzstein
Lena M. Widin Klasén
Rick Wildes
Bryan M. Williams
Williem Williem
Ole Winther
Scott Wisdom
Alex Wong
Chau-Wai Wong
Kwan-Yee K. Wong
Yongkang Wong
Scott Workman
Marcel Worring
Michael Wray
Safwan Wshah
Xiang Wu
Aming Wu
Chongruo Wu
Cho-Ying Wu
Chunpeng Wu
Chenyan Wu
Ziyi Wu
Fuxiang Wu
Gang Wu
Haiping Wu
Huisi Wu
Jane Wu

Jialian Wu
Jing Wu
Jinjian Wu
Jianlong Wu
Xian Wu
Lifang Wu
Lifan Wu
Minye Wu
Qianyi Wu
Rongliang Wu
Rui Wu
Shiqian Wu
Shuzhe Wu
Shangzhe Wu
Tsung-Han Wu
Tz-Ying Wu
Ting-Wei Wu
Jiannan Wu
Zhiliang Wu
Yu Wu
Chenyun Wu
Dayan Wu
Dongxian Wu
Fei Wu
Hefeng Wu
Jianxin Wu
Weibin Wu
Wenxuan Wu
Wenhao Wu
Xiao Wu
Yicheng Wu
Yuanwei Wu
Yu-Huan Wu
Zhenxin Wu
Zhenyu Wu
Wei Wu
Peng Wu
Xiaohe Wu
Xindi Wu
Xinxing Wu
Xinyi Wu
Xingjiao Wu
Xiongwei Wu
Yangzheng Wu
Yanzhao Wu

Yawen Wu
Yong Wu
Yi Wu
Ying Nian Wu
Zhenyao Wu
Zhonghua Wu
Zongze Wu
Zuxuan Wu
Stefanie Wuhrer
Teng Xi
Jianing Xi
Fei Xia
Haifeng Xia
Menghan Xia
Yuanqing Xia
Zhihua Xia
Xiaobo Xia
Weihao Xia
Shihong Xia
Yan Xia
Yong Xia
Zhaoyang Xia
Zhihao Xia
Chuhua Xian
Yongqin Xian
Wangmeng Xiang
Fanbo Xiang
Tiange Xiang
Tao Xiang
Liuyu Xiang
Xiaoyu Xiang
Zhiyu Xiang
Aoran Xiao
Chunxia Xiao
Fanyi Xiao
Jimin Xiao
Jun Xiao
Taihong Xiao
Anqi Xiao
Junfei Xiao
Jing Xiao
Liang Xiao
Yang Xiao
Yuting Xiao
Yijun Xiao

Yao Xiao
Zeyu Xiao
Zhisheng Xiao
Zihao Xiao
Binhui Xie
Christopher Xie
Haozhe Xie
Jin Xie
Guo-Sen Xie
Hongtao Xie
Ming-Kun Xie
Tingting Xie
Chaohao Xie
Weicheng Xie
Xudong Xie
Jiyang Xie
Xiaohua Xie
Yuan Xie
Zhenyu Xie
Ning Xie
Xianghui Xie
Xiufeng Xie
You Xie
Yutong Xie
Fuyong Xing
Yifan Xing
Zhen Xing
Yuanjun Xiong
Jinhui Xiong
Weihua Xiong
Hongkai Xiong
Zhitong Xiong
Yuanhao Xiong
Yunyang Xiong
Yuwen Xiong
Zhiwei Xiong
Yuliang Xiu
An Xu
Chang Xu
Chenliang Xu
Chengming Xu
Chenshu Xu
Xiang Xu
Huijuan Xu
Zhe Xu

Jie Xu
Jingyi Xu
Jiarui Xu
Yinghao Xu
Kele Xu
Ke Xu
Li Xu
Linchuan Xu
Linning Xu
Mengde Xu
Mengmeng Frost Xu
Min Xu
Mingye Xu
Jun Xu
Ning Xu
Peng Xu
Runsheng Xu
Sheng Xu
Wenqiang Xu
Xiaogang Xu
Renzhe Xu
Kaidi Xu
Yi Xu
Chi Xu
Qiuling Xu
Baobei Xu
Feng Xu
Haohang Xu
Haofei Xu
Lan Xu
Mingze Xu
Songcen Xu
Weipeng Xu
Wenjia Xu
Wenju Xu
Xiangyu Xu
Xin Xu
Yinshuang Xu
Yixing Xu
Yuting Xu
Yanyu Xu
Zhenbo Xu
Zhiliang Xu
Zhiyuan Xu
Xiaohao Xu

Yanwu Xu
Yan Xu
Yiran Xu
Yifan Xu
Yufei Xu
Yong Xu
Zichuan Xu
Zenglin Xu
Zexiang Xu
Zhan Xu
Zheng Xu
Zhiwei Xu
Ziyue Xu
Shiyu Xuan
Hanyu Xuan
Fei Xue
Jianru Xue
Mingfu Xue
Qinghan Xue
Tianfan Xue
Chao Xue
Chuhui Xue
Nan Xue
Zhou Xue
Xiangyang Xue
Yuan Xue
Abhay Yadav
Ravindra Yadav
Kota Yamaguchi
Toshihiko Yamasaki
Kohei Yamashita
Chaochao Yan
Feng Yan
Kun Yan
Qingsen Yan
Qixin Yan
Rui Yan
Siming Yan
Xinchen Yan
Yaping Yan
Bin Yan
Qingan Yan
Shen Yan
Shipeng Yan
Xu Yan

Yan Yan
Yichao Yan
Zhaoyi Yan
Zike Yan
Zhiqiang Yan
Hongliang Yan
Zizheng Yan
Jiewen Yang
Anqi Joyce Yang
Shan Yang
Anqi Yang
Antoine Yang
Bo Yang
Baoyao Yang
Chenhongyi Yang
Dingkang Yang
De-Nian Yang
Dong Yang
David Yang
Fan Yang
Fengyu Yang
Fengting Yang
Fei Yang
Gengshan Yang
Heng Yang
Han Yang
Huan Yang
Yibo Yang
Jiancheng Yang
Jihan Yang
Jiawei Yang
Jiayu Yang
Jie Yang
Jinfa Yang
Jingkang Yang
Jinyu Yang
Cheng-Fu Yang
Ji Yang
Jianyu Yang
Kailun Yang
Tian Yang
Luyu Yang
Liang Yang
Li Yang
Michael Ying Yang

Yang Yang
Muli Yang
Le Yang
Qiushi Yang
Ren Yang
Ruihan Yang
Shuang Yang
Siyuan Yang
Su Yang
Shiqi Yang
Taojiannan Yang
Tianyu Yang
Lei Yang
Wanzhao Yang
Shuai Yang
William Yang
Wei Yang
Xiaofeng Yang
Xiaoshan Yang
Xin Yang
Xuan Yang
Xu Yang
Xingyi Yang
Xitong Yang
Jing Yang
Yanchao Yang
Wenming Yang
Yujiu Yang
Herb Yang
Jianfei Yang
Jinhui Yang
Chuanguang Yang
Guanglei Yang
Haitao Yang
Kewei Yang
Linlin Yang
Lijin Yang
Longrong Yang
Meng Yang
MingKun Yang
Sibei Yang
Shicai Yang
Tong Yang
Wen Yang
Xi Yang

Xiaolong Yang
Xue Yang
Yubin Yang
Ze Yang
Ziyi Yang
Yi Yang
Linjie Yang
Yuzhe Yang
Yiding Yang
Zhenpei Yang
Zhaohui Yang
Zhengyuan Yang
Zhibo Yang
Zongxin Yang
Hantao Yao
Mingde Yao
Rui Yao
Taiping Yao
Ting Yao
Cong Yao
Qingsong Yao
Quanming Yao
Xu Yao
Yuan Yao
Yao Yao
Yazhou Yao
Jiawen Yao
Shunyu Yao
Pew-Thian Yap
Sudhir Yarram
Rajeev Yasarla
Peng Ye
Botao Ye
Mao Ye
Fei Ye
Hanrong Ye
Jingwen Ye
Jinwei Ye
Jiarong Ye
Mang Ye
Meng Ye
Qi Ye
Qian Ye
Qixiang Ye
Junjie Ye

Sheng Ye
Nanyang Ye
Yufei Ye
Xiaoqing Ye
Ruolin Ye
Yousef Yeganeh
Chun-Hsiao Yeh
Raymond A. Yeh
Yu-Ying Yeh
Kai Yi
Chang Yi
Renjiao Yi
Xinping Yi
Peng Yi
Alper Yilmaz
Junho Yim
Hui Yin
Bangjie Yin
Jia-Li Yin
Miao Yin
Wenzhe Yin
Xuwang Yin
Ming Yin
Yu Yin
Aoxiong Yin
Kangxue Yin
Tianwei Yin
Wei Yin
Xianghua Ying
Rio Yokota
Tatsuya Yokota
Naoto Yokoya
Ryo Yonetani
Ki Yoon Yoo
Jinsu Yoo
Sunjae Yoon
Jae Shin Yoon
Jihun Yoon
Sung-Hoon Yoon
Ryota Yoshihashi
Yusuke Yoshiyasu
Chenyu You
Haoran You
Haoxuan You
Yang You

Quanzeng You
Tackgeun You
Kaichao You
Shan You
Xinge You
Yurong You
Baosheng Yu
Bei Yu
Haichao Yu
Hao Yu
Chaohui Yu
Fisher Yu
Jin-Gang Yu
Jiyang Yu
Jason J. Yu
Jiashuo Yu
Hong-Xing Yu
Lei Yu
Mulin Yu
Ning Yu
Peilin Yu
Qi Yu
Qian Yu
Rui Yu
Shuzhi Yu
Gang Yu
Tan Yu
Weijiang Yu
Xin Yu
Bingyao Yu
Ye Yu
Hanchao Yu
Yingchen Yu
Tao Yu
Xiaotian Yu
Qing Yu
Houjian Yu
Changqian Yu
Jing Yu
Jun Yu
Shujian Yu
Xiang Yu
Zhaofei Yu
Zhenbo Yu
Yinfeng Yu

Zhuoran Yu
Zitong Yu
Bo Yuan
Jiangbo Yuan
Liangzhe Yuan
Weihao Yuan
Jianbo Yuan
Xiaoyun Yuan
Ye Yuan
Li Yuan
Geng Yuan
Jialin Yuan
Maoxun Yuan
Peng Yuan
Xin Yuan
Yuan Yuan
Yuhui Yuan
Yixuan Yuan
Zheng Yuan
Mehmet Kerim Yücel
Kaiyu Yue
Haixiao Yue
Heeseung Yun
Sangdoo Yun
Tian Yun
Mahmut Yurt
Ekim Yurtsever
Ahmet Yüzügüler
Edouard Yvinec
Eloi Zablocki
Christopher Zach
Muhammad Zaigham
   Zaheer
Pierluigi Zama Ramirez
Yuhang Zang
Pietro Zanuttigh
Alexey Zaytsev
Bernhard Zeisl
Haitian Zeng
Pengpeng Zeng
Jiabei Zeng
Runhao Zeng
Wei Zeng
Yawen Zeng
Yi Zeng

Yiming Zeng
Tieyong Zeng
Huanqiang Zeng
Dan Zeng
Yu Zeng
Wei Zhai
Yuanhao Zhai
Fangneng Zhan
Kun Zhan
Xiong Zhang
Jingdong Zhang
Jiangning Zhang
Zhilu Zhang
Gengwei Zhang
Dongsu Zhang
Hui Zhang
Binjie Zhang
Bo Zhang
Tianhao Zhang
Cecilia Zhang
Jing Zhang
Chaoning Zhang
Chenxu Zhang
Chi Zhang
Chris Zhang
Yabin Zhang
Zhao Zhang
Rufeng Zhang
Chaoyi Zhang
Zheng Zhang
Da Zhang
Yi Zhang
Edward Zhang
Xin Zhang
Feifei Zhang
Feilong Zhang
Yuqi Zhang
GuiXuan Zhang
Hanlin Zhang
Hanwang Zhang
Hanzhen Zhang
Haotian Zhang
He Zhang
Haokui Zhang
Hongyuan Zhang

Hengrui Zhang
Hongming Zhang
Mingfang Zhang
Jianpeng Zhang
Jiaming Zhang
Jichao Zhang
Jie Zhang
Jingfeng Zhang
Jingyi Zhang
Jinnian Zhang
David Junhao Zhang
Junjie Zhang
Junzhe Zhang
Jiawan Zhang
Jingyang Zhang
Kai Zhang
Lei Zhang
Lihua Zhang
Lu Zhang
Miao Zhang
Minjia Zhang
Mingjin Zhang
Qi Zhang
Qian Zhang
Qilong Zhang
Qiming Zhang
Qiang Zhang
Richard Zhang
Ruimao Zhang
Ruisi Zhang
Ruixin Zhang
Runze Zhang
Qilin Zhang
Shan Zhang
Shanshan Zhang
Xi Sheryl Zhang
Song-Hai Zhang
Chongyang Zhang
Kaihao Zhang
Songyang Zhang
Shu Zhang
Siwei Zhang
Shujian Zhang
Tianyun Zhang
Tong Zhang

Tao Zhang
Wenwei Zhang
Wenqiang Zhang
Wen Zhang
Xiaolin Zhang
Xingchen Zhang
Xingxuan Zhang
Xiuming Zhang
Xiaoshuai Zhang
Xuanmeng Zhang
Xuanyang Zhang
Xucong Zhang
Xingxing Zhang
Xikun Zhang
Xiaohan Zhang
Yahui Zhang
Yunhua Zhang
Yan Zhang
Yanghao Zhang
Yifei Zhang
Yifan Zhang
Yi-Fan Zhang
Yihao Zhang
Yingliang Zhang
Youshan Zhang
Yulun Zhang
Yushu Zhang
Yixiao Zhang
Yide Zhang
Zhongwen Zhang
Bowen Zhang
Chen-Lin Zhang
Zehua Zhang
Zekun Zhang
Zeyu Zhang
Xiaowei Zhang
Yifeng Zhang
Cheng Zhang
Hongguang Zhang
Yuexi Zhang
Fa Zhang
Guofeng Zhang
Hao Zhang
Haofeng Zhang
Hongwen Zhang

Hua Zhang
Jiaxin Zhang
Zhenyu Zhang
Jian Zhang
Jianfeng Zhang
Jiao Zhang
Jiakai Zhang
Lefei Zhang
Le Zhang
Mi Zhang
Min Zhang
Ning Zhang
Pan Zhang
Pu Zhang
Qing Zhang
Renrui Zhang
Shifeng Zhang
Shuo Zhang
Shaoxiong Zhang
Weizhong Zhang
Xi Zhang
Xiaomei Zhang
Xinyu Zhang
Yin Zhang
Zicheng Zhang
Zihao Zhang
Ziqi Zhang
Zhaoxiang Zhang
Zhen Zhang
Zhipeng Zhang
Zhixing Zhang
Zhizheng Zhang
Jiawei Zhang
Zhong Zhang
Pingping Zhang
Yixin Zhang
Kui Zhang
Lingzhi Zhang
Huaiwen Zhang
Quanshi Zhang
Zhoutong Zhang
Yuhang Zhang
Yuting Zhang
Zhang Zhang
Ziming Zhang

Zhizhong Zhang
Qilong Zhangli
Bingyin Zhao
Bin Zhao
Chenglong Zhao
Lei Zhao
Feng Zhao
Gangming Zhao
Haiyan Zhao
Hao Zhao
Handong Zhao
Hengshuang Zhao
Yinan Zhao
Jiaojiao Zhao
Jiaqi Zhao
Jing Zhao
Kaili Zhao
Haojie Zhao
Yucheng Zhao
Longjiao Zhao
Long Zhao
Qingsong Zhao
Qingyu Zhao
Rui Zhao
Rui-Wei Zhao
Sicheng Zhao
Shuang Zhao
Siyan Zhao
Zelin Zhao
Shiyu Zhao
Wang Zhao
Tiesong Zhao
Qian Zhao
Wangbo Zhao
Xi-Le Zhao
Xu Zhao
Yajie Zhao
Yang Zhao
Ying Zhao
Yin Zhao
Yizhou Zhao
Yunhan Zhao
Yuyang Zhao
Yue Zhao
Yuzhi Zhao

Bowen Zhao
Pu Zhao
Bingchen Zhao
Borui Zhao
Fuqiang Zhao
Hanbin Zhao
Jian Zhao
Mingyang Zhao
Na Zhao
Rongchang Zhao
Ruiqi Zhao
Shuai Zhao
Wenda Zhao
Wenliang Zhao
Xiangyun Zhao
Yifan Zhao
Yaping Zhao
Zhou Zhao
He Zhao
Jie Zhao
Xibin Zhao
Xiaoqi Zhao
Zhengyu Zhao
Jin Zhe
Chuanxia Zheng
Huan Zheng
Hao Zheng
Jia Zheng
Jian-Qing Zheng
Shuai Zheng
Meng Zheng
Mingkai Zheng
Qian Zheng
Qi Zheng
Wu Zheng
Yinqiang Zheng
Yufeng Zheng
Yutong Zheng
Yalin Zheng
Yu Zheng
Feng Zheng
Zhaoheng Zheng
Haitian Zheng
Kang Zheng
Bolun Zheng

Haiyong Zheng
Mingwu Zheng
Sipeng Zheng
Tu Zheng
Wenzhao Zheng
Xiawu Zheng
Yinglin Zheng
Zhuo Zheng
Zilong Zheng
Kecheng Zheng
Zerong Zheng
Shuaifeng Zhi
Tiancheng Zhi
Jia-Xing Zhong
Yiwu Zhong
Fangwei Zhong
Zhihang Zhong
Yaoyao Zhong
Yiran Zhong
Zhun Zhong
Zichun Zhong
Bo Zhou
Boyao Zhou
Brady Zhou
Mo Zhou
Chunluan Zhou
Dingfu Zhou
Fan Zhou
Jingkai Zhou
Honglu Zhou
Jiaming Zhou
Jiahuan Zhou
Jun Zhou
Kaiyang Zhou
Keyang Zhou
Kuangqi Zhou
Lei Zhou
Lihua Zhou
Man Zhou
Mingyi Zhou
Mingyuan Zhou
Ning Zhou
Peng Zhou
Penghao Zhou
Qianyi Zhou

Shuigeng Zhou
Shangchen Zhou
Huayi Zhou
Zhize Zhou
Sanping Zhou
Qin Zhou
Tao Zhou
Wenbo Zhou
Xiangdong Zhou
Xiao-Yun Zhou
Xiao Zhou
Yang Zhou
Yipin Zhou
Zhenyu Zhou
Hao Zhou
Chu Zhou
Daquan Zhou
Da-Wei Zhou
Hang Zhou
Kang Zhou
Qianyu Zhou
Sheng Zhou
Wenhui Zhou
Xingyi Zhou
Yan-Jie Zhou
Yiyi Zhou
Yu Zhou
Yuan Zhou
Yuqian Zhou
Yuxuan Zhou
Zixiang Zhou
Wengang Zhou
Shuchang Zhou
Tianfei Zhou
Yichao Zhou
Alex Zhu
Chenchen Zhu
Deyao Zhu
Xiatian Zhu
Guibo Zhu
Haidong Zhu
Hao Zhu
Hongzi Zhu
Rui Zhu
Jing Zhu

Jianke Zhu
Junchen Zhu
Lei Zhu
Lingyu Zhu
Luyang Zhu
Menglong Zhu
Peihao Zhu
Hui Zhu
Xiaofeng Zhu
Tyler (Lixuan) Zhu
Wentao Zhu
Xiangyu Zhu
Xinqi Zhu
Xinxin Zhu
Xinliang Zhu
Yangguang Zhu
Yichen Zhu
Yixin Zhu
Yanjun Zhu
Yousong Zhu
Yuhao Zhu
Ye Zhu
Feng Zhu
Zhen Zhu
Fangrui Zhu
Jinjing Zhu
Linchao Zhu
Pengfei Zhu
Sijie Zhu
Xiaobin Zhu
Xiaoguang Zhu
Zezhou Zhu
Zhenyao Zhu
Kai Zhu
Pengkai Zhu
Bingbing Zhuang
Chengyuan Zhuang
Liansheng Zhuang
Peiye Zhuang
Yixin Zhuang
Yihong Zhuang
Junbao Zhuo
Andrea Ziani
Bartosz Zieliński
Primo Zingaretti

lii   Organization

Nikolaos Zioulis
Andrew Zisserman
Yael Ziv
Liu Ziyin
Xingxing Zou
Danping Zou
Qi Zou

Shihao Zou
Xueyan Zou
Yang Zou
Yuliang Zou
Zihang Zou
Chuhang Zou
Dongqing Zou

Xu Zou
Zhiming Zou
Maria A. Zuluaga
Xinxin Zuo
Zhiwen Zuo
Reyer Zwiggelaar

Contents – Part VII

CT²: Colorization Transformer via Color Tokens

Shuchen Weng[1], Jimeng Sun[2], Yu Li[3], Si Li[2], and Boxin Shi[1(✉)]

[1] NERCVT, School of Computer Science, Peking University, Beijing, China
{shuchenweng,shiboxin}@pku.edu.cn
[2] School of Artificial Intelligence, Beijing University of Posts
and Telecommunications, Beijing, China
{sjm,lisi}@bupt.edu.cn
[3] International Digital Economy Academy, Shenzhen, China
liyu@idea.edu.cn

Abstract. Automatic image colorization is an ill-posed problem with multi-modal uncertainty, and there remains two main challenges with previous methods: incorrect semantic colors and under-saturation. In this paper, we propose an end-to-end transformer-based model to overcome these challenges. Benefited from the long-range context extraction of transformer and our holistic architecture, our method could colorize images with more diverse colors. Besides, we introduce color tokens into our approach and treat the colorization task as a classification problem, which increases the saturation of results. We also propose a series of modules to make image features interact with color tokens, and restrict the range of possible color candidates, which makes our results visually pleasing and reasonable. In addition, our method does not require any additional external priors, which ensures its well generalization capability. Extensive experiments and user studies demonstrate that our method achieves superior performance than previous works.

1 Introduction

Image colorization, a classic computer vision task, aims to convert the grayscale image into a plausible colorful one, which has broad applications in legacy image/video restoration, artistic creation, and image compression. To meet the requirement of colorization, fully automatic methods seek and cue appropriate color hints from complex image semantics (*e.g.*, shape, texture, and context).

In earlier methods, researchers focus on feature engineering, which takes handcraft approaches [6] or pyramid-shaped encoder [18] to acquire high-level image features, following a stack of convolutions to colorize images. One of them is the Colorful Image Colorization (CIC) [32], which poses colorization as a

---

S. Weng and J. Sun—Equal contributions.

Supplementary Information The online version contains supplementary material available at https://doi.org/10.1007/978-3-031-20071-7_1.

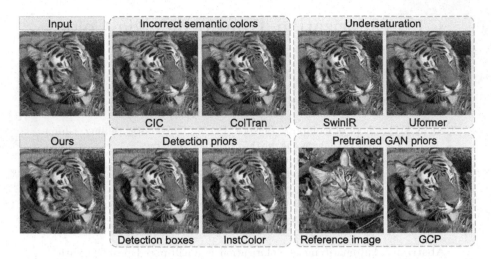

Fig. 1. *Top left*: Existing automatic colorization methods are either limited by insufficient representation ability of the network to infer colors from semantic cues (CIC [32]) or adopting staged training and aggressive sampling strategy (ColTran [17]), leading to counterintuitive colorized results. *Top right*: Advanced transformer-based image restoration methods (SwinIR [21] and Uformer [29]) produce overly conservative undersaturated results because of constructing standard regression model. *Bottom*: Methods taking external priors rely heavily on the performance of upstream models. Detection boxes as priors may be ineffective when the object covers the whole image (red boxes, 2nd column in bottom row), which limits the model performance (InstColor [26]); and pretrained GAN priors may generate inappropriate reference instances (the grey tabby cat, 4th column in bottom row), which leads to incorrect colorization (GCP [31]). We propose CT^2 to generate colorization results with reasonable semantic colors and proper saturation level without any additional external priors. (Color figure online)

classification task to make results more colorful. But limited by the content-independent interaction modeling and local inductive bias of convolutional neural network (CNN), their results have **incorrect semantic colors** (Fig. 1 CIC). To capture long-range dependency, ColTran [17] builds a probabilistic model with multiple transformer subnets which takes staged training and aggressive sampling strategies. However, as subnets of the ColTran are trained independently, the prediction error of each subnet will accumulate to a large one, which also leads to noticeable **incorrect semantic colors** in the final colorization results (Fig. 1 ColTran). Advanced transformer-based vision models have shown great success in image restoration, *e.g.*, SwinIR [21] and Uformer [29], benefited from their flexible receptive fields, coarse-to-fine feature expression, and end-to-end training. However, they bear **undersaturation** because the models they adopt are standard regression models, which encourage conservative predictions in the colorization task (Fig. 1 SwinIR and Uformer).

To overcome the aforementioned challenges, some researchers introduce external priors into colorization task, *e.g.*, object detection boxes [26], segmentation masks [35,36], and pretrained GANs [19,31]. However, these priors need additional data annotation or interaction with users, which may be ineffective or inaccurate in "out-of-distribution" scenarios (Fig. 1 InstColor and GCP).

In this paper, we propose Colorization Transformer via Color Tokens (**CT²**) to deal with incorrect semantic colors and undersaturation without any additional external priors (Fig. 1 Ours). For *(i)* **incorrect semantic colors**, we build our model based on an end-to-end transformer backbone with a newly proposed luminance-selecting module. Thanks to the long-range dependency capture ability of transformer architecture, our method copes with local nuisances in data better. In addition, the end-to-end design with the luminance-selecting module can alleviate error accumulation in staged training and avoid empirically unreasonable colors. For *(ii)* **undersaturation**, we introduce color tokens into colorization pipeline to model this task as the classification problem. We design color attention and color query modules to strengthen the interaction between grayscale image patches and color tokens, and assign vivid and plausible colors under the guidance of the luminance-selecting module.

CT² makes the following contributions:

- We develop an end-to-end colorization transformer model with the luminance-selecting module to generate semantically reasonable colorized images by narrowing the range of optional color candidates. Since no additional external priors are required, our model is applicable to more general scenarios.
- We propose color tokens into colorization task by color embedding module, with which colorization task could be treated as the classification problem for increasing saturation.
- We design color attention and color query modules to guide the interaction of grayscale image patches and optional color candidates, and generate more visually pleasing and plausible results than previous methods.

The experiments demonstrate that CT² provides higher quality colorization results both quantitatively and qualitatively, and its extensive applicability in colorizing legacy photos.

2   Related Works

Automatic Colorization. Early automatic colorization methods struggle at integrating handcraft features into deep neural network [6]. With the emergence of CNN, which significantly increases the representation ability of neural network, some works [10,16,18,32] begin to pay more attention to the network architecture and fully automatic feature extraction engineering to improve colorization performance. Later, researchers experiment with multiple advanced generative models to meet the challenges in colorization. MDN [8] takes variational autoencoder (VAE) to obtain diverse colorized results. colorGAN and ChromaGAN [3,28] take generative adversarial model (GAN) to make results vivid. CINN [2] introduces an invertible neural network to avoid mode collapse benefited from bidirectional architecture. Other works focus on using external prior knowledge to optimize the colorization algorithm. InstColor [26] utilizes the detection model to localize objects, which demonstrates that the clear figure-ground separation helps performance improve. Some works [35,36] take segmentation masks as the pixel-level object semantics to guide colorization. In addition, well-pretrained GANs [19,31] are also regarded as priors by generating reference instances as the guidance of colorization.

Vision Transformer for Low-Level Problems. Transformer [27] is firstly proposed to model sequence in natural language processing. Due to its long-range receptive field, it has made a tremendous progress in solving a diversity of computer vision problems, *e.g.*, image classification [9,22], object detection [4,38], and segmentation [25,37]. The significant performance improvement appeals researchers to introduce transformer models into low-level problems, *e.g.* image restoration, and colorization task. IPT [5] jointly trains transformer blocks with multi-heads and multi-tails on multiple low-level vision tasks, by relying on a large-scale synthesized dataset. EDT [20] proposes a novel encoder-decoder architecture to make data and computation efficient. SwinIR [21] incorporates shifted window mechanism into transformer which decreases the calculated amount. Inspired by the famous CNN architecture U-Net [23], Uformer [29] proposes a multi-scale restoration modulator to adjust on multi-scale features. For colorization problem, ColTran [17] builds a probabilistic model with transformer and samples colors from the learned distribution to make results diverse.

3   Method

The framework of CT^2 is composed of three core components: *(i)* an image encoder to extract grayscale image features and encode the sequence of patches into patch embeddings, *(ii)* a color encoder to acquire the relative position relationship of the defined color tokens in quantized ab space, *(iii)* a lightweight decoder consisting of the color transformer to interact color encodings with grayscale image features, the luminance-selecting module to narrow the range of color candidates, the upsampler to expand resolution, and the color query module to assign appropriate colors. See Fig. 2 for an overview. Next, we elaborate on the detailed designs of these modules and the losses we used for colorization.

3.1   Image Encoder

We use the standard vision transformer (ViT) [9] as our image encoder to extract long-range features of the input image. Given a single-channel grayscale image $I_L \in \mathbb{R}^{H \times W}$, we split it into a sequence of patches $I_L = [I_{L_1}, ..., I_{L_N}] \in \mathbb{R}^{N \times P^2}$, where H and W are image height and width, (P, P) is the patch size, and $N = HW/P^2$ is the number of patches. Then, with a linear projection layer, we map the input patches into a sequence of patch embeddings $I_e \in \mathbb{R}^{N \times C}$, where C is the number of channels. To capture positional information, learnable positional embeddings $I_{pos} \in \mathbb{R}^{N \times C}$ are added to the patch embeddings to get the input image tokens, written as $Z_0 = I_e + I_{pos}$.

The L-layer transformer is applied to the input tokens Z_0 to generate a sequence of contextualized embeddings Z_L. Each transformer layer consists of a

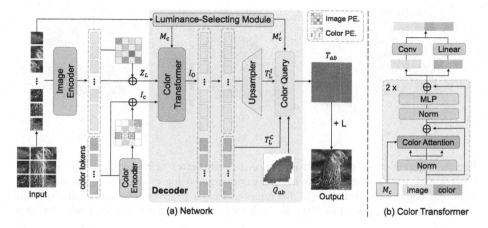

Fig. 2. (a) Overview of the proposed CT^2 network: The input grayscale image is split into image patches, and encoded into a sequence of tokens. The ab color space is quantized and extracted into multiple valid color tokens. Then all tokens are separately added with Positional Encodings (PE), and fed into the color transformer, where the color information is injected into grayscale image tokens under the guidance of the luminance-selecting module. After processed by the upsampler, the tokens are upsampled into pixel level. Color query module predicts ab pairs for every pixel conditioned on the luminance-selecting module. We concatenate predicted ab pairs with the input luminance channel to obtain colorization results. (b) The structure of the color transformer.

multi-headed self-attention (MSA) block, an MLP block with two linear layers, two LayerNorm (LN) modules, and residual connections after blocks. Finally we obtain the output $Z_L \in \mathbb{R}^{N \times C}$, a sequence containing rich long-range image semantics, which is added with the conditional positional encodings [7] and fed into the decoder (Sect. 3.3) as image features.

3.2 Color Encoder

The colorization task aims to learn the mapping from the input luminance channel L to the two associated color channels ab, which is performed in CIE Lab color space. Following CIC [32], we take samples in the training set to calculate the empirical probability distribution of ab values in ab color space (Fig. 3(a)). The distribution reveals the preference of ab pairs in natural images, $e.g.$, low saturation ab pairs (a, b values close to 0) are used more frequently while colorful ab pairs only appear in a few samples. Thus, if the model penalizes all ab pairs equally during training, the model is not capable to produce colorful results due to the dominance of low-saturation samples, resulting in undersaturated results. In addition, constructing a regression model to solve the colorization problem will produce average results, which tends to colorize images with insufficient saturation depending on empirical distribution (frequent low-saturation samples).

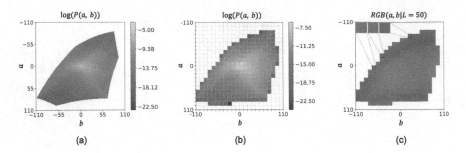

Fig. 3. Illustration of quantized ab space. (a) Statistics of empirical distribution in the training set. We show probability distribution in log scale, where darker colors represent higher probabilities. (b) 484 quantized color patches. The probability of each patch is the mean value of the 10×10 sliding window. Note that only 313 color patches are valid. (c) An example shows that the closer patches are in ab color space, the more similar their colors represent, and vice versa.

Hence, we introduce *color tokens* into CT^2 to formulate the colorization task as a classification problem to mitigate undersaturation.

We use the sliding window of size 10 and stride 10 to divide the ab color space into 484 color patches, and calculate the mean probability distribution in each color patch (Fig. 3(b)). Considering there are some color patches that never appear in empirical distribution (the white patches shown in Fig. 3(b)), we filter them out and encode the remaining valid 313 color patches by assigning a randomly initialized learnable vector to each patch in color embedding module. We define the embedded color patches as color tokens $I_c \in \mathbb{R}^{313 \times C}$. Considering that the closer the color tokens are in the quantized ab color space, the more similar the color properties are (*e.g.*, blue is more similar with cyan than green, as shown in Fig. 3(c)), we add positional information into color tokens by applying conditional positional encodings [7]. Specifically, color tokens are reshaped and zero-padded into spatial 2D quantized ab space following a convolution with 3×3 kernel, which provides relative position information and constrains the similarity between adjacent vectors in the embedded feature space. Then, we flatten the output of convolution back into the sequence as color positional encodings, which are added into the original color tokens. Finally, we obtain the embedded color tokens $I_c \in \mathbb{R}^{313 \times C}$, as color features to feed into the decoder.

3.3   Decoder

The decoder is designed to interact grayscale image features Z_L with color features I_c, and finally generate colorful images, which is the key component of CT^2. As shown in Fig. 2(a), the decoder first calculates the color mask M_c with the luminance-selecting module to construct the mapping from luminance L to the optional range of color tokens, which is used as the guidance in the following color transformer and color query module. Then the image features Z_L and color features I_c are fed into the color transformer module, where color information

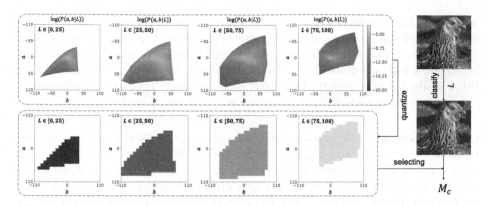

Fig. 4. The process of calculating color mask M_c with the luminance-selecting module. The top row illustrates the empirical probability distribution of ab values conditioned on L, and the bottom row illustrates the valid quantized ab patches corresponding to the different probability distributions.

is injected into grayscale image features. After that, the colorized patch-level features are upsampled to pixel-level in the upsampler module. Finally, the color query module calculates pixel-level color scores and predicts the reasonable color for each pixel. Next, we describe the proposed modules in the decoder in detail.

Luminance-Selecting Module. By observing that ab distribution varies with luminance L, we split L value into 4 non-overlapping intervals, and show the ab empirical probability distribution conditioned on different L ranges in the top row of Fig. 4. Thus we can reduce the optional quantized ab patches according to the corresponding empirical distribution, and further improve the accuracy of model prediction to avoid generating incorrect semantic colors. Specifically, we first classify the L value of the input image into 4 groups, the same as the 4 aforementioned non-overlapping intervals, which are expressed with 4 varying degrees of gray levels. Then we quantize the ab probability distribution and obtain the quantized ab patches conditioned on L, as shown in the bottom row of Fig. 4. Finally, conditioned on the classified L of the input image, we select the corresponding quantized ab patches and construct a one-hot mask $M_c \in \mathbb{R}^{H \times W \times 313}$, denoted as *color mask*, where we set the indices of optional ab patches among 313 classes as 1 and otherwise 0 for every pixel. Based on empirical distribution statistics in the training set, color mask rules out the rare strange colorization predictions and further reduces the ambiguity of colorization.

Color Transformer. The color transformer is proposed to inject color information into grayscale image features, which is composed of two transformer layers and a following projection module. The grayscale image tokens after the encoder and the embedded color tokens are concatenated firstly, and then injected into the color transformer as a whole input sequence. The transformer layer is modified from the standard version [9] by replacing the multi-headed self-attention with the color attention which we will explain later. The projection module is designed for image features and color tokens respectively, where the conventional 3×3 convolution is used to the reshaped image features after the last transformer layer, and a fully connected layer is applied to color tokens I_c, as shown in Fig. 2 (b). Finally, we concatenate the refined image features and color tokens into a sequence as the output of the color transformer, denoted as $I_O \in \mathbb{R}^{(N+313)\times C}$.

Color Attention. We propose the color attention module to bridge the gap between color tokens and image features. Specifically, color attention is essentially a masked multi-headed self-attention, which realizes the color-image interaction and injects color information into gray-scale image features under the guidance of the patch mask. To clearly illustrate it, we first describe the design of the patch mask which limits the scope of color-image interaction, and then illustrate the process of performing color attention.

Similar to the input image, we split the color mask M_c into a sequence of patches $M_c = [M_{c_1}, ..., M_{c_N}] \in \mathbb{R}^{N \times P^2 \times 313}$. For each color mask patch M_{c_i}, the model calculates the corresponding union set of the P^2 pixel values, and then concatenates all union sets as follows:

$$I_M = \text{Concat}_{i\in\{1,...,N\}} \cup_{j\in\{1,...,P^2\}} M_{c_{i,j}}, \tag{1}$$

where $M_{c_{i,j}} \in \mathbb{R}^{313}$ denotes the binary mask corresponding to the j-th luminance value in the i-th image feature patch, and $I_M \in \mathbb{R}^{N\times313}$ represents the *patch mask* which indicates inappropriate color tokens for patch-level image features. Next, considering the input sequence is the concatenation of image patch tokens and color tokens, we compose the patch mask I_M, the transpose of patch mask $I_M^\top$, and two all-1 matrices, denoted as $\mathbb{1}^{N\times N}$ and $\mathbb{1}^{313\times313}$, into the *attention mask* $I_M' \in \mathbb{R}^{(N+313)\times(N+313)}$, as follows:

$$I_M' = \begin{bmatrix} \mathbb{1}^{N\times N} & I_M \\ I_M^\top & \mathbb{1}^{313\times313} \end{bmatrix}. \tag{2}$$

To rule out the unreasonable color tokens in color attention, we convert I_M' into another binary mask $M \in \mathbb{R}^{(N+313)\times(N+313)}$, where we set the value to $-\infty$ corresponding to indicate undesirable color tokens and otherwise 0:

$$M = \begin{cases} 0 & \text{where } I_M' = 1 \\ -\infty & \text{where } I_M' = 0 \end{cases}, \tag{3}$$

After that, the binary mask M is utilized in the masked multi-headed self-attention to obtain the refined features:

$$\text{ColorAttention}(Q,K,V,M) = \text{Softmax}\left(M + \frac{QK^\top}{\sqrt{C}}\right)V, \tag{4}$$

where $Q, K, V \in \mathbb{R}^{(N+313)\times C}$ denote query, key, and value respectively, which are obtained from LayerNorm and MLP blocks processing the concatenation of image features $Z_L \in \mathbb{R}^{N\times C}$ and color tokens $I_c \in \mathbb{R}^{313\times C}$, note that both of them are added with positional encodings. C is the embedding dim of Q, K, V.

Upsampler. The upsampler is only applied on image patch tokens, which are separated from the output sequence I_O of the color transformer. The progressive upsampler is made up of 4 upsampling blocks, realizing 16 times of upsampling to achieve user-desired resolution. Each block is a stack of a BatchNorm, two ReLU functions, a conventional 3×3 convolution, and a 4×4 transposed convolution with a stride of 2 to extract features and extend spatial resolution.

Color Query. We design the color query module to estimate the correct semantic color for each image pixel and generate colorful results. Given the upsampled image features $T_L^I \in \mathbb{R}^{HW \times C}$ and refined color tokens $T_L^C \subset \mathbb{R}^{313 \times C}$ separated from I_O, the color query module calculates the cross product between the ℓ_2-normalized T_L^I and T_L^C under the guidance of the color mask M_c, where we also set the value to $-\infty$ for indices of inappropriate color tokens, and otherwise 0, denoted as $M_c' \in \mathbb{R}^{HW \times 313}$. We formulate the process as follows:

$$\hat{I}_q = \text{softmax}(\|T_L^I\|_2 \|T_L^C\|_2^\top + M_c'), \tag{5}$$

where $\hat{I}_q \in \mathbb{R}^{HW \times 313}$ is the probability distribution of the 313 color candidates. We utilized the predicted probability as the weight to summarize the quantized ab pairs $Q_{ab} \in \mathbb{R}^{313 \times 2}$ to finally obtain suitable colorized ab values, written as:

$$T_{ab} = \hat{I}_q \cdot Q_{ab}. \tag{6}$$

The final *Lab* image I_{Lab} is obtained by the concatenation of input grayscale image and estimated ab values, written as $I_{Lab} = \text{Concat}(I_L, T_{ab})$.

3.4   Optimization

Losses. We treat the colorization problem as the pixel-wise classification task to alleviate undersaturation, thus we optimize our model by minimizing the cross entropy loss L_{cl}. We quantize the ab space into 313 color candidates, and obtain the probability distribution $\hat{I}_q \in \mathbb{R}^{H \times W \times 313}$ over optional colors as the model prediction. To compare the prediction with the ground truth, we convert the ground truth I_{ab} into the quantized ab space, denoted as $I_q \in \mathbb{R}^{H \times W \times 313}$. Specifically, for every pixel, we find 5-nearest neighbors to I_{ab} among quantized ab pairs, and calculate their distance from I_{ab} as the weight to proportionally construct the normalized soft label I_q. The classification loss is formulated as:

$$L_{cl} = -\sum_{x,y,q} (\log(\hat{I}_q(x,y,q)) - \log(I_q(x,y,q))) I_q(x,y,q), \tag{7}$$

where (x, y) is the location in images, q is the index of quantized color candidates.

In addition, following Zhang *et al.* [34], a smooth-ℓ_1 loss with $\delta = 1$ is adopted to make the training process stable and reduce overly saturated color candidates:

$$L_\delta(T_{ab}, I_{ab}) = \frac{1}{2}(T_{ab} - I_{ab})^2 \mathbb{1}_{\{|T_{ab} - I_{ab}| < \delta\}} + \delta(|T_{ab} - I_{ab}| - \frac{1}{2}\delta)\mathbb{1}_{\{|T_{ab} - I_{ab}| \geq \delta\}}, \tag{8}$$

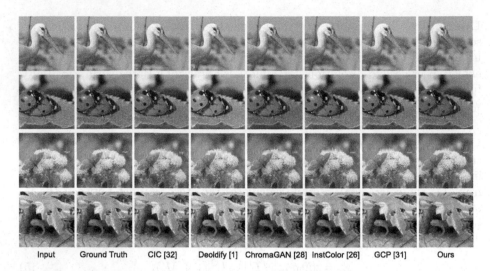

Input   Ground Truth   CIC [32]   Deoldify [1] ChromaGAN [28] InstColor [26]   GCP [31]   Ours

Fig. 5. Comparisons with CNN-based methods. Our method is superior to other comparison methods on semantic color inference, *e.g.*, the beak of the crane (first row) and the ladybug shell (second row). Our method also outperforms other comparison methods on generating colorful results, *e.g.*, flowers (third row) and geckos (last row).

where I_{ab} is the ab channels of ground truth images.

Finally, our loss function L_{total} is a combination of L_{cl} and L_δ, which can be jointly optimized as follows:

$$L_{total} = \alpha L_{cl} + \beta L_\delta, \tag{9}$$

where we set α and β as 1 and 10, respectively.

4 Experiments

Dataset. We conduct our experiments on ImageNet [24], which contains 1.3M images covering 1000 categories. We test on the first 5k images of the public validation set, which is consistent with the previous methods [2,17]. All the test images are center cropped and resized into 256×256 resolution.

Metrics. We report 6 quantitative metrics in Table 1, including Peak Signal-to-Noise Ratio (PSNR) [15], Structural Similarity Index (SSIM) [30], Learned Perceptual Image Patch Similarity (LPIPS) [33], Fréchet inception distance [14], and 2 colorfulness score [12] to reflect the vividness following GCP [31].

Implementation Details. For transformer encoder and decoder, we keep the embedding dim of the MLP block 4 times as the hidden size of the attention block. The input patch size is fixed to 16×16. The image encoder is initialized with the pretrained ViT [9] weights, and the color transformer in the decoder

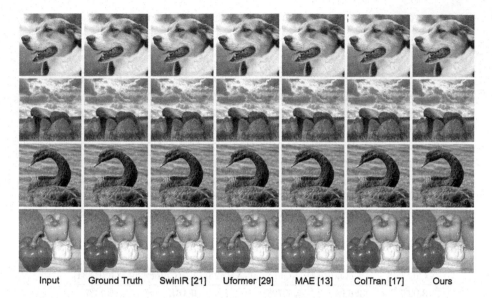

Input   Ground Truth   SwinIR [21]   Uformer [29]   MAE [13]   ColTran [17]   Ours

Fig. 6. Comparisons with transformer-based methods. Different from SwinIR [21], Uformer [29], and MAE [13], our method generates saturated colorized images, *e.g.*, the dog (first row) and the landscape scenes (second row). Our method could also generate correct semantic colors by avoiding error accumulation observed on ColTran [17], *e.g.*, the swan (third row) and vegetables (last row).

is initialized with random weights from a truncated normal distribution [11]. The details of configurations about layers, hidden size, the number of heads in attention blocks of our model are shown in the supplemental materials.

Training Details. We set the batch size to 16 and minimize our objective losses using SGD optimizer and polynomial learning rate schedule. We set the learning rate to 10^{-3} and momentum parameter to 0.9. All experiments are conducted on 8 NVIDIA GeForce RTX 3090 graphic cards and trained for 10 epochs.

4.1 Comparisons with Previous Methods

We make comparisons with 5 CNN-based methods, including CIC [32], DeOldify [1], ChromaGAN [28], InstColor [26], and GCP [31] to show our transformer-based architecture has powerful feature representation ability by capturing long-range dependencies. Note that ChromaGAN [28], InstColor [26], and GCP [31] use additional external priors, while ours without any prior.

We also compare our method with 4 advanced transformer-based methods, including: *(i)* two state-of-the-art image restoration approaches, SwinIR [21] and Uformer [29], by retraining models on the colorization task; *(ii)* the state-of-the-art self-supervised learner MAE [13], by finetuning its pretrained weights to colorization as a downstream task; and *(iii)* the state-of-the-art colorization methods ColTran [17] with same experiment settings.

Table 1. Quantitative comparison results. ↑ (↓) means higher (lower) is better.

Category	Method	FID↓	PSNR↑	SSIM↑	LPIPS↓	colorful↑	△colorful↓
CNN	CIC [32]	8.72	22.64	0.91	0.22	31.60	4.72
	DeOldify [1]	9.45	21.12	0.83	0.24	22.70	13.62
	ChromaGAN [28]	7.66	23.35	0.90	0.21	27.88	8.43
	InstColor [26]	8.06	23.28	0.91	0.21	24.87	11.44
	GCP [31]	5.95	21.68	0.88	0.23	32.98	3.34
Transformer	SwinIR [21]	12.26	21.54	0.78	0.31	16.57	19.75
	Uformer [29]	10.09	22.82	0.86	0.22	17.98	18.33
	MAE [13]	9.45	23.35	0.87	0.21	20.60	15.72
	ColTran [17]	6.44	20.95	0.80	0.29	34.50	2.24
Ours	CT^2	**5.51**	**23.50**	**0.92**	**0.19**	**38.48**	**2.17**

Table 2. User study results. Ours achieves obviously higher score than other methods.

CIC [32]	DeOldify [1]	ChromaGAN [28]	InstColor [26]	GCP [31]
3.02%	3.64%	7.72%	9.16%	15.14%
SwinIR [21]	Uformer [29]	ColTran [17]	MAE [13]	Ours
6.84%	5.48%	6.92%	2.80%	**39.28%**

Quantitative Comparisons. We show the quantitative comparisons in Table 1, where our method achieves state-of-the-art performance on all metrics. The best scores on FID, PSNR, SSIM, and LPIPS demonstrate our method colorizes images with correct semantic colors. The significant leadings in colorfulness metrics show that our method overcomes the undersaturation challenge.

Qualitative Comparisons. The qualitative comparisons demonstrate the effectiveness of our method. We show comparisons with CNN-based methods in Fig. 5. Thanks to the global interaction between features and the strong feature representation ability of transformer, our method could colorize images visually pleasing. We show comparisons with transformer-based methods in Fig. 6. Benefited from our proposed modules for colorization task, we could treat colorization as a classification task, which alleviates undersaturation appeared in other methods. In addition, the end-to-end transformer design avoids error accumulation, resulting in more plausible colors compared with ColTran [17] results.

4.2 User Study

In addition to quantitative and qualitative comparisons, we further conduct user study experiments to evaluate whether our results are favored by human observers. We provide a grayscale image and colorized images from 10 different methods: CIC [32], DeOldify [1], ChromaGAN [28], InstColor [26], GCP [31], SwinIR [21], Uformer [29], MAE [13], ColTran [17] and ours. Participants are asked to choose the most visually pleasing result with respect to the ground

Table 3. Quantitative ablation results. ↑ (↓) means higher (lower) is better.

Category	Method	FID↓	PSNR↑	SSIM↑	LPIPS↓	colorful↑	△colorful↓
Ablation	W/o LSM	7.51	20.99	0.82	0.26	**41.56**	5.24
	W/o color attention	7.76	20.93	0.82	0.27	39.53	3.22
	W/o color query	8.87	21.70	0.90	0.23	39.51	3.19
Ours	CT^2	**5.51**	**23.50**	**0.92**	**0.19**	38.48	**2.17**

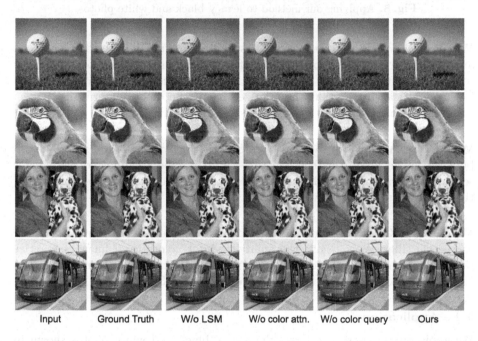

Input   Ground Truth   W/o LSM   W/o color attn.   W/o color query   Ours

Fig. 7. Ablation study. The results become counterintuitive when our proposed modules are disabled.

truth. The experiment set is composed of 100 synthetic images that are randomly selected from the testing set. We publish the experiments on Amazon Mechanical Turk (AMT), and each experiment is completed by 25 participants. We present the results of user study in Table 2, where our method outperforms other comparison methods, confirming its subjective advantages.

4.3 Ablation Study and Discussion

We disable various modules and create three baselines to study the impact of our proposed modules. We show the evaluation scores and colorized images of the ablation study experiments in Table 3 and Fig. 7, respectively. The colorfulness metrics (fifth column) of these ablation baselines are higher than ours, which is probably because the counterintuitive and mixed colors are misjudged as vivid colors by this metric, which we will explain next.

1939. "Drish House" by
Frances Benjamin Johnston.

1939. "Cow boy" by
Arthur Rothstein.

1933. "Manhattan Central Park
in New York" by Samuel Gottscho.

Fig. 8. Applying our method to legacy black and white photos.

W/o LSM. We disable the luminance-selecting module in both color attention and color query modules to study the effectiveness of narrowing optional color tokens. After the range of color candidates is expanded to include colors not in the empirical distribution, the colorized results become counterintuitive, *e.g.*, the golf ball and the parrot (first and second row in Fig. 7).

W/o Color Attention. We replace color attention with standard self-attention between image feature patches. In this way, the model cannot correctly infer semantic colors, therefore the results present mixed colors, *e.g.*, the woman and the tram (third and last row in Fig. 7).

W/o Color Query. We replace the color query module with an MLP block as the classifier. As a result, the ability to infer colors from image semantics reduces, which makes the model prediction blurred, and causes mixed colors, *e.g.*, the woman and the tram (third and last row in Fig. 7).

4.4 Application

We apply our method to colorize the legacy black and white photos shown in Fig. 8, which demonstrates the generalization capability of our proposed method.

5 Conclusion

We propose **C**olorization **T**ransformer via **C**olor **T**okens (CT^2), to deal with existing incorrect semantic colors and undersaturation challenges without additional priors. To demonstrate its effectiveness, we make comparisons with the 9 state-of-the-art methods, and the experiment results show that our method achieves highest scores on 4 image quality metrics and 2 colorfulness metrics.

Limitation. We need to calculate the empirical distribution on the training set to narrow the color candidates. Therefore, our method may degenerate if the training data are insufficient or have a clear bias. Fortunately, ImageNet [24] includes 1.3M training data and covers 1000 categories, which to some extent prevents this problem from happening in our experiments.

Acknowledgements. This project is supported by National Natural Science Foundation of China under Grant No. 62136001.

References

1. Antic, J.: A deep learning based project for colorizing and restoring old images (and video!). https://github.com/jantic/DeOldify
2. Ardizzone, L., Lüth, C., Kruse, J., Rother, C., Köthe, U.: Guided image generation with conditional invertible neural networks. arXiv (2019)
3. Cao, Y., Zhou, Z., Zhang, W., Yu, Y.: Unsupervised diverse colorization via generative adversarial networks. In: Ceci, M., Hollmén, J., Todorovski, L., Vens, C., Džeroski, S. (eds.) ECML PKDD 2017. LNCS (LNAI), vol. 10534, pp. 151–166. Springer, Cham (2017). https://doi.org/10.1007/978-3-319-71249-9_10
4. Carion, N., Massa, F., Synnaeve, G., Usunier, N., Kirillov, A., Zagoruyko, S.: End-to-end object detection with transformers. In: Vedaldi, A., Bischof, H., Brox, T., Frahm, J.-M. (eds.) ECCV 2020. LNCS, vol. 12346, pp. 213–229. Springer, Cham (2020). https://doi.org/10.1007/978-3-030-58452-8_13
5. Chen, H., et al.: Pre-trained image processing transformer. In: CVPR (2021)
6. Cheng, Z., Yang, Q., Sheng, B.: Deep colorization. In: ICCV (2015)
7. Chu, X., Zhang, B., Tian, Z., Wei, X., Xia, H.: Do we really need explicit position encodings for vision transformers? arXiv (2021)
8. Deshpande, A., Lu, J., Yeh, M.C., Chong, M.J., Forsyth, D.: Learning diverse image colorization. In: CVPR (2017)
9. Dosovitskiy, A., et al.: An image is worth 16 × 16 words: transformers for image recognition at scale. In: ICLR (2021)
10. Guadarrama, S., Dahl, R., Bieber, D., Norouzi, M., Shlens, J., Murphy, K.: PixColor: pixel recursive colorization. arXiv (2017)
11. Hanin, B., Rolnick, D.: How to start training: the effect of initialization and architecture. In: NIPS (2018)
12. Hasler, D., Suesstrunk, S.E.: Measuring colorfulness in natural images. In: Human vision and electronic imaging VIII (2003)
13. He, K., Chen, X., Xie, S., Li, Y., Dollár, P., Girshick, R.: Masked autoencoders are scalable vision learners. arXiv (2021)
14. Heusel, M., Ramsauer, H., Unterthiner, T., Nessler, B., Klambauer, G., Hochreiter, S.: GANs trained by a two time-scale update rule converge to a Nash equilibrium. In: NIPS (2017)
15. Huynh-Thu, Q., Ghanbari, M.: Scope of validity of PSNR in image/video quality assessment. Electron. Lett. (2008)
16. Iizuka, S., Simo-Serra, E., Ishikawa, H.: Let there be color! joint end-to-end learning of global and local image priors for automatic image colorization with simultaneous classification. ToG (2016)
17. Kumar, M., Weissenborn, D., Kalchbrenner, N.: Colorization transformer. In: ICLR (2021)
18. Larsson, G., Maire, M., Shakhnarovich, G.: Learning representations for automatic colorization. In: Leibe, B., Matas, J., Sebe, N., Welling, M. (eds.) ECCV 2016. LNCS, vol. 9908, pp. 577–593. Springer, Cham (2016). https://doi.org/10.1007/978-3-319-46493-0_35
19. Lei, C., Wu, Y., Chen, Q.: Towards photorealistic colorization by imagination. arXiv (2021)
20. Li, W., Lu, X., Lu, J., Zhang, X., Jia, J.: On efficient transformer and image pre-training for low-level vision. arXiv (2021)
21. Liang, J., Cao, J., Sun, G., Zhang, K., Van Gool, L., Timofte, R.: SwinIR: image restoration using swin transformer. In: ICCV (2021)

22. Liu, Z., et al.: Swin transformer: hierarchical vision transformer using shifted windows. ICCV (2021)
23. Ronneberger, O., Fischer, P., Brox, T.: U-Net: convolutional networks for biomedical image segmentation. In: Navab, N., Hornegger, J., Wells, W.M., Frangi, A.F. (eds.) MICCAI 2015. LNCS, vol. 9351, pp. 234–241. Springer, Cham (2015). https://doi.org/10.1007/978-3-319-24574-4_28
24. Russakovsky, O., et al.: ImageNet large scale visual recognition challenge. Int. J. Comput. Vis. **115**(3), 211–252 (2015). https://doi.org/10.1007/s11263-015-0816-y
25. Strudel, R., Garcia, R., Laptev, I., Schmid, C.: Segmenter: transformer for semantic segmentation. In: ICCV (2021)
26. Su, J.W., Chu, H.K., Huang, J.B.: Instance-aware image colorization. In: CVPR (2020)
27. Vaswani, A., et al.: Attention is all you need. In: NIPS (2017)
28. Vitoria, P., Raad, L., Ballester, C.: ChromaGAN: adversarial picture colorization with semantic class distribution. In: WACV (2020)
29. Wang, Z., Cun, X., Bao, J., Liu, J.: Uformer: a general u-shaped transformer for image restoration. arXiv (2021)
30. Wang, Z., Bovik, A.C., Sheikh, H.R., Simoncelli, E.P.: Image quality assessment: from error visibility to structural similarity. TIP (2004)
31. Wu, Y., Wang, X., Li, Y., Zhang, H., Zhao, X., Shan, Y.: Towards vivid and diverse image colorization with generative color prior. In: ICCV (2021)
32. Zhang, R., Isola, P., Efros, A.A.: Colorful image colorization. In: ECCV (2016)
33. Zhang, R., Isola, P., Efros, A.A., Shechtman, E., Wang, O.: The unreasonable effectiveness of deep features as a perceptual metric. In: CVPR (2018)
34. Zhang, R., et al.: Real-time user-guided image colorization with learned deep priors. ACM TOG (2017)
35. Zhao, J., Han, J., Shao, L., Snoek, C.G.: Pixelated semantic colorization. IJCV (2020). https://doi.org/10.1007/s11263-019-01271-4
36. Zhao, J., Liu, L., Snoek, C.G., Han, J., Shao, L.: Pixel-level semantics guided image colorization. In: BMVC (2018)
37. Zheng, S., et al.: Rethinking semantic segmentation from a sequence-to-sequence perspective with transformers. In: CVPR (2021)
38. Zhu, X., Su, W., Lu, L., Li, B., Wang, X., Dai, J.: Deformable DETR: deformable transformers for end-to-end object detection. In: ICLR (2020)

Simple Baselines for Image Restoration

Liangyu Chen[✉], Xiaojie Chu, Xiangyu Zhang, and Jian Sun

MEGVII Technology, Beijing, China
{chenliangyu,chuxiaojie,zhangxiangyu,sunjian}@megvii.com

Abstract. Although there have been significant advances in the field of image restoration recently, the system complexity of the state-of-the-art (SOTA) methods is increasing as well, which may hinder the convenient analysis and comparison of methods. In this paper, we propose a simple baseline that exceeds the SOTA methods and is computationally efficient. To further simplify the baseline, we reveal that the nonlinear activation functions, e.g. Sigmoid, ReLU, GELU, Softmax, etc. are not necessary: they could be replaced by multiplication or removed. Thus, we derive a Nonlinear Activation Free Network, namely NAFNet, from the baseline. SOTA results are achieved on various challenging benchmarks, e.g. 33.69 dB PSNR on GoPro (for image deblurring), exceeding the previous SOTA 0.38 dB with only 8.4% of its computational costs; 40.30 dB PSNR on SIDD (for image denoising), exceeding the previous SOTA 0.28 dB with less than half of its computational costs. The code and the pre-trained models are released at github.com/megvii-research/NAFNet.

Keywords: Image restoration · Image denoise · Image deblur

1 Introduction

With the development of deep learning, the performance of image restoration methods improve significantly. Deep learning based methods [4–7,24,30,34,35, 37] have achieved tremendous success. E.g. [7,37] achieve 40.02/33.31 dB of PSNR on SIDD [1]/GoPro [25] for image denoising/deblurring respectively.

Despite their good performance, these methods suffer from high system complexity. For a clear discussion, we decompose the system complexity into two parts: inter-block complexity and intra-block complexity. First, the inter-block complexity, as shown in Fig. 2. [6,24] introduce connections between various-sized feature maps; [4,35] are multi-stage networks and the latter stage refine the results of the previous stage. Second, the intra-block complexity, i.e. the various design choices inside the block. E.g. Multi-Dconv Head Transposed Attention

---

L. Chen and X. Chu—Equally contribution.

Supplementary Information The online version contains supplementary material available at https://doi.org/10.1007/978-3-031-20071-7_2.

© The Author(s), under exclusive license to Springer Nature Switzerland AG 2022
S. Avidan et al. (Eds.): ECCV 2022, LNCS 13667, pp. 17–33, 2022.
https://doi.org/10.1007/978-3-031-20071-7_2

Module and Gated Dconv Feed-Forward Network in [37] (as we shown in Fig. 3a), Swin Transformer Block in [21], HINBlock in [4], and etc. It is not practical to evaluate the design choices one by one.

Based on the above facts, a natural question arises: Is it possible that a network with low inter-block and low intra-block complexity can achieve SOTA performance? To accomplish the first condition (low inter-block complexity), this paper adopts the single-stage UNet as architecture (following some SOTA methods [34,37]) and focuses on the second condition. To this end, we start with a plain block with the most common components, i.e. convolution, ReLU, and shortcut [13]. From the plain block, we add/replace components of SOTA methods and verify how much performance gain do these components bring. By extensive ablation studies, we propose a simple baseline, as shown in Fig. 3c, that exceeds the SOTA methods and is computationally efficient. It has the potential to inspire new ideas and make their verification easier. The baseline, which contains GELU [14] and Channel Attention Module [15] (CA), can be further simplified: we reveal that the GELU in the baseline can be regarded as a special case of the Gated Linear Unit [9] (GLU), and from this we empirically demonstrate that it can be replaced by a simple gate, i.e. element-wise product of feature maps. In addition, we reveal the similarity of the CA to GLU in form, and the nonlinear activation functions in CA could be removed either. In conclusion, the simple baseline could be further simplified to a nonlinear activation free network, noted as NAFNet. We mainly conduct experiments on SIDD [1] for image denoising, and GoPro [25] for image deblurring, following [4,35,37]. The main results are shown in Fig. 1, our proposed baseline and NAFNet achieves SOTA results while being computationally efficient: 33.40/33.69 dB on GoPro, exceed previous SOTA [7] 0.09/0.38 dB, respectively, with 8.4% of its computational cost; 40.30 dB on SIDD, exceed [37] 0.28 dB with less than half of its computational costs. Extensive quantity and quality experiments are conducted to illustrate the effectiveness of our proposed baselines.

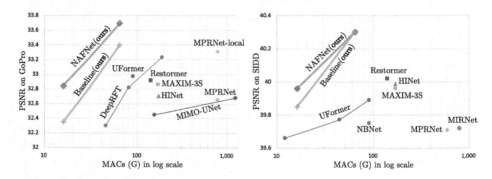

Fig. 1. PSNR vs. computational cost on Image Deblurring (left) and Image Denoising (right) tasks

The contributions of this paper are summarized as follows:

1. By decomposing the SOTA methods and extracting their essential components, we form a baseline (in Fig. 3c) with lower system complexity, which can exceed the previous SOTA methods and has a lower computational cost, as shown in Fig. 1. It may facilitate the researchers to inspire new ideas and evaluate them conveniently.

2. By revealing the connections between GELU, Channel Attention to Gated Linear Unit, we further simplify the baseline by removing or replacing the nonlinear activation functions (e.g. Sigmoid, ReLU, and GELU), and propose a nonlinear activation free network, namely NAFNet. It can match or surpass the baseline although being simplified. To the best of our knowledge, it is the first work demonstrates that the nonlinear activation functions may not be necessary for SOTA computer vision methods. This work may have the potential to expand the design space of SOTA computer vision methods.

2   Related Works

2.1   Image Restoration

Image restoration tasks aim to restore a degraded image (e.g. noisy, blur) to a clean one. Recently, deep learning based methods [4–7,24,30,34,35,37] achieve SOTA results on these tasks, and most of the methods could be viewed as variants of a classical solution, UNet [28]. It stacks blocks to a U-shaped architecture with skip-connection. The variants bring performance gain, as well as the system complexity, and we broadly categorized the complexity as inter-block complexity and intra-block complexity.

Inter-block Complexity. [4,35] are multi-stage networks, i.e. the latter stage refine the results of the previous stage, and each stage is a U-shaped architecture. This design is based on the assumption that breaking down the difficult image restoration task into several subtasks contributes to performance. Differently, [6,24] adopt the single-stage design and achieve competitive results, but they introduce complicated connections between various sized feature maps. Some methods adopt the above strategies both, e.g. [30]. Other SOTA methods, e.g. [34,37] maintain the simple structure of single-stage UNet, yet they introduce intra-block complexity, which we will discuss next.

Intra-block Complexity. There are numerous different intra-block design schemes, we pick a few examples here. [37] reduces the memory and time complexity of self-attention [32] by channelwise attention map rather than spatial-wise. Besides, gated linear units [9] and depthwise convolution are adopted in the feed-forward network. [34] introduces window-based multi-head self-attention, which is similar to [21]. In addition, it introduces locally-enhanced feed-forward network in its block, which adds depthwise convolution to feed-forward network to enhance the local information capture ability. Differently, we reveal that increasing system complexity is not the only way to improve performance: SOTA performance could be achieved by a simple baseline.

2.2   Gated Linear Units

Gated Linear Units [9] (GLU) can be interpreted by the element-wise production of two linear transformation layers, one of which is activated with the nonlinearity. GLU or its variants has verified their effectiveness in NLP [8,9,29], and there is a prosperous trend of them in computer vision [16,19,30,37]. In this paper, we reveal the non-trivial improvement brought by GLU. Different from [29], we remove the nonlinear activation function in GLU without performance degradation. Furthermore, based on the fact that the nonlinear activation free GLU contains nonlinearity itself (as the product of two linear transformations raises nonlinearity), our baseline could be simplified by replacing the nonlinear activation functions with the multiplication of two feature maps. To the best of our knowledge, it is the first computer vision model achieves SOTA performance without nonlinear activation functions.

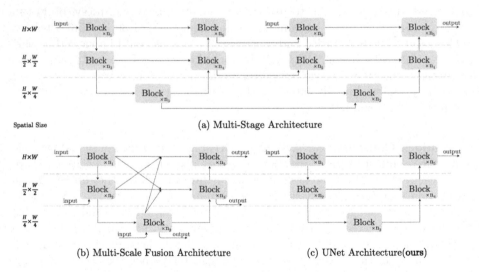

(a) Multi-Stage Architecture

(b) Multi-Scale Fusion Architecture   (c) UNet Architecture(ours)

Fig. 2. Comparison of architectures of image restoration models. Dashes to distinguish features of different sizes. (a) The multi-stage architecture [4,35] stacks UNet architecture serially. (b) The multi-scale fusion architecture [6,24] fusions the features in different scales. (c)UNet architecture, which is adopted by some SOTA methods [34,37]. We use it as our architecture. Some details have been deliberately omitted for simplicity, e.g. downsample/upsample layers, feature fusion modules, input/output shortcut, and etc.

3 Build a Simple Baseline

In this section, we build a simple baseline for image restoration tasks from scratch. To keep the structure simple, our principle is not to add entities if they are not necessary. The necessity is verified by empirical evaluation of restoration tasks. We mainly conduct experiments with the model size around 16 GMACs following HINet Simple [4], and the MACs are estimated by an input with the spatial size of 256 × 256. The results of models with different capacities, e.g. 1.1 GMACs, 65 GMACs, are in the experimental section. We mainly validate the results (PSNR) on two popular datasets for denoising (i.e. SIDD [1]) and deblurring (i.e. GoPro [25] dataset), based on the fact that those tasks are fundamental in low-level vision. The design choices are discussed in the following subsections.

3.1 Architecture

To reduce the inter-block complexity, we adopt the classic single-stage U-shaped architecture with skip-connections, as shown in Fig. 2c, following [34,37]. We believe the architecture will not be a barrier to performance. The experimental results confirmed our conjecture, in Tables 6, 7 and Fig. 1.

3.2 A Plain Block

Neural Networks are stacked by blocks. We have determined how to stack blocks in the above (i.e. stacked in a UNet architecture), but how to design the internal structure of the block is still a problem. We start from a plain block with the most common components, i.e. convolution, ReLU, and shortcut [13], and the arrangement of these components follows [12,21], as shown in Fig. 3b. We will note it as PlainNet for simplicity. Using a convolution network instead of a transformer is based on the following considerations. First, although transformers show good performance in computer vision, some works [12,22] claim that they may not be necessary for achieving SOTA results. Second, depthwise convolution is simpler than the self-attention [32] mechanism. Third, this paper is not intended to discuss the advantages and disadvantages of transformers and convolutional neural networks, but just to provide a simple baseline. The discussion of the attention mechanism is proposed in the subsequent subsection.

3.3 Normalization

Normalization is widely adopted in high-level computer vision tasks, and there is also a popular trend in low-level vision. Although [25] abandoned Batch Normalization [17] as the small batch size may bring the unstable statistics [4,36] reintroduce the Instance Normalization [31] and avoids the small batch size issue. However, [4] shows that adding instance normalization does not always bring performance gains and requires manual tuning. Differently, under the prosperity of transformers, Layer Normalization [2] is used by more and more methods, including SOTA methods [21,22,30,34,37]. Based on these facts we conjecture Layer Normalization may be crucial to SOTA restorers, thus we add Layer Normalization to the plain block described above. This change can make training smooth, even with a 10× increase in learning rate. The larger learning rate brings significant performance gain: +0.44 dB (39.29 dB to 39.73 dB) on SIDD [1], +3.39 dB (28.51 dB to 31.90 dB) on GoPro [25] dataset. To sum up, we add Layer Normalization to the plain block as it can stabilize the training process.

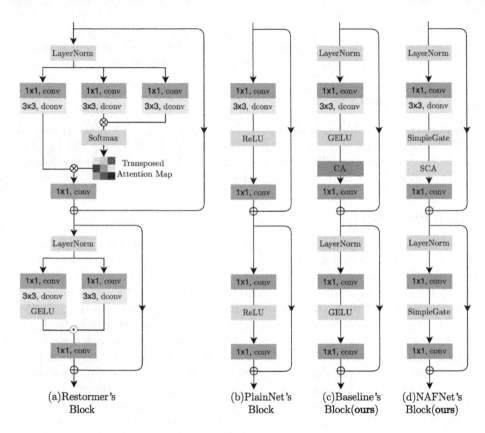

Fig. 3. Intra-block structure comparison. ⊗:matrix multiplication, ⊙/⊕:element-wise multiplication/addition. dconv: Depthwise convolution. Nonlinear activation functions are represented by yellow boxes. (a) Restormer's block [37], some details are omitted for simplicity, e.g. reshaping the feature maps. (b) PlainNet's block, which contains the most common components. (c) Our proposed baseline. Compares to (b), Channel Attention (CA) and LayerNorm are adopted. Besides, ReLU is replaced by GELU. (d) Our proposed Nonlinear Activation Free Network's block. It replaces CA/GELU with Simplified Channel Attention(SCA) and SimpleGate respectively. The details of these components are shown in Fig. 4

3.4   Activation

The activation function in the plain block, Rectified Linear Unit [27] (ReLU), is extensively used in computer vision. However, there is a tendency to replace ReLU with GELU [14] in SOTA methods [11,21,22,30,37]. This replacement is implemented in our model either. The performance stays comparable on SIDD (from 39.73 dB to 39.71 dB) which is consistent with the conclusion of [22], yet it brings 0.21 dB performance gain (31.90 dB to 32.11 dB) on GoPro. In short, we replace ReLU with GELU in the plain block, because it keeps the performance of image denoising while bringing non-trivial gain on image deblurring.

3.5   Attention

Considering the recent popularity of the transformer in computer vision, its attention mechanism is an unavoidable topic in the design of the internal structure of the block. There are many variants of attention mechanisms, and we discuss only a few of them here. The vanilla self-attention mechanism [32], which is adopted by [3,11], generate the target feature by the linear combination of all features which are weighted by the similarity between them. Therefore, each feature contains global information, while it suffers from the quadratic computational complexity with the size of the feature map. Some image restoration tasks process data at high resolution which makes the vanilla self-attention not practical. Alternatively, [20,21,34] apply self-attention only in a fix-sized local window to alleviate the issue of increased computation. While it lacks global information. We do not take the window-based attention, as the local information could be well captured by the depthwise convolution [12,22] in the plain block.

Differently, [37] modifies the spatial-wise attention to channel-wise, avoids the computation issue while maintaining global information in each feature. It could be seen as a special variant of channel attention [15]. Inspired by [37], we realize the vanilla channel attention meets the requirements: computational efficiency and brings global information to the feature map. In addition, the effectiveness of channel attention has been verified in the image restoration task [7,35], thus we add the channel attention to the plain block. It brings 0.14 dB on SIDD [1] (39.71 dB to 39.85 dB), 0.24 dB on GoPro [25] dataset (32.11 dB to 32.35 dB).

3.6   Summary

So far, we build a simple baseline from scratch, as we shown in Table 1. The architecture and the block are shown in Fig. 2c and Fig. 3c, respectively. Each component in the baseline is trivial, e.g. Layer Normalization, Convolution, GELU, and Channel Attention. But the combination of these trivial components leads to a strong baseline: it can surpass the previous SOTA results on SIDD and GoPro dataset with only a fraction of computation costs, as we shown in Fig. 1 and Tables 6, 7. We believe the simple baseline could facilitate the researchers to evaluate their ideas.

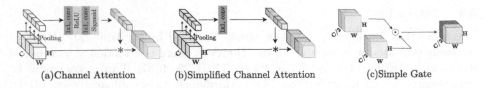

(a)Channel Attention   (b)Simplified Channel Attention   (c)Simple Gate

Fig. 4. Illustration of (a) Channel Attention [15] (CA), (b) Simplified Channel Attention (SCA), and (c) Simple Gate (SG). $\odot/*$: element-wise/channel-wise multiplication

4 Nonlinear Activation Free Network

The baseline described above is simple and competitive, but is it possible to further improve performance while ensuring simplicity? Can it be simpler without performance loss? We try to answer these questions by looking for commonalities from some SOTA methods [16,19,30,37]. We find that in these methods, Gated Linear Units [9] (GLU) are adopted. It implies that GLU might be promising. We will discuss it next.

Gated Linear Units. The gated linear units could be formulated as:

$$Gate(\mathbf{X}, f, g, \sigma) = f(\mathbf{X}) \odot \sigma(g(\mathbf{X})), \tag{1}$$

where $\mathbf{X}$ represents the feature map, f and g are linear transformers, σ is a non-linear activation function, e.g. Sigmoid, and $\odot$ indicates element-wise multiplication. As discussed above, adding GLU to our baseline may improve the performance yet the intra-block complexity is increasing as well. This is not what we expected. To address this, we revisit the activation function in the baseline, i.e. GELU [14]:

$$GELU(x) = x\Phi(x), \tag{2}$$

where Φ indicates the cumulative distribution function of the standard normal distribution. And based on [14], GELU could be approximated and implemented by:

$$0.5x(1 + tanh[\sqrt{2/\pi}(x + 0.044715x^3)]). \tag{3}$$

From Eqs. 1 and 2, it can be noticed that GELU is a special case of GLU, i.e. f, g are identity functions and take σ as Φ. Through the similarity, we conjecture from another perspective that GLU may be regarded as a generalization of activation functions, and it might be able to replace the nonlinear activation functions. Further, we note that the GLU itself contains nonlinearity and does *not* depend on σ: even if the σ is removed, $Gate(\mathbf{X}) = f(\mathbf{X}) \odot g(\mathbf{X})$ contains nonlinearity. Based on these, we propose a simple GLU variant: directly divide the feature map into two parts in the channel dimension and multiply them, as we shown in Fig. 4c, noted as SimpleGate. Compared to the complicated implementation of GELU in Eqn.3, our SimpleGate could be implemented by an element-wise multiplication, that's all:

$$SimpleGate(\mathbf{X}, \mathbf{Y}) = \mathbf{X} \odot \mathbf{Y}, \qquad\qquad (4)$$

where $\mathbf{X}$ and $\mathbf{Y}$ are feature maps of the same size.

By replacing GELU in the baseline to the proposed SimpleGate, the performance of image denoising (on SIDD [1]) and image deblurring (on GoPro [25] dataset) boost 0.08 dB (39.85 dB to 39.93 dB) and 0.41 dB (32.35 dB to 32.76 dB) respectively. The results demonstrate that GELU could be replaced by our proposed SimpleGate. At this point, only a few types of nonlinear activations left in the network: Sigmoid and ReLU in the channel attention module [15], and we will discuss the simplifications of it next.

Simplified Channel Attention. In Sect. 3, we adopt the channel attention [15] into our block as it captures the global information and it is computationally efficient. It is illustrated in Fig. 4a: it squeezes the spatial information into channels first and then a multilayer perceptual applies to it to calculate the channel attention, which will be used to weight the feature map. It could be represented as:

$$CA(\mathbf{X}) = \mathbf{X} * \sigma(W_2 max(0, W_1 pool(\mathbf{X}))), \qquad\qquad (5)$$

where $\mathbf{X}$ represents the feature map, *pool* indicates the global average pooling operation which aggregates the spatial information into channels. σ is a nonlinear activation function, Sigmoid, W_1, W_2 are fully-connected layers and ReLU is adopted between two fully-connected layers. Last, $*$ is a channelwise product operation. If we regard the channel-attention calculation as a function, noted as Ψ with input $\mathbf{X}$, Eq. 5 could be re-writed as:

$$CA(\mathbf{X}) = \mathbf{X} * \Psi(\mathbf{X}). \qquad\qquad (6)$$

It can be noticed that Eq. 6 is very similar to Eq. 1. This inspires us to consider channel attention as a special case of GLU, which can be simplified like GLU in the previous subsection. By retaining the two most important roles of channel attention, that is, aggregating global information and channel information interaction, we propose the Simplified Channel Attention:

$$SCA(\mathbf{X}) = \mathbf{X} * W pool(\mathbf{X}). \qquad\qquad (7)$$

The notations follows Eq. 5. Apparently, Simplified Channel Attention (Eq. 7) is simpler than the original one (Eq. 5), as shown in Fig. 4a and b. Although it is simpler, there is no loss of performance: +0.03 dB (39.93 dB to 39.96 dB) on SIDD and +0.09 dB (32.76 dB to 32.85 dB) on GoPro.

Summary. Starting from the baseline proposed in Sect. 3, we further simplify it by replacing the GELU with SimpleGate and Channel Attention to Simplified Channel Attention, without loss of performance. We emphasize that after the simplification, there are *no* nonlinear activation functions (e.g. ReLU, GELU,

Sigmoid, etc.) in the network. So we call this baseline Nonlinear Activation Free Network, namely NAFNet. It can match or surpass the baseline although without nonlinear activation functions, as we shown in Fig. 1 and Tables 6, 7. We can now answer the questions in the beginning of this section by yes, because of the simplicity and effectiveness of NAFNet.

5   Experiments

In this section, we analyze the effect of the design choices of NAFNet described in previous sections in detail. Next, we apply our proposed NAFNet to various image restoration applications, including RGB image denoising, image deblurring, raw image denoising, and image deblurring with JPEG artifacts.

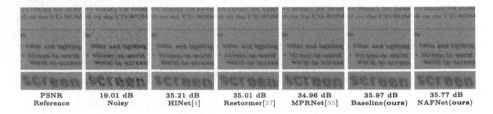

| PSNR | 19.01 dB | 35.21 dB | 35.01 dB | 34.96 dB | 35.97 dB | 35.77 dB |
| Reference | Noisy | HINet[4] | Restormer[37] | MPRNet[35] | Baseline(ours) | NAFNet(ours) |

Fig. 5. Qualitative comparison of image denoising methods on SIDD [1]

5.1   Ablations

The ablation studys are conducted on image denoising (SIDD [1]) and deblurring (GoPro [25]) tasks. We follow experiments setting of [4] if not specified, e.g. 16 GMACs of computational budget, gradient clip, and PSNR loss. We train models with Adam [18] optimizer ($\beta_1 = 0.9, \beta_2 = 0.9$, weight decay 0) for total 200K iterations with the initial learning rate $1e^{-3}$ gradually reduced to $1e^{-6}$ with the cosine annealing schedule [23]. The training patch size is 256×256 and batch size is 32. Training by patches and testing by the full image raises performance degradation [7], we solve it by adopting TLC [7] following MPRNet-local [7]. The effectiveness of TLC on GoPro[1] is shown in Table 4. We mainly compare TLC with "test by patches" strategy, which is adopted by [4,24], and etc. It brings performance gains and avoids the artifacts brought by patches. Moreover, we apply skip-init [10] to stabilize training following [22]. The default width and number of blocks are 32 and 36, respectively. We adjust the width to keep the computational budget hold if the number of blocks changed. We report Peak Signal to Noise Ratio (PSNR) and Structural SIMilarity (SSIM) in our experiments. The speed/memory/computational complexity evaluation is conducted with an input size of 256×256, on an NVIDIA 2080Ti GPU.

---

[1] SIDD test on 256×256 patches avoid the inconsistent issue.

From PlainNet to the Simple Baseline: PlainNet is defined in Sect. 3, and its block is illustrated in Fig. 3b. We find that the training of PlainNet is unstable under the default settings. As an alternative, we reduce the learning rate (lr) by a factor of 10 to make the model trainable. This issue is solved by introducing Layer Normalization (LN): the learning rate can be increased from $1e^{-4}$ to $1e^{-3}$ with a more stable training process. In PSNR, LN brings 0.46 dB and 3.39 dB on SIDD and GoPro respectively. Besides, GELU and Channel Attention (CA) also demonstrated their effectiveness in Table 1.

From the Simple Baseline to NAFNet: As described in Sect. 3, NAFNet can be obtained by simplifying the baseline. In Table 2, we show that there is no performance penalty for this simplification. Instead, the PSNR boosts 0.11 dB and 0.50 dB in SIDD and GoPro respectively. The computational complexity is consistent for a fair comparison, and details in the supplementary material. The speedup of modifications compared to Baseline is provided. In addition, no significant extra memory consumption compares to Baseline in inference.

Table 1. Build a simple baseline from PlainNet. The effectiveness of Layer Normalization (LN), GELU, and Channel Attention (CA) have been verified. $*$ indicates that the training is unstable due to the large learning rate (lr)

	lr	LN	ReLU→GELU	CA	SIDD		GoPro	
					PSNR	SSIM	PSNR	SSIM
PlainNet	$1e^{-4}$				39.29	0.956	28.51	0.907
PlainNet*	$1e^{-3}$				–	–	–	–
	$1e^{-3}$	✓			39.73	0.959	31.90	0.952
	$1e^{-3}$	✓	✓		39.71	0.958	32.11	0.954
Baseline	$1e^{-3}$	✓	✓	✓	39.85	0.959	32.35	0.956

Table 2. NAFNet is derived from the simplification of baseline, i.e. replacing GELU to SimpleGate (SG), and replacing Channel Attention (CA) to Simplified Channel Attention (SCA).

	GELU→SG	CA→SCA	SIDD		GoPro		Speedup
			PSNR	SSIM	PSNR	SSIM	
Baseline			39.85	0.959	32.35	0.956	1.00×
	✓		39.93	0.960	32.76	0.960	0.98×
		✓	39.95	0.960	32.54	0.958	1.11×
NAFNet	✓	✓	39.96	0.960	32.85	0.960	1.09×

Number of Blocks: We verify the effect of the number of blocks on NAFNet in Table 3. We mainly consider the latency at spatial size 720×1280, as this is the size of the entire GoPro image. In the process of increasing the number of blocks to 36, the performance of the model has been greatly improved, and the latency has not increased significantly (+14.5% compares to 9 blocks). When the number of blocks further increases to 72, the performance improvement of the model is not obvious, but the latency increases significantly (+30.0% compares to 36 blocks). Because 36 blocks can achieve a better performance/latency balance, we use it as the default option.

Variants of σ in SimpleGate: Vanilla gated linear unit (GLU) contains a nonlinear activation function σ as formulated in Eq. 1. Our proposed SimpleGate, as shown in Eq. 4 and Fig. 4c removes it. In other words, σ in SimpleGate is set as an identity function. We variants the σ from the identity function to different nonlinear activation functions in Table 5 to judge the importance of nonlinearity in σ. PSNR on SIDD is basically unaffected (fluctuates from 39.96 dB to 39.99 dB), while PSNR on GoPro drops significantly (-0.11 dB to -0.35 dB), which indicates that in NAFNet, the σ in SimpleGate may not be necessary.

Table 3. The effect of the number of blocks. The width is adjusted to keep the computational budget hold. Latency-256 and Latency-720 is based on the input size 256×256 and 720×1280 respectively, in milliseconds

	# of blocks	SIDD		GoPro		Latency-256	Latency-720
		PSNR	SSIM	PSNR	SSIM		
NAFNet	9	39.78	0.959	31.79	0.951	11.8	154.7
	18	39.90	0.960	32.64	0.951	19.9	151.7
	36	39.96	0.960	32.85	0.959	39.1	177.1
	72	39.95	0.960	32.88	0.961	73.8	230.1

Table 4. Effectiveness of TLC [7] on GoPro [25]

	Patches?	TLC?	PSNR	SSIM
NAFNet			33.08	0.963
	✓		33.65	0.966
		✓	33.69	0.967

Table 5. Variants of σ in $SimpleGate(\mathbf{X}, \mathbf{Y}) = \mathbf{X} \odot \sigma(\mathbf{Y})$

σ	SIDD		GoPro	
	PSNR	SSIM	PSNR	SSIM
Identity (**ours**)	39.96	0.960	32.85	0.960
ReLU	39.98	0.960	32.59	0.958
GELU	39.97	0.960	32.72	0.959
Sigmoid	39.99	0.960	32.50	0.958
SiLU	39.96	0.960	32.74	0.960

5.2   Applications

We apply NAFNet to various image restoration tasks, follow the training settings of ablation study if not specified, except that it is enlarged by increasing the width from 32 to 64. Besides, batch size and total training iterations are 64 and 400K respectively, following [4]. Random crop augmentation is applied. We report the mean of three experimental results.

RGB Image Denoising. We compare the RGB Image Denoising results with other SOTA methods on SIDD, show in Table 6. Baseline and its simplified version NAFNet, exceed the previous best result Restormer 0.28 dB with only a fraction of its computational cost, as shown in Fig. 1. The qualitative results are shown in Fig. 5. Our proposed baselines can restore more fine details compared to other methods. Moreover, we achieve SOTA result (40.15 dB) on the online benchmark, exceed previous top-ranked methods 0.23 dB.

Image Deblurring. We compare the deblurring results of SOTA methods on GoPro [25] dataset, flip and rotate augmentations are adopted. As we shown in Table 7 and Fig. 1, our baseline and NAFNet surpass the previous best method MPRNet-local [7] 0.09 dB and 0.38 dB in PSNR, respectively, with only 8.4% of its computational costs. The visualization results are shown in Fig. 6, our baselines can restore sharper results compares to other methods.

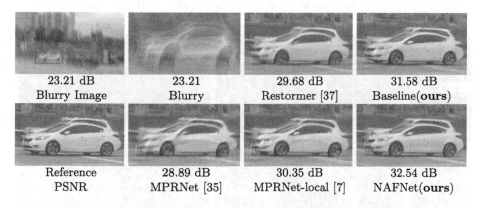

23.21 dB	23.21	29.68 dB	31.58 dB
Blurry Image	Blurry	Restormer [37]	Baseline(**ours**)
Reference	28.89 dB	30.35 dB	32.54 dB
PSNR	MPRNet [35]	MPRNet-local [7]	NAFNet(**ours**)

Fig. 6. Qualitative comparison of image deblurring methods on GoPro [25]

Table 6. Image Denoising Results on SIDD [1]

Method	MPRNet [35]	MIRNet [38]	NBNet [5]	UFormer [34]	MAXIM [30]	HINet [4]	Restormer [37]	Baseline **ours**	NAFNet **ours**
PSNR	39.71	39.72	39.75	39.89	39.96	39.99	40.02	40.30	40.30
SSIM	0.958	0.959	0.959	0.960	0.960	0.958	0.960	0.962	0.962
MACs(G)	588	786	88.8	89.5	169.5	170.7	140	65	65

Raw Image Denoising. We apply NAFNet to a raw image denoising task. The training and testing settings follow PMRID [33], and we noted the testing set as 4Scenes (as the dataset contains 39 raw images of 4 different scenes in various light conditions) for simplicity. In addition, we make fair comparison by changing the width and number of blocks of NAFNet from 32 to 16, 36 to 7, respectively, so that the computational cost is less than PMRID. The results shown in Table 8 and Fig. 7 demonstrate NAFNet can surpass PMRID quantitatively and qualitatively. In addition, this experiment indicates our NAFNet can be scaled flexibly (from 1.1 GMACs to 65 GMACs).

Image Deblurring with JPEG Artifacts. We conduct experiments on REDS [26] dataset, the training setting follows [4,30], and we evaluate the result on 300 images from the validation set (noted as REDS-val-300) following [4,30]. As shown in Table 9, our method outperforms other competing methods, including the previous winning solution (HINet) on the REDS dataset of NTIRE 2021 Image Deblurring Challenge Track2 JPEG artifacts [26].

Table 7. Image Deblurring Results on GoPro [25]

Method	MIMO-UNet [6]	HINet [4]	MAXIM [30]	Restormer [37]	UFormer [34]	DeepRFT [24]	MPRNet -local [7]	Baseline **ours**	NAFNet **ours**
PSNR	32.68	32.71	32.86	32.92	32.97	33.23	33.31	33.40	33.69
SSIM	0.959	0.959	0.961	0.961	0.967	0.963	0.964	0.965	0.967
MACs(G)	1235	170.7	169.5	140	89.5	187	778.2	65	65

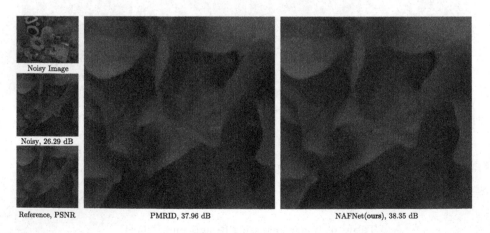

Noisy Image

Noisy, 26.29 dB

Reference, PSNR   PMRID, 37.96 dB   NAFNet(ours), 38.35 dB

Fig. 7. Qualitatively compare the noise reduction effects of PMRID [33] and our proposed NAFNet. Zoom in to see details

Table 8. Raw image denoising results on 4Scenes [33]

Method	PSNR	SSIM	MACs(G)
PMRID [33]	39.76	0.975	1.2
NAFNet(**ours**)	40.05	0.977	1.1

Table 9. Image deblurring results on REDS-val-300 [26]

Method	PSNR	SSIM	MACs(G)
MPRNet [35]	28.79	0.811	776.7
HINet [4]	28.83	0.862	170.7
MAXIM [30]	28.93	0.865	169.5
NAFNet(**ours**)	29.09	0.867	65

6 Conclusions

By decomposing the SOTA methods, we extract the essential components and adopt them on a naive PlainNet. The obtained baseline reaches SOTA performance on image denoising and image deblurring tasks. By analyzing the baseline, we reveal that it can be further simplified: The nonlinear activation functions in it can be completely replaced or removed. From this, we propose a nonlinear activation free network, NAFNet. Although simplified, its performance is equal to or better than baseline. Our proposed baselines may facilitate the researchers to evaluate their ideas. In addition, this work has the potential to influence future computer vision model design, as we demonstrate that nonlinear activation functions are not necessary to achieve SOTA performance.

Acknowledgements. This research was supported by National Key R&D Program of China (No. 2017YFA0700800) and Beijing Academy of Artificial Intelligence (BAAI).

References

1. Abdelhamed, A., Lin, S., Brown, M.S.: A high-quality denoising dataset for smartphone cameras. In: IEEE Conference on Computer Vision and Pattern Recognition (CVPR) (2018)
2. Ba, J.L., Kiros, J.R., Hinton, G.E.: Layer normalization. arXiv preprint arXiv:1607.06450 (2016)
3. Chen, H., et al.: Pre-trained image processing transformer. In: Proceedings of the IEEE/CVF Conference on Computer Vision and Pattern Recognition, pp. 12299–12310 (2021)
4. Chen, L., Lu, X., Zhang, J., Chu, X., Chen, C.: HINet: half instance normalization network for image restoration. In: Proceedings of the IEEE/CVF Conference on Computer Vision and Pattern Recognition, pp. 182–192 (2021)
5. Cheng, S., Wang, Y., Huang, H., Liu, D., Fan, H., Liu, S.: NBNet: noise basis learning for image denoising with subspace projection. In: Proceedings of the IEEE/CVF Conference on Computer Vision and Pattern Recognition, pp. 4896–4906 (2021)
6. Cho, S.J., Ji, S.W., Hong, J.P., Jung, S.W., Ko, S.J.: Rethinking coarse-to-fine approach in single image deblurring. In: Proceedings of the IEEE/CVF International Conference on Computer Vision, pp. 4641–4650 (2021)
7. Chu, X., Chen, L., Chen, C., Lu, X.: Improving image restoration by revisiting global information aggregation. arXiv preprint arXiv:2112.04491 (2021)

8. Dai, Z., Yang, Z., Yang, Y., Carbonell, J., Le, Q.V., Salakhutdinov, R.: Transformer-XL: attentive language models beyond a fixed-length context. arXiv preprint arXiv:1901.02860 (2019)
9. Dauphin, Y.N., Fan, A., Auli, M., Grangier, D.: Language modeling with gated convolutional networks. In: International Conference on Machine Learning, pp. 933–941. PMLR (2017)
10. De, S., Smith, S.: Batch normalization biases residual blocks towards the identity function in deep networks. Adv. Neural. Inf. Process. Syst. **33**, 19964–19975 (2020)
11. Dosovitskiy, A., et al.: An image is worth 16x16 words: transformers for image recognition at scale. arXiv preprint arXiv.2010.11929 (2020)
12. Han, Q., et al.: Demystifying local vision transformer: Sparse connectivity, weight sharing, and dynamic weight. arXiv preprint arXiv:2106.04263 (2021)
13. He, K., Zhang, X., Ren, S., Sun, J.: Deep residual learning for image recognition. In: Proceedings of the IEEE Conference on Computer Vision and Pattern Recognition, pp. 770–778 (2016)
14. Hendrycks, D., Gimpel, K.: Gaussian error linear units (gelus). arXiv preprint arXiv:1606.08415 (2016)
15. Hu, J., Shen, L., Sun, G.: Squeeze-and-excitation networks. In: Proceedings of the IEEE Conference on Computer Vision and Pattern Recognition, pp. 7132–7141 (2018)
16. Hua, W., Dai, Z., Liu, H., Le, Q.V.: Transformer quality in linear time. arXiv preprint arXiv:2202.10447 (2022)
17. Ioffe, S., Szegedy, C.: Batch normalization: accelerating deep network training by reducing internal covariate shift. In: International Conference on Machine Learning, pp. 448–456. PMLR (2015)
18. Kingma, D.P., Ba, J.: Adam: a method for stochastic optimization. arXiv preprint arXiv:1412.6980 (2014)
19. Liang, J., et al.: VRT: a video restoration transformer. arXiv preprint arXiv:2201.12288 (2022)
20. Liang, J., Cao, J., Sun, G., Zhang, K., Van Gool, L., Timofte, R.: SwinIR: image restoration using swin transformer. In: Proceedings of the IEEE/CVF International Conference on Computer Vision, pp. 1833–1844 (2021)
21. Liu, Z., et al.: Swin transformer: hierarchical vision transformer using shifted windows. In: Proceedings of the IEEE/CVF International Conference on Computer Vision, pp. 10012–10022 (2021)
22. Liu, Z., Mao, H., Wu, C.Y., Feichtenhofer, C., Darrell, T., Xie, S.: A convnet for the 2020s. arXiv preprint arXiv:2201.03545 (2022)
23. Loshchilov, I., Hutter, F.: SGDR: stochastic gradient descent with warm restarts. arXiv preprint arXiv:1608.03983 (2016)
24. Mao, X., Liu, Y., Shen, W., Li, Q., Wang, Y.: Deep residual Fourier transformation for single image deblurring. arXiv preprint arXiv:2111.11745 (2021)
25. Nah, S., Hyun Kim, T., Mu Lee, K.: Deep multi-scale convolutional neural network for dynamic scene deblurring. In: Proceedings of the IEEE Conference on Computer Vision and Pattern Recognition, pp. 3883–3891 (2017)
26. Nah, S., Son, S., Lee, S., Timofte, R., Lee, K.M.: NTIRE 2021 challenge on image deblurring. In: Proceedings of the IEEE/CVF Conference on Computer Vision and Pattern Recognition, pp. 149–165 (2021)
27. Nair, V., Hinton, G.E.: Rectified linear units improve restricted Boltzmann machines. In: ICML (2010)

28. Ronneberger, O., Fischer, P., Brox, T.: U-Net: convolutional networks for biomedical image segmentation. In: Navab, N., Hornegger, J., Wells, W.M., Frangi, A.F. (eds.) MICCAI 2015. LNCS, vol. 9351, pp. 234–241. Springer, Cham (2015). https://doi.org/10.1007/978-3-319-24574-4_28
29. Shazeer, N.: GLU variants improve transformer. arXiv preprint arXiv:2002.05202 (2020)
30. Tu, Z., et al.: Maxim: Multi-axis MLP for image processing. arXiv preprint arXiv:2201.02973 (2022)
31. Ulyanov, D., Vedaldi, A., Lempitsky, V.: Instance normalization: the missing ingredient for fast stylization. arXiv preprint arXiv:1607.08022 (2016)
32. Vaswani, A., et al.: Attention is all you need. In: Advances in Neural Information Processing Systems 30 (2017)
33. Wang, Y., Huang, H., Xu, Q., Liu, J., Liu, Y., Wang, J.: Practical deep raw image denoising on mobile devices. In: Vedaldi, A., Bischof, H., Brox, T., Frahm, J.-M. (eds.) ECCV 2020. LNCS, vol. 12351, pp. 1–16. Springer, Cham (2020). https://doi.org/10.1007/978-3-030-58539-6_1
34. Wang, Z., Cun, X., Bao, J., Liu, J.: Uformer: a general U-shaped transformer for image restoration. arXiv preprint arXiv:2106.03106 (2021)
35. Waqas Zamir, S., et al.: Multi-stage progressive image restoration. arXiv preprint arXiv:2102.02808 (2021)
36. Yan, J., Wan, R., Zhang, X., Zhang, W., Wei, Y., Sun, J.: Towards stabilizing batch statistics in backward propagation of batch normalization. arXiv preprint arXiv:2001.06838 (2020)
37. Zamir, S.W., Arora, A., Khan, S., Hayat, M., Khan, F.S., Yang, M.H.: Restormer: efficient transformer for high-resolution image restoration. arXiv preprint arXiv:2111.09881 (2021)
38. Zamir, S.W., et al.: Learning enriched features for real image restoration and enhancement. In: Vedaldi, A., Bischof, H., Brox, T., Frahm, J.-M. (eds.) ECCV 2020. LNCS, vol. 12370, pp. 492–511. Springer, Cham (2020). https://doi.org/10.1007/978-3-030-58595-2_30

Spike Transformer: Monocular Depth Estimation for Spiking Camera

Jiyuan Zhang[1], Lulu Tang[2,3], Zhaofei Yu[1(✉)], Jiwen Lu[3], and Tiejun Huang[1,2]

[1] Department of Computer Science, Peking University, Beijing, China
jyzhang@stu.pku.edu.cn, {yuzf12,tjhuang}@pku.edu.cn
[2] Beijing Academy of Artificial Intelligence, Beijing, China
[3] Department of Automation, Tsinghua University, Beijing, China
{lulutang,lujiwen}@tsinghua.edu.cn

Abstract. Spiking camera is a bio-inspired vision sensor that mimics the sampling mechanism of the primate fovea, which has shown great potential for capturing high-speed dynamic scenes with a sampling rate of 40,000 Hz. Unlike conventional digital cameras, the spiking camera continuously captures photons and outputs asynchronous binary spikes that encode time, location, and light intensity. Because of the different sampling mechanisms, the off-the-shelf image-based algorithms for digital cameras are unsuitable for spike streams generated by the spiking camera. Therefore, it is of particular interest to develop novel, spike-aware algorithms for common computer vision tasks. In this paper, we focus on the depth estimation task, which is challenging due to the natural properties of spike streams, such as irregularity, continuity, and spatial-temporal correlation, and has not been explored for the spiking camera. We present Spike Transformer (Spike-T), a novel paradigm for learning spike data and estimating monocular depth from continuous spike streams. To fit spike data to Transformer, we present an input spike embedding equipped with a spatio-temporal patch partition module to maintain features from both spatial and temporal domains. Furthermore, we build two spike-based depth datasets. One is synthetic, and the other is captured by a real spiking camera. Experimental results demonstrate that the proposed Spike-T can favorably predict the scene's depth and consistently outperform its direct competitors. More importantly, the representation learned by Spike-T transfers well to the unseen real data, indicating the generalization of Spike-T to real-world scenarios. To our best knowledge, this is the first time that directly depth estimation from spike streams becomes possible. Code and Datasets are available at https://github.com/Leozhangjiyuan/MDE-SpikingCamera.

Keywords: Depth estimation · Transformer · Spiking camera · Spike data

J. Zhang and L. Tang—Joint First Authors.

Supplementary Information The online version contains supplementary material available at https://doi.org/10.1007/978-3-031-20071-7_3.

1 Introduction

Traditional frame-based cameras work at a fixed rate, providing stroboscopic synchronous sequences of images by a snapshot. The concept of the exposure time window in frame-based cameras constrains their usage in some challenging scenarios, such as high-speed scenes and high dynamic range environment, leading to motion blur or over/under exposure. Compared with those cameras, the spiking camera [9,10,28], a bio-inspired visual sensor, poses a radically different sensing modality. Instead of capturing the visual signal in an exposure interval by a snapshot, each pixel on a spiking camera sensor independently and persistently captures the incoming photons, and triggers a spike only when the accumulated photons reach a dispatch threshold. Thus the spiking camera can produce a continuous spike stream at very high temporal resolution. Those recorded spatio-temporal spike streams can be used to reconstruct the dynamic scenes at any given moment [67,73]. Different from event-based camera (also called dynamic vision sensor) [15,16,38,53] that only records the relative brightness changes at each pixel, the spiking camera records the absolute light intensity, providing both static and dynamic scene information. Benefiting from the superior properties, such as full-time imaging and free dynamic range, the spiking camera poses enormous potential in autonomous driving, unmanned aerial vehicles, and mobile robots.

Depth estimation is a fundamental task in computer vision. State-of-the-art depth prediction works concentrate more on the standard frame-based cameras [5,14,21,23,33,62]. Recently, event-based depth estimation has made significant progress [18,26,48,70–72]. However, there is no investigation related to depth prediction for the spiking camera. Due to the different sampling mechanisms, the off-the-shelf depth estimation models for traditional images that only record stationary scenes are unsuitable for spike streams generated by the spiking camera. Learning depth from the asynchronous spike streams poses several challenges: 1) Lack of unified backbone for spike data: within a binary and irregular data structure, continuous spike streams capture dynamic scenes at a very high temporal resolution. There is no standard network at hand that can simultaneously mine the spatial and temporal features from the dense spike streams. 2) Lack of spike depth dataset: There is no well-annotated dataset containing spike streams and the corresponding ground truth depth. It is rather sophisticated to calibrate the imaging windows and synchronize the timestamps between spiking and depth cameras.

Inspired by prior works [1,4,41,60] that utilize Transformer [55] to model spatio-temporal correlations for videos, we attempt to explore Transformer to learn the spatio-temporal features from the irregular spike data. Transformer has been successfully applied in NLP [6,8,30,45], images [2,11,20,40], and point cloud [24,63,64,66], but very little is known about its effectiveness in binary spike data. A naive way is to convert spike streams to videos composed of sequential intensity frames so that the well-developed image-based algorithms can be used to learn the spike streams. However, when a high-temporal spike stream (40,000 HZ) is converted to typical frequency images (30 FPS), the converted images will lose some temporal continuity. When spikes are transformed to images with the same frequency (40,000 FPS), the temporal information can be preserved but with a surge of computational cost.

This work focuses on dense, monocular depth estimation (MDE) from original spike streams. Two key points are investigated: 1) How to mine the spatio-temporal features from binary, irregular, and continuous spike streams? 2) How to make full use of Transformer on the unstructured spike data? At this point, a new scheme, named Spike Transformer (Spike-T), is proposed to learn both spatial and temporal spike features and subsequently estimate depth from continuous spike streams. To our best knowledge, this is the first attempt to predict depth using only spike streams. In order to unleash the potential of the spiking camera in high-speed depth estimation, we first collect and generate one synthetic dataset, denoted as 'DENSE-spike' (see Sect. 5.1), which comprises spike streams, and the corresponding ground truth depth maps. We further collect a real dataset named 'Outdoor-spike' using the spiking camera [28], which includes various scenes of traffic roads and city streets.

Experimental results show that the proposed Spike-T performs well on our synthetic dataset and reliably predicts depth maps on the unseen real data. In summary, our main contributions include

- We dedicate to monocular depth estimation from continuous spike streams for the first time. One synthesized and one real captured spike-based depth datasets are first developed.
- We propose Spike Transformer (Spike-T), which adopts a spatio-temporal Transformer architecture to learn the unstructured spike data, mining the spatio-temporal characteristics of spike streams.
- To fit spike data to Transformer, we present an input spike embedding equipped with a spatio-temporal patch partition module to maintain features from both spatial and temporal domains.
- Qualitative and quantitative evaluations on the synthetic dataset demonstrate that the proposed Spike-T reliably predicts the scene's depth, and the representation learned by Spike-T transfers well to the unseen real data, indicating the generalization of the proposed model to the real scenarios.

2   Related Works

2.1   Bio-Inspired Spiking Camera

The spiking camera [9,10], also called Vidar camera [28], is a bio-inspired vision sensor that mimics the sampling mechanism of the primate fovea, achieving 1000× faster speed than conventional frame-based counterparts. Due to its distinct working principles, the spiking camera can continuously record the scene's texture theoretically. Given its huge potential in many applications, such as traffic surveillance and suspect identification, spike-based vision tasks have been rapidly investigated. By counting the time interval of spikes, Dong et al. [10] first provided an efficient coding method for spiking camera. Motivated by bio-realistic leaky integrate-and-fire (LIF) neurons and synapse connection with spike-timing-dependent plasticity (STDP) rules, Zhu et al. [74] constructed a three-layer spiking neural network

(SNN) to reconstruct high-quality visual images of natural scenes. Zheng et al. [69] introduced an image reconstruction model through the short-term plasticity(STP) mechanism of the brain. Zhao et al. [68] built a hierarchical CNN architecture to reconstruct dynamic scenes, exploiting the temporal correlation of the spike stream progressively. More recently, [27] presented a deep learning pipeline to estimate optical flow from continuous spike streams, where the predicted optical flow was able to alleviate motion blur. Prior works have made significant progress in developing spiking cameras. Nevertheless, one of the essential vision tasks, depth estimation, has not been fully considered. This work thus focuses on learning depth from spike streams.

2.2   Image-Based and Event-Based Monocular Depth Estimation

Image-based monocular depth estimation aims to generate a dense depth map containing 3D structure information from a single-view image. Early works on image-based depth prediction primarily based on handcrafted features related to pictorial depth cues, such as texture density and object size [50]. In more recent years, deep learning-based depth estimation models have gained traction [13, 22, 23, 34, 36, 39, 44, 56, 62]. They commonly exploit an encoder-decoder architecture with skip-connections to learn depth-related priors directly from training data, achieving impressive depth estimation performance compared to the handcrafted counterparts.

Recently, event-based monocular depth estimation has drawn increasing attention due to its unique properties [3, 7, 17, 19, 25, 26, 31, 47, 72], especially for high-speed scenes where low-latency obstacle avoidance and rapid path planning are critical. Gallego et al. [17] developed a unifying contrast maximization framework to solve several event-based vision problems, such as depth prediction and optical flow estimation, by finding the point trajectories on the image plane that are best aligned with the event-based data. Zhu et al. [72] presented a proper event representation in the form of a discretized volume and utilized an encoder-decoder mechanism to integrate several cues from the event streams. Recurrent convolutional neural networks were exploited in [26] to learn monocular depth by leveraging the temporal consistency presented in the event streams. More recently, Gehrig et al. [19] proposed a Recurrent Asynchronous Multimodal network to estimate monocular depth by combining events and frames, which generalized traditional RNNs to learn asynchronous event-based data from multiple sensors. Prior event-based works have greatly inspired our work. Unlike event-based cameras, which pay more attention to motion edges, the spiking camera captures both stationary and moving objects. Hence, spike-based vision problems need to be studied in different ways from event-based counterparts.

2.3   Transformer for Dense Prediction

Self-attention-based models, in particular Transformers [55], have recently become the dominate backbone architecture in natural language processing (NLP) [6, 8, 30, 45]. It also intrigued the vision community [2, 11, 20, 40] due to its salient benefits, including massively parallel computing, long-distance characteristics, and minimal inductive biases. As for dense prediction tasks, Transformer has a global receptive field at every stage and can work at a constant and relatively high resolution. These attractive properties can naturally lead to fine-grained and globally coherent dense predictions [46]. Transformer-based networks have been intensively investigated for dense prediction [35,37,42,57,58,65]. Ranftl et al. [46] applied ViT [11] as the encoder backbone to estimate monocular depth. Compared with CNN backbone, it showed that more coherent predictions could be learned due to the global receptive field of Transformer. Yang et al. [61] additionally used a ResNet projection layer and attention gates in the decoder to induce the spatial locality of CNNs for monocular depth estimation. Lately, Johnston et al. [29] utilized a self-attention block to explore the general contextual information and applied a discrete disparity to regularize the training procedure. More recently, Varma et al. [54] investigated self-supervised monocular depth estimation using vision Transformer. It showed that Transformer achieves comparable performance while being more robust and generalizable when compared with CNN-based architectures. The structural superiority of Transformer has been proved by both NLP and image tasks. Previous dense prediction works also justify the capability of Transformer for depth prediction. Motivated by Swin Transformer [40], we develop a spatio-temporal Transformer network for monocular depth estimation from continuous and unstructured spike streams.

3 Preliminary: Spike Generation Mechanism

Inspired by the sampling mechanism of primate fovea in retina [43,59], the spiking camera records the intensity information with spatio-temporal characteristics. It outputs binary streams in spike format, representing data with only 0 or 1. The spiking camera mainly consists of three ingredients, the photoreceptor, the accumulator, and the comparator. Specifically, an array of photosensitive pixels are spatially arranged on the photoreceptor of spiking cameras, continuously capturing photons. Secondly, the accumulator persistently converts light signals into electrical signals to increase the voltage of each unit. The comparator detects whether the accumulated voltage reaches the dispatch voltage threshold θ. When the threshold is reached, a spike is triggered, and the voltage will be reset to the preset value. To depict the spike generation mechanism, the process on one pixel can be formulated as:

$$\int_{t_{i-1}}^{t_i} \alpha I(t)dt = \theta \tag{1}$$

where $I(t)$ describes the light intensity, t_i and t_{i-1} denote the firing times of the i-th and $(i-1)$-th spikes, respectively. α is the photoelectric conversion rate. Due to the limitations of circuit technology, the unit in the output circuit read out spikes as discrete-time signals $s(x, y, n)$ periodically within a fixed interval $\Delta t = 25$ us. A spike will be read out $s(x, y, n) = 1$ $(n = 1, 2, \ldots)$ if the pixel at spatial coordinate (x, y) fires a spike at time t, with $(n - 1)\Delta t < t \leqslant n\Delta t$. Otherwise it reads out $s(x, y, n) = 0$. The sensor uses a high-speed polling to generate a spike frame with size of $H \times W$ at each discrete timestamp n. In a fixed interval $\Delta t \cdot T$, the camera would produce a binary spike stream $S = \{s(x, y, t)\}_{t=1}^{T}$ with size of $H \times W \times T$.

4 Spike Transformer for Monocular Depth Estimation

The spiking camera outputs spikes at each pixel independently and asynchronously. For simplicity, we use $S \in \{0, 1\}^{H \times W \times T}$ to denote a spike stream, and use $\mathcal{D} \in \mathbb{R}^{H \times W}$ to denote the depth map at one polling. The objective of monocular depth estimation for the spiking camera is to predict the original depth map $\mathcal{D}$ from the continuous binary spike stream S. To this end, we present Spike Transformer (Spike-T) for monocular depth prediction. The overall framework comprises three components: (a) spike embedding module, (b) spatio-temporal Transformer (STT) encoder, and (c) CNN-based decoder. The framework is illustrated in Fig. 1, which maintains the overall encoder-decoder architecture with hierarchical structures. Specifically, an input spike stream is first fed into the spike embedding module, obtaining several spike embeddings that preserve spatio-temporal characteristics for Transformer's input. Subsequently, we employ several STT blocks to learn spatio-temporal features for spike embeddings, using the adapted self-attention mechanism. The hierarchical features from the encoder are progressively fused for final depth prediction.

4.1 Spike Embedding

The spike embedding module consists of three steps: Temporal Partition, Feature Extraction, and Spatial Partition (see Fig. 2). As presented in Sect. 3, a sequence of spike frames $S = \{s(x, y, t)\}_{t=1}^{T}$ record the scene's radiance at each timestamp t. The features along the time axis are crucial to reconstruct the depth map. A multi-scale temporal window is thus introduced to maintain more temporal information.

Specifically, for each raw input S, we first partition it into n non-overlapping spike chunks along the temporal axis, using a sliding window of length $\frac{T}{n}$. Each spike chunk with shape of $H \times W \times \frac{T}{n}$ carries different local temporal features in an interval T. A lightweight feature extractor (FE), consisting of four residual blocks, is then used to project each chunk to a feature map of size $H \times W \times C$. Theoretically, the length of time window $\frac{T}{n}$ can be set as an arbitrary positive integer no more than T. Different time-scale window carries a different scale of temporal information. We thus can leverage multiple time-scale windows, e.g., $\frac{T}{1}, \frac{T}{2}, \frac{T}{4}, ... \frac{T}{n}$, to capture multi-level temporal features. Empirically, we set n to 4. Features from $\frac{T}{4}$ time window can be considered as $\frac{1}{4}$ local features. Subsequently, we set n to 1, features from $\frac{T}{1}$ time window can be seen as global features. Similarly, other time windows can be used. In our setting, only $\frac{T}{4}$ local and $\frac{T}{1}$ global features are considered. In this case, 4 spike chunks are passed through the shared local FE module separately, while the full-length spike stream

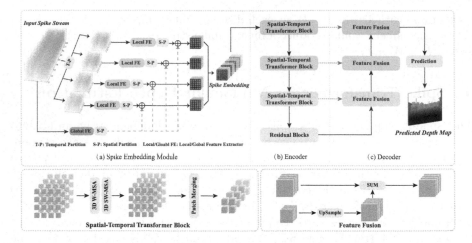

Fig. 1. The framework of Spike-T for MDE. Generally, our model is a U-shaped network consisting of three components: (a) spike embedding module, (b) spatio-temporal Transformer (STT) encoder, and (c) convolutional decoder. We first partition the input spike stream into several non-overlapping chunks by a multi-scale temporal window. Then, a spatial partition layer and Local/Global Feature Extractor (FE) are used to obtain a series of spike embeddings. Our encoder is built by several STT blocks, which implements the attention mechanism along the temporal, height, and width axes. The decoder comprises multiple feature fusion layers, in which hierarchical features are progressively fused and finally used to estimate the depth map.

is fed into the global FE module. After that, we split each feature map from FE module into $\frac{H}{2} \times \frac{W}{2}$ patches (with 2×2 patch size) in the spatial domain. By merging local and global FE features, we can obtain $\frac{H}{2} \times \frac{W}{2} \times 4$ temporal-robust feature maps. Therefore, an input spike stream with shape of $H \times W \times T$ can be partitioned into $\frac{H}{2} \times \frac{W}{2} \times 4$ spatio-temporal (ST) blocks. We treat each ST block of size $2 \times 2 \times \frac{T}{4}$ as a token. Following the practice of Transformers in NLP and image-based tasks, we term the feature of those tokens as spike embeddings, which thus can be received as inputs to Transformer.

4.2 Spatio-Temporal Transformer Encoder

The overall architecture of spatio-temporal Transformer is illustrated in Fig. 2, which is adapted from a Swin Transformer architecture [40,41]. Features from spiking embedding module are fed into the Transformer-based encoder, which includes three stages. Each stage consists of 2,2 and 6 STT blocks, respectively. A patch merging layer is added between two adjacent stages.

Spatial Patch Merging. To preserve more local temporal features, following the prior work [41], we only implement the downsampling operation in the spatial domain, maintaining the number of tokens in the temporal domain. Specifically, features from each 2×2 spatial neighboring patches are first concatenated along

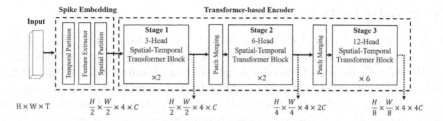

Fig. 2. Architecture of Spike Transformer.

C-channel, forming a merging feature map with $4C$ dimension. A linear layer is used to project such a $4C$-dimensional feature map to a $2C$-dimensional one. Thus, the feature dimension along C-channel will be doubled after each stage.

Spatio-Temporal Transformer Block. The key component of Spike-T is the STT block. Each STT block consists of a multi-head self-attention (MSA) module equipped with a 3D shifted window, followed by a feed-forward network (FFN) composed of a 2-layer MLP. Between each MSA module and FFN, a GELU layer is utilized, and a Layer Normalization(LN) is used before each MSA and FFN. Each module applies a residual connection.

In particular, for two consecutive STT blocks at one Transformer encoder stage, the MSA module in the former block acts on the $T_x \times H_x \times W_x$ spatio-temporal tokens. 3D windows with size of $W_t \times W_h \times W_w$ are then utilized to evenly partition these tokens into $\lceil \frac{T_x}{W_t} \rceil \times \lceil \frac{H_x}{W_h} \rceil \times \lceil \frac{W_x}{W_w} \rceil$ non-overlapping windows. In our implementation, T_x is set to be same as the temporal partition number($n = 4$). H_x and W_x are the current spatial token size. The 3D window size is set to $2 \times 7 \times 7$. For the MSA module in the latter SST block, we shift windows along the temporal, height, and width axes by (1, 3, 3) tokens from the previous STT block and perform attention among windows. Following the practice in [40,41], we term the first window-based MSA as 3D W-MSA, which uses the regular window partitioning configuration. The second window-based MSA is denoted as 3D SW-MSA, which applies a shifted window partitioning mechanism. The above two successive SST blocks can be formalized as [41]

$$
\begin{aligned}
\hat{z}^m &= \text{3DW-MSA}(LN(z^{m-1})) + z^{m-1}, \\
z^m &= \text{FFN}(LN(\hat{z}^m)) + \hat{z}^m, \\
\hat{z}^{m+1} &= \text{3DSW-MSA}(LN(z^m)) + z^m, \\
z^{m+1} &= \text{FFN}(LN(\hat{z}^{m+1})) + \hat{z}^{m+1},
\end{aligned}
\tag{2}
$$

where $\hat{z}^m$ and z^m denote the output features of the 3D(S)W-MSA module and the FFN module for block m in one stage. As for STT blocks in each stage, we use 3, 6 , and 12 attention heads, respectively. In this way, features from each Transformer encoder stage can be formed as a tuple, with sizes of $\frac{H}{2} \times \frac{W}{2} \times T \times C$, $\frac{H}{4} \times \frac{W}{4} \times T \times 2C$ and $\frac{H}{8} \times \frac{W}{8} \times T \times 4C$ separately, which thus can be used for downstream spike-based tasks.

4.3   Decoder for Depth Prediction

As shown in Fig. 1, our decoder consists of two residual blocks, three feature fusion layers, and one prediction head. The output feature maps, with size of $H_i \times W_i \times T \times C_i$ from each encoder stage, are concatenated along temporal axis, reshaping the size to $H_i \times W_i \times TC_i$. After that, a convolutional layer is used to project the reshaped features back to $H_i \times W_i \times C_i$. The last feature maps, with the size of $\frac{H}{8} \times \frac{W}{8} \times 4C$, are first passed through two residual blocks with a kernel size of 3. Subsequently, features from the previous layer are upsampled through a bilinear interpolation operation and progressively fused with the following layers. A prediction head consisting of one convolutional layer is finally used to generate a $H \times W \times 1$ depth map.

4.4   Loss Function

Following [26], we employ a scale-invariant loss to train our depth estimation network in a supervised manner. For k-th spike stream with the size of $H \times W \times T$, the model outputs the depth map with the size of $H \times W \times 1$. We denote the predicted depth map, ground truth depth map, and their residual as $\hat{\mathcal{D}}_k$, $\mathcal{D}_k$, and $\mathcal{R}_k$, respectively. The scale-invariant loss is then defined as

$$\mathcal{L}_k = \frac{1}{n} \sum_{\mathbf{p}} (\mathcal{R}_k(\mathbf{p}))^2 - \frac{1}{n^2} \left(\sum_{\mathbf{p}} \mathcal{R}_k(\mathbf{p}) \right)^2, \tag{3}$$

where $\mathcal{R}_k = \hat{\mathcal{D}}_k$ - $\mathcal{D}_k$, and n is the number of valid ground truth pixels $\mathbf{p}$.

5   Experiments

5.1   Dataset

Synthetic Dataset. We train our Spike-T in a supervised fashion, which requires a large-scale training dataset in the form of spike streams and the corresponding synchronous depth maps. Nevertheless, it is complicated to build a real dataset consisting of spike steam, gray image, and the corresponding depth map. Moreover, it is rather sophisticated to calibrate imaging windows and synchronize timestamps among a spiking camera, a frame-based camera, and a depth camera. Thus, we build a synthetic spike dataset. Specifically, we first choose the dataset named DENSE proposed in [26] as our database. The DENSE dataset was generated by CARLA simulator [12], including clear depth maps and intensity frames in 30 FPS under a variety of weather and illumination conditions. To obtain spike streams with a very high temporal resolution, we adopt a video interpolation method [52] to generate intermediate RGB frames between adjacent 30-FPS frames. With absolute intensity information among RGB frames, each sensor pixel can continuously accumulate the light intensity with the spike generation mechanism introduced in Sect. 3, producing spike streams with a high temporal resolution (128 × 30 FPS) that is 128 times of the video frame rate. The 'spike' version of DENSE dataset (namely DENSE-spike) contains eight sequences, five for training, two for validation, and one for testing. Each sequence consists 999 samples, and each sample is a tuple of one RGB image, one depth map, and one spike stream. Each spike stream is simulated between two consecutive images, generating a binary sequence with 128 spike frames (with size of 346 × 260) that depicts the continuous process of dynamic scenes.

Real Dataset. To verify the generalization of the proposed model, we further collect some natural spike sequences using a spiking camera [28]. The spatial resolution of the spiking camera is 400 × 250, and the temporal resolution is 40000 HZ. The real captured spike streams are recorded on city streets and roads. We denote this real dataset as 'Outdoor-Spike', which is only used for testing due to lack of the corresponding ground truth depth. In our 'Outdoor-Spike' dataset, 33 sequences of outdoor scenes are captured in a driving car from the first perspective. Each sequence contains 20000 spike frames.

5.2   Implementation Details

Depth Representation. Following [26], we convert the original depth $\mathcal{D}_{k,abs}$ into a logarithmic depth map $\mathcal{D}_k$, which can be calculated as

$$\mathcal{D}_k = \frac{1}{\beta} \log \frac{\mathcal{D}_{k,abs}}{\mathcal{D}_{max}} + 1, \tag{4}$$

where $\mathcal{D}_{max}$ is the maximum depth in dataset, β is a hyper-parameter empirically set to let the minimum depth closed to 0. For our synthetic dataset 'DENSE-spike', we set $\beta = 5.7$, $\mathcal{D}_{max} = 1000m$.

Training Setup. We implemented the network in PyTorch. In training, we adopt ADAM optimizer [32] to optimize the network and set the initial learning rate λ set to 0.0003. Our model is trained for 200 epochs with a batch size of 16 on 2 NVIDIA A100-SXM4-80GB GPUs. We use the exponential learning rate scheduler to adjust the learning rate after 100th epoch with γ set to 0.5.

Metrics. We adopt several important metrics, including absolute relative error (*Abs Rel.*), square relative error (*Sq Rel.*), mean absolute depth error (*MAE*), root mean square logarithmic error (*RMSE log*) and the accuracy metric (*Acc.δ*). Detailed formulations can be found in the Appendix.

5.3   Experiment Results

In this section, we evaluate the performance of our Spike-T on both synthetic and real captured datasets, and compare Spike-T with two model architectures, U-Net [49] and E2Depth [26]. Three models are all trained on the synthetic 'DENSE-spike' dataset. To verify the generalization and transferability of our Spike-T, we further utilize the real dataset 'Outdoor-Spike' for testing, and give qualitative visualization results. Finally, an ablation study of Spike-T is presented.

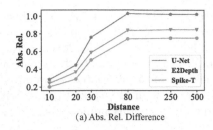 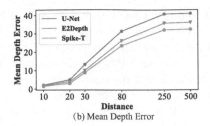

(a) Abs. Rel. Difference

(b) Mean Depth Error

Fig. 3. Results of absolute relative difference and mean depth error in different clip distances. Curves in green, red and blue represent our Spike-T, E2Depth [26] and U-Net [49], respectively. (Color figure online)

Table 1. Quantitative comparison on the DENSE-spike dataset with UNet [49] and E2Depth [26]. We present results on validation set and test set. ↓ indicates lower is better and ↑ indicates higher is better.

Dataset	Model	Abs Rel ↓	Sq Rel ↓	RMS log ↓	SI log ↓	$\delta < 1.25$ ↑	$\delta < 1.25^2$ ↑	$\delta < 1.25^3$ ↑
Test set	U-Net	0.815	27.878	0.777	0.459	0.653	0.725	0.778
	E2Depth	0.674	20.316	0.765	0.441	0.639	0.729	0.789
	Spike-T (Ours)	**0.606**	**18.388**	**0.706**	**0.395**	**0.682**	**0.762**	**0.813**
Val set	U-Net	0.306	7.101	0.394	0.139	0.833	0.909	0.939
	E2Depth	0.291	5.796	0.411	0.168	0.821	0.894	0.928
	Spike-T (Ours)	**0.262**	**4.703**	**0.364**	**0.125**	**0.850**	**0.913**	**0.944**

A. Qualitative and Quantitative Comparisons. We first compare our Spike-T with two dense prediction networks, namely U-Net and E2Depth. Both them and our Spike-T follow the encoder-decoder architecture with multi-scale fusion manner but utilize different encoding mechanisms. In particular, U-Net employs 2D convolutional layers as its encoder and focuses on spatial feature extraction, while E2Depth applies ConvLSTM [51] layers that combine CNN and LSTM to capture the spatial and temporal features. By contrast, our Spike-T employs transformer-based blocks to learn the spatio-temporal features simultaneously. Thus, both U-Net and E2Depth can be seen as our direct competitors.

Table 1 reports the quantitative comparison on 'Dense-spike' dataset. On both validation and testing sets, the proposed Spike-T consistently outperforms the other two methods on all metrics. Furthermore, our method achieves significant improvement on the metrics of Abs.Rel, which is the most convictive metric in depth estimation tasks. The major difference between the three methods lies in the encoder architecture. These experimental results indicate that our Spike-T with the Transformer-based encoder is more efficient in capturing the spatio-temporal features from irregular, continuous spike streams.

We also evaluate our method at depths of 10 m, 20 m, 30 m, 80 m, 250 m, 500 m. Figure 3 illustrates how absolute relative error and mean depth error change with depths on validating sequences. The results show that our method performs more accurate depth prediction at all distances, especially at the larger distances.

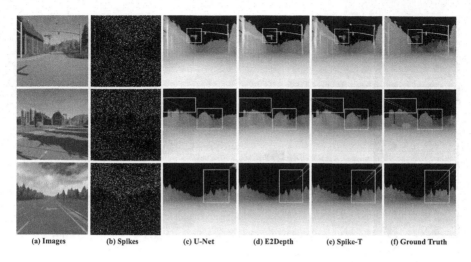

(a) Images   (b) Spikes   (c) U-Net   (d) E2Depth   (e) Spike-T   (f) Ground Truth

Fig. 4. Visualization results on synthetic dataset 'DENSE-spike'. Boxes in cyan marked in pictures provide comparisons in details. (Color figure online)

The qualitative comparison is shown in Fig. 4. For a clear comparison, we mark some cyan boxes on fine-grained objects. As we can see, more details, including tiny structures, sharp edges, and contours, can be estimated by our Spike-T. The quantitative and qualitative results demonstrate that our method is more suitable for continuous spike streams generated by the spiking camera, and can learn valid and robust features from the spatial and temporal domain.

B. Evaluation on Real-World Dataset. We evaluate our method by training networks on the synthetic dataset and testing on the real dataset 'Outdoor-Spike'. It is a more challenging dataset captured from outdoor scenes with various motions and noises from the real world. Figure 5 displays some examples with real spikes, gray images, and the predicted depth compared with the baseline U-Net and E2Depth. The visualization results verify that acceptable depth prediction results are achieved in real-world scenarios.

As shown in Fig. 5(c), depth maps predicted by U-Net and E2Depth include blur artifacts and lose some details, leading to ambiguity between foreground and background. By contrast, depth maps predicted by Spike-T are better with more details of contours, and more precise depth variation can be provided. Overall, despite the domain gap between synthetic and real data, our Spike-T can reasonably predict the real scene's depth, indicating the model's transferability to real-world scenes.

C. Comparison to Depth Estimation Methods Using Images or Events. We give more comparison with depth prediction methods that use images or events. Moreover, we captured some fast-moving and shaky scenes with a synchronized spiking camera and a traditional camera. Visualization results

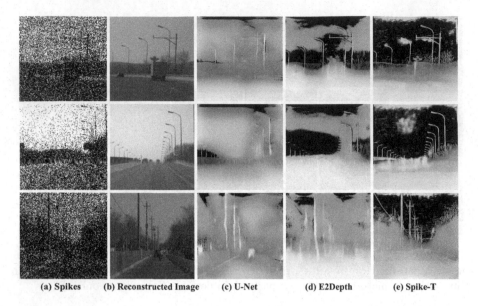

(a) Spikes   (b) Reconstructed Image   (c) U-Net   (d) E2Depth   (e) Spike-T

Fig. 5. Visualization results on real-world data (from 'Outdoor-spike'). (a) The spike frame at the predicted timestamp. (b) Reconstructed images with [69]. (c-e) Predicted depth maps with U-Net, E2Depth, and our Spike-T.

Table 2. Ablation study on different temporal window mechanisms.

Model	Abs Rel ↓	Sq Rel ↓	RMS log ↓	SI log ↓	$\delta < 1.25$ ↑	$\delta < 1.25^2$ ↑	$\delta < 1.25^3$ ↑
Global temporal	0.416	11.256	0.478	0.218	0.793	**0.867**	**0.902**
Local temporal	0.389	10.884	0.490	0.230	0.791	0.860	0.896
Multi-scale temporal	**0.376**	**9.265**	**0.478**	**0.215**	**0.794**	0.863	0.901

demonstrate the advantage of spiking cameras over conventional ones under some challenging scenarios (Refer to the Appendix).

5.4   Ablation Studies

A. Effect of Multi-scale Temporal Window. As presented in Sect. 4.1, we introduce a multi-scale temporal window at the spike embedding stage to preserve more temporal information. To verify its effectiveness, we implement three ablation studies, termed as 'Global Temporal', 'Local Temporal' and 'Multi-scale Temporal', respectively. Specifically, 'Global Temporal' means feature embedding with only global features (temporal partition number $n = 1$), which pays more attention to spatial features. 'Local Temporal' indicates feature embedding using only local features ($n = 4$), while 'Multi-scale Temporal' denotes features embedding from both local ($n = 4$) and global ($n = 1$) features. The comparison results are shown in Table 2. Spiking embedding with only 'Local Temporal' outperforms that with only 'Global Temporal' on the most crucial metric Abs

Table 3. Ablation results on different patch partitioning manner.

Dataset	Model	Abs Rel ↓	Sq Rel ↓	RMS log ↓	SI log ↓	$\delta < 1.25$ ↑	$\delta < 1.25^2$ ↑	$\delta < 1.25^3$ ↑
Test set	3D partition	0.868	31.771	0.822	0.500	0.636	0.729	0.780
	S-T partition	**0.606**	**18.388**	**0.706**	**0.395**	**0.682**	**0.762**	**0.813**
Val set	3D partition	0.310	7.458	0.386	0.139	0.841	0.907	0.938
	S-T partition	**0.262**	**4.703**	**0.364**	**0.125**	**0.850**	**0.913**	**0.944**

Rel, indicating that the spatio-temporal correlations involved in local features are more informative than that contained in global parts. Furthermore, a multi-scale temporal window combining both local and global features is superior to the above two settings. It demonstrates that more spatio-temporal features can be learned from the unstructured and successive spike streams with the multi-scale temporal window mechanism. More detailed studies on hyperparameter T and n can be found in the Appendix.

B. Effect of S-T Patch Partition. The patch partitioning operation in the standard Video Swin Transformer is implemented with a 3D convolutional layer. It splits the original input into several 3D blocks. We conduct an ablation study on the patch partitioning manner, comparing our S-T partition with standard Conv3D-based partition by replacing the spike embedding module with a Conv3D layer. The quantitative results are presented in Table. 3. Our method with S-T patch partitioning performs better on all metrics, which indicates that the S-T partition is more suitable to extract features from spike streams.

6   Conclusions

We present Spike Transformer for monocular depth estimation of the spiking camera. To favorably apply Transformer on spike data, an effective spike representation, termed as spiking embedding, is first proposed. Then a modified Swin Transformer architecture is employed to learn the spatio-temporal spike features. Furthermore, two spike-based depth datasets are carefully built. Experiments on both synthetic and real datasets show that our Spike-T can reliably predict the depth maps and express superiority to its direct competitors.

Acknowledgement. This work is supported in part by the National Natural Science Foundation of China under Grant 62176003 and No. 62088102.

References

1. Arnab, A., Dehghani, M., Heigold, G., Sun, C., Lučić, M., Schmid, C.: ViViT: a video vision transformer. In: Proceedings of the IEEE/CVF International Conference on Computer Vision (ICCV), pp. 6836–6846 (2021)
2. Bao, H., Dong, L., Wei, F.: BEiT: BERT pre-training of image transformers. arXiv preprint arXiv:2106.08254 (2021)

3. Baudron, A., Wang, Z.W., Cossairt, O., Katsaggelos, A.K.: E3D: event-based 3D shape reconstruction. arXiv preprint arXiv:2012.05214 (2020)
4. Bertasius, G., Wang, H., Torresani, L.: Is space-time attention all you need for video understanding. arXiv preprint arXiv:2102.05095 (2021)
5. Bhat, S.F., Alhashim, I., Wonka, P.: AdaBins: depth estimation using adaptive bins. In: Proceedings of the IEEE/CVF Conference on Computer Vision and Pattern Recognition (CVPR), pp. 4009–4018 (2021)
6. Brown, T., et al.: Language models are few-shot learners. Adv. Neural Inf. Process. Syst. (NeurIPS) **33**, 1877–1901 (2020)
7. Chaney, K., Zhu, A.Z., Daniilidis, K · Learning event-based height from plane and parallax. In: Proceedings of the IEEE/CVF Conference on Computer Vision and Pattern Recognition Workshops (CVPR) (2019)
8. Devlin, J., Chang, M.W., Lee, K., Toutanova, K.: BERT: pre-training of deep bidirectional transformers for language understanding. arXiv preprint arXiv:1810.04805 (2018)
9. Dong, S., Huang, T., Tian, Y.: Spike camera and its coding methods. In: 2017 Data Compression Conference (DCC), pp. 437–437 (2017)
10. Dong, S., Zhu, L., Xu, D., Tian, Y., Huang, T.: An efficient coding method for spike camera using inter-spike intervals. In: 2019 Data Compression Conference (DCC), pp. 568–568. IEEE (2019)
11. Dosovitskiy, A., et al.: An image is worth 16×16 words: transformers for image recognition at scale. arXiv preprint arXiv:2010.11929 (2020)
12. Dosovitskiy, A., Ros, G., Codevilla, F., Lopez, A., Koltun, V.: CARLA: an open urban driving simulator. In: Conference on Robot Learning, pp. 1–16 (2017)
13. Eigen, D., Fergus, R.: Predicting depth, surface normals and semantic labels with a common multi-scale convolutional architecture. In: Proceedings of the IEEE/CVF International Conference on Computer Vision (ICCV) (2015)
14. Fu, H., Gong, M., Wang, C., Batmanghelich, K., Tao, D.: Deep ordinal regression network for monocular depth estimation. In: Proceedings of the IEEE/CVF Conference on Computer Vision and Pattern Recognition (CVPR), pp. 2002–2011 (2018)
15. Gallego, G., et al.: Event-based vision: a survey. IEEE Trans. Patt. Anal. Mach. Intell. **44**(1), 154–180 (2020)
16. Gallego, G., Gehrig, M., Scaramuzza, D.: Focus is all you need: loss functions for event-based vision. In: Proceedings of the IEEE/CVF Conference on Computer Vision and Pattern Recognition (CVPR), pp. 12280–12289 (2019)
17. Gallego, G., Rebecq, H., Scaramuzza, D.: A unifying contrast maximization framework for event cameras, with applications to motion, depth, and optical flow estimation. In: Proceedings of the IEEE/CVF Conference on Computer Vision and Pattern Recognition (CVPR), pp. 3867–3876 (2018)
18. Gehrig, D., Gehrig, M., Hidalgo-Carrió, J., Scaramuzza, D.: Video to events: recycling video datasets for event cameras. In: Proceedings of the IEEE/CVF Conference on Computer Vision and Pattern Recognition (CVPR), pp. 3586–3595 (2020)
19. Gehrig, D., Rüegg, M., Gehrig, M., Hidalgo-Carrió, J., Scaramuzza, D.: Combining events and frames using recurrent asynchronous multimodal networks for monocular depth prediction. IEEE Robot. Autom. Lett. **6**(2), 2822–2829 (2021)
20. Girdhar, R., Carreira, J., Doersch, C., Zisserman, A.: Video action transformer network. In: Proceedings of the IEEE/CVF International Conference on Computer Vision (ICCV) (2019)

21. Godard, C., Mac Aodha, O., Brostow, G.J.: Unsupervised monocular depth estimation with left-right consistency. In: Proceedings of the IEEE/CVF Conference on Computer Vision and Pattern Recognition (CVPR), pp. 270–279 (2017)
22. Godard, C., Mac Aodha, O., Brostow, G.J.: Unsupervised monocular depth estimation with left-right consistency. In: Proceedings of the IEEE/CVF Conference on Computer Vision and Pattern Recognition (CVPR) (2017)
23. Godard, C., Mac Aodha, O., Firman, M., Brostow, G.J.: Digging into self-supervised monocular depth estimation. In: Proceedings of the IEEE/CVF International Conference on Computer Vision (ICCV), pp. 3828–3838 (2019)
24. Guo, M.H., Cai, J.X., Liu, Z.N., Mu, T.J., Martin, R.R., Hu, S.M.: PCT: point cloud transformer. Comput. Vis. Media **7**(2), 187–199 (2021). https://doi.org/10.1007/s41095-021-0229-5
25. Haessig, G., Berthelon, X., Ieng, S.H., Benosman, R.: A spiking neural network model of depth from defocus for event-based neuromorphic vision. Scient. Rep. **9**(1), 1–11 (2019)
26. Hidalgo-Carrió, J., Gehrig, D., Scaramuzza, D.: Learning monocular dense depth from events. In: 2020 International Conference on 3D Vision (3DV), pp. 534–542. IEEE (2020)
27. Hu, L., Zhao, R., Ding, Z., Xiong, R., Ma, L., Huang, T.: SCFlow: optical flow estimation for spiking camera. arXiv preprint arXiv:2110.03916 (2021)
28. Huang, T., et al.: 1000x faster camera and machine vision with ordinary devices. Engineering (2022)
29. Johnston, A., Carneiro, G.: Self-supervised monocular trained depth estimation using self-attention and discrete disparity volume. In: Proceedings of the IEEE/CVF Conference on Computer Vision and Pattern Recognition (CVPR), pp. 4756–4765 (2020)
30. Joshi, M., Chen, D., Liu, Y., Weld, D.S., Zettlemoyer, L., Levy, O.: SpanBERT: improving pre-training by representing and predicting spans. Trans. Assoc. Comput. Linguist. **8**, 64–77 (2020)
31. Kim, H., Leutenegger, S., Davison, A.J.: Real-time 3D reconstruction and 6-DoF tracking with an event camera. In: Leibe, B., Matas, J., Sebe, N., Welling, M. (eds.) ECCV 2016. LNCS, vol. 9910, pp. 349–364. Springer, Cham (2016). https://doi.org/10.1007/978-3-319-46466-4_21
32. Kingma, D.P., Ba, J.: Adam: a method for stochastic optimization. arXiv preprint arXiv:1412.6980 (2014)
33. Kopf, J., Rong, X., Huang, J.B.: Robust consistent video depth estimation. In: Proceedings of the IEEE/CVF Conference on Computer Vision and Pattern Recognition (CVPR), pp. 1611–1621 (2021)
34. Lee, J.H., Kim, C.S.: Monocular depth estimation using relative depth maps. In: Proceedings of the IEEE/CVF Conference on Computer Vision and Pattern Recognition (CVPR) (2019)
35. Lee, Y., Kim, J., Willette, J., Hwang, S.J.: MPVit: multi-path vision transformer for dense prediction. arXiv preprint arXiv:2112.11010 (2021)
36. Li, Z., Snavely, N.: MegaDepth: learning single-view depth prediction from internet photos. In: Proceedings of the IEEE/CVF Conference on Computer Vision and Pattern Recognition (CVPR) (2018)
37. Liang, J., Cao, J., Sun, G., Zhang, K., Van Gool, L., Timofte, R.: SwinIR: image restoration using swin transformer. In: Proceedings of the IEEE/CVF International Conference on Computer Vision (ICCV), pp. 1833–1844 (2021)

38. Lichtsteiner, P., Posch, C., Delbruck, T.: A 128×128 120db 15μs latency asynchronous temporal contrast vision sensor. IEEE J. Solid-state Circ. **43**(2), 566–576 (2008)
39. Liu, F., Shen, C., Lin, G.: Deep convolutional neural fields for depth estimation from a single image. In: Proceedings of the IEEE/CVF Conference on Computer Vision and Pattern Recognition (CVPR) (2015)
40. Liu, Z., et al.: Swin transformer: hierarchical vision transformer using shifted windows. In: Proceedings of the IEEE/CVF International Conference on Computer Vision (ICCV), pp. 10012–10022 (2021)
41. Liu, Z., et al.: Video swin transformer. arXiv preprint arXiv:2106.13230 (2021)
42. Liu, Z., et al.: ConvTransformer: a convolutional transformer network for video frame synthesis. arXiv preprint arXiv:2011.10185 (2020)
43. Masland, R.H.: The neuronal organization of the retina. Neuron **76**(2), 266–280 (2012)
44. Miangoleh, S.M.H., Dille, S., Mai, L., Paris, S., Aksoy, Y.: Boosting monocular depth estimation models to high-resolution via content-adaptive multi-resolution merging. In: Proceedings of the IEEE/CVF Conference on Computer Vision and Pattern Recognition(CVPR), pp. 9685–9694 (2021)
45. Radford, A., Wu, J., Child, R., Luan, D., Amodei, D., Sutskever, I., et al.: Language models are unsupervised multitask learners. OpenAI blog (2019)
46. Ranftl, R., Bochkovskiy, A., Koltun, V.: Vision transformers for dense prediction. In: Proceedings of the IEEE/CVF International Conference on Computer Vision (ICCV), pp. 12179–12188 (2021)
47. Rebecq, H., Gallego, G., Mueggler, E., Scaramuzza, D.: EMVS: event-based multi-view stereo-3D reconstruction with an event camera in real-time. Int. J. Comput. Vis. **126**(12), 1394–1414 (2018)
48. Rebecq, H., Gallego, G., Scaramuzza, D.: EMVS: event-based multi-view stereo. In: British Machine Vision Conference (BMVC) (2016)
49. Ronneberger, O., Fischer, P., Brox, T.: U-Net: convolutional networks for biomedical image segmentation. In: Navab, N., Hornegger, J., Wells, W.M., Frangi, A.F. (eds.) MICCAI 2015. LNCS, vol. 9351, pp. 234–241. Springer, Cham (2015). https://doi.org/10.1007/978-3-319-24574-4_28
50. Saxena, A., Sun, M., Ng, A.Y.: Make3d: learning 3d scene structure from a single still image. IEEE Trans. Patt. Anal. Mach. Intell. **31**(5), 824–840 (2008)
51. Shi, X., Chen, Z., Wang, H., Yeung, D.Y., Wong, W.K., Woo, W.C.: Convolutional LSTM network: a machine learning approach for precipitation nowcasting. Adv. Neural Inf. Process. Syst. **28**, 802–810 (2015)
52. Sim, H., Oh, J., Kim, M.: XVFi: extreme video frame interpolation. In: Proceedings of the IEEE/CVF International Conference on Computer Vision (ICCV), pp. 14489–14498 (2021)
53. Son, B., et al.: A 640× 480 dynamic vision sensor with a 9μm pixel and 300meps address-event representation. In: IEEE International Solid-State Circuits Conference (ISSCC), pp. 66–67 (2017)
54. Varma, A., Chawla, H., Zonooz, B., Arani, E.: Transformers in self-supervised monocular depth estimation with unknown camera intrinsics. arXiv preprint arXiv:2202.03131 (2022)
55. Vaswani, A., et al.: Attention is all you need. In: Advances in Neural Information Processing Systems (NeurIPS) (2017)
56. Wang, C., Buenaposada, J.M., Zhu, R., Lucey, S.: Learning depth from monocular videos using direct methods. In: Proceedings of the IEEE/CVF Conference on Computer Vision and Pattern Recognition (CVPR) (2018)

57. Wang, W., et al.: Pyramid vision transformer: a versatile backbone for dense prediction without convolutions. In: Proceedings of the IEEE/CVF International Conference on Computer Vision (ICCV), pp. 568–578 (2021)
58. Wang, Y., et al.: End-to-end video instance segmentation with transformers. In: Proceedings of the IEEE/CVF Conference on Computer Vision and Pattern Recognition (CVPR), pp. 8741–8750 (2021)
59. Wässle, H.: Parallel processing in the mammalian retina. Nat. Rev. Neurosci. 5(10), 747–757 (2004)
60. Weng, W., Zhang, Y., Xiong, Z.: Event-based video reconstruction using transformer. In: Proceedings of the IEEE/CVF International Conference on Computer Vision (ICCV), pp. 2563–2572 (2021)
61. Yang, G., Tang, H., Ding, M., Sebe, N., Ricci, E.: Transformer-based attention networks for continuous pixel-wise prediction. In: Proceedings of the IEEE/CVF International Conference on Computer Vision (ICCV), pp. 16269–16279 (2021)
62. You, Z., Tsai, Y.H., Chiu, W.C., Li, G.: Towards interpretable deep networks for monocular depth estimation. In: Proceedings of the IEEE/CVF International Conference on Computer Vision (ICCV), pp. 12879–12888 (2021)
63. Yu, X., Rao, Y., Wang, Z., Liu, Z., Lu, J., Zhou, J.: PoinTr: diverse point cloud completion with geometry-aware transformers. In: Proceedings of the IEEE/CVF International Conference on Computer Vision (ICCV), pp. 12498–12507 (2021)
64. Yu, X., Tang, L., Rao, Y., Huang, T., Zhou, J., Lu, J.: Point-BERT: pre-training 3D point cloud transformers with masked point modeling. In: Proceedings of the IEEE/CVF Conference on Computer Vision and Pattern Recognition, pp. 19313–19322 (2022)
65. Yuan, Y., et al.: HRFormer: high-resolution transformer for dense prediction. arXiv preprint arXiv:2110.09408 (2021)
66. Zhao, H., Jiang, L., Jia, J., Torr, P.H., Koltun, V.: Point transformer. In: Proceedings of the IEEE/CVF International Conference on Computer Vision (ICCV), pp. 16259–16268 (2021)
67. Zhao, J., Xie, J., Xiong, R., Zhang, J., Yu, Z., Huang, T.: Super resolve dynamic scene from continuous spike streams. In: Proceedings of the IEEE/CVF International Conference on Computer Vision (ICCV), pp. 2533–2542 (2021)
68. Zhao, J., Xiong, R., Liu, H., Zhang, J., Huang, T.: Spk2ImgNet: learning to reconstruct dynamic scene from continuous spike stream. In: Proceedings of the IEEE/CVF Conference on Computer Vision and Pattern Recognition (CVPR), pp. 11996–12005 (2021)
69. Zheng, Y., Zheng, L., Yu, Z., Shi, B., Tian, Y., Huang, T.: High-speed image reconstruction through short-term plasticity for spiking cameras. In: Proceedings of the IEEE/CVF Conference on Computer Vision and Pattern Recognition (CVPR), pp. 6358–6367 (2021)
70. Zhou, Y., Gallego, G., Rebecq, H., Kneip, L., Li, H., Scaramuzza, D.: Semi-dense 3D reconstruction with a stereo event camera. In: Proceedings of the European Conference on Computer Vision (ECCV), pp. 235–251 (2018)
71. Zhu, A.Z., Chen, Y., Daniilidis, K.: Realtime time synchronized event-based stereo. In: Proceedings of the European Conference on Computer Vision (ECCV), pp. 433–447 (2018)
72. Zhu, A.Z., Yuan, L., Chaney, K., Daniilidis, K.: Unsupervised event-based learning of optical flow, depth, and egomotion. In: Proceedings of the IEEE/CVF Conference on Computer Vision and Pattern Recognition (CVPR), pp. 989–997 (2019)

73. Zhu, L., Dong, S., Huang, T., Tian, Y.: A retina-inspired sampling method for visual texture reconstruction. In: IEEE International Conference on Multimedia and Expo (ICME), pp. 1432–1437. IEEE (2019)
74. Zhu, L., Dong, S., Li, J., Huang, T., Tian, Y.: Retina-like visual image reconstruction via spiking neural model. In: Proceedings of the IEEE/CVF Conference on Computer Vision and Pattern Recognition (CVPR) (2020)

Improving Image Restoration by Revisiting Global Information Aggregation

Xiaojie Chu, Liangyu Chen$^{(\boxtimes)}$, Chengpeng Chen, and Xin Lu

MEGVII Technology, Beijing, China
{chuxiaojie,chenliangyu}@megvii.com, chencp@live.com

Abstract. Global operations, such as global average pooling, are widely used in top-performance image restorers. They aggregate global information from input features along entire spatial dimensions but behave differently during training and inference in image restoration tasks: they are based on different regions, namely the cropped patches (from images) and the full-resolution images. This paper revisits global information aggregation and finds that the image-based features during inference have a different distribution than the patch-based features during training. This train-test inconsistency negatively impacts the performance of models, which is severely overlooked by previous works. To reduce the inconsistency and improve test-time performance, we propose a simple method called Test-time Local Converter (TLC). Our TLC converts global operations to local ones only during inference so that they aggregate features within local spatial regions rather than the entire large images. The proposed method can be applied to various global modules (e.g., normalization, channel and spatial attention) with negligible costs. Without the need for any fine-tuning, TLC improves state-of-the-art results on several image restoration tasks, including single-image motion deblurring, video deblurring, defocus deblurring, and image denoising. In particular, with TLC, our Restormer-Local improves the state-of-the-art result in single image deblurring from 32.92 dB to 33.57 dB on GoPro dataset. The code is available at https://github.com/megvii-research/tlc.

1 Introduction

Image restoration is the task of estimating the clean image from a corrupt (e.g., motion blur, noise, etc.) image. Recently, deep learning based models [7,51,55] have achieved state-of-the-art (SOTA) performance in this field. The global information, which is aggregated along entire spatial dimensions, are increasingly indispensable for the top performance restorers: HINet [7] adopts Instance Normalization (IN [43]) module which performs global normalization along the

---

Supplementary Information The online version contains supplementary material available at https://doi.org/10.1007/978-3-031-20071-7_4.

entire spatial dimension. MPRNet [55], SPDNet [51], FFA-Net [34], etc. adopt Squeeze and Excitation (SE [13]) module which learns to use global average-pooled features to selectively emphasise informative features. Restormer [53] adopt *transposed* self-attention for encoding the global information implicitly.

However, restoration models are usually trained on patches cropped from images and inference directly on full-resolution images [53,55]. In contrast to resizing the input images during both training and inference in the high-level vision task, resizing the images in the low-level vision task is avoided to preserve the image details. As a result, the regional range of the inputs for training and inference varies widely. For example, during training in MPRNet [55], the range of region for each patch is only 7% of full-resolution images (256 × 256 vs. 720 × 1280) in GoPro dataset. In this case, the model can only learn to encode a local part of the image due to the limited region of patches (Fig. 1a). It may be difficult to encode the global clues of full-resolution images, thereby providing sub-optimal performance at test time. This potential issue is severely overlooked by previous works.

This paper revisits the global information aggregation in image restoration tasks. We analyze the global avg-pooled features and find that the entire-image-based features during inference may distribute very differently from the patch-based features during training (Fig. 3a Left). This shifts in the global information distribution in training and inference can negatively impact the performance of model. To solve this issue, we proposed a novel test-time approach called Test-time Local Converter (TLC) for bridging the gap of information aggregation between training and inference. The global operation (e.g., global average pooling in SE module [13]) is converted to a local one only during inference, so that they aggregate features within local spatial regions as in the training phase (Fig. 1b). As a result, the entire-image-based "local" information during inference has similar distribution as patches-based "global" information during training (Fig. 3a Right). The proposed technique is generic in the sense that it can be applied on top of any global operation without any fine-tuning, and boost the performance of various modules (e.g., SE, IN) with negligible costs.

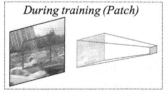
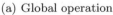
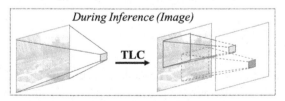

(a) Global operation   (b) Test-time Local Converter (Ours)

Fig. 1. Illustration of global operation and our TLC: (a) During training, limited by the cropped patches, global operation learns representation to local region in the original image; (b) During inference, global operation extract global representations based on full-resolution image. Our TLC convert the global operation to a local one so that it extract representations based on local spatial region of features as in training phase.

Our TLC can be conveniently applied to already trained models. We conduct extensive experiments to demonstrate the effectiveness of TLC over a variety of models and image restoration tasks. For example, for single-image motion deblurring on GoPro dataset [28], our TLC improves the PSNR of HINet [7], MPRNet [55], and Restormer [53] by 0.37 dB, 0.65 dB, and 0.65 dB, respectively. Remarkably, TLC improves the state-of-the-art results on single-image motion deblurring, video motion deblurring, defocus deblurring (single-image and dual-pixel data), and image denoising (gaussian grayscale/color denoising).

Our contributions can be summarized as follows:

1. To the best of our knowledge, we are the first to point out the inconsistency of the global information distribution in training (with cropped patches from images) and inference (with the full-resolution image) in image restoration tasks, which may harm model performance.
2. To reduce the distribution shifts between training and inference, we propose Test-time Local Converter (TLC) that converts the region of feature aggregation from global to local only at test time. Without retraining or fine-tuning, TLC significantly improves the performance of various modules with negligible costs by reducing the train-test inconsistency.
3. Extensive experiments show that our TLC improves state-of-the-art results on various image restoration tasks.

2   Related Work

Image Restoration. Image Restoration tasks, e.g. denoising, deblurring, deraining, dehazing, etc. aim to restore the degraded image to the clean one. Deep learning based restoration models have achieved state-of-the-art results [7,51,53,55] recently. The training data are cropped into patches and fed into the model in the training phase. Most methods [34,51,55] inference by the full-resolution image, which leads to a train-test inconsistency problem. Some methods [5,7] divide the input image into patches with fixed size and process each patch independently, but this strategy may introduce boundary artifacts [19,22].

Global Information in Image Restoration Models. Attention modules are designed to model long-range dependency using a single layer directly. SENet [13] and GENet [12] reweight channel dependency with global information aggregated by global average pooling. CBAM [47] uses both avg-pooled and max-pooled features to rebalance the importance of different spatial positions and channels. These channel and spatial attention modules have been successfully adopted to image restoration models for various tasks, e.g., deblurring [6,40,55] deraining [21,51], super-resolution [9,63], denoising [4,53,54] and dehazing [34].

Besides, HINet [7] introduces Instance Normalization (IN [43]) to image restoration tasks, which normalizes each channel of the features by its mean and variance. Once again, the performance improvement brought by IN proves the effectiveness of global information.

This paper mainly discusses these modules, which aggregate information from all spatial positions in input features (i.e., globally), as representatives. We find that the performance of these modules may be sub-optimal due to the train-test inconsistency mentioned above.

Local Spatial Information Modules. In local spatial schemes, the information is computed within a local spatial area for each pixel. Local Response Normalization (LRN) [15,16,26] computes the statistics in a small neighborhood for each pixel. To reduce the computational loads, SwinIR [25] and Uformer [46] apply self-attention within small spatial windows of size 8×8 around each pixel. In semantic image synthesis tasks, SPatially-Adaptive (DE)normalization (SPADE) [32] utilize the input semantic layout for modulating the activations through a spatially-adaptive, learned transformation. Spatial region-wise normalization (RN) [52], is proposed for better inpainting network training.

However, directly applying those modules to existing restoration models is not practical, as retraining or finetuning are required. Besides, these modules are designed to model local context in both the training and inference phase that they are constrained to have limited sizes of receptive field. Conversely, our proposed approach does not need to retrain or finetune the model. The region's size used for information aggregation during inference will be equal to or larger than the size of the input during training.

3   Analysis and Approach

In this section, we first introduce the image restoration pipeline and analyze the train-test inconsistency of global information aggregation induced by it. Next, to solve the inconsistency, we illustrate our novel approach, Test-time Local Converter (TLC), and the details of extending TLC to existing modules.

3.1   Revisit Global Operations in Image Restoration Tasks

Image Restoration Pipeline. We briefly describe the image restoration pipeline used in the state-of-the-art methods. For practical application, datasets for image restoration tasks (e.g., deblurring) are usually composed of high-resolution images. Due to the need for data augmentation and the limitation of GPU memory, it is common practice to train models with small patches cropped from high-resolution images (Fig. 1a). For example, MPRNet and HINet are trained on 256×256 patches cropped from 720×1280 images in GoPro datasets. During inference, the trained model directly restores high-resolution images (Fig. 1b Left). Therefore, there are train-test inconsistencies of the inputs to the model: a local region of the image during training and the entire image during inference.

Train-Test Inconsistency of Global Information Aggregation. Unlike local operations (e.g., convolution) that operate within a local spatial area for each pixel, global operations (e.g., global average pool and global attention) operate along entire spatial dimensions. As a result, global operations have global receptive fields on arbitrary input resolutions.

However, the range of receptive fields for global operation is limited by the size of input features. This property introduces significantly different behaviors for global operations during training and inference in image restoration tasks: their input features are based on different range of regions, namely the cropped patches (from images) and the full-resolution images. This inconsistency will affect the generalization of models. In training, parameters are optimized by the patches-based features. While in the test phase, the layer inference the results by the entire-image-based features. In the following, we analyze the behavior of global information aggregation, both qualitatively and statistically.

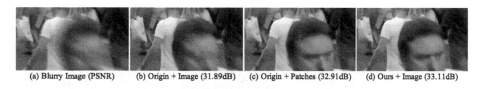

(a) Blurry Image (PSNR)   (b) Origin + Image (31.89dB)   (c) Origin + Patches (32.91dB)   (d) Ours + Image (33.11dB)

Fig. 2. Visual comparison with different test-time methods to MPRNet [55] for image deblurring. (a) Blurry image; (b) Inference with image; (c) Inference with cropped patches; (d) Ours: TLC is adopted and inference based on images. Our TLC generates sharp image without boundary artifacts in (b).

Statistical Analysis. To analyze the effects of train-test inconsistency of global information, we compare the mean statistics based on patches in the training set and full-resolution images in the test set. The mean statistics (i.e., global average-pooled features) are aggregated by the first SE layer of the second encoder in MPRNet [55]. As shown in Fig. 3a, the mean statistics distribution shifts from training (green) to inference (blue). It is hard for restorers to adapt to the severe changes in information distribution, resulting in performance degradation.

Qualitative Analysis. Intuitively, consistent with the training phase, cropping the images into patches and predicting the results independently during inference can alleviate the patch/full-image inconsistency issue described above. We conduct a visual comparison of the MPRNet deblurring results on GoPro datasets. Figure 2 shows a challenging visual example. The image-based result (Fig. 2b) fails to remove blurs completely. On the contrary, the patch-based result (Fig. 2c) is cleaner with less motion blur but introduces the artifacts at the patch boundaries. This confirms that direct inference on full-resolution results in sub-optimal performance. Though cropping images for inference improves the quality of image recovery, such a strategy will inevitably cause a new problem, i.e., patch boundary artifacts.

3.2 Test-time Local Converter

In order to reducing train-test inconsistency and improve test-time performance of model, we propose a test-time solution named Test-time Local Converter (TLC). Instead of changing the training strategy or cropping the images, our TLC directly change the range of region for information aggregation at feature level during inference phase. As shown in Fig. 1b, TLC converts the spatial information aggregation operation from global to local, i.e., each pixel of the feature aggregates its feature locally. In detail, the input feature $\mathbf{X}$ of global operation is sliced into overlapping window with size of $K_h \times K_w$ (which are treated as hyper-parameters). Then, information aggregation operation is applied independently to each overlapping window. As a result, the statistics distribution shifts are reduced by TLC as shown in Fig. 3a: the statistics distribution obtained by our MPRNet-Local (red) is close to the original MPRNet in the training phase (green). Besides, as shown in Fig. 2d, our TLC generates a sharp image without boundary artifacts.

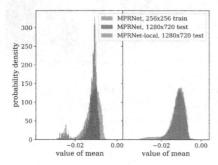 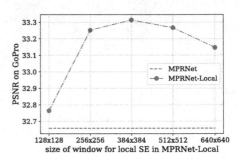

(a) TLC can reduce distribution shifts (in red) caused by the inconsistency between training and testing (green vs. blue).

(b) TLC can significantly improve the performance of MPRNet over a wide range of hyperparameters (i.e., size of local window).

Fig. 3. The effectiveness of TLC on MPRNet [55] (denoted as MPRNet-Local). (Color figure online)

An advantage of our intentionally simple design is that efficient implementations of local processing make extra computation cost negligible, allowing image restorers to use TLC feasibly. Next, we will discuss the implementations of average operation, which is an example of information aggregation and is widely used in models for image restoration.

Efficient Implementation of Information Aggregation. The (global) information aggregation of a feature layer $\mathbf{X} \in \mathbb{R}^{H \times W}$ (without loss of generality, we ignore the channel dimension), can be formulated as:

$$\Phi(\mathbf{X}, f) = \frac{1}{HW} \sum_{p=1}^{H} \sum_{q=1}^{W} f(\mathbf{X}_{p,q}). \tag{1}$$

where $f : \mathbb{R} \to \mathbb{R}$ defines how information are calculated, and $\varPhi(\mathbf{X}, f) \in \mathbb{R}$ denotes the aggregated information. It's computational complexity is $\mathcal{O}(HW)$. For local information aggregation, each pixel e.g. (i, j) aggregates the information in a local window (size $K_h \times K_w$) of feature $\mathbf{X} \in \mathbb{R}^{H \times W}$ could be formulated as:

$$\boldsymbol{\Psi}(\mathbf{X}, f)_{i,j} = \frac{1}{K_h K_w} \sum_p \sum_q f(\mathbf{X}_{p,q}), \tag{2}$$

where (p, q) in the local window of (i, j), $\boldsymbol{\Psi}(\mathbf{X}, f) \in \mathbb{R}^{H \times W}$ indicates the aggregated local information, and K_h, K_w are hyperparameters.

The edge case, e.g. (i, j) is the boundary of $\mathbf{X}$, is not considered above for simplicity. In practice, we implement $\boldsymbol{\Psi}(\mathbf{X}, f)$ by two steps. First, sliding windows (size of $K_h \times K_w$) with stride equals 1 to aggregate the local information for each pixel in non-edge case. Second, padding the result by replication of its boundary for edge case. The first step's computational complexity is $\mathcal{O}(HWK_hK_w)$. But mean/sum aggregation within each local window could be treated as *submatrix sum* problem and solved by prefix sum trick [11] with $\mathcal{O}(1)$ complexity [3]. As a result, the overall complexity could be reduced to $\mathcal{O}(HW)$ which is consistent with global information aggregation operation, i.e. Eq. (1). Therefore, our TLC do not induce a computational bottleneck.

3.3 Extending TLC to Existing Modules

In this subsection, we borrow the notations defined above (e.g., $\varPhi/\boldsymbol{\Psi}$ denotes global/local information aggregation operation, respectively). To extend TLC to existing modules, we convert the information aggregation operation from global (i.e., $\varPhi$) to local (i.e., $\boldsymbol{\Psi}$). In the following, we take Squeeze-and-Excitation(SE) and Instance Normalization(IN) as representatives, and it can be easily applied to other normalization modules such as Group Normalization (GN [48]) or variants of SE (e.g. CBAM [47], GE [12]).

Extending TLC to SE Block. We briefly revisit the squeeze-and-excitation (SE [13]) block first. For a feature map $\mathbf{X} \in \mathbb{R}^{H \times W \times C}$ with a spatial size of (H, W) and C channels, SE block first squeezes the global spatial information into channels, it could be denoted as $\varPhi(\mathbf{X}^{(c)}, id), \forall c \in [C]$, where $id(t) = t, \forall t \in \mathbb{R}$. And then, a multilayer perceptron (MLP) follows to evaluate the channel attention, which re-weights the feature map. The squeeze on the global spatial dimension could be sub-optimal as global information distribution shifts. To solve this, we extend TLC to SE by replacing $\varPhi(\mathbf{X}^{(c)}, id)$ to $\boldsymbol{\Psi}(\mathbf{X}^{(c)}, id), \forall c \in [C]$. As in SE, an MLP along the channel dimension follows. Differently, the feature map is re-weighted by the element-wise attention in this case.

Extending TLC to IN. For a feature map $\mathbf{X} \in \mathbb{R}^{H \times W}$ (we omit the channel dimension for simplicity), the normalized feature $\mathbf{Y}$ by IN is computed as: $\mathbf{Y} =$

$(\mathbf{X} - \mu)/\sigma$, where statistics μ and σ are the mean and variance computed over the global spatial of $\mathbf{X}$:

$$\mu = \Phi(\mathbf{X}, id), \ \ \sigma^2 = \Phi(\mathbf{X}, sq) - \mu^2, \tag{3}$$

where $id(t) = t, sq(t) = t^2, \forall t \in \mathbb{R}$. Besides, learnable parameters γ, β are used to scale and shift the normalized feature $\mathbf{Y}$, we omit them for simplicity. During inference, we can extend TLC to IN by replacing $\Phi(\mathbf{X}, id)$ and $\Phi(\mathbf{X}, sq)$ in Eq. (3) to $\Psi(\mathbf{X}, id)$ and $\Psi(\mathbf{X}, sq)$ respectively. As a result, each pixel is normalized by statistics in neighborhood.

Extending to Transposed Self-attention. As introduced in Sect. 3.2, our TLC can convert the *transposed* self-attention in Restormer [53] from global to local regions. However, due to inefficiency and limitation of GPU memory, i.e., different attention map for each pixel, we use a large stride rather than one to the TLC in transposed self-attention. Specifically, transposed self-attention is applied independently to each overlapping windows of $K_h \times K_w$ sliced from input features. The overlapping outputs are then fused by concatenating along spatial dimensions and averaging over the overlapping regions.

3.4 Discussion

Apart from our method, the range of input at image level also has a direct impact on train-test inconsistency. On the one hand, larger size of patches used for training pushes the patch-based information closer to image-based information. On the other, dividing the image into patches for inference can avoid the patch/entire-image inconsistency. We will discuss these two possible solutions and their drawbacks next.

Dividing the image into patches for independently inference may alleviate the inconsistency issue. However, such a strategy inevitably gives rise to two drawbacks [22]. First, border pixels cannot utilize neighbouring pixels that are out of the patch for image restoration. Second, the restored image may introduce "boundary artifacts" [19] around each patch. As shown in Fig. 2b, an obvious vertical split line is introduced by patch partition which severely damages the image quality. In contrast, our "partition" is at feature level instead of image level so that different local windows can still interact with each other through other modules (e.g., convolutions) in the network. As shown in Fig. 2d, the proposed method generates much clearer images without artifacts.

Besides, inference with overlapping patches will introduce considerable additional computational costs, as the overlapping regions are restored twice or more by the entire model. While models with our TLC directly restore whole images and TLC has low extra computing costs (Table 7). Furthermore, boundary artifacts are also found in the predictions based on overlapping patches. More details of discussion and comparison are in the supplemental material.

Training on full-images instead of patches is another straightforward idea to bridge the gap in global information distribution between training and inference, but it is not impracticable due to limited device constrains. The scaling up of resolution leads to prohibitively high GPU memory consumption with existing image restorers. For example, using V100-32G, the size of patches for training Restormer [53] can only up to 384×384, which is still significantly smaller than the original image size (e.g., 720×1280 in GoPro dataset). Furthermore, though Restormer is trained with larger patches than common practice, our TLC can significantly improve its performance (Table 1).

4 Experiments

In this section, we do quality and quantity experiments to show the effects of train-test inconsistency, and our proposed approach Test-time Local Converter (TLC) can reduce this inconsistency. Next, the extensibility of TLC and the choice of hyperparameters are discussed.

Table 1. Image motion deblurring comparisons on GoPro [28] and HIDE [36]

Dataset	Method	Gao et al. [10]	DBGAN [61]	MT-RNN [31]	DMPHN [56]	Suin et al. [40]	SPAIR [33]	MIMO-UNet+ [8]	IPT [5]
GoPro	PSNR↑	30.90	31.10	31.15	31.20	31.85	32.06	32.45	32.52
	SSIM↑	0.935	0.942	0.945	0.940	0.948	0.953	0.957	-
HIDE	PSNR↑	29.11	28.94	29.15	29.09	29.98	30.29	29.99	-
	SSIM↑	0.913	0.915	0.918	0.924	0.930	0.931	0.930	-

Dataset	Method	HINet [7]	HINet-Local (Ours)	MPRNet [55]	MPRNet-Local (Ours)	Restormer [53]	Restormer-Local (Ours)
GoPro	PSNR↑	32.71	$33.08^{+0.37}$	32.66	$33.31^{+0.65}$	32.92	$\mathbf{33.57}^{+0.65}$
	SSIM↑	0.959	$0.962^{+0.003}$	0.959	$0.964^{+0.005}$	0.961	$\mathbf{0.966}^{+0.005}$
HIDE	PSNR↑	30.33	$30.66^{+0.33}$	30.96	$31.19^{+0.23}$	31.22	$\mathbf{31.49}^{+0.27}$
	SSIM↑	0.932	$0.936^{+0.004}$	0.939	$0.942^{+0.003}$	0.942	$\mathbf{0.945}^{+0.003}$

4.1 Main Results

To verify the effectiveness of the proposed TLC, we apply it to various existing top-performing models for six image restoration tasks: (1) single-image motion deblurring, (2) video deblurring, (3) defocus deblurring, (4) image denoising, (5) image deraining and (6) image dehazing. We report the standard metrics in image restoration, including Peak Signal to Noise Ratio (PSNR) and Structural SIMilarity index (SSIM).

Implementation Details. We use the publicly available trained models with global operations (e.g., global attention, global normalization) and directly apply proposed TLC to them without any extra training. Specifically, for Restormer [53] with TLC, the forward pass of transposed attention is applied independently to each overlapping window sliced from original input features. While for SE [13] (used in MPRNet [55], RNN-MBP [67], SPDNet [51] and FFANet [34]) and Instance Normalization [43] (used in HINet [7]), TLC is extended to them as illustrated in Sect. 3.3. Models with our TLC is marked with "-Local" suffix and the local window size is set to 384×384 if not specified. We will discuss the impact of this hyper-parameter in the Sect. 4.2.

Single-image Motion Deblurring. We integrate our TLC with existing top-performing models (e.g. HINet [7], MPRNet [55], and Restormer [53]) and evaluate them on test set of GoPro [28] and HIDE [36] dataset. As shown in Table 1, the performance of both three models are significantly improved by our approach and our models achieve new state-of-the-art results on all datasets.

In detail, the PSNR on GoPro of HINet, MPRNet and Restormer are improved by 0.37 dB, 0.65 dB and 0.65 dB, respectively. And our Restormer-local exceeds the previous best result (i.e., Restormer [53]) by 0.65 dB. The PSNR on HIDE of HINet, MPRNet and Restormer are improved by 0.33 dB, 0.23 dB and 0.27 dB, respectively. And our Restormer-local exceeds the previous best result (i.e., Restormer [53]) by 0.27 dB. Visual results of our methods are shown in Fig. 4. As one can see, based on its significant quantitative improvements, TLC can help the original model generate more sharp images with clearer numeric symbols.

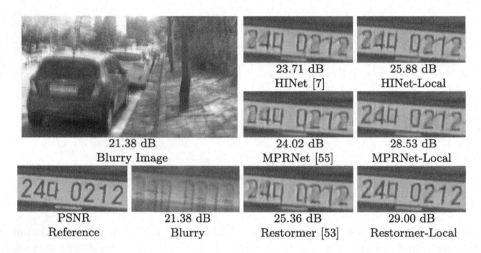

23.71 dB	25.88 dB
HINet [7]	HINet-Local

21.38 dB	24.02 dB	28.53 dB
Blurry Image	MPRNet [55]	MPRNet-Local

PSNR	21.38 dB	25.36 dB	29.00 dB
Reference	Blurry	Restormer [53]	Restormer-Local

Fig. 4. Qualitative evaluation of our TLC on single image motion deblurring methods. Models with our TLC (denoted with -Local suffix) generates sharper result than original ones.

Table 2. Video deblurring comparisons on the GoPro [28] dataset

Method	SFE [50]	IFI-RNN [29]	ESTRNN [66]	EDVR [45]	TSP [30]	PVDNet [39]	GSTA [41]	RNN-MBP [67]	RNN-MBP-Local (Ours)
PSNR↑	31.01	31.05	31.07	31.54	31.67	31.98	32.10	33.32	**33.80**$^{+0.48}$
SSIM↑	0.913	0.911	0.902	0.926	0.928	0.928	0.960	0.963	**0.966**$^{+0.003}$

Video Motion Deblurring. We apply our TLC to state-of-the-art video deblurring method (i.e., RNN-MBP [67]) and evaluate different video deblurring algorithms on GoPro datasets. As shown in Table 2, our TLC improve previous state-of-the-art method by 0.48 dB on PSNR, and set a new state-of-the-art result at 33.80 dB.

Defocus Deblurring. Table 3 shows image fidelity scores of different defocus deblurring methods on the DPDD dataset [1]. Following [1], results are reported on traditional signal processing metrics (i.e., PSNR, SSIM, and MAE) and learned perceptual image patch similarity (LPIPS) proposed by [62]. TLC are applied to the state-of-the-art method Restormer and get Restormer-Local. Our Restormer-Local significantly outperforms the state-of-the-art schemes for the single-image and dual-pixel defocus deblurring tasks on all scene categories. Take PSNR as evaluation metrics, our TLC improves Restormer by 0.21∼0.3 dB and 0.35∼0.40 dB on single-image and dual-pixel defocus deblurring, respectively. Figure 5 shows that our model recovered images of better quality on texture and edge detail.

20.72 dB	PSNR	20.72 dB	25.88 dB	27.16 dB
Blurry Image	Reference	Blurry	Restormer[53]	Restormer-Local

Fig. 5. Qualitative evaluation of our TLC for Dual-pixel defocus deblurring on the DPDD dataset [1]. Restormer with our TLC (i.e., Restormer-Local) more effectively removes blur while preserving the fine image details.

Table 3. Defocus deblurring comparisons on the DPDD testset [1] (containing 37 indoor and 39 outdoor scenes). S: single-image defocus deblurring. D: dual-pixel defocus deblurring. Our Restormer-Local sets new state-of-the-art for both single-image and dual pixel defocus deblurring

Method	Indoor Scenes				Outdoor Scenes				Combined			
	PSNR↑	SSIM↑	MAE↓	LPIPS↓	PSNR↑	SSIM↑	MAE↓	LPIPS↓	PSNR↑	SSIM↑	MAE↓	LPIPS↓
EBDB$_S$ [5]	25.77	0.772	0.040	0.297	21.25	0.599	0.058	0.373	23.45	0.683	0.049	0.336
DMENet$_S$ [17]	25.50	0.788	0.038	0.298	21.43	0.644	0.063	0.397	23.41	0.714	0.051	0.349
JNB$_S$ [37]	26.73	0.828	0.031	0.273	21.10	0.608	0.064	0.355	23.84	0.715	0.048	0.315
DPDNet$_S$ [1]	26.54	0.816	0.031	0.239	22.25	0.682	0.056	0.313	24.34	0.747	0.044	0.277
KPAC$_S$ [38]	27.97	0.852	0.026	0.182	22.62	0.701	0.053	0.269	25.22	0.774	0.040	0.227
IFAN$_S$ [18]	28.11	0.861	0.026	0.179	22.76	0.720	0.052	0.254	25.37	0.789	0.039	0.217
Restormer$_S$ [53]	28.87	0.882	0.025	0.145	23.24	0.743	0.050	0.209	25.98	0.811	0.038	0.178
Restormer-Local$_S$	**29.08**	**0.888**	**0.024**	**0.139**	**23.54**	**0.765**	**0.049**	**0.195**	**26.24**	**0.825**	**0.037**	**0.168**
DPDNet$_D$ [1]	27.48	0.849	0.029	0.189	22.90	0.726	0.052	0.255	25.13	0.786	0.041	0.223
RDPD$_D$ [2]	28.10	0.843	0.027	0.210	22.82	0.704	0.053	0.298	25.39	0.772	0.040	0.255
Uformer$_D$ [46]	28.23	0.860	0.026	0.199	23.10	0.728	0.051	0.285	25.65	0.795	0.039	0.243
IFAN$_D$ [18]	28.66	0.868	0.025	0.172	23.46	0.743	0.049	0.240	25.99	0.804	0.037	0.207
Restormer$_D$ [53]	29.48	0.895	0.023	0.134	23.97	0.773	0.047	0.175	26.66	0.833	0.035	0.155
Restormer-Local$_D$	**29.83**	**0.903**	**0.022**	**0.120**	**24.37**	**0.794**	**0.045**	**0.159**	**27.02**	**0.847**	**0.034**	**0.140**

Image Denoise. We perform denoising experiments on synthetic benchmark dataset Urban100 [14] generated with additive white Gaussian noise. Table 4a and b show PSNR scores of different approaches on several benchmark datasets for grayscale and color image denoising, respectively. Consistent with existing methods [22,53,57], we include noise levels 15, 25 and 50 in testing. The evaluated methods are divided into two experimental categories: (1) learning a single model to handle various noise levels, and (2) learning a separate model for each noise level. We apply TLC to state-of-the-art method Restormer. Our TLC brings 0.06~0.12 dB improvement on grayscale image denoising and brings 0.08~0.15 dB improvement on color image denoising. Figure 6 shows that our method clearly removes noise while maintaining fine details.

Table 4. Gaussian image denoising comparisons for two kinds of images and two categories of methods on Urban100 [14] dataset. Top super row: learning a single model to handle various noise levels. Bottom super row: training a separate model for each noise level

(a) Gaussian grayscale image denoising

Method	$\sigma=15$	$\sigma=25$	$\sigma=50$
DnCNN [58]	32.28	29.80	26.35
FFDNet [60]	32.40	29.90	26.50
IRCNN [59]	32.46	29.80	26.22
DRUNet [57]	33.44	31.11	27.96
Restormer [53]	33.67	31.39	28.33
Restormer-Local	**33.73**	**31.48**	**28.45**
MWCNN [24]	33.17	30.66	27.42
NLRN [23]	33.45	30.94	27.49
RNAN [64]	–	–	27.65
DeamNet [35]	33.37	30.85	27.53
DAGL [27]	33.79	31.39	27.97
SwinIR [22]	33.70	31.30	27.98
Restormer [53]	33.79	31.46	28.29
Restormer-Local	**33.85**	**31.55**	**28.41**

(b) Gaussian color image denoising

Method	$\sigma=15$	$\sigma=25$	$\sigma=50$
IRCNN [59]	33.78	31.2	27.7
FFDNet [60]	33.83	31.4	28.05
DnCNN [58]	32.98	30.81	27.59
DRUNet [57]	34.81	32.60	29.61
Restormer [53]	35.06	32.91	30.02
Restormer-Local	**35.14**	**33.01**	**30.16**
RPCNN [49]	–	31.81	28.62
BRDNet [42]	34.42	31.99	28.56
RNAN [64]	–	–	29.08
RDN [65]	–	–	29.38
IPT [5]	–	–	29.71
SwinIR [22]	35.13	32.90	29.82
Restormer [53]	35.13	32.96	30.02
Restormer-Local	**35.21**	**33.06**	**30.17**

Image Deraining. We compare the deraining results of SPDNet [51] and our SPDNet-local on SPA-Data [44] benchmark. As shown in Table 5, our approach brings 0.18 dB improvement to SPDNet. Figure 7 shows that our approach recovered images of better quality on both details and color fidelity.

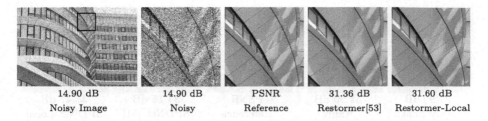

| 14.90 dB | 14.90 dB | PSNR | 31.36 dB | 31.60 dB |
| Noisy Image | Noisy | Reference | Restormer[53] | Restormer-Local |

Fig. 6. Qualitative evaluation of our TLC for Gaussian image denoising. Our Restormer-Local removes noise while preserving the fine image details.

Image Dehazing. We compare the dehazing results of FFANet [34] and our FFANet-local on Synthetic Objective Testing Set (SOTS) from RESIDE [20] dataset. The local window size is set to 416 × 416. As shown in Table 6, our approach brings 0.42 dB improvement to FFANet in outdoor scenarios. We also test the results on realistic hazy images in RESIDE [20] dataset for subjective assessment. As shown in Fig. 8, our FFANet-Local effectively removes hazy and generate visually pleasing result with high color fidelity. More high-resolution visualization results are in the supplemental material.

4.2   Size of Local Window

Size of local window is a hyper-parameter for TLC, which controls the scope of local information aggregation operation. To determinate the hyperparameter, i.e., local window size of each layer (which aggregates the spatial context) as we mentioned in Sect. 3.2, we propose a simple strategy: A calibration image is fed into the model, and the spatial sizes of these feature layers are recorded as their local window size. Therefore, the hyperparameter could be determined by the spatial size of the calibration image, and we denoted the image size as "local window size" for simplicity in the following. Besides, the calibration could be accomplished offline, thus does not increase the test latency.

Table 5. Deraining results on SPA-Data [44] dataset

Method	PSNR↑	SSIM↑
SPDNet [51]	43.55	0.988
SPDNet-Local (Ours)	43.73	0.989

Table 6. Dehazing results on outdoor scene images in SOTS [20] dataset

Method	PSNR↑	SSIM↑
FFANet [34]	33.57	0.984
FFANet-Local (Ours)	33.99	0.985

| 31.90 dB | 31.90 dB | PSNR | 34.15 dB | 38.47 dB |
| Rainy Image | Rainy | Reference | SPDNet [51] | SPDNet-Local |

Fig. 7. Qualitative evaluation of our TLC for image deraining. SPDNet with our TLC (i.e., SPDNet-Local) superior in the realistic performance of image details and color fidelity.

| Hazy Image | FFANet[34] | FFANet-Local (Ours) |

Fig. 8. Qualitative evaluation of our TLC for image dehazing on realistic hazy image. FFANet with our TLC (i.e., FFANet-Local) generate cleaner result.

We apply TLC on MPRNet [55] to investigate the impact of different size of local window on the model performance. As shown in Fig. 3b, TLC can significantly improve the performance of MPRNet over a wide range of window size (from 256×256 to 640×640). Interestingly, the optimal window size (i.e., 384×384) for the test phase is not exactly equal but may be larger than the training patch size (i.e., 256×256). We conjecture this is caused by the trade-off between the benefits of more information provided by the larger window and the side-effects of statistic inconsistency between training and inference. In addition, since our approach does not require retraining, it is easy and flexible to tune the size of local window.

Table 7. The results of applying TLC to different modules on GoPro dataset. TLC improves the performance of all models with negligible costs

Module	IN [43]		GN [48]		GE-θ^- [12]		SE [13]		CBAM [47]	
	PSNR↑	MACs↓	PSNR↑	MACs↓	PSNR↑	MACs↓	PSNR↑	MACs↓	PSNR↑	MACs↓
Origin	30.95	62.13G	30.91	62.13G	30.74	62.14G	30.82	62.14G	30.53	62.19G
+TLC	31.11	62.13G	31.03	62.13G	30.91	62.14G	31.21	62.19G	31.05	62.27G
Δ	+0.16	+0.00G	+0.12	+0.00G	+0.17	+0.00G	+0.39	+0.05G	+0.52	+0.08G

4.3 Extensibility and Complexity

We apply TLC to various modules and compare its improvement of performance and complexity of computation. We use a simple UNet model (i.e., HINet Simple without HIN [7]) as baseline (denoted as UNet). Attention modules (e.g., SE [13], GE-θ^- [12] and CBAM [47]) are added to UNet encoder following SENet [13], while Normalization modules (e.g., IN [43] and GN [48]) are added to the UNet following HINet [7].

Implementation Details. Models are trained on GoPro [28] dataset following the most training detail of HINet Simple [7]. Specially, the default size of patches for training is 256×256, and the default batch size is 64. We also use warm-up strategy in the first 5000 iterations. According to Sect. 4.2, the local window size is set to 384×384 during inference. We use MACs (i.e. multiplier-accumulator operations) to evaluate the computational cost of models, which is estimated when the input is 512×512.

Results. As shown in Table 7, our approach achieves performance gains with marginal costs. In detail, TLC improves the performance (i.e., PSNR) of IN, GN and GE-θ^- by 0.16 dB, 0.12 dB, and 0.17 dB, respectively. For SE and CBAM, TLC boosts the performance (i.e. PSNR) by 0.39 dB and 0.52 dB respectively with less than 0.2% extra MACs. It demonstrates the extensibility, effectiveness and efficiency of TLC.

5 Conclusion

In this work, we reveal the global information distribution shifts between training and inference due to train-test inconsistency of global operation, which negatively impacts the performance of restoration model. We propose simple yet test-time solutions, dubbed Test-time Local Converter, which replaces the information aggregation region from the entire spatial dimension to the local window to mitigate the inconsistency between training and inference. Our approach does not require any retraining or finetuning, and boosts the performance of models on various tasks.

Acknowledgements. This research was supported by National Key R&D Program of China (No. 2017YFA0700800) and Beijing Academy of Artificial Intelligence (BAAI).

References

1. Abuolaim, A., Brown, M.S.: Defocus deblurring using dual-pixel data. In: Vedaldi, A., Bischof, H., Brox, T., Frahm, J.-M. (eds.) ECCV 2020. LNCS, vol. 12355, pp. 111–126. Springer, Cham (2020). https://doi.org/10.1007/978-3-030-58607-2_7
2. Abuolaim, A., Delbracio, M., Kelly, D., Brown, M.S., Milanfar, P.: Learning to reduce defocus blur by realistically modeling dual-pixel data. In: Proceedings of the IEEE/CVF International Conference on Computer Vision, pp. 2289–2298 (2021)
3. Amir, A., Church, K.W., Dar, E.: The submatrices character count problem: an efficient solution using separable values. Inf. Comput. **190**(1), 100–116 (2004)

4. Anwar, S., Barnes, N.: Real image denoising with feature attention. In: Proceedings of the IEEE/CVF International Conference on Computer Vision, pp. 3155–3164 (2019)
5. Chen, H., et al.: Pre-trained image processing transformer. In: Proceedings of the IEEE/CVF Conference on Computer Vision and Pattern Recognition, pp. 12299–12310 (2021)
6. Chen, L., Chu, X., Zhang, X., Sun, J.: Simple baselines for image restoration. arXiv preprint arXiv:2204.04676 (2022)
7. Chen, L., Lu, X., Zhang, J., Chu, X., Chen, C.: HiNet: half instance normalization network for image restoration. In: IEEE/CVF Conference on Computer Vision and Pattern Recognition Workshops (2021)
8. Cho, S.J., Ji, S.W., Hong, J.P., Jung, S.W., Ko, S.J.: Rethinking coarse-to-fine approach in single image deblurring. In: Proceedings of the IEEE/CVF International Conference on Computer Vision, pp. 4641–4650 (2021)
9. Chu, X., Chen, L., Yu, W.: NAFSSR: stereo image super-resolution using NAFNet. In: Proceedings of the IEEE/CVF Conference on Computer Vision and Pattern Recognition (CVPR) Workshops, pp. 1239–1248 (2022)
10. Gao, H., Tao, X., Shen, X., Jia, J.: Dynamic scene deblurring with parameter selective sharing and nested skip connections. In: Proceedings of the IEEE/CVF Conference on Computer Vision and Pattern Recognition, pp. 3848–3856 (2019)
11. Harris, M., Sengupta, S., Owens, J.D.: Parallel prefix sum (scan) with CUDA. GPU gems **3**(39), 851–876 (2007)
12. Hu, J., Shen, L., Albanie, S., Sun, G., Vedaldi, A.: Gather-excite: exploiting feature context in convolutional neural networks. In: Advances in Neural Information Processing Systems 31 (2018)
13. Hu, J., Shen, L., Sun, G.: Squeeze-and-excitation networks. In: Proceedings of the IEEE Conference on Computer Vision and Pattern Recognition, pp. 7132–7141 (2018)
14. Huang, J.B., Singh, A., Ahuja, N.: Single image super-resolution from transformed self-exemplars. In: Proceedings of the IEEE Conference on Computer Vision and Pattern Recognition, pp. 5197–5206 (2015)
15. Jarrett, K., Kavukcuoglu, K., Ranzato, M., LeCun, Y.: What is the best multi-stage architecture for object recognition? In: 2009 IEEE 12th International Conference on Computer Vision, pp. 2146–2153. IEEE (2009)
16. Krizhevsky, A., Sutskever, I., Hinton, G.E.: ImageNet classification with deep convolutional neural networks. Adv. Neural. Inf. Process. Syst. **25**, 1097–1105 (2012)
17. Lee, J., Lee, S., Cho, S., Lee, S.: Deep defocus map estimation using domain adaptation. In: Proceedings of the IEEE/CVF Conference on Computer Vision and Pattern Recognition, pp. 12222–12230 (2019)
18. Lee, J., Son, H., Rim, J., Cho, S., Lee, S.: Iterative filter adaptive network for single image defocus deblurring. In: Proceedings of the IEEE/CVF Conference on Computer Vision and Pattern Recognition, pp. 2034–2042 (2021)
19. Lee, N.Y.: Block-iterative Richardson-Lucy methods for image deblurring. EURASIP J. Image Video Process. **2015**(1), 1–17 (2015)
20. Li, B., et al.: Benchmarking single-image dehazing and beyond. IEEE Transactions on Image Processing, pp. 492–505 (2018)
21. Li, X., Wu, J., Lin, Z., Liu, H., Zha, H.: Recurrent squeeze-and-excitation context aggregation net for single image deraining. In: Ferrari, V., Hebert, M., Sminchisescu, C., Weiss, Y. (eds.) ECCV 2018. LNCS, vol. 11211, pp. 262–277. Springer, Cham (2018). https://doi.org/10.1007/978-3-030-01234-2_16

22. Liang, J., Cao, J., Sun, G., Zhang, K., Van Gool, L., Timofte, R.: Swinir: image restoration using swin transformer. In: Proceedings of the IEEE/CVF International Conference on Computer Vision, pp. 1833–1844 (2021)
23. Liu, D., Wen, B., Fan, Y., Loy, C.C., Huang, T.S.: Non-local recurrent network for image restoration. In: Advances in Neural Information Processing Systems 31 (2018)
24. Liu, P., Zhang, H., Zhang, K., Lin, L., Zuo, W.: Multi-level wavelet-CNN for image restoration. In: Proceedings of the IEEE Conference on Computer Vision and Pattern Recognition Workshops, pp. 773–782 (2018)
25. Liu, Z., et al.: Swin transformer: hierarchical vision transformer using shifted windows. In: Proceedings of the IEEE/CVF International Conference on Computer Vision, pp. 10012–10022 (2021)
26. Lyu, S., Simoncelli, E.P.: Nonlinear image representation using divisive normalization. In: 2008 IEEE Conference on Computer Vision and Pattern Recognition, pp. 1–8. IEEE (2008)
27. Mou, C., Zhang, J., Wu, Z.: Dynamic attentive graph learning for image restoration. In: Proceedings of the IEEE/CVF International Conference on Computer Vision, pp. 4328–4337 (2021)
28. Nah, S., Hyun Kim, T., Mu Lee, K.: Deep multi-scale convolutional neural network for dynamic scene deblurring. In: Proceedings of the IEEE Conference on Computer Vision and Pattern Recognition, pp. 3883–3891 (2017)
29. Nah, S., Son, S., Lee, K.M.: Recurrent neural networks with intra-frame iterations for video deblurring. In: Proceedings of the IEEE/CVF Conference on Computer Vision and Pattern Recognition, pp. 8102–8111 (2019)
30. Pan, J., Bai, H., Tang, J.: Cascaded deep video deblurring using temporal sharpness prior. In: Proceedings of the IEEE/CVF Conference on Computer Vision and Pattern Recognition, pp. 3043–3051 (2020)
31. Park, D., Kang, D.U., Kim, J., Chun, S.Y.: Multi-temporal recurrent neural networks for progressive non-uniform single image deblurring with incremental temporal training. In: Vedaldi, A., Bischof, H., Brox, T., Frahm, J.-M. (eds.) ECCV 2020. LNCS, vol. 12351, pp. 327–343. Springer, Cham (2020). https://doi.org/10.1007/978-3-030-58539-6_20
32. Park, T., Liu, M.Y., Wang, T.C., Zhu, J.Y.: Semantic image synthesis with spatially-adaptive normalization. In: Proceedings of the IEEE/CVF Conference on Computer Vision and Pattern Recognition, pp. 2337–2346 (2019)
33. Purohit, K., Suin, M., Rajagopalan, A., Boddeti, V.N.: Spatially-adaptive image restoration using distortion-guided networks. In: Proceedings of the IEEE/CVF International Conference on Computer Vision, pp. 2309–2319 (2021)
34. Qin, X., Wang, Z., Bai, Y., Xie, X., Jia, H.: FFA-Net: feature fusion attention network for single image dehazing. In: Proceedings of the AAAI Conference on Artificial Intelligence, pp. 11908–11915 (2020)
35. Ren, C., He, X., Wang, C., Zhao, Z.: Adaptive consistency prior based deep network for image denoising. In: Proceedings of the IEEE/CVF Conference on Computer Vision and Pattern Recognition, pp. 8596–8606 (2021)
36. Shen, Z., et al.: Human-aware motion deblurring. In: Proceedings of the IEEE/CVF International Conference on Computer Vision, pp. 5572–5581 (2019)
37. Shi, J., Xu, L., Jia, J.: Just noticeable defocus blur detection and estimation. In: Proceedings of the IEEE Conference on Computer Vision and Pattern Recognition, pp. 657–665 (2015)

38. Son, H., Lee, J., Cho, S., Lee, S.: Single image defocus deblurring using kernel-sharing parallel atrous convolutions. In: Proceedings of the IEEE/CVF International Conference on Computer Vision, pp. 2642–2650 (2021)

39. Son, H., Lee, J., Lee, J., Cho, S., Lee, S.: Recurrent video deblurring with blur-invariant motion estimation and pixel volumes. ACM Trans. Graph. (TOG) **40**(5), 1–18 (2021)

40. Suin, M., Purohit, K., Rajagopalan, A.: Spatially-attentive patch-hierarchical network for adaptive motion deblurring. In: Proceedings of the IEEE/CVF Conference on Computer Vision and Pattern Recognition, pp. 3606–3615 (2020)

41. Suin, M., Rajagopalan, A.: Gated spatio-temporal attention-guided video deblurring. In: Proceedings of the IEEE/CVF Conference on Computer Vision and Pattern Recognition, pp. 7802–7811 (2021)

42. Tian, C., Xu, Y., Zuo, W.: Image denoising using deep CNN with batch renormalization. Neural Netw. **121**, 461–473 (2020)

43. Ulyanov, D., Vedaldi, A., Lempitsky, V.: Instance normalization: the missing ingredient for fast stylization. arXiv preprint arXiv:1607.08022 (2016)

44. Wang, T., Yang, X., Xu, K., Chen, S., Zhang, Q., Lau, R.W.: Spatial attentive single-image deraining with a high quality real rain dataset. In: Proceedings of the IEEE/CVF Conference on Computer Vision and Pattern Recognition, pp. 12270–12279 (2019)

45. Wang, X., Chan, K.C., Yu, K., Dong, C., Change Loy, C.: EDVR: video restoration with enhanced deformable convolutional networks. In: Proceedings of the IEEE/CVF Conference on Computer Vision and Pattern Recognition Workshops (2019)

46. Wang, Z., Cun, X., Bao, J., Zhou, W., Liu, J., Li, H.: Uformer: a general U-shaped transformer for image restoration. In: Proceedings of the IEEE/CVF Conference on Computer Vision and Pattern Recognition, pp. 17683–17693 (2022)

47. Woo, S., Park, J., Lee, J.-Y., Kweon, I.S.: CBAM: convolutional block attention module. In: Ferrari, V., Hebert, M., Sminchisescu, C., Weiss, Y. (eds.) ECCV 2018. LNCS, vol. 11211, pp. 3–19. Springer, Cham (2018). https://doi.org/10.1007/978-3-030-01234-2_1

48. Wu, Y., He, K.: Group normalization. In: Ferrari, V., Hebert, M., Sminchisescu, C., Weiss, Y. (eds.) ECCV 2018. LNCS, vol. 11217, pp. 3–19. Springer, Cham (2018). https://doi.org/10.1007/978-3-030-01261-8_1

49. Xia, Z., Chakrabarti, A.: Identifying recurring patterns with deep neural networks for natural image denoising. In: Proceedings of the IEEE/CVF Winter Conference on Applications of Computer Vision, pp. 2426–2434 (2020)

50. Xiang, X., Wei, H., Pan, J.: Deep video deblurring using sharpness features from exemplars. IEEE Trans. Image Process. **29**, 8976–8987 (2020)

51. Yi, Q., Li, J., Dai, Q., Fang, F., Zhang, G., Zeng, T.: Structure-preserving deraining with residue channel prior guidance. In: IEEE International Conference on Computer Vision (2021)

52. Yu, T., et al.: Region normalization for image inpainting. In: Proceedings of the AAAI Conference on Artificial Intelligence, pp. 12733–12740 (2020)

53. Zamir, S.W., Arora, A., Khan, S., Hayat, M., Khan, F.S., Yang, M.H.: Restormer: efficient transformer for high-resolution image restoration. In: Proceedings of the IEEE/CVF Conference on Computer Vision and Pattern Recognition, pp. 5728–5739 (2022)

54. Zamir, S.W., et al.: CycleISP: real image restoration via improved data synthesis. In: CVPR (2020)

55. Zamir, S.W., et al.: Multi-stage progressive image restoration. In: Proceedings of the IEEE/CVF Conference on Computer Vision and Pattern Recognition, pp. 14821–14831 (2021)
56. Zhang, H., Dai, Y., Li, H., Koniusz, P.: Deep stacked hierarchical multi-patch network for image deblurring. In: Proceedings of the IEEE/CVF Conference on Computer Vision and Pattern Recognition, pp. 5978–5986 (2019)
57. Zhang, K., Li, Y., Zuo, W., Zhang, L., Van Gool, L., Timofte, R.: Plug-and-play image restoration with deep denoiser prior. IEEE Transactions on Pattern Analysis and Machine Intelligence (2021)
58. Zhang, K., Zuo, W., Chen, Y., Meng, D., Zhang, L.: Beyond a gaussian denoiser: residual learning of deep CNN for image denoising. IEEE Trans. Image Process. **26**(7), 3142–3155 (2017)
59. Zhang, K., Zuo, W., Gu, S., Zhang, L.: Learning deep CNN denoiser prior for image restoration. In: Proceedings of the IEEE conference on computer vision and pattern recognition, pp. 3929–3938 (2017)
60. Zhang, K., Zuo, W., Zhang, L.: FFDNet: toward a fast and flexible solution for CNN-based image denoising. IEEE Trans. Image Process. **27**(9), 4608–4622 (2018)
61. Zhang, K., et al.: Deblurring by realistic blurring. In: Proceedings of the IEEE/CVF Conference on Computer Vision and Pattern Recognition, pp. 2737–2746 (2020)
62. Zhang, R., Isola, P., Efros, A.A., Shechtman, E., Wang, O.: The unreasonable effectiveness of deep features as a perceptual metric. In: Proceedings of the IEEE Conference on Computer Vision and Pattern Recognition, pp. 586–595 (2018)
63. Zhang, Y., Li, K., Li, K., Wang, L., Zhong, B., Fu, Y.: Image super-resolution using very deep residual channel attention networks. In: Ferrari, V., Hebert, M., Sminchisescu, C., Weiss, Y. (eds.) ECCV 2018. LNCS, vol. 11211, pp. 294–310. Springer, Cham (2018). https://doi.org/10.1007/978-3-030-01234-2_18
64. Zhang, Y., Li, K., Li, K., Zhong, B., Fu, Y.: Residual non-local attention networks for image restoration. arXiv preprint arXiv:1903.10082 (2019)
65. Zhang, Y., Tian, Y., Kong, Y., Zhong, B., Fu, Y.: Residual dense network for image restoration. IEEE Trans. Pattern Anal. Mach. Intell. **43**(7), 2480–2495 (2020)
66. Zhong, Z., Gao, Y., Zheng, Y., Zheng, B.: Efficient spatio-temporal recurrent neural network for video deblurring. In: Vedaldi, A., Bischof, H., Brox, T., Frahm, J.-M. (eds.) ECCV 2020. LNCS, vol. 12351, pp. 191–207. Springer, Cham (2020). https://doi.org/10.1007/978-3-030-58539-6_12
67. Zhu, C., et al.: Deep recurrent neural network with multi-scale bi-directional propagation for video deblurring. In: Proceedings of the AAAI Conference on Artificial Intelligence, pp. 3598–3607 (2022)

Data Association Between Event Streams and Intensity Frames Under Diverse Baselines

Dehao Zhang[1,2], Qiankun Ding[3], Peiqi Duan[1], Chu Zhou[1],
and Boxin Shi[1,2,4,5(✉)]

[1] NERCVT, School of Computer Science, Peking University, Beijing, China
shiboxin@pku.edu.cn
[2] AI Innovation Center, School of Computer Science, Peking University, Beijing,
China
[3] Yuanpei College, Peking University, Beijing, China
[4] Beijing Academy of Artificial Intelligence, Beijing, China
[5] Institute for Artificial Intelligence, Peking University, Beijing, China

Abstract. This paper proposes a learning-based framework to associate
event streams and intensity frames under diverse camera baselines, to
simultaneously benefit camera pose estimation under large baselines and
depth estimation under small baselines. Based on the observation that
event streams are globally sparse (a small percentage of pixels in global
frames are triggered with events) and locally dense (a large percentage of
pixels in local patches are triggered with events) in the spatial domain, we
put forward a two-stage architecture for matching feature maps. LSparse-
Net uses a large receptive field to find sparse matches while SDense-Net
uses a small receptive field to find dense matches. Both stages apply
Transformer modules with self-attention layers and cross-attention layers to effectively process multi-resolution features from the feature pyramid network backbone. Experimental results on public datasets show a
systematic performance improvement for both tasks compared to state-
of-the-art methods.

1 Introduction

Event cameras are biologically-inspired imaging sensors that are now experi-
encing a growing research community. Distinct from traditional cameras that
record the scene as a sequence of frames, event cameras asynchronously measure log-intensity changes for each pixel and only capture the dynamic visual
scenarios. This unique design brings high temporal resolution ($<10\,\mu s$), high
dynamic range ($>120\,dB$), and low power consumption ($<0.1\,W$) for event cameras [33,39], which give event cameras the potential to handle high-speed motion

---

Supplementary Information The online version contains supplementary material
available at https://doi.org/10.1007/978-3-031-20071-7_5.

and extreme lighting scenarios with low power consumption, *e.g.*, image reconstruction [11,12,19,38,44,55], optical flow estimation [16,48], 3D scene reconstruction [2,57], tracking [17], scene depth estimation [16], and visual SLAM [37].

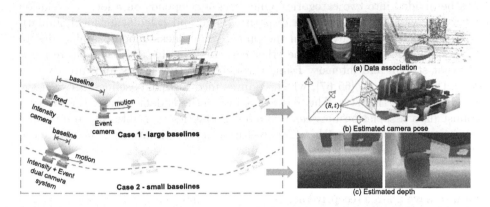

Fig. 1. This paper establishes the data association (a) between event streams and intensity frames under diverse baselines. There are two typical application scenarios: Case 1 – The intensity camera is fixed and the event camera can move freely for pose estimation (b). Case 2 – Two cameras are bundled into one system and shoot the scene in synchronization for depth estimation (c).

Autonomous driving and Augmented Reality (AR) usually adopt the map-based pose estimation to locate the camera pose [3,25,27]. A common way of existing methods is to first establish a point cloud through Structure from Motion (SfM) and obtain the camera pose for one reference image, and then establish *data association* (pixel-level correspondence as shown in Fig. 1 (a)) [67] between subsequent images and the reference image to locate camera pose of the moving device. Estimating the depth through a stereo camera system is also one of the classical topics that are tackled by establishing the data association. The disparity and depth of the scene can be recovered after calibrating the camera parameters and matching all the pixels in two views of a stereo camera system. These image-based camera pose estimation and depth estimation methods perform unsatisfyingly when suffering from over-/under-exposure and motion blur, which coincidentally match the strengths of event cameras: high temporal resolution and high dynamic range can withstand such unfriendly scenarios. This inspires researchers to introduce events to benefit and improve the performance of the two tasks mentioned above.

For camera pose estimation (Fig. 1 (b)), the probabilistic generative event model is applied to jointly process the events triggered at intensity edges and the velocity of the camera [3,14]. They first obtain the pose of the frame-based camera, and then estimate the pose of the event camera by predicting optical flow maps from event streams. These models require reliable prior information of a reference camera's initial pose and motion, and the data association between two cameras becomes unreliable as the error of the optical flow estimation accumulates with the baselines becoming larger. For depth estimation (Fig. 1 (c)), EMVS [43] first proposes the event-based multi-view stereo method, but the outputting depth maps are sparse. Subsequent deep learning-based algorithms can be divided into two categories. One category depends on a local correlation layer [10, 22–24, 50], assuming a disparity range and calculating local similarities of deep features only within the range, which lacks generalizability due to the assumed disparity range; the other category simply fuses the feature maps of event stream and intensity frame through attention layers and directly predicts the depth map [65, 67], which endures inconsistent baselines between the training and testing sets. The above existing methods demonstrate the need for robust data association between two data modalities, $i.e.$, intensity frames and event streams, whether with a large baseline (pose estimation) or a small baseline (depth estimation) between two cameras. However, existing methods such as SIFT [35, 36], ORB [47], or CNN-based ones [8, 9, 60] are not suitable to establish events and frames data association since they mainly focus on local regions. It is vital to have a large receptive field to utilize the information provided by overall edges and contours.

In this paper, we propose a learning-based framework to deal with data association between event streams and intensity frames under diverse baselines. In detail, we use the feature pyramid network (FPN) backbone [34] to extract features and make them more distinguishable. Based on the observation that event streams are globally sparse (a small percentage of pixels in global frames are triggered with events) and locally dense (a large percentage of pixels in local patches are triggered with events) at spatial perspective (as Fig. 1 (a) shows), we put forward a two-stage architecture for matching feature maps. **LSparse-Net** indicates a neural network using a **L**arge receptive field to find **Sparse** matches; **SDense-Net** indicates a neural network using a **S**mall receptive field to find **Dense** matches. Both two stages apply Transformer modules [56] with self-attention layers and cross-attention layers to process the multi-resolution features from the FPN backbone. In tasks with large baselines, where receptive fields differ largely from each other, we can match features through low-level data association; especially for pose estimation, our framework does not require the history of camera poses for estimation [3, 18] (Table 1). In tasks with small baselines, where receptive fields differ slightly from each other, our framework can provide high-level dense data association to refine the final outputs. To summarize, our primary contributions are threefold:

- We introduce Transformer modules to establish data association between event streams and intensity frames, making features more distinguishable with global information, and design a two-stage architecture according to the globally sparse and locally dense characteristics of events streams.
- Our proposed framework supports the establishment of data association between event streams and intensity frames under any baseline without requiring the history of camera poses and any extra clue.

– Our proposed framework demonstrates state-of-the-art performance for both downstream tasks with large baselines (pose estimation) and small baselines (depth estimation).

Table 1. Characteristic comparison with state-of-the-art camera pose estimation methods.

	History poses	Motion parameters
Gallego et al. [14]	Full history	Yes
Bryner et al. [3]	The Last pose	Yes
Ours	**No**	**No**

2   Related Work

Data Association. Establishing data association is a fundamental problem in the SLAM literature [41,52,53]. Most SLAM or 3D vision data association are built upon the outputs of frame-based cameras. Conventional optimization-based methods [36,47] are proposed to use handcrafted local features invariant to rotations and scales to solve this problem. With the development of neural networks, some learning-based approaches [8,9,60] can extract significant local features. The learning-based approaches significantly improve the performance on large viewpoint and illumination changes of local features. However, these detector-dependent approaches mainly focus on local regions of images, and could not make full use of global information. They are inherently unable to find similar points from different regions. Unlike other methods which aim to deal with data association between a pair of intensity frames, Gallego et al. [14] build the data association between event streams and intensity frames upon the prior knowledge by calculating the optical flow of cameras. Later, Bryner et al. [3] propose a maximum-likelihood framework, which optimizes non-linearly according to the camera poses and velocities, to establish the data association.

Event-Based Pose Estimation. Existing methods for event-based pose estimation differ in settings. Several methods [5,57,59] perform motion correcting for event streams based on depth information and the pose trajectory of cameras. Event streams are treated as intensity frames for local feature extraction and local feature matching by using RANSAC [13] for robust pose estimation. Muglikar et al. [40] adopt a similar pipeline for pose estimation with a slight difference that they directly reconstructed event streams into intensity frames. Another set of works [61,62] calculate pose by maximizing the spatio-temporal consistency of stereo event-based data for camera tracking and 3D reconstruction, without using intensity frames. The most relevant papers [3,17,18] to our work are based on a generative event model within a maximum-likelihood framework, where extra clues (*e.g.*, pose and motion of cameras, optical flow, *etc.*) are required. On the contrary, our work does not require any extra clue.

Event-Based Stereo. Existing methods for event-based depth estimation fall into two categories: two event cameras, one event camera and one frame-based camera. For the former category, Zhu *et al.* [63] propose a method which acquires a sparse depth map using a dual event camera stereo imaging system. It requires the velocity of the camera to generate a time-synchronized event disparity volume, and then applies numerical optimization methods to minimize the matching cost between two event disparity volumes. Zou *et al.* [66] recover dense depth maps from sparse event data. Ahmed *et al.* [1] design an end-to-end neural network, which first reconstructs intensity frame from event streams through learning and then calculates dense depth maps based on stereo intensity frames. The latter category is more relevant to our work [58,67]. The method proposed by Wang *et al.* [58] is similar to that of Ahmed *et al.* [1] as they both transform event streams into intensity frames for depth estimation. The method proposed by Zuo *et al.* [67] is an end-to-end approach, which directly takes event streams and intensity frames as input and outputs a disparity map through pyramid attention layers and a U-Net [46] structure. Additionally, Li *et al.* [32] propose STTR, which abandons the cost of volume construction and establishes data association between stereo intensity images using Transformer modules. This work is closely related to our work in terms of models.

3   Proposed Method

In this section, we first introduce the formulation of the problem we target and explain our overall framework in Sect. 3.1 and Fig. 2. Then, we describe our two-stage architecture in Sect. 3.2 and Sect. 3.3 in detail. Finally, we introduce our dense output decoder in Sect. 3.4 to ensure outputs consistency. The implementation details are in Sect. 3.5.

3.1   Problem Formulation and Overall Framework

We aim to establish data association between pair-wise event streams and intensity frames, captured by two separated or bundled cameras in arbitrary poses (Fig. 1), by finding pixel-level matches, without geometric constraints such as homography and epipolar constraint. Events are triggered by an event camera whenever the log intensity change d at a given pixel is larger than a threshold c. Each event is recorded as a four-attribute tuple $\{x, y, t, p\}$, where (x, y) is the coordinates, t is the timestamp, and p is the polarity given by: $p = 1$ if $d \geq c$ and $p = -1$ if $d \leq c$. An event stream is a stacking of such events generated by event cameras. We first transform event streams into four-channel time surfaces [7,29], whose first two channels record the number of positive and negative events and last two channels record the timestamp of the latest positive and negative events triggered at each pixel. Then, given an intensity frame $I_p^i \in \mathbb{R}^{H_i \times W_i \times 1}$ and the

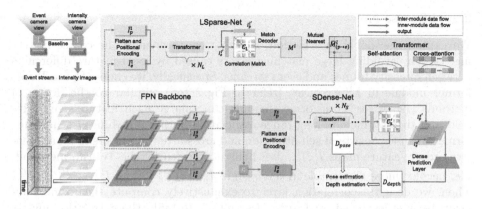

Fig. 2. The architecture of our proposed framework, which consists of three modules: FPN backbone, LSparse-Net, and SDense-Net. The backbone extracts dual-resolution feature maps from the intensity frame I_p and the time surface of the event stream I_e, respectively. LSparse-Net establishes sparse data association from coarse-level features, while SDense-Net establishes dense data association from fine-level features.

time surface $I_e^i \in \mathbb{R}^{H_i \times W_i \times 4}$ of an event stream, we formulate the problem as finding pixel-level matches between this pair of data. Specifically, the matching procedure could be expressed as $\boldsymbol{x}_e = \mathcal{F}_\Theta(\boldsymbol{x}_p | I_p^i, I_e^i)$. where $\boldsymbol{x}_p$ and $\boldsymbol{x}_e$ denote the matching pixel coordinates from I_p^i and I_e^i respectively, and $\mathcal{F}_\Theta$ denotes the matching function parameterized by Θ.

Based on the globally sparse and locally dense properties of event streams, we design the matching function as a two-stage framework: The first stage is a matching module aiming to establish sparse data association at the global level and the second stage is a matching module aiming to establish dense data association at the local level. As shown in Fig. 2, dual-resolution feature maps, $I_p^l, I_e^l \in \mathbb{R}^{H_l \times W_l \times 1}$ with coarse resolution and $I_p^s, I_e^s \in \mathbb{R}^{H_s \times W_s \times 1}$ with fine resolution, are first extracted from the intensity frame and the time surface of event streams by the FPN backbone. After the FPN backbone, regarding the difference of events in density, we design two distinct matching modules: LSparse-Net and SDense-Net. LSparse-Net takes the flattened feature maps $\bar{I}_p^l, \bar{I}_e^l$ from the large receptive fields as input and outputs sparse matches $\bar{M}z_{p \to e}^l \in \{0, 1\}^{(H_i \times W_i) \times (H_i \times W_i)}$, where $\bar{M}_{p \to e}^l(\bar{\boldsymbol{x}}_p^l, \bar{\boldsymbol{x}}_e^l) = 1$ represents the match between $\bar{I}_p^l(\bar{\boldsymbol{x}}_p^l)$ and $\bar{I}_e^l(\bar{\boldsymbol{x}}_e^l)$. Unlike LSparse-Net which aims to establish long-range data association, SDense-Net aims to find a dense, local data association. SDense-Net takes feature maps I_p^s, I_e^s from small receptive fields and outputs final dense matching results $\boldsymbol{x}_e = \mathcal{F}_\Theta(\boldsymbol{x}_p | I_p^i, I_e^i)$, where $I_p(\boldsymbol{x}_p)$ matches $I_e(\boldsymbol{x}_e)$. The final loss function then becomes the weighted sum of losses from each matching model. We further add a dense prediction layer to ensure outputs consistency and make the framework compatible with the depth estimation task. We will introduce in detail the design of two stages in the following subsections.

3.2 LSparse-Net

We exploit the global information of each view to achieve the coarse matching, thereby avoiding large matching errors caused by local feature differences between intensity frames and event streams. Specifically, we choose to use Transformer module in LSparse-Net (refer to Fig. 2 top), similar to the design of methods [49,51], as Transformer module can enlarge each feature's receptive field and thereby include long-range association during matching. Each Transformer module consists of self-attention and cross-attention layers in an alternative order. Feature maps I_p^l, I_e^l, after being forwarded by the Transformer module, become more discernible in the form of $I_p^{l'} \in \mathbb{R}^{H_l \times W_l \times D_l}, I_e^{l'} \in \mathbb{R}^{H_l \times W_l \times D_l}$. Then, we design a correlation layer to exhaustively compute the cosine similarity between each pair of feature descriptors, to build the correlation matrix $C_l \in \mathbb{R}^{H_l \times W_l \times H_l \times W_l}$. Usually, there are more matches in the vicinity of a correct match. This inspires us to design a 4-D CNN structure for matching and filtering the correlation matrix, by using the mutual nearest neighbor filter.

Transformer Module. We use linear Transformer [26] to reduce the computational complexity and apply positional encoding to encode location information into features. The original Transformer put forward by Vaswani *et al.* [56] is an encoder-decoder architecture, where the encoder consists of sequentially connected encoder layers. For each encoder layer, the most critical feature is the attention layer, which takes query vector Q, key vector K, and value vector V as input. In self-attention layers, Q, K, V are transformed from the same input vector with different weights and in cross-attention layers, Q, K, V are transformed from different input vectors.

Linear Transformer, proposed by Katharopoulos *et al.* [26], aims to reduce the computational costs caused by the dot product between Q and K. The dot product from the attention layer in the original Transformer is substituted with an alternative kernel function:

$$\text{Similarity}(Q, K) = \phi(Q) \cdot \phi(K)^\top, \tag{1}$$

where $\phi(\cdot) = \text{elu}(\cdot) + 1$. As D (the scale of $\phi(Q), \phi(K)$) is much smaller than N (the scale of Q and K), the computational complexity is reduced to $O(N)$.

Positional encoding is added to each element to encode positional information. Following DETR [4] and LoFTR [51], we apply the 2D extension of positional encoding in our Transformer module.

Our Transformer module takes feature maps $\bar{I}_p^l, \bar{I}_e^l$ as input. In the self-attention layer, the two inputs are identical: either $(\bar{I}_p^l, \bar{I}_p^l)$ or $(\bar{I}_e^l, \bar{I}_e^l)$; in cross-attention layer, the two inputs differ from each other: $(\bar{I}_e^l, \bar{I}_p^l)$. This module does not change the shape of feature map, but instead applies the attention layer to encoding more context information into the features for a better recognizability.

Correlation Layer. To acquire pairwise feature similarity, we apply a correlation layer [31] to calculate the cosine similarity between feature descriptors and normalize features with $\ell2$ norm before and after the correlation layer.

The output feature maps from the Transformer module $I_p^{l'} \in \mathbb{R}^{H_l \times W_l \times D_l}$, $I_e^{l'} \in \mathbb{R}^{H_l \times W_l \times D_l}$ have a spatial size of $H_l \times W_l$ and dimensionality D_l. Let $I_p^{l'}(i,j) \in \mathbb{R}^{D_l}$ denote the feature vector at a spatial location (i,j), then the correlation layer evaluating the pairwise similarities between all locations in feature maps $I_p^{l'}$, $I_e^{l'}$ can be calculated as

$$C_l(i,j,m,n) = I_p^{l'}(i,j) \cdot I_e^{l'}(m,n), \tag{2}$$

where $\cdot$ denotes the scalar product. The final output is the 4-D correlation matrix C_l capturing the similarities between all pairs of spatial locations.

Matching Decoder. The previous correlation layer builds a dense correlation matrix, but it is a significant challenge to determine which pairs are correct matches. To discriminate a reliable match, we apply the network proposed by Rocco *et al.* [45]. Since correct matches tend to have a coherent set of supporting matches surrounding them in the 4-D space, by processing correlation matrix with 4-D convolutional network we can establish a locality prior to the relationships between the matches. In our implementation, we apply three layers of 4-D convolutional blocks to capture the match patterns and ReLU activation function in the last layer. The output M^l has only one channel and maintains the same shape as the input.

Mutual Nearest Neighbor Filtering. If $I_p^l(i,j)$ and $I_e^l(m,n)$ matches, it simultaneously means that $I_e^l(m,n)$ is the closest feature to $I_p^l(i,j)$ in I_e^l and $I_p^l(i,j)$ is the closest feature to $I_e^l(m,n)$ in I_p^l. Therefore, we use this rule to further filter the matches and eventually acquire the final sparse results. We denote the final match matrix as $\bar{M}^l$.

Loss Function. In LSparse-Net, we acquire sparse data association. Therefore, we apply negative log-likelihood loss. With respect to each set of ground truth match $M_{gt}^l = ((i_1, j_1, m_1, n_1), ..., (i_N, j_N, m_N, n_N))$, we calculate the loss as:

$$L_l = -\frac{1}{N} \sum_{i,j,m,n} \log \bar{M}^l(i,j,m,n). \tag{3}$$

3.3 SDense-Net

LSparse-Net is a sparse matching module capable of detecting long-range association, while SDense-Net is in charge of establishing local dense data association in patches which have been matched by LSparse-Net. SDense-Net (refer to Fig. 2 bottom right) consists of Transformer modules and correlation layers similar to LSparse-Net. The distinction is that, to acquire dense matches, the matching decoder of SDense-Net differs from its counterpart in LSparse-Net.

Matching Decoder. The matching decoder in SDense-Net consists of several convolutional blocks and outputs a two-channel tensor with unchanged resolution. Given the output $C_s \in \mathbb{R}^{H_s \times W_s \times H_s \times W_s}$ from correlation layer, it is transformed to $C_s' \in \mathbb{R}^{H_s \times W_s \times (H_s \times W_s)}$ for the convenience of CNN-based processing, where the third dimension denotes channels. This decoder outputs a two-channel matrix D_{pose}, indicating the displacement of matching pixel's coordinates on X-axis and Y-axis respectively.

Loss Function. In SDense-Net, we acquire dense data association. Therefore, we apply $\ell 2$ loss. Suppose the input of this module has M points, then for each point (i, j) from $\bar{I}_p^s$, there is a corresponding point from $\bar{I}_e^s$, whose loss could be calculated as:

$$L_s = \frac{1}{M} \sum_{i,j} \|(i - m, j - n)\|_2. \tag{4}$$

3.4   Dense Prediction Layer

We add a dense prediction layer to ensure dense output consistency and make it compatible with dense outputting tasks such as predicting depth maps or disparity maps. This dense prediction layer consists of several convolution layers and a ReLU activation function at the end. We denote D_{depth} as the output of this layer.

Loss Function. We apply the L_c loss for per-pixel supervision to minimize the difference between ground truth and dense predictions. Given a batch of ground truth with pixel labels $\hat{y}$, pixel-wise dense predictions y, and the number of pixels H, L_c loss is defined as

$$L_c = \frac{1}{H} \sum_{i=1}^{H} \|\hat{y}_i - y_i\|. \tag{5}$$

3.5   Implementation Details

The resolution of event streams and intensity frames is 260×346. The entire model is trained end-to-end with randomly initialized weights. The LSparse-Net consists of two Transformer layers and SDense-Net consists of one Transformer layer. The dimension of Transformer is set to 512. The match decoder in LSparse-Net and the match decoder in SDense-Net each consists of three CNN layers.

The final loss is the weighted sum of the loss functions of LSparse-Net and SDense-Net:

$$L = L_l + \alpha \cdot L_s + \beta \cdot L_c, \tag{6}$$

where α and β are hyper parameters. For the tasks which does not require dense output, we don't use the additional dense output layer and we set $\alpha = 2$ and $\beta = 0$. Otherwise, we set both $\alpha = \beta = 2$.

All of the models are trained using Adam optimizer [28] with an initial learning rate of 1×10^{-3} and a batch size of 16. In training, the learning rate is cut in half by MultiStepLR scheduler in epoch $\{3, 9, 15\}$. All experiments are implemented on NVIDIA TITAN RTX GPUs. For all experiments, we use four GPUs for training and validating.

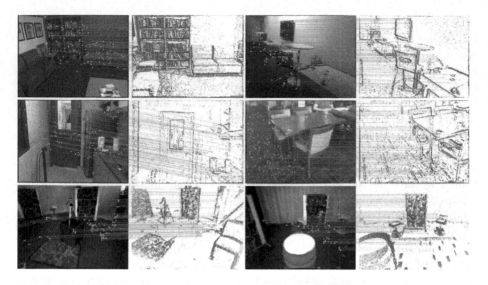

Fig. 3. Exemplars for data association. We randomly sample 100 pairs of matching pixels from all matches for visualization. The first two rows show results of data association on the synthetic data [6], whereas the last row shows results on the real data. As shown, our model can still establish sound data association even when the views of the event stream and the intensity frame differ largely from each other.

Table 2. Pose estimation evaluation on the synthetic data. We report the AUC of the pose error at thresholds (5°, 10°, 20°), where the pose error is defined as the maximum of angular error in rotation and translation.

	Pose estimation AUC		
	5°	10°	20°
Synthetic data	10.40	25.43	39.68

4 Applications

In this section, we first introduce two applications based on the data association we proposed, including pose estimation in Sect. 4.1 (for large baselines) and depth estimation in Sect. 4.2 (for small baselines). Then, we conduct several ablation studies to verify the validity of each model design choice in Sect. 4.3.

4.1 Pose Estimation

To demonstrate that our framework can establish data association under large baselines, we use it to solve the pose estimation problem. We cannot directly use existing benchmark datasets [3,14] for event-based pose estimation, because our model requires pixel-wise ground truth matches as supervision for training, but existing datasets rarely contain the information of camera poses and high-quality depth images at the same time for us to construct labels. Despite the fact that EVSEC [64] can provide both, it only contains a limited number of scenes, restricting the generalizability of the final model. Eventually, we choose Scan-Net [6], an RGB-D video dataset, and generate the corresponding event streams with the event simulator V2E [21] under the default parameter settings to generate the training dataset. ScanNet [6] contains 1613 videos with the ground truth pose and the depth map of each frame. The resolution of the images and depth maps are all 640×480, and the frame rate of videos is 30 fps. We sample a part of the synthetic dataset for training referring to [49,51] to synthesize event streams by V2E [21]. The sample indices will be provided in the supplementary materials. When generating the event stream corresponding to each intensity frame, we include the latest 20,000 events earlier than the timestamp of the intensity frame, which remains consistent in our training and testing processes on all datasets.

To evaluate the robustness to real data, we choose the scene of an actual room from Bryner et al. [3], which consists of a texture-less white wall and some rich-textured objects. The data are acquired by RGB-D cameras and motion capture system, providing depth and pose information. We compare our model (trained only on the synthetic dataset) with recent events and frame-based 6-DoF tracking methods, including the works of Gallego et al. [15], and Bryner et al. [3]. Note that our method does not require the history of camera poses like Gallego et al. [15] and Bryner et al. [3], as shown in Table 1, which makes the estimation process more convenient.

Table 3. Pose estimation evaluation on the real data. We report the median accuracy of the results. The position error (Pos.) is given by the Euclidean distance between the ground truth and the estimated event position. The orientation error (Ori.) is measured using the geodesic distance between the ground truth and the estimated event pose.

	Bryner et al. [3]		Ours	
	Pos. (cm)	Ori. (°)	Pos. (cm)	Ori. (°)
Room1	9.95	**3.08**	**8.82**	4.12
Room2	9.82	**3.84**	**8.73**	4.63

Test Setting. Referring to the test settings from Bryner et al. [3], we respectively choose 284 and 3046 pieces of event streams from trajectory 1 and trajectory 2, and choose the nearest five frames of intensity frames according to the timestamp of the last event to construct data pairs. Instead of relying on the history pose, the purpose of choosing the nearest five intensity frames is to find intensity frames that are spatially overlapped with the current events as reference frames. For a given event stream, to calculate the camera pose corresponding to the last event, we treat the five data pairs as our inputs. After matching those pairs between intensity frames and events, we can establish some correspondence between events and the intensity image. Since the 3D coordinates of intensity frame pixels are known in advance, we can build correspondences between 2D coordinates of events and the 3D coordinates of intensity frame pixels. We solve the PnP problem with the OpenCV `solvePnPRansac` to finally get the camera pose. For the parameter settings, we set `iterationsCount` = 10000, `reprojectionError` = 8.0, `confidence` = 0.99.

Evaluation Protocol and Results. For evaluation on the synthetic dataset, following [30,51], we report the area under the cumulative curve (AUC) of the pose errors at different thresholds. To recover camera poses, we solve the essential matrix from predicted matches with RANSAC. The evaluation metrics on the synthetic dataset are shown in Table 2. For evaluation on the real-world dataset, we pick the absolute and relative errors of position and rotation as evaluation metrics. As shown in Table 3, our method achieves comparable performance to

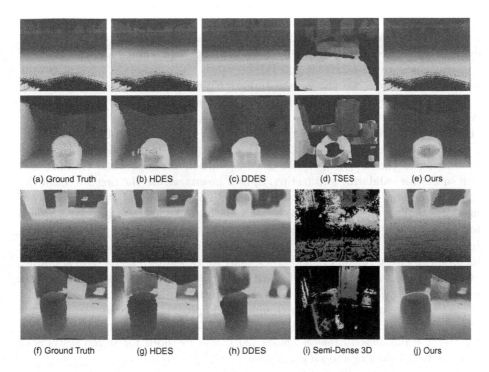

Fig. 4. Qualitative comparison against recent event-based methods on the Indoor Flying dataset. Following [54,61,63,67], we select 4 examples from the dataset and compare with HDES [67], DDES [54], TSES [63], Semi-Dense 3D [42]. From top to bottom, the rows correspond respectively to frame 100 from sequence 1, frame 340 from sequence 1, frame 1700 from sequence 3, and frame 980 from sequence 1. Following HDES [67], we add a mask in our results based on the ground truth, setting pixels as dark blue if their disparity values are missing in the ground truth. (Color figure online)

Bryner *et al.* [3] without relying on any particular initial pose. Note that as analyzed in Bryner *et al.* [3], the ground truth data contain a certain level of noise. Achieving this level of error is almost the limit for any model on this particular dataset. It is demonstrated in Fig. 3 that, for both synthetic and real data, our model is capable of establishing correct matches between event streams and intensity frames in scenes with large baselines and sparse textures, and our model is generalizable from synthetic data to real-world data.

4.2   Depth Estimation

To demonstrate that our framework can establish data association under small baselines, we use it to solve the depth estimation problem. We choose Multi Vehicle Stereo Event Camera Dataset (MVSEC) [64] for training and testing for this task. MVSEC [64] is a widely used event-based stereo dataset collected by LIDAR, IMU, and two event cameras. Each event camera can output event streams and intensity frames with a resolution of 346×260. The product of focal length and the baseline between the two cameras is 19.94. This dataset provides event streams and synchronized intensity frames, depth maps and the poses of cameras calculated by LIDAR and IMU.

For comparison, we choose the Indoor Flying dataset from MVSEC [64], which is taken by a drone in a room with several objects of irregular shapes. As the depth images are sparse on some images, referring to Zhu *et al.* [63], we choose three subsets for training and evaluation, which consist of indoor_flying1: 140–1200, indoor_flying2: 120–1420, indoor_flying3: 73–1616. Following the setup in existing methods [54,63,67], we use two subsets for supervised training and one subset for validating and testing. Split 1 means we use the first subset of the sequence as our validation and test dataset. The second and third subsets are used as training data. We use event streams for left-view and intensity frames for right-view as the input of models, and the model outputs disparity maps. Identical to the test setting of pose estimation, for each intensity frame, we include the latest 20,000 events earlier than its timestamp as its corresponding event stream. Eventually, mean disparity error, mean depth error, and one-pixel accuracy are applied to assess our results quantitatively.

We compare our framework with multiple approaches, including methods for stereo event cameras (DDES [54], Semi-Dense 3D [42], CopNet [61]), methods for stereo frame-based cameras (SGM [20]), and methods for stereo systems of a frame-based camera and an event camera (HDES [67]).

Results. Quantitative results are shown in Table 4. The results validate the capability of our framework to solve the basic problem of establishing data association between event streams and intensity frames while being adaptive to multiple tasks. Visual results for comparison are shown in Fig. 4. According to the side-by-side comparison across splits, Split 2 ranks the last. The primary reason is that some data in sequence 2 contain large depths, whereas sequences 1 and 3 do not contain such data. Compared with the state-of-the-art model HDES [67], as shown in the first row, our framework is more accurate in predicting the overall distribution of disparity, whereas HDES [67] predicts better sharp results over the edges, which might be attributed to the design of $L_{smoothness}$ in HDES [67]. As a whole, using both event streams and intensity frames to estimate depth, our model reaches the state-of-the-art performances.

Table 4. Depth estimation evaluation on the Indoor Flying dataset. Our method shows clear advantages over DDES [54], SGM [20], TSES [63], and CopNet [61]. Compared with HDES [67], our method demonstrates similar performances in most cases and is slightly ahead in the mean depth error on Split 1. The cells of mean disparity error for HDES [67], DDES [54], and SGM [20] are left blank because the metric of mean disparity error is not calculated for them in their original works.

	Mean depth error (cm)			Mean disparity error (px)			One pixel accuracy (%)		
	Split 1	Split 2	Split 3	Split 1	Split 2	Split 3	Split 1	Split 2	Split 3
HDES [67]	16.0	**28.0**	**18.0**	–	–	–	86.4	49.7	**80.1**
DDES [54]	16.7	29.4	27.8	–	–	–	**89.8**	61.0	74.8
SGM [20]	29.0	36.7	37.9	–	–	–	78.5	64.4	71.0
TSES [63]	36.0	44.0	36.0	0.89	1.98	0.88	82.3	**70.1**	82.3
CopNet [61]	61.0	100.0	64.0	1.03	1.54	1.01	70.0	52.8	70.6
Ours	**15.8**	31.8	19.7	**0.75**	1.82	**0.87**	88.1	50.3	77.4

4.3 Ablation Study

To verify the validity of each module design choice in our framework, we compare the performances of three different sets of module combinations respectively on the two tasks. For pose estimation, as shown in Table 5: 1) Removing SDense-Net while preserving LSparse-Net leads to a significant drop in performances. 2) Changing the layers of the Transformer in LSparse-Net from 2 to 1 leads to a slight drop in AUC. Note that we should not remove the whole LSparse-Net since it would lead to huge video memory consumption. For depth estimation, we conduct experiments on Split 2. As shown in Table 6: 1) Removing the dense output layer leads to a significant drop in performances. 2) Removing SDense-Net while preserving LSparse-Net also leads to a drop in performances. 3) Changing the feature dimension for the Transformer in LSparse-Net from 512 to 256 leads to a slight drop in all three metrics. These results demonstrate that our final model achieves the optimal performance with these specific design choices.

Table 5. Ablation study for pose estimation. Three variants of models are trained and evaluated on the synthetic ScanNet [6] dataset. Smaller LSparse-Net denotes that it only contains 1 Transformer layer.

	Pose estimation AUC		
	5°	10°	20°
Remove SDense-Net	2.33	14.23	25.42
Smaller LSparse-Net	9.76	23.42	32.53
Our final model	**10.40**	**25.43**	**39.68**

Table 6. Ablation study for depth estimation. The models below are trained and evaluated on Split 2 of EVSEC [64] dataset.

	Mean depth error (cm)	Mean disparity error (px)	One pixel accuracy (%)
	Split 2	Split 2	Split 2
Remove dense output layer	45.5	2.43	40.8
Remove SDense-Net	37.7	2.02	43.4
Transformer dimension = 256	32.4	1.99	47.3
Our final model	**31.8**	**1.82**	**50.3**

5   Conclusions

This paper presents an approach to establish data association between event streams and intensity frames, which not only establishes data association under large baselines and large difference in receptive fields for pose estimation of cameras, but also establishes data association under small baselines and small difference in receptive fields for depth estimation of dual camera system with bundled intensity and event cameras. We achieve this by taking the globally sparse and locally dense feature of event streams into account and establishing data association in a sparse-to-fine manner.

Limitations. Furthermore, we observe that existing real-world datasets for event-based pose estimation and depth estimation using both event streams and intensity frames with high-quality ground truth poses and depth labels are still not ready on large scales. Synthetic datasets, despite their large quantities, are not realistic enough for blur artifacts and HDR properties of events. This is one of the bottlenecks that prevents the proposed method to further explore more reliable data association.

Acknowledgements. This work was supported by National Key R&D Program of China (2021ZD0109803) and National Natural Science Foundation of China under Grant No. 62136001, 62088102.

References

1. Ahmed, S.H., Jang, H.W., Uddin, S.N., Jung, Y.J.: Deep event stereo leveraged by event-to-image translation. In: Proceedings of the AAAI Conference on Artificial Intelligence, vol. 35, pp. 882–890 (2021)
2. Alexis, B., Zihao, W.W., Oliver, C., Aggelos, K.K.: E3D: event-based 3D shape reconstruction. CoRR **abs/2012.05214** (2020). https://arxiv.org/abs/2012.05214
3. Bryner, S., Gallego, G., Rebecq, H., Scaramuzza, D.: Event-based, direct camera tracking from a photometric 3D map using nonlinear optimization. In: 2019 International Conference on Robotics and Automation (ICRA), pp. 325–331 (2019)
4. Carion, N., Massa, F., Synnaeve, G., Usunier, N., Kirillov, A., Zagoruyko, S.: End-to-end object detection with transformers. In: Vedaldi, A., Bischof, H., Brox, T., Frahm, J.-M. (eds.) ECCV 2020. LNCS, vol. 12346, pp. 213–229. Springer, Cham (2020). https://doi.org/10.1007/978-3-030-58452-8_13
5. Censi, A., Scaramuzza, D.: Low-latency event-based visual odometry. In: 2014 IEEE International Conference on Robotics and Automation (ICRA), pp. 703–710 (2014)
6. Dai, A., Chang, A.X., Savva, M., Halber, M., Funkhouser, T., Nießner, M.: ScanNet: richly-annotated 3D reconstructions of indoor scenes. In: Proceedings of Conference on Computer Vision and Pattern Recognition (CVPR), pp. 5828–5839 (2017)
7. Delbruck, T.: Frame-free dynamic digital vision. In: Proceedings of International Symposium on Secure-Life Electronics, Advanced Electronics for Quality Life and Society, vol. 1, pp. 21–26 (2008)
8. DeTone, D., Malisiewicz, T., Rabinovich, A.: Toward geometric deep slam. arXiv preprint arXiv:1707.07410 (2017)
9. DeTone, D., Malisiewicz, T., Rabinovich, A.: SuperPoint: self-supervised interest point detection and description. In: Proceedings of the IEEE Conference on Computer Vision and Pattern Recognition Workshops, pp. 224–236 (2018)
10. Dosovitskiy, A., et al.: FlowNet: learning optical flow with convolutional networks. In: Proceedings of International Conference on Computer Vision (ICCV), pp. 2758–2766 (2015)
11. Duan, P., Wang, Z., Shi, B., Cossairt, O., Huang, T., Katsaggelos, A.: Guided event filtering: synergy between intensity images and neuromorphic events for high performance imaging. IEEE Trans. Pattern Anal. Mach. Intell. **44**, 8261–8275 (2021)
12. Duan, P., Wang, Z., Zhou, X., Ma, Y., Shi, B.: EventZoom: learning to denoise and super resolve neuromorphic events. In: Proceedings of Conference on Computer Vision and Pattern Recognition (CVPR) (2021)
13. Fischler, M.A., Bolles, R.C.: Random sample consensus: a paradigm for model fitting with applications to image analysis and automated cartography. Commun. ACM **24**(6), 381–395 (1981)
14. Gallego, G., Forster, C., Mueggler, E., Scaramuzza, D.: Event-based camera pose tracking using a generative event model. arXiv preprint arXiv:1510.01972 (2015)
15. Gallego, G., Lund, J.E., Mueggler, E., Rebecq, H., Delbruck, T., Scaramuzza, D.: Event-based, 6-DoF camera tracking from photometric depth maps. IEEE Trans. Pattern Anal. Mach. Intell. **40**(10), 2402–2412 (2017)
16. Gallego, G., Rebecq, H., Scaramuzza, D.: A unifying contrast maximization framework for event cameras, with applications to motion, depth, and optical flow estimation. In: Proceedings of Conference on Computer Vision and Pattern Recognition (CVPR), pp. 3867–3876 (2018)

17. Gehrig, D., Rebecq, H., Gallego, G., Scaramuzza, D.: Asynchronous, photometric feature tracking using events and frames. In: Ferrari, V., Hebert, M., Sminchisescu, C., Weiss, Y. (eds.) ECCV 2018. LNCS, vol. 11216, pp. 766–781. Springer, Cham (2018). https://doi.org/10.1007/978-3-030-01258-8_46

18. Gehrig, D., Rebecq, H., Gallego, G., Scaramuzza, D.: EKLT: asynchronous photometric feature tracking using events and frames. Int. J. Comput. Vis. **128**, 1–18 (2019)

19. Han, J., et al: Neuromorphic camera guided high dynamic range imaging. In: Proceedings of Conference on Computer Vision and Pattern Recognition (CVPR) (2020)

20. Hirschmuller, H.: Stereo processing by semiglobal matching and mutual information. IEEE Trans. Pattern Anal. Mach. Intell. **30**(2), 328–341 (2007)

21. Hu, Y., Liu, S.C., Delbruck, T.: V2E: from video frames to realistic DVS events. In: Proceedings of Conference on Computer Vision and Pattern Recognition (CVPR), pp. 1312–1321 (2021)

22. Hui, T.W., Tang, X., Loy, C.C.: LiteFlowNet: a lightweight convolutional neural network for optical flow estimation. In: Proceedings of the IEEE Conference on Computer Vision and Pattern Recognition, pp. 8981–8989 (2018)

23. Hui, T.W., Tang, X., Loy, C.C.: A lightweight optical flow CNN-revisiting data fidelity and regularization. IEEE Trans. Pattern Anal. Mach. Intell. **43**(8), 2555–2569 (2020)

24. Ilg, E., Mayer, N., Saikia, T., Keuper, M., Dosovitskiy, A., Brox, T.: FlowNet 2.0: evolution of optical flow estimation with deep networks. In: Proceedings of Conference on Computer Vision and Pattern Recognition (CVPR), pp. 2462–2470 (2017)

25. Jin, Y., et al.: Image matching across wide baselines: from paper to practice **129**(2), 517–547 (2021)

26. Katharopoulos, A., Vyas, A., Pappas, N., Fleuret, F.: Transformers are RNNs: fast autoregressive transformers with linear attention. In: International Conference on Machine Learning, pp. 5156–5165 (2020)

27. Kendall, A., Grimes, M., Cipolla, R.: PoseNet: a convolutional network for real-time 6-DoF camera relocalization. In: Proceedings of International Conference on Computer Vision (ICCV), pp. 2938–2946 (2015)

28. Kingma, D.P., Ba, J.: Adam: a method for stochastic optimization. arXiv preprint arXiv:1412.6980 (2014)

29. Lagorce, X., Orchard, G., Galluppi, F., Shi, B.E., Benosman, R.B.: HOTS: a hierarchy of event-based time-surfaces for pattern recognition. IEEE Trans. Pattern Anal. Mach. Intell. **39**(7), 1346–1359 (2016)

30. Li, H., Li, G., Shi, L.: Super-resolution of spatiotemporal event-stream image. Neurocomputing **335**, 206–214 (2019)

31. Li, X., Han, K., Li, S., Prisacariu, V.: Dual-resolution correspondence networks. Adv. Neural. Inf. Process. Syst. **33**, 17346–17357 (2020)

32. Li, Z., et al.: Revisiting stereo depth estimation from a sequence-to-sequence perspective with transformers. In: Proceedings of International Conference on Computer Vision (ICCV), pp. 6197–6206 (2021)

33. Lichtsteiner, P., Posch, C., Delbruck, T.: A 128 × 128 120 dB 15 μs latency asynchronous temporal contrast vision sensor. IEEE J. Solid-State Circuits **43**(2), 566–576 (2008)

34. Lin, T.Y., Dollár, P., Girshick, R., He, K., Hariharan, B., Belongie, S.: Feature pyramid networks for object detection. In: Proceedings of Conference on Computer Vision and Pattern Recognition (CVPR), pp. 2117–2125 (2017)

35. Lowe, D.G.: Object recognition from local scale-invariant features. In: Proceedings of International Conference on Computer Vision (ICCV), vol. 2, pp. 1150–1157 (1999)
36. Lowe, D.G.: Distinctive image features from scale-invariant keypoints 60(2), 91–110 (2004)
37. Maqueda, A.I., Loquercio, A., Gallego, G., García, N., Scaramuzza, D.: Event-based vision meets deep learning on steering prediction for self-driving cars. In: Proceedings of Conference on Computer Vision and Pattern Recognition (CVPR) (2018)
38. Mostafavi Isfahani, S.M., Nam, Y., Choi, J., Yoon, K.J.: E2SRI: learning to super-resolve intensity images from events. IEEE Trans. Pattern Anal. Mach. Intell. 44, 6890–6909 (2021)
39. Mueggler, E., Rebecq, H., Gallego, G., Delbruck, T., Scaramuzza, D.: The event-camera dataset and simulator: Event-based data for pose estimation, visual odometry, and SLAM. Int. J. Rob. Res. 36(2), 142–149 (2017)
40. Muglikar, M., Gehrig, M., Gehrig, D., Scaramuzza, D.: How to calibrate your event camera. In: Proceedings of Conference on Computer Vision and Pattern Recognition (CVPR), pp. 1403–1409 (2021)
41. Neira, J., Tardós, J.D.: Data association in stochastic mapping using the joint compatibility test. IEEE Trans. Robot. Autom. 17(6), 890–897 (2001)
42. Piatkowska, E., Kogler, J., Belbachir, N., Gelautz, M.: Improved cooperative stereo matching for dynamic vision sensors with ground truth evaluation. In: Proceedings of the IEEE Conference on Computer Vision and Pattern Recognition Workshops, pp. 53–60 (2017)
43. Rebecq, H., Gallego, G., Mueggler, E., Scaramuzza, D.: EMVS: event-based multi-view stereo-3D reconstruction with an event camera in real-time. Int. J. Comput. Vision 126(12), 1394–1414 (2018)
44. Rebecq, H., Ranftl, R., Koltun, V., Scaramuzza, D.: Events-to-video: bringing modern computer vision to event cameras. In: Proceedings of Conference on Computer Vision and Pattern Recognition (CVPR), pp. 3857–3866 (2019)
45. Rocco, I., Cimpoi, M., Arandjelović, R., Torii, A., Pajdla, T., Sivic, J.: Neighbour-hood consensus networks. In: Advances in Neural Information Processing Systems, vol. 31 (2018)
46. Ronneberger, O., Fischer, P., Brox, T.: U-net: convolutional networks for biomedical image segmentation. In: Navab, N., Hornegger, J., Wells, W.M., Frangi, A.F. (eds.) MICCAI 2015. LNCS, vol. 9351, pp. 234–241. Springer, Cham (2015). https://doi.org/10.1007/978-3-319-24574-4_28
47. Rublee, E., Rabaud, V., Konolige, K., Bradski, G.: ORB: an efficient alternative to sift or surf. In: Proceedings of International Conference on Computer Vision (ICCV), pp. 2564–2571 (2011)
48. Rueckauer, B., Delbruck, T.: Evaluation of event-based algorithms for optical flow with ground-truth from inertial measurement sensor. Front. Neurosci. 10, 176 (2016)
49. Sarlin, P.E., DeTone, D., Malisiewicz, T., Rabinovich, A.: SuperGlue: learning feature matching with graph neural networks. In: Proceedings of Conference on Computer Vision and Pattern Recognition (CVPR), pp. 4938–4947 (2020)
50. Sun, D., Yang, X., Liu, M.Y., Kautz, J.: PWC-Net: CNNs for optical flow using pyramid, warping, and cost volume. In: Proceedings of Conference on Computer Vision and Pattern Recognition (CVPR), pp. 8934–8943 (2018)

51. Sun, J., Shen, Z., Wang, Y., Bao, H., Zhou, X.: LoFTR: detector-free local feature matching with transformers. In: Proceedings of Conference on Computer Vision and Pattern Recognition (CVPR), pp. 8922–8931 (2021)
52. Tardós, J.D., Neira, J., Newman, P.M., Leonard, J.J.: Robust mapping and localization in indoor environments using sonar data. Int. J. Rob. Res. **21**(4), 311–330 (2002)
53. Thrun, S., Burgard, W., Fox, D.: A probabilistic approach to concurrent mapping and localization for mobile robots. Auton. Robot. **5**(3), 253–271 (1998)
54. Tulyakov, S., Fleuret, F., Kiefel, M., Gehler, P., Hirsch, M.: Learning an event sequence embedding for dense event-based deep stereo. In: Proceedings of International Conference on Computer Vision (ICCV), pp. 1527–1537 (2019)
55. Tulyakov, S., et al.: Time Lens: event-based video frame interpolation. In: Proceedings of Conference on Computer Vision and Pattern Recognition (CVPR) (2021)
56. Vaswani, A., et al.: Attention is all you need. In: Advances in Neural Information Processing Systems, vol. 30 (2017)
57. Vidal, A.R., Rebecq, H., Horstschaefer, T., Scaramuzza, D.: Ultimate SLAM? Combining events, images, and IMU for robust visual SLAM in HDR and high-speed scenarios. IEEE Rob. Autom. Lett. **3**(2), 994–1001 (2018)
58. Wang, Z., Pan, L., Ng, Y., Zhuang, Z., Mahony, R.: Stereo hybrid event-frame (SHEF) cameras for 3D perception. In: 2021 IEEE/RSJ International Conference on Intelligent Robots and Systems (IROS), pp. 9758–9764 (2021)
59. Weikersdorfer, D., Adrian, D.B., Cremers, D., Conradt, J.: Event-based 3D SLAM with a depth-augmented dynamic vision sensor. In: 2014 IEEE International Conference on Robotics and Automation (ICRA), pp. 359–364 (2014)
60. Yi, K.M., Trulls, E., Lepetit, V., Fua, P.: LIFT: learned invariant feature transform. In: Leibe, B., Matas, J., Sebe, N., Welling, M. (eds.) ECCV 2016. LNCS, vol. 9910, pp. 467–483. Springer, Cham (2016). https://doi.org/10.1007/978-3-319-46466-4_28
61. Zhou, Y., Gallego, G., Rebecq, H., Kneip, L., Li, H., Scaramuzza, D.: Semi-dense 3D reconstruction with a stereo event camera. In: Ferrari, V., Hebert, M., Sminchisescu, C., Weiss, Y. (eds.) ECCV 2018. LNCS, vol. 11205, pp. 242–258. Springer, Cham (2018). https://doi.org/10.1007/978-3-030-01246-5_15
62. Zhou, Y., Gallego, G., Shen, S.: Event-based stereo visual odometry. IEEE Trans. Rob. **37**(5), 1433–1450 (2021)
63. Zhu, A.Z., Chen, Y., Daniilidis, K.: Realtime time synchronized event-based stereo. In: Ferrari, V., Hebert, M., Sminchisescu, C., Weiss, Y. (eds.) ECCV 2018. LNCS, vol. 11210, pp. 438–452. Springer, Cham (2018). https://doi.org/10.1007/978-3-030-01231-1_27
64. Zhu, A.Z., Thakur, D., Özaslan, T., Pfrommer, B., Kumar, V., Daniilidis, K.: The multivehicle stereo event camera dataset: an event camera dataset for 3D perception. IEEE Rob. Autom. Lett. **3**(3), 2032–2039 (2018)
65. Zhu, A.Z., Yuan, L., Chaney, K., Daniilidis, K.: EV-FlowNet: self-supervised optical flow estimation for event-based cameras. In: Proceedings of Robotics: Science and Systems (2018)
66. Zou, D., et al: Robust dense depth map estimation from sparse DVS stereos. In: Proceedings of British Machine Vision Conference (BMVC), vol. 1 (2017)
67. Zuo, Y.F., et al.: Accurate depth estimation from a hybrid event-RGB stereo setup. In: 2021 IEEE/RSJ International Conference on Intelligent Robots and Systems (IROS), pp. 6833–6840

D2HNet: Joint Denoising and Deblurring with Hierarchical Network for Robust Night Image Restoration

Yuzhi Zhao[1]([✉]), Yongzhe Xu[2], Qiong Yan[2], Dingdong Yang[2], Xuehui Wang[3], and Lai-Man Po[1]

[1] Department of Electrical Engineering, City University of Hong Kong, Hong Kong, China
yzzhao2-c@my.cityu.edu.hk, eelmpo@cityu.edu.hk
[2] SenseTime Research and Tetras.AI, Shenzhen, China
{xuyongzhe1,yanqiong,yangdingdong}@tetras.ai
[3] MoE Key Lab of Artificial Intelligence, AI Institute, Shanghai Jiao Tong University, Shanghai, China
wangxuehui@sjtu.edu.cn

Abstract. Night imaging with modern smartphone cameras is troublesome due to low photon count and unavoidable noise in the imaging system. Directly adjusting exposure time and ISO ratings cannot obtain sharp and noise-free images at the same time in low-light conditions. Though many methods have been proposed to enhance noisy or blurry night images, their performances on real-world night photos are still unsatisfactory due to two main reasons: 1) Limited information in a single image and 2) Domain gap between synthetic training images and real-world photos (e.g., differences in blur area and resolution). To exploit the information from successive long- and short-exposure images, we propose a learning-based pipeline to fuse them. A D2HNet framework is developed to recover a high-quality image by deblurring and enhancing a long-exposure image under the guidance of a short-exposure image. To shrink the domain gap, we leverage a two-phase DeblurNet-EnhanceNet architecture, which performs accurate blur removal on a fixed low resolution so that it is able to handle large ranges of blur in different resolution inputs. In addition, we synthesize a D2-Dataset from HD videos and experiment on it. The results on the validation set and real photos demonstrate our methods achieve better visual quality and state-of-the-art quantitative scores. The D2HNet codes and D2-Dataset can be found at https://github.com/zhaoyuzhi/D2HNet.

Keywords: Night image restoration · Image denoising · Image deblurring · Domain gap issue

---

Supplementary Information The online version contains supplementary material available at https://doi.org/10.1007/978-3-031-20071-7_6.

1   Introduction

Capturing high-quality photos at night-time on modern smartphones is troublesome due to the limitations of sensors and optical systems. It is a long-standing and practical problem in the computational photography field. Acquiring sharp and clean photos effectively and efficiently on smartphones in night conditions is in great demand. The main difficulty lies in that the image signal is too weak compared with the inherent noise in the imaging process, which yields a low signal-to-noise ratio (SNR) and degrades image quality [41,42,70]. To obtain higher SNR, there are many solutions either on the hardware level (in-camera solutions) or algorithm level, which typically fall into one of these three categories: 1) *Physical solutions*: using a larger sensor, opening the aperture, using flash, or setting longer exposure time; 2) *Single-image restoration*: deblurring the long-exposure image with motion blurs, or denoising the short-exposure image with severe noises; 3) *Burst-image restoration*: combining several photos captured in quick succession using temporal coherence within the burst.

Though these solutions improve the night image restoration quality, they might not meet the requirements of both *effectiveness* and *efficiency* for mobile photography. For *physical solutions*, larger sensor size and aperture are related to hardware design and increase the cost. The built-in flash does not help for far scenes. Long exposure time causes motion blur. To post-process the captured images, *single-image restoration* methods have been widely studied, e.g., training neural networks [36,90] on a large number of paired degraded-clean images. However, a single input image contains limited information thus restricting the restoration quality. To use more information, *burst-image restoration* methods [46,49] combine multiple continuous frames to generate a single good image. Though they have a theoretically superior SNR than single-image restoration methods, the speed is restricted by the capturing process, including multiple exposure and readout time. Meanwhile, the misalignment issue has to be solved for all captured frames. In addition, the data distribution gap (e.g., differences in blur area, resolution) between training and real images remains a key problem.

In this paper, we tackle this real-world problem by post-processing successive long- and short-exposure images through a D2HNet framework. It can produce clean and sharp photographs on mobile devices without any manual control or extra hardware support. Compared with the previous image restoration approaches, our approach has three main advantages: 1) Taking advantage of both long and short exposures; 2) Addressing the domain gap issue between training data and real-world photos by a special two-phase network; 3) Balancing image processing quality and capturing time (only 2 long- and short-exposure images are needed).

Normally, long-exposure images have regular color and fewer noises and short-exposure images are of trivial blurs. Compared with single-image restoration [36,90], fusing them helps reduce the noise level and blurriness, and improve color fidelity for night photos. Compared with burst-image restoration methods [46,49], two shots have milder misalignment issues and require a shorter capturing time. Built upon these observations, we propose the D2HNet framework.

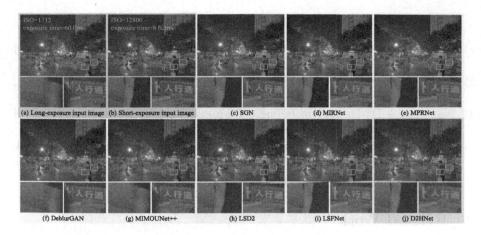

Fig. 1. Performance on real-world night photos. Input photos captured by *Xiaomi Mi Note 10* smartphone are shown in (a) and (b). Results from single image denoising methods are in (c)–(e). Results from single image deblurring methods are in (f) and (g). Results from long-short fusion methods (including our D2HNet) are in (h)–(j).

To address the domain gap between training data and real photos captured by different smartphones, we split D2HNet into sequential subnets: *DeblurNet* and *EnhanceNet*. DeblurNet runs on a small resolution at the training and a fixed resolution at the testing similar to training images. It ensures pixel shifts or blur levels between training and real-world images are comparable; therefore, the network generalizes better to different image resolutions and blur areas. EnhanceNet enhances the DeblurNet output on actual target resolutions together with short- and long-exposure inputs. We use deformable convolutions [18] in the EnhanceNet to align the features hierarchically to better extract the details and textures from the long-exposure input. In addition, we propose a *CutNoise scheme* to assist the learning of where and how to deblur and a *VarmapSelection scheme* to balance blurry and non-blurry patches during training.

To evaluate the capability of D2HNet, we synthesize a D2-Dataset from HD videos for training and validation. It contains 6853 tuples of long- and short-exposure images with corresponding sharp ground truth. It covers a wide range of scenes, e.g., cities, villages, forests, deserts, and mountains. We also capture 28 pairs of long- and short-exposure photos of real-world scenes by a smartphone for testing. Extensive experiments on both D2-Dataset and real captured photos show the state-of-the-art (SOTA) performance achieved by the proposed D2HNet. One real sample is shown in Fig. 1. D2HNet can produce clean and sharp images simultaneously, while the other methods fail to do so. It demonstrates that D2HNet better utilizes the information of dual-exposure images.

Below we summarize the main contributions of this paper:

1) We propose a two-phase D2HNet for robust real night image restoration and to address the domain gap issue between training data and real photos;
2) We propose two data augmentation schemes, CutNoise and VarmapSelection, to improve and stabilize the training of D2HNet;
3) We create a D2-Dataset including 6853 image tuples with multiple levels of blurs for benchmarking D2HNet;
4) We conduct extensive experiments with long-short fusion methods, and single image denoising or deblurring methods. The proposed D2HNet achieves better performance than other methods.

2   Related Work

Single-image Denoising. Image denoising is a fundamental topic in image processing. Previous methods such as total variation [59], wavelet coring [60], non-local means [4], BM3D [17] assumed noises and signals have specific statistical regularities. However, these methods used hand-crafted models thus not robust to real noises. Recently, CNNs have shown their advanced performance to address blind denoising issue [13,25,43,44,48,65,90,91]. Some works further extended them to reduce real noises [2,5,10–12,14,26,29,33,38,45,82,84,85,89,93]. To better simulate noise emerged on mobile ISP, many inverse algorithms [3,77,83] and real noise calibration methods [1,71,73] were proposed.

Single-image Deblurring. Image deblurring aims to generate a sharp and clean reconstruction from a blurry input. Many classical non-blind methods formulated the problem as blind deconvolutions [35,39,56]. The blur kernels are normally assumed as noisy linear operators enforced on the clean images. Recently, CNN-based approaches [6,15,21,23,30,36,37,51–54,57,63,64,66,74, 81,88,92] proposed the end-to-end deblurring with specific network architectures and loss functions. These methods are trained on large-scale blurry-sharp pairs. However, directly applying them to real-world photos may not obtain sharp results.

Burst-image Restoration. Since the overall photon counts of burst images are more than a single image, burst-image-based methods [20,22,32,46,49,76,78, 86] have theoretically superior SNR than single-image-based methods. However, burst images suffered from noises and camera shake, which increase the difficulty of implementation. To overcome that, [22] proposed a recurrent neural network to filter noises in a sequence of images. [49] combined neural network and kernel method to perform denoising and alignment jointly. Though they restore high-quality photos, their data capture occupies a major time during application.

Image Restoration by Fusing Successive Long- and Short-Exposure Images. Image restoration with dual exposures [16,24,61,62,68,75,80] is beneficial for both noise reduction and blur estimation. For instance, Yuan et al.

[80] firstly estimated blur kernels using the texture of short-exposure images, which are then used to restore the long-exposure blurry images. Recently, LSD2 [50] and LSFNet [9] used CNNs to fuse dual-exposure images and obtained better results than single-image denoising or deblurring methods on their synthetic dataset. However, they ignored the potential domain gap issue between training images and real-world photos.

Deformable Convolution. Dai et al. [18] proposed deformable convolutions, which allows the network to obtain the information away from regular local neighborhoods by learning additional offsets. It has been widely applied in computer vision tasks such as semantic segmentation [18,94], video deblurring [69], video super-resolution [7,8,67], and video restoration [19,27]. For instance, EDVR [69] used deformable convolutions to align inputs without using explicit optical flows. For the long-short fusion problem, there normally exists a misalignment issue between input long- and short-exposure images. Also, it is difficult to compute accurate optical flows from noisy and blurry inputs. Inspired by previous methods, we adopt deformable convolutions as alignment blocks.

3   Data Acquisition

D2-Dataset. We synthesize a D2-Dataset for training and benchmarking. The data synthesis pipeline is as follows:

1) We collect 30 HD videos with 1440×2560 resolution from the Internet. They are almost noise-free and cover a wide range of scenes. We sample 60 continuous frames (approximately 1 s in original 60-fps videos) every 10 s in each video to reduce repeated scenes and avoid scene switching;
2) We use a video frame interpolation model SuperSloMo [31] to increase the original 60-fps videos to 960 fps. It smooths videos to simulate realistic blurs;
3) We synthesize successive long-exposure image l and short-exposure image s by averaging interpolated frames. Meantime, we add a time gap between l and s to model hardware readout limitation. We also extract corresponding sharp single frames, i.e., the last frame of long-exposure image l_{last} and the first frame of short-exposure image s_{first}.

The pipeline results in 6853 image tuples (l, s, l_{last}, and s_{first}), where 5661 tuples are used for training and 1192 for validation. More details are presented in the supplementary material.

Testing Images. We capture 28 pairs of long- and short-exposure images with resolution 3472×4624 using a *Xiaomi Mi Note 10 smartphone*. To ensure the overall brightness of long- and short-exposure images are approximately the same, we set "ISO×exposure time" of them equal. Specifically, the exposure time of the long-exposure image is set to be 8 times of short-exposure time while its ISO is $1/8$ of the short-exposure image.

4   Methodology

4.1   Problem Formulation

Given paired noisy long- and short-exposure images denoted as l_n and s_n, we aim to recover a sharp and clean image z. We formulate it as maximizing a posteriori of the output conditioned on inputs and D2HNet parameters Θ:

$$\Theta^* = \arg\max_{\Theta} p(z|l_n, s_n, \Theta). \tag{1}$$

We train our network on the proposed D2-Dataset. From it we use l, s pair to generate noisy training inputs l_n, s_n, and s_{first} as ground truth of z here.

4.2   D2HNet Architecture and Optimization

Workflow. The workflow of D2HNet is illustrated in Fig. 2. To address the domain gap issue between synthetic training images and real-world photos (e.g.,

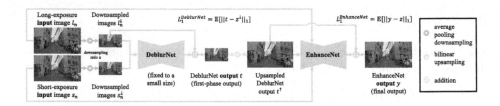

Fig. 2. Illustration of the D2HNet workflow.

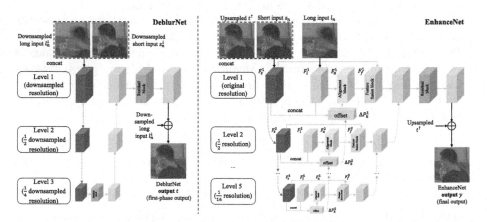

Fig. 3. Illustration of DeblurNet (left) and EnhanceNet (right). Alignment blocks, Feature fusion blocks, and Residual blocks are noted in the figure while the remaining blocks are normal convolutional layers. Offsets are learnable and as parts of Alignment blocks. Images t and y are the outputs of DeblurNet and EnhanceNet, respectively.

different resolutions and blur levels), we use a two-phase structure in our work-flow. In phase one, the two inputs are downsampled into a smaller and fixed resolution, so that motion scales and pixel shifts in the long-exposure image are restricted. Then, the DeblurNet with a certain receptive field can perform accurate deblurring based on the edge information in the short-exposure image. In phase two, to enhance the details lost during downsampling, the EnhanceNet post-process the upsampled first-phase network output together with long-short inputs in their original resolution.

DeblurNet. For the input data, DeblurNet receives the downsampled long- and short-exposure input images with a downsampling ratio α. At the training, α is set to $1/2$; while at the testing, the input resolution is fixed to 1024×1024. Therefore, the domain gap is reduced since the motion scales of testing images are controlled. We use the average pooling as the downsampling operator at both training and testing stages as it mimics the physical differences between low- and high-resolution images better. For the network architecture, DeblurNet uses 3 levels to extract features since it better balances the deblurring quality and computational complexity, where DWT [43] is used as the downsampling operator. There are two Residual blocks at the bottleneck and at the tail respectively, where each block includes 4 sequential residual layers [28]. The output t is upsampled by bilinear sampling and then as the input for the next phase, i.e., EnhanceNet.

EnhanceNet. The target of EnhanceNet is to recover the details (mostly from long-exposure input) and further remove artifacts for the upsampled Deblur-Net output $t^\uparrow$. As shown in Fig. 3, EnhanceNet has 3 modules: feature pyramid extraction (green blocks), alignment and feature fusion (pink and yellow blocks), and reconstruction (blue blocks).

The feature pyramid extraction has two branches without sharing weights. The output two feature pyramids have 5 levels, denoted as F_s^1-F_s^5 and F_l^1-F_l^5, respectively. Since inputs $s_n/y^\uparrow$ and l_n are not spatially aligned, we perform the alignment for long-exposure features (F_l^1-F_l^5) by Alignment blocks, where we use the modulated deformable convolution [94]. Alignment blocks allow the following layers to better fuse the information of two feature pyramids. Here we give a brief introduction for the modulated deformable convolution. As we have known, a 3×3 convolution kernel of dilation 1 has learnable weights $w_k \in \{1, ..., K\}$ and fixed offsets $p_k \in \{(-1,-1),(-1,0),(-1,1),(0,-1),(0,0),(0,1),(1,-1),(1,0),(1,1)\}$, where $K = 9$. Then for the modulated deformable convolution, there are learnable parameters, offsets Δp_k^i and modulation scalars Δm_k^i for each location p_k. The offsets Δp_k^i are real numbers and the modulation scalars Δm_k^i are in range of $[0, 1]$. Therefore, for such convolution result on i-th long-exposure feature F_l^i can be expressed as:

$$F_a^i(p) = \sum_{k=1}^{K} w_k^i \cdot F_l^i(p + p_k + \Delta p_k^i) \cdot \Delta m_k^i. \tag{2}$$

The modulation scalars and learnable offsets (pink blocks in Fig. 3) are learned from short- and long-exposure features hierarchically. For simplicity, we only express the learnable offsets from a series of convolutional layers c^i as:

$$\Delta P_k^i = \begin{cases} c^i(F_s^i, F_l^i, \Delta P_k^{i+1}), & i = 1, 2, 3, 4 \\ c^i(F_s^i, F_l^i), & i = 5 \end{cases} \tag{3}$$

where $\Delta P_k^i = \{\Delta p_k^i\}$. The deepest 5-th level ΔP_k^5 is first computed. Since the misalignment between two features F_s^i and F_l^i of the deepest level is small [21], the learning of offsets is relatively accurate and less challenging. We then pass the learned offsets to the upper levels to learn more precise offsets. This process is done level-by-level as a hierarchical refinement [9,47,69].

After long-exposure features F_l^1-F_l^5 are aligned, we perform the feature fusion. In i-th level's Feature fusion block, the aligned features F_a^i and short-exposure features F_s^i are concatenated and then processed by a Residual block r^i as:

$$F_f^i = r^i(F_s^i, F_a^i), \tag{4}$$

where the output features F_f^5 are connected to the first decoder layer, while F_f^1-F_f^4 serve as short-cut connections like in UNet [58]. Finally, we use a Residual block (including 4 residual layers) at the tail to further refine the features at the original resolution. The final output is added to $t^\uparrow$.

Loss. We first train DeblurNet and then train EnhanceNet. The L1 loss [90] is used for training them, as shown in Fig. 2. They are expressed as:

$$L_1^{DeblurNet} = \mathbb{E}[||t - z^\downarrow||_1], \quad L_1^{EnhanceNet} = \mathbb{E}[||y - z||_1], \tag{5}$$

where $z^\downarrow$ is the average pooling downsampled result from the ground truth z to match the resolution of t.

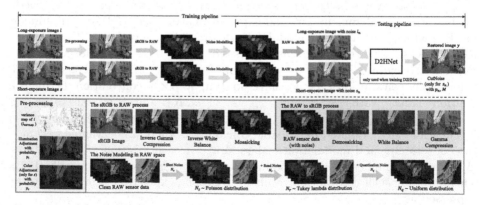

Fig. 4. Illustration of detailed procedures of training and testing pipelines (upper) and examples of every step of data processing procedures (lower).

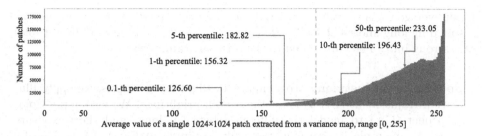

Fig. 5. Variance map patch distribution on D2-Dataset. The 5-th percentile point 182.82 is set as the threshold. If the average of a variance map patch is lower than 182.82, its corresponding long-exposure patch is regarded to be highly blurry.

4.3   Data Processing

The data processing is a key process for training the D2HNet, which includes VarmapSelection, Appearance Adjustment, Noise Modeling, and CutNoise, as shown in Fig. 4. It is designed to better model the real image distortion and balance the training data distribution.

VarmapSelection. It is a variance-map-based selection scheme to address the imbalanced blurriness issue and improve the robustness of D2HNet. Since most regions of the simulated long-exposure image l are of low levels of blur, simply randomly choosing patches at the training causes loss fluctuation and ineffective deblurring ability for large motion. VarmapSelection scheme uses the variance map to represent the blur level and choose larger motion patches for training. The variance map is calculated from both l and l_{last} as:

$$l_{varmap} = \min(\mathrm{Var}(l))/\mathrm{Var}(l_{last}), 1), \qquad (6)$$

where Var computes the variance using a $k \times k$ window, with stride k. The resulted map is $1/k \times 1/k$ of the original size, so we upsample it with the nearest interpolation. According to the definition, a smaller value means higher levels of blur. One example variance map is shown in the pink rectangle of Fig. 4, where the blurrier regions in l have clearer (darker) responses in l_{varmap}.

To determine whether a randomly chosen patch is of a large blur, we choose to define a threshold based on variance statistics on the training set. For each variance map, we randomly sample 1000 different squares of size 1024×1024 and calculate the average variance value for each square. Then, we sort all values across the dataset and use the 5-th percentile point as the threshold, as shown in Fig. 5. Afterward, we do sampling again, keep only the squares that have lower average variance values than the threshold and draw patches from the corresponding long-short-GT tuples. This process results in additional 9453 tuples of a strong blur. They are added to the original training set.

Appearance Adjustment. To simulate low-light image tuples, we apply Illumination Adjustment (IA) to lower the overall brightness. We also apply Color Adjustment (CA) to model the difference between long- and short-exposure images. An example is shown in the pink rectangle of Fig. 4. IA is done by an inverse gamma compression for long-short-GT tuples, as follows:

$$IA(u) = \max(u, \varepsilon)^g, \text{ for } u \in \{s, l, z\}, \tag{7}$$

where $\varepsilon = 10^{-8}$. The gamma value g is randomly chosen from [1/0.6, 1/0.7, 1/0.75, 1/0.8, 1/0.9]. CA is achieved by a linear transform to disturb the overall color and brightness for only the short-exposure image s. It is defined as:

$$CA(s) = a \cdot s + b, \tag{8}$$

where a and b are sampled uniformly from [0.3, 0.6] and [0.001, 0.01], respectively.

Noise Modeling. We calibrate real smartphone noises in the RAW image space following [73] and then apply the noise simulation. Since our D2-dataset contains only sRGB images, we adopt a simple reverse ISP process [3] to convert them from sRGB to RAW. It includes an inverse gamma compression (as in Eq. 7 with $g = 2.2$), an inverse white balance which simply scales R and B channels by scalar $1/w_r, 1/w_b$ separately, and the mosaic to form Bayer pattern. Note white balance gain for the G channel (w_g) is fixed to 1, while w_r and w_b are sampled uniformly from [1.9, 2.4] and [1.5, 1.9], respectively. After noise modeling, we then convert it to sRGB by a forward ISP process with corresponding parameters for inversion. The noise model is calibrated on the *Xiaomi Mi Note 10*, which we use to capture real photos.

CutNoise. To encourage the fusion and utilization of the short-exposure image, inspired by [79], we design the CutNoise scheme. It is performed after noise simulation on the short-exposure image which has stronger noise. CutNoise randomly selects a region and copies ground truth z (i.e., s_{first}) to the corresponding position of s_n. The region itself can be any shape but we fix it to square for easy implementation. With CutNoise, D2HNet will not degenerate to use only the blurrier long-exposure input but is forced to learn to fuse information from the sharper short-exposure one, therefore generating sharper output.

Table 1. Comparisons of D2HNet and other methods on D2-Dataset validation set by PSNR and SSIM [72]. The red and blue colors denote the best and second-best results, respectively.

Method	1440p val data		2880p val data	
	PSNR	SSIM	PSNR	SSIM
DenseFuse [40]	32.90	0.9484	34.70	0.9637
LSD2 [50]	33.20	0.9517	35.36	0.9675
LSFNet [9]	33.87	0.9557	36.17	0.9715
DeblurGAN [36]	33.80	0.9558	36.26	0.9701
SGN [25]	33.87	0.9567	36.25	0.9720
TP1	34.35	0.9628	36.66	0.9755
TP2	34.26	0.9599	36.54	0.9733
TP3	34.41	0.9611	36.70	0.9747
D2HNet	34.67	0.9639	36.85	0.9767

Table 2. The results of the human perceptual study on real photos for the D2HNet and other pipelines, given by preference rates (PR) for D2HNet over all the votes.

Method	PR
D2HNet > DenseFuse, LSD2, LSFNet DeblurGAN, SGN	86.07%
D2HNet > TP1	82.50%
D2HNet > TP2	81.07%
D2HNet > TP3	79.28%

5 Experiment

5.1 Implementation Details

Our training samples include original 5661 tuples of full-resolution images from the D2-Dataset and 9453 tuples of strong blurry patches selected by the VarmapSelection scheme. For DeblurNet, the input resolution is fixed to 512×512 by average pooling. The epochs are 100 and the learning rate is initialized as 1×10^{-4}. For EnhanceNet, the input resolution is 256×256 randomly cropped patches due to memory limit. The epochs are 150 and the learning rate is initialized as 5×10^{-5}. For both subnets, the learning rates are halved every 50 epochs. The batch size equals 2 and an epoch includes 5661 iterations, corresponding to the number of training tuples. The Adam optimizer [34] with $\beta_1 = 0.5$ and $\beta_2 = 0.999$ is used. The probabilities of performing Illumination Adjustment, Color Adjustment, and CutNoise are set to 0.3, 0.5, and 0.3, respectively. The size of the CutNoise square is 120. We implement the D2HNet with PyTorch 1.1.0 and train it on 2 Titan Xp GPUs. It takes approximately 2 weeks to complete the optimization.

5.2 Long-short Fusion Method Experiments

We compare the image restoration quality of D2HNet and other recent works with similar target, DenseFuse [40], LSD2 [50], and LSFNet [9], or with SOTA performance in either denoising or deblurring, SGN [25], DeblurGAN [36] (see more in Sect. 5.3). To fit the dual inputs, SGN's and DeblurGAN's input layers are changed to receive two images. In addition, we define three more two-phase pipelines for a more comprehensive evaluation: 1) image denoising by SGN + long-short fusion by SGN (denoted as TP1); 2) image deblurring by DeblurGAN

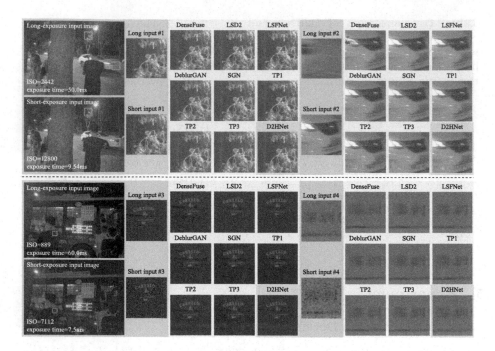

Fig. 6. Visual comparisons of the proposed D2HNet with other methods. More results on both real photos and validation images are in the supplementary material.

+ long-short fusion by SGN (denoted as TP2); 3) long-short fusion by SGN + long-short fusion refinement by SGN (the same workflow as D2HNet, denoted as TP3). The same data processing schemes are applied to other methods.

We illustrate the generated samples on real photos in Fig. 6. From image pairs ♯1 and ♯3, the black backgrounds of D2HNet results are cleaner than other methods, e.g., obvious artifacts in results of DenseFuse, DeblurGAN, and TP1-TP3. It demonstrates that D2HNet has a better denoising ability for inputs. For image pair ♯2, D2HNet can generate a clean and sharp result from extreme blurry inputs, while maintaining the denoising ability of dark regions; however, there lie in artifacts in the dark regions of others. From image pairs ♯3 and ♯4, we can see D2HNet has better edge preservation ability compared with others, e.g., letters and Chinese characters are sharper and cleaner.

The quantitative analysis is concluded in Table 1. Compared with other single-phase methods, D2HNet obtains 0.80–1.77 db PSNR gain on 1440p. It also outperforms the simple concatenated methods (TP1-TP3) on both 1440p and 2880p, which demonstrates that D2HNet is more robust to different input resolutions. Since there is no ground truth for real photos, we conduct a human perceptual study on the results generated from different methods and there are 10 observers. In each comparison, a user is presented with a pair of restored images side by side of a shuffled sequence. Then, the user chooses one result that produces cleaner and sharper images than others. The preference rates (PRs)

Table 3. Comparisons of D2HNet and other single image denoising methods.

Method	1440p val data		2880p val data	
	PSNR	SSIM	PSNR	SSIM
DnCNN [90]	32.20	0.9192	33.61	0.9265
MemNet [65]	33.74	0.9517	35.73	0.9644
MWCNN [43]	32.47	0.9372	34.71	0.9554
SGN [25]	33.94	0.9576	36.42	0.9713
RIDNet [2]	33.29	0.9462	35.55	0.9621
MIRNet [84]	33.98	0.9565	36.36	0.9708
REDI [38]	28.60	0.8964	31.54	0.9431
DeamNet [55]	33.78	0.9531	36.26	0.9685
MPRNet [85]	34.00	0.9568	36.25	0.9712
D2HNet	34.67	0.9639	36.85	0.9767

Table 4. Comparisons of D2HNet and other single image deblurring methods.

Method	1440p val data		2880p val data	
	PSNR	SSIM	PSNR	SSIM
DeepDeblur [51]	23.51	0.8252	23.80	0.8731
SRN [66]	23.99	0.8363	24.11	0.8780
DeblurGAN [36]	24.23	0.8399	24.13	0.8749
DeblurGANv2 [37]	23.88	0.8059	23.67	0.8359
DMPHN [87]	21.73	0.7807	22.38	0.8447
MPRNet [85]	22.97	0.8072	22.61	0.8438
HINet [12]	22.39	0.7586	21.93	0.7879
MIMOUNet [15]	21.11	0.7756	21.19	0.8355
MIMOUNet++ [15]	21.10	0.7753	21.25	0.8373
D2HNet	34.67	0.9639	36.85	0.9767

are concluded in Table 2, where there are 79.28%–86.07% votes for D2HNet. The majority of users thought that D2HNet achieves higher image quality than compared methods. It demonstrates that D2HNet recovers images with better details and textures and well addresses the domain gap issue.

5.3 Single-Image Denoising and Deblurring Method Experiments

We compare D2HNet and SOTA image denoising [2,25,38,43,55,65,84,85,90] and deblurring [12,15,36,37,51,66,85,87] methods. Short-exposure images serve as inputs for denoising methods and s_{first} is ground truth. Long-exposure images serve as inputs for deblurring methods and l_{last} is ground truth.

We illustrate the generated samples on real photos in Fig. 7. From ♯1 and ♯2, single image denoising methods cannot restore details of the roof (♯1) and the textures of curtains (♯2). However, D2HNet produces richer details since it fuses the information from the long-exposure input, where the textures are more distinguishable than the highly noisy short-exposure input. From ♯3 and ♯4, single image deblurring methods cannot recover either small blur or severe blur. The superiority of D2HNet comes from two reasons. On one hand, although the other methods estimate motion fields from a single long-exposure input, D2HNet utilizes the position information from the short-exposure input to guide the deblurring. On the other hand, a domain gap exists between training and testing data. Without proper handling, these methods degrade to mainly removing noises when encountering very large blurs in the testing images. Whereas, our architecture involves the DeblurNet which operates on a fixed resolution to better generalize on large blur. We also report the quantitative performance of all methods on the validation set in Tables 3 and 4. Compared with single-image-based methods, D2HNet obtains giant increases on both metrics since it fuses more information from both long- and short-exposure inputs.

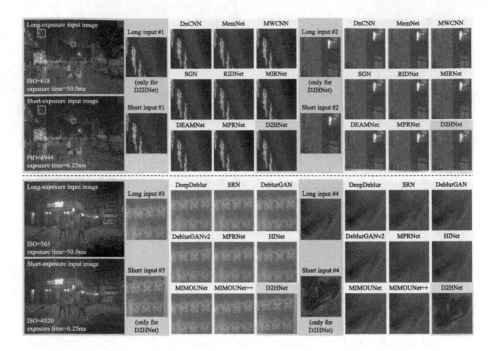

Fig. 7. Visual comparisons of the proposed D2HNet with single image denoising methods (upper ♮1 and ♮2) and single image deblurring methods (lower ♮3 and ♮4).

5.4   Ablation Study

We conduct the ablation study for the D2HNet, where the benchmark results are concluded in Table 5 and visual results are illustrated in Fig. 8[1]. The analysis for different ablation study items is as follows:

Training Strategy. Dual inputs are significant for D2HNet to get more performance gain. Compared with only using long- or short-exposure input (settings 1) and 2)), two inputs improve PSNR by 9.68 dB and 0.59 dB, respectively. Aligning the long-exposure input with short-exposure input (i.e., s_{first} as GT) also helps transfer textures from long-exposure input, which brings 4.51 db gain compared with l_{last} as GT (setting 3)). We can also see settings 1–3) cannot recover the details and remove artifacts (e.g., the face contour and eyes in ♮1).

Network Components. Alignment block makes the D2HNet better fuses features from the long-exposure input. In setting 4), we replace deformable convolutions with ordinary convolutions, forcing the network to apply rigid filters at all the spatial locations in the features, which brings a decrease of 0.24 db. In setting 5), we remove all Alignment and Feature fusion blocks, leading to a notable

---

[1] We thank Chao Wang in the SenseTime Research for helping capture the image.

performance decrease of EnhanceNet (1.4 db) since the hierarchical information is excluded. From settings 6) and 7), the tail Residual block brings 0.5 db gain, while the full EnhanceNet brings 4.19 db gain since it learns rich textures and details. In addition, settings 4–7) produce blurry outputs and vague details (i.e., the billboard in ♯2), which show the importance of every component.

Data Processing Schemes. VarmapSelection balances the training data distribution, where D2HNet better generalizes to blurry or misaligned long-exposure inputs and learns to extract textures from them, e.g., D2HNet produces sharper results than setting 8) in ♯2. Illumination Adjustment generates more low-brightness training images, helping the D2HNet obtain better performance in dark regions. Color Adjustment and CutNoise balance the usage of long-short inputs, encouraging sharper results. As shown in ♯3, if dropping each of them (settings 9–11)), the network cannot recover clear details of the black hair. Also, settings 8–11) result in the decreases of PSNR by 0.43 db, 0.36 db, 0.09 db, and 0.25 db, respectively. It is obvious that every data processing scheme is significant.

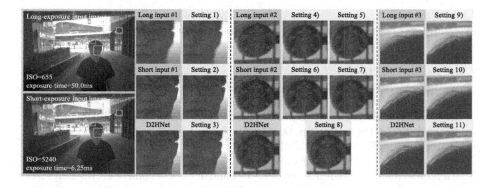

Fig. 8. Visual comparisons of D2HNet ablation study.

Table 5. Comparisons of D2HNet and ablation settings on 1440p validation data.

Ablation Study Setting	PSNR	SSIM	Ablation Study Setting	PSNR	SSIM
1) Only long input, l_{last} as ground truth	24.99	0.8610	7) w/o EnhanceNet (only DeblurNet)	30.48	0.9259
2) Only short input	34.08	0.9579	8) w/o VarmapSelection	34.24	0.9604
3) Long-short inputs, l_{last} as ground truth	30.16	0.9293	9) w/o Illumination Adjustment	34.31	0.9596
4) Replacing EnhanceNet Alignment block	34.43	0.9610	10) w/o Color Adjustment	34.58	0.9620
5) w/o EnhanceNet feature-level short-cuts	33.27	0.9530	11) w/o CutNoise	34.42	0.9616
6) w/o EnhanceNet tail Residual block	34.17	0.9602	D2HNet (full)	34.67	0.9639

6   Conclusion

In this paper, we present a D2HNet framework for robust night image restoration based on long- and short-exposure inputs. It deblurs and restores sharp outputs from the long-exposure image under the guidance of the short-exposure image to obtain accurate colors, trivial noises, and sharp edges. It includes two sequential subnets: DeblurNet to remove blur on a fixed size and EnhanceNet to refine and sharpen the output of DeblurNet. For training, we synthesize the D2-Dataset including 6853 high-quality image tuples with multiple types and levels of blur. We propose a VarmapSelection scheme to generate highly blurry patches and assist the convergence of D2HNet. We also use a CutNoise scheme to enhance textures and details by enforcing D2HNet to learn how and where to deblur. For evaluation, we compare the proposed D2HNet with SOTA long-short fusion methods, and single image denoising and deblurring methods on the D2-Dataset validation set and real-world photos. The experimental results on both validation set and real-world photos show better performance achieved by the D2HNet.

References

1. Abdelhamed, A., Brubaker, M.A., Brown, M.S.: Noise flow: noise modeling with conditional normalizing flows. In: Proceedings ICCV, pp. 3165–3173 (2019)
2. Anwar, S., Barnes, N.: Real image denoising with feature attention. In: Proceedings ICCV, pp. 3155–3164 (2019)
3. Brooks, T., Mildenhall, B., Xue, T., Chen, J., Sharlet, D., Barron, J.T.: Unprocessing images for learned raw denoising. In: Proceedings CVPR, pp. 11036–11045 (2019)
4. Buades, A., Coll, B., Morel, J.M.: A non-local algorithm for image denoising. In: Proceedings CVPR, vol. 2, pp. 60–65 (2005)
5. Byun, J., Cha, S., Moon, T.: FBI-denoiser: fast blind image denoiser for poisson-gaussian noise. In: Proceedings CVPR, pp. 5768–5777 (2021)
6. Chakrabarti, A.: A neural approach to blind motion deblurring. In: Leibe, B., Matas, J., Sebe, N., Welling, M. (eds.) ECCV 2016. LNCS, vol. 9907, pp. 221–235. Springer, Cham (2016). https://doi.org/10.1007/978-3-319-46487-9_14
7. Chan, K.C., Wang, X., Yu, K., Dong, C., Loy, C.C.: BasicVSR: the search for essential components in video super-resolution and beyond. In: Proceedings CVPR, pp. 4947–4956 (2021)
8. Chan, K.C., Zhou, S., Xu, X., Loy, C.C.: BasicVSR++: improving video super-resolution with enhanced propagation and alignment. In: Proceedings CVPR, pp. 5972–5981 (2022)
9. Chang, M., Feng, H., Xu, Z., Li, Q.: Low-light image restoration with short-and long-exposure raw pairs. IEEE Trans. Multimedia 24, 702–714 (2021)
10. Chen, C., Chen, Q., Xu, J., Koltun, V.: Learning to see in the dark. In: Proceedings CVPR, pp. 3291–3300 (2018)
11. Chen, J., Chen, J., Chao, H., Yang, M.: Image blind denoising with generative adversarial network based noise modeling. In: Proceedings CVPR, pp. 3155–3164 (2018)
12. Chen, L., Lu, X., Zhang, J., Chu, X., Chen, C.: Hinet: half instance normalization network for image restoration. In: Proceedings CVPRW, pp. 182–192 (2021)

13. Chen, Y., Pock, T.: Trainable nonlinear reaction diffusion: a flexible framework for fast and effective image restoration. IEEE Trans. Pattern Anal. Mach. Intell. **39**(6), 1256–1272 (2016)
14. Cheng, S., Wang, Y., Huang, H., Liu, D., Fan, H., Liu, S.: NbNet: noise basis learning for image denoising with subspace projection. In: Proceedings CVPR, pp. 4896–4906 (2021)
15. Cho, S.J., Ji, S.W., Hong, J.P., Jung, S.W., Ko, S.J.: Rethinking coarse-to-fine approach in single image deblurring. In: Proceedings ICCV, pp. 4641–4650 (2021)
16. Choi, B.D., Jung, S.W., Ko, S.J.: Motion-blur-free camera system splitting exposure time. IEEE Trans. Consum. Electron. **54**(3), 981–986 (2008)
17. Dabov, K., Foi, A., Katkovnik, V., Egiazarian, K.: Image denoising by sparse 3-D transform-domain collaborative filtering. IEEE Trans. Image Process. **16**(8), 2080–2095 (2007)
18. Dai, J., et al.: Deformable convolutional networks. In: Proceedings ICCV, pp. 764–773 (2017)
19. Deng, J., Wang, L., Pu, S., Zhuo, C.: Spatio-temporal deformable convolution for compressed video quality enhancement. In: Proceedings, AAAI. vol. 34, pp. 10696–10703 (2020)
20. Dudhane, A., Zamir, S.W., Khan, S., Khan, F.S., Yang, M.H.: Burst image restoration and enhancement. In: Proceedings CVPR, pp. 5759–5768 (2022)
21. Gao, H., Tao, X., Shen, X., Jia, J.: Dynamic scene deblurring with parameter selective sharing and nested skip connections. In: Proceedings CVPR, pp. 3848–3856 (2019)
22. Godard, C., Matzen, K., Uyttendaele, M.: Deep burst denoising. In: Ferrari, V., Hebert, M., Sminchisescu, C., Weiss, Y. (eds.) ECCV 2018. LNCS, vol. 11219, pp. 560–577. Springer, Cham (2018). https://doi.org/10.1007/978-3-030-01267-0_33
23. Gong, D., et al.: From motion blur to motion flow: a deep learning solution for removing heterogeneous motion blur. In: Proceedings CVPR, pp. 2319–2328 (2017)
24. Gu, C., Lu, X., He, Y., Zhang, C.: Blur removal via blurred-noisy image pair. IEEE Trans. Image Process. **30**, 345–359 (2020)
25. Gu, S., Li, Y., Gool, L.V., Timofte, R.: Self-guided network for fast image denoising. In: Proceedings ICCV, pp. 2511–2520 (2019)
26. Guo, S., Yan, Z., Zhang, K., Zuo, W., Zhang, L.: Toward convolutional blind denoising of real photographs. In: Proceedings CVPR, pp. 1712–1722 (2019)
27. Guo, S., Yang, X., Ma, J., Ren, G., Zhang, L.: A differentiable two-stage alignment scheme for burst image reconstruction with large shift. In: Proceedings CVPR, pp. 17472–17481 (2022)
28. He, K., Zhang, X., Ren, S., Sun, J.: Deep residual learning for image recognition. In: Proceedings CVPR, pp. 770–778 (2016)
29. Hu, X., et al.: Pseudo 3D auto-correlation network for real image denoising. In: Proceedings CVPR, pp. 16175–16184 (2021)
30. Ji, S.W., et al.: XYDeblur: divide and conquer for single image deblurring. In: Proceedings CVPR, pp. 17421–17430 (2022)
31. Jiang, H., Sun, D., Jampani, V., Yang, M.H., Learned-Miller, E., Kautz, J.: Super slomo: high quality estimation of multiple intermediate frames for video interpolation. In: Proceedings CVPR, pp. 9000–9008 (2018)
32. Karadeniz, A.S., Erdem, E., Erdem, A.: Burst photography for learning to enhance extremely dark images. IEEE Trans. Image Process. **30**, 9372–9385 (2021)
33. Kim, Y., Soh, J.W., Park, G.Y., Cho, N.I.: Transfer learning from synthetic to real-noise denoising with adaptive instance normalization. In: Proceedings CVPR, pp. 3482–3492 (2020)

34. Kingma, D.P., Ba, J.: Adam: a method for stochastic optimization. In: Proceedings ICLR (2014)
35. Krishnan, D., Fergus, R.: Fast image deconvolution using hyper-Laplacian priors. In: Proceedings NeurIPS, pp. 1033–1041 (2009)
36. Kupyn, O., Budzan, V., Mykhailych, M., Mishkin, D., Matas, J.: Deblurgan: blind motion deblurring using conditional adversarial networks. In: Proceedings CVPR, pp. 8183–8192 (2018)
37. Kupyn, O., Martyniuk, T., Wu, J., Wang, Z.: Deblurgan-v2: deblurring (orders-of-magnitude) faster and better. In: Proceedings ICCV, pp. 8878–8887 (2019)
38. Lamba, M., Mitra, K.: Restoring extremely dark images in real time. In: Proceedings CVPR, pp. 3487–3497 (2021)
39. Levin, A., Weiss, Y., Durand, F., Freeman, W.T.: Efficient marginal likelihood optimization in blind deconvolution. In: Proceedings CVPR, pp. 2657–2664 (2011)
40. Li, H., Wu, X.J.: DenseFuse: a fusion approach to infrared and visible images. IEEE Trans. Image Process. **28**(5), 2614–2623 (2018)
41. Li, M., Liu, J., Yang, W., Sun, X., Guo, Z.: Structure-revealing low-light image enhancement via robust retinex model. IEEE Trans. Image Process. **27**(6), 2828–2841 (2018)
42. Liba, O., et al.: Handheld mobile photography in very low light. ACM Trans. Graph. **38**(6), 1–16 (2019)
43. Liu, P., Zhang, H., Zhang, K., Lin, L., Zuo, W.: Multi-level wavelet-CNN for image restoration. In: Proceedings CVPRW, pp. 773–782 (2018)
44. Liu, W., Yan, Q., Zhao, Y.: Densely self-guided wavelet network for image denoising. In: Proceedings CVPRW, pp. 432–433 (2020)
45. Liu, Y., et al.: Invertible denoising network: a light solution for real noise removal. In: Proceedings CVPR, pp. 13365–13374 (2021)
46. Liu, Z., Yuan, L., Tang, X., Uyttendaele, M., Sun, J.: Fast burst images denoising. ACM Trans. Graph. **33**(6), 1–9 (2014)
47. Luo, Z., et al.: EBSR: feature enhanced burst super-resolution with deformable alignment. In: Proceedings CVPRW, pp. 471–478 (2021)
48. Mao, X., Shen, C., Yang, Y.B.: Image restoration using very deep convolutional encoder-decoder networks with symmetric skip connections. In: Proceedings NeurIPS, pp. 2802–2810 (2016)
49. Mildenhall, B., Barron, J.T., Chen, J., Sharlet, D., Ng, R., Carroll, R.: Burst denoising with kernel prediction networks. In: Proceedings CVPR, pp. 2502–2510 (2018)
50. Mustaniemi, J., Kannala, J., Matas, J., Särkkä, S., Heikkilä, J.: Lsd$_2$ - joint denoising and deblurring of short and long exposure images with convolutional neural networks. In: Proceedings BMVC (2020)
51. Nah, S., Hyun Kim, T., Mu Lee, K.: Deep multi-scale convolutional neural network for dynamic scene deblurring. In: Proceedings CVPR, pp. 3883–3891 (2017)
52. Nimisha, T.M., Kumar Singh, A., Rajagopalan, A.N.: Blur-invariant deep learning for blind-deblurring. In: Proceedings ICCV, pp. 4752–4760 (2017)
53. Park, D., Kang, D.U., Kim, J., Chun, S.Y.: Multi-temporal recurrent neural networks for progressive non-uniform single image deblurring with incremental temporal training. In: Vedaldi, A., Bischof, H., Brox, T., Frahm, J.-M. (eds.) ECCV 2020. LNCS, vol. 12351, pp. 327–343. Springer, Cham (2020). https://doi.org/10.1007/978-3-030-58539-6_20
54. Purohit, K., Rajagopalan, A.: Region-adaptive dense network for efficient motion deblurring. In: Proceedings AAAI, vol. 34, pp. 11882–11889 (2020)

55. Ren, C., He, X., Wang, C., Zhao, Z.: Adaptive consistency prior based deep network for image denoising. In: Proceedings CVPR, pp. 8596–8606 (2021)
56. Richardson, W.H.: Bayesian-based iterative method of image restoration. JoSA **62**(1), 55–59 (1972)
57. Rim, J., Lee, H., Won, J., Cho, S.: Real-world blur dataset for learning and benchmarking deblurring algorithms. In: Vedaldi, A., Bischof, H., Brox, T., Frahm, J.-M. (eds.) ECCV 2020. LNCS, vol. 12370, pp. 184–201. Springer, Cham (2020). https://doi.org/10.1007/978-3-030-58595-2_12
58. Ronneberger, O., Fischer, P., Brox, T.: U-net: convolutional networks for biomedical image segmentation. In: Proceedings MICCAI, pp. 234–241 (2015)
59. Rudin, L.I., Osher, S., Fatemi, E.: Nonlinear total variation based noise removal algorithms. Physica D **60**(1–4), 259–268 (1992)
60. Simoncelli, E.P., Adelson, E.H.: Noise removal via Bayesian wavelet coring. In: Proceedings ICIP, vol. 1, pp. 379–382 (1996)
61. Son, C.H., Choo, H., Park, H.M.: Image-pair-based deblurring with spatially varying norms and noisy image updating. J. Vis. Comm. Image Rep. **24**(8), 1303–1315 (2013)
62. Son, C.H., Park, H.M.: A pair of noisy/blurry patches-based PSF estimation and channel-dependent deblurring. IEEE Trans. Consum. Electron. **57**(4), 1791–1799 (2011)
63. Suin, M., Purohit, K., Rajagopalan, A.: Spatially-attentive patch-hierarchical network for adaptive motion deblurring. In: Proceedings, pp. 3606–3615 (2020)
64. Sun, J., Cao, W., Xu, Z., Ponce, J.: Learning a convolutional neural network for non-uniform motion blur removal. In: Proceedings, CVPR. pp. 769–777 (2015)
65. Tai, Y., Yang, J., Liu, X., Xu, C.: MemNet: a persistent memory network for image restoration. In: Proceedings ICCV, pp. 4539–4547 (2017)
66. Tao, X., Gao, H., Shen, X., Wang, J., Jia, J.: Scale-recurrent network for deep image deblurring. In: Proceedings CVPR, pp. 8174–8182 (2018)
67. Tian, Y., Zhang, Y., Fu, Y., Xu, C.: TDAN: temporally-deformable alignment network for video super-resolution. In: Proceedings CVPR, pp. 3360–3369 (2020)
68. Tico, M., Gelfand, N., Pulli, K.: Motion-blur-free exposure fusion. In: Proceedings ICIP, pp. 3321–3324 (2010)
69. Wang, X., Chan, K.C., Yu, K., Dong, C., Change Loy, C.: EDVR: video restoration with enhanced deformable convolutional networks. In: Proceedings CVPRW, pp. 1–10 (2019)
70. Wang, Y., et al.: Progressive retinex: mutually reinforced illumination-noise perception network for low-light image enhancement. In: Proceedings ACM MM, pp. 2015–2023 (2019)
71. Wang, Y., Huang, H., Xu, Q., Liu, J., Liu, Y., Wang, J.: Practical deep raw image denoising on mobile devices. In: Vedaldi, A., Bischof, H., Brox, T., Frahm, J.-M. (eds.) ECCV 2020. LNCS, vol. 12351, pp. 1–16. Springer, Cham (2020). https://doi.org/10.1007/978-3-030-58539-6_1
72. Wang, Z., Bovik, A.C., Sheikh, H.R., Simoncelli, E.P.: Image quality assessment: from error visibility to structural similarity. IEEE Trans. Image Process. **13**(4), 600–612 (2004)
73. Wei, K., Fu, Y., Yang, J., Huang, H.: A physics-based noise formation model for extreme low-light raw denoising. In: Proceedings CVPR, pp. 2758–2767 (2020)
74. Whang, J., Delbracio, M., Talebi, H., Saharia, C., Dimakis, A.G., Milanfar, P.: Deblurring via stochastic refinement. In: Proceedings CVPR, pp. 16293–16303 (2022)

75. Whyte, O., Sivic, J., Zisserman, A., Ponce, J.: Non-uniform deblurring for shaken images. Int. J. Comput. Vis. **98**(2), 168–186 (2012)
76. Xia, Z., Perazzi, F., Gharbi, M., Sunkavalli, K., Chakrabarti, A.: Basis prediction networks for effective burst denoising with large kernels. In: Proceedings CVPR, pp. 11844–11853 (2020)
77. Xing, Y., Qian, Z., Chen, Q.: Invertible image signal processing. In: Proceedings CVPR, pp. 6287–6296 (2021)
78. Xu, X., Li, M., Sun, W.: Learning deformable kernels for image and video denoising. arXiv preprint arXiv:1904.06903 (2019)
79. Yoo, J., Ahn, N., Sohn, K.A.: Rethinking data augmentation for image super-resolution: A comprehensive analysis and a new strategy. In: Proceedings CVPR, pp. 8375–8384 (2020)
80. Yuan, L., Sun, J., Quan, L., Shum, H.Y.: Image deblurring with blurred/noisy image pairs. ACM Trans. Graph. **26**(3), 1-es (2007)
81. Yuan, Y., Su, W., Ma, D.: Efficient dynamic scene deblurring using spatially variant deconvolution network with optical flow guided training. In: Proceedings CVPR, pp. 3555–3564 (2020)
82. Yue, Z., Yong, H., Zhao, Q., Meng, D., Zhang, L.: Variational denoising network: toward blind noise modeling and removal. Proc. NeurIPS **32**, 1690–1701 (2019)
83. Zamir, S.W., et al.: CycleISP: real image restoration via improved data synthesis. In: Proceedings CVPR, pp. 2696–2705 (2020)
84. Zamir, S.W., et al.: Learning enriched features for real image restoration and enhancement. In: Vedaldi, A., Bischof, H., Brox, T., Frahm, J.-M. (eds.) ECCV 2020. LNCS, vol. 12370, pp. 492–511. Springer, Cham (2020). https://doi.org/10.1007/978-3-030-58595-2_30
85. Zamir, S.W., et al.: Multi-stage progressive image restoration. In: Proceedings CVPR, pp. 14821–14831 (2021)
86. Zhang, B., Jin, S., Xia, Y., Huang, Y., Xiong, Z.: Attention mechanism enhanced kernel prediction networks for denoising of burst images. In: Proceedings ICASSP, pp. 2083–2087 (2020)
87. Zhang, H., Dai, Y., Li, H., Koniusz, P.: Deep stacked hierarchical multi-patch network for image deblurring. In: Proceedings CVPR, pp. 5978–5986 (2019)
88. Zhang, J., et al.: Dynamic scene deblurring using spatially variant recurrent neural networks. In: Proceedings CVPR, pp. 2521–2529 (2018)
89. Zhang, J., Cao, Y., Fang, S., Kang, Y., Wen Chen, C.: Fast haze removal for nighttime image using maximum reflectance prior. In: Proceedings CVPR, pp. 7418–7426 (2017)
90. Zhang, K., Zuo, W., Chen, Y., Meng, D., Zhang, L.: Beyond a gaussian denoiser: residual learning of deep CNN for image denoising. IEEE Trans. Image Process. **26**(7), 3142–3155 (2017)
91. Zhang, K., Zuo, W., Zhang, L.: EFDNet: toward a fast and flexible solution for CNN-based image denoising. IEEE Trans. Image Process. **27**(9), 4608–4622 (2018)
92. Zhang, Y., Wang, C., Maybank, S.J., Tao, D.: Exposure trajectory recovery from motion blur. IEEE Transactions on Pattern Analysis and Machine Intelligence (2021)
93. Zhang, Y., Tian, Y., Kong, Y., Zhong, B., Fu, Y.: Residual dense network for image restoration. IEEE Trans. Pattern Anal. Mach. Intell. **43**(7), 2480–2495 (2020)
94. Zhu, X., Hu, H., Lin, S., Dai, J.: Deformable convnets v2: more deformable, better results. In: Proceedings CVPR, pp. 9308–9316 (2019)

Learning Graph Neural Networks
for Image Style Transfer

Yongcheng Jing[1], Yining Mao[2], Yiding Yang[3], Yibing Zhan[4], Mingli Song[2,5],
Xinchao Wang[3(✉)], and Dacheng Tao[1,4]

[1] The University of Sydney, Darlington, NSW 2008, Australia
[2] Zhejiang University, Hangzhou 310027, ZJ, China
[3] National University of Singapore, Singapore, Singapore
`xinchao@nus.edu.sg`
[4] JD Explore Academy, Beijing, China
[5] Zhejiang University City College, Hangzhou 310015, ZJ, China

Abstract. State-of-the-art parametric and non-parametric style transfer approaches are prone to either distorted local style patterns due to
global statistics alignment, or unpleasing artifacts resulting from patch
mismatching. In this paper, we study a novel semi-parametric neural style
transfer framework that alleviates the deficiency of both parametric and
non-parametric stylization. The core idea of our approach is to establish accurate and fine-grained content-style correspondences using graph
neural networks (GNNs). To this end, we develop an elaborated GNN
model with content and style local patches as the graph vertices. The
style transfer procedure is then modeled as the attention-based heterogeneous message passing between the style and content nodes in a learnable manner, leading to adaptive many-to-one style-content correlations
at the local patch level. In addition, an elaborated deformable graph convolutional operation is introduced for cross-scale style-content matching.
Experimental results demonstrate that the proposed semi-parametric
image stylization approach yields encouraging results on the challenging
style patterns, preserving both global appearance and exquisite details.
Furthermore, by controlling the number of edges at the inference stage,
the proposed method also triggers novel functionalities like diversified
patch-based stylization with a single model.

Keywords: Neural style transfer · Graph neural networks ·
Attention-based message passing

1 Introduction

Image style transfer aims to automatically transfer the artistic style from a
source style image to a given content one, and has been studied for a long

Supplementary Information The online version contains supplementary material
available at https://doi.org/10.1007/978-3-031-20071-7_7.

Content+Style Huang *et al.* [14]   An *et al.* [1]   Li *et al.* [30]   Chen *et al.* [6] Sheng *et al.* [42]   Ours

Fig. 1. Existing parametric [1,14,30] and non-parametric [6,42] NST methods either barely transfer the global style appearance to the target [6], or produce distorted local style patterns [1,14,30] and undesired artifacts [42]. By contrast, the proposed GNN-based semi-parametric approach achieves superior stylization performance in the transfers of both global stroke arrangement and local fine-grained patterns.

time in the computer vision community. Conventionally, image style transfer is generally cast as the problem of non-photorealistic rendering in the domain of computer graphics. Inspired by the success of deep learning [8–10,41,55], Gatys *et al.* [11] pioneer the paradigm that leverages the feature activations from deep *convolutional neural networks (CNNs)* to extract and match the target content and style, leading to the benefits of no explicit restrictions on style types and no requirements of ground-truth training data. As such, various CNN-based style transfer methods are developed in the literature [5,13,15,22,25,34,35,47,49], establishing a novel field of *neural style transfer (NST)* [18].

State-of-the-art NST algorithms can be categorized into two streams of methods, parametric and non-parametric ones, depending on the style representation mechanisms. In particular, parametric NST approaches rely on the global summary statistics over the entire feature map from pre-trained deep CNNs to extract and match the target artistic style [11,14,21]. Non-parametric neural methods, also known as patch-based NST methods [6,42], leverage the local feature patches to represent the style information, inspired by the conventional patch-based texture modeling approaches with Markov random fields. The idea is to swap the content neural patches with the most similar style ones, through a greedy one-to-one patch matching strategy.

Both parametric and non-parametric methods, unfortunately, have their own limitations, as demonstrated in Fig. 1. Parametric stylization methods achieve good performance in transferring the overall appearance of the style images, but are incompetent in generating fine-grained local style patterns. By contrast, non-parametric style transfer algorithms allow for locally-aligned stylization; however, such patch-based methods are typically accomplished with the undesired artifacts due to content-style mismatching.

In this paper, we present a semi-parametric style transfer scheme, towards alleviating the dilemmas of existing parametric and non-parametric methods. On the one hand, our semi-parametric approach allows for the establishment of more accurate many-to-one correspondences between different content and style regions in a learnable manner. As such, our approach explicitly tackles the issue of content-style mismatching in non-parametric NST algorithms, thereby largely alleviating the deficiency of unplausible artifacts. On the other hand, the proposed semi-parametric method adaptively divides content and style features into tiny and cross-scale feature patches for stylization, thus addressing the dilemma of lacking local details in prior parametric schemes.

Towards this end, we introduce to the proposed semi-parametric NST a dedicated learning mechanism, *graph neural networks* (GNNs), to enable adaptive local patch-level interplay between the content and style. As a well-established learning paradigm for handling non-Euclidean data, GNNs are designed to explicitly account for structural relations and interdependency between nodes. Moreover, GNNs are equipped with efficacious strategies for aggregating information from multiple neighbors to a center node. Such competences make GNN an ideal tool for tackling the intricate content-style region matching challenge in style transfer, especially the many-to-one mapping between each content patch and multiple potentially-matching style patches. We therefore exploit GNNs to adaptively set up the faithful topological correspondences among the very different content and style, such that every content region is rendered with the optimal style strokes.

Specifically, we start by building a heterogeneous NST graph, with content and style feature patches as the vertices. The multi-patch parametric aggregation in semi-parametric NST can thereby be modeled as the message passing procedure among different patch nodes in the constructed stylization graph. By employing the prevalent GNN mechanisms such as the graph attention network, the k most similar patches can be aggregated in an attention-based parametric manner. The aggregated patches are then composed back into the image features, which are further aligned with the target global statistics to obtain the final stylized result. Also, a deformable graph convolutional operation is devised, making it possible for cross-scale style-content matching with spatially-varying stroke sizes in a single stylized image. Furthermore, our GNN-based NST can readily perform diversified patch-based stylization, by simply changing the number of connections during inference.

In sum, our contribution is a novel semi-parametric arbitrary stylization scheme that allows for the effective generation of both the global and local style patterns, backed by a dedicated deformable graph convolutional design. This is specifically achieved through modeling the NST process as the message passing between content and style under the framework of GNNs. Experimental results demonstrate that the proposed GNN-based stylization method yields results superior to the state of the art.

2   Related Work

Neural Style Transfer. Driven by the power of *convolutional neural networks (CNNs)* [26,57,58,62], Gatys *et al.* propose to leverage CNNs to capture and recombine the content of a given photo and the style of an artwork [11], leading to the area of *neural style transfer (NST)*. Existing NST approaches can be broadly divided into parametric and non-parametric NST methods. Specifically, parametric NST approaches leverage the global representations to transfer the target artistic style, which are obtained by computing the summary statistics in either an image-optimization-based online manner [11,28,36,40], or model-optimization-based offline manner [1,3,4,14,16,21,29,30,35,45,59]. On the other hand, non-parametric methods exploit the local feature patches to represent the image style [2,6,27,31,37,42], inspired by the conventional patch-based texture modeling approaches with Markov random fields. The idea is to search the most similar neural patches from the style image that match the semantic local structure of the content one [2,6,27,31,37,42]. This work aims to seek a balance between parametric and non-parametric NST methods by incorporating the use of GNNs.

Graph Neural Networks. GNNs have merged as a powerful tool to handle graph data in the non-Euclidean domain [19,20,24,33,43,51–54]. In particular, the seminal work of Kipf and Welling [24] proposes graph convolutional networks (GCNs), which successfully generalizes CNNs to deal with graph-structured data, by utilizing neighborhood aggregation functions to recursively capture high-level features from both the node and its neighbors. The research on GNNs leads to increasing interest in deploying GNN models in various graph-based tasks, where the input data can be naturally represented as graphs [63]. Moreover, the emerging transformers can also be treated as generalizations of GNNs [39,50,56,60,61]. Unlike these existing works where the inputs are themselves non-grid graphs, we aim to extend the use of GNN models to effectively manipulate grid-structured images, such that various image-based tasks can be benefited from GNNs.

3 Proposed Method

Towards addressing the limitations of existing parametric and non-parametric NST methods, we introduce the proposed semi-parametric style transfer framework with GNNs. In what follows, we begin by providing an overview of the proposed GNN-based approach, and then elaborating several key components, including the construction of the topological NST graph, the dedicated deformable graph convolutional operation customized for the established NST graph, and the detailed 2-hop heterogeneous message passing process for stylization. Finally, we illustrate the cascaded patch-to-image training pipeline, tailored for the proposed GNN-based stylization system.

3.1 Network Overview

The overall workflow of the proposed semi-parametric NST framework is shown in Fig. 2. There are primarily four modules in the whole pipeline, termed as *image encoding, local patch-based manipulation, global feature refinement,* and *feature decoding*. At the heart of the proposed framework is the *local patch-based manipulation* module, which will be further detailed in the following sections.

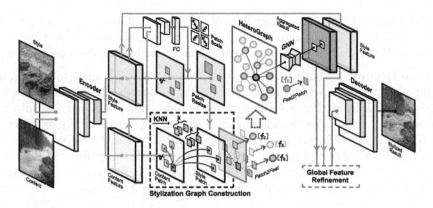

Fig. 2. Network architecture of the proposed semi-parametric style transfer network with GNNs. From left to right, the corresponding stylization pipeline comprises four subprocesses, *i.e.*, image encoding with the encoder, local patch-based manipulation based on heterogeneous GNNs, global feature refinement, and the feature decoding procedure. The symbols of scissors represent the process to divide the feature maps into feature patches. HeteroGraph denotes the established heterogeneous stylization graph with two types of content-style inter-domain connections and content-content intra-domain connections.

Image Encoding Module. The proposed semi-parametric stylization starts by receiving style and content images as inputs and encoding these images into meaningful feature maps (the green and yellow blocks in Fig. 2), by exploiting the first few layers of the pre-trained VGG network. In particular, unlike the existing work [14] that uses the layers before `relu4_1`, we leverage the VGG layers up to `relu3_1`, for the sake of more valid feature patches that can be exploited by the following local patch-based feature transformation stage.

Local Patch-Based Manipulation Module. With the embedded content and style features as inputs, the local patch-based manipulation module extracts the corresponding content and style feature patches with the stride of s and the sliding window size of $p \times p$, represented as the scissor symbol in Fig. 2. We then build a heterogeneous stylization graph (the red frame in Fig. 2) with the obtained feature patches as graph nodes and perform the dedicated deformable graph convolution to generate the locally-stylized features, which will be further detailed in the succeeding Sect. 3.2 and Sect. 3.3.

Global Feature Refinement Module. The produced style-transferred results from the stage of patch-based manipulation are effective at preserving fine-grained local style patterns; however, the global style appearance is likely to be less similar to the target style image, due to the lack of global constraint on the stroke arrangement. To alleviate this dilemma, we propose a hierarchical patch-to-image stylization scheme to yield both the exquisite brushstroke and large-scale texture patterns. This is achieved by refining the feature representations at a global level, subsequent to the local patch-based manipulation. For the specific refinement method, since there already exist several effective global feature decorated strategies in the field of NST (*e.g.*, adaptive instance normalization (AdaIN) [14] and zero-phase component analysis (ZCA) [30]), here we directly utilize AdaIN as our refinement scheme, considering its high efficiency.

Feature Decoding Module. The last stage of our semi-parametric style transfer pipeline, termed as feature decoding, aims to decode the obtained feature representations from the preceding global feature refinement module into the final stylized image. The decoder module specifically comprises a sequence of convolutional and bilinear upsampling layers with the ReLU nonlinearities.

In the following sections, we will explain more details regarding the key module of *Local Patch-based Manipulation* with GNNs, including the graph construction procedure and the deformable graph convolutional process.

3.2 Stylization Graph Construction

At the stage of local patch-based manipulation, the first challenge towards the adaptive patch-level interactions between content and style with GNNs is the establishment of topological graphs. Unlike conventional GNN-based applications where the inputs can be naturally modeled as graphs (*e.g.*, biological molecules and social networks), there is no such natural topological structure for our task of semi-parametric image style transfer. To address this issue, we develop a dedicated graph construction technique, tailored for image stylization.

We start by giving the mathematical model of general graph-structured data as: $\mathcal{G} = \{\mathcal{V}, \mathcal{E}\}$, where $\mathcal{G}$ represents a directed or undirected graph. $\mathcal{V}$ denotes the set of vertices with nodes $v_i \in \mathcal{V}$. $\mathcal{E}$ represents the edge set with $(v_i, v_j) \in \mathcal{E}$, where $\{v_j\}$ is the set of neighboring nodes of v_i. Each vertex has an associated node feature $\mathcal{X} = [x_1 \ x_2 \ ... \ x_n]$. For example, x can be defined as the 3D coordinates in the task of point cloud classification.

As can be observed from the above formulation of prevalent graph data, the key elements in a graph are the vertices with the corresponding node features as well as the edges, which are thereby identified as our target objects to instantiate in the domain of style transfer as follows:

Heterogeneous Patch Vertices. To leverage GNNs to benefit the local-level stylization, we model in our framework the content and style patches as the graph nodes. Specifically, we exploit the content and style feature activations from the pre-trained VGG encoder, shown as the green and yellow blocks in Fig. 2, respectively, to capture the corresponding feature patches with a sliding window (*i.e.*, the scissor symbol in Fig. 2), in a similar manner as what is done when performing convolutions. We set the stride as 1 by default, meaning that there exist overlaps among our extracted activation patches. Such a manner of overlapped patch generation allows for smooth transitions among different stylized regions. In particular, to achieve cross-scale patch matching, we perform multi-scale patch division, which will be demonstrated in detail as a part of the deformable convolution in Sect. 3.3.

For the definition of the associated features for each patch vertex, we use a `Patch2Feat` operation, depicted as the red fonts in Fig. 2, to produce the desired format of node features for the use of the subsequent GNN layers, as also done in [64]. The designed `Patch2Feat` operation specifically amalgamates the c-dimensional features at each position of the $p \times p$ activation patch into a 1-dimensional feature vector, which is then considered as the node feature at every patch vertex. The derived content and style node features are shown as $[f_c]$ and $[f_s]$ in Fig. 2, respectively, for the use of the latter GNN layers.

Inter- and Intra-KNN Edges. Another critical issue in building the stylization graph is the establishment of connections among different patch vertices. Customized for the task of style transfer, we formulate two types of edges, termed as *content-style inter-domain edges* and *content-content intra-domain edges*, leading to a special kind of heterogeneous graph.

In particular, the inter-domain connections between heterogeneous style and content nodes aim to attain more accurate many-to-one style-content matching for patch-based stylization. More specifically, for each content query patch $\phi_i(\mathcal{F}_c)$ with $\mathcal{F}_c$ representing the whole content feature map, we search the corresponding k-nearest ones in the set of style feature patches $\{\phi(\mathcal{F}_s)\}$, which are identified as the neighbors coupled with inter-domain edges. This process of k-nearest neighbor search (KNN) is shown in the black dotted frame in Fig. 2. We employ the distance metric of normalized cross-correlation (NCC) for pair-wise KNN, by scoring the cosine distance between a couple of content and style patches. Given a specific content patch $\phi_i(\mathcal{F}_c)$ as the query, our KNN procedure based on NCC can be specifically formulated as:

$$\mathrm{KNN}(\phi_i(\mathcal{F}_c), \{\phi(\mathcal{F}_s)\}) = \arg\max_{\substack{k \\ j \in \{1, \dots, N_s\}}} \frac{\langle \phi_i(\mathcal{F}_c), \phi_j(\mathcal{F}_s) \rangle}{\|\phi_i(\mathcal{F}_c)\| \|\phi_j(\mathcal{F}_s)\|}, i \in \{1, \dots, N_c\}, \quad (1)$$

where N_c and N_s denote the cardinalities of the corresponding content and style patch sets, respectively. $\max_k$ returns the k largest elements from the set of the computed pair-wise NCCs. $\mathrm{KNN}(\phi_i(\mathcal{F}_c))$ represents the target k nearest-neighboring style vertices for the content patch $\phi_i(\mathcal{F}_c)$.

We also introduce the intra-domain connections within the set of content activation patches in our stylization graph, shown as the brown arrows in the black dotted rectangle in Fig. 2. The goal of such content-to-content edges is to unify the transferred styles across different content patches. In other words, we utilize the devised intra-domain connections to make sure that the semantically-similar content regions will also be rendered with homogeneous style patterns. This is specifically accomplished by linking the query content patch $\phi_i(\mathcal{F}_c)$ with the top-k most similar patches $\{\phi_j(\mathcal{F}_c)\}$ where $j \in \{1, \dots, N_c\}$, by NCC-based KNN search in a similar manner with that in Eq. 1.

The ultimate heterogeneous stylization graph, with the two node types of content and style vertices and also the two edge types of inter- and intra-domain connections, is demonstrated as the red rectangle in Fig. 2. The relationship between the involved nodes is defined as the NCC-based patch similarity.

3.3 Deformable Graph Convolution

With the constructed stylization graph, we are then ready to apply GNN layers to perform heterogeneous message passing along the content-style inter-domain edges and also content-content intra-domain edges. A naïve way will be simply performing existing graph convolutions on the heterogeneous stylization graph to aggregate messages from the content and style vertices.

However, this vanilla approach is not optimal for the task of style transfer, due to a lack of considerations in feature scales. Specifically, in the process of image stylization, the proper feature scale is directly correlated with the stroke scale in the eventual output [17], which is a vital geometric primitive to characterize an artwork. The objective stylized results should have various scales of style strokes across the whole image, depending on the semantics of different content regions.

Towards this end, we propose a dedicated deformable graph convolutional network that explicitly accounts for the scale information in message passing. The devised deformable graph convolutional network comprises two components. Specifically, the first component is an elaborated *deformable scale prediction module*, with a fully-connected (FC) layer in the end, that aims to generate the optimal scale of each patch in a learnable manner before conducting message aggregation, as also done in [7]. In particular, the scale predictor receives both the content and style features as inputs, considering the potential scale mismatching between the content and style, as shown in the upper left part of Fig. 2.

As such, by adaptively performing scale adjustment according to both content and style inputs, the proposed deformable graph conventional network makes it possible for cross-scale style-content matching with spatially-varying stroke sizes across the whole image. We clarify that we only incorporate one-single predictor in our deformable graph convolutional network that produces the style scales, for the sake of computational efficiency. There is no need to also augment another predictor for content scale prediction, which is, in fact, equivalent to fixing the content scale and only changing the style one.

The second component of the proposed deformable graph convolutional network is the *general feature aggregation module* that learns to aggregate the useful features from the neighboring heterogeneous content and style nodes. Various existing message passing mechanisms can, in fact, readily be applied at this stage for message propagation. Here, we leverage the graph attention scheme to demonstrate the message flow along with the two types of stylization edges, which empirically leads to superior stylization performance thanks to its property of anisotropy.

Specifically, given an established stylization graph, our dedicated heterogeneous aggregation process is composed of two key stages, termed as *style-to-content message passing stage* and *content-to-content messing passing stage*:

Style-to-Content Message Passing. The first style-to-content stage aims to gather the useful style features from the k neighboring style vertices. For the specific message gathering method, one vanilla way is to treat the information from every style vertex equally, meaning that the aggregated result would be simply the sum of all the neighboring style node features. However, the results of such naïve approach are likely to be affected by the noisy style vertices, resulting in undesired artifacts.

To tackle this challenge, we apply an attention coefficient for each style vertex during message passing, which is learned in a data-driven manner. Given a centering content node v_c and its neighboring style nodes $\{v_s\}$ with the cardinality of k, the learned attention coefficients $w(v_c, v_s^j)$ between v_c and a specific neighbor v_s^j can be computed as:

$$w(v_c, v_s^j) = \frac{\exp\left(\text{LeakyReLU}\left(W_a[W_b\mathcal{F}_c\|W_b\mathcal{F}_s^j]\right)\right)}{\sum_{m=1}^{k} \exp\left(\text{LeakyReLU}\left(W_a[W_b\mathcal{F}_c\|W_b\mathcal{F}_s^m]\right)\right)}, \tag{2}$$

where W represents the learnable matrix in linear transformation. $\|$ is the concatenation operation.

With such an attention-based aggregation manner, our stylization GNN can adaptively collect more significant information from the best-matching style patches, and meanwhile reduce the features from the less-matching noisy ones. Furthermore, we also apply a multi-headed architecture that generates the multi-head attention, so as to stabilize the attention learning process.

Content-to-Content Message Passing. With the updated node features at the content vertices from the preceding style-to-content message passing process, we also perform a second-phase information propagation among different content nodes. The rationale behind our content-to-content message passing is to perform global patch-based adjustment upon the results of the style-to-content stage, by considering the inter-relationship between the stylized patches at different locations. As such, the global coherence can be maintained, where the content objects that share similar semantics are more likely to resemble each other in stylization, which will be further validated in the experiments.

This proposed intra-content propagation also delivers the benefit of alleviating the artifacts resulting from potential style-content patch mismatching, by combining the features from the correctly-matching results. The detailed content-to-content message passing procedure is analogous to that in style-to-content message passing, but replacing the style vertices in Eq. 2 with the neighboring content vertices with the associated updated node features.

The eventual aggregation results from the proposed inter- and intra-domain message passing are then converted back into the feature patches by a `Feat2Patch` operation, which is an inverse operation of `Patch2Feat`. The obtained patches are further transformed into the feature map for the use of the subsequent global feature alignment module and feature decoding module.

3.4 Loss Function and Training Strategy

To align the semantic content, our content loss $\mathcal{L}_c$ is defined as the perceptual loss over the features from layer $\{\texttt{relu4\_1}\}$ of the pre-trained VGG network Φ:

$$\mathcal{L}_c = \|\Phi^{\texttt{relu4\_1}}(\mathcal{I}_c) - \Phi^{\texttt{relu4\_1}}(\mathcal{I}_o)\|_2, \tag{3}$$

where $\mathcal{I}_c$ and $\mathcal{I}_o$ represent the content and the output stylized images, respectively. For the style loss, we use the BN-statistic loss to extrat and transfer the

---

Algorithm 1. Training a GNN-based stylization model that can transfer arbitrary styles in a semi-parametric manner.

Input: $\mathcal{I}_c$: the content image; $\mathcal{I}_s$: the style image; VGG: the pre-trained loss network.

Output: $\mathcal{I}_o$: Target stylized image that simultaneously preserves the appearance of $\mathcal{I}_s$ and the semantics of $\mathcal{I}_c$.

1: Perform initializations on the image encoder Enc($\cdot$), the scale predictor Prec($\cdot$), GNN parameters W_a and W_b, and the feature decoder Dec($\cdot$).
2: **for** $i = 1$ to $\mathcal{T}$ iterations **do**
3:     Feed $\mathcal{I}_s$ and $\mathcal{I}_c$ into Enc($\cdot$) and obtain the style and content features $\mathcal{F}_s$ and $\mathcal{F}_c$;
4:     Divide $\mathcal{F}_c$ into equal-size content patches $\{\phi(\mathcal{F}_c)\}$ by using a sliding window;
5:     Feed $\{\mathcal{F}_s, \mathcal{F}_c\}$ into Prec($\cdot$) and obtain the optimal scales $\{\alpha\}$ for style patches;
6:     Divide $\mathcal{F}_s$ into varying-size style patches $\{\phi(\mathcal{F}_s)\}$ with the obtained scales $\{\alpha\}$;
7:     Resize $\{\phi(\mathcal{F}_s)\}$ according to the size of the content patches $\{\phi(\mathcal{F}_c)\}$;
8:     Construct inter- and intra-domain edges by Eq. 1;
9:     Transform $\{\phi(\mathcal{F}_s)\}$ and $\{\phi(\mathcal{F}_c)\}$ into the node features by using Patch2Feat;
10:     Establish the heterogeneous graph $\mathcal{G}_{NST}$ and feed $\mathcal{G}_{NST}$ into the GNN layers;
11:     Perform heterogeneous message passing over $\mathcal{G}_{NST}$ by Eq. 2 and obtain $\mathbf{f}_c$;
12:     Convert the aggregation results $\mathbf{f}_c$ into feature map $\mathcal{F}_o$ by Feat2Patch;
13:     Feed the obtained features $\mathcal{F}_o$ into the global feature refiner and obtain $\mathcal{F}_o'$;
14:     Feed $\mathcal{F}_o'$ into the decoder Dec($\cdot$) to obtain the target stylized image $\mathcal{I}_o$;
15:     Feed $\{\mathcal{I}_o, \mathcal{I}_c, \mathcal{I}_s\}$ into VGG and compute $\mathcal{L}_c$ and $\mathcal{L}_s$ by Eq. 3 and Eq. 4;
16:     Optimize Enc($\cdot$), Prec($\cdot$), W_a, W_b, and Dec($\cdot$) with the Adam optimizer;
17: **end for**

---

style information, computed at layer $\{\texttt{relu1\_1}, \texttt{relu2\_1}, \texttt{relu3\_1}, \texttt{relu4\_1}\}$ of the VGG network $\varPhi$:

$$\mathcal{L}_s(h) = \sum_{\ell=1}^{4} \left(\left\| h \left(\varPhi^{\texttt{relu}\ell\_1} (\mathcal{I}_s) \right) - h \left(\varPhi^{\texttt{relu}\ell\_1} (\mathcal{I}_o) \right) \right\|_2 \right), \tag{4}$$

where $h(\cdot)$ denotes the mapping of computing the BN statistics over the feature maps. The style loss can then be defined as: $\mathcal{L}_s = \mathcal{L}_s(\mu) + \mathcal{L}_s(\sigma)$, with $\mu(\cdot)$ and $\sigma(\cdot)$ denoting mean and standard deviation, respectively.

Our total loss is thereby a weighted sum of the content and style loss, formulated as: $\mathcal{L} = \mathcal{L}_{content} + \lambda \mathcal{L}_{style}$ with λ as the weighting factor that balances the content and style portions.

We also derive an elaborated training pipeline, tailored for the proposed GNN-based semi-parametric style transfer framework. As a whole, the detailed process of training a GNN-based semi-parametric arbitrary stylization model with the proposed algorithm is concluded in Algorithm 1.

4   Experiments

4.1   Experimental Settings

We demonstrate here the implementation details as per the stage of the proposed semi-parametric pipeline. For the stylization graph construction stage, we set k as 5 by default for the NCC-based KNN search. The stride s for the sliding

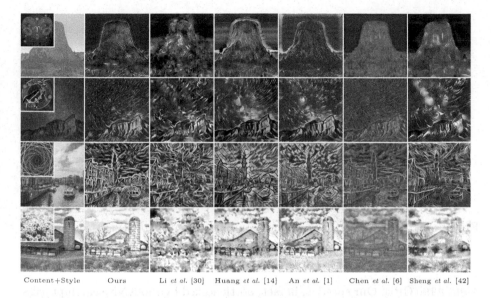

Content+Style   Ours   Li *et al.* [30]   Huang *et al.* [14]   An *et al.* [1]   Chen *et al.* [6]   Sheng *et al.* [42]

Fig. 3. Qualitative results of our proposed GNN-based semi-parametric stylization algorithm and other parametric [1,14,30] and non-parametric [6,42] methods.

window is set to 1, whereas the kernel size is set to 5×5. At the stage of deformable graph convolution, we primarily use the graph attention network (GAT) [43] for the GNN layers to validate the effectiveness of the proposed semi-parametric NST scheme. During training, we adopt the Adam optimizer [23] to optimize the whole GNN-based network. The learning rate is 1×10^{-4} with a weight decay of 5×10^{-5}. The batch size is set to 8. The weighting factor λ is set to 10. We employ a pre-trained VGG-19 as our loss network, as also done in [11,14]. The network is trained on the Microsoft COCO dataset [32] and the WikiArt [38] dataset. Our code is based on Deep Graph Library (DGL) [44]. The training takes roughly two days on an NVIDIA Tesla A100 GPU.

4.2 Results

Qualitative Comparison. Figure 3 demonstrates the results of the proposed GNN-based semi-parametric method and other arbitrary style transfer methods [1,6,14,30,42]. The results of [30] are prone to distorted patterns. By contrast, the algorithms of [1,14] generate sharper details; however, the local style patterns in their results are not well aligned with the target ones, where very few fine strokes are produced for most styles. For the non-parametric NST approaches of [6,42], their stylized results either introduce fewer style patterns or suffer from artifacts, due to the potential issue of one-to-one patch mismatching. Compared with other approaches, our semi-parametric framework leads to few artifacts, and meanwhile preserves both the global style appearance and the local fine details, thanks to the local patch-based manipulation module with GNNs.

Table 1. Average speed comparison in terms of seconds per image.

Methods	Time (s)		
	256×256	384×384	512×512
Li *et al.* [30]	0.707	0.779	0.878
Huang *et al.* [14]	0.007	0.010	0.017
An *et al.* [1]	0.069	0.108	0.169
Chen *et al.* [6]	0.017	0.051	0.218
Sheng *et al.* [42]	0.412	0.536	0.630
Ours	0.094	0.198	0.464

Efficiency Analysis. In Table 1, we compare the average stylization speed of the proposed approach with other algorithms. For a fair comparison, all the methods are implemented with PyTorch. The experiments are performed over 100 equal-size content and style images of different resolutions using an NVIDIA Tesla A100 GPU. Our speed is, in fact, bottlenecked by the KNN search process, which can be further improved with an optimized KNN implementation.

4.3   Ablation Studies

Heterogeneous Aggregation Schemes. We show in Fig. 4 the stylization results by using different neighborhood aggregation strategies in the local patch-based manipulation module. The results of the GAT aggregation scheme, as shown in the 3rd column of Fig. 4, outperform those of others in finer structures and global coherence (the areas of the sky and the human face in Fig. 4), thereby validating the superiority of the attention scheme in Eq. 2.

Stylization w/ and w/o the Deformable Scheme. Figure 5 demonstrates the results with the equal-size patch division method, and those with the proposed deformable patch splitting scheme. The devised deformable module makes it possible to adaptively control the strokes in different areas. As a result, the contrast information in the stylized results can be enhanced.

Graph w/ and w/o Intra-domain Edges. In Fig. 6, we validate the effectiveness of the proposed content-to-content message passing scheme, which typically leads to more consistent style patterns in semantically-similar content regions, as can be observed in the foreground human and fox eye areas, as well as the background regions of Fig. 6.

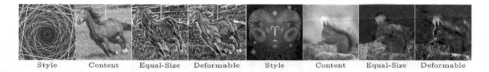

Fig. 4. Comparative results of using various aggregation mechanisms for heterogeneous message passing, including graph attention network (GAT) [43], graph convolutional network (GCN) [24], graph isomorphism network (GIN) [48], dynamic graph convolution (EdgeConv) [46], and GraphSage [12]. The GAT mechanism generally yields superior stylization results, thanks to its attention-based aggregation scheme in Eq. 2.

Fig. 5. Results of the equal-size patch division method and the proposed deformable one with a learnable scale predictor. Our deformable scheme allows for cross-scale style-content matching, thereby leading to spatially-adaptive multi-stroke stylization with an enhanced semantic saliency (*e.g.*, the foreground regions of the horse and squirrel).

Fig. 6. Results of removing the content-to-content intra-domain edges (w/o Intra) and those with the intra-domain ones (w/ Intra). The devised intra-domain connections incorporate the inter-relationship between the stylized patches at different locations, thereby maintaining the global stylization coherence (*e.g.*, the eye regions in the figure).

Euclidean Distance *vs.* Normalized Cross-Correlation. Figure 7 shows the results of using the Euclidean distance and the normalized cross-correlation (NCC) as the distance metric, respectively, in the construction of the stylization graph. The adopted metric of NCC in our framework, as observed from the 4th and 8th columns of Fig. 7, leads to superior performance than the Euclidean distance (Fig. 7, the 3rd and 7th columns) in terms of both the global stroke arrangements and local details.

Various Patch Sizes. We show in Fig. 8 the results of diversified feature patch sizes. Larger patch sizes, as shown from the left to right in the figure, generally

| Style | Content | Euclidean | NCC (Ours) | Style | Content | Euclidean | NCC (Ours) |

Fig. 7. Results obtained using Euclidean distance and normalized cross-correlation (NCC) for similarity measurement during the construction of heterogeneous edges.

Patch Size=3 Patch Size=5 Patch Size=7 Patch Size=9 Patch Size=3 Patch Size=5 Patch Size=7 Patch Size=9

Fig. 8. Results obtained using various patch sizes for constructing content and style vertices in the local patch-based manipulation module. By using a larger patch size, the stylized results can maintain an overall larger stroke size.

lead to larger strokes in the stylized results, which is especially obvious when we observe the regions of the dog and horse in Fig. 8.

4.4 Diversified Stylization Control

The proposed GNN-based arbitrary style transfer scheme, as shown in Fig. 9, can readily support diversified stylization with solely a single model. We also zoom in on the same regions (*i.e.*, the red frames in Fig. 9) to observe the details. Such diversities in Fig. 9 are specifically achieved by simply changing the numbers of node-specific connections for heterogeneous message passing, which provide users of various tastes with more stylization choices.

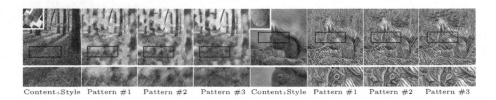

Content+Style Pattern #1   Pattern #2   Pattern #3 Content+Style Pattern #1   Pattern #2   Pattern #3

Fig. 9. Flexible control of diversified patch-based arbitrary style transfer during inference. The proposed GNN-based semi-parametric stylization scheme makes it possible to generate heterogeneous style patterns with only a single trained model.

5 Conclusions

In this paper, we introduce a semi-parametric arbitrary style transfer scheme for the effective transfers of challenging style patterns at the both local and global levels. Towards this goal, we identify two key challenges in existing parametric and non-parametric stylization approaches, and propose a dedicated GNN-based style transfer scheme to solve the dilemma. This is specifically accomplished by modeling the style transfers as the heterogeneous information propagation process among the constructed content and style vertices for accurate patch-based style-content correspondences. Moreover, we develop a deformable graph convolutional network for various-scale stroke generations. Experiments demonstrate that the proposed approach achieves favorable performance in both global stroke arrangement and local details. In our future work, we will strive to generalize the proposed GNN-based scheme to other vision tasks.

Acknowledgments. Mr Yongcheng Jing is supported by ARC FL-170100117. Dr Xinchao Wang is supported by AI Singapore (Award No.: AISG2-RP-2021-023) and NUS Faculty Research Committee Grant (WBS: A-0009440-00-00).

References

1. An, J., Huang, S., Song, Y., Dou, D., Liu, W., Luo, J.: ArtFlow: unbiased image style transfer via reversible neural flows. In: CVPR (2021)
2. Champandard, A.J.: Semantic style transfer and turning two-bit doodles into fine artworks. arXiv preprint arXiv:1603.01768 (2016)
3. Chen, D., Yuan, L., Liao, J., Yu, N., Hua, G.: StyleBank: an explicit representation for neural image style transfer. In: CVPR (2017)
4. Chen, D., Yuan, L., Liao, J., Yu, N., Hua, G.: Explicit filterbank learning for neural image style transfer and image processing. TPAMI **43**, 2373–2387 (2020)
5. Chen, H., et al.: Diverse image style transfer via invertible cross-space mapping. In: ICCV (2021)
6. Chen, T.Q., Schmidt, M.: Fast patch-based style transfer of arbitrary style. In: NeurIPS Workshop on Constructive Machine Learning (2016)
7. Chen, Z., et al.: DPT: deformable patch-based transformer for visual recognition. In: ACM MM (2021)
8. Ding, L., Wang, L., Liu, X., Wong, D.F., Tao, D., Tu, Z.: Understanding and improving lexical choice in non-autoregressive translation. In: ICLR (2021)
9. Ding, L., Wang, L., Tao, D.: Self-attention with cross-lingual position representation. In: ACL (2020)
10. Ding, L., Wang, L., Wu, D., Tao, D., Tu, Z.: Context-aware cross-attention for non-autoregressive translation. In: COLING (2020)
11. Gatys, L.A., Ecker, A.S., Bethge, M.: Image style transfer using convolutional neural networks. In: CVPR (2016)
12. Hamilton, W.L., Ying, R., Leskovec, J.: Inductive representation learning on large graphs. In: NeurIPS (2017)
13. Hong, K., Jeon, S., Yang, H., Fu, J., Byun, H.: Domain-aware universal style transfer. In: ICCV (2021)
14. Huang, X., Belongie, S.: Arbitrary style transfer in real-time with adaptive instance normalization. In: ICCV (2017)
15. Huo, J., et al.: Manifold alignment for semantically aligned style transfer. In: ICCV (2021)
16. Jing, Y., et al.: Dynamic instance normalization for arbitrary style transfer. In: AAAI (2020)

17. Jing, Y., et al.: Stroke controllable fast style transfer with adaptive receptive fields. In: Ferrari, V., Hebert, M., Sminchisescu, C., Weiss, Y. (eds.) ECCV 2018. LNCS, vol. 11217, pp. 244–260. Springer, Cham (2018). https://doi.org/10.1007/978-3-030-01261-8_15

18. Jing, Y., Yang, Y., Feng, Z., Ye, J., Yu, Y., Song, M.: Neural style transfer: a review. TVCG **26**, 3365–3385 (2019)

19. Jing, Y., Yang, Y., Wang, X., Song, M., Tao, D.: Amalgamating knowledge from heterogeneous graph neural networks. In: CVPR (2021)

20. Jing, Y., Yang, Y., Wang, X., Song, M., Tao, D.: Meta-aggregator: learning to aggregate for 1-bit graph neural networks. In: ICCV (2021)

21. Johnson, J., Alahi, A., Fei-Fei, L.: Perceptual losses for real-time style transfer and super-resolution. In: Leibe, B., Matas, J., Sebe, N., Welling, M. (eds.) ECCV 2016. LNCS, vol. 9906, pp. 694–711. Springer, Cham (2016). https://doi.org/10.1007/978-3-319-46475-6_43

22. Kalischek, N., Wegner, J.D., Schindler, K.: In the light of feature distributions: moment matching for neural style transfer. In: CVPR (2021)

23. Kingma, D., Ba, J.: Adam: a method for stochastic optimization. In: ICLR (2015)

24. Kipf, T.N., Welling, M.: Semi-supervised classification with graph convolutional networks. In: ICLR (2017)

25. Kolkin, N., Salavon, J., Shakhnarovich, G.: Style transfer by relaxed optimal transport and self-similarity. In: CVPR (2019)

26. Kong, Y., Liu, L., Wang, J., Tao, D.: Adaptive curriculum learning. In: ICCV (2021)

27. Li, C., Wand, M.: Combining Markov random fields and convolutional neural networks for image synthesis. In: CVPR, pp. 2479–2486 (2016)

28. Li, Y., Wang, N., Liu, J., Hou, X.: Demystifying neural style transfer. In: IJCAI (2017)

29. Li, Y., Chen, F., Yang, J., Wang, Z., Lu, X., Yang, M.H.: Diversified texture synthesis with feed-forward networks. In: CVPR (2017)

30. Li, Y., Fang, C., Yang, J., Wang, Z., Lu, X., Yang, M.H.: Universal style transfer via feature transforms. In: NeurIPS (2017)

31. Liao, J., Yao, Y., Yuan, L., Hua, G., Kang, S.B.: Visual attribute transfer through deep image analogy. TOG **36**, 1–15 (2017)

32. Lin, T.-Y., et al.: Microsoft COCO: common objects in context. In: Fleet, D., Pajdla, T., Schiele, B., Tuytelaars, T. (eds.) ECCV 2014. LNCS, vol. 8693, pp. 740–755. Springer, Cham (2014). https://doi.org/10.1007/978-3-319-10602-1_48

33. Liu, H., Yang, Y., Wang, X.: Overcoming catastrophic forgetting in graph neural networks. In: AAAI (2021)

34. Liu, S., et al.: Paint transformer: feed forward neural painting with stroke prediction. In: ICCV (2021)

35. Liu, S., et al.: AdaAttN: revisit attention mechanism in arbitrary neural style transfer. In: ICCV (2021)

36. Liu, X.C., Yang, Y.L., Hall, P.: Learning to warp for style transfer. In: CVPR (2021)

37. Mechrez, R., Talmi, I., Zelnik-Manor, L.: The contextual loss for image transformation with non-aligned data. In: Ferrari, V., Hebert, M., Sminchisescu, C., Weiss, Y. (eds.) Computer Vision – ECCV 2018. LNCS, vol. 11218, pp. 800–815. Springer, Cham (2018). https://doi.org/10.1007/978-3-030-01264-9_47

38. Nichol, K.: Painter by numbers (2016). https://www.kaggle.com/c/painter-by-numbers

39. Ren, S., Zhou, D., He, S., Feng, J., Wang, X.: Shunted self-attention via multi-scale token aggregation. In: CVPR (2022)
40. Risser, E., Wilmot, P., Barnes, C.: Stable and controllable neural texture synthesis and style transfer using histogram losses. arXiv preprint arXiv:1701.08893 (2017)
41. Shen, C., Yin, Y., Wang, X., Li, X., Song, J., Song, M.: Training generative adversarial networks in one stage. In: CVPR (2021)
42. Sheng, L., Shao, J., Lin, Z., Warfield, S., Wang, X.: Avatar-Net: multi-scale zero-shot style transfer by feature decoration. In: CVPR (2018)
43. Veličković, P., Cucurull, G., Casanova, A., Romero, A., Lio, P., Bengio, Y.: Graph attention networks. In: ICLR (2018)
44. Wang, M., et al.: Deep graph library: towards efficient and scalable deep learning on graphs. In: ICLR Workshop (2019)
45. Wang, P., Li, Y., Vasconcelos, N.: Rethinking and improving the robustness of image style transfer. In: CVPR (2021)
46. Wang, Y., Sun, Y., Liu, Z., Sarma, S.E., Bronstein, M.M., Solomon, J.M.: Dynamic graph CNN for learning on point clouds. TOG **38**, 1–12 (2019)
47. Wu, X., Hu, Z., Sheng, L., Xu, D.: StyleFormer: real-time arbitrary style transfer via parametric style composition. In: ICCV (2021)
48. Xu, K., Hu, W., Leskovec, J., Jegelka, S.: How powerful are graph neural networks? In: ICLR (2019)
49. Xu, W., Long, C., Wang, R., Wang, G.: DRB-GAN: a dynamic ResBlock generative adversarial network for artistic style transfer. In: ICCV (2021)
50. Xu, Y., Zhang, Q., Zhang, J., Tao, D.: ViTAE: vision transformer advanced by exploring intrinsic inductive bias. In: NeurIPS (2021)
51. Yang, Y., Feng, Z., Song, M., Wang, X.: Factorizable graph convolutional networks. In: NeurIPS (2020)
52. Yang, Y., Qiu, J., Song, M., Tao, D., Wang, X.: Distilling knowledge from graph convolutional networks. In: CVPR (2020)
53. Yang, Y., Ren, Z., Li, H., Zhou, C., Wang, X., Hua, G.: Learning dynamics via graph neural networks for human pose estimation and tracking. In: CVPR (2021)
54. Yang, Y., Wang, X., Song, M., Yuan, J., Tao, D.: SPAGAN: shortest path graph attention network. In: IJCAI (2019)
55. Ye, J., Jing, Y., Wang, X., Ou, K., Tao, D., Song, M.: Edge-sensitive human cutout with hierarchical granularity and loopy matting guidance. TIP **29**, 1177–1191 (2019)
56. Yu, W., et al.: MetaFormer is actually what you need for vision. In: CVPR (2022)
57. Zhan, Y., Yu, J., Yu, T., Tao, D.: On exploring undetermined relationships for visual relationship detection. In: CVPR (2019)
58. Zhan, Y., Yu, J., Yu, T., Tao, D.: Multi-task compositional network for visual relationship detection. IJCV **128**, 2146–2165 (2020)
59. Zhang, H., Dana, K.: Multi-style generative network for real-time transfer. arXiv preprint arXiv:1703.06953 (2017)
60. Zhang, Q., Xu, Y., Zhang, J., Tao, D.: ViTAEv2: vision transformer advanced by exploring inductive bias for image recognition and beyond. arXiv preprint arXiv:2202.10108 (2022)
61. Zhang, Q., Xu, Y., Zhang, J., Tao, D.: VSA: learning varied-size window attention in vision transformers. arXiv preprint arXiv:2204.08446 (2022)
62. Zhao, H., Bian, W., Yuan, B., Tao, D.: Collaborative learning of depth estimation, visual odometry and camera relocalization from monocular videos. In: IJCAI (2020)

63. Zhou, J., et al.: Graph neural networks: a review of methods and applications. arXiv preprint arXiv:1812.08434 (2018)
64. Zhou, S., Zhang, J., Zuo, W., Loy, C.C.: Cross-scale internal graph neural network for image super-resolution. In: NeurIPS (2020)

DeepPS2: Revisiting Photometric Stereo Using Two Differently Illuminated Images

Ashish Tiwari[1]([✉])(ID) and Shanmuganathan Raman[2](ID)

[1] IIT Gandhinagar, Gandhinagar, Gujarat, India
ashish.tiwari@iitgn.ac.in
[2] Jibaben Patel Chair in Artificial Intelligence CVIG Lab, IIT Gandhinagar,
Gandhinagar, Gujarat, India
shanmuga@iitgn.ac.in

Abstract. Estimating 3D surface normals through photometric stereo has been of great interest in computer vision research. Despite the success of existing traditional and deep learning-based methods, it is still challenging due to: (i) the requirement of three or more differently illuminated images, (ii) the inability to model unknown general reflectance, and (iii) the requirement of accurate 3D ground truth surface normals and known lighting information for training. In this work, we attempt to address an under-explored problem of photometric stereo using just two differently illuminated images, referred to as the PS2 problem. It is an intermediate case between a single image-based reconstruction method like Shape from Shading (SfS) and the traditional Photometric Stereo (PS), which requires three or more images. We propose an inverse rendering-based deep learning framework, called DeepPS2, that jointly performs surface normal, albedo, lighting estimation, and image relighting in a completely self-supervised manner with no requirement of ground truth data. We demonstrate how image relighting in conjunction with image reconstruction enhances the lighting estimation in a self-supervised setting (Supported by SERB IMPRINT 2 Grant).

Keywords: Photometric stereo · Deep learning · Inverse rendering · Image relighting

1 Introduction

Inferring the 3D shape of the objects using digital images is a fundamental and challenging task in computer vision research. It directly extends to quality control, virtual/augmented reality, medical diagnosis, e-commerce, etc. The widely used geometric approaches to shape recovery such as binocular [21,42] or multi-view stereo [11,24–26,38] methods require images from different views to

---

Supplementary Information The online version contains supplementary material available at https://doi.org/10.1007/978-3-031-20071-7_8.

triangulate the 3D points. However, they rely heavily on the success of image feature matching techniques and fall short of recovering finer details such as indentations, imprints, and scratches. The photometric methods for 3D shape reconstruction use shading cues from either a single image - *Shape from Shading (SfS)* [15] or at least three images - *Photometric Stereo (PS)* [46] to recover surface normals and are known to better preserve the finer surface details.

What are the Bottlenecks? The SfS problem is ill-posed due to the underlying convex/concave ambiguity and the fact that infinite surface normals exist to explain the intensity at each pixel [33]. The PS methods are known to handle such ambiguities and provide a unique surface normal defining the intensity at each pixel by using three or more differently illuminated images [14]. However, the well-posed traditional photometric stereo problem (as introduced by Woodhman [46]) assumes the surfaces to be purely Lambertian, which seldom is the case in the real world. Several recent methods [7–10,17,50] have also addressed shape estimation for non-Lambertian surfaces with unknown reflectance properties. However, they require more images ($\sim$50–100) as input. While there are methods that require as few as six (or even fewer) images [28], our goal is to resort to just two images under a photometric stereo setting.

Scope of the PS2 Problem. The scope of this work is to address the photometric stereo problem in an intermediate setting with two images ($m = 2$) between SfS ($m = 1$) and the traditional PS ($m \geq 3$). It can essentially be viewed as a degenerate case of lack of meaningful information due to shadows in a typical three-source photometric stereo setting [13]. Another use case of a PS2 problem arises in the 3D reconstruction of the non-rigid objects [12]. When an object is imaged under three light sources, one could be occluded by the object, and only the other two would provide meaningful cues. Further, the PS2 problem arises when $m \geq 3$ and light sources are coplanar. Such a situation typically occurs when the scene is illuminated by the sun and hence, applies to outdoor PS as well [19,37].

Constraints in Addressing the PS2 Problem. Several normal fields can offer solutions to the PS2 problem. One can perform an exhaustive search among these normal fields and find the one that best fits the underlying shape satisfying the smoothness constraint [30]. The differential PS formulation implicitly enforces such smoothness. However, it requires explicit knowledge of the surface boundary conditions [29], which is rarely available or requires regularization [13], which is generally tedious owing to heavy parameter tuning. A few methods [29,34] have put forward ways to address the PS2 problem based on the non-differential formulation by recasting it as a binary labeling problem. While such optimization problems can be solved using graph-cut-based algorithms [5], they require the albedo to be known.

Can Deep Neural Networks Offer a Solution? We use deep neural network to model unknown general surfaces with complex Bidirectional Reflectance Distribution Functions (BRDFs) while addressing the PS2 problem. The photometric stereo problem using deep neural networks has been addressed either under a *calibrated* (known lightings) or an *uncalibrated* (unknown lightings) setting. While most of these methods require 3D ground truth supervision [7–10,17,27,41,50], a little progress has been made to address PS in a self-supervised manner [20]. However, such self-supervised and uncalibrated methods still require ground truth supervision for lighting estimation.

In this work, we introduce an inverse-rendering-based deep learning framework, called DeepPS2, to address the PS2 problem and work towards developing a completely uncalibrated and self-supervised method. The core idea is to utilize the shading cues from two differently illuminated images to obtain the 3D surface normals. DeepPS2 is designed to perform albedo estimation, lighting estimation, image relighting, and image reconstruction without any ground truth supervision. While image reconstruction is commonly adopted in the existing unsupervised/self-supervised approaches, the appropriate design considerations to perform image relighting using the estimated lightings bring out several interesting insights about the proposed framework.

Contributions. The following are the key contributions of this work.

- We introduce DeepPS2, an uncalibrated inverse-rendering based photometric stereo method that jointly performs surface normal, albedo, and lighting estimation in a self-supervised setting[1].
- We propose a self-supervised lighting estimation through light space discretization and perform image relighting (using the estimated lightings) along with image reconstruction.
- We model the specularities explicitly using estimated illumination and albedo refinement.
- To the best of our knowledge, ours is the first work to introduce the PS2 problem using deep learning in a self-supervised manner.

2 Related Work

This section reviews the literature on the PS2 problem and some recent deep learning-based photometric stereo methods.

The PS2 Problem. Onn and Bruckstein [30] discussed the ambiguities in determining surface normals using two images and proposed to use integrability constraint to handle such ambiguities. Sato and Ikeuchi [37] used their method to solve the problem with $m \geq 3$ images under solar illumination, which in a sense addresses the PS2 problem [46]. Later, Yang et al. [48] studied the problem, particularly for the convex objects. Kozera provided an analytical resolution to the differential formulation of PS2 [23]. Since 1995 (for over ten years later), only Ikeda [16] addressed the PS2 problem by essentially considering the second image as an auxiliary to better solve the SFS problem. Queau et al. [34] addressed the PS2 problem using a graph cut based optimization method. Further, the problem of outdoor PS is being re-explored in several works [1,2]. While these methods attempt to provide a numerical resolution to the PS problem [29,34], we intend to address it using the capacity of deep neural networks.

---

[1] https://github.com/ashisht96/DeepPS2.

Deep Learning-Based Methods. Deep learning has seen great progress addressing photometric stereo [7,9,10,17,36,50]. Santo *et al.* [36] were the first to propose a deep learning-based method to obtain per-pixel surface normals. However, they were limited by the pre-defined order of pixels at the input. Later, Chen *et al.* in their subsequent works [7,9,10] proposed to model the spatial information using feature-extractor and features-pooling based strategies for photometric stereo. Further, the works by Yao *et al.* [49] and Wang *et al.* [44] proposed to extract and combine the local and global features for better photometric understanding. However, all these methods require ground truth surface normals for supervision which is generally difficult to obtain. Recently, Taniai & Maehara [41] proposed a self-supervised network to directly output the surface normal using a set of images and reconstruct them but with known lightings as input. Kaya *et al.* [20] expanded their method to deal with inter-reflections under an uncalibrated setting, however, the lighting estimation was still supervised. Other methods such as Lichy *et al.* [28], and Boss *et al.* [4] predicted shape and material using three or less and two images (one with and one without flash), respectively. While LERPS [43] infers lighting and surface normal from a single image, it requires multiple images (one at a time) for training. We work towards an uncalibrated photometric stereo method that uses only two differently illuminated images as the input while estimating lightings, surface normals, and albedos, all in a self-supervised manner.

3   Understanding PS2: Photometric Stereo Using Two Images

Before describing the PS2 problem, we review some key features of the SfS [15] and the traditional PS problem [46]. We assume that an orthographic camera images the surface under uniform directional lighting with viewing direction $v \in \mathbb{R}^3$ pointing along the z-direction and the image plane parallel to the XY plane of the 3D Cartesian coordinate system XYZ.

3.1   Shape from Shading (SfS)

Consider an anisotropic non-Lambertian surface f with the Bidirectional Reflectance Distribution Function (BRDF) ρ. Let the surface point (x, y) be characterized by the surface normal $n \in \mathbb{R}^3$, illuminated by the light source in the direction $\ell \in \mathbb{R}^3$, and viewed from the direction $v \in \mathbb{R}^3$. The image formation of such a surface is given as per Eq. 1.

$$I(x, y) = \rho(n, \ell, v)\psi_{f,s}(x, y) \left[n(x, y)^T \ell \right] + \epsilon \qquad (1)$$

Here, $\psi_{f,s}(x, y)$ specifies the attached and the cast shadows. It is equal to 0, if (x, y) is shadowed and equal to 1, otherwise. ϵ incorporates the global illumination and noise effect. $I(x, y)$ is the normalized gray level with respect to the light source intensity. Clearly, with albedo and lightings being known apriori, the surface normals $n(x,y)$ in the revolution cone around the lighting direction ℓ constitute the set of infinite solutions to Eq. 1. Therefore, it becomes an ill-posed problem and is difficult to solve locally.

3.2 Photometric Stereo (PS)

The simplest solution to overcome the ill-posedness of SfS is to have $m \geq 2$ differently illuminated images of the object taken from the same viewpoint. In general, for multiple light sources, Eq. 1 extends to the following.

$$I_j(x,y) = \rho(n, \ell_j, v)\psi_{f,s}(x,y)\left[n(x,y)^T\ell_j\right] + \epsilon_j \qquad (2)$$

Here, the equation is specific to the jth light source. For $m \geq 3$ and a Lambertian surface, Eq. 2 formulates a photometric stereo problem (the traditional one for $m = 3$). Solving such a system is advantageous as it is well-posed and can be solved locally, unlike SfS.

3.3 The PS2 Problem

With such a non-differential formulation (as in Eq. 2), the three unknowns (n_x, n_y, n_z) can be obtained by solving three or more linear equations. However, such a formulation is tricky to solve under two scenarios: (i) when the light sources are coplanar (rank-deficit formulation) and (ii) when $m = 2$. These scenarios lead us to the formulation of the PS2 problem - photometric stereo with two images, as described in Eq. 3.

$$\rho(n, \ell_1, v)\psi_{f,s}(x,y)\left[n(x,y)^T\ell_1\right] + \epsilon_1 = I_1(x,y)$$

$$\rho(n, \ell_2, v)\psi_{f,s}(x,y)\left[n(x,y)^T\ell_2\right] + \epsilon_2 = I_2(x,y)$$

$$n_x(x,y)^2 + n_y(x,y)^2 + n_z(x,y)^2 = 1 \qquad (3)$$

The non-linearity in the third part of Eq. 3 could give non-unique solution [18]. Adding one more image (under non-coplanar light source configuration) can straightaway solve the problem. However, it will fail when the surface is arbitrarily complex in its reflectance properties. Further, the problem becomes even more difficult to solve when albedo is unknown.

4   Method

In this section, we describe DeepPS2, a deep learning-based solution to the PS2 problem. Further, we describe several design considerations, light space sampling and discretization, and share the training strategy (Fig. 1).

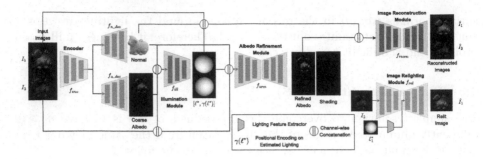

Fig. 1. The proposed inverse rendering framework, called DeepPS2, for shape, material, and illumination estimation. The encoder-decoder design is inspired by Hourglass networks [47]. Layer-wise skip connections are avoided for visual clarity

4.1   Network Architecture

Let $I_1, I_2 \in \mathbb{R}^{C \times H \times W}$ be the two images corresponding to the lighting directions ℓ_1 and ℓ_2, respectively. The two images along with the object mask $M \in \mathbb{R}^{1 \times H \times W}$ are fed to the encoder f_{enc} to obtain an abstract feature map ϕ_{img}, as described in Eq. 4.

$$\phi_{img} = f_{enc}([I_1, I_2, M]; \boldsymbol{\theta}_{enc}) \tag{4}$$

Here, $[\cdot]$ represents channel-wise concatenation and $\boldsymbol{\theta}_{enc}$ represents the parameters of the encoder.

Surface Normal and Albedo Estimation. We use ϕ_{img} to obtain an estimate of surface normal map $\hat{N}$ and the albedo $\hat{A}$ through the decoders f_{n_dec} and f_{a_dec}, respectively, as described in Eq. 5.

$$\hat{N} = f_{n\_dec}(\phi_{img}; \boldsymbol{\theta}_{n\_dec})$$

$$\hat{A} = f_{a\_dec}(\phi_{img}; \boldsymbol{\theta}_{a\_dec}) \tag{5}$$

Here, $\hat{A} = [\hat{A}_1, \hat{A}_2]$ represents the albedos of two images I_1 and I_2 together. The design of each encoder-decoder combination[2] is inspired by that of the Hourglass network [47].

Lighting Estimation. A straightforward way to estimate lighting directions could be to use another fully connected branch and train the network to regress to the desired lightings directly from ϕ_{img}. However, fully connected layers require a large number of parameters. Further, obtaining precise lighting information directly just from the image features would be difficult since it would not have the explicit knowledge of the structure and reflectance properties of the underlying surface. With an intent to keep the entire architecture fully convolutional, we propose an *illumination module* (f_{ill}) to predict the desired lighting directions by using the estimated normal map and albedos, as described in Eq. 6.

$$\hat{l}_i = f_{ill}([\hat{N}, \hat{A}_i]; \boldsymbol{\theta}_{lem}) \tag{6}$$

---

[2] The detailed layer-wise architecture can be found in our supplementary material.

Here, $i = 1, 2$ corresponding to two images I_1 and I_2, respectively.

At this stage, one straightforward approach could be to use the estimated normal, albedos, and lightings in order to reconstruct the original images through the image rendering equation (see Eq. 11). However, the estimated albedo $\hat{A}$ without lighting estimates fails to capture the complex specularities on the surface (see Fig. 4). Also, the estimated lightings were a little far from the desired ones.

Thus, the question now is - *how do we validate the accuracy of the estimated albedos and lightings*, especially when there is no ground truth supervision? The albedos and lightings go hand-in-hand and are dependent on each other as far as image rendering is considered, of course, in addition to the surface normal (see Generalized Bas Relief (GBR) ambiguity [3]). To address the aforementioned concerns, we propose two crucial resolves: (i) *albedo refinement* before image reconstruction and (ii) *image relighting* using the estimated lightings.

Albedo Refinement by Specularity Modeling. As discussed earlier, the estimated albedo $\hat{A}$ failed to represent the specularities directly from the image features. Most of the existing deep photometric stereo methods have implicitly handled specularities using multiple differently illuminated images through max-pooling and global-local feature-fusion. However, it is crucial to understand that the specularities are essentially the reflections on the surface, and information about surface geometry can help model such specularities better. Understanding surface geometry becomes even more crucial when we have just one or two images to model the surface reflection. Therefore, we choose to explicitly model these specularities and refine the albedo estimate using a few reasonable and realistic assumptions.

We assume that the specular BRDF is isotropic and is only the function of the half-vector h and the surface normal n at any point on the surface as the BRDF can be re-parameterized to a half-vector based function [35]. In doing so, we could omit the Fresnel Reflection coefficients and geometric attenuation associated with modelling BRDFs. The authors in [6,31] found that the isotropic BRDF can also be modeled simply by two parameters $\theta_h = cos^{-1}(n^T h)$ and $\theta_d = cos^{-1}(v^T h)$. Therefore, we use the estimated lighting ℓ_i to compute $cos(\theta_h)$ and $cos(\theta_d)$ to further refine the albedo. Additionally, we use positional encoding to model the high-frequency specularities in the refined albedo. In short, we construct the L_i as per Eq. 7.

$$L_i = [p_i, \gamma(p_i)]$$

$$p_i = [n^T h_i, v^T h_i] \qquad (7)$$

Here, $\gamma(\eta) = [sin(2^0 \pi \eta), cos(2^0 \pi \eta), ..., sin(2^{m-1} \pi \eta), cos(2^{m-1} \pi \eta)]$. We choose $m = 3$ in our method. Futher, $h_i = \frac{\ell_i + v}{||\ell_i + v||}$.

Following these observations, we use an encoder-decoder based *albedo refinement module* (f_{arm}) to obtain the refined albedo by considering the estimated lightings L_i, albedos $\hat{A}$, surface normal $\hat{N}$, and the underlying images as its input. Equation 8 describes the information flow.

$$\hat{A}_{i(ref)} = f_{arm}([I_i, \hat{N}, \hat{A}_i, L_i,]; \theta_{arm}) \qquad (8)$$

Image Relighting. Generally, at this stage, the existing approaches proceed further to use the rendering equation and reconstruct the input image(s). However, the lightings are either known or have been estimated with ground truth supervision. This allows stable training and offers convincing results. However, in our case, the lightings are estimated without any explicit supervision and are expected to produce learning instabilities. So the question is, *how can we ensure that the estimated lightings are close to the desired ones without any ground truth supervision?*

As an additional check on the authenticity of the estimated lightings, we propose to use them for the image relighting task. We use an *image relighting module* (f_{rel}) to relight one image into the other using the estimated lighting as the target lighting and measure the quality of the relit image, as described in Eq. 9.

$$\hat{I}_{1(rel)} = f_{rel}(I_2, \phi(\hat{\ell}_1); \theta_{rel}) \tag{9}$$

Here, $\phi(\hat{\ell}_1)$ is the lighting feature extracted from the desired target lighting $\hat{\ell}_1$. The quality of the relit image fosters the lighting estimates to be close to the desired ones.

Image Reconstruction. Having obtained the estimates of surface normal, albedo, and lightings, we finally use them to obtain the reflectance map R_i using the encoder-decoder based *image reconstruction module* (f_{recon}), as described in Eq. 10.

$$R_i = f_{recon}([I_i, \hat{N}, \hat{A}_{i(ref)}, \hat{\ell}_i]; \theta_{recon}) \tag{10}$$

The reflectance image R_i is then used to reconstruct the associated image $\hat{I}_i$, as described in Eq. 11.

$$\hat{I}_i = R_i \odot max(\hat{\ell}_i^T \hat{N}, 0) \tag{11}$$

Here, $\odot$ refers to the element-wise multiplication.

In this way, the proposed DeepPS2 produces estimates of surface normal, albedos, and lightings as well as relights the image under target lightings by using only two images as input and no additional ground truth supervision. Based on the network performance, we show that the PS2 problem can be well addressed using the benefits of deep learning framework.

4.2   More on Lighting Estimation: The Light Space Sampling

As discussed earlier, an intuitive approach to estimate light source directions would be to directly regress them from image(s). However, regressing these values to the exact ones is difficult and can cause learning difficulties [7]. Further, under the distant light source assumption, it is easier and better to specify a region in the light space rather than the exact direction while locating the light source. Additionally, this eases the light source calibration during data acquisition. Therefore, we choose to formulate the lighting estimation as a classification problem. A few methods in the recent past have adopted the classification formulation [7,10] and weak calibration setting [28] for lighting and shape estimation and have produced excellent results.

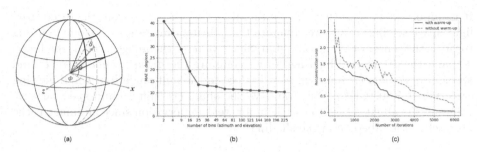

Fig. 2. (a) Light space discretization into $K = 25$ bins. $\delta = 180/2K$ is the maximum angular deviation. (b) Variation of MAE with K. (c) Effect of early stage warm-up

In this work, we discretize the light space (upper hemisphere) into $K = 25$ bins (as shown in Fig. 2(a)) i.e. 5 bins along the azimuth direction $\phi \in [0°, 180°]$ centered at $[18°, 54°, 90°, 126°, 162°]$ and 5 bins along the elevation direction $\theta \in [-90°, 90°]$ centered at $[-72°, -36°, 0°, 36°, 72°]$. While each bin suffers a maximum angular deviation of $18°$ along each direction (Fig. 2(a)), they offer a relatively simpler light source configuration during data acquisition. They can be realized using hand-held lighting devices. Further, learning under such discretized light space configuration allows the network to better tolerate errors in the estimated lightings and the subsequent downstream tasks. During training, the network must select the appropriate bin in the light space to understand the light source configuration from the input image, the estimated normal map, and the albedos.

4.3   Network Training

We use the standard DiLiGenT benchmark dataset [39] having the 10 objects imaged under 96 different light directions with complex non-Lambertian surfaces. We implement DeepPS2 in Pytorch [32] with Adam optimizer [22] and initial learning rate of 1×10^{-4} for 25 epochs and batch size 32 on NVIDIA RTX 5000 GPU. The learning rate is reduced to half after every 5 epochs. It is observed that if the object under consideration has relatively simple reflectance properties, even a randomly initialized network trained with the image reconstruction loss can lead to good solutions. However, for complex scenes, it is better to warm up the network by initializing the weights through weak supervision only at the early stages of training [20, 41]. In our case, we perform this warming up for normal, albedo, and lighting estimation through weak supervision using L_1-loss ($\mathcal{L}_{L_1}$), L_2-loss ($\mathcal{L}_{L_2}$), and the perceptual loss ($\mathcal{L}_{perp}$) for first 2000 iterations, as described in Sect. 4.4. For weak supervision, we randomly sample 10 images (preferably, each one from a different lighting bin) and estimate the normal map using the least-squares formulation [46], as per Eq. 12.

$$\hat{N}' = L^{-1}I \tag{12}$$

It is important to note that the lighting directions in L are from the discretized light space setting, where we compute the lighting direction as the one pointing towards the center of the selected bin. Since we have the images, the normal map $\hat{N}'$, and the discretized lightings L, we compute the *diffuse shading* $(\boldsymbol{n}^T \boldsymbol{\ell})$ and *specular highlights* (regions where $\boldsymbol{n}$ is close to the half-angle $\boldsymbol{h}$ of $\boldsymbol{\ell}$ and viewing direction $\boldsymbol{v} = [0, 0, 1]^T$). Once we have the shadings (diffuse and specular), we compute the albedos $(\hat{A}')$ to use them for weak supervision since an image is the product of the albedo and the shading.

4.4 Loss Functions

In this section, we describe the loss function used for training the entire framework. Equation 13 describes the combination of L_1-loss and the perceptual loss $\mathcal{L}_{perp}$ used for both image reconstruction and relighting.

$$\mathcal{L}_T(X, \hat{X}) = \lambda_1 \mathcal{L}_1(X, \hat{X}) + \lambda_2 \mathcal{L}_2(X, \hat{X}) + \lambda_{perp} \mathcal{L}_{perp}(X, \hat{X}) \qquad (13)$$

Here,

$$\mathcal{L}_1(X, \hat{X}) = \| X - \hat{X} \|_1$$

$$\mathcal{L}_2(X, \hat{X}) = \| X - \hat{X} \|_2^2$$

$$\mathcal{L}_{perp}(X, \hat{X}) = \frac{1}{WHC} \sum_{x=1}^{W} \sum_{y=1}^{H} \sum_{z=1}^{C} \| \phi(X)_{x,y,z} - \phi(\hat{X})_{x,y,z} \|_1 \qquad (14)$$

Here, ϕ is the output of VGG-19 [40] network and W, H, C are the width, height, and depth of the extracted feature ϕ, respectively. $\lambda_1 = \lambda_2 = 0.5$ and $\lambda_{perp} = 1.0$.

Weak Supervision. We use the $\mathcal{L}_T$ and the standard cross-entropy loss to provide weak supervision (for first 2000 iterations) for albedos and lightings, respectively. However, for surface normals, we use Eq. 15.

$$\mathcal{L}_{norm}(\hat{N}, \hat{N}') = \frac{1}{M} \sum_p \| \hat{N}_p - \hat{N}'_p \|_2^2 \qquad (15)$$

5 Experimental Results

In this section, we show the qualitative and quantitative comparison of the DeepPS2 with several baseline approaches. The classical methods [29,34] have provided the numerical resolution to the underlying ambiguities in PS2. However, the code and results on the DiLiGenT benchmark are not available for comparison. Moreover, since deep learning-based methods have significantly outperformed the traditional photometric stereo methods (even in handling ambiguities), we resort to comparing our work only with the state-of-the-art deep learning-based methods such as UPS-FCN [9], SDPS-Net [7], IRPS [41], Kaya et al. [20], Lichy et al. [28], and Boss et al. [4]. They have been chosen carefully

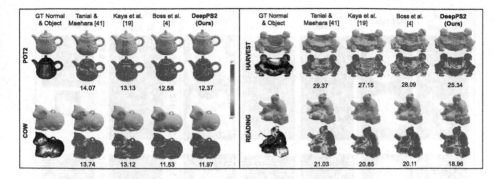

Fig. 3. Surface normal maps obtained using a randomly chosen input image pair. More results are available in the supplementary material

as they can be modified to align with our problem setting by re-training them with two images as input for a fair comparison.

Results on Normal Estimation. Table 1 shows a quantitative comparison of the proposed framework with the other deep learning-based methods. All the methods have been trained with two images as input, and the Mean Angular Error (MAE) is reported to quantify the surface normal estimation. Since IRPS [41] is designed to take two images (one with frontal flash), we evaluate it using pairs of images where one image is lit frontally i.e., from the bin corresponding to $\theta = 0°$ and $\phi = 90°$. From Table 1, we observe that the proposed DeepPS2 obtains the best average MAE value and best (or at least second best) individual scores for eight different objects (except POT1 and BEAR). Even though our framework performs best in the calibrated setting, it outperforms the other baselines under the uncalibrated setting as well. Furthermore, even with no ground truth supervision, our method outperforms other supervised (row 1–6) and self-supervised (row 7–8) methods. To appreciate the results qualitatively, we show a visual comparison of READING, HARVEST, COW, and POT2 with the self-supervised baselines [20,41], and a two-image based supervised method [4] in Fig. 3. Interestingly, DeepPS2 performs the best on objects like HARVEST and READING, having complex shadows and inter-reflections with spatially-varying material.

Results on Albedo Estimation. In Fig. 4, we present a qualitative assessment of the albedos obtained using our method. We observe that the learned albedos are able to handle the complex shadows and specular highlights, especially after refinement using the estimated lightings.

Results on Lighting Estimation. The goal of discretized lighting is to remove the network's dependence on precise lighting calibration. Therefore, we attempt to model the illumination using the weakly calibrated lighting directions such as front, front-right/left, top, top-right/left, bottom, bottom-right/left, etc. Given that the light space discretization yields an MAE of 18° numerically, we intend to establish that the network may not need precise calibration at all times. A rough and/or abstract understanding of lighting directions should help guide the

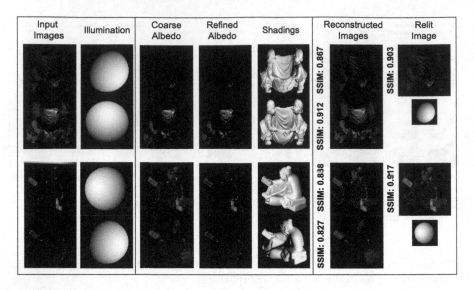

Fig. 4. Inverse rendering results on HARVEST and READING objects. The reconstruction and relighting module yield the SSIM of 0.837 and 0.779, respectively, when averaged over all the objects on the DiLiGenT Benchmark. More results are available in the supplementary material

network towards realistic shape estimation. To better evaluate the performance of the *illumination module*, we visualize the learned illumination over a sphere in Fig. 4. It is observed that the illumination module captures the distribution of light sources essential for modeling the complex specularities in the refined albedos at the later stage.

Results on Image Relighting and Reconstruction. We report the widely used Structural Similarity Index (SSIM) [45] to quantify the quality of the reconstructed and relight images. However, these results are best appreciated visually. Therefore, we use Fig. 4 to show the quality of the generated images. The quality of the results establishes that our inverse rendering results are sufficiently stable for realistic relighting and reconstruction.

5.1   Ablation Studies

In this section, we discuss several design choices in DeepPS2 under different experimental settings.

Ablation 1: *What if We Do Not Include Lighting Estimation in the Framework?* We attempt to understand the effect of including the lighting information explicitly in the surface normal estimation through such an inverse rendering-based framework. In Table 2, comparing the experiment IDs 1 and 2, we observe that lighting estimation is crucial for the task at hand. This observation is in line with the classical rendering equation that requires lighting directions to understand the reflectance properties and shadows on the surface.

Table 1. Mean Angular Error (MAE) over 10 randomly chosen image pairs per object from the DiLiGenT Benchmark [39]. GREEN and coloured cells indicate the best and the second best performing methods, respectively. Rows 1–6 and 7–8 correspond to supervised and self-supervised approaches, respectively

Type of Method	Objects → Method ↓	Ball	Cat	Pot1	Bear	Pot2	Buddha	Goblet	Reading	Cow	Harvest	Average
Calibrated	PS-FCN [9]	6.41	20.04	19.67	16.95	21.12	23.04	24.81	29.93	17.23	34.68	21.38 ± 2.05
Uncalibrated	UPS-FCN [9]	9.71	18.97	17.85	15.12	18.62	19.77	22.14	27.36	14.83	31.25	19.56 ± 1.58
Calibrated	SDPS-Net [7]	7.97	19.88	18.12	12.51	18.25	25.12	26.36	27.47	15.21	30.59	20.14 ± 1.17
Uncalibrated	SDPS-Net [7]	7.81	21.74	19.73	13.25	20.47	27.81	29.66	31.12	18.94	34.14	22.6 ± 1.02
Uncalibrated	Boss et al. [4]	7.71	14.81	10.17	8.01	12.89	15.98	18.18	21.54	11.96	27.36	14.85 ± 0.98
Uncalibrated	Lichy et al. [28]	7.42	20.34	11.87	9.94	11.12	18.75	19.38	21.51	12.93	29.52	16.27 ± 1.01
Calibrated	Taniai & Maehara [41]	7.03	10.02	11.62	8.74	12.58	18.25	16.85	21.31	14.97	28.89	15.03 ± 0.96
Uncalibrated	Kaya et al. [20]	6.97	9.57	10.14	8.69	13.81	17.57	15.93	21.87	14.81	28.72	14.81 ± 0.89
Calibrated	DeepPS2 (Ours)	6.17	9.62	10.35	8.87	12.78	14.78	13.29	18.34	10.13	25.18	12.95 ± 0.64
Uncalibrated	DeepPS2 (Ours)	6.28	9.87	10.73	9.67	12.09	14.51	14.22	19.94	11.08	26.06	13.44 ± 0.67

Further, we intended to know the deviation in MAE for surface normal estimation when actual lightings (calibrated setting) are used. Although the network performs better under the calibrated setting (see Table 1), the error difference is not very large (0.49 units). This supports our idea of using weaker calibrations for surface normal estimation under distant lightings.

Table 2. Quantitative comparison of various design choices. LE: Lighting Estimation, AR: Albedo Refinement, PE: Positional Encoding, and IR: Image Relighting. Experiments IDs 1–6 include warm-up

ID	LE	AR	PE	IR	Ball	Cat	Pot1	Bear	Pot2	Buddha	Goblet	Reading	Cow	Harvest	Average
1	✗	✗	✗	✗	9.87	36.55	19.39	12.42	14.52	13.19	20.57	58.96	19.75	55.51	26.07
2	✓	✗	✗	✗	9.32	15.62	16.41	10.96	15.77	19.93	18.37	32.34	16.17	30.26	18.51
3	✓	✓	✗	✗	7.37	15.64	10.58	9.37	14.72	15.06	18.1	23.78	16.31	27.17	15.85
4	✓	✓	✓	✗	6.88	12.16	11.13	9.79	15.11	14.89	16.07	20.46	11.85	27.22	14.55
5	✓	✓	✓	✓	6.28	9.87	10.73	9.67	12.09	14.51	14.22	19.94	11.08	26.06	13.44
6	frontally-lit image				6.74	9.38	10.13	9.08	13.18	14.58	14.63	17.84	11.98	24.87	13.24
7	w/o warm-up				12.43	25.01	22.82	15.44	20.57	25.76	29.16	52.16	25.53	44.45	27.33
8	fully supervised				5.14	8.97	10.28	8.92	9.89	12.76	12.38	18.52	9.81	23.22	11.98

Ablation 2: *Effect of Discretizing the Light Space on Normal Estimation.* Figure 2 (b) shows the effect of a different number of bins on the MAE evaluated over the DiLiGenT benchmark. We resort to choosing $K = 25$ bins as the reduction in the MAE plateaus (roughly) after that point. Further, the light space discretization not only reduces the computational overhead but also helps the network understand the lighting dynamics more holistically. This is evident from the MAE reported in Table 1 and quality of the refined albedos in Fig. 4.

Ablation 3: *Do Albedo Refinement and Image Relighting Help in Modeling the Illumination?* Qualitative results in Fig. 4 show how well the refined albedos capture the specularities on the surface. Table 2 (IDs 2 and 3) shows the performance improvement by including the *albedo refinement module*. The explicit specularity modeling is observed to produce realistic albedos. The performance is further enhanced through the use of positional encoding (Table 2 ID 4) as it helps the module to better capture the high-frequency characteristics in the refined albedo. Finally, the inclusion of the *image relighting module* further reduces the MAE (Table 2 ID 5). Since the relighting module is solely driven by the estimated lightings, relighting helps in obtaining better surface normal estimates through better lighting estimation as an additional task.

Ablation 4: *What is the Effect of Warming up the Network with Weak Supervision at the Early Stages of Training?* We also consider understanding the effect of weak supervision during the early stage warm-up. Table 2 (IDs 5 and 7) clearly establishes the benefit of warming-up. Figure 2 (c) shows the convergence with and without the warm-up. Clearly, an early-stage warm-up provides stable and faster convergence as the outliers in the images are excluded at the early stages during weak supervision.

Ablation 5: *What if the Lighting Directions of one Image at the Input is Known?* We evaluate an interesting and practical case where one of the two input images is captured with collocated light source and camera i.e., $\ell = v = [0, 0, 1]^T$. Since the lighting direction is known, we provide (auxiliary) supervision to the illumination module to obtain a better lighting estimate for the other image. Table 2 (ID 6) shows the results obtained over image pairs having one image sampled from the frontal lighting bin i.e. $\theta = 0°, \phi = 90°$. Under this setting, the method performs better than the completely self-supervised version because frontally-lit (flashed) images offer a better understanding of specularities on complex surfaces. Finally, we also show the performance of DeepPS2 under a fully supervised setting (Table 2 (ID 8)) to establish the upper bound of DeepPS2.

6   Conclusion

In this work, we address the PS2 problem (photometric stereo with two images) using a self-supervised deep learning framework called DeepPS2. In addition to surface normals, the proposed method also estimates albedos and lightings and performs image relighting, all without any ground truth supervision. Interestingly, we demonstrate that weakly calibrated lightings can be enough for the network to learn the underlying shape of an object. In conjunction with image reconstruction, image relighting helps in better lighting estimation. While other uncalibrated methods have used ground truth supervision for learning to estimate lightings, we do so entirely in a self-supervised manner. To the best of our knowledge, we are the first to address photometric stereo using two images in a deep learning setting.

References

1. Abrams, A., Hawley, C., Pless, R.: Heliometric stereo: shape from sun position. In: Fitzgibbon, A., Lazebnik, S., Perona, P., Sato, Y., Schmid, C. (eds.) ECCV 2012. LNCS, vol. 7573, pp. 357–370. Springer, Heidelberg (2012). https://doi.org/10.1007/978-3-642-33709-3_26

2. Ackermann, J., Langguth, F., Fuhrmann, S., Goesele, M.: Photometric stereo for outdoor webcams. In: 2012 IEEE Conference on Computer Vision and Pattern Recognition, pp. 262–269. IEEE (2012)

3. Belhumeur, P.N., Kriegman, D.J., Yuille, A.L.: The bas-relief ambiguity. Int. J. Comput. Vision **35**(1), 33–44 (1999)

4. Boss, M., Jampani, V., Kim, K., Lensch, H., Kautz, J.: Two-shot spatially-varying BRDF and shape estimation. In: Proceedings of the IEEE/CVF Conference on Computer Vision and Pattern Recognition, pp. 3982–3991 (2020)

5. Boykov, Y., Veksler, O., Zabih, R.: Fast approximate energy minimization via graph cuts. IEEE Trans. Pattern Anal. Mach. Intell. **23**(11), 1222–1239 (2001)

6. Burley, B., Studios, W.D.A.: Physically-based shading at Disney. In: ACM SIGGRAPH, vol. 2012, pp. 1–7 (2012)

7. Chen, G., Han, K., Shi, B., Matsushita, Y., Wong, K.Y.K.: Self-calibrating deep photometric stereo networks. In: Proceedings of the IEEE Conference on Computer Vision and Pattern Recognition, pp. 8739–8747 (2019)

8. Chen, G., Han, K., Shi, B., Matsushita, Y., Wong, K.Y.K.: Deep photometric stereo for non-Lambertian surfaces. IEEE Trans. Pattern Anal. Mach. Intell. **44**, 129–142 (2020)

9. Chen, G., Han, K., Wong, K.-Y.K.: PS-FCN: a flexible learning framework for photometric stereo. In: Ferrari, V., Hebert, M., Sminchisescu, C., Weiss, Y. (eds.) ECCV 2018. LNCS, vol. 11213, pp. 3–19. Springer, Cham (2018). https://doi.org/10.1007/978-3-030-01240-3_1

10. Chen, G., Waechter, M., Shi, B., Wong, K.-Y.K., Matsushita, Y.: What is learned in deep uncalibrated photometric stereo? In: Vedaldi, A., Bischof, H., Brox, T., Frahm, J.-M. (eds.) ECCV 2020. LNCS, vol. 12359, pp. 745–762. Springer, Cham (2020). https://doi.org/10.1007/978-3-030-58568-6_44

11. Furukawa, Y., Ponce, J.: Accurate, dense, and robust multiview stereopsis. IEEE Trans. Pattern Anal. Mach. Intell. **32**(8), 1362–1376 (2009)

12. Hernández, C., Vogiatzis, G., Brostow, G.J., Stenger, B., Cipolla, R.: Non-rigid photometric stereo with colored lights. In: 2007 IEEE 11th International Conference on Computer Vision, pp. 1–8. IEEE (2007)

13. Hernández, C., Vogiatzis, G., Cipolla, R.: Overcoming shadows in 3-source photometric stereo. IEEE Trans. Pattern Anal. Mach. Intell. **33**(2), 419–426 (2010)

14. Horn, B., Klaus, B., Horn, P.: Robot Vision. MIT Press, Cambridge (1986)

15. Horn, B.K.: Shape from shading: a method for obtaining the shape of a smooth opaque object from one view (1970)

16. Ikeda, O.: A robust shape-from-shading algorithm using two images and control of boundary conditions. In: Proceedings 2003 International Conference on Image Processing (Cat. No. 03CH37429), vol. 1, pp. 14–17. IEEE (2003)

17. Ikehata, S.: CNN-PS: CNN-based photometric stereo for general non-convex surfaces. In: Ferrari, V., Hebert, M., Sminchisescu, C., Weiss, Y. (eds.) ECCV 2018. LNCS, vol. 11219, pp. 3–19. Springer, Cham (2018). https://doi.org/10.1007/978-3-030-01267-0_1

18. Ikeuchi, K., Horn, B.K.: Numerical shape from shading and occluding boundaries. Artif. Intell. **17**(1–3), 141–184 (1981)
19. Jung, J., Lee, J.Y., So Kweon, I.: One-day outdoor photometric stereo via skylight estimation. In: Proceedings of the IEEE Conference on Computer Vision and Pattern Recognition, pp. 4521–4529 (2015)
20. Kaya, B., Kumar, S., Oliveira, C., Ferrari, V., Van Gool, L.: Uncalibrated neural inverse rendering for photometric stereo of general surfaces. In: Proceedings of the IEEE/CVF Conference on Computer Vision and Pattern Recognition, pp. 3804–3814 (2021)
21. Kendall, A., et al.: End-to-end learning of geometry and context for deep stereo regression. In: Proceedings of the IEEE International Conference on Computer Vision, pp. 66–75 (2017)
22. Kingma, D.P., Ba, J.: Adam: a method for stochastic optimization. arXiv preprint arXiv:1412.6980 (2014)
23. Kozera, R.: On shape recovery from two shading patterns. Int. J. Pattern Recogn. Artif. Intell. **6**(04), 673–698 (1992)
24. Kumar, S.: Jumping manifolds: geometry aware dense non-rigid structure from motion. In: Proceedings of the IEEE/CVF Conference on Computer Vision and Pattern Recognition, pp. 5346–5355 (2019)
25. Kumar, S., Dai, Y., Li, H.: Monocular dense 3D reconstruction of a complex dynamic scene from two perspective frames. In: Proceedings of the IEEE International Conference on Computer Vision, pp. 4649–4657 (2017)
26. Kumar, S., Dai, Y., Li, H.: Superpixel soup: monocular dense 3D reconstruction of a complex dynamic scene. IEEE Trans. Pattern Anal. Mach. Intell. **43**(5), 1705–1717 (2019)
27. Li, J., Robles-Kelly, A., You, S., Matsushita, Y.: Learning to minify photometric stereo. In: Proceedings of the IEEE/CVF Conference on Computer Vision and Pattern Recognition, pp. 7568–7576 (2019)
28. Lichy, D., Wu, J., Sengupta, S., Jacobs, D.W.: Shape and material capture at home. In: Proceedings of the IEEE/CVF Conference on Computer Vision and Pattern Recognition, pp. 6123–6133 (2021)
29. Mecca, R., Durou, J.-D.: Unambiguous photometric stereo using two images. In: Maino, G., Foresti, G.L. (eds.) ICIAP 2011. LNCS, vol. 6978, pp. 286–295. Springer, Heidelberg (2011). https://doi.org/10.1007/978-3-642-24085-0_30
30. Onn, R., Bruckstein, A.: Integrability disambiguates surface recovery in two-image photometric stereo. Int. J. Comput. Vision **5**(1), 105–113 (1990)
31. Pacanowski, R., Celis, O.S., Schlick, C., Granier, X., Poulin, P., Cuyt, A.: Rational BRDF. IEEE Trans. Visual Comput. Graphics **18**(11), 1824–1835 (2012)
32. Paszke, A., et al.: Automatic differentiation in PyTorch (2017)
33. Prados, E., Faugeras, O.: Shape from shading: a well-posed problem? In: 2005 IEEE Computer Society Conference on Computer Vision and Pattern Recognition (CVPR 2005), vol. 2, pp. 870–877. IEEE (2005)
34. Quéau, Y., Mecca, R., Durou, J.D., Descombes, X.: Photometric stereo with only two images: a theoretical study and numerical resolution. Image Vis. Comput. **57**, 175–191 (2017)
35. Rusinkiewicz, S.M.: A new change of variables for efficient BRDF representation. In: Drettakis, G., Max, N. (eds.) EGSR 1998. E, pp. 11–22. Springer, Vienna (1998). https://doi.org/10.1007/978-3-7091-6453-2_2
36. Santo, H., Samejima, M., Sugano, Y., Shi, B., Matsushita, Y.: Deep photometric stereo network. In: Proceedings of the IEEE International Conference on Computer Vision Workshops, pp. 501–509 (2017)

37. Sato, Y., Ikeuchi, K.: Reflectance analysis under solar illumination. In: Proceedings of the Workshop on Physics-Based Modeling in Computer Vision, pp. 180–187. IEEE (1995)

38. Schonberger, J.L., Frahm, J.M.: Structure-from-motion revisited. In: Proceedings of the IEEE Conference on Computer Vision and Pattern Recognition, pp. 4104–4113 (2016)

39. Shi, B., Wu, Z., Mo, Z., Duan, D., Yeung, S.K., Tan, P.: A benchmark dataset and evaluation for Non-Lambertian and uncalibrated photometric stereo. In: Proceedings of the IEEE Conference on Computer Vision and Pattern Recognition, pp. 3707–3716 (2016)

40. Simonyan, K., Zisserman, A.: Very deep convolutional networks for large-scale image recognition. arXiv preprint arXiv:1409.1556 (2014)

41. Taniai, T., Maehara, T.: Neural inverse rendering for general reflectance photometric stereo. In: International Conference on Machine Learning, pp. 4857–4866. PMLR (2018)

42. Taniai, T., Matsushita, Y., Sato, Y., Naemura, T.: Continuous 3D label stereo matching using local expansion moves. IEEE Trans. Pattern Anal. Mach. Intell. **40**(11), 2725–2739 (2017)

43. Tiwari, A., Raman, S.: LERPS: lighting estimation and relighting for photometric stereo. In: ICASSP 2022–2022 IEEE International Conference on Acoustics, Speech and Signal Processing (ICASSP), pp. 2060–2064. IEEE (2022)

44. Wang, X., Jian, Z., Ren, M.: Non-Lambertian photometric stereo network based on inverse reflectance model with collocated light. IEEE Trans. Image Process. **29**, 6032–6042 (2020)

45. Wang, Z., Simoncelli, E.P., Bovik, A.C.: Multiscale structural similarity for image quality assessment. In: The Thrity-Seventh Asilomar Conference on Signals, Systems & Computers, vol. 2, pp. 1398–1402. IEEE (2003)

46. Woodham, R.J.: Photometric method for determining surface orientation from multiple images. Opt. Eng. **19**(1), 139–144 (1980)

47. Yang, J., Liu, Q., Zhang, K.: Stacked hourglass network for robust facial landmark localisation. In: Proceedings of the IEEE Conference on Computer Vision and Pattern Recognition Workshops, pp. 79–87 (2017)

48. Yang, J., Ohnishi, N., Sugie, N.: Two-image photometric stereo method. In: Intelligent Robots and Computer Vision XI: Biological, Neural Net, and 3D Methods, vol. 1826, pp. 452–463. SPIE (1992)

49. Yao, Z., Li, K., Fu, Y., Hu, H., Shi, B.: GPS-Net: graph-based photometric stereo network. Adv. Neural. Inf. Process. Syst. **33**, 10306–10316 (2020)

50. Zheng, Q., Jia, Y., Shi, B., Jiang, X., Duan, L.Y., Kot, A.C.: SPLINE-Net: sparse photometric stereo through lighting interpolation and normal estimation networks. In: Proceedings of the IEEE/CVF International Conference on Computer Vision, pp. 8549–8558 (2019)

Instance Contour Adjustment
via Structure-Driven CNN

Shuchen Weng[1], Yi Wei[2], Ming-Ching Chang[3], and Boxin Shi[1(✉)]

[1] NERCVT, School of Computer Science, Peking University, Beijing, China
{shuchenweng,shiboxin}@pku.edu.cn
[2] Samsung Research America AI Center, New York, USA
yi.wei1@samsung.com
[3] University at Albany, State University of New York, New York, USA
mchang2@albany.edu

Abstract. Instance contour adjustment is desirable in image editing, which allows the contour of an instance in a photo to be either dilated or eroded via user sketching. This imposes several requirements for a favorable method in order to generate meaningful textures while preserving clear user-desired contours. Due to the ignorance of these requirements, the off-the-shelf image editing methods herein are unsuited. Therefore, we propose a specialized two-stage method. The first stage extracts the structural cues from the input image, and completes the missing structural cues for the adjusted area. The second stage is a structure-driven CNN which generates image textures following the guidance of the completed structural cues. In the structure-driven CNN, we redesign the context sampling strategy of the convolution operation and attention mechanism such that they can estimate and rank the relevance of the contexts based on the structural cues, and sample the top-ranked contexts regardless of their distribution on the image plane. Thus, the meaningfulness of image textures with clear and user-desired contours are guaranteed by the structure-driven CNN. In addition, our method does not require any semantic label as input, which thus ensures its well generalization capability. We evaluate our method against several baselines adapted from the related tasks, and the experimental results demonstrate its effectiveness.

1 Introduction

A photo can be considered as a composition of a certain number of instance(s), and the contour of an instance separates itself from the other instances. By adjusting instance contours, a user can achieve superior photography experience which cannot be met with the real but fixed scenery and even photography professionalism. For example, in Fig. 1 where the lake and Merlion are two instances,

---

Supplementary Information The online version contains supplementary material available at https://doi.org/10.1007/978-3-031-20071-7_9.

Fig. 1. Task comparison. The original and overlaid images are put on the left side of our results. The results of image inpainting [26] and semantic-guided (SG) inpainting [16] are shown below. The cyan dotted boxes highlight artifacts and the out-of-control contours. (Color figure online)

users hope to dilate the contour of the lake shape to be a flying pigeon; or they hope to create fantastic scenes, *e.g.*, eroding the contour of the Merlion to remove its body. These are moments when an instance contour adjustment function can turn the table.

In order to adjust the contour of an instance, users first extract the instance area (yellow in Fig. 1) with the image matting function. Then, users sketch the hypothetical contours which form two potential types of area: *(i)* **Dilated area** (refer to the left example) should be *exclusively* filled with the content of the instance area. *(ii)* **Eroded area** (refer to the right example) should be *exclusively* filled with the content external to the instance area.

These two *exclusion rules* distinguish the instance contour adjustment from the related tasks. In Fig. 1, we illustrate the differences among instance contour adjustment (ours) and the other two related tasks, *i.e.*, image inpainting and semantic-guided (SG) image inpainting. These two exclusion rules are not enforced in image inpainting, so the generated instance contours in Fig. 1 are out of user's control, and different instances tend to be mixed to cause the ambiguous structures. The semantic-guided image inpainting methods [6,16] estimate the semantic parsing mask for the input image, infer the semantic contour for the adjusted area to complete the semantic mask, and then use the completed semantic mask to guide the inpainting process. Since the inferred semantic contour is out of user's control, these two exclusion rules are not enforced in semantic-guided image inpainting either, as demonstrated by the ambiguous structures of instances in Fig. 1. Thus, it is nontrivial to study how to effectively enforce the two exclusion rules in order to generate reasonable textures for the adjusted area (dilated or eroded) while preserving the clear and desired contours that separate different instances.

In this paper, we propose a two-stage method to leverage the structural cues to address the instance contour adjustment. The dilated area and eroded area have their respective exclusion rule, so if they exist in the same image, we will handle them separately in order to avoid the potential conflicts. It is easier to complete the missing structural cues for the adjusted areas than completing the missing image textures, so we extract and complete two structural cues at the first stage, i.e., the structure image and the depth map, and use them to guide the completion of image textures at the second stage. In order to enforce the two exclusion rules, we propose a diffusion algorithm and employ a structure reconstruction model In [14] to complete the missing structural cues for the dilated area and eroded area, respectively.

At the second stage, we propose a structure-driven CNN to generate image textures based on the structural cues completed at the first stage. By "structure-driven", we mean that both the convolution operations and the attention mechanism follow the structural cues to sample potential regions of the same instance regardless of their distribution on the image plane while passing over regions of the distracting instances. Thus, different instances will not be mixed by the CNN for the adjusted area, and the clear and desired contours will be guaranteed. The structure-driven context sampling is performed as follows: given one region on the image plane, we estimate and rank the likelihoods of its contextual regions belonging to the same instance as itself, and sample the top-ranked regions as contexts. To compute the likelihood of two regions belonging to the same instance, we consider their two affinities: (i) the appearance affinity based on their inclusion relationship or color distance, and (ii) the geometry affinity based on their depth distance.

We collect a new landscape dataset to evaluate our method, and we also establish an evaluation protocol which is beneficial to the follow-up works.

2   Related Works

Semantic-guided inpainting attracts attention recently because the semantic mask can provide the structural cues for guiding image inpainting. The AIM 2020 Challenge on Image Extreme Inpainting [12] found that the introduction of the semantic mask can both increase and decrease the performance on the inpainting task, depending on how its processing was implemented. Therefore, it is nontrivial to study how to make use of the structural cues. There are only a few methods focusing on the semantic-guided inpainting. For example, Song et al. [16] proposed a two-stage network, where the first stage completes the hole regions of the semantic mask, and the second stage completes the hole of the image. Liao et al. [6,7] proposed to estimate the semantic mask on the fly, and the estimated mask is injected back to influence the intermediate feature maps.

Coarse to Fine. Many existing inpainting methods implement the coarse-to-fine pipeline with two stages. Their first stage completes the structural cues such as edge-preserved structure image [14], contour of foreground object [20], monochromic image [17], and coarse textures [2,11,13,22–24,26]. Their second stage directly takes as input the completed structural cues to generate image textures. However, we observe that it is hard to exert the influences of the structural cues effectively by processing them with the learnable parameters. Therefore, our structure-driven CNN uses them as the guidance to sample the irregularly-distributed top-ranked regions as contexts for the convolution operation and attention mechanism, which leads to user-desired contours.

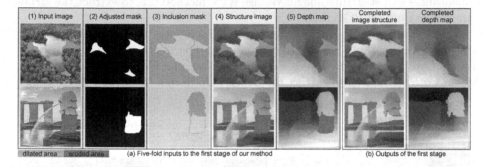

Fig. 2. Inputs and outputs of structural cue completion (first stage). (2) An adjusted mask is a binary mask which indicates the adjusted area. (3) An inclusion mask specifies correspondences between the adjusted area (enclosed in green/red dotted contour) and the others. Corresponding areas are set the same label, and visualized in the same color. (Color figure online)

Negative Influence of the Void (hole) Regions is a key factor downgrading the inpainting quality. In [9,18,24], various versions of partial convolution are proposed, which maintains or infers a mask to zero out values of the void regions. The definition of void regions in instance contour adjustment is more complicated because of higher demand for preserving desired contours. The void regions of a location are defined as those belonging to the distracting instances which need to be determined adaptively by structural cues.

Image Extrapolation by Object Completion [1] is related to completing the dilated area, but several aspects differentiate this task from the instance contour adjustment. First, this task requires an input mask with the semantic label, which harms the generalization capability. Second, the inferred contour is out of user's control. Third, the object completion model cannot complete the eroded area due to the lack of clear correspondences with the external areas.

3 Structural Cues

We employ two structural cues: *(i)* structure image and *(ii)* depth map. See Fig. 2 as an example. Based on the extracted and completed structural cues, given a region on the image plane, we can estimate and rank the likelihoods of its contextual regions belonging to the same instance as itself. Thus, the convolution operation and attention mechanism can sample the top-ranked contexts precisely regardless of their distribution on the image plane. Then, we introduce the format, extraction and completion of the structural cues.

Structure image is a kind of edge-preserved smooth image which is obtained by removing the high-frequency textures while retaining the sharp edges and the low-frequency structures. Regions of an instance tend to share similar color appearances in a structure image. We use RTV method [21] to extract the structure image from an RGB image.

Depth map is a grayscale image in which each entry represents the relative distance of an instance surface to the camera. The depth map can be used to differentiate instances at different distances from the camera. We employ the MegaDepth method [5] to extract the depth map from a monocular RGB image.

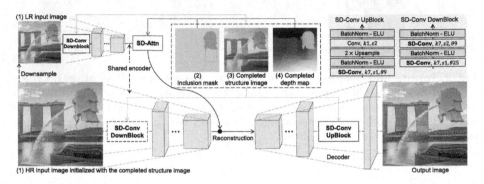

Fig. 3. Structure-driven CNN (second stage). The inputs are four-fold as shown by numbers in parentheses. "LR" and "HR" represent "low-resolution" and "high-resolution", respectively. The red dotted contour highlights the initialized adjusted area. SD-Conv and SD-Attn represent structure-driven convolution and attention, respectively. Orange and blue arrows indicate inputs to SD-Conv block and SD-Attn, respectively. The ellipsis represents Gated-Conv. The detailed architecture of SD-Conv blocks are attached at the top right corner. k and s denote the kernel size and stride, respectively. θ is a specialized parameter of SD-Conv denoting the number of contexts to be sampled. (Color figure online)

Completion. Figure 2 shows the inputs and outputs of the first stage of our method which completes the structural cues for the adjusted area (dilated or eroded). An inclusion mask specifies (potential) correspondences between the adjusted area and the others, and the corresponding areas are set the same label. For example, the dilated area (green) in Fig. 2 (a) corresponds to the instance area (lake), so both the dilated area and instance area are set the same label, *i.e.*, 1 (blue); the remaining area is set the label 0 (orange). The eroded area (red) in Fig. 2 (a) potentially corresponds to the area which is external to the instance area (Merlion), so both the eroded area and the external area are set the same label, *i.e.*, 1 (blue); the instance area is set the label 0 (orange).

The inclusion mask is not a binary mask, which enables adjusting contours for multiple instances simultaneously.

The first stage of our method completes the structural cues for the dilated and eroded areas using different approaches because of their respective exclusion rule. Specifically, we propose a diffusion algorithm based on the iterative Gaussian blur operations which under the guidance of the inclusion mask, can propagate the structural cues from the instance area to the corresponding dilated area. Due to the lack of clear correspondences between the eroded area and the external area, the hypothetical distribution of the external instances needs to be inferred for the eroded area. Thus, we modify the structure reconstruction model in [14] to complete the eroded area on the structure image and depth map. To avoid the interference from the instance area, we temporarily cut out the instance which will be pasted back after the completion, and complete the entire instance area as doing the eroded area. We put the details of the diffusion algorithm and the modified structure reconstruction model in the supplementary material.

4   Structure-Driven CNN

Figure 3 shows the pipeline of the structure-driven CNN. The inputs are four-fold including the two structural cues completed at the first stage. As highlighted by the red contour, the adjusted area on the input image is initialized with the corresponding area on the completed structure image which is smooth due to its nature. Thus, the structure-driven CNN is supposed to enrich the image texture details. The architecture consists of a shared encoder and a decoder with which the structure-driven convolution (SD-Conv) blocks are equipped. There is a structure-driven attention mechanism (SD-Attn) between the encoder and decoder. As in [27], in order to save the computational cost, we perform the attention estimation at low resolution.

4.1   Structure-Driven Convolution

Before diving into the introduction of SD-Conv, we first explain why the conventional convolutions for inpainting, *e.g.*, Gated Convolution (Gated-Conv) and Deformable Convolution (Deform-Conv), tend to mix different instances for the adjusted area, and thus cannot preserve the clear and desired contours. To this end, we prepare two baseline methods by replacing all convolutions in our method with Gated-Conv and Deform-Conv, respectively.

As illustrated in Fig. 4 (a1) and (a2), Gated-Conv and Deform-Conv sample all contexts within the receptive field regardless of whether they belong to the distracting instances. As highlighted in red, these two convolutions are prone to introduce irrelevant contexts of the distracting instances when the convolution kernels are sliding over contours separating instances. Consequently, the sampled irrelevant contexts cause the ambiguous contours between instances, as shown in Fig. 4 (a1) and (a2). The drawbacks of Gated-Conv and Deform-Conv are two-fold. First, they sample a good number of irrelevant contexts. Second, simply enlarging the kernel size might introduce more relevant contexts but it will not help to improve the ratio of relevant contexts or even worse introduce more irrelevant contexts.

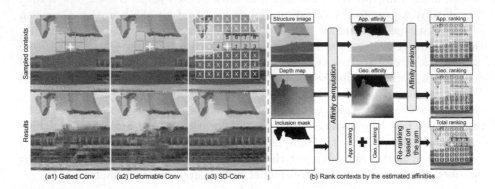

Fig. 4. (a1-3) Sampled contexts and generation results of different convolutions. The sampled contexts belonging to the same instance and the distracting ones are colored in green and red, respectively. The white cross marks the center of a convolution kernel. The numbers within boxes indicate the ranking of contexts and the priority of context sampling, and "X" marks the unsampled contexts or those belonging to the distracting instances. **(b) Rank the contexts by the computed affinities.** The appearance (App.) and geometry (Geo.) affinities are ranked in descending order, and these two rankings are summed for a re-ranking to obtain the total ranking of contexts. The top-ranked θ contexts are sampled. The brighter means the greater affinity. Please zoom in for details. (Color figure online)

In order to block the interference from the distracting instances during the context sampling process, we propose SD-Conv which can estimate and rank the likelihoods of contexts belonging to the same instance as the kernel center. As shown in Fig. 4 (a3), the SD-Conv can block the interference effectively by only sampling the top-ranked contexts.

Affinity Computation. To estimate the likelihood of a contextual region belonging to the same instance as the kernel center, as shown in Fig. 4 (b), we consider two affinities: the appearance affinity and geometry affinity.

Appearance affinity measures the appearance similarity between any contextual region and the kernel center based on the structure image, so it helps SD-Conv circumvent distracting instances of different appearances. Let i and j denote indices of the kernel center and a contextual region, and $a_{i,j}^{\mathrm{App}} \in [0, 1]$ denote their appearance affinity. There are two cases for computing $a_{i,j}^{\mathrm{App}}$ depending on the location of the kernel center. If the kernel center is within the dilated area, then $a_{i,j}^{\mathrm{App}}$ can be determined directly by the clear correspondence specified by the inclusion mask $M^{\mathrm{Inc}} \in \mathbb{Z}^{H \times W}$. Otherwise, there are no clear correspondences specified in M^{Inc} for the kernel center, so we need to estimate $a_{i,j}^{\mathrm{App}}$ based on the closeness in the HSV color space [15] of the structure image which is denoted as $c_{i,j} \in [0,1]$. Let Ω denote the index set of the dilated regions. $a_{i,j}^{\mathrm{App}}$ can be computed as follows:

$$
a_{i,j}^{\mathrm{App}} = \begin{cases} \delta(M_i^{\mathrm{Inc}} = M_j^{\mathrm{Inc}}), & \text{if } i \in \Omega \\ \delta(M_i^{\mathrm{Inc}} = M_j^{\mathrm{Inc}}) \cdot c_{i,j}, & \text{otherwise.} \end{cases} \tag{1}
$$

$\delta(\cdot)$ is an indicator function which outputs 1 when $M_i^{\mathrm{Inc}} = M_j^{\mathrm{Inc}}$ and otherwise 0. If the kernel center is outside the dilated area where only the potential correspondences are specified, the indicator function can help exclude contextual regions which definitely belong to the distracting instances, and $c_{i,j}$ determines $a_{i,j}^{\mathrm{App}}$ for contextual regions with potential correspondences, which is defined as:

$$
c_{i,j} = 1 - 1/\sqrt{5}\left((v_i - v_j)^2 + (s_i \cos h_i - s_j \cos h_j)^2 + (s_i \sin h_i - s_j \sin h_j)^2\right)^{\frac{1}{2}}, \tag{2}
$$

where h, s and v denote values of the corresponding regions on the structure image in the HSV color space.

Geometry affinity measures the proximity of a contextual region to the kernel center. The appearance affinity cannot help circumvent distracting instances with similar colors but different textures because its computation is partially based on the structure image of which the texture details are wiped off. Yet, such distracting instances can usually be differentiated by depths in the depth map. The geometry affinity $a_{i,j}^{\mathrm{Geo}}$ is computed as:

$$
a_{i,j}^{\mathrm{Geo}} = 1 - |M_i^{\mathrm{Dep}} - M_j^{\mathrm{Dep}}|/(M_{\max}^{\mathrm{Dep}} - M_{\min}^{\mathrm{Dep}} + \epsilon), \tag{3}
$$

where M^{Dep} denotes the depth map, $M_{\max}^{\mathrm{Dep}}$ and $M_{\min}^{\mathrm{Dep}}$ denote the largest and smallest value in M^{Dep}. $\epsilon = 1e^{-4}$ is used to avoid dividing zero.

Affinity Ranking. We perform the ranking over the computed affinities in order to determine a group of most relevant contextual regions for the kernel center. As shown in Fig. 4 (b), the affinity ranking is performed for the two affinities respectively in descending order. In order to combine the ranking for the two affinities, we sum their respective ranking, and re-rank the ranking sum in ascending order to form the total ranking which is used in Fig. 4 (a3). Finally, the top-ranked θ contexts are sampled.

With the ranking of contexts, we can set a large kernel size for SD-Conv boldly without worrying about blending the irrelevant contexts. Yet, we do not observe clear gains for deploying the SD-Conv for the internal levels of the encoder and decoder, so we employ the conventional Gated-Conv for them which are indicated by ellipses in Fig. 3.

4.2 Structure-Driven Attention

The convolution operations help complete image textures by aggregating local contexts. In order to exploit the useful global contexts which are far away, Yu *et al.* proposed the contextual attention mechanism [23], which aggregates and projects the information of the contextual regions for each region according to the estimated region similarities, *i.e.*, attention weights. Let h_i and h_j denote the features at region i and j from the input feature maps, respectively. Let $s_{i,j}$ denote the attention weight of region i paid to location j, which is computed as:

$$s_{i,j} = \frac{\exp\left(\alpha \cdot \cos(h_i, h_j)\right)}{\sum_k^N \exp\left(\alpha \cdot \cos(h_i, h_k)\right)}, \tag{4}$$

where α is a hyperparameter that enlarges the range of cosine similarity $\cos(\cdot, \cdot)$, and increases the attention paid to the relevant regions. In practice, α is 10.

Yet, directly applying the contextual attention in our CNN leads to the ambiguity artifact as highlighted in "w/ Context-Attn" of Fig. 6 which is caused by the inaccurate attention weights. Thus, we propose SD-Attn which addresses the ambiguity artifact effectively as shown in "Ours" of Fig. 6. SD-Attn integrates the appearance affinity $a_{i,j}^{\text{App}}$ (1) and geometry affinity $a_{i,j}^{\text{Geo}}$ (3) to estimate the attention weight in order to block the interference from the distracting instances. However, we do not directly apply $a_{i,j}^{\text{App}}$, because the color closeness $c_{i,j}$ is less reliable in differentiating instances at the global level (attention) than at the local level (convolution). Therefore, we tailor $a_{i,j}^{\text{App}}$ to attention's needs:

$$a_{i,j}^{\text{App}*} = \delta(M_i^{\text{Inc}} = M_j^{\text{Inc}}) \cdot \cos(h_i, h_j), \tag{5}$$

where the appearance similarity $\cos(h_i, h_j)$ in (4) replaces $c_{i,j}$ in (2). Though $\cos(h_i, h_j)$ is observed to be more reliable than $c_{i,j}$ in measuring the appearance similarity, computing $\cos(h_i, h_j)$ requires much higher computation than $c_{i,j}$ due to the high dimensionality of h_i. Therefore, $c_{i,j}$ is more suitable for the convolution operation which is conducted much more frequently and locally than the attention mechanism. Then, the SD-Attn weight $s_{i,j}^{\text{SD}}$ is defined as:

$$s_{i,j}^{\text{SD}} = \frac{\exp\left(\alpha \cdot a_{i,j}^{\text{App}*} \cdot a_{i,j}^{\text{Geo}}\right)}{\sum_k^N \exp\left(\alpha \cdot a_{i,j}^{\text{App}*} \cdot a_{i,j}^{\text{Geo}}\right)}. \tag{6}$$

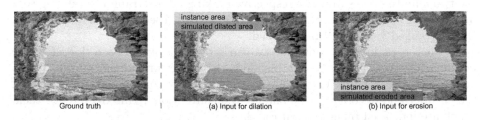

Fig. 5. Simulated inputs for training and evaluation.

Table 1. Ablation study. The higher SSIM (%) and PSNR (dB) and the lower FID, the better performance. ↑ (↓) means higher (lower) is better.

Method	Dilation			Erosion		
	FID↓	SSIM↑	PSNR↑	FID↓	SSIM↑	PSNR↑
SD-Conv $\ominus$ a^{App} (1)	12.58	95.37	28.10	11.75	95.46	29.06
SD-Conv $\ominus$ a^{Geo} (3)	12.61	95.39	28.29	12.06	95.42	29.16
w/ Gated-Conv	12.77	95.32	28.21	11.73	95.48	29.35
w/ Deform-Conv	12.99	95.37	28.07	11.82	95.43	29.23
SD-Attn $\ominus$ a^{Geo} (3)	12.57	95.40	28.29	11.78	95.44	29.35
w/ Context-Attn	13.99	95.30	27.52	13.30	95.36	28.55
Ours	**12.43**	**95.48**	**28.32**	**11.64**	**95.53**	**29.38**

5 Experiments

Implementations. We train the structure-driven CNN using L1 loss and adversarial loss, and present its training details, detailed architecture and hyperparameters in the supplementary. We implement our method using PyTorch, and train 400 epochs with batch size 48 on 3 Nvidia P100 GPUs.

Datasets. We collect landscape images from existing datasets (COCO [8] with CC-BY 4.0 licence and ADE20K [28] with BSD license) to compose our dataset, which contains nearly 53.4K training images and 1K test images. The dataset and preparation scripts will be released upon acceptance. All images are resized to 256×256. There are two settings for evaluation, *i.e.*, "Dilation" and "Erosion". To evaluate our method quantitatively, we use the collected images as the ground truth after the instance contour adjustment, and simulate the input images by overlaying the harvested instance masks onto the image plane. In Fig. 5, we show how to simulate an input image with the dilated area and eroded area, respectively. To simulate the dilated area in Fig. 5 (a), we overlay a foreground area, and treat the instances being partially occluded as those to be dilated. To simulate the eroded area in Fig. 5 (b), we put a foreground area next to the contour of an instance, and assume that the eroded area of this instance is covered by the foreground area precisely. To increase the robustness for training, we regard different category area in the segmentation mask as the instance area to simulate the image matting process, and the overlaid foreground area is treated as the adjusted area. During testing, we only need the instance area obtained by image matting function.

Quality Metrics. We adopt three widely used metrics to measure the generated image quality: Frechet Inception Distance (FID) [3], Structural Similarity Index (SSIM) [19] and Peak Signal-to-Noise Ratio (PSNR) [4]. We use FID and PSNR to measure the authenticity of the restored textures from the macroscopic and microscopic perspectives, respectively. We use SSIM to measure how well the instance contours are preserved in the generation result, so we calculate the

SSIM on the image gradient level which can better reflect the similarity and clearness of contours than the RGB images do.

Table 2. Comparison with inpainting methods. * marks baselines taking the same five-fold inputs as our method (Fig. 2). † marks the semantic-guided inpainting baseline which removes the first stage but uses the ground-truth semantic mask to replace the semantic mask completed by its first stage; we do not show its efficiency results due to the unfair shortcut. The lower Param (M) and MACs (G) are, the better efficiency. We use green and red to highlight the efficiency for "Dilation" and "Erosion", respectively. ↑ (↓) means higher (lower) is better.

Method	Dilation			Erosion			Efficiency	
	FID↓	SSIM↑	PSNR↑	FID↓	SSIM↑	PSNR↑	Param↓	MACs↓
PEN-Net*	21.01	91.89	24.79	19.67	92.35	25.13	13.38	56.93
PEN-Net	21.61	92.10	27.05	19.55	92.61	27.62	13.37	56.81
StFlow*	19.86	91.82	26.49	18.84	92.32	26.84	92.66	271.90
StFlow	21.09	91.81	25.93	20.02	92.31	26.27	92.52	262.44
FreeForm*	13.76	92.73	28.18	12.08	93.20	29.35	16.36	117.61
FreeForm	14.48	92.53	27.78	13.09	93.00	28.63	16.17	104.34
Rethink*	13.27	92.76	27.36	12.12	93.19	27.93	130.33	138.28
Rethink	16.95	92.57	26.70	15.26	93.02	27.31	130.31	137.94
ExtInt*	20.26	92.08	26.95	18.76	92.45	27.73	16.51	5.62K
ExtInt	22.42	92.09	25.99	21.10	92.35	26.60	16.16	5.60K
DivStruct*	20.48	91.50	25.33	18.48	92.04	26.12	76.28	113.9K
DivStruct	21.09	91.47	25.02	18.92	92.00	25.79	76.26	113.1K
CRFill*	29.30	90.12	21.38	28.32	91.89	22.18	4.08	27.30
CRFill	19.19	92.60	25.91	17.25	93.06	26.61	4.05	25.25
SPG-Net*	16.64	92.34	26.31	15.17	92.82	26.91	96.17	65.16
SPG-Net†	15.68	92.39	26.97	14.07	92.90	27.67	-	-
SPG-Net	16.29	92.37	26.79	14.69	92.88	27.43	96.13	64.54
SGE-Net	14.74	92.35	27.62	12.80	92.84	28.33	73.61	212.14
Ours	**12.43**	**95.48**	**28.32**	**11.64**	**95.53**	**29.38**	0.40	8.00
							47.42	270.09

Efficiency Metrics. We use THOP [29] to measure the parameter size (Param) and multiply-accumulate ops (MACs).

5.1   Ablation Study

We disable various modules to create six baselines to study the impact of SD-Conv and SD-Attn on our method.

SD-Conv. To study the impact of appearance affinity a^{App} (1) and geometry affinity a^{Geo} (3) in determining the context ranking, we create two baselines by disabling one of them, *i.e.*, "SD-Conv $\ominus$ a^{App}" and "SD-Conv $\ominus$ a^{Geo}". Table 1 and Fig. 6 show that disabling either affinity leads to lower SSIM and ambiguities along the generated contour, which shows the necessity of these two structural cues in SD-Conv.

We also replace the SD-Conv with Gated-Conv and Deform-Conv, respectively. Besides worse contour clearness, the generated image textures become less natural as shown in Fig. 6. This demonstrates the efficacy of SD-Conv in generating meaningful textures.

SD-Attn. The biggest difference between SD-Attn and contextual attention is the introduction of the geometry affinity a^{Geo} (3) into the attention estimation. In Fig. 6, we observe ambiguous contours after we disable a^{Geo} in SD-Attn. We also completely replace SD-Attn with the vanilla contextual attention, which leads to significant degradation in FID and PSNR in Table 1 and ambiguity artifacts in Fig. 6.

5.2 Comparison with Baselines

Compared baselines include PEN-Net [25], StFlow [14], FreeForm [24], Rethink [10], ExtInt [17], DivStruct [13], CRFill [26], SPG-Net [16] and SGE-Net [6].

Fig. 6. Ablation study. The cyan dotted boxes highlight the artifacts.

We modify all baselines except SGE-Net to take the same five-fold inputs as ours (Fig. 2). Specifically, we modify these methods by concatenating the additional inputs with their original ones, adjusting the input dimension of their first layer, and retraining them on our dataset. The modified methods are marked

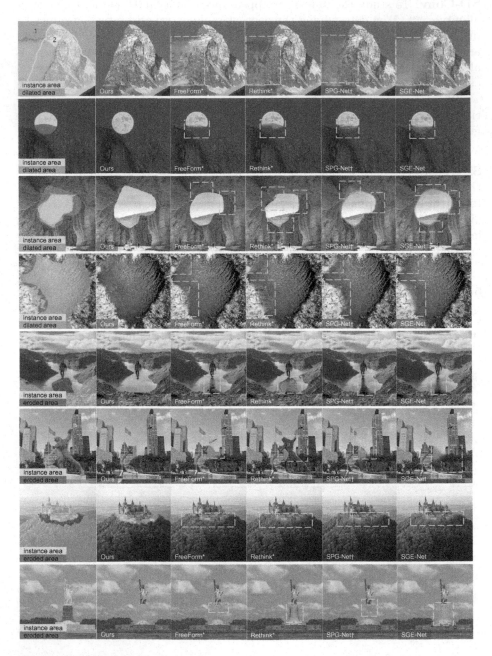

Fig. 7. Qualitative comparisons. The cyan dotted boxes highlight the artifacts. Due to the space limit, we only show comparison with four methods that with leading performance in quantitative evaluation.

with *. We cannot modify SGE-Net because it is built on a pretrained ResNet which requires exactly three input dimensions. We also show results of baselines without modification in Table 2 and Fig. 7. We prepare a stronger baseline (marked by †) for SPG-Net by replacing the semantic mask completed by its first stage with the ground-truth semantic mask which contains the user-desired semantic distribution for the adjusted area. We do not prepare such a stronger baseline for SGE-Net because its inferred semantic mask needs to be filled with activations ranging from the negative infinity to the positive infinity.

Analysis. Table 2 shows that after introducing the additional inputs, most baselines achieve better or comparable performance, but our method still outperforms them. The SSIM of all baselines are smaller than 93.3%, while our method achieves nearly 95.5% in both settings, which demonstrates the effectiveness of our method in preserving clear and user-desired contours. Such an advantage is also reflected in Fig. 7 where baselines yield non-negligible artifacts when dilating or eroding regions.

Only the performance of CRFill [26] drops drastically after the modification. As a two-stage method, its first stage is a simple CNN for generating coarse textures, and the second stage refines coarse textures. Since the additional inputs are given at the first stage, we argue that its first stage is too simple to learn processing the inputs containing such rich structural cues, and thus it causes inferior coarse textures which are too hard to be recovered by its second stage.

Efficiency and Limitation. Table 2 shows that our method is efficient for "Dilation", but is cumbersome for "Erosion". This is because we use different approaches to complete the structural cues for these two settings in the first stage (see § 3 for the motivation). For "Dilation", we propose a diffusion algorithm based on the efficient Gaussian blur (see the supplementary for details). For "Erosion", we modify the structure reconstruction model in [14] which is heavy. Our ultimate goal is to deploy our method on phones, so we need to optimize the efficiency for "Erosion". The MACs of ExtInt and DivStruct are significantly higher than the others, because they adopt iterative processing strategies.

Table 3. User study results. Our method outperforms other approaches with the highest scores on both dilation and erosion experiments.

Experiment	FreeFrom* [24]	Rethink* [10]	SPG-Net† [16]	SGE-Net [16]	Ours
Dilation	10.66%	14.41%	22.50%	20.41%	**32.01%**
Erosion	9.63%	16.47%	23.28%	21.37%	**29.25%**

5.3   User Study

We select four baselines with leading performance in the quantitative evaluation as candidates for our user study. We conduct two experiments to evaluate whether our results are more favored by human observers than other methods. Participants are shown an original image with instance with dilation/erosion area, in addition to five generated results, and asked to choose the result that matches best with the dilation/erosion area. In each experiment, 100 images are randomly selected from the testing set. Experiments are published on Amazon Mechanical Turk (AMT) and each experiment is completed by 25 participants. As shown in Table 3, our method achieves highest scores in both experiments.

6 Conclusion

We study instance contour adjustment. The first stage of our method extracts and completes the structural cues within the adjusted contours. We further propose a structure-driven CNN for the second stage which completes the image textures based on the completed structural cues. There are mainly two novel modules, SD-Conv and SD-Attn, of which the redesigned sampling strategy can estimate and rank the relevance of the contexts based on the structural cues, and sample the top-ranked contexts regardless of their distribution on the image plane. Our method could generate meaningful textures while preserving clear and user-desired contours.

Acknowledgements. This project is supported by National Natural Science Foundation of China under Grant No. 62136001. We thank Wenbo Li for the advise and discussion for this project.

References

1. Bowen, R.S., Chang, H., Herrmann, C., Teterwak, P., Liu, C., Zabih, R.: OcoNet: image extrapolation by object completion. In: CVPR (2021)
2. Guo, X., Yang, H., Huang, D.: Image inpainting via conditional texture and structure dual generation. In: ICCV (2021)
3. Heusel, M., Ramsauer, H., Unterthiner, T., Nessler, B., Hochreiter, S.: GANs trained by a two time-scale update rule converge to a local Nash equilibrium. In: NIPS (2017)
4. Huynh-Thu, Q., Ghanbari, M.: Scope of validity of PSNR in image/video quality assessment. Electron. Lett. **44**, 800–801 (2008)
5. Li, Z., Snavely, N.: MegaDepth: learning single-view depth prediction from internet photos. In: CVPR (2018)
6. Liao, L., Xiao, J., Wang, Z., Lin, C.-W., Satoh, S.: Guidance and evaluation: semantic-aware image inpainting for mixed scenes. In: Vedaldi, A., Bischof, H., Brox, T., Frahm, J.-M. (eds.) ECCV 2020. LNCS, vol. 12372, pp. 683–700. Springer, Cham (2020). https://doi.org/10.1007/978-3-030-58583-9_41
7. Liao, L., Xiao, J., Wang, Z., Lin, C., Satoh, S.: Image inpainting guided by coherence priors of semantics and textures. In: CVPR (2021)
8. Lin, T.-Y., et al.: Microsoft COCO: common objects in context. In: Fleet, D., Pajdla, T., Schiele, B., Tuytelaars, T. (eds.) ECCV 2014. LNCS, vol. 8693, pp. 740–755. Springer, Cham (2014). https://doi.org/10.1007/978-3-319-10602-1_48

9. Liu, G., Reda, F.A., Shih, K.J., Wang, T.-C., Tao, A., Catanzaro, B.: Image inpainting for irregular holes using partial convolutions. In: Ferrari, V., Hebert, M., Sminchisescu, C., Weiss, Y. (eds.) ECCV 2018. LNCS, vol. 11215, pp. 89–105. Springer, Cham (2018). https://doi.org/10.1007/978-3-030-01252-6_6

10. Liu, H., Jiang, B., Song, Y., Huang, W., Yang, C.: Rethinking image inpainting via a mutual encoder-decoder with feature equalizations. In: Vedaldi, A., Bischof, H., Brox, T., Frahm, J.-M. (eds.) ECCV 2020. LNCS, vol. 12347, pp. 725–741. Springer, Cham (2020). https://doi.org/10.1007/978-3-030-58536-5_43

11. Liu, H., Wan, Z., Huang, W., Song, Y., Han, X., Liao, J.: PD-GAN: probabilistic diverse GAN for image inpainting. In: CVPR (2021)

12. Ntavelis, E., et al.: AIM 2020 challenge on image extreme inpainting. In: ECCVW (2020)

13. Peng, J., Liu, D., Xu, S., Li, H.: Generating diverse structure for image inpainting with hierarchical VQ-VAE. In: CVPR (2021)

14. Ren, Y., Yu, X., Zhang, R., Li, T.H., Liu, S., Li, G.: StructureFlow: image inpainting via structure-aware appearance flow. In: ICCV (2019)

15. Smith, J.R., Chang, S.: VisualSeek: a fully automated content-based image query system. In: ACM MM (1996)

16. Song, Y., Yang, C., Shen, Y., Wang, P., Huang, Q., Kuo, C.J.: SPG-Net: segmentation prediction and guidance network for image inpainting. In: BMVC (2018)

17. Wang, T., Ouyang, H., Chen, Q.: Image inpainting with external-internal learning and monochromic bottleneck. In: CVPR (2021)

18. Wang, W., Zhang, J., Niu, L., Ling, H., Yang, X., Zhang, L.: Parallel multi-resolution fusion network for image inpainting. In: ICCV (2021)

19. Wang, Z., Bovik, A.C., Sheikh, H.R., Simoncelli, E.P.: Image quality assessment: from error visibility to structural similarity. TIP. **13**, 600–612 (2004)

20. Xiong, W., et al.: Foreground-aware image inpainting. In: CVPR (2019)

21. Xu, L., Yan, Q., Xia, Y., Jia, J.: Structure extraction from texture via relative total variation. TOG. **31**, 1 (2012)

22. Yi, Z., Tang, Q., Azizi, S., Jang, D., Xu, Z.: Contextual residual aggregation for ultra high-resolution image inpainting. In: CVPR (2020)

23. Yu, J., Lin, Z., Yang, J., Shen, X., Lu, X., Huang, T.S.: Generative image inpainting with contextual attention. In: CVPR (2018)

24. Yu, J., Lin, Z., Yang, J., Shen, X., Lu, X., Huang, T.S.: Free-form image inpainting with gated convolution. In: ICCV (2019)

25. Zeng, Y., Fu, J., Chao, H., Guo, B.: Learning pyramid-context encoder network for high-quality image inpainting. In: CVPR (2019)

26. Zeng, Y., Lin, Z., Lu, H., Patel, V.M.: CR-FILL: generative image inpainting with auxiliary contextual reconstruction. In: ICCV (2021)

27. Zeng, Yu., Lin, Z., Yang, J., Zhang, J., Shechtman, E., Lu, H.: High-resolution image inpainting with iterative confidence feedback and guided upsampling. In: Vedaldi, A., Bischof, H., Brox, T., Frahm, J.-M. (eds.) ECCV 2020. LNCS, vol. 12364, pp. 1–17. Springer, Cham (2020). https://doi.org/10.1007/978-3-030-58529-7_1

28. Zhou, B., Zhao, H., Puig, X., Fidler, S., Barriuso, A., Torralba, A.: Scene parsing through ADE20K dataset. In: CVPR (2017)

29. Zhu, L.: Thop: Pytorch-opcounter. https://github.com/Lyken17/pytorch-OpCounter

Synthesizing Light Field Video
from Monocular Video

Shrisudhan Govindarajan[(✉)] [ID], Prasan Shedligeri [ID], Sarah [ID],
and Kaushik Mitra [ID]

Indian Institute of Technology Madras, Chennai, India
shrisudhan07@gmail.com

Abstract. The hardware challenges associated with light-field (LF) imaging has made it difficult for consumers to access its benefits like applications in post-capture focus and aperture control. Learning-based techniques which solve the ill-posed problem of LF reconstruction from sparse (1, 2 or 4) views have significantly reduced the need for complex hardware. LF *video* reconstruction from sparse views poses a special challenge as acquiring ground-truth for training these models is hard. Hence, we propose a self-supervised learning-based algorithm for LF video reconstruction from monocular videos. We use self-supervised geometric, photometric and temporal consistency constraints inspired from a recent learning-based technique for LF video reconstruction from stereo video. Additionally, we propose three key techniques that are relevant to our monocular video input. We propose an explicit disocclusion handling technique that encourages the network to use information from adjacent input temporal frames, for inpainting disoccluded regions in a LF frame. This is crucial for a self-supervised technique as a single input frame does not contain any information about the disoccluded regions. We also propose an adaptive low-rank representation that provides a significant boost in performance by tailoring the representation to each input scene. Finally, we propose a novel refinement block that is able to exploit the available LF image data using supervised learning to further refine the reconstruction quality. Our qualitative and quantitative analysis demonstrates the significance of each of the proposed building blocks and also the superior results compared to previous state-of-the-art monocular LF reconstruction techniques. We further validate our algorithm by reconstructing LF videos from monocular videos acquired using a commercial GoPro camera. An open-source implementation is also made available (https://github.com/ShrisudhanG/Synthesizing-Light-Field-Video-from-Monocular-Video).

Keywords: Light-fields · Plenoptic function · Self-supervised learning

1 Introduction

Cameras have become cheap and ubiquitous in the modern world, giving consumers a capability to acquire photos and videos anywhere and anytime. The

Supplementary Information The online version contains supplementary material available at https://doi.org/10.1007/978-3-031-20071-7_10.

Fig. 1. We propose three novel techniques: a) disocclusion handling, b) adaptive low-rank representation for LF and c) a novel refinement block, for LF video reconstruction from monocular video. Combining these with the self-supervised cost functions inspired by [35], we can reconstruct high-fidelity LF videos, even with varying baselines. As shown in (d) this allows us to control the synthetic defocus blur using the output video.

last decade saw an accelerated improvement in image sensors and lens quality, leading to a significant improvement in the picture quality from these tiny cameras. Towards the end of the decade, the focus shifted towards more and more innovative software, pushing the limits to what can be achieved with these ubiquitous cameras [8]. This push resulted in a variety of features: ranging from simple effects like background-blur to more dramatic ones like augmented reality. Features like bokeh effects and novel view synthesis became popular as they provided a sense of '3D' to the otherwise flat pictures. However, these features have currently been limited to images and there's no straightforward way of extending them to videos. In the last few years, videos have certainly become a more powerful means of communication, knowledge-sharing and even entertainment. LF imaging could provide an intuitive way of bringing these features to videos. However, there's no easy way to capture LF videos yet. Computational photography is poised to solve this, making it easy and accessible to capture LF on small form-factor devices [20]. We instead focus on existing camera hardware and aim to reconstruct LF videos from any ordinary monocular camera.

Traditionally, LF imaging required use of bulky or complex hardware setups such as camera arrays [48] and micro-lens arrays [30]. Hence, the recent focus has been on reducing the hardware complexity through the use of learning-based techniques. Typically, these involve the reconstruction of LF from sparse input views (such as 1, 2 or 4 views) [18,22,38,52]. To solve the challenges in acquiring LF videos through commercial cameras, several techniques for LF *video* reconstruction have also been proposed [2,35,45]. SeLFVi [35] is an interesting recent work that proposes a novel self-supervised technique for LF video reconstruction from stereo videos. Being a self-supervised technique it relied on an intermediate low-rank representation for LF frames achieving high-quality reconstructions. However, it requires a stereo video input where both cameras should have identical focal lengths (identical field-of-view). This can become a limitation considering that stereo cameras are still not as widespread as monocular cameras. This is especially true for consumer applications, where mostly monocular cameras are preferred.

Motivated by the availability of large and diverse sets of high-quality monocular videos we propose a novel, self-supervised learning technique for LF video reconstruction from monocular input. To start with, we preserve the self-supervised photometric, geometric and temporal consistency constraints adopted in SeLFVi (see Sect. 3.3). Further we introduce three crucial blocks that are necessary for our case of monocular video input. These are: 1) a novel loss for handling disocclusion, 2) a scene geometry adaptive intermediate low-rank representation and 3) a novel and supervised refinement block to further refine the LF video(see Fig. 1).

The challenge with just a monocular input is that there's no information on how to fill the disoccluded regions/pixels of the predicted LF. We propose a technique to *inpaint* the disoccluded regions of the estimated LF frames. The intuition is that, in a video acquired using a moving camera, occluded regions in one frame might be visible in the neighboring temporal frames. Our disocclusion handling technique (Sect. 3.4) utilizes this existing information to fill in the disoccluded regions of the LF frame.

Next, we modify the standard tensor-display (TD) based intermediate low-rank representation so that it can adapt to any input scene. While TD model [47] uses fixed displacement between the layers, we propose a modification where this displacement can be modified for each input image (Sect. 3.2). In [47], each of the layers are shown to represent a depth-plane in the scene. Hence, by estimating the displacement values for each scene, the layers are better able to represent the given LF. This idea was inspired from a similar choice of adaptive layered representation in [22] for novel view synthesis. Unlike [22] we adopt a more sophisticated approach to predict the depth planes through global scene understanding by using transformers [3]. As shown in our experiments, the adaptive low-rank representation provides a significant boost in the quality of the predicted LF frames.

Finally, we explore the popular idea of self-supervised pre-training, followed by supervised learning on a small amount of data to boost the performance of a model [5,6,17]. We design a novel convolutional vision-transformer-based [9] refinement block that is trained via supervised learning on a small amount of LF *image* data. This helps in further refining the output around the depth-edges that are difficult to reconstruct with just self-supervised learning. The final output is a weighted combination of the refinement block output and the LF estimated by self-supervised learning (Sect. 3.5). To the best of our knowledge, this is the first time that vision transformers are used to supervise LF reconstruction by efficiently combining the spatio-angular information. In summary, we make the following contributions:

- High quality reconstruction of LF videos from monocular video with self-supervised learning.
- Handling disocclusions in rendering LFs using self-supervised consistency losses utilizing information from successive video frames.
- A modified TD-based low-rank representation that can adapt to the given input scene dynamically adjusting the distance between the layers.
- A novel supervised vision-transformer based refinement block to exploit the small amount of LF image data to further improve reconstruction on video.

2   Related Work

LF Synthesis. While the concept of LF or integral imaging is quite old [1,23], capturing these images has been complicated. While commercial LF cameras are now available in the market [30], they suffer from low spatial resolution. Over the last several years, a diverse set of camera setups and algorithms have aimed at making LF imaging simpler and more accessible. There have been setups that use coded-aperture systems [14,34,43], cameras with coded masks near the sensor [12,27] and even hybrid sensors [45]. Later, with advances in deep-learning, systems using ordinary commercial cameras such as one or more DSLRs became popular. Techniques that reconstruct LF frames from focus-defocus pair [42] or focal-stack images [4] were proposed. Several techniques were also proposed that could reconstruct LF from sparse set of views on a regular grid. The number of views could be 1-view [2,15,22,38], 2-views [35,52], 4-views [18,46,51], and even 9-views [49].

LF Synthesis from Monocular Image. As ordinary monocular cameras are ubiquitous, several techniques aim at LF reconstruction from them. As this is an ill-posed problem, learning-based techniques have been essential in this domain. A popular technique has been to first predict disparity flow [38] or appearance flow [15,54] and then warp the input image accordingly to reconstruct the LF frame. Recently, Multi-Plane Image (MPI) based representation is being used for LF prediction [13,22,28,37,53]. Li *et al.* [22] propose a modified MPI model that allowed them to significantly reduce the representation complexity. With a similar intuition, we propose a modified low-rank representation based on layered LF displays [47] for predicting the LF frames.

LF Video Reconstruction. As commercial LF cameras such as Lytro acquire videos at only 3 frames per second (fps), LF video acquisition at high angular and temporal resolution has also been challenging. In [45] a learning-based algorithm with a hybrid camera system consisting of a general DSLR camera and a light field camera was proposed. Hajisharif *et al.* [12] proposed a single sensor-based algorithm that required a coded mask to be placed in front of the sensor. As these algorithms require complex and bulky hardware setups, techniques such as [2,35] are proposed that just require ordinary cameras. Although our self-supervised algorithm is inspired from [35], the closest work to ours is [2]. Bae *et al.* [2] utilize a large set of computer-generated data to supervise a neural network for LF video reconstruction from monocular video. In contrast, our proposed technique does not require hard-to-acquire LF video data for supervision.

Learning with Layered LF Representation. Previously, layered LF display representations [47] have been used in conjunction with neural networks. [26] built an end-to-end pipeline from a coded aperture scene acquisition for display-ing the scene on a layered LF display. Similar work in [21,39] aims at capturing a focal stack and then learning to display the scene onto the LF display. Inspired by [35], we also adopt the layered LF display based intermediate low-rank repre-sentation $\mathcal{F}$ for LF estimation. We extend the standard low-rank model to adapt

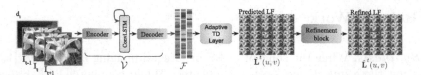

Fig. 2. Our proposed algorithm takes as input a sequence $\mathcal{I} = \{I_{t-1}, I_t, I_{t+1}, d_t\}$. A recurrent LF synthesis network $\mathcal{V}$ first predicts an intermediate low-rank representation $\mathcal{F}$ for the corresponding LF frame. An adaptive TD layer (3.2) takes the same set $\mathcal{I}$ and $\mathcal{F}$ as input and outputs the LF frame $\hat{\mathbf{L}}_t$. A set of self-supervised cost-functions (3.3, 3.4) are then imposed on $\hat{\mathbf{L}}_t$ for the end-to-end training of $\mathcal{V}$ and the adaptive TD layer. Finally, a refinement block (3.5) then takes $\ddot{\mathbf{L}}_t$ and I_t as input and outputs a refined LF.

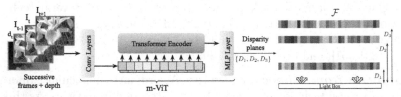

Fig. 3. We use an m-VIT block [3] to predict the displacement between the different layers of the TD based low-rank representation. Each of the layers in $\mathcal{F}$ approximately represent a scene depth plane. Instead of keeping the layers static/fixed, a scene-specific displacement value will move the layer to a depth plane where it can best represent the scene.

to the individual scene by predicting the optimal distance between the layers for each input image.

3   Monocular LF Video Estimation

We propose a self-supervised learning based technique for LF video reconstruction from a monocular video sequence. For each input frame of the monocular video, we reconstruct a corresponding LF video frame. As shown in Fig. 2, a deep neural network takes as input, a sequence of 3 input frames and a disparity map $\{I_{t-1}, I_t, I_{t+1}, d_t\}$ and estimates an intermediate low-rank representation of the current LF frame $\hat{\mathbf{L}}_t$. As shown in Fig. 3 and further elaborated in Sect. 3.2, we propose a modified intermediate low-rank representation adapted from [47]. After obtaining $\hat{\mathbf{L}}_t$ from the adaptive TD layer, we introduce the geometric, photometric and the temporal consistency constraints [35] to train our LF synthesis network (see Sect. 3.3). Being a self-supervised technique, we do not have any information about the disoccluded regions in $\hat{\mathbf{L}}_t$ from just I_t. Hence, we introduce a disocclusion handling technique that utilizes information from I_{t-1} and I_{t+1} to fill-in the disoccluded regions of $\hat{\mathbf{L}}_t$ (see Sect. 3.4). Finally, to further refine the estimated LF frame, we propose a novel residual refinement block based on vision-transformers (see Sect. 3.5) which is trained using supervised learning.

3.1   Light Field Frame Prediction

As shown in Fig. 2, we stack three successive input frames and the corresponding disparity map as $\mathcal{I} = \{I_{t-1}, I_t, I_{t+1}, d_t\}$ and feed it to the LF prediction network $\mathcal{V}$. With a monocular input, it's not possible to obtain a disparity map directly. Hence, we first estimate a relative depth map z_t of I_t using a pre-trained monocular depth estimation model [33]. We know that a disparity map is related to the depth map up to an affine transformation [10], defined here as $d_t = az_t + b$, where a and b are two scalars. During training, we randomly sample values of a and b and convert the relative depth map z_t to the disparity map d_t. The network $\mathcal{V}$ is a long short term memory (LSTM) based model consisting of an encoder and decoder with skip connections. The network $\mathcal{V}$ predicts an intermediate low-rank representation $\mathcal{F}$ for $\hat{\mathbf{L}}_t$ based on a modified tensor-display model [47]. We describe the process of obtaining $\hat{\mathbf{L}}_t$ from the low-rank representation $\mathcal{F}$ in Sect. 3.2.

3.2   Adaptive Tensor-Display Model

In the previous section, we estimated the representation $\mathcal{F}$ from the network $\mathcal{V}$, based on the low-rank model proposed in [47]. In this standard model, $\mathcal{F} = [f_{-N/2}, \ldots, f_0, \ldots, f_{N/2}]$, where $f_k = [f_k^1, f_k^2, \ldots, f_k^R]$, $f_k^r \in [0, 1]^{h \times w \times 3}$. Here N represents the number of layers in the low-rank model and R represents its corresponding rank. Given $\mathcal{F}$, the corresponding 4D LF frame can be computed as

$$L(x, y, u, v) = TD(\mathcal{F}) = \sum_{r=1}^{R} \prod_{n=-N/2}^{N/2} f_n^r(x + nu, y + nv) \tag{1}$$

where x, y and u, v respectively denote the spatial and angular coordinates. Further analysis into these representations in [47] showed that each layer approximately represents a particular depth plane in the scene. However, the standard model places these layers at a uniform distance from each other representing depth planes placed uniformly in the scene. In a natural image the objects in the scene could be distributed non-uniformly throughout the depth. This idea was exploited in [22], where the standard MPI model was adapted to each input image by assigning non-uniform disparity values for each MPI layer. This drastically reduced the number of MPI layers required to represent the scene up to a similar accuracy.

Motivated by this we use a m-VIT network [3], to predict a sequence of values, $D = \{D_{-N/2}, \ldots D_{N/2}\}$, that will be used in adapting the TD layer to each input (Fig. 3). m-VIT predicts one value for each layer in the representation $\mathcal{F}$ using the input $\mathcal{I} = \{I_{t-1}, I_t, I_{t+1}, d_t\}$. The values in D are used in the proposed adaptive TD layer as

$$L(x, y, u, v) = TD(\mathcal{F}; D) = \sum_{r=1}^{R} \prod_{n=-N/2}^{N/2} f_n^r(x + D_n u, y + D_n v), \tag{2}$$

where D_n represents the scalar value predicted by m-VIT for layer n. After computing $\hat{\mathbf{L}}_t$ from our proposed adaptive TD layer, we impose three main self-supervised cost functions to train the prediction network $\mathcal{V}$.

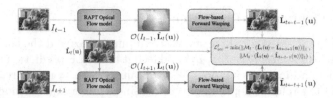

Fig. 4. We introduce disocclusion handling to constrain the synthesis network to fill in the disoccluded pixels of the LF with information from the neighboring frames. As shown, I_{t-1} is forward warped to each view of $\hat{\mathbf{L}}_t$, using the optical flow predicted from RAFT [41]. We also warp I_{t+1} to each SAIs of $\hat{\mathbf{L}}_t$, and the loss is computed as in Eq. (8).

3.3 Loss Functions

To successfully train the LF prediction network $\mathcal{V}$, we follow [35] and define three constraints that enforce the structure of the LF video on the predicted sequence of frames.

Photometric Constraint. The photometric constraint is defined on the premise that the center view of $\hat{\mathbf{L}}_t$ should match the current input frame I_t. Hence, we define the loss function reflecting this as $\mathcal{L}_{photo}^t = \|\hat{\mathbf{L}}_t(\mathbf{0}) - I_t\|_1$, where $\hat{\mathbf{L}}_t(\mathbf{0})$ represents the central angular view of $\hat{\mathbf{L}}_t$.

Geometric Constraint. To compute the cost, we first warp all sub-aperture images (SAIs) of the $\hat{\mathbf{L}}_t$ to the SAI $\mathbf{0}$ that corresponds to I_t. In essence, we warp $\hat{\mathbf{L}}_t(\mathbf{u})$ to the SAI $\mathbf{0}$ to obtain $\hat{\mathbf{L}}_t(\mathbf{u} \to \mathbf{0})$, expressed as,

$$\hat{\mathbf{L}}_t(\mathbf{u} \to \mathbf{0}) = \mathcal{W}\left(\hat{\mathbf{L}}_t(\mathbf{u}); (\mathbf{u} - \mathbf{0})\, d_t\right) . \tag{3}$$

Here, $\mathcal{W}$ denotes the bilinear inverse warping operator [16] that takes as input a displacement map and remaps the images. The geometric consistency error between the approximated current frame $\hat{\mathbf{L}}_t(\mathbf{u} \to \mathbf{0})$ and I_t is then defined as,

$$\mathcal{L}_{geo}^t = \sum_{\mathbf{u}} \|\hat{\mathbf{L}}_t(\mathbf{u} \to \mathbf{0}) - I_t\|_1 . \tag{4}$$

Temporal Consistency Constraint. In addition to an LSTM network-based [36] recurrent framework of our network $\mathcal{V}$, we impose a temporal consistency constraint on the predicted outputs. For this, we first estimate the optical flow between successive input video frames using a pre-trained RAFT [41] network, denoted as $\mathcal{O}$. The optical flow is then computed as $o_t = \mathcal{O}(I_t, I_{t+1})$. To enforce temporal consistency, we utilize the warped angular views $\hat{\mathbf{L}}_t(\mathbf{u} \to \mathbf{0})$ and again warp them to the video frame at $t+1$ using o_t. Then, the temporal consistency error is defined as the error between the known next frame I_{t+1} and these warped frames and is denoted as,

$$\mathcal{L}^t_{temp} = \sum_{\mathbf{u}} \|\mathcal{W}\left(\hat{\mathbf{L}}_t\left(\mathbf{u} \to \mathbf{0}; o_t\right)\right) - I_{t+1}\|_1 . \qquad (5)$$

Minimizing this error during training explicitly enforces temporal consistency between the successive predicted LF frames.

3.4 Disocclusion Handling

In a LF, pixels at depth boundary of objects get occluded and disoccluded between different SAIs. Due to the lack of ground truth data we face a major challenge when learning to fill-in the intensity values at the disoccluded pixels. Our objective is to use pixels in I_{t-1} and I_{t+1} to fill in the disoccluded pixels of $\hat{\mathbf{L}}_t$, as these frames could potentially have the necessary pixel values. Pixels from neighboring video frames have been used to inpaint the current frame in several video-inpainting techniques [19,50]. Here, we achieve this by bringing the informative intensity values to the disoccluded pixels through flow-based warping. As shown in Fig. 4, we use RAFT to obtain optical flow between the SAIs of $\hat{\mathbf{L}}_t$ and the input frames I_{t-1}, I_{t+1}. By including these warping based operations in a loss function, we train the network to automatically predict the disoccluded pixels.

The loss is defined on only those pixels that are disoccluded in the SAIs of the LF frame $\hat{\mathbf{L}}_t$. We obtain the disoccluded pixels by forward-warping the input frame I_t to all the SAIs of LF with the disparity map d_t. For each SAI at angular location $\mathbf{u}$, we define a binary mask $\mathcal{M}_t$ which is 1 if forward warping resulted in a hole for that particular pixel. To fill the dis-occluded pixels, we forward warp I_{t-1} to the predicted SAIs of $\hat{\mathbf{L}}_t$ using optical flow as shown in Fig. 4. The forward warped SAIs are obtained as:

$$\tilde{\mathbf{L}}_{t \leftarrow t-1}(\mathbf{u}) = \mathcal{W}\left(I_{t-1}; \mathcal{O}\left(I_{t-1}, \hat{\mathbf{L}}_t(\mathbf{u})\right)\right), \qquad (6)$$

$$\tilde{\mathbf{L}}_{t \leftarrow t+1}(\mathbf{u}) = \mathcal{W}\left(I_{t+1}; \mathcal{O}\left(I_{t+1}, \hat{\mathbf{L}}_t(\mathbf{u})\right)\right), \qquad (7)$$

where $\tilde{\mathbf{L}}_{t \leftarrow t+1}(\mathbf{u})$ and $\tilde{\mathbf{L}}_{t \leftarrow t-1}(\mathbf{u})$ represent the forwards warped SAIs from I_{t+1} and I_{t-1} respectively using optical flow. Depending on the camera motion the disoccluded pixels in $\hat{\mathbf{L}}_t$ could be visible either in I_{t-1} or I_{t+1} or both. Taking this into consideration, we define the cost function as

$$\mathcal{L}^t_{occ} = \min(\|\mathcal{M}_t \cdot \left(\hat{\mathbf{L}}_t(\mathbf{u}) - \tilde{\mathbf{L}}_{t \leftarrow t-1}(\mathbf{u})\right)\|_1 , \|\mathcal{M}_t \cdot \left(\hat{\mathbf{L}}_t(\mathbf{u}) - \tilde{\mathbf{L}}_{t \leftarrow t+1}(\mathbf{u})\right)\|_1) \quad (8)$$

$\mathcal{L}^t_{occ}$ follows the concept of minimum re-projection loss followed in monocular depth estimation techniques such as [11].

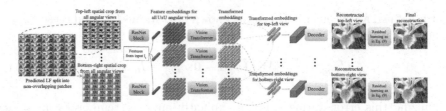

Fig. 5. A supervised residual refinement block is used to further improve the reconstruction quality of the LFs. The transformer block attends to the spatio-angular information in the estimated LF and the input frame I_t to predict the refined output.

3.5 Supervised Residual Refinement Block

Recently, self-supervised pre-training on very large unlabeled datasets followed by supervised learning on a limited labeled dataset has helped in achieving state-of-the-art results [5,6,17]. Inspired by these works, we propose to use the limited dataset of LF *images* to further refine the reconstructed LF frames. As this shouldn't affect the temporal consistency of the predicted frames, the proposed refinement module follows a residual network architecture as shown in Fig. 5. And this module can be trained as a separate block from the recurrent module in the synthesis network $\mathcal{V}$.

Vision Transformers(ViT) [9] form the backbone of our proposed refinement module. As shown in Fig. 5, we divide the predicted LF frame $\hat{\mathbf{L}}_t$ into non-overlapping patches, each of size $p \times p$. For simplicity consider all the U^2 top-left patches cropped from each angular view of $\hat{\mathbf{L}}_t$. A shallow ResNet-based neural network extracts features independently from each of the U^2 patches. Additionally, we also extract features from the top-left patch of the input image I_t. The transformer module then takes as input the $U^2 + 1$ features/embeddings as input and outputs $U^2 + 1$ tokens after applying multi-headed self-attention (MHSA) [9]. An identical procedure is repeated on all the non-overlapping patches of $\hat{\mathbf{L}}_t$ to produce $U^2 + 1$ tokens each time.

As in Fig. 5, we discard the token from the input frame and consider all the P transformed tokens from a particular angular view, say bottom-right. Here, P is the number of non-overlapping patches cropped from each angular view. These P tokens are stacked horizontally and vertically following the order of cropped patches, so as to form a larger feature map. A shallow decoder network then takes these stacked tokens as input and predicts a 4 channel output. The first 3 channels form an RGB image ($\tilde{\mathbf{L}}_t^{ref}(\mathbf{u})$) and the fourth channel is the mask $M_{ref} \in [0,1]^{h \times w}$. The final output $\hat{\mathbf{L}}_t^{ref}$ is then defined as,

$$\hat{\mathbf{L}}_t^{ref}(\mathbf{u}) = M_{ref} \odot \hat{\mathbf{L}}_t(\mathbf{u}) + (1 - M_{ref}) \odot \tilde{\mathbf{L}}_t^{ref}(\mathbf{u}). \tag{9}$$

Identical decoding step is repeated for each SAI $\mathbf{u}$ producing a refined LF frame $\hat{\mathbf{L}}_t^{ref}$. As we assume access to a LF *image* dataset, we train the refinement network by imposing L1 loss between $\hat{\mathbf{L}}_t^{ref}$ and the corresponding ground-truth

L_t as:

$$\mathcal{L}_{ref} = \sum_{\mathbf{u}} \|\hat{\mathbf{L}}_t^{ref}(\mathbf{u}) - \mathbf{L}_t(\mathbf{u})\|_1. \tag{10}$$

3.6 Overall Loss

We finally add total-variation(TV)-based smoothness constraint [35] on the predicted LF frames and Bin-center density loss [3] on disparity values predicted by m-VIT. The Bin-center density loss encourages the predicted disparity planes to be close to the disparity map d_t which is provided as input to the adaptive TD layer. Including all the cost functions, the overall loss to minimize for training $\mathcal{V}$ and the adaptive TD layer becomes,

$$\mathcal{L}_{self}^t = \lambda_1 \mathcal{L}_{photo}^t + \lambda_2 \mathcal{L}_{geo}^t + \lambda_3 \mathcal{L}_{temp}^t + \lambda_4 \mathcal{L}_{occ}^t + \lambda_5 \mathcal{L}_{bins}^t + \lambda_6 \mathcal{L}_{TV}^t, \tag{11}$$

where the parameters λ_i control the contribution of each loss term. After the self-supervised training of the main network is completed, we then freeze these weights and train the refinement block. The refinement block is trained using a supervised cost function $\mathcal{L}_{ref}$ in Eq. (10).

3.7 Implementation Details

As shown in Fig. 2, our proposed pipeline has three separate deep neural networks: (a) LF synthesis network, (b) adaptive TD layer (Fig. 3) and (c) refinement network (Fig. 5). The synthesis network $\mathcal{V}$ is a LSTM based recurrent neural network consisting of a Efficient-Net encoder [40] and a convolutional decoder with skip connections. In the adaptive TD layer, we set the low-rank representation $\mathcal{F}$ to have $N = 3$ layers and the rank $R = 12$ following [35]. The displacements $D = \{D_1, D_2, D_3\}$ are predicted from m-VIT [3] network that takes as input $\{I_{t-1}, I_t, I_{t+1}, d_t\}$. Finally, the refinement network has a backbone of the convolutional vision transformer which is supervised using a limited amount of LF *image* data. Further details of the neural networks can be found in the supplementary material.

For training our proposed synthesis network, we use the *GOPRO* monocular video dataset [29]. The *GOPRO* dataset contains monocular videos of 33 different scenes each containing 525 to 1650 monocular frames of spatial resolution 720×1280. We split the dataset into a set of 25 videos for training and 8 videos for validation. The monocular video frames are resized into frames of size 352×528 to maintain the spatial resolution of Lytro Illum light field camera. While training we obtain a monocular video of 7 frames and randomly crop a patch of size 176×264. The successive frames in the training data are 10 frames apart in the raw GoPro videos captured at 240 fps. This ensures that there's reasonable object motion between successive input frames which is crucial for the disocclusion handling technique. In one frame, closer objects show larger disocclusions in the predicted LF as they have higher disparity values. These objects also proportionally have larger displacements in successive frames, providing enough information to fill in the disoccluded pixels.

Table 1. We quantitatively compare our proposed technique with state-of-the-art algorithms on various datasets. Our algorithm consistently provides high-fidelity reconstructions. **Blue** and green represent the top-two performing algorithm in each column.

Algorithm	Hybrid		ViewSynth		TAMULF		Stanford		Average	
	PSNR	SSIM	PSNR	SSIM	PSNR	SSIM	PSNR	SSIM	PSNR	SSIM
Niklaus et al. [31]	23.87	0.873	23.19	0.903	18.12	0.811	23.19	0.892	22.10	0.870
Srinivasan et al. [38]	28.12	0.893	28.56	0.931	22.63	0.857	29.24	0.924	27.14	0.901
Li et al. [22]	31.62	0.950	29.39	0.945	25.63	0.903	30.44	0.956	29.27	0.938
Li+Ranftl [33]	31.69	0.950	29.90	0.953	25.83	0.906	31.21	0.962	29.66	0.943
Proposed (image)	32.48	0.951	30.76	0.955	27.42	0.927	34.58	0.970	31.30	0.951
Proposed	**32.66**	**0.952**	**30.97**	**0.956**	**27.24**	**0.922**	**34.98**	**0.974**	**31.47**	**0.951**

The relative depth map input to the network is obtained from [33] and then modified for various baseline factors to enable the synthesis network to generate LF outputs of various baseline. We randomly choose a value for $a \in \{0.8, 1.6, 2.4, 3.2\}$ and $b \in [0.2, 0.4]$ to obtain disparity $d_t = az_t + b$ as explained in Sect. 3.1. The network is trained in Pytorch [32] using AdamW [24] optimizer for 25 epochs, with an initial learning rate of 0.0001 and weight decay of 0.001. The learning rate is decreased to half the initial value when the validation loss plateaus for more more than 4 epochs. We empirically choose the hyperparameters as $\lambda_1 = 1.0$, $\lambda_2 = 1.0$, $\lambda_3 = 0.5$, $\lambda_4 = 0.2$, $\lambda_5 = 2$ and $\lambda_6 = 0.1$ in Eq. (11).

For training our residual refinement block, we freeze the weights of the synthesis network and train only the refinement block using supervised loss function in Eq. (10). We fix the value of a as 1.2 and b as 0.3 to estimate d_t which is provided as input to the synthesis network. For the supervised training, we use 1000 LF images from *TAMULF* [22] dataset. The network is trained using AdamW optimizer for 15 epochs, with an initial learning rate of 0.001 and weight decay of 0.001. The learning rate is decreased to half the initial value when the validation loss plateaus for more more than 4 epochs.

4   Experiments

To validate our proposed algorithm, we make several qualitative and quantitative comparisons with diverse LF datasets. For quantitative comparison, we mainly consider four different datasets: *Hybrid* [45], *ViewSynth* [18], *TAMULF* [22] and *Stanford* [7] containing 30, 25, 84 and 113 light field video sequences, respectively. From the *Hybrid* dataset we consider the central 7×7 views as the ground-truth light field videos, and the center-view of each LF forms the input monocular video. The rest three datasets are LF *image* datasets, and we simulate LF videos with 8 frames from each LF following the procedure described in [25,35]. The center-view of these 7×7 view LF videos form the monocular video sequence that is given as input to our algorithm. During inference, we first obtain the depth estimate z_t from DPT [33] and convert it to a disparity map d_t. Three

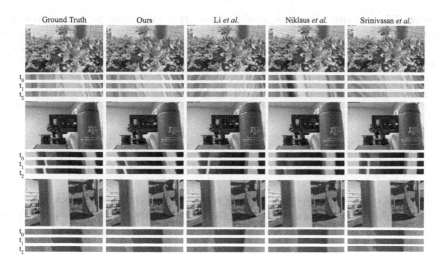

Fig. 6. We qualitatively compare our reconstruction with ground truth and other state-of-the-art techniques. We show the top-left view of t_0 and EPI images from three consecutive LF frames (t_0, t_1, t_2). As can be clearly seen from the EPI images, our technique consistently provides accurate reconstructions.

consecutive temporal frames and disparity map are stacked and input to the complete model represented in Fig. 2 to obtain the LF frame output.

4.1 Light Field Video Reconstruction

We quantitatively and qualitatively compare the results of our proposed algorithm with previously proposed monocular LF estimation techniques. For quantitative comparison, we use two metrics: peak signal-to-noise ratio (PSNR) (higher is better) and structural similarity index measure (SSIM) (higher is better). As shown in Table 1, we compare the performance of our proposed algorithm with Niklaus *et al.* [31], Srinivasan *et al.* [38] and Li *et al.* [22].

Li *et al.* [22] takes a single frame and a relative depth estimate from [44] as input. To obtain the complete LF video, we have to reconstruct each frame of the video individually. In Table 1, Li *et al.* + Ranftl *et al.* represents a modified [22], where we input a depth estimate from DPT [33] instead of the original DeepLens [44] model. This is done to ensure a fair comparison with our technique as we also use DPT, which is a state-of-the-art monocular depth estimation technique based on vision transformers. However, [22] is not trained for inputs from DPT [33]. Hence, we finetune [22] on the TAMULF dataset with depth maps from DPT [33]. Srinivasan *et al.* [38] is another single image LF estimation model. While the original network is trained on a dataset of flower images (proposed in the same work), we finetune it on a larger and diverse TAMULF dataset from [22]. Finally, we also compare our algorithm with Niklaus *et al.* [31] that takes a single frame as input. We used the default implementation provided by the authors for comparison, which is already trained on a diverse dataset. As all

Table 2. We consider a baseline model 'Base' that is trained only with the self-supervised constraints as proposed in SeLFVi [35]. We then successively enhance the 'Base' model with disocclusion handling, adaptive TD layer and the refinement block and compare the performance boost in each case.

Algorithm	Hybrid		ViewSynth		TAMULF		Stanford		Average	
	PSNR	SSIM	PSNR	SSIM	PSNR	SSIM	PSNR	SSIM	PSNR	SSIM
Base	30.76	0.945	29.07	0.947	25.74	0.918	31.70	0.963	29.32	0.943
Base+occ	31.78	0.949	29.71	0.948	26.51	0.919	32.99	0.965	30.25	0.945
Base+occ+adpt	32.26	0.950	30.69	0.954	26.96	0.919	34.45	0.973	31.09	0.949
Proposed	32.66	0.952	30.07	0.056	27.24	0.922	34.98	0.974	31.47	0.951

these techniques are image-based and don't have any temporal information, we also compare with a *downgraded* version of our algorithm 'Proposed(image)'. In this model, we repeat the current frame as three successive input frames of our proposed algorithm.

Table 1 details the quantitative comparisons of various algorithms against all 4 datasets: Hybrid, ViewSynth, TAMULF and Stanford. Our proposed reconstruction outperforms previous state-of-the-art techniques. We also notice that even our image-based model 'Proposed(image)' outperforms the previous image-based LF prediction techniques. We can also see clear distinction when we compare the images qualitatively in Fig. 6, especially when the EPI for the LF views are taken into account. We also validate our algorithm on monocular videos acquired from a commercial GoPro camera. While we show some results from GoPro dataset in Fig. 7, please refer to the supplementary material for more qualitative results.

Temporal Consistency. We evaluate and quantitatively compare the temporal consistency of the videos predicted from our proposed algorithm. For this, we first predict optical flow via [41] between all SAIs of successive ground-truth LF frames. We then compute the mean squared error between the current estimated LF and the previous LF warped to the current frame. We provide quantitative comparison in the supplementary material.

4.2   Ablation Study

Our proposed technique contains three key building blocks that enable us to work with monocular videos. Here, we evaluate the contribution of each of the three building blocks to the reconstruction quality. As shown in Table 2 we evaluate the effect of each block by successively adding the proposed blocks to the baseline model and quantitatively comparing the reconstructed LF videos. The baseline model can also be thought of as an extension of SeLFVi [35] to the case of monocular videos. Here, we utilize *only* the geometric, photometric and temporal consistency constraints proposed in SeLFVi. The LF synthesis network architecture $\mathcal{V}$ remains identical in all the models.

Fig. 7. The model trained without disocclusion handling leads to a halo-like artifact around depth-edges in the SAIs of the frames. With the proposed disocclusion handling technique, the network learns to accurately fill-in the disoccluded pixels.

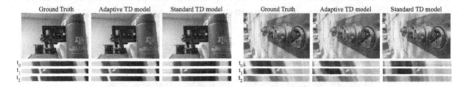

Fig. 8. As seen in the EPI images, the standard TD model is unable to represent the depth for the scene accurately compared to the proposed adaptive TD model. By separately determining the depth planes for each scene, adaptive TD model gives a more accurate reconstruction.

Disocclusion handling (Base vs Base+occ): Enforcing the disocclusion handling constraint helps the synthesis network to learn to fill in the disoccluded pixels in the estimated LF frames as shown in Fig. 7. Quantitatively, we also observe a boost of 0.9 dB PSNR in comparison to the baseline model.

Adaptive TD layer (Base+occ vs Base+occ+adpt): Our modified adaptive TD layer can accurately represent the depth planes in the LF as can be seen from the EPI images in Fig. 8. Quantitatively, we get a significant performance boost of about 0.7 dB PSNR.

Supervised refinement block (Base+occ+adpt vs Proposed): Finally, we evaluate the effect of the novel refinement block that is trained with supervised loss on ground-truth LF frames. We observe an expected improvement in the reconstruction quality, showing a boost in PSNR of nearly 0.4 dB. We also make qualitative comparison in Fig. 9, where we see that the refinement block provides more accurate SAIs around depth edges that are difficult to reconstruct with just self-supervised learning.

4.3 Variable Baseline LF Prediction

Supervised techniques using LF data from a single camera produce LF images with a fixed baseline. However, our proposed network reconstructs LF frames based on the input disparity map. By scaling the disparity map by a constant factor, we can scale the disparity values input to the network, leading to LF prediction with variable baselines. In Fig. 10 we demonstrate this with 4 different

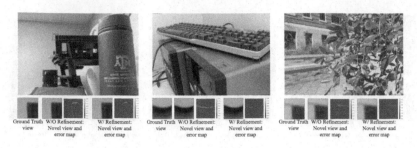

Ground Truth W/O Refinement: W/ Refinement: Ground Truth W/O Refinement: W/ Refinement: Ground Truth W/O Refinement: W/ Refinement:
view   Novel view and   Novel view and   view   Novel view and   Novel view and   view   Novel view and   Novel view and
            error map   error map   error map   error map   error map   error map

Fig. 9. The error map between the reconstructed and ground-truth shows that supervised refinement improves reconstruction at depth-edges. The refinement module corrects the baseline discrepancy The refinement block utilizes the spatial information in other SAIs through angular attention and optimizes the positioning of depth-edges correcting the baseline discrepancy between synthesized and ground truth LF.

Fig. 10. With our proposed self-supervised technique, LF frames with variable baselines can be predicted by just scaling the input disparity map. We demonstrate this on 4 different scales $\{1, 1.5, 2, 2.5\}\times$. Notice the increasing slope in the EPI images from $1\times$ to $2.5\times$.

scale factor for disparity maps, $1\times$, $1.5\times$, $2\times$, $2.5\times$. Note that our algorithm allows us to generate SAIs with higher baseline than that of the ground truth frames from Lytro.

5   Discussion

Our proposed algorithm is largely a self-supervised technique except for the refinement block that is supervised using ground-truth LF *image* data. The refinement block uses a transformer module for angular attention. To the best of our knowledge this is also the first attempt to employ vision transformers to LF data. Note that our proposed algorithm outperforms previous state-of-the-art techniques even without the supervised refinement module. Another point to note is that, during inference, we do not have any information about the true baseline of the LF. We only have access to a relative depth map obtained from a single input image. Hence, it becomes difficult to accurately compare with the ground-truth. To solve this, we choose a scale and shift factor ($\{a, b\}$) such that the mean error between the computed disparity maps (from relative depth maps) and the true disparity maps (for a given dataset such as TAMULF) is minimum. Outside of comparison with ground truth, the true disparity map is not necessary and we can generate LF of multiple baselines as needed (Fig. 10).

6   Conclusion

We propose an algorithm for LF video reconstruction from just a monocular video input. Our baseline model utilizes the intermediate layered representation for LF and the self-supervised geometric, photometric and temporal constraints [35]. Additional modifications were proposed in this work that enabled the final model to reconstruct high-fidelity LF videos from monocular input. We propose a disoclussion handling technique that is required to fill-in disoccluded regions in the estimated LF. We also propose a adaptive TD representation that can adapt to each input scene based on the layer displacements predicted by the network. Finally, we introduce a novel supervised, transformer-based refinement block that can further refine the predicted LF. Along with superior reconstruction results, our model also enables prediction of LF frames with varying baselines. Overall, our proposed algorithm facilitates a monocular camera for applications like refocusing and novel view synthesis.

Acknowledgements. This work was supported in part by Qualcomm Innovation Fellowship (QIF) India 2021.

References

1. Adelson, E.H., Bergen, J.R.: The plenoptic function and the elements of early vision. In: Computational Models of Visual Processing, pp. 3–20. MIT Press (1991)
2. Bae, K., Ivan, A., Nagahara, H., Park, I.K.: 5d light field synthesis from a monocular video. In: 2020 25th International Conference on Pattern Recognition (ICPR), pp. 7157–7164. IEEE (2021)
3. Bhat, S.F., Alhashim, I., Wonka, P.: AdaBins: depth estimation using adaptive bins. In: Proceedings of the IEEE/CVF Conference on Computer Vision and Pattern Recognition, pp. 4009–4018 (2021)
4. Blocker, C.J., Chun, Y., Fessler, J.A.: Low-rank plus sparse tensor models for light-field reconstruction from focal stack data. In: 2018 IEEE 13th Image, Video, and Multidimensional Signal Processing Workshop (IVMSP), pp. 1–5. IEEE (2018)
5. Caron, M., Misra, I., Mairal, J., Goyal, P., Bojanowski, P., Joulin, A.: Unsupervised learning of visual features by contrasting cluster assignments. Adv. Neural. Inf. Process. Syst. **33**, 9912–9924 (2020)
6. Chen, T., Kornblith, S., Norouzi, M., Hinton, G.: A simple framework for contrastive learning of visual representations. In: International Conference on Machine Learning, pp. 1597–1607. PMLR (2020)
7. Dansereau, D.G., Girod, B., Wetzstein, G.: LiFF: light field features in scale and depth. In: Computer Vision and Pattern Recognition (CVPR). IEEE, June 2019
8. Delbracio, M., Kelly, D., Brown, M.S., Milanfar, P.: Mobile computational photography: a tour. arXiv preprint arXiv:2102.09000 (2021)
9. Dosovitskiy, A., et al.: An image is worth 16x16 words: Transformers for image recognition at scale. arXiv preprint arXiv:2010.11929 (2020)
10. Garg, R., Wadhwa, N., Ansari, S., Barron, J.T.: Learning single camera depth estimation using dual-pixels. In: Proceedings of the IEEE/CVF International Conference on Computer Vision, pp. 7628–7637 (2019)

11. Godard, C., Mac Aodha, O., Firman, M., Brostow, G.J.: Digging into self-supervised monocular depth estimation. In: Proceedings of the IEEE/CVF International Conference on Computer Vision, pp. 3828–3838 (2019)
12. Hajisharif, S., Miandji, E., Guillemot, C., Unger, J.: Single sensor compressive light field video camera. In: Computer Graphics Forum, vol. 39, pp. 463–474. Wiley Online Library (2020)
13. Huang, P.H., Matzen, K., Kopf, J., Ahuja, N., Huang, J.B.: DeepMVS: learning multi-view stereopsis (2018)
14. Inagaki, Y., Kobayashi, Y., Takahashi, K., Fujii, T., Nagahara, H.: Learning to capture light fields through a coded aperture camera. In: Ferrari, V., Hebert, M., Sminchisescu, C., Weiss, Y. (eds.) ECCV 2018. LNCS, vol 11211, pp. 431–448. Springer, Cham (2018). https://doi.org/10.1007/978-3-030-01234-2_26
15. Ivan, A., et al.: Synthesizing a 4d spatio-angular consistent light field from a single image. arXiv preprint arXiv:1903.12364 (2019)
16. Jaderberg, M., Simonyan, K., Zisserman, A., Kavukcuoglu, K.: Spatial transformer networks. arXiv preprint arXiv:1506.02025 (2015)
17. Jaiswal, A., Babu, A.R., Zadeh, M.Z., Banerjee, D., Makedon, F.: A survey on contrastive self-supervised learning. Technologies 9(1), 2 (2021)
18. Kalantari, N.K., Wang, T.C., Ramamoorthi, R.: Learning-based view synthesis for light field cameras. ACM Trans. Graph. (TOG) 35(6), 1–10 (2016)
19. Kim, D., Woo, S., Lee, J.Y., Kweon, I.S.: Deep video inpainting. In: Proceedings of the IEEE/CVF Conference on Computer Vision and Pattern Recognition, pp. 5792–5801 (2019)
20. Kim, H.M., Kim, M.S., Lee, G.J., Jang, H.J., Song, Y.M.: Miniaturized 3d depth sensing-based smartphone light field camera. Sensors 20(7), 2129 (2020)
21. Kobayashi, Y., Takahashi, K., Fujii, T.: From focal stacks to tensor display: A method for light field visualization without multi-view images. In: 2017 IEEE International Conference on Acoustics, Speech and Signal Processing (ICASSP), pp. 2007–2011 (2017). https://doi.org/10.1109/ICASSP.2017.7952508
22. Li, Q., Kalantari, N.K.: Synthesizing light field from a single image with variable MPI and two network fusion. ACM Trans. Graph. 39(6), 1–229 (2020)
23. Lippmann, G.: Épreuves réversibles donnant la sensation du relief. J. Phys. Theor. Appl. 7(1), 821–825 (1908). https://doi.org/10.1051/jphystap:019080070082100
24. Loshchilov, I., Hutter, F.: Decoupled weight decay regularization. In: 7th International Conference on Learning Representations, ICLR 2019, New Orleans, LA, USA, 6–9 May 2019. OpenReview.net (2019)
25. Lumentut, J.S., Kim, T.H., Ramamoorthi, R., Park, I.K.: Deep recurrent network for fast and full-resolution light field deblurring. IEEE Signal Process. Lett. 26(12), 1788–1792 (2019)
26. Maruyama, K., Inagaki, Y., Takahashi, K., Fujii, T., Nagahara, H.: A 3-d display pipeline from coded-aperture camera to tensor light-field display through CNN. In: 2019 IEEE International Conference on Image Processing (ICIP), pp. 1064–1068 (2019). https://doi.org/10.1109/ICIP.2019.8803741
27. Marwah, K., Wetzstein, G., Bando, Y., Raskar, R.: Compressive light field photography using overcomplete dictionaries and optimized projections. ACM Trans. Graph. (TOG) 32(4), 1–12 (2013)
28. Mildenhall, B., et al.: Local light field fusion: Practical view synthesis with prescriptive sampling guidelines (2019)
29. Nah, S., Kim, T.H., Lee, K.M.: Deep multi-scale convolutional neural network for dynamic scene deblurring. In: The IEEE Conference on Computer Vision and Pattern Recognition (CVPR), July 2017

30. Ng, R., Levoy, M., Brédif, M., Duval, G., Horowitz, M., Hanrahan, P.: Light field photography with a hand-held plenoptic camera. Ph.D. thesis, Stanford University (2005)

31. Niklaus, S., Mai, L., Yang, J., Liu, F.: 3d ken burns effect from a single image. ACM Trans. Graph. (ToG) **38**(6), 1–15 (2019)

32. Paszke, A., et al.: Pytorch: An imperative style, high-performance deep learning library. In: Wallach, H., Larochelle, H., Beygelzimer, A., d' Alché-Buc, F., Fox, E., Garnett, R. (eds.) Advances in Neural Information Processing Systems, vol. 32, pp. 8024–8035. Curran Associates, Inc. (2019)

33. Ranftl, R., Bochkovskiy, A., Koltun, V.: Vision transformers for dense prediction. In: Proceedings of the IEEE/CVF International Conference on Computer Vision, pp. 12179–12188 (2021)

34. Sakai, K., Takahashi, K., Fujii, T., Nagahara, H.: Acquiring dynamic light fields through coded aperture camera. In: Vedaldi, A., Bischof, H., Brox, T., Frahm, J.-M. (eds.) ECCV 2020. LNCS, vol. 12364, pp. 368–385. Springer, Cham (2020). https://doi.org/10.1007/978-3-030-58529-7_22

35. Shedligeri, P., Schiffers, F., Ghosh, S., Cossairt, O., Mitra, K.: SelfVI: self-supervised light-field video reconstruction from stereo video. In: Proceedings of the IEEE/CVF International Conference on Computer Vision, pp. 2491–2501 (2021)

36. Shi, X., Chen, Z., Wang, H., Yeung, D.Y., Wong, W.K., Woo, W.: Convolutional LSTM network: a machine learning approach for precipitation nowcasting. Adv. Neural. Inf. Process. Syst. **28**, 1–8 (2015)

37. Srinivasan, P.P., Tucker, R., Barron, J.T., Ramamoorthi, R., Ng, R., Snavely, N.: Pushing the boundaries of view extrapolation with multiplane images. In: Proceedings of the IEEE/CVF Conference on Computer Vision and Pattern Recognition, pp. 175–184 (2019)

38. Srinivasan, P.P., Wang, T., Sreelal, A., Ramamoorthi, R., Ng, R.: Learning to synthesize a 4d RGBD light field from a single image. In: Proceedings of the IEEE International Conference on Computer Vision, pp. 2243–2251 (2017)

39. Takahashi, K., Kobayashi, Y., Fujii, T.: From focal stack to tensor light-field display. IEEE Trans. Image Process. **27**(9), 4571–4584 (2018). https://doi.org/10.1109/TIP.2018.2839263

40. Tan, M., Le, Q.: Efficientnet: Rethinking model scaling for convolutional neural networks. In: International Conference on Machine Learning, pp. 6105–6114. PMLR (2019)

41. Teed, Z., Deng, J.: RAFT: recurrent all-pairs field transforms for optical flow. In: Vedaldi, A., Bischof, H., Brox, T., Frahm, J.-M. (eds.) ECCV 2020. LNCS, vol. 12347, pp. 402–419. Springer, Cham (2020). https://doi.org/10.1007/978-3-030-58536-5_24

42. Vadathya, A.K., Girish, S., Mitra, K.: A unified learning-based framework for light field reconstruction from coded projections. IEEE Trans. Comput. Imaging **6**, 304–316 (2019)

43. Veeraraghavan, A., Raskar, R., Agrawal, A., Mohan, A., Tumblin, J.: Dappled photography: mask enhanced cameras for heterodyned light fields and coded aperture refocusing. ACM Trans. Graph. **26**(3), 69 (2007)

44. Wang, L., et al.: DeepLens: shallow depth of field from a single image. CoRR abs/1810.08100 (2018)

45. Wang, T.C., Zhu, J.Y., Kalantari, N.K., Efros, A.A., Ramamoorthi, R.: Light field video capture using a learning-based hybrid imaging system. ACM Trans. Graph. (TOG) **36**(4), 1–13 (2017)

46. Wang, Y., Liu, F., Wang, Z., Hou, G., Sun, Z., Tan, T.: End-to-end view synthesis for light field imaging with pseudo 4DCNN. In: Ferrari, V., Hebert, M., Sminchisescu, C., Weiss, Y. (eds.) ECCV 2018. LNCS, vol. 11206, pp. 340–355. Springer, Cham (2018). https://doi.org/10.1007/978-3-030-01216-8_21
47. Wetzstein, G., Lanman, D., Hirsch, M., Raskar, R.: Tensor displays: compressive light field synthesis using multilayer displays with directional backlighting. ACM Trans. Graph. **31**(4), 1–12 (2012). https://doi.org/10.1145/2185520.2185576
48. Wilburn, B., et al.: High performance imaging using large camera arrays. ACM Trans. Graph. **24**(3), 765–776 (2005). https://doi.org/10.1145/1073204.1073259
49. Wu, G., Zhao, M., Wang, L., Dai, Q., Chai, T., Liu, Y.: Light field reconstruction using deep convolutional network on EPI. In: Proceedings of the IEEE Conference on Computer Vision and Pattern Recognition, pp. 6319–6327 (2017)
50. Xu, R., Li, X., Zhou, B., Loy, C.C.: Deep flow-guided video inpainting. In: Proceedings of the IEEE/CVF Conference on Computer Vision and Pattern Recognition, pp. 3723–3732 (2019)
51. Yeung, H.W.F., Hou, J., Chen, J., Chung, Y.Y., Chen, X.: Fast light field reconstruction with deep coarse-to-fine modeling of spatial-angular clues. In: Ferrari, V., Hebert, M., Sminchisescu, C., Weiss, Y. (eds.) ECCV 2018. LNCS, vol. 11210, pp. 138–154. Springer, Cham (2018). https://doi.org/10.1007/978-3-030-01231-1_9
52. Zhang, Z., Liu, Y., Dai, Q.: Light field from micro-baseline image pair. In: Proceedings of the IEEE Conference on Computer Vision and Pattern Recognition, pp. 3800–3809 (2015)
53. Zhou, T., Tucker, R., Flynn, J., Fyffe, G., Snavely, N.: Stereo magnification: learning view synthesis using multiplane images. In: SIGGRAPH (2018)
54. Zhou, T., Tulsiani, S., Sun, W., Malik, J., Efros, A.A.: View synthesis by appearance flow. In: Leibe, B., Matas, J., Sebe, N., Welling, M. (eds.) ECCV 2016. LNCS, vol. 9908, pp. 286–301. Springer, Cham (2016). https://doi.org/10.1007/978-3-319-46493-0_18

Human-Centric Image Cropping
with Partition-Aware
and Content-Preserving Features

Bo Zhang(ID), Li Niu(✉)(ID), Xing Zhao(ID), and Liqing Zhang(ID)

MoE Key Lab of Artificial Intelligence, Shanghai Jiao Tong University,
Shanghai, China
{bo-zhang,ustcnewly,1033874657}@sjtu.edu.cn, zhang-lq@cs.sjtu.edu.cn

Abstract. Image cropping aims to find visually appealing crops in an image, which is an important yet challenging task. In this paper, we consider a specific and practical application: human-centric image cropping, which focuses on the depiction of a person. To this end, we propose a human-centric image cropping method with two novel feature designs for the candidate crop: partition-aware feature and content-preserving feature. For partition-aware feature, we divide the whole image into nine partitions based on the human bounding box and treat different partitions in a candidate crop differently conditioned on the human information. For content-preserving feature, we predict a heatmap indicating the important content to be included in a good crop, and extract the geometric relation between the heatmap and a candidate crop. Extensive experiments demonstrate that our method can perform favorably against state-of-the-art image cropping methods on human-centric image cropping task. Code is available at https://github.com/bcmi/Human-Centric-Image-Cropping.

1 Introduction

Image cropping aims to automatically find visually appealing crops in an image, which is critical in various down-stream applications, *e.g.*, photo post-processing [6], view recommendation [20,21,41], image thumbnailing [3,10], and camera view adjustment suggestion [35]. In this paper, we address a specific and practical application: human-centric image cropping, which focuses on the depiction of a person and benefits a variety of applications, including portrait enhancement [47] and portrait composition assistance [48,49]. For a human-centric image, a good crop depends on the position of the human in the crop, human information, and the content of interest, which makes human-centric image cropping challenging.

Supplementary Information The online version contains supplementary material available at https://doi.org/10.1007/978-3-031-20071-7_11.

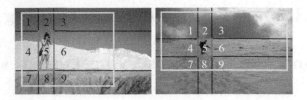

Fig. 1. Illustration of the motivation behind partition-aware feature. The whole image is divided into nine partitions based on the human bounding box (red). To produce the best crop (yellow), the aesthetic contribution of similar content in different partitions depends on its relative position to human subject. (Color figure online)

Several previous works [2,47,48] have already focused on portrait photograph cropping, which extracted hand-crafted features from the results of saliency detection, human face detection, or human pose estimation. However, extracting hand-crafted features is laborious and the hand-crafted features are generally not robust for modeling the huge aesthetic space [9]. Recently, numerous methods [15,22,23,37,40,44] addressed image cropping task in a data-driven manner, in which models are directly trained with the human-annotated datasets [5,41,43]. However, for human-centric images, these methods rarely explicitly consider human information. In contrast, we show that exploiting human information can significantly help obtain good crops. Based on the general pipeline of data-driven methods, we propose two innovations for human-centric image cropping.

In this paper, we refer to the images that meet the following conditions as human-centric images: 1) The image subject is single person, while there can be other people in the background. 2) The area of the human bounding box does not exceed 90% of the entire frame. Given a human-centric image, the whole image can be divided into nine partitions based on the human bounding box (see Fig. 1). Generally, the aesthetic contribution of similar content in different partitions depends on its relative position to the human subject. For example, in Fig. 1, partitions 4 and 6 in the left subfigure have similar content, but the best crop preserves more content in partition 6 because the person looks to the right, making the content in partition 6 visually more important [12]. Similarly, partition 4 and partition 8 in the right subfigure also have similar content, but the best crop preserves more content in partition 4, probably because the person is moving forward and the content behind him becomes less important. Therefore, when extracting features of candidate crops for aesthetic evaluation, we should consider the partition location and human information (*e.g.*, human posture, face orientation). To this end, we propose a novel partition-aware feature by incorporating partition and human information, which enables treating different partitions in a candidate crop differently conditioned on the human information.

Furthermore, a good crop should preserve the important content of source image [11], which is dubbed as "content-preserving". However, to the best of our knowledge, there is no image cropping dataset that provides the annotation of

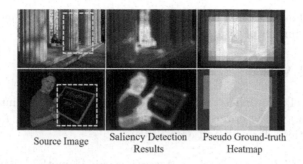

Source Image   Saliency Detection   Pseudo Ground-truth
                Results   Heatmap

Fig. 2. The comparison between saliency detection [13] and the pseudo ground-truth heatmap of important content (see Sect. 3.3). The important content of human-centric images may contain interesting objects (*e.g.*, the landmark in the top row) and the objects that person interacts with (*e.g.*, the blackboard in the bottom row). (Color figure online)

important content. Existing methods [4, 11, 25, 39] determine important content mainly based on their visual saliency by assuming that the most salient object is the most important content. In human-centric images, important content may imply key human parts (*e.g.*, face, hands), interesting objects (*e.g.*, landmark), and the objects (*e.g.*, racket, bicycle) that person interacts with. However, as shown in Fig. 2, saliency may not capture the abovementioned objects very well. Here we adopt an unsupervised saliency detection method [13]. We have also tried several supervised methods [7, 16, 50], which proves to be less effective. This is probably because that the unsupervised method has no dependence on training data and generalizes better on the image cropping datasets. Given an image with multiple annotated candidate crops [41, 43], we conjecture that the candidate crops with relatively high scores are more likely to contain important objects. Thus, we use highly scored crops to produce pseudo ground-truth heatmap of important content (see Fig. 2), which is used to supervise the heatmap prediction. Additionally, previous content-preserving methods [1, 4] typically designed a hand-crafted algorithm based on certain principles (*e.g.*, maintaining the most salient region). Differently, we automatically learn content-preserving feature to capture the geometric relation between the predicted heatmap and each candidate crop, which represents how well each candidate crop preserves the important content.

Finally, for each candidate crop, we extract its partition-aware feature and content-preserving feature to predict an aesthetic score. The main contributions of this paper can be summarized as follows: 1) We propose a novel partition-aware feature to improve human-centric image cropping by exploiting human information, which allows to treat different regions in a candidate crop differently conditioned on the human information. 2) We design a novel approach to locate important content and a novel content-preserving feature to characterize the preservation of important content in a candidate crop. 3) We demonstrate that our model outperforms the state-of-the-art image cropping methods on the human-centric images of several benchmark datasets.

2 Related Work

Following [23,44], we divide existing image cropping methods into three categories according to the criteria for evaluating candidate crops, *i.e.*, attention-guided, aesthetics-informed, and data-driven.

Attention-Guided Image Cropping: Attention-guided methods [4,11,25–27,36, 47] assumed that the best crops should preserve visually important content, which is usually determined by the saliency detection methods [17,38]. Usually, the view with the highest average saliency score is selected as the best crop. However, saliency may not accurately reflect the content of interest for human-centric images (see Fig. 2). Differently, we assume that the content that appears in multiple highly scored crops is more likely to be important content, leading to more flexible and practical important content estimation.

Aesthetics-Informed Image Cropping: The aesthetics-informed methods evaluated candidates by comparing the overall aesthetic quality of different crops. To achieve this, earlier methods [42,45,46] usually employed hand-crafted features or composition rules. However, the simple hand-crafted features may not accurately predict the complicated image aesthetics [44].

Data-Driven Image Cropping: Most recent methods address the task in a data-driven manner. Some methods [6,18,29] trained a general aesthetic evaluator on image aesthetic datasets to facilitate image cropping. With the aid of image cropping datasets [5,41,43], numerous methods [15,23,28,37,41,43] used pairwise learning to train an end-to-end model on these datasets, which can generate crop-level scores for ranking different candidate crops.

Our method is developed based on the general pipeline of the data-driven methods, but is specially tailored to human-centric image cropping with two innovations, *i.e.*, partition-aware and content-preserving features.

3 Methodology

3.1 Overview

The flowchart of the proposed method is illustrated in Fig. 3, in which we adopt a similar pipeline as [23,44]. Given an image, we first integrate multi-scale feature maps from a pretrained backbone (*e.g.*, VGG16 [34]) to obtain the basic feature map. After that, we update the basic feature map to the partition-aware feature map, based on which we extract partition-aware region feature and content-preserving feature for each candidate crop. Finally, we predict the crop-level score using the concatenation of partition-aware region feature and content-preserving feature.

3.2   Partition-Aware Feature

To acquire the human bounding box, we leverage Faster R-CNN [31] trained on Visual Genome [19] to detect human subjects for human-centric images. We check each image to ensure that the predicted bounding box correctly encloses the main human subject. We describe how to determine the main subject and discuss the robustness of our method against human detection in Supplementary. As illustrated in Fig. 1, the whole image can be divided into nine non-overlapping partitions by the human bounding box. We conjecture that the aesthetic value of similar content in different partitions often varies with its relative position to the human subject, so the feature map should be partition-aware.

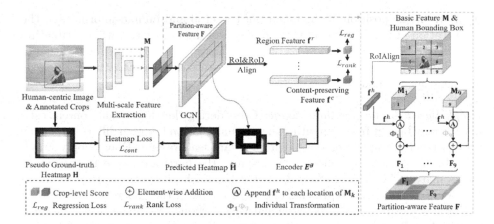

Fig. 3. The flowchart of our method for human-centric image cropping (left) and the proposed partition-aware feature (right). We use pretrained VGG16 [34] as backbone to extract basic feature map **M**, from which we derive partition-aware feature map **F**. Besides, we use the region feature obtained by RoIAlign [14] and RoDAlign [43] schemes, and content-preserving feature to predict scores for each candidate crop.

To achieve this goal, we derive partition-aware feature map from the basic feature map, as illustrated in the left subfigure in Fig. 3. Given an $H \times W$ basic feature map **M** with C channels, we partition it into nine regions $\{\mathbf{M}_k|_{k=1}^{9}\}$ with $\mathbf{M}_k$ being the k-th partition. Considering that the relative position of each partition to human subject is conditioned on the human information (*e.g.*, face orientation and posture), as exemplified in Fig. 1, we extract human feature $\mathbf{f}^h$ using RoIAlign [14] to implicitly encode the aforementioned human information and reduce its dimension to $\frac{C}{2}$, which is appended to each location of the basic feature map. The resultant feature map is represented by $\hat{\mathbf{M}}$ with $\hat{\mathbf{M}}_k$ being the k-th partition. To explicitly tackle different partitions differently, we employ nine individual nonlinear transformations for each partition to update their features with residual learning by

$$\mathbf{F}_k = \Phi_k(\hat{\mathbf{M}}_k) + \mathbf{M}_k, \tag{1}$$

where we use a 3×3 convolutional (conv) layer with C output channels followed by ReLU as the transformation function $\Phi_k(\cdot)$.

After that, we obtain a new feature map $\mathbf{F}$ by combining all updated partitions $\{\mathbf{F}_k|_{k=1}^9\}$, which has the same size as the basic feature map $\mathbf{M}$. *By integrating human feature and employing partition-specific transformations, similar contents in different partitions can produce different responses conditioned on the human information.* Thus, we refer to $\mathbf{F}$ as partition-aware feature map. Following [23,43], given a candidate crop, we employ RoIAlign [14] and RoDAlign [43] schemes to extract its partition-aware region feature based on $\mathbf{F}$, denoted as $\mathbf{f}^r$.

3.3   Content-Preserving Feature

Apart from the position of the human in the crop and human information, the preservation of important content also plays an important role when evaluating candidate crops. So we propose to predict a heatmap to indicate the location of important content and then automatically learn content-preserving features to augment our method.

Graph-Based Region Relation Mining: Considering that important content estimation may benefit from exploiting the mutual relation between different regions, we construct a graph over the partition-aware feature map $\mathbf{F}$ and apply graph convolution [24,32]. Specifically, we reshape the partition-aware feature maps into a matrix $\bar{\mathbf{F}} \in \mathcal{R}^{L \times C}$, where $L = H \times W$. Each pixel-wise feature vector in $\bar{\mathbf{F}}$ is a graph node that represents one local region in the image.

To model the relation between pairwise regions, we define the adjacency matrix $\mathbf{A} \in \mathcal{R}^{L \times L}$ according to the cosine similarity of region features following [33]. Then we perform reasoning over the graph $\bar{\mathbf{F}}$ by graph convolution [32]:

$$\bar{\mathbf{F}}' = \sigma(\mathbf{A}\bar{\mathbf{F}}\Theta), \tag{2}$$

where $\Theta \in \mathcal{R}^{C \times C}$ is the the trainable weight matrix of the graph convolution layer and $\sigma(\cdot)$ is ReLU activation. Then, we reshape $\bar{\mathbf{F}}'$ back to $\mathbf{F}' \in \mathcal{R}^{H \times W \times C}$. Compared with the conventional convolution, graph convolution allows the message flow across local regions, which is helpful for important content prediction (see Sect. 4.6).

Important Content Estimation: To obtain a high-resolution feature map for fine-grained important content localization, we upsample $\mathbf{F}'$ by four times followed by 3×3 conv and ReLU. Based on the upsampled feature map, we apply a prediction head (*i.e.*, 1×1 conv followed by Sigmoid function) to produce a heatmap $\widetilde{\mathbf{H}}$ in the range of $[0, 1]$, in which larger score indicates more important content.

There is no ground-truth heatmap for important content. Nevertheless, existing cropping datasets [41,43] are associated with multiple scored crops for each image, with a larger score indicating higher aesthetic quality. *Based on the assumption that highly scored crops are more likely to contain important content, we propose to generate pseudo ground-truth heatmap from the weighted average of highly scored crops.*

Specifically, given an image with multiple candidate crops, we suppose the score of the m-th crop to be y_m. We take the average score of all crops in the dataset as the threshold to select highly scored crops, and convert the bounding box of each selected crop to a binary map, which is resized to the same size as the predicted heatmap $\widetilde{\mathbf{H}}$. We obtain the pseudo ground-truth heatmap $\mathbf{H}$ via the weighted average of all binary maps, in which larger weight is assigned to the crop with higher score. Here, we perform softmax normalization to produce the weights for each highly scored crop: $\omega_m = \frac{\exp(y_m)}{\sum_{m=1}^{N_h} \exp(y_m)}$, in which N_h is the number of highly scored crops. In the training stage, we employ an L1 loss to supervise the heatmap learning:

$$\mathcal{L}_{cont} = \|\mathbf{H} - \widetilde{\mathbf{H}}\|_1. \tag{3}$$

As demonstrated in Fig. 2, the pseudo ground-truth heatmaps can highlight the attractive objects in the background and the objects that person interacts with, which are often ignored by saliency detection methods.

Content-Preserving Feature Extraction: To leverage the prior information of important content [41], previous content-preserving methods typically relied on certain heuristic principles (*e.g.*, minimizing the cropping area while maximizing its attention value [4]), which require extensive manual designs. *Instead, we guide the network to automatically learn how well each candidate crop preserves the important content. The idea is learning a content-preserving feature to capture the geometric relation between the heatmap and each candidate crop.* Specifically, for the m-th candidate crop, we concatenate its corresponding binary map and the predicted heatmap $\widetilde{\mathbf{H}}$ channel-wisely. Then, we apply an encoder E^g to the concatenated maps to extract the content-preserving feature $\mathbf{f}^c$.

Finally, for each candidate crop, we concatenate its partition-aware region feature $\mathbf{f}^r$ and content-preserving feature $\mathbf{f}^c$, which is passed through a fully connected (fc) layer to get the aesthetic score for this crop.

3.4   Network Optimization

We train the proposed model with a multi-task loss function in an end-to-end manner. Given an image containing N candidate crops, the ground-truth and predicted scores of the m-th crop are denoted by y_m and $\tilde{y}_m$, respectively. We first employ a smooth L1 loss [31] for the score regression considering its robustness to outliers:

$$\mathcal{L}_{reg} = \frac{1}{N} \sum_{m=1}^{N} \mathcal{L}_{s1}(y_m - \tilde{y}_m), \tag{4}$$

where $\mathcal{L}_{s1}(\cdot)$ represents the smooth L1 loss:

$$\mathcal{L}_{s1}(x) = \begin{cases} 0.5x^2, & \text{if } |x| < 1, \\ |x| - 0.5, & \text{otherwise.} \end{cases} \tag{5}$$

Besides regression loss, we also use a ranking loss [23] to learn the relative ranking order between pairwise crops explicitly, which is beneficial for enhancing the ability of ranking crops with similar content. With $e_{m,n} = y_m - y_n$ and $\tilde{e}_{m,n} = \tilde{y}_m - \tilde{y}_n$, the ranking loss is computed by

$$\mathcal{L}_{rank} = \frac{\sum_{m,n} \max\left(0, \mathrm{sign}(e_{m,n})(e_{m,n} - \tilde{e}_{m,n})\right)}{N(N-1)/2}. \tag{6}$$

After including the heatmap prediction loss in Eq.(3), the total loss is summarized as

$$\mathcal{L} = \mathcal{L}_{reg} + \mathcal{L}_{rank} + \lambda\mathcal{L}_{cont}, \tag{7}$$

in which the trade-off parameter λ is set as 1 via cross-validation (see Supplementary).

Limited by the small number of annotated human-centric images in existing image cropping datasets [41,43], only training on human-centric images would lead to weak generalization ability to the test set. Therefore, *we employ both human-centric and non-human-centric images to train our model.* For non-human-centric images, we use the basic feature map $\mathbf{M}$ to replace the partition-aware feature map $\mathbf{F}$, because there could be no dominant subject used to partition the image. Besides, we extract content-preserving features from non-human-centric images in the same way as human-centric images, because preserving important content is also crucial for non-human-centric images. In this way, our model is able to train and infer on both human-centric images and non-human-centric images.

4 Experiments

4.1 Datasets and Evaluation Metrics

We conduct experiments on the recent GAICD dataset [43], which contains 1,236 images (1,036 for training and 200 for testing). Each image has an average of 86 annotated crops. There are 339 and 50 human-centric images in the training set and test set of GAICD dataset, respectively. As described in Sect. 3.4, we employ the whole training set (1,036 images) for training and evaluate on the human-centric samples of the test set. Following [43], three evaluation metrics are employed in our experiments, including the average Spearman's rank-order correlation coefficient $(\overline{SRCC})$ and averaged top-N accuracy $(\overline{Acc_N})$ for both $N = 5$ and $N = 10$. The $\overline{SRCC}$ computes the rank correlation between the ground-truth and predicted scores of crops for each image, which is used to evaluate the ability of correctly ranking multiple annotated crops. The $\overline{Acc_N}$ measures the ability to return the best crops.

Apart from GAICD dataset, we also collect 176 and 39 human-centric images from existing FCDB [5] and FLMS [11] datasets, respectively. We evaluate our method on the collected 215 human-centric images from two datasets, following the experimental setting in [28,37]: training the model on CPC dataset [41], and using intersection of union (IoU) and boundary displacement (Disp) for performance evaluation. Note that we train on the whole CPC dataset, which contains 10,797 images including 1,154 human-centric images and each image has 24 annotated crops.

4.2 Implementation Details

Following existing methods [15,23,37], we use VGG16 [34] pretrained on ImageNet [8] as the backbone. We apply 1×1 conv to unify the channel dimensions of the last three output feature maps as 256 and add up three feature maps to produce the multi-scale feature map. We reduce the channel dimension of multi-scale feature map to 32 using a 1×1 conv, $i.e.$, $C = 32$. E^g is implemented by two 3×3 convs and pooling operations followed by a fc layer. The dimensions of partition-aware region feature $\mathbf{f}^r$ and content-preserving feature $\mathbf{f}^c$ are both 256. Similar to [23,43], the short side of input images is resized to 256 and the aspect ratios remain unchanged. We implement our method using PyTorch [30] and set the random seed to 0. More implementation details can be found in Supplementary.

Table 1. Ablation studies of the proposed method. $\mathbf{f}^h$: human feature. "res": update partition-aware feature with residual learning. K: number of partitions. "conv": replace GCN with standard convolution. $\widetilde{\mathbf{H}}$: predicted important content heatmap. "saliency": replace heatmap with saliency map [13]. $\mathbf{f}^c$: content-preserving feature.

	Partition	Content	$SRCC$ ↑	Acc_5 ↑	Acc_{10} ↑
1			0.744	52.0	70.5
2	✓		0.774	54.8	74.3
3	w/o $\mathbf{f}^h$		0.769	54.2	73.8
4	w/o res		0.764	53.9	73.5
5	$K=1$		0.746	52.1	70.8
6	$K=2$		0.756	53.2	72.4
7		✓	0.781	56.8	75.6
8		conv	0.762	54.0	73.0
9		w/o $\widetilde{\mathbf{H}}$	0.741	50.9	69.5
10		saliency	0.752	52.5	71.8
11		only $\mathbf{f}^c$	0.643	35.2	49.1
12	✓	✓	**0.795**	**59.7**	**77.0**

4.3 Ablation Study

In this section, we start from the general pipeline of existing methods [23,44] and evaluate the effectiveness of two types of features. The results are summarized in Table 1. In the baseline (row 1), we only use the region feature extracted from the basic feature map $\mathbf{M}$ to predict scores for each crop.

Partition-Aware Feature: Based on row 1, we replace the region feature with our proposed partition-aware region feature $\mathbf{f}^r$ in row 2, which verifies the effectiveness of partition-aware feature. Next, we conduct ablation studies based on row 2. First, we remove the human feature $\mathbf{f}^h$ and observe performance drop, which corroborates the importance of conditional human information. In Eq.(1), we adopt $\Phi_k(\cdot)$ to learn the residual. Based on row 2, we remove the residual strategy by using $\mathbf{F}_k = \Phi_k(\hat{\mathbf{M}}_k)$. The comparison between row 4 and row 2 demonstrates the benefit of residual learning. Recall that each image is divided into nine partitions by the human bounding box. Based on row 2, we explore using one partition ($K = 1$) and two partitions ($K = 2$). When $K = 1$, we apply the same transformation $\Phi(\cdot)$ to the whole image. When $K = 2$, we divide the image into human bounding box and the outside region. By comparing $K = 1, 2, 9$, we observe that $K = 9$ (row 2) achieves the best performance, because nine partitions can help capture more fine-grained partition-aware information. Besides, we evaluate some direct ways to leverage human bounding box for image cropping, yet producing poor results (see Supplementary).

Content-Preserving Feature: Based on row 1, we add our content-preserving feature and report the results in row 7, in which we concatenate content-preserving feature with the region feature extracted from basic feature map. The results show the effectiveness of content-preserving feature. Next, we conduct ablation studies (row 8–11) based on row 7. We first replace GCN with conventional con-

Table 2. Comparison with the state-of-the-art methods on human-centric images in GAICD [43] dataset. GAIC(ext) [44] is the extension of GAIC [43]. The results marked with * are obtained using the released models from original papers.

Method	Backbone	Training data	$SRCC \uparrow$	$Acc_5 \uparrow$	$Acc_{10} \uparrow$
VFN* [6]	AlextNet	Flickr	0.332	10.1	21.1
VFN [6]	VGG16	GAICD	0.648	41.3	60.2
VEN* [41]	VGG16	CPC	0.641	22.4	36.2
VEN [41]	VGG16	GAICD	0.683	50.1	65.1
ASM-Net [37]	VGG16	GAICD	0.680	44.8	64.5
LVRN* [28]	VGG16	CPC	0.664	30.7	49.0
LVRN [28]	VGG16	GAICD	0.716	44.8	66.0
GAIC(ext)* [44]	MobileNetV2	GAICD	0.773	54.0	73.0
GAIC(ext) [44]	VGG16	GAICD	0.741	53.3	69.6
CGS [23]	VGG16	GAICD	0.773	54.7	72.0
Ours(basic)	VGG16	GAICD	0.744	52.0	70.5
Ours	VGG16	GAICD	**0.795**	**59.7**	**77.0**

volution layers (row 8) and observe the performance drop, which proves that it is useful to exploit the mutual relation between different regions. Then, we remove the predicted heatmap $\tilde{\mathbf{H}}$ (row 9), resulting in significant performance drop, which highlights the importance of important content information. Additionally, we replace the proposed pseudo ground-truth heatmap with the saliency map detected by [13] in row 10 and obtain inferior performance. As discussed in Sect. 3.3, this can be attributed to that saliency may not accurately reflect the content of interest for human-centric images. We also try using the content-preserving feature alone. Specifically, we only use content-preserving feature $\mathbf{f}^c$ to predict the aesthetic score (row 11). The performance is even worse than row 1, because the content-preserving feature is lacking in detailed content information and thus insufficient for aesthetic prediction.

4.4   Comparison with the State-of-the-Arts

Quantitative Comparison: We compare the performance of our model with the state-of-the-art methods on 50 human-centric images of GAICD [43] dataset in Table 2. For the baselines with released models, we evaluate their models on the test set and report the results (marked with *). However, their backbone and training data may be different from our setting.

For fair comparison, we use the pretrained VGG16 [34] as the backbone for all baselines and train them on GAICD dataset, based on their released code or our own implementation. For our method, we additionally report the results of a basic version ("Ours(basic)") without using partition-aware feature or content-preserving feature (row 1 in Table 1). It can be seen that Ours(basic)

Table 3. Comparison with the state-of-the-art methods on human-centric images in FCDB [5] and FLMS [11] datasets. GAIC(ext) [44] is the extension of GAIC [43]. The results marked with * are obtained using the released models from original papers.

Method	Backbone	Training data	IoU↑	Disp↓
VFN* [6]	AlextNet	Flickr	0.5114	0.1257
VFN [6]	VGG16	CPC	0.6509	0.0876
VEN* [41]	VGG16	CPC	0.6194	0.0930
VEN [41]	VGG16	CPC	0.6670	0.0837
ASM-Net [37]	VGG16	CPC	0.7084	0.0755
LVRN* [28]	VGG16	CPC	0.7373	0.0674
GAIC(ext)* [44]	MobileNetV2	GAICD	0.7126	0.0724
GAIC(ext) [44]	VGG16	CPC	0.7260	0.0708
CGS [23]	VGG16	CPC	0.7331	0.0689
CACNet [15]	VGG16	FCDB	0.7364	0.0676
Ours(basic)	VGG16	CPC	0.7263	0.0695
Ours	VGG16	CPC	**0.7469**	**0.0648**

yields similar results with GAIC(ext) because they adopt the same region feature extractor (RoI+RoD). Among the baselines, GAIC(ext)* [44] and CGS [23] are two competitive ones, owning to the more advanced architecture and the exploitation of mutual relations between different crops. Finally, our model outperforms all the state-of-the-art methods, which demonstrates that our method is more well-tailored for the human-centric image cropping task.

Apart from GAICD dataset [43], we also collect 176 and 39 human-centric images from existing FCDB [5] and FLMS [11] datasets, respectively, and compare our method with the state-of-the-art methods on these two datasets in Table 3. Following [37,41], we train the model on CPC dataset [41], and use IoU and Disp as evaluation metrics. Additionally, we adopt the strategy in [28] to generate candidate crops and return the top-1 result as best crop without extra post-processing for all methods except CACNet [15], which is trained to regress the best crop directly. As shown in Table 3, our proposed model produces better results, but the performance gain is less significant than that on GAICD dataset. As claimed in [43], one possible reason is that the IoU based metrics used in FCDB and FLMS datasets are not very reliable for evaluating cropping performance. Furthermore, we also evaluate our method on both human-centric and non-human-centric images, and present results in Supplementary.

Source Image   VFN   VEN   ASM-Net   LVRN   GAIC(ext)   CGS   Ours

Fig. 4. Qualitative comparison of different methods on human-centric images. We show the best crops predicted by different methods, which demonstrate that our method can generate better results close to the ground-truth best crops (yellow). (Color figure online)

3.5→4.1 (4.6→4.2)   3.3→3.3 (4.2→3.8)   3.7→3.8 (4.1→3.7)   3.4→3.3 (4.3→3.9)

Fig. 5. Examples of partition-aware feature enhancing the discrimination power of basic feature. Given the ground-truth best crop of an image (yellow) and another crop with similar content (red), we show their scores predicted by using basic feature (out of bracket) and partition-aware feature (in bracket), respectively. (Color figure online)

Qualitative Comparison: We further conduct qualitative comparison to demonstrate the ability of our model in Fig. 4. For each input image, we show the source image and the returned best crops by different methods, which demonstrates that our method can perform more reliable content preservation and removal. For example, in the first row of Fig. 4, our method preserves more content on the left of human, probably because the person walks right to left, and reduces the top area that may hurt the image composition quality. In the second row, given the opposite face orientations to the first row, our model performs obviously different content preservation on the left/right sides of the human, yielding visually appealing crop. More qualitative results are shown in Supplementary.

4.5 Analysis of the Partition-Aware Feature

To take a close look at the impact of partition-aware feature on candidate crop evaluation, we use the region features extracted from basic feature map and partition-aware feature map to predict scores for crops, respectively, corresponding to row 1 and row 2 in Table 1. As shown in Fig. 5, to ensure that crop pairs have different aesthetic value yet similar content, for each image, we generate crop pair by moving its ground-truth best crop horizontally or vertically, in which the new crop still contains the human subject. We can see that using partition-aware feature consistently leads to larger and more reasonable score changes than basic feature despite the various face orientations or postures of the human in Fig. 5, which is beneficial for correctly ranking crops with similar content.

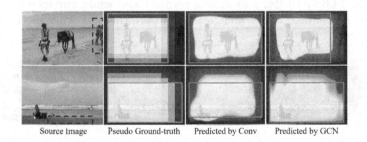

Source Image   Pseudo Ground-truth   Predicted by Conv   Predicted by GCN

Fig. 6. Visualization of the heatmap that indicates aesthetically important content. We show the source image, its pseudo ground-truth heatmap, the heatmaps estimated by conventional convolution("Conv") / graph convolution ("GCN"). We also draw the ground-truth (*resp.*, predicted) best crops in yellow (*resp.*, blue) boxes. (Color figure online)

4.6 Analysis of the Heatmap

The ablation study in Sect. 4.3 demonstrates the superiority of graph-based relation mining ("GCN") over the conventional convolution ("Conv") when predicting the heatmap of important content (see row 7,8 in Table 1). To reveal their difference qualitatively, we show the source image, its pseudo ground-truth heatmap, the heatmap predicted by "conv"/"graph" convolution in Fig. 6. With GCN learning the mutual relation between different regions, the model can make a more reasonable estimation of important content, especially the border area. For example, in the source image in the first row, we show an unpleasant outer area in the red dashed box, which should be removed for composing a good crop. The unimportant content (low values in the heatmap) predicted by "GCN" completely covers the unpleasant area, while "Conv" only covers part of the unpleasant area. In the second row, unlike "Conv" that only deems the area around person as important, "GCN" predicts relatively high values for the area behind person, indicating that preserving such area in a crop may be beneficial. In summary, "GCN" can facilitate important content localization and contributes to more informative content-preserving feature.

5   User Study

Given the subjectiveness of aesthetic assessment task, we conduct user study to compare different methods, in which we employ total 265 human-centric images, 176 from FCDB [5], 50 from GAICD [43], and 39 from FLMS [11]. For each image, we generate 7 best crops by using seven different methods: VFN [6], VEN [41], ASM-Net [37], LVRN [28], GAIC(ext) [44], CGS [23], and our proposed method. 20 experts are invited to select the best result for each image. Then we calculate the percentage that the results generated by different methods are selected as the best ones. The percentages of the abovementioned six baselines are 1.7%, 5.6%, 9.0%, 14.6%, 15.7%, and 22.5%, respectively, while our method achieves the highest percentage 30.9% and clearly outperforms the other methods.

Fig. 7. Some failure cases in the test set of GAICD dataset [43]. For each image, the ground-truth and predicted best crops are drawn in yellow and red boxes, respectively. (Color figure online)

6   Limitations

Our method can generally produce reliable crops for human-centric images, but it still has some failure cases. Some failure cases in the test set of GAICD dataset [43] are shown in Fig. 7, where the best crops produced by our method are far away from the ground-truth one and rank relatively low in the ground-truth annotations. For these examples, our method tends to preserve similar areas on the left/right side of the human subject in the best crop, probably because the complicated backgrounds and confusing human information (*e.g.*, inconsistent orientations between face and body) compromise the effectiveness of partition-aware feature and content-preserving feature.

7 Conclusion

In this paper, we have proposed a human-centric image cropping method with novel partition-aware and content-preserving features. The partition-aware feature allows to treat different regions in a candidate crop differently conditioned on the human information. The content-preserving feature represents how well each candidate crop preserves the important content. Extensive experiments have demonstrated that the proposed method can achieve the best performance on human-centric image cropping task.

Acknowledgement. The work is supported by Shanghai Municipal Science and Technology Key Project (Grant No. 20511100300), Shanghai Municipal Science and Technology Major Project, China (2021SHZDZX0102), and National Science Foundation of China (Grant No. 61902247).

References

1. Ardizzone, E., et al.: Saliency based image cropping. In: ICIAP (2013)
2. Cavalcanti, C.S.V.C., et al.: Combining multiple image features to guide automatic portrait cropping for rendering different aspect ratios. In: SITIS (2010)
3. Chen, H., Wang, B., Pan, T., Zhou, L., Zeng, H.: CropNet: real-time thumbnailing. In: ACMMM (2018)
4. Chen, J., Bai, G., Liang, S., Li, Z.: Automatic image cropping: a computational complexity study. In: CVPR (2016)
5. Chen, Y.L., Huang, T.W., Chang, K.H., Tsai, Y.C., Chen, H.T., Chen, B.Y.: Quantitative analysis of automatic image cropping algorithms: a dataset and comparative study. In: WACV (2017)
6. Chen, Y.L., Klopp, J., Sun, M., Chien, S.Y., Ma, K.L.: Learning to compose with professional photographs on the web. In: ACMMM (2017)
7. Chen, Z., Xu, Q., Cong, R., Huang, Q.: Global context-aware progressive aggregation network for salient object detection. In: AAAI (2020)
8. Deng, J., Dong, W., Socher, R., Li, L.J., Li, K., Fei-Fei, L.: ImageNet: a large-scale hierarchical image database. In: CVPR (2009)
9. Deng, Y., Loy, C.C., Tang, X., et al.: Image aesthetic assessment: an experimental survey. IEEE Signal Process. Mag. **34**(4), 80–106 (2017)
10. Esmaeili, S.A., Singh, B., Davis, L.S.: Fast-AT: fast automatic thumbnail generation using deep neural networks. In: CVPR (2017)
11. Fang, C., Lin, Z., Mech, R., Shen, X.: Automatic image cropping using visual composition, boundary simplicity and content preservation models. In: ACMMM (2014)
12. Freeman, M.: The photographer's eye: Composition and design for better digital photos. CRC Press (2007)

13. Goferman, S., Zelnik-Manor, L., Tal, A.: Context-aware saliency detection. PAMI **10**(34), 1915–1926 (2012)
14. He, K., Gkioxari, G., Dollár, P., Girshick, R.: Mask R-CNN. In: ICCV (2017)
15. Hong, C., Du, S., Xian, K., Lu, H., Cao, Z., Zhong, W.: Composing photos like a photographer. In: CVPR (2021)
16. Hou, Q., Cheng, M.M., Hu, X., Borji, A., Tu, Z., Torr, P.H.: Deeply supervised salient object detection with short connections. In: CVPR (2017)
17. Hou, X., Zhang, L.: Saliency detection: a spectral residual approach. In: CVPR (2007)
18. Kao, Y., et al.: Automatic image cropping with aesthetic map and gradient energy map. In: ICASSP (2017)
19. Krishna, R., et al.: Visual genome: connecting language and vision using crowd-sourced dense image annotations. Int. J. Comput. Vision **123**(1), 32–73 (2017)
20. Li, D., Wu, H., Zhang, J., Huang, K.: A2-RL: aesthetics aware reinforcement learning for image cropping. In: CVPR (2018)
21. Li, D., Wu, H., Zhang, J., Huang, K.: Fast A3RL: aesthetics-aware adversarial reinforcement learning for image cropping. TIP **28**(10), 5105–5120 (2019)
22. Li, D., Zhang, J., Huang, K.: Learning to learn cropping models for different aspect ratio requirements. In: CVPR (2020)
23. Li, D., Zhang, J., Huang, K., Yang, M.H.: Composing good shots by exploiting mutual relations. In: CVPR (2020)
24. Li, Q., et al.: Deeper insights into graph convolutional networks for semi-supervised learning. In: AAAI (2018)
25. Li, X., Li, X., Zhang, G., Zhang, X.: Image aesthetic assessment using a saliency symbiosis network. J. Electron. Imaging **28**(2), 023008 (2019)
26. Li, Z., Zhang, X.: Collaborative deep reinforcement learning for image cropping. In: ICME (2019)
27. Lu, P., Zhang, H., Peng, X., Jin, X.: An end-to-end neural network for image cropping by learning composition from aesthetic photos (2019)
28. Lu, W., Xing, X., Cai, B., Xu, X.: Listwise view ranking for image cropping. IEEE Access **7**, 91904–91911 (2019)
29. Mai, L., et al.: Composition-preserving deep photo aesthetics assessment. In: CVPR (2016)
30. Paszke, A., et al.: PyTorch: an imperative style, high-performance deep learning library. In: NeurIPS (2019)
31. Ren, S., He, K., Girshick, R.B., Sun, J.: Faster R-CNN: towards real-time object detection with region proposal networks. PAMI **39**, 1137–1149 (2015)
32. Scarselli, F., Gori, M., Tsoi, A.C., Hagenbuchner, M., Monfardini, G.: The graph neural network model. IEEE Trans. Neural Networks **20**(1), 61–80 (2008)
33. She, D., Lai, Y.K., Yi, G., Xu, K.: Hierarchical layout-aware graph convolutional network for unified aesthetics assessment. In: CVPR (2021)
34. Simonyan, K., Zisserman, A.: Very deep convolutional networks for large-scale image recognition (2015)
35. Su, Y.C., et al.: Camera view adjustment prediction for improving image composition. arXiv preprint arXiv:2104.07608 (2021)
36. Sun, J., Ling, H.: Scale and object aware image thumbnailing. IJCV **104**(2), 135–153 (2013)
37. Tu, Y., Niu, L., Zhao, W., Cheng, D., Zhang, L.: Image cropping with composition and saliency aware aesthetic score map. In: AAAI (2020)
38. Vig, E., Dorr, M., Cox, D.: Large-scale optimization of hierarchical features for saliency prediction in natural images. In: CVPR (2014)

39. Wang, W., Shen, J.: Deep cropping via attention box prediction and aesthetics assessment. In: ICCV (2017)
40. Wang, W., Shen, J., Ling, H.: A deep network solution for attention and aesthetics aware photo cropping. PAMI **41**(7), 1531–1544 (2018)
41. Wei, Z., et al.: Good view hunting: learning photo composition from dense view pairs. In: CVPR (2018)
42. Yan, J., Lin, S., Bing Kang, S., Tang, X.: Learning the change for automatic image cropping. In: CVPR (2013)
43. Zeng, H., Li, L., Cao, Z., Zhang, L.: Reliable and efficient image cropping: a grid anchor based approach. In: CVPR (2019)
44. Zeng, H., Li, L., Cao, Z., Zhang, L.: Grid anchor based image cropping: a new benchmark and an efficient model. PAMI PP(01) (2020)
45. Zhang, L., Song, M., Yang, Y., Zhao, Q., Zhao, C., Sebe, N.: Weakly supervised photo cropping. TMM **16**(1), 94–107 (2013)
46. Zhang, L., Song, M., Zhao, Q., Liu, X., Bu, J., Chen, C.: Probabilistic graphlet transfer for photo cropping. TIP **22**(2), 802–815 (2012)
47. Zhang, M., Zhang, L., Sun, Y., Feng, L., Ma, W.: Auto cropping for digital photographs. In: ICME (2005)
48. Zhang, X., Li, Z., Constable, M., Chan, K.L., Tang, Z., Tang, G.: Pose-based composition improvement for portrait photographs. IEEE Trans. Circuits Syst. Video Technol. **29**(3), 653–668 (2018)
49. Zhang, Y., Sun, X., Yao, H., Qin, L., Huang, Q.: Aesthetic composition represetation for portrait photographing recommendation. In: ICIP (2012)
50. Zhao, T., Wu, X.: Pyramid feature attention network for saliency detection. In: CVPR (2019)

DeMFI: Deep Joint Deblurring and Multi-frame Interpolation with Flow-Guided Attentive Correlation and Recursive Boosting

Jihyong Oh[ID] and Munchurl Kim[(⊠)][ID]

Korea Advanced Institute of Science and Technology, Daejeon, South Korea
{jhoh94,mkimee}@kaist.ac.kr

Abstract. We propose a novel joint deblurring and multi-frame interpolation (DeMFI) framework in a two-stage manner, called DeMFI-Net, which converts blurry videos of lower-frame-rate to sharp videos at higher-frame-rate based on flow-guided attentive-correlation-based feature bolstering (FAC-FB) module and recursive boosting (RB), in terms of multi-frame interpolation (MFI). Its baseline version performs feature-flow-based warping with FAC-FB module to obtain a sharp-interpolated frame as well to deblur two center-input frames. Its extended version further improves the joint performance based on pixel-flow-based warping with GRU-based RB. Our FAC-FB module effectively gathers the distributed blurry pixel information over blurry input frames in feature-domain to improve the joint performances. RB trained with recursive boosting loss enables DeMFI-Net to adequately select smaller RB iterations for a faster runtime during inference, even after the training is finished. As a result, our DeMFI-Net achieves state-of-the-art (SOTA) performances for diverse datasets with significant margins compared to recent joint methods. All source codes, including pretrained DeMFI-Net, are publicly available at https://github.com/JihyongOh/DeMFI.

Keywords: Blurry frame interpolation · Frame interpolation · Deblurring

1 Introduction

Video frame interpolation (VFI) converts a low frame rate (LFR) video to a high frame rate (HFR) one between given consecutive input frames, thereby providing a visually better motion-smoothed video which is favorably perceived by human visual systems (HVS) [24,25]. Therefore, it is widely used for diverse applications, such as adaptive streaming [50], slow motion generation [2,18,28,30,36,42] and space-time super resolution [9,15,21,22,48,49,51–53].

Supplementary Information The online version contains supplementary material available at https://doi.org/10.1007/978-3-031-20071-7_12.

On the other hand, motion blur is necessarily induced by either camera shake [1,56] or object motion [32,57] due to the accumulations of the light during the exposure period [14,16,47] when capturing videos. Therefore, eliminating the motion blur, called deblurring, is essential to synthesize sharp intermediate frames while increasing temporal resolution. The discrete degradation model for blurriness is generally formulated as follows [13,19,20,29,39,40,43]:

$$\mathbf{B} := \{B_{2i}\}_{i=0,1,\dots} = \{\frac{1}{2\tau+1}\sum_{j=iK-\tau}^{iK+\tau} S_j\}_{i=0,1,\dots}, \tag{1}$$

where S_j, $\mathbf{B}$, K and $2\tau+1$ denote latent sharp frame at time j in HFR, observed blurry frames at LFR, a factor that reduces frame rate of HFR to LFR and an exposure time period, respectively. However, a few studies have addressed the joint problem of video frame interpolation with blurred degradation namely as a joint deblurring and frame interpolation problem. To handle this problem effectively, five works [13,19,39,40,58] delicately have shown that joint approach is much better than the cascade of two separate tasks such as deblurring and VFI, which may lead to sub-optimal solutions. However, the methods [13,19,39,40] simply perform a *center*-frame interpolation (CFI) between two blurry center-input frames. This implies that they can only produce intermediate frames of time at a power of 2 in a recursive manner, not for arbitrary time. As a result, prediction errors are accumulatively propagated to the later interpolated frames.

To overcome these limitations for improving the quality in terms of multi-frame interpolation (MFI) with a temporal up-scaling factor $\times M$, we propose a novel framework for joint **De**blurring and **M**ulti-**F**rame **I**nterpolation, called DeMFI-Net, to accurately generate sharp-interpolated frames at arbitrary time t based on flow-guided attentive-correlation-based feature bolstering (FAC-FB) module and recursive boosting (RB). However, using a pretrained optical flow estimator is not optimal for blurry input frames and is computationally heavy. So, our DeMFI-Net is designed to learn *self-induced* feature-flows (f_F) and pixel-flows (f_P) in warping the blurry inputs for synthesizing a sharp-interpolated frame at arbitrary time t, without any pretrained optical flow networks.

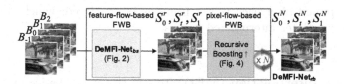

Fig. 1. Overview of our DeMFI-Net framework designed in a two-stage manner.

Direct estimation of flows for DeMFI at arbitrary t from the blurry input frames is a very challenging task. To effectively handle it, our DeMFI-Net is designed by a two-stage scheme as shown in Fig. 1: (i) the first stage (baseline version, DeMFI-Net$_{bs}$) jointly performs DeMFI based on *feature-flow-based* warping and blending (FWB) by learning f_F to obtain a sharp-interpolated frame of $t \in (0, 1)$ as well to deblur two blurry center-input frames (B_0, B_1) of $t = 0, 1$ from four blurry input frames (B_{-1}, B_0, B_1, B_2), where subscript means a corresponding time index; and (ii) the second stage (recursive boosting, DeMFI-Net$_{rb}$) further boosts the joint performance based on *pixel-flow-based* warping and blending (PWB) by iteratively updating f_P with the help of GRU-based RB. It is trained with recursive boosting loss that enables to choose smaller iterations for a faster inference during test time, even after the finished training.

On the other hand, the blurry input frames implicitly contain abundant useful latent information due to an accumulation of light [14, 16, 47], as also shown in Eq. 1. Motivated from this, we propose a novel flow-guided attentive-correlation-based feature bolstering (FAC-FB) module that can effectively bolster the source feature F_0 (or F_1) by extracting the useful information in the feature-domain from its counterpart feature F_1 (or F_0) in guidance of self-induced flow f_{01} (or f_{10}). By doing so, the distributed pixel information over four blurry input frames can be effectively gathered into the corresponding features of the two center-input frames which can then be utilized to pefrom DeMFI effectively.

In the performance evaluation, both two types of DeMFI-Nets outperform previous SOTA methods for three diverse datasets including both various real-world scenes and larger-sized blurry videos with large margins. Extensive experiments with diverse ablation studies have demonstrated the effectiveness of our framework. All source codes including pretrained DeMFI-Net are publicly available at https://github.com/JihyongOh/DeMFI.

2   Related Works

Center-Frame Interpolation (CFI). The VFI methods on CFI only interpolate a *center*-frame between two consecutive *sharp* input frames. CAIN [6] employs a channel attention module to extract motion information effectively. FeFlow [12] adopts deformable convolution [8] in a center frame generator. Ada-CoF [26] proposes a warping module in a generalized form to handle motions. However, all the above methods simply do CFI for ×2 increase in frame rates. This approach tends to limit the performance for MFI because they must be recursively applied after each center frame is interpolated, which causes error propagation into later-interpolated frames.

Multi-Frame Interpolation (MFI). To effectively synthesize an intermediate frame at arbitrary time t, many VFI methods on MFI for *sharp* videos adopt a flow-based warping operation. Quadratic video frame interpolation [27, 54] adopts the acceleration-aware approximation for the flows in a quadratic form to handle nonlinear motion. DAIN [2] proposes flow projection layer to approximate the flows according to depth information. SoftSplat [31] performs forward warping in feature space with learning-based softmax weights for the occluded region. ABME [35] proposes an asymmetric bilateral motion estimation based on bilateral cost volume [34]. XVFI [42] introduces a recursive multi-scale shared structure to capture extreme motion. However, all the above methods handle MFI problems for *sharp* input frames, which may not work well for *blurry* videos.

Joint Deblurring and Frame Interpolation. The recent studies on the *joint* deblurring and frame interpolation tasks [13,19,39,40,58] have consistently shown that the joint approaches are much better than the simple cascades of two separately pretrained networks of deblurring and VFI. TNTT [19] first extracts sharp keyframes which are then subsequently used to generate intermediate clear frames by jointly optimizing a cascaded scheme. BIN [39] and its larger-sized version PRF [40] adopts a ConvLSTM-based [41] recurrent pyramid framework to effectively propagate the temporal information over time. ALANET [13] employs the combination of both self- and cross-attention modules to adaptively fuse features in latent spaces. However, all the above four joint methods simply perform the CFI for blurry videos so their performances are limited to MFI. UTI-VFI [58] can interpolate the sharp frames at arbitrary time t in two-stage manner. It first extracts key-state frames, and then warps them to arbitrary time t. However, its performance depends on the quality of flows obtained by a pretrained optical flow network which also increases the complexity (+8.75M parameters).

Distinguished from all the above methods, our proposed framework elaborately learns self-induced f_F and f_P to effectively warp the given blurry input frames for synthesizing a sharp-interpolated frame at arbitrary time, without any pretrained optical flow network. As a result, our method not only outperforms the previous SOTA methods in structural-related metrics but also shows higher *temporal* consistency of visual quality performance for diverse datasets.

3   Proposed Method: DeMFI-Net

Design Considerations. Our proposed DeMFI-Net aims to jointly interpolate a sharp intermediate frame at arbitrary time t and deblur the blurry input frames. Most of the previous SOTA methods [13,19,39,40] only consider CFI ($\times 2$) so need to perform them recursively at the power of 2 for MFI ($\times M$) between two consecutive inputs. Therefore, later-interpolated frames must be *sequentially* created based on their previously-interpolated frames, so the errors are inherently propagated into later-interpolated frames with lower visual qualities. To avoid this, DeMFI-Net is designed to interpolate intermediate frames at multiple time instances without dependency among them. That is, the multiple intermediate frames can be *parallelly* generated. To synthesize an intermediate frame at time $t \in (0,1)$ instantaneously, we adopt a backward warping [17] which is widely used in VFI research [2,18,27,42,54] to interpolate the frames with estimated flows from time t to 0 and 1, respectively. However, direct usage of a *pretrained* optical flow network is not optimal for blurry frames and even computationally heavy. So our DeMFI-Net is devised to learn self-induced flows in both feature- and pixel-domain via an end-to-end learning. Furthermore, to effectively handle the joint task of deblurring and interpolation, DeMFI-Net is designed in a two-stage manner: baseline version (DeMFI-Net$_{bs}$) and recursive boosting version (DeMFI-Net$_{rb}$) as shown in Fig. 1. DeMFI-Net$_{bs}$ first performs feature-flow-based warping and blending (FWB) in feature-domain where the resulting learned features tend to be more sharply constructed from the blurry inputs. It produces the two deblurred center-inputs and a sharp-interpolated frame at t. Then the output of DeMFI-Net$_{bs}$ is further improved in DeMFI-Net$_{rb}$ via the residual learning, by performing pixel-flow-based warping and blending (PWB).

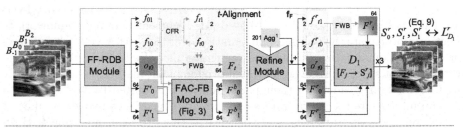

FWB: feature-flow-based warping and blending, CFR: Complementary Flow Reversal [42], Agg' : $[F_0^b, F_t, F_1^b, f_{t0}, f_{t1}, o_{t0}, f_{10}, f_{01}]$, f_F=$[f_{t0}', f_{t1}', o_{t0}']$: feature-flows

Fig. 2. DeMFI-Net$_{bs}$ based on feature-flows.

3.1   DeMFI-Net$_{bs}$

Fig. 2 shows the architecture of DeMFI-Net$_{bs}$ that first takes four consecutive blurry input frames (B_{-1}, B_0, B_1, B_2). Then, feature flow residual dense backbone (FF-RDB) module is followed which is similar to a backbone network of [39,40], described in *Supplemental*. Its modified 133 ($= 64 \times 2 + 2 \times 2 + 1$) output channels are composed of 64×2 for two feature maps (F_0', F_1') followed by tanh functions, 2×2 for two bidirectional feature-domain flows (f_{01}, f_{10}) and 1 for an occlusion map logit (o_{t0}) that is analyzed in detail in *Supplemental*.

t-**Alignment.** The intermediate flows f_{0t} (or f_{1t}) from time 0 (or 1) to time t are linearly approximated as $f_{0t} = t \cdot f_{01}$ (or $f_{1t} = (1 - t) \cdot f_{10}$) based on the f_{01}, f_{10}. Then we apply the complementary flow reversal (CFR) [42] for f_{0t} and f_{1t} to finally approximate f_{t0} and f_{t1}. Finally, we obtain t-aligned feature F_t by applying the backward warping (W_b) [17] for features F_0', F_1' followed by a blending operation with the occlusion map. This is called feature-flow-based warping and blending (FWB) (green box in Fig. 2) as follows:

$$F_t = \text{FWB}(F_0', F_1', f_{t0}, f_{t1}, o_{t0}, t)$$
$$= \frac{(1 - t) \cdot \bar{o}_{t0} \cdot W_b(F_0', f_{t0}) + t \cdot \bar{o}_{t1} \cdot W_b(F_1', f_{t1})}{(1 - t) \cdot \bar{o}_{t0} + t \cdot \bar{o}_{t1}}, \quad (2)$$

where $\bar{o}_{t0} = \sigma(o_{t0})$ and $\bar{o}_{t1} = 1 - \bar{o}_{t0}$, and σ is a sigmoid activation function.

FAC-FB Module. Since the pixel information is spread over the blurry input frames due to the accumulation of light [14,16,47] as in Eq. 1, we propose a novel FAC-FB module that can effectively bolster the source feature F'_0 (or F'_1) by extracting the useful information in the feature-domain from its counterpart feature F'_1 (or F'_0) in guidance of self-induced flow f_{01} (or f_{10}). The FAC-FB module in Fig. 3 (a) first encodes the two feature maps (F_0, F_1) by passing the outputs (F'_0, F'_1) of the FF-RDB module through its five residual blocks (ResB's). The cascade ($\mathbf{ResB}^{\times 5}$) of the five ResB's is shared for F'_0 and F'_1.

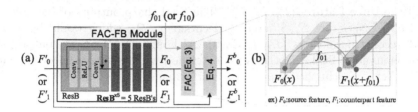

Fig. 3. Flow-guided Attentive Correlation Feature Bolstering (FAC-FB) module.

After obtaining the F_0 and F_1, the flow-guided attentive correlation (FAC) in Fig. 3 (a) computes attentive correlation of F_0 with respect to the positions of its counterpart feature F_1 pointed by the self-induced flow f_{01} as shown in Fig. 3 (b). The FAC on F_0 with respect to F_1 guided by f_{01} is calculated as:

$$\text{FAC}_{01}(F_0, F_1, f_{01})(\mathbf{x}) = [\ \textstyle\sum_{cw} \text{Conv}_1(F_0(\mathbf{x})) \odot$$
$$\text{Conv}_1(F_1(\mathbf{x} + f_{01}(\mathbf{x})))]\ \cdot \text{Conv}_1(F_1(\mathbf{x} + f_{01}(\mathbf{x}))), \qquad (3)$$

where $F_1(\mathbf{x} + f_{01}(\mathbf{x}))$ is computed by bilinear sampling on a feature location x. $\odot$, $\sum_{cw}$ and Conv_i denote element-wise multiplication, channel-wise summation and $i \times i$-sized convolution, respectively. The square bracket in Eq. 3 becomes a single-channel scaling map which is then stretched along the channel axis to be element-wise multiplied to $\text{Conv}_1(F_1(\mathbf{x} + f_{01}(\mathbf{x})))$. Finally, the FAC-FB module produces bolstered features F_0^b for F_0 as:

$$F_0^b = w_{01} \cdot F_0 + (1 - w_{01}) \cdot \underbrace{\text{Conv}_1(\text{FAC}_{01})}_{\equiv E_0} \qquad (4)$$

where w_{01} is a single channel of spatially-variant learnable weights that are dynamically generated by an embedded FAC_{01} via Conv_1 (denoted as E_0) and F_0 according to $w_{01} = (\sigma \circ \text{Conv}_3 \circ \text{ReLU} \circ \text{Conv}_3)([E_0, F_0])$. $[\cdot]$ means a concatenation along a channel axis. Similarly, FAC_{10} and F_1^b can be computed for F_1 with respect to F_0 by f_{10}. The FAC is computationally efficient because its attentive correlation is only computed in the focused locations pointed by the flows. All filter weights in the FAC-FB module are shared for both F'_0 and F'_1.

Refine Module. After the FAC-FB Module in Fig. 2, F_0^b, F_1^b, f_{t0}, f_{t1} and o_{t0} are refined via the U-Net-based [38] Refine Module (RM) as $[F_0^r, F_1^r, f_{t0}^r, f_{t1}^r, o_{t0}^r]$ = $\text{RM}(\mathbf{Agg}^1) + [F_0^b, F_1^b, f_{t0}, f_{t1}, o_{t0}]$ where $\mathbf{Agg}^1$ is the aggregation of $[F_0^b, F_t, F_1^b, f_{t0}, f_{t1}, o_{t0}, f_{01}, f_{10}]$ in the concatenated form. Then, we get the refined feature F_t^r at time t by $F_t^r = \text{FWB}(F_0^r, F_1^r, f_{t0}^r, f_{t1}^r, o_{t0}^r, t)$ as similar to Eq. 2. Here, we define a composite symbol at time t by the combination of two feature-flows and occlusion map logit as $\mathbf{f_F} \equiv [f_{t0}^r, f_{t1}^r, o_{t0}^r]$ to be used in recursive boosting.

Decoder I (D_1). D_1 is composed of $\mathbf{ResB}^{\times 5}$ and it is designed to have a function: to decode a feature F_j at a time j to a sharp frame S_j^r. D_1 is shared for all the three features (F_0^r, F_t^r, F_1^r). The final sharp outputs of baseline version DeMFI-Net$_{bs}$ are S_0^r, S_t^r and S_1^r decoded by D_1, which would be applied by L1 reconstruction loss $(L_{D_1}^r)$ (Eq. 9). Although DeMFI-Net$_{bs}$ outperforms the previous joint SOTA methods, its extension with recursive boosting, called DeMFI-Net$_{rb}$, can further improve the performance.

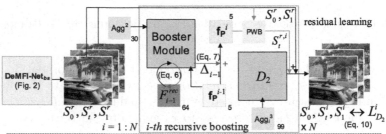

PWB: pixel-flow-based warping and blending, Agg^2: $[S_0', S_t', S_1', B_{-1}, B_0, B_1, B_2, f_{10}, f_{01}, \mathbf{f_F}]$, $\mathbf{f_P}^i$: pixel-flows, Agg$_i^3$: $[S_0', S_t^{r,i}, S_1', B_{-1}, B_0, B_1, B_2, f_{10}, f_{01}, \mathbf{f_F}, \mathbf{f_P}^i, F_i^{rec}]$, $\uparrow$: updating process, F_i^{rec}: recurrent hidden state

Fig. 4. DeMFI-Net$_{rb}$ at i-th Recursive Boosting (RB) based on pixel-flows via residual learning. The operation in the green box can recursively run $N = N_{trn}$ times during training (Eq. 8), and then it can perform $N = N_{tst}$ $(< N_{trn})$ times during testing for faster inference while maintaining high performance. (Color figure online)

3.2   DeMFI-Net$_{rb}$

Since we have already obtained sharp output frames S_0^r, S_t^r, S_1^r by DeMFI-Net$_{bs}$, they can further be sharpened based on the pixel-flows by recursive boosting via residual learning. It is known that feature-flows $(\mathbf{f_F})$ and pixel-flows $(\mathbf{f_P})$ would have similar characteristics [12,26]. Therefore, the $\mathbf{f_F}$ obtained from the DeMFI-Net$_{bs}$ are used as initial $\mathbf{f_P}$ for recursive boosting. For this, we design a GRU [5]-based recursive boosting for progressively updating $\mathbf{f_P}$ to perform PWB for two sharp frames at $t = 0, 1$ (S_0^r, S_1^r) accordingly to boost the quality of a sharp intermediate frame at t via residual learning which has been widely adopted for effective deblurring [4,10,33,37,55]. Figure 4 shows i-th recursive boosting (RB) of DeMFI-Net$_{rb}$, which is composed of Booster Module and Decoder II (D_2).

Booster Module. Booster Module iteratively updates $\mathbf{f_P}$ to perform PWB for S_0^r, S_1^r obtained from DeMFI-Net$_{bs}$. The Booster Module is composed of Mixer and GRU-based Booster (GB), and it first takes a recurrent hidden state (F_{i-1}^{rec}) and $\mathbf{f_P}^{i-1}$ at i-th recursive boosting as well as an aggregation of several components in the form of $\mathbf{Agg}^2 = [S_0^r, S_t^r, S_1^r, B_{-1}, B_0, B_1, B_2, f_{01}, f_{10}, \mathbf{f_F}]$ as an input to yield two outputs of F_i^{rec} and $\mathbf{\Delta}_{i-1}$ that is added on $\mathbf{f_P}^{i-1}$. Note that $\mathbf{f_P^0} = \mathbf{f_F}$ and $\mathbf{Agg}^2$ is not related to i-th recursive boosting. The updating process indicated by blue arrows in Fig. 4 is given as follows:

$$M_{i-1} = \text{Mixer}([\mathbf{Agg}^2, \mathbf{f_P}^{i-1}]), \tag{5}$$

$$[F_i^{rec}, \mathbf{\Delta}_{i-1}] = \text{GB}([F_{i-1}^{rec}, M_{i-1}]), \tag{6}$$

$$\mathbf{f_P}^i = \mathbf{f_P}^{i-1} + \mathbf{\Delta}_{i-1}, \tag{7}$$

where the initial feature F_0^{rec} is obtained as a 64-channel feature via channel reduction for $\text{Conv}_1([F_0^r, F_t^r, F_1^r])$ of 192 channels. More details are provided for the Mixer and the updating process of GB in *Supplemental*.

Decoder II (D_2). D_2 in Fig. 4 is composed of $\mathbf{ResB}^{\times 5}$. It fully exploits abundant information of $\mathbf{Agg}_i^3 = [S_0^r, S_t^{r,i}, S_1^r, B_{-1}, B_0, B_1, B_2, f_{01}, f_{10}, \mathbf{f_F}, \mathbf{f_P}^i, F_i^{rec}]$ to generate the refined outputs $[S_0^i, S_t^i, S_1^i] = D_2(\mathbf{Agg}_i^3) + [S_0^r, S_t^{r,i}, S_1^r]$ via residual learning, where $S_t^{r,i} = \text{PWB}(S_0^r, S_1^r, \mathbf{f_P}^i, t)$ is operated by *only* using the updated $\mathbf{f_P}^i$ after the i-th RB to enforce the flows to be better boosted.

Loss Functions. The final total loss function $\mathcal{L}_{total}$ for Fig. 1 is given as:

$$\mathcal{L}_{total} = \mathcal{L}_{D_1}^r + \underbrace{\sum_{i=1}^{N_{trn}} \mathcal{L}_{D_2}^i}_{\text{recursive boosting loss}}, \tag{8}$$

$$\mathcal{L}_{D_1}^r = (\sum_{j \in (0,t,1)} \|S_j^r - GT_j\|_1)/3, \tag{9}$$

$$\mathcal{L}_{D_2}^i = (\sum_{j \in (0,t,1)} \|S_j^i - GT_j\|_1)/3, \tag{10}$$

where GT_j and N_{trn} denote the ground-truth sharp frame at time j and total numbers of RB for training, respectively. We denote DeMFI-Net$_{rb}(N_{trn}, N_{tst})$ as DeMFI-Net$_{rb}$ that is trained with N_{trn} and is tested by N_{tst} recursive boosting. The second term in the right-hand side of Eq. 8 is called as a recursive boosting loss. It should be noted that DeMFI-Net$_{rb}$ is *jointly* trained with the architecture of DeMFI-Net$_{bs}$ in an end-to-end manner using Eq. 8 without any complex learning schedule, and DeMFI-Net$_{bs}$ is trained with only Eq. 9 *from the scratch*.

On the other hand, the design consideration for Booster Module was partially inspired from the work [46] which is here carefully modified for more complex process of DeMFI; (i) Due to the absence of ground-truth for the pixel-flows from t to 0 and 1, *self-induced* pixel-flows are instead learned by adopting D_2 and the recursive boosting loss; (ii) $\mathbf{f_P}$ is not necessarily to be learned precisely, instead to improve the final joint performance of sharpening the S_0^r, S_t^r, S_1^r via PWB and D_2 as shown in Fig. 4. So, we do not block any backpropagation to $\mathbf{f_P}$ per every RB unlike in [46], to fully focus on boosting the performance.

4 Experiments

Training Dataset. To train our network, we use Adobe240 dataset [43] which contains 120 videos of 1,280 × 720 @ 240fps. We follow a blurry formation setting of [13,39,40] by averaging 11 consecutive frames at a stride of 8 frames over time to synthesize blurry frames captured by a long exposure, which finally generates blurry frames of 30fps with $K = 8$ and $\tau = 5$ in Eq. 1. The resulting blurry frames are downsized to 640 × 352 as done in [13,39,40].

Implementation Details. Each training sample is composed of four consecutive blurry input frames (B_{-1}, B_0, B_1, B_2) and three sharp-target frames (GT_0, GT_t, GT_1) where t is randomly determined in multiple of 1/8 with $0 < t < 1$ as in [42]. The filter weights of the DeMFI-Net are initialized by the Xavier method [11] and the mini-batch size is set to 2. DeMFI-Net is trained with a total of 420K iterations (7,500 epochs) by using the Adam optimizer [23] with the initial learning rate set to 10^{-4} and reduced by a factor of 2 at the 3,750-, 6,250- and 7,250-th epochs. The total numbers of recursive boosting are empirically set to $N_{trn} = 5$ for training and $N_{tst} = 3$ for testing. We construct each training sample on the fly by randomly cropping a 256 × 256-sized patch from blurry and clean frames, and it is randomly flipped in both spatial and temporal directions for data augmentation. Training takes about five days for DeMFI-Net$_{bs}$ and ten days for DeMFI-Net$_{rb}$ by using an NVIDIA RTX^{TM} GPU with PyTorch.

4.1 Comparison to Previous SOTA Methods

We mainly compare our DeMFI-Net with five previous joint SOTA methods; TNTT [19], UTI-VFI [58], BIN [39], PRF [40] (a larger-sized version of BIN) and ALANET [13], which all have adopted joint learning for deblurring and VFI. They all have reported better performance than the cascades of separately trained VFI [2,3,18] and deblurring [45,49] networks. It should be noted that the four methods of TNTT, BIN, PRF and ALANET simply perform CFI (×2), not at arbitrary t but at the center time $t = 0.5$. So, they have to perform MFI (×8) recursively based on previously interpolated frames, which causes to propagate interpolation errors into later-interpolated frames. For experiments, we delicately compare them in two aspects of CFI and MFI. For MFI performance, *temporal* consistency is measured such that the pixel-wise difference of motions are calculated in terms of tOF [7,42] (the lower, the better) for all 7 interpolated frames and deblurred two center frames for each blurry test sequence (scene). We also retrain the UTI-VFI with the same blurry formation setting [13,39,40] for the Adobe240 for fair comparison, to be denoted as UTI-VFI*.

Test Dataset. We use three datasets for evaluation: (i) Adobe240 dataset [43], (ii) YouTube240 dataset and (iii) GoPro240 dataset (CC BY 4.0 license) [29] that contains large dynamic object motions and camera shakes. For the YouTube240, we directly selected 60 YouTube videos of 1,280 × 720 at 240fps by considering to include extreme scenes captured by diverse devices. Then they were resized to 640×352 as done in [13,39,40]. The Adobe240 contains 8 videos of $1,280 \times 720$ resolution at 240 fps and was also resized to 640×352, which is totally composed of 1,303 blurry input frames. On the other hand, the GoPro240 has 11 videos with total 1,500 blurry input frames but we used the original size of $1,280 \times 720$ for an extended evaluation in larger-sized resolution. Please note that all test datasets are also temporally downsampled to 30 fps with the blurring as [13,39,40].

Quantitative Comparison. Table 1 shows the quantitative performance comparisons for the previous SOTA methods including the cascades of deblurring and VFI methods with the Adobe240, in terms of deblurring and CFI ($\times2$). Most results of the previous methods in Table 1 are brought from [13,39,40], except those of UTI-VFI (*pretrained, newly tested*), UTI-VFI* (*retrained, newly tested*) and DeMFI-Nets (ours). Please note that all runtimes (R_t) in Table 1 were measured for 640×352-sized frames in the setting of [39,40] with one NVIDIA RTX™ GPU. As shown in Table 1, our proposed DeMFI-Net$_{bs}$ and DeMFI-Net$_{rb}$ clearly outperform all the previous methods with large margins in both

Table 1. Quantitative comparisons on Adobe240 [43] for deblurring and center-frame interpolation ($\times2$).

Method	R_t (s)	#P (M)	Deblurring		CFI ($\times2$)		Average	
			PSNR	SSIM	PSNR	SSIM	PSNR	SSIM
B_0, B_1	–	–	28.68	0.8584	–	–	–	–
SloMo [18]	–	39.6	–	–	27.52	0.8593	–	–
MEMC [3]	–	70.3	–	–	30.83	0.9128	–	–
DAIN [2]	–	24.0	–	–	31.03	0.9172	–	–
SRN [45]+ [18]	0.27	47.7	29.42	0.8753	27.22	0.8454	28.32	0.8604
SRN [45]+ [3]	0.22	78.4			28.25	0.8625	28.84	0.8689
SRN [45]+ [2]	0.79	32.1			27.83	0.8562	28.63	0.8658
EDVR [49]+ [18]	0.42	63.2	32.76	0.9335	27.79	0.8671	30.28	0.9003
EDVR [49]+ [3]	0.27	93.9			30.22	0.9058	31.49	0.9197
EDVR [49]+ [2]	1.13	47.6			30.28	0.9070	31.52	0.9203
UTI-VFI [58]	0.80	43.3	28.73	0.8656	29.00	0.8690	28.87	0.8673
UTI-VFI*	0.80	43.3	31.02	0.9168	32.67	0.9347	31.84	0.9258
TNTT [19]	0.25	10.8	29.40	0.8734	29.24	0.8754	29.32	0.8744
BIN [39]	0.28	4.68	32.67	0.9236	32.51	0.9280	32.59	0.9258
PRF [40]	0.76	11.4	33.33	0.9319	33.31	0.9372	33.32	0.9346
ALANET [13]	–	–	33.71	0.9329	32.98	0.9362	33.34	0.9355
DeMFI-Net$_{bs}$	0.38	5.96	33.83	0.9377	33.93	0.9441	33.88	0.9409
DeMFI-Net$_{rb}$(1,1)	0.51	7.41	<u>34.06</u>	<u>0.9401</u>	<u>34.35</u>	<u>0.9471</u>	<u>34.21</u>	<u>0.9436</u>
DeMFI-Net$_{rb}$(5,3)	0.61	7.41	34.19	0.9410	34.49	0.9486	34.34	0.9448

RED: Best performance, <u>BLUE</u>: Second best performance.
R_t: The runtime on 640×352-sized frames (s), UTI-VFI*: retrained version.
#P: The number of parameters (M), ALANET: no source code for testing.

deblurring and CFI performances, and the number of model parameters (#P) for our methods are the second- and third-smallest with smaller R_t compared to PRF. In particular, DeMFI-Net$_{rb}$(5,3) outperforms ALANET by 1dB and 0.0093 in terms of PSNR and SSIM, respectively for average performances of deblurring and CFI, and especially by average 1.51dB and 0.0124 for center-interpolated frames attributed to our warping-based framework with self-induced flows. Furthermore, even our DeMFI-Net$_{bs}$ is superior to all previous methods which are dedicatedly trained for CFI.

Table 2 shows quantitative comparisons of the joint methods for the three test datasets in terms of deblurring and MFI ($\times 8$). As shown in Table 2, all the three versions of DeMFI-Net significantly outperform the previous joint methods, which shows a good generalization of our DeMFI-Net framework. Figure 5 shows PSNR profiles for MFI results ($\times 8$). As shown, the CFI methods such as TNTT and PRF tend to synthesize worse intermediate frames than the methods of interpolation at arbitrary time like UTI-VFI and our DeMFI-Net. This is because the error propagation is accumulated recursively due to the inaccurate interpolations by the CFI methods, which also has been inspected in VFI for sharp input frames [42]. On the other hand, we also recursively do CFI ($\times 2$) three times to measure *sequential* inference performances of DeMFI-Net$_{rb}$(5,3), indicated by 'DeMFI-seq_' of pink color in Fig. 5, which also clearly shows that the errors are accumulatively propagated into the later interpolated frames.

Although UTI-VFI can interpolate the frames at arbitrary t by adopting the PWB combined with QVI [54], its performances inevitably depend on f_P quality obtained by PWC-Net [44], where adoption of a pretrained net brings a disadvantage in terms of both R_t and #P (+8.75M). It is worthwhile to note that our method also shows the best performances in terms of temporal consistency with tOF by help of *self-induced* flows in interpolating frames at arbitrary t.

Qualitative Comparison. Figure 6 shows the visual comparisons of deblurring and VFI performances on YouTube240 and GoPro240 datasets, respectively. As shown, the blurriness is easily visible between B_0 and B_1, which is challenging for VFI. Our DeMFI-Nets show better generalized performances for the extreme scenes (Fig. 6 (a)) and larger-sized videos (Fig. 6 (b)), also in terms of temporal consistency. Due to page limits, more visual comparisons with larger sizes are provided in *Supplemental* for all three test datasets. Also the results of deblurring and MFI ($\times 8$) of all the SOTA methods are publicly available at https://github.com/JihyongOh/DeMFI. Please note that it is laborious but worth to get results for the SOTA methods in terms of MFI ($\times 8$).

Table 2. Quantitative comparisons of joint methods on Adobe240 [43], YouTube240 and GoPro240 [29] datasets for deblurring and multi-frame interpolation (×8). R_t and FLOPS are measured on 640×352-sized frames.

Joint Method	Adobe240 [43]			YouTube240		
	deblurring PSNR/SSIM	MFI (×8) PSNR/SSIM	Average PSNR/SSIM/tOF	deblurring PSNR/SSIM	MFI (×8) PSNR/SSIM	Average PSNR/SSIM/tOF
UTI-VFI [58]	28.73/0.8657	28.66/0.8648	28.67/0.8649/0.578	28.61/0.8891	28.64/0.8900	28.64/0.8899/0.585
UTI-VFI*	31.02/0.9168	32.30/0.9292	32.13/0.9278/0.445	30.40/0.9055	31.76/0.9183	31.59/0.9167/0.517
TNTT [19]	29.40/0.8734	29.45/0.8765	29.45/0.8761/0.559	29.59/0.8891	29.77/0.8901	29.75/0.8899/0.549
PRF [40]	33.33/0.9319	28.99/0.8774	29.53/0.8842/0.882	32.37/0.9199	29.11/0.8919	29.52/0.8954/0.771
DeMFI-Net$_{bs}$	33.83/0.9377	33.79/0.9410	33.79/0.9406/0.473	32.90/0.9251	32.79/0.9262	32.80/0.9260/0.469
DeMFI-Net$_{rb}$(1,1)	34.06/0.9401	34.15/0.9440	34.14/0.9435/0.460	33.17/0.9266	33.22/0.9291	33.21/0.9288/0.459
DeMFI-Net$_{rb}$(5,3)	34.19/0.9410	34.29/0.9454	34.28/0.9449/0.457	33.31/0.9282	33.33/0.9300	33.33/0.9298/0.461

Joint Method	R_t(s)	#P(M)	FLOPS	GoPro240 [29]		
				deblurring PSNR/SSIM	MFI (×8) PSNR/SSIM	Average PSNR/SSIM/tOF
UTI-VFI [58]	0.80	43.3	3.23T	25.66/0.8085	25.63/0.8148	25.64/0.8140/0.716
UTI-VFI*	0.80	43.3	3.23T	28.51/0.8656	29.73/0.8873	29.58/0.8846/0.558
TNTT [19]	0.25	10.8	609.62G	26.48/0.8085	26.68/0.8148	26.65/0.8140/0.754
PRF [40]	0.76	11.4	3.2T	30.27/0.8866	25.68/0.8053	26.25/0.8154/1.453
DeMFI-Net$_{bs}$	0.38	5.96	748.57G	30.54/0.8935	30.78/0.9019	30.75/0.9008/0.538
DeMFI-Net$_{rb}$(1,1)	0.51	7.41	1.07T	30.63/0.8961	31.10/0.9073	31.04/0.9059/0.512
DeMFI-Net$_{rb}$(5,3)	0.61	7.41	1.71T	30.82/0.8991	31.25/0.9102	31.20/0.9088/0.500

Table 3. Ablation experiments on RB and FAC in terms of total *average* of deblurring and MFI (×8); 'w/o FAC' means $F_0^b = F_0$.

Method	R_t (s)	#P (M)	Adobe240 PSNR	SSIM	YouTube240 PSNR	SSIM
(a) w/o RB, w/o FAC	0.32	5.87	33.30	0.9361	32.54	0.9230
(b) w/o RB, $f = 0$	0.38	5.96	33.64	0.9393	32.74	0.9237
(c) w/o RB (DeMFI-Net$_{bs}$)	0.38	5.96	33.79	0.9406	32.80	0.9260
(d) w/o FAC	0.45	7.32	33.73	0.9391	32.93	0.9260
(e) $f = 0$	0.51	7.41	34.08	0.9428	33.15	0.9279
(f) DeMFI-Net$_{rb}$(1,1)	0.51	7.41	34.14	0.9435	33.21	0.9288

Table 4. Ablation study on N_{trn} and N_{tst} of DeMFI-Net$_{rb}$.

N_{trn}	N_{tst}		
	PSNR/SSIM		
	1 ($R_t = 0.51$)	3 ($R_t = 0.61$)	5 ($R_t = 0.68$)
1	34.14/0.9435	28.47/0.8695	25.99/0.8136
	33.21/0.9288	29.01/0.8845	26.56/0.8406
3	34.21/0.9439	34.21/0.9440	34.16/0.9437
	33.27/0.9290	33.27/0.9291	33.23/0.9289
5	34.27/0.9446	34.28/0.9449	34.27/0.9448
	33.32/0.9296	33.33/0.9298	33.33/0.9297

1st/2nd row: Adobe240/YouTube240 in each block.

RED: Best performance of each row, #P=7.41M.

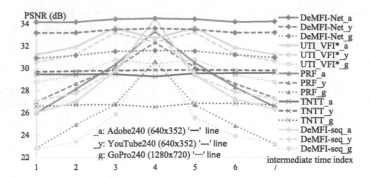

Fig. 5. PSNR profiles for multi-frame interpolation results (×8) for the *blurry* input frames on diverse three datasets; Adobe240, YouTube240 and GoPro240. The number of horizontal axis is the intermediate time index between two blurry center-input frames (0, 8). Our DeMFI-Net$_{rb}$(5,3), indicated by 'DeMFI-Net_' of red color, consistently shows best performances along all time instances.

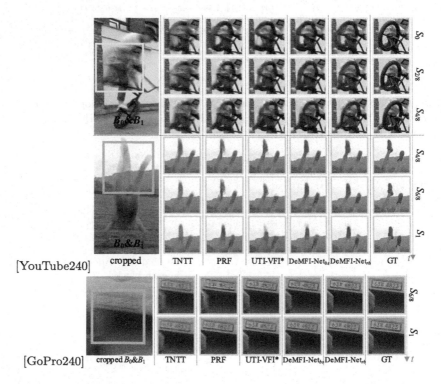

Fig. 6. Visual comparisons for MFI results of our DeMFI-Nets and joint SOTA methods on (a) YouTube240 and (b) GoPro240. *Best viewed in zoom.* Demo video is available at https://youtu.be/J93tW1uwRy0.

4.2   Ablation Studies

To analyze the effectiveness of each component in our framework, we perform ablation experiments. Table 3 shows the results of ablation experiments for FAC in Fig. 3 and RB in Fig. 4 with $N_{trn} = 1$ and $N_{tst} = 1$ for a simplicity.

FAC. By comparing the method (f) to (d) and (c) to (a) in Table 3, it is noticed that FAC can effectively improve the overall joint performances in the both cases without and with RB by taking little more runtime (+0.06s) and small number of additional parameters (+0.09M). Figure 7 qualitatively shows the effect of FAC for DeMFI-Net$_{rb}$(1,1) (f). Brighter positions with green boxes in the right-most column indicate important regions E_1 after passing Eq. 3 and Conv$_1$. The green boxes show blurrier patches that are more attentive in the counterpart feature based on f_{10} to reinforce the source feature F_1 complementally. On the other hand, the less focused regions such as backgrounds with less blurs are relatively have smaller E after FAC. In summary, FAC bolsters the source feature by complementing the important regions with blurs in the counterpart feature pointed by flow-guidance. We also show the effectiveness of FAC without flow guidance when trained with $f = 0$. As shown in Table 3, we obtained the performance higher than without FAC but lower than with FAC by flow-guidance, as expected. Therefore, we conclude that FAC works very effectively under the self-induced flow guidance to bolster the center features to improve the performance of the joint task.

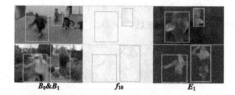

Fig. 7. Effect of FAC. The green boxes show blurrier patches that are more attentive in the counterpart feature based on flow-guidance to effectively bolster the source feature.

Fig. 8. Self-induced flows for both features $\mathbf{f_F}$ and images $\mathbf{f_P}$ ($t = 7/8$) of DeMFI-Net$_{rb}$ (1,1) show a similar tendency. *They do not have to be accurate, but help improve final joint performances.*

Recursive Boosting. By comparing the method (d) to (a), (e) to (b) and (f) to (c) in Table 3, it can be known that the RB consistently yields improved final joint results. Figure 8 shows that $\mathbf{f_F}$ and $\mathbf{f_P}$ have a similar tendency in flow characteristics. Furthermore, the $\mathbf{f_P}$ updated from $\mathbf{f_F}$ seems sharper to perform PWB in pixel domain, which may help our two-stage approach effectively handles the joint task based on warping operation. It is noted that our weakest variant (a) (w/o both RB and FAC) even outperformed the second-best joint method (UTI-VFI*) as shown in Tables 2, 3 on the both Adobe240 and YouTube240.

# of Recursive Boosting N. To inspect the relationship between N_{trn} and N_{tst} for RB, we train three variants of DeMFI-Net$_{rb}$ each for $N_{trn} = 1, 3, 5$ as shown in Table 4. Since the weight parameters in RB are shared for each recursive boosting, all the variants have same #P=7.41M and each column in Table 4 has same runtime R_t. The performances are generally boosted by increasing N_{trn}, where each recursion is attributed to the recursive boosting loss that enforces the recursively updated flows $\mathbf{f_P}^i$ to better focus on synthesis $S_t^{r,i}$ via the PWB. It should be noted that the overall performances are better when $N_{tst} \leq N_{trn}$, while they are dropped otherwise. So, we can adequately choose smaller N_{tst} ($\leq N_{trn}$) for a faster runtime by considering computational constraints while maintaining high performances, even though the training with N_{trn} is once over. That is, under the same runtime constraint of each R_t as in the column of Table 4 when testing, we can also select the model trained with larger N_{trn} to obtain better results. On the other hand, we found out that further increasing N_{trn} does not bring additional benefits due to saturated performance of DeMFI-Net$_{rb}$.

Extensibility of FAC-FB Module and RB. Both FAC-FC module in Fig. 3 and RB in Fig. 4 can be easily inserted in a flow-based network to boost its performance for a specific task. To show the extensibility for our two proposed modules, we trained two variants of the SOTA VFI method for sharp videos, XVFI-Net [42], using default training conditions in their official code by inserting (i) FAC-FB module in front of BIOF-T [42], and (ii) RB behind BIOF-T. We obtained 0.08 dB PSNR gain for the FAC-FB module and 0.07 dB gain for RB ($N_{trn} = 2$, $N_{tst} = 2$) on X-TEST test dataset [42] with $S_{tst} = 3$ [42]. This shows that FAC-FB module and RB can be inserted in *flow-based* network architectures to boost performance, showing extensibility and generalization ability of the proposed modules.

5   Conclusion

We propose a novel joint deblurring and multi-frame interpolation framework in a two-stage manner, called DeMFI-Net, based on our novel flow-guided attentive-correlation-based feature bolstering (FAC-FB) module and recursive boosting (RB), by learning the self-induced feature- and pixel-domain flows without any help of pretrained optical flow networks. FAC-FB module forcefully enriches the source feature by extracting attentive correlation from the counterpart feature at the position where self-induced feature-flow points at, to finally improve results for the joint task. RB trained with recursive boosting loss enables DeMFI-Net to adequately select smaller RB iterations for a faster runtime during inference while keeping performances, even after the training is finished. Our DeMFI-Net achieves state-of-the-art joint performances for diverse datasets with significant margins compared to the previous joint SOTA methods.

Acknowledgement. This work was supported by Institute of Information & communications Technology Planning & Evaluation (IITP) grant funded by the Korea government (MSIT) (No. 2017-0-00419, Intelligent High Realistic Visual Processing for Smart Broadcasting Media).

References

1. Bahat, Y., Efrat, N., Irani, M.: Non-uniform blind deblurring by reblurring. In: ICCV, pp. 3286–3294 (2017)
2. Bao, W., Lai, W.S., Ma, C., Zhang, X., Gao, Z., Yang, M.H.: Depth-aware video frame interpolation. In: CVPR, pp. 3703–3712 (2019)
3. Bao, W., Lai, W.S., Zhang, X., Gao, Z., Yang, M.H.: MEMC-Net: motion estimation and motion compensation driven neural network for video interpolation and enhancement. IEEE Transactions on Pattern Analysis and Machine Intelligence (2019)
4. Chi, Z., Wang, Y., Yu, Y., Tang, J.: Test-time fast adaptation for dynamic scene deblurring via meta-auxiliary learning. In: CVPR, pp. 9137–9146 (2021)
5. Cho, K., et al.: Learning phrase representations using RNN encoder-decoder for statistical machine translation. In: EMNLP (2014)
6. Choi, M., Kim, H., Han, B., Xu, N., Lee, K.M.: Channel attention is all you need for video frame interpolation. In: AAAI, pp. 10663–10671 (2020)
7. Chu, M., You, X., Jonas, M., Laura, L.T., Nils, T.: Learning temporal coherence via self-supervision for GAN-based video generation. ACM ToG **39**(4), 1–75 (2020)
8. Dai, J., et al.: Deformable convolutional networks. In: CVPR, pp. 764–773 (2017)
9. Dutta, S., Shah, N.A., Mittal, A.: Efficient space-time video super resolution using low-resolution flow and mask upsampling. In: CVPR, pp. 314–323 (2021)
10. Gao, H., Tao, X., Shen, X., Jia, J.: Dynamic scene deblurring with parameter selective sharing and nested skip connections. In: CVPR, pp. 3848–3856 (2019)
11. Glorot, X., Bengio, Y.: Understanding the difficulty of training deep feedforward neural networks. In: AISTATS, pp. 249–256 (2010)
12. Gui, S., Wang, C., Chen, Q., Tao, D.: Featureflow: robust video interpolation via structure-to-texture generation. In: CVPR, pp. 14004–14013 (2020)
13. Gupta, A., Aich, A., Roy-Chowdhury, A.K.: Alanet: adaptive latent attention network for joint video deblurring and interpolation. In: ACMMM, pp. 256–264 (2020)
14. Gupta, A., Joshi, N., Lawrence Zitnick, C., Cohen, M., Curless, B.: Single image deblurring using motion density functions. In: Daniilidis, K., Maragos, P., Paragios, N. (eds.) ECCV 2010. LNCS, vol. 6311, pp. 171–184. Springer, Heidelberg (2010). https://doi.org/10.1007/978-3-642-15549-9_13
15. Haris, M., Shakhnarovich, G., Ukita, N.: Space-time-aware multi-resolution video enhancement. In: CVPR, pp. 2859–2868 (2020)
16. Harmeling, S., Michael, H., Schölkopf, B.: Space-variant single-image blind deconvolution for removing camera shake. NeurIPS **23**, 829–837 (2010)
17. Jaderberg, M., Simonyan, K., Zisserman, A., Kavukcuoglu, K.: Spatial transformer networks. In: NeurIPS, pp. 2017–2025 (2015)
18. Jiang, H., Sun, D., Jampani, V., Yang, M.H., Learned-Miller, E., Kautz, J.: Super slomo: high quality estimation of multiple intermediate frames for video interpolation. In: CVPR, pp. 9000–9008 (2018)
19. Jin, M., Hu, Z., Favaro, P.: Learning to extract flawless slow motion from blurry videos. In: CVPR, pp. 8112–8121 (2019)

20. Jin, M., Meishvili, G., Favaro, P.: Learning to extract a video sequence from a single motion-blurred image. In: CVPR (2018)
21. Kang, J., Jo, Y., Oh, S.W., Vajda, P., Kim, S.J.: Deep space-time video upsampling networks. In: Vedaldi, A., Bischof, H., Brox, T., Frahm, J.-M. (eds.) ECCV 2020. LNCS, vol. 12355, pp. 701–717. Springer, Cham (2020). https://doi.org/10.1007/978-3-030-58607-2_41
22. Kim, S.Y., Oh, J., Kim, M.: FISR: deep joint frame interpolation and super-resolution with a multi-scale temporal loss. In: AAAI, pp. 11278–11286 (2020)
23. Kingma, D.P., Ba, J.: Adam: a method for stochastic optimization. In: ICLR (2015)
24. Kuroki, Y., Nishi, T., Kobayashi, S., Oyaizu, H., Yoshimura, S.: A psychophysical study of improvements in motion image quality by using high frame rates. J. Soc. Inform. Display 15(1), 61–68 (2007)
25. Kuroki, Y., Takahashi, H., Kusakabe, M., Yamakoshi, K.i.: Effects of motion image stimuli with normal and high frame rates on EEG power spectra: comparison with continuous motion image stimuli. J. Soc. Inf. Display 22(4), 191–198 (2014)
26. Lee, H., Kim, T., Chung, T.y., Pak, D., Ban, Y., Lee, S.: AdaCoF: adaptive collaboration of flows for video frame interpolation. In: CVPR, pp. 5316–5325 (2020)
27. Liu, Y., Xie, L., Siyao, L., Sun, W., Qiao, Yu., Dong, C.: Enhanced quadratic video interpolation. In: Bartoli, A., Fusiello, A. (eds.) ECCV 2020. LNCS, vol. 12538, pp. 41–56. Springer, Cham (2020). https://doi.org/10.1007/978-3-030-66823-5_3
28. Liu, Z., Yeh, R.A., Tang, X., Liu, Y., Agarwala, A.: Video frame synthesis using deep voxel flow. In: CVPR, pp. 4463–4471 (2017)
29. Nah, S., Hyun Kim, T., Mu Lee, K.: Deep multi-scale convolutional neural network for dynamic scene deblurring. In: CVPR, pp. 3883–3891 (2017)
30. Niklaus, S., Liu, F.: Context-aware synthesis for video frame interpolation. In: CVPR, pp. 1701–1710 (2018)
31. Niklaus, S., Liu, F.: Softmax splatting for video frame interpolation. In: CVPR, pp. 5437–5446 (2020)
32. Pan, J., Sun, D., Pfister, H., Yang, M.H.: Blind image deblurring using dark channel prior. In: CVPR, pp. 1628–1636 (2016)
33. Park, D., Kang, D.U., Kim, J., Chun, S.Y.: Multi-temporal recurrent neural networks for progressive non-uniform single image deblurring with incremental temporal training. In: Vedaldi, A., Bischof, H., Brox, T., Frahm, J.-M. (eds.) ECCV 2020. LNCS, vol. 12351, pp. 327–343. Springer, Cham (2020). https://doi.org/10.1007/978-3-030-58539-6_20
34. Park, J., Ko, K., Lee, C., Kim, C.-S.: BMBC: bilateral motion estimation with bilateral cost volume for video interpolation. In: Vedaldi, A., Bischof, H., Brox, T., Frahm, J.-M. (eds.) ECCV 2020. LNCS, vol. 12359, pp. 109–125. Springer, Cham (2020). https://doi.org/10.1007/978-3-030-58568-6_7
35. Park, J., Lee, C., Kim, C.S.: Asymmetric bilateral motion estimation for video frame interpolation. In: ICCV (2021)
36. Peleg, T., Szekely, P., Sabo, D., Sendik, O.: IM-Net for high resolution video frame interpolation. In: CVPR, pp. 2398–2407 (2019)
37. Purohit, K., Rajagopalan, A.: Region-adaptive dense network for efficient motion deblurring. In: AAAI, vol. 34, pp. 11882–11889 (2020)
38. Ronneberger, O., Fischer, P., Brox, T.: U-Net: convolutional networks for biomedical image segmentation. In: Navab, N., Hornegger, J., Wells, W.M., Frangi, A.F. (eds.) MICCAI 2015. LNCS, vol. 9351, pp. 234–241. Springer, Cham (2015). https://doi.org/10.1007/978-3-319-24574-4_28
39. Shen, W., Bao, W., Zhai, G., Chen, L., Min, X., Gao, Z.: Blurry video frame interpolation. In: CVPR, pp. 5114–5123 (2020)

40. Shen, W., Bao, W., Zhai, G., Chen, L., Min, X., Gao, Z.: Video frame interpolation and enhancement via pyramid recurrent framework. IEEE Trans. Image Process. **30**, 277–292 (2020)
41. Shi, X., Chen, Z., Wang, H., Yeung, D.Y., Wong, W.K., Woo, W.: Convolutional lstm network: a machine learning approach for precipitation nowcasting. In: NeurIPS (2015)
42. Sim, H., Oh, J., Kim, M.: XVFI: extreme video frame interpolation. In: ICCV (2021)
43. Su, S., Delbracio, M., Wang, J., Sapiro, G., Heidrich, W., Wang, O.: Deep video deblurring for hand-held cameras. In: CVPR, pp. 1279–1288 (2017)
44. Sun, D., Yang, X., Liu, M.Y., Kautz, J.: PWC-Net: CNNs for optical flow using pyramid, warping, and cost volume. In: CVPR, pp. 8934–8943 (2018)
45. Tao, X., Gao, H., Shen, X., Wang, J., Jia, J.: Scale-recurrent network for deep image deblurring. In: CVPR, pp. 8174–8182 (2018)
46. Teed, Z., Deng, J.: RAFT: recurrent all-pairs field transforms for optical flow. In: Vedaldi, A., Bischof, H., Brox, T., Frahm, J.-M. (eds.) ECCV 2020. LNCS, vol. 12347, pp. 402–419. Springer, Cham (2020). https://doi.org/10.1007/978-3-030-58536-5_24
47. Telleen, J., et al.: Synthetic shutter speed imaging. In: Computer Graphics Forum, vol. 26, pp. 591–598. Wiley Online Library (2007)
48. Tian, Y., Zhang, Y., Fu, Y., Xu, C.: TDAN: temporally-deformable alignment network for video super-resolution. In: CVPR, pp. 3360–3369 (2020)
49. Wang, X., Chan, K.C., Yu, K., Dong, C., Change Loy, C.: EDVR: video restoration with enhanced deformable convolutional networks. In: CVPRW (2019)
50. Wu, J., Yuen, C., Cheung, N.M., Chen, J., Chen, C.W.: Modeling and optimization of high frame rate video transmission over wireless networks. IEEE Trans. Wireless Commun. **15**(4), 2713–2726 (2015)
51. Xiang, X., Tian, Y., Zhang, Y., Fu, Y., Allebach, J.P., Xu, C.: Zooming slow-MO: fast and accurate one-stage space-time video super-resolution. In: CVPR, pp. 3370–3379 (2020)
52. Xiao, Z., Xiong, Z., Fu, X., Liu, D., Zha, Z.J.: Space-time video super-resolution using temporal profiles. In: ACM MM, pp. 664–672 (2020)
53. Xu, G., Xu, J., Li, Z., Wang, L., Sun, X., Cheng, M.M.: Temporal modulation network for controllable space-time video super-resolution. In: CVPR, pp. 6388–6397 (2021)
54. Xu, X., Siyao, L., Sun, W., Yin, Q., Yang, M.H.: Quadratic video interpolation. In: NeurIPS, pp. 1647–1656 (2019)
55. Zhang, H., Dai, Y., Li, H., Koniusz, P.: Deep stacked hierarchical multi-patch network for image deblurring. In: CVPR, pp. 5978–5986 (2019)
56. Zhang, K., Luo, W., Zhong, Y., Ma, L., Liu, W., Li, H.: Adversarial spatio-temporal learning for video deblurring. IEEE Trans. Image Process. **28**(1), 291–301 (2018)
57. Zhang, K., Luo, W., Zhong, Y., Ma, L., Stenger, B., Liu, W., Li, H.: Deblurring by realistic blurring. In: CVPR, pp. 2737–2746 (2020)
58. Zhang, Y., Wang, C., Tao, D.: Video frame interpolation without temporal priors. In: NeurIPS 33 (2020)

Neural Image Representations for Multi-image Fusion and Layer Separation

Seonghyeon Nam[✉], Marcus A. Brubaker, and Michael S. Brown

York University, Toronto, Canada
snam0331@gmail.com, {mab,mbrown}@eecs.yorku.ca

Abstract. We propose a framework for aligning and fusing multiple images into a single view using neural image representations (NIRs), also known as implicit or coordinate-based neural representations. Our framework targets burst images that exhibit camera ego motion and potential changes in the scene. We describe different strategies for alignment depending on the nature of the scene motion—namely, perspective planar (*i.e.*, homography), optical flow with minimal scene change, and optical flow with notable occlusion and disocclusion. With the neural image representation, our framework effectively combines multiple inputs into a single canonical view without the need for selecting one of the images as a reference frame. We demonstrate how to use this multi-frame fusion framework for various layer separation tasks. The code and results are available at https://shnnam.github.io/research/nir.

Keywords: Implicit neural representations · Coordinate-based neural representations · Multi-image fusion · Layer separation

1 Introduction and Related Work

Fusing multiple misaligned images into a single view is a fundamental problem in computer vision. The underlying assumption for this task is that the multiple images represent varying viewpoints of the same scene, perhaps with small motion in the scene. Many computer vision tasks rely on multi-image fusion, such as image stitching [7,13,16], high dynamic range (HDR) imaging [11,42,43], and image super-resolution [5,6,39]. Most existing image fusion approaches work by first aligning the multiple images based on their assumed motion—for example, homography for planar or nearly planar scenes or optical flow for nonplanar scenes, or when objects in the scene move. Traditionally, images are aligned to a reference image that is manually chosen among the input images. Since image pixels are represented in a 2D discrete sampled array, such transformations are approximated by interpolation techniques.

Supplementary Information The online version contains supplementary material available at https://doi.org/10.1007/978-3-031-20071-7_13.

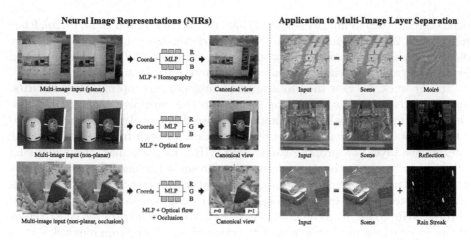

Fig. 1. This figure provides an overview of our work which fuses multiple images to a single canonical view in a continuous image representation. Our method incorporates motion models such as homography and optical flow into the formulation of implicit or coordinate-based neural representations. We demonstrate the effectiveness of our method on various applications of multi-image layer separation. Images from [4, 8, 14, 23] are used here for visualization.

Recently, implicit or coordinate-based neural representations were proposed to represent images and videos as a function of pixel coordinates parameterized by multi-layer perceptrons (MLPs) [32, 36]. This new type of image representation, which we call a neural image representation (NIR), is different from conventional discrete grid-based representations in that image signals are continuous with respect to spatial or spatio-temporal pixel coordinates. Further, the resolution of images no longer depends on the size of the discrete grid, but rather the representational complexity of the MLP. These representations have been actively studied particularly in view synthesis [15, 22, 25, 27, 28, 30, 33], 3D geometry [24, 26], and image synthesis [2, 31, 34].

This work targets multi-frame fusion by leveraging the advantages offered by NIRs. As shown on the left in Fig. 1, we propose to train MLPs to reconstruct a canonical view based on multiple images. Our approach incorporates image registration techniques into NIRs using coordinate transformations [27, 28]. Unlike existing multi-image fusion, our method does not need an explicit reference image. Instead, a virtual reference image is implicitly learned as the canonical view embedded within the neural representation. Since the space of canonical views is unbounded, all images can be fused regardless of the original image frame as shown in Fig. 1. In addition, image transformation is achieved in a real-valued coordinate space without the need for interpolation.

To demonstrate effectiveness of our NIR multi-image fusion, we apply our method to various applications of multi-image layer separation. As shown in Fig. 1, the goal of multi-image layer separation is to decompose signals from multiple images into a single underlying scene image and interference layers to improve the visibility of the underlying scene. Many approaches for different tasks have been studied, such as image demoiré [12,40], reflection removal [1,14,19,20], fence removal [19,20], and deraining [8,10,38,44]. Early works on these problems heavily rely on domain-specific priors for optimization, while recent approaches are driven by deep learning and a large amount of annotated data for supervision.

In our work, we cast the problem as an unsupervised optimization of NIRs. Specifically, we fuse the underlying scene from the multiple images using NIRs. Depending on the type of scene motion, we use different deformation strategies when computing the neural image representation for each frame. To remove the interference layer, we propose two-stream NIRs. In particular, the underlying "clean layer" image without interference is represented by one MLP, while a separate MLP is used to represent the interference layer(s). We show that standard regularization terms – for example, total variation – can be used in the optimization of these NIRs to assist in the layer separation. We demonstrate the effectiveness of our approach on moiré removal, obstruction removal, and rain removal.

Closely related to our approach is DoubleDIP [9], which also studied image layer decomposition on a single or multiple image(s) using coupled deep image priors [37]. DoubleDIP exploits self-similarity, an inductive bias in convolutional neural networks (CNNs), to separate different signals. Our approach uses the parameterization of motion as a general prior to tackle multiple tasks. Unlike semantic segmentation and matting [9,21], we focus on disentangling low-level signals rather than semantic layers.

Contribution. We describe a framework to perform multi-frame fusion and layer separation as learning a neural image representation. We describe variations on the representation and optimization for different scene and camera conditions. We also demonstrate how to apply this framework to handle several different types of layer separation tasks. To the best of our knowledge, our work is the first to explicitly address multi-image fusion with neural image representations.

2   Method Overview

Neural image representations, also known as implicit or coordinate-based neural representations, have recently been proposed [32,36] as a way to represent RGB values of an image as a function of pixel coordinates parameterized by MLPs. For multiple sequential images, this can be formulated as

$$\hat{\mathbf{I}}_{(x,y,t)} = f_{\theta_I}(x, y, t), \tag{1}$$

where $\hat{\mathbf{I}}_{(x,y,t)}$ is the value at pixel (x, y) in frame t and f_{θ_I} is an MLP with parameters θ_I. Here each frame is nearly independent due to different values of t.

In our work, we assume our multiple images are captured quickly as a burst from a single camera. Consequently, images are of approximately the same scene, but are expected to have small variations due to the motion of the camera and small amounts of motion in the scene. Furthermore, we do not expect notable variations in scene lighting, appearance, or colors due to the camera's onboard color manipulation.

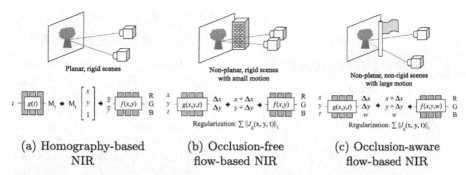

(a) Homography-based
NIR

(b) Occlusion-free
flow-based NIR

(c) Occlusion-aware
flow-based NIR

Fig. 2. Illustration of our neural image representations (NIRs). Assuming that the MLP f learns a canonical view where all burst images are fused, we render each image by projecting the canonical view to the frame-specific view, which is achieved by transforming the input coordinates fed into the f. We estimate the transform using another MLP g. According to different assumptions of the world, we formulate our framework differently; we formulate the transform of coordinates using (a) homography, (b) optical flow without occlusion/disocclusion, and (c) optical flow with occlusion/disocclusion.

Within this context of burst images, our work aims to formulate f_{θ_I} differently by learning a joint representation of multiple images using their spatio-temporal correlation. To this end, we revisit well-established image registration and motion compensation techniques within the new domain of NIRs. Specifically, our f_{θ_I} learns a canonical view of the scene shared across images. Each image in the burst sequence is modelled by a deformation of the canonical view— for instance, using a perspective planar transform (i.e., a homography) or pixel-wise optical flow. Since the function is continuous and unbounded, it not only is able store the entire scene regardless of the size of 2D image grid, but also can be easily deformed by transforming input coordinates into a real-valued space. The model is formally described as

$$\hat{\mathbf{I}}_{(x,y,t)} = f_{\theta_I}(T_g(x,y,t)), \tag{2}$$

where T applies a coordinate transformation with parameters ϕ. The parameters of the coordinate transform could be fixed or themselves a function— that is, $g = g_{\theta_T}(x,y,t)$ where g_{θ_T} is an MLP that computes the parameters of the coordinate transform. The parameters of the MLPs, θ_T and θ_I, are optimized by minimizing the following pixel reconstruction loss:

$$\mathcal{L}_{\text{Recon}} = \sum_{x,y,t} \|\hat{\mathbf{I}}_{(x,y,t)} - \mathbf{I}_{(x,y,t)}\|_2^2, \tag{3}$$

where $\mathbf{I}$ is the original image ground truth.

The explicit parameterization of motion in neural representations enables the simultaneous learning of image and motion representations. By minimizing Eq. (3), our neural representations learn the parameters of scene motion in an unsupervised manner. More importantly, unlike conventional image registration and motion compensation techniques, our approach does not require a

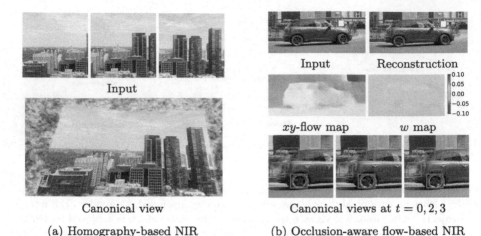

Input

Canonical view

(a) Homography-based NIR

Input   Reconstruction

xy-flow map w map

Canonical views at $t = 0, 2, 3$

(b) Occlusion-aware flow-based NIR

Fig. 3. Visualization of learned representations. In (a), the top row shows three of nine representative images used to learn a homography-based NIR, and the bottom shows a learned canonical view. In (b), the first row shows one of the input and reconstruction images, the second row shows a xy-flow map and w map learned by a occlusion-aware flow-based NIR, and the third row shows canonical views at $t = 0, 2, 3$.

reference image to be selected from the burst input. Instead, our model learns a virtual reference view of the scene implicitly.

We next show how to extend our multi-frame alignment framework for use in layer separation tasks. In particular, we target tasks where input images are modeled as a combination of two layers: (1) the desired underlying scene image and (2) the undesired corruption in the form as an interference layer. We assume that the contents of the underlying scene remains similar over the multiple images, while the interference layer changes. To do this, we propose a two-stream architecture for NIRs, with one component that captures the static scene and another that captures the interference. In the following, we describe our method in detail.

2.1 NIRs for Multi-image Fusion

Figure 2 shows the overview of the NIRs for multi-image fusion. We propose three kinds of parameterization according to the assumption of the scene: (a) homography-based NIRs, (b) occlusion-free flow-based NIRs, and (c) occlusion-aware flow-based NIRs.

Homography-Based NIRs. In case of planar, rigid scenes that are moving globally as shown in Fig. 2 (a), we can use a homography as the coordinate transformation. As shown in the figure, the function g_{θ_T} is learned to estimate parameters of a homography matrix M for each frame. Then the predicted image using the homography-based NIRs is described as:

$$\hat{\mathbf{I}}_{(x,y,t)} = f_{\theta_I}(M_t[x, y, 1]^T), \tag{4}$$

where M_t is a 3×3 linear matrix represented as $M_t = g_{\theta_T}(t)$. Since M_t is applied globally regardless of spatial coordinates, $g_{\theta_T}(t)$ only takes t as input. We omit the normalization of output coordinates in the homography transform for simplicity.

Figure 3 (a) shows a visualization of the NIR estimated from nine burst images of a distant scene, captured with a horizontally moving camera. As can be seen in the figure, the homography-based NIR automatically stitches all the images in a single view only using a reconstruction loss. A single frame t can be recreated by transforming the canonical view using the output of the $g_{\theta_I}(t)$ homography matrix.

Occlusion-Free Flow-based NIRs. In many cases, a scene will not be planar or move together rigidly. However, in burst imagery because frames are temporally close, the motions are likely to be small. To handle this, we use a dense optical flow representation to model the per-pixel displacement of scene, which is represented by the displacement of x and y coordinates as shown in Fig. 2 (b). We assume that the motion is small enough to cause minimal occlusions and disocclusions. In this case ϕ represents an xy-displacement that is computed by $g_{\theta_T}(x, y, t)$ for each (x, y, t). Formally, $T(x, y, t) = (x + \Delta x_t, y + \Delta y_t)$ where $(\Delta x_t, \Delta y_t) = g_{\theta_T}(x, y, t)$ are the displacement of x and y coordinates. An output pixel can be computed as:

$$\hat{\mathbf{I}}_{(x,y,t)} = f_{\theta_I}(x + \Delta x_t, y + \Delta y_t). \tag{5}$$

In addition to the reconstruction loss in Eq. (3), we use a total variation (TV) regularization for the flow smoothness, which is described as

$$\mathcal{L}_{\text{TVFlow}} = \sum \| J_{g_{\theta_T}}(x, y, t) \|_1, \tag{6}$$

where $J_{g_{\theta_T}}(x, y, t)$ is a Jacobian matrix that consists of gradients of g_{θ_T} with respect to x, y, and t.

Occlusion-Aware Flow-Based NIRs. Since the canonical view of the occlusion-free flow-based NIRs is in a 2D plane, it is not enough to store extra information when a scene is occluded or disoccluded. To address such cases, we add an additional dimension w to the canonical view as shown in Fig. 2 (c). Intuitively, different versions of a scene at a certain position caused by occlusion are stored at different values of w, while occlusion-irrelevant pixels are stored at the same value of w and shared across images. This is achieved by regularizing the Jacobian of g_{θ_T} in Eq. (6). With w, the output image is rendered by the following equation:

$$\hat{\mathbf{I}}_{(x,y,t)} = f_{\theta_I}(x + \Delta x_t, y + \Delta y_t, w_t). \tag{7}$$

Figure 3 (b) shows a visualization of a learned xy-flow map, w map, and canonical views at different values of w after training five consecutive images in [29]. Since the car is moving in the scene, the xy-flow map shows spatially varying optical flow on the car. The w map shows different values in regions of large motion (e.g., wheels), transient lighting effects (e.g., specularities and reflections), and regions that undergo occlusion or disocclusion. This can be seen more clearly by visualizing the canonical view, with different values of w as shown in the bottom of the figure.

2.2   Two-Stream NIRs for Layer Separation

We now extend NIRs to multi-image layer separation tasks. Figure 4 shows the overview of our two-stream NIRs. We model the images as the combination of two signals,

$$\begin{cases} \hat{\mathbf{O}}_{(x,y,t)} = f_{\theta_O}^1(T_g(x,y,t)), \\ \hat{\mathbf{U}}_{(x,y,t)} = f_{\theta_U}^2(x,y,t) \end{cases} \quad (8)$$

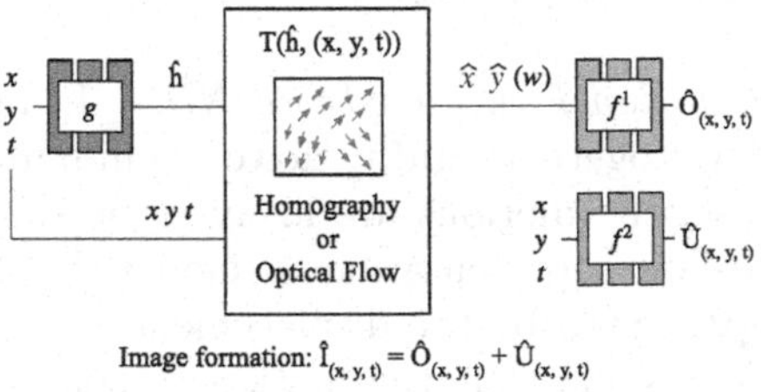

Fig. 4. Multi-image layer separation.

where $f_{\theta_O}^1$ and $f_{\theta_U}^2$ are two different MLPs used to represent the scene and corrupting interference, respectively.

Since we usually have the knowledge of scene motion, we use an explicit parameterization of motion for $f_{\theta_O}^1$—for example, a homography or a flow field. To model the interference layers, we use an unconstrained form of MLP for $f_{\theta_U}^2$ to store contents that violate the motion in $f_{\theta_O}^1$, that is beneficial for interference patterns difficult to model. The generic form of image formation is described as

$$\hat{\mathbf{I}}_{(x,y,t)} = \hat{\mathbf{O}}_{(x,y,t)} + \hat{\mathbf{U}}_{(x,y,t)}, \quad (9)$$

but the specifics can vary depending on the task. Due to the flexibility of $f_{\theta_U}^2$, it can potentially learn the full contents of the images as a "video", effectively ignoring $f_{\theta_O}^1$. To prevent this, we regularize $f_{\theta_U}^2$ using

$$\mathcal{L}_{\text{Interf}} = \sum \|\hat{\mathbf{U}}_{(x,y,t)}\|_1. \quad (10)$$

Directly incorporating a spatial alignment into the NIR optimization may appear inefficient at first glance, especially compared to methods that first apply conventional homography and or optical flow estimation and then perform some type of image fusion. However, in the case of corrupted scenes, it is often challenging to estimate the motion of the underlying clean image with the conventional methods. For instance, existing methods often rely heavily on multiple stages of refinement of motion [19] to pre-process images to assist with the alignment step. Our method tackles the problem jointly, by incorporating the scene alignment jointly with a layer separation through the benefits of NIRs.

3 Applications

We now show the effectiveness of our method on various multi-image layer separation tasks. Please refer to the supplementary material for more results.

3.1 Moiré Removal

Moiré is a common pattern of interference, often seen when taking a photo of monitor or screen using a digital camera. Moiré patterns are caused by the misalignment of the pixel grids in the display and camera sensor. Burst images usually capture temporally varying moiré patterns as camera motion changes the alignment of the sensor and screen and hence the interference pattern. Typically the movement of the scene in burst images follows homography transform as the screen is planar. We show that our two-stream NIRs are able to effectively separate the underlying scene and moiré pattern.

Formulation. We parameterize $f_{\theta_O}^1$ as a homography-based NIR in Eq. (4). The image formation follows the basic form in Eq. (9), where we use signed values in the range of $[-1, 1)$ for the output of both $\hat{\mathbf{O}}_{(x,y,t)} \in \mathbb{R}^3$ and $\hat{\mathbf{U}}_{(x,y,t)} \in \mathbb{R}^3$. The signed output for $\hat{\mathbf{U}}_{(x,y,t)}$ is particularly useful to represent color bands of moiré patterns. To further prevent scene content from appearing in both $\hat{\mathbf{O}}_{(x,y,t)}$ and $\hat{\mathbf{U}}_{(x,y,t)}$, we adopt an exclusion loss used in [9,45] to encourage the gradient structure of two signals to be decorrelated. This is formulated as

$$\mathcal{L}_{\text{Excl}} = \sum \|\Phi(J_{f^1}(x,y), J_{f^2}(x,y))\|_2^2, \tag{11}$$

where $\Phi(J_{f^1}(x,y), J_{f^2}(x,y)) = \tanh(N_1 J_{f^1}(x,y)) \otimes \tanh(N_2 J_{f^2}(x,y))$, and $\otimes$ is an element-wise multiplication. N_1 and N_2 are normalization terms [45]. We optimize θ_T, θ_O, and θ_U using the following training objective:

$$\mathcal{L}_{\text{Moire}} = \mathcal{L}_{\text{Recon}} + \lambda_{\text{Interf}}\mathcal{L}_{\text{Interf}} + \lambda_{\text{Excl}}\mathcal{L}_{\text{Excl}}, \tag{12}$$

where λ_{Interf} and λ_{Excl} are hyperparameters. We use an MLP with ReLU activation for g_{θ_T} and a SIREN [32] for $f_{\theta_O}^1$ and $f_{\theta_U}^2$.

Experiments. Since there are no publicly available datasets for multi-frame screen-captured moiré images, we synthesize a dataset from clean images. To do this, we use the Slideshare-1M [3] dataset, which consists of approximately one million images of lecture slides, to mimic content likely to be captured by students. Using this dataset, we synthesize 100 test sequences of five burst images for testing following the synthesis procedure in [17]. For comparison, we compare AFN [40] and C3Net [12], state-of-the-art deep learning methods, which are trained by our synthetic training set containing 10,000 sequences. We additionally evaluate Double DIP to compare unsupervised approaches.

Table 1 shows a quantitative comparison of methods on the synthetic test set. In addition to PSNR and SSIM, we compare a normalized cross-correlation (NCC) and structure index (SI). Even though our method does not outperform

Table 1. Quantitative evaluation of moiré removal with a synthetic dataset. AFN [40] uses a single image; other methods use five images as input.

	Supervised		Unsupervised	
	AFN [40]	C3Net [12]	Double DIP [9]	Ours
Input	Single	Burst	Burst	Burst
PSNR	43.63	27.99	18.53	38.68
SSIM	0.9952	0.8071	0.8762	0.9751
NCC	0.9963	0.7724	0.5120	0.9865
SI	0.9962	0.7721	0.4895	0.9856

AFN, the performance is significantly better than C3Net and Double DIP. However, notably our method is unsupervised—that is, it does not use a training set of images. This is in contrast to AFN and C3Net, which require explicit supervision or clean and moiré corrupted images. Figure 5 shows a qualitative evaluation on real images. As can be seen, our method outperforms all the baselines on real images. The performance of AFN and C3Net is degraded because they are not trained on real images. Double DIP fails to decompose the underlying scene and moiré pattern since it relies on an inductive bias in convolutional neural networks, which is not enough to separate complex signals. Our method removes a moiré pattern by restricting the movement of the scene to homography, which acts as a strong prior of moiré removal.

3.2 Obstruction Removal

The goal of obstruction removal [20,41] is to eliminate foreground objects or scenes that hinder the visibility of the background scene. Obstructions can be in the form of reflection on a window in front of the scene or a physical object, such as a fence. We apply the two-stream NIRs based on occlusion-free optical flow to a reflection and fence removal. In this case, the background scenes are not planar, but the movement of the scene is small enough to ignore occlusion. Similarly to moiré removal, we decompose the reflection and fence layer using the fact that they move differently to the background scene.

Formulation. We use the occlusion-free flow-based NIRs in Eq. (5) for $f^1_{\theta_O}$. For reflection removal, we use the image model in Eq. (9), where $\hat{\mathbf{O}}_{(x,y,t)} \in \mathbb{R}^3$ and $\hat{\mathbf{U}}_{(x,y,t)} \in \mathbb{R}^3$ are in the range of $[0,1)$. We use the following combination of loss functions as a training objective:

$$\mathcal{L}_{\text{Refl}} = \mathcal{L}_{\text{Recon}} + \lambda_{\text{TVFlow}} \mathcal{L}_{\text{TVFlow}} \\ + \lambda_{\text{Interf}} \mathcal{L}_{\text{Interf}} + \lambda_{\text{Excl}} \mathcal{L}_{\text{Excl}}, \tag{13}$$

where λ_{TVFlow} is a hyperparameter. For a fence removal, we use a different image model described as

$$\hat{\mathbf{I}}_{(x,y,t)} = (1 - \alpha_{(x,y,t)})\hat{\mathbf{O}}_{(x,y,t)} + \alpha_{(x,y,t)}\hat{\mathbf{U}}_{(x,y,t)}, \tag{14}$$

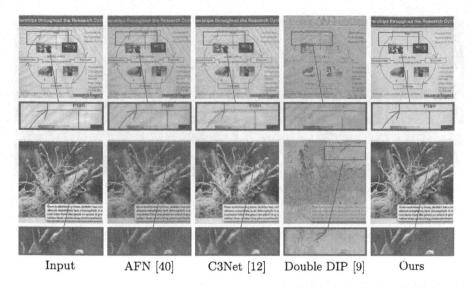

| Input | AFN [40] | C3Net [12] | Double DIP [9] | Ours |

Fig. 5. Qualitative comparison of moiré removal on real images. Our method outperforms all methods including AFN [40]. AFN was better than ours on the synthetic data in Table 1 which is unrepresentative of real-world images.

where $(\alpha_{(x,y,t)}, \hat{\mathbf{U}}_{(x,y,t)}) = f^2_{\theta_U}(x, y, t)$, and $\hat{\mathbf{O}}_{(x,y,t)} \in \mathbb{R}^3$ and $\hat{\mathbf{U}}_{(x,y,t)} \in \mathbb{R}^3$ are in the range of $[0, 1)$. $\alpha_{(x,y,t)} \in \mathbb{R}$ is an alpha map of the fence layer in the range of $[0, 1)$. The training objective is described as:

$$\mathcal{L}_{\text{Fence}} = \mathcal{L}_{\text{Recon}} + \lambda_{\text{TVFlow}}\mathcal{L}_{\text{TVFlow}} + \lambda_{\text{Interf}}\mathcal{L}_{\text{Interf}}. \tag{15}$$

We used SIREN for all coordinate functions.

Experiments. Figure 6 shows qualitative results of our method and existing approaches. We use real images in [14] for testing. The methods of Li and Brown [14] and Alayrac et al. [1] are designed for reflection removal, and the method in [20] is a general approach for obstruction removal. As can be seen, our method is able to accurately decompose the background scene and reflection compared with the baseline methods. Figure 7 shows a qualitative comparison of fence removal on real images in [20]. Our method achieves comparable quality of results to learning-based methods that heavily rely on large amounts of data and supervision.

3.3 Rain Removal

To show the effectiveness of the occlusion-aware flow-based NIRs, we address the problem of multi-image rain removal as the task deals with various kinds of scenes, from static scenes to dynamic scenes. Since rain streaks move fast and randomly, the streaks impact the smoothness of the scene motion. We exploit this prior knowledge of the randomness of rain streaks observed in multiple images by imposing a smoothness regularization on the scene flow map.

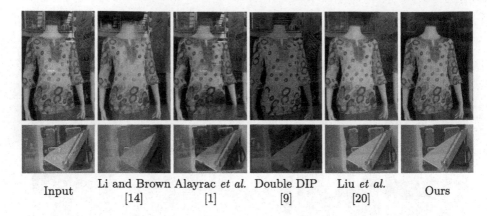

Input   Li and Brown Alayrac *et al.* Double DIP   Liu *et al.*   Ours
              [14]   [1]   [9]   [20]

Fig. 6. Qualitative results of reflection removal on real images in [14].

Input   Liu *et al.* [19]   Liu *et al.* [20]   Ours

Fig. 7. Qualitative comparison of fence removal on real images in [20].

Formulation. We use the occlusion-aware flow-based NIRs in Eq. (7) as a formulation of $f_{\theta_O}^1$. Since rain streaks are achromatic, we use the following image formation:

$$\hat{\mathbf{I}}_{(x,y,t)} = (1 - \hat{\mathbf{U}}_{(x,y,t)})\hat{\mathbf{O}}_{(x,y,t)} + \hat{\mathbf{U}}_{(x,y,t)}\mathbf{1}, \tag{16}$$

where $\hat{\mathbf{O}}_{(x,y,t)} \in \mathbb{R}^3$ and $\hat{\mathbf{U}}_{(x,y,t)} \in \mathbb{R}$ are in the range of $[0,1)$, and $\mathbf{1} = [1,1,1]^T$. In this form, $\hat{\mathbf{U}}_{(x,y,t)}$ acts as an alpha map of rain streaks. Our final training objective is described as

$$\mathcal{L}_{\text{Rain}} = \mathcal{L}_{\text{Recon}} + \lambda_{\text{TVFlow}}\mathcal{L}_{\text{TVFlow}} + \lambda_{\text{Interf}}\mathcal{L}_{\text{Interf}}. \tag{17}$$

Experiments. Figure 8 shows a qualitative evaluation on real images in NTU-Rain [8], with moving cars and pedestrians. We compare state-of-the-art video deraining methods based on optimization [10] and deep learning [8]. We take five consecutive images to run our method which clearly removes rain streaks in the scene and is qualitatively competitive with the baselines on real images. For quantitative evaluation, we must resort to synthetic data and use RainSyn-Light25 [18], consisting of 25 synthetic sequences of nine images. Table 2 shows results of ours and baseline methods: SE [38], FastDeRain [10], SpacCNN [8], and FCDN [44]. Though our method does not outperform deep learning-based methods, it achieves a comparable result to optimization-based approaches without

Table 2. Result of rain removal on RainSynLight25 [18].

	Supervised		Unsupervised		
	SpacCNN [8]	FCDN [44]	SE [38]	FastDeRain [10]	Ours
PSNR	32.78	35.80	26.56	29.42	28.61
SSIM	0.9239	0.9622	0.8006	0.8683	0.8604

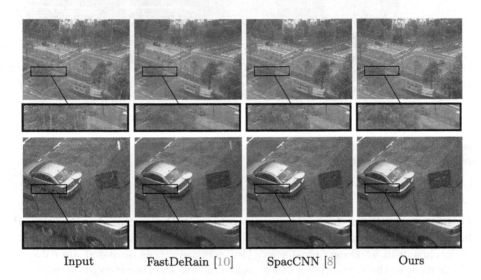

| Input | FastDeRain [10] | SpacCNN [8] | Ours |

Fig. 8. Qualitative comparison of rain removal on real images in NTURain [8].

supervision and the domain knowledge of deraining. We expect incorporating more regularization could further improve the performance.

3.4 Discussion

Ablation Study on Loss Functions. We conducted an ablation study on various loss functions. In Fig. 9, we show the decomposed background and reflection layer of different training objectives by removing each loss function. As can be seen, the background content is reconstructed in the reflection layer when we do not use $\mathcal{L}_{\text{Interf}}$ since g_{θ_U} is unconstrained. Without $\mathcal{L}_{\text{TVFlow}}$, on the other hand, both signals are reconstructed in the background layer. In this case, g_{θ_O} has enough freedom to learn the mixture of two layers moving differently. In addition to $\mathcal{L}_{\text{Interf}}$ and $\mathcal{L}_{\text{TVFlow}}$, the exclusion loss $\mathcal{L}_{\text{Excl}}$ further improves the quality by preventing the structure of two layers from being correlated.

Ablation Study on w. Fig. 10 shows an ablation study on w in the occlusion-aware flow-based NIRs using RainSynLight25 [18]. As shown in the red boxes

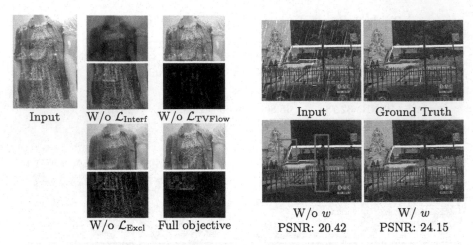

Input	W/o $\mathcal{L}_{\text{Interf}}$	W/o $\mathcal{L}_{\text{TVFlow}}$	Input	Ground Truth
	W/o $\mathcal{L}_{\text{Excl}}$	Full objective	W/o w PSNR: 20.42	W/ w PSNR: 24.15

Fig. 9. Ablation study of loss functions on reflection removal. The top and bottom images show the background and reflection layer, respectively.

Fig. 10. Ablation study on w. We show PSNRs of two outputs using the synthetic dataset RainSynLight25 [18]. (Color figure online)

on the output, the method without w produces artifacts around occlusion and disocclusion, which indicates that it is difficult to represent all contents including occlusion in a 2D canonical view. Our method stores occluded appearance information in the extra dimension w, and enables accurate reconstruction.

Can a Complex Model Take Place of a Simpler Model? Note that in principle our NIRs using a complex motion model (e.g. occlusion-aware flow) can be generalized to the scenes with a simpler motion. For layer separation, however, it is beneficial to use a simpler model that fits well with the motion of a scene as it provides a strong constraint to separate layers effectively. In Fig. 11, we compare the homography-based model and the occlusion-aware flow-based model on a demoiréing task. The PSNR and SSIM of the flow-based model on the synthetic test set are 36.72 and 0.9512, respectively. The flow-based model removes the moiré pattern to some extent, but a part of the pattern still remains. This is because constraining the representation of motion in the homography-based model is more effective than adding regularization losses in the flow-based model.

The Number of Input Images. Fig. 12 shows results of rain removal using the different number of input images. Better results are obtained with more images, as the additional images provide more information in separating two layers.

Limitations. Since our method relies on a pixel distance loss to learn the motion, it may fail when the motion of burst images is too large. Our method also fails to separate layers when the underlying scene and interference move in a similar manner. Although our method is not the top performer in all cases, it achieves

Input   Homography Optical flow

Input   2 images   5 images

Fig. 11. Analysis on different motion models. We apply homography-based (center) and occlusion-aware flow-based (right) models to demoiréing.

Fig. 12. Analysis on the number of input images. We test 2 and 5 input images on a 0rain removal task.

competitive results without the need for supervision, which is the case for many of the state-of-the-art methods.

In addition, our method requires a proper assumption of motion to tackle layer separation tasks. This is because our method relies on the motion of underlying scene as a prior to separate layers. It may be more desirable to seek a generic model that works for any example without the assumption of motion by incorporating other priors such as an inductive bias learned from a large dataset.

Finally, our method currently takes about 30 min at most for optimizing layer separation tasks, which is a limiting factor in a real-world setting. However, there is already promising research demonstrating how to improve the optimization performance of NIRs [35].

4 Conclusion

We presented a framework that uses neural image representations to fuse information from multiple images. The framework simultaneously registers the images and fuses them into a single continuous image representation. We outlined multiple variations based on the underlying scene motion: homography-based, occlusion-free optical flow, and occlusion-aware optical flow. Unlike conventional image alignment and fusion, our approach does not need to select one of the input images as a reference frame. We showed our framework can be used to address layer separation problems using two NIRs, one for the desired scene layer and the other for the interference layer.

Neural image representations are an exciting new approach to image processing. This work is a first attempt to extend NIRs to multi-frame inputs with applications to various low-level computer vision tasks. Despite making only minimal assumptions and without leveraging any supervisory training data, the NIR-based approaches described here are competitive with state-of-the-art, unsupervised methods on individual tasks. Further, because it is practically impossible to acquire supervisory data in real-world conditions, our approach often qualitatively outperforms supervised methods on real-world imagery.

230   S. Nam et al.

Acknowledgement.. This work was funded in part by the Canada First Research Excellence Fund (CFREF) for the Vision: Science to Applications (VISTA) program and the NSERC Discovery Grant program.

References

1. Alayrac, J.B., Carreira, J., Zisserman, A.: The visual centrifuge: Model-free layered video representations. In: IEEE Conference on Computer Vision and Pattern Recognition, pp. 2457–2466 (2019)
2. Anokhin, I., Demochkin, K., Khakhulin, T., Sterkin, G., Lempitsky, V., Korzhenkov, D.: Image generators with conditionally-independent pixel synthesis. In: IEEE Conference on Computer Vision and Pattern Recognition, pp. 14278–14287 (2021)
3. Araujo, A., Chaves, J., Lakshman, H., Angst, R., Girod, B.: Large-scale query-by-image video retrieval using bloom filters. arXiv preprint arXiv:1604.07939 (2016)
4. Baker, S., Scharstein, D., Lewis, J., Roth, S., Black, M.J., Szeliski, R.: A database and evaluation methodology for optical flow. Int. J. Comput. Vis. **92**(1), 1–31 (2011)
5. Bhat, G., Danelljan, M., Timofte, R.: Ntire 2021 challenge on burst super-resolution: Methods and results. In: IEEE Conference on Computer Vision and Pattern Recognition, pp. 613–626 (2021)
6. Bhat, G., Danelljan, M., Van Gool, L., Timofte, R.: Deep burst super-resolution. In: IEEE Conference on Computer Vision and Pattern Recognition, pp. 9209–9218 (2021)
7. Brown, M., Lowe, D.G.: Automatic panoramic image stitching using invariant features. Int. J. Comput. Vis. **74**(1), 59–73 (2007)
8. Chen, J., Tan, C.H., Hou, J., Chau, L.P., Li, H.: Robust video content alignment and compensation for rain removal in a CNN framework. In: IEEE Conference on Computer Vision and Pattern Recognition, pp. 6286–6295 (2018)
9. Gandelsman, Y., Shocher, A., Irani, M.: Double-DIP: unsupervised image decomposition via coupled deep-image-priors. In: IEEE Conference on Computer Vision and Pattern Recognition, pp. 11026–11035 (2019)
10. Jiang, T.X., Huang, T.Z., Zhao, X.L., Deng, L.J., Wang, Y.: FastDeRain: a novel video rain streak removal method using directional gradient priors. IEEE Trans. Image Process. **28**(4), 2089–2102 (2018)
11. Kalantari, N.K., Ramamoorthi, R., et al.: Deep high dynamic range imaging of dynamic scenes. ACM Trans. Graph. **36**(4), 144–1 (2017)
12. Kim, S., Nam, H., Kim, J., Jeong, J.: C3Net: demoireing network attentive in channel, color and concatenation. In: IIEEE Conference on Computer Vision and Pattern Recognition Workshops, pp. 426–427 (2020)
13. Levin, A., Zomet, A., Peleg, S., Weiss, Y.: Seamless image stitching in the gradient domain. In: Pajdla, T., Matas, J. (eds.) ECCV 2004. LNCS, vol. 3024, pp. 377–389. Springer, Heidelberg (2004). https://doi.org/10.1007/978-3-540-24673-2_31
14. Li, Y., Brown, M.S.: Exploiting reflection change for automatic reflection removal. In: IEEE Conference on Computer Vision and Pattern Recognition, pp. 2432–2439 (2013)
15. Li, Z., Niklaus, S., Snavely, N., Wang, O.: Neural scene flow fields for space-time view synthesis of dynamic scenes. In: IEEE Conference on Computer Vision and Pattern Recognition, pp. 6498–6508 (2021)

16. Lin, C.C., Pankanti, S.U., Natesan Ramamurthy, K., Aravkin, A.Y.: Adaptive as-natural-as-possible image stitching. In: IEEE Conference on Computer Vision and Pattern Recognition, pp. 1155–1163 (2015)
17. Liu, B., Shu, X., Wu, X.: Demoir\'eing of camera-captured screen images using deep convolutional neural network. arXiv preprint arXiv:1804.03809 (2018)
18. Liu, J., Yang, W., Yang, S., Guo, Z.: Erase or fill? deep joint recurrent rain removal and reconstruction in videos. In: IEEE Conference on Computer Vision and Pattern Recognition, pp. 3233–3242 (2018)
19. Liu, Y.L., Lai, W.S., Yang, M.H., Chuang, Y.Y., Huang, J.B.: Learning to see through obstructions. In: IEEE Conference on Computer Vision and Pattern Recognition, pp. 14215–14224 (2020)
20. Liu, Y.L., Lai, W.S., Yang, M.H., Chuang, Y.Y., Huang, J.B.: Learning to see through obstructions with layered decomposition. arXiv preprint arXiv:2008.04902 (2020)
21. Lu, E., Cole, F., Dekel, T., Zisserman, A., Freeman, W.T., Rubinstein, M.: Omnimatte: associating objects and their effects in video. In: IEEE Conference on Computer Vision and Pattern Recognition, pp. 4507–4515 (2021)
22. Martin-Brualla, R., Radwan, N., Sajjadi, M.S., Barron, J.T., Dosovitskiy, A., Duckworth, D.: NeRF in the wild: neural radiance fields for unconstrained photo collections. In: IEEE Conference on Computer Vision and Pattern Recognition, pp. 7210–7219 (2021)
23. Meneghetti, G., Danelljan, M., Felsberg, M., Nordberg, K.: Image alignment for panorama stitching in sparsely structured environments. In: Paulsen, R.R., Pedersen, K.S. (eds.) SCIA 2015. LNCS, vol. 9127, pp. 428–439. Springer, Cham (2015). https://doi.org/10.1007/978-3-319-19665-7_36
24. Mescheder, L., Oechsle, M., Niemeyer, M., Nowozin, S., Geiger, A.: Occupancy networks: learning 3D reconstruction in function space. In: IEEE Conference on Computer Vision and Pattern Recognition, pp. 4460–4470 (2019)
25. Mildenhall, B., Srinivasan, P.P., Tancik, M., Barron, J.T., Ramamoorthi, R., Ng, R.: NeRF: representing scenes as neural radiance fields for view synthesis. In: Vedaldi, A., Bischof, H., Brox, T., Frahm, J.-M. (eds.) ECCV 2020. LNCS, vol. 12346, pp. 405–421. Springer, Cham (2020). https://doi.org/10.1007/978-3-030-58452-8_24
26. Park, J.J., Florence, P., Straub, J., Newcombe, R., Lovegrove, S.: DeepSDF: learning continuous signed distance functions for shape representation. In: IEEE Conference on Computer Vision and Pattern Recognition, pp. 165–174 (2019)
27. Park, K., et al.: Nerfies: deformable neural radiance fields. In: International Conference on Computer Vision, pp. 5865–5874 (2021)
28. Park, K., et al.: HyperNeRF: a higher-dimensional representation for topologically varying neural radiance fields. ACM Trans. Graph. 40(6), 238 (2021)
29. Perazzi, F., Pont-Tuset, J., McWilliams, B., Van Gool, L., Gross, M., Sorkine-Hornung, A.: A benchmark dataset and evaluation methodology for video object segmentation. In: IEEE Conference on Computer Vision and Pattern Recognition, pp. 724–732 (2016)
30. Pumarola, A., Corona, E., Pons-Moll, G., Moreno-Noguer, F.: D-NeRF: neural radiance fields for dynamic scenes. In: IEEE Conference on Computer Vision and Pattern Recognition, pp. 10318–10327 (2021)
31. Shaham, T.R., Gharbi, M., Zhang, R., Shechtman, E., Michaeli, T.: Spatially-adaptive pixelwise networks for fast image translation. In: IEEE Conference on Computer Vision and Pattern Recognition, pp. 14882–14891 (2021)

32. Sitzmann, V., Martel, J., Bergman, A., Lindell, D., Wetzstein, G.: Implicit neural representations with periodic activation functions. In: Advances in Neural Information Processing Systems 33 (2020)

33. Sitzmann, V., Zollhoefer, M., Wetzstein, G.: Scene representation networks: Continuous 3D-structure-aware neural scene representations. Adv. Neural Inform. Process. Syst. **32**, 1121–1132 (2019)

34. Skorokhodov, I., Ignatyev, S., Elhoseiny, M.: Adversarial generation of continuous images. In: IEEE Conference on Computer Vision and Pattern Recognition, pp. 10753–10764 (2021)

35. Tancik, M., et al.: Learned initializations for optimizing coordinate-based neural representations. In: IEEE Conference on Computer Vision and Pattern Recognition, pp. 2846–2855 (2021)

36. Tancik, M., et al.: Fourier features let networks learn high frequency functions in low dimensional domains. In: Advances in Neural Information Processing Systems, vol. 33 (2020)

37. Ulyanov, D., Vedaldi, A., Lempitsky, V.: Deep image prior. In: IEEE Conference on Computer Vision and Pattern Recognition, pp. 9446–9454 (2018)

38. Wei, W., Yi, L., Xie, Q., Zhao, Q., Meng, D., Xu, Z.: Should we encode rain streaks in video as deterministic or stochastic? In: International Conference on Computer Vision, pp. 2516–2525 (2017)

39. Wronski, B., et al.: Handheld multi-frame super-resolution. ACM Trans. Graph. **38**(4), 1–18 (2019)

40. Xu, D., Chu, Y., Sun, Q.: Moiré pattern removal via attentive fractal network. In: IEEE Conference on Computer Vision and Pattern Recognition Workshops, pp. 472–473 (2020)

41. Xue, T., Rubinstein, M., Liu, C., Freeman, W.T.: A computational approach for obstruction-free photography. ACM Trans. Graph. **34**(4), 1–11 (2015)

42. Yan, Q., et al.: Attention-guided network for ghost-free high dynamic range imaging. In: IEEE Conference on Computer Vision and Pattern Recognition, pp. 1751–1760 (2019)

43. Yan, Q., et al.: Deep HDR imaging via a non-local network. IEEE Trans. Image Process. **29**, 4308–4322 (2020)

44. Yang, W., Liu, J., Feng, J.: Frame-consistent recurrent video deraining with dual-level flow. In: IEEE Conference on Computer Vision and Pattern Recognition, pp. 1661–1670 (2019)

45. Zhang, X., Ng, R., Chen, Q.: Single image reflection separation with perceptual losses. In: IEEE Conference on Computer Vision and Pattern Recognition (2018)

Bringing Rolling Shutter Images Alive with Dual Reversed Distortion

Zhihang Zhong[1,4], Mingdeng Cao[2], Xiao Sun[3], Zhirong Wu[3], Zhongyi Zhou[1], Yinqiang Zheng[1(✉)], Stephen Lin[3], and Imari Sato[1,4]

[1] The University of Tokyo, Tokyo, Japan
zhong@is.s.u-tokyo.ac.jp, yqzheng@ai.u-tokyo.ac.jp
[2] Tsinghua University, Beijing, China
[3] Microsoft Research Asia, Beijing, China
[4] National Institute of Informatics, Tokyo, Japan

Abstract. Rolling shutter (RS) distortion can be interpreted as the result of picking a row of pixels from instant global shutter (GS) frames over time during the exposure of the RS camera. This means that the information of each instant GS frame is partially, yet sequentially, embedded into the row-dependent distortion. Inspired by this fact, we address the challenging task of reversing this process, *i.e.*, extracting undistorted GS frames from images suffering from RS distortion. However, since RS distortion is coupled with other factors such as readout settings and the relative velocity of scene elements to the camera, models that only exploit the geometric correlation between temporally adjacent images suffer from poor generality in processing data with different readout settings and dynamic scenes with both camera motion and object motion. In this paper, instead of two consecutive frames, we propose to exploit a pair of images captured by dual RS cameras with reversed RS directions for this highly challenging task. Grounded on the symmetric and complementary nature of dual reversed distortion, we develop a novel end-to-end model, IFED, to generate dual optical flow sequence through iterative learning of the velocity field during the RS time. Extensive experimental results demonstrate that IFED is superior to naive cascade schemes, as well as the state-of-the-art which utilizes adjacent RS images. Most importantly, although it is trained on a synthetic dataset, IFED is shown to be effective at retrieving GS frame sequences from real-world RS distorted images of dynamic scenes. Code is available at https://github.com/zzh-tech/Dual-Reversed-RS.

Keywords: Rolling shutter correction · Frame interpolation · Dual reversed rolling shutter · Deep learning

Supplementary Information The online version contains supplementary material available at https://doi.org/10.1007/978-3-031-20071-7_14.

1 Introduction

Rolling shutter (RS) cameras are used in many devices such as smartphones and self-driving vision systems due to their low cost and high data transfer rate [19]. Compared to global shutter (GS) cameras, which capture the whole scene at a single instant, RS cameras scan the scene row-by-row to produce an image. This scanning mechanism may be viewed as sub-optimal because it leads to RS distortion, also known as the jello effect, in the presence of camera and/or object motion. However, we argue that RS photography encodes rich temporal information through its push broom scanning process. This property provides a critical cue for predicting a sequence of GS images, where distorted images are brought alive at a higher frame rate, which goes beyond the task of recovering a single snapshot as in the RS correction task [2,20,38], as shown in Fig. 1.

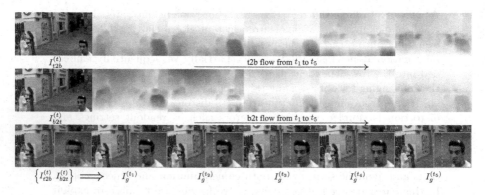

Fig. 1. Consecutive distortion-free frames extracted from a pair of images with reversed rolling shutter distortion. The 1st row presents the distorted image $I_{t2b}^{(t)}$ from top-to-bottom scanning at time t and the generated optical flows to the extracted frames. The 2nd row presents the distorted image $I_{b2t}^{(t)}$ from bottom-to-top scanning at the same time and its corresponding optical flows. The 3rd row presents the mixed input $\{I_{t2b}^{(t)} I_{b2t}^{(t)}\}$ and the extracted global shutter frames $\{I_g^{(t_i)}\}$ in chronological order.

Fan and Dai [7] proposed a Rolling Shutter temporal Super-Resolution (RSSR) pipeline for this joint interpolation and correction task. Under the assumption of constant velocity of camera motion and a static scene, RSSR combines a neural network and a manual conversion scheme to estimate undistortion flow for a specific time instance based on the temporal correlation of two adjacent frames (See Fig. 2e for a variant using three consecutive frames). However, even without object motion, the undistortion flow learned in this way tends to overfit the training dataset, because of the intrinsic uncertainty of this setup especially the readout time for each row. As proved in [5], the relative motion of two adjacent RS frames is characterized by the generalized epipolar geometry, which requires at least 17 point matches to determine camera motion.

Even worse, it suffers from non-trivial degeneracies, for example, when the camera translates along the baseline direction. In practice, both the relative motion velocity and readout setting will affect the magnitude of RS distortion, and the RSSR model and learning-based RS correction model [20] tend to fail on samples with different readout setups, especially on real-world data with complex camera and/or object motion (See details in Sect. 5 and the supplementary video).

To tackle this problem in dynamic scenes, modeling in the traditional way is particularly difficult, and the inconsistency in readout settings between training data and real test data is also challenging. Inspired by a novel dual-scanning setup [1] (bottom-to-top and top-to-bottom as shown in Fig. 2c) for rolling shutter correction, we argue that this dual setup is better constrained and bears more potential for dynamic scenes. Mathematically, it requires only 5 point matches to determine camera motion, which is much less than that required by the setup with two consecutive RS frames. The symmetric nature of the dual reversed distortion, *i.e.* the start exposure times of the same row in two images are symmetric about the center scan line, implicitly preserves the appearance of the latent undistorted images. Thus, this setup can also help to bypass the effects of inconsistent readout settings. Regarding the hardware complexity and cost, we note that synchronized dual RS camera systems can be easily realized on multi-camera smartphones [1,35] and self-driving cars. Interpolation of dual RS images into GS image sequences provides a promising solution to provide robust RS distortion-free high-fps GS images instead of directly employing expensive high-fps GS cameras. This can be further served as a high-quality image source for high-level tasks such as SfM [37], and 3D reconstruction [20].

Despite the strong geometric constraints arising from dual reversed distortion, it is still intractable to derive a video clip without prior knowledge from training data, as indicated in the large body of literature on video frame interpolation (VFI) from sparse GS frames (Fig. 2a). Therefore, grounded upon the symmetric feature of the dual-RS setup, we design a novel end-to-end **I**ntermediate **F**rames **E**xtractor using **D**ual RS images with reversed distortion (IFED) to realize joint correction and interpolation. Inspired by [20], we introduce the dual RS time cube to allow our model to learn the velocity cube iteratively, instead of regressing directly to an optical flow cube, so as to promote convergence. A mask cube and residual cube learned from an encoder-decoder network are used to merge the results of two reversely distorted images after backward warping. Taking our result in Fig. 1 as an example, the left image in the last row shows the mixed dual inputs $I_{t2b}^{(t)}$ (top-to-bottom scanning) and $I_{b2t}^{(t)}$ (bottom-to-top scanning) at time t. The rest of the row shows the extracted undistorted and smoothly moving frames by our method in chronological order.

To evaluate our method, we build a synthetic dataset with dual reversed distortion RS images and corresponding ground-truth sequences using high-fps videos from the publicly available dataset [22] and self-collected videos. Besides, we also construct a real-world test set with dual reversed distortion inputs captured by a custom-made co-axial imaging system. Although similar concept of dual-RS [1] (stereo) setup and time field [20] (2d) were proposed separately by previous works, we successfully combine and upgrade them to propose a simple yet robust architecture to solve the joint RS correction and interpolation (RS

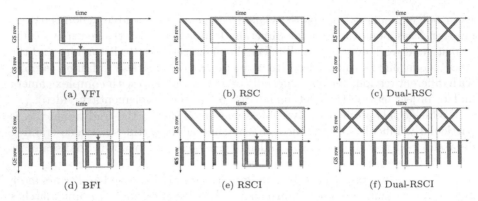

Fig. 2. Comparison of different tasks. The first row represents the input and the second row represents the output of each task. The x-axis and y-axis represent the time and the row location of the captured or generated image, respectively. (a) Video frame interpolation task (VFI). (b) RS correction task using neighboring frames (RSC). (c) RS correction task using dual frames with reversed RS distortion (Dual-RSC). (d) Blurry frame interpolation task (BFI). (e) Joint RS correction and interpolation task using neighboring frames (RSCI). (f) Joint RS correction and interpolation task using dual frames with reversed RS distortion (Dual-RSCI).

temporal super-resolution [7]) problem. The contributions of this work can be summarized as follows: 1) This is the first work that can extract video clips from distorted image in dynamic scenes. Besides, our solution can overcome the generalization problem caused by distinct readout settings. 2) We propose a novel end-to-end network architecture (IFED) that can iteratively estimate the accurate dual optical flow cube using pre-defined time cube and efficiently merges the symmetric information of the dual RS inputs for latent GS frame extraction. 3) Extensive experimental results demonstrate the superior accuracy and robustness of IFED against the state-of-the-art both on synthetic dataset and real-world data.

2   Related Works

In this section, we briefly review the closely related research on video frame interpolation and rolling shutter correction.

2.1   Video Frame Interpolation

Most existing solutions to VFI utilize optical flows to predict intermediate frames of captured images. These methods warp the input frames in a forward or backward manner based on the flow estimated by off-the-shelf networks, such as PWC-Net [32], FlowNet [6,12], and RAFT [33]. The warped frame is then refined by convolutional neural networks (CNNs) to obtain better visual quality. For example, SuperSlomo [13] uses a linear combination of two bi-directional flows from an off-the-shelf network for intermediate flow estimation and performs backward warping to infer latent frames. DAIN [3] further improves the intermediate flow estimation by employing a depth-aware flow projection layer. Recently, RIFE [11] achieves high-quality and real-time frame interpolation with an efficient flow network and a leakage distillation loss for direct flow estimation. In contrast to backward warping, Niklaus *et al.* [23] focuses on forward warping interpolation by proposing Softmax splatting to address the conflict of pixels mapped to the same target location. On the other hand, some recent works [4,17] achieve good results using flow-free methods. For example, CAIN [4] employs the PixelShuffle operation with channel attention to replace the flow computation module, while FLAVR [17] utilizes 3D space-time convolutions instead to improve efficiency and performance on non-linear motion and complex occlusions.

VFI includes a branch task, called blurry frame interpolation [14,15,28,31], which is analogous to our target problem. In this task, a blurry image is a temporal average of sharp frames at multiple instances. The goal is to deblur the video frame and conduct interpolation, as illustrated in Fig. 2d. Jin *et al.* [15] proposed a deep learning scheme to extract a video clip from a single motion-blurred image. For a better temporal smoothness in the output high-frame-rate video, Jin *et al.* [14] further proposed a two-step scheme consisting of a deblurring network and an interpolation network. Instead of using a pre-deblurring procedure, BIN [31] presents a multi-scale pyramid and recurrent architecture to reduce motion blur and upsample the frame rate simultaneously. Other works [18,25] utilize additional information from event cameras to bring a blurry frame alive with a high frame rate.

Existing VFI methods ignore the distortions in videos captured by RS cameras. In our work, instead of considering RS distortion as a nuisance, we leverage the information embedded in it to retrieve a sequence of GS frames.

2.2 Rolling Shutter Correction

RS correction itself is also a highly ill-posed and challenging problem. Classical approaches [2,9,24] work under some assumptions, such as a static scene and restricted camera motion (*e.g.*, pure rotations and in-plane translations). Consecutive frames are commonly used as inputs to estimate camera motion for distortion correction. Grundmann *et al.* [10] models the motion between two neighboring frames as a mixture of homography matrices. Zhuang *et al.* [37] develops a modified differential SfM algorithm for estimating the relative pose between consecutive RS frames, which in turn recovers a dense depth map for RS-aware warping image rectification. Vasu *et al.* [34] sequentially estimates both camera motion and the structure of the 3D scene that accounts for the RS distortion, and then infers the latent image by performing depth and occlusion-aware rectification. Rengarajan *et al.* [30] corrects the RS image according to the rule of "straight-lines-must-remain-straight". Purkait *et al.* [27] assumes that the captured 3D scene obeys the Manhattan world assumption and corrects the distortion by jointly aligning vanishing directions.

In recent years, learning-based approaches have been proposed to address RS correction in more complex cases. Rengarajan *et al.* [29] builds a CNN architecture with long rectangular convolutional kernels to estimate the camera motion

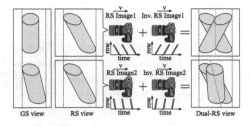

Fig. 3. RS correction ambiguity.

Table 1. Details of RS-GOPRO.

	Train	Validation	Test
Sequences	50	13	13
RS images	3554 (×2)	945 (×2)	966 (×2)
GS images	31986	8505	8694
Resolution	960 × 540		
Row exposure	1.0 ms		
Row readout	87 μs		

from a single image for RS correction. Zhuang *et al.* [38] uses two independent networks to predict a dense depth map and camera motion from a single RS image, implementing RS correction as post-processing. Liu *et al.* [20] proposes a DeepUnrollNet to realize end-to-end RS correction with a differentiable forward warping block. SUNet [8] utilizes a symmetric consistency constraint of two consecutive frames to achieve state-of-the-art performance.

The most relevant research to ours are [1,7] and the previously mentioned [20]. [7] proposed the first learning-based solution (RSSR) for latent GS video extraction from two consecutive RS images. On the other hand, [1] proposed a stereo dual-RS setup for RS correction task that infers an undistorted GS frame based on the geometric constraints among dual RS reversely distorted images. However, to the best of our knowledge, there are no methods able to achieve RS temporal super-resolution in dynamic scenes. Geometric constraints of [7] and [1] are limited to static scenes. Besides, current learning-based methods including [7,20] suffer from the inherent ambiguity of consecutive setup. We discover the merit of dual-RS to overcome distinct readout setups, which is not mentioned in [1], and we upgrade the velocity field from [20] to first time realize RS temporal SR in dynamic scenes.

3 Joint RS Correction and Interpolation

In this section, we first formulate the joint RS correction and interpolation problem. Then, we introduce the datasets for validation and comparison.

3.1 Problem Formulation

An RS camera encodes temporal visual information in an image similar to a high-frame-rate GS camera that samples the scene rapidly but only takes one row of the scene each time. In our case, we do not consider the presence of blur. Formally, given an RS video ($\{I_r^{(t)}\}$) and a GS video ($\{I_g^{(t)}\}$), we can express each row (i) in an RS image ($I_r^{(t)}[i]$) in terms of its corresponding GS image ($I_g^{(t)}[i]$) through the following equation:

$$I_r^{(t)}[i] = I_g^{(t+(i-M/2)t_r)}[i], \tag{1}$$

where t_r denotes the readout time for each RS row; M denotes the total number of rows in the image; $t + (i - M/2)t_r$ is the time instant of scanning the ith row; and $I_g^{(t+(i-M/2)t_r)}[i]$ is the portion of the GS image that will appear in the RS image. Note that we define the time t of an RS image $I_r^{(t)}$ as the midpoint of its exposure period (i.e., each RS image is captured from t_s to t_e, where $t_s = t - t_r M/2$ and $t_e = t + t_r M/2$).

The objective of the joint RS correction and interpolation is to extract a sequence of undistorted GS images ($\left\{ I_g^{(t)}, t \in [t_s, t_e] \right\}$) from the RS images. Directly feeding an RS image ($I_r^{(t)}$) into a network $\mathcal{F}\left(I_r^{(t)}; \Theta\right)$, parameterized by the weight Θ, to extract a sequence of GS images is infeasible without strong restrictions such as static scenes and known camera motions. A straightforward approach is to use temporal constraints from neighboring frames, such that the input is a concatenation of neighboring frames as $I_{inp}^{(t)} = \left\{ I_r^{(t-1/f)}, I_r^{(t)} \right\}$, where f denotes the video frame rate. This is the case of RSSR [7], which can easily overfit the readout setting of the training data. Theoretically, the generic RSC problem cannot be solved by using only consecutive frames. We show a common ambiguity of consecutive frames setup, using a toy example in Fig. 3. Suppose there are two similar cylinders, one of them is tilted, as shown in GS view. Then, two RS cameras moving horizontally at the same speed v but with different readout time setups can produce the same RS view, i.e., a short readout time RS camera for the tilted cylinder and a long readout time RS camera for the vertical cylinder. Therefore, the models based on consecutive frames are biased to the training dataset. Although these models can correct RS images, they do not know how much correction is correct facing data beyond the dataset. Instead, we introduce another constraint setting that utilizes intra-frame spatial constraints of dual images taken simultaneously but with reversed distortion captured by top-to-bottom (t2b) and bottom-to-top (b2t) scanning. Formally, the optimization process is described as:

$$\widehat{\Theta} = \arg\min_{\Theta} \left| \left\{ I_g^{(t)}, t \in [t_s, t_e] \right\} - \mathcal{F}\left(I_{t2b}^{(t)}, I_{b2t}^{(t)}; \Theta \right) \right|, \tag{2}$$

where $\widehat{\Theta}$ are optimized parameters for the joint task. $I_{t2b}^{(t)}$ denotes the t2b RS frame at time t, while $I_{b2t}^{(t)}$ denotes the b2t RS frame at the same time. We find that the dual-RS setup can avoid ambiguity because the correct correction pose can be estimated based on the symmetry, as shown in the dual-RS view.

3.2   Evaluation Datasets

Synthetic Dataset. For the pure RS correction task, the Fastec-RS [20] dataset uses a camera mounted on a ground vehicle to capture high-fps videos with only horizontal motion. Then, RS images are synthesized by sequentially copying a row of pixels from consecutive high-fps GS frames. We synthesized a dataset for the joint RS correction and interpolation task in a similar way, but with more motion patterns and multiple ground truths for one input. High-fps GS cameras with sufficient frame rate to synthesize RS-GS pairs are expensive and cumbersome to operate. Thus, we chose a GoPro (a specialized sports camera) as a trade-off. Empirically, the GoPro's tiny RS effect causes negligible impact on the learning process of our task. Specifically, we utilize the high-fps (240 fps) videos from the publicly available GOPRO [22] dataset and self-collected videos using a GoPro HERO9 to synthesize the dataset, which we refer to as RS-GOPRO. We first interpolated the original GS videos to 15 360 fps by using an off-the-shelf VFI method (RIFE [11]), and then followed the pipeline of [20] to synthesize RS videos. RS-GOPRO includes more complex urban scenes (*e.q.*, streets and building interiors) and more motion patterns, including object-only motion, camera-only motion, and joint motion. We created train/validation/test sets (50, 13, and 13 sequences) by randomly splitting the videos while avoiding images of a video from being assigned into different sets. Regarding input and target pairs, there are two kinds of input RS images which have reversed distortion, and nine consecutive GS frames are taken as ground truth for the extracted frame sequence. The image resolution is 960×540. The readout time for each row is fixed as $87\,\mu s$. Please see the details of RS-GOPRO in Table 1.

Real-World Test Set. Inspired by [36] and [1], we built a dual-RS image acquisition system using a beam-splitter and two RS cameras that are upside down from each other to collect real-world data for validation. The readout setting of the proposed dual-RS system can be changed by replacing the type of RS camera (*e.g.*, FL3-U3-13S2C, BFS-U3-63S4C). Please see details of our acquisition system in supplementary materials. We collect samples of various motion patterns, such as camera-only motion, object-only motion like moving cars and a rotating fan, and mixed motion. Each sample includes two RS distorted images with reversed distortion but without a corresponding ground truth sequence.

4   Methodology

We present the proposed architecture and implementation details in this section.

4.1   Pipeline of IFED

The proposed IFED model utilizes an architecture inherited from existing successful VFI methods [11,13], including a branch to estimate the optical flow for backward warping and an encoder-decoder branch to refine the output (see Fig. 4). However, directly estimating optical flow from the latent GS image to the input RS image is challenging due to the intra-frame temporal inconsistency of an RS image. The optical flow from GS to RS is dependent on two variables: the time difference and relative velocity of motion. As we already know the scanning mechanism of the RS camera, we are able to obtain the time difference between the input RS image and the target GS image. Thus, we propose a dual time cube as an RS prior to decouple this problem, and let the model regress the dual velocity cube to indirectly estimate the corresponding dual optical flow cube.

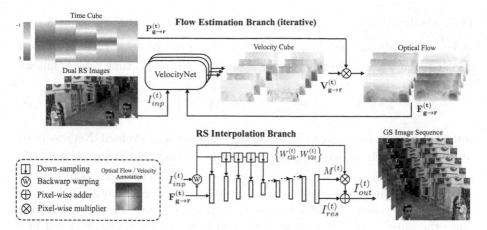

Fig. 4. Network architecture of IFED. Note that the color annotation of the dual RS time cube is different from optical flow and velocity. It represents the relative time gap between each row and the time instance of the latent GS image. This architecture first utilizes dual RS along with time cube to iteratively estimate velocity cube for better optical flow learning. Then, the warped dual frames are combined together as complementary information through the mask and residual cube learned from the encoder-decoder network to make inferences for the underlying GS image sequences.

The number of time instances per dual cube is twice the number of extracted GS frames. These time instances are sampled uniformly from the entire RS exposure time (*e.g.*, Fig. 4 shows the extraction of 5 GS frames). There is an implicit assumption that the velocity field of each row of the extracted frame is constant. Considering the short exposure time of the actual RS image and the short percentage of time corresponding to the extracted GS frames, this assumption can be basically satisfied in most scenarios. Besides, the dual warped features can be further adjusted and merged by the interpolation branch, which enables our method to handle the challenging cases of the spinning fans and wheels with row-wise non-uniform velocity.

Specifically, assuming our target latent sequence has N images, the target optical flow cube for one RS image can be expressed as follows:

$$\mathbf{F}_{\mathbf{g} \to \mathbf{r}}^{(\mathbf{t})} = \left\{ F_{g \to r}^{(t_n)} \right\}, n \in \{1, \cdots, N\}, \tag{3}$$

where $t_n = t - t_r M \left(\frac{1}{2} - \frac{n}{N} \right)$ and $F_{g \to r}^{(t_n)}$ denotes the optical flow from the GS image at time t_n to the distorted RS input $I_r^{(t)}$. Regarding the time cube, the values at row m of the time map $P_{g \to r}^{(t)}$ are given by:

$$P_{g \to r}^{(t_n)}[m] = \frac{m - 1}{M - 1} - \frac{n - 1}{N - 1}, m \in [1..M], n \in [1..N]. \tag{4}$$

Then, the RS time cube $\mathbf{P}_{\mathbf{g}\to\mathbf{r}}^{(t)} = \left\{ P_{g\to r}^{(t_n)} \right\}$ can be expressed in the same format as $\mathbf{F}_{\mathbf{g}\to\mathbf{r}}^{(t)}$. To obtain the optical flow cube, we need the network to generate a velocity cube $\mathbf{V}_{\mathbf{g}\to\mathbf{r}}^{(t)} = \left\{ V_{g\to r}^{(t_n)} \right\}$ and multiply it with the RS time cube as follows:

$$\left\{ F_{g\to r}^{(t_n)} \right\} = \left\{ P_{g\to r}^{(t_n)} V_{g\to r}^{(t_n)} \right\}. \tag{5}$$

Our flow branch uses several independent subnetworks (VelocityNet) to iteratively take dual RS images $I_{inp}^{(t)}$ and previously estimated dual optical flow cube as inputs for dual velocity cube $\mathbf{V}_{\mathbf{g}\to\mathbf{t2b}}^{(t)}$ estimation. The input scale (resolution) of the subnetwork are scaled sequentially in an iterative order following a coarse-to-fine manner (adjusted by bilinear interpolation). These sub-networks share the same structure, starting with a warping of the inputs, followed by a series of 2d convolutional layers. The initial scale velocity cube estimation is realized without the estimated optical flow cube. This branch is shown in the upper part of Fig. 4.

After obtaining the optical flow cube, we can generate a series of warped features and the warped dual RS images $W^{(t)} = \left\{ W_{b2t}^{(t)}, W_{t2b}^{(t)} \right\}$ as multi-scale inputs to an encoder-encoder network with skip connections for merging results. Specifically, a residual cube $I_{res}^{(t)}$ and a dual mask cube $M^{(t)}$ are generated to produce the final frame sequence (See the bottom part of Fig. 4) as follows:

$$I_{out}^{(t)} = I_{res}^{(t)} + M^{(t)} W_{t2b}^{(t)} + \left(1 - M^{(t)}\right) W_{b2t}^{(t)}. \tag{6}$$

4.2 Implementation Details

We implement the method using PyTorch [26]. There are three 4 sub-networks in the flow network branch for velocity cube learning, each with eight 3×3 convolutional layers. The inputs scale is gradually adjusted from $1/8$ to original size as the channel size is reduced. The network is trained in 500 epochs. The batch size and learning rate are equal to 8 and 1×10^{-4} separately. AdamW [21] is used to optimize the weights with a cosine annealing scheduler. The learning rate is gradually reduced to 1×10^{-8} throughout the whole process. 256×256 cropping is applied for both dual RS images and the time cube. Because the relative time difference between the same row of adjacent crops is constant, training with cropping does not affect the full frame inference. More details of the sub-networks and cropping are in supplementary materials. The loss function to train the model is given by:

$$\mathcal{L} = \mathcal{L}_{char} + \lambda_p \mathcal{L}_{perc} + \lambda_v \mathcal{L}_{var}, \tag{7}$$

where $\mathcal{L}_{char}$ and $\mathcal{L}_{perc}$ denote the Charbonnier loss and perceptual loss [16] for the extracted frame sequence; while $\mathcal{L}_{var}$ denotes the total variation loss for the estimated flows, to smooth the warping. λ_p and λ_v are both set to 0.1.

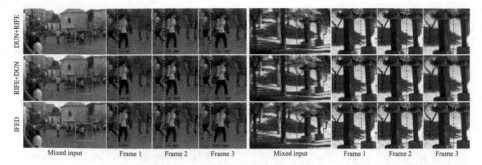

Fig. 5. Visual results on RS-GOPRO. Zoom-in results are shown chronologically on the right side of the mixed input. IFED restores the smooth moving sequence with clearer details while cascaded scheme introduced unclear artifacts.

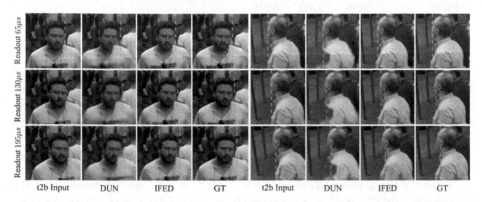

Fig. 6. Generalization ability on distinct readout time settings. Both our IFED and DUN [20] are trained on fixed readout setting, while IFED can successfully generalize to different readout settings from 65 μs to 195 μs.

5   Experimental Results

In this section, we first present comparison experiments on the synthesized dataset RS-GOPRO in Sect. 5.1. Next, we show the generality of our method on real-world data in Sect. 5.2. Finally, we present the ablation study in Sect. 5.3. Please see more additional experimental results in our appendix.

5.1   Results on Synthetic Dataset

We implemented cascade schemes with RSC model DUN (DeepUnrollNet [20]) and a VFI model RIFE [11] using adjacent frames as inputs. Both orderings were examined, *i.e.*, DUN+RIFE and RIFE+DUN ((b)+(a) and (a)+(b) in Fig. 2). We retrained DUN and RIFE on our dataset for extracting 1, 3, 5, and 9 frames for fair comparison. Quantitative results are shown in Table 2. Over the different extracted frame settings, IFED shows superiority over the cascade schemes.

Table 2. Quantitative results on RS-GOPRO. f# denotes # of frames extracted from the input RS images.

	PSNR ↑	SSIM ↑	LPIPS ↓
DUN (f1)	26.37	0.836	0.058
DUN + RIFE (f3)	25.38	0.788	0.159
DUN + RIFE (f5)	25.45	0.798	0.111
DUN + RIFE (f9)	25.31	0.795	0.102
RIFE + DUN (f3)	23.05	0.719	0.124
RIFE + DUN (f5)	22.28	0.692	0.118
RIFE + DUN (f9)	21.88	0.677	0.113
IFED (f1)	32.07	0.934	0.028
IFED (f3)	28.48	0.872	0.058
IFED (f5)	29.79	0.897	0.049
IFED (f9)	30.34	0.910	0.046

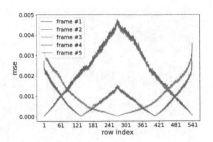

Fig. 7. Image mean squared errors based on row number in the case of IFED (f5).

The average performance of IFED is worst when the number of extracted frames is 3. Our interpretation is that the task degrades to a relatively easy RS correction task when the number of extracted frames is 1, while the greater continuity between extracted frames is better for convergence when the number of extracted frames is greater than 3. Qualitative results are shown in Fig. 5. With the cascade schemes, the details are blurry, while ours are much clearer.

To verify the generalization on distinct readout settings, we synthesized RS images with distinct readout settings such as 65 μs, 130 μs, and 195 μs. As illustrated in Fig. 6, both our IFED and DUN [20] are trained on fixed readout setting, while our IFED can successfully generalize to different readout settings without introducing artifacts and undesired distortions.

Besides, an row-wise image error analysis (f5) is shown in Fig. 7 in terms of MSE. It indicates that the performance of a given row index depends on the minimum time (the smaller the better) between the row of that extracted GS frame and the corresponding rows of dual RS frames.

5.2   Results on Real-World Data

We also compare our method to the only existing work on extracting a GS sequence from RS images RSSR [7] and the only work for dual reversed RS image correction [1]. Since the source codes of these two works are not publicly available, we sent our real-world samples from different type of cameras to the authors for testing. The comparison results with RSSR [7] are shown in Fig. 8. RSSR cannot generalize to either the case of camera-only motion (the left example) or the case of object-only motion (the right example), while IFED is robust to different motion patterns. The visual results of IFED and [1] are illustrated in Fig. 9. It demonstrates the ability of IFED to go beyond [1] by being able to

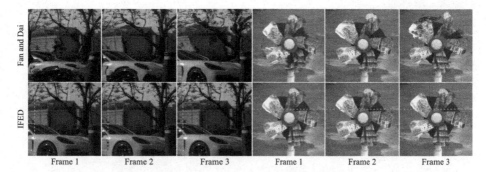

Fig. 8. Comparison with Fan and Dai [7] on real data. Our results (the 2nd row) are significantly better than Fan and Dai's for objects under both horizontal and rotational movements. Please refer to our supplementary videos.

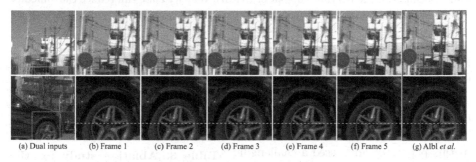

Fig. 9. Comparison with Albl *et al.* [1] on real data. Both our method and Albl *et al.*'s use the same dual inputs (the 1st column). Our method brings the dual input alive by creating a sequence of images (Frame 1–5), compared to one static image from Albl *et al.*'s.

extract a sequence of GS images in dynamic scenes, rather than just a single GS image in static scenes, from a dual reversed RS image. More results of IFED on the real dataset can be found in the supplementary materials.

5.3   Ablation Study

Table 3 shows the results of our ablation study on the RS time cube prior. It shows that IFED without the prior generally leads to worse results, and the difference increases with a larger number of frames. Note that when the number of extracted frames equals 1, IFED *w/o pr* can achieve better performance. The reason is that the task simply becomes the RSC task in this case, and the model can directly learn a precise flow for the middle time instance using dual RS inputs. When the number of extracted frames increases, the model needs the time cube to serve as an "anchor" for each time instance to improve the temporal consistency of the learned flow. We show visualizations of the flow and velocity cube with RS time cube prior

246 Z. Zhong et al.

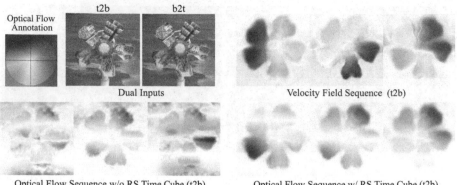

Fig. 10. Visualization of optical flow and velocity cube. Equally with dual RS frames as input, using RS time cube prior to learn velocity cube can reduce the difficulty of optical flow learning and ultimately improve the flow quality.

and the flow cube without the prior in Fig. 10. The flow sequence estimated without the RS time cube prior exhibits poor quality and consistency in time.

6 Conclusions

In this paper, we addressed a challenging task of restoring consecutive distortion-free frames from RS distorted images in dynamic scenes. We designed an end-to-end deep neural network IFED for the dual-RS setup, which has the advantages of being able to model dynamic scenes and not being affected by distinct readout times. The proposed dual RS time cube for velocity cube learning improves performance by avoiding direct flow estimation from the GS image to the RS image.

Table 3. Ablation study for the prior. *w/o pr* denotes "without RS time cube prior".

	PSNR ↑	SSIM ↑	LPIPS ↓
	Refer to IFED (f#)		
IFED *w/o pr* (f1)	+0.50	+0.006	−0.003
IFED *w/o pr* (f3)	−0.40	−0.008	0.000
IFED *w/o pr* (f5)	−0.50	−0.009	+0.001
IFED *w/o pr* (f9)	−0.70	−0.012	+0.001

Compared to the cascade scheme with existing VFI and RSC models as well as RSSR which takes temporally adjacent frames as inputs to do the same task, our IFED shows more impressive accuracy and robustness for both synthetic data and real-world data with different motion patterns.

Acknowledgement. This work was supported by D-CORE Grant from Microsoft Research Asia, JSPS KAKENHI Grant Numbers 22H00529, and 20H05951, and JST, the establishment of university fellowships towards the creation of science technology innovation, Grant Number JPMJFS2108.

References

1. Albl, C., Kukelova, Z., Larsson, V., Polic, M., Pajdla, T., Schindler, K.: From two rolling shutters to one global shutter. In: Proceedings of the IEEE/CVF Conference on Computer Vision and Pattern Recognition, pp. 2505–2513 (2020)
2. Baker, S., Bennett, E., Kang, S.B., Szeliski, R.: Removing rolling shutter wobble. In: 2010 IEEE Computer Society Conference on Computer Vision and Pattern Recognition, pp. 2392–2399. IEEE (2010)
3. Bao, W., Lai, W.S., Ma, C., Zhang, X., Gao, Z., Yang, M.H.: Depth-aware video frame interpolation. In: Proceedings of the IEEE/CVF Conference on Computer Vision and Pattern Recognition, pp. 3703–3712 (2019)
4. Choi, M., Kim, H., Han, B., Xu, N., Lee, K.M.: Channel attention is all you need for video frame interpolation. In: Proceedings of the AAAI Conference on Artificial Intelligence, vol. 34, pp. 10663–10671 (2020)
5. Dai, Y., Li, H., Kneip, L.: Rolling shutter camera relative pose: generalized epipolar geometry. In: Proceedings of the IEEE Conference on Computer Vision and Pattern Recognition, pp. 4132–4140 (2016)
6. Dosovitskiy, A., et al.: Flownet: learning optical flow with convolutional networks. In: Proceedings of the IEEE International Conference on Computer Vision, pp. 2758–2766 (2015)
7. Fan, B., Dai, Y.: Inverting a rolling shutter camera: bring rolling shutter images to high framerate global shutter video. In: Proceedings of the IEEE/CVF International Conference on Computer Vision, pp. 4228–4237 (2021)
8. Fan, B., Dai, Y., He, M.: Sunet: symmetric undistortion network for rolling shutter correction. In: Proceedings of the IEEE/CVF International Conference on Computer Vision, pp. 4541–4550 (2021)
9. Forssén, P.E., Ringaby, E.: Rectifying rolling shutter video from hand-held devices. In: 2010 IEEE Computer Society Conference on Computer Vision and Pattern Recognition, pp. 507–514. IEEE (2010)
10. Grundmann, M., Kwatra, V., Castro, D., Essa, I.: Calibration-free rolling shutter removal. In: 2012 IEEE International Conference on Computational Photography (ICCP), pp. 1–8. IEEE (2012)
11. Huang, Z., Zhang, T., Heng, W., Shi, B., Zhou, S.: Rife: real-time intermediate flow estimation for video frame interpolation. arXiv preprint arXiv:2011.06294 (2020)
12. Ilg, E., Mayer, N., Saikia, T., Keuper, M., Dosovitskiy, A., Brox, T.: Flownet 2.0: evolution of optical flow estimation with deep networks. In: Proceedings of the IEEE Conference on Computer Vision and Pattern Recognition, pp. 2462–2470 (2017)
13. Jiang, H., Sun, D., Jampani, V., Yang, M.H., Learned-Miller, E., Kautz, J.: Super slomo: high quality estimation of multiple intermediate frames for video interpolation. In: Proceedings of the IEEE Conference on Computer Vision and Pattern Recognition, pp. 9000–9008 (2018)
14. Jin, M., Hu, Z., Favaro, P.: Learning to extract flawless slow motion from blurry videos. In: Proceedings of the IEEE/CVF Conference on Computer Vision and Pattern Recognition, pp. 8112–8121 (2019)
15. Jin, M., Meishvili, G., Favaro, P.: Learning to extract a video sequence from a single motion-blurred image. In: Proceedings of the IEEE Conference on Computer Vision and Pattern Recognition, pp. 6334–6342 (2018)

16. Johnson, J., Alahi, A., Fei-Fei, L.: Perceptual losses for real-time style transfer and super-resolution. In: Leibe, B., Matas, J., Sebe, N., Welling, M. (eds.) ECCV 2016. LNCS, vol. 9906, pp. 694–711. Springer, Cham (2016). https://doi.org/10.1007/978-3-319-46475-6_43
17. Kalluri, T., Pathak, D., Chandraker, M., Tran, D.: Flavr: flow-agnostic video representations for fast frame interpolation. arXiv preprint arXiv:2012.08512 (2020)
18. Lin, S., et al.: Learning event-driven video deblurring and interpolation. In: European Conference on Computer Vision, vol. 3 (2020)
19. Litwiller, D.: CCD vs. CMOS. Photonics Spectra 35(1), 154–158 (2001)
20. Liu, P., Cui, Z., Larsson, V., Pollefeys, M.: Deep shutter unrolling network. In: Proceedings of the IEEE/CVF Conference on Computer Vision and Pattern Recognition, pp. 5941–5949 (2020)
21. Loshchilov, I., Hutter, F.: Decoupled weight decay regularization. arXiv preprint arXiv:1711.05101 (2017)
22. Nah, S., Hyun Kim, T., Mu Lee, K.: Deep multi-scale convolutional neural network for dynamic scene deblurring. In: Proceedings of the IEEE Conference on Computer Vision and Pattern Recognition, pp. 3883–3891 (2017)
23. Niklaus, S., Liu, F.: Softmax splatting for video frame interpolation. In: Proceedings of the IEEE/CVF Conference on Computer Vision and Pattern Recognition, pp. 5437–5446 (2020)
24. Oth, L., Furgale, P., Kneip, L., Siegwart, R.: Rolling shutter camera calibration. In: Proceedings of the IEEE Conference on Computer Vision and Pattern Recognition, pp. 1360–1367 (2013)
25. Pan, L., Scheerlinck, C., Yu, X., Hartley, R., Liu, M., Dai, Y.: Bringing a blurry frame alive at high frame-rate with an event camera. In: Proceedings of the IEEE/CVF Conference on Computer Vision and Pattern Recognition, pp. 6820–6829 (2019)
26. Paszke, A., et al.: Pytorch: an imperative style, high-performance deep learning library. arXiv preprint arXiv:1912.01703 (2019)
27. Purkait, P., Zach, C., Leonardis, A.: Rolling shutter correction in manhattan world. In: Proceedings of the IEEE International Conference on Computer Vision, pp. 882–890 (2017)
28. Purohit, K., Shah, A., Rajagopalan, A.: Bringing alive blurred moments. In: Proceedings of the IEEE/CVF Conference on Computer Vision and Pattern Recognition, pp. 6830–6839 (2019)
29. Rengarajan, V., Balaji, Y., Rajagopalan, A.: Unrolling the shutter: CNN to correct motion distortions. In: Proceedings of the IEEE Conference on Computer Vision and Pattern Recognition, pp. 2291–2299 (2017)
30. Rengarajan, V., Rajagopalan, A.N., Aravind, R.: From bows to arrows: rolling shutter rectification of urban scenes. In: Proceedings of the IEEE Conference on Computer Vision and Pattern Recognition, pp. 2773–2781 (2016)
31. Shen, W., Bao, W., Zhai, G., Chen, L., Min, X., Gao, Z.: Blurry video frame interpolation. In: Proceedings of the IEEE/CVF Conference on Computer Vision and Pattern Recognition, pp. 5114–5123 (2020)
32. Sun, D., Yang, X., Liu, M.Y., Kautz, J.: PWC-Net: CNNs for optical flow using pyramid, warping, and cost volume. In: Proceedings of the IEEE Conference on Computer Vision and Pattern Recognition, pp. 8934–8943 (2018)
33. Teed, Z., Deng, J.: RAFT: recurrent all-pairs field transforms for optical flow. In: Vedaldi, A., Bischof, H., Brox, T., Frahm, J.-M. (eds.) ECCV 2020. LNCS, vol. 12347, pp. 402–419. Springer, Cham (2020). https://doi.org/10.1007/978-3-030-58536-5_24

34. Vasu, S., Rajagopalan, A., et al.: Occlusion-aware rolling shutter rectification of 3D scenes. In: Proceedings of the IEEE Conference on Computer Vision and Pattern Recognition, pp. 636–645 (2018)
35. Yang, X., Xiang, W., Zeng, H., Zhang, L.: Real-world video super-resolution: a benchmark dataset and a decomposition based learning scheme. In: Proceedings of the IEEE/CVF International Conference on Computer Vision, pp. 4781–4790 (2021)
36. Zhong, Z., Gao, Y., Zheng, Y., Zheng, B.: Efficient spatio-temporal recurrent neural network for video deblurring. In: Vedaldi, A., Bischof, H., Brox, T., Frahm, J.-M. (eds.) ECCV 2020. LNCS, vol. 12351, pp. 191–207. Springer, Cham (2020). https://doi.org/10.1007/978-3-030-58539-6_12
37. Zhuang, B., Cheong, L.F., Hee Lee, G.: Rolling-shutter-aware differential SFM and image rectification. In: Proceedings of the IEEE International Conference on Computer Vision, pp. 948–956 (2017)
38. Zhuang, B., Tran, Q.H., Ji, P., Cheong, L.F., Chandraker, M.: Learning structure-and-motion-aware rolling shutter correction. In: Proceedings of the IEEE/CVF Conference on Computer Vision and Pattern Recognition, pp. 4551–4560 (2019)

FILM: Frame Interpolation for Large Motion

Fitsum Reda[1]([✉]), Janne Kontkanen[1], Eric Tabellion[1], Deqing Sun[1],
Caroline Pantofaru[1], and Brian Curless[1,2]

[1] Google Research, Mountain View, USA
{fitsumreda,jkontkanen,etabellion,deqingsun,cpantofaru}@google.com
[2] University of Washington, Seattle, USA

Abstract. We present a frame interpolation algorithm that synthesizes
an engaging slow-motion video from near-duplicate photos which often
exhibit large scene motion. Near-duplicates interpolation is an interesting
new application, but large motion poses challenges to existing methods.
To address this issue, we adapt a feature extractor that shares weights
across the scales, and present a "scale-agnostic" motion estimator. It
relies on the intuition that large motion at finer scales should be similar
to small motion at coarser scales, which boosts the number of available
pixels for large motion supervision. To inpaint wide disocclusions caused
by large motion and synthesize crisp frames, we propose to optimize
our network with the Gram matrix loss that measures the correlation
difference between features. To simplify the training process, we further
propose a unified single-network approach that removes the reliance on
additional optical-flow or depth network and is trainable from frame
triplets alone. Our approach outperforms state-of-the-art methods on
the Xiph large motion benchmark while performing favorably on Vimeo-
90K, Middlebury and UCF101. Source codes and pre-trained models are
available at https://film-net.github.io.

Keywords: Video synthesis · Interpolation · Optical flow · Feature
pyramid

1 Introduction

Frame interpolation – synthesizing intermediate images between a pair of input
frames – is an important problem with increasing reach. It is often used for
temporal up-sampling to increase refresh rate or create slow-motion videos.

Recently, a new use case has emerged. Digital photography, especially with
the advent of smartphones, has made it effortless to take several pictures within
a few seconds, and people naturally do so often in their quest for just the right

Supplementary Information The online version contains supplementary material
available at https://doi.org/10.1007/978-3-031-20071-7_15.

photo that captures the moment. These "near duplicates" create an exciting opportunity: interpolating between them can lead to surprisingly engaging videos that reveal scene (and some camera) motion, often delivering an even more pleasing sense of the moment than any one of the original photos.

Unlike video, however, the temporal spacing between near duplicates can be a second or more, with commensurately large scene motion, posing a major challenge for existing interpolation methods. Frame interpolation between consecutive video frames, which often exhibit small motion, has been studied extensively, and recent methods [3,8,18,23] show impressive results for this scenario. However, little attention has been given to interpolation for large scene motion, commonly present in near duplicates. The work of [28] attempted to tackle the large motion problem by training on an extreme motion dataset, but its effectiveness is limited when tested on small motion [23].

Fig. 1. Near-duplicate photos interpolation with ABME [23], showing large artifacts, and our FILM, showing improvements.

In this work, we instead propose a network that generalizes well to both small and large motion. Specifically, we adapt a multi-scale feature extractor from [31] that shares weights across the scales and present a "scale-agnostic" bidirectional motion estimation module. Our approach relies on the intuition that large motion at finer scales should be similar to small motion at coarser scales, thus increasing the number of pixels (as finer scale is higher resolution) available for large motion supervision. We found this approach to be surprisingly effective in handling large motion by simply training on regular frames (see Fig. 1).

We also observed that, while the state-of-the-art methods score well on benchmarks [2,16,34], the interpolated frames often appear blurry, especially in large disoccluded regions that arise from large motions. Here, we propose to optimize our models with the Gram matrix loss, which matches the *auto-correlation* of the high-level VGG features, and significantly improves the realism and sharpness of frames (see Fig. 4b).

Another drawback of recent interpolation methods [3,18,23,35] is training complexity, because they typically rely on scarce data to pre-train additional optical flow, depth, or other prior networks. Such data scarcity is even more critical for large motion. The DAIN approach [3], for example, incorporates a depth network, and the works in [18,23] use additional networks to estimate per-pixel motion. To simplify the training process, another contribution of this work is a unified architecture for frame interpolation, which is trainable from regular frame triplets alone.

In summary, the main contributions of our work are:

- We expand the scope of frame interpolation to a novel near-duplicate photos interpolation application, and open a new space for the community to tackle.
- We adapt a multi-scale feature extractor that shares weights, and propose a scale-agnostic bi-directional motion estimator to handle both small and large motion well, using regular training frames.
- We adopt a Gram matrix-based loss function to inpaint large disocclusions caused by large scene motion, leading to crisp and pleasing frames.
- We propose a unified, single-stage architecture, to simplify the training process and remove the reliance on additional optical flow or depth networks.

2   Related Work

Various CNN-based frame interpolation methods [3,6,8,11,13,18,20,22,23,32, 35] [15,26] have been proposed to up-scale frame rate of videos. To our knowledge, no prior work exists on near-duplicate photos interpolation. We, however, summarize frame interpolation methods related to our approach.

Large Motion. Handling large motion is an important yet under-explored topic in frame interpolation. The work in [28] handles large motion by training on 4K sequences with extreme motion. While this is a viable approach, it does not generalize well on regular footage as discussed in [23]. Similarly, other approaches [18,23] perform poorly when the test motion range deviates from the training motion range. We adapt a multi-scale shared feature extractor [9,10,31], and present a "scale-agnostic" motion estimation module, which allows us to learn large and small motion with equal priority, and show favorable generalization ability in various benchmarks.

Image Quality. One of our key contributions is high quality frame synthesis, especially in large disoccluded regions caused by large motion. Prior work [19–21] improves image quality by learning a per-pixel kernel instead of an offset vector, which is then convolved with the inputs. While effective at improving quality, they cannot handle large motion well. Other approaches optimize models with perceptual losses [18,20]. Some consider an adversarial loss [1], albeit with a complex training process. Our work proposes to adopt the Gram matrix loss [7], which builds up on the perceptual loss and yields high quality and pleasing frames.

Single-Stage Networks. The first CNN-based supervised frame interpolators propose UNet-like networks, trained from inputs and target frames [11,16]. Recent work [3] introduces a depth network to handle occlusions, [18,23] incorporate motion estimation modules, and [22,30,35] rely on pre-trained HED [33] features. While impressive results are achieved, multiple networks can make training processes complex. It may also need scarce data to pre-train the prior networks. Pre-training datasets, e.g. optical flows, are even more scarce for large motion. Our work introduces a single unified network, trainable from regular frame triples alone, without additional priors, and achieves state-of-the-art results.

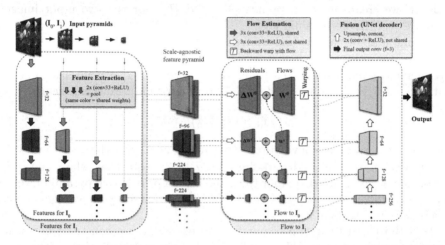

Fig. 2. FILM architecture. Our flow estimation module computes "scale agnostic" bi-directional flows based on the feature pyramids, extracted by shared weights. (Color figure online)

3 Method

Given two input images $(\mathbf{I}_0, \mathbf{I}_1)$, with large in-between motion, we synthesize a mid-image $\hat{\mathbf{I}}_t$, with time $t \in (0, 1)$, as:

$$\hat{\mathbf{I}}_t = \mathcal{M}(\mathbf{I}_0, \mathbf{I}_1), \tag{1}$$

where $\mathcal{M}$ is our FILM network trained with a ground-truth $\mathbf{I}_t$. During training, we supervise at $t = 0.5$ and we predict more in-between images by recursively invoking FILM.

A common approach to handle large motion is to employ feature pyramids, which increases receptive fields. However, a standard pyramid learning has two difficulties: 1) small fast-moving objects disappear at coarse levels, and 2) the number of pixels is drastically smaller at coarse levels (i), $(\frac{H}{2^i} \times \frac{W}{2^i})$, which means there are fewer pixels to provide large motion supervision. To overcome these challenges, we propose to share the convolution weights across the scales. Based on the intuition that large motion at finer scales should be the same as small motion at coarser scales, sharing weights allows us to boost the number of pixels available for large motion supervision.

FILM has three main stages: Shared feature extraction, scale-agnostic motion estimation, and a fusion stage that outputs the resulting color image. Figure 2 shows an overview of FILM.

Feature Extraction. We adapt a feature extractor from [31], that allows weight sharing across the scales, to create a "scale-agnostic" feature pyramid. It is constructed in three steps as follows.

First, we create image pyramids $\{\mathbf{I}_0^l\}$ and $\{\mathbf{I}_1^l\}$ for the two input images, where $l \in [1, 7]$ is the pyramid level.

Second, starting at the image at each l-th pyramid level, we build feature pyramids (the columns in Fig. 2) using a shared UNet encoder. Specifically, we extract multi-scale features $\{\mathbf{f}_0^{l,d}\}$ and $\{\mathbf{f}_1^{l,d}\}$, with $d \in [1, 4]$ being the depth at that l-th level (Fig. 2 only uses $d \in [1, 3]$ for illustration). Mathematically,

$$\mathbf{f}_0^{l,d} = \mathcal{H}^d(\mathbf{I}_0^l),   (2)$$

where $\mathcal{H}^d$ is a stack of convolutions, shown in Fig. 2 with the green arrow for $d = 1$, red for $d = 2$, and dark-blue for $d = 3$. Note that, the same $\theta^{(\mathcal{H}^d)}$ convolution weights are shared for the same d-th depth at each pyramid level, to create *compatible multiscale features*. Each $\mathcal{H}^d$ is followed by an average pooling with a size and stride of 2.

As a third and final step of our feature extractor, we construct our scale-agnostic feature pyramids, $\{\mathbf{F}_0^l\}$ and $\{\mathbf{F}_1^l\}$, by concatenating the feature maps with different depths, but the same spatial dimensions, as:

$$\mathbf{F}_0^l = \left(\mathbf{f}_0^{l-2,d=3}, \mathbf{f}_0^{l-1,d=2}, \mathbf{f}_0^{l,d=1} \right),   (3)$$

and the scale-agnostic feature, $\mathbf{F}_1^l$ of $\mathbf{I}_1$, at the l-th pyramid level, can be given in a similar way by Eq. 3. As shown in Fig. 2, the finest level feature (green) can only aggregate one feature map, the second finest level two (green+red), and the rest can aggregate three shared feature maps.

Flow Estimation. Once we extract the feature pyramids, $\{\mathbf{F}_0^l\}$ and $\{\mathbf{F}_1^l\}$, we use them to calculate a bi-directional motion at each pyramid level. Similar to [30], we start the motion estimation from the coarsest level (in our case $l = 7$). However, in contrast to other methods, we directly predict task oriented [16,34] flows, $\mathbf{W}_{t\to 0}$ and $\mathbf{W}_{t\to 1}$, from the mid-frame to the inputs.

We compute the task oriented flow at each level $\mathbf{W}_{t\to 1}^l$ as the sum of predicted residual and the upsampled flow from the coarser level $l+1$, based on the intuition that large motion at finer scales should be the same as small motion at coarser scales, as:

$$\mathbf{W}_{t\to 1}^l = \left(\mathbf{W}_{t\to 1}^{l+1}\right)_{\times 2} + \mathcal{G}^l\left(\mathbf{F}_0^l, \hat{\mathbf{F}}_{t\leftarrow 1}^l\right), \tag{4}$$

where $(\bullet)_{\times 2}$ is a bilinear up-sampling, $\mathcal{G}^l$ is a stack of convolutions that estimates the residual, and $\hat{\mathbf{F}}_{t\leftarrow 1}^l$ is the backward warped scale-agnostic feature map at $t = 1$, obtained by bilinearly warping $\mathbf{F}_1^l$ with the upsampled flow estimate, as,

$$\hat{\mathbf{F}}_{t\leftarrow 1}^l = \mathcal{T}\left(\mathbf{F}_1^l, \left(\mathbf{W}_{t\to 1}^{l+1}\right)_{\times 2}\right), \tag{5}$$

with $\mathcal{T}$ being a bilinear resample (warp) operation. Figure 2 depicts $\mathcal{G}^l$ by the blue or white arrows, depending on the pyramid level. Note that, the same residual convolution weights $\theta^{(\mathcal{G}^l)}$ are shared by levels $l \in [3, 7]$.

Finally, we create the feature pyramid at the intermediate time t, $\{\mathbf{F}_{t\leftarrow 1}^l\}$ and $\{\mathbf{F}_{t\leftarrow 0}^l\}$, by backward warping the feature pyramid, at $t = 1$ and $t = 0$, with the flows given by Eq. 4, as:

$$\mathbf{F}_{t\leftarrow 1}^l = \mathcal{T}\left(\left(\mathbf{F}_1^l, \mathbf{I}_1^l\right), \mathbf{W}_{t\to 1}^l\right), \tag{6}$$

$\mathbf{F}_{t\leftarrow 0}^l$ can be given in a similar way as Eq. 6.

Fusion. The final stage of FILM concatenates, at each l-th pyramid, the scale-agnostic feature maps at t and the bi-directional motions to t, which are then fed to a UNet-like [27] decoder to synthesize the final mid-frame $\hat{\mathbf{I}}_t$. Mathematically, the fused input at each l-th decoder level is given by,

$$\left(\mathbf{F}_{t\leftarrow 1}^l, \mathbf{F}_{t\leftarrow 0}^l, \mathbf{W}_{t\to 0}^l, \mathbf{W}_{t\to 1}^l\right). \tag{7}$$

Figure 2 illustrates the decoder's convolutions and resulting activations with a white arrow and gray boxes, respectively.

3.1 Loss Functions

We use only image synthesis losses to supervise the final output of our FILM network; we do not use auxiliary losses tapped into any intermediate stages. Our image synthesis loss is a combination of three terms.

First, we use the L1 reconstruction loss that minimizes the pixel-wise RGB difference between the interpolated frame $\hat{\mathbf{I}}_t$ and the ground-truth frame $\mathbf{I}_t$, given by:

$$\mathcal{L}_1 = \|\hat{\mathbf{I}}_t - \mathbf{I}_t\|_1. \tag{8}$$

The $\mathcal{L}_1$ loss captures the motion between the inputs $(\mathbf{I}_0, \mathbf{I}_1)$ and yields interpolation results that score well on benchmarks, as is discussed in Sect. 5.2. However, the interpolated frames are often blurry.

Second, to enhance image details, we add a perceptual loss, using the L1 norm of the VGG-19 features [29]. The perceptual loss, also called VGG-loss, $\mathcal{L}_{\mathrm{VGG}}$, is given by,

$$\mathcal{L}_{\text{VGG}} = \frac{1}{L} \sum_{l=1}^{L} \alpha_l \left\| \Psi_l(\hat{\mathbf{I}}_t) - \Psi_l(\mathbf{I}_t) \right\|_1, \tag{9}$$

where $\Psi_l(\mathbf{I}_i) \in \mathbb{R}^{H \times W \times C}$ is the features from the l-th selected layer of a pre-trained Imagenet VGG-19 network for $\mathbf{I}_i \in \mathbb{R}^{H \times W \times 3}$, L is the number of the finer layers considered, and α_l is an importance weight of the l-th layer.

Finally, we employ the Style loss [7,14,25] to further expand on the benefits of $\mathcal{L}_{\text{VGG}}$. The style loss $\mathcal{L}_{\text{Gram}}$, also called Gram matrix loss, is the L2 norm of the auto-correlation of the VGG-19 features [29]:

$$\mathcal{L}_{\text{Gram}} = \frac{1}{L} \sum_{l=1}^{L} \alpha_l \left\| M_l(\hat{\mathbf{I}}_t) - M_l(\mathbf{I}_t) \right\|_2, \tag{10}$$

where the Gram matrix of the interpolated frame at the l-th layer, $M_l(\hat{\mathbf{I}}_t) \in \mathbb{R}^{C \times C}$, is given by:

$$M_l(\hat{\mathbf{I}}_t) = \left(\Psi_l(\hat{\mathbf{I}}_t) \right)^{\mathsf{T}} \left(\Psi_l(\hat{\mathbf{I}}_t) \right), \tag{11}$$

and the Gram matrix of the ground-truth image, $M_l(\mathbf{I}_t)$, can be given in a similar way as Eq. 11.

To our knowledge, this is the first work that applies the Gram matrix loss to frame interpolation. We found this loss to be effective in synthesizing sharp images with rich details when inpainting large disocclusion regions caused by large scene motion.

To achieve high benchmark scores as well as high quality frame synthesis, we train our models with an optimally weighted combination of the RGB, VGG and Gram matrix losses. The combined loss, which we denote $\mathcal{L}_S$, is defined as,

$$\mathcal{L}_S = w_l \mathcal{L}_1 + w_{\text{VGG}} \mathcal{L}_{\text{VGG}} + w_{\text{Gram}} \mathcal{L}_{\text{Gram}}, \tag{12}$$

with the weights $(w_l, w_{\text{VGG}}, w_{\text{Gram}})$ determined empirically, as detailed in the Supplementary Materials.

3.2   Large Motion Datasets

To study FILM's ability to handle large motion, we created a "bracketed" dataset containing five training sub-sets. Each containing examples with motion disparity in the following ranges, in pixels: 0–40, 0–60, 0–80, 0–100, and 0–120.

We procedurally mine 512×512 image triplets from publicly available videos, extending the method described in [5]. We apply this procedure to generate several motion brackets, i.e.: 0–20, 20–40, ..., 100–120. The motion distribution histograms of these brackets are shown overlapped in Fig. 3. The effect of training using blends with increasing motion range is analyzed in Sect. 5.3.

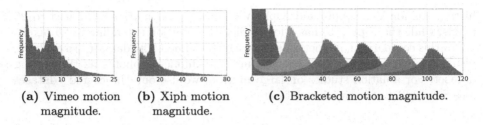

(a) Vimeo motion   (b) Xiph motion   (c) Bracketed motion magnitude.
magnitude.   magnitude.

Fig. 3. Motion magnitude histograms of datasets Vimeo-90K (a), Xiph-4K (b) and Bracketed (c).

4   Implementation Details

We implemented our model in TensorFlow 2. As training data, we use either Vimeo-90K or one of our large motion datasets described in Sect. 3.2.

For the Vimeo-90K dataset, we use a batch size of 8, with a 256×256 random crop size, distributed over 8 NVIDIA V100 GPUs. We apply data augmentation: Random rotation with $[-45°, 45°]$, rotation by multiples of $90°$, horizontal flip, and reversing triplets. We use Adam [12] optimizer with $\beta_1 = 0.9$ and $\beta_2 = 0.999$, without weight decay. We use an initial learning rate of $1e^{-4}$ scheduled (piecewise linear) with exponential decay rate of 0.464, and decay steps of 750K, for 3M iterations.

For comparison with the recent state-of-the-art models, we trained two versions: One optimized using $\mathcal{L}_1$ loss alone, which achieves higher benchmark scores, and another, that favours image quality, trained with our proposed style loss, $\mathcal{L}_S$. Our style loss optimally combines $\mathcal{L}_1$, $\mathcal{L}_{\mathrm{VGG}}$, and $\mathcal{L}_{\mathrm{Gram}}$.

To perform our qualitative evaluations, we also implement the SoftSplat [18] in TensorFlow 2, since pre-trained models were not available at the time of writing. In the Supplementary Materials, we show our faithful implementations on a DAVIS [24] image sample rendered in [18]. We found that renderings with our implementation to be quite comparable to the ones provided in the original paper. We provide additional implementation details in the Supplementary.

5   Results

Using existing benchmarks, we quantitatively compare FILM to recent methods: DAIN [3], AdaCoF [13], BMBC [22], SoftSplat [18], and ABME [23]. We additionally provide qualitative comparisons (to SoftSplat and ABME) on near-duplicate interpolation, for which no benchmarks currently exist.

Metrics. We use common quantitative metrics: Peak Signal-To-Noise Ratio (PSNR) and Structural Similarity Image Metric (SSIM). High PSNR and SSIM scores indicate better quality.

Datasets. We report metrics on Vimeo-90K [34], UCF101 [16], Middlebury [2], and on a 4K large motion dataset Xiph [17,18]. Figure 3 shows motion magnitude histograms for Vimeo-90K and Xiph. Vimeo-90K (3a) motion is limited to 25 pixels, while the Xiph (3b) has a long-tailed distribution extending to 80 pixels.

In this comparison, all methods are with the Vimeo-90K dataset. To evaluate visual quality, we use a new challenging near-duplicate photos as the testing dataset. For ablation studies on large motion, we use our "bracketed" dataset (see Sect. 3.2) as the training dataset.

5.1 Quantitative Comparisons

Small-to-Medium Motion. Table 1 shows midpoint frame interpolation comparisons with DAIN [3], AdaCoF [13], BMBC [22], SoftSplat [18], and ABME [23] on small-to-medium motion datasets: Vimeo-90K, Middlebury, and UCF101.

The SoftSplat method reports two sets of results, one set trained with color loss ($\mathcal{L}_{Lap}$), which performs better on standard benchmarks, and another trained with a perceptually-sensitive loss ($\mathcal{L}_F$), which leads to perceptually higher quality frames. The rest report results obtained by training with various color or low-level loss functions.

Based on color losses, ABME outperforms all other methods on Vimeo-90K. On Middlebury and UCF101, SoftSplat trained with color loss has the highest PSNR. We note that ABME and SoftSplat are complex to train, each consisting of multiple sub-networks dedicated to motion estimation, refinement, or synthesis. Their training processes involve multiple datasets and stage-wise pre-training. Data scarcity, which is even more critical in large motion, could also complicate pre-training. Our unified, single-stage, FILM network achieves competitive PSNR scores.

Table 1. Comparison on *small-to-medium motion* benchmarks. Best scores for color losses are in **blue**, for perceptually-sensitive losses in red. In this comparison, all methods are trained on Vimeo-90K.

	Vimeo-90K [34]		Middlebury [2]		UCF101 [16]	
	PSNR↑	SSIM↑	PSNR↑	SSIM↑	PSNR↑	SSIM↑
DAIN	34.70	0.964	36.70	0.965	35.00	0.950
AdaCoF	34.35	0.973	35.72	**0.978**	34.90	0.968
BMBC	35.01	0.976	n/a	n/a	35.15	0.969
SoftSplat-$\mathcal{L}_{Lap}$	36.10	0.970	**38.42**	0.971	**35.39**	0.952
ABME	**36.18**	**0.981**	n/a	n/a	35.38	**0.970**
Our FILM-$\mathcal{L}_1$	36.06	0.970	37.52	0.966	35.32	0.952
SoftSplat-$\mathcal{L}_F$	35.48	0.964	37.55	0.965	35.10	0.948
Our FILM-$\mathcal{L}_{VGG}$	35.76	0.967	37.43	0.966	35.20	0.950
Our FILM-$\mathcal{L}_S$	35.87	0.968	37.57	0.966	35.16	0.949

The perception-distortion tradeoff [4] proved that minimizing distortion metrics alone, like PSNR or SSIM, can have a negative effect on the perceptual quality. As such, we also optimize our model with our proposed Gram Matrix-based loss, $\mathcal{L}_S$, which optimally favours both color differences and perceptual quality.

When including perceptually-sensitive losses, FILM outperforms the state-of-the-art SoftSplat on Vimeo-90K. We also achieve the highest scores on Middlebury and UCF101. In the next Subsect. 5.2, we show visual comparisons that support the quantitative gains in PSNR with gains in image quality.

Large Motion. Table 2 presents midpoint frame interpolation comparisons on Xiph-2K and Xiph-4K, all methods (including FILM) trained on Vimeo-90K. FILM outperforms all other models for color-based losses. Note that (not shown in the table) when training FILM on a custom large motion dataset, detailed in Sect. 3.2, we can achieve an additional performance gain of +0.5 dB on Xiph-4K, the benchmark with the largest motions.

When including perceptually-sensitive losses, FILM outperforms SoftSplat-$\mathcal{L}_F$ in PSNR on Xiph-2K and both PSNR and SSIM on the larger motion Xiph-4K. Thus, FILM is better able to generalize from the small motions in the Vimeo-90K training datasets to the larger motions present in the Xiph test sets. We hope these findings will interest the greater research community, where large motion is often challenging. In the next Subsect. 5.2, we provide visual results that support the effectiveness of our method in samples with motion ranges as large as 100 pixels.

Table 2. Comparison on *large motion* benchmarks. Best scores for color losses in (**blue**), and for perceptually-sensitive losses in (red). In this comparison, all methods are trained on Vimeo-90K.

	Xiph-2K [17]		Xiph-4K [17]	
	PSNR↑	SSIM↑	PSNR↑	SSIM↑
DAIN	35.95	0.940	33.49	0.895
ToFlow	33.93	0.922	30.74	0.856
AdaCoF	34.86	0.928	31.68	0.870
BMBC	32.82	0.928	31.19	0.880
ABME	36.53	0.944	33.73	0.901
SoftSplat-$\mathcal{L}_{Lap}$	36.62	0.944	33.60	0.901
Our FILM-$\mathcal{L}_1$	**36.66**	**0.951**	**33.78**	**0.906**
SoftSplat-$\mathcal{L}_F$	35.74	0.944	32.55	0.865
Our FILM-$\mathcal{L}_S$	36.38	0.942	33.29	0.882

5.2   Qualitative Comparisons

We provide visual results that support our quantitative results. We use the version of the model that yields high image quality, i.e.: our FILM-$\mathcal{L}_S$ and SoftSplat-$\mathcal{L}_F$. For ABME[1], we create visual results using the released pre-trained models.

---

[1] https://github.com/JunHeum/ABME.

260   F. Reda et al.

For SoftSplat[2] [18], we use our faithful implementation, since neither source code nor pre-trained model was publicly available at the time of writing.

Sharpness. To evaluate the effectiveness of our Gram Matrix-based loss function (Eq. 11) in preserving image sharpness, we visually compare our results against images rendered with other methods. As seen in Fig. 4a, our method synthesizes visually superior results, with crisp image details on the face and preserving the articulating fingers.

Disocclusion Inpainting. To effectively inpaint disoccluded pixels, models must learn appropriate motions or hallucinate novel pixels, this is especially critical in large scene motion, which causes wide disocclusions. Figure 4b shows different methods, including ours, inpainting large disocclusions. Compared to the other approaches, FILM correctly paints the pixels while maintaining high fidelity. It also preserves the structure of objects, e.g. the red toy car, while SoftSplat [18] shows deformation, and ABME [23] creates blurry inpainting.

Large Motion. Large motion is one of the most challenging aspects of frame interpolation. Figure 5 shows results for different methods on a sample with 100 pixels disparity. Both SoftSplat [18] and ABME [23] were able to capture motions near the dog's nose, however they create large artifacts on the ground. FILM's strength is seen capturing the motion well and keeping the background details. Please see our Supplementary Materials for more visual results.

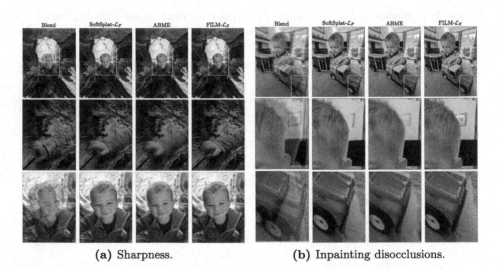

(a) Sharpness.   (b) Inpainting disocclusions.

Fig. 4. Qualitative comparison on sharpness and large disocclusion inpainting. (a) FILM produces sharp images and preserves the fingers. SoftSplat [18] shows artifacts (fingers) and ABME [23] has blurriness (the face). (b) Our method inpaints large disocclusions well, because of our proposed Gram Matrix-based (Style) loss. SoftSplat [18] and ABME [23] produce blurry inpaintings or un-natural deformations (Color figure online).

---

[2] https://github.com/sniklaus/softmax-splatting.

5.3 Ablations

In this section, we present ablation studies to analyze the design choices of FILM.

Weight Sharing. We compare our shared feature extractor with a regular UNet-like encoder [27] that uses independent weights at all scales, forcing us to also learn independent flows. Table 3 presents mid-frame results in PSNR. It is not straightforward to construct models that are fair to compare: one could either match the total number of weights or the number of filters at each level. We chose to use a UNet encoder that starts from the same number of filters as ours and then doubles the number at each level. The FILM-model we have used in this paper starts with 64 filters, so this leads to a UNet with feature counts: [64, 128, 256...]. We find that training with this configuration does not converge without weight sharing. To study this further, we construct two simpler variants of our model, starting from 32 filters. We are able to train these two models with a small loss in PSNR as compared to the equivalent model that shares weights.

To conclude, weight sharing allows training a more powerful model, reaching a higher PSNR. Additionally, sharing may be important for fitting models in GPU memory in practical applications. Further, the model with weight sharing is visually superior with substantially better generalization when testing on pairs with motion magnitude beyond the range in the training data (see Fig. 6).

Fig. 5. Qualitative comparison on large motion. Inputs with 100pixels disparity overlaid (left). Although both SoftSplat [18], ABME [23] capture the motion on the dog's nose, they appear blurry, and create a large artifact on the ground. FILM's strength is seen capturing the motion well and maintaining the background details.

Gram Matrix (Style) Loss. Figure 7 presents qualitative results of FILM trained with $\mathcal{L}_1$, adding $\mathcal{L}_{VGG}$, and with our proposed style loss $\mathcal{L}_S$, given by Eq. 12. Using $\mathcal{L}_1$ alone leads to blurry images (red box), while adding $\mathcal{L}_{VGG}$ loss reduces blurry artifacts (orange box). Our proposed loss (green box) significantly improves sharpness of our FILM method.

Motion Ranges. We study the effect of the training dataset motion range on the model's ability to handle different motions at test time, using the "bracketed dataset" (see Sect. 3.2). For this study, we use a reduced FILM-med to save compute resources. FILM-med is trained on motion ranges of 0–40, 0–60, 0–80, 0–100 and 0–120 pixels. They are evaluated on Vimeo-90K (0–25 range) and Xiph4K (0–80 range), as shown in Fig. 8. On Vimeo-90K, FILM-med trained with the smallest motion range performs the best. As larger motion is added, PSNR goes down significantly.

Table 3. Weight sharing ablation study. A model without multi-scale feature sharing achieves results that are slightly lower than those achieved with shared features, e.g. FILM-med and FILM-lite. We have not been able to train our highest quality model (FILM) without weight sharing as the training gets unstable (indicated with N/A).

Model	PSNR (w/ sharing)	PSNR (w/o sharing)
FILM	36.06	N/A
FILM-med	35.30	35.28
FILM-lite	35.09	34.93

Fig. 6. The visual impact of sharing weights. **Left**: no sharing (FILM-med), **Middle**: sharing (FILM-med), **Right**: sharing (FILM), i.e., the highest quality model. Sharing weights is clearly better. Quality and sharpness increases when going from the medium to the full model with sharing.

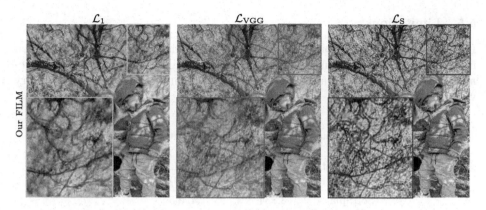

Fig. 7. Loss function comparison on our FILM. L1 loss (left), L1 plus VGG loss (middle), and our proposed style loss (right), showing significant sharpness improvements (green box). (Color figure online)

We hypothesize that this behavior is caused by two factors: 1) when training for larger motion, the model assumes a larger search window for correspondence, and thus has more chances to make errors. 2) with larger motion, the problem is simply harder and less neural capacity is left for smaller motion.

On Xiph-4K, the best performance is obtained by training with motion range 0–100 pixels. Motivated by our finding, we trained our best model (FILM) with this dataset, and achieve an additional PSNR performance gain of +0.5dB over the state-of-the-art, as described in Sect. 5.1.

In summary, our findings indicate that scale-agnostic features and shared weight flow prediction improve the model's ability to learn and generalize to a wider range of motion. In addition, we find that best results are obtained when the training data also matches the test-time motion distribution.

5.4 Performance and Memory

Table 4 presents inference times and memory comparisons on an NVIDIA V100 GPU. We report the average of 100 runs. Our FILM is 3.95× faster than ABME, and 9.75× faster than SoftSplat, while using only 1.27× and 1.01× more memory than ABME and SoftSplat, respectively. Our model is slightly larger due to its deep pyramid (7 levels), but the time performance gains are significantly large.

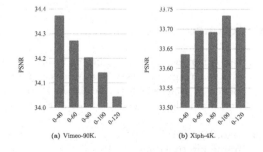

Fig. 8. A study of the effect of the training dataset's motion range on the PSNR, when evaluated on (a) Vimeo-90K, and (b) Xiph-4K.

5.5 Limitations

In some instances, FILM produces un-natural deformations when the in-between motion is extreme. Although resulting videos are appealing, the subtle movements may not look natural. We provide failure examples in our Supplementary video.

Table 4. Inference time and memory comparison for a 720p frame interpolation.

Interpolation method	Inference time (Second)↓	Peak memory (GB)↓
SoftSplat	3.834	4.405
ABME	1.554	**3.506**
Our FILM	**0.393**	4.484

6 Conclusions

We have introduced an algorithm for large motion frame interpolation (FILM), in particular, for near-duplicate photos interpolation. FILM is a simple, unified and single-stage model, trainable from regular frames, and does not require additional optical-flow or depth prior networks, or their scarce pre-training data. Its core components are a feature pyramid that shares weight across scales and a "scale-agnostic" bi-directional motion estimator that learns from frames with normal motion but generalizes well to frames with large motion. To handle wide disocclusions caused by large motion, we optimize our models with the Gram matrix loss that matches the correlation of features to generate sharp frames. Extensive experimental results show that FILM outperforms other methods on large motions while still handling small motions well, and generates high quality and temporally smooth videos. Source codes and pre-trained models are available at https://film-net.github.io.

References

1. van Amersfoort, J., et al.: Frame interpolation with multi-scale deep loss functions and generative adversarial networks. arXiv preprint arXiv:1711.06045 (2017)
2. Baker, S., Scharstein, D., Lewis, J., Roth, S., Black, M.J., Szeliski, R.: A database and evaluation methodology for optical flow. Int. J. Comput. Vision **92**(1), 1–31 (2011)
3. Bao, W., Lai, W.S., Ma, C., Zhang, X., Gao, Z., Yang, M.H.: Depth-aware video frame interpolation. In: Proceedings of the IEEE/CVF Conference on Computer Vision and Pattern Recognition, pp. 3703–3712 (2019)
4. Blau, Y., Michaeli, T.: The perception-distortion tradeoff. In: Proceedings of the IEEE Conference on Computer Vision and Pattern Recognition, pp. 6228–6237 (2018)

5. Brooks, T., Barron, J.T.: Learning to synthesize motion blur. In: Proceedings of the IEEE/CVF Conference on Computer Vision and Pattern Recognition, pp. 6840–6848 (2019)
6. Ding, T., Liang, L., Zhu, Z., Zharkov, I.: CDFI: compression-driven network design for frame interpolation. In: Proceedings of the IEEE/CVF Conference on Computer Vision and Pattern Recognition, pp. 8001–8011 (2021)
7. Gatys, L.A., Ecker, A.S., Bethge, M.: Image style transfer using convolutional neural networks. In: Proceedings of the IEEE Conference on Computer Vision and Pattern Recognition, pp. 2414–2423 (2016)
8. Huang, Z., Zhang, T., Heng, W., Shi, B., Zhou, S.: Rife: real-time intermediate flow estimation for video frame interpolation. arXiv preprint arXiv:2011.06294 (2020)
9. Hur, J., Roth, S.: Iterative residual refinement for joint optical flow and occlusion estimation. In: Proceedings of the IEEE/CVF Conference on Computer Vision and Pattern Recognition, pp. 5754–5763 (2019)
10. Jiang, H., Sun, D., Jampani, V., Lv, Z., Learned-Miller, E., Kautz, J.: Sense: a shared encoder network for scene-flow estimation. In: Proceedings of the IEEE/CVF International Conference on Computer Vision, pp. 3195–3204 (2019)
11. Jiang, H., Sun, D., Jampani, V., Yang, M.H., Learned-Miller, E., Kautz, J.: Super slomo: high quality estimation of multiple intermediate frames for video interpolation. In: Proceedings of the IEEE Conference on Computer Vision and Pattern Recognition, pp. 9000–9008 (2018)
12. KingaD, A.: A method for stochastic optimization. In: Anon. International Conference on Learning Representations, ICLR, San Dego (2015)
13. Lee, H., Kim, T., Chung, T.Y., Pak, D., Ban, Y., Lee, S.: AdaCoF: adaptive collaboration of flows for video frame interpolation. In: Proceedings of the IEEE/CVF Conference on Computer Vision and Pattern Recognition, pp. 5316–5325 (2020)
14. Liu, G., Reda, F.A., Shih, K.J., Wang, T.C., Tao, A., Catanzaro, B.: Image inpainting for irregular holes using partial convolutions. In: Proceedings of the European Conference on Computer Vision (ECCV), pp. 85–100 (2018)
15. Liu, Y.L., Liao, Y.T., Lin, Y.Y., Chuang, Y.Y.: Deep video frame interpolation using cyclic frame generation. In: Proceedings of the AAAI Conference on Artificial Intelligence, pp. 8794–8802 (2019)
16. Liu, Z., Yeh, R.A., Tang, X., Liu, Y., Agarwala, A.: Video frame synthesis using deep voxel flow. In: Proceedings of the IEEE International Conference on Computer Vision, pp. 4463–4471 (2017)
17. Montgomery, C., et al.: Xiph.org video test media (Derf's collection), the Xiph open source community, 1994, vol. 3 (1994). https://media.xiph.org/video/derf
18. Niklaus, S., Liu, F.: Softmax splatting for video frame interpolation. In: Proceedings of the IEEE/CVF Conference on Computer Vision and Pattern Recognition, pp. 5437–5446 (2020)
19. Niklaus, S., Mai, L., Liu, F.: Video frame interpolation via adaptive convolution. In: Proceedings of the IEEE Conference on Computer Vision and Pattern Recognition, pp. 670–679 (2017)
20. Niklaus, S., Mai, L., Liu, F.: Video frame interpolation via adaptive separable convolution. In: Proceedings of the IEEE International Conference on Computer Vision, pp. 261–270 (2017)
21. Niklaus, S., Mai, L., Wang, O.: Revisiting adaptive convolutions for video frame interpolation. In: Proceedings of the IEEE/CVF Winter Conference on Applications of Computer Vision, pp. 1099–1109 (2021)

22. Park, J., Ko, K., Lee, C., Kim, C.-S.: BMBC: bilateral motion estimation with bilateral cost volume for video interpolation. In: Vedaldi, A., Bischof, H., Brox, T., Frahm, J.-M. (eds.) ECCV 2020. LNCS, vol. 12359, pp. 109–125. Springer, Cham (2020). https://doi.org/10.1007/978-3-030-58568-6_7

23. Park, J., Lee, C., Kim, C.S.: Asymmetric bilateral motion estimation for video frame interpolation. In: Proceedings of the IEEE/CVF International Conference on Computer Vision, pp. 14539–14548 (2021)

24. Perazzi, F., Pont-Tuset, J., McWilliams, B., Van Gool, L., Gross, M., Sorkine-Hornung, A.: A benchmark dataset and evaluation methodology for video object segmentation. In: Proceedings of the IEEE Conference on Computer Vision and Pattern Recognition, pp. 724–732 (2016)

25. Reda, F.A., et al.: SDC-Net: video prediction using spatially-displaced convolution. In: Proceedings of the European Conference on Computer Vision (ECCV), pp. 718–733 (2018)

26. Reda, F.A., et al.: Unsupervised video interpolation using cycle consistency. In: Proceedings of the IEEE/CVF International Conference on Computer Vision, pp. 892–900 (2019)

27. Ronneberger, O., Fischer, P., Brox, T.: U-Net: convolutional networks for biomedical image segmentation. In: Navab, N., Hornegger, J., Wells, W.M., Frangi, A.F. (eds.) MICCAI 2015. LNCS, vol. 9351, pp. 234–241. Springer, Cham (2015). https://doi.org/10.1007/978-3-319-24574-4_28

28. Sim, H., Oh, J., Kim, M.: XVFI: extreme video frame interpolation. In: Proceedings of the IEEE/CVF International Conference on Computer Vision, pp. 14489–14498 (2021)

29. Simonyan, K., Zisserman, A.: Very deep convolutional networks for large-scale image recognition. arXiv preprint arXiv:1409.1556 (2014)

30. Sun, D., Yang, X., Liu, M.Y., Kautz, J.: PWC-Net: CNNs for optical flow using pyramid, warping, and cost volume. In: CVPR, June 2018

31. Trinidad, M.C., Brualla, R.M., Kainz, F., Kontkanen, J.: Multi-view image fusion. In: Proceedings of the IEEE/CVF International Conference on Computer Vision, pp. 4101–4110 (2019)

32. Xiang, X., Tian, Y., Zhang, Y., Fu, Y., Allebach, J.P., Xu, C.: Zooming slow-mo: fast and accurate one-stage space-time video super-resolution. In: Proceedings of the IEEE/CVF Conference on Computer Vision and Pattern Recognition, pp. 3370–3379 (2020)

33. Xie, S., Tu, Z.: Holistically-nested edge detection. In: Proceedings of IEEE International Conference on Computer Vision (2015)

34. Xue, T., Chen, B., Wu, J., Wei, D., Freeman, W.T.: Video enhancement with task-oriented flow. Int. J. Comput. Vision **127**(8), 1106–1125 (2019)

35. Zhang, H., Zhao, Y., Wang, R.: A flexible recurrent residual pyramid network for video frame interpolation. In: Vedaldi, A., Bischof, H., Brox, T., Frahm, J.-M. (eds.) ECCV 2020. LNCS, vol. 12370, pp. 474–491. Springer, Cham (2020). https://doi.org/10.1007/978-3-030-58595-2_29

Video Interpolation by Event-Driven Anisotropic Adjustment of Optical Flow

Song Wu[1], Kaichao You[2], Weihua He[2(✉)], Chen Yang[1], Yang Tian[2], Yaoyuan Wang[1], Ziyang Zhang[1(✉)], and Jianxing Liao[1]

[1] Advanced Computing and Storage Lab, Huawei Technologies Co. Ltd.,
Shenzhen, China
{wangyaoyuan1,zhangziyang11,liaojianx}@huawei.com
[2] Tsinghua University, Beijing, China
{ykc20,hwh20,tiany20}@mails.tsinghua.edu.cn

Abstract. Video frame interpolation is a challenging task due to the ever-changing real-world scene. Previous methods often calculate the bi-directional optical flows and then predict the intermediate optical flows under the linear motion assumptions, leading to isotropic intermediate flow generation. Follow-up research obtained anisotropic adjustment through estimated higher-order motion information with extra frames. Based on the motion assumptions, their methods are hard to model the complicated motion in real scenes. In this paper, we propose an end-to-end training method $\mathbf{A^2OF}$ for video frame interpolation with event-driven **A**nisotropic **A**djustment of **O**ptical **F**lows. Specifically, we use events to generate optical flow distribution masks for the intermediate optical flow, which can model the complicated motion between two frames. Our proposed method outperforms the previous methods in video frame interpolation, taking supervised event-based video interpolation to a higher stage.

Keywords: Video frame interpolation · Bi-directional optical flow · Event-driven distribution mask

1 Introduction

Video frame interpolation(VFI) is a challenging task in computer vision, which is widely used in slow motion video generation, high rate frame conversion and video frames recovery, etc. The goal of VFI is to synthesize nonexistent intermediate frames between two consecutive frames. However, it is hard to synthesize high-quality intermediate frames due to the lack of corresponding motion information.

S. Wu and K. You—Contribute equally to this paper. Work done while Song Wu, Kaichao You, Yang Tian are interns at Huawei.

Supplementary Information The online version contains supplementary material available at https://doi.org/10.1007/978-3-031-20071-7_16.

Optical flow is a common tool in VFI. SuperSloMo [7] linearly represent the intermediate optical flow from the target frame to original frame with bi-directional optical flow. They warp, blend and refine the original frames to obtain target frames. The key assumption in their method is uniform motion along a straight line, which runs counter to the laws of nonlinear motion in real world. Besides, they synthesize the intermediate optical flow with the same coefficient to the different directions in bi-directional optical flows. In this isotropic way, they can not obtain the inaccurate intermediate flow optical which has the different directions with bi-directional optical flow. Aiming at anisotropic adjustment of intermediate flow, some works try to extract more information through pre-trained models, such as depth information [2] and contextual information [16]. More complex motion assumptions are designed in some succeeding works, such as QVI [29] and EQVI [12]. However, it is still difficult for them to describe the actual movement under the absence of intermediate motion information. As shown in Fig. 1(d), the intermediate optical flows obtained based on this inaccurate assumption fail to describe the correct direction of football.

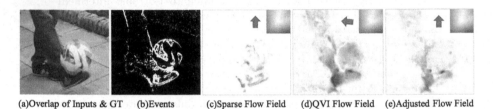

(a)Overlap of Inputs & GT   (b)Events   (c)Sparse Flow Field   (d)QVI Flow Field   (e)Adjusted Flow Field

Fig. 1. The visualization of the generated optical flow. (c) demonstrates the sparse optical flow in Time Lens [26]. (d) demonstrates the final intermediate optical flow in QVI [29]. (e) demonstrates the final intermediate optical flows generated through the proposed model. These optical flows are used to warp the original frames to get initial intermediate frames. The arrows in these pictures denote the directions of football motion.

Event streams can record accurate motion information between two consecutive frames, which help to solve the absence of information in VFI model. Time Lens [26] uses event streams to compensate for motion information. Event streams generated through event camera asynchronously record the motion information for a period of time with the merits of high temporal resolution and low latency. Time Lens directly uses event to synthesize intermediate frame and estimate intermediate optical flow. The pre-warped frames through intermediate optical flow are aligned and refined by event-driven synthesis frames to obtain the final target frames. There are some limitations: although modeling motion is avoided in the process of obtaining intermediate optical flow, the warped result is limited by the sparse flow field estimated through event streams, as shown in Fig. 1(c), which lacks the dense features of the RGB images. The predicted sparse optical flow field is also easily affected by the noise of the event itself, which affects the final result. Besides, their model is not an end-to-end training model.

In this paper, we propose a video frame interpolation method A^2OF with event-driven **A**nisotropic **A**djustment of **O**ptical **F**low in an end-to-end training manner. Specifically, our model is based on bi-directional optical flows model, such as Super SloMo [7]. Firstly, we adopt and tailor IFNet in [6] in order to better model the motion from both event streams and frames. After getting the bi-directional optical flow, instead of linearly weighting them in both horizontal and vertical directions, anisotropic weights are learnt from events to blend and generate intermediate optical flow in the orthogonal directions. As shown in Fig. 1(e), the optical flows generated from our proposed models can demonstrate the correct direction of the football. Besides, we design an event-driven motion consistency loss based on the change of intensity to further improve the performance of our proposed model. We carry out a series of experiments to evaluate our proposed model on both synthetic and real event-frame datasets. Experimental results show that our model achieves the-state-of-art performance in all evaluated datasets.

Our main contributions can be summarized as:

1. To address the limitation in video frame interpolation model based on bi-directional optical flow, we design event-driven optical flow distribution masks generation module to provide anisotropic weights for the different directions of the optical flows.
2. In order to better compensate the motion information in the event to the VFI model, we design an event-driven motion consistency loss based on the change of intensity.
3. We design an end-to-end training video frame interpolation model, which outperforms the previous methods on both synthetic and real event-frames datasets.

2 Related Works

Video Frame Interpolation. The goal of VFI is to predict the intermediate frames between the input frames. Some methods [13,14,17] mainly focused on single-frame interpolation, which is commonly ineffective and inflexible. In order to interpolate several frames at any time between consecutive frames, SuperSloMo [7] designs a video frame interpolation model based on optical flows. According to the uniform motion assumption, they linearly aggregate bi-directional optical flows to obtain intermediate optical flow from the target frame to the original frame in an isotropic way. The final synthesis intermediate frames are warped and blended from the original frames. Their uniform motion assumption does not well with nonlinear motion in real scenes. Besides, they can not model the real motion which has the different directions with bi-directional optical flow. For anisotropic adjustment of optical flow, some extra information from the pretrained model is added into VFI model, such as depth information [2] or contextual information [16]. QVI [29] and EQVI [12] design more complex motion assumptions, however, which may still deviates from the way that objects move in the real scenes. The absence of motion information between original frames is the main cause of inaccurate motion estimation and low-quality frames inter-polation. They may have poor frame interpolation ability when encountering complicated motion scenes due to inaccurate motion descriptions. We propose event-driven distribution masks generation module in the bi-directional model to obtain intermediate optical flows in an anisotropic way for the different direc-tions of optical flow. With the help of event streams, we can get more accurate motion descriptions and high-quality interpolation results.

Event Camera. Through the neuromorphic sensor like dynamic vision sensors (DVS), event camera generates the high-dynamic-range event data under low power consumption [3]. Previous works demonstrate that the event-frame based models show promising potential in visual tasks like image deblurring [8,11,18], high-dynamic-range image restoration [4,28,30], and VFI [5,26,27]. Some meth-ods [18,26,27] avoid modeling the process of motion. The former two methods mix the feature of event and frame through neural networks to directly predict intermediate frames. The disturbance of threshold in event camera has a negative influence on the performance of their models. Time Lens [26] directly predicts intermediate optical flow through event streams, which limits the accuracy of optical flows estimation due to the absence of visual detail in RGB frames. TimeReplayer [5] proposes an unsupervised learning method to aid the video frame interpolation process. Our model is designed based on bi-directional opti-cal flows model. We introduce event streams into our model for the aggregation of bi-directional optical flows in an anisotropic way. The performance of our VFI model is further improved.

3 Method

3.1 Revisiting Bi-directional Optical Flow VFI Model

Given two consecutive frames I_0 and I_1 in a video, we can obtain bi-directional optical flow $F_{0\rightarrow1}$ and $F_{1\rightarrow0}$. $F_{0\rightarrow1}$ and $F_{1\rightarrow0}$ are the optical flows from I_1 to I_0 and the optical flow from I_0 to I_1, respectively. $F_{\tau\rightarrow0}$ and $F_{\tau\rightarrow1}$ are the intermediate optical flows from the target frame to original frames I_0 and I_1, respectively. Both $F_{\tau\rightarrow0}$ and $F_{\tau\rightarrow1}$ can be represented by bi-directional optical flows $F_{0\rightarrow1}$ and $F_{1\rightarrow0}$ as shown in Eq. (1) and Eq. (2):

$$F_{\tau\rightarrow0} = g(\tau, F_{1\rightarrow0}, M_{\text{etra}}) \ or \ g(\tau, F_{0\rightarrow1}, M_{\text{etra}}), \tag{1}$$

$$F_{\tau\rightarrow1} = g(1 - \tau, F_{1\rightarrow0}, M_{\text{etra}}) \ or \ g(1 - \tau, F_{0\rightarrow1}, M_{\text{etra}}). \tag{2}$$

We can blend the optical flow obtained from $F_{1\rightarrow0}$ and $F_{0\rightarrow1}$ to get more accurate optical flows based on temporal consistency. The final intermediate optical flows can be represented as:

$$F_{\tau\rightarrow0} = \text{Blend}_F(g(\tau, F_{1\rightarrow0}, M_{\text{etra}}), g(\tau, F_{0\rightarrow1}, M_{\text{etra}}); \theta_{0-\tau}), \tag{3}$$

$$F_{\tau\rightarrow1} = \text{Blend}_F(g(1 - \tau, F_{1\rightarrow0}, M_{\text{etra}}), g(1 - \tau, F_{0\rightarrow1}, M_{\text{etra}}); \theta_{\tau-1}), \tag{4}$$

where $\text{Blend}_F(\cdot)$ denotes blending operation between initial intermediate optical flows. θ. denotes the parameters in the blending operations, such as linearly weight in temporal consistency [7] or parameters in convolution neural networks.

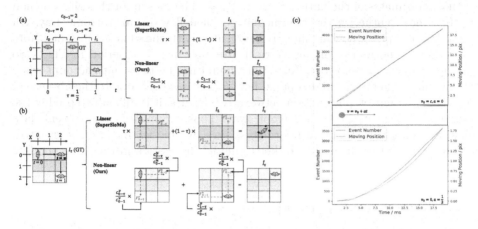

Fig. 2. (a–b) A toy example for the butterfly moving in 0–1 period in one-dimensional and two-dimensional space, respectively. For two-dimensional movements, we use the number of events to generate optical flow masks in different directions. (c) Two enlightening examples on the relationship between the motion (the right axis) and event count (the left axis) in uniform rectilinear motion (the top graph) and uniformly accelerated rectilinear motion (the bottom graph). The unit of velocity v_0 and v are pixels per time step, and the unit of acceleration a is pixels per time step squared. The time step is 3 ms.

According to the final intermediate optical flows, original frames I_0 and I_1 are warped through bilinear interpolation [31] and refined through convolution neural network to get pre-warped intermediate frames $\hat{I}_{0\to\tau}$ and $\hat{I}_{1\to\tau}$. The final intermediate frame $\hat{I}_\tau$ can be represented as the mixture of $\hat{I}_{0\to\tau}$, $\hat{I}_{1\to\tau}$ and extra pre-warped information such as visibility maps [7], depth information [2] and contextual information [16] as shown in Eq. (5):

$$\hat{I}_\tau = \text{Blend}_I(\hat{I}_{0\to\tau}, \hat{I}_{1\to\tau}, M_{\text{extra}}), \qquad (5)$$

where Blend_I denotes blending operations between pre-warped intermediate frames.

A Toy Example. We take the VFI model in SuperSloMo [7] as an example model as shown in Fig. 2(a) and Fig. 2(b) for motion in one dimension and two dimensions, respectively. For the convenience of description, we take SuperSloMo as an example model. As shown in Fig. 2(a), a butterfly rests at location Y_0 in $0 - \tau$ period and flies from location Y_0 to Y_2 in $\tau - 1$ period. I_0 records a butterfly locates in Y_0, while I_1 records a butterfly locates in Y_2. For SuperSloMo model, which assumes the butterfly moves at a constant speed along a line, the synthesized frame I_τ shows the butterfly locates in Y_1 when $\tau = \frac{1}{2}$. However, the actual coordinates of the butterfly are at Y_0. The frame interpolation of the butterfly in two-dimensional motion is similar to that in one-dimensional as shown in Fig. 2(b). The butterfly is predicted at location $Y_{(1,1)}$, while the actual coordinates of the butterfly are at $Y_{(0,2)}$. The reason for this phenomenon is that they synthesize the intermediate optical flow in an isotropic way. All directions of optical flow are linearly aggregated with the same coefficients. Note that there is no motion in the vertical direction in $0 - \tau$ period in Fig. 2. So the optical flow in the vertical direction should not be taken into account when we calculate the intermediate optical flow $F_{\tau \to 0}$. However, due to the absence of intermediate motion information between two frames, it is difficult to predict the different coefficients in an anisotropic way. Thus, we introduce the event data that records the real motion information into our model and use the event to estimate the optical flow mask to better model the motion in the corresponding period.

3.2   Event-Driven Optical Flow Mask

Let's come back to the one-dimensional condition in Fig. 2(a), no motion is observed in $0 - \tau$, leading to no event streams generated. However, the event is generated in $\tau - 1$ due to the motion of the butterfly. If we regard every change as an event, the polarities of the event data $E_{0 \to \tau}$ of such the 3×1 one-dimensional map could be encoded as $[0,\ 0,\ 0]^T$ at the timestamp $t = \tau$ in $0 - \tau$ period, and that of $E_{\tau \to 1}$ is $[-1,\ 0,\ 1]^T$ at the timestamp $t = 1$ in $\tau - 1$ period. The total event data in $0 - 1$ period could be encoded as $[-1,\ 0,\ 1]^T$, which is the same as the event data $E_{\tau \to 1}$. In this simple example, we could find that the event data could encode the ground-truth movement, which could be possibly used to distribute the bi-directional optical flows. We carry out a simulation experiment that a pixel of ball moves in uniform rectilinear motion or uniformly accelerated rectilinear motion and draw the curve of moving position and the curve of event number along the time. As shown in Fig. 2(c), the trend of the moving position curve is basically consistent with the velocity-time curve, and the event count can describe the slowness.

Herein, we propose event-driven optical flow masks ω. that anisotropically determines the weights of the bi-directional optical flows. The optical flow $F_{0 \to 1}$ contributes nothing to the synthesis frame $\hat{I}_\tau$ due to no motion and no event occurrence in $0 - \tau$ period, while the optical flow $F_{1 \to 0}$ is more important to the synthesis frame I_τ due to more motion and event from the butterfly in $\tau - 1$ period. Thus, the distribution of $F_{0 \to 1}$ should be set as 0 while the distribution of $F_{1 \to 0}$ should be set as 1 to generate the accurate intermediate flows. We find the distribution of bi-directional optical flow can be calculated by the ratio between the number of event occurrences in target period and that in the total period. Based on the above analysis, Eq. (1) and Eq. (2) can be rewritten as follows:

$$F_{\tau \to 0} = \omega_{0-\tau} \cdot F_{1 \to 0} \text{ or } -\omega_{0-\tau} \cdot F_{0 \to 1}, \qquad (6)$$

$$F_{\tau \to 1} = \omega_{1-\tau} \cdot F_{0 \to 1} \text{ or } -\omega_{1-\tau} \cdot F_{1 \to 0}, \tag{7}$$

where $\omega_{0-\tau}$ and $\omega_{1-\tau}$ denotes the optical flow mask of bi-directional optical flows in $0 - \tau$ period and $\tau - 1$. We can obtain these weight through event streams as shown in Eq. (8):

$$\omega_{0-\tau} = \frac{c_{0-\tau}}{c_{0-1}} \text{ and } \omega_{1-\tau} = \frac{c_{1-\tau}}{c_{0-1}}, \tag{8}$$

where $c.$ denotes the number of event occurrences in target period. Note that large motion does not necessarily lead to large ratio: the optical flow between two frames represent the total amount of motion, while the ratio Eq. (8) indicates how the motion distributes over time.

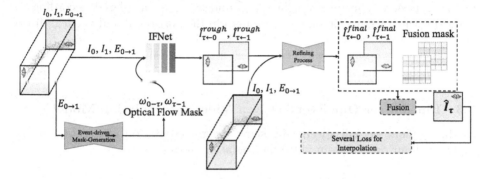

Fig. 3. The pipeline of our proposed method $\mathbf{A^2OF}$. The event is input to Event-driven Mask Generation network to get optical flow masks $\omega_{0-\tau}$ and $\omega_{\tau-1}$. We modify the structure of the IFNet [6] so that it can input event and use anisotropic flow mask as shown in supporting information. Two consecutive frames, corresponding event and optical flow mask are input to tailored IFNet to get intermediate optical flows and warp the original frames. The pre-warped frames $\hat{I}_{\tau \to 0}^{rough}$ and $\hat{I}_{\tau \to 1}^{rough}$ are fused to final intermediate frame $\hat{I}_\tau$ under the supervision of a series of loss.

In order to better analyze the motion in two-dimensional space and model the motion between two frames, we calculate different weights in the orthogonal directions as shown in Fig. 2(b). Specifically, as shown in Fig. 2(b) and Fig. 2(c), the original optical flow $F_{1 \to 0}$ can be divided into $F_{1 \to 0}^u$ in the horizontal direction and $F_{1 \to 0}^v$ in the vertical direction. $F_{0 \to 1}$ can be decomposed in the same way as $F_{0 \to 1}^u$ and $F_{0 \to 1}^v$. The subscripts of these decomposed optical flows indicate the optical flows are in which period, and the superscripts indicate the optical flows are in which direction. Note that we can still obtain intermediate optical flows in the different directions based on Eq. (6–8). Based on the time consistency, we can further combine initial intermediate optical flows $F_{\tau \to 0}^{\cdot}$ or $F_{\tau \to 1}^{\cdot}$ from $F_{1 \to 0}^{\cdot}$ and $F_{0 \to 1}^{\cdot}$, where $\cdot$ in the right corner denotes the direction of optical flow, such as horizontal or vertical direction. The final intermediate optical flows can be represented as:

$$F_{\tau \to 0}^u = -(1 - \tau) \cdot \omega_{0-\tau}^u \cdot F_{0 \to 1}^u + \tau \cdot \omega_{1-\tau}^u \cdot F_{1 \to 0}^u, \tag{9}$$

$$F^u_{\tau \to 1} = (1 - \tau) \cdot \omega^u_{1-\tau} \cdot F^u_{0 \to 1} - \tau \cdot \omega^u_{0-\tau} \cdot F^u_{1 \to 0}. \tag{10}$$

We can also obtain intermediate optical flow in the vertical direction as shown in Eq. (9–10).

Note that the event contains a certain amount of noise due to system noise and unfixed thresholds. Calculation to the weight with unprocessed events will result in inaccurate weight prediction. Thus, we propose a U-Net style convolution neural network named Event-driven Mask Generation Network to process the input event data. The architecture of Event-driven Mask Generation Network can be found in Supporting Information. As shown in Fig. 3, our event-driven mask generation network processes the input event $E_{0 \to 1}$ and outputs two channels feature map which encodes the number of events at each pixel in $0 - \tau$ or $\tau - 1$ period. The final weight $\omega_{0 \to \tau}$ and $\omega_{1 \to \tau}$ is calculated according to Eq. (8) with these two-channel feature map in the horizontal and vertical direction. The spatial size of $\omega_{0 \to \tau}$ and $\omega_{1 \to \tau}$ is with the same spatial size $H \times W$ as bi-directional optical flows. These event-driven optical flow masks are used to obtain the nonlinear intermediate flows $F_{\tau \to 0}$ and $F_{\tau \to 1}$ as shown in Eq. (9–10).

3.3   Pipeline for Our Event-Driven Video Interpolation Model

In this section, we will specifically show the representation of events and the pipeline of our event-driven video interpolation model.

Event Representation. An original event e can be represented as a four-element tuple (x_e, y_e, p_e, t_e), where x_e and y_e denote spatial coordinates. p_e denotes the polarity of the event and t_e denotes the time of occurrence for the event. We should convert those event streams into 2-D frames to input the convolution neural network. Our event streams during the target period are represented as a four-channel frame as shown in [20]. The first and second channels encode the number of positive and negative polarities of events at each pixel, respectively. The third and fourth channels encode the timestamps of the latest triggered positive and negative events, respectively. The represented event data between two consecutive frames I_0 and I_1 is set as $E_{0 \to 1}$.

Event-Driven Optical Flows Estimation. The image frames encode the details of the motion with the low temporal resolution, while the event records the motion information with high temporal resolution. A natural idea is to use these two complementary data together to predict the bi-directional optical flow. Time Lens [26] uses events to directly predict intermediate optical flow which lacks the details of the motion information from frames.

Thus, we take the frame data I_0, I_1, event $E_{0 \to 1}$ and anisotropic optical flow weights as the input to IFNet [6] to estimate the bi-directional optical flow and warp the original frames as shown in Fig. 3 and Supporting Information. We carefully tailor the IFNet and make it suitable for our task. Firstly, our tailored IFNet can process both event and image frames. In this way, the synthetic intermediate optical flow can correctly model the target motion due to the complementary of the two types of data with our anisotropic optical flow weights according to Eq. (9–10). Then, we deeper the IFNet to better process these two types of data. Our tailored IFNet has 4 blocks. Next, the optical flow mask from Event-driven Mask Generation network is input to each block in our tailored IFNet for blending and synthesizing intermediate optical flow. The output of IFNet is rough interpolated frames $\hat{I}_{\tau\leftarrow1}^{\mathrm{rough}}$ and $\hat{I}_{\tau\leftarrow0}^{\mathrm{rough}}$ which will be input to refinement network.

Refinement Network. The warped images $\hat{I}_{\tau\leftarrow0}^{\mathrm{rough}}$, $\hat{I}_{\tau\leftarrow1}^{\mathrm{rough}}$ could encode the most nonlinear motion but poorly around the stationary objects due to the absence of event data in the static regions. To make the intermediate frames better, a refining process is necessary like the previous work [7,26,29]. Except for the additional input event, the overall structure of our refinement network is similar to that in [7]. Our refinement network is a U-Net style network with 6 encoders and 5 decoders with a shortcut between encoder and decoder of the same spatial scale. The details of our refinement network are provided in supporting information.As shown in Fig. 3, we input the data I_0, I_1, $E_{0\rightarrow1}$, $\hat{I}_{\tau\leftarrow0}^{\mathrm{rough}}$, $\hat{I}_{\tau\leftarrow1}^{\mathrm{rough}}$ and bi-directional optical flow $F_{0\rightarrow1}$, $F_{1\rightarrow0}$ into a sub-network. Herein, the output is two fusion maps $V_{\tau\leftarrow0}$, $V_{\tau\leftarrow1}$ and two refined frames $\hat{I}_{\tau\leftarrow0}^{\mathrm{final}}$ and $\hat{I}_{\tau\leftarrow1}^{\mathrm{final}}$.Thus, the final intermediate frames $\hat{I}_\tau$ is defined after the Fusion process of Fusion($\cdot$):

$$\hat{I}_\tau = \mathrm{Fusion}\left(I_{\tau\leftarrow0}^{\mathrm{final}}, I_{\tau\leftarrow1}^{\mathrm{final}}, V_{\tau\leftarrow0}, V_{\tau\leftarrow1}\right)$$
$$= V_{\tau\leftarrow0} \cdot I_{\tau\leftarrow0}^{\mathrm{final}} + V_{\tau\leftarrow1} \cdot I_{\tau\leftarrow1}^{\mathrm{final}}, \tag{11}$$

where $V_{\tau\leftarrow0}$ and $V_{\tau\leftarrow1}$ are two visibility maps which encode whether the objects are occluded. The pixel-addition of two visibility map equals 1, following [7].

Loss Function. Our event-driven video frame interpolation model can be trained in an end-to-end manner under the combination of event-driven motion consistency loss $\mathcal{L}_{\mathrm{MC}}$, the reconstruction loss $\mathcal{L}_{\mathrm{rec}}$, the perceptual loss $\mathcal{L}_{\mathrm{per}}$, the warped loss $\mathcal{L}_{\mathrm{warp}}$ and the smoothness loss $\mathcal{L}_{\mathrm{smooth}}$. Note that the reconstruction loss $\mathcal{L}_{\mathrm{rec}}$, the perceptual loss $\mathcal{L}_{\mathrm{per}}$, the warped loss $\mathcal{L}_{\mathrm{warp}}$ and the smoothness loss $\mathcal{L}_{\mathrm{smooth}}$ are similar to [7].

Event-driven motion consistency loss $\mathcal{L}_{\mathrm{mc}}$ measures the gap between estimated event count map $\hat{E}^{\mathrm{count}}$ and real event count map E^{count}. We take event count map $\hat{E}_{0\rightarrow\tau}^{\mathrm{count}}$ as an example. $\hat{E}_{0\rightarrow\tau}^{\mathrm{count}}$ is calculated with the difference between two frames I_{diff} which is represented as

$$I_{\mathrm{diff}} = \log\left(\frac{I_{\tau\leftarrow0}^{\mathrm{final}}}{I_0}\right). \tag{12}$$

Due to unknown and inflexible thresholds in event camera, it is difficult to directly get event count map through Eq. (12). So, we binarize the event count to reflect whether the event appears or not in each pixel. Specifically, in the event count map, 1 denotes there is at least one event while 0 denotes there is

no event. How to binarize the I_{diff} to obtain estimated event count map $\hat{E}_{0\to\tau}^{\text{count}}$?
Firstly, we get $E_{0\to\tau}^{\text{count}}$ through the first and second channel in $E_{0\to\tau}$:

$$E_{0\to\tau}^{\text{count}} = \text{sgn}(E_{0\to\tau}[0:2]), \tag{13}$$

where $\text{sgn}(\cdot)$ denotes the sign function and $[0:2]$ denotes the first and second
channel of a tensor. Then, we sum all elements in $E_{0\to\tau}^{\text{count}}$ along each channel to
obtain binarized threshold t_{positive} and t_{negative}, respectively. These thresholds
record the number of locations where the event has occurred. Next, we sort I_{diff}
in descending order and select the top t_{positive} value $N_{t_{\text{positive}}}$ and the bottom
$N_{t_{\text{negative}}}$ value as binarized thresholds for I_{diff}.

$$\hat{E}_{0\to\tau}^{\text{count}} = [\text{sgn}(I_{\text{diff}} - N_{t_{\text{positive}}}), \text{sgn}(N_{t_{\text{negative}}} - I_{\text{diff}})], \tag{14}$$

where $[\cdot,\cdot]$ denotes concat function in tensor. $\text{sgn}(I_{\text{diff}} - N_{t_{\text{positive}}})$ represents
where there may be positive events. We want $\hat{E}_{0\to\tau}^{\text{count}}$ and $E_{\cdot}^{\text{count}}$ to be exactly
the same, which means that the motion information recorded by both is almost
the same. The definition of $\mathcal{L}_{\text{mc}}$ is

$$\mathcal{L}_{\text{mc}} = \frac{1}{N}||G(\hat{E}_{0\to\tau}^{\text{count}}) - G(E_{0\to\tau}^{\text{count}})||_1 + \frac{1}{N}||G(\hat{E}_{\tau\to1}^{\text{count}}) - G(E_{\tau\to1}^{\text{count}})||_1, \tag{15}$$

where $G(\cdot)$ denotes Gaussian Blur Function. We smooth the $\hat{E}_{\cdot}^{\text{count}}$ with $G(\cdot)$
to alleviate the effect of noise in the event. The definition of the reconstruction
loss, the perception loss, the warping loss and the smoothness loss here are the
same as SuperSloMo [7] does.

The total loss $\mathcal{L}$ of our model is

$$\mathcal{L} = \lambda_{mc} \cdot \mathcal{L}_{\text{mc}} + \lambda_{rec} \cdot \mathcal{L}_{\text{rec}} + \lambda_{per} \cdot \mathcal{L}_{\text{per}} + \lambda_{warp} \cdot \mathcal{L}_{\text{warp}} + \lambda_{smooth} \cdot \mathcal{L}_{\text{smooth}}. \tag{16}$$

Note that all the loss weights in Eq. (16) is set empirically on the validation set.
Specifically, $\lambda_{mc} = 1.0$, $\lambda_{rec} = 1.0$, $\lambda_{per} = 0.2$, $\lambda_{warp} = 0.8$ and $\lambda_{smooth} = 0.8$.

4   Experiments

4.1   Implementation Details

Our proposed model and all experiments are implemented in Pytorch [21]. We
use adam optimizer with standard settings in [9]. For training, our model is
trained end-to-end on 4 NVIDIA Tesla V100 GPUs for the total 500 epochs.
The batch size of each training step is 28. The initial learning rate is 10^{-4}
and is multiplied by 0.1 per 200 epochs. We calculate the peak-signal-to-noise
ratio (PSNR), structural similarity (SSIM), and interpolation-error (IE) as the
quantitative metric to evaluate the performance of our proposed method.

4.2   Datasets

We firstly evaluate our model on three common high-speed synthetic datasets with synthetic events: Adobe240 [25], GoPro [15] and Middlebury [1]. Besides, we also evaluate our model on the real frame-event dataset: High-Quality Frames (HQF) [24], High Speed Event-RGB(HS-ERGB) [26]. All the synthetic training sets are collected to train our model. Then, we compare with other previous state-of-the-art methods.

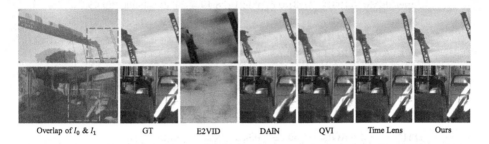

| Overlap of I_0 & I_1 | GT | E2VID | DAIN | QVI | Time Lens | Ours |

Fig. 4. Visual comparisons with different methods on the synthetic dataset Adobe240.

Synthetic Datasets. Adobe240 consists of 112 different sequences for training and 8 sequences for testing. GoPro dataset consists of 22 different videos for training and 11 videos for testing. Captured by GoPro cameras, both of them own 240 fps and 1280 × 720 resolutions in all the sequences. We use ESIM [22] to generate event streams between two consecutive frames. We crop patches with spatial size 384 × 384 for training.

Real Dataset. High-Quality Frames(HQF) is collected through the DAVIS240 event camera [24] which can generate both event streams and corresponding frames. It consists of 14 different frames sequences with the corresponding event streams. The resolutions are 240 × 180 in all sequences. We crop patches with spatial size 128 × 128 for training. HS-ERGB is collected through Gen4M 720p event camera and FLIP BackFly S RGB camera. This dataset is divided into far-away sequences and close planar scenes.

4.3   Comparisons with Previous Methods

Synthetic Datasets. We compare our proposed video frame interpolation (VFI) model with previous VFI models. Previous methods can be classified into three categories: frame-based approach, event-based approach and frame-event-based approach. For frame-based approach, we compare our model with SuperSloMo [7], DAIN [2], SepConv [17], QVI [29]. For the event-based approach, we compare our model with event-based video reconstruction method E2VID [23]. For event-frame-based approach, we compare our model with Time Lens [26]. We make a fair comparison on three synthetic datasets Adobe240 [25],

Table 1. Quantitative comparison with previous methods on the synthetic datasets Adobe240, GoPro and Middlebury. Note that we directly evaluate the released model in each method without re-training or fine-tuning.

Adobe240		All frames in 7 skips			Middle frame in 7 skips		
Method	Input	PSNR	SSIM	IE	PSNR	SSIM	IE
E2VID [23]	Event	10.40	0.570	75.21	10.32	0.573	76.01
SepConv	RGB	32.31	0.930	7.59	31.07	0.912	8.78
DAIN	RGB	32.08	0.928	7.51	30.31	0.908	8.94
SuperSloMo	RGB	31.05	0.921	8.19	29.49	0.900	9.68
QVI	RGB	32.87	0.939	6.93	31.89	0.925	7.57
Time Lens	RGB+E	35.47	0.954	5.92	34.83	0.949	6.53
Ours (A^{2}OF)	RGB+E	**36.59**	**0.960**	**5.58**	**36.21**	**0.957**	**5.96**
GoPro		All frames in 7 skips			Middle frame in 7 skips		
Method	Input	PSNR	SSIM	IE	PSNR	SSIM	IE
E2VID	Event	9.74	0.549	79.49	9.88	0.569	80.08
SepConv	RGB	29.81	0.913	8.87	28.12	0.887	10.78
DAIN	RGB	30.92	0.901	8.60	28.82	0.863	10.71
SuperSloMo	RGB	29.54	0.880	9.36	27.63	0.840	11.47
QVI	RGB	31.39	0.931	7.09	29.84	0.911	8.57
Time Lens	RGB+E	34.81	0.959	5.19	34.45	0.951	5.42
Ours (A^{2}OF)	RGB+E	**36.61**	**0.971**	**4.23**	**35.95**	**0.967**	**4.62**
Middlebury (other)		All frames in 3 skips			Middle frame in 3 skips		
Method	Input	PSNR	SSIM	IE	PSNR	SSIM	IE
E2VID	Event	11.26	0.427	69.73	11.12	0.407	70.35
SepConv	RGB	25.51	0.824	6.74	25.12	0.811	7.06
DAIN	RGB	26.67	0.838	6.17	25.96	0.793	6.54
SuperSloMo	RGB	26.14	0.825	6.33	25.53	0.805	6.85
QVI	RGB	26.31	0.827	6.58	25.72	0.798	6.73
Time Lens	RGB+E	32.13	0.908	4.07	31.57	0.893	4.62
Ours (A^{2}OF)	RGB+E	**32.59**	**0.916**	**3.92**	**31.81**	**0.903**	**4.13**

GoPro [15] and Middlebury [1]. The comparison results are as shown in Table 1. For training on Adobe240 and GoPro, we select 1 frame from every 8 frames in the original sequence, use the selected frames to form the input sequences, and use the remaining frames as the label for interpolated frames. Middlebury is only used for the test due to the sequence length. Besides, the event streams are generated through ESIM [22] between selected frames is also available to our model. For the input frames sequences from selected frames and events, the skipped frames are reconstructed through our proposed method and compared with the ground truth skipped frames. The average performance of the whole 7 skipped frames and the center one are both calculated for fair comparison. Meanwhile, only 3 frames are skipped and used to calculate reconstruction metrics due to the sequence length limitation in Middlebury. The results are summarized in Table 1. Note that we directly evaluate the released model in each comparison method without re-training or fine-tuning.

From Table 1, our proposed method outperforms all the previous methods and achieves the-state-of-art performance on Adobe240, GoPro and Middlebury. The frame-event based approaches outperform the frame-only or event-only approaches. As shown in Fig. 4, due to better use of events with event-driven optical flow mask and event-driven motion consistency loss, our model achieves the best visual quality. Specifically, for the second row in Fig. 4, all objects are static while only the intensity changes. It's a common issue in warping based interpolation method, which is also mentioned by Time Lens. The results indicate improvement by event-driven motion consistency loss in our method.

Table 2. Quantitative comparison with previous methods on the real frame-event datasets HQF. Note that we directly evaluate the released model in each comparison method without re-training or fine-tuning.

HQF		3 skips		1 skip	
Method	Input	PSNR	SSIM	PSNR	SSIM
E2VID	Event	6.70	0.315	6.70	0.315
RRIN	RGB	26.11	0.778	29.76	0.874
BMBC	RGB	26.32	0.781	29.96	0.875
DAIN	RGB	26.10	0.782	29.82	0.875
SuperSloMo	RGB	25.54	0.761	28.76	0.861
Time Lens	RGB+E	30.57	0.900	32.49	0.927
Ours (A^{2}OF)	RGB+E	**31.85**	**0.932**	**33.94**	**0.945**
HS-ERGB (far)		7 skips		5 skip	
Method	Input	PSNR	SSIM	PSNR	SSIM
E2VID	Event	7.01	0.372	7.05	0.374
RRIN	RGB	23.73	0.703	25.26	0.738
BMBC	RGB	24.14	0.710	25.62	0.742
DAIN	RGB	27.13	0.748	27.92	0.780
SuperSloMo	RGB	24.16	0.692	25.66	0.727
Time Lens	RGB+E	32.31	0.869	33.13	0.877
Ours (A^{2}OF)	RGB+E	**33.15**	**0.883**	**33.64**	**0.891**
HS-ERGB (close)		7 skips		5 skip	
Method	Input	PSNR	SSIM	PSNR	SSIM
E2VID	Event	7.68	0.427	7.73	0.432
RRIN	RGB	27.46	0.800	28.69	0.813
BMBC	RGB	27.99	0.808	29.22	0.820
DAIN	RGB	28.50	0.801	29.03	0.807
SuperSloMo	RGB	27.27	0.775	28.35	0.788
Time Lens	RGB+E	31.68	0.835	32.19	0.839
Ours (A^{2}OF)	RGB+E	**32.55**	**0.852**	**33.21**	**0.865**

Real Frame-Event Dataset. We also evaluate and compare our method with the state-of-the-art methods on the real dataset of HQF: E2VID [23], RRIN [10], BMBC [19], DAIN [2], SuperSloMo [7] and Time Lens [26]. The results are summarized in Table 2. We have two experiment settings for training on HQF: Firstly, we select 1 frame from every 4 frames in the original sequences which is viewed as '3-skip' as shown in Table 2. Second, we select 1 frame from every 2 frames in the original sequences which is viewed as '1-skip' as shown in Table 2. For HS-ERGB, we select 1 frame from every 8 frames or select 1 frame from evey 6 frames. Note that our model is finetuned with real frames-event datasets based on the model trained on synthetic datasets.

Similar results as the experiments on synthetic datasets could be indicted by quantitative comparison as shown in Table 2. As shown in Fig. 5, only our method could reconstruct the legs of the moving horse in the second row. Due to the absence of visual details from frames in E2VID, synthesized frames through the only event has a large the gap with real intermediate frames. DAIN and QVI fail to synthesize high-quality interpolated frames in the regions with complex motions such as the letters in the first row and the legs in the second row. Their methods cannot model the complicated motion in the real scenes very well.

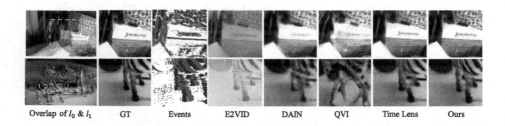

Overlap of I_0 & I_1 GT   Events   E2VID   DAIN   QVI   Time Lens   Ours

Fig. 5. Visual comparisons with different methods on HQF with real events.

Table 3. Ablation studies. EDOF denotes our proposed event-driven optical flow mask. MCL denotes our proposed event-driven Motion Consistency Loss.

EDOF	MCL	PSNR	SSIM	IE
×	✓	33.82	0.952	7.13
✓	×	35.27	0.963	5.75
✓	✓	36.61	0.971	4.23

4.4 Ablation Studies

To study the contribution of each module in our proposed model, we perform the ablation study on the GoPro dataset as shown in Table 3. Firstly, to evaluate the influence of Event-driven Optical Flow mask, we replace the mask with linear weights in SuperSloMo [7]. Experimental results show that our proposed event-driven optical flow mask has a positive effect in VFI model with the improvement of PSNR, SSIM and IE. As for our proposed event-driven motion consistency loss, we train a model without the supervision of this loss. This loss can be used to constrain the motion information coming from the change of intensity and event streams to be similar. Results show that this loss can further improve the performance of our proposed model.

5   Conclusion

In this paper, we propose a video frame interpolation method with event-driven anisotropic flow adjustment in an end-to-end training strategy. Besides, we design an event-driven motion consistency loss based on the change of intensity to constrain the gap between the estimated motion information and that from event streams. Instead of proposing complex motion assumptions like previous work, leading to isotropic intermediate flow generation or anisotropic adjustment through learned higher-order motion information, we use events to generate event-driven optical masks for the different directions, assigning the weight of bi-directional optical in intermediate optical flow in an anisotropic way. The proposed event-driven motion consistency loss further improves our method. The experiment results show that our model performs better than previous methods and achieves the state-of-the-art performance.

References

1. Baker, S., Scharstein, D., Lewis, J.P., Roth, S., Black, M.J., Szeliski, R.: A database and evaluation methodology for optical flow. Int. J. Comput. Vis. **92**(1), 1–31 (2011)
2. Bao, W., Lai, W., Ma, C., Zhang, X., Gao, Z., Yang, M.: Depth-aware video frame interpolation. In: 2019 IEEE Conference on Computer Vision and Pattern Recognition, CVPR 2019, Long Beach, CA, USA, 16–20 June 2019, pp. 3703–3712 (2019)
3. Gallego, G., et al.: Event-based vision: a survey. IEEE Trans. Pattern Anal. Mach. Intell. (2019)
4. Han, J., et al.: Neuromorphic camera guided high dynamic range imaging. In: 2020 IEEE Conference on Computer Vision and Pattern Recognition, CVPR 2020, Seattle, WA, USA, 13–19 June 2020, pp. 1730–1739 (2020)
5. He, W., et al.: TimeReplayer: unlocking the potential of event cameras for video interpolation. In: CVPR (2022)
6. Huang, Z., Zhang, T., Heng, W., Shi, B., Zhou, S.: RIFE: real-time intermediate flow estimation for video frame interpolation. CoRR abs/2011.06294 (2020)
7. Jiang, H., Sun, D., Jampani, V., Yang, M., Learned-Miller, E.G., Kautz, J.: Super slomo: high quality estimation of multiple intermediate frames for video interpolation. In: 2018 IEEE Conference on Computer Vision and Pattern Recognition, CVPR 2018, Salt Lake City, UT, USA, 18–22 June 2018, pp. 9000–9008 (2018)
8. Jiang, Z., Zhang, Y., Zou, D., Ren, J., Lv, J., Liu, Y.: Learning event-based motion deblurring. In: 2020 IEEE Conference on Computer Vision and Pattern Recognition, CVPR 2020, Seattle, WA, USA, 13–19 June 2020, pp. 3320–3329 (2020)
9. Kingma, D.P., Ba, J.: Adam: a method for stochastic optimization (2015)

10. Li, H., Yuan, Y., Wang, Q.: Video frame interpolation via residue refinement. In: 2020 IEEE International Conference on Acoustics, Speech and Signal Processing, ICASSP 2020, Barcelona, Spain, 4–8 May 2020, pp. 2613–2617 (2020)
11. Lin, S., et al.: Learning event-driven video deblurring and interpolation. In: Computer Vision - ECCV 2020–16th European Conference, Glasgow, UK, 23–28 August 2020, Proceedings, Part VIII, pp. 16155–16164 (2020)
12. Liu, Y., Xie, L., Li, S., Sun, W., Qiao, Y., Dong, C.: Enhanced quadratic video interpolation. In: Bartoli, A., Fusiello, A. (eds.) Computer Vision - ECCV 2020 Workshops - Glasgow, UK, 23–28 August 2020, Proceedings, Part IV, pp. 41–56 (2020)
13. Liu, Z., Yeh, R.A., Tang, X., Liu, Y., Agarwala, A.: Video frame synthesis using deep voxel flow. In: IEEE International Conference on Computer Vision, ICCV 2017, Venice, Italy, 22–29 October 2017, pp. 4463–4471 (2017)
14. Long, G., Kneip, L., Alvarez, J.M., Li, H., Zhang, X., Yu, Q.: Learning image matching by simply watching video. In: Leibe, B., Matas, J., Sebe, N., Welling, M. (eds.) ECCV 2016. LNCS, vol. 9910, pp. 434–450. Springer, Cham (2016). https://doi.org/10.1007/978-3-319-46466-4_26
15. Nah, S., Kim, T.H., Lee, K.M.: Deep multi-scale convolutional neural network for dynamic scene deblurring. In: 2017 IEEE Conference on Computer Vision and Pattern Recognition, CVPR 2017, Honolulu, HI, USA, 21–26 July 2017, pp. 257–265 (2017)
16. Niklaus, S., Liu, F.: Context-aware synthesis for video frame interpolation. In: 2018 IEEE Conference on Computer Vision and Pattern Recognition, CVPR 2018, Salt Lake City, UT, USA, 18–22 June 2018, pp. 1701–1710 (2018)
17. Niklaus, S., Mai, L., Liu, F.: Video frame interpolation via adaptive separable convolution. In: IEEE International Conference on Computer Vision, ICCV 2017, Venice, Italy, 22–29 October 2017 (2017)
18. Pan, L., Scheerlinck, C., Yu, X., Hartley, R., Liu, M., Dai, Y.: Bringing a blurry frame alive at high frame-rate with an event camera. In: 2019 IEEE Conference on Computer Vision and Pattern Recognition, CVPR 2019, Long Beach, CA, USA, 16–20 June 2019, pp. 6820–6829. Computer Vision Foundation/IEEE (2019)
19. Park, J., Ko, K., Lee, C., Kim, C.-S.: BMBC: bilateral motion estimation with bilateral cost volume for video interpolation. In: Vedaldi, A., Bischof, H., Brox, T., Frahm, J.-M. (eds.) ECCV 2020. LNCS, vol. 12359, pp. 109–125. Springer, Cham (2020). https://doi.org/10.1007/978-3-030-58568-6_7
20. Park, P.K.J., et al.: Performance improvement of deep learning based gesture recognition using spatiotemporal demosaicing technique. In: 2016 IEEE International Conference on Image Processing, ICIP 2016, Phoenix, AZ, USA, 25–28 September 2016, pp. 1624–1628 (2016)
21. Paszke, A., et al.: Pytorch: an imperative style, high-performance deep learning library, pp. 8024–8035 (2019)
22. Rebecq, H., Gehrig, D., Scaramuzza, D.: ESIM: an open event camera simulator. In: Proceedings of 2nd Annual Conference on Robot Learning, CoRL 2018, Zürich, Switzerland, 29–31 October 2018, pp. 969–982 (2018)
23. Rebecq, H., Ranftl, R., Koltun, V., Scaramuzza, D.: High speed and high dynamic range video with an event camera. IEEE Trans. Pattern Anal. Mach. Intell. **43**(6), 1964–1980 (2021)
24. Stoffregen, T., et al.: Reducing the sim-to-real gap for event cameras. In: Vedaldi, A., Bischof, H., Brox, T., Frahm, J.-M. (eds.) ECCV 2020. LNCS, vol. 12372, pp. 534–549. Springer, Cham (2020). https://doi.org/10.1007/978-3-030-58583-9_32

25. Su, S., Delbracio, M., Wang, J., Sapiro, G., Heidrich, W., Wang, O.: Deep video deblurring for hand-held cameras. In: 2017 IEEE Conference on Computer Vision and Pattern Recognition, CVPR 2017, Honolulu, HI, USA, 21–26 July 2017, pp. 237–246 (2017)
26. Tulyakov, S., et al.: Time lens: event-based video frame interpolation. In: 2021 IEEE Conference on Computer Vision and Pattern Recognition, CVPR 2021, virtual, 19–25 June 2021, pp. 16155–16164 (2021)
27. Wang, B., He, J., Yu, L., Xia, G.-S., Yang, W.: Event enhanced high-quality image recovery. In: Vedaldi, A., Bischof, H., Brox, T., Frahm, J.-M. (eds.) ECCV 2020. LNCS, vol. 12358, pp. 155–171. Springer, Cham (2020). https://doi.org/10.1007/978-3-030-58601-0_10
28. Wang, L., Ho, Y.S., Yoon, K.J., et al.: Event-based high dynamic range image and very high frame rate video generation using conditional generative adversarial networks. In: 2019 IEEE Conference on Computer Vision and Pattern Recognition, CVPR 2019, Long Beach, CA, USA, 16–20 June 2019, pp. 10081–10090 (2019)
29. Xu, X., Si-Yao, L., Sun, W., Yin, Q., Yang, M.: Quadratic video interpolation. In: Wallach, H.M., Larochelle, H., Beygelzimer, A., d'Alché-Buc, F., Fox, E.B., Garnett, R. (eds.) Advances in Neural Information Processing Systems 32: Annual Conference on Neural Information Processing Systems 2019, NeurIPS 2019, 8–14 December 2019, Vancouver, BC, Canada, pp. 1645–1654 (2019)
30. Zhang, S., Zhang, Yu., Jiang, Z., Zou, D., Ren, J., Zhou, B.: Learning to see in the dark with events. In: Vedaldi, A., Bischof, H., Brox, T., Frahm, J.-M. (eds.) ECCV 2020. LNCS, vol. 12363, pp. 666–682. Springer, Cham (2020). https://doi.org/10.1007/978-3-030-58523-5_39
31. Zhou, T., Tulsiani, S., Sun, W., Malik, J., Efros, A.A.: View synthesis by appearance flow. In: Leibe, B., Matas, J., Sebe, N., Welling, M. (eds.) ECCV 2016. LNCS, vol. 9908, pp. 286–301. Springer, Cham (2016). https://doi.org/10.1007/978-3-319-46493-0_18

EvAC3D: From Event-Based Apparent Contours to 3D Models via Continuous Visual Hulls

Ziyun Wang[(✉)] [ID], Kenneth Chaney[(✉)] [ID], and Kostas Daniilidis [ID]

University of Pennsylvania, Philadelphia, PA 19104, USA
{ziyunw,chaneyk}@seas.upenn.edu

Abstract. 3D reconstruction from multiple views is a successful computer vision field with multiple deployments in applications. State of the art is based on traditional RGB frames that enable optimization of photo-consistency cross views. In this paper, we study the problem of 3D reconstruction from event-cameras, motivated by the advantages of event-based cameras in terms of low power and latency as well as by the biological evidence that eyes in nature capture the same data and still perceive well 3D shape. The foundation of our hypothesis that 3D-reconstruction is feasible using events lies in the information contained in the occluding contours and in the continuous scene acquisition with events. We propose Apparent Contour Events (ACE), a novel event-based representation that defines the geometry of the apparent contour of an object. We represent ACE by a spatially and temporally continuous implicit function defined in the event x-y-t space. Furthermore, we design a novel continuous Voxel Carving algorithm enabled by the high temporal resolution of the Apparent Contour Events. To evaluate the performance of the method, we collect MOEC-3D, a 3D event dataset of a set of common real-world objects. We demonstrate EvAC3D's ability to reconstruct high-fidelity mesh surfaces from real event sequences while allowing the refinement of the 3D reconstruction for each individual event. The code, data and supplementary material for this work can be accessed through the project page: https://www.cis.upenn.edu/~ziyunw/evac3d/.

1   Introduction

Traditional 3D reconstruction algorithms are frame-based because common camera sensors output images at a fixed frame rate. The fixed frame rate assumption challenges researchers to develop complex techniques to handle undesirable situations due to discontinuity between frames, such as occlusions. Therefore, recovering the association between views of the same object has been an essential problem in 3D reconstruction with a single camera. Such challenges fundamentally arise from the discrete time sampling of visual signals, which forces

---

Supplementary Information The online version contains supplementary material available at https://doi.org/10.1007/978-3-031-20071-7_17.

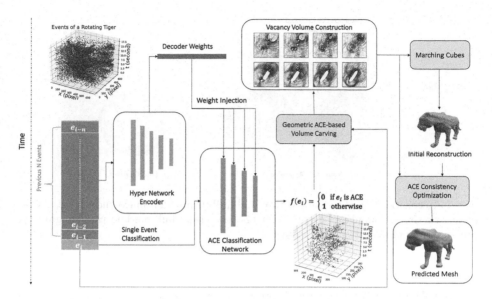

Fig. 1. EvAC3D Pipeline. We use the previous N events as conditional information to predict the label for the current event. A hyper network is used to inject the conditional information into the decoding classifier. The predicted label is then passed into a geometry-based volume event carving algorithm.

vision algorithms to recover the missing information between views. However, these problems do not exist naturally in biological systems because visual signals are encoded as a stream of temporally continuous spikes. Continuous encoding tremendously benefits humans and animals in many tasks, including estimating the 3D geometry of an object. The question is: *can a computer vision algorithm do better if it sees the same continuous world as humans do?*

In this work, we seek the answer to this question by developing a novel algorithm for bio-inspired event-based cameras. Event-based cameras are novel visual sensors that generate a continuous stream of events triggered by the change of the logarithm of the light intensity. The events are asynchronously generated without temporal binning; therefore, the high-resolution temporal information can be completely recovered from each event with minimal discontinuity. Additionally, the individual pixels of the camera do not have a global shutter speed, which gives the camera extremely high dynamic range. Due to the high dynamic range and high temporal resolution of event cameras, they have become an ideal choice for understanding fast motions. For 3D reconstruction, traditional cameras operate on a fixed frame rate. For image-based visual hull methods, the limited number of views means the smooth surfaces of the object cannot be properly reconstructed, which can be seen from the sphere reconstruction example in Fig. 2.

Ideally, one can expect to directly perform incremental updates to the geometry of an object at the same high temporal resolution as events. To this end, we

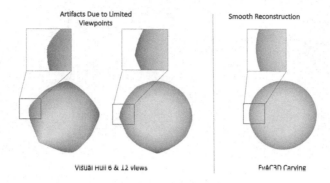

Fig. 2. Reconstruction of a sphere with visual hull (6 and 12 frames) and with EvAC3D reconstruction on simulated events. The 12-view visual hull method uses roughly the same number of operations as EvAC3D.

propose a 3D reconstruction pipeline that directly predicts a mesh from a continuous stream of events assuming known camera trajectory from a calibrated camera. We introduce a novel concept of **Apparent Contour Events** to define the boundary of an object in the continuous x-y-t space. Through Apparent Contour Events, we incrementally construct the function of a 3D object surface at the same high temporal resolution as events. Here is a list of our main contributions:

- We introduce a novel event concept of **Apparent Contour Events** that relates high-speed events to the tangent rays of the 3D surface to the viewpoint.
- We propose a learning pipeline to predict which events are Apparent Contour Events without manual annotation but using 3D models of known objects. We propose a novel event-based neural network with point-based decoding to classify the Apparent Contour Events.
- We present a continuous algorithm to reconstruct an object directly from a stream of events. The algorithm can accurately reconstruct objects with complex geometry in both synthetic and real environments.
- We collect MOEC-3D, a high-quality real 3D event dataset for evaluating the performance of 3D reconstruction techniques from events that provides events, ground-truth 3D models, and ground-truth camera trajectories.

2   Related Work

3D Reconstruction with Event Cameras. Due to the asynchronous and sparse nature of the event sensors, 3D reconstruction algorithms cannot be directly applied. Most current work in event-based 3D reconstruction uses a stereo pair of cameras [4,13,28,29]. The time coincidence of the events observed from a synchronized pair of cameras is used for stereo matching. These methods work in situations where multiple calibrated cameras are used synchronously. Zhu et al. [29] construct a cost volume based on warping using multiple disparity hypotheses. Carneiro et al. [4] use time incidence between two synchronized event streams to perform stereo matching. Chaney et al. [5] use a event single camera in motion to learn the 3D structure of the world. E3D [2] attempts to directly predict meshes from multi-view event images. This method is trained and mainly evaluated on synthetic data due to the large amount of 3D data needed for training. EMVS [20] adopts an event-based ray counting technique. Similar to our method, EMVS treats individual events as rays to take advantage of the sparse nature of the event data. In Sect. 3.3, we show how sparse processing can be extended further to work with only a particular type of events that contain rather rich geometric information.

3D Reconstruction from Occluding Contours. Reconstruction from the perspective projection of a geometric surface has been extensively studied in classical computer vision. Among different geometric representations used in such problems, apparent contour representation is most relevant to our work. Apparent contours, or extreme boundaries of the object, contain rich information about a smooth object surface. Barrow et al. [1] argue that surface orientations can be directly computed from a set of apparent contours in line drawings. Cipolla et al. [7] propose the theoretical framework from reconstructing a surface from the deformation of apparent contours. Based on the idea of contour generator [16], the projection of the apparent contours onto the image plane are used as tangent planes to the object. Furthermore, structure and motion can be simultaneously recovered from apparent contours. Wong et al. [26] propose to solve the camera poses and 3D coordinates of "frontier points", the intersection of the apparent contours in two camera views. A circular motion with a minimum of 3 image frames is assumed to solve the optimization problem.

Visual Hull. Visual hull is used to reconstruct 3D objects through Shape-From-Silhouette (SFS) techniques [3,14]. Information from multiple views are aggregated into a single volume through intersection of the projective cones described by the silhouette at each view. Voxel grid and octrees [12,23] are commonly used as discretized volumetric representations. SFS methods are particularly susceptible to false-negative labels (labeling an interior point as an exterior point).

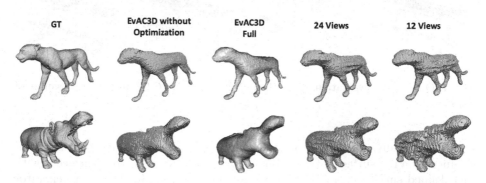

Fig. 3. Qualitative comparisons between EvAC3Dand mask based carving of 12 and 24 views respectively. Cheetah, hippo, and elephant were chosen as a subset of the animal scans.

3   Method

In this section, we explain how a continuous stream of events can be used to reconstruct the object surface. We divide the pipeline into two stages: **Apparent Contour Event Extraction** and **Continuous Volume Carving**.

3.1   Apparent Contour Event (ACE)

The main challenge in reconstructing objects from events is finding the appropriate geometric quantities that can be used for surface reconstruction. In frame-based reconstruction algorithms, silhouettes are used to encode the rays from the camera center to the object. However, computing silhouettes requires integrating frame-based representations, which limits the temporal resolution of the reconstruction updates. Additionally, since events represent the change in log of light intensity, events are only observed where the image gradients are nonzero. Therefore, one would not observe enough events on a smooth object surface. These two facts combined make traditional silhouettes non-ideal for events. To address these two shortcomings, we introduce **Apparent Contour Events (ACE)**, a novel representation that encodes the object geometry while preserving the high temporal resolution of the events.

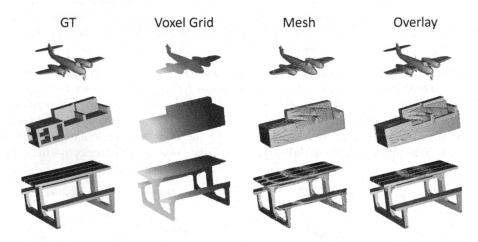

Fig. 4. Qualitative evaluations from ShapeNet using EvAC3D on three categories of objects.

Geometrically, the generator of occluding contours on image planes is constrained by a ray-surface intersection and tangency [9]. A smooth surface S with well defined surface normals at each point has an occluding contour generator for each camera center $^{w}\mathbf{p_c}$. The contour generator is composed of image rays that intersect the S at exactly one point $^{w}\mathbf{X}$. A surface point $^{o}\mathbf{x}$ with normal $^{w}\mathbf{n}$

is included in the contour generator for the camera center $^w\mathbf{p_c}$ if for an image ray $^w\mathbf{v}$ the ray-surface intersection and tangency constraints hold [9]:

$$\lambda^o\mathbf{v} + {}^w\mathbf{p_c} = {}^w\mathbf{X} \tag{1}$$
$$^w\mathbf{n}^\mathsf{T}(^w\mathbf{X} - {}^w\mathbf{p_c}) = 0 \tag{2}$$

We define Apparent Contour Events formally. ACEs are events that meet the ray-surface intersection and tangency constraints [9]. Since each event can contain a potentially unique timestamp, the constraints must be thought of in continuous time, as opposed to indexible on a per frame basis. An event e_i generates an image ray $^c\mathbf{x}(t)$ at a camera center $^w\mathbf{p_c}(t)$. e_i is an ACE if for some point $^w\mathbf{X}(t)$ on the surface $\mathcal{S}$:

$$^w\mathbf{n}(t)^\mathsf{T}(^w\mathbf{X}(t) - {}^w\mathbf{p_c}(t)) = 0 \tag{3}$$
$$\lambda(t)^w\mathbf{R_c}(t)^c\mathbf{x}(t) + {}^w\mathbf{p_c}(t) = {}^w\mathbf{X}(t) \tag{4}$$

Intuitively, ACE can be seen as the set of events $e_i = \{x_i, y_i, t_i, p_i\}$ that belong to the active contour of the object at time t_i. Due to the contrast between the active contour of an object with the background, a significant number of events are generated around the contour. Unlike silhouettes, which require filling in holes on the "eventless" areas of an integrated image, an ACE is defined purely on events. Traditional algorithms are limited by the frame rate of the input images. Projecting rays from only through the contours produces far fewer intersections of the rays. With events, we can shoot a ray for each event, which continuously refine the geometry around the active contour, as shown in Fig. 1. To fully take advantage of the continuous nature of the events, we design a novel continuous volume carving algorithm based on single events, as described in Sect. 3.3 (Fig. 5).

Circular   Const   Rand

Fig. 5. Comparison of different trajectories in simulation with ShapeNet. The circular and octahedral trajectories only move around major axes missing some contours that would improve the carving results. In comparison, the random trajectory samples evenly across the sphere providing more unique viewpoints.

3.2   Learning Apparent Contour Events

We formulate identification of Apparent Contour Events (ACEs) as a classification problem. In other words, the network learns a function $F_{E_{t_i}}$, which maps an event to whether it is an ACE conditioned on the history of events E_{t_i}. For an event $e_i = \{x_i, y_i, t_i, p_i\}$, we encode the past N events using a function θ as a K dimensional latent vector $C_i \in \mathbf{R}^K$, where K is a hyperparameter.

$$C_i = g_\phi(\{e_j := (x_j, y_j, t_j, p_j)\}) : j > \max(i - N, 0) \tag{5}$$

N is a hyperparameter that specifies the history of events as the conditional input to the classification problem. The ACE classification problem is modeled as a function that maps from the latent code and an event to the probability that it is an ACE:

$$q_i = f_\theta(e_i, C_i) \tag{6}$$
$$e_i := (x_i, y_i, t_i, p_i) \tag{7}$$
$$q_i \in [0, 1] \tag{8}$$

We use a neural network to parameterize function g_ϕ and f_θ. Note that g_ϕ takes a list of N events. In practice, we use an event volume [30] to encode past events.

$$E(x, y, t) = \sum_i p_i k_b(x - x_i) k_b(y - y_i) k_b(t - t_i^*) \tag{9}$$

We chose this representation because the values in such volumes represent the "firing rate" of visual neurons in biological systems, which preserves valuable temporal information. The temporal information is needed because labeling ACEs requires the network to predict both where the contours are in the past and how they move over time. To supervise the ACE network, we jointly optimize the encoder and the event decoder using a Binary Cross-Entropy loss directly on the predicted event labels.

$$\mathcal{L}_c = \frac{1}{N} \sum_{i=1}^{N} \mathcal{L}_{bce}(f_\theta(e_i, C_i), \hat{q}_i)) \tag{10}$$

Here $\hat{q}_i$ is the ground truth event label for e_i. In practice, the labels are extremely imbalanced especially in either low light conditions (high noise to signal ratio) or scenes where other objects are moving as well. For training, we equally sample half positive and half negative events to help overcome the imbalance of labels.

Architecture. To enable classification of individual events, we adopt an encoder-decoder architecture where the decoder maps event coordinates to probabilities. These types of architectures are widely used in learning-based single-view 3D reconstruction methods. Mapping approaches such as AtlasNet [10] and implicit approaches (Occupancy Networks [17], DeepSDF [19]) all use variants of this architecture. In our experiments, we find the decoder part of the network has

---

Algorithm 1. Event Carving Algorithm

    Input V volume initialized to zero
    Input E active contour events
    Input $^w\mathbf{R}_c(t), {}^w\mathbf{p}_c(t)$ camera trajectories
1: **procedure** CARVEEVENTS(V, E, $^w\mathbf{R}_c(t)$, $^w\mathbf{p}_c(t)$)
2:     **for** $i \leftarrow 1, |E|$ **do**
3:        $(x_i, y_i, t_i, p_i) \leftarrow E_i$
4:        $^VT_{C(t_i)} \leftarrow {}^VT_W{}^WT_{C(t_i)}$
5:        $O_i \leftarrow {}^V\mathbf{R}_W{}^w\mathbf{p}_c(t_i) + {}^V\mathbf{t}_W$
6:        $D_i \leftarrow {}^V\mathbf{R}_W{}^w\mathbf{p}_c(t_i){}^w\mathbf{x}_c(t_i)$
7:        $V_i \leftarrow bresenham3D(O_i, D_i, bounds(V))$
8:        $V[V_i] + = 1$
9:     **end for**
10:    **return** V
11: **end procedure**

---

more weight in the overall mapping performance. Rather than taking fixed-sized latent vector code, we inject the conditional information directly into the weights of the decoder, following [11,17,18,24,25]. We use the Conditional Batch Normalization to inject the encoding of the prior events into the Batch Normalization layers of the decoder network. The architecture of the network is illustrated in Fig. 1. The training details and hyperparameters of the network can be found in the Supplementary Material.

3.3 Event Based Visual Hull

In frame-based shape from silhouette and space carving approaches, the goal is to recover the visual hull, defined as the intersection of visual cones that are formed by the apparent contour in each frame. A better definition, though following the original definition by Laurentini [14] would be the largest possible volume consistent with the tangent rays arising from apparent contour events. The visual hull is always a superset of the object and a subset of the convex hull of the object. Due to the continuity of the camera trajectory and the high temporal sampling of events, we expect the obtained visual hull to be tighter to the object than the visual hull obtained from a sparse set of viewpoints that might be closer to the convex hull of the object.

Continuous Volume Carving. provides smooth continuous incremental changes to the carving volume. This is accomplished by only carving updates through the use of ACEs. This creates a more computationally efficient as shown in Table 3.

    ACEs are defined by the tangent rays to the surface at any given positional location. The time resolution of event based cameras provide ACEs that are from continuous viewpoints through the trajectory of the camera. These continuous viewpoints, $C(t)$, are from around the object in the world frame, W. Projecting

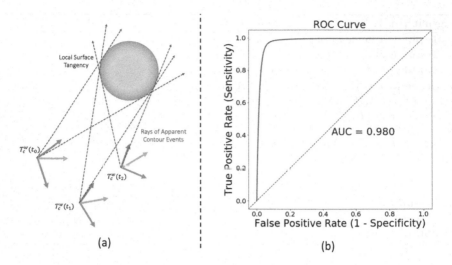

Fig. 6. (a): illustration of carving based on Apparent Contour Events. (b): ROC curve of ACE classification network.

an individual ACE, into the voxel grid coordinate system gives us a ray with origin, $^V R_W {}^w \mathbf{p}_c(t) + {}^V \mathbf{t}_W$, and direction, $^V R_W {}^w \mathbf{R}_c(t)^c \mathbf{x}(t)$. The ray in the voxel grid coordinate system allows us to project through the volume, which is illustrated in Fig. 6(a). To efficiently traverse this volume, a 3D Bresenham algorithm is used to produce a set of voxel coordinates, $\mathcal{V}_i \in \mathbb{Z}^3$, along the ray. All voxels in $\mathcal{V}_i$ are incremented. The interior of the object is left empty, as the rays trace along the continuous surface of the object. This can be seen at the bottom of Fig. 1. Algorithm 1 covers the process of generating updates to the voxel grid for every event individually. The object's mesh is then extracted from the volume (algorithm in the supplementary material) and optimized.

3.4   Global Mesh Optimization

The mesh reconstructed from volume carving can be affected by noise either from pose estimation or sensor noise. Specifically, the object will look "smaller" if some rays erroneously carve into the object due to noise. Consequently, we optimize the consistency between the proposed mesh and the high-confidence cells in the vacancy volume, which we call "high-confidence" surface points. We propose a global optimization to further refine the mesh based on these points. Recall that most rays intersect at the surface of the objects. Define point set $\hat{Y}$ as the point set of all high-confidence surface points of $V(x, y, z)$:

$$\hat{Y} = \{(x, y, z) : V(x, y, z) > \epsilon_V\} \tag{11}$$

where ϵ_V is a threshold based on the carving statistics of volume V. For a mesh reconstructed from running Marching Cubes, represented as a graph $G = (P, E)$, where P is the set of vertices and E is the set of edges that form the faces. A

Fig. 7. (Left) Comparison between options available within the optimizer. (Right) Test performance of event-based carving using predicted ACEs from our network.

deformation function f maps the original vertex set P to a deformed set $P' = f(P)$. We first optimize a one-side Chamfer distance from the high-confidence surface points (less than ϵ distance away) to the mesh vertices. In addition, we regularize the mesh by a graph Laplacian loss. The final objective can be written as:

$$L_{rf} = \lambda_1 \frac{1}{|P'|} \sum_{\substack{p'_i \in P' \\ ||p'_i - \hat{y}||_2 < \epsilon_d}} \min_{\hat{y} \in \hat{Y}} ||p'_i - \hat{y}||_2^2 + \lambda_2 \frac{1}{|P'|} \sum_{p'_i \in P'} \sum_{p'_j \in \mathcal{N}(P')} \frac{1}{\mathcal{N}(P'_i)} ||p'_j - p'_i||_2$$

where $\mathcal{N}(P'_i)$ represents all neighbors of a node P'_i, and λ_1 and λ_2 are the weights between the two losses. We find a function f that minimizes the loss. The f function can be treated as the point-wise translation of the vertices. All values used in this optimization come from our predictions without using the ground truth. We use Adam Optimizer to optimize the warping function f.

4 Experiments

In this section, we present the data collection details, evaluation of the carving algorithm, and reconstruction of real objects. To better evaluate the performance of event-based 3D reconstruction algorithms, we collect Multi Object Event Camera Dataset in 3D (MOEC-3D), a 3D event dataset of real objects. Please refer to the Supplementary Material for details about the dataset. For ground truth models, an industrial-level Artec Spider scanner is used to provide the ground truth 3D models with high accuracy. The detailed steps of data collection can be found in the Supplementary Material (Fig. 7).

4.1 Evaluation Metrics

We report both Chamfer distance and Cosine similarity of the mesh compared to the ground truth model. Chamfer distance is measuring the average distance

Table 1. Event Carving Evaluation This table contains the results using ground truth Apparent Contour Events (ACEs). Chamfer distance (lower is better) is reported in $10^{-3}m$ (millimeters). Surface normal (higher is better) is reported as cosine similarity between the ground truth and predicted surface normal. We sample 10,000 points uniformly both on the reconstructed mesh and the object mesh.

Category	Chamfer distance↓			Normal consistency↑		
	EvAC3D	Mask-24	Mask-12	EvAC3D	Mask-24	Mask-12
Mustard	**3.0164**	4.6210	5.5161	**0.9619**	0.9034	0.9035
Coffee	**2.1439**	2.2926	3.3019	0.9826	**0.9893**	0.9877
Soda (b)	1.5231	**1.4601**	2.0635	**0.9834**	0.9717	0.9735
Jello (s)	**0.9657**	2.1973	4.3524	**0.9801**	0.9766	0.9234
Jello (b)	5.9083	**4.4409**	7.7409	0.8843	**0.9541**	0.8952
Tuna	**3.2633**	3.7045	4.3070	0.9598	**0.9665**	0.9644
Soup	**1.6513**	2.0130	2.8556	0.9653	**0.9705**	0.9681
Sugar	**0.8651**	2.4071	4.9491	**0.9935**	0.9862	0.9405
Vitamin	2.6190	**1.4478**	2.4836	0.9683	**0.9947**	0.9896
Spam	**2.0398**	3.1969	4.8615	0.9739	**0.9760**	0.9479
Mean	**2.4267**	3.2652	4.3856	**0.9487**	0.9377	0.9159

between two point clouds, which reflects the positional accuracy of the reconstruction. It is defined as:

$$CD(X, \hat{X}) = \frac{1}{|X|} \sum_{x \in X} \min_{\hat{x} \in \hat{X}} ||x - \hat{x}||_2 + \frac{1}{|\hat{X}|} \sum_{\hat{x} \in \hat{X}} \min_{\hat{x} \in \hat{X}} ||\hat{x} - x||_2 \qquad (12)$$

X and $\hat{X}$ represent the points sampled from the reconstruction and the ground truth model. Surface normal is also a commonly used metric for comparing the geometry of two meshes. We report the average cosine similarity between the corresponding surface samples of two meshes, which is defined as:

$$Cos.Sim(X_{gt}, X_{pred}) = \frac{1}{|X_{gt}|} \sum_{i \in |X_{gt}|} |\vec{n}_i \cdot \vec{m}_{\theta(x, X_{pred})}| \qquad (13)$$

$$\theta(x, X_{gt} := \{(\vec{y_j}, \vec{m_j})\})) = \arg\min_{j \in |X_{gt}|} ||x - y_j||_2^2 \qquad (14)$$

We use the closest point to approximate the correspondence between two sets of oriented samples, similar to the argmin used in Eq. 12. We use a k-nearest neighbor search to estimate the normals of sampled points on the mesh, where k is 300.

4.2 Evaluating Carving Algorithm

To test the effectiveness of our continuous carving algorithm, we utilize the meshes collected as part of this dataset within a simulation environment for

Table 2. Real Object Reconstruction This table contains the results using trained network to predict Active Contour Events from real data. Chamfer distance (lower is better) is reported in $10^{-3}m$ (millimeters). Surface normal (higher is better) is reported as cosine similarity between the ground truth and predicted surface normal. "Mask" means using masks from the event mask network. "Image" means using masks predicted from reconstructed images. The number in each column name represents the number of views used for reconstruction.

| | Chamfer distance↓ /Surface normal consistency↑ | | | | | |
	EvAC3D	Mask 24	Mask 12	Image 24	Image 12	E3D [2]
Mus	**1.537/0.983**	3.034/0.968	7.061/0.926	4.192/0.868	6.947/0.926	7.986/0.713
Cof	**2.286**/0.957	2.653/**0.971**	7.771/0.915	5.733/0.840	5.930/0.821	8.354/0.756
Sod	2.239/**0.965**	**1.953**/0.957	4.611/0.929	2.380/0.914	3.865/0.884	6.762/0.703
Jel(s)	**2.889/0.928**	3.860/0.925	14.248/0.783	3.967/0.862	7.188/0.757	8.255/0.744
Jel(b)	**3.899/0.930**	4.818/0.926	13.405/0.750	3.929/0.863	6.657/0.736	14.910/0.767
Tun	**3.624/0.938**	3.518/0.937	5.552/0.753	4.254/0.863	8.545/0.734	10.850/0.704
Sou	**2.111/0.959**	2.392/0.954	5.200/0.887	2.294/0.922	5.276/0.854	6.133/0.783
Sug	**1.953**/0.970	7.904/0.854	9.929/0.833	4.000/0.939	9.724/0.775	5.924/0.691
Vit	**2.191**/0.957	2.338/**0.966**	5.772/0.949	2.226/0.958	5.710/0.915	8.462/0.715
Spa	**2.784/0.953**	3.667/0.945	9.635 /0.738	3.295/0.911	6.798/0.849	10.730/0.747
Mean	**2.551/0.954**	3.614/0.940	8.312/0.846	3.602/0.900	6.664/0.825	8.837/0.732

fair comparisons. Note that the evaluation is done with real objects and we assume the ACEs are known at every point during the camera motion. This is different than the completely synthetic environment employed in [2] because the events generated with an event simulator are not guaranteed to have the same data distribution. We observe a significant amount of noise in the real event data. The quantitative results are provided in Table 1. The mask-based carving is done with ground truth masks as well for fair comparison.

In addition to the real data simulation above, we show ShapeNet examples, Fig. 4, of our algorithm on objects with more complicated geometry to provide context for our reconstruction quality. To use these models, we use Open3D [27] to capture high frame rate images and ground truth masks. These images were then processed through ESIM [8] to generate a set of simulated events. To generate a close approximation of the real world dataset, a similar trajectory to the real world dataset was chosen.

4.3 Reconstructing Real Objects

Many network-based methods only work on simulated datasets because they require a large amount of labeled object-level 3D models. In addition, such networks cannot easily be adapted to work on real data. In comparison, the EvAC3D network can be trained on a small set of data because the labels could be obtained geometrically for events. We report the per-class performance evaluation in Table 2. For each object, we evaluate on an unseen sequence withheld

Table 3. Mean number of carving operations, mean Chamfer distance, and mean cosine similarity. With ACEs, our continuous carving method outperforms the other frame-based methods while using significantly fewer operations.

Method	Num of Ops↓	Chamfer↓	Normal ↑
GT-Mask-24	6,661,111	3.614	0.940
GT-Mask-12	3,331,536	8.312	0.846
Image-24	6,674,148	3.602	0.900
Image-12	3,345,580	6.664	0.825
E3D [2]	–	8.837	0.732
EvAC3D	**1,921,976**	**2.551**	**0.954**

from the training set. EvAC3D uses apparent contour events from the network output to perform carving. For baseline comparisons, we train two separate U-Net [22] style networks to output object masks from previous events and from reconstructed images. While they differ in input, they emulate the common situations where a fixed number of frames are used for reconstruction.

We follow the multi-view settings in 3D-R2N2 [6] where views are taken around the object. We choose 12 views as the baseline because we can reconstruct reasonable objects while keeping the computational cost close to EvAC3D. To further show the computational efficiency of EvAC3D, we also compare with 24-view carving, whose computational cost is much higher. We compare with E3D [2], the only event-based method that attempts to achieve multi-view 3D reconstruction. For fair comparison, we directly feed in the ground truth poses to E3D. E3D uses multi-view silhouette optimization over the objects, similar to PMO [15]. E3D directly uses the photometric optimization module in PMO [15] on silhouettes and removes the mesh prior from AtlasNet [10]. In our evaluation, we feed ground truth poses to E3D for fair comparison. In our experiments, we find silhouette-based optimization methods sensitive to the position and size of the mesh. To study the various components of EvAC3D, we report the performance of the ACE classification network and overall object reconstruction. For ACE classification, we provide the AUC curve of the classifier in Fig. 6 (b). The overall classification accuracy is 0.9563 (threshold = 0.5). In Table 3, we show the mean performance and the mean number of operations. We define number of operations as the number of rays that we shoot out of the camera. EvAC3D uses significantly fewer operations than both 12 and 24 views. We notice that for both mask prediction networks, the quality of reconstruction degrades quickly when the number of views decreases. In practice, the sensor frame rate is not the only limiting factor - the computational power required to carve based on masks is also significantly higher. The average number of carving operations, mean Chamfer distance, and mean normal consistency are summarized in Table 3. This means the reconstruction quality of a frame-based algorithm largely depends on the motion speed, assuming the camera sensor has a fixed frame rate. We overcome this limitation of motion speed by directly operating on a continuous stream of

events. We directly compare the qualitative results of the discussed methods in
Fig. 3.

4.4 Real Objects with Handheld Camera Trajectory

In the previous section, we present the experimental results for circular trajectories. However, camera trajectories can have more degrees of freedoms in
real life. In this section, we put EvAC3D under test of more general handheld
motions. The additional complexity of tasks comes not only from significant
background events, but also the noisy camera pose estimation from handheld
camera motion. We show a reconstructed hippo in Fig. 8. Our reconstruction
on this handheld sequence shows success in the main body of the hippo with
an average reconstruction error of 1.5 mm. The legs do not appear fully formed
likely due to the small errors in the calibration and pose, both of which rely
upon the reconstructed image to detect the AprilTags.

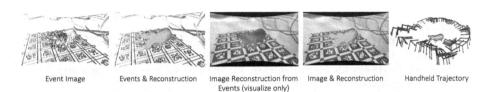

Event Image   Events & Reconstruction   Image Reconstruction from   Image & Reconstruction   Handheld Trajectory
                                                       Events (visualize only)

Fig. 8. Results from a handheld trajectory. Left to right: raw events input, raw events
overlaid with our reconstruction, image reconstruction using E2Vid [21], image reconstruction overlaid with our reconstruction, and the subsampled 3D camera trajectory
with the computed mesh.

5 Conclusions

In this work, we present a novel method for continuous 3D reconstruction using
event cameras. At the core of the method is the representation of occluding contours by Apparent Contour Events (ACE), a novel event quantity that can be
used to continuously carve out high-fidelity meshes. EvAC3D is able to update
the occupancy grid of the object on an event-to-event basis, which achieves
better performance than mask-based visual hull approaches while using significantly fewer carving operations. We evaluate the performance of the method
on both real and synthetic data. In addition, we contribute MOEC-3D, the
first high-quality event-based 3D object dataset. With these contributions, we
believe EvAC3D can provide important insights into how we can understand the
3D world through events.

Acknowledgement. We thank the support from the following grants: NSF TRIPODS
1934960, NSF CPS 2038873, ARL DCIST CRA W911NF-17-2-0181, ARO MURI
W911NF-20-1-0080, ONR N00014-17-1-2093, DARPA-SRC C-BRIC, and IARPA
ME4AI. We also thank William Sturgeon from the Fisher Fine Arts Materials Library
for providing the Artec Spider scanner and assistance.

References

1. Barrow, H.G., Tenenbaum, J.M.: Interpreting line drawings as three-dimensional surfaces. Artif. Intell. **17**(1–3), 75–116 (1981)
2. Baudron, A., Wang, Z.W., Cossairt, O., Katsaggelos, A.K.: E3D: event-based 3D shape reconstruction. arXiv preprint arXiv:2012.05214 (2020)
3. Baumgart, B.G.: Geometric modeling for computer vision. Stanford University (1974)
4. Carneiro, J., Ieng, S.H., Posch, C., Benosman, R.: Event-based 3D reconstruction from neuromorphic retinas. Neural Netw. **45**, 27–38 (2013)
5. Chaney, K., Zhu, A.Z., Daniilidis, K.: Learning event-based height from plane and parallax. In: 2019 IEEE/RSJ International Conference on Intelligent Robots and Systems (IROS), pp. 3690–3696 (2019). https://doi.org/10.1109/IROS40897.2019.8968223
6. Choy, C.B., Xu, D., Gwak, J.Y., Chen, K., Savarese, S.: 3D-R2N2: a unified approach for single and multi-view 3D object reconstruction. In: Leibe, B., Matas, J., Sebe, N., Welling, M. (eds.) ECCV 2016. LNCS, vol. 9912, pp. 628–644. Springer, Cham (2016). https://doi.org/10.1007/978-3-319-46484-8_38
7. Cipolla, R., Blake, A.: Surface shape from the deformation of apparent contours. Int. J. Comput. Vision **9**(2), 83–112 (1992)
8. Gehrig, D., Gehrig, M., Hidalgo-Carrió, J., Scaramuzza, D.: Video to events: recycling video datasets for event cameras. In: IEEE Conference on Computer Vision and Pattern Recognition (CVPR), June 2020
9. Giblin, P.: Reconstruction of surfaces from profiles. In: Proceedings of 1st International Conference on Computer Vision, London, 1987 (1987)
10. Groueix, T., Fisher, M., Kim, V.G., Russell, B.C., Aubry, M.: A papier-mâché approach to learning 3D surface generation. In: Proceedings of the IEEE Conference on Computer Vision and Pattern Recognition, pp. 216–224 (2018)
11. Ha, D., Dai, A., Le, Q.V.: Hypernetworks. arXiv preprint arXiv:1609.09106 (2016)
12. Hornung, A., Wurm, K.M., Bennewitz, M., Stachniss, C., Burgard, W.: OctoMap: an efficient probabilistic 3D mapping framework based on octrees. Autonomous Robots (2013). https://doi.org/10.1007/s10514-012-9321-0. https://octomap.github.io
13. Kim, H., Leutenegger, S., Davison, A.J.: Real-time 3D reconstruction and 6-DoF tracking with an event camera. In: Leibe, B., Matas, J., Sebe, N., Welling, M. (eds.) ECCV 2016. LNCS, vol. 9910, pp. 349–364. Springer, Cham (2016). https://doi.org/10.1007/978-3-319-46466-4_21
14. Laurentini, A.: The visual hull: a new tool for contour-based image understanding. In: Proceedings of the 7th Scandinavian Conference on Image Analysis, vol. 993, p. 1002 (1991)
15. Lin, C.H., et al.: Photometric mesh optimization for video-aligned 3D object reconstruction. In: Proceedings of the IEEE/CVF Conference on Computer Vision and Pattern Recognition, pp. 969–978 (2019)
16. Marr, D.: Analysis of occluding contour. Proc. Roy. Soc. London. Ser. B. Biol. Sci. **197**(1129), 441–475 (1977)
17. Mescheder, L., Oechsle, M., Niemeyer, M., Nowozin, S., Geiger, A.: Occupancy networks: learning 3D reconstruction in function space. In: Proceedings of the IEEE/CVF Conference on Computer Vision and Pattern Recognition, pp. 4460–4470 (2019)

18. Mitchell, E., Engin, S., Isler, V., Lee, D.D.: Higher-order function networks for learning composable 3D object representations. arXiv preprint arXiv:1907.10388 (2019)
19. Park, J.J., Florence, P., Straub, J., Newcombe, R., Lovegrove, S.: DeepSDF: learning continuous signed distance functions for shape representation. In: Proceedings of the IEEE/CVF Conference on Computer Vision and Pattern Recognition, pp. 165–174 (2019)
20. Rebecq, H., Gallego, G., Mueggler, E., Scaramuzza, D.: EMVS: event-based multi-view stereo-3D reconstruction with an event camera in real-time. Int. J. Comput. Vision **126**(12), 1394–1414 (2018)
21. Rebecq, H., Ranftl, R., Koltun, V., Scaramuzza, D.: High speed and high dynamic range video with an event camera. IEEE Trans. Pattern Anal. Mach. Intell. **43**(6), 1964–1980 (2019)
22. Ronneberger, O., Fischer, P., Brox, T.: U-Net: convolutional networks for biomedical image segmentation. In: Navab, N., Hornegger, J., Wells, W.M., Frangi, A.F. (eds.) MICCAI 2015. LNCS, vol. 9351, pp. 234–241. Springer, Cham (2015). https://doi.org/10.1007/978-3-319-24574-4_28
23. Szeliski, R.: Rapid octree construction from image sequences. CVGIP: Image Understanding **58**(1), 23–32 (1993)
24. Wang, Z., Isler, V., Lee, D.D.: Surface HOF: surface reconstruction from a single image using higher order function networks. In: 2020 IEEE International Conference on Image Processing (ICIP), pp. 2666–2670. IEEE (2020)
25. Wang, Z., Mitchell, E.A., Isler, V., Lee, D.D.: Geodesic-HOF: 3D reconstruction without cutting corners. arXiv preprint arXiv:2006.07981 (2020)
26. Wong, K.Y., Cipolla, R.: Structure and motion from silhouettes. In: Proceedings Eighth IEEE International Conference on Computer Vision, ICCV 2001, vol. 2, pp. 217–222. IEEE (2001)
27. Zhou, Q.Y., Park, J., Koltun, V.: Open3D: a modern library for 3D data processing. arXiv:1801.09847 (2018)
28. Zhou, Y., Gallego, G., Rebecq, H., Kneip, L., Li, H., Scaramuzza, D.: Semi-dense 3D reconstruction with a stereo event camera. In: Ferrari, V., Hebert, M., Sminchisescu, C., Weiss, Y. (eds.) ECCV 2018. LNCS, vol. 11205, pp. 242–258. Springer, Cham (2018). https://doi.org/10.1007/978-3-030-01246-5_15
29. Zhu, A.Z., Chen, Y., Daniilidis, K.: Realtime time synchronized event-based stereo. In: Ferrari, V., Hebert, M., Sminchisescu, C., Weiss, Y. (eds.) ECCV 2018. LNCS, vol. 11210, pp. 438–452. Springer, Cham (2018). https://doi.org/10.1007/978-3-030-01231-1_27
30. Zhu, A.Z., Yuan, L., Chaney, K., Daniilidis, K.: Unsupervised event-based learning of optical flow, depth, and egomotion. In: Proceedings of the IEEE/CVF Conference on Computer Vision and Pattern Recognition, pp. 989–997 (2019)

DCCF: Deep Comprehensible Color Filter Learning Framework for High-Resolution Image Harmonization

Ben Xue[1], Shenghui Ran[2], Quan Chen[2(✉)], Rongfei Jia[2], Binqiang Zhao[2], and Xing Tang[2]

[1] Academy for Advanced Interdisciplinary Studies, Peking University, Beijing, China
xueben@pku.edu.cn
[2] Alibaba Group, Hangzhou, China
myctllmail@163.com

Abstract. Image color harmonization algorithm aims to automatically match the color distribution of foreground and background images captured in different conditions. Previous deep learning based models neglect two issues that are critical for practical applications, namely high resolution (HR) image processing and model comprehensibility. In this paper, we propose a novel Deep Comprehensible Color Filter (DCCF) learning framework for high-resolution image harmonization. Specifically, DCCF first downsamples the original input image to its low-resolution (LR) counter-part, then learns four human comprehensible neural filters (i.e. hue, saturation, value and attentive rendering filters) in an end-to-end manner, finally applies these filters to the original input image to get the harmonized result. Benefiting from the comprehensible neural filters, we could provide a simple yet efficient handler for users to cooperate with deep model to get the desired results with very little effort when necessary. Extensive experiments demonstrate the effectiveness of DCCF learning framework and it outperforms state-of-the-art post-processing method on iHarmony4 dataset on images' full-resolutions by 7.63% and 1.69% relative improvements on MSE and PSNR, respectively. Our code is available at https://github.com/rockeyben/DCCF.

1 Introduction

Image composition, which aims at generating a realistic image with the given foreground and background, is one of the most widely used technology in photo editing. However, since the foreground and background may be captured in different conditions, simple cutting and pasting operations could not make them

---

B. Xue—Finish this work during an internship at Alibaba Group.

Supplementary Information The online version contains supplementary material available at https://doi.org/10.1007/978-3-031-20071-7_18.

S. Avidan et al. (Eds.): ECCV 2022, LNCS 13667, pp. 300–316, 2022.
https://doi.org/10.1007/978-3-031-20071-7_18

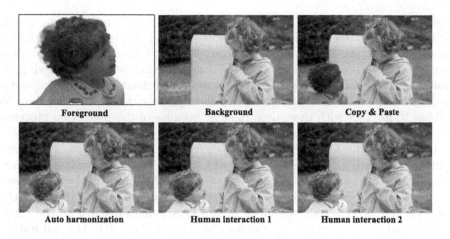

Fig. 1. Illustration of color harmonization

compatible in color space, as show in Fig. 1. Therefore, photo editors spend a lot of time in manual tuning the color distribution when they accomplish the real-world composition task.

In the past decades, a large amount of automatic color harmonization algorithms have been proposed. Traditional methods [3,17,22–25,29,30] tend to extract low-level handcrafted features to make the color statistics of the foreground to match the background, which may have poor performance when the content of foreground and background are vastly different. Since Tsai et al. [31] propose a data-driven deep learning framework for color harmonization, the research community has made a large progress rapidly over a short period of time. Deep learning based methods have become the main stream. However, we argue that previous deep learning based color harmonization methods [4,6,7,11,20,28,31] have neglected two problems which are critical for practical applications.

First, high-resolution (HR) images are rarely taken into account in previous works when deep color harmonization models are designed and evaluated. Previous deep models in color harmonization follow the evaluation system proposed by Tsai et al. [31], which resizes the original images to 256×256 or 512×512 resolution and calculate objective metrics (i.e. MSE and PSNR) in this low-resolution to evaluate the performance of models, instead of the original image resolution. The principal reason is that these methods simply employ UNet-style [26] networks to directly predict pixel level RGB values, which are memory and computational costly, and even modern GPUs could not burden for HR images. However, color harmonization needs to be frequently applied to HR images in real-world applications whose resolution is 3000×3000 or even higher. Therefore, previous deep models which perform well on low-resolutions may have poor performance when be applied to real-world HR images.

Second, model comprehensibility and manual control mechanism are rarely considered in previous works. Imagine the scenario that the harmonization result of the network is flawed, and the photo editor wants to make some modifications based on the network's prediction to avoid tuning from scratch, such as hue adjustment in Fig. 1. Thus it is essential to provide human understandable cooperation mode with the deep models for a friendly color harmonization system. However, previous methods utilize variant networks following the common image-to-image translation framework [16] that directly predicts the harmonization result. It is nearly impossible to provide comprehensible tools for humans to interact with these deep models, because of the prediction processes are "black-box" and inscrutable for photo editors.

Inspired by the idea of learning desired image transformations that could reduce computing and memory burdens by a large margin for image enhancement [8], in this paper, we propose a novel Deep Comprehensible Color Filter (DCCF) learning framework for high-resolution image harmonization. Specifically, we first downsample the input to the low-resolution (such as 256×256) counter-part, then learn four comprehensible neural filters (i.e. hue, saturation, value and attentive rendering filters) in a novel end-to-end manner with the supervisions constructed from both RGB and HSV color spaces, finally apply these filters to the original input image to get the harmonized result. Compared with previous deep learning based color harmonization methods that may fail for high-resolution images, our neural filter learning framework is insensitive to image resolution and could perform well on dataset whose resolution range from 480p to 4K. Besides, benefiting from the mechanism that parameters in the filters (especially hue, saturation and value filters) are forced to learn decoupled meaningful chromatics functions, it makes it possible to provide comprehensible tools for humans to interact with these deep models in the traditional chromatics way they familiar with. It is worth noting that learning comprehensible neural filters is not easy. Our experiments show that learning weights directly from supervisions of hue, saturation and value channels could cause poor performance. To handle this, we construct three novel supervision maps that approximate the effects of HSV color space while making the deep model converge well.

We train and evaluate our approach in the open source iHarmony4 dataset [6] on the original image resolutions, which range from 480p (HCOCO) to 4K (HAdobe5k). Since previous deep learning based color harmonization models could perform poorly when they are directly applied to HR images, we compare to them with variant post-processing methods. Extensive experiments demonstrate that our approach can make the prediction process comprehensible and outperform these methods as well. We also provide a simple handler that humans could cooperate with the learned deep model to make some desired modifications based on the network's prediction capacity to avoid tuning from scratch.

In a nutshell, our contributions are three-folds.

- We propose an effective end-to-end deep neural filter learning framework that is insensitive to image resolution, which makes deep learning based color harmonization practical for real-world high-resolution images.
- To the best of our knowledge, we are the first to design four types of novel neural filter (i.e. hue, saturation, value and attentive rendering filters) learning functions and learning strategies that make the prediction process and result comprehensible for human in image harmonization task. Meanwhile,

we provide a simple yet efficient handler for users to cooperate with deep model to get the desired results with very little effort when necessary.
- Our approach achieves state-of-the-art performance on the color harmonization benchmark for high-resolution images and outperforms state-of-the-art post-processing method by 7.63% and 1.69% relative improvements on MSE and PSNR, respectively.

2 Related Work

Image Harmonization. In this subsection, we focus on the discussion of deep learning based methods. These methods regard color harmonization as a black box image-to-image translation task. [31] apply the well-known encoder-decoder U-net structure with skip-connection and train the network with multi-task learning, simultaneously predicting pixel value and semantic segmentation. [28] insert pretrained semantic segmentation branch into encoder backbone and introduce a learnable alpha-blending mask to borrow useful information from input image. They both use semantic features in networks. [4,6] tried to make composite image harmonious via domain transfer. [7,13] both used attention mechanism in networks. [1] propose a generative adversarial network (GAN) architecture for automatic image compositing, which considers geometric, color, and boundary consistency at the same time. [11] seek to solve image harmonization via separable harmonization of reflectance and illumination, where reflectance is harmonized through material-consistency penalty and illumination is harmonized by learning and transferring light from background to foreground. Note that recently some image harmonization works start to focus on high-resolution images. [18] use self-supervised learning strategy to train network with small local patches of high resolution images, but during inference it still follow the two stage post-processing strategy. [15,27] learn global parameters to adjust image attributes such as lightness and saturation. [10] learns pixel-wise curves to perform low-light image enhancement.

Smart Upsampling. Processing high resolution image becomes difficult due to huge computational burden of deep-learning networks and limited GPU memory. A common approach to accelerate high resolution processing is to first downsample the image, apply time-consuming operator at low resolution and upsample back. To preserve edge gradients, guided filter upsampling [14] uses original high resolution input as guidance map. [9] fit transformation recipe from compressed input and output, then apply the recipe to high quality input. Bilateral guided upsampling [2] approximates the operator with grids of local affine transformations and apply them on high resolution input, thus control the operator complexity. [8] predict the local affine model with fully convolution networks, which is trained by end-to-end learning and obtain multi-scale semantic information. [32] propose a guided filter layer, using point-wise convolution to approximate median filter, thus can be plugged into networks and optimized jointly. [19] introduce extra networks to learn deformable offsets for each pixel, thus the interpolation neighbour is predicted online during upsampling. [5,33] learn 3D lookup tables (LUT) to obtain high resolution results, but the learned transformation still lacks interpretable meanings.

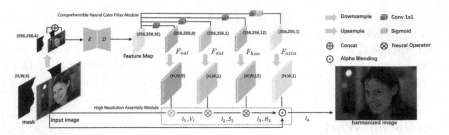

Fig. 2. An overview of our proposed color harmonization framework. It consists of two primary parts: *comprehensible neural color filter module* and *high resolution assembly module*. Given an input image and corresponding foreground mask, a low-resolution feature extraction backbone first downsamples them to a low-resolution version, such as 256×256, and employs an encoder-decoder network to extract foreground aware high-level semantic features. *Comprehensible neural color filter module* then learns value filter, saturation filter, hue filter and attentive rendering filter simultaneously based on the features extracted from the backbone. Each filter learns parameters of transformation function in per pixel manner. *High resolution assembly module* finally extracts and upsamples the specific channel of each DCCF's output to assemble the final result. In short, input image I is unharmonious, I_1 is V-harmonized, I_2 is V, S-harmonized, I_3 is V, S, H-harmonized, I_4 is the refinement of I_3 by an attention module.

3   Methodology

3.1   Framework Overview

The neural filter learning framework for high-resolution image color harmonization is illustrated in Fig. 2. It consists of two primary parts: *comprehensible neural color filter module* and *high resolution assembly module*.

Firstly, given an original input image ($H \times W \times 3$) and corresponding foreground mask ($H \times W \times 1$), low-resolution feature extraction backbone downsamples them to the low-resolution counterparts (256×256), then concatenates them as input ($256 \times 256 \times 4$) to extract foreground aware high-level semantic representations ($256 \times 256 \times 32$). The choice of backbone structure is flexible and iDIH-HRNet architecture [28] is used in this paper.

Subsequently, the *comprehensible neural color filter module* generates a series of deep comprehensible color filters (**DCCFs**) with the shape of ($256 \times 256 \times D$), where each pixel has D learnable parameters $\boldsymbol{q} = [q_1, q_2, ..., q_D]$ to construct a transformation function $f(I; \boldsymbol{q})$ which can be operated on input image I. The gathering of each pixel's functions f builds up a filter map F. The design of DCCFs and their cooperating mechanism will be detailed in Sect. 3.2.

Finally, the *high resolution assembly module* upsamples these filter maps to their full-resolution ($H \times W$) counterparts in order to be applied on the resolution of original input image. Meanwhile, since each DCCF only changes a specific aspect of image, an assembly strategy is thus required to ensure there is no conflicts between each filter's operating procedure. The details will be discussed in Sect. 3.3.

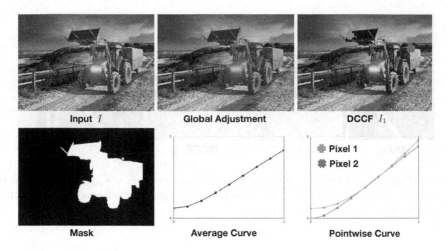

Fig. 3. Illustration of the pixel-level value adjustment function/curve. $I_1 = F_{val}(I)$ illustrated in Fig. 2 can be regarded as the result whose value is well tuned. Zoom for better view.

The entire network is trained in an end-to-end manner and benefited from the supervision of the full-resolution images. Moreover, we observe that traditional losses in RGB color space is not sufficient for achieving state-of-the-art quality. We therefore propose auxiliary losses in Sect. 3.4 for each DCCF's output to ensure that they are functioning as expected.

3.2 Comprehensible Neural Color Filter Module

The comprehensible neural color filter module plays a core rule in our proposed high-resolution image color harmonization framework. We take inspiration from the famous HSV color model which is widely used in photo editing community. Compared with RGB color space, HSV is much more intuitive and easier for humans to interact with computers for color tuning.

Our module consists of four neural filters, that is, *value filter, saturation filter, hue filter* and *attentive rendering filter* illustrated as F_{val}, F_{sat}, F_{hue} and F_{attn} respectively in Fig. 2. Each filter is generated by a 1×1 convolutional layer (expect for the attentive rendering filter has extra sigmoid layer for nomorlization) that builded on the low-resolution feature extraction backbone.

Value Filter. The customized pointwise nonlinear value transformation function f_{val} is defined as:

$$f_{val}(x; \phi, V_{min}) = V_{min} + \sum_{i=1}^{m} \phi_i * \max(x - \frac{i-1}{m}, 0) \tag{1}$$

where x indicates the V channel of input image in HSV color space, V_{min} and ϕ_i are learnable parameters and m is a hyper-parameter which we set as 8

Fig. 4. Illustration of the pixel-level saturation adjustment. $I_2 = F_{sat}(I_1)$ illustrated in Fig. 2 is the intermediate result. The change of saturation is consistent with predicted σ distributions. Zoom for better view.

in this paper. It could be considered as an arbitrary nonlinear curve which is approximated by a stack of parameterized ReLUs. V_{min} controls lower-bound of value range, m and ϕ_i control nonlinearity of the curve. Parameters V_{min} and $\phi_i(i = 1, .., 8)$ are stored for each pixel in channel direction of value filter F_{val}.

We argue that different local regions should have different adjustment curves for better harmonization quality. As illustrated in Fig. 3, two marked points have large gap in original value distribution (the left is darker, the right is brighter), our DCCF F_{val} successfully allocates proper curves for these two regions, while the global adjustment degrades the overall aesthetic.

Saturation Filter. We use a single parameter $\sigma \in [-1, 1]$ to control saturation for each pixel. The customized non-linear saturation transformation function f_{sat} for each pixel is defined as:

$$f_{sat}(x; \sigma) = x + (x - C_{med}) * clip(\sigma) \tag{2}$$

where x indicates the R, G or B values in each pixel, $C_{max} = max(R, G, B)$, $C_{min} = min(R, G, B)$, $C_{med} = (C_{min} + C_{max})/2$, σ is our learned parameter and $clip(\sigma)$ is a monotonous function to avoid saturation overflow.

If $\sigma \to 1$, the values below median will be suppressed, while the value above median will be enhanced, as a result the saturation is increased and vice versa when $\sigma \to -1$. We visualize the effectiveness of σ in Fig. 4. DCCF allocated positive σ for most of the pixels in this de-saturated input image and obtained an enhanced result.

Hue Filter. We define an affine color transformation function f_{col} for each pixel in RGB color space as:

$$
\begin{aligned}
f_{col}(x; \boldsymbol{\Delta}) &= \boldsymbol{R}x + t \\
&= \begin{bmatrix} \delta_{11} & \delta_{12} & \delta_{13} \\ \delta_{21} & \delta_{22} & \delta_{23} \\ \delta_{31} & \delta_{32} & \delta_{33} \end{bmatrix} \begin{bmatrix} x_R \\ x_G \\ x_B \end{bmatrix} + \begin{bmatrix} \delta_{14} \\ \delta_{24} \\ \delta_{34} \end{bmatrix}
\end{aligned}
\tag{3}
$$

where x indicates the RGB values for one pixel in image, and Δ is a learnable 3×4 affine transformation matrix that contains a rotation matrix R and a translation vector t.

We suppose that one could find a suitable rotation matrix R in RGB color space that is equivalent to a corresponding radian moving r on the hue ring in HSV color space [12], which is further discussed in supplementary. Based on this assumption, it is equivalent to learn an affine color transformation function $f_{col}(x; \Delta)$ in RGB color space, which contains a rotation function R that could be parameters for the corresponding hue rotation function $f_{hue}(h; R)$ in HSV color space. We suggest readers refer to [12] for technical details. Note that [12] needs extra linearization between sRGB and RGB space, which is mainly a gamma correction thus compatible with our learnable curve function f_{val}.

Attentive Rendering Filter. We employ simple yet effective attentive rendering filter F_{attn} which is similar to the attention mask in [28] to further improve the harmonization result after hue filter.

For inference, we adopt the previous filters' harmonization result I_3 and input I to perform alpha blending as illustrated in Fig. 2

$$I_4 = I * \alpha + W_{ref} * I_3 * (1 - \alpha) \tag{4}$$

where α is the per-pixel parameter on F_{attn} ranging in $[0, 1]$ to smartly borrow information from input image, W_{ref} is an extra affine matrix to refine the appearance of I_3.

3.3   High Resolution Assembly Module

The biggest reduction of computation comes from the design that each DCCF is generated at low-resolution branch. We then perform upsampling on DCCF's filter map to match the resolution of original input image. The effectiveness of this action is guaranteed by the common assumption that neighbourhood regions require similar tuning filters.

Afterwards, we propose a split-and-concat strategy to assemble the applying result of each filter. Specifically, as shown in Fig. 2, we utilize value filter F_{val}, saturation filter F_{sat} and hue filter H_{hue} to extract harmonized value channel V_1, saturation channel S_2 and hue channel H_3 respectively, then assemble V_1, S_2 and H_3 as harmonized image I_3, finally use attentive rendering filter to get the final harmonized image I_4. We illustrate the implementation details of saturation assembling as example in Fig. 5.

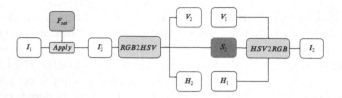

Fig. 5. Illustration of assembly module details. We take the procedure of saturation filter F_{sat} as example. The engaged channel (i.e. S_2) are colored for visualization.

3.4 Training Loss

In the following description, we will use the superscript l for low-resolution and h for high-resolution.

High Resolution Supervision. Since the area of foreground region varies a lot among training examples, we adopt foreground-normalized MSE loss [28] between ground-truth I_{gt} and intermediate result I_3, final predicted result I_4. This loss uses the area of foreground mask as a normalization factor to stablize the gradient on foreground object. Differently, our loss can be calculated on both low-resolution and high-resolution streams, namely $\mathcal{L}_{rgb}^l$ and $\mathcal{L}_{rgb}^h$.

Auxiliary HSV Loss. A straight forward solution to supervise $F_{val}, F_{sat}, F_{hue}$ is using the standard HSV decomposition equations to get HSV channels. However, we observe that this strategy could contain high frequency contents in the output channel as visualized in Fig. 6a–f, which may degrade the convergence of network according to our experiments in Fig. 6g.

Therefore we heuristically designed an approximated version of HSV loss to stabilize network training. It is mainly based on a combination of several differentiable basic image processing filters (e.g. whitening, blurring, blending) to obtain smooth approximations of these three attributes H, S, V, which benifit training procedure. The implementation details are shown in supplementary.

Auxiliary HSV losses $\mathcal{L}_{val}^l$, $\mathcal{L}_{sat}^l$, $\mathcal{L}_{hue}^l$ are calculated with MSE in low resolution stream only due to memory consideration. We also apply total variation regularization on predicted filters to increase smoothness. The overall training loss is defined as follows, where $\lambda_i(i = 1, ..., 5)$ is hyper-parameters:

$$\mathcal{L} = \lambda_1 \mathcal{L}_{rgb}^l + \lambda_2 \mathcal{L}_{rgb}^h + \lambda_3 \mathcal{L}_{val}^l + \lambda_4 \mathcal{L}_{sat}^l + \lambda_5 \mathcal{L}_{hue}^l \tag{5}$$

4 Experiments

In this section, we first describe experimental setups and implementation details, then compare our approach with the state-of-the-arts quantitatively and qualitatively. Finally, we carry out some ablation studies and provide a simple comprehensible interface to interact with our model. We also present more results and potential limitations in supplementary materials.

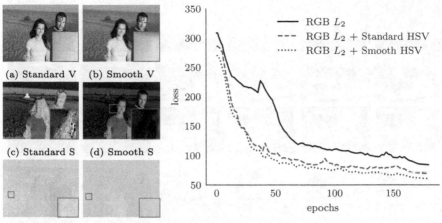

(a) Standard V   (b) Smooth V

(c) Standard S   (d) Smooth S

(e) Standard H   (f) Smooth H

(g) Ablations on loss function. Testing errors on iHarmony4 with different loss contributions.

Fig. 6. Visualization of standard HSV and our ad-hoc smoothed version. The smoothed version of V, S, H keeps global chromological properties, meanwhile makes the network converge better, which is demonstrated in sub-figure (g).

Table 1. Quantitative performance comparison on the iHarmony4 test sets. We are the first to evaluate on original resolution in this dataset. The best results are in bold. '-' means not able to obtain results due to memory limitation. Our method is trained in an end-to-end manner and outperforms post-upsampling baselines by comparison. More quantitative results with different backbones are shown in supplementary.

Method	Entire dataset		HCOCO		HAdobe5k		HFlickr		Hday2night	
	MSE ↓	PSNR ↑	MSE ↓	PSNR ↑	MSE ↓	PSNR ↑	MSE ↓	PSNR ↑	MSE ↓	PSNR ↑
Input image	177.99	31.22	73.03	33.53	354.46	27.63	270.99	28.20	113.07	33.91
iDIH-HRNet [28]	–	–	19.96	38.25	–	–	93.50	32.42	71.01	35.77
iDIH-HRNet [28]+BU	43.56	34.98	34.40	35.45	37.82	35.47	104.69	30.91	50.87	37.41
iDIH-HRNet [28]+GF [14]	35.47	36.00	25.93	36.70	34.51	36.03	85.05	32.01	**49.90**	**37.67**
iDIH-HRNet [28]+BGU [2]	26.85	37.24	18.53	37.90	26.71	37.50	66.26	33.19	51.96	37.23
DCCF	**24.65**	**37.87**	**17.07**	**38.66**	**23.34**	**37.75**	**64.77**	**33.60**	55.76	37.40

4.1 Experimental Setups

We use iHarmony4 [6] as our experiment dataset which contains 73146 images. It consists of 4 subsets: HCOCO, HFlickr, HAdobe5k, HDay2night. The image resolution varies from 640×480 to 6048×4032, which is difficult for learning based color harmonization algorithms to process on the original images' full resolution. We suggest readers refer to [6] for dataset details.

Since the lack of high-resolution process ability, previous methods [4,6,7,11, 20,28,31] resize all images in the dataset to 256×256 to process and evaluate their performance via Mean Square Error (MSE) and Peak Signal To Noise Ratio (PSNR) in this extremely low-resolution. However, we argue that evaluate

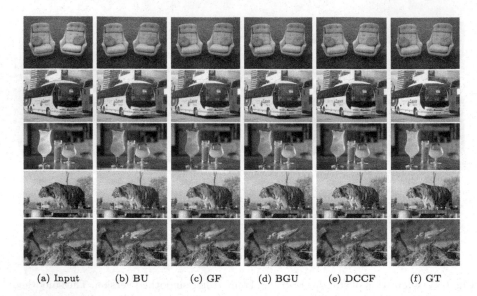

(a) Input   (b) BU   (c) GF   (d) BGU   (e) DCCF   (f) GT

Fig. 7. Visualization of high-resolution results. Foregrounds are marked in red contour. Bilinear upsampling, guided filter upsampling and bilateral guided upsampling are represented as BU, GF [14] and BGU [2] respectively. GT represents ground truths. Our method DCCF has not only better global appearance but also refined high resolution details. Zoom for better view. More visual results please refer to supplementary materials. (Color figure online)

algorithms on the image's original full-resolution is much more scientific for practical applications. In this paper, we adopt MSE and PSNR as our objective metrics on the image's original full-resolution instead of 256×256.

4.2 Implementation Details

Our DCCF learning framework is differentiable and could be stacked on the head of any deep feature extraction networks. In this paper, we adopt the recent state-of-the-art harmonization network iDIH-HRNet [28] as our backbone to carry out experiments. For feature extraction backbone, we downsample inputs (images and corresponding foreground mask) to 256×256 following the previous deep harmonization models' common setting. For detailed training procedure and hyper-parameter setting, please refer to our official Pytorch [21] code[1].

4.3 Comparison with Baselines

In order to evaluate the effectiveness of our proposed DCCF learning framework, we construct two kinds of baselines. (1) Applying recent state-of-the-art methods directly on the original input images to get the full-resolution

---

[1] https://github.com/rockeyben/DCCF.

Table 2. Qualitative results. We evaluate visual perceptual quality by DNN-based image quality assessment LPIPS [34] and a user study.

Method	iDIH-HRNet [28] +BU	iDIH-HRNet [28]+GF [14]	iDIH-HRNet [28]+BGU [2]	DCCF
LPIPS [34] ↓	0.0459	0.0291	0.0201	**0.0186**
User score ↑	2.0541	2.6583	3.3041	**3.5583**

harmonized results. (2) Applying recent state-of-the-art methods on the low-resolution inputs (256 × 256) to predict low-resolution harmonized images and adopting variates of state-of-the-art post-processing methods to get the final full-resolution harmonized results. In this paper, we choose iDIH-HRNet [28] as the deep model provided by Sofiiuk et al. [28] and Bilinear Upsampling (BU), Guided Filter Upsampling [14] (GF), Bilateral Guided Upsampling [2] (BGU) as post-processing methods. For fair comparison, we adopt the same low-resolution (i.e. 256 × 256) feature extractor as [28] for our DCCF learning framework. The performance comparison is shown in Table 1. Some harmonization results are shown in Fig. 7. For the comparison of efficiency metrics like inference time and memory usage, please refer to supplementary for details.

The method of applying [28] directly on the full-resolution (first row in Table 1) performs pooly. The principal reason is that [28] is designed and trained on the resolution of 256×256, directly applying this model in testing phase to the original image full-resolution would lead to serious feature misalignment. Moreover this strategy failed on HAdobe5k subset (max resolution: 6048 × 4032) due to memory limitation.

The method of applying post-processing after the low-resolutional prediction results from [28] with low-resolution inputs solves the memory problem. However, BU would lead to blurring effect, especially for high-resolution subset HAdobe5k, see Fig. 7. Therefore, we adopt more advanced post-processing algorithms GF [14] and BGU [2] that take original full-resolution image as detail guidance to mitigate the blurring effect from upsampling operation. Table 1 shows that these upsampling methods outperform bilinear upsampling methods by a large margin and the best one BGU [2] achieves 26.85 on MSE and 37.24 on PSNR. However, the best performance of post-processing methods is behind our approach DCCF. Our approach achieves 24.65 on MSE and 37.87 on PSNR, 7.63% and 1.69% relative improvements on MSE and PSNR respectively compared with [28]+ BGU [2].

4.4 Qualitative Results

We conduct two evaluations to compare the subjective visual quality of DCCF with other methods, which is presented in Table 2. First, we adopt LPIPS [34] to evalute visual perceptual similarity of harmonized image and ground truth reference. It computes the feature distance between two images and the lower score indicates better result. Second, we randomly select 20 images then present DCCF result with baseline results on the screen after shuffling, and ask 12 users

Table 3. Ablation studies. (a) As for filter design, DBL [8] is a "black-box" per-pixel linear filter that directly applied to RGB images. DCCFs with attention achieves the best result. (b) As for losses, supervision we constructed from HSV (i.e. smooth $\mathcal{L}_{hsv}$) is essential and improves standard HSV by 3.21 (11.65%) on MSE.

(a) Method	MSE ↓	PSNR ↑	(b) Method	MSE ↓	PSNR ↑
DBL [8]	27.92	37.48	$\mathcal{L}_{rgb}$	35.17	36.81
DCCFs w.o. attention	26.36	37.80	$\mathcal{L}_{rgb}$ + standard $\mathcal{L}_{hsv}$	27.86	37.39
DCCFs with attention	**24.65**	**37.87**	$\mathcal{L}_{rgb}$ + smooth $\mathcal{L}_{hsv}$	**24.65**	**37.87**

to judge images' global appearance and detail texture then give scores from 1 to 5, the higher the better. Our DCCF achieves the best result in both metrics which is consistent the quantitative performance.

4.5   Ablation Studies

Filter Design. An evaluation of filter design is shown in Table 3a. DBL [8] is an end-to-end "black-box" bilateral learning method that proposed in image enhancement. We adapt it to our DCCF learning framework to process high-resolution image harmonization. DCCFs w.o. attention is our DCCF learning method that exclude attentive rendering filter. Even DCCFs w.o. attention improves the performance of DBL filter [8] by 1.56 (5.58%) on MSE. It demonstrate that the performance of our model is not just from end-to-end training, our divide, conquer and assemble strategy that learns explicit meaningful parameters also benefit a lot for color harmonization task. DCCFs with attn further improve the DBL filter [8] by 3.27 (11.71%) on MSE.

Loss Functions. The impact of loss functions for our DCCF learning framework is shown in Table 3b. Note that standard H channel is an angle value while our approximated H is a scalar value, so we train standard $\mathcal{L}_h$ with cosine distance while training approximated smooth $\mathcal{L}_h$ with euclidean distance. Numerical results show that supervisions from HSV color space is essential for our DCCF learning framework, which is manifested in simply adding loss from standard HSV channels will remarkably decrease MSE from 35.17 to 27.86. The principal reason may be the parameters of our DCCFs (expect for the last attentive rendering filter) are designed from the inspiration of practical tuning criteria in HSV color space used by color artists and has explicit chromatics meaning. Therefore model converges better when supervisory signals from HSV color space are added, which is demonstrate in Fig. 6g. It is worth noting that adding smooth approximated HSV loss described in Subsect. 3.4 instead of standard HSV loss will further decrease MSE to 24.65 which demonstrates the effectiveness of proposed smoothing HSV loss.

4.6   Comprehensible Interaction with Deep Model

Benefiting from the comprehensible neural filters, we could provide a simple yet efficient handler for users to cooperate with deep model to get the desired results with very little effort when necessary. We provide two adjustable parameters in the three dimensions of hue, saturation and value respectively for users to express their color adjustment intentions. For space limitation, we only explain hue adjustment for example. The other two dimensions are similar and will be detailed in supplementary.

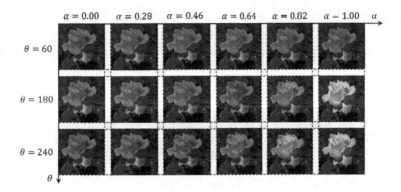

Fig. 8. Illustration of comprehensible interaction with deep harmonization model on parameter space of hue adjustment. Abscissa represents parameter α and ordinate represents parameter θ. Sampling values in (α, θ) and their results are listed. Zoom for better view.

For hue, we define parameter $\theta \in [0, 360]$ and $\alpha \in [0, 1]$ to represent the angle for Hue circle and the amount of user color intentions respectively. We calculate the desired rotation matrix R mentioned in Eq. (3) as:

$$\begin{bmatrix} \frac{1}{3} - \frac{2\cos\theta}{3} & \frac{1-\cos\theta}{3} - \frac{\sin\theta}{\sqrt{3}} & \frac{1-\cos\theta}{3} + \frac{\sin\theta}{\sqrt{3}} \\ \frac{1-\cos\theta}{3} + \frac{\sin\theta}{\sqrt{3}} & \frac{1}{3} - \frac{2\cos\theta}{3} & \frac{1-\cos\theta}{3} - \frac{\sin\theta}{\sqrt{3}} \\ \frac{1-\cos\theta}{3} + \frac{\sin\theta}{\sqrt{3}} & \frac{1-\cos\theta}{3} + \frac{\sin\theta}{\sqrt{3}} & \frac{1}{3} - \frac{2\cos\theta}{3} \end{bmatrix} \qquad (6)$$

Then we could get the final rotation matrix R: $F'_{hue} = \alpha * R + (1-\alpha) * F_{hue}$, which can be applied on image that takes global user intentions and local complex self-adaptions from deep model in mind.

In one word, users can express their color intentions by parameter $\theta \in [0, 360]$ and decide the amount of injected color by controlling $\alpha \in [0, 1]$, which is illustrated in Fig. 8. It is worth noting that when users interact with deep model in one dimension (such as hue above), they need not worry about the side-effect changes of other two dimensions from the network's prediction.

5 Conclusion

In this paper, we propose comprehensible image processing filters to deal with image harmonization problem. By gradually modifying image's attributes: value, saturation and hue, we can obtain results not only high-quality but also understandable. This also facilitate human to cooperate with deep models to perform image harmonization. We also leverage these filters to tackle high resolution images in a simple yet effective way. We hope that DCCF can set up a brand new direction for image harmonization.

References

1. Chen, B.C., Kae, A.: Toward realistic image compositing with adversarial learning. In: Proceedings of the IEEE/CVF Conference on Computer Vision and Pattern Recognition (CVPR), pp. 8415–8424 (2019)
2. Chen, J., Adams, A., Wadhwa, N., Hasinoff, S.W.: Bilateral guided upsampling. ACM Trans. Graph. (TOG) **35**(6), 1–8 (2016)
3. Cohen-Or, D., Sorkine, O., Gal, R., Leyvand, T., Xu, Y.Q.: Color harmonization. In: ACM SIGGRAPH, pp. 624–630 (2006)
4. Cong, W., Niu, L., Zhang, J., Liang, J., Zhang, L.: Bargainnet: background-guided domain translation for image harmonization. In: IEEE International Conference on Multimedia and Expo (ICME), pp. 1–6 (2021)
5. Cong, W., et al.: High-resolution image harmonization via collaborative dual transformations. In: Proceedings of the IEEE/CVF Conference on Computer Vision and Pattern Recognition (CVPR), pp. 18470–18479 (2022)
6. Cong, W., et al.: Dovenet: deep image harmonization via domain verification. In: Proceedings of the IEEE/CVF Conference on Computer Vision and Pattern Recognition (CVPR), pp. 8394–8403 (2020)
7. Cun, X., Pun, C.M.: Improving the harmony of the composite image by spatial-separated attention module. IEEE Trans. Image Process. (TIP) **29**, 4759–4771 (2020)
8. Gharbi, M., Chen, J., Barron, J.T., Hasinoff, S.W., Durand, F.: Deep bilateral learning for real-time image enhancement. ACM Trans. Graph. (TOG) **36**(4), 1–12 (2017)
9. Gharbi, M., Shih, Y., Chaurasia, G., Ragan-Kelley, J., Paris, S., Durand, F.: Transform recipes for efficient cloud photo enhancement. ACM Trans. Graph. (TOG) **34**(6), 1–12 (2015)
10. Guo, C., et al.: Zero-reference deep curve estimation for low-light image enhancement, pp. 1780–1789 (2020)
11. Guo, Z., Zheng, H., Jiang, Y., Gu, Z., Zheng, B.: Intrinsic image harmonization. In: Proceedings of the IEEE/CVF Conference on Computer Vision and Pattern Recognition (CVPR), pp. 16367–16376 (2021)
12. Haeberli, P.: Matrix operations for image processing. Grafica Obscura website (1993). http://graficaobscura.com/matrix/index.html
13. Hao, G., Iizuka, S., Fukui, K.: Image harmonization with attention-based deep feature modulation. In: British Machine Vision Conference (BMVC) (2020)
14. He, K., Sun, J., Tang, X.: Guided image filtering. IEEE Trans. Pattern Anal. Mach. Intell. (TPAMI) **35**(6), 1397–1409 (2013)

15. Hu, Y., He, H., Xu, C., Wang, B., Lin, S.: Exposure: a white-box photo post-processing framework. ACM Trans. Graph. (TOG) **37**(2), 26 (2018)
16. Isola, P., Zhu, J.Y., Zhou, T., Efros, A.A.: Image-to-image translation with conditional adversarial networks. In: Proceedings of the IEEE Conference on Computer Vision and Pattern Recognition (CVPR), pp. 1125–1134 (2017)
17. Jia, J., Sun, J., Tang, C.K., Shum, H.Y.: Drag-and-drop pasting. ACM Trans. Graph. (TOG) **25**(3), 631–637 (2006)
18. Jiang, Y., et al.: SSH: a self-supervised framework for image harmonization. In: Proceedings of the IEEE/CVF International Conference on Computer Vision (ICCV), pp. 4832–4841 (2021)
19. Kim, B., Ponce, J., Ham, B.: Deformable kernel networks for guided depth map upsampling. CoRR abs/1903.11286 (2019)
20. Ling, J., Xue, H., Song, L., Xie, R., Gu, X.: Region-aware adaptive instance normalization for image harmonization. In: Proceedings of the IEEE/CVF Conference on Computer Vision and Pattern Recognition (CVPR), pp. 9361–9370, June 2021
21. Paszke, A., et al.: Pytorch: an imperative style, high-performance deep learning library. In: Advances in Neural Information Processing Systems (NeurIPS), vol. 32, pp. 8026–8037 (2019)
22. Pérez, P., Gangnet, M., Blake, A.: Poisson image editing. In: ACM SIGGRAPH, pp. 313–318 (2003)
23. Pitié, F., Kokaram, A.: The linear monge-kantorovitch linear colour mapping for example-based colour transfer. In: Proceedings of the European Conference on Visual Media Production (CVMP), pp. 1–9 (2007)
24. Pitie, F., Kokaram, A.C., Dahyot, R.: N-dimensional probability density function transfer and its application to color transfer. In: Proceedings of the IEEE/CVF International Conference on Computer Vision (ICCV), vol. 2, pp. 1434–1439 (2005)
25. Reinhard, E., Adhikhmin, M., Gooch, B., Shirley, P.: Color transfer between images. IEEE Comput. Graph. Appl. (CG&A) **21**(5), 34–41 (2001)
26. Ronneberger, O., Fischer, P., Brox, T.: U-Net: convolutional networks for biomedical image segmentation. In: Navab, N., Hornegger, J., Wells, W.M., Frangi, A.F. (eds.) MICCAI 2015. LNCS, vol. 9351, pp. 234–241. Springer, Cham (2015). https://doi.org/10.1007/978-3-319-24574-4_28
27. Shi, J., Xu, N., Xu, Y., Bui, T., Dernoncourt, F., Xu, C.: Learning by planning: language-guided global image editing. In: Proceedings of the IEEE/CVF Conference on Computer Vision and Pattern Recognition (CVPR), pp. 13590–13599 (2021)
28. Sofiiuk, K., Popenova, P., Konushin, A.: Foreground-aware semantic representations for image harmonization. In: Proceedings of the IEEE/CVF Winter Conference on Applications of Computer Vision (WACV), pp. 1620–1629 (2021)
29. Sunkavalli, K., Johnson, M.K., Matusik, W., Pfister, H.: Multi-scale image harmonization. ACM Trans. Graph. (TOG) **29**(4), 1–10 (2010)
30. Tao, M.W., Johnson, M.K., Paris, S.: Error-tolerant image compositing. In: Daniilidis, K., Maragos, P., Paragios, N. (eds.) ECCV 2010. LNCS, vol. 6311, pp. 31–44. Springer, Heidelberg (2010). https://doi.org/10.1007/978-3-642-15549-9_3
31. Tsai, Y.H., Shen, X., Lin, Z., Sunkavalli, K., Lu, X., Yang, M.H.: Deep image harmonization. In: Proceedings of the IEEE Conference on Computer Vision and Pattern Recognition (CVPR), pp. 3789–3797 (2017)
32. Wu, H., Zheng, S., Zhang, J., Huang, K.: Fast end-to-end trainable guided filter. In: Proceedings of the IEEE Conference on Computer Vision and Pattern Recognition (CVPR), pp. 1838–1847 (2018)

33. Zeng, H., Cai, J., Li, L., Cao, Z., Zhang, L.: Learning image-adaptive 3D lookup tables for high performance photo enhancement in real-time. IEEE Trans. Pattern Anal. Mach. Intell. (TPAMI) (2020)
34. Zhang, R., Isola, P., Efros, A.A., Shechtman, E., Wang, O.: The unreasonable effectiveness of deep features as a perceptual metric. In: Proceedings of the IEEE Conference on Computer Vision and Pattern Recognition (CVPR) (2018)

SelectionConv: Convolutional Neural Networks for Non-rectilinear Image Data

David Hart$^{(\boxtimes)}$, Michael Whitney, and Bryan Morse

Brigham Young University, Provo, UT, USA
{davidmhart,mikeswhitney,morse}@byu.edu

Abstract. Convolutional Neural Networks have revolutionized vision applications. There are image domains and representations, however, that cannot be handled by standard CNNs (e.g., spherical images, super-pixels). Such data are usually processed using networks and algorithms specialized for each type. In this work, we show that it may not always be necessary to use specialized neural networks to operate on such spaces. Instead, we introduce a new structured graph convolution operator that can copy 2D convolution weights, transferring the capabilities of already trained traditional CNNs to our new graph network. This network can then operate on any data that can be represented as a positional graph. By converting non-rectilinear data to a graph, we can apply these convolutions on these irregular image domains without requiring training on large domain-specific datasets. Results of transferring pre-trained image networks for segmentation, stylization, and depth prediction are demonstrated for a variety of such data forms.

Keywords: Graph convolution · Transfer learning · Irregular images · Superpixels · Spherical images · Texture maps

1 Introduction

Convolution has been an important operator in image processing practically since its inception, long before the age of deep learning. It is the backbone of most modern deep neural networks, and learnable weights in convolution layers lead to incredible capabilities such as classification, object detection, segmentation, stylization, and many others.

Convolution is powerful, but the discrete form used for raster images requires dense rectilinear grids, typically Cartesian grids. For sparse, discontinuous, or irregular data, discrete raster convolution may not be applicable. Methods such as rasterization, interpolation, or padding are commonly used to convert the data into a form suitable for discrete convolution.

Graph convolution is more adaptable to less regularly structured data and is designed to mimic the process of 2D convolution. Instead of requiring spatial

Supplementary Information The online version contains supplementary material available at https://doi.org/10.1007/978-3-031-20071-7_19.

Fig. 1. Our method allows pre-trained 2D CNNs to operate on non-rectilinear image domains such as superpixels, spherical images, masked images, and texture maps.

adjacency, it performs convolution based on an adjacency matrix that describes the edges that connect nodes to each other in the graph. One key difference, however, between traditional and graph convolution is that graph convolution is assumed to be non-orientable, meaning that it cannot treat incoming edges differently based on spatial direction or the order they are fed into the convolution. This is called the *permutation-invariance* constraint of graph convolution [4].

In image convolution, neighboring pixels are commonly given different weights to help detect shapes and other patterns. In graph convolution, all neighbors are aggregated in the same way, removing any location-based structure in the process. Thus, the weights learned in a 2D convolutional neural network are incommensurate with the weights learned in a graph convolution neural network.

Graphs are commonly used to model abstract data that do not have positional information (social networks, individual media ratings, etc.), but when the graph data is image-based, we still wish to leverage positions, shapes, and patterns in the same manner as traditional image convolution.

This paper presents a framework for working with non-rectilinear image-based data that both traditional convolutional networks and graph networks are ill-equipped to handle natively, including the types shown in Fig. 1. We do this using a new type of selection-based graph convolution, which we name *SelectionConv*, that can retain the same shapes and patterns that a traditional convolution learns. In so doing, traditional convolution weights can be made commensurate with SelectionConv weights, allowing the transfer of weights directly from networks previously trained on standard image datasets. Thus, no special training or fine-tuning is necessary to run the network on less conventional image types. This is particularly significant because less common image types usually have far less available training data than typical image datasets.

Through this method, any network that operates on images can operate on any form of data that can be represented as a positional graph. This allows one framework to perform multiple tasks, such as depth prediction on superpixels, segmentation of spherical images, and stylization of texture maps for 3D meshes, as described in Sect. 5 and demonstrated in Sect. 6. This technique opens up a realm of possibilities for previously underused data sources.

In summary, our contributions are as follows:

- We present a selection-based graph convolution operator that assigns different weights to incoming edges without violating permutation invariance.
- We demonstrate how to transfer pre-trained 2D convolution weights to our new graph operator, thus removing the need to retrain the graph network.
- We apply this new method to various non-rectilinear image applications to demonstrate its effectiveness.

2   Related Work

2.1   Graph Convolution Networks

The explosion of deep learning in recent years has led to many developments in both Convolutional Neural Networks (CNNs) and Graph Neural Networks (GNNs). Graph Convolution Networks (GCNs) started with the work of Kipf *et al.*, which extended the ideas of CNNs to a general graph structure [18]. Improvements on the original method have been proposed including higher-order aggregation structures [6,27] and incorporating MLPs in the aggregation step [39]. For a more complete overview of this line of work, we direct the interested reader to recent surveys of both CNNs [21] and GNNs [41].

Interpolated Convolution Networks [25] and Spline Convolution Networks [10] are designed, like this work, to mimic the process of a traditional CNN on a point cloud or graph. However, these two approaches do not provide an explicit method for transferring weights to the new network. Additionally, both of these approaches require traditional position-based point clouds, whereas we show that our method is adaptable to many different data types and can be modified flexibly according to the users' specifications.

The works by Xu *et al.* [42] and Zhou *et al.* [48] both aim to use the structural and positional information inherent in graphs to improve graph learning. These are learnable components that can improve the training and performance of graph networks given sufficient suitable training data. Our approach aims to explicitly define the graph structure so that additional training is not needed.

2.2   Transfer Learning

The goal of transfer learning is to take the information or weights learned from one network and utilize them in another network in some way. One common example of transfer learning is to use a CNN backbone trained for a classification network such as VGG-19 [32] for another task such as segmentation. Many researchers have explored the effectiveness of networks trained for one task when performing another task [24,45], and a recent survey of transfer learning techniques can be found in [50]. Our work differs from the goal of previous transfer learning literature since our focus is not to transfer weights to a different task, but to a network that operates on a different domain.

It is worth noting that there has been an effort to theoretically unify the various types of neural networks and their various domains by focusing on their invariance and equivariance properties [4]. To our knowledge, though, no attempt has been made to state these operations in terms of each other and thus make them transferable.

2.3   Spherical Images, Superpixels, and Texture Maps

This paper demonstrates the effectiveness of selection-based graph convolution on various forms of non-raster data. Here we include work relevant to the tasks we perform and the types of data used.

We demonstrate working with spherical images by performing both semantic segmentation and stylization. Several groups have worked on performing semantic segmentation on spherical images [17,36,46]. Notable is the work of Tateno et al. [36] who developed distortion aware convolutions that operate in spherical space and also have the ability to transfer weights from a standard 2D CNN. However, their method is specific to spherical images where ours extends to other image domains.

Ruder et al. [30] present a method for performing style transfer on 360° images by taking the six cube-projected views and stylizing each one in turn while enforcing consistency between each previously stylized view. We also perform spherical image stylization in Sect. 6.1, but we do so in a single feed-forward step without the need of fine-tuning a specialized network.

The aim of superpixels is to group similar pixels in an image into regions, simplifying the representation of the whole image. In this work, we use SLIC, a standard baseline algorithm for generating superpixels [1]. Many other classical approaches exist for generating superpixels [34]. Recent deep learning techniques have been proposed to improve superpixels [22,38]. Superpixels have also been used to improve modern detection and segmentation methods [16,47]. Yang et al. [43] use superpixels to take low-resolution results into higher resolutions, similar to the task we perform in Sect. 6.3, but they do so by pretraining a separate network that can predict superpixel associations on a grid-based structure.

Most work on meshes has focused on learning from the geometry rather than from the color information that is provided in the texture map. Some have explored generating new texture from a smaller example texture through classical texture synthesis methods [3,8,40] and neural approaches [12,13,31,33,49]. Textures have also been manipulated through lighting-based style transfer [11,35] rather than through a purely image-based approach like the one we present in Sect. 6.4. Yin et al. [44] recently proposed a geometry and texture stylization approach that is optimization based and uses differentiable rendering, a fundamentally different approach to operating on texture map data than the one we explore in this work.

3 Selection-Based Convolution

Our method requires designing a graph convolution operator that treats incoming edges differently from one another during the aggregation step. Traditionally in graph convolution, all connecting edges are specified in a single adjacency matrix, and this matrix is used to described which nodes can influence each other after some set of transformation operations. For example, the original Graph Convolution Layer defined in [18] can be described as

$$\mathbf{X}^{(k+1)} = \tilde{\mathbf{A}}\mathbf{X}^{(k)}\mathbf{W} \qquad (1)$$

where $\mathbf{X}^{(k)}$ is the current node activations, $\tilde{\mathbf{A}}$ is a normalized adjacency matrix, and $\mathbf{W}$ is the learned weights. Note that the weight matrix is applied equally to all nodes, making the result invariant to the order that nodes are enumerated in

$\mathbf{X}^{(k)}$ as long as $\tilde{\mathbf{A}}$ changes correspondingly. This is an example of the permutation invariance constraint to which all graph convolution operations must adhere.

In comparison, while standard 2D convolution is shift invariant, it is not permutation invariant, relying heavily on orientation when assigning the weight of each connecting pixel. For example, the pixel directly above the current one might be given different weight than the pixel to the bottom right, and so on. Graph convolutions are able to assign edge weights, but they are generally static or on a node-by-node basis using a mechanism such as attention [37]. Thus, the weights learned during a 2D convolution are incommensurate with the weights learned during a graph convolution.

In order to leverage the benefits of pretrained 2D convolutional networks while having the structural flexibility of graphs, we introduce a new graph convolution layer that can preserve location information. We do so by preprocessing the graph into multiple adjacency matrices, selecting edges to be assigned to different matrices based on the spatial relationship between their two nodes. This is similar to the way we can think of different adjacency relationships between pixels and their directional neighbors. There is also a unique weight matrix for each corresponding adjacency matrix so only those edges are affected. The results for the set of adjacency and weight matrices are summed together to make the final activation. This selection-based convolution is what we call *SelectionConv*.

For each graph, a given edge e_{ij} needs to be assigned to its specific adjacency matrix. We do so using a selection function $s(v_i, v_j)$ for vertices v_i and v_j with spatial positions $\mathbf{x}_i$ and $\mathbf{x}_j$ respectively, which indicates which adjacency matrix includes the edge e_{ij} between these vertices. For m possible selections this gives m adjacency matrices respectively defined as

$$\mathbf{S}_{m_{ij}} = \begin{cases} 1 & \text{if } s(v_i, v_j) = m \\ 0 & \text{otherwise} \end{cases} \tag{2}$$

Each selection has a corresponding weight matrix. Thus our convolution becomes

$$\mathbf{X}^{(k+1)} = \sum_m \tilde{\mathbf{S}}_m \mathbf{X}^{(k)} \mathbf{W}_m \tag{3}$$

where $\tilde{\mathbf{S}}_m$ is the normalized version of $\mathbf{S}_m$ to account for nodes having multiple edges with the same selection m. With this structure, nodes can be treated differently based on location and other features relative to the current node without breaking the permutation invariance constraint. An example of this process is illustrated in Fig. 2.

We use PyTorch Geometric [9] to implement this process and use slices from 3D tensors rather than separate weight and adjacency matrices for efficiency, but the result is mathematically equivalent.

4   Selection-Based Convolution for Images

Though the process described in Sect. 3 is general enough to work with any number of selections based on any number of node attributes, we now move to

Fig. 2. A graph with a selection function that weights upwards edges differently from downwards edges. Such a selection function would give two adjacency matrices, $\mathbf{S}_1$ and $\mathbf{S}_2$, that would be applied to two different weight matrices, $\mathbf{W}_1$ and $\mathbf{W}_2$.

the specific case of working in the image domain. To start, we will establish a baseline for our method by looking at a regular image and showing that we got results identical to a 2D convolution with our selection-based convolution.

4.1   Setting Up Image Graphs

An image with pixels in a Cartesian grid can be thought of as a set of nodes at equally spaced distances. Many neural networks use 3×3 convolutions as their primary image feature extractor, which look at the pixel and its 8-connected neighbors. Thus, when we construct our graph, we will add an edge from each pixel to its 8-connected neighbors and one to itself. This means we need $m = 9$ possible selections.

For pixels in a Cartesian grid arrangement, value assignment for the respective selection functions is straightforward. For the general spatial case, we project the vector defined by the position of the two nodes onto the set $\mathbf{D}$ of unit vectors in each of the respective neighbor directions. Specifically,

$$\mathbf{D} := \begin{matrix} \langle -\sqrt{2}/2, -\sqrt{2}/2 \rangle & \langle 0, -1 \rangle & \langle \sqrt{2}/2, -\sqrt{2}/2 \rangle \\ \langle -1, 0 \rangle & & \langle 1, 0 \rangle \\ \langle -\sqrt{2}/2, \sqrt{2}/2 \rangle & \langle 0, 1 \rangle & \langle \sqrt{2}/2, \sqrt{2}/2 \rangle \end{matrix} \qquad (4)$$

Whichever directional unit vector results in the largest projection (resulting dot product) corresponds to the assigned selection. Additionally, if the positions are the same (or within some small radius), the central selection is made. Thus, our selection function becomes

$$s(v_i, v_j) = \begin{cases} 0 \text{ if } \|\mathbf{x}_j - \mathbf{x}_i\| < \epsilon \\ \underset{k}{\operatorname{argmax}} \ \mathbf{D}_k \cdot (\mathbf{x}_j - \mathbf{x}_i) \text{ otherwise} \end{cases} \qquad (5)$$

For simplicity, when assigning a selection number or index to each direction, we follow the mathematical convention of angles by making the direction to the right be the first selection and moving in the counterclockwise direction for assigning each subsequent direction. This is visualized on the left and right sides of Fig. 3.

4.2   Weight Transfer from 2D Convolutions

Once the appropriate selections have been made, transferring the weights is simply copying the appropriate slice of the convolution kernel weights to its

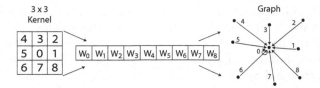

Fig. 3. Elements of a 3×3 convolution kernel are enumerated with zero for the center weight and neighboring weights from one to eight in counter-clockwise direction. The different weights from the kernel are transferred to associated weight matrices. Those weight matrices are then applied to the selected edges on the graph. Note that the points in the graph do not need to be equally spaced as in regular images. There can also be more than one node per selection.

assigned selection. For example, if selection 5 represents an edge going to the left, the left kernel convolution weights would be copied to $\mathbf{W}_5$. This process is illustrated in Fig. 3. When applied to raster data, this process leads to results that are identical to those using an image-based convolutional network.

4.3 Handling Larger Kernels

If a network uses a kernel that is larger than 3×3, more weights need to be copied over, but the same graph structure can still be used. Rather than using a larger graph that is memory inefficient, we use the edges of the simpler 3×3 graph. Through successive multiplications of the adjacency matrices, multiple edge hops (traversals) can be performed until specific kernel locations are reached. For example, if a 5×5 kernel is used, the weight associated with the bottom middle pixel would be assigned to the action of taking the bottom selection's bottom selection.

4.4 Pooling Operators and Upsampling

Many CNNs use pooling layers throughout the network to combine nearby features. While GCNs have similar pooling features, it is important that our SelectionConv network's pooling layers mimic the downsampling nature of those used in traditional CNNs.

If the network contains fully connected layers, we impose a spatial grid onto the set of nodes when pooling. This grid matches the spatial size that the original image data reduces to after pooling. If the network is fully convolutional, pooling does not require a regular grid (especially if one cannot be imposed, such as on a texture map), and any pixel-clustering algorithm can be used. In both cases, any node within a cell or cluster is made into a single node during the pooling step. The average of the positions of nodes in that cell becomes the position of the pooled node. This is similar to the meta-node approach used in [29].

Pooled nodes also need to reestablish edge connections and selections. To do so, we implement a post-pooling function that makes new edges between the aggregated cluster nodes by using the previous layer's graph edges. If any edge exists between two nodes in different clusters, the aggregated nodes of those clusters will have a corresponding edge between them. That edge is assigned the average of the previous selection values of all the edges between the original nodes in the two clusters (while properly accounting for the selection value wrap-around between 1 and 8).

If the network requires upsampling steps, we save each version of the graph before it is downsampled. When upsampling, we revert back to a previous version of the graph and copy appropriate values to each node using the defined clusters. Bilinear upsampling can also be approximated by using the average value of the connections to new nodes or through other point cloud interpolation methods.

4.5   Strides, Dilation, Padding

Traditional 2D convolution layers often have additional parameters such as the stride of the kernel, the dilation of the kernel, and the padding to be used on the border of the image. Selection-based convolution as described so far is equivalent to a stride of 1, a dilation of 1, and zero padding, but we have the ability to mimic these additional features in our SelectionConv network when needed.

Strides larger than 1 in a regular convolution layer are equivalent to a stride equal to 1 followed by downsampling by the stride amount (with no antialiasing). We use this same idea to implement large strides in the SelectionConv network. The convolution is performed as usual (equivalent to a stride of 1), then the graph is pooled using the method described in Sect. 4.4, but rather than using a max or average pooling operator, a predetermined central node in each cluster is always used as the pooled value.

Dilation is handled in a way similar to the larger kernels described in Sect. 4.3. The dilation amount defines how many times a selection is edge hopped. For example, a dilation of two would indicate that instead of taking the left selection, the left selection's left selection should be used instead. This process is repeated for each selection for the same number of times as the dilation's value.

Padding in traditional 2D CNNs helps control the size of output layers. Graph convolution layers do not change the size of the output since the number of nodes will stay the same, so padding is not usually needed. Some 2D CNN padding schemes, however, are used to help information propagate correctly along the borders of an image (such as reflective padding in stylization networks). We handle these situations not only by looking at nodes along a border, but by determining what to do with any missing selections. The following padding methods can be implemented effectively and approximate padding schemes used for images:

- **Zero**: Missing selections are not considered (default).
- **Constant**: Missing selections are assigned a predetermined value.
- **Replicate**: Missing selections are assigned the value of the current node.
- **Reflect**: Missing selections are assigned the value of the selection in the opposite direction.

Some of these steps we mimic from CNNs currently have nondifferentiable implementations. Though not needed for the scope of this work, which focuses on transferring weights from pre-trained networks, all parts of our SelectionConv network would need to be differentiable if any form of training or fine-tuning was desired for the network after weights have been transferred.

4.6   Verification

To verify that the SelectionConv network can truly be equivalent to a traditional CNN, we used a pre-trained VGG-11 network [28,32] on CIFAR-10 [19] and transferred the original weights to our network. We compared this to the original image-based network using the 10,000-image validation set. As expected, the two methods resulted in identical predictions and identical accuracies of 84.5%. This remains true even when small random spatial perturbations are introduced to the points in the graph structure.

5   Example Non-rectilinear Configurations

Section 4 describes how to configure a SelectionConv network to work on images in exactly the same way as a regular CNN. This works as a baseline but does not provide any additional power over a regular CNN. In this section, we give examples of the flexibility of our method to work with data that cannot be processed with a traditional CNN due to its irregular structure. *Importantly, our method can use the weights from a CNN pre-trained using standard image datasets without the need to retrain for specific data types.*

5.1   Panoramic and Spherical Images

Many smartphones and cameras allow users to take single or multiple pictures of their surroundings to acquire panoramic or even up to the full $360° \times 180°$ view of their environment. These panoramic and spherical images have non-simple topologies but are typically stored as simple planar images. This requires projection of the content to a surface of some kind. While there are many ways to project, including spherical, equirectangular (cylindrical), and cubic, each of these have distortion or seams of some nature that would be difficult for a traditional CNN to handle due to irregular spatial sampling or topological considerations. With our method, such seams and distortion can be handled by proper construction of the graph.

As an example, we show how to construct the graph for a cubic projection often used for environment maps in computer graphics, which we have found to be effective to work with since it has low levels of distortion compared to other projections. Seams are naturally present along each edge of the cube, and a 2D image can only represent a few of those connections. In our graph, we simply need to make the connections between the rest of the seams, as illustrated in Fig. 4a. Additionally, we orient our selection function in such a way so that the upwards selection is always pointed towards the top pole of the map.

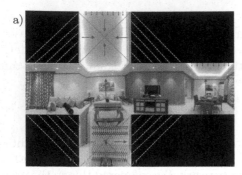 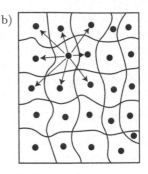

Fig. 4. a) Illustration of the graph connections for a cube map. Red arrows represent the upwards selection for nodes in that part of the graph. Green and blue lines represent connections made in the graph between faces. b) Illustration of the graph connections between the centroids of superpixels in an image. (Color figure online)

5.2 Superpixel Images

Using superpixels is a common approach for simplifying a high-resolution image by representing it as a smaller set of similar regions. Because of the irregular structure of the regions, superpixels cannot be used for standard CNNs. They can, however, be easily represented as a graph and used with our approach.

To construct the graph from the set of superpixels, the centroid of each region is treated as a node, and edges are selected using a K-nearest neighbors method. Selections are then made using the dot product method described in Sect. 4.1 and the graph is pruned so only the closest neighbor to each node for a given selection is used. This process is illustrated in Fig. 4b.

5.3 Masked Images and Texture Maps

Many applications require operating only on the foreground or a specified region of the image. Our graph construction can naturally handle these cases by simply dropping nodes and edges that are not part of the desired region, and any desired padding mode described in Sect. 4.5 can be used to handle the irregular border.

Texture maps for 3D meshes can also be thought of as masked regions. Not all pixels present on a texture map image will be used to determine colors on the actual mesh, so we can mask out the regions that contain pixels that represent some part of a face on the mesh. If we further connect these faces in the graph, we can operate on the texture map in the same fashion as any image. To do this in general, we start by determining which edges are only referenced once in the UV map, since these represent the boundaries of groups of faces on the UV map. We then find all closed loops of edges to separate each boundary. Finally, we do a polygon-contains-point test for each pixel to see if the pixel is inside any of our boundaries. This becomes the mask of relevant pixels on the texture map. An overview of this process is shown in Fig. 5.

Fig. 5. A 3D model (a) and its texture map. The model's texture seams can be determined from UV coordinates and represent boundaries on the texture map (b). From this, we construct a mask of relevant pixels (c) and connect discontiguous regions.

If it is known which geometric faces are connected to each other, this can be built into the graph construction. Otherwise, each edge boundary is paired with a corresponding edge on another face that is used to make the connections. All regions are connected regardless of where they are located on the image.

6   Results

To demonstrate transfer from image networks to SelectionConv networks, we present the results of applying this and the graph-construction methods from the previous section to various applications and image types. Additional results can be found in the accompanying supplemental materials.

6.1   Spherical Style Transfer

A simple but effective illustration of the seamless nature of a selection-based graph convolution is to perform style transfer on a spherical image. For this we use the feed-forward style transfer approach recently proposed by Li *et al.* [20]. Usually for this task, a special piece-wise optimization approach or fine-tuned network would be needed, such as that proposed by Ruder *et al.* [30]. However, by generating our spherical graph using the method shown in Sect. 5.1, we naturally avoid distortion, minimize seams, and can stylize in a single feed-forward pass. An example is shown in Fig. 6. The whole process of generating the graph, transferring the weights, and running the graph convolution can run in 15–20 s on a consumer GPU, while [30] would take 8–10 minutes per 360° image. Even the faster approach suggested in [30] requires fine-tuning a network for 120,000 iterations per style image. Our approach uses a state-of-the-art feed forward style transfer method, can be used for any style image, and still enforce consistency across the seams of the cube map.

6.2   Spherical Segmentation

We apply SelectionConv to the task of semantic segmentation on images in the Stanford 2D-3D-S [2] dataset. To do so, we first trained a standard 2D FCN [23] using a ResNet-50 [15] backbone on 2D projected views. We then

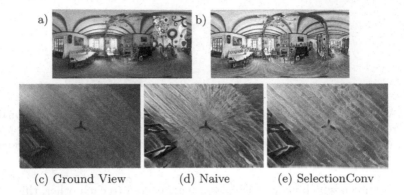

(c) Ground View   (d) Naive   (e) SelectionConv

Fig. 6. A 360° image (a) and its stylization using our feed-forward method (b). An example view looking downward at the lower pole of the image (c) has seams and distortion when naively stylizing the rectangular image (d), but those seams and distortion are minimized with our method (e). Image taken from [5].

transfer the weights to a SelectionConv-based version of FCN [23] and apply the network, with no additional training, to the standard test set, converting the data to spherical graphs using the method described in Sect. 5.1. This gives an improvement over naively applying the network to the equirectangular images, as shown in Fig. 7. When operating on the validation set, the naive approach gives an average IOU score of 32.57%. We compare our results with that of another transfer-based method, distortion-aware convolutions [36], who reported an average IOU score of 34.56% on the same dataset. Our results show an average IOU score of 36.29%. Although this is only a small improvement and is still below state-of-the-art performance for RGB spherical segmentation (45.6% [7]), we again note that other methods are designed and fine-tuned specifically for

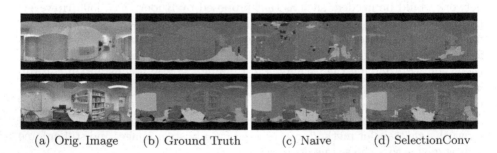

(a) Orig. Image   (b) Ground Truth   (c) Naive   (d) SelectionConv

Fig. 7. A visual comparison of semantic segmentation of images from the Stanford 2D-3D-S [2] dataset (a, b) between an FCN [23] with a ResNet-50 [15] backbone using standard convolutions (c) versus our SelectionConv operations (d). Note that the use of SelectionConv gives cleaner segmentation results along the poles of and seam of the image (located in the center of this representation).

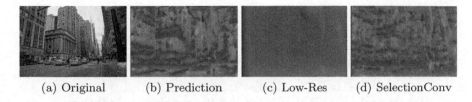

| (a) Original | (b) Prediction | (c) Low-Res | (d) SelectionConv |

Fig. 8. A high-resolution image (a) requires ~25.9 s on a CPU to create a predicted depth map (b). A lower-resolution 256 × 256 version can be processed by a network in ~0.8 s on a GPU, but with low-fidelity results when upscaled to the same resolution (c). Generating approximately the same number of superpixels as the low-resolution image then using our graph-based network requires only ~5.1 s on a GPU with higher-fidelity results (d).

spherical tasks, whereas we can achieve a performance boost through a simple design of our graph structure.

6.3   Superpixel Depth Prediction

We now illustrate possible applications using our method with superpixels for efficient processing of high-resolution images. We use a Pytorch implementation of a monocular depth estimator [14,26]. When operating on a 4K image, the amount of data is too large for a consumer-grade GPU, necessitating downsampling the input before processing. By comparison, if the image is first converted into a graph of neighboring SLIC superpixels [1], SelectionConv can process it on a GPU and output results that are of much higher quality than using a downsampled image. An example of such cases is shown in Fig. 8. We again note that Yang *et al.* [43] complete a similar task with state-of-the-art performance, but their method requires using superpixels generated by their trained network. The SelectionConv network, in comparison, can utilize any superpixel method.

6.4   Masked Image and 3D Mesh Style Transfer

Lastly, we demonstrate the ability of our network to work on data with many discontinuities by performing style transfer on masked images and texture maps.

To achieve style transfer on a masked region with a regular CNN would require stylizing the entire image or a zero-padded masked image and then reapplying the unmasked region. This means that background features can affect stylization of the foreground. In comparison, our method can handle these scenarios natively, leading to a stylization that only depends on the foreground statistics. Comparisons of these approaches are shown in Fig. 9.

As another illustration, treating a texture map as a 2D image and naively performing style transfer leads to noticeable seams in the mapped texture. In comparison, using the graph structure proposed in Sect. 5.3 leads to more continuous patterns. Visualizations of these two methods for various stylizations and meshes are shown in Fig. 10.

(a) Original   (b) Post-masking   (c) Pre-masking   (d) Ours

Fig. 9. A content image, a masked region of interest, and a given style image (a). To stylize the masked region with a traditional CNN, the entire image can be stylized (b) or the image can be masked before stylization (c) and then the masked result can be applied back to the original. In both cases, outside statistics influence the stylization inside the region of interest (making (b) darker than expected and (c) brighter than expected). In comparison, our method (d) can generate a graph just for the masked region, which more closely matches the style image statistics in the region of interest.

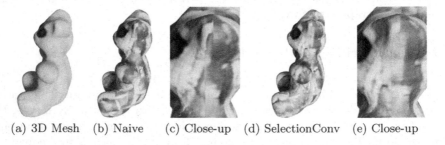

(a) 3D Mesh   (b) Naive   (c) Close-up   (d) SelectionConv   (e) Close-up

Fig. 10. 3D mesh (a), the result of naively stylizing the texture map (b) and a magnification (c), and the result of using our method (d) and a magnification (e). Note the visible seams shown in the magnifications of the naive method (c), whereas our method in (e) minimizes the visibility of those seams.

Others have attempted style transfer between two different 3D objects [11,35, 44], but we are not aware of other work attempting direct style transfer between the texture map of the 3D mesh and a 2D image.

7   Conclusion

We have presented a method that allows for information from pre-trained traditional convolutional neural networks to be transferred directly to a new kind of graph convolutional network. This makes it possible for these previously trained networks to operate on data that they could not before, such as superpixels, spherical images, and texture maps. We have demonstrated various use cases and given the general framework so that others can continue to extend this method for their needs. In theory, any set of adjacency matrices could be designed to work with the particular data of a graph. Future research could also use selection-based convolution to improve applications outside of the image domain.

References

1. Achanta, R., Shaji, A., Smith, K., Lucchi, A., Fua, P., Süsstrunk, S.: SLIC super-pixels compared to state-of-the-art superpixel methods. IEEE Trans. Pattern Anal. Mach. Intell. **34**(11), 2274–2282 (2012). https://doi.org/10.1109/TPAMI.2012.120
2. Armeni, I., Sax, A., Zamir, A.R., Savarese, S.: Joint 2D-3D-Semantic Data for Indoor Scene Understanding. arXiv:1702.01105 (2017)
3. Ashikhmin, M.: Synthesizing natural textures. In: Symposium on Interactive 3D Graphics, pp. 217–226 (2001)
4. Bronstein, M.M., Bruna, J., Cohen, T., Velickovic, P.: Geometric deep learning: grids, groups, graphs, geodesics, and gauges. arXiv:2104.13478 (2021)
5. Chou, S.H., Sun, C., Wen-Yen, C., Hsu, W.T., Sun, M., Fu, J.: 360-indoor: towards learning real-world objects in 360° indoor equirectangular images, pp. 834–842 (2020). https://doi.org/10.1109/WACV45572.2020.9093262
6. Defferrard, M., Bresson, X., Vandergheynst, P.: Convolutional neural networks on graphs with fast localized spectral filtering. In: Lee, D., Sugiyama, M., Luxburg, U., Guyon, I., Garnett, R. (eds.) Advances in Neural Information Processing Systems, vol. 29. Curran Associates, Inc. (2016)
7. Eder, M., Shvets, M., Lim, J., Frahm, J.M.: Tangent images for mitigating spherical distortion. In: Conference on Computer Vision and Pattern Recognition (CVPR), pp. 12426–12434. IEEE (2020)
8. Efros, A.A., Freeman, W.T.: Image quilting for texture synthesis and transfer. In: Proceedings of the 28th Annual Conference on Computer Graphics and Interactive Techniques, pp. 341–346 (2001)
9. Fey, M., Lenssen, J.E.: Fast graph representation learning with PyTorch Geometric. In: ICLR Workshop on Representation Learning on Graphs and Manifolds (2019)
10. Fey, M., Lenssen, J.E., Weichert, F., Müller, H.: SplineCNN: fast geometric deep learning with continuous B-spline kernels. In: Conference on Computer Vision and Pattern Recognition (CVPR), pp. 869–877. IEEE (2018)
11. Fišer, J., et al.: StyLit: illumination-guided example-based stylization of 3D renderings. ACM Trans. Graph. **35**(4), 92:1–92:11 (2016). https://doi.org/10.1145/2897824.2925948
12. Frühstück, A., Alhashim, I., Wonka, P.: TileGAN: synthesis of large-scale non-homogeneous textures. ACM Trans. Graph. (TOG) **38**(4), 1–11 (2019)
13. Gatys, L., Ecker, A.S., Bethge, M.: Texture synthesis using convolutional neural networks. Adv. Neural. Inf. Process. Syst. **28**, 262–270 (2015)
14. Godard, C., Mac Aodha, O., Brostow, G.J.: Unsupervised monocular depth estimation with left-right consistency. In: Conference on Computer Vision and Pattern Recognition (CVPR). IEEE (2017)
15. He, K., Zhang, X., Ren, S., Sun, J.: Deep residual learning for image recognition. In: Conference on Computer Vision and Pattern Recognition (CVPR), pp. 770–778 (2016)
16. Jampani, V., Sun, D., Liu, M.-Y., Yang, M.-H., Kautz, J.: Superpixel sampling networks. In: Ferrari, V., Hebert, M., Sminchisescu, C., Weiss, Y. (eds.) ECCV 2018. LNCS, vol. 11211, pp. 363–380. Springer, Cham (2018). https://doi.org/10.1007/978-3-030-01234-2_22
17. Jiang, C.M., Huang, J., Kashinath, K., Marcus, P., Niessner, M.: Spherical CNNs on unstructured grids. In: International Conference on Learning Representations (ICLR) (2019)

18. Kipf, T.N., Welling, M.: Semi-supervised classification with graph convolutional networks. In: 5th International Conference on Learning Representations, ICLR 2017, Toulon, France, 24–26 April 2017, Conference Track Proceedings (2017)
19. Krizhevsky, A., Nair, V., Hinton, G.: CIFAR-10 (Canadian institute for advanced research). http://www.cs.toronto.edu/~kriz/cifar.html
20. Li, X., Liu, S., Kautz, J., Yang, M.H.: Learning linear transformations for fast arbitrary style transfer. In: Conference on Computer Vision and Pattern Recognition (CVPR). IEEE (2019)
21. Li, Z., Yang, W., Peng, S., Liu, F.: A survey of convolutional neural networks: analysis, applications, and prospects (2020)
22. Lin, Q., Zhong, W., Lu, J.: Deep superpixel cut for unsupervised image segmentation. In: 2020 25th International Conference on Pattern Recognition (ICPR), pp. 8870–8876 (2021)
23. Long, J., Shelhamer, E., Darrell, T.: Fully convolutional networks for semantic segmentation. In: Conference on Computer Vision and Pattern Recognition (CVPR). IEEE (2015)
24. Lu, Y., et al.: Taskology: utilizing task relations at scale. In: Conference on Computer Vision and Pattern Recognition (CVPR). IEEE (2021)
25. Mao, J., Wang, X., Li, H.: Interpolated convolutional networks for 3D point cloud understanding. In: International Conference on Computer Vision (ICCV), pp. 1578–1587. IEEE (2019)
26. Monodepth. https://github.com/OniroAI/MonoDepth-PyTorch
27. Morris, C., et al.: Weisfeiler and leman go neural: higher-order graph neural networks. In: AAAI, vol. 33, no. 01, pp. 4602–4609 (2019)
28. PyTorch, Torchvision Models. https://pytorch.org/vision/stable/models.html
29. Qi, C.R., Yi, L., Su, H., Guibas, L.J.: Pointnet++: deep hierarchical feature learning on point sets in a metric space. In: Proceedings of the 31st International Conference on Neural Information Processing Systems, pp. 5105–5114. Curran Associates Inc., Red Hook (2017)
30. Ruder, M., Dosovitskiy, A., Brox, T.: Artistic style transfer for videos and spherical images. Int. J. Comput. Vision 126(11), 1199–1219 (2018)
31. Shi, W., Qiao, Y.: Fast texture synthesis via pseudo optimizer. In: Conference on Computer Vision and Pattern Recognition (CVPR), pp. 5498–5507. IEEE (2020)
32. Simonyan, K., Zisserman, A.: Very deep convolutional networks for large-scale image recognition. In: International Conference on Learning Representations (ICLR) (2015)
33. Snelgrove, X.: High-resolution multi-scale neural texture synthesis. In: SIGGRAPH Asia 2017 Technical Briefs, pp. 1–4 (2017)
34. Stutz, D., Hermans, A., Leibe, B.: Superpixels: an evaluation of the state-of-the-art. Comput. Vis. Image Underst. 166, 1–27 (2018). https://doi.org/10.1016/j.cviu.2017.03.007
35. Sýkora, D., et al.: StyleBlit: fast example-based stylization with local guidance. Comput. Graph. Forum 38(2), 83–91 (2019)
36. Tateno, K., Navab, N., Tombari, F.: Distortion-aware convolutional filters for dense prediction in panoramic images. In: Ferrari, V., Hebert, M., Sminchisescu, C., Weiss, Y. (eds.) ECCV 2018. LNCS, vol. 11220, pp. 732–750. Springer, Cham (2018). https://doi.org/10.1007/978-3-030-01270-0_43
37. Veličković, P., Cucurull, G., Casanova, A., Romero, A., Liò, P., Bengio, Y.: Graph attention networks. In: International Conference on Learning Representations (ICLR) (2018)

38. Verelst, T., Blaschko, M.B., Berman, M.: Generating superpixels using deep image representations. arXiv:1903.04586 (2019)
39. Wang, Y., Sun, Y., Liu, Z., Sarma, S.E., Bronstein, M.M., Solomon, J.M.: Dynamic graph CNN for learning on point clouds. ACM Trans. Graph. **38**(5), 1–12 (2019)
40. Wei, L.Y., Levoy, M.: Fast texture synthesis using tree-structured vector quantization. In: Proceedings of the 27th Annual Conference on Computer Graphics and Interactive Techniques, pp. 479–488 (2000)
41. Wu, Z., Pan, S., Chen, F., Long, G., Zhang, C., Yu, P.S.: A comprehensive survey on graph neural networks. IEEE Trans. Neural Netw. Learn. Syst. 1–21 (2020). https://doi.org/10.1109/tnnls.2020.2978386
42. Xu, M., Ding, R., Zhao, H., Qi, X.: Paconv: position adaptive convolution with dynamic kernel assembling on point clouds. In: Conference on Computer Vision and Pattern Recognition (CVPR). IEEE (2021)
43. Yang, F., Sun, Q., Jin, H., Zhou, Z.: Superpixel segmentation with fully convolutional networks. In: Conference on Computer Vision and Pattern Recognition (CVPR), pp. 13961–13970 (2020)
44. Yin, K., Gao, J., Shugrina, M., Khamis, S., Fidler, S.: 3DStyleNet: creating 3D shapes with geometric and texture style variations. In: International Conference on Computer Vision (ICCV). IEEE (2021)
45. Zamir, A.R., Sax, A., Shen, W.B., Guibas, L., Malik, J., Savarese, S.: Taskonomy: disentangling task transfer learning. In: Conference on Computer Vision and Pattern Recognition (CVPR). IEEE (2018)
46. Zhang, C., Liwicki, S., Smith, W., Cipolla, R.: Orientation-aware semantic segmentation on icosahedron spheres. In: International Conference on Computer Vision (ICCV). IEEE (2019)
47. Zhao, G., Ge, W., Yu, Y.: GraphFPN: graph feature pyramid network for object detection. In: International Conference on Computer Vision (ICCV), pp. 2763–2772. IEEE (2021)
48. Zhou, H., Feng, Y., Fang, M., Wei, M., Qin, J., Lu, T.: Adaptive graph convolution for point cloud analysis. In: International Conference on Computer Vision (ICCV), pp. 4945–4954 (2021)
49. Zhou, Y., Zhu, Z., Bai, X., Lischinski, D., Cohen-Or, D., Huang, H.: Non-stationary texture synthesis by adversarial expansion. ACM Trans. Graph. **37**(4) (2018). https://doi.org/10.1145/3197517.3201285
50. Zhuang, F., et al.: A comprehensive survey on transfer learning. Proc. IEEE **109**, 43–76 (2021)

Spatial-Separated Curve Rendering Network for Efficient and High-Resolution Image Harmonization

Jingtang Liang[1], Xiaodong Cun[2], Chi-Man Pun[1(✉)], and Jue Wang[2]

[1] University of Macau, Macau, China
mb05164@connect.umac.mo, cmpun@umac.mo
[2] Tencent AI Lab, Shenzhen, China

Abstract. Image harmonization aims to modify the color of the composited region according to the specific background. Previous works model this task as a pixel-wise image translation using UNet family structures. However, the model size and computational cost limit the ability of their models on edge devices and higher-resolution images. In this paper, we propose spatial-separated curve rendering network (S^{2}CRNet), a novel framework to prove that the simple global editing can effectively address this task as well as the challenge of high-resolution image harmonization for the first time. In S^{2}CRNet, we design a curve rendering module (CRM) using spatial-specific knowledge to generate the parameters of the piece-wise curve mapping in the foreground region and we can directly render the original high-resolution images using the learned color curve. Besides, we also make two extensions of the proposed framework via cascaded refinement and semantic guidance. Experiments show that the proposed method reduces more than 90% parameters compared with previous methods but still achieves the state-of-the-art performance on 3 benchmark datasets. Moreover, our method can work smoothly on higher resolution images with much lower GPU computational resources. The source codes are available at: http://github.com/stefanLeong/S2CRNet.

1 Introduction

Image composition (or image splicing in multimedia security) is a popular and necessary tool for image editing. However, in addition to the serrated edges caused by the irregular borders, the "style" disharmony occurs when we directly copy source regions (foreground) to the host image (background). The disharmony will degrade the quality of the composited images, which also can be distinguished by the human eyes easily. In general, handling this gap requires the professional editing of the well-knowledged experts. Thus, the task of image

---

J. Liang and X. Cun—Contribute equally to this work.

Supplementary Information The online version contains supplementary material available at https://doi.org/10.1007/978-3-031-20071-7_20.

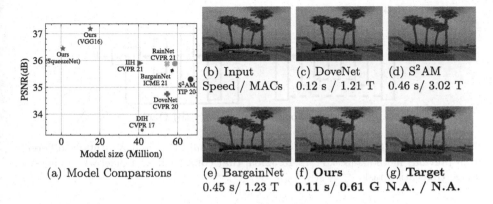

(a) Model Comparsions

(b) Input   (c) DoveNet   (d) S²AM
Speed / MACs   0.12 s / 1.21 T 0.46 s/ 3.02 T

(e) BargainNet (f) **Ours**   (g) **Target**
0.45 s/ 1.23 T **0.11 s/ 0.61 G** **N.A. / N.A.**

Fig. 1. (a) Our methods outperform other methods using much less parameters under the same setting (testing in 256 × 256 resolution). (b)–(f) Given a high-resolution image (originally 2048 × 2048 in this example), our method shows much better performance, lower computational cost (MACs) and faster speed than previous methods.

harmonization aims to squeeze this gap by leveraging some advanced algorithms, which also has a broad impact on image editing, relighting and augmented reality [22,38].

Traditional image harmonization methods intend to manually adjust and modify the specific features in the composite images, such as color [21,29], illumination [35] and texture [33], *etc.*. However, the hand-crafted and statistic low-level features cannot work well for the diverse composite images in complicated real world. Since the deep convolutional neural network (CNN) has reached impressive performance in many computer vision tasks, several attempts have also been made to address image harmonization tasks. For example, the semantic clues [32,34], the spatial differences of the neural network [5,12] and generative adversarial network (GAN [9]) based methods [3,4] have been proposed following the encoder-decoder based structures (UNet [18,30]) for pixel-wise prediction. Thus, as shown in Fig. 1(a), the speed and computational cost are sensitive to image resolution because those structures require to predict the pixel-wise results. Besides, their model sizes are too large for the edge devices, such as mobile phone. The problems mentioned above restrict the applying range of their methods since the real-world images editing are at any resolution. Furthermore, further evaluations at high-resolution images would be also downgraded from these inefficiencies.

Differently, in this paper, we rethink the image harmonization in a totally different way: Reviewing the image harmonization process in image editing software (*e.g.* PhotoShop), experts tend to adjust the global properties (color curve, illuminant, *etc.*) over the whole images rather than the pixel-wise color adjustment. Thus, the global editing can be enabled by considering those properties as the mapping function of the pixels intensities. Moreover, this global adjustment

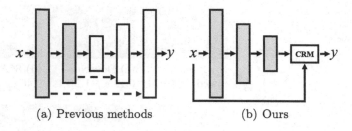

(a) Previous methods   (b) Ours

Fig. 2. We learn global mappings for image harmonization and are totally different from previous methods [3–5,11,12,23,32,34] that consider it as a pixel-wise image-to-image translation task.

is reliably efficient at any resolution images without extra expense of computational cost.

Above observation inspires us to doubt the effect of the locally-aware editing networks in previous image harmonization methods and learning the *global editing curves* of the composite foreground in terms of efficiency as shown in Fig. 2. Hence, a novel curve rendering module (CRM) is designed to produce the image-adaptive parameters of the curves that we will use to render the composite image. Specifically, we first separate the composite image into foreground/background regions using the given foreground mask. Then, we extract the global high-level features from both regions by a shared pre-trained general feature extractor (SqueezeNet [17] or VGG16 [31]). Particularly in CRM, the extracted features from foreground/background are learnt by a single layer linear projection for each region separately. Finally, the combination of these two spatial-specific features will be represented as the parameters of color curves, and we render the original foreground for each color channel with the approximate curves we learned.

Furthermore, we also make two extensions to the proposed framework. On one hand, we propose *semantic*-CRM. Since different foregrounds represent different categories, we learn the class-aware feature embeddings for each category individually by the user-guided foreground semantic encoding. On the other hand, we propose the *cascaded*-CRM, which is also inspired by the photo editing software since the image editing process generally contains multiple steps. In our implementation, we predict different domain embedding to achieve this goal via a cascaded prediction. Benefit by the proposed framework, our method shows a significantly better performance than previous state-of-the-art image harmonization networks with only 2% (25% using VGG16 backbone) of the parameters. Besides, our method can also run much faster than most previous methods with few computation cost on high-resolution images.

Our main contributions are summarized as follows:

- We find that the image harmonization can work well with the global editing method for the first time. To this end, we introduce a novel spatial-separated curve rendering network (S²CRNet), which also enables our method for efficient and high-resolution image harmonization.
- We show the extension ability of the proposed S²CRNet via better backbones or enhanced curve rendering module (CRM) via the Cascaded-CRM and Semantic-CRM.
- Experiments show that our method can achieve state-of-the-art performance and run much faster than the previous methods, while using fewer parameters and lower computational cost.

2   Related Works

Image Harmonization. Traditional image harmonization methods aim at improving composite images via low-level appearance features, such as manually adjusting global color distributions [1,2], applying gradient domain composition [19,28] or manipulating multi-scale transformation and statistical analysis [33]. Although these methods achieve preliminary results in harmonization tasks, the realism of the composite images cannot be visually guaranteed.

As the deep learning approaches has been successfully applied to the computer vision tasks, [39] back-propagate a pre-trained visual discriminator model to change the appearance harmony of the composite images. Later, further researches consider this task as an image to image translation problem. For example, additional semantic decoder [34] and pre-trained semantic feature [32] are used to ensure the semantic consistence between the composite inputs and harmonized outputs. Another noticeable idea is to model the differences between the foreground and background with the given mask. For example, novel spatial-separated attention module [5,12] under image-to-image translation framework; Domain-guided features as the discriminator of GAN [4] and as additional input [3]; masked-guided spatial normalizations [11,23] for the foreground and background respectively. However, all the previous deep networks still model this task as a pixel-wise image to image translation problem using an encoder-decoder structure, which suffers from computational inefficiency and may degrade the performance and visual quality on high-resolution inputs.

Efficient Network Design for Image Enhancement. Efficient networks designed for edge devices have also been widely-discussed in computer vision tasks [15]. For image enhancement, [8] introduce the deep bilateral learning for high-resolution and real-time image processing on mobile devices. Also, learning the image-adaptive global style features shows promising results in Exposure [16], CURL [26] and 3DLUT [36] for global image enhancement. Besides, Guo et al. [10] design a high-order pixel-wise curve function for low-light enhancement. Since our image harmonization task can be considered as a *regional* image enhancement problem, it is natural to leverage the style curve

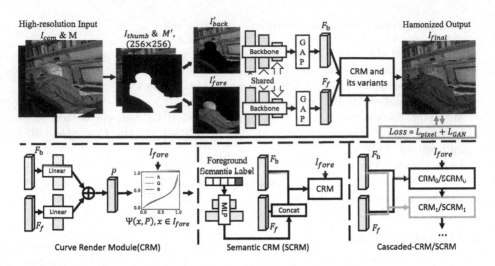

Fig. 3. The overview of the S^2CRNet, including CRM and its two variants: SCRM and Cascaded-CRM/SCRM.

to image harmonization tasks. However, different from the networks for image enhancement [16,26,36] and low-light enhancement [10], image harmonization methods rely on regional modification under the guidance of the background. Thus, we design the network structure and learn global mapping functions on this task for the first time.

3   Method

We first show the overall network structure of the proposed method. Then, we give the details of Curve Rendering Module (CRM) and its variants, which are the key components in S^2CRNet, including CRM, *Semantic*-CRM (SCRM) and their cascaded extensions. Finally, we discuss the loss functions.

3.1   Overall Network Structure

As shown in Fig. 3, given a high-resolution composite image $I_{com} \in \mathbb{R}^{3 \times H \times W}$ and its binary mask $M \in \mathbb{R}^{1 \times H \times W}$ of the corresponding foreground, we first get the thumbnail image $I_{thumb} \in \mathbb{R}^{3 \times h \times w}$ and the mask $M' \in \mathbb{R}^{1 \times h \times w}$ by down-sampling I_{com} and M with a factor of H/h for fast inference and the minimal computational cost. For the spatial-separated feature encoding, we first segment the thumbnail image I_{thumb} into foreground and background via the mask M' and inverse mask $M'_{inv} = 1 - M'$, respectively. Next, given the foreground $I_{fore} = I_{thumb} \times M'$ and background $I_{back} = I_{thumb} \times M'_{inv}$ images, we use a shared domain encoder Φ to extract the spatial-separated features for foreground and background respectively. Here, we choose the SqueezeNet [17] as the domain encoder (backbone), which is pre-trained on the ImageNet [7]

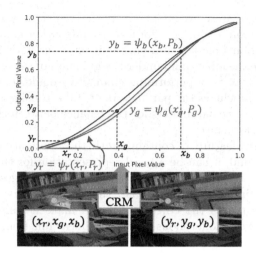

Fig. 4. CRM maps the input pixels to the target pixels using curve function $\psi(\cdot)$, where the parameters P of $\psi(\cdot)$ are learnt from the embeddings of the spatial-aware encoders.

and we only use the first 12 layers to get deeper color feature embedding. We also try different backbones (*e.g.*, VGGNet [31]) to achieve better performance as shown in Table 1. While considering the purpose of this paper is for efficient and high-resolution image harmonization, thus we use SqueezeNet as our default backbone for its good balance between the efficiency and effectiveness.

After obtaining the embedding foreground $F_{fore} \in \mathbb{R}^{D \times h' \times w'}$ and background $F_{back} \in \mathbb{R}^{D \times h' \times w'}$ features from the domain encoder, we squeeze the foreground/background feature dimensionally via the global average pooling to avoid the influence of spatial information. Then, foreground $F_f \in \mathbb{R}^D$ and background $F_b \in \mathbb{R}^D$ are learnt to generate the parameters of the color curve and render the channel-wise color curve via the proposed *Curve Rendering Module* automatically. We will discuss the details and its variants in the later sections.

3.2 Curve Rendering Modules and Its Variants

We first introduce the basic idea behind the proposed network via the *Curve Rendering Module* (CRM). Then, we discuss two different extensions using the semantic label and recurrent refinement.

Curve Rendering Module (CRM). Most previous image harmonization methods [4,5,12,32] consider this task as a pixel-wise image to image translation task, which is heavy and only works on certain resolution as we discussed in the related works. Differently, we model this task as a global region image enhancement task. Thus, our goal of CRM is try to adjust the foreground color under the given background.

To achieve the above goal, as shown in Fig. 3, after obtaining the spatial-separated foreground embedding F_f and background embedding F_b from the domain encoder separately, we first embed these spatial-aware features using two projection functions $\phi_f(\cdot)/\phi_b(\cdot)$ for foreground/background correspondingly, where each projection function is a single linear layer with ReLU activation. Then, to harmonize the foreground under the guidance of the related background features, we get $P \in \mathbb{R}^{3L}$ by performing channel-wise addition between $\phi_f(F_f)$ and $\phi_b(F_b)$. Here, L includes the parameters of R, G, B color channels and each channel has $L = 64$ piece parameters for the balance between the computational complexity and performance.

Since this hybrid feature P contains both the information from the background and foreground, it can be a good representation for the guidance of the foreground editing. To better modeling the color-wise changes, we consider the mappings between intensities rather than the semantic information. Thus, we choose the color curve as the editing tool and make it differentiable [16] by approximating L levels monotonous piece-wise linear function, and then rendering the original pixels in the foreground region. As shown in Fig. 4, for each pixels (x_r, x_g, x_b) in the foreground of the original composited image, we use CRM to map it with the learnt color curve. Here, the mappings of each intensity is identical and not related to the specific location or semantic information. The parameters of the piece-wise linear function is provided and learnt by the spatial-separated encoder and each channel is learnt individually.

Mathematically, after getting the mixed embedding for each channel $P^c = [p_0, p_1, p_2, \ldots, p_{L-1}]$, we render the foreground I_{fore}^c ($c \in \{R, G, B\}$) of the composite image via the curve rendering function $\psi(I_{fore}^c, P^c)$, which can be denoted as:

$$\psi_c(I_{fore}^c, P_c) = \frac{1}{\sum_{j=0}^{L-1} p_j} \sum_{i=0}^{L-1} p_i \xi\left(x - \frac{i}{L}\right), x \in I_{fore}^c,$$

$$\text{where} \quad \xi(y) = \begin{cases} 0, & y < 0 \\ y, & 0 \le y < \frac{1}{L} \\ 1, & y > \frac{1}{L} \end{cases} \tag{1}$$

Finally, the harmonized image can be obtained by the combination of the original background: $I_{final} = \Psi(I_{fore}, P) + I_{back}$.

Semantic CRM. Previous methods [4,5] intend to obtain a unified harmonization model for any foreground images without any specific semantic knowledge. However, the semantic information is also important for the image harmonization [32,34] and it does not make sense if we apply the same style to harmonize different categories (*e.g.* *Car* and *Person*). Since we have supposed that the linear layers in the CRM contain the domain knowledge of the foreground, we make a further step by adding extra semantic label of the foreground object to our vanilla CRM.

As shown in Fig. 3, given the semantic label d of the foreground region, we first embed the labels using a two-layer Multi-layer Perceptron (MLP), obtaining the semantic-aware embedding D. Then, we concatenate the embedded feature from the network Φ and the label embedding D to the CRM. For semantic label definition, we analyze the categories of the foreground regions in iHarmony4 and divide it into 5 classes as guidance, including *Person*, *Vehicle*, *Animal*, *Food* and others. More details can be found in the supplementary materials.

Cascaded CRM/SCRM. It is natural for the image editing tools to adjust the images with multiple steps for better visual quality. Inspired by this phenomenon, we extend our CRM (or SCRM) via the cascaded refinements. To reduce the inference time and learn a compact model, we keep the global features from the backbone unchanged and generate multi-stage heads and give the supervisions of each stage.

As shown in Fig. 3, given the global foreground features F_f and background features F_b from the backbone, we firstly generate P_0 via a CRM and get its rendered image I_0 using $\Psi_c(I_{fore}^c, P_0)$. Then, we use another set of linear layers to predict the parameters P_n from the same global features (F_f, F_b) and rendering the curve using the previous prediction I_{n-1} via $\Psi_c(I_{n-1}, P_n)$. We set n equals to 2 to ensure the high efficiency as well as the high harmonization quality.

3.3   Loss Function

We consider image harmonization as a supervised problem. Specifically, we measure the difference between the target and the corresponding rendered images (for each stage) in the composited region. Thus, we use relative L_1 loss between the predicted foreground and the target via the foreground mask M. Besides, for better visual quality, we also leverage the adversarial loss [9] to our framework. We give the details of each part as follows.

Relative L_1 Loss L_{pixel}. Another key idea to make our method work is that we only calculate the metric between the foreground of the predicted image and the target, where the differences are only measured in a single domain. Thus, inspired by recent works in watermark removal [6,14], we perform the pixel-wise L_1 loss in the foreground region M by masking out the background pixels and setting the meaningful region. Specifically, giving the rendered images I_n in each stage, we calculate the loss over the masked region:

$$L_{pixel} = \sum_{n=1}^{N} \frac{||M \times I_n - M \times I_{gt}||_1}{sum(M)} \tag{2}$$

where $N = 2$ is the number of iterations.

Adversarial Loss L_{adv}. By considering the proposed S²CRNet as the generator G, we also utilize an additional discriminator D to identify the naturalness of the color. In detail, we use a standard 5 layers CONV-BN-RELU discriminator [40] and leverage a least squares GAN [25] as criteria. Then, the generator is learnt to fool the discriminator and the discriminator is trained to identify the real or fake feed images iteratively.

Overall, our algorithm can be trained in an end-to-end function via the combination of the losses above: $L_{all} = \lambda_{pixel}L_{pixel} + \lambda_{adv}L_{adv}$, where all the hyper-parameters (λ_{pixel} and λ_{adv}) are empirically set to 1 for all our experiments.

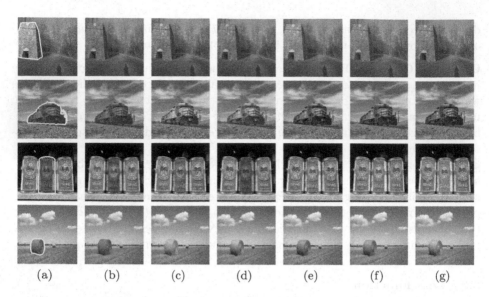

(a)   (b)   (c)   (d)   (e)   (f)   (g)

Fig. 5. Comparisons with other methods on iHarmony4 Dataset. From left to right are (a) Input (b) DoveNet [4], (c) BarGainNet [3], (d) S^2AM [5], (e) S^2CRNet-S (Ours), (f) S^2CRNet-V (Ours) and (g) Target. Here, we visualize the input mask as yellow for easy reading. S^2CRNet-S and S^2CRNet-V denote our method employs SqueezedNet and VGG16 backbone, respectively. (Color figure online)

4 Experiments

4.1 Implementation Details

We implement our method in Pytorch [27] and train on a single NVIDIA TITAN V GPU with 12 GB memory. The batch size is set to 8 and we train 20 epochs (50 epochs for VGG16 backbone) for convergence. All the images are resized to 256×256 and random cropped and flipped for fair training and evaluation as previous methods [4,5]. We leverage the AdamW optimizer [24] with the learning rate of 2×10^{-4}, the weight decay value of 10^{-2} and momentum of 0.9.

As for evaluation, we validate our approaches on the iHarmony4 using Mean-Square-Errors (MSE), Peak Signal-to-Noise Ratio (PSNR), Structural SIMilarity (SSIM) and Learned Perceptual Image Patch Similarity (LPIPS) as criteria metrics. Since DIH99 does not contain the target images, we conduct the subjective experiments.

4.2 Comparison with Existing Methods

Performance Comparison on iHarmony4. We compare our methods with other state-of-the-art image harmonization algorithms, including DoveNet, S^2AM, BargainNet, IIH [11], RainNet [23], *etc.*. In our experiments, we choose the Cascaded-SCRM model in different backbones (SqueezeNet and VGG16 as

Table 1. Comparisons on iHarmony4. The best and the second best are marked as boldface and underline respectively.

Sub-dataset		HCOCO		HAdobe5k		HFlickr		Hday2night		All	
Evaluation metric	# Param	MSE↓	PSNR↑	MSE↓	PSNR↑	MSE↓	PSNR↑	MSE↓	PSNR↑	MSE↓	PSNR↑
Input Composition	–	67.89	34.07	342.27	28.14	260.98	28.35	107.95	34.01	170.25	31.70
Lalonde & Efros [21]	–	110.10	31.14	158.90	29.66	329.87	26.43	199.93	29.80	150.53	30.16
Xue et al. [35]	–	77.04	33.32	274.15	28.79	249.54	28.32	190.51	31.24	155.87	31.40
Zhu et al. [39]	–	79.82	33.04	414.31	27.26	315.42	27.52	136.71	32.32	204.77	30.72
DIH [34]	41.76M	51.85	34.69	92.65	32.28	163.38	29.55	82.34	34.62	76.77	33.41
DoveNet [4]	54.76M	36.72	35.83	52.32	34.34	133.14	30.21	54.05	35.18	52.36	34.75
S²AM [5]	66.70M	33.07	36.09	48.22	35.34	124.53	31.00	48.78	35.60	48.00	35.29
BargainNet [3]	58.74M	24.84	37.03	39.94	35.34	**97.32**	31.34	50.98	35.67	37.82	35.88
IIH [11]	40.86M	24.92	37.16	43.02	35.20	105.13	31.34	55.53	35.96	38.71	35.90
RainNet [23]	54.75M	31.12	36.59	42.84	36.20	117.59	31.33	**47.24**	36.12	44.50	35.88
S²CRNet-SqueezeNet	**0.95M**	28.25	37.65	44.52	35.93	115.46	31.63	53.33	36.28	43.20	36.45
S²CRNet-VGG16	15.14M	**23.22**	**38.48**	**34.91**	**36.42**	98.73	**32.48**	51.67	**36.81**	**35.58**	**37.18**

shown in Table 1), where the semantic labels are generated by a pre-trained segmentation model [37]). All previous methods are tested using their official implementations and pre-trained models for fair comparison. As shown in Table 1, even training and testing on 256×256 limits the high-resolution performance, our S²CRNet-SqueezeNet only use 2% of the parameters to achieve the state-of-the-art performance in PSNR metric, which demonstrates the effectiveness of the proposed network. On the other hand, when using VGG16 backbone (S²CRNet-VGG16), our method outperforms other related methods by a clear margin and still uses only 40% of the parameters. Moreover, the proposed method also works better even on higher-resolution images, which will be discussed in later section. Besides the numeric comparison, our proposed method also obtains better visual quality than others. Qualitative examples in Fig. 5 show that the proposed method can generate harmonized results that are more realistic than other methods, which further indicates the benefits of the proposed framework. More visual comparisons are presented in the supplementary materials.

Performance on Real-World Composite Datasets. Since the real-wold image composition is still different from the synthesized dataset, we evaluate the proposed method (S²CRNet-SqueezeNet) and existing methods (DIH, DoveNet, BarginNet) by subjective experiments on DIH99. In detail, we randomly shuffle the displaying order of all the images and invite 18 users to select the most realistic results. As shown in Table 2, the proposed method gets the most votes

Table 2. User study on DIH99 [34] test set.

Method	Input	DIH	DoveNet	BargainNet	Ours
Total votes	224	385	403	328	**442**
Preference	12.57%	21.60%	22.62%	18.41%	**27.80%**

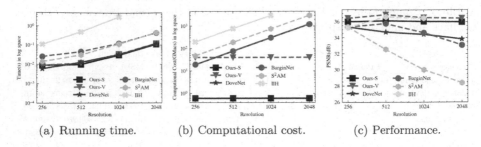

(a) Running time.   (b) Computational cost.   (c) Performance.

Fig. 6. The influence of the image resolution from different aspects. Note that all experimental values are transformed into *log* scale. IIH [11] cause out of memory error on 2048 × 2048 images.

with faster inference time and fewer model parameters as discussed previously. Additionally, we evaluate our method on RealHM dataset following [20] and summarize the qualitative results in Table 3. From Table 3, our method outperforms others at SSIM and LPIPS metrics with much less parameters and processing time. Particularly, we obtain the similar performance compared with SSH [20] at PSNR and MSE metrics while SSH is trained on 2× larger dataset with 10× lager model and stronger data augmentation. The harmonization results on DIH99 and RealHM dataset effectively demonstrate that our method has good generalization ability on the real-world applications. More details of the user study and more harmonization results of the real composite samples are shown in the supplementary.

High-Resolution Image Harmonization. We conduct extra experiments on the HAdobe5k sub-dataset in iHarmony4 to verify the speed and performance of the proposed method on higher-resolution. As experiment setup, we resize the source composite images with the square resolution of 256, 512, 1024 and 2048, and test the average processing time, computational cost and PSNR scores on the same hardware platform. Since other state-of-the-art methods (DoveNet, BargainNet, S^2AM, IIH) employ the fully convolutional encoder-decoder structures, they can be tested directly in higher resolution. As for our method, we test two backbones of the proposed S^2CRNet and donate them as Ours-S (SqueezeNet as backbone) and Ours-V (VGG16 as backbone) shown in Fig. 6.

As shown in Fig. 6(a), we plot the speed of different image harmonization methods in the *log* space. All the methods suffer a speed degradation with the

Table 3. Quantitative comparisons on RealHM dataset [20].

	PSNR↑	MSE↓	SSIM↑	LPIPS↓	Time↓	Parameters↓
DoveNet	27.41	214.11	94.14	0.049	0.081 s	54.76M
S^2AM	26.77	283.27	93.66	0.096	0.282 s	66.70M
SSH	**27.91**	**206.85**	94.79	0.039	0.153 s	15.19M
Ours	27.89	229.64	**96.16**	**0.025**	**0.012 s**	**0.95M**

resolution increasing. However, our the research quality code of Ours-S and Ours-V runs much faster (0.1s around on a 2048 × 2048 image) than all other methods and is nearly 5× faster than S²AM and BargainNet. Also, since we use a fixed size input, the required computation cost of our method still much less than previous methods as the resolution increasing as shown in Fig. 6(b). In terms of the harmonization quality, there are also some interesting phenomenons. As shown in Fig. 6(c), most of other methods confront a significant performance decline as the resolution increases. It might be because the encoder-decoder based structure will produce different reception fields of original images and then downgrade its performance. Differently, our methods maintain the higher performance at all resolutions.

4.3 Ablation Studies

We conduct the ablation experiments to demonstrate the effectiveness of each component in the proposed S²CRNet. All the experiments are performed on both HCOCO and iHarmony4 with same configurations using the SqueezeNet backbone. More ablation studies are presented in the Appendix.

Loss Function. As shown in Table 4 Model A to C, we compare the performance using different loss functions. Since background and foreground domains are different, restricting the loss function on the masked region by using relative L_1 (rL_1) rather than L_1 loss helps a lot. Besides, L_{adv} are used to improve the realism of the predicted result.

Encoder Design Φ. Extracting and learning the global foreground and background features individually (Ours in Model C in Table 4) are also the keys to facilitate the performance of the whole framework. As shown in Table 4 and Fig. 7, compared with other alternatives that extract the global features using the foreground region only (I_{fore} in Model D) and the full image (I_{com} in Model E), spatial-separated encoder shows a much better performance due to domain separation.

CRMs. The numerical metrics of different CRMs have been listed in Table 4, both *Cascaded*-CRM (Model F) and *Cascaded*-SCRM (Model G) hugely improve

Table 4. Ablation studies.

#	Loss		Network		HCOCO		iHarmony	
	L_{pixel}	L_{adv}	Φ	CRM	MSE ↓	PSNR ↑	MSE ↓	PSNR ↑
-	Original input				67.89	34.07	170.25	31.70
A	L_1		Ours	✓	67.64	34.08	114.65	32.11
B	rL_1		Ours	✓	28.43	37.59	46.79	36.20
C	rL_1	✓	Ours	✓	29.45	37.51	45.17	36.27
D	rL_1	✓	I_{fore}	✓	34.62	36.98	79.73	34.57
E	rL_1	✓	I_{com}	✓	58.53	34.69	88.61	33.88
F	rL_1	✓	Ours	C	28.47	37.60	44.08	36.41
G	rL_1	✓	Ours	CS	**27.40**	**37.72**	**43.20**	**36.45**

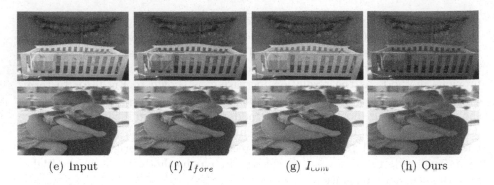

(e) Input   (f) I_{fore} (g) I_{com} (h) Ours

Fig. 7. The influence of different encoder designs.

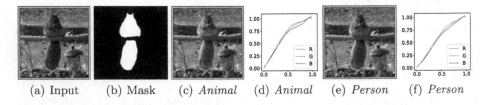

(a) Input   (b) Mask   (c) *Animal*   (d) *Animal*   (e) *Person*   (f) *Person*

Fig. 8. Results and rendering curves of SCRM using different foreground semantic labels (*Person*, *Animal*).

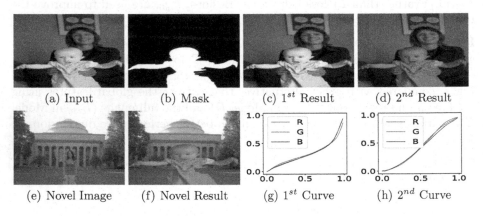

(a) Input   (b) Mask   (c) 1st Result   (d) 2nd Result

(e) Novel Image   (f) Novel Result   (g) 1st Curve   (h) 2nd Curve

Fig. 9. Given a composite image (a) and its mask (b), Cascaded-CRM learns to generate different harmonization results (c, d) via curves (g, h). Also, our method can harmonize the current foreground via novel backgrounds (e, f).

the base model (Model E). To further explore the influence of each variants, firstly, we show the importance of semantic labels. As shown in Fig. 8, different semantic labels will produce different style curves under the same input. Then, for cascaded refinement, in Fig. 9, cascaded refinement will produce different curves and achieve gradually better performance. Finally, the global color curves enable the proposed method to harmonize images with domain-aware features from novel images. In Fig. 9, a novel background can also guide the harmonization of different foreground regions, which means our method can handle two objects harmonization by generating corresponding curves for each object individually.

5   Discussion and Real-World Application

By utilizing the global editing only, the proposed framework start a new direction for image harmonization which is efficient, flexible and transparent. As for efficiency, both performance and speed are better than previous methods. With respect to flexibility, images at any resolution can be edited without additional processing, like guided filter [13,34]. As for transparency, our method is a "white-box" algorithm because the learned curves can be further edited by the user to increase/decrease the harmony. On the other hand, since the search space of the global editing is bounded, the proposed method can be used directly for video harmonization without retraining on video datasets. We show a brief video harmonization result in the supplementary to demonstrate the potential of our framework.

6   Conclusion

In this paper, we investigate the possibility of global editing only for image harmonization for the first time. To this end, we present Spatial-separated Curve Rendering Network (S²CRNet), a novel framework for efficient and high-resolution image harmonization. In detail, we utilize an efficient backbone to obtain spatial domain-aware features and the extracted features are used to generate the parameters of piece-wise curve function in the proposed curve render model. Besides, we extend the proposed curve rendering method to cascaded refinement and semantic-aware prediction. Finally, the learnt parameters are used to render the original high-resolution composite foreground. Experiments show the advantages of the proposed framework in terms of efficiency, accuracy and speed.

Acknowledgements. This work is supported in part by the University of Macau under Grant MYRG-2018-00035-FST and Grant MYRG-2019-00086-FST and in part by the Science and Technology Development Fund, Macau SAR, under Grant 0034/2019/AMJ, Grant 0087/2020/A2 and Grant 0049/2021/A.

References

1. Bychkovsky, V., Paris, S., Chan, E., Durand, F.: Learning photographic global tonal adjustment with a database of input/output image pairs. In: CVPR, pp. 97–104. IEEE (2011)

2. Cohen-Or, D., Sorkine, O., Gal, R., Leyvand, T., Xu, Y.Q.: Color harmonization. In: SIGGRAPH, pp. 624–630 (2006)
3. Cong, W., Niu, L., Zhang, J., Liang, J., Zhang, L.: BargainNet: background-guided domain translation for image harmonization. In: ICME (2021)
4. Cong, W., et al.: Dovenet: deep image harmonization via domain verification. In: CVPR, pp. 8394–8403 (2020)
5. Cun, X., Pun, C.M.: Improving the harmony of the composite image by spatial-separated attention module. TIP **29**, 4759–4771 (2020)
6. Cun, X., Pun, C.M.: Split then refine: stacked attention-guided resunets for blind single image visible watermark removal. In: AAAI (2021)
7. Deng, J., Dong, W., Socher, R., Li, L.J, Li, K, Fei-Fei, L.: Imagenet: a large-scale hierarchical image database. In: CVPR, pp. 248–255. IEEE (2009)
8. Gharbi, M., Chen, J., Barron, J.T., Hasinoff, S.W., Durand, F.: Deep bilateral learning for real-time image enhancement. TOG **36**(4), 1–12 (2017)
9. Goodfellow, I.J., et al.: Generative adversarial networks. arXiv preprint arXiv:1406.2661 (2014)
10. Guo, C., et al.: Zero-reference deep curve estimation for low-light image enhancement. In: CVPR, pp. 1780–1789 (2020)
11. Guo, Z., Zheng, H., Jiang, Y., Gu, Z., Zheng, B.: Intrinsic image harmonization. In: CVPR, pp. 16367–16376, June 2021
12. Hao, G., Iizuka, S., Fukui, K.: Image harmonization with attention-based deep feature modulation. In: BMVC (2020)
13. He, K., Sun, J., Tang, X.: Guided image filtering. TPAMI **35**(6), 1397–1409 (2012)
14. Hertz, A., Fogel, S., Hanocka, R., Giryes, R., Cohen-Or, D.: Blind visual motif removal from a single image. In: CVPR, pp. 6858–6867 (2019)
15. Howard, A.G., et al.: Mobilenets: efficient convolutional neural networks for mobile vision applications. arXiv preprint arXiv:1704.04861 (2017)
16. Hu, Y., He, H., Xu, C., Wang, B., Lin, S.: Exposure: a white-box photo post-processing framework. TOG **37**(2), 1–17 (2018)
17. Iandola, F.N., Han, S., Moskewicz, M.W., Ashraf, K., Dally, W.J., Keutzer, K.: Squeezenet: alexnet-level accuracy with 50x fewer parameters and <0.5 MB model size. arXiv preprint arXiv:1602.07360 (2016)
18. Isola, P., Zhu, J.Y., Zhou, T., Efros, A.A.: Image-to-image translation with conditional adversarial networks. In: CVPR, vol. 2017-January, pp. 5967–5976 (2017). https://doi.org/10.1109/CVPR.2017.632. http://arxiv.org/abs/1611.07004
19. Jia, J., Sun, J., Tang, C.K., Shum, H.Y.: Drag-and-drop pasting. TOG **25**(3), 631–637 (2006)
20. Jiang, Y., et al.: SSH: a self-supervised framework for image harmonization. In: ICCV, pp. 4832–4841 (2021)
21. Lalonde, J.F., Efros, A.A.: Using color compatibility for assessing image realism. In: ICCV, pp. 1–8. IEEE (2007)
22. Lee, D., Pfister, T., Yang, M.H.: Inserting videos into videos. In: CVPR, pp. 10061–10070 (2019)
23. Ling, J., Xue, H., Song, L., Xie, R., Gu, X.: Region-aware adaptive instance normalization for image harmonization. In: CVPR, pp. 9361–9370, June 2021
24. Loshchilov, I., Hutter, F.: Fixing weight decay regularization in adam (2018)
25. Mao, X., Li, Q., Xie, H., Lau, R.Y., Wang, Z., Paul Smolley, S.: Least squares generative adversarial networks. In: ICCV, pp. 2794–2802 (2017)
26. Moran, S., McDonagh, S., Slabaugh, G.: Curl: neural curve layers for global image enhancement. In: 2020 25th International Conference on Pattern Recognition (ICPR), pp. 9796–9803. IEEE (2021)

27. Paszke, A., et al.: Automatic differentiation in pytorch (2017)
28. Pérez, P., Gangnet, M., Blake, A.: Poisson image editing. In: SIGGRAPH, pp. 313–318 (2003)
29. Reinhard, E., Adhikhmin, M., Gooch, B., Shirley, P.: Color transfer between images. CG&A **21**(5), 34–41 (2001)
30. Ronneberger, O., Fischer, P., Brox, T.: U-Net: convolutional networks for biomedical image segmentation. In: Navab, N., Hornegger, J., Wells, W.M., Frangi, A.F. (eds.) MICCAI 2015. LNCS, vol. 9351, pp. 234–241. Springer, Cham (2015). https://doi.org/10.1007/978-3-319-24574-4_28
31. Simonyan, K., Zisserman, A.: Very deep convolutional networks for large-scale image recognition. arXiv preprint arXiv:1409.1556 (2014)
32. Sofiiuk, K., Popenova, P., Konushin, A.: Foreground-aware semantic representations for image harmonization. In: WACV, pp. 1620–1629 (2021)
33. Sunkavalli, K., Johnson, M.K., Matusik, W., Pfister, H.: Multi-scale image harmonization. TOG **29**(4), 1–10 (2010)
34. Tsai, Y.H., Shen, X., Lin, Z., Sunkavalli, K., Lu, X., Yang, M.H.: Deep image harmonization. In: CVPR (2017)
35. Xue, S., Agarwala, A., Dorsey, J., Rushmeier, H.: Understanding and improving the realism of image composites. TOG **31**(4), 1–10 (2012)
36. Zeng, H., Cai, J., Li, L., Cao, Z., Zhang, L.: Learning image-adaptive 3D lookup tables for high performance photo enhancement in real-time. TPAMI (2020)
37. Zhou, B., et al.: Semantic understanding of scenes through the ade20k dataset. In: IJCV (2018)
38. Zhou, H., Hadap, S., Sunkavalli, K., Jacobs, D.W.: Deep single portrait image relighting. In: ICCV (2019)
39. Zhu, J.Y., Krahenbuhl, P., Shechtman, E., Efros, A.A.: Learning a discriminative model for the perception of realism in composite images. In: ICCV, pp. 3943–3951 (2015)
40. Zhu, J.Y., Park, T., Isola, P., Efros, A.A.: Unpaired image-to-image translation using cycle-consistent adversarial networks. In: ICCV, March 2017

BigColor: Colorization Using a Generative Color Prior for Natural Images

Geonung Kim[1], Kyoungkook Kang[1], Seongtae Kim[1], Hwayoon Lee[1], Sehoon Kim[2], Jonghyun Kim[2], Seung-Hwan Baek[1], and Sunghyun Cho[1(✉)]

[1] POSTECH, Pohang, South Korea
{k2woong92,kkang831,seongtae0205,hwayoon2,shwbaek,s.cho}@postech.ac.kr
[2] Samsung Electronics, Suwon-si, South Korea
{sh0264.kim,jh015.kim}@samsung.com

Abstract. For realistic and vivid colorization, generative priors have recently been exploited. However, such generative priors often fail for in-the-wild complex images due to their limited representation space. In this paper, we propose BigColor, a novel colorization approach that provides vivid colorization for diverse in-the-wild images with complex structures. While previous generative priors are trained to synthesize both image structures and colors, we learn a generative color prior to focus on color synthesis given the spatial structure of an image. In this way, we reduce the burden of synthesizing image structures from the generative prior and expand its representation space to cover diverse images. To this end, we propose a BigGAN-inspired encoder-generator network that uses a spatial feature map instead of a spatially-flattened BigGAN latent code, resulting in an enlarged representation space. BigColor enables robust colorization for diverse inputs in a single forward pass, supports arbitrary input resolutions, and provides multi-modal colorization results. We demonstrate that BigColor significantly outperforms existing methods especially on in-the-wild images with complex structures.

Keywords: Colorization · GAN Inversion · Generative color prior

1 Introduction

Image colorization aims to hallucinate the chromatic dimension of a grayscale image and has been studied for decades in computer vision and graphics. Its application includes not only modernizing classic black-and-white films but also providing artistic control over grayscale imagery with diverse color distributions [4, 20, 25, 34, 39].

Early works propagate user-annotated color strokes based on pixel affinity [13, 22, 28, 36, 38] or find similar regions in reference images to mimic the reference color distributions [4, 6, 9]. With the advent of deep learning, data-driven

---

Supplementary Information The online version contains supplementary material available at https://doi.org/10.1007/978-3-031-20071-7_21.

(a) Input   (b) InstColor [31]   (c) ToVivid [34]   (d) BigColor

Fig. 1. We achieve robust colorization for in-the-wild images using a generative color prior. (a) For an input image with complex spatial structures, existing colorization methods suffer from (b) desaturated color and (c) unnatural color distribution. (d) In contrast, BigColor synthesizes natural colors consistent with the input structure using a learned generative color prior. (Color figure online)

colorization approaches have rapidly advanced by adopting neural networks to learn a mapping from grayscale images to trichromatic images. This trend was sparked by using a convolutional neural network (CNN) and a regression loss such as mean-squared error (MSE) [1,31,32,39], which unfortunately suffers from desaturated colors as shown in Fig. 1(b), as the MSE loss encourages to find an average of plausible color images corresponding to an input image.

To synthesize vivid colors, high-quality representations learned in pretrained generative adversarial network (GAN) models have recently been exploited as generative priors for image colorization [8,27,33,34,37]. Adopting GAN inversion, these methods invert an input grayscale image to a latent code of a pretrained GAN model by minimizing the structural discrepancy between the input gray-scale image and the generated color image from the latent code. While GAN inversion allows us to utilize the learned generative prior of natural images, it also inherits a notable problem of existing GAN models: limited representation space. Thus, existing colorization methods using generative priors fail to handle in-the-wild images with complex structures and semantics, resulting in desaturated and unnatural colors as shown in Fig. 1(c).

In this paper, we propose BigColor, a novel image colorization method that synthesizes vivid and natural colors for in-the-wild images with complex structures. For vivid colorization, we adopt the GAN-inversion approach by using a pretrained Big-GAN [2], which is a state-of-the-art class-conditional generative model. As directly using the BigGAN model hampers colorization performance for in-the-wild images due to its limited representation space, we offload the burden of the BigGAN model that was responsible for synthesizing both structures and colors to focus on color synthesis. This offloading strategy allows us to learn a generative color prior that can cover in-the-wild images with complex structures.

Specifically, we learn a generative color prior with an encoder-generator neural network. Unlike conventional GAN-inversion colorization methods, our encoder extracts a spatial feature map describing the structure of an input image better than using a spatially-flattened latent code in BigGAN. As a spatial feature map has a higher spatial resolution than an original BigGAN latent code, the representation space of the entire network can be enlarged, i.e., we can map features to a wider range of natural images. We then design our generator to directly exploit the spatial feature by using the fine-scale network layers adopted from the multi-scale BigGAN generator. We jointly train the encoder and generator networks to encourage the network to focus on color synthesis by making use of the spatial feature. As our network is fully convolutional and departs from using a fixed-size flattened latent code of BigGAN, BigColor can process images with arbitrary sizes which were not feasible for conventional GAN-inversion colorization methods that use the original latent codes of GANs [8,27,33,34,37]. Also, BigColor allows us to synthesize multi-modal colorization results by using different condition vectors for the network. We assess BigColor with extensive experiments including a user study and demonstrate that BigColor outperforms previous methods across all tested scenarios in particular for in-the-wild images.

2   Related Work

Optimization-Based Colorization. Early colorization methods utilize color annotations from users and propagate them to neighbor pixels based on pixel affinity by solving constrained optimization problems [13,22,28,36,38]. Data-driven colorization methods find reference color images with similar semantics to an input grayscale image and use the reference color distributions via optimization [4,6,9,24]. Unfortunately, the optimization-based approaches demand dense user annotations or accurate reference matching, failing to provide robust and automatic colorization.

Colorization with Regression Networks. Learning a mapping function from a grayscale image to a color image has been extensively studied with the advent of neural networks. Regression-based neural networks minimize average reconstruction error, resulting in desaturated colors [5,7,14,21]. Vivid color synthesis then became one of the core challenges in network-based image colorization methods. Notable examples in this line of research include optimizing over a quantized color space [39], detection-guided colorization [31], adversarial training [1,32], and global reasoning using a transformer [20]. While significant progress has been made, it is still challenging to synthesize vivid and natural colors for in-the-wild grayscale images with complex structures.

Colorization with Generative Prior. GANs have recently achieved remarkable success in learning low-dimensional latent representations of natural color images, enabling synthesizing high-fidelity natural images [2,17,18]. This success has led to using the learned generative prior for image restoration such as deblurring [33,37], super-resolution [3,26,27], denoising [33,37], and colorization [8,27,33,34,37]. Most previous approaches are limited to handling a single class of images, such as human faces using StyleGAN [17,18], due to the limited representation space of modern GAN models.

Recently, a few attempts [27,34] have been made to colorize natural images of multiple classes using a pretrained BigGAN generator [2]. Specifically, deep generative prior (DGP) [27] jointly optimizes the BigGAN latent code and the

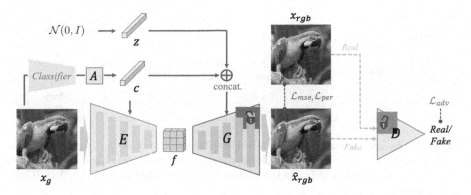

Fig. 2. We extract the spatial feature f of the input image x_g using a class-conditioned convolutional encoder E. The generator G, which is initialized with the fine levels of the pretrained BigGAN [2], takes the spatial feature f as inputs and synthesizes a colorized image $\hat{x}_{rgb}$ conditioned on the control parameters of the class code c and the random sample z. A is a class embedding layer that transforms a one-hot class vector to a class code c. Jointly training the encoder-generator model with a pretrained BigGAN discriminator D enables us to learn the generative color prior with an enlarged representation space. (Color figure online)

pretrained BigGAN generator to synthesize a color image via GAN inversion. The representation space of the DGP is still not enough to cover complex images because of the difficulty in synthesizing both structures and colors from the generator. Wu et al. [34] attempted to bypass the structural mismatch between a GAN-inverted color image and an input grayscale image by warping the synthesized color features into the input grayscale. Nonetheless, considerable mismatches between a GAN-inverted and an input image cannot be fully resolved, and thus produce colorization artifacts. In contrast to the previous methods, Big-Color effectively enlarges the representation space by using an encoder-generator architecture that uses spatial features. This allows us to handle diverse images with complex structures.

3   Colorization Using a Generative Color Prior

In this section, we describe the framework of BigColor and our strategy to learn a generative color prior. BigColor has an encoder-generator network architecture, where the encoder E estimates a spatial feature map f from an input grayscale image x_g, and the generator G synthesizes a color image $\hat{x}_{rgb}$ from the feature f. Note that different from conventional GAN-based colorization methods, we do not rely on the spatially-flattened latent code of BigGAN, but instead use a spatial feature map f that has a larger dimension. In order to exploit the effectiveness of the BigGAN architecture for image synthesis [2], we design the encoder E and the generator G by using the fine-scale layers of the BigGAN generator. Also, we use two control variables for conditioning the encoder and the generator: the class code c and the random code z sampled from a normal distribution. The class code c enables class-specific feature extraction for effective

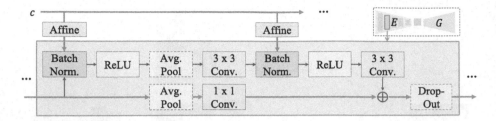

Fig. 3. We design our encoder E by inverting the fine layers of the BigGAN generator [2], consisting of the five encoder blocks shown in the top right. Each encoder block denoted as an orange box extracts the spatial features conditioned on the class (Color figure online)

colorization and the random code z accounts for the multi-modal nature of image colorization.

In the spirit of adversarial learning, we also adopt a pretrained BigGAN discriminator D. We jointly train the encoder E, the generator G, and the discriminator D, resulting in an enlarged representation space where the generator G takes the responsibility of synthesizing color on top of the spatial feature f extracted from the encoder E. See Fig. 2 for an overview of BigColor. In the following, we describe each component of BigColor and the training scheme in detail.

3.1 Encoder

Our encoder takes an input grayscale image x_g and estimates a spatial feature map f, which is fed to the generator. For an input image size of 256×256, our spatial feature f has the spatial resolution of 16×16 with the channel size of 768. To successfully extract the spatial feature f, we design our encoder inspired by an inversion of the BigGAN generator as shown in Fig. 3. The encoder consists of five blocks, where all the blocks except for the first have average pooling layers to reduce the spatial size of an input feature. We also adopt dropout layers except for the last block for better generalization on test-case inputs.

To extract class-specific spatial structures, we inject the class information of an input image into the encoder. Specifically, we obtain the scale and bias parameters of the batch-normalization layers through an affine transformation of the BigGAN class code $c \in \mathbb{R}^{128 \times 1}$ [2]. We adopt the BigGAN's class embedding layer (A in Fig. 2) to obtain the class code c from a class vector in the form of the one-hot vector representation. The class vector can be either provided by the user or estimated using an off-the-shelf classifier. In our experiments, we use a 1,000-dimensional vector for the class vector representing ImageNet-1K classes. More details on the architecture can be found in the Supplemental Document. In summary, our encoder E extracts the class-specific spatial feature map f that contains the structure information of an input image x_g as

$$f = E(x_g; c). \tag{1}$$

BigColor

| (a) Input | (b) GAN Inversion | (c) Spatial feature | (d) Spatial feature + Joint training | (e) Spatial feature + Joint training + Luminance of input |

Fig. 4. (a)&(b) Colorization with conventional GAN inversion often fail to invert in-the-wild images. (c) We exploit the spatial feature of the input and the fine-scale layers of the pretrained BigGAN generator, effectively enlarging the representation space. (d) Jointly optimizing the encoder-generator module improves the representation coverage and provides vivid and natural colorization. (e) We boost high-frequency details by replacing the luminance of synthesized image with the input luminance. (Color figure online)

3.2 Generator

Our generator G synthesizes colors given the spatial feature f of the input grayscale image x_g. Analogously to the encoder design, we design and initialize our generator G using the fine-scale layers of the pretrained BigGAN generator, specifically from the third to the last layers. The generator G uses two condition variables of the class vector c and the random vector z sampled from a normal distribution. We concatenate the class vector c and the random vector z as an input to the generator G as in the original BigGAN architecture [2]. Our generator G synthesizes a color image $\hat{x}_{rgb}$ conditioned on the class and the random codes as

$$\hat{x}_{rgb} = G(f; c, z). \tag{2}$$

We note that unlike the original BigGAN generator that uses a spatially-flattend latent code, our generator G takes the *spatial* feature f as input. To restore high-frequency spatial details, we replace the luminance of the synthesized color image $\hat{x}_{rgb}$ with the luminance of the input grayscale image x_g in the CIELAB color space [31,32,39]. See Fig. 4(e).

Generative Color Prior. We learn the generative color prior for colorizing in-the-wild images with complex structures using our generator G. To this end, we exploit our specific network architecture and training scheme. For the architecture, our generator G takes the fine-scale spatial feature map f as an input of which resolution is $16 \times 16 \times 768$ when the grayscale image has 256×256 resolution. The dimension of the feature f is higher than that of the original BigGAN latent code of which resolution is 119×1. Thus, we can effectively enlarge the representation space of our generator G compared to the conventional GAN-inversion colorization methods by utilizing the structural information provided in the large-dimensional feature f. Compare the colorization results of Fig. 4(b)&(c). We note that a similar finding was used in BDInvert [15], a recent transform-robust GAN-inversion method using a spatial feature for Style-GAN [17, 18].

In terms of training strategy, we initialize the generator G and the discriminator D with the corresponding layers of the ImageNet-pretrained BigGAN model. As such, we can leverage the learned structure-color distribution of natural images of the pretrained BigGAN. However, our generator G at the initial point is still not fully focusing on synthesizing colors as it was originally trained to synthesize both structure and color. We unlock the full potential of our network by jointly optimizing the encoder E, the generator G, and the discriminator D. The joint training allows the generator G to learn a generative color prior by focusing on synthesizing colors on top of the spatial feature f. The reduced learning complexity of the generator results in an enlarged representation space, covering in-the-wild natural images as demonstrated in Fig. 4(d).

Multi-modal Image Colorization. Image colorization is an inherently ill-posed problem as multiple potential color images could explain a single grayscale image. We handle this multi-modal nature of image colorization by injecting the random code z sampled from a normal distribution into the generator G. Sampling multiple latent code z enables synthesizing diverse color images. Note that we do not provide the random code to the encoder as the multi-modal nature only applies to the color synthesis, not the spatial feature extraction.

3.3   Training Details

Adversarial Training. We train our framework in an alternating manner for adversarial learning. We define our encoder-generator loss function $\mathcal{L}^G$ as a sum of three terms:

$$\mathcal{L}^G = \mathcal{L}^G_{mse} + \lambda_{per}\mathcal{L}^G_{per} + \lambda_{adv}\mathcal{L}^G_{adv}, \tag{3}$$

where $\mathcal{L}^G_{mse}$ and $\mathcal{L}^G_{per}$ are the MSE reconstruction losses that penalize the color and perceptual discrepancies between the synthesized image $\hat{x}_{rgb}$ and the ground truth image x_{rgb}. For the perceptual loss $\mathcal{L}^G_{per}$, we use the VGG16 [30] features at 1st, 2nd, 6th, and 9th layers. $\mathcal{L}^{\mathcal{G}}_{adv}$ is the adversarial loss, specifically the class-conditional hinge loss [23] defined as $\mathcal{L}^{\mathcal{G}}_{adv} = -D(\hat{x}_{rgb}, c)$. We use the balancing weights λ_{per} and λ_{adv} set as 0.2 and 0.03 respectively. For discriminator training, we also use the hinge loss [23]

$$\mathcal{L}^{\mathcal{D}}_{adv} = -\min(0, -1 + D(x_{rgb}, c)) + \min(0, -1 - D(\hat{x}_{rgb}, c)). \tag{4}$$

Color Augmentation. To promote synthesizing vivid color, we apply a simple color augmentation to the real color images fed to the discriminator. Specifically, we scale chromaticity of images in YUV color space as $\{U, V\} \leftarrow \{1.2\,U, 1.2\,V\}$. This color augmentation makes colors of semantically different regions in training images more distinguishable. As a result, it helps the generator learn to synthesize not only more vivid but also semantically more correct colors, which is not achievable by direct augmentation of generator output as will be shown in Sect. 4.2.

Table 1. Quantitative comparison with other colorization methods using the three metrics of colorfulness [10], FID [12], and classification accuracy [39]. BigColor outperforms all previous work with significant margins. *Aug.* denotes our color-augmentation scheme. The bold and underlined scores are the best and 2nd best results.

	Colorful ↑ [10]	FID ↓ [12]	Classification ↑
CIC [39]	33.036	11.322	69.976
ChromaGAN [32]	26.266	8.209	70.374
InstColor [31]	25.507	7.890	68.422
DeOldify [1]	23.793	3.487	72.364
ColTran [20]	34.485	3.793	67.210
ToVivid [34]	35.128	4.078	73.816
BigColor (w/o Aug.)	36.157	1.288	76.302
BigColor (w/ Aug.)	**40.006**	**1.243**	**76.516**

4 Experiments

Implementation. We train our model on 1.2M color images of the ImageNet 1K [29] training set after excluding 10% original images with low colorfulness scores [10]. We generate grayscale images based on a conventional linear-combination method[1]. We resize and crop the training images to be 256×256. For training, we use the Adam optimizer [19] with the coefficients of $\beta_1 = 0.0$ and $\beta_2 = 0.999$. The learning rates are set to 0.0001 for the encoder-generator module and 0.00003 for the discriminator with the decay rate of 0.9 per epoch. We also use the exponential moving average [16] with the coefficient of $\beta = 0.999$ for model parameter update. We set the batch size to 60 and train the entire model for 12 epochs.

4.1 Evaluation

We evaluate the effectiveness of BigColor on the ImageNet-1K validation set of 50 K images [29] that have complex spatial structures.

Comparison with Other Colorization Methods. We compare BigColor to recent automatic colorization methods including CIC [39], ChromaGAN [32], DeOldify [1], InstColor [31], ColTran [20] and ToVivid [34]. Figure 5 shows that BigColor qualitatively outperforms all the methods on six challenging images. BigColor successfully colorizes the complex structures of human faces, penguin heads, food, and buildings with semantically-natural and vivid colors. The two notable state-of-the-art methods of ToVivid [34] and ColTran [20] suffer from unnatural colorization as shown on the penguins and the human face due to their limited representation space. This clearly demonstrates the effectiveness of

---

[1] $L = 0.2989R + 0.5870G + 0.1140B$, where L is the grayscale intensity and R, G, B are the trichromatic color intensities.

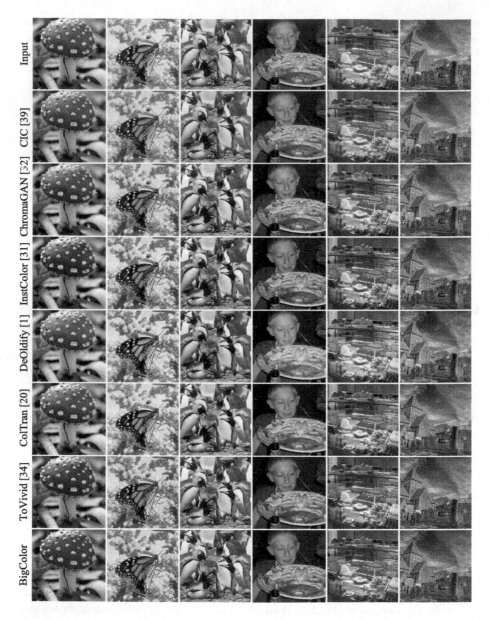

Fig. 5. Qualitative comparison with other colorization methods. For in-the-wild images with complex structure, our method synthesizes natural and vivid color images while the other methods suffer from desaturated and unnatural color distributions. (Color figure online)

our learned generative color prior to in-the-wild images. See the Supplemental Document for more qualitative results.

Table 2. BigColor is robust for colorizing complex images compared to the previous colorization methods, achieving the best performance in terms of classification accuracy with a marginal performance drop similar to the real ground-truth color images.

Dataset	Classification acc.		Performance drop
	Whole	Complex	Whole → Complex
Ground truth	78.530	76.000	−2.530
CIC [39]	69.976	64.000	−5.976
ChromaGAN [32]	70.374	60.000	−10.374
InstColor [31]	68.422	65.000	−3.422
DeOldify [1]	72.364	68.000	−4.364
ColTran [20]	67.210	65.000	−2.210
ToVivid [34]	73.816	65.000	−8.816
BigColor	**76.516**	**74.000**	−2.516

We further evaluate BigColor using the three quantitative metrics of colorfulness, FID, and classification accuracy commonly used in the image colorization field. Colorfulness measures the overall colorfulness of an image based on psychological experiments [10]. FID describes the distributional distance between the real color images and synthesized color images [12]. The classification accuracy measures whether a classifier trained on natural color images, specifically the pretrained ResNet50-based classifier [11], can predict the correct classes of synthesized color images which were used in CIC [39]. Table 1 shows that BigColor outperforms the previous methods with significant margins across all tested metrics with and without the color-augmentation scheme.

In-the-Wild Images with Complex Structures. We test the robustness of BigColor specifically on challenging in-the-wild images with complex structures. To this end, we select 100 challenging images selected from the ImageNet1K validation set which contain as many humans as possible using an off-the-shelf object detector [35], assuming the proportionality between the number of people and the image complexity. On the curated dataset with 100 samples, Table 2 shows the classification accuracy of the synthesized color images for all the methods. BigColor again achieves the best performance with only a 2.5% accuracy drop from the whole-data evaluation. Our performance drop of 2.5% is at the same level of the ground-truth case, where real color images are used to obtain the classification accuracy. We refer to the Supplemental Document for further quantitative and qualitative evaluations.

User Study. We conducted a user study to investigate the perceptual preference of colorization methods using Amazon Mechanical Turk (AMT). Specifically, 33 subjects are presented with 100 input and colorized images randomly selected from the ImageNet 1K validation set. The subjects choose the best-restored color image among the results obtained with different methods [1,20,31,32,34, 39]. Figure 6 shows that users clearly prefer BigColor over the state-of-the-art methods. More details can be found in the Supplemental Document.

4.2 Ablation Study

We conduct extensive ablation studies to assess BigColor in details by using 10% of the ImageNet training images amounting to 100 image classes.

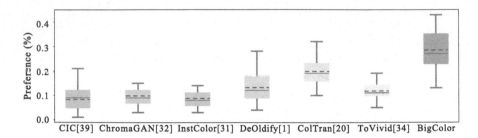

Fig. 6. We conduct a user study to evaluate the preference for colorization results. In all tested metrics, our method outperforms the other methods. The dashed green line and the bold gray line inside the bars are the mean and the median respectively. (Color figure online)

(a) Input   (b) 8 × 8   (c) 16 × 16   (d) 32 × 32   (e) 64 × 64

Fig. 7. The resolution of the spatial feature f plays an important role for maintaining a balance between keeping the spatial structure of the input and providing the degree of freedom for synthesizing color. We empirically chose 16 × 16 as the best configuration. (Color figure online)

Resolution of the Spatial Feature. We evaluate the impact of the resolution of the spatial feature f. Figure 7 shows the colorization results with varying spatial resolutions of the feature f from 8 × 8 to 64 × 64. As the spatial resolution increases, the synthesized color images can exploit more structural information of the input image for colorization. However, a large spatial resolution could harm the colorization results as it reduces the capacity of the generator with fewer layers. We chose 16 × 16 as the spatial resolution of the feature f.

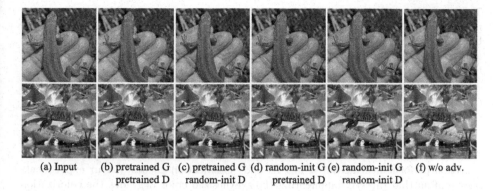

(a) Input   (b) pretrained G   (c) pretrained G   (d) random-init G   (e) random-init G   (f) w/o adv.
                  pretrained D   random-init D   pretrained D   random-init D

Fig. 8. We evaluate the impact of initializing the generator G and the discriminator D with the pretrained BigGAN model. Compared to the random initialization, pretrained initialization results in vivid and natural colorization. Also, adversarial training is critical to achieving vivid colorization without desaturation. (Color figure online)

Table 3. Initialization with the pretrained BigGAN model provides quantiatively better results in terms of FID and classification accuracy.

Model	G	D	G	D	G	D	G	D	w/o adv.
Pretrained	✓	✓	✓	-	-	✓	–	–	
FID [12]	**5.714**		8.058		6.852		7.201		7.692
Class. Acc.	**81.44**		78.96		80.78		80.60		75.52

Initialization with a Pretrained Generative Prior. We initialize our generator and discriminator using the BigGAN pretrained model in order to leverage the learned structure-color distribution of natural images. Figure 8 and Table 3 show that the pretrained initialization improves performance over the training-from-scratch alternatives with random initialization. Specifically, we test all four combinations of the generator-discriminator initialization settings with and without the pretrained initialization. The qualitative and quantitative results indicate that BigColor successfully exploits the pretrained information in the BigGAN generator and the discriminator. We also confirmed the importance of including the adversarial loss to achieve vivid colorization.

Encoder Architecture We considered two main factors for designing our encoder architecture: extracting image structure and exploiting class information. We found that the residual blocks and class-conditioned batch normalization in the original BigGAN generator are essential for robust image colorization as shown in Table 4. Specifically, residual blocks transfer structural information and the class-conditioned batch normalization extracts the class-specific spatial feature.

Color Augmentation. We experimentally evaluate the impact of color augmentation on the real color images fed to the discriminator. To this end, we

Table 4. We analyze our encoder architecture in details to provide insight on the importance of each encoder component: batch normalization (BN), class-conditioned batch normalization (CBN), residual learning (RL). The encoder with residual path and class-conditioned batch normalization shows the best result in terms of FID.

	w/o BN	w/ BN	w/ CBN
w/o RL	6.523	7.286	5.974
w/ RL	5.980	5.854	**5.714**

Table 5. Augmenting the real color image fed to the discriminator improves the colorization performance measured in FID and classification accuracy. Our experiments also confirm that directly augmenting the synthesized color degrades the colorization performance. Disc. and Gen. denote the color augmentation on the real color image fed to the discriminator and the generated color image respectively.

Color Aug.	Disc	Gen	Disc	Gen	Disc	Gen	Disc	Gen
	✓	-	✓	✓	–	–	–	✓
FID	**1.243**		1.604		1.288		1.621	
Class. Acc	**76.516**		76.282		76.302		76.238	

compare the FID score and the classification accuracy on 1000 classes of the ImageNet with and without the color augmentation, which shows clear improvements in both metrics as shown in Table 5. We also test applying the color augmentation on the synthesized image from the generator as a post-processing after training. This does not consider image semantics, resulting in unnatural colorization as indicated by the FID and the classification scores. In contrast, augmenting the discriminator input enables us to effectively learn the vivid and semantically correct color distribution of the real images. More discussion with qualitative examples of the color augmentation is provided in the Supplemental Document.

4.3 Multi-modal Colorization

BigColor is capable of synthesizing diverse colorization results for an input grayscale image as shown in Fig. 9. We can sample random code z that is injected into the generator to synthesize diverse color images. In addition, we can also alter the class vector c to generate class-specific colorization results, for instance by using the class codes of different classes of birds to colorize an input bird image as shown in the second row in Fig. 9.

4.4 Black-and-White Photo Restoration

Figure 10 shows the colorization results of BigColor for old monochromatic photographs with arbitrary resolutions and aspect ratios. Note that BigColor is not

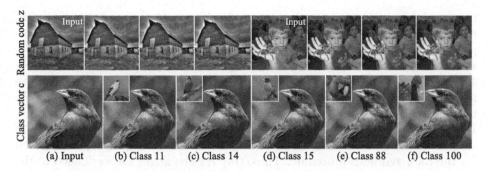

Fig. 9. BigColor supports multi-modal image colorization by sampling the random code z or using different class vectors c which can be estimated from the reference images shown in the insets. The class indices estimated from the reference images are shown below each of the colorization results. (Color figure online)

Fig. 10. We apply BigColor to old monochromatic photographs of diverse resolutions and aspect ratios. Left-top to right-bottom: *Albert Einstein at Princeton University, Charlie Chaplin on the movie 'The Kid'(1921), Marilyn Monroe, Photo by Ansel Adams of Yosemite.* (Color figure online)

limited to a specific input resolution owing to the convolutional spatial feature f with a variable spatial resolution. In contrast, conventional GAN-inversion methods [27,34] use a spatially-flattend latent code, enforcing the spatial resolution to be fixed.

5   Conclusion

We propose BigColor, a robust image colorization method using a generative color prior for in-the-wild images with complex structures. We exploit the spatial structure of an input grayscale image using a convolutional encoder, effectively enlarging the representation space of a generator compared to the conventional colorization methods using GAN inversion. Jointly optimizing the encoder-generator module with a discriminator allows us to learn a generative color prior where the generator focuses on synthesizing colors on top of the extracted spatial-structure feature. We extensively assess BigColor in qualitative and quantitative manners and demonstrate that BigColor outperforms existing state-of-the-art methods.

Limitations. Our method is not free from limitations. The spatial resolution of the extracted feature f determines the structural details that can be maintained for the color synthesis procedure. Thus, tiny regions might be overlooked in the colorization process. Also, we rely on the BigGAN class code which may not be perfectly estimated for challenging images.

Acknowledgements. This work was supported by the National Research Foundation of Korea (NRF) grant funded by the Korea government (MSIT) (NRF-2018R1A5A1060031), Institute of Information & communications Technology Planning & Evaluation (IITP) grant funded by the Korea government (MSIT) (No.2019-0-01906, Artificial Intelligence Graduate School Program (POSTECH)), and Samsung Electronics Co., Ltd.

References

1. Antic, J.: Deoldify (2019). https://github.com/jantic/DeOldify
2. Brock, A., Donahue, J., Simonyan, K.: Large scale gan training for high fidelity natural image synthesis. In: International Conference on Learning Representations (2019)
3. Chan, K.C., Wang, X., Xu, X., Gu, J., Loy, C.C.: Glean: generative latent bank for large-factor image super-resolution. In: Proceedings of the IEEE/CVF Conference on Computer Vision and Pattern Recognition, pp. 14245–14254 (2021)
4. Charpiat, G., Hofmann, M., Schölkopf, B.: Automatic image colorization via multimodal predictions. In: Forsyth, D., Torr, P., Zisserman, A. (eds.) ECCV 2008. LNCS, vol. 5304, pp. 126–139. Springer, Heidelberg (2008). https://doi.org/10.1007/978-3-540-88690-7_10
5. Cheng, Z., Yang, Q., Sheng, B.: Deep colorization. In: Proceedings of the IEEE International Conference on Computer Vision, pp. 415–423 (2015)
6. Chia, A.Y.S., et al.: Semantic colorization with internet images. ACM Trans. Graph. (TOG) **30**(6), 1–8 (2011)
7. Deshpande, A., Rock, J., Forsyth, D.: Learning large-scale automatic image colorization. In: Proceedings of the IEEE International Conference on Computer Vision, pp. 567–575 (2015)
8. Gu, J., Shen, Y., Zhou, B.: Image processing using multi-code gan prior. In: Proceedings of the IEEE/CVF Conference on Computer Vision and Pattern Recognition, pp. 3012–3021 (2020)
9. Gupta, R.K., Chia, A.Y.S., Rajan, D., Ng, E.S., Zhiyong, H.: Image colorization using similar images. In: Proceedings of the 20th ACM International Conference on Multimedia, pp. 369–378 (2012)
10. Hasler, D., Suesstrunk, S.E.: Measuring colorfulness in natural images. In: Human Vision and Electronic Imaging VIII, vol. 5007, pp. 87–95. International Society for Optics and Photonics (2003)

11. He, K., Zhang, X., Ren, S., Sun, J.: Deep residual learning for image recognition. In: Proceedings of the IEEE Conference on Computer Vision and Pattern Recognition, pp. 770–778 (2016)
12. Heusel, M., Ramsauer, H., Unterthiner, T., Nessler, B., Hochreiter, S.: Gans trained by a two time-scale update rule converge to a local nash equilibrium. In: Advances in Neural Information Processing Systems 30 (2017)
13. Huang, Y.C., Tung, Y.S., Chen, J.C., Wang, S.W., Wu, J.L.: An adaptive edge detection based colorization algorithm and its applications. In: Proceedings of the 13th Annual ACM International Conference on Multimedia, pp. 351–354 (2005)
14. Iizuka, S., Simo-Serra, E., Ishikawa, H.: Let there be color! joint end-to-end learning of global and local image priors for automatic image colorization with simultaneous classification. ACM Trans. Graph. (ToG) 35(4), 1–11 (2016)
15. Kang, K., Kim, S., Cho, S.: Gan inversion for out-of-range images with geometric transformations. In: Proceedings of the IEEE/CVF International Conference on Computer Vision, pp. 13941–13949 (2021)
16. Karras, T., Aila, T., Laine, S., Lehtinen, J.: Progressive growing of gans for improved quality, stability, and variation. arXiv preprint arXiv:1710.10196 (2017)
17. Karras, T., Laine, S., Aila, T.: A style-based generator architecture for generative adversarial networks. In: Proceedings of the IEEE/CVF Conference on Computer Vision and Pattern Recognition, pp. 4401–4410 (2019)
18. Karras, T., Laine, S., Aittala, M., Hellsten, J., Lehtinen, J., Aila, T.: Analyzing and improving the image quality of stylegan. In: Proceedings of the IEEE/CVF Conference on Computer Vision and Pattern Recognition, pp. 8110–8119 (2020)
19. Kingma, D.P., Ba, J.: Adam: A method for stochastic optimization. arXiv preprint arXiv:1412.6980 (2014)
20. Kumar, M., Weissenborn, D., Kalchbrenner, N.: Colorization transformer. In: International Conference on Learning Representations (2021)
21. Larsson, G., Maire, M., Shakhnarovich, G.: Learning representations for automatic colorization. In: Leibe, B., Matas, J., Sebe, N., Welling, M. (eds.) ECCV 2016. LNCS, vol. 9908, pp. 577–593. Springer, Cham (2016). https://doi.org/10.1007/978-3-319-46493-0_35
22. Levin, A., Lischinski, D., Weiss, Y.: Colorization using optimization. In: ACM SIGGRAPH 2004 Papers, pp. 689–694 (2004)
23. Lim, J.H., Ye, J.C.: Geometric gan. arXiv preprint arXiv:1705.02894 (2017)
24. Liu, X., et al.: Intrinsic colorization. In: ACM SIGGRAPH Asia 2008 papers, pp. 1–9 (2008)
25. Luo, X., Zhang, X., Yoo, P., Martin-Brualla, R., Lawrence, J., Seitz, S.M.: Time-travel rephotography. ACM Trans. Graph. (Proceedings of ACM SIGGRAPH Asia 2021) 40(6) (12 2021)
26. Menon, S., Damian, A., Hu, S., Ravi, N., Rudin, C.: Pulse: Self-supervised photo upsampling via latent space exploration of generative models. In: Proceedings of the IEEE/CVF Conference on Computer Vision and Pattern Recognition, pp. 2437–2445 (2020)
27. Pan, X., Zhan, X., Dai, B., Lin, D., Loy, C.C., Luo, P.: Exploiting deep generative prior for versatile image restoration and manipulation. IEEE Trans. Pattern Anal. Mach. Intell. (2021)
28. Qu, Y., Wong, T.T., Heng, P.A.: Manga colorization. ACM Trans. Graph. (TOG) 25(3), 1214–1220 (2006)
29. Russakovsky, O., Deng, J., Su, H., Krause, J., Satheesh, S., Ma, S., Huang, Z., Karpathy, A., Khosla, A., Bernstein, M., et al.: Imagenet large scale visual recognition challenge. Int. J. Comput. Vision 115(3), 211–252 (2015)

30. Simonyan, K., Zisserman, A.: Very deep convolutional networks for large-scale image recognition. arXiv preprint arXiv:1409.1556 (2014)
31. Su, J.W., Chu, H.K., Huang, J.B.: Instance-aware image colorization. In: Proceedings of the IEEE/CVF Conference on Computer Vision and Pattern Recognition, pp. 7968–7977 (2020)
32. Vitoria, P., Raad, L., Ballester, C.: Chromagan: adversarial picture colorization with semantic class distribution. In: Proceedings of the IEEE/CVF Winter Conference on Applications of Computer Vision, pp. 2445–2454 (2020)
33. Wang, X., Li, Y., Zhang, H., Shan, Y.: Towards real-world blind face restoration with generative facial prior. In: Proceedings of the IEEE/CVF Conference on Computer Vision and Pattern Recognition, pp. 9168–9178 (2021)
34. Wu, Y., Wang, X., Li, Y., Zhang, H., Zhao, X., Shan, Y.: Towards vivid and diverse image colorization with generative color prior. In: Proceedings of the IEEE/CVF International Conference on Computer Vision, pp. 14377–14386 (2021)
35. Wu, Y., Kirillov, A., Massa, F., Lo, W.Y., Girshick, R.: Detectron2 (2019). https://github.com/facebookresearch/detectron2
36. Xu, K., Li, Y., Ju, T., Hu, S.M., Liu, T.Q.: Efficient affinity-based edit propagation using KD tree. ACM Trans. Graph. (TOG) 28(5), 1–6 (2009)
37. Yang, T., Ren, P., Xie, X., Zhang, L.: Gan prior embedded network for blind face restoration in the wild. In: Proceedings of the IEEE/CVF Conference on Computer Vision and Pattern Recognition, pp. 672–681 (2021)
38. Yatziv, L., Sapiro, G.: Fast image and video colorization using chrominance blending. IEEE Trans. Image Process. 15(5), 1120–1129 (2006)
39. Zhang, R., Isola, P., Efros, A.A.: Colorful image colorization. In: Leibe, B., Matas, J., Sebe, N., Welling, M. (eds.) ECCV 2016. LNCS, vol. 9907, pp. 649–666. Springer, Cham (2016). https://doi.org/10.1007/978-3-319-46487-9_40

CADyQ: Content-Aware Dynamic Quantization for Image Super-Resolution

Cheeun Hong[1], Sungyong Baik[3], Heewon Kim[1], Seungjun Nah[1,4],
and Kyoung Mu Lee[1,2(✉)]

[1] Department of ECE and ASRI, Seoul, South Korea
{cheeun914,ghimhw,kyoungmu}@snu.ac.kr
[2] IPAI, Seoul National University, Seoul, South Korea
[3] Department of Data Science, Hanyang University, Seoul, South Korea
dsybaik@hanyang.ac.kr
[4] NVIDIA, Santa Clara, USA

Abstract. Despite breakthrough advances in image super-resolution (SR) with convolutional neural networks (CNNs), SR has yet to enjoy ubiquitous applications due to the high computational complexity of SR networks. Quantization is one of the promising approaches to solve this problem. However, existing methods fail to quantize SR models with a bit-width lower than 8 bits, suffering from severe accuracy loss due to fixed bit-width quantization applied everywhere. In this work, to achieve high average bit-reduction with less accuracy loss, we propose a novel **C**ontent-**A**ware **Dy**namic **Q**uantization (CADyQ) method for SR networks that allocates optimal bits to local regions and layers adaptively based on the local contents of an input image. To this end, a trainable bit selector module is introduced to determine the proper bit-width and quantization level for each layer and a given local image patch. This module is governed by the quantization sensitivity that is estimated by using both the average magnitude of image gradient of the patch and the standard deviation of the input feature of the layer. The proposed quantization pipeline has been tested on various SR networks and evaluated on several standard benchmarks extensively. Significant reduction in computational complexity and the elevated restoration accuracy clearly demonstrate the effectiveness of the proposed CADyQ framework for SR. Codes are available at https://github.com/Cheeun/CADyQ.

1 Introduction

Image super-resolution (SR) is a fundamental low-level vision computer problem that aims to restore the high-resolution (HR) image from its corresponding low-resolution (LR) image. Owing to the remarkable success in deep learning approaches [10, 27, 34, 40, 49, 50], high-fidelity images could be obtained using state-of-the-art super-resolution networks. Such modern deep learning models,

---

Supplementary Information The online version contains supplementary material available at https://doi.org/10.1007/978-3-031-20071-7_22.

S. Avidan et al. (Eds.): ECCV 2022, LNCS 13667, pp. 367–383, 2022.
https://doi.org/10.1007/978-3-031-20071-7_22

Fig. 1. The dynamic bit-width allocation by CADyQ. Examples from CADyQ applied to a recent SR network, CARN [2]. Our framework demonstrates a dynamic bit-width allocation per patch and layer with a minimal PSNR drop (<0.05 dB). Higher bit-widths are allocated to features containing more structural information or contours

however, rely on advanced architectures with high computational costs, thereby limiting their applications, especially in resource-limited environments.

Quantization is one of the promising approaches for reducing the computational complexity of neural networks. In particular, network quantization has greatly reduced computation loads without a significant accuracy loss, especially for high-level vision tasks (*e.g.*, classification) [7,18,51]. Recently, there have also been attempts to quantize SR networks, either by learning parameters for the binarization of each convolution weight [38] or by learning a quantization range for each layer [31]. However, unlike quantizing high-level vision networks, quantizing SR networks to bit-width lower than 8 bit while maintaining the performance remains a challenging problem [22].

As a key to the above issue, we find that the existing methods do not consider the image structure and locality information, employing a quantized network with fixed bit for all regions of given input images. This leads to processing image regions of less structural information with unnecessarily high bits. In this work, we observe that different local regions (*i.e.*, patches of a certain size) exhibit different amounts of SR performance degradation from quantization, as illustrated in Fig. 2a. In particular, patches with complex structures or contents tend to suffer more from performance degradation than patches with simple contents. Furthermore, we also observe that the quantization sensitivity varies among layers, even for the same patch, as illustrated in Fig. 2b. The observations suggest that different patches and layers require different amounts of computation and thus different bit-widths, providing motivations for a dynamic patch-and-layer-wise bit-width quantization.

Therefore, we propose a new quantization pipeline, dubbed **Content-A**ware **D**ynamic **Q**uantization (CADyQ), that dynamically selects a quantization bit-width for each convolution layer based on the quantization sensitivity of its input contents (*i.e.*, each patch and layer feature), as demonstrated in Fig. 1. However, the direct measurement of the quantization sensitivity is unsuitable as it requires ground-truth high-resolution images to measure the performance degradation. In order to estimate the quantization sensitivity, the proposed pipeline employs the

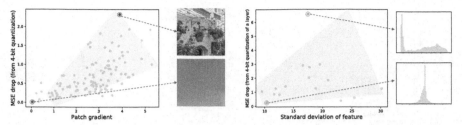

(a) Quantization sensitivity v.s. patch image gradient
(b) Quantization sensitivity v.s. standard deviation of layer features

Fig. 2. The motivation of our framework: the different quantization sensitivity per layer and per patch. Quantization sensitivity is measured with restoration performance (*e.g.*, mean-square error (MSE) between the output image and ground-truth HR image) degradation due to quantization. We observe **(a)** a correlation between the average magnitude of image gradient [13] and the quantization sensitivity of each patch. Patches with complex (simple) structures exhibit high (low) image gradient magnitude and suffer more (less) MSE drop from quantization. Also, we notice a **(b)** strong correlation between feature standard deviation and the quantization sensitivity of each layer feature for the given patch. Layers with high (low) feature standard deviation bring more (less) MSE drop from quantizing the given layer.

average gradient magnitude of the input patch and the standard deviation of the layer feature, based on the observed correlation in Fig. 2. Then, we introduce a lightweight bit selector that employs a linear layer conditioned on the estimated quantization sensitivity, to determine the bit-width of the feature for each input patch and layer.

Furthermore, a new regularization loss function is introduced to facilitate the bit-width selection process. The proposed loss function penalizes the bit selector if a high (low) bit is selected for features with a small (large) quantization sensitivity. This leads the bit selector to reserve more computation resources for features that are more critical to the restoration performance, while minimizing the resources for features with less impact on the performance.

The experimental results demonstrate the outstanding performance of the proposed quantization mechanism across various SR networks, underlining the effectiveness and importance of selecting a different bit-width for each patch and layer. Overall, our contributions can be summarized as follows:

- For the first time, we observe that the sensitivity of restoration accuracy to low-bit quantization varies across different local image regions and the SR network layers.
- Accordingly, we present a new quantization framework CADyQ that quantizes SR networks with a different bit-width for each patch and layer, by adding a lightweight bit selector module that is conditioned on the estimated quantization sensitivity.
- A novel regularization loss term is introduced to encourage the proposed framework to find a better balance between the computational complexity and overall restoration performance.

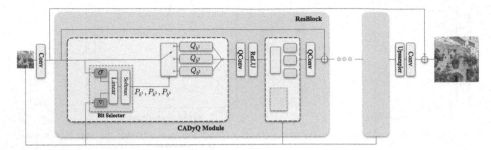

Fig. 3. The overview of the proposed quantization framework CADyQ for SR network, which we illustrate with a residual block based backbone. For each given patch and each layer, our CADyQ module introduces a light-weight bit selector that dynamically selects the bit-width and its corresponding quantization function Q_{b^k} (Eq. (3)) among the candidate quantization functions with distinct bit-widths. The bit selector is conditioned on the estimated quantization sensitivity (the average gradient magnitude $|\nabla|$ of the given patch and the standard deviation σ of the layer feature). Qconv denotes the convolution layer of the quantized features and weights

2   Related Works

Super-Resolution Neural Networks. Convolutional neural network (CNN) based approaches [29,34] have greatly improved the performance of image super-resolution (SR) methods, however, with heavy computational resources. The massive computations of SR networks have limited the application on real-world mobile devices, spurring the recent interest in lightweight SR networks. Since then, new lightweight architectures have been investigated [9,20,21,49] or searched [8,26,32,33,39]. Recently, a few works have introduced adaptive SR networks that aim to achieve efficient inference for a given input [28,36,43,45,48]. These methods mostly focus on reducing the network depth or the number of channels that still rely on heavy floating-point operations, while our focus is to lower the precision of floating-point operations with network quantization.

Neural Network Quantization. Network quantization provides an alternative approach for making networks efficient by mapping 32-bit floating point values of feature maps and weights to lower bit values [5,7,12,25,30,51,52]. Few recent works have attempted to allocate different bit-widths for different layers [6,11, 15,24,37,42,47]. However, these approaches target high-level tasks and thus do not consider the distinct local regions that we observe to play a key role in obtaining an efficient network for super-resolution.

Quantized Super-Resolution Models. In contrast to high-level vision tasks, super-resolution poses different challenges due to inherently high accuracy sensitivity to quantization [22,38,46]. A few works have attempted to recover the accuracy by modifying the network architecture [3,23,46]. However, the methods are applicable to specific models and thus not generalizable to other SR architectures. For a general quantization method for SR networks, PAMS [31] learns the quantization intervals of different layers to adapt to vastly distinct distributions in the features of SR networks (due to the absence of BN layers), and DAQ [17] further achieves ultra-low bit quantization on SR by utilizing different quantization function parameters for each feature channel. Furthermore, Wang *et al.* [41] has proposed quantizing features from all layers and skip connections of SR networks. Considering the varying degree of quantization sensitivity inside the network, Liu *et al.* [35] manually allocated a bit-width for each stage of a network. However, these works apply a fixed bit-width either throughout different input images [35] or both images and network layers [41]. In contrast, we observe that the quantization sensitivity varies throughout the network layers and images. Thus, we propose a new quantization framework that dynamically selects the appropriate bit-width for each layer feature based on its quantization sensitivity of each content (*i.e.*, patch and layer feature).

3 Proposed Method

3.1 Preliminaries

Generally, to replace the majority of floating-point operations with lower-bit operations in CNNs, the input feature and weight of each convolutional layer are respectively quantized [5,7,25]. Given an input feature of the j-th convolutional layer $x^j \in \mathbb{R}^{N \times C \times H \times W}$, where B, C, H, and W denote the mini-batch size, number of channels, height, and width of the feature, a quantization function $Q_b(\cdot)$ quantizes the feature x^j into its low-bit counterpart x_q^j of bit-width b:

$$x_q^j \equiv Q_b(x^j) = \lfloor \text{clamp}(x^j, a) \cdot \frac{s(b)}{a} \rceil \cdot \frac{a}{s(b)}. \tag{1}$$

x^j is first truncated with clamp$(\cdot, a)$ into the range of $[-a, a]$, and then scaled to $[-1, 1]$ with the scale parameter a. Then, x^j is scaled to the integer range of the given bit-width b, $[-s(b), s(b)]$ where $s(b)=2^{b-1}-1$. Consequently, the features in integer range are then rounded to integer values with $\lfloor \cdot \rceil$, and then rescaled back to range $[-a, a]$. For quantizing features of SR networks, scale parameter a is either implemented with a learnable parameter [31] or a moving average of batch-wise max values [41]. At the output of the ReLU layers, since the values are non-negative, the output values are truncated into the range of $[0, a]$ and then scaled to integer range $[0, s(b)]$ with $s(b)=2^b-1$. Similarly, a weight of the j-th convolutional layer $w^j \in \mathbb{R}^{C \times C_{out} \times F \times F}$ is quantized to w_q^j:

$$w_q^j \equiv Q_b(w^j) = \lfloor \text{clamp}(w^j, a_w^j) \cdot \frac{s(b)}{a_w^j} \rceil \cdot \frac{a_w^j}{s(b)}, \tag{2}$$

where C and C_{out} are the number of input and output channels, F is the kernel size of the convolution filter, and a_w^j is the scale parameter for the corresponding weight w^j. In quantization for SR networks, the weight scale parameter a_w^j is often determined simply by $a_w^j = \max(|w^j|)$ [31].

3.2 Motivation

Previous SR quantization works [31, 41] have quantized the network with a fixed bit-width b, as formulated in Eq. (1). However, our observations in Fig. 2 hint the disadvantages of a fixed bit-width quantization in SR. In particular, different patches and network layers exhibit different degrees of quantization sensitivity (*i.e.*, SR performance drop from a fixed-bit quantization). As such, we aim to dynamically assign bit-widths for the features based on the quantization sensitivity of *contents* (*i.e.*, the input patch *and* the layer), thereby naming our proposed framework **Contents-Aware Dynamic Quantization** (CADyQ).

3.3 Proposed Quantization Module (CADyQ)

In our proposed framework, each convolutional layer has a quantization module, which in turn consists of K bit-width quantization function candidates, one of which is selected by a bit selector, as illustrated in Fig. 3.

Dynamic Feature Quantization. To dynamically quantize features with a different bit-width for each i-th patch and j-th layer, a single quantization function will be selected in the CADyQ module among K number of candidate quantization functions with distinct bit-widths. Each quantization function $Q_{b_{i,j}^k}(\cdot)$ of bit-width $b_{i,j}^k$ ($k=1, ..., K$) will, when selected, quantize the feature of the i-th patch and j-th layer $\boldsymbol{x}_i^j$ with

$$Q_{b_{i,j}^k}(\boldsymbol{x}_i^j) = \lfloor \mathrm{clamp}(\boldsymbol{x}_i^j, a_k) \cdot \frac{s(b_{i,j}^k)}{a_k} \rceil \cdot \frac{a_k}{s(b_{i,j}^k)}, \tag{3}$$

where $s(b_k) = 2^{b_k-1} - 1$ is the integer range of the bit-width b_k and a_k is the scale parameter. Once the bit-width is selected to be $b_{i,j}^{k^*}$ for i-th input patch and j-th layer, the resulting quantized counterpart of $\boldsymbol{x}_i^j$ is

$$\boldsymbol{x}_{i,q}^j \equiv Q_{b_{i,j}^{k^*}}(\boldsymbol{x}_i^j),$$

where $Q_{b_{i,j}^{k^*}}$ is the quantization function for $\boldsymbol{x}_i^j$, corresponding to the selected bit-width $b_{i,j}^{k^*}$. Note that we simply use a linear symmetric quantization function and a learnable scale parameter a_k for each quantization function, as in [31].

Bit-Width Selection. To facilitate the bit-width selection, we use a lightweight bit selector that assigns a probability to each bit-width. Then, the bit-width with the highest probability is selected:

$$b_{i,j}^{k^*} = \begin{cases} \arg\max_{b_{i,j}^k} P_{b_{i,j}^k}(\boldsymbol{x}_i^j) & \text{forward,} \\ \sum_{k=1}^K b_{i,j}^k \cdot P_{b_{i,j}^k}(\boldsymbol{x}_i^j) & \text{backward,} \end{cases} \tag{4}$$

where $P_{b_{i,j}^k}$ is the probability assigned to the bit-width $b_{i,j}^k$ and its corresponding quantization function and $\sum_k P_{b_{i,j}^k} = 1$. We desire our bit selector network to predict a high probability to a high bit-width for features that have high quantization sensitivity (high accuracy drop from quantization) and a low bit-width for features with low quantization sensitivity. However, it is infeasible to directly measure the quantization sensitivity of each feature without access to a ground-truth HR patch for the given input LR patch. Therefore, upon the correlations observed in Fig. 2, we estimate the quantization sensitivity for each layer and the given input patch with the average magnitude of image gradient [13] of a patch and the standard deviation of a feature. Conditioned on the average gradient magnitude of a patch and the standard deviation of a feature, our bit selector assigns the probability to each bit-width candidate for $\boldsymbol{x}_i^j$, the feature of the j-th layer and input patch I_i:

$$P_{b_{i,j}^k}(\boldsymbol{x}_i^j) = \frac{\exp(f(\sigma(\boldsymbol{x}_i^j), |\nabla I_i|))}{\sum_{k=1}^K \exp(f(\sigma(\boldsymbol{x}_i^j), |\nabla I_i|))}, \tag{5}$$

where $\sigma(\boldsymbol{x}_i^j) \in \mathbb{R}^C$ measures the channel-wise standard deviation and $|\nabla I_i| \in \mathbb{R}^2$ measures the average magnitude of the image gradients from the patch I_i in horizontal and vertical directions [13]. We concatenate the two metrics and then pass it through a fully connected layer $f : \mathbb{R}^{C+2} \to \mathbb{R}^K$, based on the observed positive correlation between the measured quantization sensitivity and the feature standard deviation or the average gradient magnitude of each patch. While we make observations on the correlation using the layer-wise standard deviation for the clarity, the bit selector is conditioned on the channel-wise standard deviation, which is observed to have more fine-grained information, as discussed in the supplementary document.

Backpropagation. Selecting a quantization function of the max probability, however, is a discrete non-differentiable process and cannot be optimized end-to-end. Hence, we employ the straight-through estimator [4] to make the process differentiable. The discrete bit-width selection is replaced with its differentiable approximation, where each candidate bit-width is weighted by the probability distribution predicted by the bit selector (Eq. (5)), during backpropagation:

$$\boldsymbol{x}_{i,q}^j = \begin{cases} Q_{b_{i,j}^{k*}}(\boldsymbol{x}_i^j) & \text{forward,} \\ \sum_{k=1}^K Q_{b_{i,j}^k}(\boldsymbol{x}_i^j) \cdot P_{b_{i,j}^k}(\boldsymbol{x}_i^j) & \text{backward.} \end{cases}$$

Weight Quantization. Weights are quantized with a fixed bit-width, as in Eq. (2). While weights can be also quantized dynamically, we focus on the dynamic quantization of input features, motivated by the observations of the correlations between the quantization sensitivity and local image contents (*i.e.*, patches and layer features) in Fig. 2.

3.4 Bit Loss

Previous works [31,41] have focused on optimizing the performance of a quantized network with a fixed bit-width, by using a pixel-wise L1 loss and knowledge distillation loss [16] with the original unquantized network. On the other hand, we aim to find an efficient quantization for the given feature dynamically. Hence, we need a regularization loss term to strike a balance between the restoration performance and the quantization rate. Directed by a similar goal, few neural architecture search (NAS)-based mixed-precision quantization approaches [6,47] utilize bit regularization loss to optimize the computational resources of the quantized network. The typical bit regularization loss penalizes the total number of operations weighted by its bit-width of the currently selected network:

$$\mathcal{L}_b = \sum_{j=1}^{M} \sum_{i=1}^{N} b_{i,j}^{k^*} \cdot \text{OPs}(\boldsymbol{x}_i^j), \tag{6}$$

where N is the batch size; M is the number of quantized layers in the network; $b_{i,j}^{k^*}$ is the selected bit-width corresponding to the feature of i-th patch and j-th layer according to Eq. (4); and OPs($\cdot$) is the number of operations for convoluting the given feature. However, this standard bit regularization loss equally penalizes the quantization modules of different layers when each layer can have a different impact on the overall performance after quantization, as observed in Fig. 2b.

To achieve a better trade-off between the computational cost and restoration performance, the bit-widths of quantization modules with a larger impact on performance should be penalized less than those of the quantization modules with less impact. As a result, the layers with greater impact on the overall performance will have higher bit-width assigned. To this end, we modify the bit regularization loss by weighting each selected bit-width with the probability estimated by our bit selector, which is conditioned on the estimated quantization sensitivity (and thus estimated impact on the overall performance). Given feature $\boldsymbol{x}_i^j$ of the j-th layer for the i-th patch, our weighted bit regularization loss is

$$\mathcal{L}_{wb} = \sum_{j=1}^{M} \sum_{i=1}^{N} \frac{b_{i,j}^{k^*}}{\sum_k b_{i,j}^k \cdot \text{sg}[P_{b_{i,j}^k}(\boldsymbol{x}_i^j)]} \cdot \text{OPs}(\boldsymbol{x}_i^j), \tag{7}$$

where sg[$\cdot$] denotes stop gradient operation. Specifically, the denominator represents the expected bit-width during training, while the numerator represents the selected bit-width. When the expected bit-width is smaller than the selected bit-width, it results in a larger regularization term and hence stronger penalization. This penalization enforces a lower bit-width assignment on the feature estimated to be less sensitive to quantization. For example, when the probability distribution from the bit selector network for each bit-width 4, 6, and 8 is [0.1, 0.1, 0.8], the quantization module should be regularized less than [0.2, 0.2, 0.6]. The feature that corresponds to the former probability distribution can be considered to be more vulnerable to the performance drop from quantization. On the other hand, when the expected bit-width is larger than the selected bit-width, a larger expected bit-width is regularized less. This enables the bit selector to select a higher bit-width for more quantization-sensitive features.

Then, our final objective function becomes

$$\mathcal{L} = w_1 \mathcal{L}_1 + w_{\text{reg}} \mathcal{L}_{\text{reg}} + w_{\text{kd}} \mathcal{L}_{\text{kd}} + w_{\text{kdf}} \mathcal{L}_{\text{kdf}}, \tag{8}$$

where $w_1, w_{reg}, w_{kd}, w_{kdf}$ are the weights to balance different loss terms, respectively; $\mathcal{L}_1$ is the pixel-wise L1 loss between the output image and the ground truth; $\mathcal{L}_{reg}$ is a bit regularization loss ($\mathcal{L}_{wb}$ in our case); $\mathcal{L}_{kd}$ is the knowledge distillation loss on the last output feature using 8-bit quantized model as the teacher; $\mathcal{L}_{kdf}$ is the knowledge distillation loss on output feature of each layer using the same 8-bit teacher. As for the knowledge distillation, a teacher network has the same architecture backbone (*i.e.*, no bit selection module included) as the student SR network. A teacher network is pre-trained with uniform 8-bit weights with the activations quantized via PAMS [31].

4   Experiments

The proposed quantization framework CADyQ is evaluated on various SR networks to validate its effectiveness and flexibility. We first describe our experimental settings (Sect. 4.1) and evaluate our method on various SR networks (Sect. 4.2). We then present detailed ablation experiments to analyze each main attribute of our framework (Sect. 4.4): namely, layer-wise/patch-wise quantization, quantization sensitivity estimation, and the proposed weighted bit loss.

4.1   Implementation Details

Models. The proposed framework is applied directly to existing SR networks, including representative SR networks (EDSR-baseline [34] and SRResNet [29]) and recent efficient models (IDN [21] and CARN [2]), thereby naming the CADyQ-quantized models as EDSR-baseline-CADyQ, SRResNet-CADyQ, IDN-CADyQ, and CARN-CADyQ, respectively. Following the settings from previous works on SR quantization [31,38,46], our framework quantizes weights and feature maps in the layers of the high-level feature extraction module where most of the costly operations are concentrated in. In this work, we set the quantization bit-width candidates as $\{4, 6, 8\}$ and employ linear symmetric quantization function [31] with a learnable scale parameter for each quantization function candidate. Furthermore, we uniformly apply 8-bit linear quantization for weights. Additional experiments that demonstrate the applicability of CADyQ are provided in supplementary document Sect. A.

Training Details. Training and validation are done with DIV2K [1] dataset. For training stability, we follow [25,52] in initializing the SR network parameters with pre-trained 8-bit network weights and in controlling the bit selector to progressively decrease the bit-width. For a progressive reduction in bit-width, the weight of the proposed bit regularization loss (w_{reg}) is initially 10^{-4} and gradually increased throughout training (10^{-6} per $1K$ iteration). The weights for the loss terms w_1, w_{kd}, and w_{kdf} is respectively 1.0, 1000.0, and 100.0. Analysis on w_{reg} and other training settings are specified in Sect. C of the supplementary document.

Table 1. Quantitative comparisons on various SR networks: IDN [21], EDSR-baseline [34], SRResNet [29], and CARN [2] of scale 4. The average feature quantization rate of the feature extraction stage (FQR), PSNR, and SSIM are reported. The results demonstrate the efficiency of the proposed method that manages to reduce FQR while maintaining or improving PSNR/SSIM

Model	Urban100			Test2K			Test4K		
	FQR↓	PSNR↑	SSIM↑	FQR↓	PSNR↑	SSIM↑	FQR↓	PSNR↑	SSIM↑
IDN [21]	32.00	25.42	0.763	32.00	27.48	0.774	32.00	28.54	0.806
IDN-PAMS [31]	8.00	25.56	0.768	8.00	27.53	0.775	8.00	28.59	0.807
IDN-DAQ [17]	4.00	24.46	0.718	4.00	26.98	0.750	4.00	27.94	0.782
IDN-CADyQ (Ours)	5.78	25.65	0.771	5.16	27.54	0.776	5.03	28.61	0.808
EDSR-baseline [34]	32.00	26.04	0.784	32.00	27.71	0.782	32.00	28.80	0.814
EDSR-baseline-PAMS [31]	8.00	25.94	0.781	8.00	27.67	0.781	8.00	28.77	0.813
EDSR-baseline-DAQ [17]	4.00	25.73	0.772	4.00	27.60	0.777	4.00	28.67	0.809
EDSR-baseline-CADyQ (Ours)	6.09	25.94	0.782	5.52	27.67	0.781	5.37	28.77	0.813
SRResNet [29]	32.00	25.74	0.773	32.00	27.60	0.778	32.00	28.68	0.810
SRResNet-PAMS [31]	8.00	25.85	0.776	8.00	27.63	0.779	8.00	28.72	0.812
SRResNet-DAQ [17]	4.00	25.70	0.772	4.00	27.59	0.778	4.00	28.67	0.810
SRResNet-CADyQ (Ours)	5.73	25.92	0.781	5.14	27.64	0.781	5.02	28.72	0.812
CARN [2]	32.00	26.07	0.784	32.00	27.69	0.782	32.00	28.79	0.814
CARN-PAMS [31]	8.00	25.80	0.776	8.00	27.60	0.778	8.00	28.68	0.811
CARN-DAQ [17]	4.00	25.48	0.764	4.00	27.30	0.771	4.00	28.24	0.802
CARN-CADyQ (Ours)	5.32	25.94	0.780	4.65	27.65	0.780	4.54	28.73	0.812

Evaluation Details. We evaluate our framework on the standard benchmark (Urban100 [19]) and on more computationally demanding images of large size (e.g., 2K, 4K) in Test2K and Test4K datasets [28] which are generated via bicubic downsampling from DIV8K [14] dataset (index 1201-1400). For testing, an input test image is cropped into patches of size 96×96 with six overlapping boundary pixels. Each patch is super-resolved with our framework and then combined to produce the whole HR image. There exists a trade-off between the patch size and the overall efficiency, which is discussed in Sect. 4.5 and supplementary document Sec. B. We report peak signal-to-noise ratio (PSNR) and structural similarity index (SSIM [44]) to evaluate the SR performance, along with the average feature quantization rate (FQR) for the evaluation of efficiency. Furthermore, our ablation study is conducted consistently with CARN backbone models on Urban100 dataset.

4.2   Quantitative Results

To evaluate the effectiveness and efficiency of the proposed mechanism, we compare the results with PAMS [31] and DAQ [17] using the official code, which is similar to CADyQ in that quantization is directly applied to existing SR networks without redesigning the architecture. Specifically, we compare with PAMS (8-bit) since lower-bit quantization by PAMS results in performance degradation,

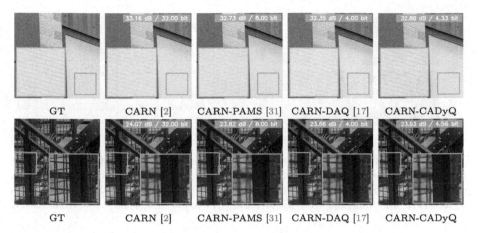

GT   CARN [2]   CARN-PAMS [31]   CARN-DAQ [17]   CARN-CADyQ

GT   CARN [2]   CARN-PAMS [31]   CARN-DAQ [17]   CARN-CADyQ

Fig. 4. Qualitative results on 'img1215' of Test4K. Quantitative measures of PSNR and average bit-width of the patch are also reported (PSNR/Average bit-width). More results are provided in Sect. E of the supplementary document

and DAQ (w4a4qq4) with 4-bit for weight and feature quantization. As shown in Table 1, DAQ reduces the computational resources but at the cost of performance degradation, which is especially severe (over -0.5dB) for IDN and CARN baseline. Also, compared with PAMS, CADyQ demonstrates a lower average precision without the performance drop, striking a better balance between computational cost and performance.

4.3 Qualitative Results

Figure 4 provides qualitative results and comparisons with the output images from CARN-based models [2]. CARN-CADyQ (ours) produces a visually clean output image, while CARN-PAMS and sometimes even original unquantized CARN suffer from a checkerboard artifact or blurred lines, even though CARN-CADyQ uses less computational resources. Moreover, CARN-DAQ, despite the low computational resources, produces various artifacts and color distortion. Also, the map of average bit-width used by our framework for each local patch in the image is visualized in Fig. 5(a). The visualized bit map demonstrates that our framework allocates more computational resources to patches with complex structures (e.g., buildings) and less to patches with simple structures (e.g., sky). Furthermore, CADyQ is shown to dynamically allocate distinct bit-widths across different network layers, as visualized in Fig. 5(b). The qualitative results stress the effectiveness and importance of the patch-and-layer-wise bit allocation.

4.4 Ablation Study

Effect of Layer-Wise and Patch-Wise Quantization. To verify the importance of layer-wise and patch-wise quantization in conjunction, we compare our

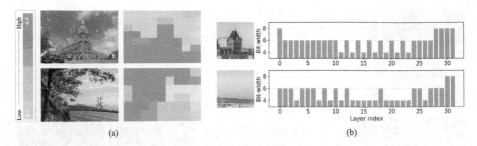

(a)   (b)

Fig. 5. Visualizations of dynamic bit-width allocation by CADyQ across patches and layers. On average, CADyQ assigns higher bit-width to (a) complex patches and to (b) important layers. Results are obtained with EDSR-CADyQ from (a) 'img1215' and 'img1222' from Test4K and (b) two patches of 'img1400' from Test2K

Table 2. Ablation study on layer-wise and patch-wise quantization

	Layer-wise	Patch-wise	FQR$_\downarrow$	PSNR$_\uparrow$	SSIM$_\uparrow$
(2a)	✗	✗	8.00	25.80	0.776
(2b)	✗	✓	6.15	25.89	0.778
(2c)	✓	✗	7.02	25.92	0.780
CADyQ	✓	✓	5.32	25.94	0.780

overall scheme CADyQ with its separate modules individually: patch-wise quantization and layer-wise quantization, as reported in Table 2. Quantization with patch-wise dynamic bit-width but fixed throughout the network (model **(2b)**) results in a performance drop. A layer-wise different bit but fixed across different patches and images (model **(2c)**) preserves the restoration accuracy but with a small improvement in efficiency (average 7.02 bit). By contrast, layer-wise and patch-wise quantization in conjunction effectively enhances the quality of the super-resolved image and reduces the average bit-width by a large amount. The results validate our claim that dynamically determining the bit-width both per layer and patch is important, corroborating our observations from Fig. 2.

Quantization Sensitivity Estimation. In this ablation study, we validate our choice of measures for quantization sensitivity, which a bit selector uses to decide the bit-width for each patch and layer, as shown in Table 3. We compare alternative measures that could estimate the quantization sensitivity and have similar computational overheads to our choice: patch gradient and channel-wise standard deviation. Although utilizing the range (the gap between max and min value) of the patch pixel values and the layer-wise feature (model **(3a)**) requires fewer computations, it induces a severe performance degradation. Also, the standard deviation of a patch and the layer-wise standard deviation of the feature (model **(3b)**) suffers from performance degradation. Notably, using the

Table 3. Ablation study on quantization sensitivity measures

	Patch	Layer	FQR$_\downarrow$	PSNR$_\uparrow$	SSIM$_\uparrow$
(3a)	max-min	max-min	4.51	25.16	0.752
(3b)	std	layer std	5.95	25.62	0.769
(3c)	gradient	layer std	6.53	25.80	0.775
CADyQ	gradient	channel std	5.32	25.94	0.780

Table 4. Ablation study on losses: bit loss and knowledge distillation loss

	Loss				FQR$_\downarrow$	PSNR$_\uparrow$	SSIM$_\uparrow$
	$\mathcal{L}_1$	$\mathcal{L}_{reg}$	$\mathcal{L}_{kd}$	$\mathcal{L}_{kdf}$			
(4a)	✓	✗	✓	✓	6.51	25.70	0.772
(4b)	✓	$\mathcal{L}_b$	✓	✓	5.75	25.68	0.772
(4c)	✓	$\mathcal{L}_{wb}$	✗	✓	4.48	25.38	0.761
(4d)	✓	$\mathcal{L}_{wb}$	✓	✗	5.25	25.51	0.766
CADyQ	✓	$\mathcal{L}_{wb}$	✓	✓	5.32	25.94	0.780

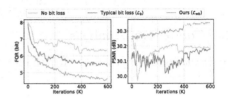

Fig. 6. Learning curves with different losses for FQR (left) and PSNR (right)

layer-wise standard deviation (model **(3c)**) results in lower performance (PSNR or SSIM) and higher average precision (FQR), compared with using channel-wise standard deviation (CADyQ). We provide further justifications for using standard deviations of each channel in the supplementary document Sec. B. In summary, the ablation study implies that the patch gradient and channel-wise standard deviation of the feature contain important information that gives a better estimate of the quantization sensitivity, thereby helping to find a better trade-off between performance and computational resources.

Ablation on Losses. We analyze the effect of the proposed weighted bit loss $\mathcal{L}_{wb}$ (Eq. (7)) by removing it (model **(4a)**) or replacing it with the conventional bit loss $\mathcal{L}_b$, formulated in Eq. (6), (model **(4b)**) in the overall objective function from Eq. (8), as displayed in Table 4 and Fig. 6. The figure shows the curves of the average bit-widths and PSNR of the validation dataset during training. Without the bit loss, the framework fails to reduce the computational resources effectively. Also, replacing our bit loss with the conventional bit loss reduces the average bit-width but with ∼0.2 dB PSNR drop. On the other hand, our proposed bit loss substantially reduces the computational resources without a PSNR drop. Then we evaluate the effect of knowledge distillation loss by removing the distillation loss on the output feature (model **(4c)**) and intermediate features (model **(4d)**), respectively. The results in the table suggest that both types of knowledge distillation play key roles in maintaining the restoration performance (Table 4).

Table 5. Complexity analysis of image-wise and patch-wise inference measured w.r.t. BitOPs of the feature extraction stage on CARN backbone models

Patch size	Full image			96×96		
Model	Baseline	PAMS	CADyQ	Baseline	PAMS	CADyQ
PSNR$_\uparrow$(dB)	26.07	25.80	**25.95**	26.07	25.80	**25.94**
BitOPs$_\downarrow$(G)	76.44	4.78	**3.24**	77.87	4.87	**3.23**

Table 6. Average GPU inference latency. GPU latency for each model is measured with EDSR backbone models on Test4K images

Model	Baseline	PAMS	**CADyQ**
GPU inference Latency (ms)	535.5	240.0	**206.5**

4.5 Complexity Analysis

Our framework can process either the full input test image at once or process, in parallel, the smaller patches, which are combined to construct the full image. For both scenarios, we analyze the complexity of our framework w.r.t. the number of operations weighted by the bit-widths of the operands (BitOPs) for generating a 720p (1820 × 720) image in Table 5. We use BitOPs as measurements for the computational complexity to better reflect the reduction in bit-width. Our framework is shown to be more effective on the patch-wise inference, as local regions with complex structures and those with simple structures are processed with different computational resources. Despite additional computational overhead from overlapping area between neighboring patches in the patch-wise inference, our framework achieves ~95.8% reduction in BitOPs compared with the baseline and ~32.2% reduction in BitOPs compared with 8-bit CARN-PAMS at image-wise inference. GPU latency is measured on NVIDIA Tesla T4 GPU with Tensor Cores supporting 4/8-bit acceleration. As hardware-acceleration for 6-bit is not supported on T4, we cast 6-bit assignments as 8-bit. On average, inference latency of Test4K images is improved to 206.5 ms for CADyQ, compared with 240.0 ms for 8-bit quantization (PAMS [31]), and 535.5 ms for 32-bit. Computational complexity of other backbone models and detailed analysis of overheads can be found in Sect. D of the supplementary document.

5 Conclusion

In this work, we study and exploit the relationship between the local image contents (*e.g.*, local patches and their features at each layer) and the super-resolution performance degradation from quantization. We thereby propose a patch-and-layer-wise bit allocation method for dynamic quantization. Experimental results demonstrate that the proposed quantization framework, CADyQ manages to reduce the computational complexity with respect to BitOPs and inference latency with negligible performance drop.

Acknowledgment. This work was supported in part by the IITP grant funded by the Korea government (MSIT) [No. 2021-0-01343, Artificial Intelligence Graduate School

Program (Seoul National University), No. 2021-0-02068, Artificial Intelligence Innovation Hub, and No. 2022-0-00156], and in part by the BK21 FOUR program of the Education and Research Program for Future ICT Pioneers, Seoul National University in 2022.

References

1. Agustsson, E., Timofte, R.: NTIRE 2017 challenge on single image super-resolution: Dataset and study. In: CVPR Workshops (2017)
2. Ahn, N., Kang, B., Sohn, K.-A.: Fast, accurate, and lightweight super-resolution with cascading residual network. In: Ferrari, V., Hebert, M., Sminchisescu, C., Weiss, Y. (eds.) ECCV 2018. LNCS, vol. 11214, pp. 256–272. Springer, Cham (2018). https://doi.org/10.1007/978-3-030-01249-6_16
3. Ayazoglu, M.: Extremely lightweight quantization robust real-time single-image super resolution for mobile devices. In: CVPR Workshops (2021)
4. Bengio, Y., Léonard, N., Courville, A.: Estimating or propagating gradients through stochastic neurons for conditional computation. arXiv preprint arXiv:1308.3432 (2013)
5. Cai, Z., He, X., Sun, J., Vasconcelos, N.: Deep learning with low precision by half-wave gaussian quantization. In: CVPR (2017)
6. Cai, Z., Vasconcelos, N.: Rethinking differentiable search for mixed-precision neural networks. In: CVPR (2020)
7. Choi, J., Wang, Z., Venkataramani, S., Chuang, P.I.J., Srinivasan, V., Gopalakrishnan, K.: Pact: Parameterized clipping activation for quantized neural networks. arXiv preprint arXiv:1805.06085 (2018)
8. Chu, X., Zhang, B., Ma, H., Xu, R., Li, Q.: Fast, accurate and lightweight super-resolution with neural architecture search. In: ICPR (2021)
9. Dong, C., Loy, C.C., He, K., Tang, X.: Learning a Deep Convolutional Network for Image Super-Resolution. In: Fleet, D., Pajdla, T., Schiele, B., Tuytelaars, T. (eds.) ECCV 2014. LNCS, vol. 8692, pp. 184–199. Springer, Cham (2014). https://doi.org/10.1007/978-3-319-10593-2_13
10. Dong, C., Loy, C.C., He, K., Tang, X.: Image super-resolution using deep convolutional networks. IEEE TPAMI **38**(2), 295–307 (2015)
11. Dong, Z., Yao, Z., Gholami, A., Mahoney, M.W., Keutzer, K.: Hawq: Hessian aware quantization of neural networks with mixed-precision. In: ICCV (2019)
12. Esser, S.K., McKinstry, J.L., Bablani, D., Appuswamy, R., Modha, D.S.: Learned step size quantization. arXiv preprint arXiv:1902.08153 (2019)
13. Fattal, R.: Image upsampling via imposed edge statistics. TOG (2007)
14. Gu, S., Lugmayr, A., Danelljan, M., Fritsche, M., Lamour, J., Timofte, R.: Div8k: diverse 8k resolution image dataset. In: ICCV Workshops (2019)
15. Habi, H.V., Jennings, R.H., Netzer, A.: HMQ: hardware friendly mixed precision quantization block for CNNs. In: Vedaldi, A., Bischof, H., Brox, T., Frahm, J.-M. (eds.) ECCV 2020. LNCS, vol. 12371, pp. 448–463. Springer, Cham (2020). https://doi.org/10.1007/978-3-030-58574-7_27
16. Hinton, G., Vinyals, O., Dean, J.: Distilling the knowledge in a neural network. arXiv preprint arXiv:1503.02531 (2015)
17. Hong, C., Kim, H., Baik, S., Oh, J., Lee, K.M.: Daq: channel-wise distribution-aware quantization for deep image super-resolution networks. In: WACV (2022)
18. Hou, L., Kwok, J.T.: Loss-aware weight quantization of deep networks. In: ICLR (2018)

19. Huang, J.B., Singh, A., Ahuja, N.: Single image super-resolution from transformed self-exemplars. In: CVPR (2015)
20. Hui, Z., Gao, X., Yang, Y., Wang, X.: Lightweight image super-resolution with information multi-distillation network. In: ACMMM (2019)
21. Hui, Z., Wang, X., Gao, X.: Fast and accurate single image super-resolution via information distillation network. In: CVPR (2018)
22. Ignatov, A., Timofte, R., Denna, M., Younes, A.: Real-time quantized image super-resolution on mobile npus, mobile ai 2021 challenge: Report. In: CVPR Workshops (2021)
23. Jiang, X., Wang, N., Xin, J., Li, K., Yang, X., Gao, X.: Training binary neural network without batch normalization for image super-resolution. In: AAAI (2021)
24. Jin, Q., Yang, L., Liao, Z.: Adabits: neural network quantization with adaptive bit-widths. In: CVPR (2020)
25. Jung, S., et al.: Learning to quantize deep networks by optimizing quantization intervals with task loss. In: CVPR (2019)
26. Kim, H., Hong, S., Han, B., Myeong, H., Lee, K.M.: Fine-grained neural architecture search. arXiv preprint arXiv:1911.07478 (2019)
27. Kim, J., Lee, J., Lee, K.M.: Accurate image super-resolution using very deep convolutional networks. In: CVPR (2016)
28. Kong, X., Zhao, H., Qiao, Y., Dong, C.: Classsr: a general framework to accelerate super-resolution networks by data characteristic. In: CVPR (2021)
29. Ledig, C., et al.: Photo-realistic single image super-resolution using a generative adversarial network. In: CVPR (2017)
30. Lee, J., Kim, D., Ham, B.: Network quantization with element-wise gradient scaling. In: CVPR (2021)
31. Li, H., et al.: PAMS: quantized super-resolution via parameterized max scale. In: Vedaldi, A., Bischof, H., Brox, T., Frahm, J.-M. (eds.) ECCV 2020. LNCS, vol. 12370, pp. 564–580. Springer, Cham (2020). https://doi.org/10.1007/978-3-030-58595-2_34
32. Li, Y., Gu, S., Zhang, K., Gool, L.V., Timofte, R.: Dhp: Differentiable meta pruning via hypernetworks. In: ECCV (2020)
33. Li, Y., et al.: The heterogeneity hypothesis: Finding layer-wise differentiated network architectures. In: CVPR (2021)
34. Lim, B., Son, S., Kim, H., Nah, S., Lee, K.M.: Enhanced deep residual networks for single image super-resolution. In: CVPR Workshops (2017)
35. Liu, J., Wang, Q., Zhang, D., Shen, L.: Super-resolution model quantized in multi-precision. Electronics 10(17), 2176 (2021)
36. Liu, M., Zhang, Z., Hou, L., Zuo, W., Zhang, L.: Deep adaptive inference networks for single image super-resolution. In: ECCV (2020)
37. Lou, Q., Guo, F., Liu, L., Kim, M., Jiang, L.: AutoQ: automated kernel-wise neural network quantization. In: ICLR (2020)
38. Ma, Y., Xiong, H., Hu, Z., Ma, L.: Efficient super resolution using binarized neural network. In: CVPR Workshops (2019)
39. Oh, J., Kim, H., Nah, S., Hong, C., Choi, J., Lee, K.M.: Attentive fine-grained structured sparsity for image restoration. In: CVPR (2022)
40. Son, S., Lee, K.M.: Srwarp: generalized image super-resolution under arbitrary transformation. In: CVPR (2021)
41. Wang, H., Chen, P., Zhuang, B., Shen, C.: Fully quantized image super-resolution networks. In: ACMMM (2021)
42. Wang, K., Liu, Z., Lin, Y., Lin, J., Han, S.: Haq: Hardware-aware automated quantization with mixed precision. In: CVPR (2019)

43. Wang, L., et al.: Exploring sparsity in image super-resolution for efficient inference. In: CVPR (2021)
44. Wang, Z., Bovik, A.C., Sheikh, H.R., Simoncelli, E.P., et al.: Image quality assessment: from error visibility to structural similarity. IEEE TIP **13**(4), 600–612 (2004)
45. Xie, W., Song, D., Xu, C., Xu, C., Zhang, H., Wang, Y.: Learning frequency-aware dynamic network for efficient super-resolution. In: ICCV (2021)
46. Xin, J., Wang, N., Jiang, X., Li, J., Huang, H., Gao, X.: Binarized neural network for single image super resolution. In: Vedaldi, A., Bischof, H., Brox, T., Frahm, J.-M. (eds.) ECCV 2020. LNCS, vol. 12349, pp. 91–107. Springer, Cham (2020). https://doi.org/10.1007/978-3-030-58548-8_6
47. Yang, L., Jin, Q.: Fracbits: Mixed precision quantization via fractional bit-widths. In: AAAI (2021)
48. Yu, K., Wang, X., Dong, C., Tang, X., Loy, C.C.: Path-restore: learning network path selection for image restoration. IEEE TPAMI (2021)
49. Zhang, Y., Li, K., Li, K., Wang, L., Zhong, B., Fu, Y.: Image super-resolution using very deep residual channel attention networks. In: Ferrari, V., Hebert, M., Sminchisescu, C., Weiss, Y. (eds.) ECCV 2018. LNCS, vol. 11211, pp. 294–310. Springer, Cham (2018). https://doi.org/10.1007/978-3-030-01234-2_18
50. Zhang, Y., Tian, Y., Kong, Y., Zhong, B., Fu, Y.: Residual dense network for image super-resolution. In: CVPR (2018)
51. Zhou, S., Wu, Y., Ni, Z., Zhou, X., Wen, H., Zou, Y.: DoReFa-Net: Training low bitwidth convolutional neural networks with low bitwidth gradients. arXiv preprint arXiv:1606.06160 (2016)
52. Zhuang, B., Shen, C., Tan, M., Liu, L., Reid, I.: Towards effective low-bitwidth convolutional neural networks. In: CVPR (2018)

Deep Semantic Statistics Matching (D2SM) Denoising Network

Kangfu Mei[1,2], Vishal M. Patel[1], and Rui Huang[2]

[1] Johns Hopkins University, Baltimore, USA
{kmei1,vpatel36}@jhu.edu
[2] The Chinese University of Hong Kong, Shenzhen, China
ruihuang@cuhk.edu.cn
https://kfmei.page/d2sm

Abstract. The ultimate aim of image restoration like denoising is to find an exact correlation between the noisy and clear image domains. But the optimization of end-to-end denoising learning like pixel-wise losses is performed in a sample-to-sample manner, which ignores the intrinsic correlation of images, especially semantics. In this paper, we introduce the Deep Semantic Statistics Matching (D2SM) Denoising Network. It exploits semantic features of pretrained classification networks, then it implicitly matches the probabilistic distribution of clear images at the semantic feature space. By learning to preserve the semantic distribution of denoised images, we empirically find our method significantly improves the denoising capabilities of networks, and the denoised results can be better understood by high-level vision tasks. Comprehensive experiments conducted on the noisy Cityscapes dataset demonstrate the superiority of our method on both the denoising performance and semantic segmentation accuracy. Moreover, the performance improvement observed on our extended tasks including super-resolution and dehazing experiments shows its potentiality as a new general plug-and-play component.

Keywords: Denoising · Semantic segmentation · Super-resolution · Dehazing · Implicit modeling · Score matching

1 Introduction

Deep learning based methods [9,24,62] have achieved a dramatic leap in the performance of various image restoration tasks. Typically, they employ a Convolutional Neural Network (CNN) on a set of image pairs, consisting of degraded images and corresponding clear images, for restoration learning. By maximizing the correspondence between each pair of the CNN-restored results and the clear image, the CNN is trained to map images from the degraded domain into the clear domain. However, blur issues always existed in such a manner. Recent

Supplementary Information The online version contains supplementary material available at https://doi.org/10.1007/978-3-031-20071-7_23.

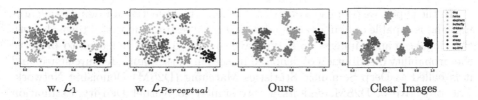

w. $\mathcal{L}_1$ w. $\mathcal{L}_{Perceptual}$ Ours   Clear Images

Fig. 1. t-SNE of Denoised Images in the Semantic Feature Space By exploiting t-SNE [34] to reduce dimensions of semantic features and project them into 2D coordinates, we visualize the distributions of denoised animal images in the semantic feature space. Ours preserves most semantics as the clear images.

work [17] called perceptual loss finds that maximizing the correspondence in the semantic feature space of pre-trained large-scale classification network (*e.g.*, VGG [50] network trained on ImageNet [8]) leads to better visual quality [35,63]. A more widely used strategy inspired by GANs [12], which employs a discriminator to implicitly enforce the distribution of restored images to be consistent with the distribution of clear images in terms of KL- and JS- divergence, can largely improve the perceptual quality of restored images. But the training procedure is often unstable, mostly because the objective is a zero-sum non-cooperative game that cannot be easily solved. Thus, it is straightforward to wonder whether it is possible to combine the pre-trained large-scale networks in an adversarial or statistical manner to bypass their drawbacks and avail their advantages together?

To answer the above question, we first look at the training procedure from a probabilistic view in the semantic feature space (the space of extracted semantic features of each images), which contains many clusters of different semantics. Figure 1 visualizes these clusters with t-SNE [34] in animals images selected from ImageNet [8]. An image that belongs to a specific cluster and owns intrinsic semantics is called Single-Semantic Image in this paper. For example, animal images are single-semantic images, because they have common semantics of species, even though individual animals with the same specie look different. Intuitively, restored single-semantic images should preserve the same distribution as the corresponding clear single-semantic images in the semantic feature space. However, the objectives of existed methods for denoising learning cannot preserve this, as w.$\mathcal{L}_1$ and w.$\mathcal{L}_{Perceptual}$ show in Fig. 1. Therefore, we argue that minimizing the divergence between the probability distributions estimated in the restored domain and the one estimated in the clear domain should be a potential promising solution. Similar idea is also validated by MMDGAN [22] and its variants for generating face and bedroom images, but the idea is rarely researched in the restoration literature.

Different from the single-semantic image, natural images like a cityscape image often consists of multiple objects, and can not be easily identified by a single semantic, here it is called Complex-Semantic image. The semantic feature extracted from such an image may not belong to any simple semantic clusters, but resides on an extremely complicated manifold in the semantic space. For example, cityscape images usually consist of objects/regions of different semantics like *road*, *sidewalk*, and *building*, as classified by the Cityscapes dataset [7]. To approximate and compare the probability distributions of complex-semantic images is nontrivial due to their unique intrinsic uncertainty of semantics.

In the paper, we propose a new distribution-wise objective for denoising learning, and is capable of being extended into general restoration tasks, towards both the single-semantic images and complex-semantic images. It learns to preserve the probability distribution of denoised images in the semantic feature space, and it is called as Deep Semantic Statistics Matching (D2SM) Denoising Network. The objective of D2SM exploits a way similar to Kernel Density Estimation (KDE) [47] to implicitly estimate the probability distributions of semantic features from a set of denoised images and clear images, and then Kullback-Leibler (KL) divergence between two distributions is used as the objective. Here, one of our major novelty comes from the way of density estimation, where we model the probability distributions based on internal patches from a single complex-semantic image or multiple single-semantic images. The way of availing internal patches tends to be more appropriate than modeling the distribution of multiple complex-semantic images. Such a phenomenon is also proved in recent work [66] suggests that the internal visual entropy of a single image is much smaller than multiple images. Therefore, we propose to use the divergence of patch distributions to guide the learning, called Patch-Wise Internal Probability.

Nevertheless, statistically estimating the density of patches conducted in a single mini-batch usually requires a great large number of samples. To maintain the trade-off between the computational cost and accuracy, another major novelty of the paper, called Memorized Historic Sampling, is proposed, inspired by recent contrastive learning related works [14,60]. By simply leveraging the statistics among the mini-batch and memorized historic mini-batch in queues, we demonstrate that D2SM significantly outperforms the same network backbone with perceptual loss and other state-of-the-art objectives, without additional information or parameters. Empirical evaluation validates that D2SM largely improves not only the effectiveness of denoising, but also super-resolution and dehazing, and hence it should be able to be generally applied to different tasks and network architectures.

Our Contributions are Therefore Three-Fold:

(i) We propose D2SM for image denoising learning, which minimizes the distribution divergence instead of the sample-to-sample distance in the semantic feature space. (ii) D2SM is adapted to complex-semantic images in a patch-wise manner, which can decompose complex semantics in natural images for efficient distribution approximation. (iii) Extensive experiments are conducted to demonstrate that D2SM substantially outperforms the original perceptual loss and other state-of-the-art losses, without modifying the network architecture or accessing the additional data. The superior accuracy in high-level vision tasks further validates that D2SM indeed transfers semantics for restoration.

2   Related Work

Resulted by the emergence of deep neural networks, recent CNN based methods have led to a dramatic leap in image restoration. Among them, most works utilize the pixel-wise similarity metrics as their objective, $e.g.$, $\mathcal{L}_1$ and $\mathcal{L}_{MSE}$. Though higher performance in metrics like PSNR or SSIM [59] is achieved by using these loss functions, recent work [63] finds that these metrics do not reflect human perceptual preferences. In contrast, results generated by CNNs trained with the perceptual objective are more closely correlated with the human judgment [35]. These methods measure the similarity of two images in the pre-trained high-level vision networks, usually VGG classification network [50] trained in ImageNet [8]. Different perceptual objectives have been proposed in this category, $e.g.$, $\mathcal{L}_{MSE}$ of features [11,17,20,38,58,63], contextual objective [35,36], and semantic label [27,28]. However, these methods lack a reasonable explanation of the effectiveness led by the perceptual objective [63]. Furthermore, the frozen network pre-trained on certain datasets, $e.g.$, ImageNet, is not appropriate for the image restoration tasks conducted on the large-scale, diverse natural image datasets [1] or specific semantic image datasets [7,19,32]. Here we hypothesize that these issues come from the objectives that estimate the sample-to-sample distance in the feature space. By exploiting the characteristics of single-semantic patches from natural images, which can be associated with an embedded manifold, we implicitly measure the divergence of the probability distributions estimated from restored images and clear images in the semantic feature space, and we use it as the objective to bypass the above issues.

Similar ideas that minimize the distribution divergence instead of the sample-to-sample distance have been proposed before. In the area of image restoration, Contextual loss [35,36] that proposed for misaligned image transformation implicitly minimizes the divergence between restored images and clear images. It approximates the divergence by the contextual relationships within patches from a single image ($i.e.$ single image statistics [66]), and hence enables image-to-image translation to be conducted on the misaligned image pairs. However, its performance is usually limited by the low accuracy of feature matching [64] and leads to worse restoration performance in aligned image restoration learning. More similar works that avail statistical features are GMMN [26] and GFMN [46]. They achieve the generative ability without adversarial learning in the problematic min/max game. Nevertheless, they are not designed for the image restoration learning that majorly consists of natural images with diverse appearance, and the desired superiority cannot be gained here. In the area of domain adaption, minimizing the statistics feature difference of the high-level vision networks can help networks adapt to unseen domain directly, like CORAL [51] and MMD [53]. However, these methods require semantic labels, which is not practical in the real-world image restoration datasets. By exploiting the internal statistics [66] of natural images, our proposed method successfully facilitates the restoration learning through more accurate divergence approximation.

3 Method

Let $\mathcal{X} \subset \mathbb{R}^{H \times W \times C}$ denotes the domain of degraded images caused by factors like noising, and $\mathcal{Y} \subset \mathbb{R}^{H \times W \times C}$ denotes the domain of corresponding clear images.

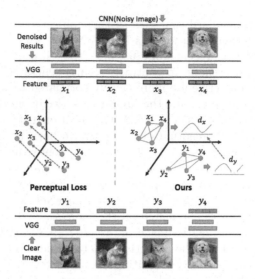

Fig. 2. Perceptual loss vs. Ours. We minimize the distribution divergence between a set of restored images and the corresponding clear images, instead of the sample-to-sample distance, in the semantic feature space (*e.g.* the penultimate layer of VGG). This procedure better simplifies the restoration learning and ameliorates underfitting compared with the perceptual loss.

We wish to restore $x \in \mathcal{X}$ to appear like its corresponding target image $y \in \mathcal{Y}$ by using a denoising network $G(\cdot)$ that outputs $\tilde{y} = G(x)$. To force the outputs $\tilde{y}$ maintains as much the perceptual detail as possible, recent works [11,17,20,35, 36] exploit the pre-trained high-level vision networks (*e.g.*, the intermediate layer of VGG), denoted as $\Phi(\cdot)$, to guide the restoration learning by minimizing the similarity between $\tilde{y}$ and y in the feature space of $\Phi(*)$. This can be formulated as the objective with the similarity metric $D(\cdot)$:

$$\mathcal{L}(x, y, G) = D(\Phi(y), \Phi(G(x))). \tag{1}$$

In practical, the similarity metric $D(\cdot)$ is usually implemented by Mean Square Error (MSE) or Contextual Distance [36].

Contrastively, we take the denoising learning as minimizing the divergence of probability distributions estimated by denoised images and clear images in the semantic feature space. Given N samples of image pairs that consist of $T_x = \{x_1, x_2, \ldots, x_N\}$ and $T_y = \{y_1, y_2, \ldots, y_N\}$, we incorporate the mutual information [54] of them in the feature space of $\Phi(G(\cdot))$ into the restoration learning. Such a manner is empirically proven to be effective to facilitate knowledge transferring [5,31,40–43,55]. By minimizing the divergence of the estimated probability distribution between samples T_x in $\Phi(G(\cdot))$ and T_y in $\Phi(\cdot)$, denoted as $\mathcal{G}'$ and $\mathcal{G}$, we force $G(\cdot)$ to better maintain the geometry of the feature space $\Phi(\cdot)$ estimated in the clear image domain $\mathcal{Y}$. In doing so, we formulate the final objective as

$$\mathcal{L}(T_x, T_y, G) = \sum_{i=1}^{N} \sum_{j=1, j\neq i}^{N} g'_{j|i} \log(\frac{g'_{j|i}}{g_{j|i}}). \tag{2}$$

To elaborate, we will detail the divergence approximation in Sect. 3.1, and the sampling strategy in Sect. 3.2 and Sect. 3.3.

3.1   Probability Distribution Divergence

Here we model the correlation of samples from the same domain in the semantic feature space as the probability distribution. Several methods have been proposed for modeling the correlation, including, but not limited to, probabilistic based [41,42], embedding based [5,43], graph based [31], and more [40]. In this work, we exploit the kernel density estimation to estimate the probability distribution of samples in the semantic feature space, which describes the probability of each sample to select its neighbors [34]. It is empirically proven to be effective for describing the geometry of feature space by Passalis et al. [41,42]. To elaborate, we denote the probability distribution between any two samples i, j from the clear domain as $g_{i|j}$ and the restored domain as $g'_{i|j}$. Based on the extracted feature f^x and f^y from $\Phi(G(\cdot)))$ and $\Phi(\cdot)$, the probability distributions are estimated by:

$$g'_{i|j} = \frac{K_{cosine}(f_i^x, f_j^x)}{\sum_{k=1, k\neq j}^{N} K_{cosine}(f_k^x, f_j^x)} \in [0, 1], \tag{3}$$

and

$$g_{i|j} = \frac{K_{cosine}(f_i^y, f_j^y)}{\sum_{k=1, k\neq j}^{N} K_{cosine}(f_k^y, f_j^y)} \in [0, 1], \tag{4}$$

where the cosine kernel function K_{cosine} is employed for estimating the probabilty distribution, formulated with two vectors a and b as:

$$K_{cosine}(a, b) = \frac{1}{2}(\frac{a^\top b}{||a||_2 ||b||_2} + 1) \in [0, 1]. \tag{5}$$

As Turlach et al. [56] suggested, this kernel function avoids the bandwidth choosing in Gaussian kernel, and it boosts performance compared with the Euclidean measures as Wang et al. [57] suggested.

To minimize the difference of two estimated probability distributions, we avail the Kullback-Leibler (KL) divergence as the similarity metric, formulated as:

$$D_{KL}(\mathcal{G}'||\mathcal{G}) = \int_t \mathcal{G}'(\mathbf{t}_x) \log \frac{\mathcal{G}'(\mathbf{t}_x)}{\mathcal{G}(\mathbf{t}_y)} d\mathbf{t}. \tag{6}$$

where $\mathbf{t}_x \in \mathcal{X}$ and $\mathbf{t}_y \in \mathcal{Y}$. In practical implementation, we avail the mini-batch that consists of N samples for approximation, aiming for acceleration in a parallel fashion.

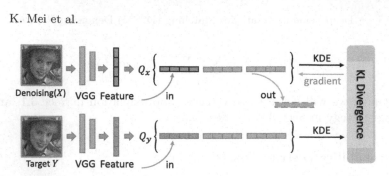

Fig. 3. Sampling with Historic Gradients. We approximate the divergence with historic sampling by using two queues to bypass the GPU memory limits.

3.2 Memorized Historic Sampling

Intuitively, the number of selected samples in a mini-batch should be as large as possible during training. However, in practical implementation, increasing the number of samples is greatly limited by the GPU memory. Such a limitation is more serious in the extracted semantic feature space, and hence greatly limits the effectiveness of our method.

To bypass the limitation, we introduce a Memorized Historic Sampling strategy, visualized in Fig. 3. It maintains two *queues* of feature samples, *i.e.*, $Q^{\mathcal{X}}$ and $Q^{\mathcal{Y}}$ that can store historic features from previous mini-batches with limited GPU memory cost. In doing so, we can estimate the probability distributions among queues instead of mini-batches. Therefore, it allows a larger number of samples and a relatively smaller mini-batch used at runtime. The queue is updated according to the First-In-First-Out rule, which enforces the historical samples in the queue are always newest, and hence it allows the probability distribution to be more consistent with the immediate state. Based on such a strategy, we can formulate Eq. 3 as below:

$$g'_{i|j} = \frac{K_{cosine}(Q_i^{\mathcal{X}}, Q_j^{\mathcal{X}})}{\sum_{k=1, k \neq j}^{q} K_{cosine}(Q_k^{\mathcal{X}}, Q_j^{\mathcal{X}})} \in [0, 1], \tag{7}$$

and

$$Q_{1...N}^{\mathcal{X}}, Q_{N...q}^{\mathcal{X}} \leftarrow f_{\{1...N\}}^x, Q_{\{1...q-N\}}^{\mathcal{X}}. \tag{8}$$

where q is the queue size of the applied queue for extracted features f_x from a single mini-batch with the number of N, and $q \gg N$.

For example, the maximum size of a mini-batch can only be 32 in a single GPU card with a memory of 12 GB, but the number of samples is usually set as 128 to ensure the accuracy of the estimation, which is not practical in a single GPU. By using the queue in the size of 128, we can directly use the current mini-batch with features from 3 historical memorized mini-batch to perform an estimation with 128 samples, while without using additional 12×3 GB memory at running time. It is because the queue that saves historical features costs less GPU memory compared with the procedure of feature extraction. Similar strategies for enlarging the number of samples also exist, *e.g.*, memory

Fig. 4. Sampling with Internal Patches. Patches cropped from a single image may consist of different semantic objects that showed in different appearances.

bank [60] and momentum encoder [14]. Compared with them, our memorized historic queue is simpler but also enlarges the maximum number of samples to be used without additional GPU memory. In the supplement we provide discussion about the effects of different queue sizes.

3.3 Patch-Wise Internal Probabilities

The most straightforward way to construct samples for the mini-batch is to randomly choose multiple images from the domains $\mathcal{X}$ and $\mathcal{Y}$, respectively. Even though it is elegant, it fails to exploit another crucial probability in the single image, *i.e.*, internal probability of patches from a single image, or internal statistics, which has been widely employed and empirically evaluated in many image restoration tasks [39,48,49,66]. As illustrated in Fig. 4, we can notice that the cropped patches from the single image, specifically the complex-semantic image, can be seen as multiple single-semantic images. In addition, the probability estimated on multiple complex-semantic images is not always accurate in some cases, *e.g.*, the denoising learning [62] in mixed noise levels. In such a case, conventional sampling results in an inaccurate estimation, because the restored images in the mini-batch come from different noisy levels. These restored images distribute in different manifolds in the semantic feature space. In contrast, by extracting patches from a single image resulted from extreme similar degradation, their similarity allows the probabilities to be accurately estimated.

In our method, a sliding window in a spatial size of $K \times K$ is availed to extract patches from the restored image $\tilde{Y}$ and clear image Y. These patches are then inputted into the high-level vision network $\Phi(\cdot)$ as a single mini-batch and transformed into feature sets, which can be formulated as:

$$f^x = \Phi(\text{sliding\_window}(\tilde{Y})). \tag{9}$$

Then we exploit Eq. 7 to estimate the probability distribution in the feature sets respectively for divergence approximation. In the empirical evaluation, shown in

Table 1, though the vanilla version achieves gains on the restoration performance, the generated images contain less semantic details (lower MIoU performance). This decreasing may boil down to incorrect probability estimation. In contrast, with the help of internal probability, our restoration network achieves a performance leap in both the restoration and semantic evaluation.

4 Experiments

Different from conventional denoising works, we focus on not only the restoration performance, but also the semantic accuracy, *i.e.*, how the denoised images can be understood by semantic segmentation networks, as well as whether the method can be extended into the other restoration tasks. Such a similar evaluation protocol is also employed in recent restoration works [21,23,52]. Therefore, our experiments are divided into three parts, including *Cityscape Denoising and Segmentation* [7], *Face Super-resolution and Alignment* [32], and *Natural Image Restoration* [2]. More details please refer to the supplemental.

4.1 Cityscape Denoising and Segmentation

To demonstrate the superiority of our method, we conduct complementary denoising and segmentation experiments on the Cityscapes dataset. The most representative denoising network, *i.e.*, FFDNet [62], as well as the state-of-the-art denoising networks, *i.e.*, CBDNet [13] and SADNet [4] are availed as the generation network $G(\cdot)$. Various objectives are applied, *i.e.*, $\mathcal{L}_1$, $\mathcal{L}_{SSIM}$ [59], $\mathcal{L}_{Perceptual}$ [17], $\mathcal{L}_{LPIPS}$ [63], $\mathcal{L}_{Contextual}$ [36], $\mathcal{L}_{CrossEntropy}$ [28], and ours. Notably, $\mathcal{L}_{CrossEntropy}$ is conducted with the HRNet48 that pre-trained on the Cityscapes dataset, which requires semantic labels during the denoising learning. In contrast, ours does not need any additional data. We then modify the original loss function of CBDNet and SADNet, *i.e.*, $\mathcal{L}_2 + \mathcal{L}_{Asymmetric} + \mathcal{L}_{TV}$ and $\mathcal{L}_2$, by attaching our proposed objective. For convenience, we set the size of the sliding window K as 224 and its stride as 56.

For denoising training, we construct noisy images by adding additive color Gaussian noise of noise level $\sigma \in [0, 75]$ to the clean images from the Cityscapes training set. The images are randomly cropped into 512×512 patches in a mini-batch size of 64. Other settings are kept the same as the settings in FFDNet. For evaluation, we first measure appearance similarities between restored images and corresponding clear images in the Cityscapes validation set, in noisy levels $\{25, 35, 50\}$, which is commonly selected by the denoising community. We then measure the semantic segmentation accuracy on restored images in the term of Mean Intersection-over-Union (MIoU) in 19 pre-defined semantic classes, i.e., *road, sidewalk, building, wall, fence, pole, traffic light, traffic sign, vegetation, terrain, sky, person, rider, car, truck, bus, train, motorcycle,* and *bicycle.*

Quantitative Comparison. In Table 1, it is easy to see that ours outperforms all compared objectives largely in PSNR, SSIM, and MIoU metrics on all noisy levels, when applied in the same backbone. Compared with the state-of-the-art

Table 1. Quantitative performance comparison on the cityscape denoising and segmentation. The comprasion is conducted with various state-of-the-art denoising objectives and ours on the representative denoising networks.

Method (Backbone)	Objective	Noise-Level $\sigma = 25$			Noise-Level $\sigma = 35$			Noise-Level $\sigma = 50$		
		PSNR ↑	SSIM ↑	MIoU (%) ↑	PSNR ↑	SSIM ↑	MIoU (%) ↑	PSNR ↑	SSIM ↑	MIoU (%) ↑
FFDNet [62]	$\mathcal{L}_1$	35.033[6]	0.925[6]	0.605[8]	34.074[6]	0.912[6]	0.537[8]	32.845[6]	0.895[6]	0.451[7]
	$+ \mathcal{L}_{SSIM}$ [59]	35.567[3]	0.935[2]	0.642[2]	34.469[4]	0.922[2]	0.584[2]	33.180[3]	0.906[2]	0.450[8]
	$+ \mathcal{L}_{Perceptual}$ [17]	34.319[7]	0.912[7]	0.629[4]	33.486[7]	0.899[7]	0.582[4]	32.383[7]	0.881[7]	0.509[2]
	$+ \mathcal{L}_{LPIPS}$ [63]	35.551[4]	0.929[4]	0.613[6]	34.463[5]	0.916[4]	0.541[7]	33.138[5]	0.899[4]	0.452[6]
	$+ \mathcal{L}_{Contextual}$ [36]	25.115[8]	0.762[8]	0.628[5]	24.938[8]	0.758[8]	0.583[3]	24.775[8]	0.753[8]	0.509[2]
	$+ \mathcal{L}_{CrossEntropy}$ [28]	35.913[2]	0.932[3]	0.630[3]	34.800[2]	0.919[3]	0.565[5]	33.477[2]	0.903[3]	0.491[4]
D2SM (Ours)	w/o. Internal	35.543[5]	0.929[4]	0.612[7]	34.475[3]	0.916[4]	0.546[6]	33.167[4]	0.899[4]	0.463[5]
	w/. Internal	**36.454**[1]	**0.936**[1]	**0.644**[1]	**35.206**[1]	**0.923**[1]	**0.587**[1]	**33.807**[1]	**0.907**[1]	**0.520**[1]
CBDNet [13]	-	36.152[3]	0.936[3]	0.655[3]	34.964[3]	0.923[3]	0.599[3]	33.613[3]	0.907[3]	0.539[3]
	w/o. Internal	36.254[2]	0.935[3]	0.679[2]	35.156[2]	0.925[2]	0.631[2]	33.904[2]	0.911[2]	0.550[2]
	w/. Internal	**36.899**[1]	**0.941**[1]	**0.691**[1]	**35.596**[1]	**0.929**[1]	**0.652**[1]	**34.172**[1]	**0.914**[1]	**0.600**[1]
SADNet [4]	-	36.310[3]	0.936[3]	0.674[3]	35.081[3]	0.924[2]	0.637[3]	33.730[3]	0.908[3]	0.581[3]
	w/o. Internal	36.822[2]	0.940[2]	0.691[2]	35.247[2]	0.924[2]	0.655[2]	34.133[2]	0.912[2]	0.600[2]
	w/. Internal	**37.130**[1]	**0.943**[1]	**0.701**[1]	**35.839**[1]	**0.931**[1]	**0.670**[1]	**34.440**[1]	**0.916**[1]	**0.634**[1]

objectives that combine high-level vision tasks, *i.e.*, $\mathcal{L}_{CrossEntropy}$ [28], which requires the semantic label of images during training, ours still outperforms it by 0.542 dB in PSNR, 1.4% in MIoU, without using any additional data. Besides, ours shows strong robustness when adopted with different network architectures and objectives, *e.g.*, it helps the original CBDNet improves 0.747dB in PSNR and 0.5% in MIoU. Also, the comparison between using and without using internal probability further demonstrates its superiority for complex-semantic images.

Qualitative Comparison. Though $\mathcal{L}_{Perceptual}$ applied in restoration methods has been proven to lead to better perceptual quality in restored images, we find that ours significantly outperforms it with more visually pleasant and exact details as shown in Fig. 5. As shown in Fig. 6, our restored results best preserve the edge of the character "**S**" in the red rectangle area. Besides, the blue rectangle area shows the best sharp details in our restored results compared with others. With regard to the segmentation evaluation, restored results from restoration networks trained with ours can best be segmented accurately. For instance, as two green rectangle areas are shown in the Fig. 6, our result is the only one that is successfully recognized into *traffic light*. This indicates that ours can best preserve semantic details during restoration in the way of divergence minimization.

Distribution Visualization. In order to get insights into the probability distribution, here we visualize the semantic feature space estimated by restored images and clear images. To elaborate, we randomly select 500 animal images that belong to 10 categories, *i.e.*, *cat, dog, chicken, cow, horse, sheep, squirrel, elephant, butterfly*, and *spider*. We then process their noisy version (*i.e.* adding additive color Gaussian noise of noise level $\sigma = 25$) with the FFDNet pre-trained on the noisy Cityscapes dataset. After that, the denoised images, as well as the clear images, are inputted into the pre-trained ResNet101 [16] to extract semantic feature maps. As such, we can visualize the distribution of semantic features with the t-SNE [34] in 2D coordinates. Compared with others, the visualized dis-

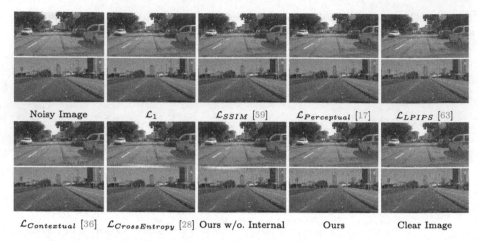

Noisy Image $\mathcal{L}_1$ $\mathcal{L}_{SSIM}$ [59] $\mathcal{L}_{Perceptual}$ [17] $\mathcal{L}_{LPIPS}$ [63]

$\mathcal{L}_{Contextual}$ [36] $\mathcal{L}_{CrossEntropy}$ [28]   Ours w/o. Internal   Ours   Clear Image

Fig. 5. Qualitative comparison on the denoising results. Ours results contain the most fine-grained high-frequency information and more visual pleasant details. (400% Zoom is recommended to see their difference in details and color bias.)

tribution from our restored images best preserves the distribution of clear images in the semantic feature space. This indicates that our proposed method indeed implicitly minimizes the probability distribution divergence between restored images and clear images in the semantic feature space.

4.2   Face Super-Resolution and Alignment

Here we extend D2SM with historic sampling as the objective and conduct face super-resolution learning under the settings of DICNet [33]. For the evaluation of high-level vision applications, we exploit the face alignment as a measurement, and its accuracy is denoted in the term of NRMSE. The queue size is set as 256 and the mini-batch size is 32, which means the probability is estimated among 32 face images instead interal patches.

In Table 2, we show the quantitative performance comparison between DIC-Net and ours, as well as the other state-of-the-art methods. Notably, the face alignment network is pre-trained on the CelebA dataset, and hence its evaluation on the Helen dataset is generally not good enough, which can only be used for reference. By combining our objective with existing $\mathcal{L}_1$ and $\mathcal{L}_{Alignment}$ proposed by DICNet, our modified version successfully outperforms the original DICNet and DICNet in the GAN manner (DICGAN), in both the distortion measurement and alignment measurement. In contrast, the original DICNet can only achieve leading performance in the distortion measurement but is poor in alignment measurement, while the DICGAN can only achieve leading performance in the alignment measurement but is bad at distortion measurement.

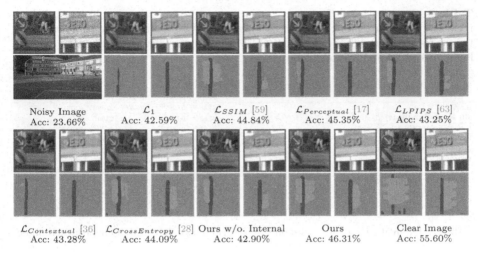

Noisy Image $\mathcal{L}_1$ $\mathcal{L}_{SSIM}$ [59] $\mathcal{L}_{Perceptual}$ [17] $\mathcal{L}_{LPIPS}$ [63]
Acc: 23.66%   Acc: 42.59%   Acc: 44.84%   Acc: 45.35%   Acc: 43.25%

$\mathcal{L}_{Contextual}$ [36] $\mathcal{L}_{CrossEntropy}$ [28]   Ours w/o. Internal   Ours   Clear Image
Acc: 43.28%   Acc: 44.09%   Acc: 42.90%   Acc: 46.31%   Acc: 55.60%

Fig. 6. Qualitative comparison on the denoising and segmentation results. Ours preserves most of the semantic details, including the human shape and font edge in the highlighted area. Additionally, in the shown segmentation results, our result is the only one that can be successfully recognized into *traffic light*.

4.3 Natural Image Restoration

Different from cityscape images collected from limited scenes, natural images contain more diverse and complex semantics. Therefore, the intrinsic semantics of natural images are more complex and diverse, which indicate a more challenging probability distribution estimation for our method. To validate our effectiveness in such cases, here we follow the settings of the state-of-the-art dehazing method, *i.e.*, MSBDN-DFF [10] on the end-to-end dehazing tasks [37], and we extend the dehazing network with our proposed objective. As the quantitative performance comparison shown in Table 3, though the density estimation is challenging, our method can successfully outperform the compared method in both the indoor scenes and outdoor scenes without additional cost. In Fig. 7, we show some randomly highlighted visual results for comparison, and all of our results contain the most clear appearance with less haze remained. Specifically, we can notice that objects, *e.g.*, *floor*, *chair*, *roof*, *toy* that contain certain semantics, are better restored with accurate color than the method trained with pixel-wise loss functions only. This phenomenon further demonstrates the semantics transferring ability of our method, which regularizes restored objects to be semantic consistent and avoids incorrect color that against its semantics.

5 Discussion

Designing Choice of KL Divergence. The way of the divergence estimation between $\mathcal{G}'$ and $\mathcal{G}$ accounts a lot in our method. We empirically employed the Kullback-Leibler (KL) divergence weighted by $\mathcal{G}'$ for D2SM. Indeed, there are

Table 2. Quantitative performance comparison on the face super-resolution and alignment. By simply attaching our objective into the DICNet, our method can outperform the state-of-the-art DICNet and DICGAN in both the distortion measurement and high-level vision application measurement.

Method (Backbone)	Objective	CelebA dataset			Helen dataset		
		PSNR ↑	SSIM ↑	NRMSE ↓	PSNR ↑	SSIM ↑	NRMSE ↓
Bicubic	-	$23.58^{(10)}$	$0.6285^{(10)}$	$0.3385^{(8)}$	$23.89^{(10)}$	$0.6751^{(10)}$	$0.4577^{(8)}*$
SRResNet [20] [CVPR-17]	$\mathcal{L}_2$	$25.82^{(6)}$	$0.7369^{(6)}$	-	$25.30^{(6)}$	$0.7297^{(7)}$	-
URDGN [61] [ECCV-16]	$\mathcal{L}_2 + \mathcal{L}_{GAN}$	$24.63^{(8)}$	$0.6851^{(9)}$	-	$24.22^{(9)}$	$0.6909^{(9)}$	-
RDN [65] [ECCV-18]	$\mathcal{L}_1$	$26.13^{(5)}$	$0.7412^{(5)}$	$0.1415^{(4)}$	$25.34^{(5)}$	$0.7249^{(8)}$	$0.4437^{(7)}*$
PFSR [18] [BMVC-18]	$\mathcal{L}_2 + \mathcal{L}_{Perceptual} + \mathcal{L}_{GAN} + \mathcal{L}_{Heatmap} + \mathcal{L}_{Attention}$	$24.43^{(9)}$	$0.6991^{(8)}$	$0.1917^{(7)}$	$24.73^{(8)}$	$0.7323^{(6)}$	$0.3498^{(4)}*$
FSRNet [6] [CVPR-18]	$\mathcal{L}_0 + \mathcal{L}_{Perceptual}$	$26.48^{(3)}$	$0.7718^{(3)}$	$0.1430^{(5)}$	$25.90^{(4)}$	$0.7759^{(3)}$	$0.3723^{(6)}*$
	$\mathcal{L}_2 + \mathcal{L}_{Perceptual} + \mathcal{L}_{GAN}$	$25.06^{(7)}$	$0.7311^{(7)}$	$0.1463^{(6)}$	$24.39^{(7)}$	$0.7191^{(5)}$	$0.3408^{(3)}*$
DICNet [33] [CVPR-20]	$\mathcal{L}_1 + \mathcal{L}_{Alignment}$	$27.28^{(2)}$	$0.7929^{(2)}$	$0.1345^{(3)}$	$26.69^{(2)}$	$0.7933^{(2)}$	$0.3674^{(5)}*$
	$\mathcal{L}_1 + \mathcal{L}_{Alignment} + \mathcal{L}_{Perceptual} + \mathcal{L}_{GAN}$	$26.34^{(4)}$	$0.7562^{(4)}$	$0.1319^{(2)}$	$25.96^{(3)}$	$0.7624^{(4)}$	$\mathbf{0.3336}^{(1)}*$
Ours	w/o. Internal	$\mathbf{27.39}^{(1)}$	$\mathbf{0.7973}^{(1)}$	$\mathbf{0.1292}^{(1)}$	$\mathbf{26.94}^{(1)}$	$\mathbf{0.8005}^{(1)}$	$0.3366^{(2)}*$

Table 3. Quantitative comparison on the natural image dehazing. Our proposed objective is capable of being extended to the dehazing task based on MSBDN-DFF, which shows superiority in both the indoor and outdoor datasets.

Method	Metric	DCP [15]	MSCNN [44]	DcGAN [25]	GFN [45]	PFFNet [37]	GDN [29]	DuRN [30]	MSBDN-DFF [10]	Ours
I-HAZE	PSNR↑	$14.43^{(9)}$	$15.22^{(8)}$	$16.06^{(5)}$	$15.84^{(7)}$	$16.01^{(6)}$	$16.62^{(4)}$	$21.23^{(3)}$	$23.93^{(2)}$	$\mathbf{24.31}^{(1)}$
	SSIM↑	$0.752^{(6)}$	$0.755^{(5)}$	$0.733^{(9)}$	$0.751^{(7)}$	$0.740^{(8)}$	$0.787^{(4)}$	$0.842^{(3)}$	$0.891^{(2)}$	$\mathbf{0.902}^{(1)}$
O-HAZE	PSNR↑	$16.78^{(9)}$	$17.56^{(8)}$	$19.34^{(4)}$	$18.16^{(7)}$	$18.76^{(6)}$	$18.92^{(5)}$	$20.45^{(3)}$	$24.36^{(2)}$	$\mathbf{24.79}^{(1)}$
	SSIM↑	$0.653^{(8)}$	$0.650^{(9)}$	$0.681^{(4)}$	$0.671^{(6)}$	$0.669^{(7)}$	$0.672^{(5)}$	$0.688^{(3)}$	$0.749^{(2)}$	$\mathbf{0.787}^{(1)}$

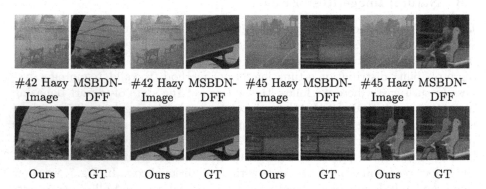

#42 Hazy MSBDN-   #42 Hazy MSBDN-   #45 Hazy MSBDN-   #45 Hazy MSBDN-
Image   DFF   Image   DFF   Image   DFF   Image   DFF

Ours   GT   Ours   GT   Ours   GT   Ours   GT

Fig. 7. Qualitative comparison on the real-world dehazing. Compared with the SOTA method that employs pixel-wise loss functions, our extended version better recover the scenes under severe ill-posed distortion.

some other ways to estimate the divergence. The most similar one, *i.e.*, inverse KL divergence weighted by $\mathcal{G}$, which is also asymmetrical. Based on KL divergence, another way to estimate the divergence is Jensen-Shannon divergence, which is symmetric and can be seen as the smoothed version of KL divergence, formulated as:

$$D_{JS}(\mathcal{G}'||\mathcal{G}) = \frac{1}{2}D_{KL}(\mathcal{G}'||\mathcal{G}) + \frac{1}{2}D_{KL}(\mathcal{G}||\mathcal{G}'). \tag{10}$$

Table 4. Performance comparison with different distribution divergence.

Method	σ	PSNR ↑	SSIM ↑	MIoU (%) ↑
FFDNet	25	35.03	0.925	0.605
$+ \mathcal{L}_{iKLD}$	25	35.97	0.931	0.638
$+ \mathcal{L}_{JSD}$	25	36.31	0.935	0.640
$+ \mathcal{L}_{GAN}$	25	35.55	0.931	0.621
Ours	25	**36.45**	**0.936**	**0.644**

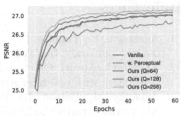

Fig. 8. Convergence visualization between different queue size.

According to [3], the optimization procedure of the optimal discriminator $D*$ in GAN yields minimizing the JS divergence, formulated as:

$$\mathcal{L}(D*, G) = 2D_{JS}(\mathcal{G}'||\mathcal{G}) - 2\log 2. \tag{11}$$

Here we present the quantitative comparison with the three additional divergence estimation or objectives in Cityscapes. The comprasion empirically proves our superiority of using KL-divergence compared with the others in the denoising tasks.

Designing Choice of Queue Size. The convergence curve visualized in the Fig. 8 further demonstrates that our proposed method significantly accelerates convergence with the proposed memorized historic sampling. From the figure we can notice that the applied historic sampling with large queue size ($Q > 64$) can greatly accelerate the learning, while the vanilla version can only achieve poor performance ($Q \leq 64$). Thus, in our practical implementation, we chose the queue size with the possible max value under the computational limitation.

6   Conclusion

We propose a simple but practical method for facilitating the restoration learning and preserving the semantic attribute. It does not rely on any external information nor introduce additional parameters. By implicitly approximating the divergence on the semantic feature space, we can force existed generation networks to learn to preserve semantic attributes during restoration learning. We further transfer the method from the single-semantic image to the complex-semantic image *i.e.* natural image by using internal statistics. Empirically evaluation validates that the proposed method can be adapted to various restoration tasks and network architectures with general performance improvement.

Acknowledgments. This work was supported in part by Shenzhen Science and Technology Program ZDSYS20211021111415025 and JCYJ20190813170601651.

References

1. Agustsson, E., Timofte, R.: Ntire 2017 challenge on single image super-resolution: dataset and study. In: CVPR Workshops (2017)
2. Ancuti, C., Ancuti, C.O., Timofte, R., De Vleeschouwer, C.: I-HAZE: a dehazing benchmark with real hazy and haze-free indoor images. In: ICACIVS (2018)
3. Arjovsky, M., Bottou, L.: Towards principled methods for training generative adversarial networks. arXiv preprint arXiv:1701.04862 (2017)
4. Chang, M., Li, Q., Feng, H., Xu, Z.: Spatial-adaptive network for single image denoising. In: Vedaldi, A., Bischof, H., Brox, T., Frahm, J.-M. (eds.) ECCV 2020. LNCS, vol. 12375, pp. 171–187. Springer, Cham (2020). https://doi.org/10.1007/978-3-030-58577-8_11
5. Chen, H., Wang, Y., Xu, C., Xu, C., Tao, D.: Learning student networks via feature embedding. TNNLS (2020)
6. Chen, Y., Tai, Y., Liu, X., Shen, C., Yang, J.: Fsrnet: end-to-end learning face super-resolution with facial priors. In: CVPR (2018)
7. Cordts, M., et al.: The cityscapes dataset for semantic urban scene understanding. In: CVPR (2016)
8. Deng, J., Dong, W., Socher, R., Li, L.J., Li, K., Fei-Fei, L.: Imagenet: a large-scale hierarchical image database. In: CVPR (2009)
9. Dong, C., Loy, C.C., He, K., Tang, X.: Image super-resolution using deep convolutional networks. TPAMI (2015)
10. Dong, H., Pan, J., Xiang, L., Hu, Z., Zhang, X., Wang, F., Yang, M.H.: Multi-scale boosted dehazing network with dense feature fusion. In: CVPR (2020)
11. Dosovitskiy, A., Brox, T.: Generating images with perceptual similarity metrics based on deep networks. In: NeurIPS (2016)
12. Goodfellow, I.J., et al.: Generative adversarial networks. In: NeurIPS (2014)
13. Guo, S., Yan, Z., Zhang, K., Zuo, W., Zhang, L.: Toward convolutional blind denoising of real photographs. In: CVPR (2019)
14. He, K., Fan, H., Wu, Y., Xie, S., Girshick, R.: Momentum contrast for unsupervised visual representation learning. In: CVPR (2020)
15. He, K., Sun, J., Tang, X.: Single image haze removal using dark channel prior. TPAMI (2010)
16. He, K., Zhang, X., Ren, S., Sun, J.: Deep Residual Learning for Image Recognition. In: CVPR (2016)
17. Johnson, J., Alahi, A., Fei-Fei, L.: Perceptual losses for real-time style transfer and super-resolution. In: Leibe, B., Matas, J., Sebe, N., Welling, M. (eds.) ECCV 2016. LNCS, vol. 9906, pp. 694–711. Springer, Cham (2016). https://doi.org/10.1007/978-3-319-46475-6_43
18. Kim, D., Kim, M., Kwon, G., Kim, D.S.: Progressive face super-resolution via attention to facial landmark. In: BMVC (2019)
19. Le, V., Brandt, J., Lin, Z., Bourdev, L., Huang, T.S.: Interactive facial feature localization. In: Fitzgibbon, A., Lazebnik, S., Perona, P., Sato, Y., Schmid, C. (eds.) ECCV 2012. LNCS, vol. 7574, pp. 679–692. Springer, Heidelberg (2012). https://doi.org/10.1007/978-3-642-33712-3_49
20. Ledig, C., et al.: Photo-realistic single image super-resolution using a generative adversarial network. In: CVPR (2017)
21. Li, B., Peng, X., Wang, Z., Xu, J., Feng, D.: Aod-net: all-in-one dehazing network. In: ICCV (2017)

22. Li, C.L., Chang, W.C., Cheng, Y., Yang, Y., Póczos, B.: Mmd gan: towards deeper understanding of moment matching network. arXiv preprint arXiv:1705.08584 (2017)
23. Li, J., Fang, F., Li, J., Mei, K., Zhang, G.: MDCN: Multi-scale Dense Cross Network for Image Super-Resolution. TCSVT (2020)
24. Li, J., Fang, F., Mei, K., Zhang, G.: Multi-scale residual network for image super-resolution. In: Ferrari, V., Hebert, M., Sminchisescu, C., Weiss, Y. (eds.) ECCV 2018. LNCS, vol. 11212, pp. 527–542. Springer, Cham (2018). https://doi.org/10.1007/978-3-030-01237-3_32
25. Li, R., Pan, J., Li, Z., Tang, J.: Single image dehazing via conditional generative adversarial network. In: CVPR (2018)
26. Li, Y., Swersky, K., Zemel, R.: Generative moment matching networks. In: ICML (2015)
27. Liu, D.: Connecting low-level image processing and high-level vision via deep learning. In: IJCAI (2018)
28. Liu, D., Wen, B., Jiao, J., Liu, X., Wang, Z., Huang, T.S.: Connecting image denoising and high-level vision tasks via deep learning. TIP (2020)
29. Liu, X., Ma, Y., Shi, Z., Chen, J.: Griddehazenet: Attention-based multi-scale network for image dehazing. In: ICCV (2019)
30. Liu, X., Suganuma, M., Sun, Z., Okatani, T.: Dual residual networks leveraging the potential of paired operations for image restoration. In: CVPR (2019)
31. Liu, Y., Cao, J., Li, B., Yuan, C., Hu, W., Li, Y., Duan, Y.: Knowledge distillation via instance relationship graph. In: CVPR (2019)
32. Liu, Z., Luo, P., Wang, X., Tang, X.: Deep learning face attributes in the wild. In: ICCV (2015)
33. Ma, C., Jiang, Z., Rao, Y., Lu, J., Zhou, J.: Deep face super-resolution with iterative collaboration between attentive recovery and landmark estimation. In: CVPR (2020)
34. Van der Maaten, L., Hinton, G.: Visualizing data using t-SNE. JMLR (2008)
35. Mechrez, R., Talmi, I., Shama, F., Zelnik-Manor, L.: Maintaining natural image statistics with the contextual loss. In: ACCV (2018)
36. Mechrez, R., Talmi, I., Zelnik-Manor, L.: The contextual loss for image transformation with non-aligned data. In: Ferrari, V., Hebert, M., Sminchisescu, C., Weiss, Y. (eds.) Computer Vision – ECCV 2018. LNCS, vol. 11218, pp. 800–815. Springer, Cham (2018). https://doi.org/10.1007/978-3-030-01264-9_47
37. Mei, K., Jiang, A., Li, J., Wang, M.: Progressive feature fusion network for realistic image dehazing. In: ACCV (2018)
38. Mei, K., Ye, S., Huang, R.: Sdan: squared deformable alignment network for learning misaligned optical zoom. In: ICME (2021)
39. Park, T., Efros, A.A., Zhang, R., Zhu, J.-Y.: Contrastive learning for unpaired image-to-image translation. In: Vedaldi, A., Bischof, H., Brox, T., Frahm, J.-M. (eds.) ECCV 2020. LNCS, vol. 12354, pp. 319–345. Springer, Cham (2020). https://doi.org/10.1007/978-3-030-58545-7_19
40. Park, W., Kim, D., Lu, Y., Cho, M.: Relational knowledge distillation. In: CVPR (2019)
41. Passalis, N., Tefas, A.: Learning deep representations with probabilistic knowledge transfer. In: Ferrari, V., Hebert, M., Sminchisescu, C., Weiss, Y. (eds.) ECCV 2018. LNCS, vol. 11215, pp. 283–299. Springer, Cham (2018). https://doi.org/10.1007/978-3-030-01252-6_17
42. Passalis, N., Tzelepi, M., Tefas, A.: Probabilistic Knowledge Transfer for Lightweight Deep Representation Learning. TNNLS (2020)

43. Peng, B., Jin, X., Liu, J., Li, D., Wu, Y., Liu, Y., Zhou, S., Zhang, Z.: Correlation congruence for knowledge distillation. In: ICCV (2019)
44. Ren, W., Liu, S., Zhang, H., Pan, J., Cao, X., Yang, M.H.: Single image dehazing via multi-scale convolutional neural networks. In: ECCV (2016)
45. Ren, W., Ma, L., Zhang, J., Pan, J., Cao, X., Liu, W., Yang, M.H.: Gated fusion network for single image dehazing. In: CVPR (2018)
46. Santos, C.N.d., Mroueh, Y., Padhi, I., Dognin, P.: Learning implicit generative models by matching perceptual features. In: CVPR (2019)
47. Scott, D.W.: Multivariate density estimation: theory, practice, and visualization (2015)
48. Shaham, T.R., Dekel, T., Michaeli, T.: Singan: learning a generative model from a single natural image. In: ICCV (2019)
49. Shocher, A., Cohen, N., Irani, M.: Zero-shot super-resolution using deep internal learning. In: CVPR (2018)
50. Simonyan, K., Zisserman, A.: Very deep convolutional networks for large-scale image recognition. In: ICLR (2015)
51. Sun, B., Saenko, K.: Deep CORAL: correlation alignment for deep domain adaptation. In: Hua, G., Jégou, H. (eds.) ECCV 2016. LNCS, vol. 9915, pp. 443–450. Springer, Cham (2016). https://doi.org/10.1007/978-3-319-49409-8_35
52. Tian, Y., Krishnan, D., Isola, P.: Contrastive Representation Distillation. In: ICLR (2019)
53. Tolstikhin, I.O., Sriperumbudur, B.K., Schölkopf, B.: Minimax estimation of maximum mean discrepancy with radial kernels. In: NeurIPS (2016)
54. Torkkola, K.: Feature extraction by non-parametric mutual information maximization. JMLR (2003)
55. Tung, F., Mori, G.: Similarity-preserving knowledge distillation. In: ICCV (2019)
56. Turlach, B.: Bandwidth Selection in Kernel Density Estimation: A Review. CORE and Institut de Statistique (1999)
57. Wang, D., Lu, H., Bo, C.: Visual tracking via weighted local cosine similarity. TCYB (2014)
58. Wang, X., Yu, K., Wu, S., Gu, J., Liu, Y., Dong, C., Qiao, Yu., Loy, C.C.: ESRGAN: enhanced super-resolution generative adversarial networks. In: Leal-Taixé, L., Roth, S. (eds.) ECCV 2018. LNCS, vol. 11133, pp. 63–79. Springer, Cham (2019). https://doi.org/10.1007/978-3-030-11021-5_5
59. Wang, Z., Bovik, A.C., Sheikh, H.R., Simoncelli, E.P.: Image quality assessment: from error visibility to structural similarity. TIP (2004)
60. Wu, Z., Xiong, Y., Yu, S.X., Lin, D.: Unsupervised feature learning via non-parametric instance discrimination. In: CVPR (2018)
61. Yu, X., Porikli, F.: Ultra-resolving face images by discriminative generative networks. In: Leibe, B., Matas, J., Sebe, N., Welling, M. (eds.) ECCV 2016. LNCS, vol. 9909, pp. 318–333. Springer, Cham (2016). https://doi.org/10.1007/978-3-319-46454-1_20
62. Zhang, K., Zuo, W., Zhang, L.: FFDNet: Toward a fast and flexible solution for CNN-based image denoising. TIP (2018)
63. Zhang, R., Isola, P., Efros, A.A., Shechtman, E., Wang, O.: The unreasonable effectiveness of deep features as a perceptual metric. In: CVPR (2018)
64. Zhang, X., Chen, Q., Ng, R., Koltun, V.: Zoom to Learn. CVPR, Learn to Zoom. In (2019)
65. Zhang, Y., Tian, Y., Kong, Y., Zhong, B., Fu, Y.: Residual dense network for image super-resolution. In: CVPR (2018)
66. Zontak, M., Irani, M.: Internal statistics of a single natural image. In: CVPR (2011)

3D Scene Inference from Transient Histograms

Sacha Jungerman$^{(\boxtimes)}$, Atul Ingle, Yin Li, and Mohit Gupta

University of Wisconsin-Madison, Madison, WI 53706, USA
{sjungerman,ingle,yin.li,mgupta37}@wisc.edu

Abstract. Time-resolved image sensors that capture light at pico-to-nanosecond timescales were once limited to niche applications but are now rapidly becoming mainstream in consumer devices. We propose low-cost and low-power imaging modalities that capture scene information from minimal time-resolved image sensors with as few as one pixel. The key idea is to flood illuminate large scene patches (or the entire scene) with a pulsed light source and measure the time-resolved reflected light by integrating over the entire illuminated area. The one-dimensional measured temporal waveform, called *transient*, encodes both distances and albedoes at all visible scene points and as such is an aggregate proxy for the scene's 3D geometry. We explore the viability and limitations of the transient waveforms by themselves for recovering scene information, and also when combined with traditional RGB cameras. We show that plane estimation can be performed from a single transient and that using only a few more it is possible to recover a depth map of the whole scene. We also show two proof-of-concept hardware prototypes that demonstrate the feasibility of our approach for compact, mobile, and budget-limited applications.

Keywords: Computational imaging · Single-photon cameras · Transient processing · Budget constrained applications · Depth estimation

1 Weak 3D Cameras

Vision and robotics systems enabled by 3D cameras are revolutionizing several aspects of our lives via technologies such as robotic surgery, augmented reality, and autonomous navigation. One catalyst behind this revolution is the emergence of depth sensors that can recover the 3D geometry of their surroundings. While a full 3D map may be needed for several applications such as industrial inspection and digital modeling, there are many scenarios where recovering high-resolution 3D geometry is not required. Imagine a robot delivering food on a college campus or a robot arm sorting packages in a warehouse. In these settings, while full 3D

Supplementary Information The online version contains supplementary material available at https://doi.org/10.1007/978-3-031-20071-7_24.

S. Avidan et al. (Eds.): ECCV 2022, LNCS 13667, pp. 401–417, 2022.
https://doi.org/10.1007/978-3-031-20071-7_24

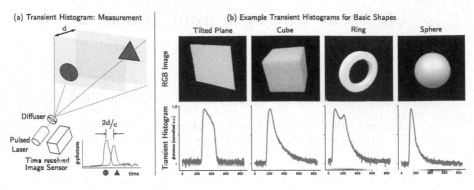

Fig. 1. Transient histogram: Measurement and examples. (a) Measuring a transient histogram involves illuminating the scene with a pulsed illumination source such as a pulsed laser which is diffused uniformly over the field of view of a time-resolved image sensor pixel such as a single-photon avalanche diode. (b) Transient histograms were captured using a hardware prototype for some basic 3D shapes. Observe that these have unique features which can help distinguish these shapes.

perception may be useful for long-term policy design, it is often unnecessary for time-critical tasks such as obstacle avoidance. There is strong evidence that many biological navigation systems such as human drivers [16] do not explicitly recover full 3D geometry for making fast, local decisions such as collision avoidance. For such applications, particularly in resource-constrained scenarios where the vision system is operating under a tight budget (e.g., low-power, low-cost), it is desirable to have *weak 3D cameras* which recover possibly low-fidelity 3D scene representations, but with low latency and limited power.

We propose a class of weak 3D cameras based on *transient histograms*, a scene representation tailored for time-critical and resource-constrained applications such as fast robot navigation. A transient histogram is a one-dimensional signal (as opposed to 2D images) that can be captured at high speeds and low-costs by re-purposing cheap proximity sensors that are now ubiquitous, everywhere from consumer electronics such as mobile phones, to cars, factories, and robots for collision safety. Most proximity sensors consist of a laser source and a fast detector and are based on the principle of time-of-flight (ToF): measuring the time it takes for a light pulse to travel to the scene and back to the sensor.

Conventionally, in a ToF sensor, both the fields of view (FoV) of the laser and that of the detector need to coincide and be highly focused (ideally at a single scene point). This ensures that the received light intensity has a single discernible peak corresponding to the round-trip time delay. We adopt a different approach. Instead of focusing the beam on a narrow region, we deliberately *diffuse* both the laser and the detector so that a large scene area is illuminated simultaneously. The received light is composed of the superposition of all scaled and shifted light pulses from all the illuminated scene points. The resulting captured waveform is called the transient histogram or simply a transient. Instead of encoding the depth of a single scene point, a transient is an *aggregate 3D scene representation* that encodes information about the 3D geometry and albedos of a large scene patch, possibly even the entire scene.

We propose a family of algorithms that can extract scene information from transients, beyond what is achieved simply via peak-finding. These methods broadly fall under two categories: parametric and non-parametric. For scenes where some prior knowledge can be explicitly modeled, we show an analysis-by-synthesis approach that can be used to recover the scene parameters. While this technique can be used for arbitrary parametric scenes, we show results for planar scenes in Sect. 4. We demonstrate the viability of plane estimation using a hardware prototype that uses a low-cost, off-the-shelf proximity sensor. Finally, for more complicated scenes, we present a learning-based method in Sect. 5 to recover a dense depth map using only a small (e.g., 20×15) array of transients. We then show how these depth maps can be further refined using an RGB image, and demonstrate these techniques on a custom hardware setup which is more flexible than a cheap off-the-shelf sensor, yet mimics its characteristics closely.

Scope and Limitations: The proposed techniques are specifically tailored for applications running on resource-constrained devices, where a low-fidelity depth representation suffices. Our methods are not meant to replace conventional depth cameras in scenarios that require dense and high-precision geometry information. Instead, the transient histograms should be considered a complementary scene representation that can be recovered with low latency and compute budgets using only low-cost proximity sensors.

Due to an inherent rotational ambiguity when estimating planes from a single transient, an analytic solution to recover depth of a piecewise planar scene is infeasible. Instead, we adopt a deep learning approach to estimate the geometry of complex scenes. Despite successful demonstration of plane estimation results with a cheap proximity sensor, using SPAD sensors to image more complex scenes is still challenging due to data bandwidth, low signal-to-noise ratio (SNR), and range issues. We instead show depth estimation results using a custom lab setup that was built to perform similarly as off-the-shelf proximity sensors, while providing us with greater flexibility and low-level access to transient histograms.

2   Related Work

3D Imaging Techniques: Traditional depth sensing methods such as stereo, structured-light, and time-of-flight are capable of acquiring high-quality depth maps. While these methods have made significant progress, such as multi-camera depth estimation [35,39,40], they still face key challenges. Certain applications such as autonomous drones, cannot support complex structured-light sensors, multiple cameras, or bulky LiDARs due to cost, power, and other constraints. We propose a method suitable for budget-constrained applications which is less resource-intensive because it can estimate depth maps from just a few transients.

Monocular Depth Estimation (MDE): A promising low-cost depth recovery technique is monocular depth estimation which aims to estimate dense depth maps from a single RGB image. Early works on MDE focus on hand-crafted appearance features [12,13,32,33] such as color, position, and texture. Modern

MDE techniques use almost exclusively learning-based approaches, including multi-scale deep networks [6,22], attention mechanisms [1,11,14], and recently vision-transformers [30]. Despite predicting ordinal depth well and providing exceptional detail, existing methods cannot resolve the inherent scale ambiguity, resulting in overall low depth accuracy as compared to LiDAR systems.

One possible approach to overcome this ambiguity is to augment the input RGB image with additional information such as the scene's average depth [2,41] or a sparse depth map [3,37]. Some approaches have also designed specialized optics that help disambiguate depth [5,36]. However, these approaches either require customized hardware that is not readily available or rely on some external information that cannot easily be procured. Sensor fusion techniques like that of Lindell et al. [19] learn to predict depth maps from dense 256×256 ToF measurements and a collocated RGB image. In contrast, our proposed method does not need an RGB image, and yields good results with as few as 4×3 transients, thus saving on power and compute requirements.

Transient-Based Scene Recovery: Recently, transient-based depth recovery methods have been proposed, including a two-step process [25] that first uses a pretrained MDE network to predict a rough depth estimate which then gets tuned as its transient gets aligned to match a captured one. This approach relies on the original MDE-based depth map to be ordinally correct for achieving high-quality depths. Further, this two-step method can only work in the presence of a collocated RGB camera. Callenberg et al. [4] use a 2-axis galvo-mirror system with a low-cost proximity sensor to scan the scene. This leads to an impractical acquisition time of more than 30 min even for a relatively low 128×128 resolution scan. Our goal is different. We aim to recover 3D scene information from a single transient or a sparse spatial grid (e.g., 20×15) of transients, with minimal acquisition times and computation costs.

Non-Line-of-Sight Imaging (NLOS): NLOS techniques aim to recover hidden geometry using indirect reflections from occluded objects [23,29,34,38]. Instead of diffusing light off a relay surface, our method diffuses the source light in a controlled manner and only captures direct scene reflections. This provides higher SNR, enables use of off-the-shelf detectors, and consumes lower power by estimating depth with orders of magnitude fewer transients than NLOS methods.

3   Transient Histograms

We consider an active imaging system that flash illuminates a large scene area by a periodic pulse train of Dirac delta laser pulses, where each pulse deposits Φ_{laser} photons into the scene over a fixed exposure time. The laser light is uniformly diffused over an illumination cone angle θ. In practice, this can be achieved with a diffuser as in Fig. 1(a). Let f denote the repetition frequency of the laser. The unambiguous depth range is given by $r_{\text{max}} = \frac{c}{2f}$ where c is the speed of light.

The imaging system also includes a single-pixel lens-less time-resolved image sensor, co-located with the laser. The sensor collects photons returning from the field of view illuminated by the laser source. Let Δ be the time resolution of

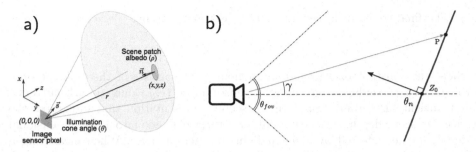

Fig. 2. Geometry for radiometric image formation model and planar parametrization. (a) The single-pixel image sensor receives light from a scene patch with albedo ρ located at a distance r. The normal vectors at the scene patch and the sensor pixel are denoted by $\vec{n}$ and $\vec{s}$. The transient response at a fixed time delay is computed by integrating the total light returning from all scene patches located in a small range corresponding to the time resolution of the sensor pixel. (b) When viewed in the $(\vec{n}, \vec{s})$ plane, the scene plane is parametrized by its distance Z_0 from the sensor and its angle θ_n measured with respect to sensor's optical axis.

the image sensor pixel, which corresponds to a distance resolution of $\frac{c\Delta}{2}$. The unambiguous depth range $r_{\max}$ is therefore discretized into $N = \lfloor 1/f\Delta \rfloor$ bins.

3.1 Image Formation

Figure 2(a) shows the imaging geometry used for deriving the radiometric image formation model, where a 3D coordinate system is fixed with the single-pixel sensor at the origin and positive z-axis pointing into the scene. The laser source is also located at the origin with its direction defined by $\vec{s}$. We assume that the scene is composed of a discrete collection of perfectly Lambertian scene patches. Each visible scene patch has a depth z parametrized by its (x, y) location. Thus, the albedo and surface normal of each patch is given by $\rho(x, y)$ and $\vec{n}(x, y)$. We assume that there are no inter-reflections within the scene and all scene patches that contribute to the signal received by the sensor are inside the unambiguous depth range $0 \leq r := \sqrt{x^2 + y^2 + [z(x, y)]^2} < r_{\max} = c/2f$.

The received laser photon flux vector consists of N bins with mean rates given by $\varphi = (\varphi_1, \varphi_2, \ldots, \varphi_N)$. We call φ the **transient histogram**. The photon flux φ_i^{laser} contributed by the laser illumination at the ith bin is given by integrating the light returning from all scene patches that lie in a range of distances satisfying $(i-1)c\Delta/2 \leq r < ic\Delta/2$. Ignoring multi-bounce paths,

$$\varphi_i^{\text{laser}} = \iint_{(x,y): \frac{(i-1)c\Delta}{2} \leq r < \frac{ic\Delta}{2}} \frac{\rho(x, y)}{4\pi^2(1 - \cos(\theta_{\text{fov}}/2))r^4}(\vec{n}(x, y) \cdot \vec{s})\Phi_{\text{laser}} \, dr$$

$$= \iint_{(x,y): \frac{(i-1)c\Delta}{2} \leq r < \frac{ic\Delta}{2}} \frac{\hat{\rho}(x, y)}{4\pi^2(1 - \cos(\theta_{\text{fov}}/2))r^4}\Phi_{\text{laser}} \, dr$$

where $\hat{\rho}$ is the cosine-angle adjusted albedo of the scene patch. Again, θ_{fov} is the illumination cone angle, $\vec{n}(x, y)$ is the surface normal of the scene patch, $\vec{s}$ is the source normal and Φ_{laser} is the number of photons in each laser pulse.

The final transient histogram at bin i is thus given by:

$$\varphi_i = \varphi_i^{\text{laser}} + \varphi^{\text{bkg}} \tag{1}$$

where the constant background component φ^{bkg} consists of the ambient photon flux (*e.g.*, sunlight) and internal sensor noise (*e.g.*, due to dark current). A transient histogram[1] thus forms a scene representation that integrates the effects of scene depth, surface normal, and surface albedo into a one dimensional signal, further affected by ambient light and sensor noise. When measuring a transient histogram, a random number of photons will be incident during each bin i according to a Poisson distribution with mean φ_i.

3.2   Measuring a Transient Histogram

The key strength of a transient histogram is its high temporal resolution. Such a scene representation can be captured using fast detectors that can operate on nano-to-picosecond timescales. One such technology is the avalanche photodiode (APD). APDs equipped with a high-sampling-rate analog-to-digital converter can be used to capture the full transient histogram in a single laser pulse. Our hardware prototypes use a different image sensing technology called single-photon avalanche diode (SPAD). SPADs have gained popularity in recent years due to their single-photon sensitivity and extreme time resolution ($\sim$100 ps). Unlike APDs, SPAD arrays can be manufactured cheaply and at scale using standard CMOS fabrication technology.

Estimating Transient Histograms Using SPADs: Unlike a conventional image sensor, a SPAD pixel can capture at most one returning photon per laser period. This is because, after each photon detection event, the SPAD pixel enters a *dead-time* during which the pixel is reset. Conventionally, a SPAD pixel is operated in synchronization with the pulsed laser; photon timestamps are acquired over many laser cycles, and a histogram of photon counts is constructed. We call this the *SPAD histogram*. We now show that the scene's transient histogram can be estimated from a measured SPAD histogram.

In each laser cycle, the probability q_i that at least one photon is incident on the SPAD pixel in bin i can be calculated using Poisson statistics[2]: $q_i = 1 - e^{-\varphi_i}$. The probability p_i that the SPAD captures a photon in the ith bin follows a geometric distribution: $p_i = q_i \prod_{j<i} q_j$. For convenience, the $(N+1)^{\text{th}}$ SPAD histogram bin stores the number of laser cycles with no photon detection: $p_{N+1} = 1 - \sum_{i=1}^{N} p_i$. If the total incident photon flux is low such that only a small fraction of the laser cycles lead to a photon detection[3], the expected

---

[1] This is different from a *transient scene response* [26] which is acquired at each (x, y) location (either by raster scanning, or a sensor pixel array) whereas a transient histogram integrates over all patches.

[2] The quantum efficiency of the SPAD pixel is absorbed into φ_i.

[3] In case of high ambient illumination, existing pile-up mitigation techniques [10,28,31] can be employed.

number of photons measured by the SPAD in bin $1 \leq i \leq N$ is proportional to the transient histogram: $\mathbf{E}[h_i] = L\varphi_i$ where L is the number of laser cycles. The transient histogram is thus $\widetilde{\varphi}_i = h_i/L$. We assume that the SPAD pixel captures 512 bins over a 10 m range corresponding to a time bin resolution of 130 ps.

3.3   Information in a Transient Histogram

A key question arises: "What information does a transient histogram contain?". Figure 1(b) shows example histograms for simple shapes, captured experimentally[4]. These histograms have unique features for different shapes. Each histogram has a sharp leading edge corresponding to the shortest distance from the sensor to the object. For a 2D tilted plane, the transient histogram also has a sharp trailing edge with a drop-off to zero. The support (width of the non-zero region) reveals the difference between the farthest and the nearest visible point on the object. For 3D shapes like the cube and the sphere, there is no sharp trailing edge, and the drop-off is more gradual. The 3D ring has a double peak, the distance between these peaks is a function of the angle of the plane of the ring with respect to the sensor.

While the leading edge of a transient histogram gives an accurate estimate of the distance to the nearest point on an object, recovering the depth map $z(x, y)$ from a histogram is severely under-determined even for very simple shapes, as a transient histogram is an integration of depth, surface normal and albedo. Physically plausible scenes with different depth maps can produce the same transient histogram.

- **Albedo-depth ambiguity:** A peak's height conflates radiometric fall-off and albedo. A small highly reflective (high albedo) object at a given distance will produce an equally strong peak as a larger but more diffuse object.
- **Albedo-normal ambiguity:** Both a tilted scene patch, and a patch with low albedo will reflect less light than a head-on, high albedo one.
- **Orientation ambiguity:** The transient histogram is insensitive to rotational symmetry; a plane tilted at 45° clockwise or counterclockwise with respect to the $x - y$ plane will produce exactly the same transient histogram.

We now present a family of techniques to recover 3D scene information from transient histograms, beyond what can be achieved via simple peak-finding.

4   Plane Estimation with Transient Histograms

As pointed out by previous works [18, 20, 21], numerous scenes especially indoor ones can be well approximated as piecewise planar. Here, we study the problem of recovering the parameters of a planar scene from a captured transient. By limiting ourselves to estimating a single plane per transient, we simplify the

---

[4] Details of experimental hardware are discussed later in Sect. 5.3.

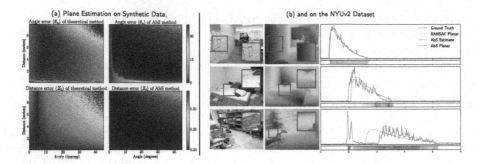

Fig. 3. Plane Estimation on Synthetic and NYUv2 data. (a) We evaluate the mean average error of estimated plane parameters produced by each approach over a wide range of parameter combinations. The first column corresponds to the theoretical approach, the second is the analysis by synthesis approach. (b) We show a few NYUv2 patches and their accompanying transients. Solid transients represent the simulated ground truth (blue) and the resulting transient produced by the AbS method (green). Dashed transients correspond to what we would observe if the scene was perfectly planar with uniform albedo with parameters as estimated by the RANSAC fitting process (orange), and with parameters estimated by the AbS approach (red). Below each transient, we show the average albedo per bin.

problem without loss of generality: one could apply our method to a small array of transients to estimate a piecewise planar scene. Solving this problem will provide insights on estimating more complex 3D geometry *e.g.*, piecewise planar scenes, and other parametric shapes.

Plane Parametrization: We parameterize a plane by its normal as given in spherical coordinates $\vec{n} = [1, \theta_n, \phi_n]^\mathsf{T}$, and the distance Z_0, at which the plane intercepts the sensor's optical axis (Fig. 2(b)). Due to rotational symmetry, it is not possible to recover the azimuth ϕ_n, so we focus on estimating θ_n and Z_0.

4.1   Plane Estimation Algorithms

Theoretical Estimator: For small FoVs, Z_0 can be directly estimated by finding the location of the largest peak in the transient. This estimator becomes less accurate as the FoV increases, but in practice, this decay can be neglected, or a better estimate can be derived from the center of the transient's support if necessary. To estimate θ_n, we refer to Fig. 2(b). The distance to a point on the plane P at a viewing angle γ, as measured from the optical axis, is given by:

$$\|P\| = Z_0 \frac{\cos(\theta_n)}{\cos(\gamma + \theta_n)}. \tag{2}$$

With the exception of when θ_n is zero, Eq. (2) reaches its extrema at $\pm\theta_{\text{fov}}/2$, corresponding to the furthest and closest visible scene points, respectively. These extrema can be directly estimated from the transient by detecting the leading and lagging edges of the peak from the 1D signal. This yields two new distances denoted D_1, D_2, which each gives an estimate of θ_n by Eq. (2). Averaging these two estimates yields our final estimate for θ_n. While such an estimator only relies on basic peak finding primitives, it may fail for large values of Z_0 and θ_n when the lagging edge of the peak falls outside the unambiguous depth range.

Analysis-by-Synthesis Algorithm: We introduce an analysis-by-synthesis (AbS) based estimator that further refines the theoretical estimator. The key idea is to directly optimize the scene parameters (θ_n, Z_0) using a differentiable forward rendering model $R(\theta_n, Z_0)$ that approximates the image formation defined in Eq. (1). This is done by discretizing the integral and replacing the transient binning operation with a soft-binning process which uses a sharp Gaussian kernel for binning. Specifically, given a measured transient histogram $\tilde{\varphi} = \{\tilde{\varphi}_i\}_{i=1}^N$, we solve the following optimization problem using gradient descent, with the initial solution of θ_n and Z_0 given by our theoretical approach:

$$\underset{\theta_n, Z_0}{\arg\min} \; ||\mathcal{F}\left(R(\theta_n, Z_0)\right) - \mathcal{F}\left(\tilde{\varphi}\right)||_2^2 \qquad (3)$$

where $\mathcal{F}$ denotes the Fourier transform. The $\mathcal{L}_2$ norm is computed on the top $k = 64$ of the 512 complex-valued Fourier coefficients. This is equivalent to low-pass filtering the signal and removes high-frequency noise. Please see the supplement for details.

4.2   Simulation Results

Quantitative Results on Synthetic Data: To evaluate the effectiveness of our approaches, we simulated transients that correspond to uniform-albedo planes with $Z_0 \in [0, 10]$ meters and $\theta_n \in [0, 45]$ degrees. For each transient, we estimated plane parameters with the theoretical and AbS methods and compare these to the ground truth. Results can be found in Fig. 3(a). We observe that the AbS method performs better than the theoretical method 87% of the time for estimating θ_n and 97% for Z_0.

Simulating Transients with RGB-D Data: We assume a Lambertian scene and simulate transients produced under direct illumination using paired RGB images and depth maps from existing RGB-D datasets. A ground truth transient histogram is generated through Monte Carlo integration for each scene. We sample rays emitted by the light source, march them until they intersect a scene surface, and weight the returning signal by scene albedo.

Qualitative Results on NYUv2 Dataset: We further test our methods on images from NYUv2 [24] — a well-known RGB-D dataset. Transient histograms of local patches were simulated, and plane fitting using RANSAC was performed on the depth map to estimate surface normals of the patches. Results of our methods with simulated transients as inputs were compared against estimated surface normals, as shown in Fig. 3(b).

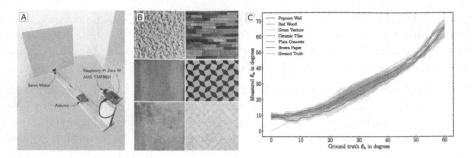

Fig. 4. Hardware prototype for plane estimation and results. (a) Our low-cost prototype consists of an AMS TMF8801 sensor that scans a planar scene from different angles. (b) We captured data from a variety of plane textures and albedos. (c) Our method successfully estimates plane parameters for a wide range of plane textures.

4.3 Hardware Prototype and Results

We built a low-cost hardware prototype using a SPAD-based proximity sensor (AMS TMF8801, retail price ~2 USD) and a Raspberry Pi Zero W mounted on a custom 3D printed mount. This sensor has a bin resolution of 200 ps and a FoV of ~20°C. As shown in Fig. 4(a) the sensor is attached to a plywood structure and scans a test plane from different angles controlled using a servo motor. The sensor and test plane are at a known distance apart. We recover the plane angle θ_n from the transient histograms. Using the servo to rotate the styrofoam backplate to all angles within $[-60°, 60°]$ in increments of $1°$, we acquired 100 transients at each angle and with each of the 6 textures shown in Fig. 4(b). We capture this range to acquire more data and correct miscalibrations.

Results: Fig. 4(c) shows the mean θ_n estimate, as well as the standard deviation, for each of the six textures. In line with the simulation results shown in Fig. 3(a), our theoretical approach gives reliable estimates with experimental data over a wide range of angles. The estimates are inaccurate when θ_n is small (*e.g.*, $\leq 5°$). Although our theoretical model assumes a Lambertian plane, in practice this method is robust to real-world albedo variations and provides reliable estimates even with non-Lambertian textured surfaces.

5   Depth Estimation via Transient Histograms

We now consider estimating depth for scenes with complex geometry and albedos. Due to the inherent rotational ambiguity of our plane estimation method, it is challenging to extend it to a small array of transient and model the scene as piecewise planar. While it is possible to estimate the remaining ϕ_n parameters from spatially-neighboring transients this method does not generalize well to more complex scenes, especially if they violate local planar assumptions. To accomplish this task without prior knowledge of the scene's overall shape we design a deep model to predict dense depth from a sparse set of transient

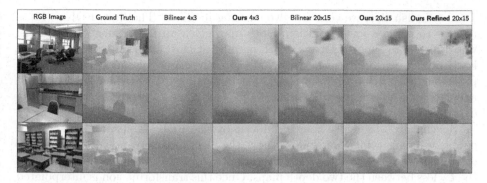

Fig. 5. Simulated Results on NYUv2 Dataset. From left to right this figure shows the RGB image, ground truth depth, bilinear upsampling followed by our method using the 4 × 3 tiling, bilinear upsampling followed by our method using the 20 × 15 tiling, and finally the refined results for the 20 × 15 grid. See supplement for more results.

histograms. We also demonstrate that the resulting depth map can be further refined with an additional RGB input image.

Multiple Transients: Recovering complex geometry from a single transient histogram is a severely ill-posed problem. So we propose to use a low spatial resolution 2D array of defocused SPAD pixels that image sub-regions of the complete FoV. Two configurations are considered: a 4 × 3 array of SPADs, each with a FoV of 25°C, and a 20 × 15 array each with a FoV of 10°C. The specific fields of view are chosen to cover the whole scene with each SPAD's FoV overlapping slightly with its neighbors. For an output resolution of 640 × 480, these arrays correspond to a downsampling ratio of 160× and 32× respectively.

5.1 Scene Depth from Transients via Deep Models

We now describe deep models for estimating depth from transient histograms and for refining the depth map with the guidance of an RGB image.

Depth Estimation: We adapt a deep convolutional neural network architecture similar to that of recent monocular depth estimation methods [8] to perform depth estimation. The model consists of repeating blocks of convolutional layers and upsampling layers which are stacked until the desired output resolution is achieved. Similar to our previous experiment on plane estimation, we compute the Fourier transform of the input transients and only keep the k coefficients with lowest frequency. We use $k = 4$ for the 4 × 3 grid and $k = 16$ for the 20 × 15 grid. We train the network using the reverse Hubert "BerHu" loss [27,42]. Details about our models and training procedures are given in the supplement.

Depth Refinement: Estimating depth from a sparse set of SPAD sensors is challenging due to the low spatial resolution. In many cases, we might have access to an RGB image of the scene which contains high-frequency spatial information that is lacking in the transients. It can be used to refine our depth prediction.

To accomplish this, we combine two existing methods. The first, FDKN [15] is trained to refine a low-resolution depth map given an RGB image. The model was designed to super-resolve a depth map by at most 16×, beyond which there is significant performance degradation. Directly using this network as a post-processing step helps yet leads to noticeable artifacts even when finetuned. To alleviate this we use the pre-trained DPT [30] model. Despite its low absolute depth accuracy, DPT provides high-resolution spatial details.

Specifically, the depth map produced by the FDKN network is used as a guidance image which determines how the depth map from DPT should be deformed. On a tile-by-tile basis, we compute the scale and shift that minimizes the $\mathcal{L}_2$ loss between the two depth maps. Once this transformation is interpolated over the whole depth map and applied to the DPT prediction, we get our final result: a depth map with greater spatial detail and higher accuracy than MDE.

5.2   Simulation Results

Dataset: We use the standard test/train split of the widely used NYUv2 dataset [24] which is a large indoor dataset with dense ground truths.

Evaluation Metrics: To quantitatively evaluate our results, we compare our approach to existing methods using the standard metrics used in prior work [7], including Absolute Relative Error (AbsRel), Root Mean Squared Error (RMSE), Average Log Error (Log10), and Threshold Accuracy ($\delta < thr$). See supplement.

Existing literature focuses on $\{1.25, 1.25^2, 1.25^3\}$ thresholds that correspond to 25%, 56%, and 95% depth error. However, we believe that many real world applications such as robot navigation and obstacle avoidance need stronger accuracy guarantees. To better quantify the gap between LiDARs and MDE-based methods, we consider three stricter thresholds $\{1.05, 1.05^2, 1.05^3\}$ that correspond to 5%, 10% and 16% error.

Baselines: A simple baseline uses bilinear upsampling of the tiled depth as computed via peak-finding. We also consider a stronger baseline that uses a deep network to super-resolve depth maps at each tile. We compare with recent MDE methods [2,9,17,30] for which some metrics were re-computed using the pre-trained models as these were not published in the original papers.

Qualitative Results: Fig. 5 compares our method against various baselines. Observe that in the first and last rows, our network can extract more information from a transient: farther scene depths that are missing in a bilinear-upsampled depth maps are visible with our method. This effect is particularly noticeable for the smaller 4 × 3 grid. The last column shows results of our depth-refinement method which adds more spatial details.

Quantitative Results: Table 1 presents our main results. As seen in the lower δ metrics, our method provides the most benefits using small grids. We observe a 5% accuracy increase over bilinear in the lowest δ metric for the small grid whereas it only boosts it by 4.1% in the larger grid. Moreover, observe that our

Table 1. Results on NYUv2 Benchmark. We show numerical results for our approaches, baselines, and well-known MDE methods. While MDE approaches can produce detailed depth maps, their absolute depth accuracy (in the lower δ metrics) is at par with our 4×3 grid. Our approach produces more accurate depth maps overall.

Grid Size	Method	$\delta < 1.05^1$ ↑	$\delta < 1.05^2$ ↑	$\delta < 1.05^3$ ↑	$\delta < 1.25^1$ ↑	$\delta < 1.25^2$ ↑	$\delta < 1.25^3$ ↑	Log_{10} ↓	$AbsRel$ ↓	$RMSE$ ↓
4×3	Ours	0.335	0.577	0.724	0.845	0.953	0.981	0.068	0.126	0.604
	Baseline	0.340	0.569	0.709	0.824	0.934	0.967	0.171	0.147	0.652
	Bilinear	0.285	0.466	0.588	0.715	0.886	0.951	0.083	0.169	0.856
20×15	Ours	0.624	0.809	0.880	0.929	0.976	0.989	0.060	0.073	0.409
	Baseline	0.576	0.786	0.867	0.923	0.973	0.988	0.066	0.084	0.450
	Bilinear	0.583	0.763	0.840	0.899	0.963	0.985	0.038	0.081	0.498
	Ours Refined	0.707	0.865	0.924	0.961	0.990	0.996	0.024	0.053	0.287
MDE	DORN [9]	0.394	0.602	0.731	0.846	0.954	0.983	0.053	0.120	0.501
	DenseDepth [2]	0.311	0.548	0.706	0.847	0.973	0.994	0.053	0.123	0.461
	BTS-DenseNet [17]	0.357	0.607	0.764	0.885	0.978	0.994	0.047	0.110	0.392
	DPT [30]	0.326	0.595	0.767	0.904	0.988	0.998	0.045	0.109	0.357

Table 2. Sensing power and compute costs. Power estimates are based on an AMS TMF8828 proximity sensor and a typical smartphone camera. Timing analysis is conducted on an Intel Core i7-9700K CPU and Nvidia RTX 2080 SUPER GPU with an input resolution of 640×480 and averaged over 300 runs.

Method	Peak Power	Bandwidth	GFLOPS	#Params	Time	$\delta < 1.25^3$ ↑
Ours 4×3	141 mW	384 B	0.811	28.6 K	2.77 ms	0.981
DORN [9]	1.98 W	900 kB	389.5	162.7 M	112.0 ms	0.983
DPT [30]	1.98 W	900 kB	280.3	120.7 M	81.4 ms	0.998

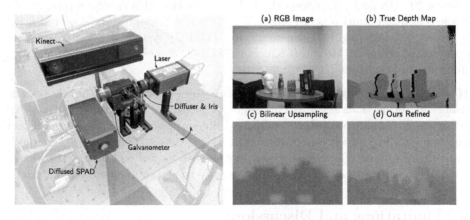

Fig. 6. Hardware prototype and experiment results. Our hardware prototype (left) scans a 20×15 grid in the scene with a diffused laser spot. A lens-less SPAD pixel captures transient histograms. (a) We imaged a table-top scene with a wide range of albedos and textured objects. (b) The true depth map captured using a Kinect v2. (c) Simple peak-finding-based depth map provides no depth details. (d) Using the RGB image and an MDE model, our method generates a higher resolution depth map.

refinement step increases the 5%-accuracy metric by more than 8%, and reaches nearly double the accuracy of some MDE approaches.

Energy, latency, and cost: Table 2 shows a comparison of our method (4×3) using a (simulated) low-cost SPAD vs. a conventional RGB camera in terms of power consumption, bandwidth, compute cost, and depth accuracy. Our method generates similar depth quality as MDE approaches while consuming $1/10^{th}$ the power, 2400× less bandwidth, and orders of magnitude less compute. We expect such low-resolution (4×3) SPAD arrays will be significantly cheaper than high resolution RGB and ToF camera modules. Table 2 does not include the optional RGB refinement step which will consume additional resources.

5.3   Hardware Prototype and Experiment Results

Our lab cart hardware prototype (Fig. 6) was designed to be similar in operation to a low-cost off-the-shelf AMS TMF8828 proximity sensor. However, this setup provides greater flexibility with reprogramming and alignment with the RGB-D camera, and allows evaluating different scanning patterns. Our setup consists of a pulsed laser (Thorlabs NPL52C) with a 6 ns pulse width, 1.2 W peak power, and 40 kHz repetition frequency. The laser spot is diffused and shaped into a $10°$ cone using a diffuser (Thorlabs ED1-C20) and an adjustable circular iris. The detector is a lens-less single-pixel SPAD (MPD InGaAs Fast Gated SPAD) operated in gated acquisition mode with a dead-time of 1µs. The FoV of the SPAD pixel covers the whole scene. A 2-axis galvanometer (Thorlabs GVS012) scans a 20×15 grid that covers the FoV. In practice, this can be replaced with a low-resolution multi-pixel SPAD array. Photon timestamps are acquired using a time-correlated single-photon counting (TCSPC) system and histograms are constructed offline. A Microsoft Kinect v2 RGB-D camera provides ground truth intensity and depth maps.

Results: Figure 6 (right panel) also shows results on an indoor table-top scene using our setup. This scene is challenging due to several objects with varying reflectances and sharp depth edges. Using bilinear upsampling from the transient peaks results in jagged edges and overall loss of detail. The proposed methods can recover fine details and accurate depths with as few as 20×15 transients. For more results and comparisons, please refer to the supplementary material.

6   Limitations and Discussion

Bottlenecks and Availability: Proximity sensors containing small arrays of SPAD pixels are already commonplace in consumer electronics. However, they only output a single depth measurement. Some off-the-shelf sensors provide limited access to low-resolution pre-processed transients. Bandwidth bottlenecks between the sensor and processing unit limit the rate at which transients can be read out. For the methods described in this paper to become widespread, sensor manufacturers need to address communication bottlenecks, and document and advertise low-level APIs that allow direct access to transients.

Future Outlook: Faster communication protocols and on-chip compression methods will enable capturing transient histograms at high frame rates using commodity hardware. These can not only be used to determine scene geometry but also help resolve objects in low-light, detect fast-moving targets, and detect subtle scene motion (e.g. heartbeat or acoustic vibrations). Transient histograms can be treated as a primitive scene representation complementary to RGB images for time-critical and resource-constrained applications.

Acknowledgments. This research was supported in part by the NSF CAREER award 1943149, NSF award CNS-2107060 and Intel-NSF award CNS-2003129. We thank Talha Sultan for help with data acquisition.

References

1. Aich, S., Vianney, J.M.U., Islam, M.A., Kaur, M., Liu, B.: Bidirectional attention network for monocular depth estimation. arXiv:2009.00743 [cs] (2020)
2. Alhashim, I., Wonka, P.: High quality monocular depth estimation via transfer learning. arXiv:1812.11941 [cs] (2019). version: 2
3. Bergman, A.W., Lindell, D.B., Wetzstein, G.: Deep adaptive LiDAR: end-to-end optimization of sampling and depth completion at low sampling rates. In: 2020 IEEE International Conference on Computational Photography (ICCP), pp. 1–11. IEEE, Saint Louis, MO, USA (2020). https://doi.org/10.1109/ICCP48838.2020.9105252, https://ieeexplore.ieee.org/document/9105252/
4. Callenberg, C., Shi, Z., Heide, F., Hullin, M.B.: Low-cost SPAD sensing for non-line-of-sight tracking, material classification and depth imaging. ACM Trans. Graph. **40**(4), 1–12 (2021). https://doi.org/10.1145/3450626.3459824, https://dl.acm.org/doi/10.1145/3450626.3459824
5. Chang, J., Wetzstein, G.: Deep Optics for Monocular Depth Estimation and 3D Object Detection. arXiv:1904.08601 [cs, eess] (2019)
6. Eigen, D., Fergus, R.: Predicting depth, surface normals and semantic labels with a common multi-scale convolutional architecture. arXiv:1411.4734 [cs] (2015)
7. Eigen, D., Puhrsch, C., Fergus, R.: Depth map prediction from a single image using a multi-scale deep network. In: Proceedings of the 27th International Conference on Neural Information Processing Systems - Volume 2, pp. 2366–2374. NIPS 2014, MIT Press, Cambridge, MA, USA (2014)
8. Fang, Z., Chen, X., Chen, Y., Van Gool, L.: Towards good practice for CNN-based monocular depth estimation. In: 2020 IEEE Winter Conference on Applications of Computer Vision (WACV), pp. 1080–1089. IEEE, Snowmass Village, CO, USA (2020). https://doi.org/10.1109/WACV45572.2020.9093334, https://ieeexplore.ieee.org/document/9093334/
9. Fu, H., Gong, M., Wang, C., Batmanghelich, K., Tao, D.: Deep ordinal regression network for monocular depth estimation. CoRR abs/1806.02446 (2018). http://arxiv.org/abs/1806.02446, _eprint: 1806.02446
10. Gupta, A., Ingle, A., Gupta, M.: Asynchronous single-photon 3D imaging. In: 2019 IEEE/CVF International Conference on Computer Vision (ICCV), pp. 7908–7917. IEEE, Seoul, Korea (South) (2019). https://doi.org/10.1109/ICCV.2019.00800, https://ieeexplore.ieee.org/document/9009520/
11. Hao, Z., Li, Y., You, S., Lu, F.: Detail preserving depth estimation from a single image using attention guided networks. arXiv:1809.00646 [cs] (2018)

12. Hoiem, D., Efros, A.A., Hebert, M.: Automatic photo pop-up. In: ACM SIG-GRAPH 2005 Papers, pp. 577–584. SIGGRAPH 2005, Association for Computing Machinery, New York, NY, USA (2005). https://doi.org/10.1145/1186822.1073232

13. Hoiem, D., Efros, A.A., Hebert, M.: Recovering surface layout from an image. Int. J. Comput. Vis. **75**(1), 151–172 (2007). https://doi.org/10.1007/s11263-006-0031-y, http://link.springer.com/10.1007/s11263-006-0031-y

14. Huynh, L., Nguyen-Ha, P., Matas, J., Rahtu, E., Heikkila, J.: Guiding monocular depth estimation using depth-attention volume. arXiv:2004.02760 [cs] (2020)

15. Kim, B., Ponce, J., Ham, B.: Deformable kernel networks for joint image filtering. Int. J. Comput. Vis. **129**(2), 579–600 (2021). https://doi.org/10.1007/s11263-020-01386-z, http://arxiv.org/abs/1910.08373, arXiv: 1910 08373

16. Lee, D.N.: A theory of visual control of braking based on information about time-to-collision. Perception **5**(4), 437–459 (1976). https://doi.org/10.1068/p050437

17. Lee, J.H., Han, M.K., Ko, D.W., Suh, I.H.: From big to small: multi-scale local planar guidance for monocular depth estimation. arXiv:1907.10326 [cs] (2020)

18. Lee, J., Gupta, M.: Blocks-world cameras. In: 2021 IEEE/CVF Conference on Computer Vision and Pattern Recognition (CVPR), pp. 11407–11417. IEEE, Nashville, TN, USA (2021). https://doi.org/10.1109/CVPR46437.2021.01125, https://ieeexplore.ieee.org/document/9578739/

19. Lindell, D.B., O'Toole, M., Wetzstein, G.: Single-photon 3D imaging with deep sensor fusion. ACM Trans. Graph. **37**(4), 113:1–113:12 (2018). https://doi.org/10.1145/3197517.3201316

20. Liu, C., Kim, K., Gu, J., Furukawa, Y., Kautz, J.: PlaneRCNN: 3D plane detection and reconstruction from a single image. arXiv:1812.04072 [cs] (2019)

21. Liu, C., Yang, J., Ceylan, D., Yumer, E., Furukawa, Y.: PlaneNet: piece-wise planar reconstruction from a single RGB image. arXiv:1804.06278 [cs] (2018). version: 1

22. Liu, F., Shen, C., Lin, G., Reid, I.: Learning depth from single monocular images using deep convolutional neural fields. IEEE Trans. Pattern Anal. Mach. Intell. **38**(10), 2024–2039 (2016). https://doi.org/10.1109/TPAMI.2015.2505283, arXiv: 1502.07411

23. Metzler, C.A., Lindell, D.B., Wetzstein, G.: Keyhole imaging: non-line-of-sight imaging and tracking of moving objects along a single optical path. IEEE Trans. Comput. Imaging **7**, 1–12 (2021). https://doi.org/10.1109/TCI.2020.3046472, conference Name: IEEE Transactions on Computational Imaging

24. Silberman, N., Hoiem, D., Kohli, P., Fergus, R.: Indoor segmentation and support inference from RGBD images. In: Fitzgibbon, A., Lazebnik, S., Perona, P., Sato, Y., Schmid, C. (eds.) ECCV 2012. LNCS, vol. 7576, pp. 746–760. Springer, Heidelberg (2012). https://doi.org/10.1007/978-3-642-33715-4_54

25. Nishimura, M., Lindell, D.B., Metzler, C., Wetzstein, G.: Disambiguating monocular depth estimation with a single transient. In: Vedaldi, A., Bischof, H., Brox, T., Frahm, J.-M. (eds.) ECCV 2020. LNCS, vol. 12366, pp. 139–155. Springer, Cham (2020). https://doi.org/10.1007/978-3-030-58589-1_9

26. O'Toole, M., Heide, F., Lindell, D.B., Zang, K., Diamond, S., Wetzstein, G.: Reconstructing transient images from single-photon sensors. In: 2017 IEEE Conference on Computer Vision and Pattern Recognition (CVPR), pp. 2289–2297 (2017). https://doi.org/10.1109/CVPR.2017.246, iSSN: 1063-6919

27. Owen, A.B.: A robust hybrid of lasso and ridge regression. In: Verducci, J.S., Shen, X., Lafferty, J. (eds.) Contemporary Mathematics, vol. 443, pp. 59–71. American Mathematical Society, Providence, Rhode Island (2007). https://doi.org/10.1090/conm/443/08555, http://www.ams.org/conm/443/

28. Pediredla, A.K., Sankaranarayanan, A.C., Buttafava, M., Tosi, A., Veeraraghavan, A.: Signal processing based pile-up compensation for gated single-photon avalanche diodes. arXiv:1806.07437 [physics] (2018)
29. Pediredla, A.K., Buttafava, M., Tosi, A., Cossairt, O., Veeraraghavan, A.: Reconstructing rooms using photon echoes: a plane based model and reconstruction algorithm for looking around the corner. In: 2017 IEEE International Conference on Computational Photography (ICCP), pp. 1–12 (2017). https://doi.org/10.1109/ICCPHOT.2017.7951478, iSSN: 2472-7636
30. Ranftl, R., Bochkovskiy, A., Koltun, V.: Vision transformers for dense prediction. arXiv:2103.13413 [cs] (2021)
31. Rapp, J., Rapp, J., Ma, Y., Dawson, R.M.A., Goyal, V.K.: High-flux single-photon lidar. Optica **8**(1), 30–39 (2021). https://doi.org/10.1364/OPTICA.403190, https://opg.optica.org/optica/abstract.cfm?uri=optica-8-1-30, publisher: Optica Publishing Group
32. Saxena, A., Sun, M., Ng, A.Y.: Make3D: learning 3D scene structure from a single still image. IEEE Trans. Pattern Anal. Mach. Intell. **31**(5), 824–840 (2009)
33. Saxena, A., Chung, S.H., Ng, A.Y.: Learning depth from single monocular images. In: Proceedings of the 18th International Conference on Neural Information Processing Systems, pp. 1161–1168. NIPS 2005, MIT Press, Cambridge, MA, USA (2005)
34. Tsai, C.Y., Kutulakos, K.N., Narasimhan, S.G., Sankaranarayanan, A.C.: The geometry of first-returning photons for non-line-of-sight imaging. In: 2017 IEEE Conference on Computer Vision and Pattern Recognition (CVPR), pp. 2336–2344 (2017). https://doi.org/10.1109/CVPR.2017.251, iSSN: 1063-6919
35. Wang, Y., Chao, W.L., Garg, D., Hariharan, B., Campbell, M., Weinberger, K.Q.: Pseudo-LiDAR from visual depth estimation: bridging the gap in 3D object detection for autonomous driving. arXiv:1812.07179 [cs] (2020)
36. Wu, Y., Boominathan, V., Chen, H., Sankaranarayanan, A., Veeraraghavan, A.: PhaseCam3D - learning phase masks for passive single view depth estimation. In: 2019 IEEE International Conference on Computational Photography (ICCP), pp. 1–12 (2019). https://doi.org/10.1109/ICCPHOT.2019.8747330, iSSN: 2472-7636
37. Xia, Z., Sullivan, P., Chakrabarti, A.: Generating and exploiting probabilistic monocular depth estimates. arXiv:1906.05739 [cs] (2019)
38. Xin, S., Nousias, S., Kutulakos, K.N., Sankaranarayanan, A.C., Narasimhan, S.G., Gkioulekas, I.: A theory of fermat paths for non-line-of-sight shape reconstruction. In: 2019 IEEE/CVF Conference on Computer Vision and Pattern Recognition (CVPR), pp. 6793–6802. IEEE, Long Beach, CA, USA (2019). https://doi.org/10.1109/CVPR.2019.00696, https://ieeexplore.ieee.org/document/8954312/
39. Zhang, F., Qi, X., Yang, R., Prisacariu, V., Wah, B., Torr, P.: Domain-invariant stereo matching networks. arXiv:1911.13287 [cs] (2019)
40. Zhang, K., Xie, J., Snavely, N., Chen, Q.: Depth sensing beyond LiDAR range. arXiv:2004.03048 [cs] (2020)
41. Zhou, T., Brown, M., Snavely, N., Lowe, D.G.: Unsupervised learning of depth and ego-motion from video. In: 2017 IEEE Conference on Computer Vision and Pattern Recognition (CVPR), pp. 6612–6619. IEEE, Honolulu, HI (2017). https://doi.org/10.1109/CVPR.2017.700, http://ieeexplore.ieee.org/document/8100183/
42. Zwald, L., Lambert-Lacroix, S.: The BerHu penalty and the grouped effect. arXiv:1207.6868 [math, stat] (2012)

Neural Space-Filling Curves

Hanyu Wang$^{(\boxtimes)}$, Kamal Gupta, Larry Davis, and Abhinav Shrivastava

University of Maryland, College Park, USA
hywang66@umd.edu, {kampta,abhinav}@cs.umd.edu, lsd@umiacs.umd.edu

Abstract. We present Neural Space-filling Curves (SFCs), a data-driven approach to infer a context-based scan order for a set of images. Linear ordering of pixels forms the basis for many applications such as video scrambling, compression, and auto-regressive models that are used in generative modeling for images. Existing algorithms resort to a fixed scanning algorithm such as Raster scan or Hilbert scan. Instead, our work learns a spatially coherent linear ordering of pixels from the dataset of images using a graph-based neural network. The resulting Neural SFC is optimized for an objective suitable for the downstream task when the image is traversed along with the scan line order. We show the advantage of using Neural SFCs in downstream applications such as image compression. Project page: https://hywang66.github.io/publication/neuralsfc.

1 Introduction

In any form of digital communication, information is transmitted via a sequence of discrete symbols. This includes images and videos, even though they are inherently signals with two spatial dimensions (2D). The modus operandi for transmitting such signals is to (1) efficiently encode and quantize their values in the spatial or spectral domain, (2) linearize the signal to a one-dimensional (1D) sequence by using a standard scanning order such as raster, zig-zag, or Hilbert Curve order [11], and finally (3) apply a Shannon [35] style entropy coding technique such as Arithmetic coding [42] or Huffman coding [13] to further compress the 1D sequence. Given the ubiquity of images and videos in our lives, a large amount of effort has gone into optimizing each of these steps of digital communication. The focus of this work is the second step of linearizing the 2D spatial signal to a 1D sequence. A continuous scan order that traverses all spatial locations in two or higher dimensional signals exactly once is also known as the space-filling curve (SFC) [31].

Prior works have proposed various space-filling curves (SFCs) in the last hundred years, most of them context-agnostic, *i.e.*, they are completely defined by the size and dimension of the space without taking into account spatial information of the space, *e.g.*, pixels in the case of two-dimensional images. These universal context-agnostic SFCs are typically defined recursively to ensure simplicity and scale. Some of the SFCs also have spatial coherence properties and have been used in various image-based applications [2,14,26,37].

Supplementary Information The online version contains supplementary material available at https://doi.org/10.1007/978-3-031-20071-7_25.

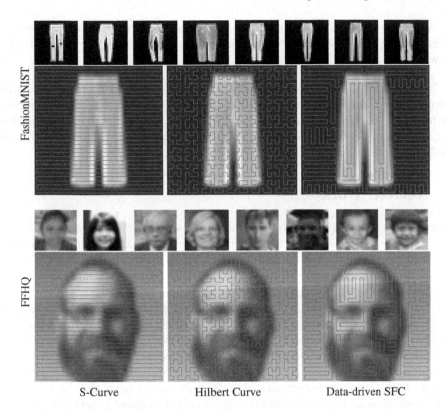

S-Curve   Hilbert Curve   Data-driven SFC

Fig. 1. Given a set of images, a gif, or a video, Neural Space-filling Curves (SFC) can provide a more spatially coherent scan order for images as compared to universal scan orders such as S-curve, or Peano-Hilbert curves. As shown in the example of a trouser and a face, the scan line tends to cover the background before moving to the foreground. (SFCs generated here using half-resolution images and resized for clarity. Best viewed in color.)

However, in many applications such as video conferencing, health-care, or social media, the images being transmitted, are often repetitive with a similar layout and content with minor variations transmitted over and over again. GIFs are another great example that consists of highly repetitive content and need to be stored efficiently and often, losslessly. Since universal SFCs do not utilize the intrinsic information of image content, they are far from optimal for a single image or a set of images with repetitive structure (refer to Fig. 1 for an example). Dafner *et al.* [5] proposed SFCs that exploit the inherent correlation between pixel values in an image. Our work improves upon Dafner *et al.*, in two aspects.

- Instead of discovering a single SFC for every image independently, we propose a data-driven technique to find optimal SFCs for a set of images. We postulate that context-based SFCs are more suitable for linearizing a group of images (or a short video/gif), since the cost of storing the SFC itself can be amortized by the number of images.

– We devise a novel alternating minimization technique to train an SFC weights generator, which allows us to optimize for any given objective function, even when not differentiable.

To the best of our knowledge, ours is the first work to propose a machine learning method for computing context-based SFCs and opens new directions for future research on optimal scanning of 2D and 3D grid-based data structures such as images, videos, and voxels. We demonstrate both quantitatively and qualitatively the benefit of our approach in various applications.

2   Related Work

Space-filling Curves (SFCs), introduced by Peano in 1890 [31] and Hilbert in 1891 [11], are injective functions that map a line segment to a continuous curve in the unit square, cube, or hypercube. Most classic SFCs such as Peano-Hilbert, Sierpinski [36], and Moore [27] curves are defined recursively which allows them to scale up to arbitrary resolution with a number of favorable properties. In fact, [21] showed that the entropy of this pixel sequence asymptotically converges to the two-dimensional entropy of the original image for a large number of images coming from sufficiently random sources. Because of their self-organizing capabilities, Hilbert curves have found applications in compression [2,14,26,37], computing [3], recognition [1,20], security [25], databases [18], electronics [46], biology [23] and even web-comics [28]. Hilbert curves have also been used to solve multidimensional task allocation problems in parallel processing [8]. This scheme is used in many job schedulers, such as the famous SLURM [44].

Dafner *et al.* [5] proposed the first context-based SFCs. Their work makes use of cover and merge algorithm [25] to compute SFC for an image. Ouni *et al.* [30] employ image gradient based method to compute context-based SFCs, and they apply their SFCs to lossless compression tasks. Zhou *et al.* [45] improve Dafner *et al.* 's method by considering both data values and location coherency. They also generalize their method to multiscale data via quadtrees and octrees.

However, computing a unique SFC specific to an image has limited applications. Compression techniques such as LZW [21] that exploit the correlation between nearby pixel values during encoding, for example, can do a better job with context-based SFCs, however, the cost of storing an SFC itself for each image gives away the advantage. Universal SFCs, such as Hilbert curves don't have this disadvantage and are frequently used in compression applications. In this work, we argue that, applications that need to store and transmit images with repetitive structures such as gifs, can benefit greatly from context-based SFC optimized for that set of images.

Finding an optimal SFC is a combinatorial optimization problem. Solving combinatorial problems have a rich history in the field of machine learning. In 1985, [12] first attempted to solve these problems using a neural network. In the deep learning era, various flavors of attention have been proposed [7,39,40] to reach an approximate solution of NP-hard problems in computer science. Since

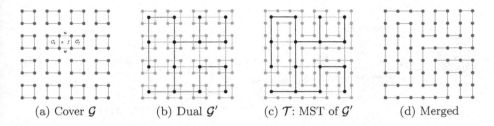

(a) Cover $\mathcal{G}$ (b) Dual $\mathcal{G}'$ (c) $\mathcal{T}$: MST of $\mathcal{G}'$ (d) Merged

Fig. 2. Cover and Merge Algorithm. (a): An 8×8 image fully covered by 2×2 circuits. (b): The dual graph $\mathcal{G}'$ (black) built on the covering circuits $\mathcal{G}$ (blue). (c): The Minimum Spanning Tree $\mathcal{T}$ (black solid lines) of $\mathcal{G}'$ (all black lines) and the Hamiltonian Circuit (blue) induced by $\mathcal{T}$. (d): A single Hamiltonian circuit merged from the covering circuits. See more details in Sect. 3.1. (Color figure online)

combinatorial optimization problems are inherently non-differentiable, reinforcement learning (RL) is also a promising alternative for addressing these problems [6,7,17,39]. In our initial experiments, we found the performance of RL approach in our use-case to be unstable and inconsistent.

3   Approach

We first describe the algorithm for computing SFC for one image as proposed by Dafner *et al.* [5] in Sect. 3.1. We then extend this treatment to a more general setting where we can optimize the SFC for any non-differential objective function for multiple images in Sect. 3.2. The rest of the Sect. 3 describes major components of our framework and training procedure in detail.

3.1   Overview of Dafner *et al.* (Single Image-Based SFC)

Given an image, [5] represents it as an undirected graph $\mathcal{G}$ whose nodes are pixel locations, and each pixel is connected to its 8 neighboring pixels by an edge. Generating a context-based SFC from the given image is then equivalent to finding a Hamiltonian path in graph $\mathcal{G}$. They use the cover and merge algorithm (initially proposed by Matias *et al.* [25] to scramble a video signal for secure transmission). As the name suggests, the algorithm works by finding a Hamiltonian path for the image-grid graph $\mathcal{G}$ in two steps - **cover** and **merge**.

In the **cover** step, a dual undirected graph $\mathcal{G}'$ is constructed from $\mathcal{G}$. The vertices of $\mathcal{G}'$ are small disjoint square circuits covering the whole of $\mathcal{G}$ as shown in Fig. 2a. Each circuit covers 4 pixels. We call these initial circuits $C_1, C_2, ..., C_k$ and connect (C_i, C_j) if the circuits C_i and C_j are adjacent in the original graph $\mathcal{G}$. Figure 2b shows a dual graph example built for an 8×8 image.

In the **merge** step, all circuits are merged to form a single Hamiltonian circuit. To merge the circuits optimally, a weight is assigned to each edge (C_i, C_j) in $\mathcal{G}'$ representing the "cost" of merging circuits C_i and C_j. The weight $w(C_i, C_j)$

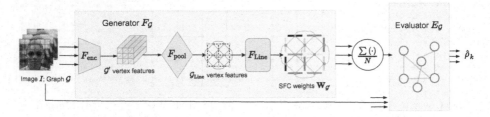

Fig. 3. Neural SFC pipeline. The Neural SFC model consists of a weight generator $F_{\mathcal{G}}$ and a weight evaluator $E_{\mathcal{G}}$. Taking one or more images as input, $F_{\mathcal{G}}$ extracts the deep features of the image and generates the SFC weights. $E_{\mathcal{G}}$ takes both the image(s) and the corresponding SFC weights as input $E_{\mathcal{G}}$ then estimates the negative autocorrelation of the image pixel sequence inferred by the input weights to evaluate the goodness of the input weights with respect to the input image. See more details in Sect. 3.2.

of the edge connecting circuits C_i and C_j is defined as the cost of exchanging the edges e and f with the edges u and w in the image graph:

$$w(C_i, C_j) = |u| + |w| - |e| - |f|, \tag{1}$$

where $|\cdot|$ corresponds to the absolute difference in pixel values at the two vertices of the edge in $\mathcal{G}$. A minimum spanning tree $\mathcal{T}$ is then constructed using these weights. Figure 2c shows what $\mathcal{T}$ might look like for $\mathcal{G}'$. Next, we start merging circuits that are part of $\mathcal{T}$. Merging two circuits corresponds to removing their adjacent edges in $\mathcal{G}$ (*e.g.*, edge e and f in Fig. 2a), and creating new edges (*e.g.*, edge u and w in Fig. 2a). Note that only adjacent circuit pairs can be merged. Given the spanning tree, all merging operations on $\mathcal{G}$ can be done in a linear time to obtain a Hamiltonian circuit as in Fig. 2d. Finally, the SFC or Hamiltonian path can be obtained by cutting the circuit at an arbitrary point.

3.2   Neural Space-Filling Curves

Dafner's approach [5] is effective at exploiting the local relationships in an image. However, it has a few limitations.

- Since the edge weights are computed using only two adjacent pixels, the receptive field is limited, and the resulting SFC does not take into account the long-range context in the image.
- Dafner's approach only works for one image at a time. The notion of context-based SFCs can be further generalized to finding an SFC for a set of images.
- In the current form, [5] cannot optimize for arbitrary objective functions. The context-based SFC obtained is closely tied to edge weights defined by Eq. 1 which encourage autocorrelation with lag-2 in the pixel sequence obtained.

We address each of these issues in our data-driven approach to infer an optimal SFC for a set of images for any objective function. For brevity, we will optimize for lag-k autocorrelation, however, in our experiments, we will show how we can modify this objective and directly optimize for a downstream application such as compression.

Setup. For the remainder of this section, we use the following notation. We are given a set of N images. Each image (color or grayscale) has a resolution of $H \times W$. For a given image I, we define graph $\mathcal{G}$ over its HW pixel locations. The dual graph $\mathcal{G}'$ consists of 2×2 disjoint circuits covering all the vertices of $\mathcal{G}$ as defined in the previous section. We first note that the whole cover and merge algorithm is context-agnostic barring the step where we assign weights to the edges of the dual graph. Therefore, a context-based SFC can be completely parameterized by these weights, denoted by $\mathbf{W}_{\mathcal{G}'}$. For a given set of weights of image I, the merge operation provides us with a Hamiltonian circuit. A Hamiltonian path, or an SFC, can be obtained by breaking the merged Hamiltonian circuit at any point. Hence, the problem of finding an SFC can be reduced to finding the optimal weights $\mathbf{W}_{\mathcal{G}'}$. We propose to learn a neural network, $F_{\mathcal{G}}$, to approximate $\mathbf{W}_{\mathcal{G}'}$. Once we have the optimized weights, the merge operation is fast and efficient in terms of both memory and speed, and we exploit it to get our desired SFC.

3.3   Weight Generator

The weight generator $F_{\mathcal{G}}$ is designed to take as input a single image I, and output the edge weights $\mathbf{W}_{\mathcal{G}'}$ of its dual graph, *i.e.*, $\mathbf{W}_{\mathcal{G}'} = F_{\mathcal{G}}(I)$. While the input dimension is $H \times W$, the output $\mathbf{W}_{\mathcal{G}'}$, has a size equal to the number of edges in the dual graph $\mathcal{G}'$. It is trivial to show that for the dual graph $\mathcal{G}'$ consisting of $\frac{H}{2} \times \frac{W}{2}$ vertices (or circuits), the corresponding number of edges will be $\frac{HW - H - W}{2}$. Further, the edges of $\mathcal{G}'$ do not conform to a 2D grid structure as the input image I. To address this, we decompose the weight generator $F_{\mathcal{G}}$ further in three modules.

$$\mathbf{W}_{\mathcal{G}'} = F_{\mathcal{G}}(I) = F_{\mathrm{Line}} \circ F_{\mathrm{pool}} \circ F_{\mathrm{enc}}(I). \tag{2}$$

Figure 3 shows the architecture of the weight generator. The first submodule is a dual graph encoder F_{enc}, which takes I as the input and extracts a deep representation of the vertices of dual graph $\mathcal{G}'$, resulting in a $\frac{H}{2} \times \frac{W}{2} \times d$ dimensional output, where d is the number of output feature maps. In this work, F_{enc} is implemented using a fully convolutional neural network with residual connections.

The second submodule F_{pool} consists of two pooling filters (and no trainable weights) of dimension 1×2 and 2×1 applied sequentially. F_{pool} imitates the graph operations by aggregating the features of vertices, and hence forming edge features of $\mathcal{G}'$. Given a d-dimensional representation of edges, we want to compute a scalar weight for each edge in $\mathcal{G}'$. It is desirable that this scalar weight can exploit not only the edge features, but also long-range relationships among the edges. Hence we construct a Line graph [10] $\mathcal{G}_{\mathrm{Line}}$ to represent the adjacency between edges of $\mathcal{G}'$. Each vertex in $\mathcal{G}_{\mathrm{Line}}$ corresponds to an edge in $\mathcal{G}'$. For every two edges in $\mathcal{G}'$ that have a vertex in common, there is an edge between their corresponding vertices in $\mathcal{G}_{\mathrm{Line}}$.

Using the Line graph, the edge features of $\mathcal{G}'$ becomes the vertex feature of $\mathcal{G}_{\text{Line}}$, and the adjacent relations of edges of $\mathcal{G}'$ are represented by edges of $\mathcal{G}_{\text{Line}}$. To compute the scalar weights on $\mathcal{G}_{\text{Line}}$, we introduce the third submodule, a weights regressor F_{Line} to run on $\mathcal{G}_{\text{Line}}$. F_{Line} can be implemented using Graph Neural Network modules. In this work, we use GCN [16] in MNIST experiments and GAT [38] in FFHQ Faces experiments.

3.4   Objective Functions

The weight generator described above can generate edge weights for a given image. For every mini-batch of images, we take an expected value of the weights for all the images to get $\overline{W}_{\mathcal{G}'}$. Given $\overline{W}_{\mathcal{G}'}$, we can compute an SFC for the mini-batch of images. The quality or 'goodness' of an SFC can be different for different applications. In this paper, we consider two plausible objectives: the 1D autocorrelation and the LZW sequence length. For both of them, the first step is to flatten the given image I to the 1D pixel sequence $\{y_i\}$ based on the SFC defined by $\overline{W}_{\mathcal{G}'}$.

Autocorrelation. The 1D autocorrelation measures the internal local similarity of a 1D sequence. Therefore, the smaller the 1D autocorrelation is, the better the SFC is. The lag-k 1D autocorrelation of a pixel sequence $\{y_i\}$ of length HW is defined as

$$\rho_k = \frac{\sum_{i=1}^{HW-k} y_i y_{i+k}}{\sum_{i=1}^{HW} y_i^2}. \tag{3}$$

Code Length. Another SFC quality metric, the LZW sequence length, is inspired from the Lempel-Ziv Welch (LZW) encoding [41,47], which is popularly used to encode GIFs losslessly. Its performance depends on the amount of redundant data in a given sequence. Given a pixel sequence $\{y_i\}$, it's LZW length is defined as

$$L = \text{length}(\text{Encode}(\{y_i\})), \tag{4}$$

where Encode is the LZW-encoding function, and length measures the length of a sequence.

Note that computing ρ_k or L requires us to first obtain a minimum spanning tree to infer the SFC from I and $\overline{W}_{\mathcal{G}'}$, which is a non-differentiable operation. Therefore, these metrics, by themselves, cannot be directly used to optimize a neural network. Hence we can't simply backpropagate gradient information to update $F_{\mathcal{G}}$.

To overcome the problem of non-differentiability of SFC computation, we train an evaluator neural network, $E_{\mathcal{G}}$, as a differentiable proxy to estimate the resulting autocorrelation of SFC weights computed by $F_{\mathcal{G}}$ from the context image(s). By carefully designing the training procedure, our model $E_{\mathcal{G}}$ is able to approximate any non-differentiable metric, hence serving as an effective loss function of the weight generator. Figure 3 summarizes our approach.

Also note that, while we refer to the lag-k autocorrelation and the LZW length as our objective functions, we can replace them with any loss (or reward) suitable for a given application, even if it is not differentiable.

3.5   Weight Evaluator

The weight evaluator, denoted by $E_{\mathcal{G}}$, acts as a differentiable proxy to estimate the objective Φ. Depending on the task, we choose $\Phi = -\rho_k$ for minimizing the negative autocorrelation or $\Phi = L$ for minimizing LZW length.

Given the average SFC weights $\overline{W}_{\mathcal{G}}$ and an image I, we compute

$$\hat{\Phi} = E_{\mathcal{G}}(\overline{W}_{\mathcal{G}}, I), \tag{5}$$

$$\mathcal{L}_E = \mathbb{E}\left[\|\Phi - \hat{\Phi}\|\right], \tag{6}$$

where $\mathcal{L}_E$ denotes the expected value of l-2 error between groundtruth lag-k autocorrelation and the predicted autocorrelation by $E_{\mathcal{G}}$ computed for the entire batch. $\mathcal{L}_E$ serves as the objective function for training the evaluator.

The inputs to the weight evaluator $E_{\mathcal{G}}$ are $\overline{W}_{\mathcal{G}}$ and I. Similar to Sect. 3.3, we again decompose the weight evaluator $E_{\mathcal{G}}$ into submodules,

$$\hat{\Phi} = E_{\mathcal{G}}(\overline{W}_{\mathcal{G}}, I) = E_{\text{Line}}(\overline{W}_{\mathcal{G}} \| E_{\text{pool}} \circ E_{\text{enc}}(I)), \tag{7}$$

where $\|$ denotes the concatenation along the feature dimension. Following the graph encoding procedure of the weight generator $F_{\mathcal{G}}$, E_{pool} and E_{enc} are functionally identical to F_{pool} and F_{enc}, respectively. The final submodule E_{Line}, which takes similar input to F_{Line}, has a different head to predict the estimated objective value $\hat{\Phi}$. The backbone of E_{Line} is also implemented using a GCN or GAT, followed by an average pooling operation and a simple MLP to predict $\hat{\Phi}$ as a single value.

3.6   Training

We adopt an alternating optimization procedure for training the core components of our architecture $F_{\mathcal{G}}$ and $E_{\mathcal{G}}$. Algorithm 1 gives an overview of the training schema. The weight evaluator $E_{\mathcal{G}}$ solves the regression task of computing the estimated objective $\hat{\Phi}$ for a given set of SFC weights $\overline{W}_{\mathcal{G}}$. Given the context image I and SFC weights $\overline{W}_{\mathcal{G}}$, we can get the groundtruth objective by first running Prim's algorithm [32] to get the desired SFC followed by Eq. 3 or Eq. 4.

Once we have the groundtruth Φ, we optimize a standard L2 loss commonly used in regression methods to train $E_{\mathcal{G}}$, as we described in Eq. 6. Since we eventually need to use $E_{\mathcal{G}}$ to train the upstream network F, we would like $E_{\mathcal{G}}$ to be trained on a diverse range of input SFC weights $W_{\mathcal{G}}$.

The $F_{\mathcal{G}}$ can be trained trivially using a fixed $E_{\mathcal{G}}$. We empirically observed that training them alternately improves the training dynamics thus boosting the SFC quality.

Algorithm 1: Training Neural SFC

    Data: A set of N images each of resolution $H \times W$
    Result: SFC weights $\overline{\mathbf{W}}_{\mathcal{G}'}$ for the image set

1 Randomly initialize $\mathrm{F}_{\mathcal{G}}$ and $\mathrm{E}_{\mathcal{G}}$;
2 **repeat**
      // training $\mathrm{F}_{\mathcal{G}}$
3   Sample a minibatch of B images;
4   Forward pass for the weight generator $\mathrm{F}_{\mathcal{G}}$, $\mathbf{W}_{\mathcal{G}'} \leftarrow \mathrm{F}_{\mathcal{G}}(I)$;
5   Expected weights for the mini-batch $\overline{\mathbf{W}}_{\mathcal{G}'} \leftarrow \mathbb{E}(\mathbf{W}_{\mathcal{G}'})$;
6   Forward pass for the weight evaluator $\hat{\Phi} \leftarrow \mathrm{E}_{\mathcal{G}}(\overline{\mathbf{W}}_{\mathcal{G}'}, I)$;
7   SGD update for $\mathrm{F}_{\mathcal{G}}$ keeping $\mathrm{E}_{\mathcal{G}}$ fixed, $\nabla_{\mathrm{F}_{\mathcal{G}}} \mathbb{E}\left[\hat{\Phi}\right]$;

      // training $\mathrm{E}_{\mathcal{G}}$
8   For each example in B, with a probability p_1, get $\mathbf{W}_{\mathcal{G}'}$ using Eq. 1, with a probability p_2, sample $\mathbf{W}_{\mathcal{G}'} \sim \mathcal{N}(0, 1)$ and with a probability $1 - p_1 - p_2$, keep $\mathbf{W}_{\mathcal{G}'} = \mathrm{F}_{\mathcal{G}}(I)$;
9   Run a forward pass for the weight evaluator $\hat{\Phi} \leftarrow \mathrm{E}_{\mathcal{G}}(\overline{\mathbf{W}}_{\mathcal{G}'}, I)$;
10   For the whole batch, compute the ground truth Φ using Eq. 3 or Eq. 4;
11   SGD update for $\mathrm{E}_{\mathcal{G}}$ with $\nabla_{\mathrm{E}_{\mathcal{G}}} \mathcal{L}_{\mathrm{E}}$;
12 **until** $\mathcal{L}_E \rightarrow 0$;

---

4 Experiments

In this section, we evaluate the ability of the proposed training scheme to generate optimized Space-filling Curves (SFC) for a set of images. We further validate the efficacy of the Neural SFCs on real-world applications such as image or gif compression. We compare with standard Raster scan and Hilbert curves. Note that even though Raster scan is not an SFC mathematically speaking, we use it for benchmarking in our experiments due to its prevalence.

4.1 Datasets

We trained the Neural SFC model on four different datasets. Both **MNIST** [19] and **Fashion-MNIST** [43] comprise of 60000 training images, and 10000 test images. Each image is a 28×28 grayscale image, which we resize to 32×32 to do a fair comparison with Hilbert curves which can be defined only when the image resolution is a power of 2. Resizing is done by a simple zero padding around the image. We observe a lot of intra-class similarity in the case of both MNIST and Fashion-MNIST, *i.e.*, the images within the same class are similar in layout and content to each other, and hence we train a single SFC for each MNIST and Fashion-MNIST class.

We also consider **FFHQ** [15] dataset. We downsample all the images to size 32×32 using bilinear interpolation. FFHQ is a dataset of celebrity faces and contains less noise compared to datasets like CelebA [24]. We split the dataset into 60000 training and 10000 test images. We train a single SFC for all the images in the data.

Lastly, in order to demonstrate a real-world application of SFCs designed for a set of images, we use a large-scale GIF dataset **TGIF** [22]. The dataset consists of 80,000 training gifs, and 11,360 test gifs. We train a single Neural SFC model that takes a gif as an input and outputs an optimized SFC for the gif. We evaluate it on every gif in the test dataset. Average numbers are reported.

4.2   Training Details

We consider two different objective functions for training Neural SFC. First, in order to compare our method with Dafner *et al.* [5], we train our model using the autocorrelation objective function. Since Dafner's method cannot generate SFCs for an image-set trivially, we compute Dafner's image-set SFC by taking the expected value of $\mathbf{W}_{\mathcal{G}}$, defined in their method for all the images in the training set. Another possible choice is to calculate an average image for the entire image set, then run Dafner's method on it to generate an image-set SFC. We use the first setting in all experiments in our main paper because it empirically performs better. In all our experiments, we set $k = 6$, such that lag-6 autocorrelation is used to train the weight evaluator $E_{\mathcal{G}}$.

Second, we also provide quantitative results on the compression of images and gifs using a Lempel-Ziv encoder (LZW) encoding scheme. Specifically, we optimize the SFC separately for each gif, although, it is possible to train a large SFC encoder on the entire gif dataset. We leave the study for evaluating context-based SFC for large- gifs or video datasets for future work.

4.3   Qualitative Evaluation

Visualizing the 1D Sequence. In Fig. 4, we show a few examples to illustrate the difference between Neural SFCs and Hilbert Curve on the MNIST, Fashion-MNIST, and FFHQ images. We look at the SFC (red curve overlayed on the image of the digits/clothing/faces). While the Hilbert Curve outputs the same SFC for any 32×32 image in the world, Neural SFC optimizes the SFC for a given set of images. To see this difference, we flatten the SFCs into a 1D sequence (images on the right of the digits/clothing/faces), and observe that Neural SFCs tend to keep better long-range spatial coherence than Hilbert Curve. In both cases, Neural SFCs show pixels in fewer clusters as compared to Hilbert curves. Specifically, Neural SFCs are able to roughly stay in the bright regions until they all get covered. Therefore, bright pixels will mostly gather in one contiguous segment in the 1D sequence inferred from a Neural SFC. In contrast, Hilbert curves often result in multiple clusters of contiguous structures in the 1D sequence. We provide more examples in the supplementary material.

SFCs Obtained with Different Objectives. Figure 5 shows two different SFCs obtained by our approach when trained with different objective functions. The figure on the left corresponds to SFC optimized for LZW encoding length,

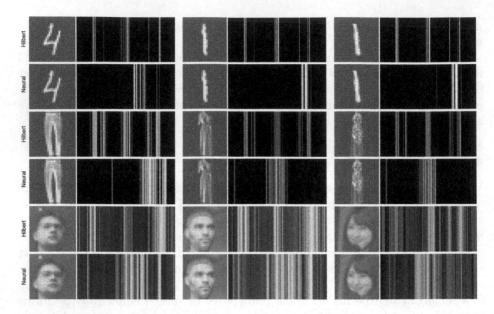

Fig. 4. Qualitative comparison between Hilbert curves and Neural SFCs. Left: SFC (in red color) overlayed on the image. Right: Image flattened according to the SFC and visualized in 1-dimension. Images in the top two rows are from MNIST, the ones in the middle two rows are from Fashion-MNIST, and the ones in the bottom two rows are from FFHQ Faces. Neural SFCs on images from MNIST and Fashion-MNIST are class-conditional, *i.e.*, computed for each class. Therefore, for MNIST and Fashion-MNIST, Neural SFCs in the right two columns are the same since the two images have the same class label. In all datasets, Neural SFCs are more spatially coherent and produce fewer clusters when visualized in 1-dimension. Best viewed in color. (Color figure online)

while the figure on the right corresponds to SFC optimized for auto-correlation. We observe that generally, SFCs optimized for LZW encoding length are better at short-lag auto-correlation (as compared to SFCs optimized for lag-6 as in most of our experiments). This results in an SFC with fewer turns and straighter paths.

4.4   Optimizing Autocorrelation

To quantitatively evaluate the generated SFCs, we plot lag-k autocorrelations of pixel sequences obtained from test sets of three different datasets MNIST, Fashion-MNIST, and FFHQ. Note that even though, we trained our models only to optimize the lag-6 autocorrelation, we plot them for a range of values of lag-k. From Fig. 6, we first observe that the trend is somewhat consistent across multiple datasets, even though they are very different in nature. Neural SFC performs the same or slightly worse than other SFCs at lower values of k. However, for $k > 4$, it outperforms other SFCs by a wider margin. This is intuitive since our model was optimized to increase the autocorrelation for a large value of lag. This also reflects our model's ability to capture long-range

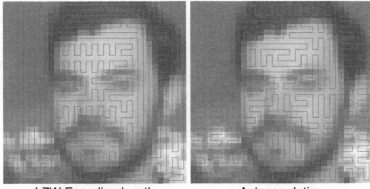

LZW Encoding length   Autocorrelation

Fig. 5. We visualize the Neural SFCs training with two objectives considered in this paper – autocorrelation and LZW encoding.

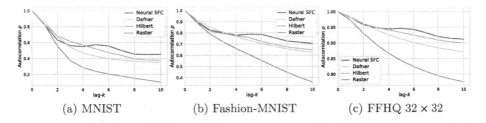

(a) MNIST   (b) Fashion-MNIST   (c) FFHQ 32×32

Fig. 6. lag-k autocorrelation for MNIST, Fashion-MNIST and FFHQ datasets. While Dafner *et al.* provide higher autocorrelation for small lag, *i.e.*, from $k = 2$ to $k = 4$, Neural SFCs outperform Dafner *et al.* for $k > 4$ in all the datasets. Note that we trained our model for $k = 6$, and hence this behaviour is expected.

and global information. We believe that higher gains can be obtained if we train and test using the same k value.

In the second and the third columns of Table 1, we show the autocorrelation values for MNIST, Fashion-MNIST, and FFHQ. We observe that the performance of Dafner's SFCs is even worse than the Hilbert Curve in most cases. This indicates that the naive average of several good SFCs may not be a good way to compute the SFC for a set of images.

4.5 Optimizing Code Length

In this section, we study how Neural SFC can improve image compression results. Specifically, we use the LZW length objective to optimize $E_{\mathcal{G}}$. This means we set $\Phi = L$ in Algorithm 1, where L is defined in Eq. 4. We evaluate our model's performance on all 4 datasets. On MNIST and Fashion-MNIST, Neural SFC model is trained for each class label. FFHQ has no labels, therefore all images are used together to learn a Neural SFC. On the TGIF dataset, Neural SFC

Table 1. Comparison of performance of lag-k autocorrelation and LZW Encoding length for different orders. For autocorrelation, we consistently outperform both the universal and context-based SFC computation approaches at high values of k. For LZW Encoding length, we measure the average size per frame in bytes as well as the relative improvement compared to the raster scan order, in the case of each of the datasets. We consistently outperform compression performance for other order schemes.

Dataset	Method	$\rho_6 \uparrow$	$\rho_{10} \uparrow$	Size in bytes (Δ) $\downarrow$
MNIST	Raster	0.206	0.102	175.4
	Hilbert	0.475	0.378	182.7 (+7.3)
	Dafner [5]	0.401	0.348	–
	Neural SFC (Ours)	**0.558**	**0.451**	**171.1 (−4.3)**
FMNIST	Raster	0.552	0.360	425.8
	Hilbert	0.7 23	0.647	427.3(+1.5)
	Dafner [5]	0.704	0.627	–
	Neural SFC (Ours)	**0.786**	**0.705**	**412.4 (−13.4)**
FFHQ	Raster	0.824	0.775	688.0
	Hilbert	0.924	0.899	689.6(+1.6)
	Dafner [5]	0.901	0.871	–
	Neural SFC (Ours)	**0.943**	**0.911**	**678.3 (−9.7)**
TGIF	Raster	–	–	563.9
	Hilbert	–	–	567.0 (+3.1)
	Neural SFC (Ours)	–	–	**556.9 (−7.0)**

model is trained on all gifs but generates a unique SFC for each gif, *i.e.*, all frames in a gif share the same Neural SFC.

The last column of Table 1 shows the average file size required to store an image in the test data and its relative improvement compared to the Raster scan. Specifically, in the TGIF section, the number represents the average size to save a single frame instead of the entire gif file. It is worth noting that this size does not include the order itself. One order can be shared by many images, thus the cost of it can be amortized. We observe that the Neural SFC results in smaller a sequence size on all 4 datasets, showing consistent improvement on the Raster scan or Hilbert Curve. Interestingly, as compared to the Raster scan, even though Hilbert Curve results in higher autocorrelation (see Fig. 6), it is always worse in terms of LZW encoding length. This finding suggests that there is no simple relation between an order's autocorrelation performance and LZW encoding length performance.

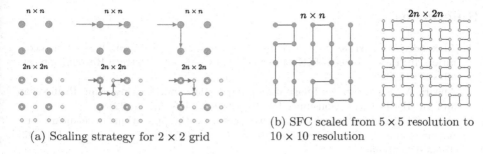

(a) Scaling strategy for 2 × 2 grid

(b) SFC scaled from 5 × 5 resolution to 10 × 10 resolution

Fig. 7. Scaling up SFC. The top row (blue circles) shows a 2 × 2 crop of an image grid of resolution $n \times n$. The bottom row (red circles) shows how we can scale the SFC path from $n \times n$ grid to $2n \times 2n$ grid. For every incoming SFC to a pixel location, there are 3 possible 'next' pixels, straight ahead, left, or right. Column 2 and 3 consider the cases where the SFC goes 'straight' or 'right'. The image on the right shows a toy example of scaling up SFC for a 5 × 5 image. (Color figure online)

4.6 Scaling Up SFC

Although in the current work, we only train Neural SFC models for 32 × 32 images to demonstrate their effectiveness, there are no theoretical restrictions of our approach for higher resolution images. It is trivial to either (1) train SFC for higher resolution itself or (2) scale an SFC computed for a low-resolution image to a high-resolution image, preserving the locality properties as shown in Fig. 7.

5   Conclusions and Future Work

We propose Neural SFC, the first data-driven approach to finding a context-based SFC for a set of images. We parameterize the SFCs as a set of weights over a graph defined using an image grid, and train a neural network to generate the weights. Neural SFC can be trained for any objective function defined for a set of images, even when not differentiable. We show the performance of Neural SFC on four real-world datasets on two different objective functions - (1) Pixel autocorrelations in the pixel sequences obtained from an image (2) Compressing a set of images or a short video such as a gif using LZW encoding.

While our work takes the first steps towards finding 1D sequences in 2D data, it opens up a number of directions for future research such as learning SFC for higher dimensional data such as 3D objects or in the case when the 2D space is in a latent space instead of pixels (VQ-VAE [29,34], dVAE [33]). Applying Neural SFCs to large video compression tasks [4,9] is also promising given their success on gifs. We will explore these exciting directions and more in future work.

Acknowledgements. This work was partially supported by the Amazon Research Award to AS.

References

1. Alexandrov, V., Alexeev, A., Gorsky, N.: A recursive algorithm for pattern recognition. In: Proceedings of IEEE International Conference Pattern Recognition, pp. 431–433 (1982)
2. Ansari, A., Fineberg, A.: Image data compression and ordering using Peano scan and lot. IEEE Trans. Consumer Electron. **38**(3), 436–445 (1992)
3. Bader, M.: Space-filling curves: an introduction with applications in scientific computing, vol. 9. Springer Science & Business Media (2012). https://doi.org/10.1007/978-3-642-31046-1
4. Chen, H., He, B., Wang, H., Ren, Y., Lim, S.N., Shrivastava, A.: NeRV: neural representations for videos. Adv. Neural Inf. Process. Syst. **34**, 21557–21568 (2021)
5. Dafner, R., Cohen-Or, D., Matias, Y.: Context-based space filling curves. In: Computer Graphics Forum, vol. 19, pp. 209–218. Wiley Online Library (2000)
6. Dai, H., Khalil, E.B., Zhang, Y., Dilkina, B., Song, L.: Learning combinatorial optimization algorithms over graphs. NIPS (2017)
7. Deudon, M., Cournut, P., Lacoste, A., Adulyasak, Y., Rousseau, L.-M.: Learning heuristics for the TSP by policy gradient. In: van Hoeve, W.-J. (ed.) CPAIOR 2018. LNCS, vol. 10848, pp. 170–181. Springer, Cham (2018). https://doi.org/10.1007/978-3-319-93031-2_12
8. Drozdowski, M.: Scheduling for parallel processing, vol. 18. Springer (2009). https://doi.org/10.1007/978-1-84882-310-5
9. Ehrlich, M., et al.: Leveraging bitstream metadata for fast and accurate video compression correction. arXiv preprint arXiv:2202.00011 (2022)
10. Harary, F., Norman, R.Z.: Some properties of line digraphs. Rendiconti del Circolo Matematico di Palermo **9**(2), 161–168 (1960)
11. Hilbert, D.: Über die stetige abbildung einer linie auf ein flächenstück. In: Dritter Band: Analysis· Grundlagen der Mathematik· Physik Verschiedenes, pp. 1–2. Springer (1935). https://doi.org/10.1007/978-3-662-38452-7_1
12. Hopfield, J.J., Tank, D.W.: "neural" computation of decisions in optimization problems. Biol. Cybern. **52**(3), 141–152 (1985). https://doi.org/10.1007/BF00339943
13. Huffman, D.A.: A method for the construction of minimum-redundancy codes. Proc. IRE **40**(9), 1098–1101 (1952)
14. Kamata, S., Eason, R.O., Kawaguchi, E.: An implementation of the Hilbert scanning algorithm and its application to data compression. IEICE Trans. Inf. Syst. **76**(4), 420–428 (1993)
15. Karras, T., Laine, S., Aila, T.: A style-based generator architecture for generative adversarial networks. In: Proceedings of the IEEE/CVF Conference on Computer Vision and Pattern Recognition, pp. 4401–4410 (2019)
16. Kipf, T.N., Welling, M.: Semi-supervised classification with graph convolutional networks. ICLR (2016)
17. Kool, W., Van Hoof, H., Welling, M.: Attention, learn to solve routing problems! ICLR (2019)
18. Lawder, J.K.: Calculation of mappings between one and n-dimensional values using the Hilbert space-filling curve. School of Computer Science and Information Systems, Birkbeck College, University of London, London Research Report BBKCS-00-01 August (2000)
19. LeCun, Y., Bottou, L., Bengio, Y., Haffner, P.: Gradient-based learning applied to document recognition. Proc. IEEE **86**(11), 2278–2324 (1998)

20. Lee, J.H., Hsueh, Y.C.: Texture classification method using multiple space filling curves. Patt. Recogn. Lett. **15**(12), 1241–1244 (1994)
21. Lempel, A., Ziv, J.: Compression of two-dimensional data. IEEE Trans. Inf. Theory **32**(1), 2–8 (1986)
22. Li, Y., et al.: TGIF: a new dataset and benchmark on animated gif description. In: Proceedings of the IEEE Conference on Computer Vision and Pattern Recognition, pp. 4641–4650 (2016)
23. Lieberman-Aiden, E., et al.: Comprehensive mapping of long-range interactions reveals folding principles of the human genome. Science **326**(5950), 289–293 (2009)
24. Liu, Z., Luo, P., Wang, X., Tang, X.: Deep learning face attributes in the wild. In: Proceedings of International Conference on Computer Vision (ICCV) (December 2015)
25. Matias, Y., Shamir, A.: A video scrambling technique based on space filling curves. In: Conference on the Theory and Application of Cryptographic Techniques, pp. 398–417. Springer (1987). https://doi.org/10.1007/3-540-48184-2_35
26. Moon, B., Jagadish, H.V., Faloutsos, C., Saltz, J.H.: Analysis of the clustering properties of the Hilbert space-filling curve. IEEE Trans. knowl. Data Eng **13**(1), 124–141 (2001)
27. Moore, E.H.: On certain crinkly curves. Trans. Am. Math. Soc. **1**(1), 72–90 (1900)
28. Munroe, R.: xkcd: Map of the internet. https://xkcd.com/195 (2006-12-11). Accessed 16 Nov 2021
29. Oord, A.V.D., Vinyals, O., Kavukcuoglu, K.: Neural discrete representation learning. NIPS (2017)
30. Ouni, T., Lassoued, A., Abid, M.: Gradient-based space filling curves: application to lossless image compression. In: 2011 IEEE International Conference on Computer Applications and Industrial Electronics (ICCAIE), pp. 437–442. IEEE (2011)
31. Peano, G.: Sur une courbe, qui remplit toute une aire plane. Mathematische Annalen **36**(1), 157–160 (1890)
32. Prim, R.C.: Shortest connection networks and some generalizations. Bell Syst. Tech. J. **36**(6), 1389–1401 (1957)
33. Ramesh, A., et al.: Zero-shot text-to-image generation. ICML (2021)
34. Razavi, A., Oord, A.V.D., Vinyals, O.: Generating diverse high-fidelity images with VQ-VAE-2. NeurIPS (2019)
35. Shannon, C.E.: A mathematical theory of communication. Bell Syst. Tech. J. **27**(3), 379–423 (1948)
36. Sierpínski, W.: Sur une nouvelle courbe continue qui remplit toute une aire plane. Bull. Acad. Sci. Cracovie (Sci. math. et nat. Serie A), pp. 462–478 (1912)
37. Thyagarajan, K., Chatterjee, S.: Fractal scanning for image compression. In: Conference Record of the Twenty-Fifth Asilomar Conference on Signals, Systems & Computers, pp. 467–468. IEEE Computer Society (1991)
38. Veličković, P., Cucurull, G., Casanova, A., Romero, A., Lió, P., Bengio, Y.: Graph attention networks. In: International Conference on Learning Representations (2018). https://openreview.net/forum?id=rJXMpikCZ
39. Vinyals, O., Bengio, S., Kudlur, M.: Order matters: sequence to sequence for sets. ICLR (2015)
40. Vinyals, O., Fortunato, M., Jaitly, N.: Pointer networks. NIPS (2015)
41. Welch, T.A.: Technique for high-performance data compression. Computer (1984)
42. Witten, I.H., Neal, R.M., Cleary, J.G.: Arithmetic coding for data compression. Commun. ACM **30**(6), 520–540 (1987)

43. Xiao, H., Rasul, K., Vollgraf, R.: Fashion-MNIST: a novel image dataset for bench-marking machine learning algorithms. arXiv preprint arXiv:1708.07747 (2017)

44. Yoo, A.B., Jette, M.A., Grondona, M.: SLURM: simple Linux utility for resource management. In: Feitelson, D., Rudolph, L., Schwiegelshohn, U. (eds.) JSSPP 2003. LNCS, vol. 2862, pp. 44–60. Springer, Heidelberg (2003). https://doi.org/10.1007/10968987_3

45. Zhou, L., Johnson, C.R., Weiskopf, D.: Data-driven space-filling curves. IEEE Trans. Visual. Comput. Graph. **27**(2), 1591–1600 (2020)

46. Zhu, J., Hoorfar, A., Engheta, N.: Bandwidth, cross-polarization, and feed-point characteristics of matched Hilbert antennas. IEEE Antennas Wireless Propag. Lett. **2**, 2–5 (2003)

47. Ziv, J., Lempel, A.: Compression of individual sequences via variable-rate coding. IEEE Trans. Inf. Theory **24**(5), 530–536 (1978)

Exposure-Aware Dynamic Weighted Learning for Single-Shot HDR Imaging

An Gia Vien🆔 and Chul Lee$^{(\boxtimes)}$🆔

Department of Multimedia Engineering, Dongguk University, Seoul, Korea
viengiaan@mme.dongguk.edu, chullee@dongguk.edu

Abstract. We propose a novel single-shot high dynamic range (HDR) imaging algorithm based on exposure-aware dynamic weighted learning, which reconstructs an HDR image from a spatially varying exposure (SVE) raw image. First, we recover poorly exposed pixels by developing a network that learns local dynamic filters to exploit local neighboring pixels across color channels. Second, we develop another network that combines only valid features in well-exposed regions by learning exposure-aware feature fusion. Third, we synthesize the raw radiance map by adaptively combining the outputs of the two networks that have different characteristics with complementary information. Finally, a full-color HDR image is obtained by interpolating missing color information. Experimental results show that the proposed algorithm significantly outperforms conventional algorithms on various datasets. The source codes and pretrained models are available at https://github.com/viengiaan/EDWL.

Keywords: HDR imaging · SVE image · Exposure-aware fusion

1 Introduction

The luminance intensity range of real-world scenes is significantly higher than the range that conventional cameras can capture [33, 37]. Therefore, conventional cameras typically acquire low dynamic range (LDR) images, which contain under- and/or over-exposed regions. To overcome the limitations of the conventional imaging systems, high dynamic range (HDR) imaging techniques have been developed to represent, store, and reproduce the full visible luminance range of real-world scenes. Due to its practical importance, various algorithms have been developed to acquire high-quality HDR images [20, 26, 34, 36, 48, 51, 52].

A common approach to HDR imaging is to merge a set of LDR images of a scene captured with different exposure times [7, 28]. Whereas this approach works well with static scenes, camera or object motion across LDR images leads to ghosting artifacts in the synthesized HDR images. Although there has been much effort to develop deghosting algorithms for HDR image synthesis [13, 16, 48, 51, 52], developing an efficient, robust, and reliable algorithm that can handle complex motions

Supplementary Information The online version contains supplementary material available at https://doi.org/10.1007/978-3-031-20071-7_26.

remains a significant challenge. Another approach, called inverse tone mapping, attempts to reconstruct an HDR image from a single LDR image [8,9,17,20,25,36]. Although this approach can prevent ghosting artifacts, it often fails to reconstruct texture details in large poorly exposed regions due to the lack of underlying information in the regions in a single LDR image.

Another effective approach to HDR imaging that does not result in ghosting artifacts is spatially varying exposure (SVE) [31]. SVE-based HDR imaging, also known as single-shot HDR imaging, algorithms capture a scene with pixel-wise varying exposures in a single image and then computationally synthesize an HDR image, which benefits from the multiple exposures of the single image. Because of this merit, various SVE-based HDR imaging algorithms have recently been developed to improve synthesis performance by recovering poorly exposed pixels by exploiting information from pixels with different exposures [4–6,10,38,40,44, 50]. However, such algorithms are still susceptible to providing visible artifacts in the synthesized HDR images, since they fail to faithfully recover the missing pixels and texture information in poorly exposed regions.

To alleviate the aforementioned issues, we propose a novel single-shot HDR imaging algorithm that recovers missing information by learning weights to take advantage of the benefits of both neighboring pixels and learned deep features. The proposed algorithm is composed of the dynamic interpolation network (DINet), exposure-aware reconstruction network (ExRNet), and fusion network (FusionNet). DINet recovers poorly exposed pixels by learning local dynamic filters. ExRNet combines only valid features in well-exposed regions. Specifically, we develop the multi-exposure fusion (MEF) block for exposure-aware feature fusion that learns local and channel weights to exploit the complementarity between these features. Finally, FusionNet generates the reconstructed radiance map by adaptively merging the results from DINet and ExRNet. Experimental results demonstrate that the proposed algorithm outperforms the state-of-the-art single-shot HDR imaging algorithms [5,6,40,44,50] on various datasets.

The main contributions of this paper are as follow:

- We propose a learning-based single-shot HDR imaging algorithm that can recover poorly exposed pixels by exploiting both local neighboring pixels across color channels and exposure-aware feature fusion.
- We develop the MEF block, which learns adaptive local and channel weights to effectively fuse valid deep features by exploiting the complementary information of the well-exposed regions.
- We experimentally show that the proposed algorithm significantly outperforms state-of-the-art single-shot HDR imaging algorithms on multiple datasets.

2   Related Work

2.1   SVE-Based HDR Imaging

An approach to SVE-based HDR imaging is to use spatial light modulators in camera sensors to capture SVE images. Various such techniques have been developed, including learned optical coding [2,27,41], focus pixel sensors [47], and programmable sensors for per-pixel shutter [26,42]. However, these approaches are too complex and expensive for use in practical applications.

An alternative approach to capturing SVE images is to control the per-pixel exposure time or camera gain. Algorithms in this approach can be divided into two categories according to how they synthesize HDR images from captured SVE images. The first category of algorithms attempts to first reconstruct multiple images with different exposures from a single SVE image and then merges them to synthesize an HDR image. Interpolation [10], sparse representation [5], and deep learning [6,40] have been employed to recover the different exposures. However, artifacts in the reconstructed images remain in the synthesized HDR images and degrade their visual quality. The algorithms in the second category directly reconstruct HDR images from SVE images using neighboring pixels with different exposures. Interpolation-based algorithms [4,11] and learning-based algorithms [44,50] have been developed to exploit pixels with different exposures for synthesis. However, they may fail to produce textures in poorly exposed regions due to the spatial inconsistency among neighboring pixels with different exposures.

2.2   Image Inpainting with Partial Convolution

Both single-shot HDR imaging and image inpainting attempt to fill in missing regions of an image with visually plausible content. Recent learning-based approaches [18,32,46,55,56] have shown excellent inpainting performance. However, since these algorithms use convolutional layers, which apply identical filters to the entire image for feature extraction, they may extract invalid information in irregular missing regions. For better handling of those irregular missing regions, the partial convolutional (PConv) layer [19] was developed to ensure the use of only valid information during convolution through a binary mask, which is updated at each layer. In [49], the PConv was generalized by learnable masks for convolution. We also adopt the masks, but the outputs of the learnable mask convolutions are used as local weight maps that represent the relative importance of each value in features for HDR image synthesis.

3   Proposed Algorithm

3.1   Overview

In this work, we assume the SVE pattern in Fig. 1, which consists of row-wise varying exposures with two exposure times: a short exposure time Δt_S and a long exposure time Δt_L, in a single raw Bayer image with the 2×2 RGGB color filter array. This pattern has been commonly employed in single-shot HDR imaging [5,6,44,50]. Specifically, the input SVE image $\mathbf{Z}$ with a resolution of $W \times H$ and bit-depth of 8 is modeled as

$$\mathbf{Z} = \begin{cases} \mathbf{Z}_S, & \text{on } 4n+1 \text{ and } 4n+2\text{-th rows,} \\ \mathbf{Z}_L, & \text{on } 4n+3 \text{ and } 4n+4\text{-th rows,} \end{cases} \tag{1}$$

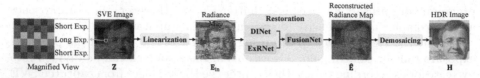

Fig. 1. An overview of the proposed single-shot HDR imaging algorithm. Given a linearized radiance map $\mathbf{E}_{in}$, DINet, ExRNet, and FusionNet jointly recover missing pixels to output the reconstructed radiance map $\hat{\mathbf{E}}$. Next, a demosaicing algorithm synthesizes a full-color HDR image $\mathbf{H}$. Missing values in $\mathbf{E}_{in}$ are illustrated in white.

where $\mathbf{Z}_S$ and $\mathbf{Z}_L$ denote the short- and long-exposure subimages, respectively, and $n = 0, 1, \ldots, \frac{H}{4}$. We then linearize the input $\mathbf{Z}$ into the radiance map $\mathbf{E}_{in}$ using the camera response function (CRF) [7], which is known *a priori*. As $\mathbf{Z}$ contains poorly exposed pixels, $\mathbf{E}_{in}$ contains invalid values at the corresponding pixel locations, which are represented by white in Fig. 1.

We synthesize an HDR image by recovering missing information in $\mathbf{E}_{in}$ through two procedures: restoration and demosaicing. In restoration, missing information in $\mathbf{E}_{in}$ is recovered using DINet, ExRNet, and FusionNet. Then, given a reconstructed output $\hat{\mathbf{E}}$, we obtain the full-color HDR image $\mathbf{H}$ using a demosaicing algorithm. We describe each stage subsequently.

3.2 Restoration

Figure 2 shows the restoration procedure, which is composed of three networks: DINet, ExRNet, and FusionNet. DINet and ExRNet recover missing information by learning dynamic weights in the image and feature domains, respectively. Then, FusionNet fuses the restored results from DINet and ExRNet by exploiting their complementarity to generate the reconstructed radiance map $\hat{\mathbf{E}}$.

DINet: Interpolation-based single-shot HDR imaging algorithms recover missing information from the neighboring pixels in each color channel using different weighting strategies, such as bicubic interpolation [10], bilateral filtering [4], and polynomial interpolation [11]. However, valid information may not be found in the neighboring pixels in each color channel, especially in large missing regions. To solve this issue, DINet exploits the neighboring pixels across color channels to consider inter-channel correlations for more accurate recovery.

We first rearrange the radiance map $\mathbf{E}_{in} \in \mathbb{R}^{W \times H}$ into a set of single-color subimages $\{\mathbf{E}_{in}^c\} \in \mathbb{R}^{\frac{W}{2} \times \frac{H}{2} \times 4}$, where $c \in \{R, G_1, G_2, B\}$ denotes color channels in an SVE image. It is easier to encode long-range dependencies across color channels in the subimages $\{\mathbf{E}_{in}^c\}$ than in $\mathbf{E}_{in}$, and the subimages contain structurally similar information. DINet consists of four dynamic filter networks (DFNs) [12] that generate local filters for each color channel. Each DFN[1] takes the four subimages $\{\mathbf{E}_{in}^c\}$ as input and generates local filter coefficients $\mathbf{k}^c \in \mathbb{R}^{3 \times 3 \times 4}$ dynamically for each color channel c to fuse the 3×3 local neighboring pixels

---

[1] The details of the DFN architecture are provided in the supplemental document.

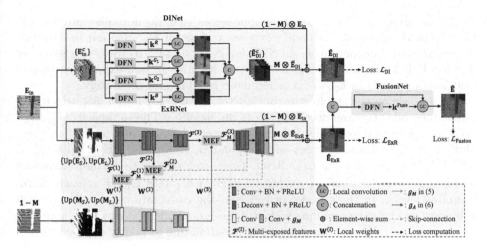

Fig. 2. An overview of the proposed restoration algorithm, consisting of DINet, ExR-Net, and FusionNet. DINet learns dynamic local filters for restoration. ExRNet combines only valid features in well-exposed regions for restoration. FusionNet fuses the outputs of DINet and ExRNet to form the reconstructed radiance map $\widehat{\mathbf{E}}$.

in the four subimages. For each pixel (x, y) of the input $\{\mathbf{E}_{in}^c\}$, we obtain the filtered output for channel c via local convolution (LC) as

$$\widetilde{E}_{DI}^c(x,y) = \sum_{c'} \sum_{i=-1}^{1} \sum_{j=-1}^{1} k^c(i,j,c') E_{in}^{c'}(x+i, y+j), \tag{2}$$

where (i, j) are local coordinates around (x, y), and c' is the color channel index. The filter coefficients are normalized, $\sum_{c'} \sum_i \sum_j k^c(i,j,c') = 1$. Next, we rearrange the filtered outputs $\{\widetilde{E}_{DI}^c\}$ into a single image $\widetilde{\mathbf{E}}_{DI} \in \mathbb{R}^{W \times H}$

Instead of the entire filtered radiance map $\widetilde{\mathbf{E}}_{DI}$, we use restored radiance values only on the poorly exposed regions and use those in $\mathbf{E}_{in}$ on well-exposed regions. To this end, we first define a soft mask $\mathbf{M}$ with values in the range of $[0, 1]$ to reveal poorly exposed regions as

$$\mathbf{M} = \min\left(\frac{\max(0, \mathbf{Z} - \tau) + \max(0, 255 - \tau - \mathbf{Z})}{255 - \tau}, 1\right), \tag{3}$$

where τ is a threshold to determine the over-exposure. We then obtain the reconstructed image $\widehat{\mathbf{E}}_{DI}$ in an exposure-aware manner as

$$\widehat{\mathbf{E}}_{DI} = \mathbf{M} \otimes \widetilde{\mathbf{E}}_{DI} + (1 - \mathbf{M}) \otimes \mathbf{E}_{in}, \tag{4}$$

where $\otimes$ is element-wise multiplication.

ExRNet: As the radiance map $\mathbf{E}_{in}$ is formed by interlacing two subimages $\{\mathbf{E}_S, \mathbf{E}_L\}$ for long and short exposures, respectively, poorly exposed regions in $\mathbf{E}_{in}$ are irregular. Thus, previous approaches that do not take into account the spatial characteristic of poorly exposed regions in $\mathbf{E}_{in}$ may fail to faithfully restore missing information in an SVE image [6,40,44]. To solve this issue, we develop ExRNet, which combines only valid features in well-exposed regions so that missing pixels in $\mathbf{E}_{in}$ are restored more reliably and accurately.

Figure 2 shows the architecture of ExRNet. We employ U-Net [35], which contains an encoder G_E and decoder G_D, as the baseline. The subimages $\{\mathbf{E}_S, \mathbf{E}_L\}$ are first upsampled vertically using linear interpolation $\mathrm{Up}(\cdot)$ to the same resolution as $\mathbf{E}_{in}$. Then, the set of interpolated images $\{\mathrm{Up}(\mathbf{E}_S), \mathrm{Up}(\mathbf{E}_L)\} \in \mathbb{R}^{W \times H \times 1 \times 2}$ is used as input to ExRNet. The encoder G_E extracts multi-exposure features $\boldsymbol{\mathcal{F}}^{(l)} = \{\boldsymbol{\mathcal{F}}_S^{(l)}, \boldsymbol{\mathcal{F}}_L^{(l)}\} = \{G_E^{(l)}(\mathrm{Up}(\mathbf{E}_S)), G_E^{(l)}(\mathrm{Up}(\mathbf{E}_L))\}$ at each downsampling level l. In the encoder of ExRNet, the convolution is applied to each subimage and its corresponding feature maps independently. However, note that the feature map $\boldsymbol{\mathcal{F}}^{(l)}$ contains invalid information due to poorly exposed regions in $\mathbf{E}_{in}$. Thus, we develop the MEF block as shown in Fig. 3, which enables the network to fuse two feature maps with different exposures by exploiting the information of the well-exposed regions in $\mathbf{E}_{in}$.

Because the two feature maps $\{\boldsymbol{\mathcal{F}}_S^{(l)}, \boldsymbol{\mathcal{F}}_L^{(l)}\}$ contain irregular missing regions, their fusion using convolution with local weights, which exploits only spatial information, may cause inaccurate restoration with large errors. In this scenario, global contexts across channels may contain meaningful information of a scene. Therefore, to exploit both spatial and global information, the MEF block fuses $\{\boldsymbol{\mathcal{F}}_S^{(l)}, \boldsymbol{\mathcal{F}}_L^{(l)}\}$ by learning local and channel weights for the spatial fusion and channel fusion, respectively.

First, for spatial fusion, we construct two local weight maps $\mathbf{W}^{(l)} = \{\mathbf{W}_S^{(l)}, \mathbf{W}_L^{(l)}\}$ by considering the information on poorly exposed regions. To this end, we use the encoder G_E with learnable mask convolution [49] to effectively exploit the well-exposed information. Specifically, as shown in Fig. 2, we first extract multi-exposure submasks $\{\mathbf{M}_S, \mathbf{M}_L\}$ from a mask $(1 - \mathbf{M})$ and then vertically upsample them to obtain $\{\mathrm{Up}(\mathbf{M}_S), \mathrm{Up}(\mathbf{M}_L)\}$, which are used as input to the encoder. After each convolution, to constrain each mask value in the range of $[0, 1]$, the mask-updating function g_M is used as an activation function, given by

$$g_M(x) = \big(\mathrm{ReLU}(x)\big)^\alpha, \tag{5}$$

where $\alpha > 0$ is a hyper-parameter. At each downsampling level l, we obtain two adaptive local weight maps $\mathbf{W}^{(l)} = \{\mathbf{W}_S^{(l)}, \mathbf{W}_L^{(l)}\}$ by using the learnable attention function g_A [49] as an activation function as

$$g_A(x) = \begin{cases} a \cdot e^{-\gamma_l(x-\beta)^2}, & \text{if } x < \beta \\ 1 + (a-1) \cdot e^{-\gamma_r(x-\beta)^2}, & \text{otherwise,} \end{cases} \tag{6}$$

where a, β, γ_l, and γ_r are the learnable parameters. We then obtain the fused feature map $\boldsymbol{\mathcal{F}}_{\mathrm{Sp}}^{(l)}$ by spatial fusion in an exposure-aware manner as

$$\boldsymbol{\mathcal{F}}_{\mathrm{Sp}}^{(l)} = \frac{\boldsymbol{\mathcal{F}}_S^{(l)} \otimes \mathbf{W}_S^{(l)} + \boldsymbol{\mathcal{F}}_L^{(l)} \otimes \mathbf{W}_L^{(l)}}{\mathbf{W}_S^{(l)} + \mathbf{W}_L^{(l)}}, \tag{7}$$

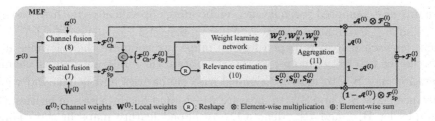

Fig. 3. Architecture of the MEF block.

where the division is component-wise.

Next, assuming that each channel of features represents different visual content, at each downsampling level l, the MEF block learns two channel weight maps $\boldsymbol{\alpha}^{(l)} = \{\boldsymbol{\alpha}_S^{(l)}, \boldsymbol{\alpha}_L^{(l)}\} \in \mathbb{R}^{C^{(l)} \times 1 \times 1}$, where $C^{(l)}$ is the number of channels. Then, the fused feature map $\mathcal{F}_{\mathrm{Ch}}^{(l)}$ by channel fusion is obtained by

$$\mathcal{F}_{\mathrm{Ch}}^{(l)} = \frac{\mathcal{F}_S^{(l)} \odot \boldsymbol{\alpha}_S^{(l)} + \mathcal{F}_L^{(l)} \odot \boldsymbol{\alpha}_L^{(l)}}{\boldsymbol{\alpha}_S^{(l)} + \boldsymbol{\alpha}_L^{(l)}}, \tag{8}$$

where $\odot$ denotes channel-wise multiplication, and the division is channel-wise.

Although the two feature maps $\{\mathcal{F}_{\mathrm{Ch}}^{(l)}, \mathcal{F}_{\mathrm{Sp}}^{(l)}\}$ are obtained by fusing multi-exposure features by learning local and channel weights in (7) and (8), respectively, the feature representations in $\mathcal{F}_{\mathrm{Ch}}^{(l)}$ and $\mathcal{F}_{\mathrm{Sp}}^{(l)}$ may become inconsistent due to independent weight learning. Thus, a straightforward fusion of those feature maps using local convolutions may fail to convey essential information in the feature maps, because local convolutions can capture only local information from a small region. To address the limitation of local convolutions by capturing the long-range dependencies in an entire image, transformers [43] or a non-local module [45] have been employed [53,54] that can exploit the correlations between features. In this work, we develop an element-wise weighting scheme that can consider the relationship between $\mathcal{F}_{\mathrm{Ch}}^{(l)}$ and $\mathcal{F}_{\mathrm{Sp}}^{(l)}$ in both spatial and channel domains inspired by transformers and non-local module, as shown in Fig. 3. Specifically, the output of the MEF block $\mathcal{F}_{\mathrm{M}}^{(l)}$ is obtained as the element-wise weighted sum of the two features, given by

$$\mathcal{F}_{\mathrm{M}}^{(l)} = \mathcal{A}^{(l)} \otimes \mathcal{F}_{\mathrm{Ch}} + (1 - \mathcal{A}^{(l)}) \otimes \mathcal{F}_{\mathrm{Sp}}, \tag{9}$$

where $\mathcal{A}^{(l)}$ is the learnable weight map.

In (9), the weight map $\mathcal{A}^{(l)}$ is obtained so that the merged feature map carries the complementary information from the two feature maps. To this end, we employ a neural network[2] to learn three weight maps $\boldsymbol{\mathcal{W}}_W^{(l)}$, $\boldsymbol{\mathcal{W}}_H^{(l)}$, and $\boldsymbol{\mathcal{W}}_C^{(l)}$ of the size $C^{(l)} \times W^{(l)} \times H^{(l)}$ for each dimension of the feature maps. Next, the similarities (relevance) between the two fused features across spatial and channel

---

[2] The details of the network are provided in the supplemental document.

domains are computed for relevance embedding. Specifically, we first reshape $\mathcal{F}_{\text{Ch}}^{(l)}$ and $\mathcal{F}_{\text{Sp}}^{(l)}$ into matrices in $\mathbb{R}^{C^{(l)} \times W^{(l)} H^{(l)}}$, $\mathbb{R}^{H^{(l)} \times W^{(l)} C^{(l)}}$, and $\mathbb{R}^{W^{(l)} \times H^{(l)} C^{(l)}}$. Then, for each pair of reshaped feature maps, we compute the relevance map between the two feature maps; we thereby obtain three relevance maps: channel relevance map $\mathbf{S}_C^{(l)}$ to measure channel-wise similarities and height and width relevance maps $\mathbf{S}_W^{(l)}$ and $\mathbf{S}_H^{(l)}$ to measure width- and height-wise similarities. For example, let $\mathbf{R}_{\text{Ch}}^C$ and $\mathbf{R}_{\text{Sp}}^C$ denote the reshaped feature maps in the channel domain, then the channel relevance map $\mathbf{S}_C^{(l)}$ is obtained by

$$\mathbf{S}_C^{(l)} = \left(\frac{\mathbf{R}_{\text{Ch}}^C}{\|\mathbf{R}_{\text{Ch}}^C\|} \right) \left(\frac{\mathbf{R}_{\text{Sp}}^C}{\|\mathbf{R}_{\text{Sp}}^C\|} \right)^T. \tag{10}$$

Then, the weight map $\mathcal{A}^{(l)}$ is obtain by aggregating the weight maps with the relevance maps as

$$\mathcal{A}^{(l)}(i,j,c) = \frac{s_W \cdot \mathcal{W}_W^{(l)}(i,j,c) + s_H \cdot \mathcal{W}_H^{(l)}(i,j,c) + s_C \cdot \mathcal{W}_C^{(l)}(i,j,c)}{\mathcal{W}_W^{(l)}(i,j,c) + \mathcal{W}_H^{(l)}(i,j,c) + \mathcal{W}_C^{(l)}(i,j,c)}, \tag{11}$$

where $s_W = \sum_{k=1}^{W^{(l)}} \mathbf{S}_W^{(l)}(i,k)$, $s_H = \sum_{k=1}^{H^{(l)}} \mathbf{S}_H^{(l)}(j,k)$, and $s_C = \sum_{k=1}^{C^{(l)}} \mathbf{S}_C^{(l)}(c,k)$, and (i,j,c) are the indices of $W^{(l)}$, $H^{(l)}$, and $C^{(l)}$, respectively. For each channel c, the weights are normalized, $\sum_i \sum_j \mathcal{A}^{(l)}(i,j,c) = 1$.

Finally, similarly to DINet, we reconstruct the output image $\widehat{\mathbf{E}}_{\text{ExR}}$ of ExRNet in an exposure-aware manner as

$$\widehat{\mathbf{E}}_{\text{ExR}} = \mathbf{M} \otimes \widetilde{\mathbf{E}}_{\text{ExR}} + (\mathbf{1} - \mathbf{M}) \otimes \mathbf{E}_{\text{in}}. \tag{12}$$

FusionNet: In Fig. 2, FusionNet synthesizes an output image $\widehat{\mathbf{E}}$ by combining two reconstructed images, $\widehat{\mathbf{E}}_{\text{DI}}$ and $\widehat{\mathbf{E}}_{\text{ExR}}$, from DINet and ExRNet, respectively. Since the two images are reconstructed in the image and feature domains, respectively, they have different characteristics with complementary information, as will be discussed in Sect. 4.4. We adopt DFN in DINet as FusionNet, which learns local filters $\mathbf{k}^{\text{Fuse}} \in \mathbb{R}^{3 \times 3 \times 2}$ for combining the two images, $\widehat{\mathbf{E}}_{\text{DI}}$ and $\widehat{\mathbf{E}}_{\text{ExR}}$, and then obtains the filtered image $\widehat{\mathbf{E}}$ via the LC in (2).

3.3   Demosaicing

As mentioned above, the reconstructed image $\widehat{\mathbf{E}}$ is the Bayer pattern image, as shown in Fig. 1. It therefore requires the interpolation of missing color information to obtain a full-color HDR image $\mathbf{H}$. In this work, we employ the existing demosaicing algorithms [1,21,39,57]. The choice of the demosaicing algorithm affects the synthesis performance, as will be discussed in Sect. 4.4.

3.4   Loss Functions

To train DINet, ExRNet, and FusionNet, we define the DI loss $\mathcal{L}_{\text{DI}}$, ExR loss $\mathcal{L}_{\text{ExR}}$, and fusion loss $\mathcal{L}_{\text{Fusion}}$, respectively, as will be described subsequently.

DI Loss: To train DINet, we define the DI loss $\mathcal{L}_{\text{DI}}$ as the weighted sum of the reconstruction loss $\mathcal{L}_r$ and the multi-scale contrast loss $\mathcal{L}_{\text{MC}}$ between a ground-truth radiance map $\mathbf{E}_{\text{gt}}$ and reconstructed radiance map $\widehat{\mathbf{E}}_{\text{DI}}$ as

$$\mathcal{L}_{\text{DI}} = \mathcal{L}_r(\mathbf{E}_{\text{gt}}, \widehat{\mathbf{E}}_{\text{DI}}) + \lambda_{\text{MC}}\mathcal{L}_{\text{MC}}(\mathbf{E}_{\text{gt}}, \widehat{\mathbf{E}}_{\text{DI}}), \tag{13}$$

where λ_{MC} is a hyper-parameter to balance the two losses. To define the losses, we compress the range of radiance values using the μ-law function $\mathcal{T}$ [13] as

$$\mathcal{T}(x) = \frac{\log(1 + \mu x)}{\log(1 + \mu)}, \tag{14}$$

where the parameter μ controls the amount of compression. We employ the ℓ_1-norm as the reconstruction loss $\mathcal{L}_r$ in poorly-exposed regions as

$$\mathcal{L}_r = \left\| \mathbf{M}_{\text{h}} \otimes \left(\mathcal{T}(\mathbf{E}_{\text{gt}}) - \mathcal{T}(\widehat{\mathbf{E}}_{\text{DI}}) \right) \right\|_1, \tag{15}$$

where $\mathbf{M}_{\text{h}}$ denotes a hard binary mask. A mask value of 1 indicates that the corresponding pixel in $\mathbf{Z}$ is poorly exposed, $i.e..$, $Z(x,y) < \tau$ or $Z(x,y) > 255 - \tau$ with the threshold τ. The multi-scale contrast loss [58] is defined as

$$\mathcal{L}_{\text{MC}} = 1 - \prod_{j=1}^{M} cs_j \left(\mathcal{T}(\mathbf{E}_{\text{gt}}), \mathcal{T}(\widehat{\mathbf{E}}_{\text{DI}}) \right), \tag{16}$$

where M is the number of scales, and cs_j denotes the contrast and structure term at the j-th scale of SSIM.

ExR Loss: We define the ExR loss $\mathcal{L}_{\text{ExR}}$ to train ExRNet as a weighted sum of the DI loss $\mathcal{L}_{\text{DI}}$ and the adversarial loss $\mathcal{L}_{\text{Adv}}$ between $\mathbf{E}_{\text{gt}}$ and a reconstructed map $\widehat{\mathbf{E}}_{\text{ExR}}$ as

$$\mathcal{L}_{\text{ExR}} = \mathcal{L}_{\text{DI}}(\mathbf{E}_{\text{gt}}, \widehat{\mathbf{E}}_{\text{ExR}}) + \lambda_{\text{Adv}}\mathcal{L}_{\text{Adv}}(\mathbf{E}_{\text{gt}}, \widehat{\mathbf{E}}_{\text{ExR}}), \tag{17}$$

where λ_{Adv} is a hyper-parameter that controls the relative impacts of the two losses. The adversarial loss $\mathcal{L}_{\text{Adv}}$ penalizes the semantic difference estimated by the discriminator network D,[3] which is defined as

$$\mathcal{L}_{\text{Adv}} = -\log D\left(\mathbf{M}_{\text{h}} \otimes \mathcal{T}(\widehat{\mathbf{E}}_{\text{ExR}}) \right). \tag{18}$$

Fusion Loss: To train FusionNet, we define the fusion loss $\mathcal{L}_{\text{Fusion}}$ between $\mathbf{E}_{\text{gt}}$ and $\widehat{\mathbf{E}}$ similarly to the DI loss $\mathcal{L}_{\text{DI}}$ in (13) but without $\mathbf{M}_{\text{h}}$ in $\mathcal{L}_r$.

4   Experiments

4.1   Datasets

Since there is no publicly available SVE image dataset with ground-truths, we evaluate the performance of the proposed algorithm on synthetic images

---

[3] The details of the network architecture is provided in the supplemental document.

from various datasets. Specifically, we define a set of exposure values as EV = $\{-1, +1\}$ for short and long exposures and then generate Bayer pattern images. The images in the datasets are either calibrated in units of cd/m^2 or non-calibrated. We multiply non-calibrated HDR images by a single constant to approximate luminance values, as done in [22,24,44].

Fairchild's Dataset[4]: It contains 105 HDR images of the resolution 2848×4288; 36 images are calibrated and 69 images are non-calibrated.

Kalantari's Dataset [13]: Its test set contains 12 non-calibrated HDR images of the resolution 1500 × 1000.

HDM-HDR[5]: It contains 10 non-calibrated videos of the resolution 1856×1024. We randomly selected 12 HDR frames for the test, and they are provided in the supplemental document.

HDR-Eye[6]: It contains 46 HDR images of the resolution 1920 × 1056, of which 16 are calibrated and 30 are non-calibrated.

HDRv [15]: It contains four calibrated HDR videos of HD (1280 × 720) resolution. For each video, we chose four different frames; thus, there are 16 calibrated HDR images in total.

4.2 Training

We first train DINet and ExRNet separately and then, after fixing them, train FusionNet. Next, we train the demosaicing networks with optimized DINet, ExR-Net, and FusionNet in an end-to-end manner.

DINet, ExRNet, and FusionNet: We use the Adam optimizer [14] with $\beta_1 = 0.9$ and $\beta_2 = 0.999$ and a learning rate of 10^{-4} for 150 epochs. The threshold τ in (3) and (15) is set to 15, and the hyper-parameters α in (5), λ_{MC} in (13), λ_{Adv} in (17), and μ in (14) are fixed to 0.8, 0.75, 10^{-3}, and 5000, respectively.

Demosaicing: We retrain conventional demosaicing networks [39,57] using the robust loss in [44] with the same settings as those in DINet and ExRNet training.

Training Dataset: We use only 36 calibrated images from the Fairchild's dataset in Sect. 4.1 for training. We augment the dataset by rotating and flipping images, and then we divided all training HDR images into non-overlapping patches with the size of 32 × 32.

4.3 Performance Comparison

We evaluate the synthesis performance of the proposed algorithm with those of conventional algorithms: Choi *et al.*'s [5], Suda *et al.*'s [40], Çoğalan and Akyüz's [6], Vien and Lee's [44], and Xu *et al.*'s [50]. We retrained the learning-based algorithms [6,40,44,50] with the parameter settings recommended by the

---

[4] http://markfairchild.org/HDRPS/HDRthumbs.html.

[5] https://www.hdm-stuttgart.de/vmlab/hdm-hdr-2014.

[6] https://mmspg.epfl.ch/hdr-eye.

Table 1. Quantitative comparison of the proposed algorithm with the conventional algorithms on the test sets using six quality metrics. For each metric, the best result is boldfaced, while the second best is underlined.

Kalantari's dataset

	pu-MSSSIM	pu-PSNR	log-PSNR	HDR-VDP		HDR-VQM
				Q	P	
Choi et al. [5]	0.9750	36.17	35.47	69.35	0.4559	0.9266
Suda et al. [40]	0.9833	37.19	36.27	71.48	0.5103	0.8826
Çoğalan and Akyüz [6]	0.9870	38.96	37.67	70.25	0.7694	0.9296
Vien and Lee [44]	0.9964	45.10	42.22	73.72	0.3930	0.9696
Xu et al. [50]	0.9957	44.62	42.01	73.00	0.5593	0.9700
Proposed	0.9969	46.17	43.04	74.03	0.3889	0.9718

HDM-HDR

	pu-MSSSIM	pu-PSNR	log-PSNR	HDR-VDP		HDR-VQM
Choi et al. [5]	0.9540	33.71	27.20	66.13	0.4523	0.5677
Suda et al. [40]	0.9594	32.41	25.62	66.33	0.5989	0.4418
Çoğalan and Akyüz [6]	0.9399	35.61	27.15	67.07	0.6711	0.6246
Vien and Lee [44]	0.9769	38.58	29.52	68.34	0.4580	0.6520
Xu et al. [50]	0.9758	38.68	29.89	68.05	0.4878	0.6533
Proposed	0.9759	39.44	30.87	68.70	0.4340	0.6948

HDR-Eye

	pu-MSSSIM	pu-PSNR	log-PSNR	HDR-VDP		HDR-VQM
Choi et al. [5]	0.9522	34.49	33.56	67.95	0.5334	0.8633
Suda et al. [40]	0.9823	39.78	37.23	71.80	0.5481	0.8452
Çoğalan and Akyüz [6]	0.9728	37.43	34.87	70.15	0.7952	0.8894
Vien and Lee [44]	0.9937	42.06	39.32	72.68	0.4902	0.9209
Xu et al. [50]	0.9933	41.28	38.28	72.42	0.6039	0.9149
Proposed	0.9950	43.35	40.16	73.02	0.4053	0.9354

HDRv

	pu-MSSSIM	pu-PSNR	log-PSNR	HDR-VDP		HDR-VQM
Choi et al. [5]	0.9886	45.30	44.16	71.71	0.1809	0.9782
Suda et al. [40]	0.9954	47.87	44.36	74.27	0.3088	0.9731
Çoğalan and Akyüz [6]	0.9935	45.20	43.88	69.79	0.4352	0.9816
Vien and Lee [44]	0.9979	50.75	48.00	74.96	0.1290	0.9841
Xu et al. [50]	0.9976	50.99	47.49	74.13	0.3366	0.9835
Proposed	0.9983	54.58	49.83	75.74	0.0978	0.9854

authors using the training dataset in Sect. 4.2. We use six quality metrics: pu-MSSSIM, pu-PSNR, log-PSNR [3], Q and P scores of HDR-VDP [23,29], and HDR-VQM [30]. The pu-MSSSIM and pu-/log-PSNR metrics are extensions of the MS-SSIM and PSNR, respectively, that consider human perception.

Table 1 compares the synthesis performances quantitatively on various datasets. First, the proposed algorithm outperforms the conventional algorithms in terms of pu-MSSSIM and pu-/log-PSNR in all cases by large margins, except for pu-MSSSIM on the HDM-HDR dataset, where the proposed algorithm achieves the second-best results. For example, the proposed algorithm achieves a 3.59 dB higher pu-PSNR and a 1.83 dB higher log-PSNR scores on HDRv dataset, and a 0.0013 higher pu-MSSSIM score on the HDR-Eye dataset in comparison with the second best, Vien and Lee's. Second, the proposed algorithm

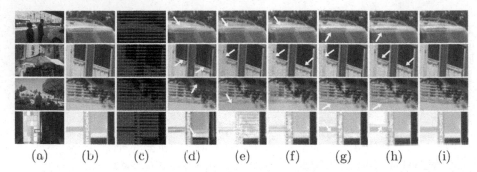

(a)   (b)   (c)   (d)   (e)   (f)   (g)   (h)   (i)

Fig. 4. Qualitative comparison of synthesized HDR images. (a) Ground-truths and the magnified parts for the red rectangles in (b) ground-truths, (c) synthetic SVE images, and synthesized images obtained by (d) Choi *et al.*'s [5], (e) Suda *et al.*'s [40], (f) Çoğalan and Akyüz's [6], (g) Vien and Lee's [44], (h) Xu *et al.*'s [50], and (i) the proposed algorithm.

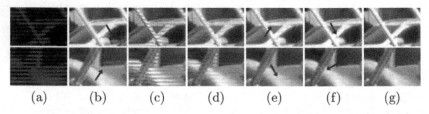

(a)   (b)   (c)   (d)   (e)   (f)   (g)

Fig. 5. Synthesis results of the captured images. The magnified parts in (a) SVE images, and synthesized images obtained by (b) Choi *et al.*'s [5], (c) Suda *et al.*'s [40], (d) Çoğalan and Akyüz's [6], (e) Vien and Lee's [44], (f) Xu *et al.*'s [50], and (g) the proposed algorithm.

also provides the best results for perceptual quality metrics HDR-VDP and HDR-VQM, with no exception. In particular, on the HDRv dataset, the proposed algorithm yields a 0.79 higher HDR-VDP Q score than the second best, Vien and Lee's. These results indicate that the proposed algorithm synthesizes high-quality HDR images by recovering missing pixels accurately and in consideration of semantic information.

Figure 4 qualitatively compares the synthesis results obtained by each algorithm. The conventional algorithms in Figs. 4(d)–(h) fail to synthesize textures and, thus, produce results with blurring, jaggy, and false-color artifacts in poorly exposed regions. In contrast, the proposed algorithm in Fig. 4(i) synthesizes high-quality HDR images without visible artifacts by restoring textures faithfully. For example, the conventional algorithms yield strong visible artifacts around the edges of the red light bar in the first row, which are effectively suppressed by the proposed algorithm. More qualitative comparisons are provided in the supplemental document.

Finally, we compare the synthesis results for the captured image dataset, provided in [44]. The synthesized results in Fig. 5 exhibit similar tendencies to

Table 2. Impacts of the multi-domain learning in the restoration algorithm on the synthesis performance.

	pu-MSSSIM	pu-PSNR	log-PSNR
DINet	0.9969	44.84	45.11
ExRNet	0.9965	46.96	47.01
FusionNet	**0.9973**	**47.72**	**47.75**

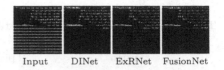

Input   DINet   ExRNet   FusionNet

Fig. 6. Comparison of the error maps for different networks.

Table 3. Impacts of the mask **M** in DINet and ExRNet on the restoration performance.

	M	pu-MSSSIM	pu-PSNR	log-PSNR
DINet		0.9960	38.18	38.53
	✓	**0.9969**	**44.84**	**45.11**
ExRNet		0.9893	42.86	42.96
	✓	**0.9965**	**46.96**	**47.01**

those in Fig. 4. These results indicate that the proposed algorithm can effectively process real SVE images with real noise captured by real-world cameras, providing a superior generalization ability.

4.4 Model Analysis

We analyze the contributions of key components in the proposed algorithm: multi-domain learning, exposure-aware reconstruction, and the MEF block. We also analyze the effects of the demosaicing algorithms on the synthesis performance. All experiments are performed using the Kalantari's dataset.

Multi-domain Learning: To analyze the effects of DINet, ExRNet, and FusionNet in Fig. 2 on the synthesis performance, we train the proposed network with different settings. Table 2 compares the average scores. ExRNet yields significantly higher pu-PSNR and log-PSNR scores but a slightly worse pu-MSSSIM score than DINet. This indicates that, while ExRNet faithfully recovers missing pixels, its ability to preserve consistency between poorly and well-exposed regions is inferior to that of DINet. Finally, combining the results of DINet and ExRNet using FusionNet further improves the synthesis performance by exploiting complementary information from the two networks. In addition, Fig. 6 shows the error maps for each network, which indicates that DINet and ExRNet yield complementary results, and FusionNet combines the complementary information to improve the synthesis performance.

Exposure-Aware Reconstruction: We analyze the effectiveness of the exposure-aware reconstruction using a mask **M** in (4) and (12) in DINet and ExRNet, respectively. Table 3 compares the average scores of these settings for

Table 4. Impacts of fusion schemes in the MEF block on the restoration performance.

Fusion			pu-MSSSIM	pu-PSNR	log-PSNR
Channel	Spatial	$\mathcal{A}^{(l)}$			
			0.9962	46.05	46.24
✓			0.9963	46.67	46.77
	✓		0.9963	46.63	46.80
✓	✓		0.9964	46.85	46.88
✓	✓	✓	**0.9965**	**46.96**	**47.01**

Table 5. Impacts of different demosaicing algorithms on the synthesis performance.

Demosaicing	pu-MSSSIM	pu-PSNR	log-PSNR	HDR-VDP		HDR-VQM
				Q	P	
Adams [1]	0.9963	45.22	42.29	70.96	**0.2252**	0.9697
Malvar *et al.* [21]	0.9962	44.99	41.21	73.61	0.4707	0.9675
Sharif *et al.* [39]	0.9968	46.01	42.91	73.98	0.4627	0.9713
Zhang *et al.* [57]	**0.9969**	**46.17**	**43.04**	**74.03**	0.3889	**0.9718**

both networks. The exposure-aware reconstruction using **M** improves the performances of both DINet and ExRNet significantly by enabling the networks to recover only missing regions.

MEF Block: To analyze the effectiveness of the proposed MEF block, we train ExRNet with different settings. Table 4 compares the results. ExRNet without the MEF block provides the worst performance because valid information in multi-exposed features cannot be fully exploited. Using either of the channel and spatial fusions improves the restoration performance by exploiting the exposure information, and the use of both fusion strategies further improves the performance. Finally, the element-wise weighting scheme using the weight $\mathcal{A}^{(l)}$ yields the best performance.

Demosaicing: To analyze the effects of demosaicing algorithms on the synthesis performance, we test four demosaicing algorithms: two model-based algorithms [1,21], which were employed in conventional algorithms [4–6], and two learning-based algorithms [39,57]. Table 5 compares the results. The choice of demosaicing algorithm significantly affects the synthesis performance. In particular, Zhang *et al.*'s [57] yields the best overall performance.

5   Conclusions

We proposed a learning-based single-shot HDR imaging algorithm that recovers poorly exposed regions via exposure-aware dynamic weighted learning. The proposed algorithm consists of three networks: DINet, ExRNet, and FusionNet. DINet recovers poorly exposed pixels by learning local dynamic filters. ExRNet combines only valid features in well-exposed regions. To achieve this, we developed the MEF block to learn local and channel weights for exposure-aware feature fusion. FusionNet aggregates the outputs from DINet and ExRNet to produce the reconstructed images. Extensive experiments demonstrated that the proposed algorithm outperforms conventional algorithms on various datasets.

Acknowledgements. This work was supported in part by the Institute of Information & Communications Technology Planning & Evaluation (IITP) grant funded by the Korea government (MSIT) (No. 2020-0-00011, Video Coding for Machine) and in part by the National Research Foundation of Korea (NRF) grant funded MSIP (No. NRF-2022R1F1A1074402).

References

1. Adams, J.E.: Design of practical color filter array interpolation algorithms for digital cameras. In: Proceedings of the SPIE, pp. 117–125, February 1997
2. Alghamdi, M., Fu, Q., Thabet, A., Heidrich, W.: Transfer deep learning for reconfigurable snapshot HDR imaging using coded masks. Comput. Graph. Forum **40**(6), 90–103 (2021)
3. Aydın, T.O., Mantiuk, R., Seidel, H.P.: Extending quality metrics to full dynamic range images. In: Proceedings of the SPIE, Human Vision and Electronic Imaging XIII, pp. 6806–6810, January 2008
4. Cho, H., Kim, S.J., Lee, S.: Single-shot high dynamic range imaging using coded electronic shutter. Comput. Graph. Forum **33**(7), 329–338 (2014)
5. Choi, I., Baek, S.H., Kim, M.H.: Reconstructing interlaced high-dynamic-range video using joint learning. IEEE Trans. Image Process. **26**(11), 5353–5366 (2017)
6. Çoğalan, U., Akyüz, A.O.: Deep joint deinterlacing and denoising for single shot dual-ISO HDR reconstruction. IEEE Trans. Image Process. **29**, 7511–7524 (2020)
7. Debevec, P., Malik, J.: Recovering high dynamic range radiance maps from photographs. In: Proceedings of the ACM SIGGRAPH, pp. 369–378, August 1997
8. Eilertsen, G., Kronander, J., Denes, G., Mantiuk, R.K., Unger, J.: HDR image reconstruction from a single exposure using deep CNNs. ACM Trans. Graph. **36**(6), 178:1–178:15 (2017)
9. Endo, Y., Kanamori, Y., Mitani, J.: Deep reverse tone mapping. ACM Trans. Graph. **36**(6), 177:1–177:10 (2017)
10. Gu, J., Hitomi, Y., Mitsunaga, T., Nayar, S.K.: Coded rolling shutter photography: flexible space-time sampling. In: Proceedings of the ICCP, pp. 1–8, March 2010
11. Hajisharif, S., Kronander, J., Unger, J.: HDR reconstruction for alternating gain (ISO) sensor readout. In: Eurograph, pp. 25–28, April 2014
12. Jia, X., De Brabandere, B., Tuytelaars, T., Gool, L.V.: Dynamic filter networks. In: Proceedings NeurIPS, December 2016

13. Kalantari, N.K., Ramamoorthi, R.: Deep high dynamic range imaging of dynamic scenes. ACM Trans. Graph. **36**(4), 144:1–144:12 (2017)

14. Kingma, D.P., Ba, J.: Adam: A method for stochastic optimization. In: Proceedings of the ICLR, September 2015

15. Kronander, J., Gustavson, S., Bonnet, G., Unger, J.: Unified HDR reconstruction from raw CFA data. In: Proceedings of ICCP, pp. 1–9, April 2013

16. Lee, C., Lam, E.Y.: Computationally efficient truncated nuclear norm minimization for high dynamic range imaging. IEEE Trans. Image Process. **25**(9), 4145–4157 (2016)

17. Lee, S., An, G.H., Kang, S.J.: Deep recursive HDRI: Inverse tone mapping using generative adversarial networks. In: Proceedings of the ECCV, pp. 613–628, September 2018

18. Li, J., Wang, N., Zhang, L., Du, B., Tao, D.: Recurrent feature reasoning for image inpainting. In: Proceedings of the CVPR, pp. 7757–7765, June 2020

19. Liu, G., Reda, F.A., Shih, K.J., Wang, T.C., Tao, A., Catanzaro, B.: Image inpainting for irregular holes using partial convolutions. In: Proceedings of ECCV, pp. 89–105, September 2018

20. Liu, Y.L., et al.: Single-image HDR reconstruction by learning to reverse the camera pipeline. In: Proceedings of CVPR, pp. 1651–1660, June 2020

21. Malvar, H.S., He, L.W., Cutler, R.: High-quality linear interpolation for demosaicing of Bayer-patterned color images. In: Proceedings of ICASSP, pp. 2274–2282, May 2004

22. Mantiuk, R., Efremov, A., Myszkowski, K., Seidel, H.P.: Backward compatible high dynamic range MPEG video compression. ACM Trans. Graph. **25**(3), 713–723 (2006)

23. Mantiuk, R., Kim, K.J., Rempel, A.G., Heidrich, W.: HDR-VDP-2: A calibrated visual metric for visibility and quality predictions in all luminance conditions. ACM Trans. Graph. **30**(4), 1–14 (2011)

24. Mantiuk, R., Myszkowski, K., Seidel, H.P.: Lossy compression of high dynamic range images and video. In: Proceedings of SPIE, Human Vision and Electronic Imaging, pp. 6057–6057-10, February 2006

25. Marnerides, D., Bashford-Rogers, T., Hatchett, J., Debattista, K.: ExpandNet: A deep convolutional neural network for high dynamic range expansion from low dynamic range content. Comput. Graph. Forum **37**(2), 37–49 (2018)

26. Martel, J.N.P., Müller, L.K., Carey, S.J., Dudek, P., Wetzstein, G.: Neural sensors: Learning pixel exposures for HDR imaging and video compressive sensing with programmable sensors. IEEE Trans. Pattern Anal. Mach. Intell. **42**(7), 1642–1653 (2020)

27. Metzler, C.A., Ikoma, H., Peng, Y., Wetzstein, G.: Deep optics for single-shot high-dynamic-range imaging. In: Proceedings of CVPR, pp. 1372–1382, June 2020

28. Mitsunaga, T., Nayar, S.K.: Radiometric self calibration. In: Proceedings of CVPR, pp. 374–380, August 1999

29. Narwaria, M., Mantiuk, R., Perreira Da Silva, M., Le Callet, P.: HDR-VDP-2.2: a calibrated method for objective quality prediction of high dynamic range and standard images. J. Electron. Imaging **24**(1), 010501 (2015)

30. Narwaria, M., Da Silva, M.P., Le Callet, P.: HDR-VQM: An objective quality measure for high dynamic range video. Signal Process. Image Commun. **35**, 46–60 (2015)

31. Nayar, S.K., Mitsunaga, T.: High dynamic range imaging: spatially varying pixel exposures. In: Proceedings of the CVPR, pp. 472–479, June 2000

32. Pathak, D., Krähenbühl, P., Donahue, J., Darrell, T., Efros, A.A.: Context encoders: Feature learning by inpainting. In: Proceedings of CVPR, pp. 2536–2544, June 2016
33. Reinhard, E., Ward, G., Pattanaik, S., Debevec, P., Heidrich, W., Myszkowski, K.: High Dynamic Range Imaging: Acquisition, Display, and Image-Based Lighting. Morgan Kaufmann Publishers, second edn. (2010)
34. Robidoux, N., Capel, L.E.G., Seo, D.E., Sharma, A., Ariza, F., Heide, F.: End-to-end high dynamic range camera pipeline optimization. In: Proceedings of CVPR, pp. 6297–6307, June 2021
35. Ronneberger, O., Fischer, P., Brox, T.: U-Net: Convolutional networks for biomedical image segmentation. In: Navab, N., Hornegger, J., Wells, W.M., Frangi, A.F. (eds.) MICCAI 2015. LNCS, vol. 9351, pp. 234–241. Springer, Cham (2015). https://doi.org/10.1007/978-3-319-24574-4_28
36. Santos, M.S., Ren, T.I., Kalantari, N.K.: Single image HDR reconstruction using a CNN with masked features and perceptual loss. ACM Trans. Graph. **39**(4), 80:1–80:10 (2020)
37. Sen, P., Aguerrebere, C.: Practical high dynamic range imaging of everyday scenes: photographing the world as we see it with our own eyes. IEEE Signal Process. Mag. **33**(5), 36–44 (2016)
38. Serrano, A., Heide, F., Gutierrez, D., Wetzstein, G., Masia, B.: Convolutional sparse coding for high dynamic range imaging. Comput. Graph. Forum **35**(2), 153–163 (2016)
39. Sharif, S.M.A., Naqvi, R.A., Biswas, M.: Beyond joint demosaicking and denoising: An image processing pipeline for a pixel-bin image sensor. In: Proceedings of the CVPRW, pp. 233–242, June 2021
40. Suda, T., Tanaka, M., Monno, Y., Okutomi, M.: Deep snapshot HDR imaging using multi-exposure color filter array. In: Proceedings of the ACCV, pp. 353–370, November 2020
41. Sun, Q., Tseng, E., Fu, Q., Heidrich, W., Heide, F.: Learning rank-1 diffractive optics for single-shot high dynamic range imaging. In: Proceedings of CVPR, pp. 1383–1393, June 2020
42. Vargas, E., Martel, J.N., Wetzstein, G., Arguello, H.: Time-multiplexed coded aperture imaging: learned coded aperture and pixel exposures for compressive imaging systems. In: Proceedings of ICCV, pp. 2692–2702, October 2021
43. Vaswani, A., et al.: Attention is all you need. In: Proceedings of NeurIPS, pp. 6000–6010, December 2017
44. Vien, A.G., Lee, C.: Single-shot high dynamic range imaging via multiscale convolutional neural network. IEEE Access **9**, 70369–70381 (2021)
45. Wang, X., Girshick, R., Gupta, A., He, K.: Non-local neural networks. In: Proceedings of CVPR, pp. 7794–7803, June 2018
46. Wang, Y., Tao, X., Qi, X., Shen, X., Jia, J.: Image inpainting via generative multi-column convolutional neural networks. In: Proceedings of NeurIPS, pp. 329–338, December 2018
47. Woo, S.M., Ryu, J.H., Kim, J.O.: Ghost-free deep high-dynamic-range imaging using focus pixels for complex motion scenes. IEEE Trans. Image Process. **30**, 5001–5016 (2021)
48. Wu, S., Xu, J., Tai, Y.W., Tang, C.K.: Deep high dynamic range imaging with large foreground motions. In: Proceedings of ECCV, pp. 120–135, September 2018
49. Xie, C., et al.: Image inpainting with learnable bidirectional attention maps. In: Proceedings of the ICCV, pp. 8857–8866, October 2019

50. Xu, Y., Liu, Z., Wu, X., Chen, W., Wen, C., Li, Z.: Deep joint demosaicing and high dynamic range imaging within a single shot. IEEE Trans. Circ. Syst. Video Technol. **32**(7), 4255–4270 (2022)
51. Yan, Q., Gong, D., Shi, Q., van den Hengel, A., Shen, C., Reid, I., Zhang, Y.: Attention-guided network for ghost-free high dynamic range imaging. In: Proceedings of CVPR, pp. 1751–1760, June 2019
52. Yan, Q., et al.: Deep HDR imaging via a non-local network. IEEE Trans. Image Process. **29**, 4308–4322 (2020)
53. Yan, Q., et al.: Deep HDR imaging via a non-local network. IEEE Trans. Image Process. **29**, 4308–4322 (2020)
54. Yang, F., Yang, H., Fu, J., Lu, H., Guo, B.: Learning texture transformer network for image super-resolution. In: Proceedings of the CVPR, pp. 5790–5799, June 2020
55. Yu, J., Lin, Z., Yang, J., Shen, X., Lu, X., Huang, T.: Free-form image inpainting with gated convolution. In: Proceedings of the ICCV, pp. 4470–4479, October 2019
56. Yu, J., Lin, Z., Yang, J., Shen, X., Lu, X., Huang, T.S.: Generative image inpainting with contextual attention. In: Proceedings of the CVPR, pp. 5505–5514, June 2018
57. Zhang, Y., Li, K., Li, K., Zhong, B., Fu, Y.: Residual non-local attention networks for image restoration. In: Proceedings of the ICLR, May 2019
58. Zhao, H., Gallo, O., Frosio, I., Kautz, J.: Loss functions for image restoration with neural networks. IEEE Trans. Comput. Imaging **3**(1), 47–57 (2017)

Seeing Through a Black Box: Toward High-Quality Terahertz Imaging via Subspace-and-Attention Guided Restoration

Wen-Tai Su[1], Yi-Chun Hung[2], Po-Jen Yu[1], Shang-Hua Yang[1]📷,
and Chia-Wen Lin[1(✉)]📷

[1] Department of EE, National Tsing Hua University, Hsinchu 300044, Taiwan
cwin@ee.nthu.edu.tw
[2] Department of ECE, University of California, Los Angeles, USA

Abstract. Terahertz (THz) imaging has recently attracted significant attention thanks to its non-invasive, non-destructive, non-ionizing, material-classification, and ultra-fast nature for object exploration and inspection. However, its strong water absorption nature and low noise tolerance lead to undesired blurs and distortions of reconstructed THz images. The performances of existing restoration methods are highly constrained by the diffraction-limited THz signals. To address the problem, we propose a novel **S**ubspace-**A**ttention-guided **R**estoration **Net**work (SARNet) that fuses multi-spectral features of a THz image for effective restoration. To this end, SARNet uses multi-scale branches to extract spatio-spectral features of amplitude and phase which are then fused via shared subspace projection and attention guidance. Here, we experimentally construct a THz time-domain spectroscopy system covering a broad frequency range from 0.1 THz to 4 THz for building up temporal/spectral/spatial/phase/material THz database of hidden 3D objects. Complementary to a quantitative evaluation, we demonstrate the effectiveness of SARNet on 3D THz tomographic reconstruction applications.

Keywords: THz imaging · THz tomography · Deep learning · Image restoration

1 Introduction

Ever since the first camera's invention, imaging under different bands of electro-magnetic (EM) waves, especially X-ray and visible lights, has revolutionized our daily lives [16,29,39]. X-ray imaging plays a crucial role in medical diagnosis, such as cancer, odontopathy, and COVID-19 symptom [1,30,35], based on X-ray's high penetration depth to great varieties of materials; visible-light imaging

---

Supplementary Information The online version contains supplementary material available at https://doi.org/10.1007/978-3-031-20071-7_27.

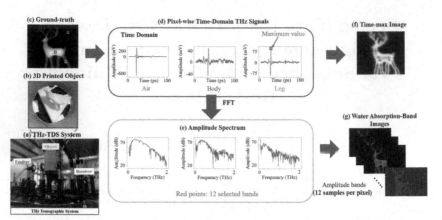

Fig. 1. THz data collection flow. (a) Our THz-TDS tomographic imaging system, (b) the 3D printed object, (c) the ground-truth of one projected view, (d) the time-domain THz signals of three different pixels (on the body and leg of the object and in the air), (e) the magnitude spectra of the three signals, (f) the time-max image (the maximums of each pixel's THz signal, (g) the images at the water-absorption frequencies.

has not only changed the way of recording lives but contributes to the development of artificial intelligence (AI) applications, such as surveillance security and surface defect inspection [38]. However, X-ray and visible-light imaging still face tough challenges. X-ray imaging is ionizing, which is harmful to biological objects and thus severely limits its application scope [9]. On the other hand, although both non-ionizing and non-destructive, visible-light imaging cannot retrieve most optically opaque objects' interior information due to the highly absorptive and intense scattering behaviors between light and matter in the visible light band. To visualize the 3D information of objects in a remote but accurate manner, terahertz (THz) imaging has become among the most promising candidates among all EM wave-based imaging techniques [3,4].

THz radiation, in between microwave and infrared, has often been regarded as the last frontier of EM wave [31], which provides its unique functionalities among all EM bands. Along with the rapid development of THz technology, THz imaging has recently attracted significant attention due to its non-invasive, non-destructive, non-ionizing, material-classification, and ultra-fast nature for advanced material exploration and engineering. As THz waves can partially penetrate through varieties of optically opaque materials, it carries hidden material tomographic information along the traveling path, making this approach a desired way to see through black boxes without damaging the exterior [13,21,22]. By utilizing light-matter interaction within the THz band, multifunctional tomographic information of a great variety of materials can also be retrieved even at a remote distance. In the past decades, THz time-domain spectroscopy (THz-TDS) has become one of the most representative THz imaging modalities to achieve non-invasive evaluation because of its unique capability of extracting geometric and multi-functional information of objects. Owing to its unique material interaction information in multi-dimensional domains—space, time, frequency, and

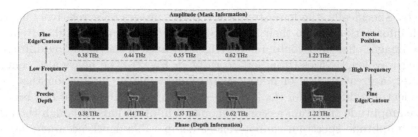

Fig. 2. THz multi-spectral amplitude and phase images measured from **Deer**.

phase, THz-TDS imaging has found applications in many emerging fields, including drug detection [18], industrial inspection, cultural heritage inspection [7], advanced material exploration [34], and cancer detection [2].

To retrieve temporal-spatio-spectral information of each object voxel, our THz imaging experiment setup is based on a THz-TDS system as shown in Fig. 1(a). Our measured object (a covered 3D printed deer, see Fig. 1(b)) is placed on the rotation stage in the THz path between the THz source and detector of the THz-TDS system. During the scanning, the THz-TDS system profiles each voxel's THz temporal signal (Fig. 1(d)) with 0.1 ps temporal resolution, whose amplitude corresponds to the strength of THz electric field. Based on the dependency between the amplitude of a temporal signal and THz electric field, in conventional THz imaging, the maximum peak of the signal (`Time-max`) is extracted as the feature for a voxel. The reconstructed image based on `Time-max` features can deliver great signal-to-noise ratio and a clear object contour. However, as shown in Fig. 1(f), the conventional THz imaging based on `Time-max` features suffers from several drawbacks, such as the undesired contour in the boundary region, the hollow in the body region, and the blurs in high spatial-frequency regions. To break this limitation, we utilize the spectral information (Fig. 1(g)) of THz temporal signals to supplement the `Time-max` features since the voxel of the material behaviors are encoded in both the phase and amplitude of different frequency components, according to the Fresnel equation [6].

Due to the large number of spectral bands with measured THz image data, it is required to sample a subset of the spectral bands to reduce the training parameters. The THz beam is significantly attenuated at water absorption frequencies (*i.e.*, the valleys indicated in Fig. 1(e)). Thus, the reconstructed THz images based on water absorption lines offer worse details. Besides, our THz-TDS system offers more than 20 dB SNR in a frequency range of 0.3 THz–1.3 THz. Considering the water absorption in THz regime [33,36] and the superior SNR in the range of 0.3 THz–1.3 THz, we select 12 frequencies at 0.380, 0.448, 0.557, 0.621, 0.916, 0.970, 0.988, 1.097, 1.113, 1.163, 1.208, and 1.229 THz. The spectral information including both amplitude and phase at the selected frequencies is extracted and used to restore clear 2D images. Figure 2 depicts multiple 2D THz images of the same object at the selected frequencies, showing very different contrasts and spatial resolutions as these hyperspectral THz image sets have different physical characteristics through the interaction of THz waves with objects. Specifically, the lower-frequency phase images offer relatively accurate depth information due to their higher SNR level, whereas the higher-frequency phase images offer finer contours and edges because of the shrinking diffraction-limited wavelength sizes (from left to right in Fig. 2). The phase also contains, however, a great variety of information of light-matter interaction that could cause learning difficulty for the image restoration task. To address this issue, we utilize amplitude spectrum as complementary information. Although the attenuated amplitude spectrum cannot reflect comparable depth accuracy levels as phase spectrum, amplitude spectrum still present superior SNR and more faithful contours of a measured object. Besides, as complementary information to phase, the lower-frequency amplitude offers higher contrast, while the higher-frequency amplitude offers a better object mask.

In sum, the amplitude complements the shortcomings of phase. The advantages of fusing the two signals from low to high frequencies are as follows: Since the low-frequency THz signal provides precise depth (the thickness of an object) and fine edge/contour information in the phase and amplitude, respectively, they together better delineate and restore the object. In contrast, the high-frequency feature maps of amplitude and phase respectively provide better edges/contours and precise position information, thereby constituting a better object mask from the complementary features. With these multi-spectral properties of THz images, we can extract rich information from a wide spectral range in the frequency domain to restore 2D THz images without additional computational cost or equipment, which is beneficial for practical THz imaging systems.

We propose a **S**ubspace-**A**ttention-guided **R**estoration **Net** (SARNet) that fuses complementary THz amplitude and phase spectral features to supplement the Time-max image for restoring clear 2D images. To this end, SARNet learns common representations in a latent subspace shared between the amplitude and phase components, and then adopts a Self-Attention mechanism to learn the wide-range dependencies of the spectral features for guiding the restoration task. Finally, from clear 2D images restored from corrupted images of an object captured from different angles, we can reconstruct high-quality 3D tomography via inverse Radon transform. Our main contributions are summarized as follows:

- We merge the THz temporal-spatio-spectral data, physics-guided data-driven models, and material properties for high-precision THz tomographic imaging. The proposed SARNet has demonstrated the capability in extracting and fusing features from the light-matter interaction data in THz spectral regime, which inherently contains interior 3D object information and its material behaviors. Based on the designed architecture of SARNet on feature fusion, SARNet delivers state-of-the-art performance on THz image restoration.
- With our established THz tomography dataset, we provide comprehensive quantitative/qualitative analyses among SARNet and SOTAs. SARNet significantly outperforms Time-max, baseline U-Net, and multi-band U-Net by 11.17 dB, 2.86 dB, and 1.51 dB in average PSNR.
- This proof-of-concept work shows that computer vision techniques can significantly contribute to the THz community and further open up a new inter-

disciplinary research field to boost practical applications, e.g., non-invasive evaluation, gas tomography, industrial inspection, material exploration, and biomedical imaging.

2   Related Work

2.1   Deep Learning-Based Image Restoration

In recent years, deep learning methods were first popularized in high-level visual tasks, and then gradually penetrated into many tasks such as image restoration and segmentation. Convolutional neural network (CNNs) have proven to achieve the state-of-the-art performances in fundamental image restoration problem [19, 28,41–43]. Several network models for image restoration were proposed, such as U-Net [28], hierarchical residual network [19] and residual dense network [43]. Notably, DnCNN [41] uses convolutions, BN, and ReLU to build 17-layer network for image restoration which was not only utilized for blind image denoising, but was also employed for image super-resolution and JPEG image deblocking. FFDNet [42] employs noise level maps as inputs and utilizes a single model to develop variants for solving problems with multiple noise levels. In [19] a very deep residual encoding-decoding (RED) architecture was proposed to solve the image restoration problem using skip connections. [43] proposed a residual dense network (RDN), which maximizes the reusability of features by using residual learning and dense connections. NBNet [5] employs subspace projection to transform learnable feature maps into the projection basis, and leverages non-local image information to restore local image details. Similarly, the `Time-max` image obtained from a THz imaging system can be cast as an image-domain learning problem which was rarely studied due to the difficulties in THz image data collection. Research works on image-based THz imaging include [24,25,37], and THz tomographic imaging works include [10,11].

2.2   Tomographic Reconstruction

Computer tomographic (CT) imaging methods started from X-ray imaging, and many methods of THz imaging are similar to those of X-ray imaging. One of the first works to treat X-ray CT as an image-domain learning problem was [17], that adopts CNN to refine tomographic images. In [14], U-Net was used to refine image restoration with significantly improved performances. [44] further projects sinograms measured directly from X-ray into higher-dimensional space and uses domain transfer to reconstruct images. The aforementioned works were specially designed for X-ray imaging.

Hyperspectral imaging [8,23,32] constitutes image modalities other than THz imaging. Different from THz imaging, Hyperspectral imaging collects continuous spectral band information of the target sample. Typically, the frequency bands fall in the visible and infrared spectrum; hence, most hyperspectral imaging modalities can only observe the surface characteristics of targeted objects.

3   Physics-Guided Terahertz Image Restoration

3.1   Overview

As different EM bands interact with objects differently, THz waves can partially penetrate through various optically opaque materials and carry hidden material tomographic information along the traveling path. This unique feature provides a new approach to visualize the essence of 3D objects, which other imaging modalities cannot achieve. Although existing deep neural networks can learn spatio-spectral information from a considerable amount of spectral cube data, we found that directly learning from the **full spectral information** to restore THz images usually leads to an unsatisfactory performance. The main reason is that the full spectral bands of THz signals involve diverse characteristics of materials, noises, and scattered signal, which causes difficulties in model training. To address this problem, our work is based on extracting **complementary information** from both the amplitude and phase of a THz signal. That is, as illustrated in Fig. 2, in the low-frequency bands, the amplitude images delineate finer edges and object contours while the phase images offer relatively precise depths of object surfaces. In contrast, in the high-frequency bands, the amplitude images offer object mask information while the phase images delineate finer edges and object contours. Therefore, the amplitude and phase complement to each other in both the low and high frequency bands.

Motivated by the above findings, we devise a novel multi-scale SARNet to capture such complementary spectral characteristics of materials to restore damaged

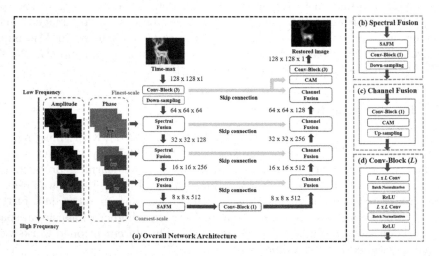

Fig. 3. (a) Overall network architecture of SARNet consisting of five scale-branches, where the finest-scale takes the feature tensor of one view's Time-max image as input. Additionally, each scale of the second to fifth takes 6 images of spectral frequencies (3 amplitude bands and 3 phase bands) as inputs. The three gray blocks show the detailed structures of (b) Spectral Fusion, (c) Channel Fusion, and (d) Conv-Block.

2D THz images effectively. The key idea of SARNet is to fuse spatio-spectral features with different characteristics on a common ground via deriving the shared latent subspace and discovering the short/long-range dependencies between the amplitude and phase to guide the feature fusion. To this end, SARNet is based on U-Net [28] to perform feature extraction and fusion in a multi-scale manner.

3.2 Network Architecture

On top of U-Net [28], the architecture of SARNet is depicted in Fig. 3. Specifically, SARNet is composed of an encoder (spectral-fusion module) with 5 branches of different scales (from the finest to the coarsest) and a decoder (channel fusion module) with 5 corresponding scale branches. Each scale branch of the encoder involves a Subspace-Attention-guided Fusion module (SAFM), a convolution block (Conv-block), and a down-sampler, except for the finest-scale branch that does not employ SAFM. To extract and fuse multi-spectral features of both amplitude and phase in a multi-scale manner, the encoder takes a THz 2D Time-max image as the input of the finest-scale branch as well as receives to its second to fifth scale branches 24 images of additional predominant spectral frequencies extracted from the THz signal, where each branch takes 6 images of different spectral bands (3 bands of amplitude and 3 bands of phase) to extract learnable features from these spectral bands. To reduce the number of model parameters, these 24 amplitude and phase images (from low to high frequencies) are downsampled to 4 different resolutions and fed into the second to fifth scale branches in a fine-to-coarse manner as illustrated in Fig. 3. We then fuse the multi-spectral amplitude and phase feature maps in each scale via the proposed SAFM that learns a common latent subspace shared between the amplitude and phase features to facilitate associating the short/long-range amplitude-phase dependencies. Projected into the shared latent subspace, the spectral features of amplitude and phase components, along with the down-sampled features of the upper layer, can then be properly fused together on a common ground in a fine-to-coarse fashion to obtain the final latent code.

The Conv-block(L) contains two stacks of $L \times L$ convolution, batch normalization, and ReLU operations. Because the properties of the spectral bands of amplitude and phase can be significantly different, we partly use $L = 1$ to learn the best linear combination of multi-spectral features to avoid noise confusion and reduce the number of model parameters. The up-sampler and down-sampler perform $2\times$ and $\frac{1}{2}\times$ scaling, respectively. The skip connections (SC) directly pass the feature maps of different spatial scales from individual encoder branches to the Channel Attention Modules (CAMs) of their corresponding branches of the decoder. The details of SAFM and CAM will be elaborated later.

In the decoder path, each scale-branch for channel fusion involves a up-sampler, a CAM, and a Conv-block. The Conv-block has the same functional blocks as that in the encoder. Each decoding-branch receives a "shallower-layer" feature map from the corresponding encoding-branch via the skip-connection shortcut and concatenates the feature map with the upsampled version of the decoded "deeper-layer" feature map from its coarser-scale branch. Besides, the concatenated feature map is then processed by CAM to capture the cross-channel interaction to complement the local region for restoration.

Note, a finer-scale branch of SARNet extracts shallower-layer features which tend to capture low-level features, such as colors and edges. To complement the Time-max image for restoration, we feed additional amplitude and phase images of low to high spectral-bands into the fine- to coarse-scale branches of SARNet. Since the spectral bands of THz amplitude and phase offer complementary information, as mentioned in Sect. 3.1, besides the Time-max image SARNet also extracts multi-scale features from the amplitude and phase images of 12 selected THz spectral bands, which are then fused by the proposed SAFM.

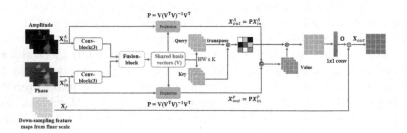

Fig. 4. Block diagram of Subspace-and-Attention guided Fusion Module (SAFM).

3.3   Subspace-Attention Guided Fusion Module

How to properly fuse the spectral features of THz amplitude and phase are, however, not trivial, as their characteristics are very different. To address the problem, inspired by [5] and [40], we propose the SAFM as shown in Fig. 4.

Let $\mathbf{X}_{in}^{A}$, $\mathbf{X}_{in}^{P} \in \mathbb{R}^{H \times W \times 3}$ denote the spectral bands of the THz amplitude and phase, respectively. The Conv-block $f_C(\cdot)$ extracts two intermediate feature maps $f_C(\mathbf{X}_{in}^{A})$, $f_C(\mathbf{X}_{in}^{P}) \in \mathbb{R}^{H \times W \times C_1}$ from $\mathbf{X}_{in}^{A}$ and $\mathbf{X}_{in}^{P}$, respectively. As a result, we then derive the K shared basis vectors $\mathbf{V} = [\mathbf{v}_1, \mathbf{v}_2, ..., \mathbf{v}_K]$ from $f_C(\mathbf{X}_{in}^{A})$ and $f_C(\mathbf{X}_{in}^{P})$, where $\mathbf{V} \in \mathbb{R}^{N \times K}$, $N = HW$ denotes the dimension of each basis vector, and K is the rank of the shared subspace. The basis set of the shared common subspace is expressed as

$$\mathbf{V} = f_F(f_C(\mathbf{X}_{in}^{A}), f_C(\mathbf{X}_{in}^{P})), \qquad (1)$$

where we first concatenate the two feature maps in the channel dimension and then feed the concatenated feature into the fusion-block $f_F(\cdot)$. The structure of the fusion-block is the same as that of the Conv-block with K output channels as indicated in the red block in Fig. 4. The weights of the fusion-block are learned in the end-to-end training stage. The shared latent-subspace learning mainly serves two purposes: 1) learning the common latent representations between the THz amplitude and phase bands, and 2) learning the subspace projection matrix to project the amplitude and phase features into a shared subspace such that they can be analyzed on a common ground. These both help identify wide-range dependencies of amplitude and phase features for feature fusion.

To find wide-range dependencies between the amplitude and phase features on a common ground, we utilize the orthogonal projection matrix $\mathbf{V}$ in (1) to estimate the self-attentions in the shared feature subspace as

$$\beta_{j,i} = \frac{\exp(s_{ij})}{\sum_{i=1}^{N} \exp(s_{ij})} \ , \ s_{ij} = \mathbf{v}_i^T \mathbf{v}_j \tag{2}$$

where $\beta_{j,i}$ represents the model attention in the i-th location of the j-th region.

The projection matrix $\mathbf{P}$ is derived from the subspace basis $\mathbf{V}$ as follows [20]:

$$\mathbf{P} = \mathbf{V}(\mathbf{V}^T\mathbf{V})^{-1}\mathbf{V}^T \tag{3}$$

where $(\mathbf{V}^T\mathbf{V})^{-1}$ is the normalization term to make the basis vectors orthogonal to each other during the basis generation process. As a result, the output of the self-attention mechanism becomes

$$\mathbf{o}_j = \left(\sum_{i=1}^{N} \beta_{j,i}\mathbf{s}_i\right), \ \ \mathbf{s}_i = \text{Concate}(\mathbf{PX}_{\text{in}}^A, \mathbf{PX}_{\text{in}}^P) \tag{4}$$

where the key of $\mathbf{s}_i \in \mathbb{R}^{HW \times 6}$ is obtained by concatenating the two feature maps $\mathbf{PX}_{\text{in}}^A$ and $\mathbf{PX}_{\text{in}}^P$ projected by orthogonal projection matrix $\mathbf{P} \in \mathbb{R}^{HW \times HW}$, and $\mathbf{X}_{\text{in}}^A$ and $\mathbf{X}_{\text{in}}^P$ are reshaped to $HW \times 3$. Since the operations are purely linear with some proper reshaping, they are differentiable.

Finally, we further fuse cross-scale features in the self-attention output by adding the down-sampled feature map $\mathbf{X}_f$ from the finer scale as

$$\mathbf{X}_{\text{out}} = f_s(\mathbf{o}) + \mathbf{X}_f \tag{5}$$

where f_s is the 1×1 convolution to keep the channel number consistent with $\mathbf{X}_f$.

3.4 Channel Attention Module

To fuse multi-scale features from different spectral bands in the channel dimension, we incorporate the efficient channel attention mechanism proposed in [26] in the decoder path of SARNet. In each decoding-branch, the original U-Net directly concatenates the up-sampled feature from the coarser scale with the feature from the corresponding encoding-branch via the skip-connection shortcut, and then fuses the intermediate features from different layers by convolutions. This, however, leads to poor image restoration performances in local regions such as incorrect object thickness or details. To address this problem, we propose a channel attention module (CAM) that adopts full channel attention in the dimensionality reduction operation by concatenating two channel attention groups. CAM first performs global average pooling to extract the global spatial information in each channel:

$$G_t = \frac{1}{H \times W} \sum_{i=1}^{H} \sum_{j=1}^{W} X_t(i,j) \tag{6}$$

462   W.-T. Su et al.

where $X_t(i,j)$ is the t-th channel of X_t at position (i,j) obtained by concatenating the up-sampled feature map $\mathbf{X}_c$ of the coarser-scale and the skip-connection feature map $\mathbf{X}_s$. The shape of G is from $C \times H \times W$ to $C \times 1 \times 1$.

We directly feed the result through two 1×1 convolution, sigmoid, and ReLU activation function as:

$$\mathbf{w} = \sigma\left(\text{Conv}_{1\times1}\left(\delta\left(\text{Conv}_{1\times1}(G)\right)\right)\right), \tag{7}$$

where $\text{Conv}_{1\times1}(\cdot)$ denotes a 1×1 convolution, σ is the sigmoid function, and δ is the ReLU function. In order to better restore a local region, we divide the weights $\mathbf{w}$ of different channels into two groups $\mathbf{w} = [\mathbf{w}_1, \mathbf{w}_2]$ corresponding to two different sets of input feature maps, respectively. Finally, we element-wise multiply the input X_c and X_s of the weights $\mathbf{w}$ and add these two group features.

3.5 Loss Function for THz Image Restoration

To effectively train SARNet, we employ the following mean squared error (MSE) loss function to measure the dissimilarity between the restored image $\mathbf{X}_{\text{rec}}$ and its ground-truth $\mathbf{X}_{\text{GT}}$:

$$\mathcal{L}_{\text{MSE}}(\mathbf{X}_{\text{GT}}, \mathbf{X}_{\text{rec}}) = \frac{1}{HW} \sum_{i=1}^{H} \sum_{j=1}^{W} (\mathbf{X}_{\text{GT}}(i,j) - \mathbf{X}_{\text{rec}}(i,j))^2, \tag{8}$$

where H and W are the height and width of the image.

3.6 3D Tomography Reconstruction

The 3D tomography of an object can then be reconstructed from the restored THz 2D images of the object scanned in different angles. To this end, we can directly apply the inverse Radon transform to obtain the 3D tomography, using methods like filtered back-projection [15] or the simultaneous algebraic reconstruction technique [27].

4 Experiments

We conduct experiments to evaluate the effectiveness of SARNet against existing state-of-the-art restoration methods. We first present our experiment settings and then evaluate the performances of SARNet and the competing methods on THz image restoration.

4.1 THz-TDS Image Dataset

As shown in Fig. 1, we prepare the sample objects by a Printech 3D printer and use the material of high impact polystyrene (HIPS) for 3D-printing the objects due to its high penetration of THz waves. We then use our in-house

Table 1. Quantitative comparison (PSNR and SSIM) of THz image restoration performances with different methods on seven test objects. ($\uparrow$: higher is better)

Method	PSNR $\uparrow$							SSIM $\uparrow$						
	Deer	DNA	Box	Eevee	Bear	Robot	Skull	Deer	DNA	Box	Eevee	Bear	Robot	Skull
Time-max	12.42	12.07	11.97	11.20	11.21	11.37	10.69	0.05	0.05	0.14	0.14	0.12	0.08	0.09
DnCNN-S [41]	19.94	23.95	19.13	19.69	19.44	19.72	17.33	0.73	0.77	0.73	0.72	0.63	0.77	0.36
RED [19]	19.30	24.17	20.18	19.97	19.17	19.76	16.28	0.81	0.83	0.74	0.77	0.75	0.80	0.74
NBNet [5]	20.24	25.10	20.21	19.84	20.12	20.01	19.69	0.81	0.85	0.75	0.77	0.80	0.80	0.78
U-Net$_{base}$ [28]	19.84	24.15	19.77	19.95	19.09	18.80	17.49	0.55	0.78	0.77	0.76	0.56	0.76	0.51
U-Net$_{MB}$	22.46	25.05	20.81	20.34	19.86	20.64	19.43	0.76	0.73	0.78	0.76	0.78	0.79	0.78
SARNet (Ours)	**22.98**	**26.05**	**22.67**	**20.87**	**21.42**	**22.66**	**22.48**	**0.84**	**0.90**	**0.83**	**0.82**	**0.82**	**0.83**	**0.84**

Asynchronous Optical Sampling (ASOPS) THz-TDS system [12] to measure the sample objects. Although the speed of our mechanical scanning stage limits the number and the size of the objects in the dataset, we carefully designed 7 objects to increase the dataset variety for the generalization to unseen objects. For example, the antler of Deer and the tilted cone of Box are designed for high spatial frequency and varying object thickness. Each sample object is placed on a motorized stage between the source and the receiver. With the help of the motorized stage, raster scans are performed on each object in multiple view angles. In the scanning phase, we scan the objects covering a rotational range of 180° (step-size: 6°), a horizontal range of 72 mm (step-size: 0.25 mm), and a variable vertical range corresponding to the object height (step-size: 0.25 mm). In this way, we obtain 30 projections of each object, which are then augmented to 60 projections by horizontal flipping. The ground-truths of individual projections are obtained by converting the original 3D printing files into image projections in every view-angle. We use markers to indicate the center of rotation to align the ground truths with the measured THz data. In this paper, a total of 7 objects are printed, measured, and aligned for evaluation.

4.2 Data Processing and Augmentation

In our experiments, we train SARNet using the 2D THz images collected from our THz imaging system shown in Fig. 2. The seven sample objects are consisting of 60 projections per object and 420 2D THz images in total. To evaluate the effectiveness of SARNet, we adopt the leave-one-out strategy: using the data of 6 objects as the training set, and that of the remaining object as the testing set. Due to the limited space, we only present part of the results in this section, and the complete results in the supplementary material. We will release our code (Link) and the THz image dataset (Link) after the work is accepted.

4.3 Quantitative Evaluations

To the best of our knowledge, there is no method specially designed for restoring THz images besides Time-max. Thus, we compare our method against several representative CNN-based image restoration models, including DnCNN [41],

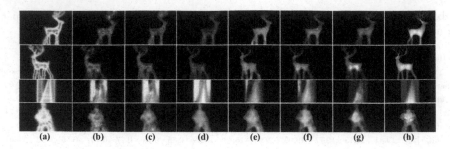

Fig. 5. Qualitative comparison of THz image restoration results for **Deer**, **Box**, and **Robot** from left to right: (a) `Time-max`, (b) `DnCNN-S` [41], (c) `RED` [19], (d) `NBNet` [5], (e) `U-Net`$_{base}$ [28], (f) `U-Net`$_{MS}$, (g) `SARNet`, and (h) the ground-truth.

Fig. 6. Illustration of 3D tomographic reconstruction results on **Deer** and **Robot** from left to right: (a) `Time-max`, (b) `DnCNN-S` [41], (c) `RED` [19], (d) `NBNet` [5], (e) `U-Net`$_{base}$ [28], (f) `U-Net`$_{MB}$, (g) `SARNet`, and (h) the ground-truth.

RED [19], and NBNet [5]. Moreover, we also compare two variants of U-Net [28]: baseline U-Net (`U-Net`$_{base}$) and multi-band U-Net (`U-Net`$_{MB}$). `U-Net`$_{base}$ extracts image features in five different scales following the original setting in U-Net [28], whereas `U-Net`$_{MB}$ incorporates multi-spectral features by concatenating the features of `Time-max` image with additional 12 THz bands for amplitude as the input (i.e., $12 + 1$ channels) of the finest scale of U-Net. For objective quality assessment, we adopt two widely-used metrics including the Peak Signal-to-Noise Ratio (PSNR) and Structural SIMilarity (SSIM) to respectively measure the pixel-level and structure-level similarities between a restored image and its ground-truth. To estimate the 3D tomographic reconstruction, we adopt the Mean-Square Error (MSE) between the cross-sections of a reconstructed 3D tomography and the corresponding ground-truths for assessing the 3D reconstruction accuracy as compared in Table 2.

Table 1 shows that our `SARNet` significantly outperforms the competing methods on all sample objects in both metrics. Specifically, `SARNet` outperforms `Time-max`, baseline U-Net (`U-Net`$_{base}$), and the multi-band U-Net (`U-Net`$_{MB}$) by 11.17 dB, 2.86 dB, and 1.51 dB in average PSNR, and 0.744, 0.170, and 0.072 in average SSIM for 7 objects. Similarly, in terms of 3D reconstruction accuracy, Table 2 demonstrates that our models both stably achieve significantly

Table 2. Quantitative comparison of MSE between the cross-sections of reconstructed 3D objects and the ground-truths with different methods on 7 objects. ($\downarrow$: lower is better)

Method	MSE $\downarrow$						
	Deer	DNA	Box	Eevee	Bear	Robot	Skull
Time-max	0.301	0.026	0.178	0.169	0.084	0.203	0.225
DnCNN-S [41]	0.153	0.162	0.309	0.149	0.056	0.223	0.293
RED [19]	0.139	0.238	0.300	0.179	0.070	0.215	0.324
NBNet [5]	0.240	0.184	0.305	0.134	0.088	0.128	0.138
U-Net$_{base}$ [28]	0.227	0.166	0.266	0.157	0.077	0.093	0.319
U-Net$_{MB}$	0.183	0.043	0.205	0.114	0.089	0.196	0.080
SARNet (Ours)	**0.107**	**0.015**	**0.041**	**0.105**	**0.050**	**0.065**	**0.052**

Table 3. Quantitative comparison (PSNR and SSIM) of THz image restoration performances on seven test objects with the different variants of SARNet based on different settings. ($\uparrow$: higher is better)

Method	PSNR $\uparrow$							SSIM $\uparrow$						
	Deer	DNA	Box	Eevee	Bear	Robot	Skull	Deer	DNA	Box	Eevee	Bear	Robot	Skull
U-Net$_{base}$	19.84	25.63	19.77	19.95	19.09	18.80	10.69	0.55	0.78	0.77	0.76	0.56	0.76	0.51
Amp-Unet w/o SAFM	22.05	25.84	20.32	20.21	20.48	20.63	20.70	0.80	0.83	0.77	0.79	0.80	0.78	0.77
Phase-Unet w/o SAFM	21.14	24.98	20.42	20.26	20.15	20.58	21.36	0.82	0.72	0.78	0.78	0.81	0.74	0.75
Mix-Unet w/o SAFM	21.44	25.78	20.00	20.32	20.44	21.12	21.18	0.81	0.81	0.78	0.80	0.79	0.81	0.82
Amp-Unet w/ SAFM	20.97	26.00	21.83	20.22	20.30	21.11	20.18	0.84	0.90	0.78	0.80	0.79	0.83	0.79
Phase-Unet w/ SAFM	22.66	25.52	21.65	20.63	20.18	21.50	21.42	0.83	0.86	0.79	0.74	0.81	0.83	0.82
SARNet (Ours)	**22.98**	**26.05**	**22.67**	**20.87**	**21.42**	**22.66**	**22.48**	**0.84**	**0.90**	**0.83**	**0.82**	**0.82**	**0.83**	**0.84**

lower average MSE of tomographic reconstruction than the competing methods on all the seven objects. For qualitative evaluation, Fig. 5 illustrates a few restored views for **Deer**, **Box**, and **Robot**, demonstrating that SARNet can restore objects with much finer and smoother details (e.g., the antler and legs of **Deer**, the depth and shape of **Box**, and the body of **Robot**), faithful thickness of material (e.g., the body and legs of **Deer** and the correct edge thickness of **Box**), and fewer artifacts (e.g., holes and broken parts). Both the quantitative and qualitative evaluations confirm a significant performance leap with SARNet over the competing methods.

4.4 Ablation Studies

To verify the effectiveness of multi-spectral feature fusion, we evaluate the restoration performances with SARNet under different settings in Table 3. The compared methods include (1) U-Net$_{base}$ using a single channel of data (Time-max) without using features of multi-spectral bands; (2) **Amp-Unet w/o SAFM** employing multi-band amplitude feature (without the SAFM mechanism) in each of the four spatial-scale branches, except for the finest scale (that accepts the Time-max image as the input), where 12 spectral bands of amplitude (3 bands/scale) are fed into the four spatial-scale branches with the assignment of the highest-frequency band to the coarsest scale, and vice versa; (3) **Phase-Unet w/o SAFM** employing multi-spectral phase features with the same spectral arrangements as (2), and without the SAFM mechanism; (4) **Mix-Unet w/o SAFM** concatenating multi-spectral amplitude and phase features (without the SAFM mechanism) in each of the four spatial-scale branches, except for the finest scale (that accepts the Time-max image as the input), where totally 24 additional spectral bands of amplitude and phase (3 amplitude plus 3 phase bands for each scale) are fed into the four branches; (5) **Amp-Unet with SAFM** utilizing attention-guided multi-spectral amplitude features with the same spectral arrangements as specified in (2); and (6) **Phase-Unet with SAFM** utilizing attention-guided multi-spectral phase features with the same spectral arrangements as in (2).

The results clearly demonstrate that the proposed SAFM can benefit fusing the spectral features of both amplitude and phase with different characteristics for THz image restoration. Specifically, employing additional multi-spectral features of either amplitude or phase as the input of the multi-scale branches in the network (i.e., Amp-Unet or Phase-Unet w/o SAFM) can achieve performance improvement over U-Net$_{base}$. Combining both the amplitude and phase features without the proposed subspace-and-attention guided fusion (i.e., **Mix-Unet w/o SAFM**) does not outperform **Amp-Unet w/o SAFM** and usually leads to worse performances. The main reason is that the characteristics of the amplitude and phase features are too different to be fused to extract useful features with direct fusion methods. This motivates our subspace-and-attention guided fusion scheme, that learns to effectively identify and fuse important and complementary features on a common ground.

4.5   3D Tomography Reconstruction

Our goal is to reconstruct clear and faithful 3D object shapes through our THz tomographic imaging system. In our system, the tomography of an object is reconstructed from 60 views of 2D THz images of the object, each being restored by SARNet, via the inverse Radon transform. Figure 6 illustrates the 3D reconstructions of our reconstruct results much clearer and more faithful 3D images with finer details such as the thickness of body and clear antlers of **Deer** and the gun in **Robot**'s hand, achieving by far the best 3D THz tomography reconstruction quality in the literature. Complete 3D reconstruction results are provided in the supplementary material.

5   Conclusion

We proposed a 3D THz imaging system that is the first to merge THz spatio-spectral data, data-driven models, and material properties to restore corrupted THz images. Based on the physical characteristics of THz waves passing through different materials, our SARNet efficiently fuses spatio-spectral features with different characteristics on a common ground via deriving a shared latent subspace and discovering the wide-range dependencies between the amplitude and phase to guide the feature fusion for boosting restoration performance. Our results have confirmed a performance leap from the relevant state-of-the-art techniques in the area. We believe our findings in this work will stimulate further applicable research for THz imaging with advanced computer vision techniques.

References

1. Abbas, A., Abdelsamea, M., Gaber, M.: Classification of COVID-19 in chest x-ray images using DeTraC deep convolutional neural network. Appl. Intell. **51**(2), 854–864 (2021)
2. Bowman, T., et al.: Pulsed terahertz imaging of breast cancer in freshly excised murine tumors. J. Biomed. Opt. **23**(2), 026004 (2018)
3. braham, E., Younus, A., Delagnes, T.C., Mounaix, P.: Non-invasive investigation of art paintings by terahertz imaging. Appl. Phys. A **100**(3), 585–590 (2010)
4. Calvin, Y., Shuting, F., Yiwen, S., Emma, P.M.: The potential of terahertz imaging for cancer diagnosis: a review of investigations to date. Quant. Imaging Med. Surg. **2**(1), 33 (2012)
5. Cheng, S., Wang, Y., Huang, H., Liu, D., Fan, H., Liu, S.: NBNet: noise basis learning for image denoising with subspace projection. In: Proceedings of IEEE/CVF International Conference on Computer Vision and Pattern Recognition, pp. 4896–4906 (2021)
6. Dorney, T.D., Baraniuk, R.G., Mittleman, D.M.: Material parameter estimation with terahertz time-domain spectroscopy. JOSA A **18**(7), 1562–1571 (2001)
7. Fukunaga, K.: THz Technology Applied to Cultural Heritage in Practice. CHS, Springer, Tokyo (2016). https://doi.org/10.1007/978-4-431-55885-9
8. Geladi, P., Burger, J., Lestander, T.: Hyperspectral imaging: calibration problems and solutions. Chemom. Intell. Lab. Syst. **72**(2), 209–217 (2004)
9. de Gonzalez, A.B., Darby, S.: Risk of cancer from diagnostic x-rays: estimates for the UK and 14 other countries. Lancet **363**(9406), 345–351 (2004)
10. Hung, Y.C., Yang, S.H.: Kernel size characterization for deep learning terahertz tomography. In: Proc. IEEE International Conference on Infrared, Millimeter, and Terahertz Waves (IRMMW-THz), pp. 1–2 (2019)
11. Hung, Y.C., Yang, S.H.: Terahertz deep learning computed tomography. In: Proceedings of International Infrared, Millimeter, and Terahertz Waves, pp. 1–2. IEEE (2019)
12. Janke, C., Först, M., Nagel, M., Kurz, H., Bartels, A.: Asynchronous optical sampling for high-speed characterization of integrated resonant terahertz sensors. Opt. Lett. **30**(11), 1405–1407 (2005)
13. Jansen, C., et al.: Terahertz imaging: applications and perspectives. Appl. Opt. **49**(19), E48–E57 (2010)
14. Jin, K.H., McCann, M.T., Froustey, E., Unser, M.: Deep convolutional neural network for inverse problems in imaging. IEEE Trans. Image Process. **26**(9), 4509–4522 (2017)
15. Kak, A.C.: Algorithms for reconstruction with nondiffracting sources. In: Principles of Computerized Tomographic Imaging, pp. 49–112 (2001)

16. Kamruzzaman, M., ElMasry, G., Sun, D.W., Allen, P.: Application of NIR hyperspectral imaging for discrimination of lamb muscles. J. Food Engineer. **104**(3), 332–340 (2011)
17. Kang, E., Min, J., Ye, J.C.: A deep convolutional neural network using directional wavelets for low-dose x-ray CT reconstruction. J. Medical Phys. **44**(10), e360–e375 (2017)
18. Kawase, K., Ogawa, Y., Watanabe, Y., Inoue, H.: Non-destructive terahertz imaging of illicit drugs using spectral fingerprints. Opt. Express **11**(20), 2549–2554 (2003)
19. Mao, X., Shen, C., Yang, Y.B.: Image restoration using very deep convolutional encoder-decoder networks with symmetric skip connections. In: Proceedings of Advances in Neural Information Processing Systems, pp. 2802–2810 (2016)
20. Meyer, C.D.: Matrix Analysis and Applied Linear Algebra. SIAM (2000)
21. Mittleman, D., Gupta, M., Neelamani, R., Baraniuk, R., Rudd, J., Koch, M.: Recent advances in terahertz imaging. Appl. Phys. B **68**(6), 1085–1094 (1999)
22. Mittleman, D.M.: Twenty years of terahertz imaging. Opt. Express **26**(8), 9417–9431 (2018)
23. Ozdemir, A., Polat, K.: Deep learning applications for hyperspectral imaging: a systematic review. J. Inst. Electron. Comput. **2**(1), 39–56 (2020)
24. Popescu, D.C., Ellicar, A.D.: Point spread function estimation for a terahertz imaging system. EURASIP J. Adv. Sig. Process. **2010**(1), 575817 (2010)
25. Popescu, D.C., Hellicar, A., Li, Y.: Phantom-based point spread function estimation for terahertz imaging system. In: Blanc-Talon, J., Philips, W., Popescu, D., Scheunders, P. (eds.) ACIVS 2009. LNCS, vol. 5807, pp. 629–639. Springer, Heidelberg (2009). https://doi.org/10.1007/978-3-642-04697-1_59
26. Qin, X., Wang, X., Bai, Y., Xie, X., Jia, H.: FFA-net: feature fusion attention network for single image dehazing. In: Proceedings of the AAAI Conference on Artificial Intelligence, pp. 11908–11915 (2020)
27. Recur, B., et al.: Investigation on reconstruction methods applied to 3D terahertz computed tomography. Opt. Express **19**(6), 5105–5117 (2011)
28. Ronneberger, O., Fischer, P., Brox, T.: U-net: convolutional networks for biomedical image segmentation. In: Proceedings of Interenaional Conference on Medical Image Computer and Computing.-Assisted Intervention, pp. 234–241 (2015)
29. Rotermund, H.H., Engel, W., Jakubith, S., Von Oertzen, A., Ertl, G.: Methods and application of UV photoelectron microscopy in heterogenous catalysis. Ultramicroscopy **36**(1–3), 164–172 (1991)
30. Round, A.R., et al.: A preliminary study of breast cancer diagnosis using laboratory based small angle x-ray scattering. Phys. Med. Biol. **50**(17), 4159 (2005)
31. Saeedkia, D.: Handbook of Terahertz Technology for Imaging, Sensing and Communications. Elsevier, Amsterdam (2013)
32. Schultz, R., Nielsen, T., Zavaleta, R.J., Wyatt, R., Garner, H.: Hyperspectral imaging: a novel approach for microscopic analysis. Cytometry **43**(4), 239–247 (2001)
33. Slocum, D.M., Slingerland, E.J., Giles, R.H., Goyette, T.M.: Atmospheric absorption of terahertz radiation and water vapor continuum effects. J. Quant. Spectrosc. Radiat. Transf. **127**, 49–63 (2013)
34. Spies, J.A., et al.: Terahertz spectroscopy of emerging materials. J. Phys. Chem. C **124**(41), 22335–22346 (2020)
35. Tuan, T.M., Fujita, H., Dey, N., Ashour, A.S., Ngoc, T.N., Chu, D.T., et al.: Dental diagnosis from x-ray images: an expert system based on fuzzy computing. Biomed. Sig. Process. Control **39**, 64–73 (2018)

36. Van Exter, M., Fattinger, C., Grischkowsky, D.: Terahertz time-domain spectroscopy of water vapor. Opt. Lett. **14**(20), 1128–1130 (1989)
37. Wong, T.M., Kahl, M., Bolívar, P.H., Kolb, A.: Computational image enhancement for frequency modulated continuous wave (FMCW) THZ image. J. Infrared Millimeter Terahertz Waves **40**(7), 775–800 (2019)
38. Xie, X.: A review of recent advances in surface defect detection using texture analysis techniques. ELCVIA: Electron. Lett. Comput. Vis. Iimage Ana. 1–22 (2008)
39. Yujiri, L., Shoucri, M., Moffa, P.: Passive millimeter wave imaging. IEEE Microwave Mag. **4**(3), 39–50 (2003)
40. Zhang, H., Goodfellow, I., Metaxas, D., Odena, A.: Self-attention generative adversarial networks. In: Proceedings of International Conference on Machine learning, pp. 7354–7363 (2019)
41. Zhang, K., Ana Y. Chen, W.Z., Meng, D., Zhang, L.: Beyond a Gaussian denoiser: residual learning of deep CNN for image denoising. IEEE Trans. Image Process. **26**(7), 3142–3155 (2017)
42. Zhang, K., Zuo, W.M., Zhang, L.: FFDNet: toward a fast and flexible solution for CNN-based image denoising. IEEE Trans. Image Process. **27**(9), 4608–4622 (2018)
43. Zhang, Y., Tian, Y., Kong, Y., Zhong, B., Fu, Y.: Residual dense network for image restoration. IEEE Trans. Pattern Anal. Mach. Intell. (2020)
44. Zhu, B., Liu, J.Z., Cauley, S.F., Rosen, R.B., Rosen, M.S.: Image reconstruction by domain-transform manifold learning. Nature **555**(7697), 487–492 (2018)

Tomography of Turbulence Strength Based on Scintillation Imaging

Nir Shaul[(✉)] [iD] and Yoav Y. Schechner [iD]

Viterbi Faculty of Electrical and Computers Engineering,
Technion - Israel Institute of Technology, Haifa, Israel
nir.ohaul@gmail.com, yoav@ee.technion.ac.il

Abstract. Developed areas have plenty of artificial light sources. As the stars, they appear to twinkle, i.e., scintillate. This effect is caused by random turbulence. We leverage this phenomenon in order to reconstruct the spatial distribution of the turbulence strength (TS). Sensing is passive, using a multi-view camera setup in a city scale. The cameras sense the scintillation of light sources in the scene. The scintillation signal has a linear model of a line integral over the field of TS. Thus, the TS is recovered by linear tomography analysis. Scintillation offers measurements and TS recovery, which are more informative than tomography based on angle-of-arrival (projection distortion) statistics. We present the background and theory of the method. Then, we describe a large field experiment to demonstrate this idea, using distributed imagers. As far as we know, this work is the first to propose reconstruction of a TS horizontal field, using passive optical scintillation measurements.

Keywords: Computational photography · Multi-view imaging · Atmospheric remote sensing

1 Introduction

A beautiful visual scene is that of twinkling stars. Twinkling is even stronger when observing by the naked eye artificial light sources (bulbs) at a distance. This effect is formally termed *scintillation* [8,24], and it is caused by atmospheric turbulence. Prior computer vision art on turbulence mostly seeks image enhancement [12,25, 49], and simulations [34]. However, turbulence *encodes* information about scenes, such as distance to background objects [41,48] and crosswind [1,28].

We deal with sensing of the turbulence itself, specifically the field of turbulence strength (TS). It is important to quantify and model turbulence due to its effect on wind turbine farms [26], meteorology, aviation [39], free space communication and other technologies [10,45]. To quantify TS, the main methods recover a *single* value which averages [41,47] the TS over a single line of sight (LOS). The LOS is between a fixed laser source and fixed detector (a scintillometer), or

Supplementary Information The online version contains supplementary material available at https://doi.org/10.1007/978-3-031-20071-7_28.

Fig. 1. Scintillating light sources over Haifa Bay, imaged on a winter evening. [Left] A preliminary capture of a twilight scene consists of lights and landmarks. [Right] Operational imaging optimized for turbulence scintillation sensing. Colors encode processed results: valid measurements are in green; red denotes signals that are either saturated or too dim. (Color figure online)

that of a camera [23,44]. However, the TS generally varies spatially [13]. There are methods that resolve the TS over a LOS, using high definition correlation of objects around the LOS [6,15,27,32,37]. At a laboratory scale, TS can be spatially resolved by active coherent illumination [17] (holography).

We suggest a method for reconstructing the TS in a wide horizontal field. The sensing is passive, relying on scintillation of bulbs that happen to be in the scene. The bulbs are observed from multiple cameras in a wide breadth of locations and fields of view (FOV). Data analysis is that of linear tomography, i.e., multi-view imaging for volumetric reconstruction. The main idea is that a scintillation index of an observation is linearly related to the spatially varying TS.[1] Our work is related to [3]. In [3], measurement linearly weight TS in a way that is mostly sensitive to air near a camera. However, usually we are interested in remote sensing of TS in a wide, deep domain, rather than the air adjacent to a camera. Our method, in contrast, is most sensitive around the domain core. We therefore yield better sensing of regions that are inaccessible.

The reason for this is that the sensing principle of [3] is temporal geometric distortion, caused by turbulence mainly near the camera. On the other hand, our sensing principle is scintillation, which is mostly affected by air away from a camera and the objects it observes. We provide the theory of this tomographic principle. We further demonstrate it in a city-scale real experiment, which includes a set of cameras dispersed in the domain. This adds-up to other recent work in computer vision, which seeks new ways for sensing of the atmosphere, particularly using new types of tomography [2,16,21,22,40].

2   Background on Turbulence

Denote a spatial location in a refractive medium by $\mathbf{X} = (X, Y, Z)$. In our case, the medium is air. Uppercase Z denotes *vertical location* in 3D. Over time t,

---

[1] Note that tomography to sense properties of atmospheric scatterers is non-linear in the unknowns [21,22,30,35].

the medium changes due to eddies having variable temperatures, pressure and humidity. The eddies are created by winds or local heating sources on the ground. The eddies are chaotic and constitute *turbulence*. The said medium variations lead to changes in the medium's refractive index, denoted as the unit-less $n(\mathbf{X}, t)$. The changes are chaotic, but have established statistics. For temporally stationary turbulence [3], a *structure function* [20,41] is defined by

$$\mathcal{D}_n(\mathbf{X}_1, \mathbf{X}_2) = \langle [n(\mathbf{X}_1, t) - n(\mathbf{X}_2, t)]^2 \rangle_t \tag{1}$$

for any two points $\mathbf{X}_1, \mathbf{X}_2$ in the medium. Typical times scales of turbulence in air are 1 s to 1 h, corresponding to length scales from 1 mm up to the order of 1 km. Within these scales, $\mathcal{D}_n$ is spatially wide-sense-stationary, according to Kolmogorov [18,19]. Let us approximate the structure function as space-invariant, depending only on the distance $\rho = ||\mathbf{X}_1 - \mathbf{X}_2||$, in units of meters. Then

$$\mathcal{D}_n(\rho) = C_n^2 \rho^{2/3}. \tag{2}$$

Here C_n^2 is termed the refractive index *structure constant* [20,41]. The units of C_n^2 are $m^{-2/3}$. The structure constant is non-negative and has typical values in the range $10^{-17} m^{-2/3}$ to $10^{-13} m^{-2/3}$.

The TS is quantified by C_n^2. Suppose $C_n^2 = 0$ in Eq. (2). Then Eq. (1) means that the refractive index is spatially uniform, which occurs when the medium is still. The higher C_n^2 is, the higher the spatiotemporal variability of the refractive index. This leads to observable optical effects [13]. In large scales, some regions are more turbulent than others, due to spatial variations of temperature gradients and winds. Thus we denote TS by $C_n^2(\mathbf{X})$. Locally, nature it is quasi-stationary, allowing the use of space-invariant correlations as Eq. (2). Indeed, the form $C_n^2(\mathbf{X})$ is prevalent in prior art [15,32], including theory [20,38].

Vertical vs. Horizontal Imaging

There is a clear distinction between imaging of celestial objects (e.g., stars) and low-altitude objects. The atmosphere is thin: air pressure falls to half that of sea-level at 5 km. Moreover, local topographic features (which affect wind) and sources of temperature gradients and moisture are mainly on the ground. Thus turbulence effects are strongest at very low altitudes. In a vertical observation of a celestial object, the LOS is mostly [27] affected by the lowest 3 km (see Fig. 2). The situation is very different [27,46] when observing objects near ground (horizontal views). Then, the entire LOS passes through the densest air, rich in turbulence sources. Moreover, horizontal paths can extend far beyond 3 km. Hence, horizontal imaging easily expresses strong visual effects of turbulence.

One of visual effects of turbulence is termed *Seeing*. In this effect, random refraction perturbs the angle of arrival (AOA) of a ray from an object to the camera [33]. Thus, the LOS of each pixel wiggles, creating spatiotemporal geometric distortions in image sequences. For an object at distance L and a camera having a lens aperture diameter D, the AOA of a LOS has variance given by

$$\sigma_{\text{AOA}}^2 = 2.914 D^{-1/3} \int_0^L C_n^2[\mathbf{X}(z)] w_{\text{AOA}}(z|L) dz, \qquad \mathbf{X} \in \text{LOS} \tag{3}$$

Fig. 2. Vertical and horizontal turbulence paths. For vertical paths, approximately 60% of the turbulence is located 3 km near the sensor [27], and the propagation model is that of a collimated beam (plane wave). In horizontal imaging, turbulence can be strong all along the LOS, and the propagation model is that of a point source (spherical wave).

where

$$w_{\mathrm{AOA}}(z|L) = \left(\frac{z}{L}\right)^{5/3}. \tag{4}$$

Note that $z \in [0, L]$ is a *location parameter* along a LOS. Here $z = 0$ corresponds to the object location, while the camera is at $z = L$ (Fig. 2). The term $w_{\mathrm{AOA}}(z|L)$ weights the contribution of $C_n^2[\mathbf{X}(z)]$ along the LOS. From Eq. (4), clearly, the contribution is maximal by a turbulent air parcel right near the camera lens. The farther the turbulent air parcel (lower z), the smaller is its effect on σ_{AOA}^2.

Another visual effects of turbulence is termed *Scintillation*. It is the reason that stars twinkle. Similarly, it is the reason that distant bulbs on horizontal paths twinkle. In scintillation, the measured light intensity fluctuates. We provide more details about this effect in Sect. 3.

3   Scintillation by Turbulence

There are several theories of scintillation, based on different approximations of light propagation [29,31]. Here we provide an intuitive illustration of how a turbulent medium creates twinkling, in a camera observing a single isotropic point source. Consider a very simplified case, where an air parcel has a shape of a lens, and its refractive index is slightly lower than that of calm steady air. Then, the air parcel acts as a very weak diverging lens (Fig. 3).

If the air parcel is adjacent to the camera lens ($z = L$), then it has a negligible effect on the light flux gathered by the camera. A similar outcome occurs if the air parcel is adjacent to the isotropic point object ($z = 0$). As a result, no matter what is the random refractive index of the air parcel, it does not change

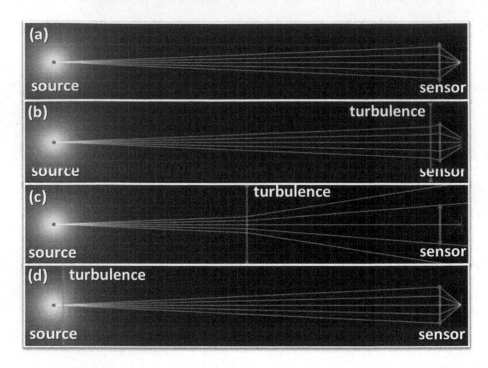

Fig. 3. Ray tracing simulation, modeling turbulence phenomena as defocusing by a lens. The influence of the turbulence is minor if it is located close to the sensor (**b**) or to the point source (**d**). The influence becomes major while located in the middle (**c**). Based on a ray-tracing simulator [50].

the measured intensity in these two cases. However, if the air parcel is at the center of the LOS, ($z = L/2$), it has a significant effect: some light rays miss the camera aperture, leading to loss of light gathered by the camera. Because the air-parcel has a random refractive index, the loss of gathered light power is random. This leads to observed scintillation. In analogy to Eqs. (3, 4), we thus expect that in scintillation[2] of an isotropic source (marked ●), there is a weight of $C_n^2[\mathbf{X}(z)]$ along a LOS, which satisfies

$$w_{\text{scint}}^{\bullet}(z = 0\,L) = 0, \quad w_{\text{scint}}^{\bullet}(z = L|L) = 0, \quad L/2 = \arg\max_z w_{\text{scint}}^{\bullet}(z|L). \quad (5)$$

An isotropic light source emits a spherical wave. Rigorous wave-optics analysis of scintillation of a spherical wave yields the following result. Let the intensity observed by the camera at time t be $I(t)$. Its expectation value is $\langle I(t) \rangle_t$. Define

---

[2] From the illustration, despite beam spread caused by turbulence, if the camera lens is large enough, the lens gathers the light power as in non-turbulent air. This inhibits the scintillation signal, and termed *aperture filtering*. In practice, the aperture filters scintillation if $D > 5\,\text{cm}$. In our work, this is negligible because $D < 5\,\text{cm}$.

a unit-less normalized variance by

$$\sigma_I^2 = \left\langle \left[\frac{I - \langle I(t)\rangle_t}{\langle I(t)\rangle_t}\right]^2 \right\rangle_t = \frac{\langle I^2(t)\rangle_t - [\langle I(t)\rangle_t]^2}{[\langle I(t)\rangle_t]^2} = \frac{\langle I^2(t)\rangle_t}{[\langle I(t)\rangle_t]^2} - 1. \qquad (6)$$

In our context, σ_I^2 is termed a *scintillation index*. For a spherical wave having wavelength λ propagating in a turbulent medium, the scintillation index is modelled [20, 24, 38] by

$$\sigma_{I\bullet}^2 = 2.24 \left(\frac{2\pi}{\lambda}\right)^{7/6} \int_0^L C_n^2[\mathbf{X}(z)] w_{\text{scint}}^\bullet(z|L) dz, \qquad \mathbf{X} \in \text{LOS} \qquad (7)$$

where

$$w_{\text{scint}}^\bullet(z|L) = (L - z)^{5/6} \left(\frac{z}{L}\right)^{5/6}. \qquad (8)$$

Note that Eq. (8) is consistent with Eq. (5).

There is an additional model of scintillation, where the object is a star [5, 7, 27], far away from the turbulent medium, observed vertically from Earth (Fig. 2), or a laser-based scintillometer [42]. Each can be approximated as a plane wave source, marked ‖. Then, the scintillation index is modelled by

$$\sigma_{I\|}^2 = 2.24 \left(\frac{2\pi}{\lambda}\right)^{7/6} \int_0^L C_n^2[\mathbf{X}(z)] w_{\text{scint}}^\|(z|L) dz, \qquad \mathbf{X} \in \text{LOS} \qquad (9)$$

where

$$w_{\text{scint}}^\|(z|L) = (L - z)^{5/6}. \qquad (10)$$

The weight functions $w_{\text{AOA}}(z|L)$, $w_{\text{scint}}^\bullet(z|L)$, $w_{\text{scint}}^\|(z|L)$ are plotted in Fig. 4. According to Ref. [8], in a weak scintillation regime, $\sigma_I^2 < 0.2$, while $I(t)$ is sampled from approximately a log normal distribution. In a very weak regime, $\sigma_I^2 < 0.1$, while $I(t)$ is sampled approximately from a normal distribution.

4   TS Tomography from Scintillation

We formalize an inverse problem, of reconstructing C_n^2 from scintillation measurements of point sources. The formulation is that of a linear tomography problem. As seen in Eq. (7), over a single LOS, the scintillation index is a linear (weighted) integral of $C_n^2(\mathbf{X})$. Linear path integrals are the basis of linear tomography as used in medical imaging.

Analogously, we formulate TS tomography based on scintillation of point sources at horizontal views. As in medical imaging, we need multi-view projections. Then, different LOSs yield a set of independent linear equations as (7), modeling how the unknown field $C_n^2(\mathbf{X})$ leads to the set of measured σ_I^2.

Empirically, Eq. (6) uses a sequence of images. Each image is affected by image noise, including photon noise. This aspect needs to be accounted for.

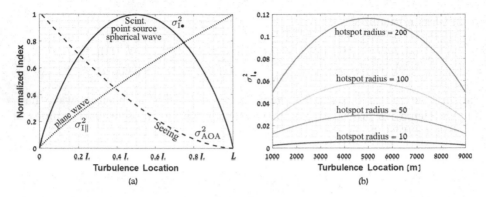

Fig. 4. (a) Spherical wave, plane wave, and AOA theoretical Weights. (b) Simulation results, for a set of hot-spot locations and radii. Here $C_n^2 = 1e^{-15}m^{-2/3}$. The sensor and source are located at $X = 0$ and $X = 10\,\text{km}$, respectively.

Let p denote a specific pixel observing a point object (bulb) **O** from a specific viewpoint. Without turbulence, in a lab, the variance of imaging noise (VAR$_\text{noise}$) can be calibrated per expected graylevel $\langle I(t)\rangle_t$. Imaging noise is independent of turbulence-induced scintillation, whose variance is VAR$_\text{scint}(p)$. Therefore, the empirical variance VAR$_\text{data}$ of the measured intensity of **O** satisfies

$$\text{VAR}_\text{data}(p) = \text{VAR}_\text{scint}(p) + \text{VAR}_\text{noise} . \qquad (11)$$

Therefore, from Eqs. (6, 7, 11), a datum at p is

$$y(p) \equiv \sigma_{\mathbf{I}\bullet}^2(p) = \frac{\text{VAR}_\text{data}(p) - \text{VAR}_\text{noise}}{[\langle I(p,t)\rangle_t]^2} . \qquad (12)$$

Now, the continuous model of Eqs. (7, 8) is discretized. The domain is divided into a set of N_voxels voxels, $\{V_k\}_{k=1}^{N_\text{voxels}}$. TS is approximated as a constant within each voxel. We follow some of the notations of Ref. [3]. Pixel p observes object **O** through LOS$_p$ (Fig. 5). As p relates to a specific viewpoint (camera) which observes **O**, the distance of the camera from **O** is denoted $L(p)$. The intersection of LOS$_p$ with voxel V_k is denoted $\Psi_{p,k} \equiv \text{LOS}_p \cap V_k$. If LOS$_p$ does not intersect voxel V_k, then $\Psi_{p,k}$ is empty. The intersection is a line segment between two points $s_{p,k}^\text{min}, s_{p,k}^\text{max}$, defined by

$$s_{p,k}^\text{min} = \min_{\mathbf{X}\in\Psi_{p,k}} \|\mathbf{X} - \mathbf{O}\| \qquad s_{p,k}^\text{max} = \max_{\mathbf{X}\in\Psi_{p,k}} \|\mathbf{X} - \mathbf{O}\|. \qquad (13)$$

Using Eq. (8), define

$$a(p,k) = 2.24 \left(\frac{2\pi}{\lambda}\right)^{7/6} \int_{s_{p,k}^\text{min}}^{s_{p,k}^\text{max}} w_\text{scint}^\bullet[z|L(p)]\,dz . \qquad (14)$$

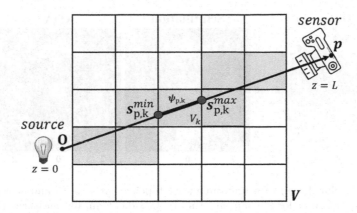

Fig. 5. Line of sight ray-voxel intersection. Points $s_{p,k}^{min}$ and $s_{p,k}^{max}$ are the intersection points of the ray with voxel V_k. We used the ray tracing algorithm of [4].

There is a closed form for the integral in Eq. (14), using the hypergeometric [14] function $_2F_1$

$$\int_{s_{p,k}^{min}}^{s_{p,k}^{max}} \dot{w}_{\mathrm{scint}}[z|L(p)]\, dz = \frac{6z[L(p)-z]^{5/6}[\frac{z}{L(p)}]^{5/6}\,_2F_1(-\frac{5}{6},\frac{11}{6};\frac{17}{6};\frac{z}{L(p)})}{11[1-\frac{z}{L(p)}]^{5/6}}\Bigg|_{s_{p,k}^{min}}^{s_{p,k}^{max}},$$

(15)

where

$$_2F_1(\alpha,\beta;\gamma;\xi) = \sum_{m=0}^{\infty} \frac{(\alpha)_m(\beta)_m}{(\gamma)_m} \frac{\xi^m}{m!}.$$

(16)

Because TS is approximated as a constant within each voxel k, Eq. (7) is discretized to a sum:

$$\sigma_{\mathrm{I}\bullet}^2(p) \approx \sum_{\Psi_{p,k}\neq\emptyset} a(p,k)C_n^2(k).$$

(17)

This sum can be approximated also using linear interpolation.

The total number of pixels in all viewpoints is N_{pixels}. Define a $N_{\mathrm{pixels}}\times N_{\mathrm{voxels}}$ matrix $\mathbf{A}$, whose element (p,k) is

$$A(p,k) = \begin{cases} 0 & \text{if } \Psi_{p,q}=\emptyset \\ a(p,k) & \text{otherwise} \end{cases}.$$

(18)

Based on Eq. (12), concatenate the values $y(p)$ for all p into a column vector $\mathbf{y}$. Concatenate the variables $C_n^2(k)$ for all k into a column vector $\mathbf{c}$. Then Eq. (17) has the form

$$\mathbf{y} \approx \mathbf{A}\mathbf{c}.$$

(19)

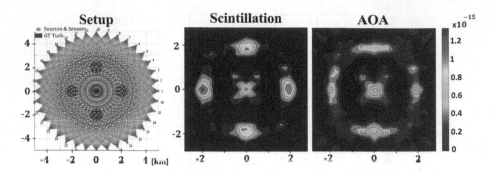

Fig. 6. [Left] Simulation of a uniform radial topology of sources and sensors. Each sensor acts as a source for the opposite sensors. [Middle] Scintillation-based TS tomography result (NRMSE = 0.158). Notice all five TS blobs were reconstructed. [Right] Results of AOA-based TS tomography (NRMSE = 0.217).

The tomographic inverse problem can then be solved using

$$\hat{\mathbf{c}} = \arg \min_{\mathbf{c}} \left\{ \|\mathbf{y} - \mathbf{Ac}\|^2 + \mu R(\mathbf{c}) \right\} \qquad s.t. \quad \mathbf{c} \geq 0 \,. \qquad (20)$$

Here μ is a regularization parameter and $R(\mathbf{c})$ is a regularization term. Here we chose a spatial smoothness prior $R(\mathbf{c}) = \|\nabla^2 \mathbf{c}\|^2$ as an example. We use the simultaneous algebraic reconstruction technique (SART) [11] as a solver. Other priors can also be used.

5 Simulation

Consider Fig. 6. A simulated circular domain has a diameter of 10 km. It is surrounded by 36 cameras. Each camera location has a bulb, to be observed by the other cameras. Each camera has a fixed FOV of 80°. A camera has 15 pixels, each observing a bulb. Thus $N_{\text{pix}} = 540$. The domain includes five turbulent circular hot-spots, at and around the domain center, Each hot-spot has a 500 m radius and TS $C_n^2 = 10^{-15} \text{m}^{-2/3}$.

Each pixel has full-well of 3000 photoelectrons and 8-bit quantization, i.e., the expected number of photoelectrons per graylevel is 11.8. Using these specifications, each noisy measurement is drawn from a Poisson distribution of photoelectrons, and then quantized. A sequence of 1000 frames was then used for tomography. From this sequence, we estimated both $\sigma^2_{\text{AOA}}(p)$ and $\sigma^2_{\text{I}_\bullet}(p)$, for each pixel p. The values of σ^2_{AOA} are used to run the method of Ref. [3], to which we compare. Fig. 6 shows our result, in comparison to that obtained by the principle of Ref. [3]. In Fig. 7 we simulate a scene of one blob, in a sensors' configuration as that of the field experiment (Sect. 6).

We studied how N_{pix} affects the results. We changed the number of cameras in the range 9 to 88, but keeping the FOV of each at 80°. Each camera has a bulb to be observed by the other cameras. This way N_{pix} varies in the range

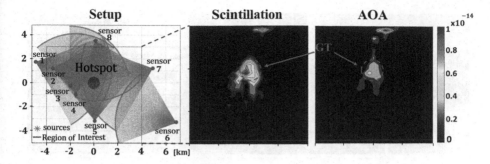

Fig. 7. TS simulated recovery. Cameras are placed as in the field experiment.

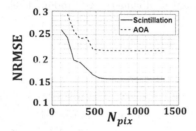

Fig. 8. TS Reconstruction NRMSE over N_{pix}.

[108, 1332]. Results of the estimated $\hat{C}_n^2$ are quantitatively compared to the true C_n^2 using the normalized root mean square error (NRMSE),

$$\text{NRMSE} = \frac{\sqrt{\langle [\hat{C}_n^2(k) - C_n^2(k)]^2 \rangle_k}}{\max_k C_n^2(k)} , \tag{21}$$

where k is the voxel index. The results are plotted in Fig. 8.

We also checked the influence of the distance of the hot-spots from the camera ring, and the radius of each hot-spot. The results appear in Fig. 4b. The dependency on distance is consistent with the theory [24]. Note that the scintillation index is in the range $0 \leq \sigma_{\text{I}\bullet}^2(p) \leq 0.2$.

6   Field Experiment

Turbulence effects typically require very long ranges. Hence, we conducted a field experiment in a greater-city scale, at the Haifa Bay, Israel. This is a domain which is about 10 km across. The experiment included the following elements:

Building Imaging Systems. We need to simultaneously image a field of a large scale, yet with high angular resolution, in order to resolve individual bulbs at large distances. For this purpose, we custom-built a set of untethered imaging systems (see Fig. 9). Each integrates power, embedded computing, communications, electro-mechanics, a camera, a lens and a dedicated software.

Fig. 9. [**Left**] Sample images from the outdoor experiment. [**Right**] A custom-built imager. It consists of an industrial camera, a C-mount lens, a raspberry-pi controller and a motorized pan and tilt head.

Table 1. Components of the imaging system

Component	Model	Spec.
Machine vision camera	IDS UI-3480LE-M-G	2560×1920, $2.2\,\mu m^2$
Lens	Fujinon HF75SA-1	$f/11$, $f = 75\,mm$
Controller	Raspberry Pi 4B	8 GB RAM, WiFi
Motorized pan & Tilt Head	Bescor MP-101	$0\text{–}340°$, $\pm15°$
Power bank	Xiaomi Redmi 18 W	20,000 mAh, 3.6 A
Housing	Nisko T2 IP55	$90 \times 150 \times 80\,mm$
Cellular modem	Boon	WiFi-cellular

Table 1 lists hardware components. An industrial machine vision camera provides radiometric reliability. The lens provides high angular resolution (0.035 mrad/pixel), but limits the FOV (4.301°). So, a motorized pan-tilt unit head scans the FOV. A baffle attached to the lens reduces stray light from peripheral bulbs. Remote control and verification is by cellular communication. The camera, pan-tilt-unit and communications are automatically controlled by a raspberry-pi controller running the software. Scintillation degrades by *aperture filtering* [9]. So, a small aperture is used ($f/11$). Light bulbs flicker due to alternating-current (AC) in the power grid [36]. This flicker may overwhelm the scintillation signal. This disturbance is filtered out using a 80 ms exposure time (an integer multiple of the period of the grid's AC). At 80 ms, the exposure of distant bulbs was sufficient. In each view angle, 50 frames were acquired, for latter processing. From Eq. (8), wavelengths scale the scintillation index, but add no information regarding the TS. Night capture requires maximal light sensitivity. So, no spectral filter was added to the panchromatic camera. The sensitivity of IDS UI-3480LE-M-G peaks at $\lambda = 500\,nm$, which we used in (14).

Waiting for a Feasible Experiment Opportunity: a night having no rain, fog or pandemic lock-downs, while a team is available to cover the region.

Simultaneous Imaging by a Team. At dusk, natural lighting makes the landscape visible in conjunction to the lit-up bulbs. This enables identification and localization of each bulb of interest in the FOV. On 02/02/2022, a team of volunteers went to eight viewpoint locations, setting an untethered imaging system in each. Preliminary imaging started at dusk (5:15PM local time), for bulb localization, Then, at night (5:45PM to 6:10PM), imaging of bulb scintillation took place. We make the raw data, codes and system design of the field experiment publicly available in: https://github.com/nirshaul/ScintillationTomography.

Sensor Calibration: The IDS UI-3480LE-M-G is radiometrically linear. We did not need intrinsic geometric calibration: any bulb we used in p was registered to a specific LOS by recognizing this bulb on a landmark in our known domain. Nevertheless we calibrated the focal length by observing the pixel coordinates of several recognizable bulbs in the FOV, while knowing their corresponding LOS (thus relative LOS angles) in the real world.

Image Analysis included several steps:

(a) Filtering out all bulbs whose scintillation approached or reached the graylevel saturation level, or those who were too weak (marked as red in Fig. 1).
(b) Bulbs appear as blobs. The intensity of a bulb was estimated by summing I in each blob. Using $I(p,t)$, potential sources are mapped by $B(p) \equiv 1$ if $[\max_t I(p,t)] > 20$, else $B(p) = 0$. MATLAB's `bwconncomp` finds connected components in $B(p)$: each is an individual blob, where $I(p,t)$ is spatially integrated. This yields a time sequence (for 50 frames), per blob. When possible, longer sequences are measured.
(c) Per spatially-integrated bulb, $\langle I(t) \rangle_t$, $\langle I^2(t) \rangle_t$ are calculated, leading to (6).
(d) Each bulb of interest was registered to ground location coordinates. This was done using dusk images and maps of the region.
(e) The GPS coordinates of each viewpoint defined the LOS to each bulb. In total, we marked 327 LOSs, each with a corresponding σ_I^2 value (Fig. 10).
(f) In our outdoor field, viewpoints and the ground vary vertically by 50 m at most, over a horizontal span of 6–12 km. So, we do not attempt vertical resolution. The domain was divided horizontally to 15×27 voxels, each 500 m long. This way, the number of unknowns is comparable the 327 measured LOSs to recognized landmarks. The voxel-size order of magnitude is consistent with prior art (200 m in [32]; 600 m in [3]). We ran Eqs. (13–20), using $\mu = 0.3$.

The result is shown in Fig. 12. Major TS hostspots are consistent with major heavy-industry plants, specifically oil refineries having a cluster of chimneys and a fertilizer plant. There was medium-TS in an industrial suburban area, and very low TS in vegetated regions. The maximum in TS values were $2.3e^{-16}\mathrm{m}^{-2/3}$ and $2.45e^{-16}\mathrm{m}^{-2/3}$ (at the refineries and the Kiryat-Ata town, respectively). These values are consistent with typical values in a winter evening [43,46] (Fig. 11).

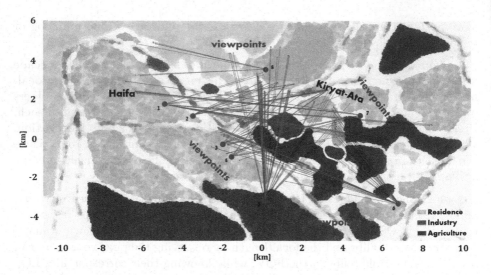

Fig. 10. Outdoor experiment setup: Eight viewpoints spread around Haifa Bay. Several dozens of lines of sight measurements were associated to each sensor.

7   Discussion

We present a novel approach for resolving turbulence strength spatially. We rely on the phenomenon of scintillating point light sources. As this approach is based on passive imaging using a basic machine vision tools, it can be easily utilized for a wide area of interests and applications.

The analysis and the experiment here were geared to night-time. Nevertheless, there is an adaptation of scintillation imaging for daytime [48]. This can thus enable our tomographic approach to work in daytime. We believe that far better resolution can be obtained *using the same video data*, if many more LOSs are analyzed. This requires computer vision methods for automatically finding correspondences of solitude bulbs observed at night from very different multiple views, and registering them to the topography. Hence the TS problem can stimulate further computer vision studies.

In medical CT, there is a missing cone (MC) of frequencies, which is the *null subspace* of multi-angular linear projection *across the domain*. TS-by-scintillation may have a null space too, which is fascinating to explore in future work. It is different from medical MC, because our LOSs can begin/end arbitrarily *inside the domain* (to bulbs), and because of $w_{\text{scint}}^{\bullet}$.

Fig. 11. Sample images from the outdoor experiment. These images from multiple viewpoints were collected as preliminary data. At twilight, we thus capture light sources and landmarks, for registration.

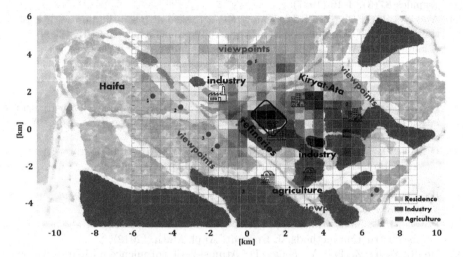

Fig. 12. The estimated TS parameter C_2^n, shown in a 2D map overlaid with regional places of interest. Deep-red areas represent high values, while unsaturated red areas represent low values. Notice the hottest spot is located at the oil refineries. (Color figure online)

Acknowledgments. We thank Uri, Ofra, Dor, Dvir and Inbar Shaul, Roi Ronen, Alon Preger, Haran Man, Vadim Holodovsky and Chanoch Kalifa for participating in the field experiment. Yoav Schechner is the Mark and Diane Seiden Chair in Science at the Technion. He is a Landau Fellow - supported by the Taub Foundation. His work was conducted in the Ollendorff Minerva Center. Minvera is funded through the BMBF. This project has received funding from the European Research Council (ERC) under the European Union's Horizon 2020 research and innovation program (CloudCT, grant agreement No. 810370).

References

1. Afanasiev, A.L., Banakh, V.A., Rostov, A.P.: Crosswind measurements from image flutter of remote objects. In: International Symposium on Atmospheric and Ocean Optics: Atmospheric Physics, vol. 9292, p. 929237 (2014)
2. Aides, A., Schechner, Y.Y., Holodovsky, V., Garay, M.J., Davis, A.B.: Multi sky-view 3D aerosol distribution recovery. Opt. Express (2013)
3. Alterman, M., Schechner, Y.Y., Vo, M., Narasimhan, S.G.: Passive tomography of turbulence strength. In: Fleet, D., Pajdla, T., Schiele, B., Tuytelaars, T. (eds.) ECCV 2014. LNCS, vol. 8692, pp. 47–60. Springer, Cham (2014). https://doi.org/10.1007/978-3-319-10593-2_4
4. Amanatides, J., Woo., A.: A fast voxel traversal algorithm for ray tracing. Eurographics **87**(3), 3–10 (1987)
5. Andrews, L.C., Phillips, R.L., Young, C.Y.: Laser beam scintillation with applications. In: Laser Beam Scintillation with Applications, chap. 3. SPIE (2009)
6. Campbell, M.: Atmospheric turbulence and its influence on adaptive optics (2009)
7. Dravins, D., Lindegren, L., Mezey, E., Young, A.T.: Atmospheric intensity scintillation of stars. II. Dependence on optical wavelength. Publ. Astron. Soc. Pac. **109**, 725 (1997)
8. Dravins, D., Lindegren, L., Mezey, E., Young, A.T.: Atmospheric intensity scintillation of stars, I. Statistical distributions and temporal properties. Publ. Astron. Soc. Pac. **109**, 173 (1997)
9. Dravins, D., Lindegren, L., Mezey, E., Young, A.T.: Atmospheric intensity scintillation of stars. III. Effects for different telescope apertures: erratum. Publ. Astron. Soc. Pac. **110**(751) (1998)
10. Fedorovich, E., Rotunno, R., Stevens, B.: Atmospheric Turbulence and Mesoscale Meteorology. Cambridge University Press, Cambridge (2004)
11. Hansen, P.C., Saxild-Hansen, M.: AIR tools MATLAB package of algebraic iterative reconstruction methods. J. Comput. Appl. Math. (2012)
12. He, R., Wang, Z., Fan, Y., Fengg, D.: Atmospheric turbulence mitigation based on turbulence extraction. In: IEEE ICASSP (2016)
13. Holtslag, A.A.: Atmospheric turbulence. In: Meyers, R.A. (ed.) Encyclopedia of Physical Science and Technology, 3rd edn, vol. 11. Academic Press, New York (2003)
14. Inc., W.R.: Wolfram Alpha. https://www.wolframalpha.com/. Accessed Mar 2022
15. Johnston, R.A., Wooder, N.J., Reavell, F.C., Bernhardt, M., Dainty, C.: Horizontal scintillation detection and ranging Cn2(z) estimation. Appl. Opt. **42** (2003)
16. Karypidou, S., Georgousis, I., Papakostas, G.A.: Computer vision for astronomical image analysis. In: IEEE PIC (2021)
17. Klee, A., Thurman, S.T., Alley, T.: Digital holographic tomography for path-resolved turbulence measurements. In: Dolne, J.J., Spencer, M.F. (eds.) Unconventional Imaging and Adaptive Optics 2021. SPIE (2021)
18. Kolmogorov, A.N.: Dissipation of energy in locally isotropic turbulence. In: Dokl. Akad. Nauk SSSR, vol. 32, pp. 16–18 (1941)
19. Kolmogorov, A.N.: The local structure of turbulence in incompressible viscous fluid for very large reynolds numbers. In: Dokl. Akad. Nauk SSSR (1941)
20. Kopeika, N.: A System Engineering Approach to Imaging. SPIE Press (1998)
21. Levis, A., Davis, A.B., Loveridge, J.R., Schechner, Y.Y.: 3D cloud tomography and droplet size retrieval from multi-angle polarimetric imaging of scattered sunlight from above. In: Polarization Science and Remote Sensing X. SPIE (2021)

22. Loeub, T., Levis, A., Holodovsky, V., Schechner, Y.Y.: Monotonicity prior for cloud tomography. In: Vedaldi, A., Bischof, H., Brox, T., Frahm, J.-M. (eds.) ECCV 2020. LNCS, vol. 12363, pp. 283–299. Springer, Cham (2020). https://doi.org/10.1007/978-3-030-58523-5_17

23. McKechnie, T.S.: General Theory of Light Propagation and Imaging Through the Atmosphere. Springer Series in Optical Sciences, vol. 196. Springer, Cham (2015). https://doi.org/10.1007/978-3-319-18209-4

24. Meijninger, W.M.L.: Surface fluxes over natural landscapes using scintillometry. Ph.D. thesis, Wageningen University (2003)

25. Nair, N.G., Patel, V.M.: Confidence guided network for atmospheric turbulence mitigation. In: IEEE ICIP (2021)

26. Oberlack, M., Peinke, J., Talamelli, A., Castillo, L., Hölling, M.: Progress in turbulence wind energy IV. In: Proceedings of iTi Conference in Turbulence (2010)

27. Osborn, J., et al.: Optical turbulence profiling with stereo-SCIDAR for VLT and ELT. MNRAS 478(1), 825–834 (2018)

28. Porat, O., Shapira, J.: Crosswind sensing from optical-turbulence-induced fluctuations measured by a video camera. Appl. Opt. 49(28), 5236–5244 (2010)

29. Rino, C.: The Theory of Scintillation with Applications in Remote Sensing. Wiley, Hoboken(2011)

30. Ronen, R., Schechner, Y.Y., Eytan, E.: 4D cloud scattering tomography. In: Proceedings of ICCV (2021)

31. Sasiela, R.J.: Electromagnetic Wave Propagation in Turbulence: Evaluation and Application of Mellin Transforms, 2nd edn. SPIE Press (2007)

32. Sauvage, C., et al.: Near ground horizontal high rresolution Cn2 profiling from shack-Hartmann slope and scintillation data. Appl. Opt. 60 (2021)

33. Schroeder, D.J.: Adaptive optics: an introduction. In: Astronomical Optics, chap. 16, pp. 409–424. Elsevier (2000)

34. Schwartzman, A., Alterman, M., Zamir, R., Schechner, Y.Y.: Turbulence-Induced 2D Correlated Image Distortion. In: IEEE ICCP, pp. 1–13 (2017)

35. Sde-Chen, Y., Schechner, Y.Y., Holodovsky, V., Eytan, E.: 3DeepCT: learning volumetric scattering tomography of clouds. In: Proceedings of ICCV (2021)

36. Sheinin, M., Schechner, Y.Y., Kutulakos, K.N.: Computational imaging on the electric grid. In: Proceedings of IEEE CVPR (2017)

37. Shepherd, H.W., et al.: Stereo-SCIDAR: optical turbulence profiling with high sensitivity using a modified SCIDAR instrument. MNRAS 437(4) (2014)

38. Smith, F.G.: The Infrared & Electro-Optical Systems Handbook: Volume 2 Atmospheric Propagation of Radiation, vol. 2. Infrared Information and Analysis Center, Ann Arbor, MI (1993)

39. Storer, L.N., Williams, P.D., Gill, P.G.: Aviation turbulence: dynamics, forecasting, and response to climate change. Pure Appl. Geophys. (2019)

40. Thomas, H.E., Prata, A.J.: Computer vision for improved estimates of SO 2 emission rates and plume dynamics. IJRS (2018)

41. Tian, Y., Narasimhan, S., Vannevel, A.: Depth from optical turbulence. In: Proceedings of IEEE CVPR (2012)

42. Toselli, I., Gladysz, S., Filimonov, G.: Scintillation analysis of LIDAR systems operating in weak-to-strong non-kolmogorov turbulence: unresolved target case. JARS 12(04), 1 (2018)

43. Venet, B.P.: Optical scintillometry over a long elevated horizontal path. Airborne Laser Adv. Technol. 3381(September 1998) (1998)

44. Vorontsov, A.M., Vorontsov, M.A., Filimonov, G.A., Polnau, E.: Atmospheric turbulence study with deep machine learning of intensity scintillation patterns. Appl. Sci. (2020)
45. Ward, H.C.: Scintillometry in urban and complex environments: a review. Meas. Sci. Technol. (2017)
46. Wilcox, C.C., Santiago, F., Martinez, T., Judd, K.P., Restaino, S.R.: Horizontal atmospheric turbulence, beam propagation, and modeling. In: Micro-and Nanotechnology Sensors, Systems, and Applications IX (2017)
47. Wu, C., et al.: Near ground surface turbulence measurements and validation: a comparison between different systems. In: Laser Communication and Propagation through the Atmosphere and Oceans VII. SPIE (2018)
48. Wu, C., et al.: Using turbulence scintillation to assist object ranging from a single camera viewpoint. Appl. Opt. **57**(9), 2177 (2018)
49. Yasarla, R., Patel, V.M.: Learning to restore images degraded by atmospheric turbulence using uncertainty. In: IEEE ICIP. IEEE (2021)
50. Tu, J.Y.-T.: Ray Optics Simulation. https://ricktu288.github.io/ray-optics/

Realistic Blur Synthesis for Learning Image Deblurring

Jaesung Rim, Geonung Kim, Jungeon Kim, Junyong Lee, Seungyong Lee, and Sunghyun Cho[✉]

POSTECH, Pohang, Korea
{jsrim123,k2woong92,jungeonkim,junyonglee,leesy,s.cho}@postech.ac.kr
http://cg.postech.ac.kr/research/RSBlur

Abstract. Training learning-based deblurring methods demands a tremendous amount of blurred and sharp image pairs. Unfortunately, existing synthetic datasets are not realistic enough, and deblurring models trained on them cannot handle real blurred images effectively. While real datasets have recently been proposed, they provide limited diversity of scenes and camera settings, and capturing real datasets for diverse settings is still challenging. To resolve this, this paper analyzes various factors that introduce differences between real and synthetic blurred images. To this end, we present RSBlur, a novel dataset with real blurred images and the corresponding sharp image sequences to enable a detailed analysis of the difference between real and synthetic blur. With the dataset, we reveal the effects of different factors in the blur generation process. Based on the analysis, we also present a novel blur synthesis pipeline to synthesize more realistic blur. We show that our synthesis pipeline can improve the deblurring performance on real blurred images.

Keywords: Realistic blur synthesis · Dataset and analysis · Deblurring

1 Introduction

Motion blur is caused by camera shake or object motion during exposure, especially in a low-light environment that requires long exposure time. Image deblurring is the task of enhancing image quality by removing blur. For the past several years, numerous learning-based deblurring methods have been introduced and significantly improved the performance [8,15,16,22,30,31,34–36].

Training learning-based deblurring methods demands a significant amount of blurred and sharp image pairs. Since it is hard to obtain real-world blurred and sharp image pairs, a number of synthetically generated datasets have been proposed, whose blurred images are generated by blending sharp video frames

Supplementary Information The online version contains supplementary material available at https://doi.org/10.1007/978-3-031-20071-7_29.

captured by high-speed cameras [11,20–22,27,28,43]. Unfortunately, such synthetic images are not realistic enough, so deblurring methods trained on them often fail to deblur real blurred images [25].

To overcome such a limitation, Rim *et al.* [25] and Zhong *et al.* [40,41] recently presented the RealBlur and BSD datasets, respectively. These datasets consist of real blurred and sharp ground truth images captured using specially designed dual-camera systems. Nevertheless, coverage of such real datasets are still limited. Specifically, both RealBlur and BSD datasets are captured using *a single camera model*, Sony A7R3, and a machine vision camera, respectively [25,40,41]. As a result, deblurring models trained on each of them show significantly low performance on the other dataset, as shown in Sect. 6. Moreover, it is not easy to expand the coverage of real datasets as collecting such datasets require specially designed cameras and a tremendous amount of time.

In this paper, we explore ways to synthesize more realistic blurred images for training deblurring models so that we can improve deblurring quality on real blurred images without the burden of collecting a broad range of real datasets. To this end, we first present *RSBlur*, a novel dataset of real and synthetic blurred images. Then, using the dataset, we analyze the difference between the generation process of real and synthetic blurred images and present a realistic blur synthesis method based on the analysis.

Precise analysis of the difference between real and synthetic blurred images requires pairs of synthetic and real blurred images to facilitate isolating factors that cause the difference. However, there exist no datasets that provide both synthetic and real blurred images of the same scenes so far. Thus, to facilitate the analysis, the *RSBlur* dataset provides pairs of a real blurred image and a sequence of sharp images captured by a specially-designed high-speed dual-camera system. With the dataset, we can produce a synthetic blurred image by averaging a sequence of sharp images and compare it with its corresponding real blurred image. This allows us to analyze the difference between real and synthetic blurred images focusing on their generation processes. In particular, we investigate several factors that may degrade deblurring performance of synthetic datasets on real blurred images, such as noise, saturated pixels, and camera ISP. Based on the analysis, we present a method to synthesize more realistic blurred images. Our experiments show that our method can synthesize more realistic blurred images, and our synthesized training set can greatly improve the deblurring performance on real blurred images compared to existing synthetic datasets.

Our contributions are summarized as follows:

- We propose *RSBlur*, the first dataset that provides pairs of a real blurred image and a sequence of sharp images, which enables accurate analysis of the difference between real and synthetic blur.
- We provide a thorough analysis of the difference between the generation processes of real and synthetic blurred images.
- We present a novel synthesis method to synthesize realistic blurred images for learning image deblurring. While collecting large-scale real datasets for different cameras is challenging, our method offers a convenient alternative.

2   Related Work

Deblurring Methods. Traditional deblurring methods rely on restrictive blur models, thus they often fail to deblur real-world images [7,9,18,19,23,26,29,33]. To overcome such limitations, learning-based approaches that restore a sharp image from a blurred image by learning from a large dataset have recently been proposed [8,15,16,22,30,31,34–36]. However, they require a large amount of training data.

Deblurring Datasets. For evaluation of deblurring methods, Levin *et al.* [18] and Köhler *et al.* [14] collected real blurred images by capturing images on the wall while shaking the cameras. Sun *et al.* [29] generate 640 synthetic blurred images by convolving 80 sharp images with eight blur kernels. Lai *et al.* [17] generate spatially varying blurred images from 6D camera trajectories and construct a dataset including 100 real blurred images. However, due to the small number of images, these datasets cannot be used for learning-based methods.

Several synthetic datasets using high-speed videos have been proposed for training learning-based methods. They capture high-speed videos and generate synthetic blurred images by averaging sharp frames. GoPro [22] is the most widely used dataset for learning-based deblurring methods. REDS [21] and DVD [28] provide synthetically blurred videos for learning video deblurring. Stereo Blur [43] consists of stereo blurred videos generated by averaging high-speed stereo video frames. HIDE [27] provides synthetic blurred images with bounding box labels of humans. To expand deblurring into high-resolution images, 4KRD [11] is presented, which consists of synthetically blurred UHD video frames. All the datasets discussed above, except for GoPro, use frame interpolation before averaging sharp images to synthesize more realistic blur [11,21,27,28,43]. HFR-DVD [20] uses high-speed video frames captured at 1000 FPS to synthesize blur without frame interpolation. However, all the aforementioned datasets are not realistic enough, thus deblurring networks trained with them often fail to deblur real-world blurred images.

Recently, real-world blur datasets [25,40,41] have been proposed. They simultaneously capture a real blurred image and its corresponding sharp image using a dual-camera system. Rim *et al.* [25] collected a real-world blur dataset in low-light environments. Zhong *et al.* [40,41] proposed the BSD dataset containing pairs of real blurred and sharp videos. However, their performances degrade on other real images captured in different settings due to their limited coverage.

Synthesis of Realistic Degraded Images. In the denoising field, synthesizing more realistic noise for learning real-world denoising has been actively studied [1, 4,6,12,13,32]. Abdelhamed *et al.* [1], Chang *et al.* [6], and Jang *et al.* [13] use generative models to learn a mapping from a latent distribution to a real noise distribution. Zhang *et al.* [39] and Wei *et al.* [32] propose realistic noise generation methods based on the physical properties of digital sensors. Guo *et al.* [12] and Brooks *et al.* [4] generate realistic noise by unprocessing arbitrary clean sRGB images, adding Poisson noise, and processing them back to produce noisy sRGB images. These methods show that more realistically synthesized noise datasets greatly improve the denoising performance of real-world noisy images.

Synthesis of Blurred Images. A few methods have been proposed to synthesize blur without using high-speed videos [3,38]. Brooks *et al.* [3] generate a blurred image from two sharp images using a line prediction layer, which estimates spatially-varying linear blur kernels. However, linear blur kernels cannot express a wide variety of real-world blur. Zhang *et al.* [38] use real-world blurred images without their ground-truth sharp images to train a GAN-based model to generate a blurred image from a single sharp image. However, their results are not realistic enough as their generative model cannot accurately reflect the physical properties of real-world blur.

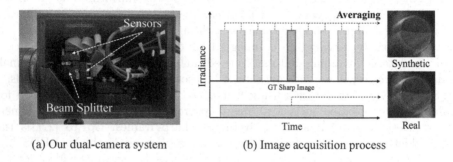

(a) Our dual-camera system   (b) Image acquisition process

Fig. 1. The dual-camera system and the acquisition process for simultaneously capturing a real blurred image and sharp images.

3   RSBlur Dataset

Our proposed RSBlur dataset provides real blurred images of various outdoor scenes, each of which is paired with a sequence of nine sharp images to enable the analysis of the difference between real and synthetic blur. The dataset includes a total of 13,358 real blurred images of 697 scenes. For our analysis, we split the dataset into training, validation, and test sets with 8,878, 1,120, and 3,360 blurred images of 465, 58, and 174 scenes, respectively. Below, we explain the acquisition process and other details of the RSBlur dataset.

To collect the dataset, we built a dual camera system (Fig. 1(a)) as done in [25,40–42]. The system consists of one lens, one beam splitter, and two camera modules with imaging sensors so that the camera modules can capture the same scene while sharing one lens. The shutters of the camera modules are carefully synchronized in order that the modules can capture images simultaneously (Fig. 1(b)). Specifically, one camera module captures a blurred image with a long exposure time. During the exposure time of a blurred image, the other module captures nine sharp images consecutively with a short exposure time. The shutter for the first sharp image opens when the shutter for the blurred image opens, and the shutter for the last sharp image closes when the shutter for the blurred image closes. The exposure time of the fifth sharp image matches with the center of the exposure time of the blurred image so that the fifth sharp image can be used as a ground-truth sharp image for the blurred one.

The blurred images are captured with a 5% neutral density filter installed in front of a camera module to secure a long exposure time as done in [40,41]. The exposure times for the blurred and sharp images are 0.1 and 0.005 s, respectively. We capture images holding our system in hand so that blurred images can be produced by hand shakes. The captured images are geometrically and photometrically aligned to remove misalignment between the camera modules as done in [25]. We capture all images in the camera RAW format, and convert them into the nonlinear sRGB space using a simple image signal processing (ISP) pipeline similar to [2] consisting of four steps: 1) white balance, 2) demosaicing, 3) color correction, and 4) conversion to the sRGB space using a gamma correction of sRGB space as a camera response function (CRF). More details on our dual-camera system and ISP are in the supplement.

4   Real *vs* Synthetic Blur

Using the RSBlur dataset, we analyze the difference between the generation process of real and synthetic blur. Specifically, we first compare the overall generation process of real and synthetic blur, and discover factors that can introduce the dominant difference between them. Then, we analyze each factor one by one and discuss how to address them by building our blur synthesis pipeline.

In the case of real blur, camera sensors accumulate incoming light during the exposure time to capture an image. During this process, blur and photon shot noise are introduced due to camera and object motion, and due to the fluctuation of photons, respectively. The limited dynamic range of sensors introduces saturated pixels. The captured light is converted to analog electrical signals and then to digital signals. During this conversion, additional noise such as dark current noise and quantization noise is added. The image is then processed by a camera ISP, which performs white balance, demosaicing, color space conversion, and other nonlinear operation that distort the blur pattern and noise distribution.

During this process, an image is converted through multiple color spaces. Before the camera ISP, an image is in the camera RAW space, which is device-dependent. The image is then converted to the linear sRGB space, and then to the nonlinear sRGB space. In the rest of the paper, we refer to the linear sRGB space as the linear space, and the nonlinear sRGB space as the sRGB space.

On the other hand, the blurred image generation processes of the widely used datasets, e.g., GoPro [22], DVD [28], and REDS [21], are much simpler. They use sharp images in the sRGB space consecutively captured by a high-speed camera. The sharp images are optionally interpolated to increase the frame rate [21,28]. Then, they are converted to the linear space, and averaged together to produce a blurred image. The blurred image is converted to the sRGB space. For conversion between the linear to sRGB spaces, GoPro uses a gamma curve with $\gamma = 2.2$ while REDS uses a CRF estimated from a GOPRO6 camera.

Between the two processes described above, the main factors that cause the gap between synthetic and real blur include 1) discontinuous blur trajectories in synthetic blur, 2) saturated pixels, 3) noise, and 4) the camera ISP. In this paper, we analyze the effect of these factors one by one. Below, we discuss these factors in more detail.

Discontinuous Blur Trajectories. The blur generation process of the GoPro dataset [22], which is the most popular dataset, captures sharp video frames at a high frame rate and averages them to synthesize blur. However, temporal gaps between the exposure of consecutive frames cause unnatural discontinuous blur (Fig. 2(b)). While DVD [28] and REDS [21] use frame interpolation to fill such gaps, the effects of discontinuous blur and frame interpolation on the deblurring performance have not been analyzed yet.

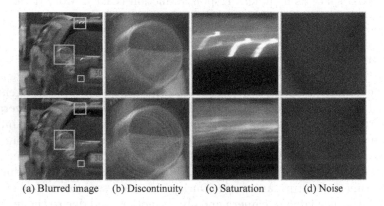

(a) Blurred image   (b) Discontinuity   (c) Saturation   (d) Noise

Fig. 2. The top row shows real blurred images and the bottom row shows the corresponding synthetic blurred images. Best viewed in zoom in.

Saturated Pixels. While real-world blurred images may have saturated pixels (Fig. 2(c)) due to the limited dynamic range, previous synthetic datasets do not have such saturated pixels as they simply average sharp images. As saturated pixels in real blurred images form distinctive blur patterns from other pixels, it is essential to reflect them to achieve high-quality deblurring results [10].

Noise. Noise is inevitable in real-world images including blurred images, especially captured by a low-end camera at night (Fig. 2(d)). Even for high-end sensors, noise cannot be avoided due to the statistical property of photons and the circuit readout process. In the denoising field, it has been proven important to model the realistic noise for high-quality denoising of real-world images [1,4,6,13,32,39]. On the other hand, noise is ignored by the blur generation processes of the previous synthetic datasets [11,20–22,27,28,43], and its effect on deblurring has not been investigated. Our experiments in Sect. 6 show that accurate modeling of noise is essential even for the RealBlur dataset, which consists of images mostly captured from a high-end camera with the lowest ISO.

Camera ISP. ISPs perform various operations, including white balancing, color correction, demosaicing, and nonlinear mapping using CRFs, which affect the noise distribution and introduce distortions [4,5]. However, they are ignored by the previous synthetic datasets [11,20–22,27,28,43].

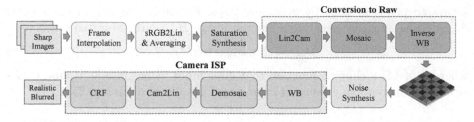

Fig. 3. Overview of our realistic blur synthesis pipeline. Lin2Cam: Inverse color correction, i.e., color space conversion from the linear space to the camera RAW space. WB: White balance. Cam2Lin: Color correction.

5   Realistic Blur Synthesis

To synthesize more realistic blur while addressing the factors discussed earlier, we propose a novel blur synthesis pipeline. The proposed pipeline will also serve as a basis for the experiments in Sect. 6 that study effect of each factor that degrades the quality of synthetic blur. Figure 3 shows an overview of our blur synthesis pipeline. Our pipeline takes sharp video frames captured by a high-speed camera as done in [21,22,28], and produces a synthetic blurred image. Both input and output of our pipeline are in the sRGB space. Below, we explain each step in more detail.

Frame Interpolation. To resolve the discontinuity of blur trajectory, our pipeline adopts frame interpolation as done in [21,28]. We increase nine sharp images to 65 images using ABME [24], a state-of-the-art frame interpolation method. In this step, we perform frame interpolation in the sRGB space to use an off-the-shelf frame interpolation method without modification or fine-tuning.

sRGB2Lin and Averaging. To synthesize blur using the interpolated frames, we convert the images into the linear space, and average them to precisely mimic the real blur generation process. While the actual accumulation of incoming light happens in the camera RAW space, averaging in the camera RAW space and in the linear space are equivalent to each other as the two spaces can be converted using a linear transformation. Figure 4(a) shows an example of the averaging of interpolated frames.

Saturation Synthesis. In this step, we synthesize saturated pixels. To this end, we propose a simple approach. For a given synthetic blurred image B_{syn} from the previous step, our approach first calculates a mask M_i of the saturated pixels in the i-th sharp source image S_i of B_{syn} as follows:

$$M_i(x, y, c) = \begin{cases} 1, & \text{if } S_i(x, y, c) = 1 \\ 0, & \text{otherwise,} \end{cases} \quad (1)$$

where (x, y) is a pixel position, and $c \in \{R, G, B\}$ is a channel index. S_i has a normalized intensity range $[0, 1]$. Then, we compute a mask M_{sat} of potential saturated pixels in B_{syn} by averaging M_i's. Figure 4(b) shows an example of M_{sat}. Using M_{sat}, we generate a blurred image B_{sat} with saturated pixels as:

$$B_{sat} = \text{clip}(B_{syn} + \alpha M_{sat}) \tag{2}$$

where $\text{clip}(\cdot)$ is a clipping function that clips input values into $[0, 1]$, and α is a scaling factor randomly sampled from a uniform distribution $\mathcal{U}(0.25, 1.75)$.

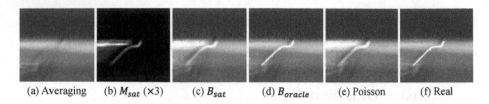

(a) Averaging   (b) M_{sat} (×3)   (c) B_{sat} (d) B_{oracle} (e) Poisson   (f) Real

Fig. 4. Generated images from our synthesis pipeline. (a) Averaging image of interpolated frames. (b) M_{sat} scaled by three times. (c)–(d) Examples of saturated images. (e)–(f) Synthetic noisy image and real image. The images except for (b) are converted into the sRGB space for visualization.

For the sake of analysis, we also generate blurred images with oracle saturated pixels. An oracle image B_{oracle} is generated as:

$$B_{oracle}(x, y, c) = \begin{cases} B_{real}(x, y, c), & \text{if } M_{sat}(x, y, c) > 0 \\ B_{syn}(x, y, c), & \text{otherwise.} \end{cases} \tag{3}$$

Our approach is simple and heuristic, and cannot reproduce the saturated pixels in real images due to missing information in sharp images. Specifically, while we resort to a randomly-sampled uniform scaling factor α, for accurate reconstruction of saturated pixels, we need pixel-wise scaling factors, which are impossible to estimate. Figure 4(c) and (d) show examples of B_{sat} and B_{oracle} where the image in (c) looks different from the one in (d). Nevertheless, our experiments in Sect. 6 show that our approach still noticeably improves the deblurring performance on real blurred images.

Conversion to RAW. In the next step, we convert the blurred image from the previous step, which is in the linear space, into the camera RAW space to reflect the distortion introduced by the camera ISP. In this step, we apply the inverse of each step of our ISP except for the CRF step in the reverse order. Specifically, we apply the inverse color correction transformation, mosaicing, and inverse white balance sequentially. As the color correction and white balance operations are invertible linear operations, they can be easily inverted. More details are provided in the supplement.

Noise Synthesis. After the conversion to the camera RAW space, we add noise to the image. Motivated by [32,39], we model noise in the camera RAW space as a mixture of Gaussian and Poisson noise as:

$$B_{noisy} = \beta_1(I + N_{shot}) + N_{read} \tag{4}$$

where B_{noisy} is a noisy image, and I is the number of incident photons. β_1 is the overall system gain determined by digital and analog gains. N_{shot} and N_{read} are photon shot and read noise, respectively. We model $(I + N_{shot})$ as a Poisson distribution, and N_{read} as a Gaussian distribution with standard deviation β_2. Mathematically, $(I + N_{shot})$ and N_{read} are modeled as:

$$(I + N_{shot}) \sim \mathcal{P}\left(\frac{B_{raw}}{\beta_1}\right)\beta_1, \quad \text{and} \tag{5}$$

$$N_{read} \sim \mathcal{N}(0, \beta_2) \tag{6}$$

where $\mathcal{P}$ and $\mathcal{N}$ denote Poisson and Gaussian distributions, respectively. B_{raw} is a blurred image in the camera RAW space from the previous step.

To reflect the noise distribution in the blurred images in the RSBlur dataset, we estimate the parameters β_1 and β_2 of our camera system as done in [39], where β_1 and β_2 are estimated using flat-field and dark-frame images, respectively. Refer to [39] for more details. The estimated values of β_1 and β_2 are 0.0001 and 0.0009, respectively. To cover a wider range of noise in our synthetic blurred images, we sample random parameter values β_1' and β_2' from $\mathcal{U}(0.5\beta_1, 1.5\beta_1)$ and $\mathcal{U}(0.5\beta_2, 1.5\beta_2)$, respectively. Then, using Eq. (5) and Eq. (6) with β_1' and β_2', we generate a noisy blurred image in the camera RAW space.

For the analysis in Sect. 6, we also consider Gaussian noise, which is the most widely used noise model. We obtain a noisy image with Gaussian noise as:

$$B_{noisy} = B + N_{gauss} \tag{7}$$

where B is an input blurred image and N_{gauss} is Gaussian noise sampled from $\mathcal{N}(0, \sigma)$, and σ is the standard deviation. As we include Gaussian noise in our analysis to represent the conventional noise synthesis, we skip the ISP-related steps (conversion to RAW, and applying camera ISP), but directly add noise to a blurred image in the sRGB space, i.e., we apply gamma correction to B_{sat} from the previous step, and add Gaussian noise to produce the final results. In our experiments, we randomly sample standard deviations of Gaussian noise from $\mathcal{U}(0.5\sigma', 1.5\sigma')$ where $\sigma' = 0.0112$ is estimated using a color chart image.

Applying Camera ISP. Finally, after adding noise, we apply the camera ISP to the noisy image to obtain a blurred image in the sRGB space. We apply the same ISP described in Sect. 3, which consists of white balance, demosaicing, color correction, and CRF steps. Figure 4(e) shows our synthesis result with Poisson noise and ISP distortions. As the example shows, our synthesis pipeline can synthesize a realistic-looking blurred image.

6   Experiments

In this section, we evaluate the performance of our blur synthesis pipeline, and the effect of its components on the RSBlur and other datasets. To this end, we synthesize blurred images using variants of our pipeline, and train a learning-based deblurring method using them. We then evaluate its performance on real blur datasets. In our analysis, we use SRN-DeblurNet [30] as it is a strong base-line [25], and requires a relatively short training time. We train the model for 262,000 iterations, which is half the iterations suggested in [30], with additional augmentations including random horizontal and vertical flip, and random rota-tion, which we found improve the performance. We also provide additional anal-ysis results using another state-of-the-art deblurring method, MIMO-UNet [8], in the supplement.

6.1   Analysis Using the RSBlur Dataset

We first evaluate the performance of the blur synthesis pipeline, and analyze the effect of our pipeline using the RSBlur dataset. Table 1 compares different variants of our blur synthesis pipeline. The method 1 uses real blurred images for training SRN-DeblurNet model [30], while the others use synthetic images for training. To study the effect of saturated pixels, we divide the RSBlur test set into two sets, one of which consists of images with saturated pixels, and the other does not, based on whether a blurred image has more than 1,000 non-zero pixels in M_{sat} computed from its corresponding sharp image sequence. The numbers of images in the sets with and without saturated pixels are 1,626 and 1,734, respectively. Below, we analyze the effects of different methods and com-ponents based on Table 1. As the table includes a large number of combinations of different components, we include the indices of methods that each analysis compares in the title of each paragraph.

Naïve Averaging (2 & 3). We first evaluate the performance of the naïve averaging approach, which is used in the GoPro dataset [22]. The GoPro dataset provides two sub-datasets: one of which applies gamma-decoding and encoding before and after averaging, and the other performs averaging without gamma-decoding and encoding. Thus, in this analysis, we also include two versions of naïve averaging. The method 2 in Table 1 is the most naïve approach, which uses naïve averaging and ignores CRFs. The method 3 also uses naïve averaging, but it uses a gamma correction of sRGB space as a CRF. The table shows that both methods perform significantly worse than the real dataset. This proves that there is a significant gap between real blur and synthetic blur generated by the naïve averaging approach of the previous synthetic dataset. The table also shows that considering CRF is important for the deblurring performance of real blurred images.

Frame Interpolation (3, 4, 5 & 6). We then study the effect of frame inter-polation, which is used to fill the temporal gap between consecutive sharp frames by the REDS [21] and DVD [28] datasets. Methods 5 and 6 in Table 1 use frame interpolation. The method 6 adds synthetic Gaussian noise to its images as described in Sect. 5. Interestingly, the table shows that the method 5 performs worse than the method 3 without frame interpolation. This is because of the different amounts of noise in blurred images of methods 3 and 5. As frame inter-polation increases the number of frames, more frames are averaged to produce a blurred image. Thus, a resulting blurred image has much less noise. The results of methods 6 and 4, both of which add Gaussian noise, verify this. The results show that frame interpolation performs better than naïve averaging when Gaussian noise is added.

Saturation (6, 7, 8, 9 & 10). To analyze the effect of saturated pixels, we first compare the method 6, which does not include saturated pixels whose values are clipped, and the method 7, which uses oracle saturated pixels. As shown by the results, including saturated pixels improves the deblurring quality by 0.12 dB. Especially, the improvement is large for the test images with saturated pixels (0.30 dB). Methods 8 and 10 use our saturation synthesis approach. The result of the method 8 shows that, while it is worse than the method 7 (the oracle method), it still performs better the method 6, which does not perform saturation synthesis, especially for the test images with saturated pixels. Also, our final method (method 10) performs comparably to the oracle method (method 9). Both methods 9 and 10 achieve 32.06 dB for all the test images. This confirms the effectiveness of our saturation synthesis approach despite its simplicity.

Table 1. Performance comparison among different blur synthesis methods on the RSBlur test set. Interp.: Frame interpolation. Sat.: Saturation synthesis. sRGB: Gamma correction of sRGB space. G: Gaussian noise. G+P: Gaussian and Poisson noise.

Blur synthesis methods						PSNR/SSIM		
No.	Real	CRF	Interp.	Sat.	Noise	ISP	All	Saturated	No Saturated
1	✓						32.53/0.8398	31.20/0.8313	33.78/0.8478
2		Linear					30.12/0.7727	28.67/0.7657	31.47/0.7793
3		sRGB					30.90/0.7805	29.60/0.7745	32.13/0.7861
4		sRGB			G		31.69/0.8258	30.18/0.8174	33.11/0.8336
5		sRGB	✓				30.20/0.7468	29.06/0.7423	31.27/0.7511
6		sRGB	✓		G		31.77/0.8275	30.28/0.8194	33.17/0.8352
7		sRGB	✓	Oracle	G		31.89/0.8267	30.58/0.8191	33.12/0.8338
8		sRGB	✓	Ours	G		31.83/0.8265	30.47/0.8187	33.12/0.8339
9		sRGB	✓	Oracle	G+P	✓	32.06/0.8315	30.79/0.8243	33.25/0.8384
10		sRGB	✓	Ours	G+P	✓	32.06/0.8322	30.74/0.8248	33.30/0.8391

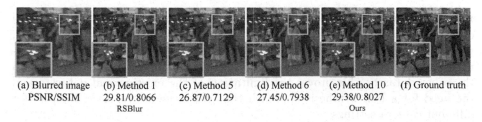

| (a) Blurred image PSNR/SSIM | (b) Method 1 29.81/0.8066 RSBlur | (c) Method 5 26.87/0.7129 | (d) Method 6 27.45/0.7938 | (e) Method 10 29.38/0.8027 Ours | (f) Ground truth |

Fig. 5. Qualitative comparison of deblurring results on the RSBlur test set produced by models trained with different synthesis methods. (b)–(e) Methods 1, 5, 6 and 10 in Table 1. Best viewed in zoom in.

Noise & ISP (5, 6, 7, 8, 9 & 10). We study the effect of noise and the ISP. To this end, we compare three different approaches: 1) ignoring noise, 2) adding Gaussian noise, and 3) adding Gaussian and Poisson noise with an ISP. The first approach corresponds to previous synthetic datasets that do not consider noise, such as GoPro [22], REDS [21] and DVD [28]. The second is the most widely used approach for generating synthetic noise in many image restoration tasks [37]. The third one reflects real noise and distortion caused by an ISP.

The table shows that, compared to the method 5 (No noise), the method 6 (Gaussian noise) performs significantly better by 1.57 dB. Moreover, a comparison between methods 7 and 8 (Gaussian noise) and methods 9 and 10 (Gaussian+Poisson noise with an ISP) shows that adding more realistic noise and distortion further improves the deblurring performance consistently.

Finally, our final method (method 10) achieves 32.06 dB, which is more than 1 dB higher than those of the naïve methods 2, 3, and 5. In terms of SSIM, our final method outperforms the naïve methods by more than 0.05. Compared to all the other methods, our final method achieves the smallest difference against the method 1 which uses real blurred images. In terms of SSIM, our final method achieves 0.8332, which is only 0.0076 lower than that of the method 1. This proves the effectiveness of our method, and the importance of realistic blur synthesis.

Qualitative Examples. Fig. 5(b)–(e) show qualitative deblurring results produced by models trained with different methods in Table 1. As Fig. 5(c) shows, a deblurring model trained with images synthesized using frame interpolation without noise synthesis fails to remove blur in the input blurred image. Adding Gaussian noise improves the quality (Fig. 5(d)), but blur still remains around the lights. Meanwhile, the method trained with our full pipeline (Fig. 5(e)) produces a comparable result to the method trained with real blurred images.

6.2 Application to Other Datasets

We evaluate the proposed pipeline on other datasets. Specifically, we apply several variants of our pipeline to the sharp source images of the GoPro dataset [22] to synthesize more realistic blurred images. Then, we train a deblurring model on synthesized images, and evaluate its performance on the RealBlur_J [25] and BSD [40,41] datasets. The BSD dataset consists of three subsets with different shutter speeds. We use all of them as a single set, which we denote by BSD_All.

Limited Coverage of Real Datasets. We examine the performance of real datasets on other real datasets to study the coverage of real datasets. To this end, we compare methods 1 and 2 in Table 2. The comparison shows that the performance of a deblurring model on one dataset significantly drops when trained on the other dataset. This proves the limitation of the existing real datasets and the need for a blur synthesis approach that can generate realistic datasets for different camera settings.

Improving GoPro. The method 3 in Table 2 performs naïve averaging to the sharp source images in the GoPro dataset [22] without gamma correction. The method 4 performs gamma decoding, naïve averaging, and then gamma encoding. These two methods correspond to the original generation processes of GoPro. As the images in both RealBlur_J [25] and BSD [40,41] datasets have blur distorted by the CRFs, the method 4 performs better. However, both of them perform much worse than the real-world blur training sets for both RealBlur_J and BSD_All.

The method 5 performs 0.01 dB worse than the method 4 on RealBlur_J. This again shows that frame interpolation without considering noise may degrade the deblurring performance as it reduces noise as discussed in Sect. 6.1. Adding Gaussian noise (method 6), and saturated pixels (method 7) further improves the deblurring performance on both test sets. For Gaussian noise, we simply add Gaussian noise with standard deviation $\sigma = 0.0112$.

The method 8 uses the noise and ISP parameters estimated for the RealBlur_J dataset [25]. The RealBlur_J dataset was captured using a Sony A7R3 camera, of which we can estimate the noise distribution, color correction matrix, and CRF. We use the method described in Sect. 5 for noise estimation. For the color correction matrix and CRF estimation, we refer the readers to our supplementary material. As the CRFs of the training set and RealBlur_J are different, the method 8 uses different CRFs in different steps. Specifically, it uses gamma decoding with sharp source images of the GoPro dataset into the linear space, and in the last step of our pipeline, it applies the estimated CRF of Sony A7R3. The method 8 achieves 30.32 dB for the RealBlur_J dataset, which is much higher

Table 2. Performance comparison of different blur synthesis methods on the RealBlur_J [25] and BSD_All [40,41] test sets. Interp.: Frame interpolation. Sat.: Saturation synthesis. sRGB: Gamma correction of sRGB space. G: Gaussian noise. G+P: Gaussian and Poisson noise. A7R3: Using camera ISP parameters estimated from a Sony A7R3 camera, which was used for collecting the RealBlur dataset.

Blur synthesis methods							PSNR/SSIM	
No.	Training set	CRF	Interp.	Sat.	Noise	ISP	RealBlur_J	BSD_All
1	RealBlur_J						30.79/0.8985	29.67/0.8922
2	BSD_All						28.66/0.8589	33.35/0.9348
3	GoPro	Linear					28.79/0.8741	29.17/0.8824
4	GoPro	sRGB					28.93/0.8738	29.65/0.8862
5	GoPro	sRGB	✓				28.92/0.8711	30.09/0.8858
6	GoPro	sRGB	✓		G		29.17/0.8795	31.19/0.9147
7	GoPro	sRGB	✓	Ours	G		29.95/0.8865	31.41/0.9154
8	GoPro	sRGB, A7R3	✓	Ours	G+P	A7R3	30.32/0.8899	30.48/0.9060
9	GoPro_U	Linear					29.09/0.8810	29.22/0.8729
10	GoPro_U	sRGB					29.28/0.8766	29.72/0.8773
11	GoPro_U	sRGB			G		29.50/0.8865	30.22/0.8973
12	GoPro_U	sRGB		Ours	G		30.40/0.8970	30.31/0.8995
13	GoPro_U	sRGB, A7R3		Ours	G+P	A7R3	30.75/0.9019	29.72/0.8925

(a) Blurred image   (b) Method 1   (c) Method 5   (d) Method 6   (e) Method 8
PSNR/SSIM   28.27/0.8562   26.00/0.8218   26.69/0.8430   28.16/0.8562
                      RealBlur_J   Ours (GoPro)

(f) Ground truth   (g) Method 2   (h) Method 10   (i) Method 11   (j) Method 13
                      24.68/0.7471   26.27/0.8191   26.50/0.8534   28.67/0.8870
                      BSD_All   Ours (GoPro_U)

Fig. 6. Qualitative comparison of deblurring results on the RealBlur_J test set produced by models trained with different synthesis methods. (b)–(e) Methods 1, 5, 6 and 8 in Table 2. (g)–(j) Methods 2, 10, 11 and 13 in Table 2. Best viewed in zoom in.

than 28.93 dB of the method 4. This proves that our blur synthesis pipeline reflecting the noise distribution and distortion caused by the ISP improves the quality of synthetic blur. It is also worth mentioning that the method 8 performs worse than the method 7 on the BSD_All dataset because the camera ISP of BSD_All is different from that of RealBlur_J. This also shows the importance of correct camera ISP parameters including CRFs, and explains why real datasets perform poorly on other real datasets. Figure 6(c)–(e) show results of deblurring methods trained on the GoPro dataset with different methods in Table 2.

Convolution-Based Blur Synthesis. Our pipeline also applies to convolution-based blur synthesis and improves its performance as well. To verify this, we build a dataset with synthetic blur kernels as follows. For each sharp image in the GoPro dataset, we randomly generate ten synthetic blur kernels following [25] in order that we can convolve them with sharp images to synthesize blurred images instead of frame interpolation and averaging. We also compute saturation masks M_{sat} by convolving the masks of saturated pixels in each sharp image with the synthetic blur kernels. We denote this dataset as GoPro_U. Methods 9 to 13 in Table 2 show different variants of our pipeline using GoPro_U. For these methods, except for the frame interpolation and averaging, all the other steps in our pipeline are applied in the same manner.

In Table 2, methods 9 and 10 perform much worse than methods 1 and 2, which use real blurred images. Methods 11 and 12 show that considering Gaussian noise ($\sigma = 0.0112$) and saturated pixels significantly improves the performance. Finally, the method 13 that uses our full pipeline, achieves 30.75 dB in PSNR, which is only 0.04 dB lower than that of the method 1, and achieves 0.9019 in SSIM, which is 0.003 higher than that of the method 1. This shows that our pipeline is also effective for the convolution-based blur model.

Figure 6(h)–(j) show results of deblurring methods trained on the GoPro_U dataset with different methods in Table 2.

7 Conclusion

In this paper, we presented the RSBlur dataset, which is the first dataset that provides pairs of a real-blurred image and a sequence of sharp images. Our dataset enables accurate analysis of the difference between real and synthetic blur. We analyzed several factors that introduce the difference between them with the dataset and presented a novel blur synthesis pipeline, which is simple but effective. Using our pipeline, we quantitatively and qualitatively analyzed the effect of each factor that degrades the deblurring performance on real-world blurred images. We also showed that our blur synthesis pipeline could greatly improve the deblurring performance on real-world blurred images.

Limitations and Future Work. Our method consists of simple and heuristic steps including a simple ISP and a mask-based saturation synthesis. While they improve the deblurring performance, further gains could be obtained by adopting sophisticated methods for each step. Also, there is still the performance gap between real blur datasets and our synthesized datasets, and some other factors may exist that cause the gap. Investigating that is an interesting future direction.

Acknowledgements. This work was supported by Samsung Research Funding & Incubation Center of Samsung Electronics under Project Number SRFC-IT1801-05 and Institute of Information & communications Technology Planning & Evaluation (IITP) grants (2019-0-01906, Artificial Intelligence Graduate School Program (POSTECH)) funded by the Korea government (MSIT) and the National Research Foundation of Korea (NRF) grants (2020R1C1C1014863) funded by the Korea government (MSIT).

References

1. Abdelhamed, A., Brubaker, M.A., Brown, M.S.: Noise flow: noise modeling with conditional normalizing flows. In: ICCV, October 2019
2. Abdelhamed, A., Lin, S., Brown, M.S.: A high-quality denoising dataset for smartphone cameras. In: CVPR, June 2018
3. Brooks, T., Barron, J.T.: Learning to synthesize motion blur. In: CVPR, June 2019
4. Brooks, T., Mildenhall, B., Xue, T., Chen, J., Sharlet, D., Barron, J.T.: Unprocessing images for learned raw denoising. In: CVPR, June 2019
5. Cao, Y., Wu, X., Qi, S., Liu, X., Wu, Z., Zuo, W.: Pseudo-ISP: learning pseudo in-camera signal processing pipeline from A color image denoiser. arXiv preprint arXiv:2103.10234 (2021)
6. Chang, K.-C., et al.: Learning camera-aware noise models. In: Vedaldi, A., Bischof, H., Brox, T., Frahm, J.-M. (eds.) ECCV 2020. LNCS, vol. 12369, pp. 343–358. Springer, Cham (2020). https://doi.org/10.1007/978-3-030-58586-0_21
7. Cho, S., Lee, S.: Convergence analysis of map based blur kernel estimation. In: ICCV, pp. 4818–4826, October 2017

8. Cho, S.J., Ji, S.W., Hong, J.P., Jung, S.W., Ko, S.J.: Rethinking coarse-to-fine approach in single image deblurring. In: ICCV, pp. 4641–4650, October 2021

9. Cho, S., Lee, S.: Fast motion deblurring. ACM TOG **28**(5), 145:1–145:8 (2009)

10. Cho, S., Wang, J., Lee, S.: Handling outliers in non-blind image deconvolution. In: ICCV (2011)

11. Deng, S., Ren, W., Yan, Y., Wang, T., Song, F., Cao, X.: Multi-scale separable network for ultra-high-definition video deblurring. In: ICCV, pp. 14030–14039, October 2021

12. Guo, S., Yan, Z., Zhang, K., Zuo, W., Zhang, L.: Toward convolutional blind denoising of real photographs. In: CVPR, June 2019

13. Jang, G., Lee, W., Son, S., Lee, K.M.. C2n. Practical generative noise modeling for real-world denoising. In: ICCV, pp. 2350–2359, October 2021

14. Köhler, R., Hirsch, M., Mohler, B., Schölkopf, B., Harmeling, S.: Recording and playback of camera shake: benchmarking blind deconvolution with a real-world database. In: Fitzgibbon, A., Lazebnik, S., Perona, P., Sato, Y., Schmid, C. (eds.) ECCV 2012. LNCS, vol. 7578, pp. 27–40. Springer, Heidelberg (2012). https://doi.org/10.1007/978-3-642-33786-4_3

15. Kupyn, O., Budzan, V., Mykhailych, M., Mishkin, D., Matas, J.: DeblurGAN: blind motion deblurring using conditional adversarial networks. In: CVPR, pp. 8183–8192 (June 2018)

16. Kupyn, O., Martyniuk, T., Wu, J., Wang, Z.: Deblurgan-v2: Deblurring (orders-of-magnitude) faster and better. In: ICCV, October 2019

17. Lai, W.S., Huang, J.B., Hu, Z., Ahuja, N., Yang, M.H.: A comparative study for single image blind deblurring. In: CVPR, June 2016

18. Levin, A., Weiss, Y., Durand, F., Freeman, W.T.: Understanding and evaluating blind deconvolution algorithms. In: CVPR, pp. 1964–1971 (2009)

19. Levin, A., Weiss, Y., Durand, F., Freeman, W.T.: Efficient marginal likelihood optimization in blind deconvolution. In: CVPR, pp. 2657–2664 (2011)

20. Li, D., et al.: ARVO: learning all-range volumetric correspondence for video deblurring. In: CVPR, pp. 7721–7731, June 2021

21. Nah, S., et al.: Ntire 2019 challenge on video deblurring and super-resolution: dataset and study. In: CVPRW, June 2019

22. Nah, S., Kim, T.H., Lee, K.M.: Deep multi-scale convolutional neural network for dynamic scene deblurring. In: CVPR, July 2017

23. Pan, J., Sun, D., Pfister, H., Yang, M.H.: Blind image deblurring using dark channel prior. In: CVPR, pp. 1628–1636 (2016)

24. Park, J., Lee, C., Kim, C.S.: Asymmetric bilateral motion estimation for video frame interpolation. In: ICCV, pp. 14539–14548, October 2021

25. Rim, J., Lee, H., Won, J., Cho, S.: Real-world blur dataset for learning and benchmarking deblurring algorithms. In: Vedaldi, A., Bischof, H., Brox, T., Frahm, J.-M. (eds.) ECCV 2020. LNCS, vol. 12370, pp. 184–201. Springer, Cham (2020). https://doi.org/10.1007/978-3-030-58595-2_12

26. Shan, Q., Jia, J., Agarwala, A.: High-quality motion deblurring from a single image. ACM TOG **27**(3), 73:1–73:10 (2008)

27. Shen, Z., et al.: Human-aware motion deblurring. In: ICCV, October 2019

28. Su, S., Delbracio, M., Wang, J., Sapiro, G., Heidrich, W., Wang, O.: Deep video deblurring for hand-held cameras. In: CVPR, pp. 237–246, July 2017

29. Sun, L., Cho, S., Wang, J., Hays, J.: Edge-based blur kernel estimation using patch priors. In: ICCP (2013)

30. Tao, X., Gao, H., Shen, X., Wang, J., Jia, J.: Scale-recurrent network for deep image deblurring. In: CVPR, June 2018

31. Wang, Z., Cun, X., Bao, J., Zhou, W., Liu, J., Li, H.: Uformer: a general u-shaped transformer for image restoration. In: CVPR, June 2022
32. Wei, K., Fu, Y., Yang, J., Huang, H.: A physics-based noise formation model for extreme low-light raw denoising. In: CVPR, June 2020
33. Xu, L., Jia, J.: Two-phase kernel estimation for robust motion deblurring. In: Daniilidis, K., Maragos, P., Paragios, N. (eds.) ECCV 2010. LNCS, vol. 6311, pp. 157–170. Springer, Heidelberg (2010). https://doi.org/10.1007/978-3-642-15549-9_12
34. Zamir, S.W., Arora, A., Khan, S., Hayat, M., Khan, F.S., Yang, M.H.: Restormer: efficient transformer for high-resolution image restoration. In: CVPR, June 2022
35. Zamir, S.W., et al.: Multi-stage progressive image restoration. In: CVPR, pp. 14821–14831, June 2021
36. Zhang, H., Dai, Y., Li, H., Koniusz, P.: Deep stacked hierarchical multi-patch network for image deblurring. In: CVPR, June 2019
37. Zhang, K., Zuo, W., Chen, Y., Meng, D., Zhang, L.: Beyond a gaussian denoiser: residual learning of deep CNN for image denoising. IEEE TIP **26**(7), 3142–3155 (2017)
38. Zhang, K., et al.: Deblurring by realistic blurring. In: CVPR, June 2020
39. Zhang, Y., Qin, H., Wang, X., Li, H.: Rethinking noise synthesis and modeling in raw denoising. In: ICCV, pp. 4593–4601, October 2021
40. Zhong, Z., Gao, Y., Zheng, Y., Zheng, B.: Efficient spatio-temporal recurrent neural network for video deblurring. In: Vedaldi, A., Bischof, H., Brox, T., Frahm, J.-M. (eds.) ECCV 2020. LNCS, vol. 12351, pp. 191–207. Springer, Cham (2020). https://doi.org/10.1007/978-3-030-58539-6_12
41. Zhong, Z., Gao, Y., Zheng, Y., Zheng, B., Sato, I.: Efficient spatio-temporal recurrent neural network for video deblurring. arXiv preprint arXiv:2106.16028 (2021)
42. Zhong, Z., Zheng, Y., Sato, I.: Towards rolling shutter correction and deblurring in dynamic scenes. In: CVPR, pp. 9219–9228, June 2021
43. Zhou, S., Zhang, J., Zuo, W., Xie, H., Pan, J., Ren, J.S.: DavaNet: stereo deblurring with view aggregation. In: CVPR, June 2019

Learning Phase Mask for Privacy-Preserving Passive Depth Estimation

Zaid Tasneem[2], Giovanni Milione[1], Yi-Hsuan Tsai[1], Xiang Yu[1],
Ashok Veeraraghavan[2], Manmohan Chandraker[1,3],
and Francesco Pittaluga[1(✉)]

[1] NEC Laboratories America, Princeton, USA
francescopittaluga@nec-labs.com
[2] Rice University, Houston, USA
[3] University of California San Diego, San Diego, USA

Abstract. With over a billion sold each year, cameras are not only becoming ubiquitous, but are driving progress in a wide range of domains such as mixed reality, robotics, and more. However, severe concerns regarding the privacy implications of camera-based solutions currently limit the range of environments where cameras can be deployed. The key question we address is: Can cameras be enhanced with a scalable solution to preserve users' privacy without degrading their machine intelligence capabilities? Our solution is a novel end-to-end adversarial learning pipeline in which a phase mask placed at the aperture plane of a camera is jointly optimized with respect to privacy and utility objectives. We conduct an extensive design space analysis to determine operating points with desirable privacy-utility tradeoffs that are also amenable to sensor fabrication and real-world constraints. We demonstrate the first working prototype that enables passive depth estimation while inhibiting face identification.

Keywords: Privacy · Optics · Deep learning · Adversarial training

1 Introduction

Computer vision is increasingly enabling automatic extraction of task-specific insights from images, but its use in ubiquitously deployed cameras poses significant privacy concerns [3,35]. These concerns are further heightened by the fact that most cameras today are connected to the internet, leaving them vulnerable to data sniffing attacks. Existing solutions for improving visual privacy include post-capture image sanitization (blurring, resolution loss, etc.), or post-capture image encryption. Unfortunately, these solutions are vulnerable to typical sniffing attacks that can get direct access to the original captures rich in sensitive information.

Supplementary Information The online version contains supplementary material available at https://doi.org/10.1007/978-3-031-20071-7_30.

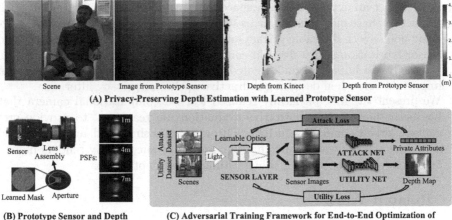

Fig. 1. Learning phase mask for privacy-preserving passive depth estimation

This leads to two fundamental questions: Can computational cameras for machine intelligence be designed to excel at particular tasks while ensuring *pre-capture privacy* with respect to specific sensitive information? And, can such cameras be realized in practice, to achieve advantageous privacy-utility trade-offs despite non-idealities in the modeling and fabrication process? This paper answers both the questions in the affirmative.

Unlike conventional post-capture visual privacy methods, our learned camera optics filter out privacy sensitive information prior to image capture, directly from the incident light-field – ensuring that private data never reaches the digital domain where it's susceptible to sniffing and other attacks. The learned filter can be optically implemented using a single phase mask inserted in the aperture plane of a normal camera – making the design practical and scalable. Development of our pre-capture privacy aware computational camera is driven by a novel adversarial-learning-based design principle for jointly optimizing the phase mask and downstream neural networks that enables us to achieve flexible tradeoffs for the utilitiy task of depth estimation and privacy task of avoiding face recognition.

Since, many downstream computer vision applications such as scene understanding, action recognition, planning and navigation have depth as a prerequisite, it serves as an information rich utility objective. We validate this notion by showing depth-based action recognition using private depth estimates from our learned sensor. Our optimized phase masks filter out high frequency information to obfuscate face identity while the resulting depth dependent encodings enable depth estimation.

We make the following contributions:

1. We present an end-to-end adversarial learning framework for optimizing the sensor optics with respect to utility and privacy objectives. We demonstrate the application of this design principle by optimizing the phase mask of a sensor to enable depth estimation while inhibiting face recognition.

2. We conduct an extensive design space analysis of sensor configurations with respect to phase mask design, focus settings and resolution to determine operating points with desirable privacy-utility tradeoffs that are also amenable to sensor fabrication and real-world constraints.
3. We study the impact of undiffracted light and demonstrate that it plays an important role when designing diffractive optics for privacy filtering.
4. We present the first physically realized learned computational camera that has been shown, via quantitative evaluations on real data, to provide pre-capture privacy and high utility. Through both simulated and real world experiments, we demonstrate that our prototype successfully renders human faces unidentifiable while enabling estimation of depth maps.

2 Related Work

The intersection of privacy, computer vision and computational imaging is related to many research areas. Here we summarize related works and explain how our framework is distinct. With respect to privacy, the focus of this paper is on visual privacy [37], i.e., on inhibiting estimation of sensitive attributes from imagery data. Other forms of privacy, such differential privacy [14] and federated learning [63] that aim to publish aggregate information about a database while limiting disclosure of database records are outside the scope of this paper.

In recent years, concerns regarding data sniffing attacks have led to development of pre-capture privacy cameras that apply privacy encodings at the sensor level via a trusted-hardware layer [15,34,42,56] and/or filtering optics [36,40,41,55]. Our approach, like [20,49], is a generalization of these methods in that de-identification is driven through automatic inference rather than manually designed strategies. However, we employ a more realistic physics model, which enables us to reproduce our simulated results in a fully working hardware prototype. To our knowledge, we are the first to successfully port a learned pre-capture privacy sensor to a real prototype device and demonstrate, via quantitative evaluations on real data, that it provides both privacy and utility. Finally, we also show an in-depth analysis of the sensor design space that provides critical insight into how privacy is being achieved.

Many prior visual privacy methods have relied on domain knowledge and hand-crafted heuristics—such as pixelation, blurring, face replacement, etc.—to degrade sensitive information [37]. Such approaches usually fail to achieve privacy-utility trade-offs comparable to that of more recent learning-based visual privacy methods. The most successful learning-based visual privacy methods [9,39,58,61], leverage adversarial training to learn encoding functions that inhibit estimation of private attributes by downstream discriminator models, yet still enable estimation of utility attributes by downstream utility models. This is a natural formulation, as an effective attack method to estimate the value of a private attribute is to train a neural network on a large set of encoded images. A similar approach has also been used to learn encoding functions that produce fair or unbiased encodings [2,24,25]. Such encodings can be thought of as private representations invariant to sensitive attributes such as ethnicity or gender. Adversarial training has also been used to learn adversarial perturbations that fool classifiers that expect natural images, but such classifiers recover when retrained on examples with the perturbations [10,31,32,45]. Finally, [38] learns adversarial perturbations for specific camera optics and image processing pipelines. We seek image transformations that inhibit estimation of the private attributes even after a classifier is retrained on encoded images.

Recent works have shown that modern deep learning tools can be used to efficiently model and optimize the end-to-end computational imaging process. This approach has been successfully leveraged to design computational sensors with improved performance across a range of tasks: demoisaicing [7], monocular depth estimation [4,8,18,19,57], extended depth of field and super-resolution [47], non-paraxial imaging [23], object detection [51] and high dynamic range imaging [30,48]. We present a computational imaging design principle that not only enables improved performance on a target utility task, but also inhibits estimation of private attributes.

3   Method

Our goal is end-to-end optimization of a sensor's optical elements with respect to privacy and utility objectives. To achieve this, we employ an adversarial learning formulation in which a sensor layer with learnable parameters is trained to simultaneously (a) promote the success of UTILITYNET, a downstream neural network aims to solve a target vision task, e.g., depth estimation, and (b) inhibit the success of ATTACKNET, a downstream neural network that seeks to infer private information from sensor images, e.g., face identification. See Fig. 7 of the appendix for a summary of the entire optimization scheme.

3.1   Sensor Layer

Like [57], our sensor layer consists of a conventional imaging system with a fixed focusing lens and learnable phase mask positioned in the aperture plane. Accordingly, we follow [57] and employ computational Fourier optics [17] to model the sensor via a pupil function:

$$P_{\lambda,z}(x_1, y_1) = A(x_1, y_1) \underbrace{e^{-jk_\lambda \left(\frac{x_1^2 + y_1^2}{2}\right)\left(\frac{1}{z} - \frac{1}{u}\right)}}_{\phi_{lens}} \left[\underbrace{e^{-jk_\lambda \Delta_n h(x_1, y_1)}}_{\phi_{mask}} + \nu \right] \qquad (1)$$

where $A, \phi_{mask}, \phi_{lens}, h \in \mathbb{R}^{W_1 \times H_1}$ denote the amplitude modulation due to the aperture, the phase modulations due to the phase mask and lens, and the learnable heights of the phase mask pixels respectively; z denotes the scene point distance; u the focal plane distance of the lens; f the focal length the lens; $k_\lambda = \frac{2\pi}{\lambda}$ the wave number; and Δ_n the difference between the refractive indices of air and the phase mask material. In an important deviation from [8], we introduce a new variable $\nu > 0$ into the sensor model to account for the portion of light that travels through the phase mask undiffracted. The reason for this is that undiffracted light may, as we show in Sect. 4.1, leak privacy-sensitive information if not accounted for. Since our goal is to design a sensor that optically filters out privacy-sensitive information, keeping track of the undiffracted light is critical. Finally, let $I_\lambda \in \mathbb{R}^{W_2 \times H_2}$ and $M \in \mathbb{R}^{W_2 \times H_2}$ denote an all-in-focus image and its corresponding depth map respectively. Then, the image formed by the sensor layer is

$$I'_\lambda(x_2, y_2) = \sum_{i=1}^{N} \left[I_\lambda(x_2, y_2) \cdot B_s(\mathbf{1}_{M(x_2,y_2)=z_i}) \right] * \underbrace{\left| \mathcal{F}\left\{ P_{\lambda,z}\left(\frac{x_2}{\lambda f}, \frac{y_2}{\lambda f} \right) \right\} \right|^2}_{PSF_{\lambda, z}} \quad (2)$$

where $\mathcal{F}$ denotes the discrete Fourier transform; $*$ the convolution operator; $z_1, ..., z_N$ a set of discrete depths; s the size of PSF_{λ,z_i}; $\mathbf{1}_{M(x_2,y_2)=z_i} \in \mathbb{R}^{W_2 \times H_2}$ an indicator function that is true when $M(x_2, y_2) = z_i$; and B_j a max-pool operation with a kernel of size $j \times j$. Note, we normalize over all N depths such that $\sum_{i=1}^{N} B_s(\mathbf{1}_{M(x_2,y_2)=z_i}) = 1$.

Optimization. The sensor layer $S : \mathbb{R}^{W_2 \times H_2 \times 3} \rightarrow \mathbb{R}^{W_2 \times H_2 \times 3}$ maps an all-in-focus image I to a sensor image $I' = S(I)$. Our goal is to optimize heights of the phase mask $h \in \mathbb{R}^{W_1 \times H_1}$ such that the sensor images I' cannot be used for estimation of sensitive attributes $g(I) \in \mathbf{G}$, but can be used for estimation of the target attributes $t(I) \in \mathbf{T}$. To achieve this, we employ an adversarial training formulation in which the sensor layer is trained to simultaneously promote the success of UTILITYNET $U : \mathbb{R}^{W_2 \times H_2 \times 3} \rightarrow \mathbf{T}$ while inhibiting the success of ATTACKNET $A : \mathbb{R}^{W_2 \times H_2 \times 3} \rightarrow \mathbf{G}$.

Let L_U and L_A denote the loss functions for UTILITYNET and ATTACKNET respectively. Then, the objective function for the sensor layer is given by

$$L_S(I) = \min_h L_U\big(t(I), U(I')\big) - \eta L_A\big(g(I), A(I')\big), \quad (3)$$

where η denotes a weight parameter to balance the privacy and utility trade off. To implement this loss function, we apply alternating gradient updates to the height map (sensor layer) and the weights of the downstream networks: In step 1, we update the height map and weights of UTILITYNET together and in step 2, we update the weights of ATTACKNET while the sensor layer and UTILITYNET are fixed. For our experiments, we set $\eta = 0.01$ and we used the Adam optimizer [26] with $\beta_1 = 0.9$, $\beta_2 = 0.999$, $\epsilon = 1\text{e-}8$ and a learning rate of 0.001. We also bound the heights of the phase mask pixels between $[0, 1.525]\,\mu\text{m}$ by applying a *hardsigmoid* function and then a scaling operation to the height map h.

3.2   Downstream Neural Networks

Downstream of the sensor layer, we have two neural networks, UTILITYNET and ATTACKNET. We define the utility task as monocular depth estimation and the attack task as face identification. Thus, the expected effect of our learned phase mask is to obfuscate identifiable facial information, while boosting the depth estimation accuracy.

For UTILITYNET, we adopt the ResNet-based multi-scale network proposed by [60] and we initialize the model with the pre-trained weights from [44]. For optimization of UTILITYNET, we follow [1] and adopt an objective function consisting of a weighted sum of losses on the depth, gradient and perceptual quality:

$$L_U(y, \hat{y}) = \frac{1 - \text{SSIM}(y, \hat{y})}{2} + \frac{1}{n}\left[\xi|y - \hat{y}| + |\mathbf{g_x}(y, \hat{y})| + |\mathbf{g_y}(y, \hat{y})| \right] \quad (4)$$

where $y = 10/y_{\text{gt}}$ denotes the reciprocal of the ground-truth depth map, $\hat{y}$ the estimated depth map, and ξ a weighting parameter (which we set to 0.1), n the number of pixels in the depth map, $SSIM$ structural similarity [54] and $\mathbf{g_x}$ and $\mathbf{g_y}$ compute the differences of the x and y components of gradients of y and $\hat{y}$.

For ATTACKNET, we use the EfficientNet-b0 [50] architecture and adopt a softmax activation followed by a cross-entropy loss for n-way classification as in [5]. For testing, we remove the final layer of the network and learn one-vs-all SVM classifiers for each test subject, using a held-out subset of the evaluation set, as in [5]. Finally, we train both UTILITYNET and ATTACKNET until saturation using the Adam optimizer [26] with $\beta_1 = 0.9$, $\beta_2 = 0.999$, $\epsilon = 1\text{e}{-8}$ and a learning rate of 0.001.

3.3 Prototype Sensor

The prototyping pipeline accepts a learned phase mask height map and culminates with fine-tuning of UTILITYNET and ATTACKNET with the calibrated PSFs (Fig. 8 of appendix). The phase mask is fabricated using two-photon lithography and inserted into the aperture plane of a conventional lens system. Section A of the appendix includes the fabrication details of the prototype for interested readers.

4 Experimental Results

This section includes both simulation and real results with our prototype sensor. For all reported results, attack models are retrained after adversarial optimization is complete, i.e., after the learnable parameters of the sensor layer have been permanently fixed. This ensures that the sensor layer cannot be overcome by an adversary with access to a large set of labeled sensor images. Utility models are also retrained after the sensor layer is fixed. The full details about the datasets, evaluation protocols and image formation model are available in Sects.B1, B2 and B3 of the appendix respectively.

4.1 Design Space Analysis

We show a systematic analysis of the sensor design space which is essential in designing any optical pre-capture privacy sensor. The utility task is fixed to monocular depth estimation on the NYUv2 dataset [33] and the attack task to face identification on the VGGFace2 dataset [5]. For face identification, the faces were resized, as discussed in Sect. B3, to simulate different camera-to-subject distance between 1–10 m and the face identification performance was averaged over these depth ranges.

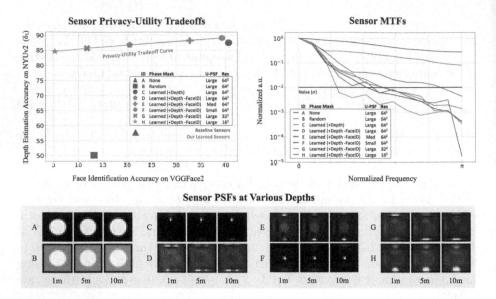

Fig. 2. Design space analysis. The plot on the top left shows depth estimation (utility) vs face identification (privacy) accuracy for multiple sensor designs (A–H), with varying phase mask designs, undiffracted PSF sizes and sensor resolutions. The sensors optimized using our approach (D–H), have a better privacy utility trade-off (smaller slope) compared to the traditional sensor designs (A–C). The corresponding modulus-transfer-function (MTF) plots, shown in the top right plot, give an intuition into the privacy performance of the different sensor designs based on their respective cut-off frequencies. Lower cut-off frequency corresponds to better privacy (filtering of facial details). The PSFs of each sensor designs for 3 different depths are shown at the bottom of the figure. Note, the PSFs corresponding to learned sensors vary significantly over different depths, which results in better depth estimation performance.

Impact of Phase Mask Design. This section examines how the goal of balancing privacy and utility objectives can be achieved by optimizing the phase mask. We compare four sensors with identical parameters, but with four different phase mask designs. The four phase mask designs that we consider are: (A) none; (B) random; (C) optimized to maximize depth estimation performance; and (D) optimized to maximize depth estimation performance while inhibiting face identification. At the top left of Fig. 2, we show the privacy-utility trade-off of each sensor, i.e., the performance of downstream depth estimation and face identification models for each sensor. At the top right of Fig. 2, we show the modulation-transfer-function (MTFs) corresponding to the PSFs of each sensor at 1 m. The MTFs are computed as the radially averaged magnitude of the frequency spectrum of the PSFs. The cut-off frequencies are determined by the noise level of $\sigma = 0.01$, which we assume to be Gaussian. At the bottom of Fig. 2, we show pixel-space visualizations of the depth-dependent point-spread-functions (PSFs) of each sensor. The presence of the large defocus spot in the

PSFs of sensors A, B, C, and D is due to fact that all four sensors are focused at 10cm and a portion of the light travels through the phase masks undiffracted [52]. For all four sensors, focal length $f = 16$ mm, focal distance $u = 10$ cm, sensor size of 8.8×6.6 mm, sensor resolution of 64×64 pixels, aperture diameter $d = 8.7$ mm, phase mask pitch $4.25 \, \mu$m, and we considered a working range of $z = [1, 10]$ m.

Consider sensor A (no phase mask/naive defocus). Since it is focused at 10 cm and does not have a phase mask, faces located in the working range of 1–10 m with be heavily out-of-focus. This is advantageous for privacy as high frequency facial details will be optically filtered out. This is consistent with Fig. 2, as the PSFs of sensor A resemble a large Gaussian filter and the MTF a low-pass filter. Finally, privacy-utility curve in Fig. 2 shows that sensor A succeeds at reducing face identification accuracy from 80.1% (all-in-focus) images to 21.7%, but fails to provide satisfactory depth estimation performance, as the PSFs remain constant over depth, and thus fails to provide a desirable privacy-utility trade-off.

Consider sensor B (random phase mask). Due to the fact that approximately 10% of the incident light passes through the phase mask undiffracted, its PSF consist of a linear combination of a diffracted and an undiffracted PSF, as shown in Fig. 2. The undiffracted PSFs exactly match the PSFs of sensor A, which resemble a Gaussian filter. The diffracted PSFs are the result of light passing through the random phase mask, which disperses light uniformly to the entire receptive field, so the diffracted PSF is effectively a square average filter. Comparing the MTFs of sensors A and B in Fig. 2, we can observe that the cut-off frequency of sensor B is much lower than sensor A. As expected, this results in sensor B having worse downstream depth estimation and face identification performance compared to sensor A. Overall, sensor B fails to provide a desirable privacy-utility trade-off.

Consider sensor C (phase mask optimized to maximize depth estimation performance as in [57]). Although its PSFs also consist of a linear combination of diffracted and undiffracted PSFs, this is obscured in Fig. 2, by the fact that the diffracted PSFs are very sparse, which results in the "activated" pixels having a much higher magnitude than the undiffracted PSFs. Looking now at the MTF of sensor C in Fig. 2, we observe that optimizing the phase mask for depth estimation resulted in PSFs that don't filter out any information, which is consistent with what one would expect. Interestingly, we also see from Fig. 2 that the PSFs vary with depth, which is also what we would expect if our goal is to maximize downstream depth estimation performance. Finally, looking at Fig. 2, we see that depth estimation performance is comparable to the state-of-the-art, but that it comes at the cost of face identification accuracy also being high (40%). Note, the reason face identification accuracy is not higher than 40% is that sensor C has a resolution of 64×64 pixels.

Consider sensor D (learned using our proposed adversarial optimization algorithm to maximize depth estimation performance while minimizing face identification performance). Its PSFs filter out high frequency facial details, yet also vary significantly with depth, as shown in the PSFs and MTF of sensor D in Fig. 2. Both of these outcomes are intuitively consistent with our goal of balancing privacy and utility. The privacy-utility plot in Fig. 2 confirms this intuition by showing that downstream depth estimation performance is comparable to the state-of-the-art and that face identification is limited to an accuracy of 20.5%.

Impact of Undiffracted Light Vis-á-vis Focus Settings. In practice, ν from Eq. 1 typically varies usually between 0.08 to 0.2 [52], which results in a non-insignificant amount of undiffracted light reaching the sensor. Previous deep optics works for depth estimation [8,57] have simply ignored this issue. This was possible because they were not concerned with leakage of privacy sensitive information. For our setting, preventing leakage of privacy sensitive information is crucial, so the undiffracted light must be modeled. We illustrate this by optimizing the phase masks of three sensors (D, E and F) with undiffracted PSFs of different sizes and comparing the resulting privacy-utility trade-offs of the respective sensors. Note, since the undiffracted PSFs don't depend on the phase mask design, they can be fixed prior to optimizing the masks. We vary the size of the undiffracted PSFs by setting the focal distance $u = \{0.1, 0.17, 1.0\}$m to produce sensors with "large", "medium", and "small" undiffracted PSFs. For all three sensors, we fix $\nu = 0.1$, focal length $f = 16$ mm, sensor size of 8.8×6.6 mm, sensor resolution of 64×64 pixels, aperture diameter $d = 8.7$ mm, phase mask pitch $4.25\,\mu$m, and we considered a working range of $z = [1, 10]$ m. The PSFs of each sensor are shown at the bottom of Fig. 2. In the MTF plot in Fig. 2, we see that larger undiffracted PSFs result in less leakage of privacy sensitive information. Intuitively, this is reasonable as a larger defocus kernel corresponds to a lower cut-off frequency, so more information will be filtered out, and this is consistent with the results shown in privacy-utility trade-off plot in Fig. 2. Thus, when designing our final sensor, we utilize a large undiffracted PSF.

Impact of Sensor Resolution. Our goal is to design a sensor that inhibits recovery of privacy sensitive information from encoded sensor images. From an attacker's perspective, recovery of sensitive information from encoded images can be modeled as a conventional inverse problem, so the number of observations (or sensor resolution) naturally plays an important role. We study this role by optimizing the phase masks of three sensors with identical parameters, but different resolutions. The three sensor resolutions we consider are 16×16, 32×32 and 64×64, and the resulting privacy-utility trade-offs are shown in the top left of Fig. 2. As expected, the lower the sensor resolution, the lower the face identification accuracy. Interestingly, the ability of the downstream depth estimation models to produce high quality depths maps of size 256×256 is not meaningfully impacted by the sensor resolution as scene depth in most natural settings tends to be a low frequency signal. This is highly advantageous for our setting as we are able to reduce face identification performance by reducing the sensor resolution without sacrificing significant depth estimation performance. Note, for ease of comparison, we display all the sensor PSFs and MTFs using a

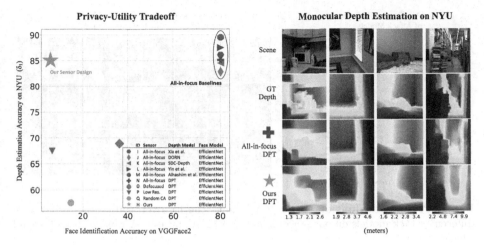

Fig. 3. Comparisons with existing methods. On the left, we compare the privacy-utility trade-off of our learned sensor design against four other sensors: a conventional all-in-focus sensor, a defocused privacy sensor [40], a low resolution privacy sensor [11] and a random coded aperture privacy sensor [55]. For all sensors, we show the corresponding face identification accuracy of EfficientNet-b0 [50] on the VGGFace2 dataset, along the x-axis, and the depth estimation accuracy (δ_1) of DPT [43] on the NYU Depth v2 dataset, along the y-axis. For the all-in-focus sensor, we additionally show the depth estimation performance of [1,16,53,59,64]. On the right, we compare the monocular depth estimation predictions of DPT operating on conventional all-in-focus images vs private images from our learned sensor design.

sensor resolution of 64×64. For all three sensors, focal length $f = 16$ mm, sensor size of 8.8×6.6 mm, aperture diameter $d = 8.7$ mm, phase mask pitch 4.25 μm, and we considered a working range of $z = [1, 10]$ m.

4.2 Simulation Results

Comparisons with Pre-capture Privacy Sensors. We compare the privacy-utility trade-off provided by our optimized sensor design (sensor H from Fig. 2) to an all-in-focus sensor and three existing pre-capture privacy sensors: a heavily defocused sensor [40], an extremely low-resolution sensor [11], and a sensor with a random coded aperture mask [55]. For all four sensors, the focal length $f = 16$ mm, the sensor size was 8.8×6.6mm, and a working range of $z = [1, 10]$ m was considered. For the all-in-focus sensor (N), the focal distance $u = \infty$, the sensor resolution was 256×256 pixels, and the aperture diameter $d = 1$ mm. For the defocused sensor (O), the focal distance $u = 10$ cm, the sensor resolution was 256×256 pixels, and the aperture diameter $d = 8.7$ mm. For the low resolution sensor (P), the focal distance $u = \infty$, the sensor resolution was 16×16 pixels, and the aperture diameter $d = 1$ mm. Lastly, for the coded aperture camera (Q), the focal distance $u = 10$ cm, the sensor resolution was 256×256 pixels, and the aperture diameter $d = 8.7$ mm. For fair evaluation, new copies of UTILITYNET

514   Z. Tasneem et al.

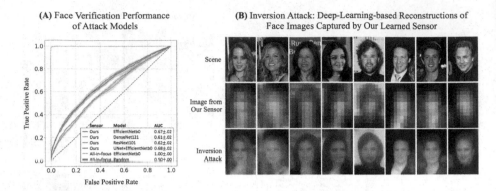

Fig. 4. Privacy evaluation. Figure **(A)** shows the face verification performance of different attack models on our sensor simulated LFW dataset. A random classifier and EfficientNet-b0 [50] trained on an all-in-focus LFW dataset serve as our lower and upper bounds respectively. For figure **(B)**, we train a U-Net [29] style neural network to reconstruct the original source images from simulated sensor images. The results show that the U-Net learns to reconstruct low frequency information such as hair color and skin pigment, but fails to reconstruct the same identity as the original person, as the high frequency identity information is filtered out by our optimized sensor.

and ATTACKNET were trained from scratch to test each sensor, using only images produce by the respective sensor. As shown on the left of Fig. 3, our data-driven approach (H), achieves a far better privacy-utility trade-off compared to the three pre-capture sensors (O, P and Q) and the all-in-focus baseline (N). It is important to note that the sensor resolution and defocus settings of our learned sensor (H) are the same as the low-res (P) and defocused (O) sensors respectively. This clearly demonstrates the advantage of our learning based approach over the fixed sensors.

For completeness, we also compare our learned sensor design against six state-of-the-art monocular depth estimation methods that operate on all-in-focus images from conventional sensors. The six methods we compare against are Xie et al. [59], DORN [16], SDC-depth [53], Yin et al. [64], Alhashim et al. [1] and DPT [43]. As illustrated in Fig. 3, our approach limits face identification performance to 5.3% compared to 80.1% for the all-in-focus sensor, while still achieving depth estimation performance comparable to the state-of-the-art. On the right side of Fig. 3, we qualitatively compare the predicted depth maps of DPT [43] when operating on all-in-focus sensor images vs private images from our learned sensor. Here we note the limitation of our approach as the depth maps produced by our approach doesn't preserve very high frequency details.

Privacy Evaluation. In this section, we assess the efficacy of our learned sensor design (H) at inhibiting facial identification attacks by four different models: EfficientNetb0 [50], DenseNet121 [21], ResNext101 [62], and UNet+EfficientNetb0. All models are retrained on the private images from our sensor. In the fourth

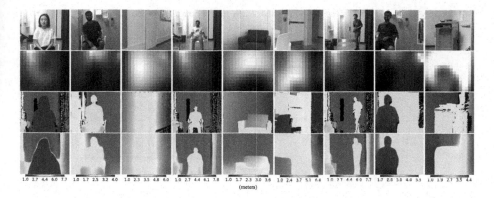

1.0 2.7 4.4 6.0 7.7   1.0 1.7 2.5 3.2 4.0   1.0 2.3 3.5 4.8 6.0   1.0 2.7 4.4 6.1 7.8   1.0 1.7 2.3 3.0 3.6   1.0 2.4 3.7 5.1 6.4   1.0 7.7 4.4 6.0 7.7   1.7 2.6 3.0 4.0 5.5   1.0 1.9 2.7 3.5 4.4
(meters)

Fig. 5. Private depth etimation with prototype sensor. We show the depth reconstruction performance of our prototype sensor in the wild. Row 1: all-in-focus images of the scene. Row 2: Images captured by our prototype sensor (16 × 16 pixels). Row 3: Depth map captured by Microsoft Kinect v2. Row 4: Depth maps predicted from images captured by our prototype sensor. The mean depth estimation accuracy (δ_1) of our predicted depth maps is 83.73%. This is consistent with the 84.69% accuracy of our simulated results on the NYUv2 Dataset.

model (UNet+EfficientNetb0), the UNet [29] precedes EfficientNetb0 and is trained to reconstruct the original face images from their encoded counterparts (i.e., from simulated captures from our learned sensor). Figure 4(A) shows the performance of the four models in the form of receiver operating characteristic (ROC) curves and Fig. 4(B) shows some sample reconstructions from the UNet. Our learned sensor limits face verification performance to an area-under-the-curve (AUC) of 0.67 ± 0.02 for the best performing model. This represents a significant obfuscation of face identity information using our sensor design, considering that the same network, when learned on images from a conventional sensor, achieves an AUC of 0.99 ± 0.05. Regarding the reconstructions shown in Fig. 4(B), we can see that while it's possible to recover some low frequency information, such hair color and skin pigment, from a sensor image, key high frequency features, such as the lips, eyes and nose, are incorrectly reconstructed, which prevents successful facial identification. The full details of the evaluation are provided in Sect. B4 of the appendix.

Privacy-Preserving Action Recognition. We further evaluate the utility of our learned sensor design (H) by training a 3D-fused two-stream model (I3D) [6] for action recognition using simulated color images and predicted depth maps from our learned sensor. For comparison, we also train an I3D model on conventional all-in-focus color images and "ground-truth" depth maps from a Microsoft Kinect v2. Both models are trained on the NTURGBD120 [28] dataset using the cross-setup training and testing protocol. The model trained on outputs from the Kinect achieved a top 1 and top 5 accuracy of 79.1% and 94.0% respectively. The model trained on outputs from our learned sensor achieved a top 1

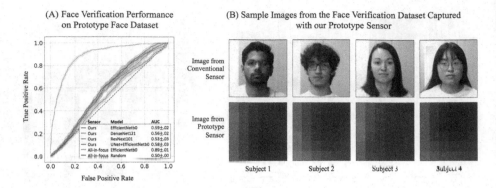

Fig. 6. Privacy evaluation of prototype sensor. (A) Face verification performance of different attack models on the face images from a dataset of 20 individuals captured by our sensor prototype. A random classifier and the EfficientNet-b0 attack on all-in-focus images serve as our lower-bound and upper-bound respectively. **(B)** Sample Images from the face verification dataset captured with our prototype sensor (row 2) with corresponding all-in-focus images (row 1).

and top 5 accuracy of 70.5% and 91.5% respectively. These results demonstrate that out optimized sensor has the potential impact a range of applications for which privacy is a major concern, such as elder care, remote health monitoring, surveillance of sensitive environments (schools, hospitals, etc.), and more.

4.3   Results with Real Prototype Sensor

To demonstrate the viability of our approach, we build a physical prototype (shown in Fig. 1) of our optimized sensor design (sensor H from Fig. 2) and evaluate it's performance along a range of dimensions. In order to avoid fabricating a low resolution sensor we simply downsample a high resolution sensor to 16×16 pixels. The consequences of such a choice are discussed in detail along with the prototyping pipeline in Sect. A of the appendix.

Privacy-Preserving Depth Estimation with Prototype Sensor. We present qualitative depth estimation results on real captures from our prototype sensor in row 4 of Fig. 5. The mean depth estimation accuracy (δ_1) for these results is 83.73%, which is consistent with the 84.69% accuracy of our simulated results on the NYUv2 Dataset. Images of the corresponding scene captured with a Kinect color camera and our prototype sensor (16×16 pixels) are shown in rows 1 and 2 respectively, and depth images captured from a stereo calibrated time-of-flight Kinect sensor are shown in row 3. Qualitatively, the depth estimates from our sensor are comparable to the Kinect measurements, but lack some of the high frequency details.

Privacy Evaluation of Prototype Sensor. To validate our prototype sensor's ability to inhibit face identification, we capture a novel face verification dataset using our prototype sensor, consisting of 100 images of 20 subjects (5 images per subject at different depths). As an upper bound, we also capture an identical dataset using a conventional all-in-focus color camera. For the evaluation, we generate 10 sets of 200 pairs of face images for 10-fold cross-validation. Sample images from our dataset are shown in Fig. 6(B).

For the evaluation, we assume a white-box attack model and use the same protocol as for our previous simulation-based privacy analysis. The results of the evaluation, presented in Fig. 6(A), show that our prototype sensor limits face verification performance to an area-under-the-curve (AUC) of 0.59 ± 0.02 for the best performing model. The same model, when operating on images from a conventional sensor, achieves an AUC of 0.89 ± 0.01. These results demonstrate that we are able to reproduce our simulated results with a real hardware prototype.

5   Conclusions

We believe our framework and prototype sensor design represent a first and significant advance towards enabling a new generation of pre-capture privacy aware computational cameras that will greatly expand the range of environments, technologies, and applications where computer-vision-based solutions can be deployed. Thus, it becomes important to discuss what other possible utility and privacy tasks our proposed framework can be applied to, to get good privacy-utility trade-offs. Based on our analysis of the MTFs of various sensor designs (Fig. 2), a good pair of privacy-utility tasks would be one with contrasting requirements for frequency/detail preservation. For example, for a privacy task of inhibiting face identification, a utility task of object classification is likely to work best for objects that are larger than a human face, such as a human body, furniture, cars, etc.

Our choice of utility and privacy objectives is a rather interesting one. The optimization makes sure that the psfs produced vary over depth, but still act as a low pass filter. This enables us to estimate high quality depth maps, while inhibiting face identification. However, it's also important to note a limitation of our choice of privacy-utility tasks. Namely, that the objective of acquiring high-frequency depth maps comes into direct conflict with the objective of preventing accurate face identification, resulting in over smoothed depth estimates. Nevertheless, as shown in Sect. 4.2, our estimated depth maps have enough detail for many downstream vision tasks such as depth-based activity recognition.

References

1. Alhashim, I., Wonka, P.: High quality monocular depth estimation via transfer learning. arXiv preprint arXiv:1812.11941 (2018)

518   Z. Tasneem et al.

2. Alvi, M., Zisserman, A., Nellåker, C.: Turning a blind eye: explicit removal of biases and variation from deep neural network embeddings. In: Leal-Taixé, L., Roth, S. (eds.) ECCV 2018. LNCS, vol. 11129, pp. 556–572. Springer, Cham (2019). https://doi.org/10.1007/978-3-030-11009-3_34
3. Beach, S., Schulz, R., Downs, J., Matthews, J., Barron, B., Seelman, K.: Disability, age, and informational privacy attitudes in quality of life technology applications: results from a national web survey. ACM Trans. Access. Comput. **2**(1), 5 (2009)
4. Boominathan, V., Adams, J.K., Robinson, J.T., Veeraraghavan, A.: PhlatCam: designed phase-mask based thin lensless camera. IEEE Trans. Pattern Anal. Mach. Intell. **42**(7), 1618–1629 (2020)
5. Cao, Q., Shen, L., Xie, W., Parkhi, O.M., Zisserman, A.: Vggface2: a dataset for recognising faces across pose and age. In: 2018 13th IEEE International Conference on Automatic Face & Gesture Recognition (FG 2018), pp. 67–74 (2018)
6. Carreira, J., Zisserman, A.: Quo vadis, action recognition? A new model and the kinetics dataset. In: Proceedings of the IEEE Conference on Computer Vision and Pattern Recognition, pp. 6299–6308 (2017)
7. Chakrabarti, A.: Learning sensor multiplexing design through back-propagation. In: 30th Conference on Advances in Neural Information Processing Systems, pp. 3081–3089 (2016)
8. Chang, J., Wetzstein, G.: Deep optics for monocular depth estimation and 3D object detection. In: Proceedings of the IEEE International Conference on Computer Vision, pp. 10193–10202 (2019)
9. Chen, J., Konrad, J., Ishwar, P.: VGAN-based image representation learning for privacy-preserving facial expression recognition. In: Proceedings of the IEEE Conference on Computer Vision and Pattern Recognition Workshops, pp. 1570–1579 (2018)
10. Chhabra, S., Singh, R., Vatsa, M., Gupta, G.: Anonymizing k-facial attributes via adversarial perturbations. arXiv preprint arXiv:1805.09380 (2018)
11. Dai, J., Wu, J., Saghafi, B., Konrad, J., Ishwar, P.: Towards privacy-preserving activity recognition using extremely low temporal and spatial resolution cameras. In: Proceedings of the IEEE Conference on Computer Vision and Pattern Recognition Workshops, pp. 68–76 (2015)
12. Deng, J., Dong, W., Socher, R., Li, L.J., Li, K., Fei-Fei, L.: ImageNet: a large-scale hierarchical image database. In: IEEE Conference on Computer Vision and Pattern Recognition, 2009. CVPR 2009, pp. 248–255 (2009)
13. Dosovitskiy, A., Brox, T.: Generating images with perceptual similarity metrics based on deep networks. In: Advances in Neural Information Processing Systems, pp. 658–666 (2016)
14. Dwork, C.: Differential privacy: a survey of results. In: International Conference on Theory and Applications of Models of Computation, pp. 1–19 (2008)
15. Erdélyi, A., Barát, T., Valet, P., Winkler, T., Rinner, B.: Adaptive cartooning for privacy protection in camera networks. In: 2014 11th IEEE International Conference on Advanced Video and Signal Based Surveillance (AVSS), pp. 44–49 (2014)
16. Fu, H., Gong, M., Wang, C., Batmanghelich, K., Tao, D.: Deep ordinal regression network for monocular depth estimation. In: Proceedings of the IEEE Conference on Computer Vision and Pattern Recognition, pp. 2002–2011 (2018)
17. Goodman, J.W.: Introduction to Fourier Optics. Roberts and Company Publishers, Englewood (2005)
18. Haim, H., Elmalem, S., Giryes, R., Bronstein, A.M., Marom, E.: Depth estimation from a single image using deep learned phase coded mask. IEEE Trans. Comput. Imag. **4**(3), 298–310 (2018)

19. He, L., Wang, G., Hu, Z.: Learning depth from single images with deep neural network embedding focal length. IEEE Trans. Image Process. **27**(9), 4676–4689 (2018)
20. Hinojosa, C., Niebles, J.C., Arguello, H.: Learning privacy-preserving optics for human pose estimation. In: Proceedings of the IEEE/CVF International Conference
21. Hinojosa, C., Niebles, J.C., Arguello, H.: Learning privacy-preserving optics for human pose estimation. In: Proceedings of the IEEE/CVF International Conference
22. Huang, G.B., Ramesh, M., Berg, T., Learned-Miller, E.: Labeled faces in the wild: a database for studying face recognition in unconstrained environments. Tech. Rep. 07–49, University of Massachusetts, Amherst, October 2007
23. Jeong, Y., Yoo, D.H., Cho, J., Lee, B.: Optic design and image processing considering angle of incidence via end-to-end optimization method. Ultra-High-Defi. Imag Syst. II **10943**, 109430U (2019)
24. Jia, S., Lansdall-Welfare, T., Cristianini, N.: Right for the right reason: training agnostic networks. In: International Symposium on Intelligent Data Analysis, pp. 164–174 (2018)
25. Kim, B., Kim, H., Kim, K., Kim, S., Kim, J.: Learning not to learn: training deep neural networks with biased data. In: Proceedings of the IEEE Conference on Computer Vision and Pattern Recognition, pp. 9012–9020 (2019)
26. Kingma, D.P., Ba, J.: Adam: a method for stochastic optimization. arXiv preprint arXiv:1412.6980 (2014)
27. Ledig, C., et al.: Photo-realistic single image super-resolution using a generative adversarial network. In: CVPR, vol. 2 (2017)
28. Liu, J., Shahroudy, A., Perez, M.L., Wang, G., Duan, L.Y., Chichung, A.K.: Ntu RGB+ D 120: a large-scale benchmark for 3D human activity understanding. IEEE Trans. Pattern Anal. Mach. Intell. (2019)
29. Long, J., Shelhamer, E., Darrell, T.: Fully convolutional networks for semantic segmentation. In: Proceedings of the IEEE Conference on Computer Vision and Pattern Recognition (2014)
30. Metzler, C.A., Ikoma, H., Peng, Y., Wetzstein, G.: Deep optics for single-shot high-dynamic-range imaging. In: Proceedings of the IEEE/CVF Conference on Computer Vision and Pattern Recognition, pp. 1375–1385 (2020)
31. Mirjalili, V., Raschka, S., Ross, A.: Gender privacy: an ensemble of semi adversarial networks for confounding arbitrary gender classifiers. In: 2018 IEEE 9th International Conference on Biometrics Theory, Applications and Systems (BTAS), pp. 1–10 (2018)
32. Mirjalili, V., Raschka, S., Ross, A.: Flowsan: privacy-enhancaing semi-adversarial networks to confound arbitrary face-based gender classifiers. IEEE Access **7**, 99735–99745 (2019)
33. Silberman, N., Hoiem, D., Kohli, P., Fergus, R.: Indoor segmentation and support inference from rgbd images. In: Fitzgibbon, A., Lazebnik, S., Perona, P., Sato, Y., Schmid, C. (eds.) ECCV 2012. LNCS, vol. 7576, pp. 746–760. Springer, Heidelberg (2012). https://doi.org/10.1007/978-3-642-33715-4_54
34. Nawaz, T., Rinner, B., Ferryman, J.: User-centric, embedded vision-based human monitoring: a concept and a healthcare use case. In: Proceedings of the 10th International Conference on Distributed Smart Camera, pp. 25–30 (2016)
35. Neustaedter, C.G., Greenberg, S.: Balancing privacy and awareness in home media spaces. In: Citeseer (2003)

36. Nguyen Canh, T., Nagahara, H.: Deep compressive sensing for visual privacy protection in Flatcam imaging. In: Proceedings of the IEEE International Conference on Computer Vision Workshops, pp. 0–0 (2019)
37. Padilla-López, J.R., Chaaraoui, A.A., Flórez-Revuelta, F.: Visual privacy protection methods: A survey. Expert Syst. Appl. **42**(9), 4177–4195 (2015)
38. Phan, B., Mannan, F., Heide, F.: Adversarial imaging pipelines. In: Proceedings of the IEEE/CVF Conference on Computer Vision and Pattern Recognition, pp. 16051–16061 (2021)
39. Pittaluga, F., Koppal, S., Chakrabarti, A.: Learning privacy preserving encodings through adversarial training. In: 2019 IEEE Winter Conference on Applications of Computer Vision (WACV), pp. 791–799 (2019)
40. Pittaluga, F., Koppal, S.J.: Privacy preserving optics for miniature vision sensors. In: Proceedings of the IEEE Conference on Computer Vision and Pattern Recognition, pp. 314–324 (2015)
41. Pittaluga, F., Koppal, S.J.: Pre-capture privacy for small vision sensors. IEEE Trans. Pattern Anal. Mach. Intell. **39**(11), 2215–2226 (2016)
42. Pittaluga, F., Zivkovic, A., Koppal, S.J.: Sensor-level privacy for thermal cameras. In: 2016 IEEE International Conference on Computational Photography (ICCP), pp. 1–12 (2016)
43. Ranftl, R., Bochkovskiy, A., Koltun, V.: Vision transformers for dense prediction. ArXiv preprint (2021)
44. Ranftl, R., Lasinger, K., Hafner, D., Schindler, K., Koltun, V.: Towards robust monocular depth estimation: mixing datasets for zero-shot cross-dataset transfer. IEEE Trans. Pattern Anal. Mach. Intell.**44**, 1623–1637 (2020)
45. Sattar, H., Krombholz, K., Pons-Moll, G., Fritz, M.: Shape evasion: Preventing body shape inference of multi-stage approaches. arXiv preprint arXiv:1905.11503 (2019)
46. Simonyan, K., Zisserman, A.: Very deep convolutional networks for large-scale image recognition. arXiv preprint arXiv:1409.1556 (2014)
47. Sitzmann, V., et al.: End-to-end optimization of optics and image processing for achromatic extended depth of field and super-resolution imaging. ACM Trans. Graph. **37**(4), 1–13 (2018)
48. Sun, Q., Tseng, E., Fu, Q., Heidrich, W., Heide, F.: Learning rank-1 diffractive optics for single-shot high dynamic range imaging. In: Proceedings of the IEEE/CVF conference on Computer Vision and Pattern Recognition, pp. 1386–1396 (2020)
49. Tan, J., et al.: Canopic: Pre-digital privacy-enhancing encodings for computer vision. In: 2020 IEEE International Conference on Multimedia and Expo (ICME), pp. 1–6 (2020)
50. Tan, M., Le, Q.: EfficientNet: rethinking model scaling for convolutional neural networks. In: International Conference on Machine Learning, pp. 6105–6114 (2019)
51. Tseng, E., et al.: Differentiable compound optics and processing pipeline optimization for end-to-end camera design. ACM Trans. Graph. **40**(2), 1–19 (2021)
52. Wang, H., et al.:Off-axis holography with uniform illumination via 3D printed diffractive optical elements. Adv. Opt. Mater.**7**(12), 1900068 (2019)
53. Wang, L., Zhang, J., Wang, O., Lin, Z., Lu, H.: SDC-depth: semantic divide-and-conquer network for monocular depth estimation. In: Proceedings of the IEEE/CVF Conference on Computer Vision and Pattern Recognition, pp. 541–550 (2020)

54. Wang, Z., Bovik, A.C., Sheikh, H.R., Simoncelli, E.P.: Image quality assessment: from error visibility to structural similarity. IEEE Trans. Image Process. **13**(4), 600–612 (2004)
55. Wang, Z.W., Vineet, V., Pittaluga, F., Sinha, S.N., Cossairt, O., Bing Kang, S.: Privacy-preserving action recognition using coded aperture videos. In: Proceedings of the IEEE Conference on Computer Vision and Pattern Recognition Workshops (2019)
56. Winkler, T., Erdélyi, A., Rinner, B.: TrustEYE. M4: protecting the sensor-not the camera. In: 2014 11th IEEE International Conference on Advanced Video and Signal Based Surveillance (AVSS), pp. 159–164 (2014)
57. Wu, Y., Boominathan, V., Chen, H., Sankaranarayanan, A., Veeraraghavan, A.: Phasecam3d-learning phase masks for passive single view depth estimation. In: 2019 IEEE International Conference on Computational Photoagraphy (ICCP), pp. 1–12. IEEE (2019)
58. Wu, Y., Yang, F., Ling, H.: Privacy-protective-GAN for face de-identification. arXiv preprint arXiv:1806.08906 (2018)
59. Xia, Z., Sullivan, P., Chakrabarti, A.: Generating and exploiting probabilistic monocular depth estimates. In: Proceedings of the IEEE/CVF Conference on Computer Vision and Pattern Recognition, pp. 65–74 (2020)
60. Xian, K., et al.: Monocular relative depth perception with web stereo data supervision. In: Proceedings of the IEEE Conference on Computer Vision and Pattern Recognition, pp. 311–320 (2018)
61. Xiao, T., Tsai, Y.H., Sohn, K., Chandraker, M., Yang, M.H.: Adversarial learning of privacy-preserving and task-oriented representations. In: Proceedings of the AAAI Conference on Artificial Intelligence (2020)
62. Xie, S., Girshick, R., Dollár, P., Tu, Z., He, K.: Aggregated residual transformations for deep neural networks. In: Proceedings of the IEEE Conference on Computer Vision and Pattern Recognition, pp. 1492–1500 (2017)
63. Yang, Q., Liu, Y., Chen, T., Tong, Y.: Federated machine learning: Concept and applications. ACM Trans. Intell. Syst. Technol. **10**(2), 1–19 (2019)
64. Yin, W., Liu, Y., Shen, C., Yan, Y.: Enforcing geometric constraints of virtual normal for depth prediction. In: Proceedings of the IEEE/CVF International Conference on Computer Vision, pp. 5684–5693 (2019)
65. Zhang, K., Zhang, Z., Li, Z., Qiao, Y.: Joint face detection and alignment using multitask cascaded convolutional networks. IEEE Signal Proacess. Lett. **23**(10), 1499–1503 (2016)
66. Zhuang, Z., Bradtmiller, B.: Head-and-face anthropometric survey of us respirator users. J. Occup. Environ. Hyg. **2**(11), 567–576 (2005)

LWGNet - Learned Wirtinger Gradients
for Fourier Ptychographic Phase Retrieval

Atreyee Saha[✉], Salman S. Khan, Sagar Sehrawat, Sanjana S. Prabhu,
Shanti Bhattacharya, and Kaushik Mitra

Indian Institute of Technology Madras, Chennai 600036, India
sat3ee.17@gmail.com

Abstract. Fourier Ptychographic Microscopy (FPM) is an imaging procedure that overcomes the traditional limit on Space-Bandwidth Product (SBP) of conventional microscopes through computational means. It
utilizes multiple images captured using a low numerical aperture (NA)
objective and enables high-resolution phase imaging through frequency
domain stitching. Existing FPM reconstruction methods can be broadly
categorized into two approaches: iterative optimization based methods,
which are based on the physics of the forward imaging model, and data-
driven methods which commonly employ a feed-forward deep learning
framework. We propose a hybrid model-driven residual network that
combines the knowledge of the forward imaging system with a deep
data-driven network. Our proposed architecture, LWGNet, unrolls traditional Wirtinger flow optimization algorithm into a novel neural network design that enhances the gradient images through complex convolutional blocks. Unlike other conventional unrolling techniques, LWGNet
uses fewer stages while performing at par or even better than existing
traditional and deep learning techniques, particularly, for low-cost and
low dynamic range CMOS sensors. This improvement in performance for
low-bit depth and low-cost sensors has the potential to bring down the
cost of FPM imaging setup significantly. Finally, we show consistently
improved performance on our collected real data (We have made the
code avaiable at: https://github.com/at3e/LWGNet.git).

Keywords: Fourier ptychography · Physics-based network ·
Computational imaging

1 Introduction

One of the main challenges in medical computational imaging is to make imaging
technology accessible for point of care diagnostics in resource constrained communities. One way to make these techniques accessible includes designing cheaper
and portable hardware. [6,18] have used smartphone cameras for microscopy,

---

Supplementary Information The online version contains supplementary material
available at https://doi.org/10.1007/978-3-031-20071-7_31.

S. Avidan et al. (Eds.): ECCV 2022, LNCS 13667, pp. 522–537, 2022.
https://doi.org/10.1007/978-3-031-20071-7_31

while [1] have used 3D printed microscopes for wide field of view high resolution imaging. However, the use of cheaper and inefficient hardware introduces limits on the imaging capabilities of these systems through various degradations which can only be dealt by designing effective computational algorithms.

In this work, we will be focusing on a particular microscopy technique called Fourier Ptychographic Microscopy (FPM) [23]. It is a computational microscopy technique that allows us to perform high resolution and wide field of view (FOV) imaging. It circumvents the limit on SBP of conventional microscope by relying on multiple low-resolution captures of the sample under programmed illumination and reconstruction via phase retrieval algorithms. Development in FPM in the recent years has included improving the temporal resolution through multiplexed illumination [20], designing better reconstruction algorithms [2,4,5], and designing better illumination codes [9].

Despite the above-mentioned progress, there hasn't been enough work done to make these FPM systems accessible for point of care diagnostics. Some of the works on making FPM accessible are [1,10,12]. However, the authors rely on extensive hardware modifications without much changes to the algorithmic aspects. The following fundamental challenges have been the main reason behind that. First, the existing FPM systems, like most low-light imaging modalities, suffer from significant noise and dynamic range problems especially for darkfield images. These FPM systems rely on expensive optics and scientific grade sCMOS sensors to increase the SNR and dynamic range of the low-resolution darkfield captures which increases the system cost significantly [20]. Second, existing reconstruction algorithms designed for FPM systems have shown results only for these expensive systems and are unlikely to perform optimally when the quality of sensor degrades. Third, the existing reconstruction techniques are either slow or are model-independent data-driven techniques that ignore the forward imaging process completely.

Keeping the above challenges in mind, we propose 'LWGNet' for sequential FPM reconstruction. LWGNet is a novel physics-driven unrolled neural network that combines the expressiveness of data-driven techniques with the interpretability of iterative Wirtinger flow based techniques [2]. Previous unrolling works perform their operation in the image or object field space, while LWGNet perform these operations in the gradient of the object fields. LWGNetlearns a non-linear mapping from complex stochastic gradients to intermediate object fields through complex-valued neural networks. Such a learned mapping helps preserve the high frequency details in the peripheral darkfield images, especially for low dynamic range sensor. LWGNet outperforms both traditional and deep-learning methods in terms of reconstruction quality, especially for low-cost machine vision sensors with poor dynamic range. We show this by performing extensive evaluations on simulated and real histopathological data captured under different bit depths. In summary, we make the following contributions:

- We propose LWGNet which is a physics-inspired complex valued feed-forward network for FPM reconstructions that exploits the physics of the FPM model and data-driven methods.

- The proposed approach uses a learned complex-valued non-linear mapping from gradients to object field that helps restore the finer details under a low dynamic range scenario thereby reducing the gap in reconstruction quality between expensive HDR sCMOS cameras and low cost 8-bit CMOS sensors. This enables reducing the cost of the experimental setup to a large extent.
- We collect a real dataset of 8, 12 and 16 bit low resolution measurements using a CMOS sensor along with the corresponding aligned groundtruth for finetuning our method. To the best of our knowledge, this is the only FPM dataset captured with multiple bit depth settings using a low cost CMOS sensor. This dataset will be made public upon acceptance.
- The proposed network outperforms existing traditional and learning based algorithms in terms of reconstruction quality for both simulated and real data as verified through extensive experiments on challenging histopathological samples.

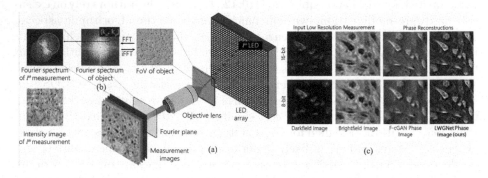

Fig. 1. Overview of FPM phase reconstruction. (a) The object is placed between a planar LED array and objective of the inverted microscope. Low resolution images corresponding to ℓ^{th} LED is captured. (b) Representation of the equivalent forward model, comprises of down-sampling the object spectrum by the system pupil function centred at $(k_{x\ell}, k_{y\ell})$. (c) Examples of input low resolution measurements under different sensor quantization and corresponding reconstructions using F-cGAN and the proposed LWGNet.

2   Background

2.1   The Nature of Phase Retrieval Problem

We are interested in the case of phase recovery from intensity measurements only. The experimental setup for FPM involves illuminating the object from multiple angles and is described in detail in [23]. Mathematically, the phase retrieval problem while using multiple structured illuminations for intensity measurement is as follows:

$$\text{Find } \mathbb{O}, \quad \text{subject to} \quad I_\ell = |\mathcal{F}^{-1}\{P_\ell \odot \mathcal{F}\{\mathbb{O}(\mathbf{k} - \mathbf{k}_\ell)\}\}|^2, \text{for } \ell = 1, 2, \ldots, L, \tag{1}$$

where $\mathcal{F}$ is the 2D spatial Fourier transform and $\mathcal{F}^{-1}$ is the corresponding inverse transform. $P_\ell \in \mathbb{C}^{N \times N}$ is the pupil function for $\mathbf{k}_\ell = (k_{x\ell}, k_{y\ell})$, the unique spatial frequency corresponding to the ℓth illumination source. It is assumed that $\mathcal{O}$ is an optically thin sample, i.e. its transmittance is close to unity. Classical retrieval algorithms seek to solve the following minimization problem,

$$\min_{\mathcal{O}} \sum_{\ell=1}^{L} \||I_\ell - |A_\ell\{\mathcal{O}\}|^2\|_2^2, \tag{2}$$

where $A\{.\} \triangleq \mathcal{F}^{-1} \circ P_\ell \odot \mathcal{F}\{.\}$.

The objective is a non-convex, real-valued function of complex-valued object field. Conventional approaches like gradient descent will converge to a stationary point.

2.2 Related Works

There have been numerous works on FPM reconstruction. Ou et al. [15] successfully performed whole slide high-resolution phase and amplitude imaging using a first-order technique based on alternate projections (AP). Song et al. [19] proposed algorithms to overcome system aberration in FPM reconstruction. In [3], the authors proposed sample motion correction for dynamic scenes. The work by Tian et al. [20] extended the AP algorithm for multiplexed illumination in FPM setup. Besides AP, Wirtinger flow based methods are shown to perform well under low SNR [2]. The Wirtinger flow algorithm is also extended to the multiplexed scheme by Bostan et al. [5].

Recently, deep learning techniques have also been explored to solve the FPM reconsruction problem. Jiang et al. [7] show a novel approach by treating the object as a learnable network parameter. However, as it requires optimization for each patch, it has a large inference time. Kappeler et al. [8] have performed high-resolution amplitude recovery using a CNN architecture. Nguyen et al. [14] have performed time-lapse high-resolution phase imaging via adversarial training of a U-Net architecture [13]. The authors performed phase imaging using a limited set of low-resolution images. They train (transfer learn in the case of new biological type of cells) U-Net on a subset of low resolution video measurements. While testing, they predict phase of dynamic cell samples on the subsequent frames. FPM phase reconstruction under various overlap conditions between adjacent low-resolution images in the frequency domain has been studied by Boominathan et al. [4]. However, they show results only on simulated samples. Kellman et al. [9] have designed a Physics-based Neural Network (PbNN) that learns patterns for multiplexed illumination by optimizing the weights of the LEDs.

An important line of work is the employment of high-resolution phase imaging using low-cost components. To our best knowledge, the only attempt made so far is by Aidukas et al. [1], who employed traditional reconstruction algorithm accompanied with an elaborate calibration and pre-processing of low-resolution images taken from a commercial-grade camera. The authors performed amplitude reconstruction, but their system has fundamental limitations due to sensor size and optical aberrations.

3   Proposed Method: LWGNet

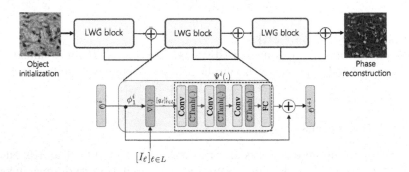

Fig. 2. Model architecture of LWGNet comprises of three stages of the LWG update block. The inputs are object, pupil initialization and measurement images for every stage. LWG block comprises of a Gradient computation block followed by three stages of Conv+$Tanh$ layers followed by a Fully Connected(FC) layer. The adder block updates the input object field using the modified gradients.

The naive Wirtinger flow algorithm seeks to minimize the following objective [2],

$$f(\mathbb{O}) = \sum_{\ell=1}^{L} \| I_\ell - |A_\ell\{\mathbb{O}\}|^2 \|_2^2 \tag{3}$$

$$= \sum_{\ell=1}^{L} \| I_\ell - A_\ell\{\mathbb{O}\} \odot \overline{A_\ell\{\mathbb{O}^i\}} \|_2^2, \tag{4}$$

where $A\{.\} \triangleq \mathcal{F}^{-1} \circ P_\ell \odot \mathcal{F}\{.\}$, $\mathcal{F}$ is the 2D spatial Fourier transform, $\mathcal{F}^{-1}$ is the corresponding inverse transform, P_ℓ is the pupil function corresponding to the ℓth illumination source and I_ℓ is the capture ℓ^{th} measurement for the same illumination source. Minimizing Eq. (4) with respect to $\mathbb{O}$ using gradient descent leads to the following i^{th} step update,

$$\mathbb{O}^{i+1} = \mathbb{O}^i - \eta \frac{1}{L} \sum_{\ell=1}^{L} \nabla_{\mathbb{O}} f_\ell^i, \tag{5}$$

where η is the step-size and,

$$\nabla_{\mathbb{O}} f_\ell^i = A_\ell^H \{ (|A_\ell\{\mathbb{O}^i\}|^2 - I_\ell) \odot A_\ell\{\mathbb{O}^i\} \}. \tag{6}$$

A naive way to unroll the above gradient descent Wirtinger flow algorithm could be to design a neural network with each stage performing the gradient update step of Eq. (5) followed by convolutional block. However, we found that such a naive unrolling doesn't converge to any meaningful solution. To overcome this, we design a K-stage unrolled network with the ith stage performing the following operation

$$\mathcal{O}^{i+1} = \mathcal{O}^i + \Psi^i([q_\ell]^i_{\ell \in L}), \tag{7}$$

where

$$q_\ell^i = A_\ell^H \{(|A_\ell\{\phi^i_{\ell-1}\}|^2 - I_\ell) \odot A_\ell\{\phi^i_{\ell-1}\}\}, \tag{8}$$

$$\phi^i_\ell = \phi^i_{\ell-1} - \eta q^i_{\ell-1}, \tag{9}$$

and $\Psi(.)$ is a learned complex neural network. , ϕ^i_ℓ is an intermediate object field that is estimated at the i−th stage using the gradients obtained with respect to the ℓ−th LED measurement. We initialize $\phi^i_1 as \mathcal{O}^i$. q^i_ℓ in the above equations can be interpreted as stochastic gradients corresponding to each illumination source. $\Psi(.)$ then learns to non-linearly combine these stochastic gradients and update the object field as shown in Eq. (7). Experimentally, we found that such an unrolled network converged faster with fewer K than naively unrolled wirtinger flow. $\Psi(.)$ consists of three 3×3 complex convolutions followed by complex Tanh non-linearity, instance norm, and a fully connected layer. The learned non-linear $\Psi(.)$ helps combine the stochastic gradients in a more effective way especially for peripheral darkfield images which are typically degraded due to lower bit depth and noise.

We simulate complex arithmetic using real-valued entities [22] in $\Psi(.)$. We perform equivalent 2D complex-valued convolution using real-valued CNN blocks as follows: let there be M input channels and N output channels for a given CNN layer. Then, complex-valued filter matrix weight for m^{th} input channel and n^{th} output channel is $\mathbf{w}_{mn} = \mathbf{a}_{mn} + j\mathbf{b}_{mn}$ that convolves with a 2D complex input $\mathbf{z}_m = \mathbf{x}_m + j\mathbf{y}_m$. Here, $\mathbf{a}_{mn}$ and $\mathbf{b}_{mn}$ are real-valued kernels, and $\mathbf{x}_m$ and $\mathbf{y}_m$ are also real.

$$\mathbf{w}_{mn} * \mathbf{z}_m = \mathbf{a}_{mn} * \mathbf{x}_m + j\mathbf{b}_{mn} * \mathbf{y}_m. \tag{10}$$

We initialize filter weights as a uniform distribution. The CNN layer is followed by an 2D instance normalization layer. An amplitude-phase type non-linear activation function for and complex-valued $z = x + jy$ is defined as follows

$$\mathbb{C}\text{Tanh}(z) = \text{Tanh}(|z|)e^{i\theta_z} \tag{11}$$

acts on the normalised outputs.

Finally, after 3 convolutional and non-linearity blocks, we use a fully connected block that acts on the channel dimension.

3.1 Loss Functions

Let O be the ground truth object and $\hat{O}$ be the reconstruction. We use the following weighted combination of loss functions to optimize our network,

$$\mathscr{L} = \lambda_1 \mathscr{L}_{MSE} + \lambda_2 \mathscr{L}_{FMAE} + \lambda_3 \mathscr{L}_{VGG} \tag{12}$$

where,

$$\mathscr{L}_{MSE} = \|\angle(\hat{O}) - \angle(O)\|_2^2 + \||\hat{O}| - |O|\|_2^2 \tag{13}$$

$$\mathscr{L}_{FMAE} = \||\mathscr{F}(\hat{O})| - |\mathscr{F}(O)|\|_1 \tag{14}$$

$$\mathscr{L}_{VGG/i,j} = \beta_1 \|\psi_{i,j}(|\hat{O}|) - \psi_{i,j}(|O|)\|_2^2 + \beta_2 \|\psi_{i,j}(\angle\hat{O}) - \psi_{i,j}(\angle O)\|_2^2 \tag{15}$$

$\|\cdot\|_p$ represents the p-norm. Eq. (13) defines the pixel-wise Mean Squared Error (MSE) loss over amplitude and phase components. The VGG loss function is a perceptual loss function, as defined by [11]. It minimizes the MSE from the output of the feature maps of the pre-trained VGG-19 network. $\psi_{i,j}(.)$ is the feature map obtained by the j-th convolution (after activation) before the i-th max-pooling layer in the network, which we consider given. Here, we use ReLU output $\psi_{2,2}$ and $\psi_{4,3}$ the VGG-19 network. The output feature maps corresponding to the reconstruction and ground truth amplitudes are compared. Equation (14) minimizes the L_1-norm of the magnitude Fourier spectrum between reconstruction and ground truth.

4 Experiments and Results

4.1 Simulated Dataset

Images in Iowa histology dataset [17] are used for simulating objects fields with uncorrelated amplitude and phase. The FoV of the entire histology slide is divided into 320×320 pixels; the amplitude images are normalised, such that the values lie in the range $[0, 1]$. The pixel values of the phase image are linearly mapped to the range $[-\pi, \pi]$. These objects are further divided into training, validation and test splits. Then the FPM forward model [23], is used to generates low resolution intensity images of 64×64 pixels from these object field samples.

4.2 Our Captured Real Dataset

The experimental setup to capture real data consists of a Nikon Eclipse TE300 inverted microscope and a 10X/0.25 NA objective lens for imaging. An AdaFruit programmable RGB LED array (32×32, planar) is used to illuminate the sample from various angles using Red LED with a wavelength of 630nm. By using central 225 LEDs, we captured sequential low-resolution images using a High Dynamic Range (HDR) scientific grade sCMOS camera (PCO Edge 5.5) and a low cost machine vision CMOS camera (FLIR FLEA3). The sCMOS camera allows us to capture only 16-bit images while the CMOS allows to capture 8, 12 and 16-bit images. The sCMOS camera has a resolution of 2560 × 2160 pixels and a pixel pitch 6.5 μm while the CMOS sensor has a resolution of 1552 × 2080 pixels and pixel pitch of 2.5 μm. Both the sensors are monochromatic. The sCMOS camera is used on the front port of the inverted microscope while the CMOS camera is used on the side port of the same microscope.

The LEDs on the array have a grid spacing of 4mm and the array is placed at a distance of 80 mm from the sample plane of the microscope. The illumination from the LED array is controlled using an Arduino MEGA 2560 microcontroller, and simultaneously sends a clock signal to external exposure start port of the sCMOS camera for controlling the camera shutter speed with respect to LED illumination.

Before testing our network on real data, we finetune our network on a small set of real training data. To capture a training set, first low resolution images are captured in a sequential manner using the sCMOS sensor and the CMOS sensor. To generate the groundtruth data for training, FPM phase reconstructions using the algorithm in [21] is used on the captured low resolution sCMOS images. To compensate for the misalignment between sCMOS and CMOS images, image registration is also performed. In total 8 slides of cervical, cerebral cortical, lung carcinoma and osteosarcoma cells were used for real data. 4 slides were kept for training and 4 for testing. We show the capture setup and few real captured data in the supplementary.

We implement our neural network using PyTorch [16], and train the same on 2 GTX 1080Ti GPUs of 12 GB capacity, for 100 epochs. The loss function parameters as described in Eq. (3.1) are $(\lambda_1, \lambda_2, \lambda_3) = (0.1, 0.05, 1)$ and $(\beta_1, \beta_2) = (0.5, 1)$. We use Adam optimizer with an initial learning rate (LR) of 10^{-4} and a learning rate scheduler that reduces the LR by a factor of 0.1 when the overall loss does not improve. On the simulated data, we use 3 stages of the update block as described in Fig. 2 for 16-bit and 12-bit depth images, and increase the number of stages to 5 for 8-bit images.

4.3   Comparison on Simulated Data

We compare our simulated and experimental results against existing iterative procedure and deep-learning techniques. Under iterative methods, we have compared with the alternate projections (AP) algorithm proposed by Tian et al. [20]. Another class of iterative method for phase retrieval is the Wirtinger Flow Optimization proposed by [2]. Under data-driven techniques, we consider the conditional deep image prior (cDIP) architecture proposed by Boominathan et al. [4]. We also compare against Fourier-loss cGAN (F-cGAN) architecture provided by Nguyen et al. [14] and modify the input layer dimension of the U-Net architecture to take into account the difference in number of illumination LEDs.

Table 1 shows image quality with two metrics, namely Peak Signal to Noise Ratio (PSNR) and Structural SIMilarity (SSIM) against existing FPM phase retrieval algorithms. The proposed LWGNet is shown to perform at par for

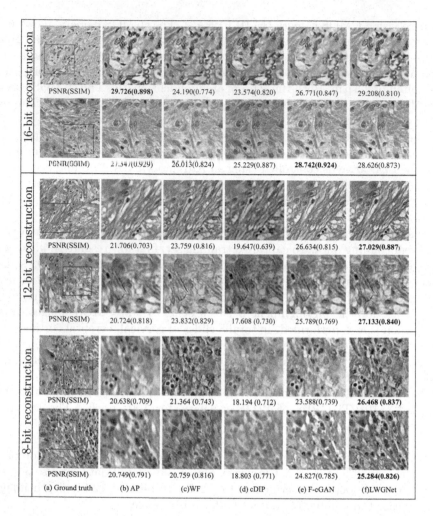

Fig. 3. Phase reconstruction on simulated data using proposed LWGNet method are perceptually superior at lower-bit depth depths compared to existing methods. Traditional algorithms WF and AP do not perform well under lower bit-depths. Among deep methods, cDIP performs poorly at lower bit depths.

Table 1. Compared to previous works, the proposed LWGNet achieves a better reconstruction quality at lower bit-depths using fewer trainable parameters.

Method	16		12		8		Memory	Inference time	Parameters
	PSNR	SSIM	PSNR	SSIM	PSNR	SSIM	*(in GiB)*	*(in ms)*	*(in millions)*
AP	24.346	0.835	21.764	0.728	20.500	0.594	NA	NA	NA
WF	23.172	0.769	22.706	0.744	21.621	0.730	NA	NA	NA
cDIP	25.654	0.815	22.563	0.718	20.951	0.712	3.24	5	54.9
F-cGAN	**29.021**	**0.907**	26.325	0.797	25.715	0.765	3.52	29	7.88
LWGNet	28.745	0.829	**27.726**	**0.807**	**26.035**	**0.802**	2.26	341	0.39

the 16-bit simulation results and outperforms the baseline methods at lower bit depths of 12-bit and 8-bit in terms of both PSNR and SSIM. Although the F-cGAN [14] baseline performs better on 16-bit simulated data, the proposed method performs perceptually better on real data, as shown later in Sect. 4.4. Figure 3 shows a few phase reconstructions from simulated data at three bit depths. For 16-bit measurement images, both traditional and neural network based methods perform competitively well. Figure 3(b) shows AP-based reconstruction method [20] suffers the most from degradation of peripheral LED measurements at lower bit-depths. Gradient-based methods [2] display poor contrast and blurring at the edges as shown in Fig. 3(c). Consequently, this is corrected for in the proposed method as shown in Fig. 3(f). cDIP [4] shows checkerboard artifacts that become more prominent with under lower bit depth. Similarly, F-cGAN [14] model successfully preserves finer details at higher bit-depths, but shows blur artifacts with increase in quantization. Additionally, LWGNet involves fewer trainable parameters and requires about 100 epochs of training. LWGNet is shown to be less memory intensive compared to the deep-learning based models, cDIP and F-cGAN. However, the gradient computation block is computationally intensive taking longer inference time, compared to matrix computations of fully convolutional networks. The memory and inference time reported in Table 1 are for a 3 stage proposed network.

4.4   Comparison on Real Data

We test our model on real experimental data and compare the results against two deep-learning techniques, cDIP and F-cGAN. Prior to evaluation, we fine-tune all the methods on real dataset described in Sect. 4.2. Figure 4 show the visual results for 16, 12 and 8 bit depths respectively. For our experiments, we use histological sample slides, specifically Lung carcinoma and Osteosarcoma (H&E stained). Phase reconstruction obtained from cDIP show low contrast and are prone to checkerboard artifacts. F-cGAN reconstructs the cellular structures but performs relatively poor in reconstruction of finer background details. However, the proposed algorithm successfully preserves edges and background details compared to the other approaches consistently for all bit depths. The computed gradients of peripheral LED images contain high-frequency details. We hypothesize that the learned complex-valued neural network parameters are optimized to map these useful gradients to desired object field more effectively than neural networks that use just the intensity images as input. Moreover, due to the extremely small parameter count of our proposed method, finetuning on a small dataset of real data doesn't lead to any overfitting.

4.5   Sensor Quantization Analysis

In this section, we experimentally verify that the proposed method shows little perceptual variation over reconstruction with increasing quantization noise or decrease in the bit depth of the input data. We finetune our proposed approach using the dataset described in Sect. 4.2 prior to evaluation. Figure 5 shows

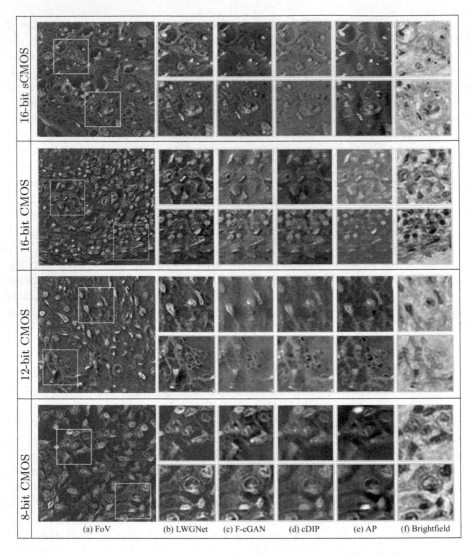

Fig. 4. Phase reconstruction for *real* 16-bit Lung carcinoma (sCMOS and CMOS), 12-bit Osteosarcoma, and 8-bit Osteosarcoma (CMOS). (a) FoV reconstruction using LWGNet and inset shown in (b). (c) reconstruction obtained from F-cGAN, (d) reconstruction obtained from cDIP, (e) reconstruction obtained from AP, and (f) input brightfield image.

reconstruction for Osteosarcoma (top) and Lung carcinoma (bottom) samples at different bit-depth settings of the camera. The reconstructions obtained are perceptually indistinguishable in the first case as shown in the inset. In the second case, we observe minor changes at reconstructions of sharp edge features with the bit-depth setting.

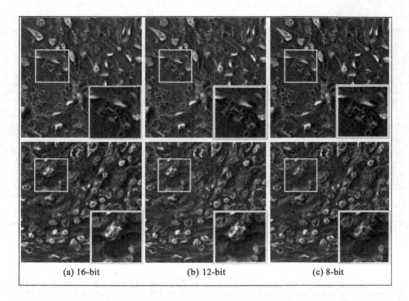

Fig. 5. Comparison of phase reconstruction using the proposed LWGNet on Osteosarcoma (top) and Lung carcinoma (bottom) at various bit depth settings. The reconstruction quality is consistent even under high quantization noise.

4.6   Ablation Study

In this subsection, we analyse the impact of different components of our proposed network on simulated data.

Effect of Complex-Valued Operations. Here we verify the necessity of the complex-valued operations described in Sect. 3. To do that, we replace the complex-valued operation of our proposed network with real-valued operations acting individually on the real and imaginary channels of the complex gradient. We keep the rest of the architecture and loss functions the same. Top row of Fig. 6 presents the visual comparison between reconstructions obtained from complex-valued and real-valued networks. Our experiments show that the use of complex valued operations increases the average PSNR by 5 dB.

Effect of Processing Gradients. To verify that processing gradients through a learned network actually helps, we train a variant of the proposed architecture with the following update stage where the learned neural network acts on the estimated object field,

$$\mathbb{O}_f = \hat{\Psi}(\mathbb{O}^K) \tag{16}$$

where,

$$\mathbb{O}^{i+1} = (\mathbb{O}^i + \frac{1}{L}\sum_{\ell=1}^{L} g_\ell^i), i \in \{0, 1, .., K-1\} \tag{17}$$

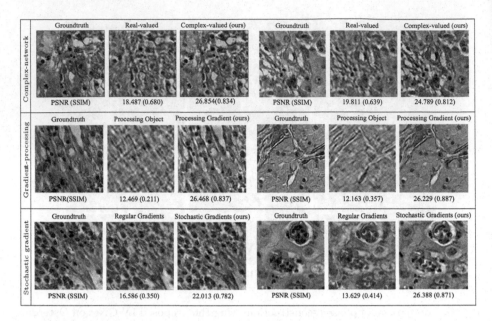

Fig. 6. Ablation experiments: First row shows the using complex-valued operations leads to improved reconstruction. Second row shows that the proposed method of learning the network on gradient leads to effective utilization of gradient information than learning a network on estimated object field. Third row shows that using stochastic gradient improves our results compared to regular gradients.

and $\hat{\Psi}(.)$ is N numbers of $\Psi^i(.)$ (described in Sect. 3) stacked together. We used $K = 5$ iterations of Wirtinger flow and stack $N = 3$ numbers of $\Psi(.)$ for this purpose to compare against 3 stages of proposed approach. The rest of the architecture and loss functions are kept the same as proposed method. Second row in Fig. 6 shows the visual results highlighting the effect of processing the gradients. The proposed way of learning a mapping from the stochastic gradients to object fields leads to more effective use of the gradient information compared to a enhancing an object field using a neural network after wirtinger updates.

Effect of Stochastic Gradients. In this experiment, we verify the efficacy of the stochastic gradients estimated in Eq. (8). To do that, we train a variant of the proposed network where regular gradients are used instead of the stochastic gradients and each stage is given by,

$$\mathbb{O}^{i+1} = \mathbb{O}^i + \Psi^i([\nabla_\mathbb{O} f_\ell^i]_{\ell \in L}). \tag{18}$$

where $\nabla_\mathbb{O} f_\ell^i$ is given by Eq. (6). The rest of the network and loss functions are kept the same as the proposed LWGNet. The third row of Fig. 6 shows visual results for this experiment. The use of stochastic gradient clearly outperforms the use of regular gradients.

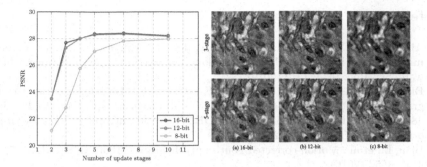

Fig. 7. Left: PSNR vs Number of unrolled stages. Right: corresponding reconstructions for 3 and 5 stage LWGNet under different bit depths. For 16 and 12 bit data, after just 3 stages the performance saturates while 5 stages are needed for 8 bit data.

Effect of Number of Unrolled Stages. In this section, we analyse the effect of the number of unrolled iterative stages (K in Sect. 3). Figure 7 represents the variation of PSNR with the number of update blocks in the proposed architecture varied between 2 to 10 blocks. We found that the PSNR saturates after 3 stages for 16-bit and 12-bit data, while it takes at least 5 stages to achieve a similar performance for 8 bit data.

5   Discussion and Conclusion

We propose a novel physics based neural network for FPM reconstructions. Our network derives inspiration from conventional wirtinger flow phase retrieval and combines it with data-driven neural networks. Unlike naive wirtinger flow, our network learns a non-linear mapping from stochastic gradients to object field intermediates. We use complex-valued neural networks to learn this non-linear mapping. We perform extensive experiments on simulated and real data to validate the proposed architecture's efficacy. Our method performs at par or even better than existing FPM reconstruction techniques especially for difficult scenarios like low dynamic range. We attribute the success of our network on such challenging conditions to the novel non-linear physics-based mapping. Moreover, we also collect a dataset of real samples using a low cost sensor under different sensor bit depths which will be made public upon acceptance of the paper. The ability to perform high-resolution wide-field of view microscopy using low-cost sensor through physics inspired data-driven techniques can significantly bring down the system cost and is a step towards making point of care diagnostics more accessible.

Acknowledgement. We gratefully acknowledge the funding from DST IMPRINT-2 (IMP/2018/001168).

References

1. Aidukas, T., Eckert, R., Harvey, A.R., Waller, L., Konda, P.C.: Low-cost, sub-micron resolution, wide-field computational microscopy using opensource hardware. Sci. Rep. **9**(1), 1–12 (2019)
2. Bian, L., Suo, J., Zheng, G., Guo, K., Chen, F., Dai, Q.: Fourier ptychographic reconstruction using wirtinger flow optimization. Opt. Exp. **23**(4), 4856–4866 (2015). https://doi.org/10.1364/OE.23.004856, http://www.opticsexpress.org/abstract.cfm?URI=oe-23-4-4856
3. Bian, L., et al.: Motion-corrected Fourier ptychography. Biomed. Opt. Exp. **7**(11), 4543–4553 (2016)
4. Boominathan, L., Maniparambil, M., Gupta, H., Baburajan, R., Mitra, K.: Phase retrieval for Fourier ptychography under varying amount of measurements. arXiv preprint arXiv:1805.03593 (2018)
5. Bostan, E., Soltanolkotabi, M., Ren, D., Waller, L.: Accelerated wirtinger flow for multiplexed Fourier ptychographic microscopy. In: 2018 25th IEEE International Conference on Image Processing (ICIP), pp. 3823–3827. IEEE (2018)
6. Breslauer, D.N., Maamari, R.N., Switz, N.A., Lam, W.A., Fletcher, D.A.: Mobile phone based clinical microscopy for global health applications. PLoS ONE **4**(7), e6320 (2009)
7. Jiang, S., Guo, K., Liao, J., Zheng, G.: Solving Fourier ptychographic imaging problems via neural network modeling and tensorflow. Biomed. Opt. Exp. **9**(7), 3306–3319 (2018). https://doi.org/10.1364/BOE.9.003306, http://www.osapublishing.org/boe/abstract.cfm?URI=boe-9-7-3306
8. Kappeler, A., Ghosh, S., Holloway, J., Cossairt, O., Katsaggelos, A.: PtychNet: CNN based Fourier ptychography. In: 2017 IEEE International Conference on Image Processing (ICIP), pp. 1712–1716. IEEE (2017)
9. Kellman, M., Bostan, E., Chen, M., Waller, L.: Data-driven design for fourier ptychographic microscopy. In: 2019 IEEE International Conference on Computational Photography (ICCP), pp. 1–8. IEEE (2019)
10. Kim, J., Henley, B.M., Kim, C.H., Lester, H.A., Yang, C.: Incubator embedded cell culture imaging system (emsight) based on Fourier ptychographic microscopy. Biomed. Opt. Exp. **7**(8), 3097–3110 (2016)
11. Ledig, C., et al.: Photo-realistic single image super-resolution using a generative adversarial network (2017)
12. Lee, K.C., Lee, K., Jung, J., Lee, S.H., Kim, D., Lee, S.A.: A smartphone-based Fourier ptychographic microscope using the display screen for illumination. ACS Phot. **8**(5), 1307–1315 (2021)
13. Mirza, M., Osindero, S.: Conditional generative adversarial nets. arXiv preprint arXiv:1411.1784 (2014)
14. Nguyen, T., Xue, Y., Li, Y., Tian, L., Nehmetallah, G.: Deep learning approach for fourier ptychography microscopy. Opt. Exp. **26**(20), 26470–26484 (2018). https://doi.org/10.1364/OE.26.026470,http://www.opticsexpress.org/abstract.cfm?URI=oe-26-20-26470
15. Ou, X., Horstmeyer, R., Yang, C., Zheng, G.: Quantitative phase imaging via fourier ptychographic microscopy. Opt. Lett. **38**(22), 4845–4848 (2013). https://doi.org/10.1364/OL.38.004845,http://ol.osa.org/abstract.cfm?URI=ol-38-22-4845

16. Paszke, A., et al.: Pytorch: An imperative style, high-performance deep learning library. In: Wallach, H., Larochelle, H., Beygelzimer, A., d'Alché-Buc, F., Fox, E., Garnett, R. (eds.) Advances in Neural Information Processing Systems 32, pp. 8024–8035. Curran Associates, Inc. (2019). http://papers.neurips.cc/paper/9015-pytorch-an-imperative-style-high-performance-deep-learning-library.pdf
17. Dee, F.R., Leaven, T.: Department of Pathology: Iowa Virtual Slidebox, http://www.path.uiowa.edu/virtualslidebox/
18. Smith, Z., et al.: Cell-phone-based platform for biomedical device development and education applications. PloS one **6**(3), e17150 (2011)
19. Song, P., Jiang, S., Zhang, H., Huang, X., Zhang, Y., Zheng, G.: Full-field Fourier ptychography (Ffp): spatially varying pupil modeling and its application for rapid field-dependent aberration metrology. APL Photon. **4**(5), 050802 (2019)
20. Tian, L., Li, X., Ramchandran, K., Waller, L.: Multiplexed coded illumination for Fourier ptychography with an led array microscope. Biomed. Opt. Exp. **5**(7), 2376–2389 (2014). https://doi.org/10.1364/BOE.5.002376,http://www.osapublishing.org/boe/abstract.cfm?URI=boe-5-7-2376
21. Tian, L., Liu, Z., Yeh, L.H., Chen, M., Zhong, J., Waller, L.: Computational illumination for high-speed in vitro fourier ptychographic microscopy. Optica **2**(10), 904–911 (2015). http://www.osapublishing.org/optica/abstract.cfm?URI=optica-2-10-904, https://www.laurawaller.com/opensource/
22. Trabelsi, C., et al.: Deep complex networks. In: ICLR (2018)
23. Zheng, G., Horstmeyer, R., Yang, C.: Wide-field, high-resolution Fourier ptychographic microscopy. Nat. Photon. **7**(9), 739–745 (2013)

PANDORA: Polarization-Aided Neural Decomposition of Radiance

Akshat Dave[(✉)] , Yongyi Zhao , and Ashok Veeraraghavan

Rice University, Houston, TX 77005, USA
{ad74,yongyi,vashok}@rice.edu

Abstract. Reconstructing an object's geometry and appearance from multiple images, also known as inverse rendering, is a fundamental problem in computer graphics and vision. Inverse rendering is inherently ill-posed because the captured image is an intricate function of unknown lighting, material properties and scene geometry. Recent progress in representing scene through coordinate-based neural networks has facilitated inverse rendering resulting in impressive geometry reconstruction and novel-view synthesis. Our key insight is that polarization is a useful cue for neural inverse rendering as polarization strongly depends on surface normals and is distinct for diffuse and specular reflectance. With the advent of commodity on-chip polarization sensors, capturing polarization has become practical. We propose PANDORA, a polarimetric inverse rendering approach based on implicit neural representations. From multiview polarization images of an object, PANDORA jointly extracts the object's 3D geometry, separates the outgoing radiance into diffuse and specular and estimates the incident illumination. We show that PANDORA outperforms state-of-the-art radiance decomposition techniques. PANDORA outputs clean surface reconstructions free from texture artefacts, models strong specularities accurately and estimates illumination under practical unstructured scenarios.

Keywords: Polarization · Inverse rendering · Multi-view reconstruction · Implicit neural representations

1 Introduction

Inverse rendering involves reconstructing an object's appearance and geometry from multiple images of the object captured under different viewpoints and/or lighting conditions. It is important for many computer graphics and vision applications such as re-lighting, synthesising novel views and blending real objects with virtual scenes. Inverse rendering is inherently challenging because the object's 3D shape, surface reflectance and incident illumination are intermixed in the captured images. A diverse array of techniques have been proposed

---

Supplementary Information The online version contains supplementary material available at https://doi.org/10.1007/978-3-031-20071-7_32.

to alleviate this challenge by incorporating prior knowledge of the scene, optimizing the scene parameters iteratively with differentiable rendering, and exploiting the unique properties of light such as spectrum, polarization and time.

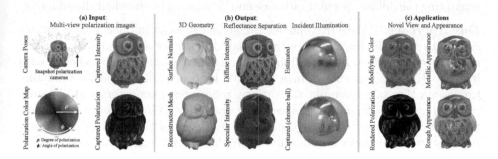

Fig. 1. PANDORA overview: PANDORA utilizes multi-view polarization images with known poses (a) and outputs the object's 3D geometry, separation of radiance in to diffuse and specular along with incident illumination (b). The learned PANDORA model can be applied to render the object under novel views and edit the object's appearance (c). Please refer to the supplementary video for renderings of these outputs and applications under varying viewpoints.

Neural Inverse Rendering. Recent works demonstrate that modelling the outgoing radiance and object shape as coordinate-based neural networks results in impressive novel-view synthesis (NeRF) [26] and surface reconstruction (VolSDF) [47] from multi-view captures. The outgoing radiance from the object is a combination of different components of surface reflectance and illumination incident on the object. As a result, separation and modification of components of the captured object's reflectance is not possible with works such as NeRF and VolSDF. Moreover, the diffuse and specular components of object reflectance have different view dependence. Using the same network to model a combination of difuse and specular radiance results in inaccurate novel view synthesis.

Radiance Decomposition. Decomposition of the outgoing radiance into reflectance parameters and incident illumination is inherently ill-posed. Recent works such as PhySG [52] and NeuralPIL [7] aim to address the ill-posed nature of radiance decomposition by employing spherical Gaussians and data-driven embeddings respectively to model the reflectance and lighting. While these approach provides plausible decomposition in simple settings under large number of measurements, the decomposition is inaccurate in challenging scenarios such as strong specularities and limited views (Fig. 4) leading to blurrier specular reconstructions and artefacts in surface reconstruction.

Key Idea: Polarization as a Cue for Reflectance Decomposition. Our key insight is that polarimetric cues aid in radiance decomposition. Polarization has a strong dependence on surface normals. The diffuse and specular reflectance components have different polarimetric properties: the specular is more polarized than diffuse and the polarization angle for the two components are orthogonal. The advent of snapshot polarimetric cameras has made it pratical to capture this polarization information. In this work, we present our approach PANDORA that exploits multi-view polarization images for jointly recovering the 3D surface, separating the diffuse-specular radiance and estimating the incident illumination.

Our Approach. PANDORA models the geometry as an implicit neural surface similar to VolSDF. Implicit coordinate based networks are used to model the reflectance properties. Incident lighting is modelled as an implicit network with integrated directional embeddings [42]. We propose a differentiable rendering framework that takes as input the surface, reflectance parameters and illumination and renders polarization images under novel views. Given a set of multi-view polarization images, we jointly optimize parameters of the surface, reflectance parameters and incident illumination to minimize rendering loss.

Contributions. Our contributions are as follows:

- Polarized neural rendering: We propose a framework to render polarization images from implicit representations of the object geometry, surface reflectance and illumination.
- 3D surface reconstruction: Equipped with implicit surface representation and polarization cues, PANDORA outputs high quality surface normal, signed distance field and mesh representations of the scene.
- Diffuse-specular separation: We demonstrate accurate diffuse-specular radiance decomposition on real world scenes under unknown illumination.
- Incident illumination estimation: We show that PANDORA can estimate the illumination incident on the object with high fidelity.

Assumptions. In this work, we assume that the incident illumination is completely unpolarized. The object is assumed to be opaque and to be made up of dielectric materials such as plastics, ceramics etc. as our polarimetric reflectance model doesn't handle metals. We focus on direct illumination light paths. Indirect illumination and self-occlusions are currently neglected.

2   Related Work

Inverse Rendering. The goal of inverse rendering is to recover scene parameters from a set of associated images. Inverse rendering approaches traditionally rely on multi-view geometry [36,37], photometry [4] and structured lighting [29,31] for 3D reconstruction [43], reflectance separation [22,29], material characterization [15] and illumination estimation [11,35]. Due to the ill-posed nature of inverse rendering, these approaches often require simplifying assumptions on the scene such as textured surfaces, Lambertian reflectance, direct illumination and simple geometry. Methods that aim to work in generalized scene settings involve incorporating scene priors [8,17,50], iterative scene optimization using differentiable rendering [21,51] and exploiting different properties of light such as polarization [53], time-of-flight [49] and spectrum [20].

Neural Inverse Rendering. Recent emergence of neural implicit representations [45] has led to an explosion of interest in neural inverse rendering [41]. Neural implicit representations use a coordinate-based neural network to represent a visual signals such as images, videos, and 3D objects [25,32,38]. These representations are powerful because the resolution of the underlying signal is limited only by the network capacity, rather than the discretization of the signal. Interest from the vision community originated largely due to neural radiance field (NeRF) [26], which showed that modelling radiance using implicit representations leads to high-quality novel view synthesis.

Since the advent of NeRF, several works have exploited neural implicit representations for inverse rendering applications. IDR [48], UNISURF [30], NeuS [44] and VolSDF [47] demonstrate state-of-the-art 3D surface reconstruction from multi-view images by extending NeRF's volume rendering framework to handle implicit surface representations. Accurate surface normals are crucial for modelling polarization and reflectance. Thus, we use ideas from one such work, VolSDF [47], as a build block in PANDORA.

NeRF models the net outgoing radiance from a scene point in which both the material properties and the lighting are mixed. Techniques such as NeRV [40], NeRD [6], NeuralPIL [7], PhySG [52], RefNeRF [42] have looked at decomposing this radiance into reflectance and illumination. PhySG and NeuralPIL employ spherical Gaussian and data-driven embeddings to model the scene's illumination and reflectance. RefNeRF introduces integrated directional embeddings (IDEs) to model radiance from specular reflections and illumination and demonstrates improved novel view synthesis. Inspired from RefNeRF, we incorporate IDEs in our framework. Equipped with IDEs, implicit surface representation and polarimetric acquisition, PANDORA demonstrate better radiance decomposition than the state-of-the-art, NeuralPIL and PhySG (Fig. 4,5, Table 1)

Polarimetric Inverse Rendering. Polarization strongly depends on the surface geometry leading to several single view depth and surface normal imaging approaches [2,3,19,27,39]. Inclusion of polarization cues has also led to enhancements in multi-view stereo [10,13,14,53], SLAM [46] and time-of-flight imaging [16]. The diffuse and specular components of reflectance have distinct polarization properties and this distinction has been utilized for reflectance seperation [10,18,24], reflection removal [23] and spatially varying BRDF estimation [12]. PANDORA exploits these polarimetric cues for 3D reconstruction, diffuse-specular separation and illumination estimation.

Traditionally acquiring polarization information required capturing multiple measurements by rotating a polarizer infront of the camera, unfortunately prohibiting fast acquisition. The advent of single-shot polarization sensors, such as the Sony IMX250MZR (monochrome) and IMX250MYR (color) [1] in commercial-grade off-the-shelf machine vision cameras has made polarimetric acquisition faster and more practical. These sensors have a grid of polarizers oriented at different angles attached on the CMOS sensor enabling the capture of polarimetric cues at the expense of spatial resolution. Various techniques have been proposed for polarization and color demosaicking of the raw sensor mea-

surements [28,34]. In PANDORA we use such a camera FLIR BFS-U3-51S5P-C
to capture polarization information for every view in a single shot.

3   Polarization as Cue for Radiance Separation

Here we introduce our key insight on how polarimetric cues aid in decomposing
radiance into the diffuse and specular components. First we derive the polarimetric properties of diffuse and specular reflectance. Then we demonstrate how
these cues can aid in separating the combined reflectance in a simple scene.

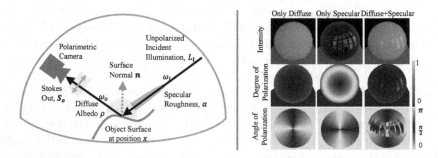

Fig. 2. Polarization as a cue for radiance decomposition. Left: Notations for
our polarized image formation model. Right: Polarimetric cues for different radiance
components. Diffuse radiance has a lower degree of polarization than the specular
radiance. The diffuse and specular components have orthogonal polarization angles.
We utilize these polarization cues for radiance decomposition.

3.1   Theory of Polarized Reflectance

Stokes Vector. The polarization state of a light ray at $\mathbf{x}$ along direction ω is
modelled as Stokes vector containing four components, $S(\mathbf{x}, \omega) = [S_0, S_1, S_2, S_3]$
[9]. We assume there is no circular polarization and thus neglect S_3. The Stokes
vector can be parametrized as a function of three polarimetric cues: the total
intensity, $L_o = S_0$, degree of polarization (DoP), $\beta_o = \sqrt{S_1^2 + S_2^2}/S_0$ and angle
of polarization (AoP), $\phi_o = \tan^{-1}(S_2/S_1)/2$.

Mueller Matrix. Upon interaction with a surface, the polarization of light
changes. The resulting Stokes vector is modelled as the matrix multiplication of
the input Stokes vector with a 4×4 matrix, known as the Mueller matrix.

Polarimetric BRDF (pBRDF) Model. The interaction of object for diffuse
and specular components of the reflectance are different. The diffuse reflectance
involves sub-surface scattering into the surface and then transmission out of the
surface. The specular component can be modelled as a direct reflection from
specular microfacets on the surface. The pBRDF model [3] model these interactions as Mueller matrices for the diffuse and specular polarized reflectance,
which we denoted as H_d and H_s respectively.

Incident Stokes Vector. Considering illumination is from far away sources, the dependance of S_i on $\mathbf{x}$ can be dropped. Assuming the polarization to be completely unpolarized:

$$S_i(\mathbf{x}, \omega_i) = L_i(\mathbf{x}, \omega_i)[1 \quad 0 \quad 0]^T , \tag{1}$$

Exitant Stokes Vector. From the pBRDF model, the output Stokes vector at every point can be decomposed into the matrix multiplication of diffuse and specular Mueller matrices, H_d and H_s, with the illumination Stokes vector S_i,

$$S_o(\mathbf{x}, \omega_i) = \int_\Omega H_d \cdot S_i(\mathbf{x}, \omega_i)d\omega + \int_\Omega H_s \cdot S_i(\mathbf{x}, \omega_i)d\omega \tag{2}$$

From S_i and the pBRDF model, we derive that the outgoing Stokes vector at every point depends on the diffuse radiance L_d, specular radiance L_s and the incident illumination L_i as,

$$S_o(\mathbf{x}, \omega_i) = L_d \begin{bmatrix} 1 \\ \beta_d(\theta_n)\cos(2\phi_n) \\ -\beta_d(\theta_n)\sin(2\phi_n) \end{bmatrix} + L_s \begin{bmatrix} 1 \\ \beta_s(\theta_n)\cos(2\phi_n) \\ -\beta_s(\theta_n)\sin(2\phi_n) \end{bmatrix} , \tag{3}$$

where we terms β_d/β_s depend on Fresnel transmission/reflection coefficients for the polarization components parallel and perpendicular to the plane of incidence, $T^\|/R^\|$ and $T^\perp/R^\perp$

$$\beta_d = \frac{T^\perp - T^\|}{T^\perp + T^\|} , \quad \beta_s = \frac{R^\perp - R^\|}{R^\perp + R^\|} , \tag{4}$$

The Fresnel coefficients, T/R solely depend on the elevation angle of the viewing ray with respect to the surface normal, $\theta_n = \cos^{-1}(\mathbf{n} \cdot \omega_o)$. ϕ_o denotes the azimuth angle of the viewing ray with respect to the surface normals, $\phi_n = \cos^{-1}(\mathbf{n}_o, \mathbf{y}_o)$, where $\mathbf{n}_o$ is the normal vector perpendicular to the viewing ray and $\mathbf{y}_o$ is the y axis of camera coordinate system. Please refer to the supplementary material for the detailed derivation and functional forms for Fresnel coefficients.

Next we show how these polarimetric cues depend on the diffuse and specular reflectance and aid in radiance decomposition.

3.2 Polarimetric Properties of Diffuse and Specular Radiance

From Eq. 3, the polarimetric cues of the captured Stokes vector are

$$L_o = L_d + L_s , \quad \beta_o = L_d\beta_d + L_s\beta_s , \quad \phi_o = \tan^{-1}(-\tan(2\phi_n))/2$$

Figure 2 shows polarimetric cues for a sphere scene for different reflectance properties. For only diffuse case (left), the degree of polarization increases with elevation angle and the angle of polarization is equal to the azimuth angle. For only specular case (middle), the degree of polarization increases with elevation angle until the Brewster's angle after which it reduces. The angle of polarization is shifted from azimuth angle by 90°. When both diffuse and specular reflectance are present (right), the polarimetric cues indicate if a region is dominated by diffuse or specular radiance. The specular areas have higher degree of polarization than diffuse areas. The two components have orthogonal angle of polarization.

4   Our Approach

We aim to recover the object shape, diffuse and specular radiance along with the incident illumination from multi-view images captured from a consumer-grade snapshot polarization camera. Figure 3 summarizes our pipeline.

4.1   Input

PANDORA relies on the following inputs to perform radiance decomposition: 1) *Polarization Images.* We capture multiple views around the object with a 4 MP snapshot polarization camera [1] (Fig. 3(a)). These cameras comprise of polarization and Bayer filter arrays on the sensor to simultaneously capture color images for four different polarizer orientations at the expense of spatial resolution. We employ the demosaicking and post-processing techniques utilized in [53] to convert the raw sensor measurements into 4 MP RGB Stokes vector images. 2) *Camera poses.* We use COLMAP Structure-from-motion technique [37], [36] to calibrate the camera pose from the intensity measurements of the polarization images. Thus for any pixel in the captured images, the camera position **o** and camera ray direction **d** are known. An optional binary mask can also be used to remove signal contamination from the background. To create masks for real-world data, We use an existing object segmentation approach [33] for creating the object masks. The binary mask values are denoted as, $M(\mathbf{o}, \mathbf{d})$.

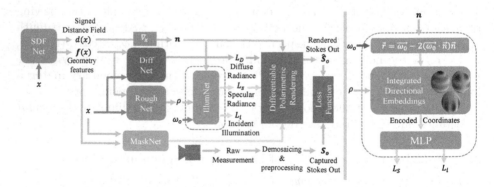

Fig. 3. PANDORA Pipeline: Left: Our pipeline. We use coordinate-based networks to estimate surface normals, diffuse and specular radiance and incident illumination. From these parameters, we render exitant Stokes vector that is compared with captured Stokes vector and the loss is backpropagated to train the networks. Right: Detailed schematic of the Illumination Net

4.2   Implicit Surface Estimation

The Stokes vector measured by camera ray given by **o** and **d**, the ray is sampled at $\mathcal{T}$ points. For a sample on the ray with travel distance t, its location is denoted at $\mathbf{r}(t) = \mathbf{o} + t\mathbf{d}$. The Stokes vector contribution of this sample depends on the scene opacity, $\sigma(\mathbf{r}(t))$ and exitant Stokes vector $S_o(\mathbf{r}(t), \mathbf{d})$. The observed Stokes vector, $S(\mathbf{o}, \mathbf{d})$ is denoted by the integral,

$$S(\mathbf{o}, \mathbf{d}) = \int_0^\infty T(t)\sigma(\mathbf{r}(t))S_o(\mathbf{r}(t), \mathbf{d})dt , \qquad (5)$$

where $T(t) = exp\left(-\int_0^\infty \sigma(\mathbf{r}(t))\right)$ is the probablity that the ray travels to t without getting occluded.

For rendering surfaces, the ideal opacity should have a sharp discontinuity at the ray surface intersection. Thus accurately sampling T points for reconstructing sharp surfaces is challenging. High quality surface estimation is crucial for our approach as the polarization cues depend on the surface normals, (Eq. 3).

VolSDF [47] has demonstrated significant improvements in surface estimation by modelling the signed distance field d with a coordinate-based neural network. The opacity is then estimated as $\sigma(x) = \alpha\psi_\beta(-d(x))$ where α, β are learnable parameters and Ψ is the Cumulative Distribution Function of the Laplace distribution with zero mean and scale β. They also propose a better sampling algorithm for T points utilizing the SDF representation. We follow the same algorithm as VolSDF for opacity generation. Similar to VolSDF, our pipeline comprises of an MLP, which we term SDFNet, that takes as input the position $\mathbf{x}$ and outputs the signed distance field at that position $\mathbf{x}$ along with geometry feature vectors $\mathbf{f}$ useful for radiance estimation. The SDF model also provides surface normals that we use to estimate specular radiance and polarimetric cues.

4.3   Neural Rendering Architecture

Diffuse Radiance Estimation. Diffuse radiance is invariant of the viewing direction and only depends on the spatial location. The geometry features from SDFNet and the position are passed through another coordinate-based MLP, denoted as DiffuseNet, to output the diffuse radiance at that position $L_D(\mathbf{x})$.

Specular Radiance Estimation. Unlike the diffuse radiance, the specular radiance depends on the viewing angle $\mathbf{d}$ and the object roughness $\alpha\mathbf{x}$. First we estimate the object roughness using an coordinate-based MLP, RoughNet, similar in architecture to the DiffuseNet. For a certain object roughness, the obtained specular radiance involves integrating the specular BRDF along an incident direction factored by the incident illumination [5], which is a computationally expensive procedure that generally requires Monte Carlo. Inspired by [42], we instead use an IDE-based neural network to output the specular radiance, L_D from the estimated roughness, α and surface normals, $\mathbf{n}$. Moreover, on setting roughness close to zero, IllumNet also provides us the incident illumination, L_i.

Volumetric Masking. We exploit object masks to ensure only the regions in the scene corresponding to the target object are used for radiance decomposition. Even when the background is zero, VolSDF estimates surface normals which have

546   A. Dave et al.

to be masked out to avoid incorrect quering of the IllumNet. Rather than using the 2D masks on the rendered images, we found that learning a 3D mask of the target object helps in training, especially in the initial interations. This 3D mask $m(\mathbf{x})$ is 1 only for the positions $\mathbf{x}$ that the object occupies and represent's the object's visual hull. We use this 3D mask to obtain the diffuse and specular radiance that is clipped to zero at background values,

$$L_D^m(\mathbf{x}) = m(\mathbf{x}) \cdot L_D(\mathbf{x}) \quad L_S^m(\mathbf{x}, \mathbf{d}) = m(\mathbf{x}) \cdot L_S(\mathbf{x}, \mathbf{d}) \tag{6}$$

The 3D mask is estimated using a coordinate-based MLP that we term MaskNet. This network is trained with the supervision of the input 2D object masks under different views. Similar to Eq. 5, the 3D mask values are accumulated along the ray and compared to the provided mask M using the binary cross entropy loss:

$$\mathcal{L}_{\text{mask}} = \mathbb{E}_{\mathbf{o},1}\text{BCE}\left(M(\mathbf{o}, \mathbf{d}), \hat{M}(\mathbf{o}, \mathbf{d})\right), \tag{7}$$

where $\hat{M}(\mathbf{o}, \mathbf{d}) = \int_0^\infty T(t)\sigma(\mathbf{r}(t))m(\mathbf{r}(t))dt$.

Neural Polarimetric Rendering. Using the masked diffuse L_D^m, masked specular L_S^m and the estimated surface normals $\mathbf{n}$, we can render the outgoing Stokes vector, $S_o(\mathbf{x}, \mathbf{d})$ from Eq. 3. On integrating outgoing Stokes vectors for points along the ray according to Eq. 5, we obtain the rendered Stokes vector $\hat{S}(\mathbf{x}, \mathbf{d})$.

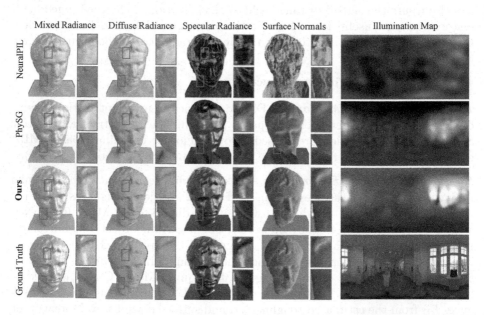

Fig. 4. Comparison of reflectance separation and surface normals with baselines on rendered dataset: NeuralPIL fails to estimate correct normals and illumination on this challenging scene with strong specularities and 45 views. PhySG exhibits blurrier speculars and illumination along with artifacts in the reconstructed normals. PANDORA outputs sharp specularities, cleaner surface and more accurate illumination.

4.4 Loss Function

We compare the rendered Stokes vector $\hat{S} = [\hat{s_0}, \hat{s_1}, \hat{s_2}]^T$ with the captured Stokes vector $S = [s_0, s_1, s_2]^T$ (Sect. 4.1) using an L1 loss. The loss is masked to remove the effect of background values. The s_1 and s_2 could have low values in regions having low degree of polarization (Fig. 2). We apply a weightage factor w_s on the loss for s_1 and s_2 outputs to further encourage the network to consider polarimetric cues in the training. The Stokes loss is modelled as:

$$\mathcal{L}_{\text{stokes}} = \mathbb{E}_{\mathbf{o},\mathbf{l}} \left[M \cdot \|\hat{s_0} - s_0\| + w_s \cdot M \cdot (\|\hat{s_1} - s_1\| + \|\hat{s_2} - s_2\|) \right] \qquad (8)$$

Additionally, similar to VolSDF [47], we have the Eikonal loss, $\mathcal{L}_{\text{SDF}}$ to encourage the SDFNet to approximate a signed distance field.

$$\mathcal{L}_{\text{SDF}} = \mathbb{E}_{\mathbf{o},\mathbf{l}} \left(\|\mathbf{n}\| - 1 \right)^2 \qquad (9)$$

The net loss used to train all the networks described in the pipeline:

$$\mathcal{L}_{\text{net}} = \mathcal{L}_{\text{stokes}} + 0.1\mathcal{L}_{\text{SDF}} + \mathcal{L}_{\text{mask}} \qquad (10)$$

4.5 Implementation Details

All the networks are standard MLPs with 4 layers each. SDFNet has 256 hidden units per layer and the other networks have 512 hidden units. ReLU activations are used in intermediate layers. Final activation in DiffNet and MaskNet and the final activation in IllumNet and RoughNet is softplus. Please refer to the supplementary material for additional implementation details of our framework.

5 Results and Evaluation

5.1 Datasets

We generate the following datasets for evaluating radiance decomposition.

1. Rendered Polarimetric Dataset (Fig. 4): Using Mitsuba2, we apply pBRDF on objects with complicated geometry and perform polarimetric rendering of multiple camera views under realistic environment lighting.
2. Real Polarimetric Dataset (Figs. 5, 6 and 7): Using a snapshot polarimetric camera, we acquire multi-view polarized images of complex objects composed of materials with varying roughness, such as ceramics, glass, resin and plastic, under unstructured lighting conditions such as an office hallway. We also acquire the ground truth lighting using a chrome ball.

Please refer to supplementary material for additional details on the generation of these datasets and more examples from the datasets.

Table 1. Quantiative evaluation on rendered scenes. We evaluate PANDORA and state-of-the-art methods on held-out testsets of 45 images for two rendered scenes. We report the peak average signal-to-noise ratio (PSNR) and structured similarity (SSIM) of diffuse, specular and net radiance, mean angular error (MAE) of surface normals and the Hausdorff distance (HD) of the reconstructed mesh. PANDORA outperforms state-of-the-art in radiance separation and geometry estimation.

Scene	Approach	Diffuse PSNR ↑ (dB)	Diffuse SSIM ↑	Specular PSNR ↑ (dB)	Specular SSIM ↑	Mixed PSNR ↑ (dB)	Mixed SSIM ↑	Normals MAE ↓ (°)	Mesh HD ↓
Bust	NeuralPIL	23.90	0.87	18.04	0.87	**26.71**	**0.87**	15.36	N/A
	PhySG	22.64	**0.94**	**23.00**	**0.94**	19.94	0.72	9.81	0.012
	Ours	**25.82**	0.81	22.96	0.75	22.79	0.79	**3.91**	**0.003**
Sphere	NeuralPIL	13.09	0.55	12.92	0.55	20.04	0.66	38.73	N/A
	PhySG	21.76	0.76	18.90	0.76	17.93	0.70	8.42	0.011
	Ours	**24.33**	**0.77**	**22.70**	**0.89**	**21.76**	**0.81**	**1.41**	**0.003**

5.2 Comparisons with Baselines

We demonstrate that PANDORA excels in 3D reconstruction, diffuse-specular separation and illumination estimation compared to two existing state-of-the-art radiance decomposition baselines, NeuralPIL [7] and PhySG [52]. These baselines cannot exploit polarization and are run on radiance-only images using the public code implementations provided by the authors. Note that NeuralPIL achieves higher PSNR than PhySG and PANDORA for the mixed-radiance on the bust

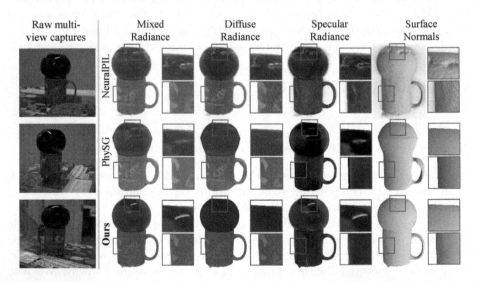

| Raw multi-view captures | Mixed Radiance | Diffuse Radiance | Specular Radiance | Surface Normals |

Fig. 5. Reflectance separation and surface normal estimation on real data. Left: Raw muli-view captures from the polarization camera. Right: Reflectance separation and surface normal estimation using baselines and our technique. The decomposition using PhySG and NeuralPIL on intensity-only images has artifacts such as the specular highlights bleeding into the diffuse component and surface normals. PANDORA on polarized images produces accurate diffuse radiance, and accurately reconstructs the specular components and geometry.

images. However, this is likely due to overfitting since the baseline comparisons are all trained on the mixed-radiance images. As a result, NeuralPIL performs very poorly for the diffuse-specular separation, achieving worse performance than PANDORA in estimating both the diffuse and specular components. We then show additional applications of PANDORA and an ablation study to analyse the crucial aspects of our algorithm.

3D Reconstruction. The polarization cues directly depend on the surface normals (Sect.3.2). Thus, inclusion of polarization cues, enhances multi-view 3D reconstruction. PANDORA reconstructs cleaner and more accurate surfaces such as jaw of the bust in Fig. 4 and the glass ball in Fig. 5. In Table 1, we show that the mesh reconstructed by PANDORA has much lower Hausdorff distance with the ground truth mesh as compared to state-of-the-art. PANDORA also estimates more accurate surface normals as evaluated on a held-out test set.

Diffuse-Specular Separation. The inherent ambiguity in separating diffuse and specular radiance components from intensity-only measurements leads to artefacts in existing techniques. For example, the black sphere in diffuse radiance reconstructed by NeuralPIL and PhySG contain faint specular highlights. Difference in polarization of diffuse and specular components enables PANDORA to obtain more accurate separation along with better combined radiance Fig. 4,5. In Table 1, we show that PANDORA consistent outperforms state-of-the-art in peak signal-to-noise ratio (PSNR) and the structural similarity index measure (SSIM) of diffuse, specular and the net radiance images. We also provide the video of multi-view renderings from these diffuse, specular and mixed radiance fields that highlight the high quality of PANDORA's separation.

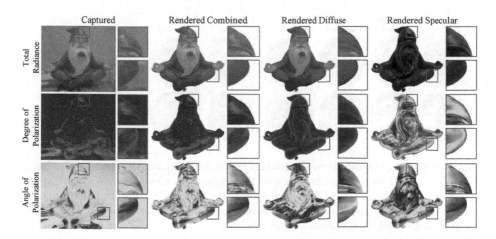

Fig. 6. Polarimetric diffuse-specular separation on real-world objects. PANDORA can separate out diffuse and specular polarimetric properties from captured polarized images. As expected, rendered specular component has higher DoP and AoP is orthogonal to the diffuse component. Polarization properties of the PANDORA rendered image match the captured image.

Apart from the radiance, PANDORA can also separate polarization properties of the object's diffuse and specular components (Fig. 6). Here, we see predicted cues match with our physical intuition: AoP is orthogonal for the diffuse and specular components, while DoP is higher for the specular component.

Illumination Estimation. In addition to reflectance separation, our method can also estimate the illumination incident on the object. The rendered bust in Fig. 4 has blurry specular highlights that make illumination estimation challenging. Here, NeuralPIL fails to estimate the correct lighting. PhySG employs spherical Gaussians that result in blurrier and more sparse reconstruction. PANDORA provides the best reconstruction with sharper walls and window edges.

There are still limitations to illumination estimation. For example, our method may have difficulties distinguishing between point diffuse illumination versus sharp illumination with a rough surface. However, this is also challenging for prior work. For example Miyazaki et al. [27] resolved this by assuming light sources were point sources; as another example, in PhySG increased roughness led to a blurred illumination map [52]. In future work, our method could resolve this ambiguity by incorporating priors about the environment.

Similarly, we also perform illumination estimation on real-world data (Fig. 7). We show results on data captured in two different environments. Figure 7(left) is captured on a lab table with a long bright linear LED with dim ambient light. Figure 7(right) is captured in a office hallway with many small tube-lights and bright walls. PhySG reconstruction is blurrier especially for the walls and comprises of color artifacts. PANDORA can recover high quality illumination that accurately matches the ground truth illumination as captured by replacing the object with a chrome ball.

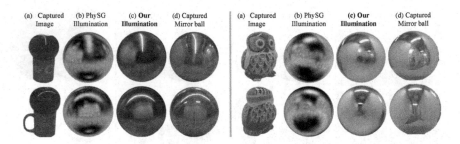

Fig. 7. Incident illumination estimated from real object. We visualize the illumination estimated on a mirror ball viewed from two train viewpoints. We also capture a mirror ball placed at a similar viewpoints. PhySG models the illumination using spherical Gaussians and leads to blurrier reconstruction with artefacts. PANDORA's estimation has higher sharpness and accuracy.

5.3 Additional Applications

The decomposed radiance field from PANDORA enables not only to render the object under novel views but also to change the object's appearance under novel views by altering the separated diffuse and specular radiance fields. We demonstrate this application under Fig. 1(c). We perform polarimetric rendering from the learned PANDORA model under a novel view. The rendered polarization (Fig. 1(c) bottom left) is consistent with the captured polarization. As PANDORA decomposes radiances, we can alter the diffuse component without affecting the specular reflections. For example, we assign pink albedo to the object by removing the G component of radiance without altering the specularities in (Fig. 1(c) top left). To create a metallic appearance, we render only the specular component with the Fresnel reflectance R^+ set to 1 (Fig 1(c) top right). To obtain rougher appearance (Fig 1(c) bottom right), we multiply the roughness parameter with a factor 3 before passing to the IllumNet. Please refer to the supplementary video for multi-view renderings of the changed appearance.

5.4 Ablation Study: Role of Polarization and IllumNet

Polarization and illumination modelling are key aspects of PANDORA. Here we analyse the role of these components by devising the following experiments

Ours w\o IllumNet w\o pol: We set Stokes loss weightage factor w_s (Eq. 8) as 0 to constrain PANDORA to just use S_o component, i.e., intensities for radiance decomposition. Also, instead of modelling illumination and roughness with neural networks, we directly model the specular radiance with a neural network same as the conventional RadianceNet in VolSDF.

Ours w\o pol: We set w_s as 0. But keep the IllumNet. So, this model has the same architecture as PANDORA. But it is trained on only the intensity. We then train these two models and PANDORA on the same data with the same training scheme. As shown in Fig. 8, inclusion of the illumination modelling and polarization information significantly improves PANDORA's performance. The model without IllumNet and polarization, exhibits strong artefacts of specular highlights in the diffuse and fails to capture the smaller specularites. Removing just polarization leads to worse illumination estimation, bleeding of diffuse into the specular and texture artefacts in the normals. These artefacts are more prominent at sharp specular highlights and can be problematic in critical applications such as 3D scanning objects for quality inspection. Equipped with polarization information and correct illumination modelling, PANDORA outputs sharper diffuse texture, accurately handles the small specularities and even captures the subtle bumps on the object's back.

552   A. Dave et al.

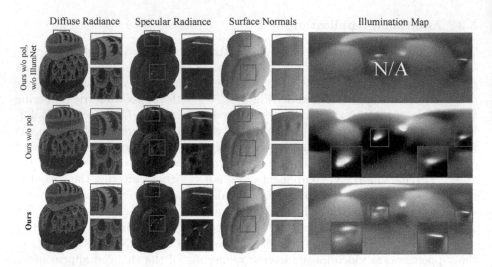

Fig. 8. Ablation study: Role of polarization and IllumNet. We devise two ablation experiments by training on intensity-only images without IllumNet(top row) and
with IllumNet(middle row). Without polarization and correct illumination modelling,
there are texture artefacts in specular and surface normals due to ambiguities in texture
decomposition. Polarimetric cues and IllumNet help resolve such ambiguities resulting
in higher quality reconstructions, sharper diffuse texture, and more accurate surface
normals and lighting estimation.

6 Conclusion and Discussion

We have proposed PANDORA a novel neural inverse rendering algorithm that
achieves state-of-the-art performance in reflectance separation and illumination
estimation. PANDORA achieves this by using polarimetric cues and an SDF-
based implicit surface representation. We have demonstrated the success of our
approach on both simulated data that was generated by a physics based renderer,
and real-world data captured with a polarization camera. Finally, we compared
against similar approaches and demonstrated superior surface geometry reconstruction and illumination estimation. We believe PANDORA would pave the
way for exciting ideas in the space of polarimetric and neural inverse rendering.

Acknowledgements. We acknowledge the support of DARPA Contract No. N66001-
19-C-4020, NSF Expeditions in Computing Grant #1730147, NSF CAREER Grant
#1652633; Y. Zhao was supported by a training fellowship from the NLM Training
Program (T15LM007093).

References

1. Sony polarization image sensors. https://www.sony-semicon.co.jp/e/products/IS/industry/product/polarization.html (2021), accessed: 2021-09-25
2. Ba, Y., et al.: Deep Shape from polarization. In: Vedaldi, A., Bischof, H., Brox, T., Frahm, J.-M. (eds.) ECCV 2020. LNCS, vol. 12369, pp. 554–571. Springer, Cham (2020). https://doi.org/10.1007/978-3-030-58586-0_33
3. Baek, S.H., Jeon, D.S., Tong, X., Kim, M.H.: Simultaneous acquisition of polarimetric SVBRDF and normals. ACM Trans. Graph. **37**(6), 1–15 (2018)
4. Barron, J.T., Malik, J.: Shape, illumination, and reflectance from shading. IEEE Trans. Pattern Anal. Mach. Intell. **37**(8), 1670–1687 (2014)
5. Barron, J.T., et al.: Mip-NeRF: a multiscale representation for anti-aliasing neural radiance fields (2021)
6. Boss, M., Braun, R., Jampani, V., Barron, J.T., Liu, C., Lensch, H.P.: NeRD: neural reflectance decomposition from image collections. In: IEEE International Conference on Computer Vision (ICCV) (2021)
7. Boss, M., Jampani, V., Braun, R., Liu, C., Barron, J., Lensch, H.: Neural-PIL: Neural pre-integrated lighting for reflectance decomposition. In 34th Proceedings of the conference on Advances in Neural Information Processing Systems (2021)
8. Chen, Z., Nobuhara, S., Nishino, K.: Invertible neural brdf for object inverse rendering. In: Vedaldi, A., Bischof, H., Brox, T., Frahm, J.-M. (eds.) ECCV 2020. LNCS, vol. 12350, pp. 767–783. Springer, Cham (2020). https://doi.org/10.1007/978-3-030-58558-7_45
9. Collett, E.: Polarized Light: Fundamentals and Applications. CRC Press, New York (1992)
10. Cui, Z., Gu, J., Shi, B., Tan, P., Kautz, J.: Polarimetric multi-view stereo. In: 2017 IEEE Conference on Computer Vision and Pattern Recognition (CVPR), pp. 369–378 (2017). https://doi.org/10.1109/CVPR.2017.47
11. Debevec, P.E., Malik, J.: Recovering high dynamic range radiance maps from photographs. In: Proceedings of the 24th Annual Conference on Computer Graphics and Interactive Techniques, SIGGRAPH 1997, pp. 369–378. ACM Press/Addison-Wesley Publishing Co., USA (1997). https://doi.org/10.1145/258734.258884, https://doi.org/10.1145/258734.258884
12. Deschaintre, V., Lin, Y., Ghosh, A.: Deep polarization imaging for 3D shape and SVBRDF acquisition. In: Proceedings of the IEEE/CVF Conference on Computer Vision and Pattern Recognition (CVPR), June 202
13. Ding, Y., Ji, Y., Zhou, M., Kang, S.B., Ye, J.: Polarimetric helmholtz stereopsis. In: Proceedings of the IEEE/CVF International Conference on Computer Vision, pp. 5037–5046 (2021)
14. Fukao, Y., Kawahara, R., Nobuhara, S., Nishino, K.: Polarimetric normal stereo. In: 2021 IEEE/CVF Conference on Computer Vision and Pattern Recognition (CVPR), pp. 682–690 (2021). https://doi.org/10.1109/CVPR46437.2021.00074
15. Gkioulekas, I., Zhao, S., Bala, K., Zickler, T., Levin, A.: Inverse volume rendering with material dictionaries. ACM Trans. Graph. **32**(6) (2013). https://doi.org/10.1145/2508363.2508377, https://doi.org/10.1145/2508363.2508377
16. Kadambi, A., Taamazyan, V., Shi, B., Raskar, R.: Polarized 3D: High-quality depth sensing with polarization cues. In: Proceedings of the IEEE International Conference on Computer Vision, pp. 3370–3378 (2015)
17. Kim, H., Zollöfer, M., Tewari, A., Thies, J., Richardt, C., Theobalt, C.: Inverse-faceNet: deep single-shot inverse face rendering from a single image. In: Proceedings of the IEEE Conference on Computer Vision and Pattern Recognition (2018)

18. Kim, J., Izadi, S., Ghosh, A.: Single-shot layered reflectance separation using a polarized light field camera. In: Proceedings of the Eurographics Symposium on Rendering: Experimental Ideas & Implementation (2016)
19. Lei, C., et al.: Shape from polarization for complex scenes in the wild. arXiv preprint arXiv:2112.11377 (2021)
20. Li, C., Manno, Y., Okutomi, M.: Spectral MVIR: joint reconstruction of 3D shape and spectral reflectance. In: 2021 IEEE International Conference on Computational Photography (ICCP), pp. 1–12. IEEE (2021)
21. Li, T.M., Aittala, M., Durand, F., Lehtinen, J.: Differentiable Monte Carlo ray tracing through edge sampling. ACM Trans. Graph. (Proc. SIGGRAPH Asia) **37**(6), 222:1–222:11 (2018)
22. Lin, S., Li, Y., Kang, S.B., Tong, X., Shum, H.-Y.: Diffuse-specular separation and depth recovery from image sequences. In: Heyden, A., Sparr, G., Nielsen, M., Johansen, P. (eds.) ECCV 2002. LNCS, vol. 2352, pp. 210–224. Springer, Heidelberg (2002). https://doi.org/10.1007/3-540-47977-5_14
23. Lyu, Y., Cui, Z., Li, S., Pollefeys, M., Shi, B.: Reflection separation using a pair of unpolarized and polarized images. In: Wallach, H., Larochelle, H., Beygelzimer, A., d'Alché-Buc, F., Fox, E., Garnett, R. (eds.) Advances in Neural Information Processing Systems, vol. 32. Curran Associates, Inc. (2019), https://proceedings.neurips.cc/paper/2019/file/d47bf0af618a3523a226ed7cada85ce3-Paper.pdf
24. Ma, W.C., Hawkins, T., Peers, P., Chabert, C.F., Weiss, M., Debevec, P.E., et al.: Rapid acquisition of specular and diffuse normal maps from polarized spherical gradient illumination. Rend. Techn. **2007**(9), 10 (2007)
25. Mescheder, L., Oechsle, M., Niemeyer, M., Nowozin, S., Geiger, A.: Occupancy networks: learning 3D reconstruction in function space. In: Proceedings IEEE Conf. on Computer Vision and Pattern Recognition (CVPR) (2019)
26. Mildenhall, B., Srinivasan, P.P., Tancik, M., Barron, J.T., Ramamoorthi, R., Ng, R.: NeRF: Representing scenes as neural radiance fields for view synthesis. In: Vedaldi, A., Bischof, H., Brox, T., Frahm, J.-M. (eds.) ECCV 2020. LNCS, vol. 12346, pp. 405–421. Springer, Cham (2020). https://doi.org/10.1007/978-3-030-58452-8_24
27. Miyazaki, T., Hara, I.: Polarization-based inverse rendering from a single view. In: Proceedings Ninth IEEE International Conference on Computer Vision, vol. 2, pp. 982–987 (2003). https://doi.org/10.1109/ICCV.2003.1238455
28. Morimatsu, M., Monno, Y., Tanaka, M., Okutomi, M.: Monochrome and color polarization demosaicking using edge-aware residual interpolation. In: 2020 IEEE International Conference on Image Processing (ICIP), pp. 2571–2575. IEEE (2020)
29. Nayar, S.K., Krishnan, G., Grossberg, M.D., Raskar, R.: Fast separation of direct and global components of a scene using high frequency illumination. ACM Trans. Graph. **25**(3), 935–944 (2006). https://doi.org/10.1145/1141911.1141977, https://doi.org/10.1145/1141911.1141977
30. Oechsle, M., Peng, S., Geiger, A.: UNISURF: unifying neural implicit surfaces and radiance fields for multi-view reconstruction. In: Proceedings of the IEEE/CVF International Conference on Computer Vision, pp. 5589–5599 (2021)
31. OToole, M., Mather, J., Kutulakos, K.N.: 3D shape and indirect appearance by structured light transport. IEEE Trans. Pattern Anal. Mach. Intell. **38**(07), 1298–1312 (2016). https://doi.org/10.1109/TPAMI.2016.2545662
32. Park, J.J., Florence, P., Straub, J., Newcombe, R., Lovegrove, S.: DeepSDF: learning continuous signed distance functions for shape representation. In: The IEEE Conference on Computer Vision and Pattern Recognition (CVPR), June 2019

33. Qin, X., Zhang, Z., Huang, C., Dehghan, M., Zaiane, O.R., Jagersand, M.: U2-net: Going deeper with nested u-structure for salient object detection. Pattern Recogn. **106**, 107404 (2020)
34. Qiu, S., Fu, Q., Wang, C., Heidrich, W.: Linear polarization demosaicking for monochrome and colour polarization focal plane arrays. Comput. Graph. Forum **40**. (2021), Wiley Online Library
35. Ramamoorthi, R., Hanrahan, P.: A signal-processing framework for inverse rendering. In: Proceedings of the 28th Annual Conference on Computer Graphics and Interactive Techniques, SIGGRAPH 2001, pp. 117–128. Association for Computing Machinery, New York, NY, USA (2001). https://doi.org/10.1145/383259.383271, https://doi.org/10.1145/383259.383271
36. Schönberger, J.L., Frahm, J.M.: Structure-from-motion revisited. In: Conference on Computer Vision and Pattern Recognition (CVPR) (2016)
37. Schönberger, J.L., Zheng, E., Frahm, J.-M., Pollefeys, M.: Pixelwise view selection for unstructured multi-view stereo. In: Leibe, B., Matas, J., Sebe, N., Welling, M. (eds.) ECCV 2016. LNCS, vol. 9907, pp. 501–518. Springer, Cham (2016). https://doi.org/10.1007/978-3-319-46487-9_31
38. Sitzmann, V., Martel, J.N., Bergman, A.W., Lindell, D.B., Wetzstein, G.: Implicit neural representations with periodic activation functions. arXiv (2020)
39. Smith, W.A., Ramamoorthi, R., Tozza, S.: Height-from-polarisation with unknown lighting or albedo. IEEE Trans. Pattern Anal. Mach. Intell. **41**(12), 2875–2888 (2018)
40. Srinivasan, P.P., Deng, B., Zhang, X., Tancik, M., Mildenhall, B., Barron, J.T.: NeRV: neural reflectance and visibility fields for relighting and view synthesis. In: CVPR (2021)
41. Tewari, A., et al.: Advances in neural rendering. arXiv preprint arXiv:2111.05849 (2021)
42. Verbin, D., Hedman, P., Mildenhall, B., Zickler, T., Barron, J.T., Srinivasan, P.P.: Ref-NeRF: structured view-dependent appearance for neural radiance fields. arXiv preprint arXiv:2112.03907 (2021)
43. Vlasic, D., et al.: Dynamic shape capture using multi-view photometric stereo. In: ACM SIGGRAPH Asia 2009 Papers. SIGGRAPH Asia '09, Association for Computing Machinery, New York, NY, USA (2009). https://doi.org/10.1145/1661412.1618520, https://doi.org/10.1145/1661412.1618520
44. Wang, P., et al.: Neus: learning neural implicit surfaces by volume rendering for multi-view reconstruction. In: NeurIPS (2021)
45. Xie, Y., et al.: Neural fields in visual computing and beyond. arXiv preprint arXiv:2111.11426 (2021)
46. Yang, L., Tan, F., Li, A., Cui, Z., Furukawa, Y., Tan, P.: Polarimetric dense monocular slam. In: 2018 IEEE/CVF Conference on Computer Vision and Pattern Recognition, pp. 3857–3866 (2018). https://doi.org/10.1109/CVPR.2018.00406
47. Yariv, L., Gu, J., Kasten, Y., Lipman, Y.: Volume rendering of neural implicit surfaces. In: 34th Proceedings Conference on Advances in Neural Information Processing Systems (2021)
48. Yariv, L., et al.: Multiview neural surface reconstruction by disentangling geometry and appearance. Adv. Neural. Inaf. Process. Syst. **33**, 2492–2502 (2020)
49. Yi, S., Kim, D., Choi, K., Jarabo, A., Gutierrez, D., Kim, M.H.: Differentiable transient rendering. ACM Trans. Graph. **40**(6), 1–11 (2021)
50. Yu, Y., Smith, W.A.: InverserenderNet: learning single image inverse rendering. In: Proceedings of the IEEE/CVF Conference on Computer Vision and Pattern Recognition (CVPR) (2019)

51. Zhang, C., Wu, L., Zheng, C., Gkioulekas, I., Ramamoorthi, R., Zhao, S.: A differential theory of radiative transfer. ACM Trans. Graph. **38**(6), 227:1–227:16 (2019)
52. Zhang, K., Luan, F., Wang, Q., Bala, K., Snavely, N.: Physg: inverse rendering with spherical gaussians for physics-based material editing and relighting. In: The IEEE/CVF Conference on Computer Vision and Pattern Recognition (CVPR) (2021)
53. Zhao, J., Monno, Y., Okutomi, M.: Polarimetric multi-view inverse rendering (2020)

HuMMan: Multi-modal 4D Human Dataset for Versatile Sensing and Modeling

Zhongang Cai[1,2,3], Daxuan Ren[2], Ailing Zeng[4], Zhengyu Lin[3],
Tao Yu[5], Wenjia Wang[3], Xiangyu Fan[3], Yang Gao[3], Yifan Yu[3],
Liang Pan[2], Fangzhou Hong[2], Mingyuan Zhang[2], Chen Change Loy[2],
Lei Yang[1,3(✉)], and Ziwei Liu[2(✉)]

[1] Shanghai AI Laboratory, Shanghai, China
[2] S-Lab, Nanyang Technological University, Singapore, Singapore
`ziwei.liu@ntu.edu.sg`
[3] SenseTime Research, Hong Kong, China
`yanglei@sensetime.com`
[4] The Chinese University of Hong Kong, Hong Kong, China
[5] Tsinghua University, Beijing, China

Abstract. 4D human sensing and modeling are fundamental tasks in vision and graphics with numerous applications. With the advances of new sensors and algorithms, there is an increasing demand for more versatile datasets. In this work, we contribute **HuMMan**, a large-scale multi-modal 4D human dataset with 1000 human subjects, 400k sequences and 60M frames. HuMMan has several appealing properties: **1)** multi-modal data and annotations including color images, point clouds, keypoints, SMPL parameters, and textured meshes; **2)** popular mobile device is included in the sensor suite; **3)** a set of 500 actions, designed to cover fundamental movements; **4)** multiple tasks such as action recognition, pose estimation, parametric human recovery, and textured mesh reconstruction are supported and evaluated. Extensive experiments on HuMMan voice the need for further study on challenges such as fine-grained action recognition, dynamic human mesh reconstruction, point cloud-based parametric human recovery, and cross-device domain gaps (Homepage: https://caizhongang.github.io/projects/HuMMan/).

1 Introduction

Sensing and modeling humans are longstanding problems for both computer vision and computer graphics research communities, which serve as the fundamental technology for a myriad of applications such as animation, gaming, augmented, and virtual reality. With the advent of deep learning, significant

---

Z. Cai, D. Ren, A. Zeng, Z. Lin, T. Yu and W. Wang—Co-first authors.

Supplementary Information The online version contains supplementary material available at https://doi.org/10.1007/978-3-031-20071-7_33.

S. Avidan et al. (Eds.): ECCV 2022, LNCS 13667, pp. 557–577, 2022.
https://doi.org/10.1007/978-3-031-20071-7_33

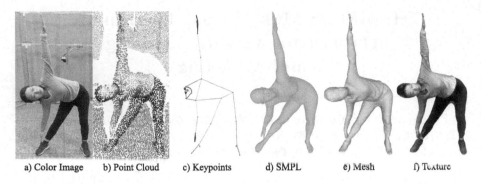

a) Color Image   b) Point Cloud   c) Keypoints   d) SMPL   e) Mesh   f) Texture

Fig. 1. HuMMan features multiple modalities of data format and annotations. We demonstrate a) color image, b) point cloud, c) keypoints, d) SMPL parameters and e) mesh geometry with f) texture. Each sequence is also annotated with an action label from 500 actions. Each subject has two additional high-resolution scans of naturally and minimally clothed body.

progress has been made alongside the introduction of large-scale datasets in human-centric sensing and modeling [29,53,60,62,103,113]. In this work, we present **HuMMan**, a comprehensive human dataset consisting of 1000 human subjects, captured in total 400k sequences and 60M frames. More importantly, HuMMan features four main properties listed below.

- **Multiple Modalities.** HuMMan provides a basket of data formats and annotations in the hope to assist exploration in their potential complementary nature. We build HuMMan with a set of 10 synchronized RGB-D cameras to capture both video and depth sequences. Our toolchain then post-process the raw data into sequences of colored point clouds, 2D/3D keypoints, statistical model (SMPL) parameters, and model-free textured mesh. Note that all data and annotations are temporally synchronized, while 3D data and annotations are spatially aligned. In addition, we provide a high-resolution scan for each of the subjects in a canonical pose (Fig. 1).
- **Mobile Device.** With the development of 3D sensors, it is common to find depth cameras or low-power LiDARs on a mobile device in recent years. In view of the surprising gap between emerging real-life applications and the insufficiency of data collected with mobile devices, we add a mobile phone with built-in LiDAR in the data collection to facilitate the relevant research.
- **Action Set.** We design HuMMan to empower comprehensive studies on human actions. Instead of empirically selecting daily activities, we propose to take an anatomical point of view and systematically divide body movements by their driving muscles. Specifically, we design 500 movements by categorizing major muscle groups to achieve a more complete and fundamental representation of human actions.
- **Multiple Tasks.** To facilitate research on HuMMan, we provide a whole suite of baselines and benchmarks for action recognition, 2D and 3D pose estimation, 3D parametric human recovery, and textured mesh reconstruction. Popular methods are implemented and evaluated using standard metrics. Our

Table 1. Comparisons of HuMMan with published datasets. HuMMan has a competitive scale in terms of the number of subjects (#Subj), actions (#Act), sequences (#Seq) and frames (#Frame). Moreover, HuMMan features multiple modalities and supports multiple tasks. Video: sequential data, not limited to RGB sequences; Mobile: mobile device in the sensor suite; D/PC: depth image or point cloud, only genuine point cloud collected from depth sensors are considered; Act: action label; K2D: 2D keypoints; K3D: 3D keypoints; Param: statistical model (*e.g.* SMPL) parameters; Txtr: texture. -: not applicable or not reported.

Dataset	#Subj	#Act	#Seq	#Frame	Video	Mobile	Modalities RGB	D/PC	Act	K2D	K3D	Param	Mesh	Txtr
UCF101 [87]	-	101	13k	-	✓	-	✓	-	✓	-	-	-	-	-
AVA [21]	-	80	437	-	✓	-	✓	-	✓	-	-	-	-	-
FineGym [84]	-	530	32k	-	✓	-	✓	-	✓	-	-	-	-	-
HAA500 [15]	-	500	10k	591k	✓	-	✓	-	✓	-	-	-	-	-
SYSU 3DHOI [27]	40	12	480	-	✓	-	✓	✓	✓	-	✓	-	-	-
NTU RGB+D [83]	40	60	56k	-	✓	-	✓	✓	✓	-	✓	-	-	-
NTU RGB+D 120 [55]	106	120	114k	-	✓	-	✓	✓	✓	-	✓	-	-	-
NTU RGB+D X [93]	106	120	113k	-	✓	-	✓	✓	✓	-	✓	✓	-	-
MPII [4]	-	410	-	24k	-	-	✓	-	✓	✓	-	-	-	-
COCO [53]	-	-	-	104k	-	-	✓	-	-	✓	-	-	-	-
PoseTrack [3]	-	-	>1.35k	>46k	✓	-	✓	-	-	✓	-	-	-	-
Human3.6M [29]	11	17	839	3.6M	✓	-	✓	✓	✓	✓	✓	-	-	-
CMU Panoptic [35]	8	5	65	154M	✓	-	✓	✓	-	✓	✓	-	-	-
MPI-INF-3DHP [64]	8	8	16	1.3M	✓	-	✓	-	-	✓	✓	-	-	-
3DPW [62]	7	-	60	51k	✓	✓	✓	-	-	-	✓	✓	-	-
AMASS [61]	344	-	>11k	>16.88M	✓	-	-	-	-	-	✓	✓	-	-
AIST++ [49]	30	-	1.40k	10.1M	✓	-	✓	-	-	✓	✓	✓	-	-
CAPE [60]	15	-	>600	>140k	✓	-	-	-	-	✓	-	✓	✓	-
BUFF [107]	6	3	>30	>13.6k	✓	-	✓	✓	✓	-	✓	✓	✓	✓
DFAUST [7]	10	>10	>100	>40k	✓	-	✓	✓	✓	✓	✓	✓	✓	✓
HUMBI [103]	772	-	-	~26M	✓	-	✓	-	-	✓	✓	✓	✓	✓
ZJU LightStage [78]	6	6	9	>1k	✓	-	✓	-	✓	-	✓	✓	✓	✓
THuman2.0 [101]	200	-	-	>500	-	-	-	-	-	-	-	✓	✓	✓
HuMMan (ours)	1000	500	400k	60M	✓	✓	✓	✓	✓	✓	✓	✓	✓	✓

experiments demonstrate that HuMMan would be useful for multiple fields of study, such as fine-grained action recognition, point cloud-based parametric human recovery, dynamic mesh sequence reconstruction, and transferring knowledge across devices (Table 1).

In summary, HuMMan is a large-scale multi-modal dataset for 4D (spatio-temporal) human sensing and modeling, with four main features: **1)** multi-modal data and annotations; **2)** mobile device included in the sensor suite; **3)** action set with atomic motions; **4)** standard benchmarks for multiple vision tasks. We hope HuMMan would pave the way towards more comprehensive sensing and modeling of humans.

2   Related Works

Action Recognition. As an important step towards understanding human activities, action recognition is the task to categorize human motions into predefined classes. RGB videos [16,17,91,92] with additional information such as optical flow and estimated poses and 3D skeletons typically obtained from RGB-D sequences [85,86,100,105] are the common input to existing methods.

Datasets for RGB video-based action recognition are often collected from the Internet. Some have a human-centric action design [15,21,39,46,84,87] whereas others introduce interaction and diversity in the setup [11,67,111]. Recently, fine-grained action understanding [15,21,84] is drawing more research attention. However, these 2D datasets lack 3D annotations. As for RGB-D datasets, earlier works are small in scale [27,50,96]. As a remedy, the latest NTU RGB-D series [55,83,93] features 60–120 actions. However, the majority of the actions are focused on the upper body. We develop a larger and more complete action set in HuMMan.

2D and 3D Keypoint Detection. Estimation of a human pose is a vital task in computer vision, and a popular pose representation is human skeletal keypoints. The field is categorized by output format: 2D [12,47,71,88] and 3D [63,77,104–106,112] keypoint detection, or by the number of views: single-view [12,63,71,77,88,105,112] and multi-view pose estimation [28,30,80]. For 2D keypoint detection, single-frame datasets such as MPII [4] and COCO [53] provide diverse images with 2D keypoints annotations, whereas video datasets such as J-HMDB [32], Penn Action [108] and PoseTrack [3] provide sequences of 2D keypoints. However, they lack 3D ground truths. In contrast, 3D keypoint datasets are typically built indoor data to accommodate sophisticated equipment, such as Human3.6M [29], CMU Panoptic [35], MPI-INF-3DHP [64], TotalCapture [94], and AIST++ [49]. Compared to these datasets, HuMMan not only supports 2D and 3D keypoint detection but also textured mesh reconstruction assist in more holistic modeling of humans.

3D Parametric Human Recovery. Also known as human pose and shape estimation, 3D parametric human recovery leverages human parametric model representation (such as SMPL [58], SMPL-X [75], STAR [73] and GHUM [99]) that achieves sophisticated mesh reconstruction with a small amount of parameters. Existing methods take keypoints [6,75,109], images [20,22,44,45,48,72,76], videos [13,37,59,65,68,89], and point clouds [5,33,54,97] as the input to obtain the parameters. Joint limits [1] and contact [69] are also important research topics. Apart from those that provide keypoints, various datasets also provide ground-truth SMPL parameters. MoSh [57] is applied on Human3.6M [29] to generate SMPL annotations. CMU Panoptic [35] and HUMBI [103] leverages keypoints from multiple camera views. 3DPW [62] combines a mobile phone and inertial measurement units (IMUs). Synthetic dataset such as AGORA [74] renders high-quality human scans in virtual environments and fits SMPL to the original mesh. Video games have also become an alternative source of data [9,10]. In addition to SMPL parameters that do not model clothes or texture, HuMMan also provides textured meshes of clothed subjects.

Textured Mesh Reconstruction. To reconstruct the 3D surface, common methods include multi-view stereo [18], volumetric fusion [31,70,102], Poisson surface reconstruction [40,41], and neural surface reconstruction [79,82]. To reconstruct texture for the human body, popular approaches include texture mapping or montage [19], deep neural rendering [56], deferred neural rendering [90], and NeRF-like methods [66]. Unfortunately, existing datasets for

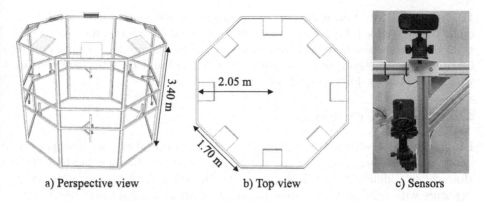

a) Perspective view   b) Top view   c) Sensors

Fig. 2. Hardware setup. a) and b) we build a octagonal prism-shaped framework to accommodate the data collection system. c) sensors used to collect sequential data include ten Azure Kinects and an iPhone 12 Pro Max. Besides, an Artec Eva is used to produce high-resolution static scans of the subjects.

textured human mesh reconstruction typically provide no sequential data [101, 113], which is valuable to the reconstruction of animatable avatars [81,98]. Moreover, many have only a limited number of subjects [2,7,23–25,60,78,107]. In contrast, HuMMan includes diverse subjects with high-resolution body scans and a large amount of dynamic 3D sequences.

3   Hardware Setup

We customize an octagonal prism-shaped multi-layer framework to accommodate calibrated and synchronized sensors. The system is 1.7 m in height and 3.4 m in side length of its octagonal cross-section as illustrated in Fig. 2.

3.1   Sensors

RGB-D Sensors. Azure Kinect is popular with both academia and the industry with a color resolution of 1920×1080, and a depth resolution of 640×576. We deploy ten Kinects to capture multi-view RGB-D sequences. The Kinects are strategically placed to ensure a uniform spacing, and a wide coverage such that any body part of the subject, even in most expressive poses, is visible to at least two sensors. We develop a program that interfaces with Kinect's SDK to obtain a data throughput of 74.4 MB per frame and 2.2 GB per second at 30 FPS before data compression.

Mobile Device. An iPhone 12 Pro Max is included in the sensor suite to allow for the study on a mobile device. Besides the regular color images of resolution 1920×1440, the built-in LiDAR produces depth maps of resolution 256×192. We develop an iOS app upon ARKit to retrieve the data.

High-Resolution Scanner. To supplement our sequential data with high-quality body shape information, a professional handheld 3D scanner, Artec Eva, is used to produce a body scan of resolution up to 0.2 mm and accuracy up to 0.1 mm. A typical scan consists of $300k$ to $500k$ faces and $100k$ to $300k$ vertices, with a 4K (4096×4096) resolution texture map.

3.2   Two-Stage Calibration

Image-Based Calibration. To obtain a coarse calibration, we first perform image-based calibration following the general steps in Zhang's method [110]. However, we highlight that Kinect's active IR depth cameras encounter over-exposure with regular chessboards. Hence, we customize a light absorbent material to cover the black squares of the chessboard pattern. In this way, we acquire reasonably accurate extrinsic calibration for Kinects and iPhones.

Geometry-Based Calibration. Image-based calibration is unfortunately not accurate enough to reconstruct good-quality mesh. Hence, we propose to take advantage of the depth information in a geometry-based calibration stage. We empirically verify that image-based calibration serves as a good initialization for geometry-based calibration. Hence, we randomly place stacked cubes inside the framework. After that, we convert captured depth maps to point clouds and apply multi-way ICP registration [14] to refine the calibration.

3.3   Synchronization

Kinects. As the Azure Kinect implements the Time-of-Flight principle, it actively illuminates the scene multiple times (nine exposures in our system) for depth computation. To avoid interference between individual sensors, we use the synchronization cables to propagate a unified clock in a daisy chain fashion, and reject any image that is 33 ms or above out of synchronization. We highlight that there is only a 1450-μs interval between exposures of 160 μs; our system of ten Kinects reaches the theoretical maximum number.

Kinect-iPhone. Due to hardware limitations, we cannot apply the synchronization cable to the iPhone. We circumvent this challenge by implementing a TCP-based communication protocol that computes an offset between the Kinect clock and the iPhone ARKit clock. As iPhone is recording at 60 FPS, we then use the offset to map the closest iPhone frames to Kinect frames. Our test shows the synchronization error is constrained below 33 ms.

4   Toolchain

To handle the large volume of data, we develop an automatic toolchain to provide annotations such as keypoints and SMPL parameters. Moreover, dynamic sequences of textured mesh are also reconstructed. The pipeline is illustrated in Fig. 3. Note that there is a human inspection stage to reject low-quality data with erroneous annotations.

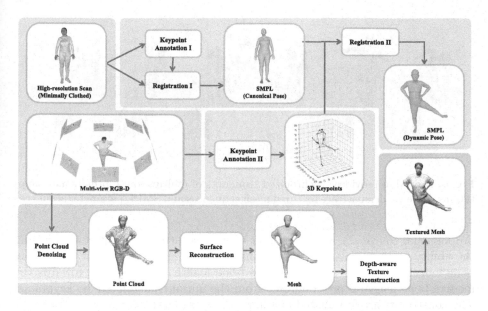

Fig. 3. Our toolchain produces multiple annotation formats such as 3D keypoint sequences, SMPL parameter sequences, and textured mesh sequences

4.1   Keypoint Annotation

There are two stages of keypoint annotation (I and II) in the toolchain. For stage I, virtual cameras are placed around the minimally clothed body scan to render multi-view images. For stage II, the color images from multi-view RGB-D are used. The core ideas of the keypoint annotation are demonstrated below, with the detailed algorithm in the Supplementary Material.

Multi-view 2D Keypoint Detection. We employ the whole-body pose model that includes body, hand and face 2D keypoints $\hat{\mathcal{P}}_{2D} \in \mathbb{R}^{P \times 2}$, where $P = 133$. A large deep learning model HRNet-w48 [88] is used which achieves AP 66.1 and AR 74.3 on COCO whole-body benchmark [34].

3D Keypoint Triangulation. As the camera intrinsic and extrinsic parameters are available, we triangulate 3D keypoints $\mathcal{P}_{3D} \in \mathbb{R}^{P \times 3}$ with the multi-view 2D estimated keypoints $\hat{\mathcal{P}}_{2D}$. However, 2D keypoints from any single view may not be always reliable. Hence, we use the following strategies to improve the quality of 3D keypoints. 1) *Keypoint selection.* To avoid the influence of poor-quality estimated 2D keypoints, we use a threshold τ_k to remove keypoints with a low confidence score. 2) *Camera selection.* As our system consists of ten Kinects, we exploit the redundancy to remove low-quality views. We only keep camera views with reprojection errors that are top-k smallest [38] and no larger than a threshold τ_c. 3) *Smoothness constraint.* Due to inevitable occlusion in the single view, the estimated 2D keypoints often have jitters. To alleviate the issue, we develop a smoothness loss to minimize the difference between consecutive triangulated 3D keypoints. Note that we design the loss weight to be inversely

564   Z. Cai et al.

Fig. 4. HuMMan provides synchronized sequences of multiple data formats and annotations. Here we demonstrate textured mesh sequences and SMPL parameter sequences

proportional to average speed, in order to remove jitters without compromising the ability to capture fast body motions. 4) *Bone length constraint.* As human bone length is constant, the per-frame bone length is constrained towards the median bone length $\mathcal{B}$ pre-computed from the initial triangulated 3D keypoints. The constraints are formulated as Eq. 1:

$$E_{tri} = \lambda_1 \sum_{t=0}^{T-1} \|\mathcal{P}_{3D}(t+1) - \mathcal{P}_{3D}(t)\| + \lambda_2 \sum_{(i,j)\in\mathcal{I}_\mathcal{B}} \|\mathcal{B}_{i,j} - f_\mathcal{B}(\mathcal{P}_{3D}(i,j))\| \quad (1)$$

where $\mathcal{I}_\mathcal{B}$ contains the indices of connected keypoints and $f_\mathcal{B}(\cdot)$ calculates the average bone length of a given 3D keypoint sequence. Note that 3) and 4) are jointly optimized.

2D Keypoint Projection. To obtain high-quality 2D keypoints $\mathcal{P}_{2D} \in \mathbb{R}^{P\times 2}$, we project the triangulated 3D keypoints to image space via calibrated camera parameters. Note that this step is only needed for stage II keypoint annotation.

Keypoint Quality. We use $\mathcal{P}_{2D}$ and $\mathcal{P}_{3D}$ as keypoint annotations for 2D Pose Estimation and 3D Pose Estimation, respectively. To gauge the accuracy of the automatic keypoint annotation pipeline, we manually annotate a subset of data. The average Euclidean distance between annotated 2D keypoints and reprojected 2D keypoints $\mathcal{P}_{2D}$ is 15.13 pixels on the resolution of 1920 × 1080.

4.2   Human Parametric Model Registration

We select SMPL [58] as the human parametric model for its popularity. There are two stages of registration (I and II). Stage I is used to obtain accurate shape parameters from the static high-resolution scan, whereas stage II is used to obtain pose parameters from the dynamic sequence, with shape parameters from stage I. The registration is formulated as an optimization task to obtain SMPL pose parameters $\theta \in \mathbb{R}^{n\times 72}$, shape parameters $\beta \in \mathbb{R}^{n\times 10}$ (stage I only) and translation parameters $t \in \mathbb{R}^{n\times 3}$ where n is the number of frames ($n = 1$ for stage I), with the following energy terms and constraints. We show a sample sequence of SMPL models with reconstructed textured mesh in Fig. 4.

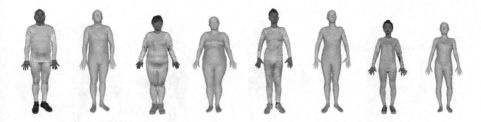

Fig. 5. Examples of SMPL registered on high-resolution static body scans for accurate shape parameters. The subjects are instructed to wear tight clothes for this scan. Note that each subject has another naturally clothed scan

Keypoint Energy. SMPLify [6] estimates camera parameters to leverage 2D keypoint supervision, which may be prone to depth and scale ambiguity. Hence, we develop the keypoint energy on 3D keypoints. For simplicity, we denote P_{3D} as P, the global rigid transformation derived from the SMPL kinematic tree as T, the joint regressor as J. We formulate the energy term (Fig. 5):

$$E_P(\theta, \beta, t) = \frac{1}{|\mathcal{P}|} \sum_i^{|\mathcal{P}|} \|T(J(\beta)_i, \theta), t) - \mathcal{P}_i\| \qquad (2)$$

Surface Energy. To supplement 3D keypoints that do not provide sufficient constraint for shape parameters, we add an additional surface energy term for registration on the high-resolution minimally clothed scans in stage I only. We use bi-directional Chamfer distance to gauge the difference between two mesh surfaces:

$$E_S = \frac{1}{|\mathcal{V}_H|} \sum_{v_H \in \mathcal{V}_H} \min_{v_S \in \mathcal{V}_S} \|v_H - v_S\| + \frac{1}{|\mathcal{V}_S|} \sum_{v_S \in \mathcal{V}_S} \min_{v_H \in \mathcal{V}_H} \|v_H - v_S\| \qquad (3)$$

where $\mathcal{V}_H$ and $\mathcal{V}_S$ are the mesh vertices of the high-resolution scan and SMPL.

Shape Consistency. Unlike existing work [74] that enforces an inter-beta energy term due to the lack of minimally clothed scan of each subject, we obtain accurate shape parameters from the high-resolution scan that allow us to apply constant beta parameters in the registration in stage II.

Full-Body Joint Angle Prior. Joint rotation limitations serve as an important constraint to prevent unnaturally twisted poses. We extend existing work [6,75] that only applies constraints on elbows and knees to all $J = 23$ joints in SMPL. The constraint is formulated as a strong penalty outside the plausible rotation range (with more details included in the Supplementary Material):

$$E_a = \frac{1}{J \times 3} \sum_j^{J \times 3} exp(\max(\theta_i - \theta_i^u, 0) + \max(\theta_i^l - \theta_i, 0)) - 1 \qquad (4)$$

where θ_i^u and θ_i^l are the upper and lower limit of a rotation angle. Note that each joint rotation is converted to three Euler angles which can be interpreted as a series of individual rotations to decouple the original axis-angle representation.

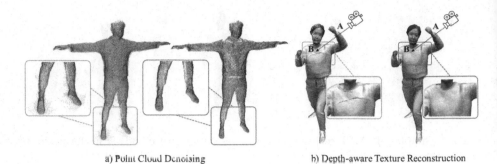

a) Point Cloud Denoising   h) Depth-aware Texture Reconstruction

Fig. 6. Key steps to textured mesh reconstruction. a) Point cloud denoising removes noisy points. b) Depth-aware texture reconstruction prevents texture miss projection artifacts (such as projecting texture at point A to point B) due to misalignment between the actual subject and the reconstructed geometry

4.3   Textured Mesh Reconstruction

Point Cloud Reconstruction and Denoising. We convert depth maps to point clouds and transform them into a world coordinate system with camera extrinsic parameters. However, the depth images captured by Kinect contain noisy pixels, which are prominent at subject boundaries where the depth gradient is large. To solve this issue, we first generate a binary boundary mask through edge finding with Laplacian of Gaussian Filters. Since our cameras have highly overlapped views to supplement points for one another, we apply a more aggressive threshold to remove boundary pixels. After the point cloud is reconstructed from the denoised depth images, we apply Statistical Outlier Removal [26] to further remove sprinkle noises.

Geometry and Depth-Aware Texture Reconstruction. With complete and dense point cloud reconstructed, we apply Poisson Surface Reconstruction with envelope constraints [42] to reconstruct the watertight mesh. However, due to inevitable self-occlusion in complicated poses, interpolation artifacts arise from missing depth information, which leads to a shrunk or a dilated geometry. These artifacts are negligible for geometry reconstruction. However, a prominent artifact appears when projecting a texture onto the mesh even if the inconsistency between the true surface and the reconstructed surface is small. Hence, we extend MVS-texturing [95] to be depth-aware in texture reconstruction. We render the reconstructed mesh back into the camera view and compare the rendered depth map with the original depth map to generate the difference mask. We then mask out all the misalignment regions where the depth difference exceeds a threshold τ_d. The masked regions do not contribute to texture projection. As shown in Fig. 6(b), the depth-aware texture reconstruction is more accurate and visually pleasing.

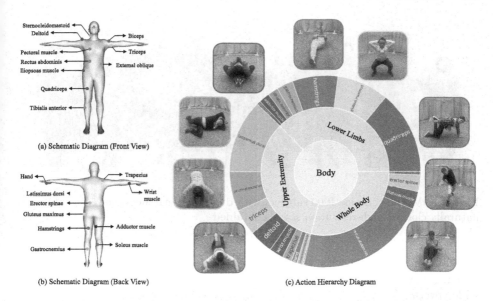

Fig. 7. Schematic diagram of muscles from a) front and b) back views. c) HuMMan categorizes 500 actions hierarchically, first by body parts to achieve *complete* body coverage, then by driving muscles for *unambiguous* action definition

5   Action Set

Understanding human actions is a long-standing computer vision task. In this section, we elaborate on the two principles, following which we design the action set of 500 actions: *completeness* and *unambiguity*. More details are included in the Supplementary Material.

Completeness. We build the action set to cover plausible human movements as much as possible. Compared to the popular 3D action recognition dataset NTU-RGBD-120 [55] whose actions are focused on upper body movements, we employ a hierarchical design to first divide possible actions into upper extremity, lower limbs, and whole-body movements. Such design allows us to achieve a balance between various body parts instead of over-emphasizing a specific group of movements. Note that we define whole body movements to be actions that require multiple body parts to collaborate, including different poses of the body trunk (*e.g.* lying down and sprawling). Figure 7(c) demonstrates the action hierarchy and examples of interesting actions that are vastly diverse.

Unambiguity. Instead of providing a general description of the motions [11,29,39,62,64,67,87], we argue that the action classes should be clearly defined and are easy to identify and reproduce. Inspired by the fact that all human actions are the result of muscular contractions, we propose a *muscle-driven* strategy to systematically design the action set from the perspective of human anatomy. As illustrated in Fig. 7(a)(b), 20 major muscles are identified by professionals in fitness and yoga training, who then put together a list of standard

Fig. 8. HuMMan contains 1000 subjects with diverse appearances. For each subject, a naturally clothed high-resolution scan is obtained

movements associated with these muscles. Moreover, we cross-check with the action definitions from existing datasets [8,11,15,21,35,39,51,55] to ensure a wide coverage.

6 Subjects

HuMMan consists of 1000 subjects with a wide coverage of genders, ages, body shapes (heights, weights), and ethnicity. The subjects are instructed to wear their personal daily clothes to achieve a large collection of natural appearances. We demonstrate examples of high-resolution scans of the subjects in Fig. 8. We include statistics in the Supplementary Material.

7 Experiments

In this section, we evaluate popular methods from various research fields on HuMMan. To constrain the training within a reasonable computation budget, we sample 10% of data and split them into training and testing sets for both Kinects and iPhone. The details are included in the Supplementary Material.

Action Recognition. HuMMan provides action labels and 3D skeletal positions, which can verify its usefulness on 3D action recognition. Specifically, we train popular graph-based methods (STGCN [100] and 2s-AGCN [85]) on HuMMan. Results are shown in

Table 2. Action recognition

Method	Top-1 (%)↑	Top-5 (%)↑
ST-GCN	72.5	94.3
2s-AGCN	74.1	95.4

Table 2. Compared to NTU RGB+D, a large-scale 3D action recognition dataset and a standard benchmark that contains 120 actions [55], HuMMan may be more challenging since 2s-AGCN [85] achieves Top-1 accuracy of 88.9% and 82.9% on NTU RGB+D 60 and 120 respectively, but 74.1% only on HuMMan. The difficulties come from the whole-body coverage design in our action set, instead of

over-emphasis on certain body parts (*e.g.* NTU RGB+D has a large proportion of upper body movements). Moreover, we observe a significant gap between Top-1 and Top-5 accuracy (~30%). We attribute this phenomenon to the fact that there are plenty of *intra-actions* in HuMMan. For example, there are similar variants of push-ups such as quadruped push-ups, kneeling push-ups, and leg push-ups. This challenges the model to pay more attention to the fine-grained differences in these actions. Hence, we find HuMMan would serve as an indicative benchmark for fine-grained action understanding.

3D Keypoint Detection. With the well-annotated 3D keypoints, HuMMan supports 3D keypoint detection. We employ popular 2D-to-3D lifting backbones [63,77] as single-frame and multi-frame baselines on HuMMan. We experiment with different training and test settings to obtain the baseline results in Table 3. First, in-domain training and testing on HuMMan are provided. The values are slightly higher than the same baselines on Human3.6M [29] (on which FCN obtains

Table 3. 3D keypoint detection. PA: PA-MPJPE. Row 1–3: FCN [63]; Row 4–6: Video3D [77]

Train	Test	MPJPE ↓	PA ↓
HuMMan	HuMMan	78.5	46.3
H36M	AIST++	133.9	73.1
HuMMan	AIST++	116.4	67.2
HuMMan	HuMMan	73.1	43.5
H36M	AIST++	128.5	72.0
HuMMan	AIST++	109.2	63.5

MPJPE of 53.4 mm). Second, methods trained on HuMMan tend to generalize better than on Human3.6M. This may be attributed to HuMMan's diverse collection of subjects and actions.

3D Parametric Human Recovery. HuMMan provides SMPL annotations, RGB and RGB-D sequences. Hence, we evaluate HMR [36], not only one of the first deep learning approaches towards 3D parametric human recovery but a fundamental component for follow-up works [43,45], to represent image-

Table 4. 3D parametric human recovery. Image- and point cloud-based methods are evaluated

Method	MPJPE ↓	PA ↓
HMR	54.78	36.14
VoteHMR	144.99	106.32

based methods. In addition, we employ VoteHMR [54], a recent work that takes point clouds as the input. In Table 4, we find that HMR has achieved low MPJPE and PA-MPJPE, which may be attributed to the clearly defined action set and the training set already includes all action classes. However, VoteHMR is not performing well. We argue that existing point cloud-based methods [33,54,97] rely heavily on synthetic data for training and evaluation, whereas HuMMan provides genuine point clouds from commercial RGB-D sensors that remain challenging.

Textured Mesh Reconstruction. We gauge mesh geometry reconstruction quality of PIFu, PIFuHD, and Function4D (F4D) in Table 5 with Chamfer distance (CD) as the metric. Note that benefiting from the multi-

Table 5. Geometry reconstruction

Method	PIFu	PIFuHD	F4D
CD (10^{-2} m)	7.92	7.73	1.80

modality signals, HuMMan supports a wide range of surface reconstruction methods that leverage various input types like PIFu [82] (RGB-only), 3D Self-Portrait [52] (single-view RGBD video), and CON [79] (multi-view depth point cloud).

Mobile Device. It is under-explored that if model trained with the regular device is readily transferable to the mobile device. In Table 6, we study the performance gaps across devices. For the image-based method, we find that there exists a considerable domain gap across devices, despite that they have similar resolutions. Moreover, for the point cloud-based method, the domain gap is much more significant as the mobile device tends to have much sparser

Table 6. Mobile device. The models are trained with different training sets, and evaluated on HuMMan iPhone test set. Kin.: Kinect training set. iPh.: iPhone training set.

Method	Kin.	iPh.	MPJPE ↓	PA ↓
HMR	✓	–	97.81	52.74
HMR	–	✓	72.62	41.86
VoteHMR	✓	–	255.71	162.00
VoteHMR	–	✓	83.18	01.09

point clouds as a result of lower depth map resolution. Hence, it remains a challenging problem to transfer knowledge across devices, especially for point cloud-based methods.

8 Discussion

We present HuMMan, a large-scale 4D human dataset that features multi-modal data and annotations, inclusion of mobile device, a comprehensive action set, and support for multiple tasks. Our experiments point out interesting directions that await future research, such as fine-grained action recognition, point cloud-based parametric human estimation, dynamic mesh sequence reconstruction, transferring knowledge across devices, and potentially, multi-task joint training. We hope HuMMan would facilitate the development of better algorithms for sensing and modeling humans.

Acknowledgements. This work is supported by NTU NAP, MOE AcRF Tier 2 (T2EP20221-0033), NSFC No. 62171255, and under the RIE2020 Industry Alignment Fund - Industry Collaboration Projects (IAF-ICP) Funding Initiative, as well as cash and in-kind contribution from the industry partner(s).

References

1. Akhter, I., Black, M.J.: Pose-conditioned joint angle limits for 3D human pose reconstruction. In: Proceedings of the IEEE Conference on Computer Vision and Pattern Recognition, pp. 1446–1455 (2015)
2. Alldieck, T., Magnor, M., Xu, W., Theobalt, C., Pons-Moll, G.: Video based reconstruction of 3D people models. In: Proceedings of the IEEE Conference on Computer Vision and Pattern Recognition, pp. 8387–8397 (2018)
3. Andriluka, M., et al.: PoseTrack: a benchmark for human pose estimation and tracking. In: Proceedings of the IEEE Conference on Computer Vision and Pattern Recognition, pp. 5167–5176 (2018)
4. Andriluka, M., Pishchulin, L., Gehler, P., Schiele, B.: 2D human pose estimation: new benchmark and state of the art analysis. In: Proceedings of the IEEE Conference on Computer Vision and Pattern Recognition, pp. 3686–3693 (2014)

5. Bhatnagar, B.L., Sminchisescu, C., Theobalt, C., Pons-Moll, G.: Combining implicit function learning and parametric models for 3D human reconstruction. In: Vedaldi, A., Bischof, H., Brox, T., Frahm, J.-M. (eds.) ECCV 2020. LNCS, vol. 12347, pp. 311–329. Springer, Cham (2020). https://doi.org/10.1007/978-3-030-58536-5_19

6. Bogo, F., Kanazawa, A., Lassner, C., Gehler, P., Romero, J., Black, M.J.: Keep it SMPL: automatic estimation of 3D human pose and shape from a single image. In: Leibe, B., Matas, J., Sebe, N., Welling, M. (eds.) ECCV 2016. LNCS, vol. 9909, pp. 561–578. Springer, Cham (2016). https://doi.org/10.1007/978-3-319-46454-1_34

7. Bogo, F., Romero, J., Pons-Moll, G., Black, M.J.: Dynamic FAUST: registering human bodies in motion. In: Proceedings of the IEEE Conference on Computer Vision and Pattern Recognition, pp. 6233–6242 (2017)

8. Caba Heilbron, F., Escorcia, V., Ghanem, B., Carlos Niebles, J.: ActivityNet: a large-scale video benchmark for human activity understanding. In: Proceedings of the IEEE Conference on Computer Vision and Pattern Recognition, pp. 961–970 (2015)

9. Cai, Z., et al.: Playing for 3D human recovery. arXiv preprint arXiv:2110.07588 (2021)

10. Cao, Z., Gao, H., Mangalam, K., Cai, Q.-Z., Vo, M., Malik, J.: Long-term human motion prediction with scene context. In: Vedaldi, A., Bischof, H., Brox, T., Frahm, J.-M. (eds.) ECCV 2020. LNCS, vol. 12346, pp. 387–404. Springer, Cham (2020). https://doi.org/10.1007/978-3-030-58452-8_23

11. Carreira, J., Noland, E., Hillier, C., Zisserman, A.: A short note on the kinetics-700 human action dataset. arXiv preprint arXiv:1907.06987 (2019)

12. Chen, Y., Wang, Z., Peng, Y., Zhang, Z., Yu, G.G., Sun, J.: Cascaded pyramid network for multi-person pose estimation. In: Proceedings of the IEEE Conference on Computer Vision and Pattern Recognition, pp. 7103–7112 (2018)

13. Choi, H., Moon, G., Lee, K.M.: Beyond static features for temporally consistent 3D human pose and shape from a video. In: Conference on Computer Vision and Pattern Recognition (CVPR) (2021)

14. Choi, S., Zhou, Q.Y., Koltun, V.: Robust reconstruction of indoor scenes. In: Proceedings of the IEEE Conference on Computer Vision and Pattern Recognition, pp. 5556–5565 (2015)

15. Chung, J., Wuu, C.H., Yang, H.R., Tai, Y.W., Tang, C.K.: HAA500: human-centric atomic action dataset with curated videos. In: Proceedings of the IEEE/CVF International Conference on Computer Vision, pp. 13465–13474 (2021)

16. Feichtenhofer, C.: X3D: expanding architectures for efficient video recognition. In: Proceedings of the IEEE/CVF Conference on Computer Vision and Pattern Recognition, pp. 203–213 (2020)

17. Feichtenhofer, C., Fan, H., Malik, J., He, K.: SlowFast networks for video recognition. In: Proceedings of the IEEE/CVF International Conference on Computer Vision, pp. 6202–6211 (2019)

18. Furukawa, Y., Ponce, J.: Accurate, dense, and robust multiview stereopsis. IEEE Trans. Pattern Anal. Mach. Intell. 32(8), 1362–1376 (2010). https://doi.org/10.1109/TPAMI.2009.161

19. Gal, R., Wexler, Y., Ofek, E., Hoppe, H., Cohen-Or, D.: Seamless montage for texturing models. In: Computer Graphics Forum, vol. 29, no. 2, pp. 479–486 (2010). https://doi.org/10.1111/j.1467-8659.2009.01617.x. https://onlinelibrary.wiley.com/doi/abs/10.1111/j.1467-8659.2009.01617.x

20. Georgakis, G., Li, R., Karanam, S., Chen, T., Košecká, J., Wu, Z.: Hierarchical kinematic human mesh recovery. In: Vedaldi, A., Bischof, H., Brox, T., Frahm, J.-M. (eds.) ECCV 2020. LNCS, vol. 12362, pp. 768–784. Springer, Cham (2020). https://doi.org/10.1007/978-3-030-58520-4_45

21. Gu, C., et al.: AVA: a video dataset of spatio-temporally localized atomic visual actions. In: Proceedings of the IEEE Conference on Computer Vision and Pattern Recognition, pp. 6047–6056 (2018)

22. Guler, R.A., Kokkinos, I.: HoloPose: holistic 3D human reconstruction in-the-wild. In: Proceedings of the IEEE/CVF Conference on Computer Vision and Pattern Recognition, pp. 10884–10894 (2019)

23. Habermann, M., Liu, L., Xu, W., Zollhoefer, M., Pons-Moll, G., Theobalt, C.: Real-time deep dynamic characters. ACM Trans. Graph. (TOG) **40**(4), 1–16 (2021)

24. Habermann, M., Xu, W., Zollhoefer, M., Pons-Moll, G., Theobalt, C.: LiveCap: real-time human performance capture from monocular video. ACM Trans. Graph. (TOG) **38**(2), 1–17 (2019)

25. Habermann, M., Xu, W., Zollhofer, M., Pons-Moll, G., Theobalt, C.: DeepCap: monocular human performance capture using weak supervision. In: Proceedings of the IEEE/CVF Conference on Computer Vision and Pattern Recognition, pp. 5052–5063 (2020)

26. Hodge, V., Austin, J.: A survey of outlier detection methodologies. Artif. Intell. Rev. **22**(2), 85–126 (2004). https://doi.org/10.1023/B:AIRE.0000045502.10941.a9

27. Hu, J.F., Zheng, W.S., Lai, J., Zhang, J.: Jointly learning heterogeneous features for RGB-D activity recognition. In: Proceedings of the IEEE Conference on Computer Vision and Pattern Recognition, pp. 5344–5352 (2015)

28. Huang, F., Zeng, A., Liu, M., Lai, Q., Xu, Q.: DeepFuse: an IMU-aware network for real-time 3D human pose estimation from multi-view image. arXiv preprint arXiv:1912.04071 (2019)

29. Ionescu, C., Papava, D., Olaru, V., Sminchisescu, C.: Human3.6M: large scale datasets and predictive methods for 3D human sensing in natural environments. IEEE Trans. Pattern Anal. Mach. Intell. **36**(7), 1325–1339 (2013)

30. Iskakov, K., Burkov, E., Lempitsky, V., Malkov, Y.: Learnable triangulation of human pose. In: Proceedings of the IEEE International Conference on Computer Vision, pp. 7718–7727 (2019)

31. Izadi, S., et al.: KinectFusion: real-time 3D reconstruction and interaction using a moving depth camera. In: Proceedings of the 24th Annual ACM Symposium on User Interface Software and Technology, pp. 559–568 (2011)

32. Jhuang, H., Gall, J., Zuffi, S., Schmid, C., Black, M.J.: Towards understanding action recognition. In: Proceedings of the IEEE International Conference on Computer Vision, pp. 3192–3199 (2013)

33. Jiang, H., Cai, J., Zheng, J.: Skeleton-aware 3D human shape reconstruction from point clouds. In: Proceedings of the IEEE/CVF International Conference on Computer Vision, pp. 5431–5441 (2019)

34. Jin, S., et al.: Whole-body human pose estimation in the wild. In: Vedaldi, A., Bischof, H., Brox, T., Frahm, J.-M. (eds.) ECCV 2020. LNCS, vol. 12354, pp. 196–214. Springer, Cham (2020). https://doi.org/10.1007/978-3-030-58545-7_12

35. Joo, H., et al.: Panoptic studio: a massively multiview system for social motion capture. In: Proceedings of the IEEE International Conference on Computer Vision, pp. 3334–3342 (2015)

36. Kanazawa, A., Black, M.J., Jacobs, D.W., Malik, J.: End-to-end recovery of human shape and pose. In: Proceedings of the IEEE Conference on Computer Vision and Pattern Recognition, pp. 7122–7131 (2018)

37. Kanazawa, A., Zhang, J.Y., Felsen, P., Malik, J.: Learning 3D human dynamics from video. In: Proceedings of the IEEE/CVF Conference on Computer Vision and Pattern Recognition, pp. 5614–5623 (2019)

38. Karashchuk, P., et al.: Anipose: a toolkit for robust markerless 3D pose estimation. Cell Rep. **36**(13), 109730 (2021)

39. Karpathy, A., Toderici, G., Shetty, S., Leung, T., Sukthankar, R., Fei-Fei, L.: Large-scale video classification with convolutional neural networks. In: Proceedings of the IEEE Conference on Computer Vision and Pattern Recognition, pp. 1725–1732 (2014)

40. Kazhdan, M., Hoppe, H.: Screened Poisson surface reconstruction. ACM Trans. Graph. **32**(3) (2013). https://doi.org/10.1145/2487228.2487237

41. Kazhdan, M., Chuang, M., Rusinkiewicz, S., Hoppe, H.: Poisson surface reconstruction with envelope constraints. In: Computer Graphics Forum (Proceedings of the Symposium on Geometry Processing), vol. 39, no. 5, July 2020

42. Kazhdan, M., Chuang, M., Rusinkiewicz, S., Hoppe, H.: Poisson surface reconstruction with envelope constraints. In: Computer Graphics Forum, vol. 39, pp. 173–182. Wiley Online Library (2020)

43. Kocabas, M., Athanasiou, N., Black, M.J.: VIBE: video inference for human body pose and shape estimation. In: Proceedings of the IEEE/CVF Conference on Computer Vision and Pattern Recognition, pp. 5253–5263 (2020)

44. Kocabas, M., Huang, C.H.P., Hilliges, O., Black, M.J.: PARE: part attention regressor for 3D human body estimation. arXiv preprint arXiv:2104.08527 (2021)

45. Kolotouros, N., Pavlakos, G., Black, M.J., Daniilidis, K.: Learning to reconstruct 3D human pose and shape via model-fitting in the loop. In: Proceedings of the IEEE/CVF International Conference on Computer Vision, pp. 2252–2261 (2019)

46. Kuehne, H., Jhuang, H., Garrote, E., Poggio, T., Serre, T.: HMDB: a large video database for human motion recognition. In: 2011 International Conference on Computer Vision, pp. 2556–2563. IEEE (2011)

47. Li, J., et al.: Human pose regression with residual log-likelihood estimation. In: ICCV (2021)

48. Li, J., Xu, C., Chen, Z., Bian, S., Yang, L., Lu, C.: HybrIK: a hybrid analytical-neural inverse kinematics solution for 3D human pose and shape estimation. In: CVPR, pp. 3383–3393. Computer Vision Foundation/IEEE (2021)

49. Li, R., Yang, S., Ross, D.A., Kanazawa, A.: AI choreographer: music conditioned 3D dance generation with AIST++. In: Proceedings of the IEEE/CVF International Conference on Computer Vision, pp. 13401–13412 (2021)

50. Li, W., Zhang, Z., Liu, Z.: Action recognition based on a bag of 3D points. In: 2010 IEEE Computer Society Conference on Computer Vision and Pattern Recognition-Workshops, pp. 9–14. IEEE (2010)

51. Li, Y.L., et al.: HAKE: a knowledge engine foundation for human activity understanding (2022)

52. Li, Z., Yu, T., Zheng, Z., Liu, Y.: Robust and accurate 3D self-portraits in seconds. IEEE Trans. Pattern Anal. Mach. Intell. 1 (2021). https://doi.org/10.1109/TPAMI.2021.3113164

53. Lin, T.-Y., et al.: Microsoft COCO: common objects in context. In: Fleet, D., Pajdla, T., Schiele, B., Tuytelaars, T. (eds.) ECCV 2014. LNCS, vol. 8693, pp. 740–755. Springer, Cham (2014). https://doi.org/10.1007/978-3-319-10602-1_48

54. Liu, G., Rong, Y., Sheng, L.: VoteHMR: occlusion-aware voting network for robust 3D human mesh recovery from partial point clouds. In: Proceedings of the 29th ACM International Conference on Multimedia, pp. 955–964 (2021)
55. Liu, J., Shahroudy, A., Perez, M., Wang, G., Duan, L.Y., Kot, A.C.: NTU RGB+D 120: a large-scale benchmark for 3D human activity understanding. IEEE Trans. Pattern Anal. Mach. Intell. **42**(10), 2684–2701 (2019)
56. Lombardi, S., Saragih, J., Simon, T., Sheikh, Y.: Deep appearance models for face rendering **37**(4) (2018). https://doi.org/10.1145/3197517.3201401
57. Loper, M., Mahmood, N., Black, M.J.: MoSh: motion and shape capture from sparse markers. ACM Trans. Graph. (TOG) **33**(6), 1–13 (2014)
58. Loper, M., Mahmood, N., Romero, J., Pons-Moll, G., Black, M.J.: SMPL: a skinned multi-person linear model. ACM Trans. Graph. (TOG) **34**(6), 1–16 (2015)
59. Luo, Z., Golestaneh, S.A., Kitani, K.M.: 3D human motion estimation via motion compression and refinement. In: Proceedings of the Asian Conference on Computer Vision (2020)
60. Ma, Q., et al.: Learning to dress 3D people in generative clothing. In: Proceedings of the IEEE/CVF Conference on Computer Vision and Pattern Recognition, pp. 6469–6478 (2020)
61. Mahmood, N., Ghorbani, N., Troje, N.F., Pons-Moll, G., Black, M.J.: AMASS: archive of motion capture as surface shapes. In: Proceedings of the IEEE/CVF International Conference on Computer Vision, pp. 5442–5451 (2019)
62. von Marcard, T., Henschel, R., Black, M.J., Rosenhahn, B., Pons-Moll, G.: Recovering accurate 3D human pose in the wild using IMUs and a moving camera. In: Ferrari, V., Hebert, M., Sminchisescu, C., Weiss, Y. (eds.) ECCV 2018. LNCS, vol. 11214, pp. 614–631. Springer, Cham (2018). https://doi.org/10.1007/978-3-030-01249-6_37
63. Martinez, J., Hossain, R., Romero, J., Little, J.J.: A simple yet effective baseline for 3D human pose estimation. In: Proceedings of the IEEE International Conference on Computer Vision, pp. 2640–2649 (2017)
64. Mehta, D., et al.: Monocular 3D human pose estimation in the wild using improved CNN supervision. In: 2017 International Conference on 3D Vision (3DV), pp. 506–516. IEEE (2017)
65. Mehta, D., et al.: XNect: real-time multi-person 3D motion capture with a single RGB camera. ACM Trans. Graph. (TOG) **39**(4), 82-1 (2020)
66. Mildenhall, B., Srinivasan, P.P., Tancik, M., Barron, J.T., Ramamoorthi, R., Ng, R.: NeRF: representing scenes as neural radiance fields for view synthesis. In: Vedaldi, A., Bischof, H., Brox, T., Frahm, J.-M. (eds.) ECCV 2020. LNCS, vol. 12346, pp. 405–421. Springer, Cham (2020). https://doi.org/10.1007/978-3-030-58452-8_24
67. Monfort, M., et al.: Moments in time dataset: one million videos for event understanding. IEEE Trans. Pattern Anal. Mach. Intell. **42**(2), 502–508 (2019)
68. Moon, G., Lee, K.M.: I2L-MeshNet: image-to-lixel prediction network for accurate 3D human pose and mesh estimation from a single RGB image. In: Vedaldi, A., Bischof, H., Brox, T., Frahm, J.-M. (eds.) ECCV 2020. LNCS, vol. 12352, pp. 752–768. Springer, Cham (2020). https://doi.org/10.1007/978-3-030-58571-6_44
69. Muller, L., Osman, A.A., Tang, S., Huang, C.H.P., Black, M.J.: On self-contact and human pose. In: Proceedings of the IEEE/CVF Conference on Computer Vision and Pattern Recognition, pp. 9990–9999 (2021)
70. Newcombe, R.A., Fox, D., Seitz, S.M.: DynamicFusion: reconstruction and tracking of non-rigid scenes in real-time. In: Proceedings of the IEEE Conference on Computer Vision and Pattern Recognition, pp. 343–352 (2015)

71. Newell, A., Yang, K., Deng, J.: Stacked hourglass networks for human pose esti-mation. In: Leibe, B., Matas, J., Sebe, N., Welling, M. (eds.) ECCV 2016. LNCS, vol. 9912, pp. 483–499. Springer, Cham (2016). https://doi.org/10.1007/978-3-319-46484-8_29

72. Omran, M., Lassner, C., Pons-Moll, G., Gehler, P., Schiele, B.: Neural body fit-ting: unifying deep learning and model based human pose and shape estimation. In: 2018 International Conference on 3D Vision (3DV), pp. 484–494. IEEE (2018)

73. Osman, A.A.A., Bolkart, T., Black, M.J.: STAR: sparse trained articulated human body regressor. In: Vedaldi, A., Bischof, H., Brox, T., Frahm, J.-M. (eds.) ECCV 2020. LNCS, vol. 12351, pp. 598–613. Springer, Cham (2020). https://doi.org/10.1007/978-3-030-58539-6_36

74. Patel, P., Huang, C.H.P., Tesch, J., Hoffmann, D.T., Tripathi, S., Black, M.J.: AGORA: avatars in geography optimized for regression analysis. In: Proceedings of the IEEE/CVF Conference on Computer Vision and Pattern Recognition, pp. 13468–13478 (2021)

75. Pavlakos, G., et al.: Expressive body capture: 3D hands, face, and body from a single image. In: Proceedings of the IEEE/CVF Conference on Computer Vision and Pattern Recognition, pp. 10975–10985 (2019)

76. Pavlakos, G., Zhu, L., Zhou, X., Daniilidis, K.: Learning to estimate 3D human pose and shape from a single color image. In: Proceedings of the IEEE Conference on Computer Vision and Pattern Recognition, pp. 459–468 (2018)

77. Pavllo, D., Feichtenhofer, C., Grangier, D., Auli, M.: 3D human pose estimation in video with temporal convolutions and semi-supervised training. In: Proceedings of the IEEE Conference on Computer Vision and Pattern Recognition, pp. 7753–7762 (2019)

78. Peng, S., et al.: Neural body: implicit neural representations with structured latent codes for novel view synthesis of dynamic humans. In: CVPR (2021)

79. Peng, S., Niemeyer, M., Mescheder, L., Pollefeys, M., Geiger, A.: Convolutional occupancy networks. In: Vedaldi, A., Bischof, H., Brox, T., Frahm, J.-M. (eds.) ECCV 2020. LNCS, vol. 12348, pp. 523–540. Springer, Cham (2020). https://doi.org/10.1007/978-3-030-58580-8_31

80. Qiu, H., Wang, C., Wang, J., Wang, N., Zeng, W.: Cross view fusion for 3D human pose estimation. In: Proceedings of the IEEE International Conference on Computer Vision, pp. 4342–4351 (2019)

81. Raj, A., Tanke, J., Hays, J., Vo, M., Stoll, C., Lassner, C.: ANR-articulated neural rendering for virtual avatars. arXiv:2012.12890 (2020)

82. Saito, S., Huang, Z., Natsume, R., Morishima, S., Kanazawa, A., Li, H.: PIFu: pixel-aligned implicit function for high-resolution clothed human digitization. In: Proceedings of the IEEE International Conference on Computer Vision, pp. 2304–2314 (2019)

83. Shahroudy, A., Liu, J., Ng, T.T., Wang, G.: NTU RGB+D: a large scale dataset for 3D human activity analysis. In: Proceedings of the IEEE Conference on Com-puter Vision and Pattern Recognition, pp. 1010–1019 (2016)

84. Shao, D., Zhao, Y., Dai, B., Lin, D.: FineGym: a hierarchical video dataset for fine-grained action understanding. In: Proceedings of the IEEE/CVF Conference on Computer Vision and Pattern Recognition, pp. 2616–2625 (2020)

85. Shi, L., Zhang, Y., Cheng, J., Lu, H.: Skeleton-based action recognition with multi-stream adaptive graph convolutional networks. arXiv preprint arXiv:1912.06971 (2019)

86. Shi, L., Zhang, Y., Cheng, J., Lu, H.: Skeleton-based action recognition with multi-stream adaptive graph convolutional networks. IEEE Trans. Image Process. **29**, 9532–9545 (2020)
87. Soomro, K., Zamir, A.R., Shah, M.: UCF101: a dataset of 101 human actions classes from videos in the wild. arXiv preprint arXiv:1212.0402 (2012)
88. Sun, K., Xiao, B., Liu, D., Wang, J.: Deep high-resolution representation learning for human pose estimation. In: Proceedings of the IEEE/CVF Conference on Computer Vision and Pattern Recognition, pp. 5693–5703 (2019)
89. Sun, Y., Ye, Y., Liu, W., Gao, W., Fu, Y., Mei, T.: Human mesh recovery from monocular images via a skeleton-disentangled representation. In: Proceedings of the IEEE/CVF International Conference on Computer Vision, pp. 5349–5358 (2019)
90. Thies, J., Zollhöfer, M., Nießner, M.: Deferred neural rendering: image synthesis using neural textures. ACM Trans. Graph. **38**(4) (2019). https://doi.org/10.1145/3306346.3323035
91. Tran, D., Wang, H., Torresani, L., Feiszli, M.: Video classification with channel-separated convolutional networks. In: Proceedings of the IEEE/CVF International Conference on Computer Vision, pp. 5552–5561 (2019)
92. Tran, D., Wang, H., Torresani, L., Ray, J., LeCun, Y., Paluri, M.: A closer look at spatiotemporal convolutions for action recognition. In: Proceedings of the IEEE Conference on Computer Vision and Pattern Recognition, pp. 6450–6459 (2018)
93. Trivedi, N., Thatipelli, A., Sarvadevabhatla, R.K.: NTU-X: an enhanced large-scale dataset for improving pose-based recognition of subtle human actions. arXiv preprint arXiv:2101.11529 (2021)
94. Trumble, M., Gilbert, A., Malleson, C., Hilton, A., Collomosse, J.P.: Total capture: 3D human pose estimation fusing video and inertial sensors. In: BMVC, vol. 2, pp. 1–13 (2017)
95. Waechter, M., Moehrle, N., Goesele, M.: Let there be color! Large-scale texturing of 3D reconstructions. In: Fleet, D., Pajdla, T., Schiele, B., Tuytelaars, T. (eds.) ECCV 2014. LNCS, vol. 8693, pp. 836–850. Springer, Cham (2014). https://doi.org/10.1007/978-3-319-10602-1_54
96. Wang, J., Nie, X., Xia, Y., Wu, Y., Zhu, S.C.: Cross-view action modeling, learning and recognition. In: Proceedings of the IEEE Conference on Computer Vision and Pattern Recognition, pp. 2649–2656 (2014)
97. Wang, S., Geiger, A., Tang, S.: Locally aware piecewise transformation fields for 3D human mesh registration. In: Proceedings of the IEEE/CVF Conference on Computer Vision and Pattern Recognition, pp. 7639–7648 (2021)
98. Xiang, D., et al.: Modeling clothing as a separate layer for an animatable human avatar. ACM Trans. Graph. **40**(6) (2021). https://doi.org/10.1145/3478513.3480545
99. Xu, H., Bazavan, E.G., Zanfir, A., Freeman, W.T., Sukthankar, R., Sminchisescu, C.: GHUM & GHUML: generative 3D human shape and articulated pose models. In: Proceedings of the IEEE/CVF Conference on Computer Vision and Pattern Recognition, pp. 6184–6193 (2020)
100. Yan, S., Xiong, Y., Lin, D.: Spatial temporal graph convolutional networks for skeleton-based action recognition. arXiv preprint arXiv:1801.07455 (2018)
101. Yu, T., Zheng, Z., Guo, K., Liu, P., Dai, Q., Liu, Y.: Function4D: real-time human volumetric capture from very sparse consumer RGBD sensors. In: IEEE Conference on Computer Vision and Pattern Recognition (CVPR 2021), June 2021

102. Yu, T., et al.: DoubleFusion: real-time capture of human performances with inner body shapes from a single depth sensor. In: IEEE Conference on Computer Vision and Pattern Recognition (CVPR), Salt Lake City, pp. 7287–7296. IEEE, June 2018

103. Yu, Z., et al.: HUMBI: a large multiview dataset of human body expressions. In: 2020 IEEE/CVF Conference on Computer Vision and Pattern Recognition (CVPR), pp. 2987–2997 (2020)

104. Zeng, A., Sun, X., Huang, F., Liu, M., Xu, Q., Lin, S.: SRNet: improving generalization in 3D human pose estimation with a split-and-recombine approach. In: Vedaldi, A., Bischof, H., Brox, T., Frahm, J.-M. (eds.) ECCV 2020. LNCS, vol. 12359, pp. 507–523. Springer, Cham (2020). https://doi.org/10.1007/978-3-030-58568-6_30

105. Zeng, A., Sun, X., Yang, L., Zhao, N., Liu, M., Xu, Q.: Learning skeletal graph neural networks for hard 3D pose estimation. In: Proceedings of the IEEE International Conference on Computer Vision (2021)

106. Zeng, A., Yang, L., Ju, X., Li, J., Wang, J., Xu, Q.: SmoothNet: a plug-and-play network for refining human poses in videos. arXiv preprint arXiv:2112.13715 (2021)

107. Zhang, C., Pujades, S., Black, M.J., Pons-Moll, G.: Detailed, accurate, human shape estimation from clothed 3D scan sequences. In: Proceedings of the IEEE Conference on Computer Vision and Pattern Recognition, pp. 4191–4200 (2017)

108. Zhang, W., Zhu, M., Derpanis, K.G.: From actemes to action: a strongly-supervised representation for detailed action understanding. In: Proceedings of the IEEE International Conference on Computer Vision, pp. 2248–2255 (2013)

109. Zhang, Y., Li, Z., An, L., Li, M., Yu, T., Liu, Y.: Lightweight multi-person total motion capture using sparse multi-view cameras. In: Proceedings of the IEEE/CVF International Conference on Computer Vision (ICCV), pp. 5560–5569, October 2021

110. Zhang, Z.: A flexible new technique for camera calibration. IEEE Trans. Pattern Anal. Mach. Intell. **22**(11), 1330–1334 (2000)

111. Zhao, H., Torralba, A., Torresani, L., Yan, Z.: HACS: human action clips and segments dataset for recognition and temporal localization. In: Proceedings of the IEEE/CVF International Conference on Computer Vision, pp. 8668–8678 (2019)

112. Zhao, L., Peng, X., Tian, Y., Kapadia, M., Metaxas, D.N.: Semantic graph convolutional networks for 3D human pose regression. In: Proceedings of the IEEE Conference on Computer Vision and Pattern Recognition, pp. 3425–3435 (2019)

113. Zheng, Z., Yu, T., Wei, Y., Dai, Q., Liu, Y.: DeepHuman: 3D human reconstruction from a single image. In: The IEEE International Conference on Computer Vision (ICCV), October 2019

DVS-Voltmeter: Stochastic Process-Based Event Simulator for Dynamic Vision Sensors

Songnan Lin[1], Ye Ma[2], Zhenhua Guo[3], and Bihan Wen[1]($\boxtimes$)

[1] Nanyang Technological University, 50 Nanyang Ave, Singapore, Singapore
bihan.wen@ntu.edu.sg
[2] McGill University, Montreal, Canada
[3] Alibaba Group, Hangzhou, China
https://github.com/Lynn0306/DVS-Voltmeter

Abstract. Recent advances in deep learning for event-driven applications with dynamic vision sensors (DVS) primarily rely on training over simulated data. However, most simulators ignore various physics-based characteristics of real DVS, such as the fidelity of event timestamps and comprehensive noise effects. We propose an event simulator, dubbed DVS-Voltmeter, to enable high-performance deep networks for DVS applications. DVS-Voltmeter incorporates the fundamental principle of physics - (1) voltage variations in a DVS circuit, (2) randomness caused by photon reception, and (3) noise effects caused by temperature and parasitic photocurrent - into a stochastic process. With the novel insight into the sensor design and physics, DVS-Voltmeter generates more realistic events, given high frame-rate videos. Qualitative and quantitative experiments show that the simulated events resemble real data. The evaluation on two tasks, *i.e.*, semantic segmentation and intensity-image reconstruction, indicates that neural networks trained with DVS-Voltmeter generalize favorably on real events against state-of-the-art simulators.

Keywords: Event camera · Dataset · Simulation

1 Introduction

Dynamic Vision Sensors (DVS) [17] and related sensors are novel biologically-inspired cameras that mimic human visual perceptual systems. Unlike conventional cameras capturing intensity frames at a fixed rate, DVS respond to brightness changes in the scene asynchronously and independently for every pixel. Once a brightness change exceeds a preset threshold, a DVS triggers an event recording its spatiotemporal coordinate and polarity (sign) of the change. And thus, DVS are endowed with low power consumption, high temporal resolution, and

---

S. Lin and Y. Ma—Equal contribution.

Supplementary Information The online version contains supplementary material available at https://doi.org/10.1007/978-3-031-20071-7_34.

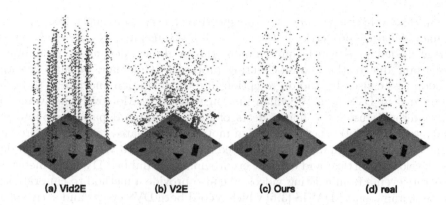

Fig. 1. Visualization of event data and the existing event generation model. (a)–(c) Synthetic events from Vid2E [11], V2E [6], and the proposed DVS-Voltmeter, respectively. (d) Real events. The color pair (red, blue) represents their polarity (1, −1) throughout this paper. Our simulator integrates circuit properties of DVS in a unified stochastic process and can provide more realistic events. (Color figure online)

high dynamic range, which attract much attention [9] for challenging scenarios for conventional cameras, such as low latency [24], high-speed motion [12,19], and broad illumination range [27]. Recent works propose to apply deep learning models for event-based vision applications, which have achieved superior results. However, compared to conventional camera images, DVS data are much less accessible and more difficult to obtain. Thus, most of the deep algorithms for event-based applications primarily rely on simulated training data.

DVS simulators utilize the brightness changes calculated from video datasets to simulate event datasets. Existing DVS simulators are like black boxes, modeling the relationship between the brightness changes and the event amount within adjacent frames rather than the attribute changes in the DVS circuit. For example, prior works [16,20] adopt a simple model to determine the event amount by counting the predefined triggering threshold given brightness changes. As they do not consider noise effects, prototyping on simulated data transfers more difficultly to real data. Some attempts have been made to incorporate noises into the simple model. Based on the observation that the triggering threshold is not constant [17], ESIM [23] and Vid2E [11] replace the threshold with Gaussian-distributed one. As shown in Fig. 1(a), the threshold only varies spatially rather than spatiotemporally, resulting in an apparent artificial pattern with rare noises. Furthermore, V2E [6] incorporates shot noises caused by photon counting into the event model. It randomly adds a certain number of temporal-uniformly distributed noises, which is inconsistent with the distribution of the real ones (see Fig. 1(b)(d)). Besides, all the algorithms mentioned above adopt linear interpolation to determine the timestamp of events after calculating the event amount between two consecutive frames, resulting in equal-spacing distribution. This simple timestamp sampling strategy inevitably causes overfitting in neural networks and makes them less effective on real data.

In this paper, we provide a new perspective on event simulation from the fundamental voltage properties in the circuit of DVS. Inspired by the conventional-image modeling [7] which approximates the brightness-dependent randomness essentially due to the photon-counting process as Gaussian, we also take the randomness caused by photon reception into consideration and model the voltage signal in DVS as a Brownian motion with drift. Moreover, motivated by [22] which discusses the noise effects of temperature and parasitic photocurrent, we further introduce a Brownian motion term related to temperature and light brightness to simulate noises. Based on the proposed voltage signal model, we develop a practical and efficient event simulator, dubbed DVS-Voltmeter, to generate events from existing videos. We also provide a method to calibrate the model parameters of DAVIS [3,5] which record both DVS events and active pixel sensor (APS) intensity frames. Unlike existing simulators generating events in uniform intervals, the proposed DVS-Voltmeter hinges on the stochastic process, and thus it outputs events at random timestamps. Moreover, as DVS-Voltmeter is based on the circuit principle of DVS, the simulated events resemble real ones (see Fig. 1(c)(d)) and benefit event-driven applications.

The main contributions of this paper are summarized as follows:

- We offer a novel insight into event modeling based on the fundamental principle of the DVS circuit. Our model utilizes a stochastic process to integrate the circuit properties into a unified representation.
- We propose a practical and efficient event simulator (DVS-Voltmeter) to generate realistic event datasets from existing high frame-rate videos.
- We qualitatively and quantitatively evaluate the proposed simulator and show that our simulated events resemble real ones.
- We validate our simulated events by training neural networks for semantic segmentation and intensity-image reconstruction, which generalize well to real scenes.

2   DVS Pixel Circuit

Considering that the proposed event simulator hinges on the fundamental voltage properties in the DVS circuit, we revisit the working principle of the DVS circuit to better motivate our event model. As each pixel in DVS independently responds to local brightness changes to generate spike events, we take a pixel circuit of a DVS 128 camera [17] as an example to illustrate the event triggering process.

As shown in Fig. 2(a), when light signal L hits a pixel on the photoreceptor, it is transduced to a photocurrent with a dark current $I = I_p + I_{dark}$ ($I_p \propto L$) and then logarithmically converted to a voltage V_p. After that, it is amplified to a voltage change $\Delta V_d(t)$ memorized after the last event triggered at the time t_0, which can be ideally formulated as

$$\Delta V_d(t) = -\frac{C_1 \kappa_p U_T}{C_2 \kappa_n}(\ln I(t) - \ln I(t_0)), \tag{1}$$

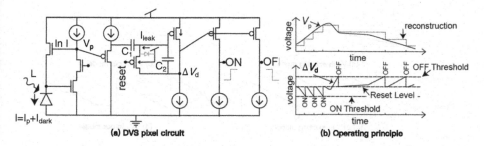

Fig. 2. Pixel circuit and operation of DVS 128. (a) DVS receives a pixel light signal L and transduces it to a photocurrent I, a voltage V_p, and a voltage change ΔV_d sequentially. (b) Once ΔV_d reaches an ON or OFF threshold, the DVS triggers an ON or OFF event and resets ΔV_d. This figure is adapted from [17,22]. Please see these papers for more details.

where C_1, C_2, κ_p, and κ_n are the parameters of the circuit components, and U_T denotes a thermal voltage [17]. Once the DVS detects that ΔV_d reaches ON threshold $-\Theta_{ON}$ or OFF threshold Θ_{OFF}, it records an ON or OFF event and resets ΔV_d by a pulse as illustrated in Fig. 2(b), formulated as

$$
\begin{cases}
\Delta V_d(t) \leq -\Theta_{ON} & ON\ events \\
\Delta V_d(t) \geq \Theta_{OFF} & OFF\ events \\
-\Theta_{ON} < \Delta V_d(t) < \Theta_{OFF} & no\ events.
\end{cases}
\tag{2}
$$

Like conventional cameras, DVS event cameras suffer from complex electromagnetic interference, so it is inappropriate to model the voltage change ΔV_d in the simple way above. As shown in Fig. 2(a), there is an inevitable junction leakage current named I_{leak}, which affects ΔV_d as

$$
\Delta V_d(t) = -\frac{C_1 \kappa_p U_T}{C_2 \kappa_n} (\ln I(t) - \ln I(t_0)) - \int_{t_0}^{t} \frac{1}{C_2} I_{leak}\ du,
\tag{3}
$$

resulting in a background of activity of ON events.

Prior work [22] validates that the junction leakage current is influenced by the temperature and parasitic photocurrent $I_{leak} = I_{leak\_T} + I_{leak\_pp}$. As for the temperature factor, I_{leak_T} exponentially increases with temperature as

$$
I_{leak\_T} \propto \exp(-E_a/k_T T),
\tag{4}
$$

where E_a is an activation energy, k_T is Boltzmann's constant, and T is the absolute temperature. Meantime, the lighting condition causes parasitic photocurrent like a leakage current

$$
I_{leak\_pp} \propto L.
\tag{5}
$$

3   Stochastic Process-Based Event Model

Based on the circuit principle of dynamic vision sensors, we propose to model the time-series voltage change ΔV_d as a stochastic process. We start by constructing

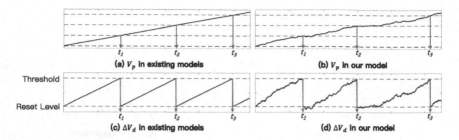

Fig. 3. Comparison of principles of operation with a same brightness change. (a) Existing models assume that the voltage change $\Delta V_d(t)$ increases linearly, resulting in clean events with equal spaces. (b) The proposed model introduces randomness in timestamps by modeling the process of $\Delta V_d(t)$ as Brownian motion with drift.

a noiseless event model considering the randomness only caused by photon reception. And then, we propose a practical model along with the noises caused by the leakage current.

3.1   Noiseless Event Model

We propose to model the voltage change ΔV_d in Eq. (1) considering the randomness only caused by photon reception. During a short period, we assume that local brightness changes linearly with a constant speed k_{dL}. Then, the electrical current ΔI_p transduced from the light signal can be represented by

$$\Delta I_p(t) = k_L k_{dL} \Delta t + N_p(t), \tag{6}$$

where k_L is the transduce rate from light signal to electrical current, $\Delta t = t - t_0$ is a short time after the last event triggered, and $N_p(t)$ is the randomness mainly due to photon reception. The design of $N_p(t)$ is inspired by the model of raw images in conventional cameras [7] that involves a Poissonian component for brightness-dependent randomness essentially due to the photon-counting process. In practice, conventional-image signal processing treats the Poissonian distribution as a special heteroskedastic Gaussian with its variances proportional to brightness. As for the event data, we attempt to model the stochastic process of $N_p(t)$ as a collection of special heteroskedastic Gaussian random variables in the temporal domain. For simplification, we use the Wiener process $W(\cdot)$, also called Brownian motion, to represent the random term by $N_p = \sqrt{m_L \bar{L}} W(\Delta t)$, where m_L is a constant parameter, $\bar{L}$ is the brightness regarded as a constant value within a short time. Thus, the distribution of randomness at every timestamp is Gaussian with its variance proportional to brightness $\bar{L}$.

Then, by combining Eq. (6) and Eq. (1), the voltage change ΔV_d, which determines event triggering, is modeled as a Brownian motion with drift according to the formula[1]:

$$\Delta V_d = -\frac{C_1 \kappa_p U_T}{C_2 \kappa_n} \cdot \frac{1}{I_p(t) + I_{dark}} (k_L k_{dL} \Delta t + \sqrt{m_L \bar{L}} W(\Delta t)). \tag{7}$$

---

[1] Equation (7) uses first-order Taylor approximation $\ln I(t) - \ln I(t_0) \approx \frac{1}{I(t)} \Delta I(t)$.

As shown in Fig. 3(b), our model based on a stochastic process introduces randomness in timestamps and generates events with varying time intervals.

3.2 Event Model with Noises

We further model the voltage change ΔV_d in Eq. (3) considering the noises caused by the leakage current. As discussed above, leakage current is influenced by the temperature and parasitic photocurrent, which affects the voltage ΔV_d and eventually causes noises. According to Eq. (4)(5), we reformulate the leakage current by

$$I_{leak} = m_T \exp(-E_u/k_T) + m_{pp}\bar{L} + N_{leak}, \tag{8}$$

where $m_T > 0$ and $m_{pp} > 0$ are camera-related constants, and N_{leak} is a noise term in the leakage current. Here, we assume N_{leak} is white noise. As the temporal integral of a white noise signal is Brownian Motion $W(\cdot)$ [14], we can rewrite the noise term in Eq. (3) as

$$\Delta V_{d\_leak} = -\frac{1}{C_2}(m_T \exp(-E_a/k_T)\Delta t + m_{pp}\bar{L}\Delta t + \sigma_{leak}W(\Delta t)). \tag{9}$$

Overall, the model for dynamic vision sensors is formulated as

$$\begin{aligned}
\Delta V_d &= -\frac{C_1\kappa_p U_T}{C_2\kappa_n} \cdot \frac{1}{I_p + I_{dark}}(k_L k_{dL}\Delta t + \sqrt{m_L \bar{L}}W(\Delta t)) \\
&\quad - \frac{1}{C_2}(m_T \exp(-E_a/k_T)\Delta t + m_{pp}\bar{L}\Delta t + \sigma_{leak}W(\Delta t)) \\
&= \frac{k_1}{\bar{L}+k_2}k_{dL}\Delta t + \frac{k_3}{\bar{L}+k_2}\sqrt{\bar{L}}W(\Delta t) + k_4\Delta t + k_5\bar{L}\Delta t + k_6 W(\Delta t),
\end{aligned} \tag{10}$$

where k_1, k_2, ..., k_6 are calibrated parameters, I_p is replaced by $\bar{L}$ due to their proportional relationship. It can be noticed that the final model can be summarized as a Brownian motion with drift parameter μ and scale parameter σ:

$$\Delta V_d = \mu\Delta t + \sigma W(\Delta t). \tag{11}$$

4 Event Simulation Strategy

As the proposed model considers the event generating process as a Brownian motion with drift, a simple idea to simulate events is to sample from Gaussian distribution at dense timestamps. However, it is computation-intensive, if not impossible, due to the high temporal resolution of event cameras. Therefore, we analyze the property of this stochastic process and propose an efficient event simulator, dubbed DVS-Voltmeter, to decide how and when to trigger events. The overall framework of DVS-Voltmeter is illustrated in Algorithm 1, which alternates between two parts:

– *Polarity Selection:* it determines the polarity of the next triggered event at each pixel based on the hitting probability of the Brownian motion model.

Algorithm 1. Event Simulation (DVS-Voltmeter).

Input: Frames $F_1, F_2, \ldots, F_n$ and according timestamps $t_1, t_2, \ldots, t_n$
Output: Events generated.
  for each pixel in frames with location x, y **do**
    Obtain pixel series $P_j = F_j(x,y), j = 1, 2, \ldots, n$
    Initialize: $\Delta V_d^{res} \leftarrow 0, t_{now} \leftarrow t_1$
    for $i = 2$ to n **do**
      $k_{dL} \leftarrow \frac{P_i - P_{i-1}}{t_i - t_{i-1}}, \bar{L} \leftarrow \frac{P_i + P_{i-1}}{2}$
      Compute μ and σ in Eq. (11)
      while $t_{now} < t_i$ **do**
        Select polarity $p = ON/OFF$ for next event using probability in Eq. (12)
        $\hat{\Theta}_{ON} \leftarrow \Theta_{ON} + \Delta V_d^{res}, \hat{\Theta}_{OFF} \leftarrow \Theta_{OFF} - \Delta V_d^{res}$
        Sample time interval τ with Eq. (13)(14)
        if $t_{now} + \tau > t_i$ **then**
          $\Delta V_d^{res} \leftarrow \Theta_p(t_i - t_{now})/\tau, t_{now} \leftarrow t_i$
        else
          $\Delta V_d^{res} \leftarrow 0, t_{now} \leftarrow t_{now} + \tau$
          Record event with t_{now}, p, x, y
        end if
      end while
    end for
  end for

- *Timestamp Sampling:* it samples the timestamp of the next triggered event at each pixel using the first hitting time distribution of Brownian motion.

Polarity Selection. Given a pair of adjacent video frames F_i and F_{i-1} at timestamps t_i and t_{i-1}, respectively, we can obtain an approximated brightness within the capture of two frames by $\bar{L} = (F_i + F_{i-1})/2$ and a brightness changing speed $k_{dL} = \frac{F_i - F_{i-1}}{t_i - t_{i-1}}$. Furthermore, μ and σ in the proposed noise model Eq. (11) can be calculated with a set of well-calibrated parameters of DVS. According to the property of a Brownian motion model, the chance of triggering an ON event next time can be mathematically modeled as the probability of the voltage ΔV_d hitting $-\Theta_{ON}$ before Θ_{OFF}, formulated as

$$P(ON) = \frac{\exp(-2\mu\Theta_{ON}/\sigma^2) - 1}{\exp(-2\mu\Theta_{ON}/\sigma^2) - \exp(2\mu\Theta_{OFF}/\sigma^2)}. \tag{12}$$

And the chance of triggering an OFF event next time is $P(OFF) = 1 - P(ON)$.

  Specifically, DVS-Voltmeter performs a uniform sampling within the range $[0, 1]$ at each pixel and compares the samples with the corresponding $P(ON)$. As for the pixel where the sample is smaller than $P(ON)$, DVS-Voltmeter triggers an ON event next; otherwise, an OFF one.

Timestamp Sampling. After determining the polarity of the next event, we sample its triggering time interval from the distribution of the first hitting time

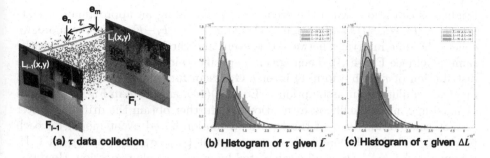

(a) τ data collection   **(b)** Histogram of τ given $\bar{L}$ **(c)** Histogram of τ given ΔL

Fig. 4. Model calibration operation and statistical analysis. (a) Given real captured DAVIS data consisting of frames and events, we collect the time interval τ between two adjacent events at each pixel. τ has an inverse Gaussian distribution/Lévy distribution. (b) The larger the brightness change ΔL, the more compressed the distribution. (c) The larger the average brightness $\bar{L}$, the more spread out the distribution. This statistical result is consistent with the proposed model in Eq. (13)(14).

τ of Brownian Motion with Drift. τ follows an inverse Gaussian distribution [8] with non-zero drift parameter μ,

$$\tau_{ON} \sim IG(-\frac{\Theta_{ON}}{\mu}, \frac{\Theta_{ON}^2}{\sigma^2}); \qquad \tau_{OFF} \sim IG(\frac{\Theta_{OFF}}{\mu}, \frac{\Theta_{OFF}^2}{\sigma^2}), \qquad (13)$$

or a Lévy distribution when $\mu = 0$:

$$\tau_{ON} \sim Levy(\mu, \frac{\Theta_{ON}^2}{\sigma^2}); \qquad \tau_{OFF} \sim Levy(\mu, \frac{\Theta_{OFF}^2}{\sigma^2}). \qquad (14)$$

The timestamp sampling uses transformation with multiple roots [18]. For simplification, we set both Θ_{ON} and Θ_{OFF} as 1.

DVS-Voltmeter repeats the polarity selection and timestamp sampling, and updates the timestamp of a new event by $t_{now} = t_{now} + \tau$. The simulator ends until the timestamp of a new event is beyond the frame timestamp t_i. At this moment, we neither record a new event nor update a new timestamp. Instead, we save the residual voltage change ΔV_d^{res} related to the remaining time $t_i - t_{now}$ for follow-up event simulation during the subsequent two adjacent frames.

5   Model Calibration

To train networks generalizing to a specific DVS camera, it is necessary to accurately calibrate k_1, k_2, ..., k_6 in the model in Eq. (10) and generate realistic events for this DVS camera. Ideally, we can look up the camera's specification and conduct a statistical experiment on noise effects to determine the parameters, similar to V2E [6]. However, statistical experiments need complex equipment and, thus, are hard to implement. We provide a calibration method for DAVIS [3,5], which record both events and active pixel sensor (APS) intensity frames.

Specifically, given a sequence of APS frames and corresponding events, for every event recorded between two adjacent frames F_i and F_{i+1}, we can get the brightness conditions when the event occurs, including an approximate brightness $\bar{L} = (F_i + F_{i-1})/2$ and a brightness change $\Delta L = F_i - F_{i-1}$. Furthermore, we collect the time interval τ between this event and the last event triggered at the same pixel (see Fig. 4(a)). Then, given a specific pair of $\bar{L}$ and ΔL, we find the distribution of τ with a form of inverse Gaussian function or Lévy distribution function similar to our assumption in Eq. (13)(14), as shown in Fig. 4(b)(c) and fit it by maximum-likelihood estimation. We further obtain the drift parameter μ and scale parameter σ of the Brownian motion-based event model for each pair of $\bar{L}$ and ΔL. Theoretically, given a set of $\{(\mu_m, \sigma_m, \bar{L}_m, \Delta L_m)\}, m \in \mathbb{N}$, parameters $k_1, k_2, ..., k_6$ can be calculated by multivariable regression. However, this auto-calibration method is limited by the quality of APS, image quantization, and the assumption of constant brightness changes in our model, so it introduces large errors on σ-related parameters, including k_3 and k_6, in challenging scenes, such as high dynamic range and fast motion. Therefore, we only auto-calibrate μ-related parameters by regression and determine the σ-related parameters manually. Details are provided in our supplementary material.

6 Evaluation

In this section, we provide qualitative and quantitative results on the fidelity of the proposed DVS-Voltmeter and compare it to existing methods [6,11].

6.1 Qualitative Comparison

We exhibit a side-by-side comparison of a real public DAVIS dataset [20] and its simulated reproductions from Vid2E [11], V2E [6], and our DVS-Voltmeter. For a fair comparison, all simulators firstly interpolate the videos by 10 times to reach a high frame rate using *Super-SloMo* [13], similar to V2E [6]. After that, the simulators generate synthetic events using the interpolated video sequences. Figure 5 shows the events between two adjacent frames. In addition to illustration in the form of spatiotemporal event clouds, the events are visualized using an exponential time surface [15] with exponential decay of 3.0 ms.

As illustrated in Fig. 5, Vid2E [11], which only considers the noises of triggering threshold in DVS, shows an apparent artificial pattern with relatively equal-spacing timestamps. Most events in Vid2E locate around moving edges, resulting in a sharp exponential time surface. Although V2E [6] injects more noises, its strategy of timestamp sampling makes events cluster to limited numbers of time intervals, and most events appear close to the timestamp of frames, leading to unrealistic results. Instead, the proposed DVS-Voltmeter adopts a more flexible timestamp sampling solution based on the stochastic process so that the event clouds spread out and seem realistic. As for the exponential time surface, although there are some differences between the real and simulated events, the result generated from DVS-Voltmeter resembles real data more.

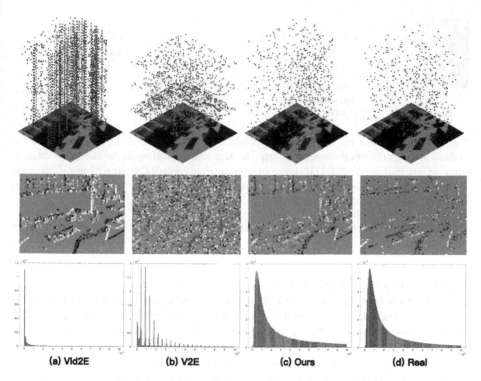

(a) Vid2E   (b) V2E   (c) Ours   (d) Real

Fig. 5. Qualitative and quantitative comparison among Vid2E [11], V2E [6], our DVS-Voltmeter, and real data 'office_zigzag' in [20]. We illustrate 3D clouds, 2D time surfaces, and probability density function histograms of event data from top to bottom. Our DVS-Voltmeter gains more randomness, and the generated events resemble real data. More results are provided in our supplementary material.

6.2   Effectiveness of Event Model

To quantify the proposed model, we conduct some experiments to compare our simulated events' distribution and noise effects with the statistical results from real DVS. The temperature effect is provided in our supplementary material.

Event Distribution: To validate the accuracy of event simulators, one might directly compare generated events against the captured 'ground truth' events. However, there is no clear metric for the similarity between two event clouds, making the evaluation an ill-posed problem [23]. Therefore, we instead measure the distribution of events. For each event, we calculate the time interval τ after the last event triggered at the same pixel and create a histogram of τ.

Figure 5 shows the probability density function of the time intervals from the synthetic data and the real one. Vid2E [11] generates events only when encountering brightness changes, and thus, most of the time intervals are within two consecutive interpolated frames (about 4500 μs). V2E [6] considers more complex noises but tends to assign events to the timestamps clustered to frames, causing a discrete-like distribution of time intervals. The proposed DVS-Voltmeter is designed with a stochastic process-based model, and thus the time intervals

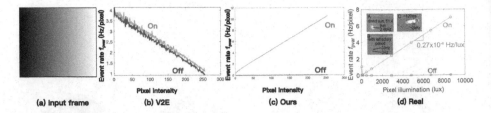

Fig. 6. Comparisons on the effects of brightness-related parasitic photocurrent. We continuously feed a single image (a) into the simulators and measure the noise rates at different intensities. Vid2E [11] does not generate any events. (b)(c)(d) are the results of V2E [6], our DVS-Voltmeter, and real data from DAVIS240C [22]. Our noise rate is similar to the real statistical analysis.

are spread out. Moreover, it hinges on the circuit principle and noise analysis of DVS so that the event distribution of our simulator resembles that of real data more.

Parasitic Photocurrent: As mentioned in Sect. 2, leak activity caused by parasitic photocurrent increases with light illumination and introduces unintended noises. We measure this noise by continuously inputting a single image with intensity increasing from left to right (see Fig. 6(a)) and counting the noise rate for each intensity.

As there are no brightness changes over the period, previous event simulators [10,16,20,23], including Vid2E [11], do not generate any events. Although V2E [6] considers complex noises, the distribution of generated events (see Fig. 6(b)) is different from the one of real event data provided in [22]. However, our simulator is designed based on the DVS pixel circuit and incorporates a Brownian motion-based noise term to model the noises from parasitic photocurrent, which naturally represents the distribution of real events. As shown in Fig. 6(c), the number of ON events increases with the pixel intensity, and the OFF rate is nearly zero for all points, similar to the real statistical analysis in Fig. 6(d).

7   Example Application

In this section, we validate the proposed simulator on two tasks: semantic segmentation and intensity-image reconstruction. Compared with existing simulators, the deep learning networks trained on our synthetic events perform favorably on real event data.

7.1   Semantic Segmentation

Event-driven semantic segmentation shows the potential for processing challenging scenarios for conventional cameras. In this section, we attempt to train a segmentation network on simulated event datasets and validate its generalization capacity on real data.

Table 1. Semantic segmentation performance on the test Ev-Seg data [1] in terms of average accuracy and MIoU (Mean Intersection over Union). The networks are firstly trained on the simulated events and then fine-tuned using 20 real samples.

Training data	Before fine-tuning		After fine-tuning	
	Accuracy	MIoU	Accuracy	MIoU
Vid2E [11]	84.95	46.67	86.41	47.81
V2E [6]	84.11	42.25	84.41	44.32
Ours	**87.88**	**50.60**	**88.51**	**51.20**
Real (20 samples)	67.68	24.39		
Real (all samples)	89.76	54.81		

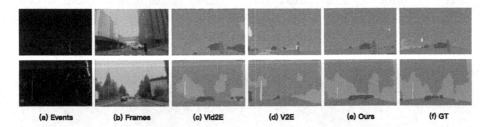

(a) Events   (b) Frames   (c) Vid2E   (d) V2E   (e) Ours   (f) GT

Fig. 7. Visual comparisons on semantic segmentation on Ev-Seg data [1]. The network trained on our simulated events generates more accurate and detailed results. More results are provided in our supplementary material.

Specifically, we reproduce synthetic event datasets from a publicly available DAVIS Driving Dataset (DDD17) [4] captured with a DAVIS346 sensor. As the quality of APS intensity frames limits our model calibration, we utilize the 'LabSlow' sequence in DVSNOISE20 dataset [2], which is captured with slower and stabler camera movement of a static scene, rather than DDD17 to calibrate DAVIS346 sensors. For a fair comparison, we use the same interpolation strategy on frames in DDD17 by 10 times to generate high frame-rate videos and then generate events by Vid2E [11], V2E [6], and the proposed DVS-Voltmeter. The semantic annotations are provided by [1] for training and testing. The experiment settings, such as event representation, network architecture, and training details, are the same as [1].

We evaluate accuracy and MIoU (Mean Intersection over Union) on semantic segmentation in Table 1. Although the network trained on our simulated data presents slightly lower accuracy than that trained on the whole real event data directly, it performs favorably against state-of-the-art simulators. Figure 7 provides some examples in the testing set. Our method can give a more accurate and detailed segmentation, which indicates the good resemblance between our events and real ones.

Moreover, we fine-tune the networks given a small-scale real training dataset containing 20 samples for further performance improvement. As shown in Table 1, the network trained only on 20 real samples is overfitted and cannot perform accurately on the testing dataset. However, pre-training on synthetic

Table 2. Intensity-image reconstruction performance on the Event Camera Dataset [20] in terms of mean squared error (MSE), structural similarity (SSIM) [25], and the calibrated perceptual loss (LPIPS) [26].

	MSE ↓			SSIM ↑			LPIPS ↓		
	Vid2E [11]	V2E [6]	Ours	Vid2E [11]	V2E [6]	Ours	Vid2E [11]	V2E [6]	Ours
dynamic_6dof	0.093	0.177	**0.052**	0.365	0.231	**0.430**	**0.367**	0.437	0.405
boxes_6dof	0.044	0.112	**0.033**	0.509	0.281	**0.521**	0.474	0.590	**0.465**
poster_6dof	0.075	0.158	**0.044**	0.433	0.227	**0.495**	**0.354**	0.511	0.371
shapes_6dof	0.020	0.053	**0.007**	0.707	0.634	**0.790**	0.352	0.375	**0.275**
office_zigzag	0.057	0.125	**0.035**	0.427	0.232	**0.464**	0.507	0.597	**0.483**
slider_depth	0.048	0.108	**0.030**	0.406	0.336	**0.458**	0.523	0.558	**0.501**
calibration	0.051	0.115	**0.036**	0.541	0.393	**0.550**	0.467	0.545	**0.423**
Mean	0.056	0.122	**0.034**	0.505	0.346	**0.550**	0.413	0.501	**0.397**

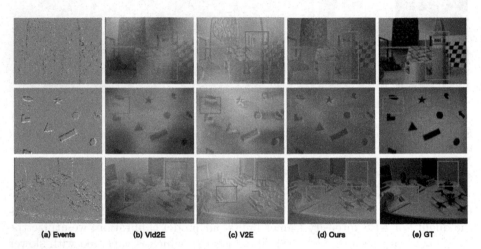

(a) Events   (b) Vid2E   (c) V2E   (d) Ours   (e) GT

Fig. 8. Visual comparisons on intensity-image reconstruction on Event Camera Dataset [20]. The network trained on our simulated events generates sharper results with fewer artifacts. More results are provided in our supplementary material.

data and fine-tuning on limited real samples can avoid overfitting and generalize well when testing. Compared to other simulators, our method achieves the highest quantitative results. And it shows a comparable result with the model trained with a large-scale real dataset (All samples). Therefore, using our simulator is more effective and makes it possible to learn a good segmentation given few or no real training samples.

7.2   Intensity-Image Reconstruction

Intensity-image reconstruction aims to generate a high-quality video image from a stream of sparse events, enabling various downstream applications for event-based cameras. Training reconstruction networks requires a large-scale dataset in the form of event streams and the corresponding ground-truth images. However, directly using images captured by DAVIS is inappropriate due to their poor quality, for example, limited dynamic range and blur. Therefore, existing algorithms simulate events from videos to supervise networks.

In this section, we evaluate the effectiveness of our simulator on intensity-image reconstruction by training on synthetic datasets generated from GoPro [21], which provides sharp videos at a frame rate of 240 fps, and testing on Event Camera Dataset [20] recorded by a DAVIS240C sensor. Specifically, we calibrate the proposed Brownian motion event model for DAVIS240C with the 'office_zigzag' sequence in the testing dataset. Moreover, we use the same frame interpolation strategy to increase the frame rate 10 times and then generate events by Vid2E [11], V2E [6], and the proposed DVS-Voltmeter. Every 1/120 s of events are stacked into a 5 channel spatiotemporal voxel and fed into a recurrent network to reconstruct an image, similar to [24]. The network is trained for 120,000 iterations with a batch size of 2 and a learning rate of 0.0001. Other training details are the same as suggested in [24]. As for testing, because the frame rates of ground truth images in the testing dataset are different among scenes, we generate 4 voxels between two adjacent images and reconstruct 4× frame-rate videos for quantitative evaluation.

We measure mean squared error (MSE), structural similarity (SSIM) [25], and the calibrated perceptual loss (LPIPS) [26] in Table 2. Our simulator shows better generalization capacity on almost all real datasets with an average 39% decrease in MSE, 9% increase in SSIM, and 4% decrease in LPIPS. Figure 8 shows some qualitative comparisons side by side. As the proposed simulator is designed based on the statistics and circuit principle of events, it naturally encourages the reconstructed images to have natural image statistics. The results show that the network trained on our simulated events reconstructs more visually pleasing images with finer details and fewer artifacts.

8   Conclusions and Future Work

In this paper, we propose an event model with a novel perspective from the fundamental circuit properties of DVS. The whole model incorporates the voltage variation, the randomness caused by photon reception, and the noises caused by leakage current into a unified stochastic process. Based on the proposed model, we develop a practical and efficient event simulator (DVS-Voltmeter) to generate events from high frame-rate videos. Benefiting from this design, simulated events bear a strong resemblance to real event data. The applications on semantic segmentation and intensity-image reconstruction demonstrate that the proposed simulator achieves superior generalization performance against the existing event simulators.

For future work, one of the main challenges is a more comprehensive characterization of noise effects in DVS, such as temporal noises at low illumination and refractory periods. Besides, a more robust auto-calibration for our model is necessary to mitigate manual calibration.

Acknowledgement. This work was supported in part by the Ministry of Education, Republic of Singapore, through its Start-Up Grant and Academic Research Fund Tier 1 (RG137/20).

References

1. Alonso, I., Murillo, A.C.: EV-SegNet: semantic segmentation for event-based cameras. In: IEEE Computer Vision and Pattern Recognition Workshops (CVPRW) (2019)
2. Baldwin, R., Almatrafi, M., Asari, V., Hirakawa, K.: Event probability mask (EPM) and event denoising convolutional neural network (EDnCNN) for neuromorphic cameras. In: IEEE Computer Vision and Pattern Recognition (CVPR), pp. 1701–1710 (2020)
3. Berner, R., Brandli, C., Yang, M., Liu, S.C., Delbruck, T.: A 240 × 180 10 mw 12 us latency sparse-output vision sensor for mobile applications. In: Symposium on VLSI Circuits, pp. C186–C187. IEEE (2013)
4. Binas, J., Neil, D., Liu, S.C., Delbruck, T.: DDD17: end-to-end DAVIS driving dataset (2017)
5. Brandli, C., Berner, R., Yang, M., Liu, S.C., Delbruck, T.: A 240 × 180 130 db 3 μs latency global shutter spatiotemporal vision sensor. IEEE J. Solid-State Circ. **49**(10), 2333–2341 (2014)
6. Delbruck, T., Hu, Y., He, Z.: V2E: from video frames to realistic DVS event camera streams. arXiv preprint arXiv:2006.07722
7. Foi, A., Trimeche, M., Katkovnik, V., Egiazarian, K.: Practical Poissonian-Gaussian noise modeling and fitting for single-image raw-data. IEEE Trans. Image Process. (TIP) **17**(10), 1737–1754 (2008)
8. Folks, J.L., Chhikara, R.S.: The inverse Gaussian distribution and its statistical application-a review. J. Roy. Stat. Soc.: Ser. B (Methodol.) **40**(3), 263–275 (1978)
9. Gallego, G., et al.: Event-based vision: a survey. IEEE Trans. Pattern Anal. Mach. Intell. (TPAMI) **44**(1), 154–180 (2020)
10. Garca, G.P., Camilleri, P., Liu, Q., Furber, S.: pyDVS: an extensible, real-time dynamic vision sensor emulator using off-the-shelf hardware. In: IEEE Symposium Series on Computational Intelligence (SSCI), pp. 1–7. IEEE (2016)
11. Gehrig, D., Gehrig, M., Hidalgo-Carrió, J., Scaramuzza, D.: Video to events: recycling video datasets for event cameras. In: IEEE Computer Vision and Pattern Recognition (CVPR), pp. 3586–3595 (2020)
12. Gehrig, M., Millhäusler, M., Gehrig, D., Scaramuzza, D.: E-RAFT: dense optical flow from event cameras. In: International Conference on 3D Vision (3DV), pp. 197–206. IEEE (2021)
13. Jiang, H., Sun, D., Jampani, V., Yang, M.H., Learned-Miller, E., Kautz, J.: Super SloMo: high quality estimation of multiple intermediate frames for video interpolation. In: IEEE Computer Vision and Pattern Recognition (CVPR), pp. 9000–9008 (2018)
14. Kuo, H.H.: White Noise Distribution Theory. CRC Press (2018)
15. Lagorce, X., Orchard, G., Galluppi, F., Shi, B.E., Benosman, R.B.: HOTS: a hierarchy of event-based time-surfaces for pattern recognition. IEEE Trans. Pattern Anal. Mach. Intell. (TPAMI) **39**(7), 1346–1359 (2016)
16. Li, W., et al.: InteriorNet: mega-scale multi-sensor photo-realistic indoor scenes dataset (2018)
17. Lichtsteiner, P., Posch, C., Delbruck, T.: A 128 × 128 120db 15 μs latency asynchronous temporal contrast vision sensor. IEEE J. Solid-State Circ. **43**(2), 566–576 (2008)
18. Michael, J.R., Schucany, W.R., Haas, R.W.: Generating random variates using transformations with multiple roots. Am. Stat. **30**(2), 88–90 (1976)

19. Mitrokhin, A., Hua, Z., Fermuller, C., Aloimonos, Y.: Learning visual motion segmentation using event surfaces. In: Proceedings of the IEEE/CVF Conference on Computer Vision and Pattern Recognition, pp. 14414–14423 (2020)
20. Mueggler, E., Rebecq, H., Gallego, G., Delbruck, T., Scaramuzza, D.: The event-camera dataset and simulator: event-based data for pose estimation, visual odometry, and SLAM. Int. J. Robot. Res. (IJRR) **36**(2), 142–149 (2017)
21. Nah, S., Hyun Kim, T., Mu Lee, K.: Deep multi-scale convolutional neural network for dynamic scene deblurring. In: IEEE Computer Vision and Pattern Recognition (CVPR), pp. 3883–3891 (2017)
22. Nozaki, Y., Delbruck, T.: Temperature and parasitic photocurrent effects in dynamic vision sensors. IEEE Trans. Electron Dev. **64**(8), 3239–3245 (2017)
23. Rebecq, H., Gehrig, D., Scaramuzza, D.: ESIM: an open event camera simulator. In: Conference on Robot Learning (CoRL), pp. 969–982. PMLR (2018)
24. Rebecq, H., Ranftl, R., Koltun, V., Scaramuzza, D.: High speed and high dynamic range video with an event camera. IEEE Trans. Pattern Anal. Mach. Intell. (TPAMI) **43**(6), 1964–1980 (2019)
25. Wang, Z., Bovik, A.C., Sheikh, H.R., Simoncelli, E.P.: Image quality assessment: from error visibility to structural similarity. IEEE Trans. Image Process. (TIP) **13**(4), 600–612 (2004)
26. Zhang, R., Isola, P., Efros, A.A., Shechtman, E., Wang, O.: The unreasonable effectiveness of deep features as a perceptual metric. In: IEEE Computer Vision and Pattern Recognition (CVPR), pp. 586–595 (2018)
27. Zhang, S., Zhang, Yu., Jiang, Z., Zou, D., Ren, J., Zhou, B.: Learning to see in the dark with events. In: Vedaldi, A., Bischof, H., Brox, T., Frahm, J.-M. (eds.) ECCV 2020. LNCS, vol. 12363, pp. 666–682. Springer, Cham (2020). https://doi.org/10.1007/978-3-030-58523-5_39

Benchmarking Omni-Vision Representation Through the Lens of Visual Realms

Yuanhan Zhang[1](ID), Zhenfei Yin[2](ID), Jing Shao[2](✉)(ID), and Ziwei Liu[1](ID)

[1] S-Lab, Nanyang Technological University, Singapore, Singapore
{yuanhan002,ziwei.liu}@ntu.edu.sg
[2] SenseTime Research, Shatin, Hong Kong
{yinzhenfei,shaojing}@sensetime.com

Abstract. Though impressive performance has been achieved in specific visual realms (*e.g.* faces, dogs, and places), an omni-vision representation generalizing to many natural visual domains is highly desirable. But, existing benchmarks are biased and inefficient to evaluate the omni-vision representation—these benchmarks either only include several specific realms, or cover most realms at the expense of subsuming numerous datasets that have extensive realm overlapping. In this paper, we propose Omni-Realm Benchmark (**OmniBenchmark**). It includes 21 realm-wise datasets with 7,372 concepts and 1,074,346 images. Without semantic overlapping, these datasets cover most visual realms comprehensively and meanwhile efficiently. In addition, we propose a new supervised contrastive learning framework, namely **R**elational **C**ontrastive learning (**ReCo**), for a better omni-vision representation. Beyond pulling two instances from the same concept closer—the typical supervised contrastive learning framework—ReCo also pulls two instances from the same semantic realm closer, encoding the semantic relation between concepts, facilitating omni-vision representation learning. We benchmark ReCo and other advances in omni-vision representation studies that are different in architectures (from CNNs to transformers) and in learning paradigms (from supervised learning to self-supervised learning) on OmniBenchmark. We illustrate the superior of ReCo to other supervised contrastive learning methods, and reveal multiple practical observations to facilitate future research. The code and models are available at https://zhangyuanhan-ai.github.io/OmniBenchmark.

Keywords: Representation learning · Visual realm

1 Introduction

Large-scale pre-trained models, either trained in a supervised [24,63,67] or unsupervised manner [7,23,41], have become a foundation [4] for modern com-

Supplementary Information The online version contains supplementary material available at https://doi.org/10.1007/978-3-031-20071-7_35.

S. Avidan et al. (Eds.): ECCV 2022, LNCS 13667, pp. 594–611, 2022.
https://doi.org/10.1007/978-3-031-20071-7_35

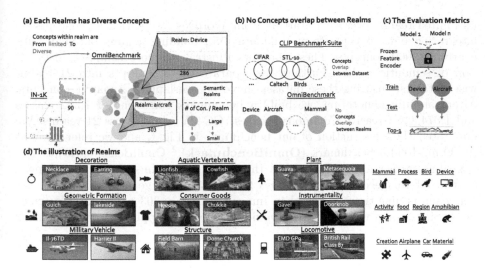

Fig. 1. A overview of OmniBenchmark. (a) Compared with ImageNet-1k, OmniBenchmark covers more realms and annotate more images of each realm. (b) Included datasets in OmniBenchmark have no semantic concepts overlap. (c) OmniBenchmark diagnoses pre-trained models through linear probing. (d) We present 21 semantic realm-wise datasets and the sampled concepts of 9 datasets.

puter vision [9,19,28,29,41,43,48,69]. The generalization quality of pre-trained models—whether models are helpful for various downstream tasks—typically determines models' quality. Recent benchmarks for evaluating model generalization mainly collect downstream tasks belonging to two facets: across image domains (*e.g.* from natural domain to synthetic domain) [69]; across vision tasks (*e.g.* from image classification to instance segmentation) [7,23]. In this study, we focus on the third facet: across semantic super-concepts/realms (*e.g.* across pets to scenes). We found that current benchmarks focusing on the last facet either cover a limited range of the semantic realms or are overly cumbersome for evaluation. For example, ImageNet-1k [44] only focuses on the mammal, instrumentality, devices, and consumer goods. But these realms struggle to describe the complete realms in the natural domain. Meanwhile, though CLIP [41] builds a significant benchmark that consists of 24 datasets across a large spectrum of realms, several datasets included have an extensive concept overlapping (*e.g.* CIFAR100 [31], Caltech101 [18], and STL-10 [12] all have bird class) as shown in Fig. 1(b), resulting in benchmarking on its benchmark suite is less efficient than on an ideal benchmark where datasets included do not conceptually overlap with each other.

In this work, we systematically investigates how to build a benchmark for evaluating omni-vision representation that can generalize to a wide range of semantic realms. This benchmark focuses the classification task on the natural image domain. Through the analysis of ImageNet-1k, we find that the limited number of concepts in its concepts resource, *i.e.* WordNet [38], results in its limited realm coverage.[1] Starting from WordNet, we enrich its concepts by integrating new concepts from Wikidata [55], building a large ontology with nearly 100,000 concepts. These concepts illustrate a more complete distribution of semantic realms. Further, we separate these concepts into 21 realm-wise datasets, ensuring these datasets have no overlapping semantic concepts. After carefully annotation, we build a benchmark consisting of 7,372 classes and 1,074,346 Creative Commons licenses (CC-BY) data across 21 realms. We illustrated the construction of our benchmark in Fig. 1, and we refer to it as the Omni-Realm benchmark (**OmniBenchmark**).[2] OmniBenchmark has two appealing properties. **1) Diversity.** the number of realms of OmniBenchmark is twice of ImageNet-1k's, *i.e.* 21 *v.s* 9, and the average number of concepts per realm is nine times bigger than ImageNet-1k, *i.e.* 263 *v.s* 29. **2) Conciseness.** Since realm-wise datasets have no concept overlapping, OmniBenchmark is concise.

We further investigate how to learn a better omni-vision representation. We purpose an omni-vision representation should not only cluster instances of the *same* concept but also cluster the instances of *related* semantic concept—two concepts within the same realm should imply closer relation than two concepts across the realm, *e.g.* the relation between husky and labrador (two dog species) should be closer than husky and Ferrari 488 (a sports car). However, current representative representation learning methods, *e.g.* supervised contrastive learning [13,26], commonly construct negative pairs by exhaustive sampling without considering their semantic relation, *e.g.* husky and labrador should have the same possibility of being the negative pair than husky and Ferrari 488. Motivated by this limitation, we present a novel supervised contrastive learning framework called **R**elational **C**ontrastive Learning (**ReCo**). ReCo selects the high-quality negative pairs, which belong to different semantic realms, for supervised contrastive learning. ReCo improves the state-of-the-art (SOTA) supervised contrastive learning method (PaCo [13]) on the ImageNet-1k by 0.7 points gain.

We conduct extensive studies on OmniBenchmark to diagnose ReCo and other advances in the omni-vision representation learning including architectures (from CNNs [24] to transformers [15]); learning paradigms (from fully-supervised learning to self-supervised learning); pre-training data volume (from ImageNet-1k [14] to IG-1B [63]). We reveal several valuable observations and prove the priority of ReCo: ReCo outperforms PaCo with an average 0.5 points gain on OmniBenchmark.

We summarize the contributions of this work as follows.

- We propose OmniBenchmark with 21 semantic realm-wise datasets. OmniBenchmark focus on evaluating the concept generalization ability of omni-vision representation thoroughly and efficiently.
- We evaluate 22 recent representation learning approaches on OmniBenchmark, uncovering several interesting insights for future research.

---

[1] Annotation budget also limits its realm coverage.
[2] We use "Omni" to emphasize the diversity of semantic realms.

– A novel supervised contrastive learning method, ReCo, is proposed for encoding the semantic relation information in the supervised contrastive learning framework, achieving competitive performance on ImageNet1k and OmniBenchmark.

2   Related Work

Representation Learning Methods. Representation learning has advanced thanks to improvements in various learning paradigms. To avoid the need for supervision, self-supervised leaning [6,7,10,16,23,32,34,39,59,70] has been proposed. Recently, Guo *et al.* [21] proposed hierarchical contrastive selective coding (HCSC) that improves conventional contrastive learning by implicitly coding the semantic similarity between instances. Inspired by HCSC, ReCo explicitly encodes the semantic similarity, using the label information in the hierarchical concepts structure. In addition, weakly supervised learning [62,63,76] focuses on learning from unlabeled data by self-training. The success of representation learning should also owe to architecture designs breakthrough, *e.g.* Vision Transformer (ViT) [15]. This paper benchmark the most recent methods that have public implementations available. Moreover, there have extensive studies that explore to use semantic structure in various ways. Specifically, Bertinetto *et al.* [3] use the information in the class hierarchy to achieve competitive performance on several datasets. Wang *et al.* [58] model the classification process on the semantic hierarchy as a sequential decision-making task. In addition, Wang *et al.* [57] propose a deep fuzzy tree model for learning the semantic hierarchy better. Wang *et al.* [56] and Guo *et al.* [20] propose very insightful frameworks for leveraging semantic relation information in tasks other than image classification. Ma *et al.* [37] propose contrastive learning that compares images with the same visual concepts with a help of a concept-feature dictionary.

Evaluations and Benchmarks. The importance of empirical evaluation of representation learning is highlighted by the growing number of major evaluation papers [9,19,29,43,48]. CLIP [41] proposes a significant benchmark that consists of 24 datasets across different semantic realms. However, CLIP benchmark suite struggles to select the most valuable set of datasets for the benchmark. In particular, several datasets have an extensive concept overlapping, making their benchmark suite cumbersome for evaluation. Visual Decathlon [42] evaluates the ability of representations to capture simultaneously ten very different visual domains and measures their ability to perform well uniformly. Visual Task Adaptation Benchmark (VTAB) [69] includes datasets from several different domains (natural, specialized, and structured) and annotation information (classification, counting, and *etc.*) to evaluate methods of varying learning paradigms. We argue that the motivation and evaluation protocol of OmniBenchmark are different from VTAB and Visual Decathlon. First, the Visual Decathlon studies the multi-task learning ability of models. Its evaluation protocol is train-test. By contrast, OmniBenchmark explores the generalization ability of pre-trained models. Its evaluation protocol is pretrain-train-test. Secondly, VTAB quantifies the generalization ability of representation to transfer to different image domains and different annotation information (The first and second facet of quantifying representation quality as mentioned in Sect. 1). OmniBenchmark focuses explicitly on evaluating concept generalization of the classification task in the natural domain. Beyond that, ImageNet-COG [45] also studies concept generalization. It evaluates the generalization of models from ImageNet-1k to other unseen concepts for ImageNet-1k. OmniBenchmark evaluates the generalization of models from any open pre-trained source to extensive categories organized by semantic realms.

3   The Construction of Omni-Realm Bechmark

In this section, we describe the construction of OmniBenchmark. First, we integrate new concepts from Wikidata into WordNet, enlarging the concept storage of WordNet extensively (Sect. 3.1). For the all concepts of this larger "WordNet", we secondly crawl raw images of each of them from Flickr (Sect. 3.1). Thirdly, we select valid concepts from the whole concepts, following multiple steps (Sect. 3.2). Fourthly we split WordNet into 21 sub-trees, each sub-tree represents a semantic realm and covers a set of valid concepts (Sect. 3.3). Fifthly, we annotate all the raw images of the valid concepts of these 21 semantic realms (Sect. 3.4), forming the 21 realm-wise datasets for benchmarking. In addition, we present detail information of the statistics (Sect. 3.5), and the evaluation protocols of OmniBenchmark (Sect. 3.6).

3.1   Integrating New Concepts

Wikidata [65] contains a large number of concepts, such as different kinds of foods and structures. As the number of concepts in Wikidata continues to grow, we have integrated 170,586 concepts from it so far. These concepts are the leaf nodes in the taxonomy of the Wikidata. Referred to [51], we link Wikidata leaf node concepts to the WordNet through leveraging on the "sub-classOf" attribute of Wikidata. This attribute denotes the hypernyms relation. Further, we obtain raw images for each concept by using the Flickr API.[3]

3.2   Concept Filtering

After integrating 170,586 new concepts into WordNet, there are nearly 210K concepts in the WordNet. However, not all these concepts are valid for the image classification benchmark. Thus, we manually filter the 210K concepts by the following steps. 1) We ask annotators to identify and then discard concepts that are related to the offensive content, such as drugs and blood. 2) Referred to Yang

---

[3] https://www.flickr.com/, All the crawled images are strictly followed the CC-BY license.

et al. [64], we only keep the visual concepts that are highly concrete words. 3) Referred to ImageNet [44], We suggest ensuring the label in our benchmark is mutually exclusive. We thus only keep annotate leaf node in the larger "Word-Net" created in Sect. 3.1. 4) In our trial annotation, *i.e.* annotation for randomly selected 200 concepts, only 50% of the crawled data of a specific concept are semantic related to this concept. Since we plan to have 50 images for the test-set of the concept, and 50 images for its train set, we thus discard concepts that have less than 200 crawled data. We illustrate these steps in Fig. 2(b).

3.3 Realm Selection

In WordNet, concepts are organized by the hierarchical structure with many sub-trees. We select semantic realms from these sub-trees by following three principles. 1) We select sub-trees that cover at least 20 valid concepts. 2) We discard the sub-tree that is covered by another sub-tree. 3) We discard the sub-tree that most of their concepts imply non-natural images and personal information. For example, we discard the chemical material realm because most of its concepts can only be related to the structural formula image. In addition, we also discard person because its related images contain personal information such as IDs, names. We illustrate these three principles in the Fig. 2(c).

3.4 Image Annotation and De-duplication

For each candidate raw image, we ask five annotators whether this image conforms to its query concept. An image is annotated only if at least 3 out of 5 annotators consider its semantic information closely related to its query concept. More detail information, *e.g.* the annotation interface, is described in the *Supplementary Material.*

To enable a meaningful test of generalization, OmniBenchmark remove duplicates with potential pre-training datasets that includes Bamboo-CLS [46,71], ImageNet-22K [14], PASCAL-VOC [17], MS-COCO [35] and Places [72]. Specifically, we firstly utilize Difference Hash (DHash) [2] to calculate the hash-code of images of both OmniBenchmark and these pre-training datasets. Then we delete the image that has the same hash-code as any image in these pre-training datasets.

3.5 Benchmark Statistics

In Fig. 2(a), we compare the distribution of the concepts of each realm of OmniBenchmark and ImageNet-1k. Specifically, 815 concepts of ImageNet-1k are included in these 21 realms, which can fairly reflect the distribution of the ImageNet-1k.[4] Fig. 2(a) presents that ImageNet-1k covers a very limited number of *ImageNet-1k-seen-realms*, *e.g.* Device, instrumentality consumer_goods and

---

[4] The other 185 concepts are included in realm that are filtered in Sect. 3.3.

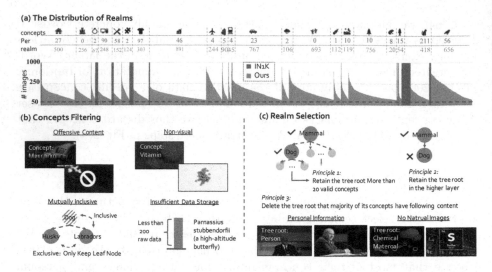

Fig. 2. (a) **The statistic of OmniBenchmark.** We compare the distribution of the concepts of each realm in OmniBenchmark and ImageNet-1k. For ImageNet-1k, 12 out of 21 realms are unseen-realm because ImageNet-1k has less than 20 concepts in these realms. We report the number of concepts per realm of ImageNet-1k and OmniBenchmark in a different color. (b) **Four principles of filtering concepts.** We discard the concept when it implies offensive content, is a non-visual word, is not a leaf node, and has less than 200 raw data. (c) **Three principles of selecting realms.** We illustrate three principles to select semantic realms from numerous sub-trees.

mammal.[5] Therefore, ImageNet-1k hardly becomes an ideal benchmark to evaluate the generalization ability of the omni-vision representation. In contrast, the number of OmniBenchmark-seen-realms is 21 that is twice of ImageNet-1k-seen-realms'. We believe the large spectrum of realms included in OmniBenchmark can relatively thoroughly represents the distribution of realms in the natural domain.

We carefully discuss the potential legal issue of OmniBenchmark, *e.g.* the copyright and privacy issue, in the *supplementary material*.

3.6   Evaluation Protocol

We now present the protocol for OmniBenchmark, and summarize the metrics for the experiments presented in Sect. 5.

Linear Probing. Our benchmark quantifies the generalization ability of visual representation on different semantic realms. We build the evaluation protocol based on the assumption that a good representation is an omni-vision representation that can generalize any specific realm without updating the feature

---

[5] In the following material, the dataset-seen-realms/dataset-unseen-realms is a set of realms. Each dataset-seen-realm/dataset-unseen-realm in it has at least 20 concepts/fewer than 20 concepts.

extractor. Therefore, we keep the pre-trained backbone frozen and use it as the feature extractor. Then, we learn linear logistic regression classifiers for realm-wise datasaets, following the linear probing setting [19].

Metrics. We report the top-1 accuracy for all experiments. In addition, to makes the plots clearer and the differences easier to grasp, we follow the metric setting in the ImageNet-CoG [45] that plots accuracy relative to the baseline ResNet-50 model pre-trained on ImageNet-1k.

4   Methodology

4.1   Preliminaries

Self-supervised Contrastive Learning. A widely-used way to achieve self-supervised learning is contrastive learning, which is proposed in InfoNCE [52]. InfoNCE loss works for pulling positive pairs belonging to the same classes closer and push negative pairs belonging to different classes away is an effective way to achieve self-supervised learning. Specifically, for a set of N sampled pairs, $\{x_k, y_k\}_{k=1...N}$, the corresponding batch used for training consists of $2N$ pairs, $\{\tilde{x}_i, \tilde{y}_i\}_{i=1...2N}$, where $\tilde{x}_{2k}$ and $\tilde{x}_{2k-1}$ are two random augmentations of x_k and $\tilde{y}_{2k} = \tilde{y}_{2k-1} = y_k$. Finally, a N samples batch forms a $2N$ multiview batch, let $i \in I \equiv \{1...2N\}$ be the index of an augmented sample, and let $j(i)$ be the index of the other augmented sample originating from the same source sample. For a given sample i, the loss takes the following form:

$$\mathcal{L}_i = -\log \frac{\exp(z_i \cdot z_{j(i)})}{\sum_{a \in A(i)} \exp(z_i \cdot z_a)}. \tag{1}$$

Here, $z_i = Encoder(x_i)$, $A(i) \equiv I \setminus \{i\}$, the index i is called the anchor, index $j(i)$ is called the positive, and the other $2(N-1)$ indexes ($A(i) \equiv I \setminus \{i\}$) are called the negative.

Supervised Contrastive Learning. To add label information into the self-supervised representation learning, Khosla *et al.* [26] proposed the supervised contrastive learning (Supcon) in the following way:

$$\mathcal{L}_i = -\sum_{z_+ \in P(i)} \log \frac{\exp(z_i \cdot z_+)}{\sum_{z_k \in A(i)} \exp(z_i \cdot z_k)}, \quad P(i) \equiv \{p \in A(i) : \tilde{y}_p = \tilde{y}_i\}. \tag{2}$$

Parametric Contrastive Learning. Cui *et al.* [13] introduce a set of para-metric class-wise learnable center $\mathbf{C} = \{c_1, c_2, ..., c_n\}$ into the original supervised contrastive learning, and named a new framework: Parametric Contrastive learn-ing (PaCo). Here, n is the number of the classes. Specifically, the loss is change to.

$$\mathcal{L}_i = -\sum_{z_+ \in P(i) \cup \{c_{\tilde{y}}\}} \log \frac{\exp(z_i \cdot z_+)}{\sum_{z_k \in A(i) \cup \mathbf{C}} \exp(z_i \cdot z_k)}. \tag{3}$$

PaCo boosts the performance of Supcon on several datasets.

4.2 Motivation

Previous Supcon and PaCo methods sample negative samples uniformly over the datasets. However, some negative samples are semantics closely to the query sample, *e.g.* the husky and labrador in the Fig. 3(a). Wrongly expelling these negative samples from query samples could break the semantic structure to some extent, hampering the representation learning.

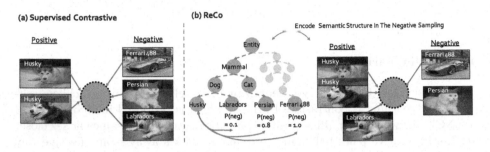

Fig. 3. Supervised contrastive losses *v.s* ReCo. The supervised contrastive loss (left, Eq. 2) contrasts the set of all samples from the same class as positives against the negatives from the remainder of the batch. The ReCo (right, Eq. 6), however, contrasts the set of all samples from the same class as positives against the *real semantic dissimilar* negatives from the remainder of the batch. Leverage semantic relation when sampling negative samples, ReCo provides an embedding space where elements of similar classes (husky and labrador) are aligned closer than in the supervised case.

Motivated by this limitation, we aim to carefully select semantic irrelevant negative samples to the query sample instead of selecting negative samples uniformly. In particular, We propose a novel hierarchical instance contrastive learning framework called Relational Contrastive Learning (ReCo). ReCo captures the semantic relation and then transforms this relation into the probability of being sampled as negative samples, as shown in Fig. 3(b).

4.3 Relational Contrastive Learning

The gist of ReCo is to pulling instances of similar semantic classes closer while pushing instances of dissimilar semantic classes far apart. For a specific query image x, we select real semantic dissimilar negative samples for the contrastive learning by performing Bernoulli sampling on each negative candidate, which is inspired by HCSC [21]. To achieve this goal, we first define a similarity $s(m,n)$ measure between two classes m,n as follows.

$$s(m,n) = -\log \frac{d_{\min}(m,n)+1}{2*\max(l^m,l^n)+1},\tag{4}$$

m,n lie in the hierarchical depth l^m, l^n, and $d_{\min}(m,n)$ denotes the shortest path that connects the m and n in the hypernym/hyponym taxonomy. As shown in Fig. 3(b), since the dog is the father node of the husky, their shortest distance equals one, and the shortest distance between husky and labrador equals two because they are in sibling relation. In addition, $\max(\cdot)$ in the denominator makes the $s(m,q) > s(m,n)$ if q is another class that lies in deeper depth than n and $d_{\min}(m,n) = d_{\min}(m,q)$. We ensure that m should be more related to node that lies in deeper depth because as the hierarchical depth is deeper, the nodes in that depth are more concrete. For example, as shown in Fig. 3(b), the dog should be semantic closer to the husky than to the mammal. Moreover, we normalize the similarity between m and other classes for ensuring $s(m,\cdot) \in [0,1]$.

On such bases, we conduct negative sample selection for a specific instance x_i. For the negative candidate $z_k \in A(i)$, we are more likely to select it if its $S(\widetilde{y}_i, \widetilde{y}_k)$ is low. The negative sampling follows the Bernoulli sampling:

$$A_{select}(i) = \{ß(z_k; P = 1 - s(\widetilde{y}_i, \widetilde{y}_k))|z_k \in A(i)\}, \tag{5}$$

where $ß(z; s)$ denotes a Bernoulli trail of accepting z with similarity S. By using these refined negative samples selection, we define the objective function of ReCo as below

$$\mathcal{L}_i(ReCo) = -\sum_{z_+ \in P(i)} \log \frac{\exp(z_i \cdot z_+)}{\sum_{z_k \in A_{select}(i)} \exp(z_i \cdot z_k)}. \tag{6}$$

In general, ReCo injects the advantages of semantic relation from the hierarchical structure into the negative pairs sampling, and it can effectively regularize the overall contrastive learning:

$$\min_{f(\theta)} \mathcal{L}_{Supcon/PaCo} + \alpha \mathcal{L}_{ReCo}. \tag{7}$$

We note that ReCo is not sensitive to the weight α. We empirically set $\alpha = 1$.

5   Systematic Investigation on OmniBenchmark

We now report our thorough experimental studies on OmniBenchmark. These studies evaluate an extensive suite of recent representation learning methods. We first introduce these methods briefly (Sect. 5.1). Then, we quantify existing intuitions and reveal new insights from the results of the experiments (Sect. 5.2). Finally, we present the ablation studies of ReCo (Sect. 5.3), indicating that ReCo can boost the performance of the state-of-the-art supervised contrastive learning on both the ImageNet-1k and OmniBenchmark.

5.1   Models

We benchmark 22 current models that are split into the following four categories referred to [45].

Self-supervised. We benchmark four types of self-supervised models, including contrastive (MoCov2 [11]), clustering-based (SwAV [7], DINO [8]), feature de-correlation (BarlowTwins [68]), masked autoencoder (MAE [22], BeiT [1]) models. These models are based on the ResNet-50 structure.

Table 1. Up: linear classification result on OmniBenchmark. We present the Top-1 linear probing accuracy on each realm dataset for 25 models listed in Sect. 5.1. **Down: Accuracy relative to the baseline ResNet50.** Accuracy relative to the baseline ResNet50 for the all models, split across the four model categories. For the limited space, we only report the performance of models on 15 out of 21 realms. The complete results are shown in *Supplementary Material*. ImageNet-1k-seen-realms are marked in underline. Consumer. denotes consumer goods, Locom. denotes locomotive.

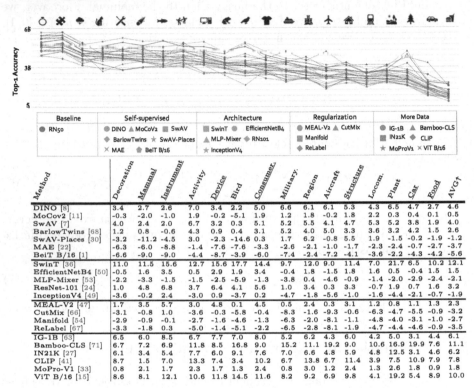

Baseline	Self-supervised		Architecture		Regularization		More Data	
● RN50	● DINO ▲ MoCoV2 ◆ SwAV	◼ SwinT ● EfficientNetB4	● MEAL-V2 ▲ CutMix	● IG-1B ▲ Bamboo-CLS	
	◆ BarlowTwins ★ SwAV-Places	▲ MLP-Mixer ◆ RN101	◼ Manifold	◼ IN21K ◆ CLIP	
	✕ MAE ● BeiT B/16	★ InceptionV4	◆ ReLabel	★ MoProV1 ✕ ViT B/16	

Method	Decoration	Mammal	Instrument	Activity	Device	Bird	Consumer.	Military.	Region	Aircraft	Structure	Locom.	Plant	Car	Food	AVGf
DINO [8]	3.4	2.7	2.6	7.0	3.4	2.2	5.0	6.6	6.1	6.1	5.3	4.3	6.5	4.7	2.7	4.6
MoCov2 [11]	-0.3	-2.0	-1.0	1.9	-0.2	-5.1	1.9	1.2	1.8	-0.2	1.8	2.2	0.3	0.4	0.1	0.5
SwAV [7]	4.0	2.4	2.0	6.7	3.2	0.3	5.1	5.2	5.5	4.1	4.7	5.3	5.2	3.8	1.9	4.0
BarlowTwins [68]	1.2	0.8	-0.6	4.3	0.9	0.4	3.1	5.2	4.0	5.0	3.3	3.6	3.2	4.2	1.5	2.6
SwAV-Places [30]	-3.2	-11.2	-4.5	3.0	-2.3	-14.6	0.3	1.7	6.2	-0.8	5.5	1.9	-1.5	-0.2	-1.9	-1.2
MAE [22]	-6.3	-6.0	-8.8	-1.4	-7.6	-7.6	-3.3	-2.6	-2.1	-1.0	-1.7	-2.3	-2.4	-0.7	-2.7	-3.7
BeiT B/16 [1]	-6.6	-9.0	-9.0	-4.4	-8.7	-3.9	-6.0	-7.4	-2.4	-7.2	-4.1	-3.6	-2.2	-4.3	-4.2	-5.6
SwinT [36]	11.0	11.5	15.6	12.7	15.6	17.7	14.4	9.7	12.0	9.0	11.4	7.0	21.7	6.5	10.2	12.1
EfficientNetB4 [50]	-0.5	1.6	3.5	0.5	2.9	1.9	3.4	-0.4	1.8	-1.5	1.8	1.6	0.5	-0.4	1.5	1.5
MLP-Mixer [53]	-2.2	-3.3	-1.5	-1.5	-2.5	-5.9	-1.3	-3.8	0.4	-4.6	-0.9	-1.4	-2.0	-2.9	-2.4	-2.1
ResNet-101 [24]	1.0	4.8	6.8	3.7	6.4	4.1	5.6	1.0	3.4	0.3	3.3	-0.7	1.9	0.7	1.6	3.2
InceptionV4 [49]	-3.6	-0.2	2.4	-3.0	0.9	-3.7	0.2	-4.7	-1.8	-5.6	-1.0	-1.6	-4.4	-2.1	-0.7	-1.9
MEAL-V2 [47]	1.7	3.5	5.7	3.0	4.8	0.1	4.5	0.5	2.4	0.3	3.1	1.2	0.8	1.1	1.3	2.3
CutMix [66]	-3.1	-0.8	1.0	-3.6	-0.3	-5.8	-0.4	-8.3	-1.6	-9.3	-0.6	-6.3	-4.7	-5.5	-0.9	-3.2
Manifold [54]	-2.9	-0.9	-0.1	-2.7	-1.6	-4.6	-1.3	-6.3	-2.0	-8.1	-1.1	-4.8	-4.0	-3.1	-1.0	-2.7
ReLabel [67]	-3.3	-1.8	0.3	-5.0	-1.4	-5.1	-2.2	-6.5	-2.8	-8.1	-1.9	-4.7	-4.4	-4.6	-0.9	-3.5
IG-1B [63]	6.5	6.0	8.5	6.7	7.7	7.0	8.0	5.2	6.2	4.3	6.0	4.2	5.0	3.1	4.4	6.1
Bamboo-CLS [71]	6.7	7.2	6.9	11.8	8.5	16.8	9.0	15.2	11.1	19.2	9.0	10.6	16.9	19.9	7.6	11.1
IN21K [27]	6.1	3.4	5.4	7.7	6.0	9.1	7.6	7.0	6.6	4.8	5.9	4.8	12.5	3.1	4.6	6.2
CLIP [41]	8.7	1.5	7.0	13.3	7.4	3.4	10.2	6.7	13.8	6.7	11.4	3.9	7.5	10.9	7.9	7.8
MoPro-V1 [33]	0.8	2.1	1.7	2.3	1.7	1.3	2.4	0.8	3.0	1.2	2.4	1.3	2.6	1.8	0.9	1.8
ViT B/16 [15]	8.6	8.1	12.1	10.6	11.8	14.5	11.6	8.2	9.2	6.9	9.8	4.1	19.2	5.4	8.9	10.0

Architecture. We consider several architectures that include CNN based (ResNet-50 [24], ResNet-101 [24], EfficientNet-B4 [50] and Inception-v4 [49]), MLP based (MLP-Mixer [53]), Transformer based (Swin-T [36]). All these models are pre-trained on ImageNet-1k [44].

Regularization. ResNet-50 sized models with regularization techniques applied during the training phase include distillation (MEAL-V2 [47]), label augmentation (Manifold-MixUp [54], CutMix [66] and ReLabel [67]).

Larger Scale Data. ResNet-50 Model pre-trained on the larger scale data (compared with ImageNet-1k (1M)) includes IG-1B [63] that is first pre-trained on IG-1B (1000×) and then fine-tuning on ImageNet-1k; CLIP that is image-text models pre-trained on WebImageText (400×); MoProV1 [33] that is pre-trained on the WebVision-V1 (2×); ViT-B/16 that is pre-trained on the ImageNet-22K

(14×) [14] and then fine-tune on the ImageNet-1k; Bamboo-CLS [71] that is pre-trained on the Bamboo-CLS (65×).

5.2   Benchmarking Results

Table 1 (up) reports top-1 accuracy of all models on different realms. Table 1 (down) presents the performance of four model categories relative to the baseline ResNet50. Our main observations are as follows.

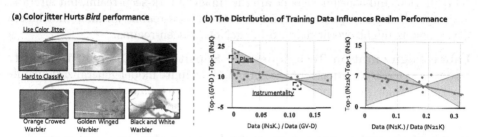

Fig. 4. The highlighted observation of benchmark results. (a) Though color jitters make models insensitive to color, it causes the model unable to classify among *Orange Crowed Warbler*, *Golden Winged Warbler* and *Black and White Warbler*. (b) On the *plant*, the amount of data in IN-1K is 0.08% of Bamboo-CLS; and on the *instrumentality*, the amount of data in IN-1K is 12.5% of Bamboo-CLS. Therefore, when it is compared with IN-1K model, the Bamboo-CLS model obtains larger top-1 accuracy gains on the *plant* than on the *instrumentality*. Each points denotes a realm. (Color figure online)

The Selection of Pertaining Data Affects the Realm Performance. We hypothesize that using a pre-training dataset more similar than ImageNet-1k to a specific end realm dataset will produce a better encoder that performs better on that end realm dataset. We choose one model to test this hypothesis: SwAV-Places. Specifically, SwAV-Places is pre-trained on Places [72] for 200 epochs based on the SwAV framework, and we download the SwAV-Places from [30]. In Table 1 (down) Self-supervised split, we find that for realms (*i.e.* structure and region) that are semantic similar to the Places dataset, SwAV-Places achieves the best performance compared with other Self-supervised learning (SSL) methods. This observation justifies our hypothesis.

Strong Augmentation of SSL Hurts Fine-Grained Realm Performance. SSL relies on strong data augmentation [7,8,11,68] (*e.g.* color jitters) to learn visual representation, encouraging inductive bias. However, some data augmentation strategies may hurt the performance of fine-grain realm [61], *i.e.* Bird. As shown in Table 1 (down) Self-supervised split, except for masked encoder-based methods that use cropping-only augmentation, four out of five SSL methods achieve the worst performance on the bird realm. As illustrated in Fig. 4(a), models that are insensitive to color transformation could struggle to classify between different warbler species.

Larger CNN Models Overfit to ImageNet-1k-Seen-Realms. As shown in Table 1 (down) Architecture split, we compare ResNet-50 with other CNN models with larger parameters. This figure illustrates that larger CNN models, *i.e.* Inception-v4 [49], EfficientNet-B4 [50] and ResNet-101 [24], achieve higher performance than ResNet-50 among most of realms. However, compared to the ResNet-50, we see larger gains that the these models exhibit on the realm: mammal, instrumentality, device, and consumer_goods are practically lost for the realm: aircraft, military_vehicle, and plant. We noted that mammal, instrumentality, device, and consumer_goods are the ImageNet-1k-seen-realm, but aircraft, military_vehicle, and plant are ImageNet-1k-unseen-realm, we infer that larger CNN models might overfit more to ImageNet-1k-seen-realms.

Label Augmentation Techniques are Sensitive to Distribution Shift. Robustness to distribution shift is essential to evaluate model generalization ability [73]. Regularization methods exhibit strong performance gains over ResNet-50 on ImageNet-1k [54,66,67]. However, on the OmniBenchmark, these methods neither achieve good performance in the ImageNet-1k-unseen-realms nor show performance gain in the ImageNet-1k-seen-realms (*e.g.* instrumentality, consumer_goods, device), as shown in Table 1 (down) Regularization split. We note that the ImageNet-1k and OmniBenchmark are built at different times, and the distribution shift thus exists in their data. Poor performance of label augmentation methods even on the ImageNet-1k-seen-realms of OmniBenchmark indicates that augmentation techniques are sensitive to the distribution shift. Unlike the larger parameters models that overfit to ImageNet-1k-seen-realm, which performs well on ImageNet-1k-seen-realm but lag in ImageNet-1k-unseen-realm, label augmentation techniques appear to overfit to ImageNet-1k instead of ImageNet-1k-seen-realm.

The Distribution of Training Data Influences Realm Performance. As shown in Fig. 4(b), we argue that the distribution of training Data influences realm performance on OmniBenchmark. For example, ImageNet-1k has 1,250 times fewer data than Bamboo-CLS on the plant realm, when compared to ResNet-50, Bamboo-CLS obtains 16.9 points gain on that realm of OmniBenchmark. However, since ImageNet-1k has only 8 times fewer data than Bamboo-CLS on the instrumentality realm, Bamboo-CLS obtains only 6.9 points gain. Each point represents a specific realm.

OmniBenchmark is a Better Indicator for Generalization Ability. As shown in Bamboo-CLS paper [71], though DINO outperforms Bamboo-CLS on ImageNet-1k by 5.1%, Bamboo-CLS outperforms DINO by a large margin on other 9 out of 10 downstream tasks that include Food101 [5], SUN397 [60], OxfordPets [40] and *etc.*, which indicate that the ImageNet-1k performance could not accurately indicates pre-trained models' generalization ability in most downstream tasks. Surprisingly, Bamboo-CLS shows its better generalization ability than DINO on OmniBenchmark with 6.5 points gain. This observation align with the benchmarking results in Bamboo-CLS paper, and thus indicates that OmniBenchmark is a better indicator than ImageNet-1k for benchmarking pre-trained mode generalization ability.

5.3   Ablation Study of ReCo

We compare the performance of ReCo, and the state-of-the-art supervised contrastive learning method: parametric contrastive learning (PaCo) on both the pre-training dataset, *i.e.* ImageNet-1k, and OmniBenchmark. Better performance of ReCo indicates that it can effectively boost the current contrastive learning.

Implementation Details. Recently, parametric contrastive learning (PaCo) [13] achieves better ImageNet-1k performance than the conventional supervised contrastive learning (Supcon). To fair comparison, we reproduce PaCo and train ReCo. Specifically, we use ResNet-50 [24] and ResNet-101 [24] as our backbones for experiments. The learning rate decays by a cosine scheduler from 0.1 to 0 with batch size 4096 on 32 GPUs in 200 epochs. These two models are trained using SGD optimizer with momentum $\mu = 0.9$.

Table 2. The performance of SupCon, PaCo and ReCo on ImageNet-1k and OmniBenchmark. On the pre-training dataset, *i.e.* ImageNet-1k, both ReCo ResNet-50 and ResNet-101 models achieve 0.7 top-1 accuracy gain from the state-of-the-art supervised contrastive learning methods, *i.e.* PaCo. On the OmniBenchmark, ReCo ResNet-50 achieves 0.5 top-1 average performance gain from PaCo. Numbers in red are the performance gain on the same backbone network.

Method	Model	IN1K Top-1 ↑	IN1K Top-5 ↑	Omni. AVG↑
Supcon	ResNet-50	75.1	92.0	35.8
PaCo	ResNet-50	75.9	92.5	36.4
ReCo	ResNet-50	**76.6** (+0.7)	**93.0** (+0.5)	**36.9** (+0.5)
Supcon	ResNet-101	78.9	94.4	37.9
PaCo	ResNet-101	79.1	94.4	38.4
ReCo	ResNet-101	**79.8** (+0.7)	**94.8** (+0.4)	**38.7** (+0.3)

Results on IN-1K and OmniBenchmark. The experimental results are summarized in Table 2. Our ResNet-50 model outperforms PaCo baseline models by 0.7%. And ReCo ResNet-50 improves the average top-1 performance of ReCo on the OmniBenchmark with a 0.5 point gain.

6   Conclusion

In our work, we develop a methodology for constructing a large-scale omni-realm benchmark, namely OmniBenchmark. Especially, as the basic building block of the OmniBenchmark, we define the visual realm indicated by expert knowledge, *i.e.* WordNet. Through extensive studies of recent representation learning methods, we find several insights. For example, the distribution of training data influences realm performance on our OmniBenchamrk. Besides, we propose a novel supervised contrastive learning, *i.e.* ReCo. ReCo selects the semantic dissimilar negative pairs rather than exhaustive sampling, boosting the performance of state-of-the-art supervised contrastive learning methods not only on ImageNet-1k but also on the OmniBenchmark. With the advent of the parameter-efficient tuning methods [25,74,75] in the vision task, we plan to evaluate various representation learning paradigm in the parameter-efficient tuning setting in the future. Overall, we hope our work could facilitate future research in omni-vision.

Acknowledgement. This work is supported by NTU NAP, MOE AcRF Tier 2 (T2EP20221-0033), and under the RIE2020 Industry Alignment Fund—Industry Collaboration Projects (IAF-ICP) Funding Initiative, as well as cash and in-kind contribution from the industry partner(s).

References

1. Bao, H., Dong, L., Wei, F.: BEiT: BERT pre-training of image transformers (2021)
2. Ben, H.: Duplicate image detection with perceptual hashing in python (2017). https://benhoyt.com/writings/duplicate-image-detection/#difference-hash-dhash
3. Bertinetto, L., Mueller, R., Tertikas, K., Samangooei, S., Lord, N.A.: Making better mistakes: leveraging class hierarchies with deep networks. In: CVPR, pp. 12506–12515 (2020)
4. Bommasani, R., et al.: On the opportunities and risks of foundation models. arXiv preprint arXiv:2108.07258 (2021)
5. Bossard, L., Guillaumin, M., Van Gool, L.: Food-101 – mining discriminative components with random forests. In: Fleet, D., Pajdla, T., Schiele, B., Tuytelaars, T. (eds.) ECCV 2014. LNCS, vol. 8694, pp. 446–461. Springer, Cham (2014). https://doi.org/10.1007/978-3-319-10599-4_29
6. Caron, M., Bojanowski, P., Joulin, A., Douze, M.: Deep clustering for unsupervised learning of visual features. In: Ferrari, V., Hebert, M., Sminchisescu, C., Weiss, Y. (eds.) Computer Vision – ECCV 2018. LNCS, vol. 11218, pp. 139–156. Springer, Cham (2018). https://doi.org/10.1007/978-3-030-01264-9_9
7. Caron, M., Misra, I., Mairal, J., Goyal, P., Bojanowski, P., Joulin, A.: Unsupervised learning of visual features by contrasting cluster assignments. arXiv preprint arXiv:2006.09882 (2020)
8. Caron, M., et al.: Emerging properties in self-supervised vision transformers (2021)
9. Chatfield, K., Simonyan, K., Vedaldi, A., Zisserman, A.: Return of the devil in the details: delving deep into convolutional nets. arXiv preprint arXiv:1405.3531 (2014)
10. Chen, T., Kornblith, S., Norouzi, M., Hinton, G.: A simple framework for contrastive learning of visual representations. In: ICML, pp. 1597–1607. PMLR (2020)
11. Chen, X., Fan, H., Girshick, R., He, K.: Improved baselines with momentum contrastive learning. arXiv preprint arXiv:2003.04297 (2020)

12. Coates, A., Ng, A., Lee, H.: An analysis of single-layer networks in unsupervised feature learning. In: Proceedings of the Fourteenth International Conference on Artificial Intelligence and Statistics. JMLR Workshop and Conference Proceedings, pp. 215–223 (2011)

13. Cui, J., Zhong, Z., Liu, S., Yu, B., Jia, J.: Parametric contrastive learning (2021)

14. Deng, J., Dong, W., Socher, R., Li, L.J., Li, K., Fei-Fei, L.: ImageNet: a large-scale hierarchical image database. In: CVPR, pp. 248–255. IEEE (2009)

15. Dosovitskiy, A., et al.: An image is worth 16×16 words: transformers for image recognition at scale. arXiv preprint arXiv:2010.11929 (2020)

16. Dosovitskiy, A., Fischer, P., Springenberg, J.T., Riedmiller, M., Brox, T.: Discriminative unsupervised feature learning with exemplar convolutional neural networks. TPAMI **38**(9), 1734–1747 (2015)

17. Everingham, M., Van Gool, L., Williams, C.K., Winn, J., Zisserman, A.: The Pascal visual object classes (VOC) challenge. IJCV **88**(2), 303–338 (2010). https://doi.org/10.1007/s11263-009-0275-4

18. Fei-Fei, L., Fergus, R., Perona, P.: Learning generative visual models from few training examples: an incremental Bayesian approach tested on 101 object categories. In: CVPR Workshop, pp. 178–178. IEEE (2004)

19. Goyal, P., Mahajan, D., Gupta, A., Misra, I.: Scaling and benchmarking self-supervised visual representation learning. In: ICCV, pp. 6391–6400 (2019)

20. Guo, J.N., Mao, X.L., Wei, W., Huang, H.: Intra-category aware hierarchical supervised document hashing. IEEE Trans. Knowl. Data Eng. (2022)

21. Guo, Y., et al.: HCSC: hierarchical contrastive selective coding. arXiv preprint arXiv:2202.00455 (2022)

22. He, K., Chen, X., Xie, S., Li, Y., Dollár, P., Girshick, R.: Masked autoencoders are scalable vision learners (2021)

23. He, K., Fan, H., Wu, Y., Xie, S., Girshick, R.: Momentum contrast for unsupervised visual representation learning. In: CVPR, pp. 9729–9738 (2020)

24. He, K., Zhang, X., Ren, S., Sun, J.: Deep residual learning for image recognition. In: CVPR, pp. 770–778 (2016)

25. Jia, M., et al.: Visual prompt tuning. arXiv preprint arXiv:2203.12119 (2022)

26. Khosla, P., et al.: Supervised contrastive learning. In: Advances in Neural Information Processing Systems, vol. 33, pp. 18661–18673 (2020)

27. Kolesnikov, A., et al.: Big transfer (BiT): general visual representation learning. In: Vedaldi, A., Bischof, H., Brox, T., Frahm, J.-M. (eds.) ECCV 2020. LNCS, vol. 12350, pp. 491–507. Springer, Cham (2020). https://doi.org/10.1007/978-3-030-58558-7_29

28. Kolesnikov, A., Zhai, X., Beyer, L.: Revisiting self-supervised visual representation learning. In: CVPR, pp. 1920–1929 (2019)

29. Kornblith, S., Shlens, J., Le, Q.V.: Do better ImageNet models transfer better? In: CVPR, pp. 2661–2671 (2019)

30. Kotar, K., Ilharco, G., Schmidt, L., Ehsani, K., Mottaghi, R.: Contrasting contrastive self-supervised representation learning models. arXiv preprint arXiv:2103.14005 (2021)

31. Krizhevsky, A., Hinton, G., et al.: Learning multiple layers of features from tiny images (2009)

32. Larsson, G., Maire, M., Shakhnarovich, G.: Learning representations for automatic colorization. In: Leibe, B., Matas, J., Sebe, N., Welling, M. (eds.) ECCV 2016. LNCS, vol. 9908, pp. 577–593. Springer, Cham (2016). https://doi.org/10.1007/978-3-319-46493-0_35

33. Li, J., Xiong, C., Hoi, S.C.: MoPro: webly supervised learning with momentum prototypes. In: ICLR (2021)
34. Li, J., Zhou, P., Xiong, C., Socher, R., Hoi, S.C.: Prototypical contrastive learning of unsupervised representations. arXiv preprint arXiv:2005.04966 (2020)
35. Lin, T.-Y., et al.: Microsoft COCO: common objects in context. In: Fleet, D., Pajdla, T., Schiele, B., Tuytelaars, T. (eds.) ECCV 2014. LNCS, vol. 8693, pp. 740–755. Springer, Cham (2014). https://doi.org/10.1007/978-3-319-10602-1_48
36. Liu, Z., et al.: Swin transformer: hierarchical vision transformer using shifted windows (2021)
37. Ma, X., et al.: RelViT: concept-guided vision transformer for visual relational reasoning. In: International Conference on Learning Representations (2022). https://openreview.net/forum?id=afoV8W3-IYp
38. Miller, G.A.: WordNet: An Electronic Lexical Database. MIT Press, Cambridge (1998)
39. Misra, I., van der Maaten, L.: Self-supervised learning of pretext-invariant representations. In: CVPR, pp. 6707–6717 (2020)
40. Parkhi, O.M., Vedaldi, A., Zisserman, A., Jawahar, C.: Cats and dogs. In: CVPR, pp. 3498–3505. IEEE (2012)
41. Radford, A., et al.: Learning transferable visual models from natural language supervision. arXiv preprint arXiv:2103.00020 (2021)
42. Rebuffi, S.A., Bilen, H., Vedaldi, A.: Learning multiple visual domains with residual adapters (2017)
43. Recht, B., Roelofs, R., Schmidt, L., Shankar, V.: Do ImageNet classifiers generalize to ImageNet? In: International Conference on Machine Learning, pp. 5389–5400. PMLR (2019)
44. Russakovsky, O., et al.: ImageNet large scale visual recognition challenge. IJCV 115(3), 211–252 (2015). https://doi.org/10.1007/s11263-015-0816-y
45. Sariyildiz, M.B., Kalantidis, Y., Larlus, D., Alahari, K.: Concept generalization in visual representation learning (2021)
46. Shao, J., et al.: INTERN: a new learning paradigm towards general vision. arXiv preprint arXiv:2111.08687 (2021)
47. Shen, Z., Savvides, M.: MEAL V2: boosting vanilla ResNet-50 to 80%+ top-1 accuracy on ImageNet without tricks (2021)
48. Simonyan, K., Zisserman, A.: Very deep convolutional networks for large-scale image recognition. arXiv preprint arXiv:1409.1556 (2014)
49. Szegedy, C., Ioffe, S., Vanhoucke, V., Alemi, A.: Inception-v4, inception-ResNet and the impact of residual connections on learning (2016)
50. Tan, M., Le, Q.V.: EfficientNet: rethinking model scaling for convolutional neural networks (2020)
51. Pellissier Tanon, T., Weikum, G., Suchanek, F.: YAGO 4: a reason-able knowledge base. In: Harth, A., et al. (eds.) ESWC 2020. LNCS, vol. 12123, pp. 583–596. Springer, Cham (2020). https://doi.org/10.1007/978-3-030-49461-2_34
52. Tian, Y., Sun, C., Poole, B., Krishnan, D., Schmid, C., Isola, P.: What makes for good views for contrastive learning? (2020)
53. Tolstikhin, I., et al.: MLP-Mixer: an all-MLP architecture for vision (2021)
54. Verma, V., et al.: Manifold mixup: better representations by interpolating hidden states. In: ICML (2019)
55. Vrandečić, D., Krötzsch, M.: Wikidata: a free collaborative knowledgebase. Commun. ACM 57(10), 78–85 (2014)
56. Wang, W., Zhou, T., Qi, S., Shen, J., Zhu, S.C.: Hierarchical human semantic parsing with comprehensive part-relation modeling. TPAMI 44(7), 3508–3522 (2022)

57. Wang, Y., et al.: Deep fuzzy tree for large-scale hierarchical visual classification. IEEE Trans. Fuzzy Syst. **28**(7), 1395–1406 (2019)
58. Wang, Y., Wang, Z., Hu, Q., Zhou, Y., Su, H.: Hierarchical semantic risk minimization for large-scale classification. IEEE Trans. Cybern. **52**(9), 9546–9558 (2022)
59. Wu, Z., Xiong, Y., Yu, S.X., Lin, D.: Unsupervised feature learning via nonparametric instance discrimination. In: CVPR, pp. 3733–3742 (2018)
60. Xiao, J., Ehinger, K.A., Hays, J., Torralba, A., Oliva, A.: SUN database: exploring a large collection of scene categories. IJCV **119**(1), 3–22 (2016). https://doi.org/10.1007/s11263-014-0748-y
61. Xiao, T., Wang, X., Efros, A.A., Darrell, T.: What should not be contrastive in contrastive learning (2021)
62. Xie, Q., Luong, M.T., Hovy, E., Le, Q.V.: Self-training with noisy student improves ImageNet classification. In: CVPR, pp. 10687–10698 (2020)
63. Yalniz, I.Z., Jégou, H., Chen, K., Paluri, M., Mahajan, D.: Billion-scale semi-supervised learning for image classification. arXiv preprint arXiv:1905.00546 (2019)
64. Yang, K., Qinami, K., Fei-Fei, L., Deng, J., Russakovsky, O.: Towards fairer datasets: filtering and balancing the distribution of the people subtree in the ImageNet hierarchy. In: Proceedings of the 2020 Conference on Fairness, Accountability, and Transparency, pp. 547–558 (2020)
65. Yang, S., Luo, P., Loy, C.C., Tang, X.: Wider face: a face detection benchmark. In: CVPR, pp. 5525–5533 (2016)
66. Yun, S., Han, D., Oh, S.J., Chun, S., Choe, J., Yoo, Y.: CutMix: regularization strategy to train strong classifiers with localizable features (2019)
67. Yun, S., Oh, S.J., Heo, B., Han, D., Choe, J., Chun, S.: Re-labeling ImageNet: from single to multi-labels, from global to localized labels. arXiv preprint arXiv:2101.05022 (2021)
68. Zbontar, J., Jing, L., Misra, I., LeCun, Y., Deny, S.: Barlow twins: self-supervised learning via redundancy reduction (2021)
69. Zhai, X., et al.: A large-scale study of representation learning with the visual task adaptation benchmark. arXiv preprint arXiv:1910.04867 (2019)
70. Zhang, R., Isola, P., Efros, A.A.: Colorful image colorization. In: Leibe, B., Matas, J., Sebe, N., Welling, M. (eds.) ECCV 2016. LNCS, vol. 9907, pp. 649–666. Springer, Cham (2016). https://doi.org/10.1007/978-3-319-46487-9_40
71. Zhang, Y., et al.: Bamboo: building mega-scale vision dataset continually with human-machine synergy. arXiv preprint arXiv:2203.07845 (2022)
72. Zhou, B., Lapedriza, A., Khosla, A., Oliva, A., Torralba, A.: Places: a 10 million image database for scene recognition. TPAMI **40**(6), 1452–1464 (2018)
73. Zhou, K., Liu, Z., Qiao, Y., Xiang, T., Loy, C.C.: Domain generalization: a survey (2021)
74. Zhou, K., Yang, J., Loy, C.C., Liu, Z.: Conditional prompt learning for vision-language models. In: Proceedings of the IEEE/CVF Conference on Computer Vision and Pattern Recognition (CVPR) (2022)
75. Zhou, K., Yang, J., Loy, C.C., Liu, Z.: Learning to prompt for vision-language models. Int. J. Comput. Vis. (IJCV) **130**, 2337–2348 (2022). https://doi.org/10.1007/s11263-022-01653-1
76. Zoph, B., et al.: Rethinking pre-training and self-training. arXiv preprint arXiv:2006.06882 (2020)

BEAT: A Large-Scale Semantic and Emotional Multi-modal Dataset for Conversational Gestures Synthesis

Haiyang Liu[1]([✉]), Zihao Zhu[2], Naoya Iwamoto[3], Yichen Peng[4], Zhengqing Li[4], You Zhou[3], Elif Bozkurt[5], and Bo Zheng[3]

[1] The University of Tokyo, Tokyo, Japan
liuhaiyang@kmj.iis.u-tokyo.ac.jp
[2] Keio University, Tokyo, Japan
[3] Digital Human Lab, Huawei Technologies Japan K.K., Tokyo, Japan
[4] Japan Advanced Institute of Science and Technology, Nomi, Japan
[5] Huawei Turkey R&D Center, Istanbul, Turkey

Fig. 1. Overview. BEAT is a large-scale, multi-modal mo-cap human gestures dataset with semantic, emotional annotations, diverse speakers and multiple languages.

Abstract. Achieving realistic, vivid, and human-like synthesized conversational gestures conditioned on multi-modal data is still an unsolved problem due to the lack of available datasets, models and standard evaluation metrics. To address this, we build **B**ody-**E**xpression-**A**udio-**T**ext dataset, **BEAT**, which has i) 76 h, high-quality, multi-modal data captured from 30 speakers talking with eight different emotions and in four different languages, ii) 32 millions frame-level emotion and semantic relevance annotations. Our statistical analysis on BEAT demonstrates the correlation of conversational gestures with *facial expressions*, *emotions*, and *semantics*, in addition to the known correlation with *audio*, *text*, and *speaker identity*. Based on this observation, we propose a baseline

Supplementary Information The online version contains supplementary material available at https://doi.org/10.1007/978-3-031-20071-7_36.

model, **C**ascaded **M**otion **N**etwork (**CaMN**), which consists of above six modalities modeled in a cascaded architecture for gesture synthesis. To evaluate the semantic relevancy, we introduce a metric, Semantic Relevance Gesture Recall (**SRGR**). Qualitative and quantitative experiments demonstrate metrics' validness, ground truth data quality, and baseline's state-of-the-art performance. To the best of our knowledge, BEAT is the largest motion capture dataset for investigating human gestures, which may contribute to a number of different research fields, including controllable gesture synthesis, cross-modality analysis, and emotional gesture recognition. The data, code and model are available on https://pantomatrix.github.io/BEAT/.

1   Introduction

Synthesizing conversational gestures can be helpful for animation, entertainment, education and virtual reality applications. To accomplish this, the complex relationship between speech, facial expressions, emotions, speaker identity and semantic meaning of gestures has to be carefully considered in the design of the gesture synthesis models.

While synthesizing conversational gestures based on audio [20,32,52] or text [3,5,8,53] has been widely studied, synthesizing realistic, vivid, human-like conversational gestures is still unsolved and challenging for several reasons. i) **Quality and scale of the dataset.** Previously proposed methods [32,52] were trained on limited mo-cap datasets [17,46] or on pseudo-label [20,21,52] datasets (*cf.* Table 1), which results in limited generalization capability and lack of robustness. ii) **Rich and paired multi-modal data.** Previous works adopted one or two modalities [20,52,53] to synthesize gestures and reported that conversational gestures are determined by multiple modalities together. However, due to the lack of paired multi-modal data, the analysis of other modalities, *e.g.*, facial expression, for gesture synthesis is still missing. iii) **Speaker style disentanglement.** All available datasets, as shown in Table 1, either have only a single speaker [17], or many speakers but different speakers talk about different topics [20,21,52]. Speaker-specific styles were not much investigated in previous studies due to the lack of data. iv) **Emotion annotation.** Existing work [7] analyzes the emotion-conditioned gestures by extracting implicit sentiment features from texts. Due to the unlabeled, limited emotion categories in the dataset [52], it cannot cover enough emotion in daily conversations. v) **Semantic relevance.** Due to the lack of semantic relevance annotation, only a few works [31,52] analyze the correlation between generated gestures and semantics though listing subjective visualization examples. It will enable synthesizing context-related meaningful gestures if existing semantic labels of gestures. In conclusion, the absence of a large-scale, high-quality multi-modal dataset with semantic and emotional annotation is the main obstacle to synthesizing human-like conversational gestures.

There are two design choices for collecting unlabeled multi-modal data, i) the pseudo-label approach [20,21,52], *i.e.*, extracting conversational gestures, facial landmark from in-the-wild videos using 3D pose estimation algorithms [12] and

Table 1. Comparison of Datasets. We compare with all 3D conversational gesture and face datasets. "#", "LM" and "BSW" indicate the number, landmark and blendshape weight, respectively. best and second are highlighted. Our dataset is the largest mocap dataset with multi-modal data and annotations

dataset	Quailty	Modality						Annotation		Scale	
		#body	#hand	face	audio	text	#speaker	#emo	sem	#seq	dura
TED [52]	pseudo	9	–	–	En	✓	>100	–	–	1400	97 h
S2G [20,21]	label	14	42	2D LM	En	–	6	–	–	N/A	33 h
MPI [47]		23	–	–	–	✓	1	11	–	1408	1.5 h
VOCA [16]		–	–	3D Mesh	En	–	12	–	–	480	0.5 h
Takechi [46]	mo-cap	24	38	–	Jp	–	2	–	–	1049	5 h
Trinity [17]		24	38	–	En	✓	1	–	–	23	4 h
BEAT (Ours)	mo-cap	27	48	3D BSW	E/C/S/J	✓	30	8	✓	2508	76 h

ii) the motion capture approach [17], *i.e.*, recording the data of speakers through predefined themes or texts. In contrast to the pseudo-labeling approach, which allows for low-cost, semi-automated access to large-scale training data, *e.g.*, 97h [52], motion-captured data requires a higher cost and more manual work resulting in smaller dataset sizes, *e.g.*, 4h [17]. However, Due to the motion capture can be strictly controlled and designed in advance, it is able to ensure the quality and diversity of the data, e.g., eight different emotions of the same speaker, and different gestures of 30 speakers talking in the same sentences. Besides, high-quality motion capture data are indispensable to evaluate the effectiveness of pseudo-label training.

Based on the above analysis, to address these data-related problems, we built a mo-cap dataset **BEAT** containing semantic and eight different emotional annotations (*cf.* Fig. 1), from 30 speakers in four modalities of **B**ody-**E**xpression-**A**udio-**T**ext, annotated in total of 30M frames. The motion capture environment is strictly controlled to ensure quality and diversity, with 76 h and more than 2500 topic-segmented sequences. Speakers with different language mastery provided data in three other languages at different durations and in pairs. The ratio of actors/actresses, range of phonemes, and variety of languages are carefully designed to cover natural language characteristics. For emotional gestures, feedback on the speakers' expressions was provided by professional instructors during the recording process and re-recorded in case of non-expressive gesturing to ensure the expressiveness and quality of the entire dataset. After statistical analysis on BEAT, we observed the correlation of conversational gestures with *facial expressions*, *emotions*, and *semantics*, in addition to the known correlation with *audio*, *text*, and *speaker identity*.

Additionally, we propose a baseline neural network architecture, **C**ascaded **M**otion **N**etwork (**CaMN**), which learns synthesizing body and hand gestures by inputting all six modalities mentioned above. The proposed model consists of cascaded encoders and decoders for enhancing the contribution of audio and facial modalities. Besides, in order to evaluate the semantic relevancy, we propose **S**emantic-**R**elevant **G**esture **R**ecall (**SRGR**), which weights Probability of

Correct Keypoint (PCK) based on semantic scores of the ground truth data. Overall, our contributions can be summarized as follows:

- We release BEAT, which is the first gesture dataset with semantic and emotional annotation, and the largest motion capture dataset in terms of duration and available modalities to the best of our knowledge.
- We propose CaMN as a baseline model that inputs audio, text, facial blendweight, speaker identity, emotion and semantic score to synthesize conversational body and hand gestures through cascaded network architecture.
- We introduce SRGR to evaluate the semantic relevancy as well as the human preference for conversational gestures.

Finally, qualitative and quantitative experiments demonstrate the data quality of BEAT, the state-of-the-art performance of CaMN and the validness of SRGR.

2   Related Work

Conversational Gestures Dataset. We first review mo-cap and pseudo-label conversational gestures datasets. Volkova *et al.* [47] built a mo-cap emotional gestures dataset in 89 mins with text annotation, Takeuchi *et al.* [45] captured an interview-like audio-gesture dataset in total 3.5-h with two Japanese speakers. Ferstl and Mcdonnell [17] collected a 4-hour dataset, Trinity, with a single male speaker discussing hobbies, *etc.*, which is the most common used mo-cap dataset for conversational gestures synthesis. On the other hand, Ginosar *et al.* [20] used OpenPose [12] to extract 2D poses from YouTube videos as training data for 144 h, called S2G Dataset. Habibie *et al.* [21] extended it to a full 3D body with facial landmarks, and the last available data is 33 h. Similarly, Yoon *et al.* [52] used VideoPose3D [39] to build on the TED dataset, which is 97 h with 9 joints on upper body. The limited data amount of mo-cap and noise in ground truth makes a trade-off for the trained network's generalization capability and quality. Similar to our work, several datasets are built for talking-face generation and the datasets can be divided into 3D scan face, *e.g.*, VOCA [46] and MeshTalk [42] or RGB images [4,11,15,26,49]. However, these datasets cannot be adopted to synthesize human gestures.

Semantic or Emotion-Aware Motion Synthesis. Semantic analysis of motion has been studied in the action recognition and the sign-language analysis/synthesis research domains. For example, in some of action recognition datasets [9,13,14,25,28,34,40,43,44,48] clips of action with the corresponding label of a single action, *e.g.*, running, walking [41] is used. Another example is audio-driven sign-language synthesis [27], where hand gestures have specific semantics. However, these datasets do not apply to conversational gestures synthesis since gestures used in natural conversations are more complex than single actions, and their semantic meaning differs from sign-language semantics. Recently, Bhattacharya [7] extracted emotional cues from text and used them for gesture synthesis. However, the proposed method has limitations in the accuracy of the emotion classification algorithm and the diversity of emotion categories in the dataset.

Conditional Conversational Gestures Synthesis. Early baseline models were released with datasets such as text-conditioned gesture [53], audio-conditioned gesture [17,20,45], and audio-text-conditioned gesture [52]. These baseline models were based on CNN and LSTM for end-to-end modelling. Several efforts try to improve the performance of the baseline model by input/output representation selection [19,30], adversarial training [18] and various types of generative modeling techniques [1,36,50,51], which can be summarized by "Estimating a better distribution of gestures based on the given conditions.". As an example, StyleGestures [2] uses Flow-based model [23] and additional control signal to sample gesture from the distribution. Probabilistic gesture generation enables generating diversity based on noise, which is achieved by CGAN [51], WGAN [50]. However, due to the lack of paired multi-modal data, the analysis of other modalities, *e.g.*, facial expression, for gesture synthesis is still missing.

3   BEAT: Body-Expression-Audio-Text Dataset

In this section, we introduce the proposed Body-Expression-Audio-Text (BEAT) Dataset. First, we describe the dataset acquisition process and then introduce text, emotion, and semantic relevance information annotation. Finally, we use BEAT to analyze the correlation between conversational gestures and emotions and show the distribution of semantic relevance.

3.1   Data Acquisition

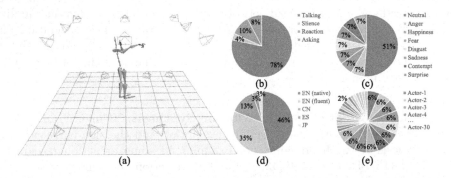

Fig. 2. Capture System and Subject Distribution of BEAT. (a) A 16-camera motion capture system is adopted to record data in Conversation and Self-Talk sessions. (b) Gestures are divided into four categories in Conversation session. (c) Seven additional emotion categories are set in equal proportions in the self-talk session. Besides, (d) our dataset includes four languages which mainly consist of English, (e) by 30 speakers from ten countries with different recording duration.

Motion Capture System. The motion capture system shown in Fig. 2a, is based on 16 synchronized cameras recording motion 120 Hz. We use Vicon's suits with 77 markers (*cf.* supplementary materials for the location of markers on the body). The facial capture system uses ARKit with a depth camera on iPhone 12 Pro, which extracts 52 blendshape weights 60 Hz. The blendshape targets are designed based on Facial Action Coding System (FACS) and are widely used by industry novice users. The audio is recorded in a 48 KHz stereo.

Design Criteria. BEAT is equally divided into *conversation* and *self-talk* sessions, which consist of 10-min and 1-min sequences, respectively. The conversation is between the speaker and the instructor remotely, *i.e.*, to ensure only the speaker's voice is recorded. As shown in Fig. 2b, The speaker's gestures are divided into four categories talking, instantaneous reactions to questions, the state of thinking (silence) and asking. We timed each category's duration during the recording process. Topics were selected from 20 predcfined topics, which cover 33% and 67% debate and description topics, respectively. *Conversation* sessions would record the neutral conversations without acting to ensure the diversity of the dataset. The *self-talk* sessions consist of 120 1-minute self-talk recordings, where speakers answer questions about daily conversation topics, *e.g.*, personal experiences or hobbies. The answers were written and proofread by three English native speakers, and the phonetic coverage was controlled to be similar to the frequently used 3000 words [24]. We covered 8 emotions, *neutral, anger, happiness, fear, disgust, sadness, contempt* and *surprise*, in the dataset referring to [35] and the ratio of each emotion is shown in Fig. 2c. Among the 120 questions, 64 were for neutral emotions, and the remaining seven had eight questions each. Different speakers were asked to talk about the same content with their personalized gestures. Details about predefined answers and pronunciation distribution are available in the supplementary materials.

Speaker Selection and Language Ratio. We strictly control the proportion of languages as well as accents to ensure the generalization capability of the dataset. As shown in Fig. 2d, the dataset consists mainly of English data: 60 h (81%), 12 h of Chinese, 2 h of Spanish and Japanese. The Spanish and Japanese are also 50% of the size of the previous mo-cap dataset [17]. The English component includes 34 h of 10 native English speakers, including the US, UK, and Australia, and 26 h of 20 fluent English speakers from other countries. As shown in Fig. 2e, 30 speakers (including 15 females) from different ethnicities can be grouped into two depending on their total recording duration as 4-h (10 speakers) and 1-h (20 speakers), where the 1-h data is proposed for few-shot learning experiments. It is recommended to check the supplementary material for details of the speakers.

Recording. Speakers were asked to read answers in self-talk sections proficiently. However, they were not guided to perform a specific style of gesture but were encouraged to show a natural, personal, daily style of conversational gestures. Speakers would watch 2–10 mins of emotionally stimulating videos corresponding to different emotions before talking with the particular emotion. A professional speaker would instruct them to elicit the corresponding emotion correctly. We re-record any unqualified data to ensure the data's correctness and quality.

3.2 Data Annotation

Text Alignment. We use an in-house-built Automatic Speech Recognizer (ASR) to obtain the initial text for the conversation session and proofread it by annotators. Then, we adopt Montreal Forced Aligner (MFA) aligner [37] for temporal alignment of the text with audio.

Emotion and Semantic Relevance. The 8-class emotion label of self-talk is confirmed, and the on-site supervision guarantees the correctness. For the conversation session, annotators would watch the video with corresponding audio and gestures to perform frame-level annotation. For the semantic relevance, we get the score on a scale of 0–10 from assigned 600 annotators from Amazon Mechanical Turk (AMT). The annotators were asked to annotate a small amount of test data as a qualification check, of which only 118 annotators succeeded in the qualification phase for the final data annotation. We paid ∼ $10 for each annotator per hour in this task.

(a) (b)

Fig. 3. Emotional Gesture Clustering and Examples. (a) T-SNE visualization for gestures in eight emotion categories. Gestures with different emotions are basically distinguished into different groups, *e.g.*, the Happiness (blue) and Anger (orange). (b) Examples of Happiness (top) and Anger gestures from speaker-2. (Color figure online)

3.3 Data Analysis

The collection and annotation of BEAT have made it possible to analyze correlations between conversational gestures and other modalities. While the connection between gestures and audio, text and speaker identity has been widely studied. We further discuss the correlations between gestures, facial expressions, emotions, and semantics.

Facial Expression and Emotion. Facial expressions and emotions were strongly correlated (excluding some of the lip movements), and we first analyze the correlation between conversational gestures and emotional categories here. As shown in Fig. 3a, We visualized the gestures in T-SNE based on a 2s-rotation representation, and the results showed that gestures have different characteristics in different emotions. For example, as shown in Fig. 3b, speaker-2 has different gesture styles when angry and happy, e.g., the gestures are larger and faster when angry. The T-SNE results also significantly differ between happy (blue) and angry (yellow). However, the gestures for the different emotions are still not perfectly separable by the rotation representation. Furthermore, the gestures of the different emotions appear to be confounded in each region, which is also consistent with subjective perceptions.

Distribution of Semantic Relevance. There is large randomness for the semantic relevance between gestures and texts, which is shown in Fig. 4, where the frequency, position and content of the semantic-related gestures vary from speaker to speaker when the same text content is uttered. In order to better understand the distribution of the semantic relevance of the gestures, we conducted a semantic relevance study based on four hours of two speakers' data. As shown in Figure 4b, for the overall data, 83% of the gestures have low semantic scores (≤ 0.2). For the words-level, the semantic distribution varied between words, e.g., i and was which are sharing a similar semantic score but different

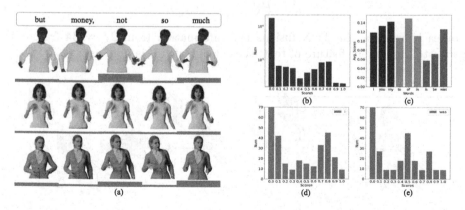

Fig. 4. Distribution of semantic labels. (a) Different speaker ID speaks in a same phase happens different levels of semantic relevance and different styles of gesture. (b) The overall semantic distribution of BEAT. (c) The semantic relevance of the high frequency words which are grouped by their lexical in different color. (d, e) Different distribution of semantic relevance happens in words i and was even sharing almost the same level of semantic relevance. (Color figure online)

in the score distribution. Besides, Figure 4c shows the average semantic scores of nine high-frequency words in the text corpus. It is to be mentioned that the scores of the *Be-verbs* showed are comparatively lower than that *Pronouns* and *Prepositions* which are shown in blue and yellow, respectively. Ultimately, it presents a different probability distribution to the semantically related gestures.

4   Multi-modal Conditioned Gestures Synthesis Baseline

In this section, we propose a baseline that inputs all the modalities for generating vivid, human-like conversational gestures. The proposed baseline, Cascaded Motion Network (CaMN), is shown in Fig. 5, which encodes text, emotion condition, speaker identity, audio and facial blendshape weights to synthesize body and hands gestures in a multi-stage, cascade structure. In addition, semantic relevancy is adopted as a loss weight to make the network generate more semantic-relevant gestures. The text, audio and speaker ID encoders network selection are referred to [52] and customized for better performance. All input data have the same time resolution as the output gestures so that the synthesized gestures can be processed frame by frame through a sequential model. The gesture and facial blendshape weights are downsampled to 15 FPS, and the word sentence is inserted with padding tokens to correspond to the silence time in the audio.

Text Encoder. First, words are converted to word embedding set $\mathbf{v}^{\mathrm{T}} \in \mathbb{R}^{300}$ by pre-trained model in FastText [10] to reduce dimensions. Then, the word sets are fine-tuned by customized encoder E_{T}, which is a 8-layer temporal convolution network (TCN) [6] with skip connections [22], as

$$z_i^{\mathrm{T}} = E_{\mathrm{T}}(v_{i-f}^{\mathrm{T}}, ..., v_{i+f}^{\mathrm{T}}), \tag{1}$$

For each frame i, the TCN fusions the information from $2f = 34$ frames to generate final latent feature of text, the set of features is note as $\mathbf{z}^{\mathrm{T}} \in \mathbb{R}^{128}$.

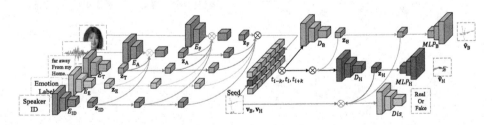

Fig. 5. Cascaded Motion Network (CaMN). As a multi-modal gesture synthesis baseline, CaMN inputs *text, emotion label, speaker ID, audio* and *facial blendweight* in a cascaded architecture, the audio and facial feature will be extracted by concatenating the features of previous modalities. The fused feature will be reconstructed to body and hands gestures by two cascaded LSTM+MLP decoders.

Speaker ID and Emotion Encoders. The initial representation of speaker ID and emotion are both one-hot vectors, as $\mathbf{v}^{\text{ID}} \in \mathbb{R}^{30}$ and $\mathbf{v}^{\text{E}} \in \mathbb{R}^{8}$. Follow the suggestion in [52], we use embedding-layer as speaker ID encoder, E_{ID}. As the speaker ID does not change instantly, we only use the current frame speaker ID to calculate its latent features. On the other hand, we use a combination of embedding-layer and 4-layer TCN as the emotion encoder, E_{E}, to extract the temporal emotion variations.

$$z_i^{\text{ID}} = E_{\text{ID}}(v_i^{\text{ID}}), z_i^{\text{E}} = E_{\text{E}}(v_{i-f}^{\text{E}}, ..., v_{i+f}^{\text{E}}), \tag{2}$$

where $\mathbf{z}^{\text{ID}} \in \mathbb{R}^8$ and $\mathbf{z}^{\text{E}} \in \mathbb{R}^8$ is the latent feature for speaker ID and emotion, respectively.

Audio Encoder. We adopt the raw wave representation of audio and down-sample it to $16\,\text{KHZ}$, considering audio as $15\,\text{FPS}$, for each frame, we have $\mathbf{v}^{\text{A}} \in \mathbb{R}^{1067}$. We feed the audio joint with the text, speakerID and emotion features into audio encoder E_{A} to learn better audio features. As

$$z_i^{\text{A}} = E_{\text{A}}(v_{i-f}^{\text{A}}, ..., v_{i+f}^{\text{E}}; v_i^{\text{T}}; v_i^{\text{E}}; v_i^{\text{ID}}), \tag{3}$$

The E_{A} consists of 12-layer TCN with skip connection and 2-layer MLP, features in other modifies are concatenated with the 12th layer audio features thus the final MLP layers are for audio feature refinement, and the final latent audio feature is $\mathbf{z}^{\text{A}} \in \mathbb{R}^{128}$.

Facial Expression Encoder. We take the $\mathbf{v}^{\text{F}} \in \mathbb{R}^{52}$ as initial representation of facial expression. 8-layer TCN and 2-layer MLP based encoder E_{F} is adopt to extract facial latent feature $\mathbf{z}^{\text{F}} \in \mathbb{R}^{32}$, as

$$z_i^{\text{F}} = E_{\text{F}}(v_{i-f}^{\text{F}}, ..., v_{i+f}^{\text{F}}; v_i^{\text{T}}; v_i^{\text{E}}; v_i^{\text{ID}}; v_i^{\text{A}}), \tag{4}$$

the features are concatenated at 8th layer and the MLP is for refinement.

Body and Hands Decoders. We implement the body and hands decoders in a separated, cascaded structure, which is based on [38] conclusion that the body gestures can be used to estimate hand gestures. These two decoders, D_{B} and D_{F} are based on the LSTM structure for latent feature extraction and 2-layer MLP for gesture reconstruction. They would combine the features of five modalities with previous gestures, $i.e.$, seed pose, to synthesis latent gesture features $\mathbf{z}^{\text{B}} \in \mathbb{R}^{256}$ and $\mathbf{z}^{\text{H}} \in \mathbb{R}^{256}$. The final estimated body $\hat{\mathbf{v}}^{\text{B}} \in \mathbb{R}^{27 \times 3}$ and hands $\hat{\mathbf{v}}^{\text{H}} \in \mathbb{R}^{48 \times 3}$ are calculated as,

$$z_i^{\text{M}} = z_i^{\text{T}} \otimes z_i^{\text{ID}} \otimes z_i^{\text{E}} \otimes z_i^{\text{A}} \otimes z_i^{\text{F}} \otimes v_i^{\text{B}} \otimes v_i^{\text{H}}, \tag{5}$$

$$\mathbf{z}^{\text{B}} = D_{\text{B}}(z_0^{\text{M}}, ..., z_n^{\text{M}}), \mathbf{z}^{\text{H}} = D_{\text{H}}(z_0^{\text{M}}, ..., z_n^{\text{M}}; \mathbf{z}^{\text{B}}), \tag{6}$$

$$\hat{\mathbf{v}}^{\text{B}} = MLP_{\text{B}}(\mathbf{z}^{\text{B}}), \hat{\mathbf{v}}^{\text{H}} = MLP_{\text{H}}(\mathbf{z}^{\text{H}}), \tag{7}$$

$\mathbf{z}^{\text{M}} \in \mathbb{R}^{549}$ is the merged features for all modalities. For Eq. 5, the length for the seed pose is four frames.

Loss Functions. The final supervision of our network is based on gesture recon-struction and the adversarial loss

$$\ell_{\text{Gesture Rec.}} = \mathbb{E}\left[\left\|\mathbf{v}^B - \hat{\mathbf{v}}^B\right\|_1\right] + \alpha\mathbb{E}\left[\left\|\mathbf{v}^H - \hat{\mathbf{v}}^H\right\|_1\right], \tag{8}$$

$$\ell_{\text{Adv.}} = -\mathbb{E}[\log(Dis(\hat{\mathbf{v}}^B; \hat{\mathbf{v}}^H))], \tag{9}$$

where the discriminator input to the adversarial training is only the gesture itself. We also adopt a weight α to balance the body and hands penalties. After that, during training, we adjust the weights of L1 loss, and adversarial loss using the semantic-relevancy label λ The final loss function is

$$\ell = \lambda\beta_0\ell_{\text{Gesture Rec.}} + \beta_1\ell_{\text{Adv}}, \tag{10}$$

where β_0 and β_1 are predefined weight for L1 and adversarial loss. When semantic relevancy is high, we encourage the network to generate gestures spatially similar to ground truth as much as possible, thus strengthening the L1 penalty and decreasing the adversarial penalty.

5 Metric for Semantic Relevancy

We propose the Semantic-Relevant Gesture Recall (SRGR) to evaluate the semantic relevancy of gestures, which can also be interpreted as whether the gestures are vivid and diverse. We utilize the semantic scores as a weight for the Probability of Correct Keypoint (PCK) between the generated gestures and the ground truth gestures. Where PCK is the number of joints successfully recalled against a specified threshold δ. The SRGR metric can be calculated as follows:

$$D_{SRGR} = \lambda \sum \frac{1}{T \times J} \sum_{t=1}^{T} \sum_{j=1}^{J} \mathbf{1}\left[\left\|p_t^j - \hat{p}_t^j\right\|_2 < \delta\right], \tag{11}$$

where $\mathbf{1}$ is the indicator function and T, J is the set of frames and number of joints. We think the SRGR, which emphasizes recalling gestures in the clip of interest, is more in line with the subjective human perception of gesture's valid diversity than the L1 variance of synthesized gestures.

6 Experiments

In this section, we first evaluate the SRGR metric's validity, then demonstrate our dataset's data quality based on subjective experiments. Next, we demon-strate the validity of our baseline model using subjective and objective experi-ments, and finally, we discuss the contribution of each modality based on ablation experiments.

6.1   Validness of SRGR

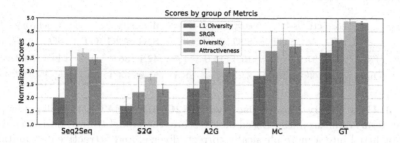

Fig. 6. Comparison of Metrics by Group. SRGR shows the consistence with human perception, and lower variance comparing with L1 Diversity in evaluation.

A user study is conducted to evaluate the validity of SRGR. Firstly, we randomly trim the motion sequences with rendered results into clips which are around 40 s. For each clip, the participants are asked to evaluate the gesture based on its diversity which is the number of non-repeated gestures. Besides, the participants then need to score its attractiveness which should be based on the motion itself instead of the content of the speech. Totally 160 participants took part in the evaluation study, and each of them evaluated 15 random clips of gestures. There are totally 200 gesture clips including the results generated by using the methods from Seq2Seq [53], S2G [20], A2G [32], MultiContext [52], and ground truth, 40 clips for each with the same speaker data. Both of the questions follow a 5-points Likert scale. As shown in Fig. 6, we found a large variance in L1 diversity even though we used 100 gesture segments to calculate the average L1 distance, (usually around 40 segments [32,33]). Secondly, generated results with strong semantic relevance but a smaller motion range, such as Seq2Seq, obtained a lower L1 diversity than A2G, which has a larger motion range, yet the statistical evidence that humans feel that Seq2Seq has higher diversity than A2G. An explanation is a human evaluating diversity not only on the range of motion but also on some other implicit features, such as expressiveness and semantic relevancy of the motion.

6.2   Data Quality

To evaluate the captured ground truth motion data quality, we compare our proposed dataset with the widely used mocap dataset Trinity [17] and in-the-wild dataset S2G-3D [20, 21]. We conducted the user study by comparing clips sampled from ground truth and generated results using motion synthesis networks trained in each dataset. The Trinity dataset has a total of 23 sequences, with 10 minutes each. We randomly divide the data into 19:2:2 for train/valid/test since there is no standard for splitting.

Table 2. User Study Comparison with Trinity for Data Quality. Comparing with Trinity [17], BEAT get higher user preference score in terms of ground truth data quality. "-b" and "-h" indicate body and hands, respectively.

	correctness-b			correctness-h			diversity			synchrony		
	S2G	A2G	GT	S2G	A2G	GT	S2G	A2G	GT	S2G	A2G	GT
Trinity [17]	38.8	37.0	43.8	15.3	14.6	11.7	42.1	36.7	40.2	40.9	36.3	46.4
BEAT (Ours)	61.2	63.0	56.2	84.7	85.4	88.3	57.9	63.3	59.8	59.1	63.7	53.6

Table 3. User Study Comparison with S2G 3D. BEAT get similar user preferences in terms of naturalness. Based on the score, the model trained on BEAT dataset would be fitted into a more physically correct, diverse, and attractive distribution.

	naturalness	correctness	diversity	attractiveness
S2G-3D [20,21]	33.03 ± 1.93	21.17 ± 2.84	29.17 ± 1.81	28.79 ± 2.53
BEAT (conversation)	34.16 ± 2.16	39.94 ± 3.97	34.69 ± 1.76	29.90 ± 2.19
BEAT (self-talk)	32.81 ± 1.79	38.89 ± 3.75	36.14 ± 1.99	42.31 ± 2.40

We used S2G [20], as well as the SoTA algorithm A2G [32], to cover both GAN and VAE models. The output layer of the S2G model was adapted for outputting 3D coordinates. In the ablation study, the final generated 3D skeleton results were rendered and composited with audio for comparison in the user study. A total of 120 participant subjects compared the clips randomly sampled from Trinity and our dataset, with 5–20s in length. The participants were asked to evaluate gestures correctness, i.e., physical correctness, diversity and gesture-audio synchrony. Furthermore, the body and hands were evaluated separately for the gesture correctness test. The results are shown in Table 2, demonstrating that our dataset received higher user preference in all aspects. Especially for the hand movements, we outperformed the Trinity dataset by a large margin. This is probably due to the noise of the past motion capture devices and the lack of markers on the hands. Table 3 shows preference ratios (%) of 60 subjects who watch 20 random rendered 3D skeletons pairs per subjective test. Based on the score, the model trained on the BEAT dataset would be fitted into a more physically correct, diverse, and attractive distribution.

6.3 Evaluation of the Baseline Model

Training Setting. We use the Adam optimizer [29] to train at a learning rate of 2e-4, and the 4-speaker data is trained in an NVIDIA V100 environment. For evaluation metrics, L1 has been demonstrated unsuitable for evaluating the gesture performance [32,52] thus, we adopt FGD [52] to evaluate the generated gestures' distribution distance with ground truth. It computes the distance between latent features extracted by a pretrained network, we use an LSTM-based autoencoder as the pretrained network. In addition, we adopt SRGR and

Table 4. Evaluation on BEAT. Our CaMN performs best in the term of FGD, SRGR and BeatAlign, all methods are trained on our dataset (BEAT)

	FGD ↓	SRGR ↑	BeatAlign ↑
Seq2Seq [53]	261.3	0.173	0.729
S2G [20]	256.7	0.092	0.751
A2G [32]	223.8	0.097	0.766
MultiContext [52]	176.2	0.196	0.776
CaMN (Ours)	123.7	0.239	0.783

Table 5. Results of Ablation Study.

	FGD ↓	BGSR ↑	BeatAlign ↑
full cascated	123.7	0.239	0.783
w/o cascaded	137.2	0.207	0.776
w/o text	149.4	0.171	0.781
w/o audio	155.7	0.225	0.733
w/o speaker ID	159.1	0.207	0.774
w/o face	163.3	0.217	0.767
w/o emotion	151.7	0.231	0.775
w/o semantic	151.8	0.194	0.786

BeatAlign to evaluate diversity and synchrony. BeatAlign [33] is a Chamfer Distance between audio and gesture beats to evaluate gesture-audio beat similarity.

Quantitative Results. The final results are shown in Table 4. In addition to S2G and A2G, we also compare our results with text-to-gesture and audio&test-to-gesture algorithm, Seq2Seq [53] and MultiContext [52]. The results show that both our end2end model and cascaded model archive SoTA performance in all metrics (*cf.* supplementary materials for video results).

6.4   Ablation Study

Effectiveness of Cascaded Connection. As shown in Table 5, in contrast to the end-to-end approach, the cascaded connection can achieve better performance because we introduce prior human knowledge to help the network extract features of different modalities.

Effectiveness of Each Modality. We gradually removed the data of one modality during the experiment (*cf.* Table 5). Synchrony would significantly be reduced after removing the audio, which is intuitive. However, it still maintains some synchronizations, such as the padding and time-align annotation of the text and the lip motion of the facial expression. In contrast, eliminating weighted semantic loss improves synchrony, which means that semantic gestures are usually not strongly aligned with audio perfectly. There is also a relationship between emotion and synchrony, but speaker ID only has little effect on synchrony. The removal of audio, emotion, and facial expression does not significantly affect the semantic relevant gesture recall, which depends mainly on the text and the speaker ID. Data from each modality contributed to improving the FGD, which means using different modalities of data enhances the network's mapping ability. The unities of audio and facial expressions, especially facial expressions, improve the FGD significantly. We found that removing emotion and speaker ID also impacts the FGD scores. This is because using the integrated network increases the diversity of features, which leads to a diversity of results, increasing the variance of the distribution and making it more like the original data.

Emotional Gestures. As shown in Table 6, we train a classifier by an additional 1DCNN + LSTM network and invite 60 subjects each to classify 12 random real test clips (with audio). The classifier is trained and tested on speaker-4's ground truth data.

Table 6. Emotional Gesture Classification. The classification accuracy (%) gap between the test real and generated data (1344 clips, 10 s each) is 15.85.

	Neutral	Happiness	Sadness	Anger	Surprise	Contempt	Fear	Disgust	Avg
Human	84.29	74.86	82.65	88.36	76.12	71.59	80.94	72.33	78.89
Real	51.06	98.68	85.08	38.78	99.39	81.08	99.95	99.62	83.26
Generated	36.95	76.83	62.17	37.46	77.91	70.61	81.32	83.03	67.41

6.5   Limitation

Impact of Acting. Self-Talk sessions might reflect the impact of acting, which is inevitable and controlled. *Inevitable:* The impact is probably caused by predefined content. However, to explore the semantic-relevancy and personality, it is necessary to control the variables, *i.e.*, different speakers should talk in the same text and emotion so that the personality can be carefully explored. *Controlled.* Speakers recorded the conversation session first and were encouraged to keep the same style as the conversation. We also filtered out about 21h of data and six speakers due to inconsistencies in their styles.

Calculation of SRGR. SRGR now is calculated based on semantic annotation, which has a limitation for an un-labelled dataset. To solve this problem, training a scoring network or semantic discriminator is a possible direction.

7   Conclusion

We build a large-scale, high-quality, multi-modal, semantic and emotional annotated dataset to generate more human-like, semantic and emotional relevant conversational gestures. Together with the dataset, we propose a cascade-based baseline model for gesture synthesis based on six modalities and achieve SoTA performance. Finally, we introduce SRGR for evaluating semantic relevancy. In the future, we plan to expand cross-data checks for AU and emotion recognition benchmarks. Our dataset and the related statistical experiments could benefit a number of different research fields, including controllable gesture synthesis, cross-modality analysis and emotional motion recognition in the future.

Acknowledgements. This work was conducted during Haiyang Liu, Zihao Zhu, and Yichen Peng's internship at Tokyo Research Center. We thank Hailing Pi for communicating with the recording actors of the BEAT dataset.

References

1. Ahuja, C., Lee, D.W., Nakano, Y.I., Morency, L.-P.: Style transfer for co-speech gesture animation: a multi-speaker conditional-mixture approach. In: Vedaldi, A., Bischof, H., Brox, T., Frahm, J.-M. (eds.) ECCV 2020. LNCS, vol. 12363, pp. 248–265. Springer, Cham (2020). https://doi.org/10.1007/978-3-030-58523-5_15
2. Alexanderson, S., Henter, G.E., Kucherenko, T., Beskow, J.: Style-controllable speech-driven gesture synthesis using normalising flows. In: Computer Graphics Forum. Wiley Online Library, vol. 39, pp. 487–496 (2020)
3. Alexanderson, S., Székely, É., Henter, G.E., Kucherenko, T., Beskow, J.: Generating coherent spontaneous speech and gesture from text. In: Proceedings of the 20th ACM International Conference on Intelligent Virtual Agents, pp. 1–3 (2020)
4. Alghamdi, N., Maddock, S., Marxer, R., Barker, J., Brown, G.J.: A corpus of audio-visual lombard speech with frontal and profile views. J. Acoust. Soc. Am. 143(6), EL523-EL529 (2018)
5. Ali, G., Lee, M., Hwang, J.I.: Automatic text-to-gesture rule generation for embodied conversational agents. Comput. Anim. Virtual Worlds 31(4–5), e1944 (2020)
6. Bai, S., Kolter, J.Z., Koltun, V.: An empirical evaluation of generic convolutional and recurrent networks for sequence modeling. arXiv preprint arXiv:1803.01271 (2018)
7. Bhattacharya, U., Childs, E., Rewkowski, N., Manocha, D.: Speech2AffectiveGestures: synthesizing co-speech gestures with generative adversarial affective expression learning. In: Proceedings of the 29th ACM International Conference on Multimedia, pp. 2027–2036 (2021)
8. Bhattacharya, U., Rewkowski, N., Banerjee, A., Guhan, P., Bera, A., Manocha, D.: Text2Gestures: a transformer-based network for generating emotive body gestures for virtual agents** this work has been supported in part by aro grants w911nf1910069 and w911nf1910315, and intel. code and additional materials available at: https://gamma.umd.edu/t2g. In: 2021 IEEE Virtual Reality and 3D User Interfaces (VR), pp. 1-10. IEEE (2021)
9. Bloom, V., Makris, D., Argyriou, V.: G3D: a gaming action dataset and real time action recognition evaluation framework. In: 2012 IEEE Computer Society Conference on Computer Vision and Pattern Recognition Workshops. IEEE, pp. 7–12 (2012)
10. Bojanowski, P., Grave, E., Joulin, A., Mikolov, T.: Enriching word vectors with subword information. Trans. Assoc comput. linguist 5, 135–146 (2017)
11. Cao, H., Cooper, D.G., Keutmann, M.K., Gur, R.C., Nenkova, A., Verma, R.: CREMA-D: crowd-sourced emotional multimodal actors dataset. IEEE Trans. Affect. Comput. 5(4), 377–390 (2014)
12. Cao, Z., Hidalgo, G., Simon, T., Wei, S.E., Sheikh, Y.: Openpose: realtime multi-person 2D pose estimation using part affinity fields. IEEE Trans. Pattern Anal. Mach. Intell. 43(1), 172–186 (2019)
13. Carreira, J., Zisserman, A.: Quo vadis, action recognition? A new model and the kinetics dataset. In: Proceedings of the IEEE Conference on Computer Vision and Pattern Recognition, pp. 6299–6308 (2017)
14. Chen, C., Jafari, R., Kehtarnavaz, N.: UTD-MHAD: a multimodal dataset for human action recognition utilizing a depth camera and a wearable inertial sensor. In: 2015 IEEE International conference on image processing (ICIP), IEEE, pp. 168–172 (2015)

15. Cooke, M., Barker, J., Cunningham, S., Shao, X.: An audio-visual corpus for speech perception and automatic speech recognition. J. Acoust. Soc. Am. **120**(5), 2421–2424 (2006)
16. Cudeiro, D., Bolkart, T., Laidlaw, C., Ranjan, A., Black, M.J.: Capture, learning, and synthesis of 3D speaking styles. In: Proceedings of the IEEE/CVF Conference on Computer Vision and Pattern Recognition, pp. 10101–10111 (2019)
17. Ferstl, Y., McDonnell, R.: Investigating the use of recurrent motion modelling for speech gesture generation. In: Proceedings of the 18th International Conference on Intelligent Virtual Agents, pp. 93–98 (2018)
18. Ferstl, Y., Neff, M., McDonnell, R.: Adversarial gesture generation with realistic gesture phasing. Comput. Graph. **89**, 117–130 (2020)
19. Ferstl, Y., Neff, M., McDonnell, R.: ExpressGesture: expressive gesture generation from speech through database matching. Comput. Anim. Virtual Worlds **32**, e2016 (2021)
20. Ginosar, S., Bar, A., Kohavi, G., Chan, C., Owens, A., Malik, J.: Learning individual styles of conversational gesture. In: Proceedings of the IEEE/CVF Conference on Computer Vision and Pattern Recognition, pp. 3497–3506 (2019)
21. Habibie, I., et al.: Learning speech-driven 3D conversational gestures from video. arXiv preprint arXiv:2102.06837 (2021)
22. He, K., Zhang, X., Ren, S., Sun, J.: Deep residual learning for image recognition. In: Proceedings of the IEEE Conference on Computer Vision and Pattern Recognition, pp. 770–778 (2016)
23. Henter, G.E., Alexanderson, S., Beskow, J.: MoGlow: probabilistic and controllable motion synthesis using normalising flows. ACM Trans. Graph. (TOG) **39**(6), 1–14 (2020)
24. Hornby, A.S., et al.: Oxford Advanced Learner's Dictionary of Current English. Oxford University Press, Oxford (1974)
25. Ionescu, C., Papava, D., Olaru, V., Sminchisescu, C.: Human3.6M: large scale datasets and predictive methods for 3D human sensing in natural environments. IEEE Trans. Pattern Anal. Mach. Intell. **36**(7), 1325–1339 (2013)
26. Jackson, P., Haq, S.: Surrey Audio-Visual Expressed Emotion (SAVEE) Database. University of Surrey, Guildford, UK (2014)
27. Kapoor, P., Mukhopadhyay, R., Hegde, S.B., Namboodiri, V., Jawahar, C.: Towards automatic speech to sign language generation. arXiv preprint arXiv:2106.12790 (2021)
28. Kay, W., et al.: The kinetics human action video dataset. arXiv preprint arXiv:1705.06950 (2017)
29. Kingma, D.P., Ba, J.: Adam: a method for stochastic optimization. arXiv preprint arXiv:1412.6980 (2014)
30. Kucherenko, T., Hasegawa, D., Kaneko, N., Henter, G.E., Kjellström, H.: Moving fast and slow: analysis of representations and post-processing in speech-driven automatic gesture generation. Int. J. Hum-Comput. Interact. **37**, 1–17 (2021)
31. Kucherenko, T., et al.: Gesticulator: a framework for semantically-aware speech-driven gesture generation. In: Proceedings of the 2020 International Conference on Multimodal Interaction, pp. 242–250 (2020)
32. Li, J., et al.: Audio2Gestures: generating diverse gestures from speech audio with conditional variational autoencoders. In: Proceedings of the IEEE/CVF International Conference on Computer Vision, pp. 11293–11302 (2021)
33. Li, R., Yang, S., Ross, D.A., Kanazawa, A.: AI choreographer: music conditioned 3D dance generation with AIST++. In: Proceedings of the IEEE/CVF International Conference on Computer Vision, pp. 13401–13412 (2021)

34. Liu, A.A., Xu, N., Nie, W.Z., Su, Y.T., Wong, Y., Kankanhalli, M.: Benchmarking a multimodal and multiview and interactive dataset for human action recognition. IEEE Trans. Cybern. **47**(7), 1781–1794 (2016)
35. Livingstone, S.R., Russo, F.A.: The Ryerson audio-visual database of emotional speech and song (RAVDESS): a dynamic, multimodal set of facial and vocal expressions in north American english. PLoS ONE **13**(5), e0196391 (2018)
36. Lu, J., Liu, T., Xu, S., Shimodaira, H.: Double-DCCCAE: estimation of body gestures from speech waveform. In: ICASSP 2021–2021 IEEE International Conference on Acoustics, Speech and Signal Processing (ICASSP). IEEE, pp. 900–904 (2021)
37. McAuliffe, M., Socolof, M., Mihuc, S., Wagner, M., Sonderegger, M.: Montreal forced aligner: trainable text-speech alignment using kaldi. In: Interspeech, vol. 2017, pp. 498–502 (2017)
38. Ng, E., Ginosar, S., Darrell, T., Joo, H.: Body2Hands: learning to infer 3D hands from conversational gesture body dynamics. In: Proceedings of the IEEE/CVF Conference on Computer Vision and Pattern Recognition, pp. 11865–11874 (2021)
39. Pavllo, D., Feichtenhofer, C., Grangier, D., Auli, M.: 3D human pose estimation in video with temporal convolutions and semi-supervised training. In: Proceedings of the IEEE/CVF Conference on Computer Vision and Pattern Recognition, pp. 7753–7762 (2019)
40. Perera, A.G., Law, Y.W., Ogunwa, T.T., Chahl, J.: A multiviewpoint outdoor dataset for human action recognition. IEEE Trans Hum-Mach. Syst **50**(5), 405–413 (2020)
41. Punnakkal, A.R., Chandrasekaran, A., Athanasiou, N., Quiros-Ramirez, A., Black, M.J.: BABEL: bodies, action and behavior with english labels. In: Proceedings of the IEEE/CVF Conference on Computer Vision and Pattern Recognition, pp. 722–731 (2021)
42. Richard, A., Zollhöfer, M., Wen, Y., De la Torre, F., Sheikh, Y.: MeshTalk: 3D face animation from speech using cross-modality disentanglement. In: Proceedings of the IEEE/CVF International Conference on Computer Vision, pp. 1173–1182 (2021)
43. Singh, S., Velastin, S.A., Ragheb, H.: Muhavi: A multicamera human action video dataset for the evaluation of action recognition methods. In: 2010 7th IEEE International Conference on Advanced Video and Signal Based Surveillance, pp. 48–55. IEEE (2010)
44. Song, S., Lan, C., Xing, J., Zeng, W., Liu, J.: An end-to-end spatio-temporal attention model for human action recognition from skeleton data. In: Proceedings of the AAAI Conference on Artificial Intelligence, vol. 31 (2017)
45. Takeuchi, K., Hasegawa, D., Shirakawa, S., Kaneko, N., Sakuta, H., Sumi, K.: Speech-to-gesture generation: a challenge in deep learning approach with bi-directional LSTM. In: Proceedings of the 5th International Conference on Human Agent Interaction, pp. 365–369 (2017)
46. Takeuchi, K., Kubota, S., Suzuki, K., Hasegawa, D., Sakuta, H.: Creating a gesture-speech dataset for speech-based automatic gesture generation. In: Stephanidis, C. (ed.) HCI 2017. CCIS, vol. 713, pp. 198–202. Springer, Cham (2017). https://doi.org/10.1007/978-3-319-58750-9_28
47. Volkova, E., De La Rosa, S., Bülthoff, H.H., Mohler, B.: The MPI emotional body expressions database for narrative scenarios. PLoS ONE **9**(12), e113647 (2014)
48. Wang, J., Liu, Z., Chorowski, J., Chen, Z., Wu, Y.: Robust 3D action recognition with random occupancy patterns. In: Fitzgibbon, A., Lazebnik, S., Perona, P.,

Sato, Y., Schmid, C. (eds.) ECCV 2012. LNCS, vol. 7573, pp. 872–885. Springer, Heidelberg (2012). https://doi.org/10.1007/978-3-642-33709-3_62

49. Wang, K., et al.: MEAD: a large-scale audio-visual dataset for emotional talking-face generation. In: Vedaldi, A., Bischof, H., Brox, T., Frahm, J.-M. (eds.) ECCV 2020. LNCS, vol. 12366, pp. 700–717. Springer, Cham (2020). https://doi.org/10.1007/978-3-030-58589-1_42

50. Wu, B., Ishi, C., Ishiguro, H., et al.: Probabilistic human-like gesture synthesis from speech using GRU-based WGAN. In: GENEA: Generation and Evaluation of Non-verbal Behaviour for Embodied Agents Workshop 2021 (2021)

51. Wu, B., Liu, C., Ishi, C.T., Ishiguro, H.: Modeling the conditional distribution of co-speech upper body gesture jointly using conditional-GAN and unrolled-GAN. Electronics 10(3), 228 (2021)

52. Yoon, Y.: Speech gesture generation from the trimodal context of text, audio, and speaker identity. ACM Trans. Graph. (TOG) 39(6), 1–16 (2020)

53. Yoon, Y., Ko, W.R., Jang, M., Lee, J., Kim, J., Lee, G.: Robots learn social skills: end-to-end learning of co-speech gesture generation for humanoid robots. In: 2019 International Conference on Robotics and Automation (ICRA), pp. 4303–4309. IEEE (2019)

Neuromorphic Data Augmentation for Training Spiking Neural Networks

Yuhang Li[(⊠)] , Youngeun Kim , Hyoungseob Park , Tamar Geller ,
and Priyadarshini Panda

Yale University, New Haven, CT 06511, USA
{yuhang.li,youngeun.kim,hyoungseob.park,
tamar.geller,priya.panda}@yale.edu

Abstract. Developing neuromorphic intelligence on event-based datasets with Spiking Neural Networks (SNNs) has recently attracted much research attention. However, the limited size of event-based datasets makes SNNs prone to overfitting and unstable convergence. This issue remains unexplored by previous academic works. In an effort to minimize this generalization gap, we propose Neuromorphic Data Augmentation (NDA), a family of geometric augmentations specifically designed for event-based datasets with the goal of significantly stabilizing the SNN training and reducing the generalization gap between training and test performance. The proposed method is simple and compatible with existing SNN training pipelines. Using the proposed augmentation, for the first time, we demonstrate the feasibility of unsupervised contrastive learning for SNNs. We conduct comprehensive experiments on prevailing neuromorphic vision benchmarks and show that NDA yields substantial improvements over previous state-of-the-art results. For example, the NDA-based SNN achieves accuracy gain on CIFAR10-DVS and N-Caltech 101 by 10.1% and 13.7%, respectively. Code is available on GitHub (URL).

Keywords: Data augmentation · Event-based vision · Spiking neural networks

1 Introduction

Spiking Neural Networks (SNNs), a representative category of models in neuromorphic computing, have received attention as a prospective candidate for low-power machine intelligence [52]. Unlike the standard Artificial Neural Networks (ANNs), SNNs deal with binarized spatial-temporal data. A popular example of this data is the DVS event-based dataset.[1] Each pixel inside a DVS camera is operated independently and asynchronously, reporting new brightness when it changes, and staying silent otherwise [61]. The spatial-temporal information

---

[1] In this paper, most event-based datasets we use are collected with Dynamic Vision Sensor (DVS) cameras, therefore we also term them as DVS data for simplicity.

© The Author(s), under exclusive license to Springer Nature Switzerland AG 2022
S. Avidan et al. (Eds.): ECCV 2022, LNCS 13667, pp. 631–649, 2022.
https://doi.org/10.1007/978-3-031-20071-7_37

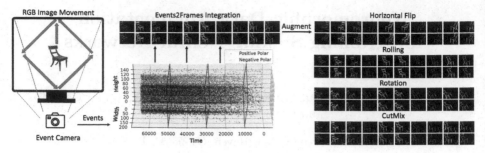

Fig. 1. *Left*: Event data collection of a chair image from N-Caltech101 [47], these events are too sparse to process, thus we integrate them into frames of sparse tensors. *Right*: Our neuromorphic data augmentation on events data.

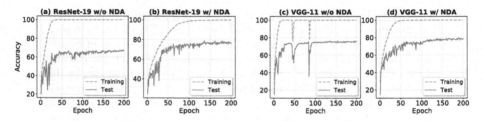

Fig. 2. Training/test accuracy curves of ResNet-19 and VGG-11 on CIFAR10-DVS dataset. Networks trained with NDA tends to have better convergence.

encoded in DVS data can be suitably leveraged by the temporally evolving spiking neurons in SNNs. In Fig. 1, we describe the process of data recording with a DVS camera. First, an RGB image is programmed to move in a certain trajectory (or the camera moves in a reverse way), and then the event camera records the brightness change and outputs an event stream. Note that the raw event-based DVS data is too sparse to extract features. Thus, we integrate the events into multiple frames and we study this sparse frame-based data [63] (see the events2frames integration in Fig. 1).

Due to the high cost of collecting DVS data [43], existing DVS datasets usually contain limited data instances [37]. Consequently, models trained on raw DVS datasets exhibit large training-test performance gaps due to overfitting. For instance, CIFAR10-DVS [37] only contains 10k data points while CIFAR-10 RGB dataset contains 60k data points. In Fig. 2, we plot the training-test accuracies on CIFAR10-DVS using VGG-11 [56] and ResNet-19 [28]. It is obvious that training accuracy increases swiftly and smoothly. On the contrary, the test accuracy oscillates and remains at half of the training accuracy. Although advanced training algorithms [17,69] have been proposed to improve the generalization of SNNs, data scarcity remains a major challenge and needs to be addressed. A naive way to increase DVS data samples is using the DVS camera to record additional augmented RGB images. However, during training, this carries prohibitively high latency overhead due to the cost of DVS recording.

Because of this, we focus on a data augmentation technique that can be directly applied to DVS data in order to balance efficiency and effectiveness.

We propose Neuromorphic Data Augmentation (NDA) to transform the off-the-shelf recorded DVS data in a way that prevents overfitting. To ensure the consistency between augmentation and event-stream generation, we extensively investigate various possible augmentations and identify the most beneficial family of augmentations. In addition, we show that the proposed data augmentation techniques lead to a substantial gain of training stability and generalization performance (cf. Figure 2). Even more remarkably, NDA enables SNNs to be trained through unsupervised contrastive learning without the usage of labels. Figure 1 (right) demonstrates four examples where NDA is applied.

The main contributions of this paper are:

1. We propose Neuromorphic Data Augmentation for training Spiking Neural Networks on event datasets. Our proposed augmentation policy significantly improves the test accuracy of the model with negligible cost. Furthermore, NDA is compatible with existing training algorithm.
2. We conduct extensive experiments to verify the effectiveness of our proposed NDA on several benchmark DVS datasets like CIFAR10-DVS, N-Caltech 101, N-Cars, and N-MNIST. NDA brings a significant accuracy boost when compared to the previous state-of-the-art results.
3. In a first of its kind analysis, we show the suitability of NDA for unsupervised contrastive learning on the event-based datasets, enabling SNN feature extractors to be trained without labels.

2 Related Work

2.1 Data Augmentation

Today, deep learning is a prevalent technique in various commercial, scientific, and academic applications. Data augmentation [54] plays an indispensable role in the deep learning model, as it forces the model to learn invariant features, and thus helps generalization. The data augmentation is applied in many areas of vision tasks including object recognition [8,9,42], objection detection [71], and semantic segmentation [51]. Apart from learning invariant features, data augmentation also has other specific applications in deep learning. For example, adversarial training [19,59] leverages data augmentation to create adversarial samples and thereby improves the adversarial robustness of the model. Data augmentation is also used in generative adversarial networks (GAN) [1,3,23, 31], neural style transfer [20,30], and data inversion [41,68]. For event-based data, there are few data augmentation techniques. EventDrop [22], for example, randomly removes several events due to noise produced in the DVS camera. Our work, on the other hand, tackles the consistency problem of directly applying data augmentations to event-based data. A related augmentation technique is video augmentation [4], which also augmentation spatial-temporal data. The main difference is that video augmentation can utilize photometric and color augmentations while our NDA can only adopt geometric augmentations.

2.2 Spiking Neural Networks

Spiking Neural Networks (SNNs) are often recognized as the third generation of generalization methods for artificial intelligence [2]. Unlike traditional Artificial Neural Networks (ANNs), SNNs apply the spiking mechanism inside the network. Therefore, the activation in SNNs is binary and adds a temporal dimension. Current practices consist of two approaches for obtaining an SNN: *Direct training* and *ANN-to-SNN conversion*. Conversion from a pre-trained ANN can guarantee good performance [11,15,25,38,39,53], however, in this paper, we do not study conversion since our topic is a neuromorphic dataset that requires direct training. Training SNNs [12,24,26,40,63,64] requires spatial-temporal backpropagation. Recently, more methods and variants for such spatio-temporal training have been proposed: [50] present hybrid training, [32,69] propose a variant of batch normalization [29] for SNN; [17,49] propose training threshold and potential for better accuracy. However, most of these works focus on algorithm or architecture optimization to achieve improved performance. Because of their sparse nature, DVS datasets present an orthogonal problem of overfitting that is not addressed by the previously mentioned works.

3 Conventional Augmentations for RGB Data

We generally divide the current data augmentation techniques for ANN training on natural RGB image datasets into two types, namely photometric & color augmentations and geometric augmentations.

Photometric and Color Augmentations. This type indicates any augmentations that can transform the image illumination and color space. Figure 3 (2nd-5th examples) demonstrates some examples of increasing contrast, saturation, and imposing gray scale as well as Gaussian blur. Typically, photometric augmentation is applied to an image by changing each pixel value. For instance, the contrast enhancement will use $f(x) = \mathrm{clip}(ax - \frac{1}{2}a + \frac{1}{2}, 0, 1)$ where $a > 1$, to push pixel values close to black (zero value) and white (one value) and is applied in a pixel-wise manner. The color augmentation includes some color space transformation by casting more red, blue, or green colors on the image (*e.g.* saturation and grayscale). Generally, both Photometric and Color augmentations can be categorized as value-based augmentation where a transformation $f(x)$ applies to all pixels. Therefore, we also categorize augmentations like a Gaussian filter where a convolution with a Gaussian kernel is applied to this class.

Geometric Augmentations. Unlike *value-based* augmentations, geometric augmentations do not seek to alter every pixel value with a certain criterion. Rather, they change the images based on the coordinate of each pixel, *i.e.* the index of each element. In Fig. 3 (6th-9th examples), we visualize several geometric augmentation examples of horizontal flipping, resizing, rotation and cutout. For example, horizontal flipping reverses the order of each pixel and turns the image by 180°C. Rotation can be viewed as moving the location of pixels to another place. Cutout [13] applies a 0/1 mask to the original image. All of these augmentations are *index-based*.

| Original | Contrast | Saturation | Gray scale | Gaussian filter | Flipping | Resizing | Rotation | Cutout |

Fig. 3. Types of RGB data augmentation. The 2–5th examples include the photometric & color augmentations and the 6–9th examples contain the geometric augmentations.

4 Neuromorphic Augmentations for Event-Based Data

The event-based datasets contain sparse, discrete, and time-series samples, which have fundamentally different formats when compared to RGB images. As a result, the above conventional augmentations cannot all be directly applied. To explore which augmentation is useful for event data, we study the case of photometric and geometric augmentations separately. We also discuss the potential application of neuromorphic data augmentation.

4.1 DVS Data and Augmentation

DVS cameras are data-driven sensors: their output depends on the amount of motion or brightness change in the scene [18]. Mathematically, the output of event camera $x_E \in \mathbb{B}^{t \times p \times w \times h}$ is a 4-D tensor ($\mathbb{B}$ is the binary domain $\{0, 1\}$ and here we treat it as a sparse binary tensor, *i.e.* we also record 0 if there are no events), where t is the time step, p is the polarity ($p = 2$ corresponding to positive and negative polars) and w, h are the width and the height of the event tensor. The event generation (see details in [18]) can be modeled as

$$x_E(t, 1, x, y) = \begin{cases} 1 & \text{if } \log V(t, x, y) - \log V(t - \Delta t, x, y) > \alpha \\ 0 & \text{otherwise} \end{cases}, \quad (1)$$

$$x_E(t, 0, x, y) = \begin{cases} 1 & \text{if } \log V(t, x, y) - \log V(t - \Delta t, x, y) < -\alpha \\ 0 & \text{otherwise} \end{cases}, \quad (2)$$

where, $x_E(t, 1, x, y)$ is the generated event stream at time step t, spatial coordinate (x, y) and positive polarity. V is the photocurrent (or "brightness") of the original RGB image. Δt is the time elapsed since the last event generated at the same coordinate. During DVS data recording, the RGB images are programmed to move in a certain trajectory (or the camera moves in a reverse way). As time evolves, if the pixel value changes fast and exceeds a certain threshold α, an event will be generated, otherwise it will stay silent, meaning that the output is 0 in x_E. The event stream will be split into two channels, *i.e.* two polarities. Positive events are integrated into positive polarity and vice versa.

Consider the RGB data as $x \in \mathbb{C}^{3 \times w \times h}$ ($\mathbb{C}$ is the continuous domain in $[0, 1]$). We use the function $f(x) : \mathbb{C}^{3 \times w \times h} \to \mathbb{C}^{3 \times w \times h}$ to augment the RGB data. Note that $f(x)$ can be both photometric or geometric augmentation, and is randomly sampled from a set of augmentations. The optimization objective of training an ANN with RGB augmented data can be given by $\min_w \frac{1}{n} \sum_{i=1}^{n} \ell(\boldsymbol{w}, f(\boldsymbol{x}_i), \boldsymbol{y}_i)$.

Now consider event-based data $\boldsymbol{x}_E$. We define RGB to DVS data function $\boldsymbol{x}_E = g(\boldsymbol{x}) : \mathbb{C}^{3 \times w \times h} \rightarrow \mathbb{B}^{t \times p \times w \times h}$.[2] A naive approach to augment DVS data when training SNN is to first augment RGB data and then translate them to event-stream form, *i.e.* $g \circ f(\boldsymbol{x})$. This method can ensure the augmentation is correctly implemented as well as yield the event-stream data. In fact, training with Poisson encoding [14,52] uses such form $g \circ f(\boldsymbol{x})$ where g is the encoding function that translates the RGB images to spike trains. However, unlike Poisson encoding which can be implemented with one line of code, it would be very time-consuming and expensive to generate a large amount of DVS augmented data, *i.e.* $g \circ f(\boldsymbol{x})$. We propose a more efficient method, the neuromorphic data augmentation f_{NDA} which is directly applied to the DVS data $f_{\text{NDA}} \circ g(\boldsymbol{x})$. As a result, we avoid the expensive $g \circ f(\boldsymbol{x})$ in the training phase Table 1.

Table 1. Comparison among all potential augmentation for DVS data. f_P and f_G mean photometric and geometric augmentations. $\mathbb{C}$ stands for the continuous domain in $[0,1]$ and $\mathbb{B}$ stands for the binary domain $\{0,1\}$.

Aug.	Combination	Input-output	Pros	Cons
f_P	$g \circ f_P(\boldsymbol{x})$	$\mathbb{C}^{3 \times w \times h} \rightarrow \mathbb{B}^{t \times p \times w \times h}$	i. Effective augmentation	i. Impractical to record huge amount of DVS data
f_P	$f_P \circ g(\boldsymbol{x})$	$\mathbb{C}^{3 \times w \times h} \rightarrow \mathbb{C}^{t \times p \times w \times h}$	i. Practical	i. Not effective, ii. Creates continuous data
f_G	$g \circ f_G(\boldsymbol{x})$	$\mathbb{C}^{3 \times w \times h} \rightarrow \mathbb{B}^{t \times p \times w \times h}$	i. Effective augmentation	i. Impractical to record huge amount of DVS data
f_G	$f_G \circ g(\boldsymbol{x})$	$\mathbb{C}^{3 \times w \times h} \rightarrow \mathbb{B}^{t \times p \times w \times h}$	i. Practical and effective, ii. Approximates $g \circ f_G(\boldsymbol{x})$	None

Ideally, NDA is supposed to satisfy $f_{\text{NDA}} \circ g(\boldsymbol{x}) \approx g \circ f(\boldsymbol{x})$. To fulfill this commutative law, the NDA data augmentation function must have the mapping of $f_{\text{NDA}} : \mathbb{B}^{t \times p \times w \times h} \rightarrow \mathbb{B}^{t \times p \times w \times h}$. Without loss of generality, a core component is to evaluate whether an arbitrary augmentation $f(\cdot)$ can achieve

$$f(H_\alpha [\log V(t) - \log V(t - \Delta t)]) \approx H_\alpha [\log f(V(t)) - \log f(V(t - \Delta t))], \quad (3)$$

where $H_\alpha[\cdot]$ is the Heaviside step function (*i.e.* returns 1 when the input is greater than α otherwise 0). Note that we omit the spatial coordinate here. Recall that photometric & color augmentation are *value-based* augmentation schemes. This brings two problems: first, on the left hand side of Eq. (3), the augmented DVS data is not event-stream since the *value-based* transformation outputs continuous values. Second, on the right hand side of Eq. (3), predicting the event is intractable. Due to brightness difference change, it is unclear whether the event

---

[2] Note that using event camera $g(\boldsymbol{x})$ to generate DVS data is expensive and impractical during run-time. It is easier to pre-collect the DVS data with a DVS camera and, then work with the DVS data during runtime.

is activated or remains silent after augmentation ($f(\log V(t)) - f(\log V(t-1))$). Therefore, we cannot use this type of augmentation in NDA.

It turns out that *index-based* geometric augmentation is suitable for NDA. First, the geometric transformation only changes the position, and therefore the augmented data is still maintained in event-stream. Second, assume an original event which has $\log V(t) - \log V(t-1) > \alpha$ is still generated in the case of geometric augmentation $f(\log V(t)) - f(\log V(t-1))$. The only difference is position change which can be effectively predicted by the left hand side of Eq. (3). For example, rotating a generated set of DVS data and generating a rotated set of DVS data have the same output. Therefore, our NDA consists of several geometric augmentations:

Horizontal Flipping. Flipping is widely used in computer vision tasks. It turns the order of horizontal dimension w. Note that for DVS data, the polarity and the time dimension are kept intact. We set the probability of flipping to 0.5.

Rolling. Rolling means randomly shifting the geometric position of the DVS image. Similar to a bit shift, rolling can move the pixels left or right in the horizontal dimension. In the vertical dimension, we can also shift the pixels up or down. Note that both circular and non-circular shifts are acceptable since DVS image borders are likely to be 0. Each time we apply rolling, the horizontal shift value a and the vertical shift value b are sampled from an integer uniform distribution $\mathcal{U}(-c, c)$, where c is a hyper-parameter.

Rotation. The DVS data will be randomly rotated in the clockwise or counter-clockwise manner. Similar to rolling, each time we apply rotation, the degree of rotation is sampled from a uniform distribution $\mathcal{U}(-d, d)$, where positive degree means clockwise rotation and vice versa. d is a hyperparameter.

Cutout. Cutout was originally proposed in [13] to address overfitting. This method randomly erases a small area of the image, with a similar effect of dropout [58]. Mathematically, first, a square is generated with random size and random position. The side length is sampled from an integer uniform distribution $\mathcal{U}(1, e)$, and then a center inside the image is randomly chosen to place the square. All pixels inside the square are masked off.

Shear. Shear mapping originated from plane geometry. It is a linear map that displaces each point in a fixed direction [62]. Mathematically, a horizontal shear (or ShearX) is a function that takes point (x, y) to point $(x + my, y)$. All pixels above x-axis are displaced to the right if $m > 0$, and to the left if $m < 0$. Note that we do not use vertical shear (ShearY) following prior arts [8,9]. The shear factor m is also sampled from some uniform distribution $\mathcal{U}(n, n)$.

CutMix. Proposed in [67], CutMix is an effective linear interpolation of two input data and labels. Consider two input data samples $\boldsymbol{x}_{N1}$ and $\boldsymbol{x}_{N2}$ and their corresponding label $\boldsymbol{y}_1, \boldsymbol{y}_2$. CutMix is formulated as

$$\tilde{\boldsymbol{x}}_n = \boldsymbol{M}\boldsymbol{x}_{N1} + (1 - \boldsymbol{M})\boldsymbol{x}_{N2}, \quad \tilde{\boldsymbol{y}} = \beta\boldsymbol{y}_1 + (1 - \beta)\boldsymbol{y}_2, \tag{4}$$

where $\boldsymbol{M}$ is a binary mask (similar to the one used in Cutout), and β is the ratio between the area of one and the area of zero in that mask.

Table 2. Look-up table for exchanging N with augmentation hyper-parameters.

N	Rolling c	Rotation d	Cutout e	Shear n
1	3	15	8	0.15
2	5	30	16	0.30
3	7	45	24	0.45

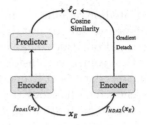

Fig. 4. NDA for SSL-SNN.

4.2 Augmentation Policy

With each above augmentation, one can generate more training samples. In this section, we explore the combination and intensity of the considered augmentations. We first set flipping and CutMix as the default augmentation, which means they are always enabled. The flipping probability is set to 0.5 and the CutMix interpolation factor is sampled from $\beta(1,1)$. Second, for all time step of input data, we randomly sample several augmentations from {Rolling, Rotation, Cutout, ShearX}, inspired by prior work [9,46,70]. We define two hyper-parameters: M for the number of augmentations and N for the intensity of augmentations. That is, before each forward pass, we randomly sample M augmentations with N-level intensity (the higher the N, the greater the difference between augmented and original data). M can be set from 1 to 4. In Table 2, we describe the corresponding relationship between N and the augmentation hyper-parameters. For instance, using M2N3 policy during a forward pass yields 2 randomly sampled augmentations with $N = 3$ intensity as shown in Table 2. Our algorithm can be simply implemented and can be an add-on extension to existing SNN training methods. In the following experiments, we will show how the number of augmentations and the intensity of augmentations impact test accuracy.

4.3 Application to Unsupervised Contrastive Learning

Besides improving the supervised learning of SNNs, we show another application of NDA, *i.e.* unsupervised contrastive learning for SNNs. Unsupervised contrastive learning [5,6,21,27] is a widely used and well-performing learning algorithm without the requirement of labels. The idea of contrastive learning is to learn the similarity between paired input images. Each paired output can be either similar or different. It would be easy to identify different images, as they are naturally distinct. However, for a similar image pair, it is required to augment the same image to different tensors and optimize the network to output the same feature. This task is a simpler task that doesn't require any labels as compared to image classification or segmentation, which makes it perfect for learning some low-level features and transferring the model to some high-level vision tasks.

In this paper, we implement unsupervised contrastive learning for SNNs based on a recent work Simple Siamese Network [7] with our proposed NDA, as illustrated in Fig. 4. First, a DVS data input x_E is augmented into two samples: $f_{NDA1}(x_E)$ and $f_{NDA2}(x_E)$. Our goal is to maximize the similarity of two outputs and one output is further processed by a predictor head to make the final prediction. The contrastive loss is defined as the cosine similarity between the predictor output and the encoder output. In contrastive learning, there is a problem called *latent space collapsing*, meaning that the output of a network is the same, irrespective of different inputs which can render the network useless. This collapsing can always yield minimum loss. To address this problem, gradient detach is applied to the branch without predictor. It is noteworthy to mention that all the contrastive learning schemes require data augmentation to make model learn invariant features. As a broader impact, this could be helpful when the event camera collects new data that is not easy to be labeled because of raw events.

After the unsupervised pre-training stage, we drop the predictor and only save the encoder part. This encoder is used for transfer learning, *i.e.* construct a new head (the last fully-connected layer *a.k.a* the classifier) and finetune the model. We will provide transfer results in the experiments section below.

5 Experiments

In this section, we will verify the effectiveness and efficiency of our proposed NDA. In Sect. 5.2, we compare our model with existing literature. In Sect. 5.3, we analyze our method in terms of sharpness and efficiency. In Sect. 5.1, we give an ablation study of our methods. In Sect. 5.4, we provide the results of unsupervised contrastive learning.

Implementation details. We implement our experiments with the Pytorch package. All our experiments are run on 4 GPUs. We use ResNet-19 [28,69] and VGG-11 [17,56] as baseline models. Note that all ReLU layers are changed to the Leaky integrate-and-fire module and all max-pooling layers are changed to average pooling. We use tdBN [69] as our baseline SNN training method. For our own implementation, we only change the data augmentation part and keep other training hyper-parameters aligned. We use M1N2 NDA configuration for all our experiments. The total batch size is set to 256 and we use Adam optimizer. For all our experiments, we train the model for 200 epochs and the learning rate is set to 0.001 followed by a cosine annealing decay [45]. The weight decay is $1e-4$. We verify our method on the following DVS benchmarks:

CIFAR10-DVS [37]. CIFAR10-DVS contains 10K DVS images recorded from the original CIFAR10 dataset. We apply a $9:1$ train-valid split (*i.e.* 9k training images and 1k validation images). The resolution is 128×128, we resize all of them to 48×48 in our training and we integrate the event data into 10 frames per sample.

N-Caltech 101 [47]. N-Caltech 101 contains 8831 DVS images recorded from the original Caltech 101 dataset. Similarly, we apply $9:1$ train-valid split and resize

Table 3. Ablation study: comparison between photometric/color augmentation and geometric augmentation, and comparison with the intensity and the number of the augmentation per data.

Dataset	Photo/Color	Geo−M1N1	Geo−M1N2	Geo−M2N2	Geo−M3N3
CIFAR10-DVS	62.8	73.4	78.0	75.1	71.4
N−Caltech101	64.0	74.4	78.6	72.7	65.1

all images to 48×48. We use the spikingjelly package [16] to process the data and integrate them into 10 frames per sample.

N-MNIST [47]. The neuromorphic MNIST dataset is a converted dataset from MNIST. It contains 50K training images and 10K validation images. We pre-process it in the same way as in N-Caltech 101.

N-Cars [57]. Neuromorphic cars dataset is a binary classification dataset with labels either from *cars* or from *background*. It contains 7940 car and 7482 background training samples, 4396 car and 4211 background test samples. We pre-process it in the same way as in N-Caltech 101.

5.1   Ablation Study

Augmentation Choice. In theory, photometric & color augmentations are not supposed to be used for DVS data. To verify this, we **compulsorily cast Color-Jitter and GaussianBlur augmentation to the DVS data** (note that the data is not event-stream after these augmentations) and compare the results with geometric augmentation. The results are shown in Table 3 (all entries are results trained with ResNet-19). We find that photometric and color augmentation (Jitter + GaussianBlur) performs much worse than geometric augmentation, regardless of the dataset. This confirms our analysis that *value-based* augmentations are not suitable for NDA.

Augmentation Policy. We also test the augmentation intensity as well as the number of the augmentation. In Table 3, we show that the intensity of the augmentation satisfies some bias-variance trade-off. The augmentation can become neither too simple so that the data is not diverse enough, nor too complex so that the data does not contain useful event information.

5.2   Comparison with Existing Literature

We first compare our NDA method on the CIFAR10-DVS dataset. The results are shown in Table 4. We compare our method with Gabor-SNN, Streaming roll-out, tdBN, and PLIF [17,34,44,57,64,69]. Among these baselines, tdBN and PLIF achieve better accuracy. We reproduce tdBN with our own implementations. When training with NDA, we use the best practice M1N2 for sampling augmentations. With NDA, our ResNet-19 reaches 78.0% top-1 accuracy, outperforming the baseline without augmentation by a large margin. After scaling the

Table 4. Accuracy comparison with different methods on CIFAR10-DVS, N-Caltech 101, N-Cars, we use tdBN in our model. Acc. is referred as the top-1 accuracy.

Method	Model	CIFAR10-DVS		N Caltech-101		N-Cars	
		T Step	Acc.	T Step	Acc.	T Step	Acc.
HOTS [35]	N/A	N/A	27.1	N/A	21.0	10	54.0
Gabor-SNN [57]	2-layer CNN	N/A	28.4	N/A	28.4	–	–
HATS [57]	N/A	N/A	52.4	N/A	64.2	10	81.0
DART [48]	N/A	N/A	65.8	N/A	66.8	–	–
CarSNN [60]	4-layer CNN	–	–	–	–	10	77.0
CarSNN [60]	4-layer CNN[2]	–	–	–	–	10	86.0
BNTT [32]	6-layer CNN	20	63.2	–	–	–	–
Rollout [34]	VGG-16	48	66.5	–	–	–	–
SALT [33]	VGG11	20	67.1	20	55.0	–	–
LIAF-Net [65]	VGG-like	10	70.4	–	–	–	–
tdBN [69]	ResNet-19[1]	10	67.8	–	–	–	–
PLIF [17]	VGG-11[2]	20	74.8	–	–	–	–
tdBN (w/o NDA)[3]	ResNet-19[1]	10	67.9	10	62.8	10	82.4
tdBN (w/. NDA)	ResNet-19[1]	10	**78.0**	10	**78.6**	10	**87.2**
tdBN (w/o NDA)[3]	VGG-11	10	76.2	10	67.2	10	84.4
tdBN (w/. NDA)	VGG-11	10	**79.6**	10	**78.2**	10	**90.1**
tdBN (w/o NDA)[3]	VGG-11[2]	10	76.3	10	72.9	10	87.4
tdBN (w/. NDA)	VGG-11[2]	10	**81.7**	10	**83.7**	10	**91.9**

[1] Quadrupled channel number,
[2] 128 × 128 resolution,
[3] Our implementation.

data to a resolution of 128, our method gets 81.7% accuracy on VGG-11 model. We also compare our method on N-Caltech 101 dataset. There aren't many SNN works on this dataset. Most of them are non-neural network based methods using hand-crafted processing [35,48,57]. NDA can obtain a high accuracy network with 15.8% absolute accuracy improvement over the baseline without NDA. Our VGG-11 even reaches 83.7% accuracy with full 128×128 resolution. This indicates that only improving the network training strategy is less effective. Next, we test our algorithm on the N-Cars dataset. The primary comparison work is CarSNN [60] which optimizes a spiking network and deploys it on the Loihi chip [10]. tdBN trained ResNet-19 achieve 82.4% using 48×48 resolution. Simply applying NDA improves the accuracy by 4.8% without any additional modifications. When training with full resolution, we have 4.5% accuracy improvement with VGG-11.

Finally, we validate our method on the N-MNIST dataset (as shown in Table 5). N-MNIST is harder than the original MNIST dataset, but most base-

Table 5. N-MNIST accuracy comparison with different methods, we use tdBN in our model.

Method	Model	Time Step	Top-1 Acc.
Lee *et al.* [36]	2-layer CNN	N/A	98.61
SLAYER [55]	3-layer CNN	N/A	99.20
Gabor-SNN [57]	2-layer CNN	N/A	83.70
HATS [57]	N/A	N/A	99.10
STBP [64]	6-layer CNN	10	99.53
PLIF [17]	4-layer CNN	10	99.61
tdBN (w/o NDA)	4-layer CNN	10	99.58
tdBN (w/. NDA)	4-layer CNN	10	**99.70**

Table 6. Comparison with Event-Drop [22] using ANNs for DVS datasets. EventDrop models are ImageNet pre-trained.

Model	Method	N-Caltech 101	N-Cars
ResNet-34	Baseline [22][1]	77.4	91.8
	EventDrop [22][1]	78.2	94.0
	Ours (w/o NDA)	67.7	90.5
	Ours (w/. NDA)	81.2	**95.5**
VGG-19	Baseline [22][1]	72.3	91.6
	EventDrop [22][1]	75.0	92.7
	Ours (w/o. NDA)	65.4	90.3
	Ours (w/. NDA)	**82.8**	**94.5**

lines get over 99% accuracy. We use the same architecture as PLIF. Our NDA uplifts the model by 0.12% in terms of accuracy. Although this is a marginal improvement, the final test accuracy is quite close to the 100% mark.

Evaluating NDA on ANN. We also evaluate if our method is applicable to ANNs. We mainly compare our method with EventDrop on frame data [22], another work that augments the event data by random dropping some events (like Cutout used in NDA). In Table 6, we find NDA can greatly improve the performance of ANN. For VGG-19, our NDA can boost the accuracy to 82.8%. For N-Cars dataset, we adopt the same pre-processing as EventDrop, *i.e.* using 8 : 2 train-validation split to optimize the model, and our method attains 1.8% higher accuracy even without any ImageNet pre-training.

5.3 Analysis

Model Sharpness. Apart from the test accuracy, we can measure the *sharpness* of a model to estimate its generalizability. A sharp loss surface implies that a model has a higher probability of mispredicting unseen samples. In this section, we will use two simple and popular metrics: (1) Hessian spectra and (2) Noise injection. Hessian matrix is the second-order gradient matrix. The second-order gradient contains the curvature information of the model. Here, we measure the topk Hessian eigenvalues and the trace to estimate the sharpness. Low eigenvalue and low trace lead to low curvature and better performance. We compute the 1st, 5th eigenvalues as well as the trace of the Hessian in ResNet-19 using PyHessian [66]. The model is trained on CIFAR10-DVS with and without NDA. We summarize the results in Table 7. We show that the Hessian spectra of the model trained with NDA is significantly lower than that without NDA. Moreover, the trace of the Hessian also satisfies this outcome.

Another way to measure the sharpness is noise injection. We randomly inject Gaussian noise sampled from $\mathcal{N}(0, \gamma)$ into the model weights, where γ is a hyper-parameter controlling the range of the noise. We run 5 times for each γ and record the mean & standard deviation, which are summarized in Fig. 5. It can

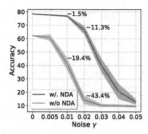

Fig. 5. Comparison of robustness under Gaussian noise injected to weights.

Table 7. Hessian spectra comparison. λ_1, λ_5, Tr refer to the 1st, 5th highest eigenvalue and the trace of the Hessian matrix. We record the model at 100, 200, 300 epochs. (The lower the Hessian spectrum, the flatter the converged minimum is).

Epoch	w/o NDA			w/. NDA		
	λ_1	λ_5	Tr	λ_1	λ_5	Tr
100	910.7	433.4	6277	424.3	73.87	1335
200	3375	1416	21342	516.4	155.3	1868
300	3404	1686	20501	639.7	187.5	2323

be seen that the model with NDA is much more robust to the noise we imposed on the weights. For example, when we set the noise to $\mathcal{N}(0, 0.01)$, the model with NDA only suffers a slight 1.5% accuracy drop, while the model without NDA has a 19.4% accuracy drop. More evidently, when casting $\mathcal{N}(0, 0.02)$ noise, our NDA model suffers 11.3% accuracy decline, while the counterpart suffers a drastic 43.4% accuracy decline. This indicates that NDA serves a similar effect with regularization technique.

Algorithm Efficiency. Our NDA is efficient and easy to implement. To demonstrate its efficiency, we hereby report the time cost of NDA. We use Intel XEON(R) E5-2620 v4 CPU to test the data loader. When loading CIFAR10-DVS, the CPU expends additional 15.2873 s seconds in applying NDA to 9000 DVS training images. The average cost basically amounts to 1.7 ms per image.

We also estimate the energy consumption of the model using NDA. Specifically, we use the number of operations and roughly assume energy consumption is linearly proportional to the number of operations [49,69]. We do not count the operation if the spike does not fire. Thus, the number of operations can be computed as $FireRate \times MAC$. In Fig. 6, we visualize the $FireRate$ of several layers in the trained model with and without NDA. We can find that the $FireRate$ is similar (note, NDA is slightly higher) and the final number of operations are very close in both cases. Model with NDA only expends a 10% higher number of operations than the model without NDA, demonstrating the efficiency of NDA.

Training with validation dataset. Following [17], we test our algorithm on a challenging task. We take 15% of the data from the training dataset to build a *validation dataset*. Then, we report the *test accuracy* when the model reaches best *validation accuracy*. We run experiments on CIFAR10-DVS with ResNet-19. In this case (Table 8), our NDA model yields 16.3% accuracy improvement over a model without NDA.

5.4 Unsupervised Contrastive Learning

In this section, we test our NDA algorithm with unsupervised contrastive learning. Usually, the augmentation in unsupervised contrastive learning requires

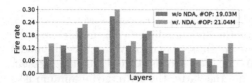

Fig. 6. Fire Rate of several LIF layers of ResNet-19 trained on CIFAR10-DVS.

Table 8. Ablation Study: the effect of validation dataset.

Method	Acc. No Valid.	Acc. 15% Valid.
PLIF [17]	74.8	69.0
w/o NDA	63.4	58.5
w/. NDA	78.0	**74.4**

stronger augmentation than that in supervised learning [5]. Thus we use NDA-M3N2 for augmentation. We pre-train a VGG-11 on the N-Caltech 101 dataset with SimSiam learning (cf. Section 4.3, Fig. 4). N-Caltech 101 contains more visual categories and can be a good pre-training dataset. In this experiment, we use the original 128 × 128 resolution DVS data, and use the simple-siamese method to train the network for 600 epochs. The batch size is set to 256.

After pre-training, we replace the predictor with a zero-initialized fully-connected classifier and finetune the model for 100/300 epochs on CIFAR10-DVS. We also add supervised pre-training with NDA and no pre-training (*i.e.* directly train a model on downstream task) as our baselines. We show the transferability results in Table 9. Interestingly, we find supervised pre-training has no effect on transfer learning with such DVS datasets, which is different from conventional natural image classification transferability results. This may be attributed to the distance between dataset domains that is larger in DVS than that in RGB dataset. The model pre-trained on N-Caltech 101 with supervised learning only achieves 80.9% accuracy, which is even 0.8% lower than the no pre-training method. The unsupervised learning with NDA achieves significantly better transfer results: finetuning only for 100 epochs takes the model to 80.8% accuracy on CIFAR10-DVS, and 300 epochs finetuning yields 82.1% test accuracy, establishing a new state of the art.

Table 9. Unsupervised transfer learning results on CIFAR10-DVS. All the model is pre-trained on N-Caltech 101.

Pre-training Method	Finetuning Method	Test Acc.
No Pre-training	Train@300	81.7
Supervised	Finetune@100	77.4
Supervised	Finetune@300	80.9
Unsupervised	Finetune@100	80.8
Unsupervised	Finetune@300	**82.1**

6   Conclusions

We introduce the Neuromorphic Data Augmentation technique (NDA), a simple yet effective method that improves the generalization of SNNs on event-based data. NDA allows users to generate new high-quality event-based data instances that force the model to learn invariant features. Furthermore, we show that NDA acts like regularization that achieves an improved bias-variance trade-off. Extensive experimental results validate that NDA is able to find a flatter minimum with the higher test accuracy and enable unsupervised pre-training for transfer learning. However, the current NDA lacks value-based augmentations for events, which may be realized by logical operations and studied in the future.

Acknowledgment. This work was supported in part by C-BRIC, a JUMP center sponsored by DARPA and SRC, Google Research Scholar Award, the National Science Foundation (Grant#1947826), TII (Abu Dhabi), and the DARPA AI Exploration (AIE) program.

References

1. Arjovsky, M., Chintala, S., Bottou, L.: Wasserstein generative adversarial networks. In: International Conference on Machine Learning, pp. 214–223. PMLR (2017)
2. Basegmez, E.: The next generation neural networks: Deep learning and spiking neural networks. In: Advanced Seminar in Technical University of Munich, pp. 1–40. Citeseer (2014)
3. Brock, A., Donahue, J., Simonyan, K.: Large scale GAN training for high fidelity natural image synthesis. arXiv preprint arXiv:1809.11096 (2018)
4. Budvytis, I., Sauer, P., Roddick, T., Breen, K., Cipolla, R.: Large scale labelled video data augmentation for semantic segmentation in driving scenarios. In: Proceedings of the IEEE International Conference on Computer Vision Workshops, pp. 230–237 (2017)
5. Chen, T., Kornblith, S., Norouzi, M., Hinton, G.: A simple framework for contrastive learning of visual representations. In: International conference on machine learning, pp. 1597–1607. PMLR (2020)
6. Chen, X., Fan, H., Girshick, R., He, K.: Improved baselines with momentum contrastive learning. arXiv preprint arXiv:2003.04297 (2020)
7. Chen, X., He, K.: Exploring simple Siamese representation learning. In: Proceedings of the IEEE/CVF Conference on Computer Vision and Pattern Recognition, pp. 15750–15758 (2021)
8. Cubuk, E.D., Zoph, B., Mane, D., Vasudevan, V., Le, Q.V.: AutoAugment: learning augmentation policies from data. arXiv preprint arXiv:1805.09501 (2018)
9. Cubuk, E.D., Zoph, B., Shlens, J., Le, Q.V.: RandAugment: practical automated data augmentation with a reduced search space. In: Proceedings of the IEEE/CVF Conference on Computer Vision and Pattern Recognition Workshops, pp. 702–703 (2020)
10. Davies, M., et al.: Loihi: a neuromorphic manycore processor with on-chip learning. IEEE Micro **38**(1), 82–99 (2018)
11. Deng, S., Gu, S.: Optimal conversion of conventional artificial neural networks to spiking neural networks. arXiv preprint arXiv:2103.00476 (2021)

12. Deng, S., Li, Y., Zhang, S., Gu, S.: Temporal efficient training of spiking neural network via gradient re-weighting. arXiv preprint arXiv:2202.11946 (2022)
13. DeVries, T., Taylor, G.W.: Improved regularization of convolutional neural networks with cutout. arXiv preprint arXiv:1708.04552 (2017)
14. Diehl, P.U., Neil, D., Binas, J., Cook, M., Liu, S.C., Pfeiffer, M.: Fast-classifying, high-accuracy spiking deep networks through weight and threshold balancing. In: 2015 International joint conference on neural networks (IJCNN), pp. 1–8. IEEE (2015)
15. Diehl, P.U., Zarrella, G., Cassidy, A., Pedroni, B.U., Neftci, E.: Conversion of artificial recurrent neural networks to spiking neural networks for low-power neuromorphic hardware. In: 2016 IEEE International Conference on Rebooting Computing (ICRC), pp. 1–8. IEEE (2016)
16. Fang, W., et al.: Spikingjelly (2020). https://github.com/fangwei123456/spikingjelly
17. Fang, W., Yu, Z., Chen, Y., Masquelier, T., Huang, T., Tian, Y.: Incorporating learnable membrane time constant to enhance learning of spiking neural networks. In: Proceedings of the IEEE/CVF International Conference on Computer Vision, pp. 2661–2671 (2021)
18. Gallego, G., et al.: Event-based vision: a survey. arXiv preprint arXiv:1904.08405 (2019)
19. Ganin, Y., et al.: Domain-adversarial training of neural networks. J. Mach. Learn. Res. **17**(1), 1–35 (2016)
20. Gatys, L.A., Ecker, A.S., Bethge, M.: Image style transfer using convolutional neural networks. In: Proceedings of the IEEE Conference on Computer Vision and Pattern Recognition, pp. 2414–2423 (2016)
21. Grill, J.B., et al.: Bootstrap your own latent: a new approach to self-supervised learning. arXiv preprint arXiv:2006.07733 (2020)
22. Gu, F., Sng, W., Hu, X., Yu, F.: EventDrop: data augmentation for event-based learning. arXiv preprint arXiv:2106.05836 (2021)
23. Gulrajani, I., Ahmed, F., Arjovsky, M., Dumoulin, V., Courville, A.: Improved training of wasserstein gans. arXiv preprint arXiv:1704.00028 (2017)
24. Guo, Y., Tong, X., Chen, Y., Zhang, L., Liu, X., Ma, Z., Huang, X.: RecDis-SNN: rectifying membrane potential distribution for directly training spiking neural networks. In: Proceedings of the IEEE/CVF Conference on Computer Vision and Pattern Recognition, pp. 326–335 (2022)
25. Han, B., Roy, K.: Deep spiking neural network: energy efficiency through time based coding. In: European Conference on Computer Vision (2020)
26. Hazan, H., et al.: BindsNET: a machine learning-oriented spiking neural networks library in Python. Front. Neuroinform. **12**, 89 (2018)
27. He, K., Fan, H., Wu, Y., Xie, S., Girshick, R.: Momentum contrast for unsupervised visual representation learning. In: Proceedings of the IEEE/CVF Conference on Computer Vision and Pattern Recognition, pp. 9729–9738 (2020)
28. He, K., Zhang, X., Ren, S., Sun, J.: Deep residual learning for image recognition. In: Proceedings of the IEEE Conference on Computer Vision and Pattern Recognition, pp. 770–778 (2016)
29. Ioffe, S., Szegedy, C.: Batch normalization: accelerating deep network training by reducing internal covariate shift. In: International Conference on Machine Learning, pp. 448–456. PMLR (2015)
30. Jing, Y., Yang, Y., Feng, Z., Ye, J., Yu, Y., Song, M.: Neural style transfer: a review. IEEE Trans. Vis. Comput. Graph. **26**(11), 3365–3385 (2019)

31. Karras, T., Aila, T., Laine, S., Lehtinen, J.: Progressive growing of GANs for improved quality, stability, and variation. arXiv preprint arXiv:1710.10196 (2017)
32. Kim, Y., Panda, P.: Revisiting batch normalization for training low-latency deep spiking neural networks from scratch. arXiv preprint arXiv:2010.01729 (2020)
33. Kim, Y., Panda, P.: Optimizing deeper spiking neural networks for dynamic vision sensing. Neural Networks (2021)
34. Kugele, A., Pfeil, T., Pfeiffer, M., Chicca, E.: Efficient processing of spatio-temporal data streams with spiking neural networks. Front. Neurosci. **14**, 439 (2020)
35. Lagorce, X., Orchard, G., Galluppi, F., Shi, B.E., Benosman, R.B.: HOTS: a hierarchy of event-based time-surfaces for pattern recognition. IEEE Trans. Pattern Anal. Mach. Intell. **39**(7), 1346–1359 (2016)
36. Lee, J.H., Delbruck, T., Pfeiffer, M.: Training deep spiking neural networks using backpropagation. Front. Neurosci. **10**, 508 (2016)
37. Li, H., Liu, H., Ji, X., Li, G., Shi, L.: CIFAR10-DVS: an event-stream dataset for object classification. Front. Neurosci. **11**, 309 (2017)
38. Li, Y., Deng, S., Dong, X., Gong, R., Gu, S.: A free lunch from ANN: towards efficient, accurate spiking neural networks calibration. arXiv preprint arXiv:2106.06984 (2021)
39. Li, Y., Deng, S., Dong, X., Gu, S.: Converting artificial neural networks to spiking neural networks via parameter calibration. arXiv preprint arXiv:2205.10121 (2022)
40. Li, Y., Guo, Y., Zhang, S., Deng, S., Hai, Y., Gu, S.: Differentiable spike: Rethinking gradient-descent for training spiking neural networks. Adv. Neural. Inf. Process. Syst. **34**, 23426–23439 (2021)
41. Li, Y., et al.: MixMix: all you need for data-free compression are feature and data mixing. In: Proceedings of the IEEE/CVF International Conference on Computer Vision, pp. 4410–4419 (2021)
42. Lim, S., Kim, I., Kim, T., Kim, C., Kim, S.: Fast autoaugment. Adv. Neural. Inf. Process. Syst. **32**, 6665–6675 (2019)
43. Lin, Y., Ding, W., Qiang, S., Deng, L., Li, G.: ES-ImageNet: a million event-stream classification dataset for spiking neural networks. Front. Neurosci., 1546 (2021)
44. Liu, Q., Ruan, H., Xing, D., Tang, H., Pan, G.: Effective AER object classification using segmented probability-maximization learning in spiking neural networks. In: Proceedings of the AAAI Conference on Artificial Intelligence, vol. 34, pp. 1308–1315 (2020)
45. Loshchilov, I., Hutter, F.: SGDR: stochastic gradient descent with warm restarts. arXiv preprint arXiv:1608.03983 (2016)
46. Munoz-Bulnes, J., Fernandez, C., Parra, I., Fernández-Llorca, D., Sotelo, M.A.: Deep fully convolutional networks with random data augmentation for enhanced generalization in road detection. In: 2017 IEEE 20th International Conference on Intelligent Transportation Systems (ITSC), pp. 366–371. IEEE (2017)
47. Orchard, G., Jayawant, A., Cohen, G.K., Thakor, N.: Converting static image datasets to spiking neuromorphic datasets using saccades. Front. Neurosci. **9**, 437 (2015)
48. Ramesh, B., Yang, H., Orchard, G., Le Thi, N.A., Zhang, S., Xiang, C.: DART: distribution aware retinal transform for event-based cameras. IEEE Trans. Pattern Anal. Mach. Intell. **42**(11), 2767–2780 (2019)
49. Rathi, N., Roy, K.: DIET-SNN: direct input encoding with leakage and threshold optimization in deep spiking neural networks. arXiv preprint arXiv:2008.03658 (2020)

50. Rathi, N., Srinivasan, G., Panda, P., Roy, K.: Enabling deep spiking neural networks with hybrid conversion and spike timing dependent backpropagation. arXiv preprint arXiv:2005.01807 (2020)
51. Ronneberger, O., Fischer, P., Brox, T.: U-Net: convolutional networks for biomedical image segmentation. In: Navab, N., Hornegger, J., Wells, W.M., Frangi, A.F. (eds.) MICCAI 2015. LNCS, vol. 9351, pp. 234–241. Springer, Cham (2015). https://doi.org/10.1007/978-3-319-24574-4_28
52. Roy, K., Jaiswal, A., Panda, P.: Towards spike-based machine intelligence with neuromorphic computing. Nature **575**(7784), 607–617 (2019)
53. Rucckauer, B., Lungu, I.A., Hu, Y., Pfeiffer, M.: Theory and tools for the conversion of analog to spiking convolutional neural networks. arXiv: Statistics/Machine Learning (1612.04052) (2016)
54. Shorten, C., Khoshgoftaar, T.M.: A survey on image data augmentation for deep learning. J. Big Data **6**(1), 1–48 (2019)
55. Shrestha, S.B., Orchard, G.: SLAYER: spike layer error reassignment in time. arXiv preprint arXiv:1810.08646 (2018)
56. Simonyan, K., Zisserman, A.: Very deep convolutional networks for large-scale image recognition. arXiv preprint arXiv:1409.1556 (2014)
57. Sironi, A., Brambilla, M., Bourdis, N., Lagorce, X., Benosman, R.: HATS: histograms of averaged time surfaces for robust event-based object classification. In: Proceedings of the IEEE Conference on Computer Vision and Pattern Recognition, pp. 1731–1740 (2018)
58. Srivastava, N., Hinton, G., Krizhevsky, A., Sutskever, I., Salakhutdinov, R.: Dropout: a simple way to prevent neural networks from overfitting. J. Mach. Learn. Res. **15**(1), 1929–1958 (2014)
59. Tramèr, F., Kurakin, A., Papernot, N., Goodfellow, I., Boneh, D., McDaniel, P.: Ensemble adversarial training: Attacks and defenses. arXiv preprint arXiv:1705.07204 (2017)
60. Viale, A., Marchisio, A., Martina, M., Masera, G., Shafique, M.: CarSNN: an efficient spiking neural network for event-based autonomous cars on the Loihi neuromorphic research processor. In: 2021 International Joint Conference on Neural Networks (IJCNN), pp. 1–10. IEEE (2021)
61. Wikipedia: event camera – Wikipedia, the free encyclopedia. https://en.wikipedia.org/wiki/Event_camera (2021)
62. Wikipedia: shear mapping – Wikipedia, the free encyclopedia. https://en.wikipedia.org/wiki/Shear_mapping (2021)
63. Wu, Y., Deng, L., Li, G., Zhu, J., Shi, L.: Spatio-temporal backpropagation for training high-performance spiking neural networks. Front. Neurosci. **12**, 331 (2018)
64. Wu, Y., Deng, L., Li, G., Zhu, J., Xie, Y., Shi, L.: Direct training for spiking neural networks: faster, larger, better. In: Proceedings of the AAAI Conference on Artificial Intelligence, vol. 33, pp. 1311–1318 (2019)
65. Wu, Z., Zhang, H., Lin, Y., Li, G., Wang, M., Tang, Y.: LIAF-NET: leaky integrate and analog fire network for lightweight and efficient spatiotemporal information processing. IEEE Trans. Neural Netw. Learn. Syst. (2021)
66. Yao, Z., Gholami, A., Keutzer, K., Mahoney, M.W.: PyHessian: neural networks through the lens of the Hessian. In: 2020 IEEE International Conference on Big Data (Big Data), pp. 581–590. IEEE (2020)
67. Yun, S., Han, D., Oh, S.J., Chun, S., Choe, J., Yoo, Y.: CutMix: regularization strategy to train strong classifiers with localizable features. In: Proceedings of the IEEE/CVF International Conference on Computer Vision, pp. 6023–6032 (2019)

68. Zhang, X., et al.: Diversifying sample generation for accurate data-free quanti-zation. In: Proceedings of the IEEE/CVF Conference on Computer Vision and Pattern Recognition, pp. 15658–15667 (2021)
69. Zheng, H., Wu, Y., Deng, L., Hu, Y., Li, G.: Going deeper with directly-trained larger spiking neural networks. arXiv preprint arXiv:2011.05280 (2020)
70. Zhong, Z., Zheng, L., Kang, G., Li, S., Yang, Y.: Random erasing data augmenta-tion. In: Proceedings of the AAAI conference on artificial intelligence, vol. 34, pp. 13001–13008 (2020)
71. Zoph, B., Cubuk, E.D., Ghiasi, G., Lin, T.-Y., Shlens, J., Le, Q.V.: Learning data augmentation strategies for object detection. In: Vedaldi, A., Bischof, H., Brox, T., Frahm, J.-M. (eds.) ECCV 2020. LNCS, vol. 12372, pp. 566–583. Springer, Cham (2020). https://doi.org/10.1007/978-3-030-58583-9_34

CelebV-HQ: A Large-Scale Video Facial Attributes Dataset

Hao Zhu[1], Wayne Wu[1(✉)], Wentao Zhu[2], Liming Jiang[3],
Siwei Tang[1], Li Zhang[1], Ziwei Liu[3], and Chen Change Loy[3]

[1] SenseTime Research, Hong Kong, China
wuwenyan0503@gmail.com
[2] Peking University, Beijing, China
[3] S-Lab, Nanyang Technological University, Singapore, Singapore

Abstract. Large-scale datasets have played indispensable roles in the recent success of face generation/editing and significantly facilitated the advances of emerging research fields. However, the academic community still lacks a video dataset with diverse facial attribute annotations, which is crucial for the research on face-related videos. In this work, we propose a large-scale, high-quality, and diverse video dataset with rich facial attribute annotations, named the High-Quality Celebrity Video Dataset (CelebV-HQ). CelebV-HQ contains $35,666$ video clips with the resolution of 512×512 at least, involving $15,653$ identities. All clips are labeled manually with 83 facial attributes, covering appearance, action, and emotion. We conduct a comprehensive analysis in terms of age, ethnicity, brightness stability, motion smoothness, head pose diversity, and data quality to demonstrate the diversity and temporal coherence of CelebV-HQ. Besides, its versatility and potential are validated on two representative tasks, *i.e.*, unconditional video generation and video facial attribute editing. We finally envision the future potential of CelebV-HQ, as well as the new opportunities and challenges it would bring to related research directions. Data, code, and models are publicly available (Project page: https://celebv-hq.github.io/ Code and models: https://github.com/CelebV-HQ/CelebV-HQ).

Keywords: Large-scale video dataset · Facial attribute annotation · Face video generation and editing

1 Introduction

The rapid development of Generative Adversarial Networks (GANs) [17,34–37,55] has demonstrably promoted advances in face generation and editing. This progress relies heavily on the contribution of large-scale datasets, *e.g.*,

---

H. Zhu and W. Wu—Equal Contribution.

Supplementary Information The online version contains supplementary material available at https://doi.org/10.1007/978-3-031-20071-7_38.

(a) Appearance   (b) Action   (c) Emotion

Fig. 1. Overview of CelebV-HQ. CelebV-HQ contains 35,666 videos, including 15,653 identities. Each video was manually labeled with 83 facial attributes, covering appearance, action, and emotion attributes.

CelebA [45], CelebA-HQ [34], and FFHQ [36]. These datasets, with high-quality facial images, have facilitated the development of a series of face generation and editing tasks, such as unconditional face generation [17,31,36,37,55,63,65,81], facial attribute editing [8,26,61,66,77] and neural rendering [3,4,6,14,18,19,24, 52,52]. However, most of these efforts are based on static *image modality*. In industry, with the booming development of mobile internet [10], *video modality* data begins to take a bigger and bigger share in customers' daily shootings [28,48]. A well-suited dataset, which is capable of supporting the face generation and editing tasks in video modality, is eagerly asked.

Recent works [2,37] have shown that the *scale* and *quality* are essential factors for a facial dataset in image modality. A more sufficient utilization of large-scale datasets would improve model generalization [58], while the quality of the dataset largely determines the limit of the generative models [36,37,55,63,65,81]. In addition, facial *attribute* provides effective information to help researchers go more deeply into the face-related topics [8,26,45,61]. However, the current public facial datasets consist of either static images with attribute labels [34,45] or videos with insufficient scale [72] and quality [9,51].

Constructing a large-scale and high-quality face video dataset with diverse facial attribute's annotations is still an open question, given the challenges brought by the nature of video data. 1) Scale. The collected videos need to meet several requirements, such as temporal consistency, high-resolution and full-head. The strict standards together with the limited sources, make the expansion of dataset's scale both time and labor consuming. 2) Quality. The quality is not only reflected in the high fidelity and resolution, but also in the diverse and natural distribution of data samples. It asks for a well-designed data-filtering process to ensure all of the requirements of fidelity, resolution and data distribution. 3) Attribute Annotation. The coverage of the facial attribute set need to be sufficient to describe a human face thoroughly, both in the time-invariant and time-variant perspective. Also, the annotation process need to be accurate and highly efficient.

In order to tackle the challenges discussed above, we carefully devise a procedure for dataset construction. First, to ensure the scale of the collected video, we build a large and diverse set of Internet queries. The designed queries cover a rich set of scenarios and thus successfully enable a huge raw data pool with millions of clips. Then, to filter out high-quality data from the raw data pool, we introduce an automatic pre-processing pipeline. In this pipeline, we leverage face detection and alignment tools to ensure the high fidelity and resolution. Finally, we propose a facial attributes set with extensive coverage, including appearance, action and emotion. To ensure the accuracy and efficiency of the annotation, we design a systematic attributes annotation process, including annotator training, automatic judgment and quality check steps.

To this end, we successfully create the High-Quality Celebrity Video (CelebV-HQ) Dataset, a large-scale, diverse, and high-quality video facial dataset with abundant attributes' annotations. CelebV-HQ contains $35,666$ in-the-wild video clips with the resolution of 512×512 at least, involving $15,653$ person identities and 83 manually labeled facial attributes. Our labeling comprises a comprehensive set of face-related attributes, including 40 appearance attributes, 35 action attributes, and 8 emotion attributes. Samples on CelebV-HQ are shown in Fig. 1.

We perform a comprehensive analysis of data distribution to demonstrate CelebV-HQ's statistical superiority to existing image and video datasets. First, compared to image datasets with attribute annotations [34,45], CelebV-HQ has much higher resolution ($2\times$) than CelebA [45] and comparable scale to high-quality dataset [34]. Also, by comparing CelebV-HQ with CelebA-HQ [34] in the *time-invariant* aspects, we demonstrate that CelebV-HQ has a reasonable distribution on appearance and facial geometry. Furthermore, we compare CelebV-HQ with a representative video face dataset VoxCeleb2 [9] in the *time-variant* aspects, such as temporal data quality, brightness variation, head pose distribution, and motion smoothness, suggesting that CelebV-HQ has superior video quality.

Besides, to demonstrate the effectiveness and potential of CelebV-HQ, we evaluate representative baselines in two typical tasks: unconditional video generation and video facial attribute editing. For the task of unconditional video generation, we train state-of-the-art unconditional video GANs [65,81] on CelebV-HQ fullset and its subsets that divided by different actions. When trained on different subsets of CelebV-HQ, the corresponding actions can be successfully generated. Further, we explore the video facial attribute editing task using temporal constrained image-to-image baselines [8,26]. Thanks to the rich sequential information included in CelebV-HQ dataset, We show that simple modification of current image-based methods can bring remarkable improvement in the

Table 1. Face datasets comparison. The symbol "#" indicates the number. The abbreviations "Id.", "Reso.", "Dura.", "App.", "Act.", "Emo.", "Env.", and "Fmt." stand for Identity, Resolution, Duration, Appearance, Action, Emotion, Environment, and Format, respectively. The "*" denotes the estimated resolution.

Datasets	Meta infomation				Attributes			Env.	Fmt.
	#Samples	#Id.	Reso.	Dura.	App.	Act.	Emo.		
CelebA [45]	202,599	10,177	178×218	N/A	✓	✗	✗	Wild	IMG
CelebA-HQ [34]	30,000	6,217	1024×1024	N/A	✓	✗	✗	Wild	IMG
FFHQ [36]	70,000	N/A	1024×1024	N/A	✗	✗	✗	Wild	IMG
CelebV [76]	5	5	256×256	2hrs	✗	✗	✗	Wild	VID
FaceForensics [56]	1,004	1,004	256×256*	4hrs	✗	✗	✗	Wild	VID
VoxCeleb [51]	21,245	1,251	224×224	352hrs	✗	✗	✗	Wild	VID
VoxCeleb2 [9]	150,480	6,112	224×224	2,442hrs	✗	✗	✗	Wild	VID
MEAD [72]	281,400	60	1980×1080	39hrs	✗	✗	✓	Lab	VID
CelebV-HQ	35,666	15,653	512×512	68hrs	✓	✓	✓	Wild	VID

temporal consistency of generated videos. The experiments conducted above empirically demonstrate the effectiveness of our proposed CelebV-HQ dataset. Additionally, CelebV-HQ could potentially benefit the academic community in many other fields. We provide several empirical insights during constructing CelebV-HQ dataset and make an exhaustive discussion of the potential of CelebV-HQ in research community.

In summary, our contributions are threefold: 1) We contribute the first large-scale face video dataset, named CelebV-HQ, with high-quality video data and diverse manually annotated attributes. Corresponding to CelebA-HQ [34], CelebV-HQ fills in the blank on video modality and facilitates future research. 2) We perform a comprehensive statistical analysis in terms of attributes diversity and temporal statistics to show the superiority of CelebV-HQ. 3) We conduct extensive experiments on typical video generation/editing tasks, demonstrating the effectiveness and potential of CelebV-HQ.

2   Related Work

2.1   Video Face Generation and Editing

Recent advances in face video generation typically focused on unconditional video generation [57,63,65,67,70,81] and conditional face video generation [5, 30,62,73,76,82,85,86,88]. Conventional unconditional video face generation [57, 67,70,81] are mainly based on GANs [17]. These models usually decompose the latent code into content and motion codes to control the corresponding signals. Some recent efforts [63,65] aimed to extend high-quality pre-trained image generators to a video version to exploit the rich prior information. Conditional face video generation mainly including face reenactment [62,73,76,82] and talking face generation [5,30,85,86,88]. The motivation of these tasks is to use visual and audio modalities to guide the motion of a face video.

Face video editing is another emerging field [68,79]. The common characteristic of these works is to edit face attributes on the StyleGAN [37] latent space. Nevertheless, due to the lack of large-scale high-quality video datasets, these video-based editing efforts are still trained on images, exploiting the rich information of a pre-trained image model [37]. This leads to the main problem of having to solve for temporal consistency. The face video dataset proposed in this paper would help to address such hurdles and facilitate more interesting research in video face generation and editing.

2.2 Face Datasets

Face datasets can be divided into two categories: image datasets and video datasets. Many face image datasets are initially proposed for face recognition, like LFW [25] and CelebFaces [64] which largely promote the development of related fields. To analyze facial attributes, datasets like CelebA and LFWA [45] have been proposed. Both of them have 40 facial attribute annotations and have advanced the research field to a finer level of granularity. CelebA-HQ [34] improves 30k images in CelebA to 1024×1024 resolution. CelebAMask-HQ [38] further labels 19 classes of segmentation masks. CelebA-Dialog [32] labels captions describing the attributes.

In addition to the above image datasets, many video datasets have also been released. CelebV [76] was proposed for face reenactment. Audiovisual datasets such as VoxCeleb [51] and VoxCeleb2 [9] were originally released for speaker recognition, and further stimulated the development of audiovisual speaker separation and talking face generation domains. There are also several face video datasets with emotion attributes, such as RAVDESS [46] and MEAD [72]. MEAD [72] is the largest emotional video dataset, which includes 60 actors recorded from seven view directions. However, all of these datasets either contains only images with attribute annotations or are unlabeled videos with insufficient diversity. The rapidly growing demand for video facial attribute editing cannot be met. A video version of the dataset like CelebA-HQ [34] is urgently needed.

3   CelebV-HQ Construction

A dataset lies the foundation for model training, and its quality greatly affects the downstream tasks. The principle of building CelebV-HQ is to reflect real-world distribution with large-scale, high-quality, and diverse video clips. Hence, we design a rigorous and efficient pipeline to construct CelebV-HQ dataset, including Data Collection, Data Pre-processing, and Data Annotation.

3.1 Data Collection

The data collection process consists of the following steps. We start by creating various queries in order to retrieve human videos that are diverse in content and rich in attributes. The queries are designed to include keywords of different categories such as celebrity names, movie trailers, street interviews and vlogs, all in different languages, with 8376 entities, and 3717 actions. Then, we use these queries to collect the raw videos from the Internet. During the collection process, we introduce several constraints to discard unsatisfactory videos. For each query, we only collect the first 30 results to reduce duplicate human IDs, and the raw videos are required to have a resolution greater than 1080p with a normal bitrate. Consequently, we obtain a raw data pool with millions of video clips.

3.2   Data Pre-processing

In order to sample high-quality face video clips from the raw data pool, we develop an automatic video pre-processing pipeline. Please refer to the supplementary materials for more details.

We choose 512^2 as the normalized resolution due to the following reasons. 1) The face regions of web videos usually do not reach the resolution of 1024^2 or higher, and it is difficult to obtain super high-resolution videos and ensure their diversity. Before the rescaling, the percentage of video resolution: 0.6% for $450^2\sim512^2$, 76.6% for $512^2\sim1024^2$, and 22.7% for 1024^2+. 2) We need to make sure that all the videos are of the same resolution when training models. We choose 512^2 to ensure that all the clips are not upsampled significantly, which would affect the video quality. Also, to meet different usage scenario, a tool is provided on our project page that offers options to keep the original resolution.

3.3   Data Annotation

Data annotation is the core part of CelebV-HQ, and the annotation accuracy is vital. We first describe how we select the attributes to be annotated, then present the standard protocol of manual annotation.

Attribute Selection. We decouple a face video into three factors, *i.e.*, appearance, action, and emotion. Appearance describes the facial attributes that do not change along with the video sequence, such as hair color and gender. Action describes facial attributes that are related with video sequence, such as laugh and talk. Emotion describes the high-level mental status of human, such as neutral and happy. These three categories serve as important feature dimensions to characterize face video clips. We provide the design details and the complete list of all the attributes in the supplementary materials.

Attribute Annotation. To ensure the accuracy of the annotations, our entire annotation process includes the training of annotators, annotation, and quality control. Before the labeling begins, training courses are provided to help annotators understand each attribute and to have the same criteria for judging each attribute. We set up a Multi-label Annotation Table for each video, the table contains all labels that need to be labeled. Each video clip is independently annotated by 5 trained annotators. We select the annotation that has been agreed the most. If the annotation is only marginally agreed (3 vs 2), the sample will

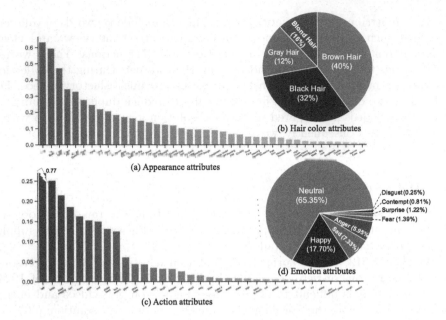

Fig. 2. The distributions of each attribute. CelebV-HQ has a diverse distribution on each attribute category. (Please zoom in for details).

be re-labeled. Finally, we additionally take a Quality Check process, in which the annotated data is further inspected by a professional quality inspector. If the annotated data does not meet the standard, it will also be re-labeled.

4   Statistics

In this section, we present the statistics of CelebV-HQ to demonstrate its statistical superiority. Then, we make comparison of CelebV-HQ with two most related and representative image and video datasets (*i.e.*, CelebA-HQ [34] and VoxCeleb2 [9]) respectively, in which we verify that the proposed CelebV-HQ has a natural distribution and better quality.

4.1   Analysis of CelebV-HQ

CelebV-HQ consists of 35, 666 video clips of 3 to 20 s each, involving 15, 653 identities, with a total video duration of about 65 h. For facial attributes, the attribute distribution of CelebV-HQ covers time-invariant (*i.e.*, appearance), time-variant attributes (*i.e.*, action and emotion).

As shown in Table 1, compared to the image datasets that contain facial attribute annotations [34,45], the resolution of CelebV-HQ is more than twice that of CelebA [34], and has a comparable scale to the high-quality dataset, CelebA-HQ [45]. More importantly, CelebV-HQ, as a video dataset, contains not only appearance attribute annotations, but also action and emotion attribute annotations, which make it contains richer information than image datasets. Other than the diverse annotations, compared to the recent in-the-wild video datasets (CelebV [76], FaceForensics [56], VoxCeleb [51] and VoxCeleb2 [9]), CelebV-HQ has a much higher resolution. Specifically, VoxCeleb2 [9] and MEAD [72], as two representative face video datasets, are the largest audio-visual video face datasets under in-the-wild and lab-controlled environments respectively. Although the data volume of VoxCeleb2 [9] and MEAD [72] is relatively large, the videos on these two datasets are homogeneous and in limited distributions. The videos on VoxCeleb2 are mainly talking face, while MEAD was collected in a constrained laboratory environment. In contrast, CelebV-HQ is collected in real-world scenarios with a diverse corpus, making it more natural and rich in the distribution of attributes.

We start our analysis of CelebV-HQ with the attribute distribution.
1) CelebV-HQ contains a total of 40 appearance attributes, as shown in Fig. 2 (a), of which 10 attributes account for more than 20% each, while there are more than 10 attributes accounting for about 10% each. Meanwhile, the overall attribute distribution has a long tail, with 10 attributes accounting for less than 3% each. We compare the hair colors separately, as they are mutually exclusive. From Fig. 2 (b), the distribution in hair color is even, and there are no significant deviations. 2) There are diverse action attributes in CelebV-HQ as shown in Fig. 2 (c). The common actions, such as "talk", "smile", and "head wagging", account for over 20% each. About 20 uncommon actions, such as "yawn", "cough" and "sneeze", account for less than 1% each. This result is in line with our expectation that these uncommon attributes remain open challenges for the academic community. 3) The proportion of emotion attributes also varies as shown in Fig. 2 (d), with "neutral" accounting for the largest proportion, followed by "happiness" and "sadness" emotions. Unlike the data collected in the laboratory, we do not strictly control the proportion of each attribute, so the overall distribution is more in line with the natural distribution. Overall, the CelebV-HQ is a real-world dataset with diverse facial attributes in a *natural distribution*, bringing new opportunities and challenges to the community.

4.2 Comparison with Image Dataset

Due to CelebV-HQ can be considered as a video version of CelebA-HQ [34] which is a commonly used dataset and its facial attributes annotation is successful in many works [8,11,21,36,37,60,66,80]. We argue that a face video dataset that has similar distribution with CelebA-HQ would also effective.

To show a reasonable distribution of CelebV-HQ, we compare the proposed CelebV-HQ with CelebA-HQ [34] in face attribute aspects such as age, ethnicity, and face shape. Face shape comparisons are provided in the supplementary materials. These factors reflect the basic face information in terms of facial appearance and geometry. Since ethnicity and age attributes are not explicitly labeled, we estimate them for both datasets using an off-the-shelf facial attribute analysis framework [59].

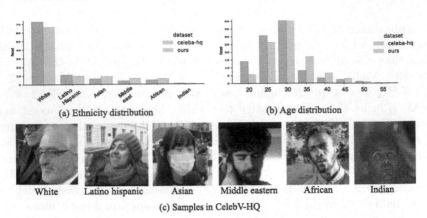

(a) Ethnicity distribution   (b) Age distribution

(c) Samples in CelebV-HQ

Fig. 3. Distributions of age and ethnicity compared with CelebA-HQ [34]. (a) and (b) show that CelebV-HQ has a similar distribution compared to CelebA-HQ [34].

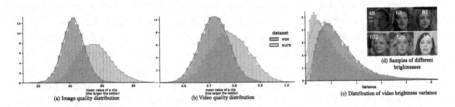

(a) Image quality distribution   (b) Video quality distribution   (c) Distribution of video brightness variance   (d) Samples of different brightnesses

Fig. 4. Distributions of image and video quality, and brightness variance. (a) Image quality and (b) video quality are measured by BRISQUE [49] and VSFA [40], the higher score, the better quality. (c) The video brightness is measured by [1], the low variance reflects the more stable in brightness aspect. (d) Samples at different brightness, with brightness values in the upper right corner.

Age Distribution. We evaluate whether the dataset is biased towards certain age groups. From Fig. 3 (a), we can see that the age in CelebA-HQ is mainly distributed below 35 years old, while the age distribution of CelebV-HQ is smoother.

Ethnic Distribution. The ethnic distribution roughly reflects the data distribution in terms of geography. As shown in Fig. 3 (b), CelebV-HQ achieves a distribution close to CelebA-HQ [34], and has a more even distribution in Latino Hispanic, Asian, Middle-eastern, and African. As shown in Fig. 3 (c), we show a random sample of each ethnic group in the CelebV-HQ.

4.3 Comparison with Video Dataset

As stated before, VoxCeleb2 [9] is one of the largest in-the-wild face video datasets, and it contains massive face videos, that have contributed to the development of many fields [5,13,16,30,85,86,88,89]. However, CelebV-HQ not only contains speech-based videos, we believe that if it is more diverse and of higher quality than the videos in VoxCeleb2 [9], this can be used to further improve the

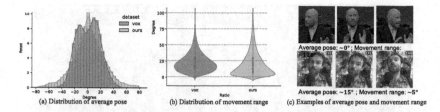

(a) Distribution of average pose   (b) Distribution of movement range   (c) Examples of average pose and movement range

Fig. 5. Distributions of average head pose and movement range. There is a wide range of head movement in CelebV-HQ, including both stable videos (less than 20° of movement) and videos with significant movement (from 75° to 100°).

performance of the related models. To demonstrate the superiority of CelebV-HQ and its ability to better support relevant studies, we compare with VoxCeleb2 [9] in terms of the data quality and temporal smoothness. For temporal smoothness, we conduct a comprehensive evaluation in brightness and head pose. We also provide a comparison of the richness and smoothness of the action units in the supplementary material.

Data Quality. We use BRISQUE [49] as a static quality evaluation metric, which is a non-reference evaluation algorithm. For each video clip, we average the BRISQUE [49] value between frames. For the comparison of video quality distributions, we apply the VSFA [40] measurement, a non-reference evaluation method that scores content dependency and temporal memory effects. The distributions are shown in Fig. 4, and CelebV-HQ offers higher quality than Vox-Celeb2 [9] at both image and video levels.

Brightness Variation. We also compare video brightness variance distribution with VoxCeleb2 [9]. We first obtain the brightness of each frame and compute the standard deviation in the temporal dimension. The brightness is calculated by averaging the pixels and then converting them to "perceived brightness" [1]. The lower variance of brightness indicates more similar luminance within the video clip, *i.e.*, better brightness uniformity. Figure 4 (c) shows that CelebV-HQ contains more low variance videos, that demonstrates the brightness change during videos in CelebV-HQ is more stable in the temporal dimension. As shown in Fig. 4 (c), CelebV-HQ contains videos of diverse brightness conditions, we categorized the videos in terms of brightness to further facilitate the usage of CelebV-HQ.

Head Pose Distribution. The head pose distribution is compared in two aspects: the average head pose of a video and the range of head pose movement. These two are used to show the diversity of head poses across the dataset and within the videos, respectively. As stated before, we leverage [75] to detect the head pose in the yaw direction. As shown in Fig. 5 (a), CelebV-HQ is more diverse and smoother than VoxCeleb2 [9] in the overall distribution. From Fig. 5 (b), we see that we have about 75% of the data with movements less than 30°, which means that most of the data are stable, while there are still 25% of movements between 30° and 100°, indicating the overall distribution is diverse. The illustration of average head pose and movement range is shown in Fig. 5 (c).

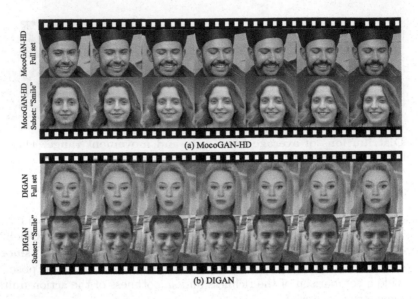

Fig. 6. Qualitative results of unconditional video generation. We present "Full set" and "Subset" settings of MoCoGAN-HD [65] and DIGAN [81] respectively.

5 Evaluation

In this section, we describe our experimental setups and the implementation details of baseline methods. We report the results on state-of-the-art baselines in two typical video generation/editing tasks, *i.e.*, unconditional video generation and video facial attribute editing.

5.1 Unconditional Video Generation

Settings. We employ four unconditional video generation methods, *i.e.*, VideoGPT [78], MoCoGAN-HD [65], DIGAN [81], and StyleGAN-V [63]. We chose these methods based on their performance and code availability. Furthermore, since CelebV-HQ contains action annotations, the models are evaluated under two settings, *i.e.*, the full set of data and the subsets split by different action attributes, *e.g.*, smile. We followed the original authors' setting. To evaluate the model performance, we leverage FVD [69] and FID [22] to access video quality and image quality, respectively.

Results. As shown in Fig. 6, MoCoGAN-HD [65] and DIGAN [81] can generate consistent videos trained on CelebV-HQ. Besides, all methods can successfully produce the desire actions when trained on different subsets of CelebV-HQ with specific attributes. Satisfactory results achieved on the these state-of-the-art methods, demonstrating the effectiveness of CelebV-HQ. More results of different methods are provided in the supplementary materials.

Table 2. Quantitative results of unconditional video generation. We evaluate VideoGPT [78], MoCoGAN-HD [65], DIGAN [81], and StyleGAN-V [63] on different datasets and report the FVD and FID scores. "↓" means a lower value is better.

	FaceForensics [56]		Vox [51]		MEAD [72]		CelebV-HQ	
	FVD (↓)	FID (↓)	FVD (↓)	FID (↓)	FVD (↓)	FID (↓)	FVD (↓)	FID (↓)
VideoGPT [78]	185.90	38.19	187.95	65.18	233.12	75.32	177.89	52.95
MoCoGAN-HD [65]	111.80	**7.12**	314.68	**55.98**	245.63	32.54	212.41	21.55
DIGAN [81]	62.50	19.10	201.21	72.21	165.90	43.31	72.98	19.39
StyleGAN-V [63]	**47.41**	9.45	**112.46**	60.44	**93.89**	**31.15**	**69.17**	**17.95**

Table 3. Quantitative results of video facial attribute editing. The "Video" version achieves lower FVD scores and comparable FID performance than "Original".

Metrics	StarGAN-v2 (Gender)				MUNIT (Gender)	
	Original		Video		Original	Video
	Reference	Label	Reference	Label		
FVD (↓)	284.80	258.36	262.01	189.40	219.96	211.45
FID (↓)	**80.61**	65.70	82.99	**55.73**	58.58	**57.01**

Benchmark. We construct a benchmark of unconditional video generation task, for four currently prevalent models (VideoGPT [78], MoCoGAN-HD [65], DIGAN [81], and StyleGAN-V [63]) on 4 face video datasets (FaceForensics [56], Vox [51], MEAD [72] and CelebV-HQ). The benchmark is presented in Table 2. Firstly, it can be observed that the ranking achieved by CelebV-HQ is similar to other prevalent datasets within different methods, which indicates the effectiveness of CelebV-HQ. In addition, the current video generation models [63,65,78,81] obtained good FVD/FID metrics compared to the Vox [51] dataset with similar data size. This illustrates that CelebV-HQ further exploits the potential of the current work, allowing it to generate more diverse and higher quality results. However, CelebV-HQ as a challenging real-world dataset, still has room for community to make improvement.

5.2   Video Facial Attribute Editing

Settings. We employ two representative facial editing baselines, *i.e.*, StarGAN-v2 [8] and MUNIT [26], to explore the potential of CelebV-HQ on video facial attribute editing task. The canonical StarGAN-v2 [8] and MUNIT [26] are designed for image data. We also modify these models by simply adding a vanilla temporal constraint, *i.e.*, estimating the optical flows for adjacent frames in different domains by LiteFlowNet [27] and enforcing L2 Loss between flows. Other losses the original authors proposed remain unchanged. To demonstrate the practical value of our dataset, we select a commonly used appearance attribute, *i.e.*, "Gender", for different baselines.

Results. The baseline methods achieve good results when editing the Gender attribute. The main difference lies in the temporal consistency. In Fig. 7, we

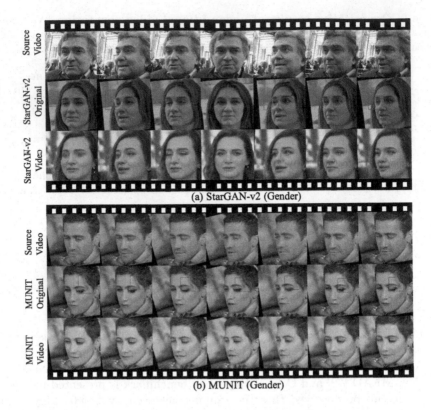

Fig. 7. Qualitative results of video facial attribute editing. Results of "Original" tend to have a jittering in the hair area, while results of "Video" are more stable.

observe that the results generated by the original image models are sometimes unstable in the hair area. As reported in Table 3, the "Video" version outperform the "Original" one with respect to the FVD metric in all cases (highlighted in blue), with comparable FID scores. These results indicate that a simple modification using the temporal cues in video dataset can bring performance improvement.

6   Discussion

6.1   Empirical Insights

Some empirical insights are drawn during the construction of CelebV-HQ and the baseline benchmarking. 1) We observe a trend in the growing demand for video facial editing due to the prevalence of short videos [28,48]. However current applications are mainly based on static images [28,47]. Therefore, the research on transforming face editing from images to videos would be an emerging direction. 2) An effective video alignment strategy is important for coherent video generation. In most image generation studies, faces are usually aligned by key points. And the quality might degrade if faces are not aligned. This suggests a new method that can simultaneously retain temporal information and align the face may improve the video face generation.

6.2   Future Work

Finally, we envision the research areas that may benefit from CelebV-HQ.

Video Generation/Editing. CelebV-HQ provides the possibility of improving Video Generation/Editing, such as unconditional face generation [17,36,55,63], text-to-video generation [23,43,74], video facial attributes editing [77], face reenactment [62,76,82], and face swapping [15,41,87]. These tasks rely heavily on the scale and quality of the dataset. CelebV-HQ also contains rich facial annotations, this would allow researcher to go deeper when using this information, e.g., synthesize text description with templates and learning disentanglement of facial attributes.

Neural Rendering. CelebV-HQ has great potential for applications in Neural Rendering. Current tasks, such as novel view synthesis [7,18,24,44,52] and 3d generation [3,4,6,14,19,52], are trained on in-the-wild image datasets [34,36] which lacks facial dynamics to provide natural geometries. CelebV-HQ provides diverse natural facial dynamics and 3D geometries. These features on video modality could not only be further exploited to improve the quality of current models, but also stimulate the emerging of several budding topics, such as Dynamic NeRF [54] and Animatable NeRF [53].

Face Analysis. Face Analysis tasks, such as Attribute Recognition [11,33,84], Action Recognition [29,71], Emotion Recognition [12,39], Forgery Detection [20, 42,90], and Multi-modal Recognition [50,83]. These tasks usually require the dataset to have diverse attribute coverage and natural distribution. CelebV-HQ not only meets these requirements, but also could help to transfer previous image tasks to the video version by learning spatio-temporal representations.

7   Conclusion

In this paper, we propose a large-scale, high-quality, and diverse video dataset with rich facial attributes, called CelebV-HQ. CelebV-HQ contains 35, 666 video clips involving 15, 653 identities, accompanied by 40 appearance attributes, 35 action attributes, and 8 emotion attributes. Through extensive statistical analysis of the dataset, we show the rich diversity of CelebV-HQ in terms of age, ethnicity, brightness, motion smoothness, pose diversity, data quality, etc.. The effectiveness and future potential of CelebV-HQ are also demonstrated via the unconditional video generation and video facial attribute editing tasks. We finally provide an outlook on the future prospects of CelebV-HQ, which we believe can bring new opportunities and challenges to the academic community. In the future, we are going to maintain a continued evolution of CelebV-HQ, including the scale, quality and annotations.

Acknowledgement. This work is supported by Shanghai AI Laboratory and Sense-Time Research. It is also supported by NTU NAP, MOE AcRF Tier 1 (2021-T1-001-088), and under the RIE2020 Industry Alignment Fund - Industry Collaboration Projects (IAF-ICP) Funding Initiative, as well as cash and in-kind contribution from the industry partner(s).

References

1. Bezryadin, S., Bourov, P., Ilinih, D.: Brightness calculation in digital image processing. In: TDPF (2007)
2. Brock, A., Donahue, J., Simonyan, K.: Large scale GAN training for high fidelity natural image synthesis. In: ICLR (2018)
3. Chan, E.R., et al.: Efficient geometry-aware 3D generative adversarial networks. In: CVPR (2022)
4. Chan, E.R., Monteiro, M., Kellnhofer, P., Wu, J., Wetzstein, G.: pi-GAN: periodic implicit generative adversarial networks for 3D-aware image synthesis. In: CVPR (2021)
5. Chen, L., Maddox, R.K., Duan, Z., Xu, C.: Hierarchical cross-modal talking face generation with dynamic pixel-wise loss. In: CVPR (2019)
6. Chen, Y., Wu, Q., Zheng, C., Cham, T.J., Cai, J.: Sem2NeRF: converting single-view semantic masks to neural radiance fields. In: ECCV (2022)
7. Cheng, W., et al.: Generalizable neural performer: Learning robust radiance fields for human novel view synthesis. arXiv preprint arxiv:2204.11798 (2022)
8. Choi, Y., Uh, Y., Yoo, J., Ha, J.W.: StarGAN v2: diverse image synthesis for multiple domains. In: CVPR (2020)
9. Chung, J.S., Nagrani, A., Zisserman, A.: VoxCeleb2: deep speaker recognition. In: INTERSPEECH (2018)
10. Da Xu, L., He, W., Li, S.: Internet of things in industries: a survey. IEEE TII **10**, 2233–2243 (2014)
11. Ding, H., Zhou, H., Zhou, S., Chellappa, R.: A deep cascade network for unaligned face attribute classification. In: AAAI (2018)
12. Dzedzickis, A., Kaklauskas, A., Bucinskas, V.: Human emotion recognition: review of sensors and methods. Sensors **20**, 592 (2020)
13. Ephrat, A., et al.: Looking to listen at the cocktail party: a speaker-independent audio-visual model for speech separation. ACM TOG **37**, 1–11 (2018)
14. Gafni, G., Thies, J., Zollhöfer, M., Nießner, M.: Dynamic neural radiance fields for monocular 4D facial avatar reconstruction. In: CVPR (2021)
15. Gao, G., Huang, H., Fu, C., Li, Z., He, R.: Information bottleneck disentanglement for identity swapping. In: CVPR (2021)
16. Gao, R., Grauman, K.: VisualVoice: audio-visual speech separation with cross-modal consistency. In: CVPR (2021)
17. Goodfellow, I., et al.: Generative adversarial nets. In: NeurIPS (2014)
18. Gu, J., Liu, L., Wang, P., Theobalt, C.: StyleNeRF: a style-based 3D aware generator for high-resolution image synthesis. In: ICLR (2021)
19. Guo, Y., Chen, K., Liang, S., Liu, Y., Bao, H., Zhang, J.: AD-NeRF: audio driven neural radiance fields for talking head synthesis. In: ICCV (2021)
20. Haliassos, A., Vougioukas, K., Petridis, S., Pantic, M.: Lips don't lie: a generalisable and robust approach to face forgery detection. In: CVPR (2021)

21. Han, H., Jain, A.K., Wang, F., Shan, S., Chen, X.: Heterogeneous face attribute estimation: a deep multi-task learning approach. IEEE TPAMI **40**, 2597–2609 (2017)

22. Heusel, M., Ramsauer, H., Unterthiner, T., Nessler, B., Hochreiter, S.: GANs trained by a two time-scale update rule converge to a local nash equilibrium. In: NeurIPS (2017)

23. Hong, W., Ding, M., Zheng, W., Liu, X., Tang, J.: CogVideo: large-scale pretraining for text-to-video generation via transformers. arXiv preprint arXiv:2205.15868 (2022)

24. Hong, Y., Peng, B., Xiao, H., Liu, L., Zhang, J.: HeadNeRF: a real-time nerf-based parametric head model. In: CVPR (2022)

25. Huang, G.B., Mattar, M., Berg, T., Learned-Miller, E.: Labeled faces in the wild: a database for studying face recognition in unconstrained environments. In: ECCV Workshop (2008)

26. Huang, X., Liu, M.Y., Belongie, S., Kautz, J.: Multimodal unsupervised image-to-image translation. In: ECCV (2018)

27. Hui, T.W., Loy, C.C.: LiteFlowNet3: resolving correspondence ambiguity for more accurate optical flow estimation. In: ECCV (2020)

28. Inc., S.: Snapchat. In: https://www.snapchat.com/ (2022)

29. Jegham, I., Khalifa, A.B., Alouani, I., Mahjoub, M.A.: Vision-based human action recognition: an overview and real world challenges. Forensic Sci. Int.: Digit. Invest. **32**, 200901 (2020)

30. Ji, X., et al.: Audio-driven emotional video portraits. In: CVPR (2021)

31. Jiang, L., Dai, B., Wu, W., Loy, C.C.: Deceive D: adaptive pseudo augmentation for GAN training with limited data. In: NeurIPS (2021)

32. Jiang, Y., Huang, Z., Pan, X., Loy, C.C., Liu, Z.: Talk-to-edit: fine-grained facial editing via dialog. In: ICCV (2021)

33. Karkkainen, K., Joo, J.: FairFace: Face attribute dataset for balanced race, gender, and age for bias measurement and mitigation. In: WACV (2021)

34. Karras, T., Aila, T., Laine, S., Lehtinen, J.: Progressive growing of GANs for improved quality, stability, and variation. In: ICLR (2018)

35. Karras, T., et al.: Alias-free generative adversarial networks. In: NeurIPS (2021)

36. Karras, T., Laine, S., Aila, T.: A style-based generator architecture for generative adversarial networks. In: CVPR (2019)

37. Karras, T., Laine, S., Aittala, M., Hellsten, J., Lehtinen, J., Aila, T.: Analyzing and improving the image quality of styleGAN. In: CVPR (2020)

38. Lee, C.H., Liu, Z., Wu, L., Luo, P.: MaskGAN: towards diverse and interactive facial image manipulation. In: CVPR (2020)

39. Lee, J., Kim, S., Kim, S., Park, J., Sohn, K.: Context-aware emotion recognition networks. In: ICCV (2019)

40. Li, D., Jiang, T., Jiang, M.: Quality assessment of in-the-wild videos. In: ACM MM (2019)

41. Li, L., Bao, J., Yang, H., Chen, D., Wen, F.: FaceShifter: towards high fidelity and occlusion aware face swapping. arXiv preprint arxiv:1912.13457 (2019)

42. Li, L., Bao, J., Zhang, T., Yang, H., Chen, D., Wen, F., Guo, B.: Face X-Ray for more general face forgery detection. In: CVPR (2020)

43. Li, Y., Min, M., Shen, D., Carlson, D., Carin, L.: Video generation from text. In: AAAI (2018)

44. Liang, B., et al.: Expressive talking head generation with granular audio-visual control. In: CVPR (2022)

45. Liu, Z., Luo, P., Wang, X., Tang, X.: Deep learning face attributes in the wild. In: ICCV (2015)
46. Livingstone, S.R., Russo, F.A.: The Ryerson audio-visual database of emotional speech and song (Ravdess): a dynamic, multimodal set of facial and vocal expressions in north American english. PLoS ONE **13**, e0196391 (2018)
47. Ltd., F.T.: Faceapp. In: https://www.faceapp.com/ (2022)
48. Ltd., T.P.: Tiktok. In: https://www.tiktok.com (2022)
49. Mittal, A., Moorthy, A.K., Bovik, A.C.: No-reference image quality assessment in the spatial domain. IEEE TIP **21**, 4695–4708 (2012)
50. Munro, J., Damen, D.: Multi modal domain adaptation for fine-grained action recognition. In: CVPR (2020)
51. Nagrani, A., Chung, J.S., Zisserman, A.: VoxCeleb: a large-scale speaker identification dataset. In: INTERSPEECH (2017)
52. Or-El, R., Luo, X., Shan, M., Shechtman, E., Park, J.J., Kemelmacher-Shlizerman, I.: StyleSDF: high-resolution 3D-consistent image and geometry generation. In: CVPR (2022)
53. Peng, S., et al.: Animatable neural radiance fields for modeling dynamic human bodies. In: ICCV (2021)
54. Pumarola, A., Corona, E., Pons-Moll, G., Moreno-Noguer, F.: D-NeRF: neural radiance fields for dynamic scenes. In: CVPR (2021)
55. Radford, A., Metz, L., Chintala, S.: Unsupervised representation learning with deep convolutional generative adversarial networks. arXiv preprint arxiv:1511.06434 (2015)
56. Rössler, A., Cozzolino, D., Verdoliva, L., Riess, C., Thies, J., Nießner, M.: FaceForensics: a large-scale video dataset for forgery detection in human faces. arXiv preprint arxiv:1803.09179 (2018)
57. Saito, M., Matsumoto, E., Saito, S.: Temporal generative adversarial nets with singular value clipping. In: ICCV (2017)
58. Schmidt, L., Santurkar, S., Tsipras, D., Talwar, K., Madry, A.: Adversarially robust generalization requires more data. In: NeurIPS (2018)
59. Serengil, S.I., Ozpinar, A.: Hyperextended lightface: a facial attribute analysis framework. In: ICEET (2021)
60. Shen, W., Liu, R.: Learning residual images for face attribute manipulation. In: CVPR (2017)
61. Shen, Y., Yang, C., Tang, X., Zhou, B.: InterfaceGAN: interpreting the disentangled face representation learned by GANs. IEEE TPAMI **44**(4), 2004–2018 (2022)
62. Siarohin, A., Lathuilière, S., Tulyakov, S., Ricci, E., Sebe, N.: First order motion model for image animation. In: NeurIPS (2019)
63. Skorokhodov, I., Tulyakov, S., Elhoseiny, M.: StyleGAN-v: a continuous video generator with the price, image quality and perks of styleGAN2. In: CVPR (2022)
64. Sun, Y., Chen, Y., Wang, X., Tang, X.: Deep learning face representation by joint identification-verification. In: NeurIPS (2014)
65. Tian, Y., et al.: A good image generator is what you need for high-resolution video synthesis. In: ICLR (2020)
66. Tov, O., Alaluf, Y., Nitzan, Y., Patashnik, O., Cohen-Or, D.: Designing an encoder for styleGAN image manipulation. ACM TOG **40**(4), 1–14 (2021)
67. Tulyakov, S., Liu, M.Y., Yang, X., Kautz, J.: MoCoGAN: decomposing motion and content for video generation. In: CVPR (2018)
68. Tzaban, R., Mokady, R., Gal, R., Bermano, A.H., Cohen-Or, D.: Stitch it in time: GAN-based facial editing of real videos. arXiv preprint arxiv:2201.08361 (2022)

69. Unterthiner, T., van Steenkiste, S., Kurach, K., Marinier, R., Michalski, M., Gelly, S.: Towards accurate generative models of video: a new metric & challenges. arXiv preprint arxiv:1812.01717 (2018)
70. Vondrick, C., Pirsiavash, H., Torralba, A.: Generating videos with scene dynamics. In: NeurIPS (2016)
71. Wang, H., Schmid, C.: Action recognition with improved trajectories. In: ICCV (2013)
72. Wang, K., et al.: Mead: a large-scale audio-visual dataset for emotional talking-face generation. In: ECCV (2020)
73. Wang, T.C., Mallya, A., Liu, M.Y.: One-shot free-view neural talking-head synthesis for video conferencing. In: CVPR (2021)
74. Wu, C., et al.: N\" uwa: visual synthesis pre-training for neural visual world creation. arXiv preprint arXiv:2111.12417 (2021)
75. Wu, W., Qian, C., Yang, S., Wang, Q., Cai, Y., Zhou, Q.: Look at boundary: a boundary-aware face alignment algorithm. In: CVPR (2018)
76. Wu, W., Zhang, Y., Li, C., Qian, C., Loy, C.C.: ReenactGAN: learning to reenact faces via boundary transfer. In: ECCV (2018)
77. Xu, Y., et al.: Transeditor: transformer-based dual-space GAN for highly controllable facial editing. In: CVPR (2022)
78. Yan, W., Zhang, Y., Abbeel, P., Srinivas, A.: VideoGPT: video generation using VQ-VAE and transformers. arXiv preprint arxiv:2104.10157 (2021)
79. Yao, X., Newson, A., Gousseau, Y., Hellier, P.: A latent transformer for disentangled face editing in images and videos. In: ICCV (2021)
80. Yao, X., Newson, A., Gousseau, Y., Hellier, P.: A latent transformer for disentangled face editing in images and videos. In: ICCV (2021)
81. Yu, S., et al.: Generating videos with dynamics-aware implicit generative adversarial networks. In: ICLR (2021)
82. Zakharov, E., Ivakhnenko, A., Shysheya, A., Lempitsky, V.: Fast Bi-layer neural synthesis of one-shot realistic head avatars. In: ECCV (2020)
83. Zhang, J., Yin, Z., Chen, P., Nichele, S.: Emotion recognition using multi-modal data and machine learning techniques: a tutorial and review. Inf. Fusion 59, 103–126 (2020)
84. Zhong, Y., Sullivan, J., Li, H.: Face attribute prediction using off-the-shelf CNN features. In: ICB (2016)
85. Zhou, H., Liu, Y., Liu, Z., Luo, P., Wang, X.: Talking face generation by adversarially disentangled audio-visual representation. In: AAAI (2019)
86. Zhou, H., Sun, Y., Wu, W., Loy, C.C., Wang, X., Liu, Z.: Pose-controllable talking face generation by implicitly modularized audio-visual representation. In: CVPR (2021)
87. Zhu, H., Fu, C., Wu, Q., Wu, W., Qian, C., He, R.: AOT: appearance optimal transport based identity swapping for forgery detection. In: NeurIPS (2020)
88. Zhu, H., Huang, H., Li, Y., Zheng, A., He, R.: Arbitrary talking face generation via attentional audio-visual coherence learning. In: IJCAI (2021)
89. Zhu, H., Luo, M.D., Wang, R., Zheng, A.H., He, R.: Deep audio-visual learning: a survey. IJAC 18, 351–376 (2021)
90. Zhu, X., Wang, H., Fei, H., Lei, Z., Li, S.Z.: Face forgery detection by 3D decomposition. In: CVPR (2021)

MovieCuts: A New Dataset and Benchmark for Cut Type Recognition

Alejandro Pardo[1](✉) (iD), Fabian Caba Heilbron[2] (iD), Juan León Alcázar[1] (iD), Ali Thabet[1,3] (iD), and Bernard Ghanem[1] (iD)

[1] King Abdullah University of Science and Technology, KAUST,
Thuwal, Saudi Arabia
{alejandro.pardo,juancarlo.alcazar,
ali.thabet,bernard.ghanem}@kaust.edu.sa
[2] Adobe Research, San Jose, USA
caba@adobe.com
[3] Facebook Reality Labs, Redmond, USA
thabetak@fb.com

Abstract. Understanding movies and their structural patterns is a crucial task in decoding the craft of video editing. While previous works have developed tools for general analysis, such as detecting characters or recognizing cinematography properties at the shot level, less effort has been devoted to understanding the most basic video edit, *the Cut*. This paper introduces the Cut type recognition task, which requires modeling multi-modal information. To ignite research in this new task, we construct a large-scale dataset called MovieCuts, which contains $173,967$ video clips labeled with ten cut types defined by professionals in the movie industry. We benchmark a set of audio-visual approaches, including some dealing with the problem's multi-modal nature. Our best model achieves 47.7% mAP, which suggests that the task is challenging and that attaining highly accurate Cut type recognition is an open research problem. Advances in automatic Cut-type recognition can unleash new experiences in the video editing industry, such as movie analysis for education, video re-editing, virtual cinematography, machine-assisted trailer generation, machine-assisted video editing, among others. Our data and code are publicly available: https://github.com/PardoAlejo/MovieCuts.

Keywords: Video editing · Cut-types · Recognition · Shot transition · Cinematography · Movie understanding

1 Introduction

Professionally edited movies use the film grammar [1] as a convention to tell visual stories. Through the lenses of the film grammar, a movie can be deconstructed into a hierarchical structure: a string of contiguous frames form a shot,

---

Supplementary Information The online version contains supplementary material available at https://doi.org/10.1007/978-3-031-20071-7_39.

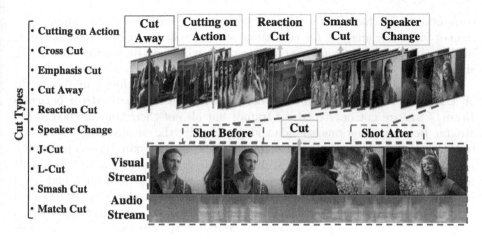

Fig. 1. Cut Type Recognition Task. Within a movie scene, most of the shot transitions use the *Straight Cut*, or Cut. Cuts are designed to preserve audio-visual continuity [45] across time, space, or story, and can be classified by their the semantic meaning [46]. This figure illustrates a scene with different cut types happening one after the other. Towards the end of the scene, there is a dialogue portrayed by cutting when the active speaker changes. Understanding this task requires audio-visual analysis. The visual stream helps detect the camera change to focus on one of the two actors. The audio stream exhibits a clear change of frequencies when the cut happens. Combining these two cues allows us to predict the cut type: *Speaker Change*.

a sequence of shots build a scene, and a series of scenes compose the movie. Typically, scenes portray events that happen in single locations using shots recorded with a multi-camera setup [28]. Like punctuation in the written grammar, careful transition between shots is also an important component of the film grammar. Indeed, shot transitions can be viewed as the most basic video editing device [30,52]. They create changes of perspective, highlight emotions, and help to advance stories [30,52]. Several types of *soft* shot transitions like wipes, or fades are commonly used between scenes. However, within a scene, the most used transition between shots [13] is the Cut, which simply joins two shots without any special effect.

Cuts in professionally edited movies are not random but rather have language, structure, and a taxonomy [1]. Each cut in a movie has a purpose and a specific meaning. Thus, to understand movie editing styles, one has to understand the cuts. Tsivian *et al.* introduced a platform called Cinemetrics to analyze movies by analysing their cut frequency [13]. While Cinemetrics is helpful in characterizing the rhythm and pace of cuts, analyzing and understanding the semantic meaning of these cuts remains a rather difficult task. In the computer vision community, recent works have tackled the problem of analyzing different cinematography components at the shot level [24,41,56,58] for automatic film analysis. However, only a few works, have focused on shot transitions for film analysis [57] and continuity editing [16,37]. We argue that automatically recognizing and understanding cut types would make an important step towards computationally characterize the principles of video editing, enabling new experiences for movie analysis for education, video re-editing, virtual cinematography, machine-assisted trailer generation, and machine-assisted video editing. We showcase one example of the latter in Sect. 4.5.

Figure 1 illustrates the cut type recognition task introduced in this work. *A Cut is composed of two adjacent shots and the transition between them.* Cuts are not only made of frames but also of their time-aligned sound stream. In many situations, sounds and speech drive the cut and shape its meaning. Our goal is then to recognize the cut type by analyzing the clip's audio-visual information across shots. Multiple research challenges emerge from this new multi-shot video understanding task. First, there is a need for a high-level understanding of visual and audio relationships over time to identify the intended cut type. To identify Speaker Change in Fig. 1, one needs a detailed audio-visual inspection to associate the sounds before and after the cut to the corresponding actor's voice. Although it sounds trivial, small changes in the signal can change the cut type. For instance, if the speakers are in different locations, the cut type would no longer be Speaker Change but rather a Cross Cut (see Fig. 2). If the active speaker does not change after the cut, the cut type would be Reaction Cut instead. Thus, it is essential to understand the fine-grained details of both signals. We argue that these challenges can promote the development of new techniques to address the multi-modal and multi-shot nature of the problem.

Understanding the audio-visual properties of movies has a long-standing track of interest [17,32,42,53]. The community has developed methods to recognize characters and speaker [9,15,36], events and actions [17,21,33], storylines [2,24,53], shot-level cinematography properties such as shot-scale and camera motion [11,40], and mine shot-sequencing patterns [52,57,58]. While these approaches have set an initial framework for understanding editing in movies, there is still a lack of automated tools that understand the most basic and used editing technique, the Cut.

This work aims to study and bootstrap research in Cut type recognition. To do so, we introduce MovieCuts, a new large-scale dataset with manually curated Cut type annotations. Our new dataset contains 173, 967 clips (with cuts) labeled with ten different cut categories taken from the literature [5,51] and movie industry [50]. We hired professional and qualified annotators to label the cut type categories. MovieCuts offers the opportunity to benchmark core research tasks such as multi-modal analysis, long-tailed distribution learning, and multi-label classification. Furthermore, the study of this task, might benefit other areas like machine-assited video editing. While we observe improvements by leveraging recent techniques for audio-visual blending [55], there is ample room for improvement, and the task remains an open research problem.

Contributions. Our contributions are threefold: **(1)** We introduce the cut type recognition task. To the best of our knowledge, our work is the first to address and formalize the task from a machine learning perspective. **(2)** We collect a large-scale dataset containing qualified human annotations that verify the presence of different cut types. We do an extensive analysis of the dataset to highlight its properties and the challenges it presents. We call this dataset MovieCuts (Sect. 3). **(3)** We implement multiple audio-visual baselines and establish a benchmark in cut type recognition (Sect. 4).

2   Related Work

The Anatomy of a Movie Scene. Scenes are key building blocks for storytelling in film. They are built from a sequence of shots to depict an event, action, or element of film narration. Extensive literature in film studies has analyzed and characterized the structure of a scene. It includes (among others) the properties and categorization of shots and, to the interest of our work, the type of shot transitions [1,10,35]. There are four basic shot transitions: the wipe, the fade, the dissolve, and the cut. Each one of these four transitions has its purpose and appropriate usage. For instance, soft transitions like wipe, fade, and dissolve, are commonly used to transition between scenes and evoke a passage of time or change in location. Our work studies the cut, the instantaneous (hard) change from one shot to another, which is arguably the most frequently used.

Film theory has developed multiple taxonomies to organize the types of cuts [1,5,48]. Case in point, Thompson and Bowen [48] divide the types of cuts (or edits) into five different categories: action edit, screen position edit, form edit, concept edit, and combined edit. While such categorization provides a high-level grouping, it is too coarse. The categorization centers around the emotional aspects of the edit rather than the audio-visual properties of the cut. Film courses [51] and practitioners [50] have also developed a taxonomy of cut types. These tend to be more specific and closely describe the audio-visual properties of the shot pair forming the cut. We choose our list of Cut types based on the existing literature and narrow it down to categories that video editors recognize in their daily routine.

Edited Content in Video Understanding. Edited video content such as movies has been a rich source of data for general video understanding. Such video sources contain various human actions, objects, and situations occurring in people's daily life. In the early stages of action recognition, the Hollywood Human Actions (HOHA) [32] and HMDB51 [31], introduced human action recognition benchmarks using short clips from Hollywood movies. Another group of works used a limited number of films to train, and test methods for character recognition [43], human action localization [14], event localization [33], and spatio-temporal action and character localization [4]. With the development of deep-learning techniques and the need for large-scale datasets to train deep models, Gu *et al.* proposed the AVA dataset [17]. AVA is a large-scale dataset with spatio-temporal annotations, actors, and actions, whose primary data sources are movies and TV shows. Furthermore, other works have focused on action, and event recognition across shots [21,33]. Finally, Pavlakos *et al.* leverage information across shots from TV shows to do human mesh reconstruction [38]. Instead of leveraging movie data to learn representations for traditional tasks, we propose a new task to analyze movie cut types automatically.

672   A. Pardo et al.

Stories, Plots, and Cinematography. Movies and TV shows are rich in complexity and content, which makes their analysis and understanding a challenging task. Movies are a natural multi-modal source of data, with audio, video, and even transcripts being often available. Several works in the literature focus on the task of understanding movie content. Recent works have addressed the task of movie trailer creation [20,27,44,62], TV show summarization [6,7], and automated video editing [37]. Moreover, Vicol *et al.* proposed MovieGraphs [53], a dataset that uses movies to analyze human-centric situations. Rohrbach *et al.* presented a Movie Description dataset [42], which contains audio narratives and movie scripts aligned to the movies' full-length. Using this dataset, a Large Scale Movie Description Challenge (LSMDC) has hosted competitions for a variety of tasks, including Movie Fill-In-The-Blank [34], and movie Q&A [47], among others. Like LSMDC, MovieNet [24] and Condensed Movies [2] are big projects that contain several tasks, data, and annotations related to movie understanding. MovieNet includes works related to person re-identification [22,23,26,60], Movie Scene Temporal Segmentation [41], and trailer and synopsis analysis [25,61]. All these works have shown that movies have rich information about human actions, including their specific challenges. However, only a few of them have focused on artistic aspects of movies, such as shot scales [3,11,40], shot taxonomy and classification [54], and their editing structure and cinematography [56–58]. These studies form the foundations to analyze movie editing properties but miss one of the most used techniques, the Cut. Understanding cuts is crucial for decoding the grammar of the film language. Our work represents a step towards that goal.

3   The MovieCuts Dataset

3.1   Building MovieCuts

Cut Type Categories. Our goal is to find a set of cut type categories often used in movie editing. Although there exists literature in the grammar of film language [1,46] and the taxonomy of shot types [3,11,54], there is no gold-standard categorization of cuts. As mentioned earlier in the related work, there exist categorization of cut types [48] but it focuses on the emotional aspects of the cuts rather than the audio-visual properties of the shots composing the cut. We gathered an initial taxonomy (17 cut types) from film-making courses (*e.g.* [51]), textbooks [5], and blogs [50]. We then hired ten different editors to validate the taxonomy. All the editors studied film-making, two have been nominated for the Emmys, and most have over 10 years of experience. Some of the original categories were duplicated and some of them were challenging to mine from movies. Our final taxonomy includes 10 categories. Figure 2 illustrates each cut type along with their visual and audio signals:

1. **Cutting on Action:** Cutting from one shot to another while the subject is still in motion.
2. **Cross Cut:** Cutting back and forth within locations.

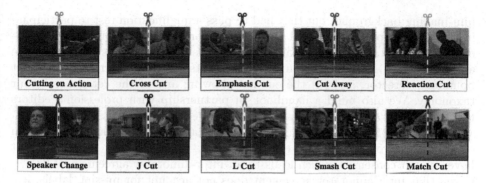

Fig. 2. MovieCuts Dataset. MovieCuts contains 173,967 video clips labeled with 10 different Cut types. Each sample in the dataset is composed of two shots (with a cut) and their audio spectogram. Our cuts are grouped into two major categories, visual (top) and audio-visual (bottom) driven.

3. **Emphasis Cut:** Cut from wide to close within the same shot, or the other way around.
4. **Cut Away:** Cutting into an insert shot of something and then back.
5. **Reaction Cut:** A cut to the reaction of a subject (facial expression or single word) to the comments/actions of other actors, or a cut after the reaction.
6. **Speaker Change:** A cut that changes the shot to the current speaker.
7. **J Cut:** The audio of the next shot begins before you can see it. You hear what is going on before you actually see what is going on.
8. **L Cut:** The audio of the current shot carries over to the next shot.
9. **Smash Cut:** Abrupt cut from one shot to another for aesthetic, narrative, or emotional purpose.
10. **Match Cut:** Cut from one shot to another by matching a concept, an action or a composition of both.

Video Collection and Processing. We need professionally edited videos containing diverse types of cuts. Movies are a perfect source to gather and collect such data. As pointed out by Bain *et al.* [2], there are online video channels[1] that distribute *individual* movie scenes, thus facilitating access to movie data for research. We downloaded 9,363 scenes, which come from 1,986 movies. However, these movie scenes come untrimmed, and further processing is required to obtain cuts from them. We automatically detect all the cuts in the dataset with a highly accurate shot boundary detector [18] (97.3% precision and 98.5% recall), which yields a total of 195,000 candidate cuts for annotation.

Human Annotations and Verification. Our goal at this stage is to collect expert annotations for 195,000 candidate cuts. To do so, we hired Hive AI to run our annotation campaign. We choose them given their experience in labeling data for the entertainment industry. Annotators did not necessarily have a

---

[1] MovieClips YouTube Channel is the source of scenes in MovieCuts.

film-making background, but they had to pass a qualification test to participate in the labeling process. At least three annotators reviewed each cut/label candidate pair, and only the annotations with more than two votes were kept. The annotators also have the option to discard cuts due to: (i) errors in the shot boundary detector, and (ii) the cut not showing any of the categories in our taxonomy. We also build a handbook in partnership with professional editors to include several examples per class and guidelines on addressing edge cases. We discarded 21,033 cuts, which left us with a total of 173,967 cuts to form our dataset. From the 21,073 discarded clips, we found that 12,090 did not have enough consensus, which leads to an inter-annotator agreement of 93.8%. Given that inter-annotator agreement does not account for missing labels, five professional editors labelled a small subset of two thousand cuts and created a high-consensus ground truth. We found that our annotations exhibited a 90.5% precision and 88.2% recall when contrasted with such a gold standard.

3.2   MovieCuts Statistics

Cut Label Distribution. Figure 3a shows the distribution of cut types in MovieCuts. The distribution is long-tailed, which may reflect the editors' preferences for certain types of cuts. It is not a surprise that *Reaction Cut* is the most abundant label given that emotion and human reactions play a central role in storytelling. Beyond human emotion, dialogue and human actions are additional key components to advance movie storylines. We observe this in the label distribution, where *Speaker Change* and *Cutting on Action* are the second and third most abundant categories in the dataset. While classes such as *Smash Cut* and *Match Cut* emerge scarcely in the dataset, it is still important to recognize these types of cuts, which can be considered the most creative ones. We also show the distribution of cut types per movie genre in the *supplementary material*.

Multi-label Distribution and Co-occurrences. We plot in Fig. 3b the distribution of labels per cut and the co-occurrence matrix. On one hand, we observe that a significant number of cuts contain more than one label. On the other, we observe that certain pair of classes co-occur more often, *e.g. Reaction Cut / L Cut*. The multi-label properties of the dataset suggest that video editors compose and combine cut types quite often.

Duration of Shot Pairs. We study the duration of the shot pairs that surround (and form) the cuts. Figure 3c shows the distribution of such shot pair duration. The most typical length is about 3.5 s. Moreover, we observe that the length of shot pairs ranges from 2 s to more than 30 s. In Sect. 4, we study the effect of sampling different context around the cut.

Cut Genre, Year of Production, and Cuts Per Scene. Figures. 3d, 3e, 3f show statistics about the productions from where the cuts are sampled. First, we observe that the cuts are sampled across a diverse set of genres, with Comedy being the most frequent one. Second, we sourced the cuts from old and contemporary movie scenes. While many cuts come from the last decade, we also

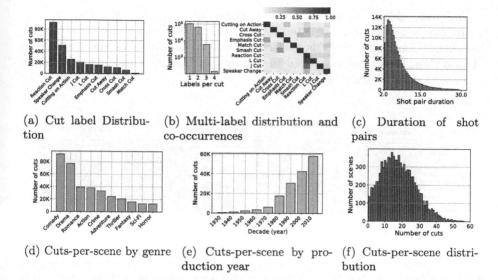

(a) Cut label Distribution

(b) Multi-label distribution and co-occurrences

(c) Duration of shot pairs

(d) Cuts-per-scene by genre

(e) Cuts-per-scene by production year

(f) Cuts-per-scene distribution

Fig. 3. MovieCuts statistics. Figure 3a shows the number of instances per cut type. Labels follow a long-tail distribution. Figure 3b indicates that a large number of instances contain more than a single cut type. Moreover, certain pairs of cut types co-occur more often. Figure 3c plots the distribution of lengths (in seconds) of all the dataset instances. Figure 3d summarizes the production properties of the movie scenes and cuts used in our study. Figure 3e shows the distribution based on year of production. Finally, Fig. 3f shows the distribution of number of cuts per scene.

scouted cuts from movie scenes from the 1930's. Finally, we observe that the number of cuts per scene roughly follows a normal distribution with a mean of 15 cuts per scene. Interestingly, few movie scenes have a single cut, while others may contain more than 60 cuts. These statistics highlight the editing diversity in MovieCuts.

3.3   MovieCuts Attributes

Sound Attributes. We leverage an off-the-shelf audio classifier [12] to annotate the sound events in the dataset. Figure 4a summarizes the distribution of three super-groups of sound events: Speech, Music, and Other. Dialogue related cuts such as *Speaker Change* and *J Cut* contain a large amount of speech. Contrarily, visual-driven cuts *e.g. Match Cut* and *Smash Cut* hold a larger number of varied sounds and background music. These attributes suggest that, while analyzing speech is crucial for recognizing cut types, it is also beneficial to model music and general sounds.

Subject Attributes. We build a zero-shot classifier using CLIP [39], a neural network trained on 400M image-text pairs, to tag the subjects present in our dataset samples (4b).

Interestingly, dialogue and emotion-driven cuts (*e.g. Reaction Cut*) contain many face tags, which can be interpreted as humans framed in medium-to-close-up shots. Contrarily, Body is the most common attribute in the *Cutting on Action* class, which suggests editors often opt for framing humans in long shots when actions are occurring.

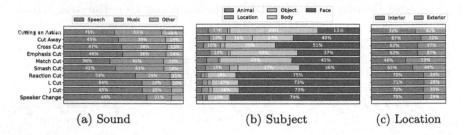

(a) Sound   (b) Subject   (c) Location

Fig. 4. MovieCuts attributes. MovieCuts contains diverse sounds (4a), subjects (4b), and locations (4c). Some sounds co-occur more often in particular cut types. For instance, Speech is the predominant sound for dialogue related cut types such as Speaker Change or J Cut. Similarly, there exists correlation between cut types and the subjects depicted in the movie clip.

Location Attributes. We reuse CLIP [39] to construct a zero-shot classifier of locations on our dataset. Figure 4c summarizes the distribution of locations (Interior/Exterior) per cut type. On one hand, we observe that most cut types contain instances shot in Interior locations 60%-70% of the time. On the other hand, *Match Cuts* reverse this trend with the majority (53%) of cuts shot in Exterior places. The obtained distribution suggests that stories in movies (as in real-life) develop (more often) in indoor places.

4 Experiments

4.1 Audio-Visual Baseline

Our base architecture is shown in Fig. 5. Similar to [55], it takes as input the audio signal and a set of frames (clip), which are then processed by a late-fusion multi-modal CNN. We use a visual encoder and an audio encoder to extract audio and visual features per clip. Then, we form an audio-visual feature by concatenating them. Finally, a Multi Layer Perceptron (MLP) computes the final predictions on the audio-visual features. We optimize a binary cross-entropy (BCE) loss $\mathcal{L}$ per modality and for their combination in a one-vs-all manner to deal with the problem's multi-label nature. Our loss is summarized as:

$$\text{loss} = \omega_a \mathcal{L}\left(\hat{y}_a, y\right) + \omega_v \mathcal{L}\left(\hat{y}_v, y\right) + \omega_{av} \mathcal{L}\left(\hat{y}_{av}, y\right), \tag{1}$$

where ω_a, ω_v, and ω_{av} are the weights for the audio, visual, and audio-visual losses, respectively. Using this architecture, we propose several baselines:

MLP Classifier. We use the backbone as a feature extractor for each stream and train an MLP to predict on top of them and their concatenation.

Encoder Fine-Tuning. We train the whole backbone starting from Kinetics-400 [29] weights for the visual stream and from VGGSound [12] weights for the audio.

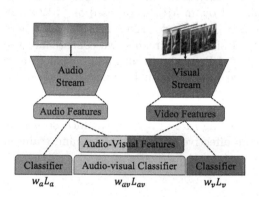

Fig. 5. Audio-visual pipeline. A late-fusion multi-modal network processes audio and visual streams. We train both networks jointly using audio loss L_a, visual loss L_v, and audio-visual loss L_{av}, weighted with w_a, w_v, and w_{av}, respectively.

Modality Variants. We train our model using the different modalities: audio only, visual only, and audio-visual. For audio-visual, we combine the losses in a naive way giving each one of them the same weight, *i.e.* $\omega_a = \omega_v = \omega_{av}$.

Modality Blending. To combine losses from multiple modalities in a more effective way, Wang *et al.* [55] proposed *Gradient Blending* (GB), a strategy to compute the weight of each modality loss at training time. We use the offline GB algorithm to calculate ω_a, ω_v, and ω_{av}. For further details, refer to Algorithms 1 and 2 of the paper [55].

4.2 Experimental Setup

Dataset Summary. We divide our dataset into training, validation, and test sets by using 70%, 10%, and 20% percent of the data, respectively. Thus, we use $121,423$ clips for training, $17,505$ clips for validation, and $35,039$ clips for testing. We make sure that the sets are *i.i.d.*w.r.t. the movie genre, we show distributions per genre for each split in the supplementary material. We report all experiments on the validation set unless otherwise mentioned.

Metrics. Following [59], we choose the mean Average Precision (mAP) across all classes and per-class AP to summarize and compare baseline performances. This metric helps to deal with MovieCuts' multi-label nature. We also report Precision-Recall curves in supplementary material.

Implementation Details. For all experiments, we use ResNet-18 [19] as the backbone for both visual and audio streams. **For the audio stream**, we use a ResNet with 2D convolutions pre-trained on VGGSound [12]. This backbone takes as input a spectrogram of the audio signal and processes it as an image. To compute the spectogram we take the audios of each pair of clips, and apply consecutive Fourier Transforms with 512 points windows with 353 overlapping points between them. If the audio is longer than 10 s we trim it to 10 s only. **For the visual stream**, we use a ResNet-(2+1)D [49] pre-trained on Kinetics-400 [29]. We sample 16 frames from a window centered around the cut as the input to the network Using single streams, *i.e.* only audio or only visual, we use the features after the average pooling followed by an MLP composed of a 512×128 Fully-Connected (FC) layer followed by a ReLU and a $128 \times N$ FC-layer, where N is the number of classes ($N = 10$). Using two streams, we concatenate the features after the first FC-layer of the MLP to obtain an audio-visual feature per clip of size $128 \times 2 = 256$. Then, we pass it through a second FC-layer of size $256 \times N$ to compute the predictions. We train using SGD with momentum 0.9 and weight decay of 10^{-4}. We also use a linear warm-up for the first epoch. We train for 8 epochs with an initial learning rate of 3×10^{-2}, which decays by a factor of 10 after 4 epochs. We use an effective batch-size of 112 and train on one NVIDIA A100 GPU.

4.3   Results and Analysis

As described in Sect. 4.1, we benchmark the MovieCuts dataset using several combinations of modalities. Results are reported in Table 1.

Linear Classifier *vs.* Fine-Tune: We evaluate the performance of using frozen *vs.* fine-tuned features. As one might expect, the fine-tuning of the backbone shows consistent improvement over all the classes regardless of the modality used. For instance, the Audio-Visual backbone performance increases from 30.82% to 46.57%. These results validate the value of the dataset for improving the audio and visual representations encoded by the backbones.

Modality Variants: Consistently across training strategies, we observe a common pattern in the results: the visual modality performs better (43.98%) at the task than its audio counterpart (27.24%). Nonetheless, combining both modalities still provides enhanced results for several classes and the overall mAP (46.57%). We observe that cuts driven mainly by visual cues, such as Cutting on Action, Cut Away, and Cross Cut, do not improve their performance when audio is added. However, the rest of the classes improve when using both modalities. In particular, L Cut, J Cut, and Speaker Change improve drastically, since these types of cuts are naturally driven by audio-visual cues.

Gradient Blending: The second-to-last row in Table 1 shows the results of using the three modalities combined with the GB weights $\omega_a = 0.08$, $\omega_v = 0.57$ and $\omega_{av} = 0.35$. GB performs slightly better (47.43%) than combining the losses naively (46.57%), where $\omega_a = \omega_v = \omega_{av}$.

Scaled Gradient Blending: By experimenting with the Gradient Blending weights, we found that scaling them all by a constant factor can help. We empirically found that scaling the weights by a factor of 3 ($\omega_a = 1.31$, $\omega_v = 4.95$ and $\omega_{av} = 2.74$) improves the results to 47.91% mAP.

Frame Sampling: In addition to these experiments, we explore how to pick the frames to feed into the visual network. For all the previous experiments and as mentioned, we use *Fixed Sampling* by sampling frames from a window centered around the cut. However, this is not the only strategy to sample frames. We explore two other strategies: *Uniform Sampling* that takes sample frames from a uniform distribution across the two shots forming the cut, and *Gaussian Sampling*, which samples the frames from a Gaussian centered around the cut. We fit both audios up to 10 s into the audio stream.

Table 1. Baseline comparison on MovieCuts. We show the results of our different baselines using visual, audio, and audio-visual modalities. The last two rows use both modalities combined with Gradient Blending (GB) [55] and Scaled Gradient Blending (SGB). All the reported results are % AP. We observe three key findings. (1) Fine-tuning on MovieCuts provides clear benefits over the linear classifier trained on frozen features. (2) Audio-visual information boosts the performance of the visual only stream. (3) Gradient Blending provides further performance gains by an optimal combination of both modalities. Showing classes: Cutting on Action (**CA**), Cut Away (**CW**), Cross Cut (**CC**), Emphasis Cut (**EC**), Match Cut (**MC**), Smash Cut (**SC**), Reaction Cut (**RC**), L Cut (**LC**), J Cut (**JC**), Speaker Chance (**SC**).

	Model	mAP	CA	CW	CC	EC	MC	SC	RC	LC	JC	SC
Linear	Audio(A)	23.9	36.7	14.8	11.8	14.6	1.5	10.7	65.3	15.3	18.4	50.0
	Visual(V)	28.8	53.8	36.3	16.9	19.4	1.1	13.3	69.7	12.9	16.2	48.0
	AV	30.8	55.5	32.8	16.0	20.3	1.7	13.2	73.7	17.4	21.6	56.0
Fine-tune	Audio	27.2	42.6	19.0	14.6	15.8	1.5	12.9	69.4	18.5	21.3	56.7
	Visual	44.0	64.8	60.8	33.2	30.7	1.5	21.5	81.2	33.7	42.0	70.3
	AV	46.6	65.2	62.5	31.1	30.5	2.0	22.3	82.9	43.3	50.0	75.1
	AV+GB	47.4	64.8	62.4	32.5	31.6	1.8	23.8	83.1	45.6	51.0	77.4
	AV+SGB	47.9	65.6	63.0	34.9	31.8	2.3	24.3	83.3	45.0	51.6	77.1

Fixed Sampling gives the best results with 47.91% mAP, followed by *Gaussian Sampling* with 47.44%, and *Uniform Sampling* gives the lowest mAP among them with 47.17%. These results suggest that the most critical information lays around the cut. We hypothesize that the model is not good enough at handling context, architectures better at handling sequential inputs may benefit from the context of the *Gaussian* or *Uniform* sampling.

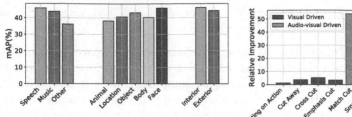

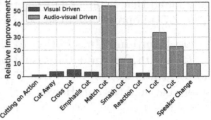

(a) Performance breakdown per attribute.   (b) Audio-visual improvements per type.

Fig. 6. Performance breakdown. Here, we showcase a detailed performance analysis. Figure 6a shows the performance breakdown according to attributes of MovieCuts, such as type of sound, subjects, locations, duration per clip, and production year. Figure 6b shows the performance gain of the audio-visual model versus the visual-only model. For this analysis, we group the cut classes into visual-driven and audio-visual driven.

Test Set Results. After obtaining the best-performing model on the validation set, we evaluate this model on the test set. We obtain 47.70% mAP, which is slightly lower than the results on the validation set 47.91% mAP. For the full test set results, and experiments using Distribution-Balanced loss [59], refer to the **supplementary material**.

4.4   Performance Breakdown

Attributes and Dataset Characteristics. Figure 6a summarizes the performance of our best audio-visual model from Table 1 for different attributes and dataset characteristics. In most cases, the model exhibits robust performance across attributes. The largest performance gap is observed between Speech and Other sounds. We associate this result with the fact that cuts with complex audio editing, *e.g.* those that include sound effects, often employ abstract editing such as Smash Cuts and Match Cuts, which are harder for the model to recognize. We also observe that the model is better at classifying cuts when there are faces in the scene, which aligns with the fact that it was trained on movies, which are mainly human-centered. These findings showcase the multi-modal nature of MovieCuts. Thus, the results can be improved by studying better audio-visual backbones.

Audio-Visual Improvements Per Cut Type. Figure 6b shows the relative improvement of the audio-visual model w.r.t. using the visual stream only. It highlights whether the type of cut is driven by visual or audio-visual information. We observe that the audio-visual driven cuts generally benefit the most from training a joint audio-visual model. Match cuts show a relative 50% improvement when adding audio. These types of cuts use audiovisual concepts to match the two shots. The second-largest gains are for cuts related to dialogue and conversations (L cut, J cut). For instance, L Cuts improve by 30%; this class typically involves a person on screen talking in the first shot while only their voice is heard in the second shot. By encoding audio-visual information, the model disambiguates predictions that would otherwise be confused by the visual-only model. Finally, all classes show a relative improvement w.r.t. the visual baseline. This suggests that the GB [55] strategy allows the model to optimize modality weights. In the worst-case scenario, GB achieves slight improvements over the visual-only baseline. In short, we empirically demonstrate the importance of modeling audio-visual information to recognize cut types.

4.5   Machine-Assisted Video Editing with MovieCuts

We argue that recognizing cut types can enable many applications in video editing. In this section, we leverage the knowledge of our Audio-Visual model to attempt automated video editing. Inspired by [37], we use EditStock[2] to gather raw footage of edited movies and perform video editing on them. Specifically, we use our model to create cuts (shot transitions) between two long sequences of shots. Further details can be found in **supplementary material**. We measure qualitatively and quantitatively our model's editing by comparing it with different automated editing methods: (1) **Random baseline frame by frame RF:** Every frame, we perform a cut with a probability of 0.5. (2) **Random baseline snippet by snippet RS:** Similar to how the model is trained, every 16 frames snippet we cut with a probability of 0.5. This restriction allows each shot to be on screen for at least 16 frames. (3) **Biased Random BR:** Similar to (2), we cut every 16 snippets. However, this time we use the expected number of cuts prior. Thus, we ensure that the number of random cuts is the same as the ground truth. (4) **MovieCuts' AV model AV:** We use our audio-visual model's scores to score all possible cuts between the two sequences. Then, we use the top-k cuts, where k is given by the expected number of cuts. (5) **Human Editor GT:** From EditStock we collect the actual edited sequence edited by professional editors. We use these sequences as a reference for the quantitative study, and ground-truth for the qualitative evaluation.

In the qualitative evaluation we ask 63 humans to pick between our method and all the other methods. We observe that users picked our method (AV) over the human editor 38% of the times while the BR was picked 34% of the times – RF and RS were picked only 15.7% and 1.8%, respectively. Furthermore, for the quantitative results we use the human edit as ground-truth and measure Purity, Coverage, and F1 for each method. These metrics were implemented by [8] and measure the similarity between the segmentation of two different sequences. The results are consistent with the qualitative study and show that MovieCuts' edits have an F1 of 81% while BR, RS, and RF have only 77%, 63% 17%, respectively. A more in-depth analysis of this study can be found in **supplementary material**. This simple experiment suggests that the MovieCuts dataset allows

---

[2] EditStock.com.

the model to learn about video editing by learning cut-type recognition. Thus, we argue that further improvement in Cut-type recognition tasks can translate into advances in tasks related to machine-assisted video editing.

5   Conclusion

We introduced the cut-type recognition task in movies and started research in this new area by providing a new large-scale dataset, MovieCuts accompanied with a benchmark of multiple audio-visual baselines.. We collect $173,967$ annotations from qualified human workers. We analyze the dataset diversity and uniqueness by studying its properties and audio-visual attributes. We propose audio-visual baselines by using learning approaches that address the multi-modal nature of the problem. Although we established a strong research departure point, we hope that more research pushes the envelope of cut-type recognition by leveraging MovieCuts.

Acknowledgements. This work was supported by the King Abdullah University of Science and Technology (KAUST) Office of Sponsored Research through the Visual Computing Center (VCC) funding.

References

1. Arijon, D.: Grammar of the Film Language. Focal Press London (1976)
2. Bain, M., Nagrani, A., Brown, A., Zisserman, A.: Condensed movies: story based retrieval with contextual embeddings (2020)
3. Benini, S., Svanera, M., Adami, N., Leonardi, R., Kovács, A.B.: Shot scale distribution in art films. Multimedia Tools Appl. **75**(23), 16499–16527 (2016). https://doi.org/10.1007/s11042-016-3339-9
4. Bojanowski, P., Bach, F., Laptev, I., Ponce, J., Schmid, C., Sivic, J.: Finding actors and actions in movies. In: Proceedings of the IEEE International Conference on Computer Vision, pp. 2280–2287 (2013)
5. Bordwell, D., Thompson, K., Smith, J.: Film Art: An Introduction, vol. 7. McGraw-Hill, New York (1993)
6. Bost, X., et al.: Remembering winter was coming. Multimedia Tools Appl. **78**(24), 35373–35399 (2019). https://doi.org/10.1007/s11042-019-07969-4
7. Bost, X., Labatut, V., Linares, G.: Serial speakers: a dataset of tv series. arXiv preprint arXiv:2002.06923 (2020)
8. Bredin, H.: pyannote.metrics: a toolkit for reproducible evaluation, diagnostic, and error analysis of speaker diarization systems. In: Interspeech 2017, 18th Annual Conference of the International Speech Communication Association. Stockholm, Sweden (2017). http://pyannote.github.io/pyannote-metrics/
9. Brown, A., Huh, J., Nagrani, A., Chung, J.S., Zisserman, A.: Playing a part: speaker verification at the movies. arXiv preprint arXiv:2010.15716 (2020)
10. Burch, N.: Theory of Film Practice. Princeton University Press (2014)
11. Canini, L., Benini, S., Leonardi, R.: Classifying cinematographic shot types. Multimedia Tools Appl. **62**(1), 51–73 (2013). https://doi.org/10.1007/s11042-011-0916-9

12. Chen, H., Xie, W., Vedaldi, A., Zisserman, A.: Vggsound: a large-scale audio-visual dataset. In: International Conference on Acoustics, Speech, and Signal Processing (ICASSP) (2020)
13. Cutting, J.E.: The evolution of pace in popular movies. Cogn. Res. Principles Implications **1**(1), 1–21 (2016). https://doi.org/10.1186/s41235-016-0029-0
14. Duchenne, O., Laptev, I., Sivic, J., Bach, F., Ponce, J.: Automatic annotation of human actions in video. In: 2009 IEEE 12th International Conference on Computer Vision, pp. 1491–1498. IEEE (2009)
15. Everingham, M., Sivic, J., Zisserman, A.: Hello! my name is... buffy"-automatic naming of characters in tv video. In: BMVC, vol. 2, p. 6 (2006)
16. Galvane, Q., Ronfard, R., Lino, C., Christie, M.: Continuity editing for 3D animation. In: Proceedings of the AAAI Conference on Artificial Intelligence, vol. 29 (2015)
17. Gu, C., et al.: Ava: a video dataset of spatio-temporally localized atomic visual actions. In: Proceedings of the IEEE Conference on Computer Vision and Pattern Recognition, pp. 6047–6056 (2018)
18. Gygli, M.: Ridiculously fast shot boundary detection with fully convolutional neural networks. In: 2018 International Conference on Content-Based Multimedia Indexing (CBMI), pp. 1–4. IEEE (2018)
19. He, K., Zhang, X., Ren, S., Sun, J.: Deep residual learning for image recognition. In: Proceedings of the IEEE Conference on Computer Vision and Pattern Recognition, pp. 770–778 (2016)
20. Hesham, M., Hani, B., Fouad, N., Amer, E.: Smart trailer: automatic generation of movie trailer using only subtitles. In: 2018 First International Workshop on Deep and Representation Learning (IWDRL), pp. 26–30. IEEE (2018)
21. Hoai, M., Zisserman, A.: Thread-safe: towards recognizing human actions across shot boundaries. In: Cremers, D., Reid, I., Saito, H., Yang, M.-H. (eds.) ACCV 2014. LNCS, vol. 9006, pp. 222–237. Springer, Cham (2015). https://doi.org/10.1007/978-3-319-16817-3_15
22. Huang, Q., Liu, W., Lin, D.: Person search in videos with one portrait through visual and temporal links. In: Proceedings of the European Conference on Computer Vision (ECCV), pp. 425–441 (2018)
23. Huang, Q., Xiong, Y., Lin, D.: Unifying identification and context learning for person recognition. In: The IEEE Conference on Computer Vision and Pattern Recognition (CVPR) (2018)
24. Huang, Q., Xiong, Yu., Rao, A., Wang, J., Lin, D.: MovieNet: a holistic dataset for movie understanding. In: Vedaldi, A., Bischof, H., Brox, T., Frahm, J.-M. (eds.) ECCV 2020. LNCS, vol. 12349, pp. 709–727. Springer, Cham (2020). https://doi.org/10.1007/978-3-030-58548-8_41
25. Huang, Q., Xiong, Y., Xiong, Y., Zhang, Y., Lin, D.: From trailers to storylines: an efficient way to learn from movies. arXiv preprint arXiv:1806.05341 (2018)
26. Huang, Q., Yang, L., Huang, H., Wu, T., Lin, D.: Caption-supervised face recognition: training a state-of-the-art face model without manual annotation. In: Vedaldi, A., Bischof, H., Brox, T., Frahm, J.-M. (eds.) ECCV 2020. LNCS, vol. 12362, pp. 139–155. Springer, Cham (2020). https://doi.org/10.1007/978-3-030-58520-4_9
27. Irie, G., Satou, T., Kojima, A., Yamasaki, T., Aizawa, K.: Automatic trailer generation. In: Proceedings of the 18th ACM international conference on Multimedia, pp. 839–842 (2010)
28. Katz, E., Klein, F.: The film encyclopedia. Collins (2005)
29. Kay, W., et al.: The kinetics human action video dataset. arXiv preprint arXiv:1705.06950 (2017)

30. Kozlovic, A.K.: Anatomy of film. Kinema A J. Film Audiov. Media (2007)
31. Kuehne, H., Jhuang, H., Garrote, E., Poggio, T., Serre, T.: Hmdb: a large video database for human motion recognition. In: 2011 International Conference on Computer Vision, pp. 2556–2563. IEEE (2011)
32. Laptev, I., Marszalek, M., Schmid, C., Rozenfeld, B.: Learning realistic human actions from movies. In: 2008 IEEE Conference on Computer Vision and Pattern Recognition, pp. 1–8. IEEE (2008)
33. Liu, X., Hu, Y., Bai, S., Ding, F., Bai, X., Torr, P.H.: Multi-shot temporal event localization: a benchmark. arXiv preprint arXiv:2012.09434 (2020)
34. Maharaj, T., Dallas, N., Rohrbach, A., Courville, A., Pal, C..: A dataset and exploration of models for understanding video data through fill-in-the-blank question-answering. In: Proceedings of the IEEE Conference on Computer Vision and Pattern Recognition, pp. 6884–6893 (2017)
35. Murch, W.: In the Blink of an Eye, vol. 995. Silman-James Press Los Angeles (2001)
36. Nagrani, A., Zisserman, A.: From benedict cumberbatch to sherlock holmes: character identification in tv series without a script. arXiv preprint arXiv:1801.10442 (2018)
37. Pardo, A., Caba, F., Alcazar, J.L., Thabet, A.K., Ghanem, B.: Learning to cut by watching movies. In: Proceedings of the IEEE/CVF International Conference on Computer Vision (ICCV), pp. 6858–6868 (2021)
38. Pavlakos, G., Malik, J., Kanazawa, A.: Human mesh recovery from multiple shots. arXiv preprint arXiv:2012.09843 (2020)
39. Radford, A., et al.: Learning transferable visual models from natural language supervision. arXiv preprint arXiv:2103.00020 (2021)
40. Rao, A., et al.: A unified framework for shot type classification based on subject centric lens. In: Vedaldi, A., Bischof, H., Brox, T., Frahm, J.-M. (eds.) ECCV 2020. LNCS, vol. 12356, pp. 17–34. Springer, Cham (2020). https://doi.org/10.1007/978-3-030-58621-8_2
41. Rao, A., et al.: A local-to-global approach to multi-modal movie scene segmentation. In: Proceedings of the IEEE/CVF Conference on Computer Vision and Pattern Recognition, pp. 10146–10155 (2020)
42. Rohrbach, A., et al.: Movie description. Int. J. Comput. Vis. 123(1), 94–120 (2017). https://doi.org/10.1007/s11263-016-0987-1
43. Sivic, J., Everingham, M., Zisserman, A.: "Who are you?"-learning person specific classifiers from video. In: 2009 IEEE Conference on Computer Vision and Pattern Recognition, pp. 1145–1152. IEEE (2009)
44. Smith, J.R., Joshi, D., Huet, B., Hsu, W., Cota, J.: Harnessing ai for augmenting creativity: Application to movie trailer creation. In: Proceedings of the 25th ACM international conference on Multimedia, pp. 1799–1808 (2017)
45. Smith, T.J., Henderson, J.M.: Edit blindness: the relationship between attention and global change blindness in dynamic scenes. J. Eye Mov. Res. 2(2) (2008)
46. Smith, T.J., Levin, D., Cutting, J.E.: A window on reality: perceiving edited moving images. Curr. Dir. Psychol. Sci. 21(2), 107–113 (2012)
47. Tapaswi, M., Zhu, Y., Stiefelhagen, R., Torralba, A., Urtasun, R., Fidler, S.: MovieQA: understanding stories in movies through question-answering. In: IEEE Conference on Computer Vision and Pattern Recognition (CVPR) (2016)
48. Thompson, R., Bowen, C.J.: Grammar of the Edit, vol. 13. Taylor & Francis (2009)
49. Tran, D., Wang, H., Torresani, L., Ray, J., LeCun, Y., Paluri, M.: A closer look at spatiotemporal convolutions for action recognition. In: Proceedings of the IEEE conference on Computer Vision and Pattern Recognition, pp. 6450–6459 (2018)

50. http://www.cuvideoedit.com/types-of-edits.php
51. https://filmanalysis.yale.edu/editing/#transitions
52. Tsivian, Y.: Cinemetrics, part of the humanities' cyberinfrastructure (2009)
53. Vicol, P., Tapaswi, M., Castrejon, L., Fidler, S.: Moviegraphs: towards understanding human-centric situations from videos. In: IEEE Conference on Computer Vision and Pattern Recognition (CVPR) (2018)
54. Wang, H.L., Cheong, L.F.: Taxonomy of directing semantics for film shot classification. IEEE Trans. Circ. Syst. Video Technol. **19**(10), 1529–1542 (2009)
55. Wang, W., Tran, D., Feiszli, M.: What makes training multi-modal classification networks hard? In: Proceedings of the IEEE/CVF Conference on Computer Vision and Pattern Recognition, pp. 12695–12705 (2020)
56. Wu, H.Y., Christie, M.: Analysing cinematography with embedded constrained patterns. In: WICED-Eurographics Workshop on Intelligent Cinematography and Editing (2016)
57. Wu, H.Y., Galvane, Q., Lino, C., Christie, M.: Analyzing elements of style in annotated film clips. In: WICED 2017-Eurographics Workshop on Intelligent Cinematography and Editing, pp. 29–35. The Eurographics Association (2017)
58. Wu, H.Y., Palù, F., Ranon, R., Christie, M.: Thinking like a director: film editing patterns for virtual cinematographic storytelling. ACM Trans. Multimedia Comput. Commun. Appl. (TOMM) **14**(4), 1–22 (2018)
59. Wu, T., Huang, Q., Liu, Z., Wang, Yu., Lin, D.: Distribution-balanced loss for multi-label classification in long-tailed datasets. In: Vedaldi, A., Bischof, H., Brox, T., Frahm, J.-M. (eds.) ECCV 2020. LNCS, vol. 12349, pp. 162–178. Springer, Cham (2020). https://doi.org/10.1007/978-3-030-58548-8_10
60. Xia, J., Rao, A., Huang, Q., Xu, L., Wen, J., Lin, D.: Online multi-modal person search in videos. In: Vedaldi, A., Bischof, H., Brox, T., Frahm, J.-M. (eds.) ECCV 2020. LNCS, vol. 12357, pp. 174–190. Springer, Cham (2020). https://doi.org/10.1007/978-3-030-58610-2_11
61. Xiong, Y., Huang, Q., Guo, L., Zhou, H., Zhou, B., Lin, D.: A graph-based framework to bridge movies and synopses. In: The IEEE International Conference on Computer Vision (ICCV) (2019)
62. Xu, H., Zhen, Y., Zha, H.: Trailer generation via a point process-based visual attractiveness model. In: Twenty-Fourth International Joint Conference on Artificial Intelligence (2015)

LaMAR: Benchmarking Localization and Mapping for Augmented Reality

Paul-Edouard Sarlin[1]([⊠]), Mihai Dusmanu[1], Johannes L. Schönberger[2],
Pablo Speciale[2], Lukas Gruber[2], Viktor Larsson[1], Ondrej Miksik[2],
and Marc Pollefeys[1,2]

[1] Department of Computer Science, ETH Zürich, Zürich, Switzerland
psarlin@ethz.ch, mihai.dusmanu@inf.ethz.ch
[2] Microsoft Mixed Reality & AI Lab, Zürich, Switzerland

Abstract. Localization and mapping is the foundational technology for augmented reality (AR) that enables sharing and persistence of digital content in the real world. While significant progress has been made, researchers are still mostly driven by unrealistic benchmarks not representative of real-world AR scenarios. In particular, benchmarks are often based on small-scale datasets with low scene diversity, captured from stationary cameras, and lacking other sensor inputs like inertial, radio, or depth data. Furthermore, ground-truth (GT) accuracy is mostly insufficient to satisfy AR requirements. To close this gap, we introduce a new benchmark with a comprehensive capture and GT pipeline, which allow us to co-register realistic AR trajectories in diverse scenes and from heterogeneous devices at scale. To establish accurate GT, our pipeline robustly aligns the captured trajectories against laser scans in a fully automatic manner. Based on this pipeline, we publish a benchmark dataset of diverse and large-scale scenes recorded with head-mounted and hand-held AR devices. We extend several state-of-the-art methods to take advantage of the AR specific setup and evaluate them on our benchmark. Based on the results, we present novel insights on current research gaps to provide avenues for future work in the community.

1 Introduction

Placing virtual content in the physical 3D world, persisting it over time, and sharing it with other users are typical scenarios for Augmented Reality (AR). In order to reliably overlay virtual content in the real world with pixel-level precision, these scenarios require AR devices to accurately determine their 6-DoF pose at any point in time. While visual localization and mapping is one of the most studied problems in computer vision, its use for AR entails specific challenges and opportunities. First, modern AR devices, such as mobile phones or the Microsoft HoloLens or MagicLeap One, are often equipped with multiple cameras and additional inertial or radio sensors. Second, they exhibit characteristic hand-held or head-mounted motion patterns. The on-device real-time tracking systems provide spatially-posed sensor streams. However, many AR

P.-E. Sarlin and M. Dusmanu—Equal contribution.
V. Larsson—Now at Lund University, Sweden.

S. Avidan et al. (Eds.): ECCV 2022, LNCS 13667, pp. 686–704, 2022.
https://doi.org/10.1007/978-3-031-20071-7_40

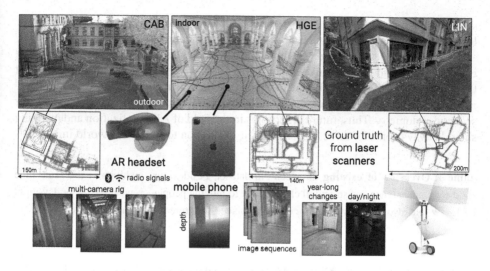

Fig. 1. We revisit localization and mapping in the context of Augmented Reality by introducing LaMAR, a large-scale dataset captured using AR devices (HoloLens2, iPhone) and laser scanners.

scenarios require positioning beyond local tracking, both indoors and outdoors, and robustness to common temporal changes of appearance and structure. Furthermore, given the plurality of temporal sensor data, the question is often not whether, but how quickly can the device localize at any time to ensure a compelling end-user experience. Finally, as AR adoption grows, crowd-sourced data captured by users with diverse devices can be mined for building large-scale maps without a manual and costly scanning effort. Crowd-sourcing offers great opportunities but poses additional challenges on the robustness of algorithms, e.g., to enable cross-device localization [21], mapping from incomplete data with low accuracy [8,67], privacy-preservation of data [23,25,26,71,73], etc.

However, the academic community is mainly driven by benchmarks that are disconnected from the specifics of AR. They mostly evaluate localization and mapping using single still images and either lack temporal changes [56,72] or accurate ground truth (GT) [37,65,76], are restricted to small scenes [6,37,70,72,83] or landmarks [34,68] with perfect coverage and limited viewpoint variability, or disregard temporal tracking data or additional visual, inertial, or radio sensors [12,40,65,66,75,76].

Our first contribution is to introduce **a large-scale dataset captured using AR devices in diverse environments**, notably a historical building, a multi-story office building, and part of a city center. The initial data release contains both indoor and outdoor images with illumination and semantic changes as well as dynamic objects. Specifically, we collected multi-sensor data streams (images, depth, tracking, IMU, BT, WiFi) totalling more than 100 h using head-mounted HoloLens 2 and hand-held iPhone/iPad devices covering 45'000 square meters over the span of one year (Fig. 1).

Second, we develop **a GT pipeline to automatically and accurately register AR trajectories** against large-scale 3D laser scans. Our pipeline does not require any manual labelling or setup of custom infrastructure (e.g., fiducial markers). Furthermore, the system robustly handles crowd-sourced data from heterogeneous devices captured over longer periods of time and can be easily extended to support future devices.

Finally, we present **a rigorous evaluation of localization and mapping in the context of AR** and provide **novel insights for future research**. Notably, we show that the performance of state-of-the-art methods can be drastically improved by considering additional data streams generally available in AR devices, such as radio signals or sequence odometry. Thus, future algorithms in the field of AR localization and mapping should always consider these sensors in their evaluation to show real-world impact.

Table 1. Overview of existing datasets. No dataset, besides ours, exhibits at the same time short-term appearance and structural changes due to moving people, 👤 weather ☁, or day-night cycles ●, but also long-term changes due to displaced furniture 🪑 or construction work ⏊.

dataset	out/indoor	changes	scale	density	camera motion	imaging devices	additional sensors	ground truth	accuracy
Aachen [66,65]	✓✗	●⏊	★★★	★★☆	still images	DSLR	✗	SfM	>dm
Phototourism [34]	✓✗	👤⏊	★☆☆	★★★	still images	DSLR, phone	✗	SfM	~m
San Francisco [14]	✓✗	👤⏊	★★★	★☆☆	still images	DSLR, phone	GNSS	SfM+GNSS	~m
Cambridge [37]	✓✗	👤☁	★☆☆	★★☆	handheld	mobile	✗	SfM	>dm
7Scenes [72]	✗✓	✗	★☆☆	★★★	handheld	mobile	depth	RGB-D	~cm
RIO10 [83]	✗✓	🪑	★☆☆	★★★	handheld	Tango tablet	depth	VIO	>dm
InLoc [76]	✗✓	🪑	★★☆	★☆☆	still images	panoramas, phone	lidar	manual+lidar	>dm
Baidu mall [75]	✗✓	👤	★★☆	★★☆	still images	DSLR, phone	lidar	manual+lidar	~dm
Naver Labs [40]	✗✓	👤🪑	★★☆	★★☆	robot-mounted	fisheye, phone	lidar	lidar+SfM	~dm
NCLT [12]	✓✓	☁🪑	★★☆	★★☆	robot-mounted	wide-angle	lidar, IMU, GNSS	lidar+VIO	~dm
ADVIO [56]	✓✓	👤	★★☆	★☆☆	handheld	phone, Tango	IMU, depth, GNSS	manual+VIO	~m
ETH3D [70]	✓✓	✗	★☆☆	★★★	handheld	DSLR, wide-angle	lidar	manual+lidar	~mm
LaMAR (ours)	✓✓	👤●🪑⏊	★★☆ 3 locations 45'000 m²	★★★ 100 hours 40 km	handheld head-mounted	phone, headset backpack, trolley	lidar, IMU, 📶🔋 depth, infrared	lidar+SfM+VIO automated	~cm

The LaMAR dataset, benchmark, GT pipeline, and the implementations of baselines integrating additional sensory data are all publicly available at lamar.ethz.ch. We hope that this will spark future research addressing the challenges of AR.

2   Related Work

Image-Based Localization. is classically tackled by estimating a camera pose from correspondences established between sparse local features [7,43,47,59] and a 3D Structure-from-Motion (SfM) [67] map of the scene [24,42,64]. This pipeline scales to large scenes using image retrieval [2,11,33,55,57,78,79]. Recently, many of these steps or even the end-to-end pipeline have been successfully learned with neural networks [3,20,22,32,49,61–63,69,77,88]. Other approaches regress absolute camera pose [36,37,50] or scene coordinates [9,10,41,45,46,72,82,85]. However, all these approaches typically fail whenever there is lack of context (e.g., limited field-of-view) or the map has repetitive elements. Leveraging the sequential ordering of video frames [35,48] or modelling the problem as a generalized camera [29,53,65,73] can improve results.

Radio-Based Localization: Radio signals, such as WiFi and Bluetooth, are spatially bounded (logarithmic decay) [5,28,38], thus can distinguish similarly looking (spatially distant) locations. Their unique identifiers can be uniquely hashed which makes them computationally attractive (compared with high-dimensional image descriptors). Several methods use the signal strength, angle, direction, or time of arrival [13,18,51] but the most popular is model-free map-based fingerprinting [28,38,39], as it only requires to collect unique identifiers of nearby radio sources and received signal strength. GNSS provides absolute 3-DoF positioning but is not applicable indoors and has insufficient accuracy for AR scenarios, especially in urban environments due to multi-pathing, etc.

Datasets and Ground-Truth: Many of the existing benchmarks (cf. Table 1) are captured in small-scale environments [19,30,72,83], do not contain sequential data [6, 14,34,66,68,70,75,76], lack characteristic hand-held/head-mounted motion patterns [4,44,65,86], or their GT is not accurate enough for AR [37,56]. None of these datasets contain WiFi or Bluetooth data (Table 1). The closest to our work are Naver Labs [40], NCLT [12] and ETH3D [70]. Both, Naver Labs [40] and NCLT [12] are less accurate than ours and do not contain AR specific trajectories or radio data. The Naver Labs dataset [40] also does not contain any outdoor data. ETH3D [70] is highly accurate, however, it is only small-scale, does not contain significant changes, or any radio data.

Table 2. Sensor specifications. Our dataset has visible light images (global shutter GS, rolling shutter RS, auto-focus AF), depth data (ToF, lidar), radio signals (*, if partial), dense lidar point clouds, and poses with intrinsics from on-device tracking.

device	motion type	cameras				radios	other data	poses
		# FOV	frequency	resolution	specs			
M6	trolley	6 113°	1-3m	1080p	RGB, sync	📶🔵	lidar points+mesh	lidar SLAM
VLX	backpack	4 90°	1-3m	1080p	RGB, sync	🔵	lidar points+mesh	lidar SLAM
HoloLens2	head-mounted	4 83°	30Hz	VGA	gray, GS	📶🔵	ToF depth/IR 1Hz, IMU	head-tracking
iPad/iPhone	hand-held	1 64°	10Hz	1080p	RGB, RS, AF	🔵*	lidar depth 10Hz, IMU	ARKit

To establish ground-truth, many datasets rely on off-the-shelf SfM algorithms [67] for unordered image collections [34,37,56,66,75,76,83]. Pure SfM-based GT generation has limited accuracy [8] and completeness, which biases the evaluations to scenarios in which visual localization already works well. Other approaches rely on RGB(-D) tracking [72,83], which usually drifts in larger scenes and cannot produce GT in crowd-sourced, multi-device scenarios. Specialized capture rigs of an AR device with a more accurate sensor (lidar) [12,40] prevent capturing of realistic AR motion patterns. Furthermore, scalability is limited for these approaches, especially if they rely on manual selection of reference images [75], laborious labelling of correspondences [66,76], or placement of fiducial markers [30]. For example, the accuracy of ETH3D [70] is achieved by using single stationary lidar scan, manual cleaning, and aligning very few images captured by tripod-mounted DSLR cameras. Images thus obtained are not representative for AR devices and the process cannot scale or take advantage of crowd-sourced data. In contrast, our fully automatic approach does not require any manual labelling or special capture setups, thus enables light-weight and repeated scanning of large locations.

3 Dataset

We first give an overview of the setup and content of our dataset.

Locations: The initial release of the dataset contains 3 large locations representative of AR use cases: 1) HGE ($18'000\,\text{m}^2$) is the ground floor of a historical university building composed of multiple large halls and large esplanades on both sides. 2) CAB ($12'000\,\text{m}^2$) is a multi-floor office building composed of multiple small and large offices, a kitchen, storage rooms, and 2 courtyards. 3) LIN ($15'000\,\text{m}^2$) is a few blocks of an old town with shops, restaurants, and narrow passages. HGE and CAB contain both indoor and outdoor sections with many symmetric structures. Each location underwent structural changes over the span of a year, e.g., the front of HGE turned into a construction site and the indoor furniture was rearranged. See Fig. 2 for a visualization of the locations.

Fig. 2. The locations feature diverse indoor and outdoor spaces. High-quality meshes, obtained from lidar, are registered with numerous AR sequences, each shown here as a different color.

Data Collection: We collected data using Microsoft HoloLens 2 and Apple iPad Pro devices with custom raw sensor recording applications. 10 participants were each given one device and asked to walk through a common designated area. They were only given the instructions to freely walk through the environment to visit, inspect, and find their way around. This yielded diverse camera heights and motion patterns. Their trajectories were not planned or restricted in any way. Participants visited each location, both during the day and at night, at different points in time over the course of up to 1 year. In total, each location is covered by more than 100 sessions of 5 min. We did not need to prepare the capturing site in any way before recording. This enables easy barrier-free crowd-sourced data collections. Each location was also captured twice by NavVis M6 trolley and VLX backpack mapping platforms, which generate textured dense 3D models of the environment using laser scanners and panoramic cameras.

Privacy: We paid special attention to comply with privacy regulations. Since the dataset is recorded in public spaces, our pipeline anonymizes all visible faces and licence plates.

Sensors: We provide details about the recorded sensors in Table 2. The HoloLens has a specialized large field-of-view (FOV) multi-camera tracking rig (low resolution, global shutter) [81], while the iPad has a single, higher-resolution camera with rolling shutter and more limited FOV. We also recorded outputs of the real-time AR tracking algorithms available on each device, which includes relative camera poses and sensor calibration. All images are undistorted. All sensor data is registered into a common reference frame with accurate absolute GT poses using the pipeline described in the next section.

4   Ground-Truth Generation

The GT estimation process takes as input the raw data from the different sensors. The entire pipeline is fully automated and does not require any manual alignment or input.

Overview: We start by aligning different sessions of the laser scanner by using the images and the 3D lidar point cloud. When registered together, they form the GT reference map, which accurately captures the structure and appearance of the scene. We then register each AR sequence individually to the reference map using local feature matching and relative poses from the on-device tracker. Finally, all camera poses are refined jointly by optimizing the visual constraints within and across sequences.

Notation: We denote $_i\mathbf{T}_j \in \text{SE}(3)$ the 6-DoF pose, encompassing rotation and translation, that transforms a point in frame j to another frame i. Our goal is to compute globally-consistent absolute poses $_w\mathbf{T}_i$ for all cameras i of all sequences and scanning sessions into a common reference world frame w.

4.1   Ground-Truth Reference Model

Each capture session $S \in \mathcal{S}$ of the NavVis laser-scanning platform is processed by a proprietary inertial-lidar SLAM that estimates, for each image i, a pose $_0\mathbf{T}_i^S$ relative to the beginning of the session. The software filters out noisy lidar measurements, removes dynamic objects, and aggregates the remainder into a globally-consistent colored 3D point cloud with a grid resolution of 1 cm. To recover visibility information, we compute a dense mesh using the Advancing Front algorithm [17].

Our first goal is to align the sessions into a common GT reference frame. We assume that the scan trajectories are drift-free and only need to register each with a rigid transformation $_w\mathbf{T}_0^S$. Scan sessions can be captured between extensive periods of time and therefore exhibit large structural and appearance changes. We use a combination of image and point cloud information to obtain accurate registrations without any manual initialization. The steps are inspired by the reconstruction pipeline of Choi et al. [15, 89].

Pair-Wise Registration: We first estimate a rigid transformation $_A\mathbf{T}_B$ for each pair of scanning sessions $(A, B) \in \mathcal{S}^2$. For each image I_i^A in A, we select the r most similar images $(I_j^B)_{1\leq j \leq r}$ in B based on global image descriptors [3,33,57], which helps the registration scale to large scenes. We extract sparse local image features and establish 2D-2D correspondences $\{\mathbf{p}_i^A, \mathbf{p}_j^B\}$ for each image pair (i, j). The 2D keypoints $\mathbf{p}_i \in \mathbb{R}^2$ are lifted to 3D, $\mathbf{P}_i \in \mathbb{R}^3$, by tracing rays through the dense mesh of the corresponding session. This yields 3D-3D correspondences $\{\mathbf{P}_i^A, \mathbf{P}_j^B\}$, from which we estimate an initial relative pose [80] using RANSAC [24]. This pose is refined with the point-to-plane Iterative Closest Point (ICP) algorithm [60] applied to the pair of lidar point clouds.

We use state-of-the-art local image features that can match across drastic illumination and viewpoint changes [20,58,61]. Combined with the strong geometric constraints in the registration, our system is robust to long-term temporal changes and does not require manual initialization. Using this approach, we have successfully registered building-scale scans captured at more than a year of interval with large structural changes.

Global Alignment: We gather all pairwise constraints and jointly refine all absolute scan poses $\{_w\mathbf{T}_0^S\}$ by optimizing a pose graph [27]. The edges are weighted with the covariance matrices of the pair-wise ICP estimates. The images of all scan sessions are finally combined into a unique reference trajectory $\{_w\mathbf{T}_i^{\mathrm{ref}}\}$. The point clouds and meshes are aligned according to the same transformations. They define the reference representation of the scene, which we use as a basis to obtain GT for the AR sequences.

Ground-Truth Visibility: The accurate and dense 3D geometry of the mesh allows us to compute accurate visual overlap between two cameras with known poses and calibration. Inspired by Rau et al. [55], we define the overlap of image i wrt. a reference image j by the ratio of pixels in i that are visible in j:

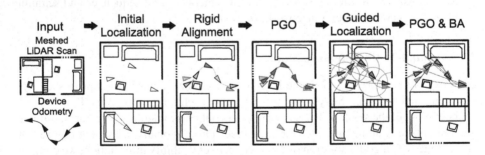

Fig. 3. Sequence-to-scan alignment. We first estimate the absolute pose of each sequence frame using image retrieval and matching. This initial localization prior is used to obtain a single rigid alignment between the input trajectory and the reference 3D model via voting. The alignment is then relaxed by optimizing the individual frame poses in a pose graph based on both relative and absolute pose constraints. We bootstrap this initialization by mining relevant image pairs and re-localizing the queries. Given these improved absolute priors, we optimize the pose graph again and finally include reprojection errors of the visual correspondences, yielding a refined trajectory.

$$O(i \to j) = \frac{\sum_{k \in (W,H)} \mathbb{1} \left[\Pi_j(_w\mathbf{T}_j, \Pi_i^{-1}(_w\mathbf{T}_i, \mathbf{p}_k^i, z_k)) \in (W,H) \right] \alpha_k}{W \cdot H} , \quad (1)$$

where Π_i projects a 3D point k to camera i, Π_i^{-1} conversely backprojects it using its known depth z_k with (W, H) as the image dimensions. The contribution of each pixel is weighted by the angle $\alpha_k = \cos(\mathbf{n}_{i,k}, \mathbf{n}_{j,k})$ between the two rays. To handle scale changes, it is averaged both ways $i \to j$ and $j \to i$. This score is efficiently computed by tracing rays through the mesh and checking for occlusion for robustness.

This score $O \in [0, 1]$ favors images that observe the same scene from similar viewpoints. Unlike sparse co-visibility in an SfM model [54], our formulation is independent of the amount of texture and the density of the feature detections. This score correlates with matchability – we thus use it as GT when evaluating retrieval and to determine an upper bound on the theoretically achievable performance of our benchmark.

4.2 Sequence-to-Scan Alignment

We now aim to register each AR sequence individually into the dense GT reference model (see Fig. 3). Given a sequence of n frames, we introduce a simple algorithm that estimates the per-frame absolute pose $\{_w\mathbf{T}_i\}_{1 \leq i \leq n}$. A frame refers to an image taken at a given time or, when the device is composed of a camera rig with known calibration (e.g., HoloLens), to a collection of simultaneously captured images.

Inputs: We assume given trajectories $\{_0\mathbf{T}_i^{\text{track}}\}$ estimated by a visual-inertial tracker – we use ARKit for iPhone/iPad and the on-device tracker for HoloLens. The tracker also outputs per-frame camera intrinsics $\{\mathbf{C}_i\}$, which account for auto-focus or calibration changes and are for now kept fixed.

Initial Localization: For each frame of a sequence $\{I_i^{\text{query}}\}$, we retrieve a fixed number r of relevant reference images $(I_j^{\text{ref}})_{1 \leq j \leq r}$ using global image descriptors. We match sparse local features [20,43,58] extracted in the query frame to each retrieved image I_j^{ref} obtaining a set of 2D-2D correspondences $\{\mathbf{p}_{i,k}^q, \mathbf{p}_{j,k}^{\text{ref}}\}_k$. The 2D reference keypoints are lifted to 3D by tracing rays through the mesh of the reference model, yielding a set of 2D-3D correspondences $\mathcal{M}_{i,j} := \{\mathbf{p}_{i,k}^q, \mathbf{P}_{j,k}^{\text{ref}}\}_k$. We combine all matches per query frame $\mathcal{M}_i = \cup_{j=1}^r \mathcal{M}_{i,j}$ and estimate an initial absolute pose $_w\mathbf{T}_i^{\text{loc}}$ using the (generalized) P3P algorithm [29] within a LO-RANSAC scheme [16] followed by a non-linear refinement [67]. Because of challenging appearance conditions, structural changes, or lack of texture, some frames cannot be localized in this stage. We discard all poses that are supported by a low number of inlier correspondences.

Rigid Alignment: We next recover a coarse initial pose $\{_w\mathbf{T}_i^{\text{init}}\}$ for all frames, including those that could not be localized. Using the tracking, which is for now assumed drift-free, we find the rigid alignment $_w\mathbf{T}_0^{\text{init}}$ that maximizes the consensus among localization poses. This voting scheme is fast and effectively rejects poses that are incorrect, yet confident, due to visual aliasing and symmetries. Each estimate is a candidate transformation $_w\mathbf{T}_0^i = {}_w\mathbf{T}_i^{\text{loc}} \left(_0\mathbf{T}_i^{\text{track}} \right)^{-1}$, for which other frames can vote, if they are consistent within a threshold τ_{rigid}. We select the candidate with the highest count of inliers:

$$_w\mathbf{T}_0^{\text{init}} = \arg\max_{\mathbf{T}\in\{_w\mathbf{T}_0^i\}_{1\le i\le n}} \sum_{1\le j\le n} \mathbb{1}\left[\text{dist}\left(_w\mathbf{T}_j^{\text{loc}}, \mathbf{T}\cdot {_0}\mathbf{T}_j^{\text{track}}\right) < \tau_{\text{rigid}}\right], \qquad (2)$$

where $\mathbb{1}[\cdot]$ is the indicator function and $\text{dist}(\cdot,\cdot)$ returns the magnitude, in terms of translation and rotation, of the difference between two absolute poses. We then recover the per-frame initial poses as $\{_w\mathbf{T}_i^{\text{init}} := {_w}\mathbf{T}_0^{\text{init}} \cdot {_0}\mathbf{T}_i^{\text{track}}\}_{1\le i\le n}$.

Pose Graph Optimization: We refine the initial absolute poses by maximizing the consistency of tracking and localization cues within a pose graph. The refined poses $\{_w\mathbf{T}_i^{\text{PGO}}\}$ minimize the energy function

$$E(\{_w\mathbf{T}_i\}) = \sum_{i=1}^{n-1}\mathcal{C}_{\text{PGO}}\left(_w\mathbf{T}_{i+1}^{-1}\,{_w}\mathbf{T}_i,\,{_{i+1}}\mathbf{T}_i^{\text{track}}\right) + \sum_{i=1}^{n}\mathcal{C}_{\text{PGO}}\left(_w\mathbf{T}_i,\,{_w}\mathbf{T}_i^{\text{loc}}\right), \qquad (3)$$

where $\mathcal{C}_{\text{PGO}}(\mathbf{T}_1, \mathbf{T}_2) := \left\|\text{Log}\left(\mathbf{T}_1\,\mathbf{T}_2^{-1}\right)\right\|_{\Sigma,\gamma}^2$ is the distance between two absolute or relative poses, weighted by covariance matrix $\Sigma \in \mathbb{R}^{6\times 6}$ and loss function γ. Here, Log maps from the Lie group $\text{SE}(3)$ to the corresponding algebra $\mathfrak{se}(3)$.

We robustify the absolute term with the Geman-McClure loss function and anneal its scale via a Graduated Non-Convexity scheme [87]. This ensures convergence in case of poor initialization, e.g., when the tracking exhibits significant drift, while remaining robust to incorrect localization estimates. The covariance of the absolute term is propagated from the preceding non-linear refinement performed during localization. The covariance of the relative term is recovered from the odometry pipeline, or, if not available, approximated as a factor of the motion magnitude.

This step can fill the gaps from the localization stage using the tracking information and conversely correct for tracker drift using localization cues. In rare cases, the resulting poses might still be inaccurate when both the tracking drifts and the localization fails.

Guided Localization via Visual Overlap: To further increase the pose accuracy, we leverage the current pose estimates $\{_w\mathbf{T}_i^{\text{PGO}}\}$ to mine for additional localization cues. Instead of relying on global visual descriptors, which are easily affected by aliasing, we select reference images with a high overlap using the score defined in Sect. 4.1. For each sequence frame i, we select r reference images with the largest overlap and again match local features and estimate an absolute pose. These new localization priors improve the pose estimates in a second optimization of the pose graph.

Bundle Adjustment: For each frame i, we recover the set of 2D-3D correspondences $\mathcal{M}_i$ used by the guided re-localization. We now refine the poses $\{_w\mathbf{T}_i^{\text{BA}}\}$ by jointly minimizing a bundle adjustment problem with relative pose graph costs:

$$\begin{aligned}
E(\{_w\mathbf{T}_i\}) = &\sum_{i=1}^{n-1}\mathcal{C}_{\text{PGO}}\left(_w\mathbf{T}_{i+1}^{-1}\,{_w}\mathbf{T}_i,\,{_{i+1}}\mathbf{T}_i^{\text{track}}\right) \\
&+ \sum_{i=1}^{n}\sum_{\mathcal{M}_{i,j}\in\mathcal{M}_i}\sum_{(\mathbf{p}_k^{\text{ref}},\mathbf{P}_k^q)\in\mathcal{M}_{i,j}}\left\|\Pi(_w\mathbf{T}_i, \mathbf{P}_{j,k}^{\text{ref}}) - \mathbf{p}_{i,k}^q\right\|_{\sigma^2}^2,
\end{aligned} \qquad (4)$$

where the second term evaluates the reprojection error of a 3D point $\mathbf{P}^{\text{ref}}_{j,k}$ for observation k to frame i. The covariance is the noise σ^2 of the keypoint detection algorithm. We pre-filter correspondences that are behind the camera or have an initial reprojection error greater than $\sigma\,\tau_{\text{reproj}}$. As the 3D points are sampled from the lidar, we also optimize them with a prior noise corresponding to the lidar specifications. We use the Ceres [1] solver.

4.3 Joint Global Refinement

Once all sequences are individually aligned, we refine them jointly by leveraging sequence-to-sequence visual observations. This is helpful when sequences observe parts of the scene not mapped by the LiDAR. We first triangulate a sparse 3D model from scan images, aided by the mesh. We then triangulate additional observations, and finally jointly optimize the whole problem.

Reference Triangulation: We estimate image correspondences of the reference scan using pairs selected according to the visual overlap defined in Sect. 4.2. Since the image poses are deemed accurate and fixed, we filter the correspondences using the known epipolar geometry. We first consider feature tracks consistent with the reference surface mesh before triangulating more noisy observations within LO-RANSAC using COLMAP [67]. The remaining feature detections, which could not be reliably matched or triangulated, are lifted to 3D by tracing through the mesh. This results in an accurate, sparse SfM model with tracks across reference images.

Sequence Optimization: We then add each sequence to the sparse model. We first establish correspondences between images of the same and of different sequences. The image pairs are again selected by highest visual overlap computed using the aligned poses $\{_w\mathbf{T}^{\text{BA}}_i\}$. The resulting tracks are sequentially triangulated, merged, and added to the sparse model. Finally, all 3D points and poses are jointly optimized by minimizing the joint pose-graph and bundle adjustment (Eq. 4). As in COLMAP [67], we alternate optimization and track merging. To scale to large scenes, we subsample keyframes from the full frame-rate captures and only introduce absolute pose and reprojection constraints for keyframes while maintaining all relative pose constraints from tracking.

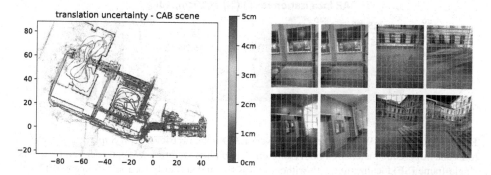

Fig. 4. Uncertainty of the GT poses for the CAB scene. Left: The overhead map shows that the uncertainties are larger in long corridors and outdoor spaces. Right: Pixel-aligned renderings at the estimated camera poses confirm that the poses are sufficiently accurate for our evaluation.

4.4   Ground-Truth Validation

Potential Limits: Brachmann et al. [8] observe that algorithms generating pseudo-GT poses by minimizing either 2D or 3D cost functions alone can yield noticeably different results. We argue that there exists a single underlying, true GT. Reaching it requires fusing large amounts of redundant data with sufficient sensors of sufficiently low noise. Our GT poses optimize complementary constraints from visual and inertial measurements, guided by an accurate lidar-based 3D structure. Careful design and propagation of uncertainties reduces the bias towards one of the sensors. All sensors are factory- and self-calibrated during each recording by the respective commercial, production-grade SLAM algorithms. We do not claim that our GT is perfect but analyzing the optimization uncertainties sheds light on its degree of accuracy.

Pose Uncertainty: We estimate the uncertainties of the GT poses by inverting the Hessian of the refinement. To obtain calibrated covariances, we scale them by the empirical keypoint detection noise, estimated as $\sigma = 1.33$ pixels for the CAB scene. The maximum noise in translation is the size of the major axis of the uncertainty ellipsoids, which is the largest eivenvalue σ_t^2 of the covariance matrices. Figure 4 shows its distribution for the CAB scene. We retain images whose poses are correct within 10 cm with a confidence of 99.7%. For normally distributed errors, this corresponds to a maximum uncertainty $\sigma_t = 3.33$ cm and discards 3.9% of the queries. For visual inspection, we render images at the estimated GT camera poses using the colored mesh. They appear pixel-aligned with the original images, supporting that the poses are accurate.

4.5   Selection of Mapping and Query Sequences

We divide the set of sequences into two disjoint groups for mapping (database) and localization (query). Database sequences are selected such that they have a minimal overlap between each other yet cover the area visited by all remaining sequences. This simulates a scenario of minimal coverage and maximizes the number of query sequences. We cast this as a combinatorial optimization problem solved with a depth-first search guided by some heuristics. We provide more details in the supp. material.

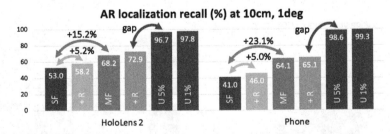

Fig. 5. Main results. We show results for NetVLAD image retrieval with SuperPoint local features and SuperGlue matcher on both HoloLens 2 and phone queries. We consider several tracks: single-frame (SF) localization with/without radios (R) and similarly for multi-frame (MF) localization. In addition, we report a theoretical upper bound (U): the percentage of queries with at least 5%/1% ground-truth overlap with respect to the best database image.

5   Evaluation

We evaluate state-of-the-art approaches in both single- and multi-frame settings and summarize our results in Fig. 5.

Single-Frame: We first consider in Sect. 5.1 the classical academic setup of single-frame queries (single image for phones and single rig for HoloLens 2) without additional sensor. We then look at how radio signals can be beneficial. We also analyze the impact of various settings: FOV, type of mapping images, and mapping algorithm.

Multi-frame: Second, by leveraging the real-time AR tracking poses, we consider the problem of multi-frame localization in Sect. 5.2. This corresponds to a real-world AR application retrieving the content attached to a target map using the real-time sensor stream from the device. In this context, we not only care about accuracy and recall but also about the time required to localize accurately, which we call the *time-to-recall*.

5.1   Single-Frame Localization

We first evaluate several algorithms representative of the state of the art in the classical single-frame academic setup. We consider the hierarchical localization framework with different approaches for image retrieval and matching. Each of them first builds a sparse SfM map from reference images. For each query frame, we then retrieve relevant reference images, match their local features, lift the reference keypoints to 3D using the sparse map, and finally estimate a pose with PnP+RANSAC. We report the recall of the final pose at two thresholds [65]: 1) a fine threshold at $\{1°, 10\,cm\}$, which we see as the minimum accuracy required for a good AR user experience in most settings. 2) a coarse threshold at $\{5°, 1\,m\}$ to show the room for improvement for current approaches.

We evaluate global descriptors computed by NetVLAD [3] and by a fusion [31] of NetVLAD and APGeM [57], which are representative of the field [52]. We retrieve the 10 most similar images. For matching, we evaluate handcrafted SIFT [43], SOS-Net [77] as a learned patch descriptor extracted from DoG [43] keypoints, and a robust deep-learning based joint detector and descriptor R2D2 [58]. Those are matched by exact mutual nearest neighbor search. We also evaluate SuperGlue [62] – a learned matcher based on SuperPoint [20] features. To build the map, we retrieve neighboring images using NetVLAD filtered by frustum intersection from reference poses, match these pairs, and triangulate a sparse SfM model using COLMAP [67].

We report the results in Table 3 (left). Even the best methods have a large gap to perfect scores and much room for improvement. In the remaining ablation, we solely rely on SuperPoint+SuperGlue [20, 62] for matching as it clearly performs the best.

Leveraging Radio Signals: In this experiment, we show that radio signals can be used to constrain the search space for image retrieval. This has two main benefits: 1) it reduces the risk of incorrectly considering visual aliases, and 2) it lowers the compute requirements by reducing that numbers of images that need to be retrieved and matched. We

Table 3. Left: single-frame localization. We report the recall at $(1°, 10\,\text{cm})/(5°, 1\,\text{m})$ for baselines representative of the state of the art. Our dataset is challenging while most others are saturated. There is a clear progress from SIFT but also large room for improvement. **Right: localization with radio signals.** Increasing the number $\{5, 10, 20\}$ of retrieved images increases the localization recall at $(1°, 10\,\text{cm})$. The best-performing visual retrieval (Fusion, orange) is however far worse than the GT overlap. Filtering with radio signals (blue) improves the performance in all settings.

Hierarchical localization		Query device	
Retrieval	Matching	HL2	Phone
NetVLAD	SIFT	30.3 / 41.4	28.6 / 42.3
	DoG+SOSNet	31.6 / 43.3	29.8 / 45.7
	R2D2	38.9 / 51.3	40.6 / 57.3
	SP+SG	46.3 / 59.8	49.3 / 62.8
Fusion	SIFT	32.8 / 47.0	29.0 / 43.6
	DoG+SOSNet	34.5 / 48.9	30.4 / 46.4
	R2D2	43.0 / 57.8	40.4 / 57.7
	SP+SG	52.4 / 67.3	50.2 / 64.3

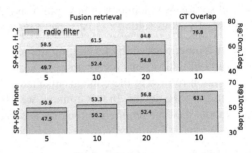

implement this filtering as follows. We first split the scene into a sparse 3D grid considering only voxels containing at least one mapping frame. For each frame, we gather all radio signals in a $\pm 10\,\text{s}$ window and associate them to the corresponding voxel. If the same endpoint is observed multiple times in a given voxel, we average the received signal strengths (RSSI) in dBm. For a query frame, we similarly aggregate signals over the past 10 s and rank voxels by their L2 distance between RSSIs, considering those with at least one common endpoint. We thus restrict image retrieval to 5% of the map.

Table 3 (right) shows that radio filtering always improves the localization accuracy over vanilla vision-only retrieval, irrespective of how many images are matches. The upper bound based on the GT overlap (defined in Sect. 4.1) shows that there is still much room for improvement for both image and radio retrieval. As the GT overlap baseline is far from the perfect 100% recall, frame-to-frame matching and pose estimation have also much room to improve.

Varying Field-of-View: We study the impact of the FOV of the HoloLens 2 device via two configurations: 1) Each camera in a rig is seen as a single-frame and localized using LO-RANSAC + P3P. 2) We consider all four cameras in a frame and localize them together using the generalized solver GP3P. NetVLAD retrieval with SuperPoint and SuperGlue only achieves 36.6%/45.8% recall, compared to the results from Table 3 (46.3%/59.8%). Rig localization thus provides much better performance, mainly in hard cases where single cameras face texture-less areas, such as the ground and walls.

Mapping Modality: We study whether the high-quality lidar mesh can be used for localization. We consider two approaches to obtain a sparse 3D point cloud: 1) By triangulating sparse visual correspondences across multiple views. 2) By lifting 2D keypoints in reference images to 3D by tracing rays through the mesh. Lifting can leverage dense correspondences, which cannot be efficiently triangulated with conventional multi-view geometry. We thus compare 1) and 2) with SuperGlue to 2) with LoFT [74], a state-of-the-art dense matcher. The results (Table 4 right) show that the mesh brings

Table 4. Impact of mapping. Left: Scenarios. Building the map with sparse HD 360 images from the NavVis rig, instead of or with dense AR sequences, boosts the localization performance for HL2 as it makes image retrieval easier – NetVLAD tends to incorrectly retrieve same-device HL images over same-location phone images. This does not help phone localization, likely due to the viewpoint sparsity. **Right: Modalities.** Lifting 2D points to 3D using the lidar mesh instead of triangulating with SfM is beneficial. This can also leverage dense matching, e.g. with LoFTR.

Mapping images →	HL2 + Phone			HD 360	Both	
Image pairs from →	Retrieval		GT	Retrieval	Retrieval	
Matching Device	NetVLAD	+ Poses	overlap	+ Poses	+ Poses	
SP + SG HL2	46.6 / 59.6	46.3 / 59.8	47.4 / 60.2	69.3 / 81.8	68.6 / 80.3	
Phone	48.8 / 63.3	49.3 / 62.8	49.9 / 63.0	48.2 / 63.3	51.1 / 65.4	

Chart (recall @ $(5°, 1m)$): HL2: 59.8, 60.9, 60.4. Phone: 62.8, 64.3, 64.2. Legend: SP+SG, SfM | SP+SG, lift | LoFTR, lift

some improvements. Points could also be lifted by dense depth from multi-view stereo. We however did not obtain satisfactory results with a state-of-the-art approach [84] as it cannot handle very sparse mapping images.

Mapping Scenario: We study the accuracy of localization against maps built from different types of images: 1) crowd-sourced, dense AR sequences; 2) curated, sparser HD 360 images from the NavVis device; 3) a combination of the two. The results are summarized in Table 4 (left), showing that the mapping scenario has a large impact on the final numbers. On the other hand, image pair selection for mapping matters little. Current crowd-sourcing approaches do not yield as good results as capturing a space using a specialized scanning device at high density. Further, crowd-sourcing and manual scans can complement each other. We hope that future work can close the gap between the scenarios to achieve better metrics from crowd-sourced data without curation.

5.2 Multi-frame Localization

Inspired by typical AR use cases, we consider the problem of multi-frame localization in this section. The task is to align multiple consecutive frames of varied lengths and aggregated radio signals against the database map. Our baseline for this task is based on the ground-truthing pipeline and has as such relatively high compute requirements. However, we are primarily interested to demonstrate the potential performance gains by leveraging multiple frames. First, we run image retrieval and single-frame localization, followed by a first PGO with tracking and localization poses. Then, we do a second localization with retrieval guided by the poses of the first PGO, followed by a second PGO. Finally, we run a pose refinement by considering reprojections to query frames and tracking cost. Additionally, we can also use radio to restrict image retrieval throughout the pipeline. We keep the same accuracy metric as before, considering only the last frame in each multi-frame query, which is the one that influences the current AR user experience in a real-time scenario.

We evaluate various query sizes and introduce the *time-to-recall* metric as: sequence length (time) until successful localization at X% (recall) for a tight threshold (1°, 10 cm) (TTR@X%). Methods should aim to minimize this metric to render retrieved content as quickly as possible after starting an AR experience. We show the results for the CAB scene in Fig. 6. While the performance of current methods is not satisfactory yet to achieve a TTR@90% under 20 s, using multi-frame localization leads to significant gains of 20–40%. The radio signals improve the performance in particular with shorter sequences and thus effectively reduce time-to-recall.

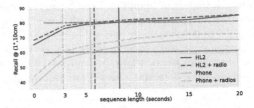

Fig. 6. Multi-frame localization. We report the localization recall of SuperPoint+SuperGlue as we increase the duration of each sequence. The pipeline leverages both on-device tracking and absolute retrieval, as vision-only (solid) or combined with radio signals (dashed). We show the TTR@80% for HL2 (blue) and TTR@60% for phone queries (orange). Using radio signals reduce the TTR from 8 s to 5 s and from 5 s to 3 s, respectively. (Color figure online)

6 Conclusion

In this paper, we identified several key limitations of current localization and mapping benchmarks that make them unrealistic in the context of AR. To address these limitations, we developed a new GT pipeline to accurately and robustly register realistic AR scenario captures in large and diverse scenes against laser scans without any manual labelling or setup of custom infrastructure. With this new benchmark, initially consisting of 3 large locations (note that we will add more locations over time), we revisited the traditional academic setup and showed a large performance gap for existing state-of-the-art methods when evaluated using our more realistic and challenging dataset. By implementation of simple yet representative baselines to take advantage of the AR specific setup, we present novel insights and pave several avenues of future work. In particular, we showed huge potential for leveraging query sequences instead of single frames as well as leveraging other sensor modalities like radio signals or depth data in the localization and mapping problem. Furthermore, we hope to direct research attention to not only tackle the localization problem in isolation but also improve map representations as well as consider the currently largely ignored time-to-recall metric. The dataset and the source code of the GT pipeline will be available to the community. We will also host an evaluation server to facilitate benchmarking of future work.

Acknowledgements. This paper would not have been possible without the hard work and contributions of Gabriela Evrova, Silvano Galliani, Michael Baumgartner, Cedric Cagniart, Jeffrey Delmerico, Jonas Hein, Dawid Jeczmionek, Mirlan Karimov, Maximilian Mews, Patrick Misteli, Juan Nieto, Sònia Batllori Pallarès, Rémi Pautrat, Songyou Peng, Iago Suarez, Rui Wang, Jeremy Wanner, Silvan Weder and our colleagues in CVG at ETH Zürich and the wider Microsoft Mixed Reality & AI team.

References

1. Agarwal, S., Mierle, K., et al.: Ceres solver. http://ceres-solver.org
2. Arandjelovic, R.: Three things everyone should know to improve object retrieval. In: CVPR (2012)
3. Arandjelovic, R., Gronat, P., Torii, A., Pajdla, T., Sivic, J.: NetVLAD: CNN architecture for weakly supervised place recognition. In: Proceedings of the CVPR (2016)
4. Badino, H., Huber, D., Kanade, T.: The CMU visual localization data set (2011). http://3dvis.ri.cmu.edu/data-sets/localization
5. Bahl, P., Padmanabhan, V.N.: RADAR: an in-building RF-based user location and tracking system. In: INFOCOM (2000)
6. Balntas, V., Lenc, K., Vedaldi, A., Mikolajczyk, K.: HPatches: a benchmark and evaluation of handcrafted and learned local descriptors. In: Proceedings of the CVPR (2017)
7. Bay, H., Ess, A., Tuytelaars, T., Van Gool, L.: Speeded-up robust features (SURF). CVIU **110**, 346–359 (2008)
8. Brachmann, E., Humenberger, M., Rother, C., Sattler, T.: On the limits of pseudo ground truth in visual camera re-localisation. In: Proceedings of the ICCV (2021)
9. Brachmann, E., Rother, C.: Expert sample consensus applied to camera re-localization. In: ICCV (2019)
10. Brachmann, E., Rother, C.: Visual camera re-localization from RGB and RGB-D images using DSAC. T-PAMI **44**, 5847–5865 (2021)
11. Cao, B., Araujo, A., Sim, J.: Unifying deep local and global features for image search. In: Vedaldi, A., Bischof, H., Brox, T., Frahm, J.-M. (eds.) ECCV 2020. LNCS, vol. 12365, pp. 726–743. Springer, Cham (2020). https://doi.org/10.1007/978-3-030-58565-5_43
12. Carlevaris-Bianco, N., Ushani, A.K., Eustice, R.M.: University of Michigan North Campus long-term vision and lidar dataset. Int. J. Robot. Res. **35**, 1023–1035 (2015)
13. Chan, Y.T., Tsui, W.Y., So, H.C., Chung Ching, P.: Time-of-arrival based localization under NLOS conditions. IEEE Trans. Veh. Technol. **55**, 17–24 (2006)
14. Chen, D.M., et al.: City-scale landmark identification on mobile devices. In: CVPR (2011)
15. Choi, S., Zhou, Q.Y., Koltun, V.: Robust reconstruction of indoor scenes. In: CVPR, pp. 5556–5565 (2015)
16. Chum, O., Matas, J., Kittler, J.: Locally optimized RANSAC. In: Joint Pattern Recognition Symposium, pp. 236–243 (2003)
17. Cohen-Steiner, D., Da, F.: A greedy Delaunay-based surface reconstruction algorithm. Vis. Comput. **20**(1), 4–16 (2004)
18. Comsa, C.R., Luo, J., Haimovich, A., Schwartz, S.: Wireless localization using time difference of arrival in narrow-band multipath systems. In: 2007 International Symposium on Signals, Circuits and Systems (2007)
19. Dai, A., Chang, A.X., Savva, M., Halber, M., Funkhouser, T., Nießner, M.: ScanNet: richly-annotated 3D reconstructions of indoor scenes. In: CVPR (2017)
20. DeTone, D., Malisiewicz, T., Rabinovich, A.: SuperPoint: self-supervised interest point detection and description. In: CVPR workshops (2018)
21. Dusmanu, M., Miksik, O., Schönberger, J.L., Pollefeys, M.: Cross-descriptor visual localization and mapping. In: ICCV (2021)
22. Dusmanu, M., et al.: D2-Net: a trainable CNN for joint detection and description of local features. In: CVPR (2019)
23. Dusmanu, M., Schönberger, J.L., Sinha, S., Pollefeys, M.: Privacy-preserving image features via adversarial affine subspace embeddings. In: CVPR (2021)
24. Fischler, M.A., Bolles, R.C.: Random sample consensus: a paradigm for model fitting with applications to image analysis and automated cartography. Commun. ACM **24**, 381–395 (1981)

25. Geppert, M., Larsson, V., Speciale, P., Schönberger, J.L., Pollefeys, M.: Privacy preserving structure-from-motion. In: Vedaldi, A., Bischof, H., Brox, T., Frahm, J.-M. (eds.) ECCV 2020. LNCS, vol. 12346, pp. 333–350. Springer, Cham (2020). https://doi.org/10.1007/978-3-030-58452-8_20

26. Geppert, M., Larsson, V., Speciale, P., Schonberger, J.L., Pollefeys, M.: Privacy preserving localization and mapping from uncalibrated cameras. In: CVPR (2021)

27. Grisetti, G., Kümmerle, R., Stachniss, C., Burgard, W.: A tutorial on graph-based slam. IEEE Intell. Transp. Syst. Mag. **2**(4), 31–43 (2010)

28. He, S., Chan, S.H.G.: Wi-fi fingerprint-based indoor positioning: recent advances and comparisons. IEEE Commun. Surv. Tutor. **18**, 466–490 (2016)

29. Hee Lee, G., Li, B., Pollefeys, M., Fraundorfer, F.: Minimal solutions for pose estimation of a multi-camera system. In: Inaba, M., Corke, P. (eds.) Robotics Research. STAR, vol. 114, pp. 521–538. Springer, Cham (2016). https://doi.org/10.1007/978-3-319-28872-7_30

30. Hodaň, T., et al.: BOP: benchmark for 6D object pose estimation. In: Ferrari, V., Hebert, M., Sminchisescu, C., Weiss, Y. (eds.) ECCV 2018. LNCS, vol. 11214, pp. 19–35. Springer, Cham (2018). https://doi.org/10.1007/978-3-030-01249-6_2

31. Humenberger, M., et al.: Robust image retrieval-based visual localization using kapture. arXiv preprint arXiv:2007.13867 (2020)

32. Hyeon, J., Kim, J., Doh, N.: Pose correction for highly accurate visual localization in large-scale indoor spaces. In: ICCV (2021)

33. Jégou, H., Douze, M., Schmid, C., Pérez, P.: Aggregating local descriptors into a compact image representation. In: CVPR (2010)

34. Jin, Y., et al.: Image matching across wide baselines: from paper to practice. Int. J. Comput. Vis. **129**, 517–547 (2020)

35. Johns, E., Yang, G.Z.: Feature co-occurrence maps: appearance-based localisation throughout the day. In: ICRA (2013)

36. Kendall, A., Cipolla, R.: Geometric loss functions for camera pose regression with deep learning. In: CVPR (2017)

37. Kendall, A., Grimes, M., Cipolla, R.: PoseNet: a convolutional network for real-time 6-DoF camera relocalization. In: ICCV (2015)

38. Khalajmehrabadi, A., Gatsis, N., Akopian, D.: Modern WLAN fingerprinting indoor positioning methods and deployment challenges (2016)

39. Laoudias, C., Michaelides, M.P., Panayiotou, C.G.: Fault detection and mitigation in WLAN RSS fingerprint-based positioning. J. Locat. Based Serv. **6**, 101–116 (2012)

40. Lee, D., et al.: Large-scale localization datasets in crowded indoor spaces. In: CVPR (2021)

41. Li, X., Ylioinas, J., Verbeek, J., Kannala, J.: Scene coordinate regression with angle-based reprojection loss for camera relocalization. In: ECCV workshop (2018)

42. Li, Y., Snavely, N., Huttenlocher, D., Fua, P.: Worldwide pose estimation using 3D point clouds. In: Fitzgibbon, A., Lazebnik, S., Perona, P., Sato, Y., Schmid, C. (eds.) ECCV 2012. LNCS, vol. 7572, pp. 15–29. Springer, Heidelberg (2012). https://doi.org/10.1007/978-3-642-33718-5_2

43. Lowe, D.G.: Distinctive image features from scale-invariant keypoints. IJCV **60**, 91–110 (2004)

44. Maddern, W., Pascoe, G., Linegar, C., Newman, P.: 1 year, 1000 km: the Oxford RobotCar dataset. IJRR **36**, 3–15 (2017)

45. Massiceti, D., Krull, A., Brachmann, E., Rother, C., Torr, P.H.S.: Random forests versus neural networks - what's best for camera localization? In: ICRA (2017)

46. Meng, L., Chen, J., Tung, F., Little, J.J., Valentin, J., de Silva, C.W.: Backtracking regression forests for accurate camera relocalization. In: IROS (2017)

47. Mikolajczyk, K., Schmid, C.: Scale and affine invariant interest point detectors. IJCV **60**, 63–86 (2004)

48. Milford, M.J., Wyeth, G.F.: SeqSLAM: visual route-based navigation for sunny summer days and stormy winter nights. In: ICRA (2012)
49. Mishchuk, A., Mishkin, D., Radenovic, F., Matas, J.: Working hard to know your neighbor's margins: local descriptor learning loss. In: NeurIPS (2017)
50. Ng, T., Lopez-Rodriguez, A., Balntas, V., Mikolajczyk, K.: Reassessing the limitations of CNN methods for camera pose regression. arXiv (2021)
51. Peng, R., Sichitiu, M.L.: Angle of arrival localization for wireless sensor networks. In: 2006 3rd Annual IEEE Communications Society on Sensor and Ad Hoc Communications and Networks (2006)
52. Pion, N., Humenberger, M., Csurka, G., Cabon, Y., Sattler, T.: Benchmarking image retrieval for visual localization. In: 3DV (2020)
53. Pless, R.: Using many cameras as one. In: CVPR (2003)
54. Radenović, F., Tolias, G., Chum, O.: Fine-tuning CNN image retrieval with no human annotation. T-PAMI 41(7), 1655–1668 (2018)
55. Rau, A., Garcia-Hernando, G., Stoyanov, D., Brostow, G.J., Turmukhambetov, D.: Predicting visual overlap of images through interpretable non-metric box embeddings. In: Vedaldi, A., Bischof, H., Brox, T., Frahm, J.-M. (eds.) ECCV 2020. LNCS, vol. 12350, pp. 629–646. Springer, Cham (2020). https://doi.org/10.1007/978-3-030-58558-7_37
56. Reina, S.C., Solin, A., Rahtu, E., Kannala, J.: ADVIO: an authentic dataset for visual-inertial odometry. In: ECCV (2018). http://arxiv.org/abs/1807.09828
57. Revaud, J., Almazán, J., de Rezende, R.S., de Souza, C.R.: Learning with average precision: training image retrieval with a listwise loss. In: ICCV (2019)
58. Revaud, J., Weinzaepfel, P., de Souza, C.R., Humenberger, M.: R2D2: repeatable and reliable detector and descriptor. In: NeurIPS (2019)
59. Rublee, E., Rabaud, V., Konolige, K., Bradski, G.: ORB: an efficient alternative to SIFT or SURF. In: ICCV (2011)
60. Rusinkiewicz, S., Levoy, M.: Efficient variants of the ICP algorithm. In: 3DIM (2001)
61. Sarlin, P.E., Cadena, C., Siegwart, R., Dymczyk, M.: From coarse to fine: robust hierarchical localization at large scale. In: CVPR (2019)
62. Sarlin, P.E., DeTone, D., Malisiewicz, T., Rabinovich, A.: SuperGlue: learning feature matching with graph neural networks. In: CVPR (2020)
63. Sarlin, P.E., et al.: Back to the feature: learning robust camera localization from pixels to pose. In: CVPR (2021)
64. Sattler, T., Leibe, B., Kobbelt, L.: Improving image-based localization by active correspondence search. In: Fitzgibbon, A., Lazebnik, S., Perona, P., Sato, Y., Schmid, C. (eds.) ECCV 2012. LNCS, vol. 7572, pp. 752–765. Springer, Heidelberg (2012). https://doi.org/10.1007/978-3-642-33718-5_54
65. Sattler, T., et al.: Benchmarking 6DOF outdoor visual localization in changing conditions. In: CVPR (2018)
66. Sattler, T., Weyand, T., Leibe, B., Kobbelt, L.P.: Image retrieval for image-based localization revisited. In: BMVC (2012)
67. Schönberger, J., Frahm, J.M.: Structure-from-motion revisited. In: CVPR (2016)
68. Schönberger, J.L., Hardmeier, H., Sattler, T., Pollefeys, M.: Comparative evaluation of hand-crafted and learned local features. In: Proceedings of the CVPR (2017)
69. Schönberger, J.L., Pollefeys, M., Geiger, A., Sattler, T.: Semantic visual localization. In: CVPR (2018)
70. Schops, T., et al.: A multi-view stereo benchmark with high-resolution images and multi-camera videos. In: CVPR (2017)
71. Shibuya, M., Sumikura, S., Sakurada, K.: Privacy preserving visual SLAM. In: Vedaldi, A., Bischof, H., Brox, T., Frahm, J.-M. (eds.) ECCV 2020. LNCS, vol. 12367, pp. 102–118. Springer, Cham (2020). https://doi.org/10.1007/978-3-030-58542-6_7

72. Shotton, J., Glocker, B., Zach, C., Izadi, S., Criminisi, A., Fitzgibbon, A.: Scene coordinate regression forests for camera relocalization in RGB-D images. In: CVPR (2013)
73. Speciale, P., Schönberger, J.L., Kang, S.B., Sinha, S.N., Pollefeys, M.: Privacy preserving image-based localization. In: CVPR (2019)
74. Sun, J., Shen, Z., Wang, Y., Bao, H., Zhou, X.: LoFTR: detector-free local feature matching with transformers. In: CVPR (2021)
75. Sun, X., Xie, Y., Luo, P., Wang, L.: A dataset for benchmarking image-based localization. In: CVPR (2017)
76. Taira, H., et al.: InLoc: indoor visual localization with dense matching and view synthesis. In: CVPR (2018)
77. Tian, Y., Yu, X., Fan, B., Wu, F., Heijnen, H., Balntas, V.: SOSNet: second order similarity regularization for local descriptor learning. In: CVPR (2019)
78. Tolias, G., Avrithis, Y., Jégou, H.: To aggregate or not to aggregate: selective match kernels for image search. In: ICCV (2013)
79. Torii, A., Arandjelović, R., Sivic, J., Okutomi, M., Pajdla, T.: 24/7 place recognition by view synthesis. In: CVPR (2015)
80. Umeyama, S.: Least-squares estimation of transformation parameters between two point patterns. IEEE Trans. Pattern Anal. Mach. Intell. **13**(04), 376–380 (1991)
81. Ungureanu, D., et al.: HoloLens 2 research mode as a tool for computer vision research (2020)
82. Valentin, J., Niessner, M., Shotton, J., Fitzgibbon, A., Izadi, S., Torr, P.H.S.: Exploiting uncertainty in regression forests for accurate camera relocalization. In: CVPR (2015)
83. Wald, J., Sattler, T., Golodetz, S., Cavallari, T., Tombari, F.: Beyond controlled environments: 3D camera re-localization in changing indoor scenes. In: Vedaldi, A., Bischof, H., Brox, T., Frahm, J.-M. (eds.) ECCV 2020. LNCS, vol. 12352, pp. 467–487. Springer, Cham (2020). https://doi.org/10.1007/978-3-030-58571-6_28
84. Wang, F., Galliani, S., Vogel, C., Speciale, P., Pollefeys, M.: PatchMatchNet: learned multi-view patchmatch stereo (2021)
85. Wang, S., Laskar, Z., Melekhov, I., Li, X., Kannala, J.: Continual learning for image-based camera localization. In: ICCV (2021)
86. Wenzel, P., et al.: 4Seasons: a cross-season dataset for multi-weather SLAM in autonomous driving. In: GCPR (2020)
87. Yang, H., Antonante, P., Tzoumas, V., Carlone, L.: Graduated non-convexity for robust spatial perception: from non-minimal solvers to global outlier rejection. RA-L **5**(2), 1127–1134 (2020)
88. Yi, K.M., Trulls, E., Lepetit, V., Fua, P.: LIFT: learned invariant feature transform. In: Leibe, B., Matas, J., Sebe, N., Welling, M. (eds.) ECCV 2016. LNCS, vol. 9910, pp. 467–483. Springer, Cham (2016). https://doi.org/10.1007/978-3-319-46466-4_28
89. Zhou, Q.Y., Park, J., Koltun, V.: Open3D: a modern library for 3D data processing. arXiv:1801.09847 (2018)

Unitail: Detecting, Reading, and Matching in Retail Scene

Fangyi Chen[1]([⊠]), Han Zhang[1], Zaiwang Li[2], Jiachen Dou[1], Shentong Mo[1], Hao Chen[1], Yongxin Zhang[3], Uzair Ahmed[1], Chenchen Zhu[1], and Marios Savvides[1]

[1] Carnegie Mellon University, Pittsburgh, PA 15213, USA
{fangyic,hanz3,jiachend,shentonm,haoc3,uzaira,marioss}@andrew.cmu.edu,
chenchez@alumni.cmu.edu
[2] University of Pittsburgh, Pittsburgh, PA 15213, USA
zal17@pitt.edu
[3] Tsinghua University, Beijing 100084, China
yx-zhang20@mails.tsinghua.edu.cn

Abstract. To make full use of computer vision technology in stores, it is required to consider the actual needs that fit the characteristics of the retail scene. Pursuing this goal, we introduce the United Retail Datasets (Unitail), a large-scale benchmark of basic visual tasks on products that challenges algorithms for detecting, reading, and matching. With 1.8M quadrilateral-shaped instances annotated, the Unitail offers a detection dataset to align product appearance better. Furthermore, it provides a gallery-style OCR dataset containing 1454 product categories, 30k text regions, and 21k transcriptions to enable robust reading on products and motivate enhanced product matching. Besides benchmarking the datasets using various start-of-the-arts, we customize a new detector for product detection and provide a simple OCR-based matching solution that verifies its effectiveness. The Unitail and its evaluation server is publicly available at https://unitedretail.github.io.

Keywords: Product detection · Product recognition · Text detection · Text recognition

1 Introduction

With the rise of deep learning, numerous computer vision algorithms have been developed and have pushed many real-world applications to a satisfactory level. Currently, various visual sensors (fixed cameras, robots, drones, mobile phones, etc.) are deployed in retail stores, enabling advanced computer vision methods in shopping and restocking. Scene Product Recognition (SPR) is the foundation

Supplementary Information The online version contains supplementary material available at https://doi.org/10.1007/978-3-031-20071-7_41.

module in most of these frameworks, such as planogram compliance, out-of-stock managing, and automatic check-out.

SPR refers to the automatic detection and recognition of products in complex retail scenes. It comprises steps that first localize products and then recognize them via the localized appearance, analogous to many recognition tasks. However, scene products have their characteristics: *they are densely-packed, low-shot, fine-grained, and widely-categorized*. These innate characteristics result in obvious challenges and will be a continuing problem. Recent datasets in retail scenes follow the typical setting in the common scene to initiate the momentum of research in SPR. For instance, the SKU110k dataset [17], which has recently enabled large-scale product detection, is following the MS-COCO [33] style annotation and evaluation metric. Despite their significant value, the underpaid attention to the SPR's characteristics leads us to the question: what is the next advance towards SPR?

Firstly, traditional detection targets poorly comply with the actual needs, causing improper image alignment of the product appearances. Detection targets in common scenes [9,11,33,57] are usually defined as covering the utmost visible entirety of an object with a minimal rectangle box. This format is inherited by most existing retail datasets [2,14,17,52,55]. However, because occlusion occurs more frequently between products (the densely-packed characteristic), improper alignments can easily hinder the detection performance. Detectors equipped with Non-Maximum Suppression (NMS) suffer from the overlaps among the axis-aligned rectangular bounding boxes (AABB) and rotated rectangular bounding boxes (RBOX). Moreover, poor alignment leads to inconsistent image registration of the same products, which brings extra difficulties to accurate recognition.

Secondly, even in the well-aligned cases, products from intra-classes require discriminative features due to their fine-grained characteristic. On the one hand, a slight variation in the product packaging can significantly change the product price, especially for the visually similar but textually different regions such as brand/model, flavour/version, ingredient/material, count/net weight. This requires SPR algorithms to pay attention to the particular text patterns. On the other hand, due to the labelling effort on thousands of categories per store (the widely-categorized characteristic), the available samples per category are scarce (the low-shot characteristic), which degrades the SPR robustness. These two constraints are in conjunction with our empirical observation that visual classifiers could frequently make mistakes when products look similar but vary in text information.

In this paper, we introduce the United Retail Datasets (Unitail) that responds to these issues. The Unitail is a comprehensive benchmark composed of two datasets: *Unitail-Det* and *Unitail-OCR*, and currently supports four tasks in real-world retail scene: *Product Detection, Text Detection, Text Recognition,* and *Product Matching* (Fig. 1).

Unitail-Det, as one of the largest quadrilateral object detection datasets in terms of instance number and the only existing product dataset in quadrilateral annotations by far, is designed to support well-aligned product detection. Unitail-Det enjoys two key features: 1. Bounding boxes of products are densely

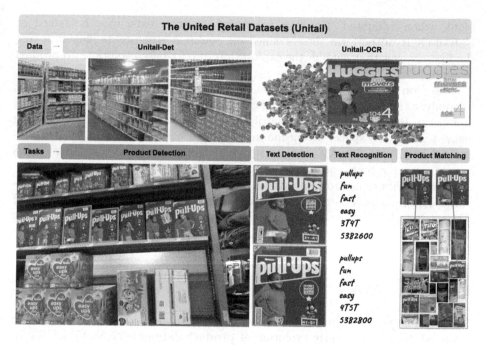

Fig. 1. The Unitail is a large-scale benchmark in retail scene that consists of two sub-datasets and supports four basic tasks.

annotated in the quadrilateral style that cover the frontal face of products. Practically, Quadrilaterals (QUADs) adequately reflect the shapes and poses of most products regardless of the viewing angles, and efficiently cover the irregular shapes. The frontal faces of products provide distinguishable visual information and keep the appearances consistent. 2. In order to evaluate the robustness of the detectors across stores, the test set consists of two subsets to support both origin-domain and cross-domain evaluation. While one subset shares the domain with the training set, the other is independently collected from other different stores, with diverse optical sensors, and from various camera perspectives.

Unitail-OCR (Optical Character Recognition) aims to drive research and applications using visual texts as representations for products. This direction is partially inspired by the customers' behavior: people can glance and recognize ice cream but need to scrutinize the flavor and calories to make a purchase. It is organized into three tasks: text detection, text recognition, and product matching. Product images in Unitail-OCR are selected from the Unitail-Det and benefit from the quadrilateral aligned annotations. Each is equipped with on-product text location and textual contents together with its category. Due to the product's low-shot and widely-categorized characteristics, product recognition is operated by matching within an open-set gallery. To the best of our knowledge, Unitail-OCR is the first dataset to support OCR models' training and evaluation on the retail products, and it is experimentally verified to fill in the domain blank; when evaluated on a wide variety of product texts, models trained on Unitail-OCR outperform those trained on common scene texts [24]. It is also the first dataset that enables the exploration of text-based solutions to product matching.

Based on the proposed Unitail, we design two baselines. To detect products, we analyze the limitation of applying generic object detectors in the retail scene and design RetailDet to detect quadrilateral products. To match products using visual texts on 2D space, we encode text features with spatial positional encoding and use Hungarian Algorithm [28] that calculates optimal assignment plans between varying text sequences.

Our contributions are summarized in three folds: **(1)** we introduce the Unitail, a comprehensive benchmark for well-aligned textually enhanced SPR. **(2)** We benchmark the tasks of Unitail with various off-the-shelf methods, including [12, 19–21, 29–31, 36, 39, 42, 47, 48, 50, 53, 54, 56, 60, 64]. **(3)** we design two baselines for product detection and text-based product matching.

2   Related Work

The retail scene has drawn attention to the computer vision community for an extended period. The early evolution of product datasets [27, 35, 45] facilitates reliable training and evaluation and drives research in this challenging field. Recently, large-scale datasets [5, 17] has enabled deep learning based approaches. Datasets related to SPR can be split into two groups: product detection and product recognition. We address each in this section.

Product Detection Datasets. Detection is the first step in SPR entailing the presence of products that are typically represented by rectangular bounding boxes. The GroZi-120 [35] was created using in situ and in vitro data to study the product detection and recognition with 120 grocery products varying in color, size, and shape. The D2S [13] is an instance segmentation benchmark for sparsely-placed product detection, with 21000 images and 72447 instances. The SKU110k [17] and the SKU110k-r [40] provide 11762 images with 1.7M on-shelf product instances; they are annotated with axis-aligned bounding boxes and rotated bounding boxes, respectively.

For the detection of coarsely categorized products, The RPC [55] is designed for checkout scenarios containing 0.4M instances and 200 products. The Grocery Shelves dataset [52] took 354 shelf images and 13k instances, and around 3k instances are noted in 10 brand classes. The Locount [2] simultaneously considers the detection and counting for groups of products, with an impressive number of 1.9M instances and 140 categories.

Despite the significant values of these datasets, we are still challenged by the availability of optimal bounding boxes. In the proposed Unitail-Det, we aim to shape products into quadrilaterals whose appearances are well aligned. The dataset also provides evaluation targets in the origin-domain and cross-domain, bringing algorithms closer to practical deployment.

Product Recognition Datasets. Multiple product recognition datasets have been built over the past decades. Early ones have limitations in the diversity of categories and amount of images, such as the SOIL-47 [27] containing 47 categories, the Supermarket Produce Datasets [45] with 15 categories, and the Freiburg Groceries [23] covering 25 categories. Recent collections like Products-6K [16] and Products-10K [1] focus on large-scale data, which satisfy the training of deep learning algorithms. AliProducts [5] is crawled from web sources by searching 50K product names, consequently containing 2.5 million noisy images without human annotations. The ABO [7] dataset covers 576 categories that studies the 3D object understanding. The Grozi-3.2K [14] contains 80 fine-grained grocery categories and 8350 images for multi-label classification. To the best of our knowledge, there is a lack of a dataset that encourages leveraging both visual and textual information for product recognition.

OCR on Retail Products. Product recognition by texts is challenging. The lack of datasets obstructs the relevant research on this topic. The most relevant dataset is Products-6K [16] where the Google Cloud Vision API is employed to extract the textual information to enhance products' descriptions. But the texts were not labelled by human annotators, and text location information is missing, so it is infeasible to support any advance to OCR related tasks.

There are a couple of attempts that use off-the-shelf OCR models for assisted shopping. [15] presented a system on which users search products by name and OCR models return the texts on products so that a product list ranked by word histogram is generated for the users. [38] recognize texts and then apply text embedding and language models to extract features for product verification.

Other Related Datasets. Many OCR datasets [6, 18, 22, 24, 25, 34, 37, 44, 49, 59] exist prior to Unitail-OCR. Typically, an OCR dataset supports text detection and text recognition and so enables text spotting. The ICDAR2015 [24] and CTW1500 [34] are two widely applied benchmarks for training and evaluating OCR models in common scene. The ICDAR2015 has 1,000 training and 500 testing images causally shot indoor and outdoor with word-level annotations for each text. The CTW1500 contains 10k text (3.5k of them are curved boxes) in 1500 images collected from the internet. Compared to them, Unitail-OCR is the first that focuses on product texts and supports object-level matching task at the same time. Product texts are usually artistic words with substantial character distortions, which are hard to be localize and recognize.

3   The Unitail

3.1   Unitail-Det

Image Collection. Practically, the industry utilizes a variety of sensors under different conditions for product detection. The resolution and camera angles cover an extensive range by different sensors. For example, fixed cameras are

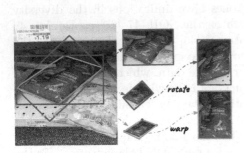

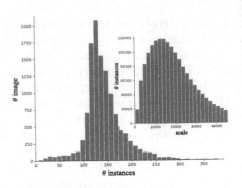

Fig. 2. Quadrilateral (in green) is a nature fit to product in real scene, removing more noisy contexts than AABB (in violet) and RBOX (in red)). (Color figure online)

Fig. 3. Unitail-Det statistics. Left: instance density. Right: instance scale

mounted on the ceiling in most cases, and customers prefer to photograph with mobile devices. The product categories in different stores also span a great range. With these factors in mind, we collect images from two sources to support origin-domain and cross-domain detection. *In the origin domain*, training and testing images are supposed to share the same domain and are taken from similar perspectives in the same stores by the same sensors. As a result, we select the 11,744 images from the prior largest product dataset, SKU110k [17], to form the origin domain. *In the cross domain*, we collect 500 images in different stores through multiple sensors, covering unseen categories and camera angles.

Annotation. We annotate each product with a quadrilateral style bounding box, denoted as QUAD. Figure 2 is an illustration of its advance. A QUAD refers to 4 points p_{tl}, p_{tr}, p_{br}, p_{bl} with 8 degrees of freedom (x_{tl}, y_{tl}, x_{tr}, y_{tr}, x_{br}, y_{br}, x_{bl}, y_{bl}). For regular products shaped mainly in cuboid and cylinder, the (x_{tl},y_{tl}) is defined as the top-left corners of their frontal faces, and the other points represent the rest 3 corners in clockwise order. For spherical, cones, and other shapes whose corners are difficult to identify, and for irregularly shaped products where so defined quadrilateral box cannot cover the entire frontal face, we first draw the minimum AABB and then adjust the four corners according to the camera perspective. As belabored, the frontal face of a product has the most representative information and is also critical for appearance consistency, but we still annotate the side face if the front face is invisible.

Totally, 1,777,108 QUADs are annotated by 13 well-trained annotators in 3 rounds of verification. The origin-domain is split to training (8,216 images, 1,215,013 QUADs), validation (588 images, 92,128 QUADs), and origin-domain testing set (2,940 images, 432,896 QUADs). The cross-domain supports a testing set (500 images, 37,071 QUADs). Their density and scale are shown in Fig. 3

3.2   Unitail-OCR

Gallery and Testing Suite. A product gallery setup is a common practice in the retail industry for product matching applications. All known categories are first registered in the gallery. In case of a query product, the matching algorithms find the top ranked category in the gallery. The gallery of Unitail-OCR contains 1454 fine-grained and one-shot product categories. Among these products, 10709 text regions and 7565 legible text transcriptions (words) are annotated. This enables the gallery to act as the training source and the matching reference.

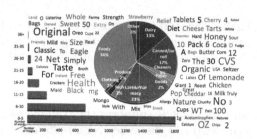

Fig. 4. Unitail-OCR statistical graphic. The pie chart reflects sections that source images were collected from. The bar chart is a histogram for the count of words on products. The font size of the words reflects the frequency of occurrence.

The testing suite contains four components: 1. 3012 products labeled with 18972 text regions for text detection. 2. Among the pre-localized text regions, 13416 legible word-level transcriptions for text recognition. 3. 10k product samples from the 1454 categories for general evaluation on product matching. 4. From the 10k products, we select 2.4k fine-grained samples (visually similar for humans) for hard-example evaluation on product matching.

Image Collection and Annotation. Images are gathered from the Unitail-Det cross-domain and cropped and affine transformed according to the quadrilateral bounding boxes to form an upright appearance. We remove the low-quality images with low resolution and high blurriness. Some products kept in the Unitail-OCR might exclude text regions, like those from the produce and clothes departments. We randomly select one sample from each category to form the product gallery, and the remaining is further augmented by randomly adjusting the brightness and cropping for matching purposes.

We annotate 29681 text regions from 4466 products as quadrilateral text boxes. Figure 4 shows the statistics. The bounding boxes are first classified as *legible* or *illegible*. For the 20981 legible ones, the alphanumeric transcriptions are annotated ignoring letter case and symbols. Numerical values with units are commonly seen on products such as *120mg*, and we regard them as entire words. We also provide a vocabulary that covers all words present. The usage of vocabulary is more practical in our case than in other scenes [24], because the presence of products and texts are usually known in advance by the store owner.

3.3   Tasks and Evaluation Metrics

Product Detection Task. The goal is to detect products as quadrilaterals from complex backgrounds. Unitail-Det supports the training and evaluation.

We use the geometric mean of mean average precision (mAP) calculated on the origin-domain test set and cross-domain test set as the primary metric for the product detection, where the mAP is calculated in MS-COCO style [33]. Compared to arithmetic mean, the geometric mean is more sensitive when the model overfits to origin-domain but gains low performance on the cross-domain.

Text Detection Task. The goal is to detect text regions from pre-localized product images. Unitail-OCR supports the training and evaluation.

We adopt the widely used precision, recall and hmean [24,34] for evaluation.

Text Recogniton Task. The goal is to recognize words over a set of pre-localized text regions. Unitail-OCR supports the training and evaluation.

We adopt the normalized edit distance (NED) [25] and word-level accuracy for evaluation. The edit distance between two words is defined by the minimum number of characters edited (insert, delete or substitute) required to change one into the other, then it is normalized by the length of the word and averaged on all ground-truths.

Product Matching Task. The goal is to recognize products by matching a set of query samples to the Unitail-OCR gallery. The task is split into two tracks: **Hard Example Track**, which is evaluated on 2.5k selected hard examples; this track is designed for scenarios in which products are visually similar (for example pharmacy stores). And **General Track**, which is conducted on all 10k samples.

We adopt the top-1 accuracy as the evaluation metric.

4   Two Baselines Designed for the Unitail

4.1   A Customized Detector for Product Detection

Recent studies [4,26,51,61,62] on generic object detection apply prior-art DenseBox-style head [21] to multiple feature pyramid levels. The feature pyramid is generated via feature pyramid network (FPN) [32] and contains different levels that are gradually down-sampled but semantically enhanced. An anchor-free detection head is then attached to classify each pixel on the feature pyramid and predict axis-aligned bounding boxes (AABB).

During training, assigning ground-truths to each feature pixels on the feature pyramid plays a key role. *On each pyramid level*, the centerness [51] is widely used. It is an indicator to value how far a pixel locates from the center of a ground-truth: the farther, the more likely it is to predict an inaccurate box, and the lower centerness score it gains. *Across pyramid levels*, various strategies are proposed to determine which level should be assigned, and they are grouped into scale-based and loss-based strategies. The scale-based [26, 32, 43, 51] assigns ground-truths to different levels in terms of their scales. The larger scale, the higher level is assigned so that the needs of receptive field and resolution of feature maps are balanced. The loss-based like Soft Selection [62] assigns ground-truths by calculating their losses on all levels, and trains an auxiliary network that re-weights the losses. Our design, RetailDet, adopts the DenseBox style architecture but predicts the four corners of quadrilateral by 8-channel regression head. During training, we found the prior assignment strategies unsuitable for quadrilateral products, which is specified below.

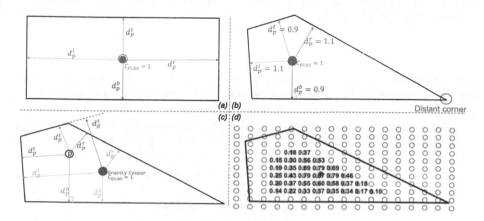

Fig. 5. (a): C_{FCOS} on AABB. (b): C_{FCOS} on QUAD. (c) and (d): C_{QUAD}.

Centerness. The previous definition of the centerness [51,62] is shown in Eq. 1,

$$C_{FCOS}(p) = [\frac{\min(d_p^l, d_p^r)}{\max(d_p^l, d_p^r)} \cdot \frac{\min(d_p^t, d_p^b)}{\max(d_p^t, d_p^b)}]^{0.5} \qquad (1)$$

by the Eq. 1 and Fig. 5(a), a location p keeps the same distance to the left/right boundaries $(d_p^l = d_p^r)$ and to the top/bottom boundaries $(d_p^t = d_p^b)$ will gain the highest centerness 1, and other pixels gain degraded score by Eq. 1.

Limitation. When adopting the same centerness to quadrilaterals, as shown in Fig. 5(b), the center can be far away from a distant corner, which leads to unbalanced regression difficulty and lack of receptive field from that corner.

Our Solution. We first re-define the *center* as the center of gravity (Fig. 5(c)), because it is the geometric center and represents the mean position of all the points in the shape, which mitigates the unbalanced regression difficulties. We then propose Eq. 2 to calculate the quad-centerness for any p,

$$C_{QUAD}(p) = [\frac{\min(d_p^l, d_g^l)}{\max(d^l, d_g^l)} \cdot \frac{\min(d_p^r, d_g^r)}{\max(d_p^r, d_g^r)} \cdot \frac{\min(d_p^t, d_g^t)}{\max(d_p^t, d_g^t)} \cdot \frac{\min(d_p^b, d_g^b)}{\max(d_p^b, d_g^b)}]^{0.5} \qquad (2)$$

where the $d_g^{l/r/t/b}$ denotes the distances between the gravity center g and the left/right/top/bottom boundaries. The $d_p^{l/r/t/b}$ denotes the distances between the p and the boundaries. If p locates on the gravity center, its quad-centerness gains the highest value as 1. Otherwise, it is gradually degraded (See Fig. 5(d)).

It is mentionable that when applied to AABB, Eq. 2 is mathematically equivalent to Eq. 1, which is proved in supplementary.

Soft Selection. The loss-based Soft Selection in [62] outperforms scale-based strategies on generic objects because it assigns ground-truths to multiple levels and re-weights their losses. This is achieved by calculating losses for each object on all levels and using the losses to train an auxiliary network that predicts the re-weighting factors.

Limitation. Instances per image are numerous in densely-packed retail scene, and Soft Selection is highly inefficient (5×slower) due to the auxiliary network.

Our Solution. Can we maintain the merit of Soft Selection while accelerating the assignment? We approach this issue by mimicking the loss re-weighting mechanism of the auxiliary network using scale-based calculation. This is feasible because we find the Soft Selection, in essence, follows scale-based law (detailed in supplementary). Thus, we design Soft Scale (SS) in Eq. 3, 4, 5 and 6. For an arbitrary shaped object O with area $area_O$, SS assigns it to two adjacent levels l_i and l_j by Eq. 3 and 4 and calculates the loss-reweighting factors F_{li}, F_{lj} by Eq. 5 and 6.

$$l_i = \lceil l_{org} + log_2(\sqrt{area_O}/224) \rceil \tag{3}$$

$$l_j = \lfloor l_{org} + log_2(\sqrt{area_O}/224) \rfloor \tag{4}$$

$$F_{l_i} = log_2(\sqrt{area_O}/224) - \lfloor log_2(\sqrt{area_O}/224) \rfloor \tag{5}$$

$$F_{l_j} = 1 - F_{l_i} \tag{6}$$

where 224 is the ImageNet pre-training size. Objects with exact area 224^2 is assigned to l_{org}, in which case $l_i = l_j = l_{org}$. If an object is with area 223^2, SS assigns it to l_{org} with $F_{l_{org}} = 0.994$, and also to $(l_{org} - 1)$ with $F_{(l_{org}-1)} = 0.006$. In this work we fix l_{org} to be level 5 of feature pyramid. SS operates rapidly as scale-based strategies and keeps the loss-reweighting like Soft Selection.

4.2   A Simple Baseline for Product Matching

A number of directions can be explored on this new task, while in this paper, we design the simplest solution to verify the motivation: *people glance and recognize the product, and if products looks similar, they further scrutinize the text (if appears) to make decision.* To this end, we first apply a well-trained image classifier that extracts visual features $f_{g_i}^v$ from each gallery image g_i and feature f_p^v from query image p, and calculate the cosine similarity between each pair $(f_{g_i}^v, f_p^v)$ (termed as sim_i^v). If the highest ranking value sim_1^v and the second highest sim_2^v are close ($sim_1^v - sim_2^v \leq t$), we then read on products and calculate the textual similarity (termed as sim^t) to make decision by Eq. 7,

$$Decision = \underset{i \in [1,2]}{\text{argmax}} \left[w \cdot sim^t(g_i, p) + (1 - w) \cdot sim_i^v \right] \qquad (7)$$

where threshold t and coefficient w are tuned on validation set.

Our design focuses on how to calculate sim^t. We denote the on-product texts obtained from ground-truth or OCR prediction as $S = \{s^1, s^2, \ldots, s^N\}$ where N varies. People may propose to utilize sequence-to-one models (like BERT [8]) to encode S into a fixed length feature vector $f \in \mathbb{R}^d$. As shown in Fig. 6(a), a text detector is followed by a text recognizer predicting $n = 5$ words, and the 5 words are fed into the BERT to encode a feature vector $f_p \in \mathbb{R}^d$. For each gallery image g, the same process is operated to get a feature vector $f_g \in \mathbb{R}^d$, and $sim^t(f_p, f_g)$ is calculated by the cosine similarity.

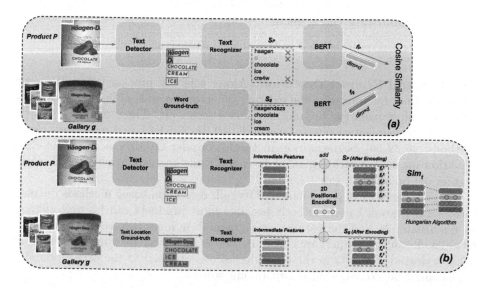

Fig. 6. (a) Pipeline with BERT encoded features, (b) Pipeline with positional encoding and Hungarian Algorithm based textual similarity.

But this design does not perform well because errors from OCR models (especially from text recognizer) are propagated to the BERT causing poor feature encoding. Moreover, the positional information of text boxes is lost in the sequence. So we design a new method in Fig. 6(b). Rather than using the n recognized words, we use the n intermediate feature vectors from the text recognizer to mitigate propagated errors. For example, *CREAM* is confused as *CRE4w*, but the intermediate feature should maintain information on A and M, which is more robust than the false prediction. Each feature is then added by a 2D positional encoding [3,41] whose calculation is based on the location of the corresponding text. It encodes the spatial information into the feature and it is predefined to keep the same dimension as the intermediate feature. Finally, we get a sequence that contains the n encoded features $f^{1 \sim n}$. As shown we get

716 F. Chen et al.

$S_p = \{f_p^1, f_p^2, f_p^3, f_p^4, f_p^5\}$ from a query product and $S_g = \{f_g^1, f_g^2, f_g^3, f_g^4\}$ from a gallery reference. Inspired by the Hungarian Algorithm [28], we design Eq. 8 to directly calculate the similarity between two sequence with varying length:

$$sim^t(p,g) = sim^t(S_p, S_g) = \max_X \sum_{i=1}^{n} \sum_{j=1}^{m} \left(\frac{f_p^i \cdot f_g^j}{|f_p^i| \cdot |f_g^j|} X_{ij} \right) \tag{8}$$

where the X is a $n \times m$ boolean matrix where $\sum_j X_{ij} = 1, \sum_i X_{ij} = 1$. Equation 8 maximizes the summation of cosine similarities from assigned feature pairs, and the assignment is optimized by X.

5 Experiments

5.1 Benchmarking the Unitail

The implementation is detailed in the supplementary materials.

Quadrilateral Product Detection. Along with the proposed RetailDet, we build baselines by borrowing the existing detectors capable of detecting quadrilaterals, mainly from the textual and aerial scenes [9]. These methods can be grouped into segmentation based methods [19,31,53,54,64] and regression based methods [36,42,56]. Segmentation methods consider QUADs as per-pixel classification masks for each region of interest, while regression methods directly regress the bounding boxes.

Table 1 shows their performances. Overall, regression based methods outperform segmentation based methods because most products can be well aligned by quadrilaterals, and the learning on segmentation mask involves extra difficulties. The RetailDet outperforms other detectors by a large margin. All detectors achieve degraded results in the cross-domain as opposed to the origin-domain, confirming that domain shift exists among stores.

Table 1. Benchmarking product detection on the Unitail. All methods are trained and tested under same setting. g-mAP is the geometric mean of mAPs.

#	Method	Backbone	g-mAP	Origin-domain			Cross-domain		
				mAP	AP50	AP75	mAP	AP50	AP75
1	FCENet [64]	ResNet50	32.0	36.8	76.0	31.2	27.9	60.1	22.6
2	PANet [54]	ResNet50	35.0	40.5	72.8	41.9	30.3	53.3	31.6
3	PSENet [53]	ResNet50	39.4	45.3	77.5	49.5	34.4	58.7	36.9
4	DBNet [31]	ResNet50	45.3	51.0	86.8	55.4	40.3	71.6	42.7
5	RIDet [36]	ResNet50	45.7	51.2	82.9	58.5	40.8	70.3	43.2
6	Gliding Vertex [56]	ResNet50	46.0	52.3	89.0	56.9	40.5	76.7	38.6
7	RSDet [42]	ResNet50	46.1	51.4	83.6	58.8	41.4	71.1	44.4
8	Mask-RCNN [19]	ResNet50	52.4	57.3	91.6	66.0	48.0	77.9	53.2
9	RetailDet (ours)	ResNet50	54.7	58.7	91.6	68.4	50.9	80.6	56.7
10	RetailDet	ResNet101	57.1	60.3	92.8	70.6	54.1	83.5	60.6

Text Detection & Text Recognition. We benchmark the tasks of text detection and text recognition in Table 2 and Table 3, respectively. For each of the listed algorithms, it is trained under two setting: one is following a common setting that trained on SynthText [18] and ICDAR2015(IC15) [24] for text detection and on Synth90K [22] and SynthText for text recognition, another is trained/finetuned on the Unitail. As shown all algorithms achieve better performance if trained on the Unitail, this verifies that texts in the retail domain are better handled by the proposed dataset.

Table 2. Benchmarking text detection on Unitail. P and R stand for Precision and Recall, respectively. hmean is the harmonic mean of precision and recall.

Method	Training Set	R	P	hmean
DBNet [31]	SynthText+IC15	0.541	0.866	0.666
DBNet	Unitail	0.773	0.871	0.819
FCENet [64]	SynthText+IC15	0.420	0.745	0.538
FCENet	Unitail	0.795	0.857	0.825
PSENet [53]	SynthText+IC15	0.421	0.750	0.539
PSENet	Unitail	0.705	0.789	0.744

Table 3. Benchmarking text recognition on Unitail. S90k: Synth90k. ST: SynthText. PW: methods use public available weights. NED: Normalized Edit Distance, the lower the better. Acc: word top-1 Accuracy, the higher the better.

Method	Training Set	PW	NED	Acc (%)
CRNN [48]	S90k+ST	✓	0.36	40.0
CRNN	S90k+ST+Unitail		0.25	51.4
NRTR [47]	S90k+ST	✓	0.28	55.7
NRTR	S90k+ST+Unitail		0.16	69.4
RobustScanner [60]	S90k+ST	✓	0.25	56.3
RobustScanner	S90k+ST+Unitail		0.18	65.9
SAR [30]	S90k+ST	✓	0.25	56.2
SAR	S90k+ST+Unitail		0.18	66.5
SATRN [29]	S90k+ST	✓	0.23	62.7
SATRN	S90k+ST+Unitail		0.13	74.9
ABINet [12]	S90k+ST	✓	0.17	69.2
ABINet	S90k+ST+Unitail		0.11	77.2

Product Matching. The product matching results are shown in Table 4. With just texts across all 1454 categories, the method in Fig. 6(b) reaches 31.71% and 47.81% on the Hard Example Track and the General Track, respectively. The result is convincing that only textual information is a strong representation for the product, but this new direction clearly requires further exploration.

Moreover, the textual information improves the regular visual classifier using the method proposed in Sect. 4.2. In the hard example track, the improvement of textual information is significant (+1.76−2.75%) since the similar-looking products which are hard for regular classifier could be easier distinguished by texts. In the general track, the improvement drops (+0.56−0.94%) due to the limited ability of the textual matching algorithm.

5.2   Discussion

RetailDet. Table 5 shows that the RetailDet achieves state-of-the-art results on product detection benchmark SKU110k [17]. The SKU110k and the Unitail-Det share the same training images but with different annotations (QUAD vs AABB), and the origin-domain mAP on the SKU110k is 59.0 and 61.3 on the Unitail-Det (not included in Table 1). The difference is mainly for the reason that QUAD is a natural fit for products as a smoother regression target, and it avoids densely-packed overlaps which makes post-processing easier. We also provide ablation study on the quad-centerness and soft selection in supplementary materials.

Table 4. Benchmarking on the product matching task.

Method	Acc (%)
Hard example:	
Only text (Fig. 6(b))	31.71
EfficientNetV2 [50]	56.49
EfficientNetV2+Text	59.24 (+2.75)
ResNet101 [20, 39]	58.37
ResNet101+Text	60.52 (+2.15)
General:	
Only Text (Fig. 6(a))	30.37
Only Text (Fig. 6(b))	47.81 (+17.44)
EfficientNetV2	83.81
EfficientNetV2+Text	84.62 (+0.81)
ResNet101	85.03
ResNet101+Text	86.19 (+1.16)

Table 5. Results on SKU110k. RetailDet++ is an enhanced variant where a box refinement module is added (see supplementary for details)

Method	mAP
RetinaNet+EM [17]	49.2
FSAF [63]	56.2
CenterNet [10]	55.8
ATSS [61]	57.4
FCOS [51]	54.4
SAPD [62]	55.7
Faster-RCNN+FPN [43]	54.0
Reppoints [58]	55.6
Cascade-RCNN+Rong [46]	58.7
RetailDet++ (Ours)	**59.0**

Difficulty of the Text Based Product Matching. Since the proposed matching pipeline is not end-to-end trained, errors are accumulated by the text detector (0.773 recall and 0.871 precision for DBNet) and text recognizer (0.772 for ABINet). Some products in the dataset do not contain texts (2%), and many words are partially or fully illegible. This requires further study on topics such as: attention mechanism on text regions, end-to-end framework for text spotting based product recognition, and one-shot learning based sequence matching.

Inference Speed. The inference speed is tested on a single 2080Ti GPU, with 6.3 FPS for RetailDet, 27.6 FPS for DBNet, 41.4 FPS for ABINet, and 65.1 FPS for text+visual matching.

6   Conclusions

In this work, we introduce the United Retail Datasets (Unitail), a large-scale benchmark aims at supporting well-aligned textually enhanced scene product recognition. It involves quadrilateral product instances, on-product texts, product matching gallery, and testing suite. We also design two baselines that take advantages of the Unitail and provide comprehensive benchmark experiments on various state-of-the-art methods.

References

1. Bai, Y., Chen, Y., Yu, W., Wang, L., Zhang, W.: Products-10K: a large-scale product recognition dataset. CoRR abs/2008.10545 (2020). https://arxiv.org/abs/2008.10545
2. Cai, Y., Wen, L., Zhang, L., Du, D., Wang, W.: Rethinking object detection in retail stores. In: Proceedings of the AAAI Conference on Artificial Intelligence, vol. 35, pp. 947–954 (2021)
3. Carion, N., Massa, F., Synnaeve, G., Usunier, N., Kirillov, A., Zagoruyko, S.: End-to-end object detection with transformers. CoRR abs/2005.12872 (2020). https://arxiv.org/abs/2005.12872
4. Chen, F., Zhu, C., Shen, Z., Zhang, H., Savvides, M.: NCMS: towards accurate anchor free object detection through l2 norm calibration and multi-feature selection. Comput. Vis. Image Underst. **200**, 103050 (2020)
5. Cheng, L., et al.: Weakly supervised learning with side information for noisy labeled images. CoRR abs/2008.11586 (2020). https://arxiv.org/abs/2008.11586
6. Chng, C.K., Chan, C.S.: Total-text: a comprehensive dataset for scene text detection and recognition. CoRR abs/1710.10400 (2017). http://arxiv.org/abs/1710.10400
7. Collins, J., et al.: ABO: dataset and benchmarks for real-world 3D object understanding. CoRR abs/2110.06199 (2021). https://arxiv.org/abs/2110.06199
8. Devlin, J., Chang, M., Lee, K., Toutanova, K.: BERT: pre-training of deep bidirectional transformers for language understanding. CoRR abs/1810.04805 (2018). http://arxiv.org/abs/1810.04805
9. Ding, J., et al.: Object detection in aerial images: a large-scale benchmark and challenges (2021)
10. Duan, K., Bai, S., Xie, L., Qi, H., Huang, Q., Tian, Q.: CenterNet: object detection with keypoint triplets. arXiv preprint arXiv:1904.08189 (2019)
11. Everingham, M., Gool, L.V., Williams, C.K.I., Winn, J.M., Zisserman, A.: The pascal visual object classes (VOC) challenge. Int. J. Comput. Vis. **88**(2), 303–338 (2010). https://doi.org/10.1007/s11263-009-0275-4

12. Fang, S., Xie, H., Wang, Y., Mao, Z., Zhang, Y.: Read like humans: autonomous, bidirectional and iterative language modeling for scene text recognition (2021)
13. Follmann, P., Böttger, T., Härtinger, P., König, R., Ulrich, M.: MVTec D2S: densely segmented supermarket dataset. CoRR abs/1804.08292 (2018). http://arxiv.org/abs/1804.08292
14. George, M., Floerkemeier, C.: Recognizing products: a per-exemplar multi-label image classification approach. In: Fleet, D., Pajdla, T., Schiele, B., Tuytelaars, T. (eds.) ECCV 2014. LNCS, vol. 8690, pp. 440–455. Springer, Cham (2014). https://doi.org/10.1007/978-3-319-10605-2_29
15. George, M., Mircic, D., Soros, G., Floerkemeier, C., Mattern, F.: Fine-grained product class recognition for assisted shopping (2015). https://doi.org/10.48550/arxiv.1510.04074. https://arxiv.org/abs/1510.04074
16. Georgiadis, K., et al.: Products-6K: a large-scale groceries product recognition dataset. In: The 14th PErvasive Technologies Related to Assistive Environments Conference, PETRA 2021, pp. 1–7. Association for Computing Machinery, New York (2021). https://doi.org/10.1145/3453892.3453894
17. Goldman, E., Herzig, R., Eisenschtat, A., Goldberger, J., Hassner, T.: Precise detection in densely packed scenes. In: Proceedings of Conference on Computer Vision Pattern Recognition (CVPR) (2019)
18. Gupta, A., Vedaldi, A., Zisserman, A.: Synthetic data for text localisation in natural images. In: IEEE Conference on Computer Vision and Pattern Recognition (2016)
19. He, K., Gkioxari, G., Dollár, P., Girshick, R.: Mask R-CNN. In: Proceedings of the IEEE International Conference on Computer Vision, pp. 2961–2969 (2017)
20. He, K., Zhang, X., Ren, S., Sun, J.: Deep residual learning for image recognition. In: Proceedings of the IEEE Conference on Computer Vision and Pattern Recognition, pp. 770–778 (2016)
21. Huang, L., Yang, Y., Deng, Y., Yu, Y.: DenseBox: unifying landmark localization with end to end object detection. arXiv preprint arXiv:1509.04874 (2015)
22. Jaderberg, M., Simonyan, K., Vedaldi, A., Zisserman, A.: Synthetic data and artificial neural networks for natural scene text recognition. In: Workshop on Deep Learning, NIPS (2014)
23. Jund, P., Abdo, N., Eitel, A., Burgard, W.: The Freiburg groceries dataset. CoRR abs/1611.05799 (2016). http://arxiv.org/abs/1611.05799
24. Karatzas, D., et al.: ICDAR 2015 competition on robust reading. In: Proceedings of the 2015 13th International Conference on Document Analysis and Recognition (ICDAR), ICDAR 2015, pp. 1156–1160. IEEE Computer Society, New York (2015). https://doi.org/10.1109/ICDAR.2015.7333942
25. Karatzas, D., et al.: ICDAR 2013 robust reading competition. In: 2013 12th International Conference on Document Analysis and Recognition, pp. 1484–1493 (2013). https://doi.org/10.1109/ICDAR.2013.221
26. Kong, T., Sun, F., Liu, H., Jiang, Y., Shi, J.: FoveaBox: beyond anchor-based object detector. arXiv preprint arXiv:1904.03797 (2019)
27. Koubaroulis, D., Matas, J., Kittler, J.: Evaluating colour-based object recognition algorithms using the SOIL-47 database. In: in Asian Conference on Computer Vision, pp. 840–845 (2002)
28. Kuhn, H.W.: The Hungarian method for the assignment problem. Naval Res. Logist. Q. **2**(1–2), 83–97 (1955). https://doi.org/10.1002/nav.3800020109. https://onlinelibrary.wiley.com/doi/abs/10.1002/nav.3800020109

29. Lee, J., Park, S., Baek, J., Oh, S.J., Kim, S., Lee, H.: On recognizing texts of arbitrary shapes with 2D self-attention. CoRR abs/1910.04396 (2019). http://arxiv.org/abs/1910.04396
30. Li, H., Wang, P., Shen, C., Zhang, G.: Show, attend and read: a simple and strong baseline for irregular text recognition. In: Proceedings of the AAAI Conference on Artificial Intelligence, vol. 33, pp. 8610–8617 (2019)
31. Liao, M., Wan, Z., Yao, C., Chen, K., Bai, X.: Real-time scene text detection with differentiable binarization. In: Proceedings of the AAAI Conference on Artificial Intelligence, pp. 11474–11481 (2020)
32. Lin, T.Y., Dollár, P., Girshick, R., He, K., Hariharan, B., Belongie, S.: Feature pyramid networks for object detection. In: CVPR (2017)
33. Lin, T.-Y., et al.: Microsoft COCO: common objects in context. In: Fleet, D., Pajdla, T., Schiele, B., Tuytelaars, T. (eds.) ECCV 2014. LNCS, vol. 8693, pp. 740–755. Springer, Cham (2014). https://doi.org/10.1007/978-3-319-10602-1_48
34. Liu, Y., Jin, L., Zhang, S., Zhang, S.: Detecting curve text in the wild: new dataset and new solution. CoRR abs/1712.02170 (2017). http://arxiv.org/abs/1712.02170
35. Merler, M., Galleguillos, C., Belongie, S.: Recognizing groceries in situ using in vitro training data. In: 2007 IEEE Conference on Computer Vision and Pattern Recognition, pp. 1–8 (2007). https://doi.org/10.1109/CVPR.2007.383486
36. Ming, Q., Miao, L., Zhou, Z., Yang, X., Dong, Y.: Optimization for arbitrary-oriented object detection via representation invariance loss. IEEE Geosci. Remote Sens. Lett., 1–5 (2021). https://doi.org/10.1109/LGRS.2021.3115110
37. Mishra, A., Alahari, K., Jawahar, C.: Scene text recognition using higher order language priors. In: BMVC - British Machine Vision Conference. BMVA, Surrey, UK, September 2012. https://doi.org/10.5244/C.26.127. https://hal.inria.fr/hal-00818183
38. Oucheikh, R., Pettersson, T., Löfström, T.: Product verification using OCR classification and Mondrian conformal prediction. Expert Syste. Appl. **188**, 115942 (2022). https://doi.org/10.1016/j.eswa.2021.115942. https://www.sciencedirect.com/science/article/pii/S0957417421012963
39. Pan, X., Luo, P., Shi, J., Tang, X.: Two at once: enhancing learning and generalization capacities via IBN-Net. In: Ferrari, V., Hebert, M., Sminchisescu, C., Weiss, Y. (eds.) ECCV 2018. LNCS, vol. 11208, pp. 484–500. Springer, Cham (2018). https://doi.org/10.1007/978-3-030-01225-0_29
40. Pan, X., et al.: Dynamic refinement network for oriented and densely packed object detection, pp. 1–8 (2020)
41. Parmar, N., Vaswani, A., Uszkoreit, J., Kaiser, L., Shazeer, N., Ku, A.: Image transformer. CoRR abs/1802.05751 (2018). http://arxiv.org/abs/1802.05751
42. Qian, W., Yang, X., Peng, S., Yan, J., Guo, Y.: Learning modulated loss for rotated object detection. In: Proceedings of the AAAI Conference on Artificial Intelligence, vol. 35, no. 3, pp. 2458–2466, May 2021. https://ojs.aaai.org/index.php/AAAI/article/view/16347
43. Ren, S., He, K., Girshick, R., Sun, J.: Faster R-CNN: towards real-time object detection with region proposal networks. In: Advances in Neural Information Processing Systems, pp. 91–99 (2015)
44. Risnumawan, A., Shivakumara, P., Chan, C.S., Tan, C.L.: A robust arbitrary text detection system for natural scene images. Expert Syst. Appl. **41**(18), 8027–8048 (2014). https://doi.org/10.1016/j.eswa.2014.07.008. https://www.sciencedirect.com/science/article/pii/S0957417414004060

722   F. Chen et al.

45. Rocha, A., Hauagge, D.C., Wainer, J., Goldenstein, S.: Automatic fruit and vegetable classification from images. Comput. Electro. Agric. **70**(1), 96–104 (2010). https://doi.org/10.1016/j.compag.2009.09.002. https://www.sciencedirect.com/science/article/pii/S016816990900180X
46. Rong, T., Zhu, Y., Cai, H., Xiong, Y.: A solution to product detection in densely packed scenes (2021)
47. Sheng, F., Chen, Z., Xu, B.: NRTR: a no-recurrence sequence-to-sequence model for scene text recognition. In: 2019 International Conference on Document Analysis and Recognition (ICDAR), pp. 781–786. IEEE (2019)
48. Shi, B., Bai, X., Yao, C.: An end-to-end trainable neural network for image-based sequence recognition and its application to scene text recognition. IEEE Trans. Pattern Anal. Mach. Intell. **39**, 2298–2304 (2016)
49. Singh, A., Pang, G., Toh, M., Huang, J., Galuba, W., Hassner, T.: TextOCR: towards large-scale end-to-end reasoning for arbitrary-shaped scene text (2021)
50. Tan, M., Le, Q.V.: EfficientNetV2: smaller models and faster training. CoRR abs/2104.00298 (2021). https://arxiv.org/abs/2104.00298
51. Tian, Z., Shen, C., Chen, H., He, T.: FCOS: fully convolutional one-stage object detection. arXiv preprint arXiv:1904.01355 (2019)
52. Varol, G., Kuzu, R.: Toward retail product recognition on grocery shelves. In: International Conference on Graphic and Image Processing (2015)
53. Wang, W., et al.: Shape robust text detection with progressive scale expansion network. In: Proceedings of the IEEE/CVF Conference on Computer Vision and Pattern Recognition, pp. 9336–9345 (2019)
54. Wang, W., et al.: Efficient and accurate arbitrary-shaped text detection with pixel aggregation network. In: ICCV, pp. 8439–8448 (2019)
55. Wei, X., Cui, Q., Yang, L., Wang, P., Liu, L.: RPC: a large-scale retail product checkout dataset. CoRR abs/1901.07249 (2019). http://arxiv.org/abs/1901.07249
56. Xu, Y., et al.: Gliding vertex on the horizontal bounding box for multi-oriented object detection. IEEE Trans. Pattern Anal. Mach. Intell. **4**, 1452–1459 (2020)
57. Yang, S., Luo, P., Loy, C.C., Tang, X.: Wider face: a face detection benchmark. In: IEEE Conference on Computer Vision and Pattern Recognition (CVPR) (2016)
58. Yang, Z., Liu, S., Hu, H., Wang, L., Lin, S.: RepPoints: point set representation for object detection. arXiv preprint arXiv:1904.11490 (2019)
59. Yao, C., Bai, X., Liu, W., Ma, Y., Tu, Z.: Detecting texts of arbitrary orientations in natural images. In: 2012 IEEE Conference on Computer Vision and Pattern Recognition, pp. 1083–1090 (2012). https://doi.org/10.1109/CVPR.2012.6247787
60. Yue, X., Kuang, Z., Lin, C., Sun, H., Zhang, W.: RobustScanner: dynamically enhancing positional clues for robust text recognition. In: Vedaldi, A., Bischof, H., Brox, T., Frahm, J.-M. (eds.) ECCV 2020. LNCS, vol. 12364, pp. 135–151. Springer, Cham (2020). https://doi.org/10.1007/978-3-030-58529-7_9
61. Zhang, S., Chi, C., Yao, Y., Lei, Z., Li, S.Z.: Bridging the gap between anchor-based and anchor-free detection via adaptive training sample selection (2020)
62. Zhu, C., Chen, F., Shen, Z., Savvides, M.: Soft anchor-point object detection. In: Vedaldi, A., Bischof, H., Brox, T., Frahm, J.-M. (eds.) ECCV 2020. LNCS, vol. 12354, pp. 91–107. Springer, Cham (2020). https://doi.org/10.1007/978-3-030-58545-7_6
63. Zhu, C., He, Y., Savvides, M.: Feature selective anchor-free module for single-shot object detection. In: The IEEE Conference on Computer Vision and Pattern Recognition (CVPR), June 2019
64. Zhu, Y., Chen, J., Liang, L., Kuang, Z., Jin, L., Zhang, W.: Fourier contour embedding for arbitrary-shaped text detection. In: CVPR (2021)

Not Just Streaks: Towards Ground Truth for Single Image Deraining

Yunhao Ba[1], Howard Zhang[1], Ethan Yang[1], Akira Suzuki[1],
Arnold Pfahnl[1], Chethan Chinder Chandrappa[1], Celso M. de Melo[2],
Suya You[2], Stefano Soatto[1], Alex Wong[3], and Achuta Kadambi[1(✉)]

[1] University of California, Los Angeles, Los Angeles, USA
{yhba,hwdz15508,eyang657,asuzuki100,ajpfahnl,chinderc}@ucla.edu,
soatto@cs.ucla.edu, achuta@ee.ucla.edu
[2] DEVCOM Army Research Laboratory, Adelphi, USA
{celso.m.demelo.civ,suya.you.civ}@army.mil
[3] Yale University, New Haven, USA
alex.wong@yale.edu

Abstract. We propose a large-scale dataset of real-world rainy and clean image pairs and a method to remove degradations, induced by rain streaks and rain accumulation, from the image. As there exists no real-world dataset for deraining, current state-of-the-art methods rely on synthetic data and thus are limited by the sim2real domain gap; moreover, rigorous evaluation remains a challenge due to the absence of a real paired dataset. We fill this gap by collecting a real paired deraining dataset through meticulous control of non-rain variations. Our dataset enables paired training and quantitative evaluation for diverse real-world rain phenomena (e.g. rain streaks and rain accumulation). To learn a representation robust to rain phenomena, we propose a deep neural network that reconstructs the underlying scene by minimizing a rain-robust loss between rainy and clean images. Extensive experiments demonstrate that our model outperforms the state-of-the-art deraining methods on real rainy images under various conditions. Project website: https://visual.ee.ucla.edu/gt_rain.htm/.

Keywords: Single-image rain removal · Real deraining dataset

1 Introduction

Single-image deraining aims to remove degradations induced by rain from images. Restoring rainy images not only improves their aesthetic properties, but also supports reuse of abundant publicly available pretrained models across

---

Y. Ba and H. Zhang—Equal contribution.

Supplementary Information The online version contains supplementary material available at https://doi.org/10.1007/978-3-031-20071-7_42.

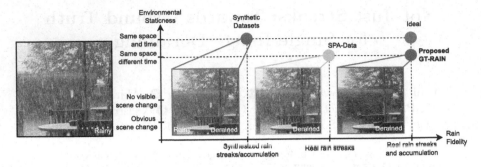

Fig. 1. The points above depict datasets and their corresponding outputs from models trained on them. These outputs come from a real rain image from the Internet. Our opinion* is that GT-RAIN can be the right dataset for the deraining community to use because it has a smaller domain gap to the ideal ground truth. * Why an asterisk? The asterisk emphasizes that this is an "opinion". It is impossible to quantify the domain gap because collecting true real data is infeasible. To date, deraining is largely a viewer's imagination of what the derained scene should look like. Therefore, we present the derained images above and leave it to the viewer to judge the gap. Additionally, GT-RAIN can be used in complement with the litany of synthetic datasets [12,19,27,29,50,56,57], as illustrated in Table 4.

computer vision tasks. Top performing methods use deep networks, but suffer from a common issue: it is not possible to obtain ideal real ground-truth pairs of rain and clean images. The same scene, in the same space and time, cannot be observed both with and without rain. To overcome this, deep learning based rain removal relies on synthetic data.

The use of synthetic data in deraining is prevalent [12,19,27,29,50,56,57]. However, current rain simulators cannot model all the complex effects of rain, which leads to unwanted artifacts when applying models trained on them to real-world rainy scenes. For instance, a number of synthetic methods add *rain streaks* to clean images to generate the pair [12,29,50,56,57], but rain does not only manifest as streaks: If raindrops are further away, the streaks meld together, creating *rain accumulation*, or *veiling* effects, which are exceedingly difficult to simulate. A further challenge with synthetic data is that results on real test data can only be evaluated qualitatively, for no real paired ground truth exists.

Realizing these limitations of synthetic data, we tackle the problem from another angle by relaxing the concept of ideal ground truth to a sufficiently short time window (see Fig. 1). We decide to conduct the experiment of obtaining short time interval paired data, particularly in light of the timely growth and diversity of landscape YouTube live streams. We strictly filter such videos with objective criteria on illumination shifts, camera motions, and motion artifacts. Further correction algorithms are applied for subtle variations, such as slight movements of foliage. We call this dataset GT-RAIN, as it is a first attempt to provide real paired data for deraining. Although our dataset relies on streamers, YouTube's fair use policy allows its release to the academic community.

Defining "Real, Paired Ground Truth": Clearly, obtaining real, paired ground truth data by capturing a rain and rain-free image pair at the exact same space and time is not feasible. However, the dehazing community has accepted several test sets [1–4] following these guidelines as a satisfactory replacement for evaluation purposes:

- A pair of degraded and clean images is captured as real photos at two different timestamps;
- Illumination shifts are limited by capturing data on cloudy days;
- The camera configuration remains identical while capturing the degraded and clean images.

We produce the static pairs in GT-RAIN by following the above criterion set forth by the dehazing community while enforcing a stricter set of rules on sky and local motion. More importantly, as a step closer towards obtaining real ground truth pairs, we capture natural weather effects instead, which address problems of scale and variability that inherently come with simulating weather through man-made methods. In the results of the proposed method, we not only see quantitative and qualitative improvements, but also showcase a unique ability to handle diverse rain physics that was not previously handled by synthetic data.

Contributions: In summary, we make the following contributions:

- We propose a real-world paired dataset: GT-RAIN. The dataset captures *real* rain phenomena, from rain streaks to accumulation under various rain fall conditions, to bridge the domain gap that is too complex to be modeled by synthetic [12,19,27,29,50,56,57] and semi-real [44] datasets.
- We introduce an avenue for the deraining community to now have standardized quantitative and qualitative evaluations. Previous evaluations were quantifiable only wrt. simulations.
- We propose a framework to reconstruct the underlying scene by learning representations robust to the rain phenomena via a rain-robust loss function. Our approach outperforms the state of the art [55] by 12.1% PSNR on average for deraining real images.

2   Related Work

Rain Physics: Raindrops exhibit diverse physical properties while falling, and many experimental studies have been conducted to investigate them, i.e. equilibrium shape [5], size [35], terminal velocity [10,14], spatial distribution [34], and temporal distribution [58]. A mixture of these distinct properties transforms the photometry of a raindrop into a complex mapping of the environmental radiance which considers refraction, specular reflection, and internal reflection [13]:

$$L(\hat{n}) = L_r(\hat{n}) + L_s(\hat{n}) + L_p(\hat{n}), \tag{1}$$

where $L(\hat{n})$ is the radiance at a point on the raindrop surface with normal $\hat{n}$, $L_r(\cdot)$ is the radiance of the refracted ray, $L_s(\cdot)$ is the radiance of the specularly reflected

Table 1. Our proposed large-scale dataset enables paired training and quantitative evaluation for real-world deraining. We consider SPA-Data [44] as a semi-real dataset since it only contains real rainy images, where the pseudo ground-truth images are synthesized from a rain streak removal algorithm.

Dataset	Type	Rain effects	Size
Rain12 [29]	Simulated	Synth. streaks only	12
Rain100L [50]	Simulated	Synth. streaks only	300
Rain800 [57]	Simulated	Synth. streaks only	800
Rain100H [50]	Simulated	Synth. streaks only	1.9K
Outdoor-Rain [27]	Simulated	Synth. streaks & Synth. accumulation	10.5K
RainCityscapes [19]	Simulated	Synth. streaks & Synth. accumulation	10.62K
Rain12000 [56]	Simulated	Synth. streaks only	13.2K
Rain14000 [12]	Simulated	Synth. streaks only	14K
NYU-Rain [27]	Simulated	Synth. streaks & Synth. accumulation	16.2K
SPA-Data [44]	Semi-real	Real streaks only	29.5K
Proposed	Real	Real streaks & Real accumulation	31.5K

ray, and $L_p(\cdot)$ is the radiance of the internally reflected ray. In real images, the appearance of rain streaks is also affected by motion blur and background intensities. Moreover, the dense rain accumulation results in sophisticated veiling effects. Interactions of these complex phenomena make it challenging to simulate realistic rain effects. Until GT-RAIN, previous works [15,20,22,27,42,44,55] have relied heavily on simulated rain and are limited by the sim2real gap.

Deraining Datasets: Most data-driven deraining models require paired rainy and clean, rain-free ground-truth images for training. Due to the difficulty of collecting real paired samples, previous works focus on synthetic datasets, such as Rain12 [29], Rain100L [50], Rain100H [50], Rain800 [57], Rain12000 [56], Rain14000 [12], NYU-Rain [27], Outdoor-Rain [27], and RainCityscapes [19]. Even though synthetic images from these datasets incorporate some physical characteristics of real rain, significant gaps still exist between synthetic and real data [51]. More recently, a "paired" dataset with real rainy images (SPA-Data) was proposed in [44]. However, their "ground-truth" images are in fact a product of a video-based deraining method – synthesized based on the temporal motions of raindrops which may introduce artifacts and blurriness; moreover, the associated rain accumulation and veiling effects are not considered. In contrast, we collect pairs of real-world rainy and clean ground-truth images by enforcing rigorous selection criteria to minimize the environmental variations. To the best of our knowledge, our dataset is the first large-scale dataset with real paired data. Please refer to Table 1 for a detailed comparison of the deraining datasets.

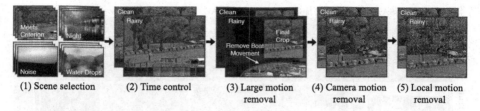

(1) Scene selection   (2) Time control   (3) Large motion removal   (4) Camera motion removal   (5) Local motion removal

Fig. 2. We collect the a real paired deraining dataset by rigorously controlling the environmental variations. First, we remove heavily degraded videos such as scenes without proper exposure, noise, or water droplets on the lens. Next, we carefully choose the rainy and clean frames as close as possible in time to mitigate illumination shifts before cropping to remove large movement. Lastly, we correct for small camera motion (due to strong wind) using SIFT [31] and RANSAC [9] and perform elastic image registration [40,41] by estimating the displacement field when necessary.

Single-Image Deraining: Previous methods used model-based solutions to derain [7,23,29,33]. More recently, deep-learning based methods have seen increasing popularity and progress [11,15,20,22,27,38,39,42,44,50,55,56]. The multi-scale progressive fusion network (MSPFN) [22] characterizes and reconstructs rain streaks at multiple scales. The rain convolutional dictionary network (RCDNet) [42] encodes the rain shape using the intrinsic convolutional dictionary learning mechanism. The multi-stage progressive image restoration network (MPRNet) [55] splits the image into different sections in various stages to learn contextualized features at different scales. The spatial attentive network (SPANet) [44] learns physical properties of rain streaks in a local neighborhood and reconstructs the clean background using non-local information. Efficient-DeRain (EDR) [15] aims to derain efficiently in real time by using pixel-wise dilation filtering. Other than rain streak removal, the heavy rain restorer (HRR) [27] and the depth-guided non-local network (DGNL-Net) [20] have also attempted to address rain accumulation effects. All of these prior methods use synthetic or semi-real datasets, and show limited generalizability to real images. In contrast, we propose a derainer that learns a rain-robust representation directly.

3   Dataset

We now describe our method to control variations in a real dataset of paired images taken at two different timestamps, as illustrated in Fig. 2.

Data Collection: We collect rain and clean ground-truth videos using a Python program based on FFmpeg to download videos from YouTube live streams across the world. For each live stream, we record the location in order to determine whether there is rain according to the OpenWeatherMap API [32]. We also determine the time of day to filter out nighttime videos. After the rain stops, we continue downloading in order to collect clean ground-truth frames. Note: while our dataset is formatted for single-image deraining, it can be re-purposed for video deraining as well by considering the timestamps of the frames collected.

Fig. 3. Our proposed dataset contains diverse rainy images collected across the world. We illustrate several representative image pairs with various rain streak appearances and rain accumulation strengths at different geographic locations.

Collection Criteria: To minimize variations between rainy and clean frames, videos are filtered based on a strict set of collection criteria. Note that we perform realignment for camera and local motion only when necessary – with manual oversight to filter out cases where motion still exists after realignment. Please see examples of motion correction and alignment in the supplement.

- **Heavily degraded scenes** that contain excessive noise, webcam artifacts, poor resolution, or poor camera exposure are filtered out as the underlying scene cannot be inferred from the images.
- **Water droplets** on the surface of the lens occlude large portions of the scene and also distort the image. Images containing this type of degradation are filtered out as it is out of the scope of this work – we focus on rain streak and rain accumulation phenomena.
- **Illumination shifts** are mitigated by minimizing the time difference between rainy and clean frames. Our dataset has an average time difference of 25 min, which drastically limits large changes in global illumination due to sun position, clouds, etc.
- **Background changes** containing large discrepancies (e.g. cars, people, swaying foliage, water surfaces) are cropped from the frame to ensure that clean and rainy images are aligned. By limiting the average time difference between scenes, we also minimize these discrepancies before filtering. All sky regions are cropped out as well to ensure proper background texture.
- **Camera motion.** Adverse weather conditions, i.e. heavy wind, can cause camera movements between the rainy and clean frames. To address this, we use the Scale Invariant Feature Transform (SIFT) [31] and Random Sample Consensus (RANSAC) [9] to compute the homography to realign the frames.
- **Local motion.** Despite controlling for motion whenever possible, certain scenes still contain small local movements that are unavoidable, especially in areas of foliage. To correct for this, we perform elastic image registration when necessary by estimating the displacement field [40,41].

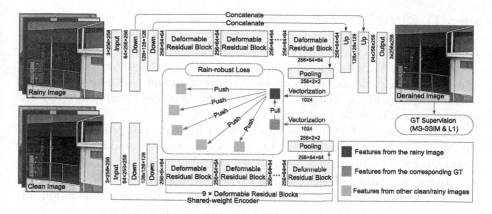

Fig. 4. By minimizing a rain-robust objective, our model learns robust features for reconstruction. When training, a shared-weight encoder is used to extract features from rainy and ground-truth images. These features are then evaluated with the rain-robust loss, where features from a rainy image and its ground-truth are encouraged to be similar. Learned features from the rainy images are also fed into a decoder to reconstruct the ground-truth images with MS-SSIM and $\ell 1$ loss functions.

Dataset Statistics: Our large-scale dataset includes a total of 31,524 rainy and clean frame pairs, which is split into 26,124 training frames, 3,300 validation frames, and 2,100 testing frames. These frames are taken from 101 videos, covering a large variety of background scenes from urban locations (e.g. buildings, streets, cityscapes) to natural scenery (e.g. forests, plains, hills). We span a wide range of geographic locations (e.g. North America, Europe, Oceania, Asia) to ensure that we capture diverse scenes and rain fall conditions. The scenes also include varying degrees of illumination from different times of day and rain of varying densities, streak lengths, shapes, and sizes. The webcams cover a wide array of resolutions, noise levels, intrinsic parameters (focal length, distortion), etc. As a result, our dataset captures diverse rain effects that cannot be accurately reproduced by SPA-Data [44] or synthetic datasets [12,19,27,29,50,56,57]. See Fig. 3 for representative image pairs in GT-RAIN.

4   Learning to Derain Real Images

To handle greater diversity of rain streak appearance, we propose to learn a representation (illustrated in Fig. 4) that is robust to rain for real image deraining.

Problem Formulation: Most prior works emphasize on the rain streak removal and rely on the following equation to model rain [8,12,26,29,42,44,52,56,61]:

$$\mathbf{I} = \mathbf{J} + \sum_{i}^{n} \mathbf{S}_i, \tag{2}$$

where $\mathbf{I} \in \mathbb{R}^{3 \times H \times W}$ is the observed rainy image, $\mathbf{J} \in \mathbb{R}^{3 \times H \times W}$ is the rain-free or "clean" image, and $\mathbf{S}_i$ is the i-th rain layer. However, real-world rain can be more complicated due to the dense rain accumulation and the rain veiling effect [27, 28,49]. These additional effects, which are visually similar to fog and mist, may cause severe degradation, and thus their removal should also be considered for single-image deraining. With GT-RAIN, it now becomes possible to study and conduct optically challenging, real-world rainy image restoration.

Given an image $\mathbf{I}$ of a scene captured during rain, we propose to learn a function $\mathcal{F}(\cdot, \theta)$ parameterized by θ to remove degradation induced by the rain phenonmena. This function is realized as a neural network (see Fig. 4) that takes as input a rainy image $\mathbf{I}$ and outputs a "clean" image $\hat{\mathbf{J}} = \mathcal{F}(\mathbf{I}, \theta) \in \mathbb{R}^{3 \times H \times W}$, where undesirable characteristics, i.e. rain streaks and rain accumulation, are removed from the image to reconstruct the underlying scene $\mathbf{J}$.

Rain-Robust Loss: To derain an image $\mathbf{I}$, one may directly learn a map from $\mathbf{I}$ to $\hat{\mathbf{J}}$ simply by minimizing the discrepancies between $\hat{\mathbf{J}}$ and the ground truth $\mathbf{J}$, i.e. an image reconstruction loss – such is the case for existing methods. Under this formulation, the model must explore a large hypothesis space, e.g. any region obfuscated by rain streaks is inherently ambiguous, making learning difficult.

Unlike previous works, we constrain the learned representation such that it is robust to rain phenomena. To "learn away" the rain, we propose to map both the rainy and clean images of the same scene to an embedding space where they are close to each other by optimizing a similarity metric. Additionally, we minimize a reconstruction objective to ensure that the learned representation is sufficient to recover the underlying scene. Our approach is inspired by the recent advances in contrastive learning [6], and we aim to distill rain-robust representations of real-world scenes by directly comparing the rainy and clean images in the feature space. But unlike [6], we do not define a positive pair as augmentation to the same image, but rather any rainy image and its corresponding clean image from the same scene.

When training, we first randomly sample a mini-batch of N rainy images with the associated clean images to form an augmented batch $\{(\mathbf{I}_i, \mathbf{J}_i)\}_{i=1}^{N}$, where $\mathbf{I}_i$ is the i-th rainy image, and $\mathbf{J}_i$ is its corresponding ground-truth image. This augmented batch is fed into a shared-weight feature extractor $\mathcal{F}_E(\cdot, \theta_E)$ with weights θ_E to obtain a feature set $\{(\mathbf{z}_{\mathbf{I}_i}, \mathbf{z}_{\mathbf{J}_i})\}_{i=1}^{N}$, where $\mathbf{z}_{\mathbf{I}_i} = \mathcal{F}_E(\mathbf{I}_i, \theta_E)$ and $\mathbf{z}_{\mathbf{J}_i} = \mathcal{F}_E(\mathbf{J}_i, \theta_E)$. We consider every $(\mathbf{z}_{\mathbf{I}_i}, \mathbf{z}_{\mathbf{J}_i})$ as the positive pairs. This is so that the learned features from the same scene should be close to each other regardless of the rainy conditions. We treat the other $2(N-1)$ samples from the same batch as negative samples. Based on the noise-contrastive estimation (NCE) [16], we adopt the following InfoNCE [37] criterion to measure the rain-robust loss for a positive pair $(\mathbf{z}_{\mathbf{J}_i}, \mathbf{z}_{\mathbf{I}_i})$:

$$\ell_{\mathbf{z}_{\mathbf{J}_i}, \mathbf{z}_{\mathbf{I}_i}} = -\log \frac{\exp\left(\mathrm{sim}_{\cos}(\mathbf{z}_{\mathbf{I}_i}, \mathbf{z}_{\mathbf{J}_i})/\tau\right)}{\sum_{\mathbf{k} \in \mathcal{K}} \exp\left(\mathrm{sim}_{\cos}(\mathbf{z}_{\mathbf{J}_i}, \mathbf{k})/\tau\right)}, \tag{3}$$

where $\mathcal{K} = \{\mathbf{z}_{\mathbf{I}_j}, \mathbf{z}_{\mathbf{J}_j}\}_{j=1,j\neq i}^{N}$ is a set that contains the features extracted from other rainy and ground-truth images in the selected mini-batch, $\text{sim}_{\cos}(\mathbf{u}, \mathbf{v}) = \mathbf{u}^{\mathsf{T}}\mathbf{v}/\|\mathbf{u}\|\|\mathbf{v}\|$ is the cosine similarity between two feature vectors $\mathbf{u}$ and $\mathbf{v}$, and τ is the temperature parameter [48]. We set τ as 0.25, and this loss is calculated across all positive pairs within the mini-batch for both $(\mathbf{z}_{\mathbf{I}_i}, \mathbf{z}_{\mathbf{J}_i})$ and $(\mathbf{z}_{\mathbf{J}_i}, \mathbf{z}_{\mathbf{I}_i})$.

Full Objective: While minimizing Eq. (3) maps features of clean and rainy images to the same subspace, we also need to ensure that the representation is sufficient to reconstruct the scene. Hence, we additionally minimize a Multi-Scale Structural Similarity Index (MS-SSIM) [46] loss and a $\ell1$ image reconstruction loss to prevent the model from discarding useful information for the reconstruction task. Our full objective $\mathcal{L}_{\text{full}}$ is as follows:

$$\mathcal{L}_{\text{full}}(\hat{\mathbf{J}}, \mathbf{J}) = \mathcal{L}_{\text{MS-SSIM}}(\hat{\mathbf{J}}, \mathbf{J}) + \lambda_{\ell1}\mathcal{L}_{\ell1}(\hat{\mathbf{J}}, \mathbf{J}) + \lambda_{\text{robust}}\mathcal{L}_{\text{robust}}(\mathbf{z}_{\mathbf{J}}, \mathbf{z}_{\mathbf{I}}), \quad (4)$$

where $\mathcal{L}_{\text{MS-SSIM}}(\cdot)$ is the MS-SSIM loss that is commonly used for image restoration [59], $\mathcal{L}_{\ell1}(\cdot)$ is the $\ell1$ distance between the estimated clean images $\hat{\mathbf{J}}$ and the ground-truth images $\mathbf{J}$, $\mathcal{L}_{\text{robust}}(\cdot)$ is the rain-robust loss in Eq. (3), and $\lambda_{\ell1}$ and λ_{robust} are two hyperparameters to control the relative importance of different loss terms. In our experiments, we set both $\lambda_{\ell1}$ and λ_{robust} as 0.1.

Network Architecture & Implementation Details: We design our model based on the architecture introduced in [24,60]. As illustrated in Fig. 4, our network includes an encoder of one input convolutional block, two downsampling blocks, and nine residual blocks [18] to yield latent features $\mathbf{z}$. This is followed by a decoder of two upsampling blocks and one output layer to map the features to $\mathbf{J}$. We fuse skip connections into the decoder using 3×3 up-convolution blocks to retain information lost in the bottleneck. Note: normal convolution layers are replaced by deformable convolution [62] in our residual blocks – in doing so, we enable our model to propagate non-local spatial information to reconstruct local degradations caused by rain effects. Latent features $\mathbf{z}$ are used for the rain-robust loss described in Eq. (3). Since these features are high dimensional ($256 \times 64 \times 64$), we use an average pooling layer to condense the feature map of each channel to 2×2. The condensed features are flattened into a vector of length 1024 for the rain-robust loss. It is worth noting that our rain-robust loss does not require additional modifications on the model architectures.

Our deraining model is trained on 256×256 patches and a mini-batch size $N = 8$ for 20 epochs. We use the Adam optimizer [25] with $\beta_1 = 0.9$ and $\beta_2 = 0.999$. The initial learning rate is 2×10^{-4}, and it is steadily modified to 1×10^{-6} based on a cosine annealing schedule [30]. We also use a linear warm-up policy for the first 4 epochs. For data augmentation, we use random cropping, random rotation, random horizontal and vertical flips, and RainMix augmentation [15]. More details can be found in the supplementary material.

Table 2. Quantitative comparison on GT-RAIN. Our method outperforms the existing state-of-the-art derainers. The preferred results are marked in **bold**.

Data split	Metrics	Rainy images	SPANet [44] (CVPR'19)	HRR [27] (CVPR'19)	MSPFN [22] (CVPR'20)	RCDNet [42] (CVPR'20)	DGNL-Net [20] (IEEE TIP'21)	EDR [15] (AAAI'21)	MPRNet [55] (CVPR'21)	Ours
Dense rain streaks	PSNR↑	18.46	18.87	17.86	19.58	19.50	17.33	18.86	19.12	**20.84**
	SSIM↑	0.6284	0.6314	0.5872	0.6342	0.6218	0.5947	0.6296	0.6375	**0.6573**
Dense rain accumulation	PSNR↑	20.87	21.42	14.82	21.13	21.27	20.75	21.07	21.38	**24.78**
	SSIM↑	0.7706	0.7696	0.4675	0.7735	0.7765	0.7429	0.7766	0.7808	**0.8279**
Overall	PSNR↑	19.49	19.96	16.55	20.24	20.26	18.80	19.81	20.09	**22.53**
	SSIM↑	0.6893	0.6906	0.5359	0.6939	0.6881	0.6582	0.6926	0.6989	**0.7304**

5   Experiments

We compare to state-of-the-art methods both quantitatively and qualitatively on GT-RAIN, and qualitatively Internet rainy images [47]. To quantify the difference between the derained results and ground-truth, we adopt peak signal-to-noise ratio (PSNR) [21] and structure similarity (SSIM) [45].

Quantitative Evaluation on GT-RAIN: To quantify the sim2real gap of the existing datasets, we test seven representative existing state-of-the-art methods [15,20,22,27,42,44,55] on our GT-RAIN test set.[1] Since there exist numerous synthetic datasets proposed by previous works [12,19,27,29,50,56,57], we found it intractable to train our method on each one; whereas, it is more feasible to take the best derainers for each respective dataset and test on our proposed dataset as a proxy (Table 2). This follows the conventions of previous deraining dataset papers [11,20,29,44,51,56,57] to compare with top performing methods from each existing dataset.

SPANet [44] is trained on SPA-Data [44]. HRR [27] utilizes both NYU-Rain [27] and Outdoor-Rain [27]. MSPFN [22] and MPRNet [55] are trained on a combination of multiple synthetic datasets [12,29,50,57]. DGNL-Net [20] is trained on RainCityscapes [19]. For RCDNet [42] and EDR [15], multiple weights from different training sets are provided. We choose RCDNet trained on SPA-Data and EDR V4 trained on Rain14000 [12] due to superior performance.

Compared to training on GT-RAIN (ours), methods trained on other data perform worse, with the largest domain gap being in NYU-Rain and Outdoor-Rain (HRR) and RainCityscapes (DGNL). Two trends do hold: training on (1) more synthetic data gives better results (MSPFN, MPRNet) and (2) semi-real data also helps (SPANet). However, even when multiple synthetic [12,29,50,57] or semi-real [44] datasets are used, their performance on real data is still around 2 dB lower than training on GT-RAIN (ours).

Figure 5 illustrates some representative derained images across scenarios with various rain appearance and rain accumulation densities. Training on GT-RAIN enables the network to remove most rain streaks and rain accumulation; whereas, training on synthetic/semi-real data tends to leave visible rain streaks. We note that HRR [27] and DGNL [20] may seem like they remove rain accumulation, but they in fact introduce undesirable artifacts, e.g. dark spots on the back of

---

[1] We use the original code and network weights from the authors for comparison. Code links for all comparison methods are provided in the supplementary material.

the traffic sign, tree, and sky. The strength of having ground-truth paired data is demonstrated by our 2.44 dB gain compared to the state of the art [55]. On test images with dense rain accumulation, the boost improves to 3.40 dB.

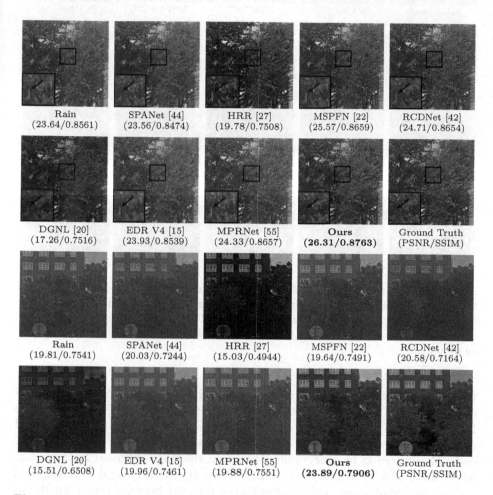

Fig. 5. **Our model simultaneously removes rain streaks and rain accumulation, while the existing models fail to generalize to real-world data.** The red arrows highlight the difference between the proposed and existing methods on the GT-RAIN test set (zoom for details, PSNR and SSIM scores are listed below the images). (Color figure online)

Qualitative Evaluation on Other Real Images: Other than the models described in the above section, we also include EDR V4 [15] trained on SPA-Data [44] for the qualitative comparison, since it shows more robust rain streak removal results as compared the version trained on Rain14000 [12]. The derained results on Internet rainy images are illustrated in Fig. 6. The model trained on

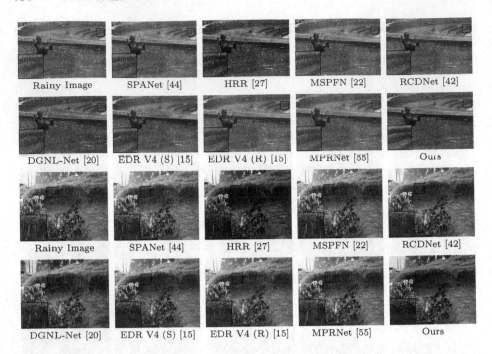

Fig. 6. Our model can generalize across real rainy images with robust performance. We select representative real rainy images with various rain patterns and backgrounds for comparison (zoom for details). EDR V4 (S) [15] denotes EDR trained on SPA-Data [44], and EDR V4 (R) [15] denotes EDR trained on Rain14000 [12].(Color figure online)

the proposed GT-RAIN (i.e. ours) deals with large rain streaks of various shapes and sizes as well as the associated rain accumulation effects, while preserving the features present in the scene. In contrast, we observe that models [20,27] trained on data with synthetic rain accumulation introduce unwanted color shifts and residual rain streaks in their results. Moreover, the state-of-the-art methods [22, 42,55] are unable to remove the majority of rain streaks in general as highlighted in the red zoom boxes. This demonstrates the gap between top methods on synthetic versus one that can be applied to real data.

Retraining Other Methods on GT-RAIN: We additionally train several state-of-the-art derainers [15,42,55] on the GT-RAIN training set to demonstrate that our real dataset leads to more robust real-world deraining and benefits all models. We have selected the most recent derainers for this retraining study.[2] All the models are trained from scratch, and the corresponding PSNR and SSIM scores on the GT-RAIN test set are provided in Table 3. For all the retrained models, we can observe a PSNR and SSIM gain by using the proposed

---

[2] Both DGNL-Net [20] and HRR [27] cannot be retrained on our real dataset, as both require additional supervision, such as transmission maps and depth maps.

Table 3. Retraining comparison methods on GT-RAIN. The improvement of these derainers further demonstrates the effectiveness of real paired data.

Data split	Metrics	Rainy images	RCDNet [42] (Original)	RCDNet [42] (GT-RAIN)	EDR [15] (Original)	EDR [15] (GT-RAIN)	MPRNet [55] (Original)	MPRNet [55] (GT-RAIN)	Ours
Dense rain streaks	PSNR↑	18.46	19.50	19.60	18.86	19.95	19.12	20.19	**20.84**
	SSIM↑	0.6284	0.6218	0.6492	0.6296	0.6436	0.6375	0.6542	**0.6573**
Dense rain accumulation	PSNR↑	20.87	21.27	22.74	21.07	23.42	21.38	23.38	**24.78**
	SSIM↑	0.7706	0.7765	0.7891	0.7766	0.7994	0.7808	0.8009	**0.8279**
Overall	PSNR↑	19.49	20.26	20.94	19.81	21.44	20.09	21.56	**22.53**
	SSIM↑	0.6893	0.6881	0.7091	0.6926	0.7104	0.6989	0.7171	**0.7304**

Table 4. Fine-tuning comparison methods on GT-RAIN. (F) denotes the fine-tuned models, and (O) denotes the original models trained on synthetic/real data.

Data split	Metrics	Rainy images	RCDNet [42] (O)	RCDNet [42] (F)	EDR [15] (O)	EDR [15] (F)	MPRNet [55] (O)	MPRNet [55] (F)	Ours (O)	Ours (F)
Dense rain streaks	PSNR↑	18.46	19.50	19.33	18.86	20.03	19.12	20.65	**20.84**	20.79
	SSIM↑	0.6284	0.6218	0.6463	0.6296	0.6433	0.6375	0.6561	0.6573	**0.6655**
Dense rain accumulation	PSNR↑	20.87	21.27	22.50	21.07	23.57	21.38	24.37	24.78	**25.20**
	SSIM↑	0.7706	0.7765	0.7893	0.7766	0.8016	0.7808	0.8250	0.8279	**0.8318**
Overall	PSNR↑	19.49	20.26	20.69	19.81	21.55	20.09	22.24	22.53	**22.68**
	SSIM↑	0.6893	0.6881	0.7076	0.6926	0.7111	0.6989	0.7285	0.7304	**0.7368**

GT-RAIN dataset. In addition, with all models trained on the same dataset, our model still outperforms others in all categories.

Fine-Tuning Other Methods on GT-RAIN: To demonstrate of the effectiveness of combining real and synthetic datasets, we also fine-tune several more recent derainers [15,42,55] that are previously trained on synthetic datasets with the proposed GT-RAIN dataset. We fine-tune from the official weights as described in the above quantitative evaluation section, and the fine-tuning learning rate is 20% of the original learning rate for each method. For the proposed method, we pretrain the model on the synthetic dataset used by MSPFN [22] and MPRNet [55]. The corresponding PSNR and SSIM scores on the GT-RAIN test set are listed in Table 4. In the table, we can observe a further boost as compared with training the models from scratch with just real or synthetic data.

Table 5. Ablation study. Our rain-robust loss improves both PSNR and SSIM.

Metrics	Rainy images	Ours w/o $\mathcal{L}_{robust}$	Ours w/ $\mathcal{L}_{robust}$
PSNR↑	19.49	21.82	**22.53**
SSIM↑	0.6893	0.7148	**0.7304**

Ablation study: We validate the effectiveness of the rain-robust loss with two variants of the proposed method: (1) the proposed network with the full objective as describe in Sect. 4; and (2) the proposed network with just MS-SSIM loss and ℓ_1 loss. The rest of the training configurations and hyperparameters remain identical. The quantitative metrics for these two variants on the proposed GT-RAIN test set are listed in Table 5. Our model trained with the proposed rain-robust loss produces a normalized correlation between rainy and clean latent

| Rainy | EDR V4 (R) [15] | MPRNet [55] | Ours | Ground Truth |

Fig. 7. Deraining is still an open problem. Both the proposed method and the existing work have difficulty in generalizing the performance to some challenging scenes.

vectors of $.95 \pm .03$; whereas it is $.85 \pm .10$ for the one without. These rain-robust features help the model to show improved performance in both PSNR and SSIM.

Failure Cases: Apart from the successful cases illustrated in Fig. 5, we also provide some of the failure cases in the GT-RAIN test set in Fig. 7. Deraining is still an open problem, and we hope future work can take advantages of both real and synthetic samples to make derainers more robust in diverse environments.

6   Conclusions

Many of us in the deraining community probably wish for the existence of parallel universes, where we could capture the exact same scene with and without weather effects at the exact same time. Unfortunately, however, we are stuck with our singular universe, in which we are left with two choices: (1) synthetic data at the same timestamp with simulated weather effects or (2) real data at different timestamps with real weather effects. Though it is up to opinion, it is our belief that the results of our method in Fig. 6 reduce the visual domain gap more than those trained with synthetic datasets. Additionally, we hope the introduction of a real dataset opens up exciting new pathways for future work, such as the blending of synthetic and real data or setting goalposts to guide the continued development of existing rain simulators [17,36,43,53,54].

Acknowledgements. The authors thank members of the Visual Machines Group for their feedback and support, as well as Mani Srivastava and Cho-Jui Hsieh for technical discussions. This research was partially supported by ARL W911NF-20-2-0158 under the cooperative A2I2 program. A.K. was also partially supported by an Army Young Investigator Award.

References

1. Ancuti, C.O., Ancuti, C., Sbert, M., Timofte, R.: Dense-haze: a benchmark for image dehazing with dense-haze and haze-free images. In: 2019 IEEE international conference on image processing (ICIP), pp. 1014–1018. IEEE (2019)
2. Ancuti, C.O., Ancuti, C., Timofte, R.: NH-haze: an image dehazing benchmark with non-homogeneous hazy and haze-free images. In: Proceedings of the IEEE/CVF Conference on Computer Vision and Pattern Recognition Workshops, pp. 444–445 (2020)
3. Ancuti, C.O., Ancuti, C., Timofte, R., De Vleeschouwer, C.: O-haze: a dehazing benchmark with real hazy and haze-free outdoor images. In: Proceedings of the IEEE Conference on Computer Vision and Pattern Recognition Workshops, pp. 754–762 (2018)
4. Ancuti, C., Ancuti, C.O., Timofte, R., De Vleeschouwer, C.: I-HAZE: a dehazing benchmark with real hazy and haze-free indoor images. In: Blanc-Talon, J., Helbert, D., Philips, W., Popescu, D., Scheunders, P. (eds.) ACIVS 2018. LNCS, vol. 11182, pp. 620–631. Springer, Cham (2018). https://doi.org/10.1007/978-3-030-01449-0_52
5. Beard, K.V., Chuang, C.: A new model for the equilibrium shape of raindrops. J. Atmosp. Sci. **44**(11), 1509–1524 (1987)
6. Chen, T., Kornblith, S., Norouzi, M., Hinton, G.: A simple framework for contrastive learning of visual representations. In: International Conference on Machine Learning, pp. 1597–1607. PMLR (2020)
7. Chen, Y.L., Hsu, C.T.: A generalized low-rank appearance model for spatio-temporally correlated rain streaks. In: Proceedings of the IEEE International Conference on Computer Vision, pp. 1968–1975 (2013)
8. Deng, L.J., Huang, T.Z., Zhao, X.L., Jiang, T.X.: A directional global sparse model for single image rain removal. Appl. Math. Model. **59**, 662–679 (2018)
9. Fischler, M.A., Bolles, R.C.: Random sample consensus: a paradigm for model fitting with applications to image analysis and automated cartography. Commun. ACM **24**(6), 381–395 (1981)
10. Foote, G.B., Du Toit, P.S.: Terminal velocity of raindrops aloft. J. Appl. Meteorol. **8**(2), 249–253 (1969)
11. Fu, X., Huang, J., Ding, X., Liao, Y., Paisley, J.: Clearing the skies: a deep network architecture for single-image rain removal. IEEE Trans. Image Process. **26**(6), 2944–2956 (2017)
12. Fu, X., Huang, J., Zeng, D., Huang, Y., Ding, X., Paisley, J.: Removing rain from single images via a deep detail network. In: Proceedings of the IEEE/CVF Conference on Computer Vision and Pattern Recognition, pp. 3855–3863 (2017)
13. Garg, K., Nayar, S.K.: Vision and rain. Int. J. Comput. Vis. **75**(1), 3–27 (2007)
14. Gunn, R., Kinzer, G.D.: The terminal velocity of fall for water droplets in stagnant air. J. Atmos. Sci. **6**(4), 243–248 (1949)
15. Guo, Q., et al.: EfficientDeRain: learning pixel-wise dilation filtering for high-efficiency single-image deraining. In: Proceedings of the AAAI Conference on Artificial Intelligence, vol. 35, pp. 1487–1495 (2021)
16. Gutmann, M., Hyvärinen, A.: Noise-contrastive estimation: a new estimation principle for unnormalized statistical models. In: Proceedings of the Thirteenth International Conference on Artificial Intelligence and Statistics, pp. 297–304. JMLR Workshop and Conference Proceedings (2010)

17. Halder, S.S., Lalonde, J.F., de Charette, R.: Physics-based rendering for improving robustness to rain. In: Proceedings of the IEEE/CVF International Conference on Computer Vision, pp. 10203–10212 (2019)
18. He, K., Zhang, X., Ren, S., Sun, J.: Deep residual learning for image recognition. In: Proceedings of the IEEE/CVF Conference on Computer Vision and Pattern Recognition, pp. 770–778 (2016)
19. Hu, X., Fu, C.W., Zhu, L., Heng, P.A.: Depth-attentional features for single-image rain removal. In: Proceedings of the IEEE/CVF Conference on Computer Vision and Pattern Recognition, pp. 8022–8031 (2019)
20. Hu, X., Zhu, L., Wang, T., Fu, C.W., Heng, P.A.: Single-image real-time rain removal based on depth-guided non-local features. IEEE Trans. Image Process. **30**, 1759–1770 (2021)
21. Huynh-Thu, Q., Ghanbari, M.: Scope of validity of PSNR in image/video quality assessment. Electron. Lett. **44**(13), 800–801 (2008)
22. Jiang, K., et al.: Multi-scale progressive fusion network for single image deraining. In: Proceedings of the IEEE/CVF Conference on Computer Vision and Pattern Recognition, pp. 8346–8355 (2020)
23. Jiang, T.X., Huang, T.Z., Zhao, X.L., Deng, L.J., Wang, Y.: FastDeRain: a novel video rain streak removal method using directional gradient priors. IEEE Trans. Image Process. **28**(4), 2089–2102 (2018)
24. Johnson, J., Alahi, A., Fei-Fei, L.: Perceptual losses for real-time style transfer and super-resolution. In: Leibe, B., Matas, J., Sebe, N., Welling, M. (eds.) ECCV 2016. LNCS, vol. 9906, pp. 694–711. Springer, Cham (2016). https://doi.org/10.1007/978-3-319-46475-6_43
25. Kingma, D.P., Ba, J.: Adam: a method for stochastic optimization. arXiv preprint arXiv:1412.6980 (2014)
26. Li, G., He, X., Zhang, W., Chang, H., Dong, L., Lin, L.: Non-locally enhanced encoder-decoder network for single image de-raining. In: Proceedings of the 26th ACM international conference on Multimedia, pp. 1056–1064 (2018)
27. Li, R., Cheong, L.F., Tan, R.T.: Heavy rain image restoration: integrating physics model and conditional adversarial learning. In: Proceedings of the IEEE/CVF Conference on Computer Vision and Pattern Recognition, pp. 1633–1642 (2019)
28. Li, R., Tan, R.T., Cheong, L.F.: All in one bad weather removal using architectural search. In: Proceedings of the IEEE/CVF Conference on Computer Vision and Pattern Recognition, pp. 3175–3185 (2020)
29. Li, Y., Tan, R.T., Guo, X., Lu, J., Brown, M.S.: Rain streak removal using layer priors. In: Proceedings of the IEEE/CVF Conference on Computer Vision and Pattern Recognition, pp. 2736–2744 (2016)
30. Loshchilov, I., Hutter, F.: SGDR: stochastic gradient descent with warm restarts. In: 5th International Conference on Learning Representations, ICLR 2017, Toulon, France, 24–26 April 2017. Conference Track Proceedings. OpenReview.net (2017), https://openreview.net/forum?id=Skq89Scxx
31. Lowe, D.: Sift-the scale invariant feature transform. Int. J. **2**(91–110), 2 (2004)
32. Ltd., O.: OpenWeatherMap API. https://openweathermap.org/. Accessed 05 Nov 2021
33. Luo, Y., Xu, Y., Ji, H.: Removing rain from a single image via discriminative sparse coding. In: Proceedings of the IEEE International Conference on Computer Vision, pp. 3397–3405 (2015)
34. Manning, R.M.: Stochastic Electromagnetic Image Propagation. McGraw-Hill Companies, New York (1993)

35. Marshall, J., Palmer, W.M.: The distribution of raindrops with size. J. Meteorol. **5**(4), 165–166 (1948)
36. Ni, S., Cao, X., Yue, T., Hu, X.: Controlling the rain: from removal to rendering. In: Proceedings of the IEEE/CVF Conference on Computer Vision and Pattern Recognition, pp. 6328–6337 (2021)
37. Oord, A.v.d., Li, Y., Vinyals, O.: Representation learning with contrastive predictive coding. arXiv preprint arXiv:1807.03748 (2018)
38. Pan, J., et al.: Learning dual convolutional neural networks for low-level vision. In: Proceedings of the IEEE/CVF Conference on Computer Vision and Pattern Recognition, pp. 3070–3079 (2018)
39. Ren, D., Shang, W., Zhu, P., Hu, Q., Meng, D., Zuo, W.: Single image deraining using bilateral recurrent network. IEEE Trans. Image Process. **29**, 6852–6863 (2020)
40. Thirion, J.P.: Image matching as a diffusion process: an analogy with Maxwell's demons. Med. Image Anal. **2**(3), 243–260 (1998)
41. Vercauteren, T., Pennec, X., Perchant, A., Ayache, N.: Diffeomorphic demons: efficient non-parametric image registration. NeuroImage **45**(1), S61–S72 (2009)
42. Wang, H., Xie, Q., Zhao, Q., Meng, D.: A model-driven deep neural network for single image rain removal. In: Proceedings of the IEEE/CVF Conference on Computer Vision and Pattern Recognition, June 2020
43. Wang, H., Yue, Z., Xie, Q., Zhao, Q., Zheng, Y., Meng, D.: From rain generation to rain removal. In: Proceedings of the IEEE/CVF Conference on Computer Vision and Pattern Recognition, pp. 14791–14801 (2021)
44. Wang, T., Yang, X., Xu, K., Chen, S., Zhang, Q., Lau, R.W.: Spatial attentive single-image deraining with a high quality real rain dataset. In: Proceedings of the IEEE/CVF Conference on Computer Vision and Pattern Recognition, pp. 12270–12279 (2019)
45. Wang, Z., Bovik, A.C., Sheikh, H.R., Simoncelli, E.P.: Image quality assessment: from error visibility to structural similarity. IEEE Trans. Image Process. **13**(4), 600–612 (2004)
46. Wang, Z., Simoncelli, E.P., Bovik, A.C.: Multiscale structural similarity for image quality assessment. In: The Thrity-Seventh Asilomar Conference on Signals, Systems and Computers, vol. 2, pp. 1398–1402. IEEE (2003)
47. Wei, W., Meng, D., Zhao, Q., Xu, Z., Wu, Y.: Semi-supervised transfer learning for image rain removal. In: Proceedings of the IEEE/CVF Conference on Computer Vision and Pattern Recognition, pp. 3877–3886 (2019)
48. Wu, Z., Xiong, Y., Yu, S.X., Lin, D.: Unsupervised feature learning via non-parametric instance discrimination. In: Proceedings of the IEEE/CVF Conference on Computer Vision and Pattern Recognition, pp. 3733–3742 (2018)
49. Yang, W., Tan, R.T., Feng, J., Guo, Z., Yan, S., Liu, J.: Joint rain detection and removal from a single image with contextualized deep networks. IEEE Trans. Pattern Anal. Mach. Intell. **42**(6), 1377–1393 (2019)
50. Yang, W., Tan, R.T., Feng, J., Liu, J., Guo, Z., Yan, S.: Deep joint rain detection and removal from a single image. In: Proceedings of the IEEE/CVF Conference on Computer Vision and Pattern Recognition, pp. 1357–1366 (2017)
51. Yang, W., Tan, R.T., Wang, S., Fang, Y., Liu, J.: Single image deraining: from model-based to data-driven and beyond. IEEE Trans. Pattern Anal. Mach. Intell. **43**, 4059–4077 (2020)
52. Yasarla, R., Patel, V.M.: Uncertainty guided multi-scale residual learning-using a cycle spinning CNN for single image de-raining. In: Proceedings of the IEEE/CVF Conference on Computer Vision and Pattern Recognition, pp. 8405–8414 (2019)

53. Ye, Y., Chang, Y., Zhou, H., Yan, L.: Closing the loop: joint rain generation and removal via disentangled image translation. In: Proceedings of the IEEE/CVF Conference on Computer Vision and Pattern Recognition, pp. 2053–2062 (2021)

54. Yue, Z., Xie, J., Zhao, Q., Meng, D.: Semi-supervised video deraining with dynamical rain generator. In: Proceedings of the IEEE/CVF Conference on Computer Vision and Pattern Recognition, pp. 642–652 (2021)

55. Zamir, S.W., et al.: Multi-stage progressive image restoration. In: Proceedings of the IEEE/CVF Conference on Computer Vision and Pattern Recognition, pp. 14821–14831 (2021)

56. Zhang, H., Patel, V.M.: Density-aware single image de-raining using a multi-stream dense network. In: Proceedings of the IEEE/CVF Conference on Computer Vision and Pattern Recognition, pp. 695–704 (2018)

57. Zhang, H., Sindagi, V., Patel, V.M.: Image de-raining using a conditional generative adversarial network. IEEE Trans. Circuits Syst. Video Technol. **30**(11), 3943–3956 (2019)

58. Zhang, X., Li, H., Qi, Y., Leow, W.K., Ng, T.K.: Rain removal in video by combining temporal and chromatic properties. In: 2006 IEEE International Conference on Multimedia and Expo, pp. 461–464. IEEE (2006)

59. Zhao, H., Gallo, O., Frosio, I., Kautz, J.: Loss functions for image restoration with neural networks. IEEE Trans. Comput. Imaging **3**(1), 47–57 (2016)

60. Zhu, J.Y., Park, T., Isola, P., Efros, A.A.: Unpaired image-to-image translation using cycle-consistent adversarial networks. In: Proceedings of the IEEE International Conference on Computer Vision, pp. 2223–2232 (2017)

61. Zhu, L., Fu, C.W., Lischinski, D., Heng, P.A.: Joint bi-layer optimization for single-image rain streak removal. In: Proceedings of the IEEE International Conference on Computer Vision, pp. 2526–2534 (2017)

62. Zhu, X., Hu, H., Lin, S., Dai, J.: Deformable ConvNets v2: more deformable, better results. In: Proceedings of the IEEE/CVF Conference on Computer Vision and Pattern Recognition, pp. 9308–9316 (2019)

Author Index

Printed in the United States
by Baker & Taylor Publisher Services